GARDNER'S
ART
THROUGH THE
AGES

TWELFTH EDITION

Volume I

FRED S. KLEINER

CHRISTIN J. MAMIYA

THOMSON

WADSWORTH

AUSTRALIA • CANADA • MEXICO • SINGAPORE • SPAIN
UNITED KINGDOM • UNITED STATES

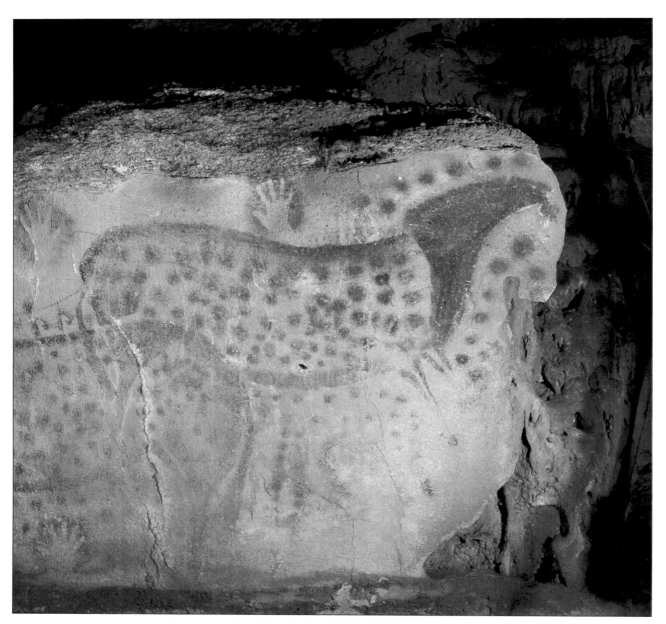

Spotted horses and negative hand imprints, wall painting in the cave at Pech-Merle, Lot, France, ca. 22,000 BCE. Approx. 11′ 2″ long.

About the Cover Art

Created almost 25,000 years ago, the Old Stone Age mural paintings in the cave at Pech-Merle, France, are among the earliest artworks known. Our detail of spotted horses appropriately serves as the cover of the first volume of *Gardner's Art through the Ages*. Animals (always shown in profile) are the almost exclusive subject of these early paintings and the Pech-Merle horses are no exception. Here, however, the horses are accompanied by painted hands, which the prehistoric painter produced by placing one hand against the wall and then brushing or blowing pigment around it. Some scholars think these handprints are "signatures" of cult or community members or, less likely, of individual painters.

THOMSON

WADSWORTH

Acquisitions Editor
JOHN R. SWANSON

Senior Development Editor
STACEY SIMS

Assistant Editor
AMY MCGAUGHEY

Editorial Assistant
BRIANNA BRINKLEY

Technology Project Manager
MELINDA NEWFARMER

Marketing Manager
MARK ORR

Marketing Assistant
ANNABELLE YANG

Advertising Project Manager
VICKY WAN

Project Manager, Editorial Production
KATHRYN M. STEWART

Print/Media Buyer
BARBARA BRITTON

Permissions Editor
JOOHEE LEE

Production Service
JOAN KEYES, DOVETAIL PUBLISHING SERVICES

Text Designer
JOHN WALKER

Photo Researchers
CARRIE WARD, IMAGE SELECT INTERNATIONAL

Copy Editor
MICHELE JONES

Illustrator
DARTMOUTH PUBLISHING

Cover Designer
BRIAN SALISBURY

Cover Image
SPOTTED HORSES AND NEGATIVE HAND IMPRINTS (DETAIL), WALL PAINTING IN THE CAVE AT PECH-MERLE, LOT, FRANCE, CA. 22,000 BCE. APPROX. 11′ 2″ LONG. PHOTOGRAPH: JEAN VERTUT.

Cover Printer
THE LEHIGH PRESS, INC.

Compositor
PROGRESSIVE INFORMATION TECHNOLOGIES

Printer
R.R. DONNELLEY/WILLARD

Printed in the United States of America
2 3 4 5 6 7 08 07 06 05

For more information about our products, contact us at:
Thomson Learning Academic Resource Center
1-800-423-0563

For permission to use material from this text or product, submit a request online at http://www.thomsonrights.com. Any additional questions about permissions can be submitted by e-mail to thomsonrights@thomson.com

Wadsworth/Thomson Learning
10 Davis Drive, Belmont, CA 94002-3098
USA

Asia
Thomson Learning
5 Shenton Way #01-01, UIC Building
Singapore 068808

Australia
Nelson Thomson Learning
102 Dodds Street, South Melbourne, Victoria 3205
Australia

Canada
Nelson Thomson Learning
1120 Birchmount Road, Toronto, Ontario M1K 5G4
Canada

Europe/Middle East/Africa
Thomson Learning
High Holborn House, 50/51 Bedford Row, London WC1R 4LR
United Kingdom

Library of Congress Control Number
2003111627

ISBN 0-534-64095-8

CONTENTS IN BRIEF

CONTENTS

PREFACE

We take great pleasure in presenting the Twelfth Edition of *Gardner's Art through the Ages*, the most widely read introduction to the history of art in the English language. When Helen Gardner published the first edition of her classic global survey of art and architecture in 1926, she could not have imagined that eight decades later instructors all over the world would still be using her textbook in their classrooms. She would no doubt have been especially proud that the Eleventh Edition of *Art through the Ages* was awarded both the 2001 Texty and McGuffey Book Prizes of the Text and Academic Authors Association as the best college textbook in the humanities and social sciences—the first art history book to win either award and the only title ever to win both prizes in the same year.

The fundamental belief that guided Helen Gardner—that the history of art is essential to a liberal education—is one that we also embrace. The study of art history has as its aim the appreciation and understanding of works of high aesthetic quality and historical significance produced throughout the world and across thousands of years of human history. We think, as she did, that the most effective way to tell the story of art through the ages, especially for those who are studying art history for the first time, is to organize the vast array of artistic monuments according to the civilizations that produced them and to consider each work in roughly chronological order. This approach has not only stood the test of time; it is the most appropriate for narrating the *history* of art. We believe that the enormous variation in the form and meaning of paintings, sculptures, buildings, and other artworks is largely the result of the constantly changing historical, social, economic, religious, and cultural context in which artists and architects worked. A historically based narrative is therefore best suited for a global history of art.

Yet, in other ways, Helen Gardner would not recognize the Twelfth Edition of *Art through the Ages* as her book. Most obvious, perhaps, Pablo Picasso and Arthur B. Davies are no longer treated in a chapter entitled "Contemporary Art in Europe and America." More significantly, however, the discipline of art history has changed markedly in recent decades, and so too has this book. The Twelfth Edition fully reflects the latest art historical research emphases, while maintaining the traditional strengths that have made all the previous editions of *Art through the Ages* so successful. While sustaining attention to style, chronology, iconography, and technique, we pay greater attention than ever before to function and context. We consider artworks with a view toward their purpose and meaning in the society that produced them at the time at which they were produced. We also address the very important role of patronage in the production of art and examine the role of the individuals or groups who paid the artists and influenced the shape the monuments took. We devote more space to the role of women and women artists in societies worldwide over time. Throughout, we have aimed to integrate the historical, political, and social context of art and architecture with the artistic and intellectual aspects. Consequently, we often treat painting, sculpture, architecture, and the so-called minor arts together, highlighting how they all reflect the conventions and aspirations of a common culture, rather than treating them as separate and distinct media. And we feature many works that until recently art historians would not have considered to be "art" at all. In every chapter, we have tried in our choice of artworks and buildings to reflect the increasingly wide range of interests of scholars today, while not rejecting the traditional list of "great" works or the very notion of a "canon." The selection of works encompasses every artistic medium and almost every era and culture.

The changes we have made even with respect to the Eleventh Edition are notable and will be immediately apparent to anyone who examines the Eleventh and Twelfth Editions side by side. Both editions feature more than 1400 photographs, plans, and drawings, but in the new edition nearly every photograph is in color. The only exceptions are works that were created in black-and-white, such as prints or photographs, and a small number of other monuments of which we were unable to obtain a color view that met our very high standards for reproduction.

Every edition of *Art through the Ages* has gone through a rigorous process of review, and the Twelfth Edition is no exception. Each of its 34 chapters has been read by experts in the respective fields. Some chapters were reviewed by as many as six scholars in order to ensure that the text lived up to the Gardner reputation for accuracy as well as readability. Every chapter has been revised. Some have been rewritten almost in their entirety. All feature superb new color illustrations, including a full-page, chapter-opening image reproducing a characteristic work of each period.

The rich illustration program is not, however, confined to the printed page. Every copy of the Twelfth Edition of *Art through the Ages* comes with a complimentary copy of *ArtStudy 2.0*, a CD-ROM that contains hundreds of high-quality digital images of the works discussed in the text. To facilitate the coordinated use of the CD-ROM and the book itself, every monument illustrated on the CD-ROM has an identifying icon appended to the caption of the corresponding figure in the text.

In response to student requests, every chapter of the new edition of *Art through the Ages* now ends with a short Conclusion summarizing the major themes discussed. These summaries face a full-page Chronological Overview of the material presented in the chapter, organized as a vertical timeline, with four "thumb-nail" illustrations of characteristic works in a variety of media, generally including at least one painting, sculpture, and building. Each thumbnail is numbered; the corresponding number appears on the time rule to the left so that the chronological sequence of production is clear.

The most popular features of previous editions of *Art through the Ages* have, of course, been retained. Especially noteworthy are the boxed essays that we introduced in the Eleventh Edition and which were so enthusiastically received by students and instructors alike. As before, these essays are presented in six broad categories.

Architectural Basics provide students with a sound foundation for the understanding of architecture. These discussions are concise primers, with drawings and diagrams of the major aspects of design and construction. The information included is essential to an understanding of architectural technology and terminology. The boxes address questions of how and why various forms developed, the problems architects confronted, and the solutions they used to resolve them. Topics discussed include how the Egyptians built the pyramids, the orders of classical architecture, Roman concrete construction, and the design and terminology of mosques, stupas, and Gothic cathedrals.

Materials and Techniques essays explain the various media artists employed from prehistoric to modern times. Since materials and techniques often influence the character of works of art, these discussions also contain essential information on why many monuments look the way they do. Hollow-casting bronze statues, fresco painting, Chinese silk, Andean weaving, Islamic tilework, embroidery and tapestry, woodblock prints, and perspective are among the many subjects treated.

Written Sources present and discuss key historical documents illuminating important monuments of art and architecture and the careers of some of the world's leading artists, architects, and patrons. The passages we quote permit voices from the past to speak directly to the reader, providing vivid and unique insights into the creation of artworks in all media. Examples include Bernard of Clairvaux's treatise on sculpture in medieval churches, Sinan the Great's commentary on the mosque he built for Selim II, Jean François Marmontel's account of 18th-century salon culture, as well as texts that bring the past to life, such as eyewitness accounts of the volcanic eruption that buried Roman Pompeii and of the fire that destroyed Canterbury Cathedral in medieval England.

Religion and Mythology boxes introduce students to the principal elements of the world's great religions, past and present, and to the representation of religious and mythological themes in painting and sculpture of all periods and places. These discussions of belief systems and iconography give readers a richer understanding of some of the greatest artworks ever created. The topics include the gods and goddesses of Egypt, Mesopotamia, Greece, and Rome; the life of Jesus in art; Buddha and Buddhism; Muhammad and Islam; and Aztec religion.

Art and Society essays treat the historical, social, political, cultural, and religious context of art and architecture. In some instances, specific monuments are the basis for a discussion of broader themes, as when we use the Hegeso stele to serve as the springboard for an exploration of the role of women in ancient Greek society. In other cases, we discuss how people's evaluation today of artworks can differ from those of the society that produced them, as when we examine the problems created by the contemporary market for undocumented archaeological finds. Other subjects include Egyptian mummification, the art of freed Roman slaves, the Mesoamerican ball game, the shifting fortunes of Vincent van Gogh, Japanese court culture, and Native American artists.

Art in the News boxes present accounts of the latest archaeological finds and discussions of current controversies in the history of art. Among the discoveries and issues we highlight are the excavation of the tomb of the sons of the pharaoh Ramses and the restoration of Michelangelo's frescoes in the Sistine Chapel.

As in the past, the Twelfth Edition of *Art through the Ages* is published in a single hardcover version and as two paperbound volumes. Because many students taking the second half of a year-long introductory art history survey course will only have the second volume of the paperbound edition, we have again provided a feature not found in any other textbook currently available: a special set of Volume II boxes on religion, mythology, and architecture entitled *Before 1300*. These discussions immediately follow the Preface to Volume II and provide concise primers on religion and mythology and on architectural terminology and construction methods in the ancient and medieval worlds—information that is essential for understanding the history of art after 1300, both in the West and the East. The subjects of these special boxes are The Gods and Goddesses of Mount Olympus; Buddhism and Hinduism; The Life of Jesus in Art; Greco-Roman Temple Design and the Classical Orders; Arches and Vaults; The Basilican Church; and The Central-Plan Church.

Full-color maps also remain an important element of every chapter of *Art through the Ages*. As in previous editions, we have taken great care to make sure that every site discussed in the text appears on our maps. These maps vary widely in both geographical and chronological scope. Some focus on a small region or even a single city, while others encompass a vast territory and occasionally bridge two or more continents. Several maps plot the art-producing sites of a given area over hundreds, even thousands, of years. In every instance, our aim has been to provide readers with maps that will easily allow them to locate the places where works of art originated or were found and where buildings were erected. To this end we have regularly placed the names of modern nations on maps of the territories of past civilizations.

In addition, in order to aid our readers in mastering the vocabulary of art history, we have italicized and defined all art historical terms and other unfamiliar words at their first occurrence in the text—and at later occurrences too, whenever the term has not been used again for several chapters. Definitions of all terms introduced in the text appear once more in the Glossary at the back of the book, which includes pronunciations, a feature introduced in the Eleventh Edition. *Art through the Ages* also has a comprehensive bibliography of books in English, including both general works and a chapter-by-chapter list of more focused studies.

The captions to our more than 1400 illustrations contain a wealth of information, including the name of the artist or architect, if known; the formal title (printed in italics), if assigned, description of the work, or name of the building; the findspot or place of production of the object or location of the building; the date; the material or materials used; the size; and the present location if the work is in a museum or private collection. We urge readers to pay attention to the scales provided on all plans and to all dimensions given in the captions. The objects we illustrate vary enormously in size, from colossal sculptures carved into mountain cliffs and paintings that cover entire walls or ceilings to tiny figurines, coins, and jewelry that one can hold in the hand. Note too the location of the monuments discussed. Although many buildings and museums may be in cities or countries that a reader may never visit, others are likely to be close to home.

Nothing can substitute for walking through a building, standing in the presence of a statue, or inspecting the brushwork of a painting close up. Consequently, we have made a special effort to illustrate artworks in geographically wide-ranging public collections.

A work as extensive as a global history of art could not be undertaken or completed without the counsel of experts in all areas of world art. We are especially grateful to Herbert Cole of the University of California, Santa Barbara, for contributing the two chapters on African art, reprising a role he played in the Tenth Edition of *Art through the Ages*. And we remain grateful to Robert L. Brown (University of California, Los Angeles), George Corbin (Lehman College of the City University of New York), Virginia E. Miller (University of Illinois, Chicago), and Quitman Eugene Phillips (University of Wisconsin, Madison) for their contributions to the Eleventh Edition on India and Southeast Asia; Africa and Oceania; the native arts of the Americas; and China, Korea, and Japan, respectively, which laid the foundation for much of the treatment of non-Western art in the Twelfth Edition.

For contributions in the form of extended critiques of the Eleventh Edition or of the penultimate drafts of the Twelfth Edition chapters, as well as other assistance of various sorts, we wish to thank Stanley K. Abe, Duke University; C. Edson Armi, University of California, Santa Barbara; Frederick M. Asher, University of Minnesota; Cynthia Atherton, Middlebury College; Paul G. Bahn, Hull, England; Janis Bergman-Carton, Southern Methodist University; Janet Berlo, University of Rochester; Anne Bertrand, Bard College; Jonathan M. Bloom, Boston College; Kendall H. Brown, California State University, Long Beach; Andrew L. Cohen, University of Central Arkansas; Harry A. Cooper, Fogg Art Museum, Harvard University; Roger J. Crum, University of Dayton; LouAnn Faris Culley, Kansas State University; Thomas E. A. Dale, University of Wisconsin, Madison; Anne D'Alleva, University of Connecticut; Eve D'Ambra, Vassar College; Cindy Bailey Damschroder, University of Cincinnati; Abraham A. Davidson, Temple University; Carolyn Dean, University of California, Santa Cruz; William Diebold, Reed College; Erika Doss, University of Colorado; Daniel Ehnbom, University of Virginia; David Ehrenpreis, James Madison University; Jerome Feldman, Hawaii Pacific University; Peter Fergusson, Wellesley College; Barbara Frank, State University of New York, Stony Brook; Rita E. Freed, Museum of Fine Arts, Boston; Eric G. Garbersen, Virginia Commonwealth University; Clive F. Getty, Miami University; Paula Girshick, Indiana University; Carma R. Gorman, Southern Illinois University, Carbondale; Elizabeth ten Grotenhuis, Boston University; Melinda K. Hartwig, Georgia State University; Marsha Haufler, University of Kansas; Mary Beth Heston, College of Charleston; Hannah Higgins, University of Illinois, Chicago; Charlotte Houghton, The Pennsylvania State University; Aldona Jonaitis, University of Alaska Museum; Adrienne Kaeppler, Smithsonian Institution; Padma Kaimal, Colgate University; Stacy L. Kamehiro, University of Redlands; Thomas DaCosta Kaufmann, Princeton University; Dale Kinney, Bryn Mawr College; Sandy Kita, University of Maryland, College Park; Cecelia F. Klein, University of California, Los Angeles; James Kornwolf, College of William and Mary; Andrew Ladis, University of Georgia, Athens; Ellen Johnston Laing, University of Michigan; Joseph Lamb, Ohio University; Dana Leibsohn, Smith College; Janice Leoshko, University of Texas at Austin; Henry Maguire, Johns Hopkins University; Joan Marter, Rutgers University; Michael Meister, University of Pennsylvania; Samuel C. Morse, Amherst College; Susan E. Nelson, Indiana University; Irene Nero, Southeastern Louisiana University; Esther Pasztory, Columbia University; Jeanette F. Peterson, University of California, Santa

Barbara; Elizabeth Piliod, Oregon State University; Martin Powers, University of Michigan; Ingrida Raudzens, Salem State College; Paul Rehak, University of Kansas; Margaret Cool Root, University of Michigan; Lisa Rosenthal, University of Illinois, Urbana-Champaign; Jonathan M. Reynolds, University of Southern California; Conrad Rudolph, University of California, Riverside; Denise Schmandt-Besserat, University of Texas at Austin; Ellen C. Schwartz, Eastern Michigan University; Michael Schwartz, Augusta State University; Raymond A. Silverman, Michigan State University; Jeffrey Chipps Smith, University of Texas at Austin; Anne Rudloff Stanton, University of Missouri, Columbia; Rebecca Stone-Miller, Emory University; Mary C. Sturgeon, University of North Carolina at Chapel Hill; Peter C. Sturman, University of California, Santa Barbara; Melinda Takeuchi, Stanford University; Woodman Taylor, University of Illinois at Chicago; Jehanne Teilhet-Fisk, Florida State University; John Turner, Butler University, Dorothy Verkerk, University of North Carolina at Chapel Hill; Monica Blackmun Visonà, Metro State College; Gerald Walker, Clemson University; Martha Ward, University of Chicago; Gregory Warden, Southern Methodist University; Kent R. Weeks, American University in Cairo; Victoria Weston, University of Massachusetts, Boston; Deborah B. Waite, University of Hawaii; Catherine Wilkinson Zerner, Brown University. Innumerable other instructors and students have also sent us helpful reactions, comments, and suggestions for ways to improve the book. We are grateful for their interest and their insights.

Among those at Thomson Wadsworth who worked with us to make the new edition of *Art through the Ages* the best ever are the CEO and president, Susan Badger; senior vice president, editorial, Sean Wakely; vice president and editor-in-chief, Marcus Boggs; publisher, Clark Baxter; executive editor, David Tatom; acquisitions editor, John Swanson; technology project manager, Melinda Newfarmer; our development editors, Helen Triller and Stacey Sims; assistant editor, Amy McGaughey; and editorial assistants, Rebecca Jackson and Brianna Brinkley. This edition of *Art through the Ages* is the most ambitious ever, and the production schedule was the tightest ever. We therefore want to acknowledge the extraordinary efforts of our editorial production manager, Kathryn Stewart, and her team of dedicated professionals: Joan Keyes of Dovetail Publishing Services, our production service; our copy editors, Michele Jones and Gail Nelson-Bonebrake; interior designer, John Walker; cover designer, Brian Salisbury; and photo researchers Carrie Ward, Lili Weiner, and Image Select International. We are also grateful to the marketing staff for their dedication to making this edition a success: senior vice president, marketing, Jonathan Hulbert; director of marketing, Elana Dolberg; executive marketing manager, Diane Wenckebach; executive director of advertising and marketing communications, Margaret Parks; senior channel manager, school, Wadsworth Group, Pat Murphree; marketing manager, Mark Orr; and marketing assistant, Annabelle Yang. Recognition and thanks are also due to our proofreaders, Katherine Hyde and Pete Shanks, and our indexer, Nancy Ball.

We also owe a deep debt of gratitude to our colleagues at Boston University and the University of Nebraska, Lincoln, and to the thousands of students and the scores of teaching fellows in our art history courses over many years in Boston and Lincoln, and at the University of Virginia and Yale University. From them we have learned much that has helped determine the form and content of *Art through the Ages*.

FRED S. KLEINER
CHRISTIN J. MAMIYA

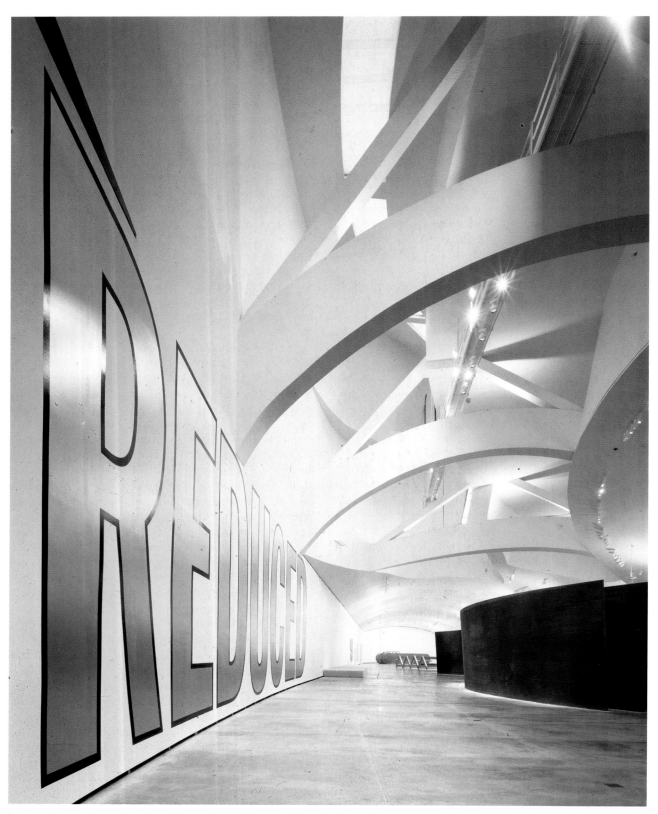

Intro-1 FRANK GEHRY, interior of Guggenheim Museum, Bilbao, Spain, 1997.

INTRODUCTION

THE SUBJECTS AND VOCABULARY OF ART HISTORY

People do not often juxtapose the terms *art* and *history*. They tend to think of history as the record and interpretation of past human actions, particularly social and political actions. Most think of art, quite correctly, as part of the present—as something people can see and touch. People cannot, of course, see or touch history's vanished human events. But a visible and tangible artwork is a kind of persisting event. One or more artists made it at a certain time and in a specific place, even if no one now knows just who, when, where, or why. Although created in the past, an artwork continues to exist in the present, long surviving its times. The first painters and sculptors died 30,000 years ago, but their works remain, some of them exhibited in glass cases in museums built only a few years ago.

Modern museum visitors can admire these relics of the remote past and the countless other objects humankind has produced over the millennia without any knowledge of the circumstances that led to the creation of those works. The beauty or sheer size of an object can impress people, the artist's virtuosity in the handling of ordinary or costly materials can dazzle them, or the subject depicted can move them. Viewers can react to what they see, interpret the work in the light of their own experience, and judge it a success or a failure. These are all valid responses to a work of art. But the enjoyment and appreciation of artworks in museum settings (FIG. **Intro-1**) are relatively recent phenomena, as is the creation of artworks solely for museum-going audiences to view.

Today, it is common for artists to work in private studios and to create paintings, sculptures, and other objects commercial art galleries will offer for sale. Usually, someone the artist has never met will purchase the artwork and display it in a setting the artist has never seen. But although this is not a new phenomenon in the history of art—an ancient potter decorating a vase for sale at a village market stall also probably did not know who would buy the pot or where it would be housed—it is not at all typical. In fact, it is exceptional. Throughout history, most artists created the paintings, sculptures, and other objects exhibited in museums today for specific patrons and settings and to fulfill a specific purpose. Often, no one knows the original contexts of those artworks.

Although people may appreciate the visual and tactile qualities of these objects, they cannot understand why they were made or why they look the way they do without knowing the circumstances of their creation. *Art appreciation* does not require knowledge of the historical context of an artwork (or a building). *Art history* does.

Thus, a central aim of art history is to determine the original context of artworks. Art historians seek to achieve a full understanding not only of why these "persisting events" of human history look the way they do but also of why the artistic events happened at all. What unique set of circumstances gave rise to the erection of a particular building or led a specific patron to commission an individual artist to fashion a singular artwork for a certain place? The study of history is therefore vital to art history. And art history is often very important to the study of history. Art objects and buildings are historical documents that can shed light on the peoples who made them and on the times of their creation in a way other historical documents cannot. Furthermore, artists and architects can affect history by reinforcing or challenging cultural values and practices through the objects they create and the structures they build. Thus, the history of art and architecture is inseparable from the study of history, although the two disciplines are not the same. In the following pages, we outline some of the distinctive subjects art historians address and the kinds of questions they ask, and explain some of the basic terminology art historians use when answering their questions. Armed with this arsenal of questions and terms, you will be ready to explore the multifaceted world of art through the ages.

ART HISTORY IN THE 21ST CENTURY

Art historians study the visual and tangible objects humans make and the structures humans build. Scholars traditionally have classified such works as architecture, sculpture, the pictorial arts (painting, drawing, printmaking, and photography), and the craft arts, or arts of design. The craft arts comprise utilitarian objects, such as ceramics, metalwares, textiles, jewelry, and similar accessories of ordinary living. Artists of every age have blurred the boundaries between these categories, but this is especially true today, when *multimedia* works abound.

From the earliest Greco-Roman art critics on, scholars have studied objects that their makers consciously manufactured as "art" and to which the artists assigned formal titles. But today's art historians also study a vast number of objects that their creators and owners almost certainly did not consider to be "works of art." Few ancient Romans, for example, would have regarded a coin bearing their emperor's portrait as anything but money. Today, an art museum may exhibit that coin in a locked case in a climate-controlled room, and scholars may subject it to the same kind of art historical analysis as a portrait by an acclaimed Renaissance or modern sculptor or painter.

The range of objects art historians study is constantly expanding and now includes, for example, computer-generated images, whereas in the past almost anything produced using a machine would not have been regarded as art. Most people still consider the performing arts—music, drama, and dance—as outside art history's realm because these arts are fleeting, impermanent media. But recently even this distinction between "fine art" and performance art has become blurred. Art historians, however, generally ask the same kinds of questions about what they study, whether they employ a restrictive or expansive definition of art.

The Questions Art Historians Ask

HOW OLD IS IT? Before art historians can construct a history of art, they must be sure they know the date of each work they study. Thus, an indispensable subject of art historical inquiry is *chronology*, the dating of art objects and buildings. If researchers cannot determine a monument's age, they cannot place the work in its historical context. Art historians have developed many ways to establish, or at least approximate, the date of an artwork.

Physical evidence often reliably indicates an object's age. The material used for a statue or painting—bronze, plastic, or oil-based pigment, to name only a few—may not have been invented before a certain time, indicating the earliest possible date someone could have fashioned the work. Or artists may have ceased using certain materials—such as specific kinds of inks and papers for drawings and prints—at a known time, providing the latest possible dates for objects made of such materials. Sometimes the material (or the manufacturing technique) of an object or a building can establish a very precise date of production or construction. Studying tree rings, for instance, usually can determine within a narrow range the date of a wood statue or a timber roof beam.

Documentary evidence also can help pinpoint the date of an object or building when a dated written document mentions the work. For example, official records may note when church officials commissioned a new altarpiece—and how much they paid to which artist.

Visual evidence, too, can play a significant role in dating an artwork. A painter might have depicted an identifiable person or a kind of hairstyle, clothing, or furniture fashionable only at a certain time. If so, the art historian can assign a more accurate date to that painting.

Stylistic evidence is also very important. The analysis of *style*—an artist's distinctive manner of producing an object, the way a work looks—is the art historian's special sphere. Unfortunately, because it is a subjective assessment, stylistic evidence is by far the most unreliable chronological criterion. Still, art historians sometimes find style a very useful tool for establishing chronology.

WHAT IS ITS STYLE? Defining artistic style is one of the key elements of art historical inquiry, although the analysis of artworks solely in terms of style no longer dominates the field the way it once did. Art historians speak of several different kinds of artistic styles.

Period style refers to the characteristic artistic manner of a specific time, usually within a distinct culture, such as "Archaic Greek" or "Late Byzantine." But many periods do not display any stylistic unity at all. How would someone define the artistic style of the opening decade of the new millennium in North America? Far too many crosscurrents exist in contemporary art for anyone to describe a period style of the early 21st century—even in a single city such as New York.

Regional style is the term art historians use to describe variations in style tied to geography. Like an object's date, its *provenance*, or place of origin, can significantly determine its character. Very often two artworks from the same place made centuries apart are more similar than contemporaneous works from two different regions. To cite one example, usually only an expert can distinguish between an Egyptian statue carved in 2500 BCE and one made in 500 BCE. But no one would mistake an Egyptian statue of 500 BCE for one of the same date made in Greece or Mexico.

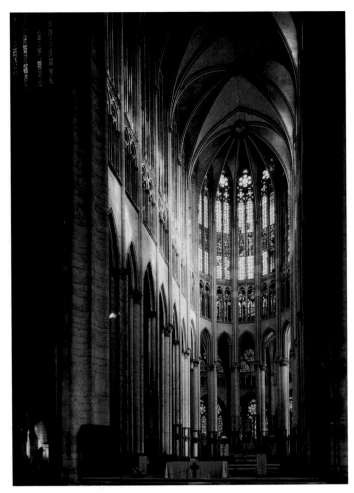

Intro-2 Choir of Beauvais Cathedral, Beauvais, France, rebuilt after 1284.

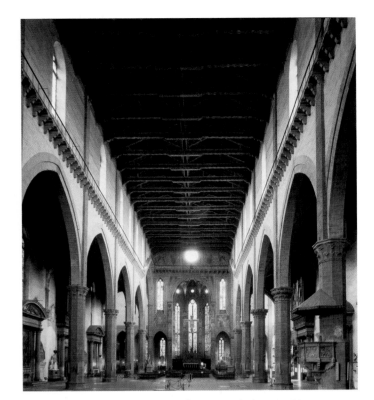

Intro-3 Interior of Santa Croce, Florence, Italy, begun 1294.

Intro-4 GEORGIA O'KEEFFE, *Jack-in-the-Pulpit No. 4*, 1930. Oil on canvas, 3′ 4″ × 2′ 6″. National Gallery of Art, Washington (Alfred Stieglitz Collection, bequest of Georgia O'Keeffe).

Considerable variations in a given area's style are possible, however, even during a single historical period. In late medieval Europe during the so-called Gothic age, French architecture differed significantly from Italian architecture. The interiors of Beauvais Cathedral (FIG. **Intro-2**) and Santa Croce in Florence (FIG. **Intro-3**) typify the architectural styles of France and Italy, respectively, at the end of the 13th century. The rebuilding of the choir of Beauvais Cathedral began in 1284. Construction commenced on Santa Croce only 10 years later. Both structures employ the characteristic Gothic pointed arch, yet they contrast strikingly. The French church has towering stone vaults and large expanses of stained-glass windows, whereas the Italian building has a low timber roof and small, widely separated windows. Because the two contemporaneous churches served similar purposes, regional style mainly explains their differing appearance.

Personal style, the distinctive manner of individual artists or architects, often decisively explains stylistic discrepancies among monuments of the same time and place. In 1930 the American painter GEORGIA O'KEEFFE produced a series of paintings of flowering plants. One of them was *Jack-in-the-Pulpit No. 4* (FIG. **Intro-4**), a sharply focused close-up view of petals and leaves. O'Keeffe captured the growing plant's slow, controlled motion while converting the plant into a powerful abstract composition of lines, forms, and colors (see the discussion of art historical vocabulary in the next section). Only a year later, another American artist, BEN SHAHN, painted *The Passion of Sacco and Vanzetti*

The different kinds of artistic styles are not mutually exclusive. For example, an artist's personal style may change dramatically during a long career. Art historians then must distinguish among the different period styles of a particular artist, such as the "Blue Period" and the "Cubist Period" of the prolific 20th-century artist Pablo Picasso.

WHAT IS ITS SUBJECT? Another major concern of art historians is, of course, subject matter, encompassing the story, or *narrative;* the scene presented; the action's time and place; the persons involved; and the environment and its details. Some artworks, such as modern abstract paintings, have no subject, not even a setting. But when artists represent people, places, or actions, viewers must identify these aspects to achieve complete understanding of the work. Art historians traditionally separate pictorial subjects into various categories, such as religious, historical, mythological, *genre* (daily life), portraiture, *landscape* (a depiction of a place), *still life* (an arrangement of inanimate objects), and their numerous subdivisions and combinations.

Iconography—literally, the "writing of images"—refers both to the *content,* or subject of an artwork, and to the study of content in art. By extension, it also includes the study of *symbols,* images that stand for other images or encapsulate ideas. In Christian art, two intersecting lines of unequal length or a simple geometric cross can serve as an emblem of the religion as a whole, symbolizing the cross of Jesus Christ's crucifixion. A symbol also can be a familiar object the artist imbued with greater meaning. A balance or scale, for example, may symbolize justice or the weighing of souls on Judgment Day (FIG. **Intro-6**).

Artists also may depict figures with unique *attributes* identifying them. In Christian art, for example, each of the authors of the New Testament Gospels, the Four Evangelists (FIG. **Intro-7**), has a

Intro-5 BEN SHAHN, *The Passion of Sacco and Vanzetti,* 1931–1932. Tempera on canvas, $7' \frac{1}{2}'' \times 4'$. Whitney Museum of American Art, New York (gift of Edith and Milton Lowenthal in memory of Juliana Force).

(FIG. **Intro-5**), a stinging commentary on social injustice inspired by the trial and execution of two Italian anarchists, Nicola Sacco and Bartolomeo Vanzetti. Many people believed Sacco and Vanzetti had been unjustly convicted of killing two men in a holdup in 1920. Shahn's painting compresses time in a symbolic representation of the trial and its aftermath. The two executed men lie in their coffins. Presiding over them are the three members of the commission (headed by a college president wearing academic cap and gown) that declared the original trial fair and cleared the way for the executions. Behind, on the wall of a columned government building, hangs the framed portrait of the judge who pronounced the initial sentence. Personal style, not period or regional style, sets Shahn's canvas apart from O'Keeffe's. The contrast is extreme here because of the very different subjects the artists chose. But even when two artists depict the same subject, the results can vary widely. The *way* O'Keeffe painted flowers and the *way* Shahn painted faces are distinctive and unlike the styles of their contemporaries. (See the "Who Made It?" discussion on page 5.)

Intro-6 GISLEBERTUS, The weighing of souls, detail of Last Judgment, west tympanum of Saint-Lazare, Autun, France, ca. 1120–1135.

Intro-7 The Four Evangelists, folio 14 verso of the *Aachen Gospels*, ca. 810. Ink and tempera on vellum, $1' \times 9\frac{1}{2}''$. Cathedral Treasury, Aachen.

Intro-8 ALBRECHT DÜRER, *The Four Horsemen of the Apocalypse*, ca. 1498. Woodcut, approx. $1' 3\frac{1}{4}'' \times 11''$. Metropolitan Museum of Art, New York (gift of Junius S. Morgan, 1919).

distinctive attribute. Saint John is known by his eagle, Luke by an ox, Mark by a lion, and Matthew by a winged man.

Throughout the history of art, artists also used *personifications*—abstract ideas codified in bodily form. Worldwide, people visualize Liberty as a robed woman with a torch because of the fame of the colossal statue set up in New York City's harbor in the 19th century. *The Four Horsemen of the Apocalypse* (FIG. **Intro-8**) is a terrifying late-15th-century depiction of the fateful day at the end of time when, according to the Bible's last book, Death, Famine, War, and Pestilence will cut down the human race. The artist, ALBRECHT DÜRER, personified Death as an emaciated old man with a pitchfork. Dürer's Famine swings the scales that will weigh human souls (compare FIG. Intro-6), War wields a sword, and Pestilence draws a bow.

Even without considering style and without knowing a work's maker, informed viewers can determine much about the work's period and provenance by iconographical and subject analysis alone. In *The Passion of Sacco and Vanzetti* (FIG. Intro-5), for example, the two coffins, the trio headed by an academic, and the robed judge in the background are all pictorial clues revealing the painting's subject. The work's date must be after the trial and execution, probably while the event was still newsworthy. And because the deaths of the two men caused the greatest outrage in the United States, the painter–social critic was probably American.

WHO MADE IT? If Ben Shahn had not signed his painting of Sacco and Vanzetti, an art historian could still assign, or *attribute*,

the work to him based on knowledge of the artist's personal style. Although signing (and dating) works is quite common (but by no means universal) today, in the history of art countless works exist whose artists remain unknown. Because personal style can play a large role in determining the character of an artwork, art historians often try to attribute anonymous works to known artists. Sometimes they attempt to assemble a group of works all thought to be by the same person, even though none of the objects in the group is the known work of an artist with a recorded name. Art historians thus reconstruct the careers of people such as "the Andokides Painter," the anonymous ancient Greek artist who painted the vases produced by the potter Andokides. Scholars base their attributions on internal evidence, such as the distinctive way an artist draws or carves drapery folds, earlobes, or flowers. It requires a keen, highly trained eye and long experience to become a *connoisseur*, an expert in assigning artworks to "the hand" of one artist rather than another. Attribution is, of course, subjective and ever open to doubt. At present, for example, international debate rages over attributions to the famous Dutch painter Rembrandt.

Sometimes a group of artists works in the same style at the same time and place. Art historians designate such a group as a *school*. "School" does not mean an educational institution. The term connotes only chronological, stylistic, and geographic similarity. Art historians speak, for example, of the Dutch school of the 17th century and, within it, of subschools such as those of the cities of Haarlem, Utrecht, and Leyden.

Intro-9 Augustus wearing the *corona civica* (civic crown), early first century CE. Marble, approx. 1′ 5″ high. Glyptothek, Munich.

WHO PAID FOR IT? The interest many art historians show in attribution reflects their conviction that the identity of an artwork's maker is the major reason the object looks the way it does. For them, personal style is of paramount importance. But in many times and places, artists had little to say about what form their work would take. They toiled in obscurity, doing the bidding of their *patrons,* those who paid them to make individual works or employed them on a continuing basis. The role of patrons in dictating the content and shaping the form of artworks is also an important subject of art historical inquiry.

In the art of portraiture, to name only one category of painting and sculpture, the patron has often played a dominant role in deciding how the artist represented the subject, whether the patron or another person, such as a spouse, son, or mother. Many Egyptian pharaohs and some Roman emperors, for example, insisted that artists depict them with unlined faces and perfect youthful bodies no matter how old they were when portrayed. In these cases, the state employed the sculptors and painters, and the artists had no choice but to depict their patrons in the officially approved manner. This is why Augustus, who lived to age 76, looks so young in his portraits (FIG. **Intro-9**). Although Roman emperor for more than 40 years, Augustus demanded that artists always represent him as a young, godlike head of state.

All modes of artistic production reveal the impact of patronage. Learned monks provided the themes for the sculptural decoration of medieval church portals (FIG. Intro-6). Renaissance princes and popes dictated the subject, size, and materials of artworks destined, sometimes, for buildings constructed according to their specifications. An art historian could make a very long list along these lines, and it would indicate that throughout the history of art, patrons have had diverse tastes and needs and demanded different kinds of art. Whenever a patron contracts an artist or architect to paint, sculpt, or build in a prescribed manner, personal style often becomes a very minor factor in how the painting, statue, or building looks. In such cases, the identity of the patron reveals more to art historians than does the identity of the artist or school. The portrait of Augustus illustrated here (FIG. Intro-9) was the work of a virtuoso sculptor, a master wielder of hammer and chisel. But scores of similar portraits of that emperor exist today. They differ in quality but not in kind from this one. The patron, not the artist, determined the character of such artworks. Augustus's public image never varied.

The Words Art Historians Use

Like all specialists, art historians have their own specialized vocabulary. That vocabulary consists of hundreds of words, but certain basic terms are indispensable for describing artworks and buildings of any time and place, and we use those terms throughout this book. They make up the essential vocabulary of *formal analysis,* the visual analysis of artistic form. We define the most important of these art historical terms here. For a much longer list, consult the Glossary in this book's end material.

FORM AND COMPOSITION *Form* refers to an object's shape and structure, either in two dimensions (for example, a figure painted on a canvas) or in three dimensions (such as a statue carved from a marble block). Two forms may take the same shape but may differ in their color, texture, and other qualities. *Composition* refers to how an artist organizes (composes) forms in an artwork, either by placing shapes on a flat surface or by arranging forms in space.

MATERIAL AND TECHNIQUE To create art forms, artists shape materials (pigment, clay, marble, gold, and many more) with tools (pens, brushes, chisels, and so forth). Each of the materials and tools available has its own potentialities and limitations. Part of all artists' creative activity is to select the medium and instrument most suitable to the artists' purpose—or to pioneer the use of new media and tools, such as bronze and concrete in antiquity and cameras and computers in modern times. The processes artists employ, such as applying paint to canvas with a brush, and the distinctive, personal ways they handle materials constitute their *technique*. Form, material, and technique interrelate and are central to analyzing any work of art.

LINE *Line* is one of the most important elements defining an artwork's shape or form. A line can be understood as the path of a point moving in space, an invisible line of sight or a visual *axis*. But, more commonly, artists and architects make a line concrete by drawing (or chiseling) it on a *plane*, a flat and two-dimensional surface. A line may be very thin, wirelike, and delicate; it may be thick and heavy; or it may alternate quickly from broad to narrow, the strokes jagged or the outline broken. When a continuous line defines an object's outer shape, art historians call it a *contour line*.

One can observe all of these line qualities in Dürer's *Four Horsemen of the Apocalypse* (FIG. Intro-8). Contour lines define the basic shapes of clouds, human and animal limbs, and weapons. Within the forms, series of short broken lines create shadows and textures. An overall pattern of long parallel strokes suggests the dark sky on the frightening day when the world is about to end.

COLOR *Light* reveals all colors. Light in the world of the painter and other artists differs from natural light. Natural light, or sunlight, is whole or *additive* light. As the sum of all the wavelengths composing the visible *spectrum*, it may be disassembled or fragmented into the individual colors of the spectral band. The painter's light in art—the light reflected from pigments and objects—is *subtractive* light. Paint pigments produce their individual colors by reflecting a segment of the spectrum while absorbing all the rest. Green pigment, for example, subtracts or absorbs all the light in the spectrum except that seen as green, which it reflects to the eyes.

Hue is the property giving a color its name. Although the spectrum colors merge into each other, artists usually conceive of their hues as distinct from one another. Color has two basic variables—the apparent amount of light reflected and the apparent purity. A change in one must produce a change in the other. Some terms for these variables are *value* or *tonality* (the degree of lightness or darkness) and *intensity* or *saturation* (the purity of a color, its brightness or dullness).

The *color triangle* (FIG. **Intro-10**) JOSEF ALBERS and SEWELL SILLMAN developed clearly shows the relationships among the six main colors. Red, yellow, and blue, the *primary colors,* are the vertexes of the large triangle. Orange, green, and purple, the *sec-*

Intro-10 JOSEF ALBERS and SEWELL SILLMAN, color triangle. Yale University Art Gallery, New Haven.

ondary colors resulting from mixing pairs of primaries, lie between them. Colors opposite each other in the spectrum—red and green, purple and yellow, and orange and blue here—are *complementary colors.* They "complement," or complete, each other, one absorbing colors the other reflects. When painters mix complementaries in the right proportions, a neutral tone or gray (theoretically, black) results.

TEXTURE *Texture* is the quality of a surface (such as rough or shiny) that light reveals. Art historians distinguish between *actual* texture, or the tactile quality of the surface, and *represented* texture, as when painters depict an object as having a certain texture, even though the pigment is the actual texture. Sometimes artists combine different materials of different textures on a single surface, juxtaposing paint with pieces of wood, newspaper, fabric, and so forth. Art historians refer to this mixed-media technique as *collage*. Texture is, of course, a key determinant of any sculpture's character. People's first impulse is usually to handle a piece of sculpture—even though museum signs often warn "Do not touch!" Sculptors plan for this natural human response, using surfaces varying in texture from rugged coarseness to polished smoothness. Textures are often intrinsic to a material, influencing the type of stone, wood, plastic, clay, or metal sculptors select.

SPACE, MASS, AND VOLUME *Space* is the bounded or boundless "container" of objects. For art historians, space can be *actual,* the three-dimensional space occupied by a statue or a vase or contained within a room or courtyard. Or it can be *illusionistic,* as when painters depict an image (or illusion) of the three-dimensional spatial world on a two-dimensional surface.

Mass and *volume* describe three-dimensional space. In both architecture and sculpture, mass is the bulk, density, and weight of matter in space. Yet the mass need not be solid. It can be the exterior form of enclosed space. "Mass" can apply to a solid Egyptian pyramid or wooden statue, to a church, synagogue, or mosque—architectural shells enclosing sometimes vast spaces—and to a hollow metal statue or baked clay pot. Volume is the space that mass organizes, divides, or encloses. It may be a building's interior spaces, the intervals between a structure's masses, or the amount of space occupied by three-dimensional objects such

Intro-11 CLAUDE LORRAIN, *Embarkation of the Queen of Sheba,* 1648. Oil on canvas, approx. 4′ 10″ × 6′ 4″. National Gallery, London.

as sculpture, pottery, or furniture. Volume and mass describe both the exterior and interior forms of a work of art—the forms of the matter of which it is composed and the spaces immediately around the work and interacting with it.

PERSPECTIVE AND FORESHORTENING *Perspective* is one of the most important pictorial devices for organizing forms in space. Throughout history, artists have used various types of perspective to create an illusion of depth or space on a two-dimensional surface. The French painter CLAUDE LORRAIN employed several perspectival devices in *Embarkation of the Queen of Sheba* (FIG. **Intro-11**), a painting of a biblical episode set in a 17th-century European harbor with a Roman ruin in the left foreground. For example, the figures and boats on the shoreline are much larger than those in the distance. Decreasing the size of an object makes it appear farther away from the viewer. Also, the top and bottom of the port building at the painting's right side are not parallel horizontal lines, as they are in an actual building. Instead, the lines converge beyond the structure, leading the viewer's eye toward the hazy, indistinct sun on the horizon. These perspectival devices—the reduction of figure size, the convergence of diagonal lines, and the blurring of distant forms—have been familiar features of Western art since the ancient Greeks. But it is important to note at the outset that all kinds of perspective

are only pictorial conventions, even when one or more types of perspective may be so common in a given culture that they are accepted as "natural" or as "true" means of representing the natural world.

In *White and Red Plum Blossoms* (FIG. **Intro-12**), a Japanese landscape painting on two folding screens, OGATA KORIN used none of these Western perspective conventions. He showed the two plum trees as seen from a position on the ground, while viewers look down on the stream between them from above. Less concerned with locating the trees and stream in space than with composing shapes on a surface, the painter played the water's gently swelling curves against the jagged contours of the branches and trunks. Neither the French nor the Japanese painting can be said to project "correctly" what viewers "in fact" see. One painting is not a "better" picture of the world than the other. The European and Asian artists simply approached the problem of picture-making differently.

Artists also represent single figures in space in varying ways. When PETER PAUL RUBENS painted *Lion Hunt* (FIG. **Intro-13**) in the early 17th century, he used *foreshortening* for all the hunters and animals—that is, he represented their bodies at angles to the picture plane. When in life one views a figure at an angle, the body appears to contract as it extends back in space. Foreshortening is a kind of perspective. It produces the illusion that one part of the

Intro-12 OGATA KORIN, *White and Red Plum Blossoms,* Edo period, ca. 1710–1716. Pair of twofold screens. Ink, color, and gold leaf on paper, each screen 5′ 1⅝″ × 5′ 7⅞″. MOA Art Museum, Shizuoka-ken.

body is farther away than another, even though all the forms are on the same surface. Especially noteworthy in *Lion Hunt* are the gray horse at the left, seen from behind with the bottom of its left rear hoof facing viewers and most of its head hidden by its rider's shield, and the fallen hunter at the painting's lower right corner, whose barely visible legs and feet recede into the distance.

The artist who carved the portrait of the ancient Egyptian official Hesire (FIG. **Intro-14**) did not employ foreshortening. That artist's purpose was to present the various human body parts as clearly as possible, without overlapping. The lower part of Hesire's body is in profile to give the most complete view of the legs, with both the heels and toes of the foot visible. The frontal torso, however, allows the viewer to see its full shape, including both shoulders, equal in size, as in nature. (Compare the shoulders of the

hunter on the gray horse or those of the fallen hunter in *Lion Hunt*'s left foreground.) The result, an "unnatural" 90-degree twist at the waist, provides a precise picture of human body parts. Rubens and the Egyptian sculptor used very different means of depicting forms in space. Once again, neither is the "correct" manner.

PROPORTION AND SCALE *Proportion* concerns the relationships (in terms of size) of the parts of persons, buildings, or objects. "Correct proportions" may be judged intuitively ("that statue's head seems the right size for the body"). Or proportion may be formalized as a mathematical relationship between the size of one part of an artwork or building and the other parts within the work. Proportion in art implies using a *module,* or basic unit of measure. When an artist or architect uses a formal

Intro-13 PETER PAUL RUBENS, *Lion Hunt,* 1617–1618. Oil on canvas, approx. 8′ 2″ × 12′ 5″. Alte Pinakothek, Munich.

Intro-14 Hesire, from his tomb at Saqqara, Egypt, Dynasty III, ca. 2650 BCE. Wood, approx. 3′ 9″ high. Egyptian Museum, Cairo.

system of proportions, all parts of a building, body, or other entity will be fractions or multiples of the module. A module might be a column's diameter, the height of a human head, or any other component whose dimensions can be multiplied or divided to determine the size of the work's other parts.

In certain times and places, artists have formulated *canons,* or systems, of "correct" or "ideal" proportions for representing human figures, constituent parts of buildings, and so forth. In ancient Greece, many sculptors formulated canons of proportions so strict and all-encompassing that they calculated the size of every body part in advance, even the fingers and toes, according to mathematical ratios. The ideal of human beauty the Greeks created based on "correct" proportions influenced the work of countless later artists in the Western world (for example, FIG. **Intro-15**) and endures to this day. Proportional systems can differ sharply from period to period, culture to culture, and artist to artist. Part of the task art history students face is to perceive and adjust to these differences.

Intro-15 MICHELANGELO, unfinished captive, 1527–1528. Marble, 8′ 7½″ high. Accademia, Florence.

In fact, many artists have used *disproportion* and distortion deliberately for expressive effect. In the medieval French depiction of the weighing of souls on Judgment Day (FIG. Intro-6), the devilish figure yanking down on the scale has distorted facial features and stretched, lined limbs with animal-like paws for feet. Disproportion and distortion make him appear "inhuman," precisely as the sculptor intended.

In other cases, artists have used disproportion to focus attention on one body part (often the head) or to single out a group member (usually the leader). These intentional "unnatural" discrepancies in proportion constitute what art historians call *hierarchy of scale,* the enlarging of elements considered the most important. On a bronze plaque from Benin, Nigeria (FIG. **Intro-16**), the sculptor enlarged all the heads for emphasis and also varied the size of each figure according to its social status. Central, largest, and therefore most important is the Benin king, mounted on horseback. The horse has been a symbol of power and wealth in many societies from prehistory to the present. That the Benin king is disproportionately larger than his horse, contrary to nature, further aggrandizes him. Two large attendants fan the king. Other figures of smaller size and lower status at the Benin court stand on the king's left and right and in the plaque's upper corners. One tiny figure next to the horse is almost hidden from view beneath the king's feet.

CARVING AND CASTING Sculptural technique falls into two basic categories, *subtractive* and *additive. Carving* is a subtractive technique. The final form is a reduction of the original mass of a

Intro-16 King on horseback with attendants, from Benin, Nigeria, ca. 1550–1680. Bronze, 1′ 7½″ high. Metropolitan Museum of Art, New York (Michael C. Rockefeller Memorial Collection, gift of Nelson A. Rockefeller).

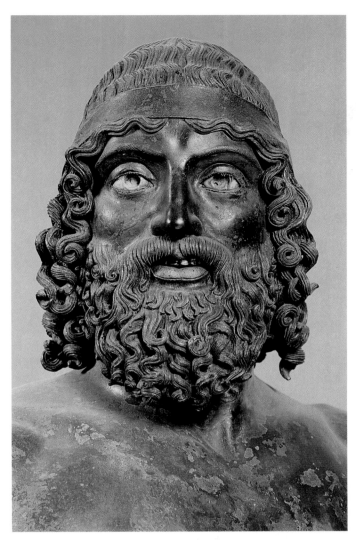

Intro-17 Head of a warrior, detail of a statue from the sea off Riace, Italy, ca. 460–450 BCE. Bronze, statue approx. 6′ 6″ high. Archaeological Museum, Reggio Calabria.

block of stone, a piece of wood, or another material. Wooden statues were once tree trunks, and stone statues began as blocks pried from mountains. In an unfinished 16th-century marble statue of a bound slave (FIG. Intro-15) by MICHELANGELO, the original shape of the stone block is still visible. Michelangelo thought of sculpture as a process of "liberating" the statue within the block. All sculptors of stone or wood cut away (subtract) "excess material." When they finish, they "leave behind" the statue—in our example, a twisting nude male form whose head Michelangelo never freed from the stone block.

In additive sculpture, the artist builds up the forms, usually in clay around a framework, or *armature*. Or a sculptor may fashion a *mold*, a hollow form for shaping, or *casting*, a fluid substance such as bronze. The ancient Greek sculptor who made the bronze statue of a warrior found in the sea near Riace, Italy, cast the head (FIG. **Intro-17**), limbs, torso, hands, and feet in separate molds and then *welded* them (joined them by heating). Finally, the artist added features, such as the pupils of the eyes (now missing), in other materials. The warrior's teeth are silver, and his lower lip is copper.

RELIEF SCULPTURE Statues or busts that exist independent of any architectural frame or setting and that viewers can walk around are *freestanding sculptures*, or *sculptures in the round*, whether the piece was carved (FIG. Intro-9) or cast (FIG. Intro-17). In *relief sculptures*, the subjects project from the background but remain part of it. In *high relief* sculpture, the images project boldly. In some cases, such as the weighing-of-souls relief at Autun (FIG. Intro-6), the relief is so high that not only do the forms

cast shadows on the background, but some parts are actually in the round. The arms of the scale are fully detached from the background in places—which explains why some pieces broke off centuries ago. In *low relief*, or *bas-relief*, such as the wooden relief of Hesire (FIG. Intro-14), the projection is slight. In a variation of both techniques, *sunken relief*, the sculptor cuts the design into the surface so that the image's highest projecting parts are no higher than the surface itself. Relief sculpture, like sculpture in the round, can be produced either by carving or casting. The plaque from Benin (FIG. Intro-16) is an example of bronze casting in high relief. Artists also can make reliefs by hammering a sheet of metal from behind, pushing the subject out from the background in a technique called *repoussé*.

ARCHITECTURAL DRAWINGS Buildings are groupings of enclosed spaces and enclosing masses. People experience architecture both visually and by moving through and around it, so they perceive architectural space and mass together. These spaces and masses can be represented graphically in several ways, including as plans, sections, elevations, and cutaway drawings.

A *plan*, essentially a map of a floor, shows the placement of a structure's masses and, therefore, the spaces they bound and

Intro-18 Plan *(left)* and lateral section *(right)* of Beauvais Cathedral, Beauvais, France, rebuilt after 1284.

enclose. A *section*, like a vertical plan, depicts the placement of the masses as if the building were cut through along a plane. Drawings showing a theoretical slice across a structure's width are *lateral sections.* Those cutting through a building's length are *longitudinal sections.* Illustrated here are the plan and lateral section of Beauvais Cathedral (FIG. **Intro-18**), which may be compared to the photograph of the church's choir (FIG. Intro-2). The plan shows not only the choir's shape and the location of the piers dividing the aisles and supporting the *vaults* above but also the pattern of the crisscrossing vault *ribs.* The lateral section shows not only the interior of the choir with its vaults and tall stained-glass windows but also the structure of the roof and the form of the exterior *buttresses* that hold the vaults in place.

Other types of architectural drawings appear throughout this book. An *elevation* drawing is a head-on view of an external or internal wall. A *cutaway* combines an exterior view with an interior view of part of a building in a single drawing.

This overview of the art historian's vocabulary is not exhaustive, nor have artists used only painting, drawing, sculpture, and architecture as media over the millennia. Ceramics, jewelry, textiles, photography, and computer art are just some of the numerous other arts. All of them involve highly specialized techniques described in distinct vocabularies. These are considered and defined where they arise in the text.

Art History and Other Disciplines

By its very nature, the work of art historians intersects with that of others in many fields of knowledge, not only in the humanities but also in the social and natural sciences. To "do their job" well

today, art historians regularly must go beyond the boundaries of what the public and even professional art historians of previous generations traditionally have considered the specialized discipline of art history. Art historical research in the 21st century is frequently *interdisciplinary* in nature. To cite one example, in an effort to unlock the secrets of a particular statue, an art historian might conduct archival research hoping to uncover new documents shedding light on who paid for the work and why, who made it and when, where it originally stood, how its contemporaries viewed it, and a host of other questions. Realizing, however, that the authors of the written documents often were not objective recorders of fact but observers with their own biases and agendas, the art historian may also use methodologies developed in such fields as literary criticism, philosophy, sociology, and gender studies to weigh the evidence the documents provide.

At other times, rather than attempting to master many disciplines at once, art historians band together with other specialists in *multidisciplinary* inquiries. Art historians might call in chemists to date an artwork based on the composition of the materials used or might ask geologists to determine which quarry furnished the stone for a particular statue. X-ray technicians might be enlisted in an attempt to establish whether or not a painting is a forgery. Of course, art historians often contribute their expertise to the solution of problems in other disciplines. A historian, for example, might ask an art historian to determine—based on style, material, iconography, and other criteria—if any of the portraits of a certain king were made after his death. That would help establish the ruler's continuing prestige during the reigns of his successors. (Some portraits of Augustus, FIG. Intro-9, the founder of the Roman Empire, postdate his death by decades, even centuries.)

Intro-19 John Sylvester *(left)* and Te Pehi Kupe *(right),* portraits of Maori chief Te Pehi Kupe, 1826. From *The Childhood of Man,* by Leo Frobenius (New York: J. B. Lippincott, 1909).

DIFFERENT WAYS OF SEEING

The history of art can be a history of artists and their works, of styles and stylistic change, of materials and techniques, of images and themes and their meanings, and of contexts and cultures and patrons. The best art historians analyze artworks from many viewpoints. But no art historian (or scholar in any other field), no matter how broad-minded in approach and no matter how experienced, can be truly objective. Like artists, art historians are members of a society, participants in its culture. How can scholars (and museum visitors and travelers to foreign locales) comprehend cultures unlike their own? They can try to reconstruct the original cultural contexts of artworks, but they are bound to be limited by their distance from the thought patterns of the cultures they study and by the obstructions to understanding — the assumptions, presuppositions, and prejudices peculiar to their own culture — their own thought patterns raise. Art historians may reconstruct a distorted picture of the past because of culture-bound blindness.

A single instance underscores how differently people of diverse cultures view the world and how various ways of seeing can cause sharp differences in how artists depict the world. We illustrate two contemporaneous portraits of a 19th-century Maori chieftain side by side (FIG. **Intro-19**) — one by an Englishman, JOHN SYLVESTER, and the other by the New Zealand chieftain himself, TE PEHI KUPE. Both reproduce the chieftain's facial tattooing. The European artist included the head and shoulders and underplayed the tattooing. The tattoo pattern is one aspect of the likeness among many, no more or less important than the chieftain's dressing like a European. Sylvester also recorded his subject's momentary glance toward the right and the play of light on his hair, fleeting aspects that have nothing to do with the figure's identity.

In contrast, Te Pehi Kupe's self-portrait — made during a trip to Liverpool, England, to obtain European arms to take back to New Zealand — is not a picture of a man situated in space and bathed in light. Rather, it is the chieftain's statement of the supreme importance of the tattoo design that symbolizes his rank among his people. Remarkably, Te Pehi Kupe created the tattoo patterns from memory, without the aid of a mirror. The splendidly composed insignia, presented as a flat design separated from the body and even from the head, is Te Pehi Kupe's image of himself. Only by understanding the cultural context of each portrait can viewers hope to understand why either looks the way it does.

As noted at the outset, the study of the context of artworks and buildings is one of the central aims of art history. Our purpose in writing *Art through the Ages* is to present a history of art and architecture that will help you understand not only the subjects, styles, and techniques of paintings, sculptures, buildings, and other art forms created in all parts of the world for 30 millennia but also their cultural and historical contexts. That story now begins.

Bison, detail of a painted ceiling in the Altamira cave, Santander, Spain, ca. 12,000–11,000 BCE. Each bison approx. 5′ long.

1

THE BIRTH OF ART

AFRICA, EUROPE, AND THE NEAR EAST IN THE STONE AGE

Humankind seems to have originated in Africa in the very remote past. From that great continent also comes the earliest evidence of human recognition of abstract images in the natural environment, if not the first examples of what people generally call "art." In 1925, explorers of a cave at Makapansgat in South Africa (see MAP 15-1) discovered bones of *Australopithecus,* a predecessor of modern humans who lived some three million years ago. Associated with the bones was a waterworn reddish brown jasperite pebble (FIG. **1-1**) that bears an uncanny resemblance to a human face. The nearest known source of this variety of ironstone is 20 miles away from the cave. One of the early humans who took refuge in the rock shelter at Makapansgat must have noticed the pebble in a streambed and, awestruck by the "face" on the stone, brought it back for safekeeping.

Is the Makapansgat pebble art? In modern times, many artists have created works people universally consider art by removing objects from their normal contexts, altering them, and then labeling them. In 1917, for example, Marcel Duchamp took a ceramic urinal, set it on its side, called it *Fountain* (see FIG. 33-23), and declared his "ready-made" worthy of exhibition among more conventional artworks. But the artistic environment of the past century cannot be projected into the remote past. For art historians to declare a found object such as the Makapansgat pebble an "artwork," it must have been modified by human intervention beyond mere selection—and it was not. In fact, evidence indicates that, with few exceptions, it was not until three million years later, around 30,000 BCE, that humans *intentionally manufactured* sculptures and paintings. That is when the story of art through the ages really begins.

PALEOLITHIC ART

The several millennia following 30,000 BCE saw a powerful outburst of creativity. The works produced by the peoples of the Old Stone Age or *Paleolithic* period (from the Greek *paleo,* old, and *lithos,* stone) are of an astonishing variety. They range from

MAP 1-1 Prehistoric Europe and the Near East.

simple shell necklaces to human and animal forms in ivory, clay, and stone to monumental paintings, engravings, and relief sculptures covering the huge wall surfaces of caves. During the Paleolithic period, humankind went beyond the *recognition* of human and animal forms in the natural environment to the *representation* (literally, the presenting again—in different and substitute form—of something observed) of humans and animals. The immensity of this achievement cannot be exaggerated.

Africa

NAMIBIAN ANIMALS Some of the earliest paintings yet discovered come from Africa, and, like the treasured pebble in the form of a face found at Makapansgat, the oldest African paintings were portable objects. Between 1969 and 1972, scientists working in the Apollo 11 Cave in Namibia (see MAP 15-1) found seven fragments of stone plaques with paint on them, including four or five recognizable images of animals. In most cases, including the example we illustrate (FIG. **1-2**), the species is uncertain, but the forms are always carefully rendered. One plaque depicts a striped beast, possibly a zebra. The charcoal from the archaeological layer in which the Namibian plaques were found has been dated to around 23,000 BCE.

Like every artist in every age in every medium, the painter of the Apollo 11 plaque had to answer two questions before beginning work: *What* shall be my subject? *How* shall I represent it? In Paleolithic art, the almost universal answer to the first question was an animal—bison, mammoth, ibex, and horse were most common. In fact, Paleolithic painters and sculptors depicted humans infrequently and men almost never. In equally stark contrast to today's world, there was also agreement on the best answer to the second question. Virtually every animal in every Paleolithic, *Mesolithic* (Middle Stone Age), and *Neolithic* (New Stone Age) painting was presented in the same manner—in strict profile. The profile is the only view of an animal wherein the head, body, tail, and all four legs can be seen. A frontal view would have concealed most of the body,

1-1 Waterworn pebble resembling a human face, from Makapansgat, South Africa, ca. 3,000,000 BCE. Reddish brown jasperite, approx. $2\frac{3}{8}''$ wide.

1-2 Animal facing left, from the Apollo 11 Cave, Namibia, ca. 23,000 BCE. Charcoal on stone, approx. 5″ × 4¼″. State Museum of Namibia, Windhoek.

and a three-quarter view would not have shown either the front or side fully. Only the profile view is completely informative about the animal's shape, and this is why the Stone Age painter always chose it. A very long time passed before artists placed any premium on "variety" or "originality," either in subject choice or in representational manner. These are quite modern notions in the history of art. The aim of the earliest painters was to create a convincing image of the subject, a kind of pictorial definition of the animal capturing its very essence, and only the profile view met their needs.

Western Europe

EUROPE'S FIRST SCULPTURES Even older than the Namibian painted plaques are some of the first sculptures and paintings of western Europe (MAP 1-1), although examples of still greater antiquity may yet be found in Africa, bridging the gap between the Makapansgat pebble and the Apollo 11 painted plaques. One of the earliest sculptures discovered to date is an extraordinary ivory statuette (FIG. 1-3), which may be as old as 30,000 BCE, from a cave at Hohlenstein-Stadel in Germany. Carved out of mammoth ivory and nearly a foot tall—a truly huge image for its era—the statuette represents something that existed only in the vivid imagination of the unknown sculptor who conceived it. It is a human (whether male or female is debated) with a feline head.

Such composite creatures with animal heads and human bodies (and vice versa) were common in the art of the ancient Near East and Egypt (compare, for example, FIGS. 2-10 and 3-39). In those civilizations, surviving texts usually allow historians to name the figures and describe their role in contemporary religion and mythology. But for Stone Age representations, no one knows what their makers had in mind. The animal-headed humans of Paleolithic art sometimes have been called sorcerers and described as magicians wearing masks. Similarly, Paleolithic human-headed animals have been interpreted as humans dressed up as animals. In the absence of any Stone Age written explanations—this is a time before writing, before (or pre-) history—researchers can only speculate on the purpose and function of a statuette such as that from Hohlenstein-Stadel.

Art historians are certain, however, that such statuettes were important to those who created them, because manufacturing an ivory figure, especially one a foot tall, was a complicated process. First, a tusk had to be removed from the dead animal by cutting into the ivory where it joined the head. The sculptor then cut the tusk to the desired size and rubbed it into its approximate final shape with sandstone. Finally, a sharp stone blade was used to carve the body, limbs, and head, and a stone *burin* (a pointed engraving tool) to *incise* (scratch) lines into the surfaces, as on the Hohlenstein-Stadel creature's arms. All this probably required at least several days of skilled work.

WOMEN IN PALEOLITHIC ART The composite feline-human from Germany is exceptional for the Stone Age. The vast majority of prehistoric sculptures depict either animals or humans. In the earliest art, humankind consists almost exclusively of women as opposed to men, and the painters and sculptors almost invariably showed them nude, although scholars generally assume that in life both women and men wore garments covering parts of their bodies. When archaeologists first discovered Paleolithic statuettes of women, they dubbed them "Venuses," after the Greco-Roman goddess of beauty and love, whom artists usually depicted nude (see FIG. 5-60). The nickname is inappropriate and misleading. Not only does no evidence exist for named gods and goddesses in human form during the Old Stone Age, but also it is doubtful these figurines represented deities of any kind.

One of the oldest and the most famous of the prehistoric female figures is the tiny (only slightly more than four inches tall) limestone figurine of a woman that long has been known as the

1-3 Human with feline head, from Hohlenstein-Stadel, Germany, ca. 30,000–28,000 BCE. Mammoth ivory, 11⅝″ high. Ulmer Museum, Ulm.

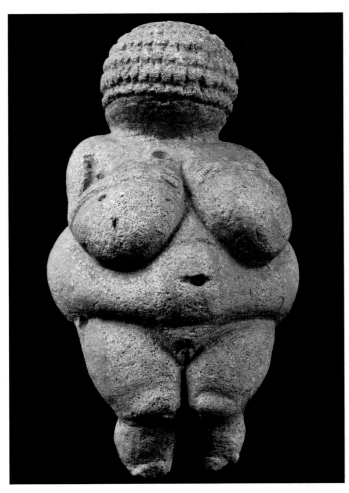

1-4 Nude woman *(Venus of Willendorf),* from Willendorf, Austria, ca. 28,000–25,000 BCE. Limestone, approx. $4\frac{1}{4}''$ high. Naturhistorisches Museum, Vienna.

Venus of Willendorf (FIG. **1-4**) after its findspot in Austria. Its cluster of almost ball-like shapes is unusual, the result in part of the sculptor's response to the natural shape of the stone selected for carving. The anatomical exaggeration has suggested to many that this and similar statuettes served as fertility images. But other Paleolithic stone women of far more slender proportions exist, and the meaning of these images is as elusive as everything else about Paleolithic art. Yet the preponderance of female over male figures in the Old Stone Age seems to indicate a preoccupation with women, whose childbearing capabilities ensured the survival of the species.

One thing at least is clear. The *Venus of Willendorf* sculptor did not aim for naturalism in shape and proportion. As with most Paleolithic figures, the sculptor did not carve any facial features. Here the carver suggested only a mass of curly hair or, as some researchers have recently argued, a hat woven from plant fibers—evidence for the art of textile manufacture at a very early date. In either case, the emphasis is on female fertility. The breasts of the Willendorf woman are enormous, far larger than the tiny forearms and hands that rest upon them. The carver also took pains to scratch into the stone the outline of the pubic triangle. Sculptors often omitted this detail in other early figurines, leading some scholars to question the nature of these figures as fertility images. Whatever the purpose of such statuettes, the makers' intent seems to have been to represent not a specific woman but the female form.

THE LAUSSEL SHELTER Because precision in dating is impossible for the Paleolithic era, art historians usually can be no more specific than assigning a range of several thousand years to each artifact. But probably later in date than the *Venus of Willendorf* is another female figure (FIG. **1-5**), from Laussel in France. The Willendorf and Hohlenstein-Stadel figures were sculpted in the round (that is, they are freestanding objects). The Laussel woman is one of the earliest relief sculptures known. The sculptor employed a stone chisel to cut into the relatively flat surface of a large rock and create an image that projects from its background.

Today the Laussel relief is exhibited in a museum, divorced from its original context, a detached piece of what once was a much more imposing monument. When the relief was discovered, the Laussel woman (who is about $1\frac{1}{2}$ feet tall, much larger than the Willendorf statuette) was part of a great stone block that measured about 140 cubic feet. The carved block stood in the open air in front of a Paleolithic rock shelter. Such shelters were a common type of dwelling for early humans, along with huts and the mouths of caves. The Laussel relief is one of many examples of open-air art in the Old Stone Age. The popular notions that early humans dwelled exclusively in caves and that all Paleolithic art comes from mysterious dark caverns are false.

After chiseling out the female form and etching the details with a sharp burin, the Laussel sculptor applied red ocher to the body. (The same color is also preserved on parts of the *Venus of Willendorf.*) Contrary to modern misconceptions about ancient art, stone sculptures were frequently painted in antiquity, not only in prehistoric times and in the ancient Near East and Egypt

1-5 Woman holding a bison horn, from Laussel, Dordogne, France, ca. 25,000–20,000 BCE. Painted limestone, approx. 1' 6" high. Musée d'Aquitaine, Bordeaux.

1-6 Reclining woman, rock-cut relief, La Magdelaine cave, Tarn, France, ca. 12,000 BCE. Approx. half life-size.

but in the Greco-Roman era as well. The Laussel woman has the same bulbous forms as the earlier Willendorf figurine, with a similar exaggeration of the breasts, abdomen, and hips. The head is once again featureless, but the arms have taken on greater importance. The left arm draws attention to the midsection and pubic area, and the raised right hand holds a bison horn. The meaning of the horn is debated.

ROCK-CUT WOMEN At La Magdelaine in France, archaeologists have discovered relief sculptures of nude women on cave walls. The rock-cut reliefs are about half life-size. The example we illustrate (FIG. **1-6**) is typical of many Paleolithic reliefs in that the sculptor used the natural contours of the stone wall as the basis for the representation. Old Stone Age painters and sculptors frequently and skillfully used the caves' naturally irregular surfaces—the projections, recessions, fissures, and ridges—to help give the illusion of real presence to their forms. Once

an appropriate rock formation was selected, the sculptor then accentuated the outlines and added internal details to the figure with a stone chisel. The La Magdelaine woman reclines with extended arms and her left leg crossed over her right one. She lacks a head, but the sculptor carefully delineated her large breasts and pubic triangle.

CLAY BISON Other Paleolithic sculptors created reliefs by building up forms out of clay rather than by cutting into stone blocks or stone walls. Sometime 12,000 to 17,000 years ago in the low-ceilinged circular space at the end of a succession of cave chambers at Le Tuc d'Audoubert, a master sculptor modeled a pair of bison in clay against a large, irregular freestanding rock (FIG. **1-7**). The two bison, like the much older painted animal from the Apollo 11 Cave in Namibia (FIG. 1-2), are in strict profile. Each is about two feet long. They are among the largest Paleolithic sculptures known. The sculptor brought the clay from

1-7 Two bison, reliefs in cave at Le Tuc d'Audoubert, Ariège, France, ca. 15,000–10,000 BCE. Clay, each approx. 2′ long.

1-8 Bison with turned head, fragmentary spearthrower, from La Madeleine, Dordogne, France, ca. 12,000 BCE. Reindeer horn, approx. 4″ long. Réunion des Musées Nationaux.

another chamber in the cave complex and modeled it by hand into the overall shape of the animals. The artist then smoothed the surfaces with a spatula-like tool and finally used fingers to shape the eyes, nostrils, mouths, and manes. The cracks in the two animals resulted from the drying process and probably appeared within days of the sculptures' completion.

ANTLER SCULPTURE As already noted, sculptors fashioned ivory mammoth tusks into human and animal forms from very early times (FIG. 1-3). Prehistoric carvers also used antlers as a sculptural medium, even though it meant they were forced to work on a very small scale. Our example (FIG. **1-8**), found at La Madeleine in France, is a broken spearthrower in the form of a bison. It is only four inches long and was carved from reindeer antler. The sculptor incised lines into the bison's mane using a sharp burin. Compared to the bison in the cave at Le Tuc d'Audoubert (FIG. 1-7), the engraving is much more detailed and extends to the horns, eye, ear, nostrils, mouth, and the hair on the face. Especially interesting is the engraver's decision to represent the bison with the head turned. The small size of the reindeer horn may have been the motivation for this space-saving device. Whatever the reason, it is noteworthy that the sculptor turned the neck a full 180 degrees to maintain the strict profile Paleolithic sculptors and painters insisted on for the sake of clarity and completeness.

THE DISCOVERY OF ALTAMIRA The works examined here thus far, whether portable or fixed to rocky outcroppings or cave walls, are all small. They are dwarfed by the "herds" of painted animals that roam the cave walls of southern France and northern Spain, where some of the most spectacular prehistoric art has been discovered. The first examples of cave paintings were found accidentally by an amateur archaeologist in 1879 at Altamira, Spain. Don Marcelino Sanz de Sautuola was exploring on his estate a cave where he had already found specimens of flint and carved bone. His little daughter Maria was with him when they reached a chamber some 85 feet from the cave's entrance. Because it was dark and the ceiling of the debris-filled cavern was only a few inches above the father's head, the child was the first to discern, from her lower vantage point, the shadowy forms of painted beasts on the cave roof (FIG. **1-9**, a detail of a much larger painting approximately 60 feet long).

Sanz de Sautuola was certain the bison painted on the Altamira ceiling dated back to prehistoric times. Professional

1-9 Bison, detail of a painted ceiling in the Altamira cave, Santander, Spain, ca. 12,000–11,000 BCE. Each bison approx. 5′ long.

archaeologists, however, doubted the authenticity of these works, and at the Lisbon Congress on Prehistoric Archaeology in 1880, they officially dismissed the paintings as forgeries. But by the close of the century, other caves had been discovered with painted walls partially covered by mineral deposits that would have taken thousands of years to accumulate. Skeptics were finally persuaded that the first paintings were of an age far more remote than they had ever dreamed. Examples of Paleolithic painting now have been found at more than 200 sites (see "Paleolithic Cave Painting," page 21). Prehistorians still regard painted caves as rare occurrences, though, because the images in them, even if they number in the hundreds, were created over a period of some 10,000 to 20,000 years.

"FLOATING" BISON The bison at Altamira are 13,000 to 14,000 years old, but the painters of Paleolithic Spain approached the problem of representing an animal in essentially the same way as the painter of the stone plaque from Namibia (FIG. 1-2), who worked in Africa more than 10,000 years earlier. Every one of the Altamira bison is in profile, whether alive and standing or curled up on the ground (probably dead, although this is disputed). To maintain the profile in the latter case, the painter had to adopt a viewpoint above the animal, looking down, rather than the view a person standing on the ground would have.

Modern critics often refer to the Altamira animals as a *group* of bison, but that is very likely a misnomer. The several bison in our illustration do not stand on a common *ground line* (a painted or carved baseline on which figures appear to stand in paintings and reliefs), nor do they share a common orientation. They seem

Paleolithic Cave Painting

The caves of Altamira (FIG. 1-9), Lascaux (FIGS. 1-11 and 1-13), and other sites in prehistoric Europe had served as underground water channels, a few hundred to several thousand feet long. They are often choked, sometimes almost impassably, by deposits, such as stalactites and stalagmites. Far inside these caverns, well removed from the cave mouths early humans sometimes chose for habitation, painters made pictures on the walls. For light, they used stone lamps filled with marrow or fat, perhaps with a wick of moss. For drawing, they used chunks of red and yellow ocher. For painting, they ground these same ochers into powders they mixed with water before applying. Recent analyses of the pigments used show that Paleolithic painters used many different minerals, attesting to a technical sophistication surprising at so early a date.

Large flat stones served as palettes. The painters made brushes from reeds, bristles, or twigs, and may have used a blowpipe of reeds or hollow bones to spray pigments on out-of-reach surfaces. Some caves have natural ledges on the rock walls upon which the painters could have stood in order to reach the upper surfaces of the naturally formed "rooms" and corridors. One Lascaux gallery has holes in one of the walls that once probably anchored a scaffold made of saplings lashed together.

Despite the difficulty of making the tools and pigments, modern attempts at replicating the techniques of Paleolithic painting have demonstrated that skilled workers could cover large surfaces with images in less than a day.

almost to float above viewers' heads, like clouds in the sky. And the dead(?) bison are seen in an "aerial view," while the others are seen from a position on the ground. The painting has no setting, no background, no indication of place. The Paleolithic painter was not at all concerned with *where* the animals were or with how they related to one another, if at all. Instead, several *separate* images of a bison adorn the ceiling, perhaps painted at different times, and each is as complete and informative as possible — even if their meaning remains a mystery (see "Art in the Old Stone Age," page 22).

SIGNS AND HANDS That the paintings did have meaning to the Paleolithic peoples who made and observed them cannot, however, be doubted. In fact, signs consisting of checks, dots, squares, or other arrangements of lines often accompany the pictures of animals. Several observers have seen a primitive writing form in these representations of nonliving things. Representations of human hands also are common. At Pech-Merle (FIG. **1-10**) in France, painted hands accompany representations of spotted horses. These and the majority of painted hands at other sites are "negative," that is, the painter placed one hand against the wall and then brushed

or blew or spat pigment around it. Occasionally, the painter dipped a hand in the pigment and then pressed it against the wall, leaving a "positive" imprint. These handprints, too, must have had a purpose. Some scholars have considered them "signatures" of cult or community members or, less likely, of individual painters. But like everything else in Paleolithic art, their meaning is unknown.

The *mural* (wall) paintings at Pech-Merle also allow some insight into the reason certain subjects may have been chosen for a specific location. One of the horses (at the right in our illustration) may have been inspired by the rock formation in the wall surface resembling a horse's head and neck. Like the reclining woman at La Magdelaine (FIG. 1-6), the Pech-Merle representations may have been created after someone noticed a resemblance between a chance configuration in nature and an animal or person. The perceived forms were then "finished" by accentuating the outlines with stone tools, as at La Magdelaine, or by the addition of color, as at Pech-Merle. Prehistorians also have observed that nearly all horses and hands are painted on concave surfaces, whereas bison and cattle appear almost exclusively on convex surfaces. What this signifies has yet to be determined.

1-10 Spotted horses and negative hand imprints, wall painting in the cave at Pech-Merle, Lot, France, ca. 22,000 BCE. Approx. 11′ 2″ long.

Art in the Old Stone Age

From the moment in 1879 that cave paintings were discovered at Altamira (FIG. 1-9), scholars have wondered why the hunters of the Old Stone Age decided to cover the walls of dark caverns with animal images. Various theories have been proposed, including that the painted and engraved animals were mere decoration, but this explanation cannot account for the narrow range of subjects or the inaccessibility of many of the representations. In fact, the remoteness and difficulty of access of many of the images, and indications that the caves were used for centuries, are precisely why many scholars have suggested that the prehistoric hunters attributed magical properties to the images they painted and sculpted. According to this argument, by confining animals to the surfaces of their cave walls, the Paleolithic hunters believed they were bringing the beasts under their control. Some have even hypothesized that rituals or dances were performed in front of the images and that these rites served to improve the hunters' luck. Still others have stated that the animal representations may have served as teaching tools to instruct new hunters about the character of the various species they would encounter or even to serve as targets for spears!

In contrast, some scholars have argued that the magical purpose of the paintings and reliefs was not to facilitate the *destruction* of bison and other species. Instead, they believe prehistoric painters and sculptors created animal images to assure the *survival* of the herds on which Paleolithic peoples depended for their food supply and for their clothing.

A central problem for both the hunting-magic and food-creation theories is that the animals that seem to have been diet staples of Old Stone Age peoples are not those most frequently portrayed. At Altamira, for example, faunal remains show that red deer, not bison, were eaten.

Other scholars have sought to reconstruct an elaborate mythology based on the cave paintings and sculptures, suggesting that Paleolithic humans believed they had animal ancestors. Still others have equated certain species with men and others with women and postulated various meanings for the abstract signs that sometimes accompany the images. Almost all of these theories have been discredited over time, and most prehistorians admit that no one knows the intent of these representations. In fact, a single explanation for all Paleolithic animal images, even ones similar in subject, style, and composition (how the motifs are arranged on the surface), is unlikely to apply universally. The works remain an enigma—and always will, because before the invention of writing, no contemporary explanations could be recorded.

THE BULLS OF LASCAUX Perhaps the best-known Paleolithic cave is that at Lascaux, near Montignac, France. It is extensively decorated, but most of the paintings are hundreds of feet from any entrance. The most magnificent is a large circular gallery, characteristically far removed from the daylight, called the Hall of the Bulls (FIG. **1-11**). Not all of the painted animals are bulls, despite the modern nickname, and the several species depicted vary in size. Many are represented using colored silhouettes, as in the cave at Altamira (FIG. 1-9) and on the Namibian plaque (FIG. 1-2). Others—such as the great bull at the right in our illustration—were created by outline alone, as were the Pech-Merle horses (FIG. 1-10). On the walls of the Lascaux cave one sees, side by side, the two basic approaches to drawing and painting found repeatedly in the history of art. These differences in style and

1-11 Hall of the Bulls (left wall), Lascaux, Dordogne, France, ca. 15,000–13,000 BCE. Largest bull approx. 11′ 6″ long.

The World's Oldest Paintings?

One of the most spectacular archaeological finds of the past century came to light in December 1994 at Vallon-Pont-d'Arc, France, and was announced at a dramatic press conference in Paris on January 18, 1995. The next day, people around the world were startled when they picked up their morning newspapers or turned on their televisions and saw a sampling of pictures of extraordinary Paleolithic cave paintings. Unlike some other recent "finds" of prehistoric art that proved to be forgeries, the paintings in the Chauvet Cave (named after the leader of the exploration team, Jean-Marie Chauvet) seemed to be authentic. But no one, including Chauvet and his colleagues, guessed at the time of their discovery that *radiocarbon dating* (a measure of the rate of degeneration of carbon 14 in organic materials) of the paintings might establish that the murals in the cave were more than 15,000 years older than those at Altamira (FIG. 1-9). When the scientific tests were completed, the French archaeologists announced that the Chauvet Cave paintings were the oldest yet found anywhere, datable around 30,000–28,000 BCE. Such an early date immediately caused scholars to reevaluate the scheme of "stylistic development" from simple to more complex forms that had been nearly universally accepted for decades.

Many species of animals appear on the Chauvet Cave walls, including several ferocious animals that were never part of the Paleolithic human diet, such as lions and bears. Bears, in fact,

hibernated in the cave, and more than 50 bear skulls are still there. When the bears resided in the cave, it was a dangerous place for anyone to venture into.

Several of the paintings discovered by Chauvet's team occupy a special place in the history of art. In the Chauvet Cave, in contrast to Lascaux (FIG. 1-11), the horns of the aurochs (extinct long-horned wild oxen) are shown naturalistically, one behind the other, not in the twisted perspective thought to be universally characteristic of Paleolithic art. Moreover, the two rhinoceroses at the lower right of FIG. 1-12 appear to confront each other, suggesting to some observers that a narrative was intended, another "first" in either painting or sculpture. If the paintings are twice as old as those of Lascaux, Altamira (FIG. 1-9), and Pech-Merle (FIG. 1-10), the assumption that Paleolithic art "evolved" from simple to more sophisticated representations is wrong.

Much research remains to be conducted in the Chauvet Cave, but already the paintings have become the subject of intense controversy. Recently, some archaeologists have contested the early dating of the Chauvet paintings on the grounds that the tested samples were contaminated. The paintings, therefore, may not be revolutionary after all. The dispute exemplifies the frustration—and the excitement—of studying the art of an age so remote that almost nothing remains and almost every new find causes art historians to reevaluate what had previously been taken for granted.

technique alone suggest that the animals in the Hall of the Bulls were painted at different times, and the modern impression of a rapidly moving herd of beasts was probably not the original intent. In any case, the "herd" consists of several different kinds of animals of various sizes moving in different directions.

Another feature of the Lascaux paintings deserves attention. The bulls there show a convention of representing horns that has been called *twisted perspective,* because viewers see the heads in profile but the horns from the front. Thus, the painter's approach

is not strictly or consistently *optical* (seen from a fixed viewpoint). Rather, the approach is *descriptive* of the fact that cattle have two horns. Two horns are part of the concept "bull." In strict optical-perspective profile, only one horn would be visible, but to paint the animal in that way would, as it were, amount to an incomplete definition of it. This kind of twisted perspective was the norm in prehistoric painting, but it was not universal. In fact, the recent discovery of Paleolithic paintings in the Chauvet Cave (FIG. **1-12**) at Vallon-Pont-d'Arc in France, where the painters

1-12 Aurochs, horses, and rhinoceroses, wall painting in Chauvet Cave, Vallon-Pont-d'Arc, Ardèche, France, ca. 30,000–28,000 or ca. 15,000–13,000 BCE. Approx. half life-size.

1-13 Rhinoceros, wounded man, and disemboweled bison, painting in the well, Lascaux, Dordogne, France, ca. 15,000–13,000 BCE. Bison approx. 3′ 8″ long.

represented horns in a more natural way, has caused art historians to rethink many of the assumptions they had made about Paleolithic art (see "The World's Oldest Paintings?" page 23).

PALEOLITHIC NARRATIVE ART? Perhaps the most perplexing painting in all the Paleolithic caves is the one deep in the well shaft at Lascaux (FIG. **1-13**), where man (as opposed to woman) makes one of his earliest appearances in prehistoric painting. At the left is a rhinoceros, rendered with all the skilled attention to animal detail customarily seen in cave art. Beneath its tail are two rows of three dots of uncertain significance. At the right is a bison, more schematically painted, probably by someone else. The second painter nonetheless successfully suggested the bristling rage of the animal, whose bowels are hanging from it in a heavy coil. Between the two beasts is a bird-faced (masked?) man (compare the feline-headed human from Hohlenstein-Stadel, FIG. 1-3) with outstretched arms and hands with only four fingers. The man is depicted with far less care and detail than either animal, but the painter made the hunter's gender explicit by the prominent penis. The position of the man is ambiguous. Is he wounded or dead or merely tilted back and unharmed? Do the staff(?) with the bird on top and the spear belong to him? Is it he or the rhinoceros who has gravely wounded the bison—or neither? Which animal, if either, has knocked the man down, if indeed he is on the ground? Are these three images related at all? Researchers can be sure of nothing, but if the figures were placed beside each other to tell a story, then this is evidence for the creation of complex narrative compositions involving humans and animals at a much earlier date than anyone had imagined only a few generations ago. Yet it is important to remember that even if a story was intended, very few people would have been able to "read" it. The painting, in a deep shaft, is very difficult to reach and could have been viewed only in flickering lamplight. Like all Paleolithic art, the scene in the Lascaux well shaft remains enigmatic.

NEOLITHIC ART

THE ICE RECEDES Around 9000 BCE, the ice that covered much of northern Europe during the Paleolithic period melted as the climate grew warmer. The reindeer migrated north, and the woolly mammoth and rhinoceros disappeared. The Paleolithic gave way to a transitional period, the Mesolithic, when Europe became climatically, geographically, and biologically much as it is today. Then, for several thousand years at different times in different parts of the globe, a great new age, the Neolithic, dawned. Human beings began to settle in fixed abodes and to domesticate plants and animals. Their food supply assured, many groups changed from hunters to herders, to farmers, and finally to townspeople. Wandering hunters settled down to organized community living in villages surrounded by cultivated fields.

The conventional division of prehistory into the Paleolithic, Mesolithic, and Neolithic periods is based on the development of stone implements. However, a different kind of distinction may be made between an age of food gathering and an age of food production. In this scheme, the Paleolithic period corresponds roughly to the age of food gathering, and the Mesolithic period, the last phase of that age, is marked by intensified food gathering and the taming of the dog. In the Neolithic period, agriculture and stock raising became humankind's major food sources. The transition to the Neolithic occurred first in the ancient Near East (MAP 1-1).

Ancient Near East

THE BEGINNING OF AGRICULTURE The remains of the oldest known settled communities have been found in the grassy uplands bordering the Tigris and Euphrates Rivers in Mesopotamia (parts of modern Syria and Iraq). These regions provided the necessary preconditions for the development of agriculture. Species of native plants, such as wild wheat and barley, were plentiful, as were herds of animals (goats, sheep, and pigs) that could be domesticated. Sufficient rain occurred for the raising of crops. When village farming life was well developed, some settlers, attracted by the greater fertility of the soil and perhaps also by the need to find more land for their rapidly growing populations, moved into the river valleys and deltas of the two rivers.

NEOLITHIC INNOVATIONS The new sedentary societies of the Neolithic age originated systematic agriculture, weaving, metalworking, pottery, and counting and recording with tokens. Soon, these innovations spread from Mesopotamia to northern Syria, Anatolia (Turkey), and Egypt. Village farming communities such as Jarmo in Iraq and Çatal Höyük in southern Anatolia date back to the mid-seventh millennium BCE. The remarkable fortified town of Jericho, before whose walls the biblical Joshua appeared thousands of years later, is even older. Archaeologists are constantly uncovering surprises, and the discovery and exploration of new sites each year is compelling them to revise their views about the emergence of Neolithic society. But three sites known for some time—Jericho, Ain Ghazal, and Çatal Höyük—offer a fascinating picture of the rapid and exciting transformation of human society—and of art—during the Neolithic period.

JERICHO'S STONE FORTIFICATIONS By 7000 BCE, agriculture was well established in at least three Near Eastern regions: ancient Palestine, Iran, and Anatolia. Although no remains of domestic cereals have been found that can be dated before 7000 BCE, the advanced state of agriculture at that time presupposes a long development. Indeed, the very existence of a town such as Jericho gives strong support to this assumption. The site of

Jericho—a plateau in the Jordan River valley with an unfailing spring—was occupied by a small village as early as the ninth millennium BCE. This village underwent spectacular development around 8000 BCE, when a new Neolithic town covering about 10 acres was built. Its mud-brick houses sat on round or oval stone foundations and had roofs of branches covered with earth.

As the town's wealth grew and powerful neighbors established themselves, the need for protection resulted in the first known permanent stone fortifications. By approximately 7500 BCE, the town, estimated to have had a population of more than 2,000 people, was surrounded by a wide rock-cut ditch and a 5-foot-thick wall. Into this wall, which has been preserved to a height of almost 13 feet, was built a great circular stone tower (FIG. **1-14**), 28 feet high. Almost 33 feet in diameter at the base, the tower has an inner stairway leading to its summit. Not enough of the site has been excavated to determine whether this tower was solitary or one of several similar towers that formed a complete defense system. In either case, a structure such as this, built with only simple stone tools, was a tremendous technological achievement. It constitutes the beginning of the long history of monumental architecture.

SCULPTURE AT AIN GHAZAL Near Amman, Jordan, the construction of a highway in 1974 revealed another important Neolithic settlement in ancient Palestine at the site of Ain Ghazal, occupied from the late eighth through the late sixth millennium BCE. The inhabitants built houses of irregularly shaped stones, but carefully plastered and then painted their floors and walls red. The most striking finds at Ain Ghazal, however, are two caches containing three dozen plaster statuettes (FIG. **1-15**) and

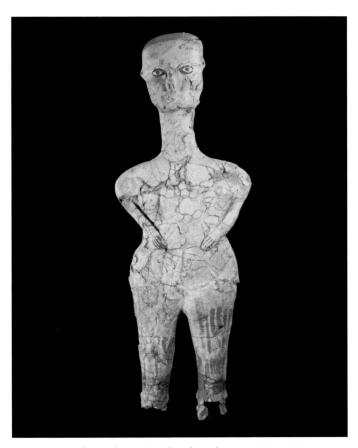

1-15 Human figure, from Ain Ghazal, Jordan, ca. 6750–6250 BCE. Plaster, painted and inlaid with cowrie shell and bitumen, 3′ 5⅜″ high. Louvre, Paris.

1-14 Great stone tower built into the settlement wall, Jericho, ca. 8000–7000 BCE.

busts, some with two heads, datable to the mid-seventh millennium BCE. The sculptures appear to have been ritually buried. The figures were fashioned of white plaster, which was built up over a core of reeds and twine. Black bitumen, a tarlike substance, was used to delineate the pupils of the eyes, which are inset cowrie shells. Painters added orange and black hair, clothing, and, in some instances, body paint or tattooing. Only rarely did the sculptors indicate the gender of the figures. Whatever their purpose, by their size (as much as three feet tall) and sophisticated technique, the Ain Ghazal statuettes and busts are distinguished from Paleolithic figurines such as the tiny *Venus of Willendorf* (FIG. 1-4) and even the foot-tall ivory statuette from Hohlenstein-Stadel (FIG. 1-3). They mark the beginning of monumental sculpture in the ancient Near East.

A TOWN WITHOUT STREETS Remarkable discoveries also have been made in Anatolia. Excavations at Hacilar, Çatal Höyük, and elsewhere have shown that the central Anatolian plateau was the site of a flourishing Neolithic culture between 7000 and 5000 BCE. Twelve successive building levels excavated at Çatal Höyük between 1961 and 1965 have been dated between 6500 and 5700 BCE. On a single site, it is possible to retrace, in an unbroken sequence, the evolution of a Neolithic culture over a period of 800 years. (Only 1 of 32 acres had been explored before the recent resumption of excavations. The new project promises to expand and perhaps revise the current picture of Neolithic life.)

The source of Çatal Höyük's wealth was trade, especially in obsidian, a glasslike volcanic stone Neolithic toolmakers and weapon makers valued highly because it could be chipped into fine cutting edges. Along with Jericho, Çatal Höyük seems to have been one of the first experiments in urban living. The regularity of its plan suggests that the town was built according to some predetermined scheme. A peculiar feature is the settlement's complete lack of streets (FIG. **1-16**). The houses adjoin one another and have no doors. Openings in the roofs provided access to the interiors. The openings also served as chimneys to ventilate the hearth in the combination living room and kitchen that formed the core of the house. Impractical as such an arrangement may

1-16 Schematic reconstruction drawing of a section of Level VI, Çatal Höyük, Turkey, ca. 6000–5900 BCE (after J. Mellaart).

appear today, it did offer some advantages. The attached buildings were more stable than freestanding structures and, at the limits of the town site, formed a perimeter wall well suited to defense against human or natural forces. Thus, if enemies managed to breach the exterior wall, they would find themselves not inside the town but above the houses with the defenders waiting there on the roof.

The houses, constructed of mud brick strengthened by sturdy timber frames, varied in size but repeated the same basic plan. Walls and floors were plastered and painted, and platforms along walls served as sites for sleeping, working, and eating. The dead were buried beneath the floors. A great number of decorated rooms have been found at Çatal Höyük. The excavators called these rooms shrines, but their function is uncertain. Their number suggests that these rooms played an important role in the life of Çatal Höyük's inhabitants.

The "shrines" are distinguished from the house structures by the greater richness of their interior decoration, which consisted of wall paintings, plaster reliefs, animal heads, and *bucrania* (bovine skulls). Bulls' horns, widely thought to be symbols of masculine potency, are the most common motif in these rooms. In some cases they are displayed next to plaster breasts, symbols of female fertility, projecting from the walls. Many statuettes of stone or *terracotta* (baked clay) also have been found at Çatal Höyük. Most are quite small (2 to 8 inches high) and primarily depict female figures. Only a few reach 12 inches.

NARRATIVE PAINTING Although at Çatal Höyük animal husbandry was well established, hunting continued to play an important part in the early Neolithic economy. The importance of hunting as a food source (until about 5700 BCE) is reflected also in wall paintings, where, in the older decorated rooms, hunting scenes predominate. In style and concept, however, the deer hunt mural at Çatal Höyük (FIG. **1-17**) is worlds apart from the wall paintings the hunters of the Paleolithic period produced. Perhaps what is most strikingly new about the Çatal Höyük painting and others like it is the regular appearance of the human figure—not only singly but also in large, coherent groups with a wide variety of poses, subjects, and settings. As noted earlier, humans were unusual in Paleolithic cave paintings, and pictorial narratives have almost never been found. Even the "hunting scene" in the well at Lascaux (FIG. 1-13) is doubtful as a narrative. In Neolithic paintings, human themes and concerns and action scenes with humans dominating animals are central.

In the Çatal Höyük hunt, the group of hunters—and no one doubts it is, indeed, an organized hunting party, not a series of individual figures—shows a tense exaggeration of movement and a rhythmic repetition of basic shapes customary for the period. The painter took care to distinguish important descriptive details—for example, bows, arrows, and garments—and the heads have clearly defined noses, mouths, chins, and hair. The Neolithic painter placed all the heads in profile for the same reason Paleolithic painters universally chose the profile view for representations of animals. Only the side view of the human head shows all its shapes clearly. However, at Çatal Höyük the torsos are presented from the front—again, the most informative viewpoint—while the profile view was chosen for the legs and arms. This *composite view* of the human body is quite artificial because the human body cannot make an abrupt 90-degree shift at the hips. But it is very descriptive of what a human body is—as opposed to what it looks like from a particular viewpoint. The composite view is another manifestation of the twisted perspective of Paleolithic paintings that combined a frontal view of an animal's two horns with a profile view of the head (FIGS. 1-11 and 1-13). The technique of painting also changed dramatically since Paleolithic times. The pigments were applied with a brush to a white background of dry plaster. The careful preparation of the wall surface is in striking contrast to the direct application of pigment to the rock face.

THE FIRST LANDSCAPE? More remarkable still is a painting in one of the older rooms at Çatal Höyük (FIG. **1-18**) that gener-

ally has been acclaimed as the world's first landscape (a picture of a natural setting in its own right, without any narrative content). As such, it remained unique for thousands of years. According to radiocarbon dating, the painting was executed around 6150 BCE. In the foreground is a town, with rectangular houses neatly laid out side by side, probably representing Çatal Höyük itself. Behind the town appears a mountain with two peaks. Many archaeologists think that the dots and lines issuing from the higher of the two cones represent a volcanic eruption, and have suggested that the mountain is the 10,600-foot-high Hasan Dağ. It is located within view of Çatal Höyük and is the only twin-peaked volcano in central Anatolia. The conjectured

1-18 Landscape with volcanic eruption(?), detail of a watercolor copy of a wall painting from Level VII, Çatal Höyük, Turkey, ca. 6150 BCE.

1-19 Aerial view of Stonehenge, Salisbury Plain, Wiltshire, England, ca. 2550–1600 BCE. Circle is 97′ in diameter; trilithons approx. 24′ high.

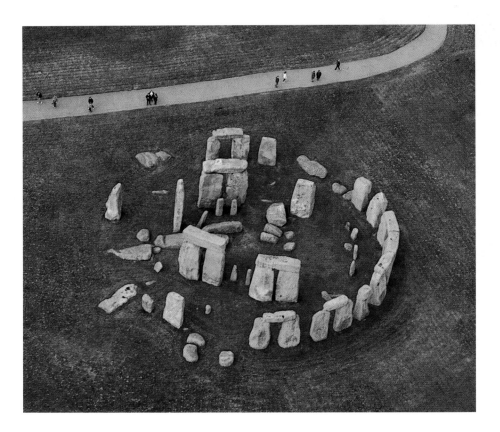

volcanic eruption shown in the mural does not necessarily depict a specific historical event. If, however, the Çatal Höyük painting relates a story, even a recurring one, then it cannot be considered a pure landscape. Nonetheless, this mural is the first depiction of a place devoid of both humans and animals.

The rich finds at Çatal Höyük give the impression of a prosperous and well-ordered society that practiced a great variety of arts and crafts. In addition to painting and sculpture, weaving and pottery were well established, and even the technique of smelting copper and lead in small quantities was known before 6000 BCE. The conversion to an agricultural economy appears to have been completed by about 5700.

Western Europe

MEGALITHS AND HENGES In western Europe, where Paleolithic paintings and sculptures abound, no comparably developed towns of the time of Çatal Höyük have been found. However, in succeeding millennia, perhaps as early as 4000 BCE, the local Neolithic populations in several areas developed a monumental architecture employing massive rough-cut stones. The very dimensions of the stones, some as high as 17 feet and weighing as much as 50 tons, have prompted historians to call them *megaliths* (great stones) and to designate the culture that produced them *megalithic.*

Although megalithic monuments are plentiful throughout Europe, the arrangement of huge stones in a circle (called a *cromlech* or *henge*), often surrounded by a ditch, is almost entirely limited to Britain. The most imposing today is Stonehenge (FIG. **1-19**) on the Salisbury Plain in southern England. Stonehenge is a complex of rough-cut sarsen (a form of sandstone) stones and smaller "bluestones" (various volcanic rocks). Outermost is a ring, almost 100 feet in diameter, of large monoliths of sarsen stones capped by

lintels (a stone "beam" used to span an opening; see FIG. 4-18). Next is a ring of bluestones, which, in turn, encircles a horseshoe (open end facing east) of *trilithons* (three-stone constructions)—five lintel-topped pairs of the largest sarsens, each weighing 45 to 50 tons. Standing apart and to the east (outside our photograph at the lower right corner) is the "heel-stone," which, for a person looking outward from the center of the complex, would have marked the point where the sun rose at the summer solstice.

Stonehenge probably was built in several phases in the centuries before and after 2000 BCE. It seems to have been a kind of astronomical observatory. The mysterious structures were believed in the Middle Ages to have been the work of the magician Merlin of the King Arthur legend, who spirited them from Ireland. Most archaeologists now consider Stonehenge a remarkably accurate solar calendar. This achievement is testimony to the rapidly developing intellectual powers of Neolithic humans as well as to their capacity for heroic physical effort.

CONCLUSION

The first sculptures and paintings antedate the invention of writing by tens of thousands of years. No one knows why the first "artists" began to paint and carve images of animals and humans or what role those images played in the lives of Paleolithic hunters. All that is certain is that the statuettes, reliefs, and mural paintings were not created as "art" in the modern sense of the word. But the Paleolithic artists *were* the first to represent the world around them in stone and paint, initiating an intellectual revolution of enormous consequences. They and their Neolithic successors also invented many of the techniques and established many of the conventions that would characterize sculpture and painting for millennia.

30,000 BCE

| FIRST PALEOLITHIC PAINTINGS AND SCULPTURES, CA. 30,000–28,000 BCE

1

25,000 BCE

1   Nude woman
    (*Venus of Willendorf*),
    ca. 28,000–25,000 BCE

15,000 BCE

2

12,000 BCE

| FINAL RECESSION OF ICE AND ONSET
  OF TEMPERATE CLIMATE, CA. 9000 BCE

2   Hall of the Bulls, Lascaux, ca. 15,000–13,000 BCE

| NEOLITHIC PERIOD BEGINS IN THE NEAR EAST, CA. 8000 BCE

7500 BCE

| EARLIEST FARMING COMMUNITIES, CA. 7000 BCE

3

5000 BCE

| NEOLITHIC PERIOD BEGINS IN EUROPE, CA. 4000 BCE

3   Plaster figurine from Ain Ghazal,
    ca. 6750–6250 BCE

4

2000 BCE

4   Stonehenge, Salisbury Plain,
    ca. 2550–1600 BCE

Statuettes of two worshipers, from the Square Temple at Eshnunna (modern Tell Asmar), Iraq, ca. 2700 BCE. Gypsum inlaid with shell and black limestone, male figure approx. 2′ 6″ high. Iraq Museum, Baghdad.

2

THE RISE OF
CIVILIZATION

THE ART OF THE ANCIENT NEAR EAST

When humans first gave up the dangerous and uncertain life of the hunter and gatherer for the more predictable and stable life of the farmer and herder, the change in human society was so astounding, so fundamental, that it justly has been called the Neolithic Revolution. This revolutionary change in the nature of daily life first occurred in Mesopotamia—a Greek word that means "the land between the [Tigris and Euphrates] rivers." Mesopotamia is at the core of the region often called the Fertile Crescent, a land mass that forms a huge arc from the mountainous border between Turkey and Syria through Iraq to Iran's Zagros Mountains (MAP **2-1**). There, humans first learned how to use the wheel and the plow and how to control floods and construct irrigation canals. The land became a giant oasis, the presumed locale of the biblical Garden of Eden.

As the region that gave birth to three of the world's great modern faiths—Judaism, Christianity, and Islam—the Near East has long been of interest to historians. But not until the 19th century did systematic excavation open the world's eyes to the extraordinary art and architecture of the ancient land between the rivers. After the first discoveries, the great museums of Europe quickly began to acquire Mesopotamian artworks. The instructions the British Museum gave to Austen Henry Layard, one of the pioneers of Near Eastern archaeology, were typical of the treasure-hunting spirit of the era: Obtain as many well-preserved artworks as you can while spending the least possible amount of time and money doing so. Interest heightened with each new find, and soon North American museums also began to collect Near Eastern art.

The most popular 19th-century acquisitions were the stone reliefs depicting warfare and hunting (FIGS. 2-22 and 2-24) and the colossal statues of monstrous human-headed bulls (FIG. 2-21) from the palaces of the Assyrians, rulers of a northern Mesopotamian empire during the ninth to the seventh centuries BCE. But nothing that emerged from the Near Eastern soil attracted as much attention as the treasures Leonard Woolley discovered in the 1920s at the Royal Cemetery at Ur in southern Mesopotamia. The interest in his unearthing of lavish third-millennium Sumerian

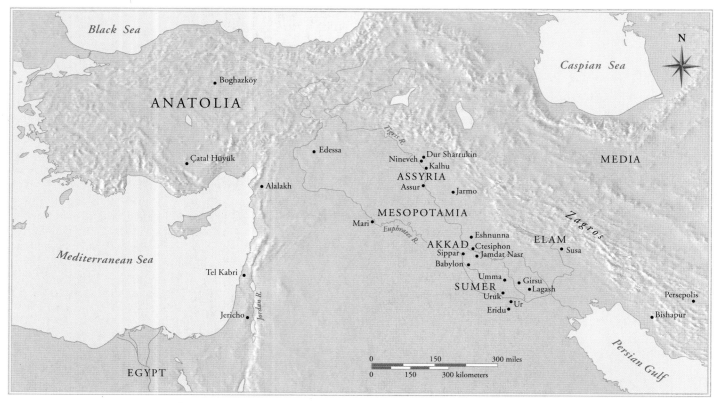

MAP 2-1 The ancient Near East.

burials rivaled the public fascination with the 1922 discovery of the tomb of the Egyptian boy-king Tutankhamen (see FIGS. 3-36 to 3-38). The Ur cemetery yielded gold objects, jewelry, artworks, and musical instruments (FIGS. 2-8 to 2-11) of the highest quality. Europe's royalty and elite frequently visited the site. One of the visitors was the mystery writer Agatha Christie, who later married one of the British archaeologists working at Ur. Her 1936 novel *Murder in Mesopotamia* centers on an excavation in Iraq.

SUMERIAN ART

The discovery of the treasures of ancient Ur put the Sumerians once again in a prominent position on the world stage. They had been absent for more than 4,000 years. The Sumerians were the people who transformed the vast, flat lower valley between the Tigris and Euphrates into the Fertile Crescent of the ancient world. Sparsely inhabited before the Sumerians, this area is now southern Iraq. In the fourth millennium BCE, the Sumerians established the

2-1 White Temple and ziggurat, Uruk (modern Warka), Iraq, ca. 3200–3000 BCE.

The Invention of Writing

The oldest written documents are Mesopotamian records of administrative acts and commercial transactions. At first, around 3400–3200 BCE, the Sumerians (in Iraq) and their contemporaries, the Elamites (in Iran), made inventories of cattle, food, and other items by scratching *pictographs* (simplified pictures standing for words) into soft clay with a sharp tool, or *stylus*. The clay plaques hardened into breakable, yet nearly indestructible, tablets. This accounts for the existence today of thousands of documents dating back nearly five millennia. The Sumerians wrote their pictorial signs from the top down and arranged them in boxes they read from right to left. By 3000–2900 BCE, they had further simplified the pictographic signs by reducing them to a group of wedge-shaped *(cuneiform)* signs. The development of cuneiform marked the beginning of writing, as historians strictly define it. By 2600, cuneiform texts were sophisticated enough to express complex grammatical constructions.

The Sumerian and Elamite languages do not belong to any of the major linguistic groups of antiquity and are unrelated to each other, yet historians do not doubt that these early peoples were a major force in the spread of civilization. Thousands of cuneiform tablets, for example, testify to the far-flung network of Sumerian contacts reaching from southern Mesopotamia eastward to the Iranian plateau, northward to Assyria, and westward to Syria. Trade was essential for the Sumerians, because despite their land's fertility, it was poor in such vital natural resources as metal, stone, and wood.

The Sumerians also produced great literature. Their most famous work, known from fragmentary cuneiform texts, is the late-third-millennium *Epic of Gilgamesh*, which antedates Homer's *Iliad* and *Odyssey* by some 1,500 years. It recounts the heroic story of Gilgamesh, legendary king of Uruk and slayer of the monster Huwawa. Translations of the Sumerian epic into several other ancient Near Eastern languages attest to the fame of the original version.

---

first great urban communities and developed the earliest known writing system (see "The Invention of Writing," above).

THE FIRST CITY-STATES Ancient Sumer was not a unified nation; rather, it was made up of a dozen or so independent *city-states*. Each was thought to be under the protection of a different Mesopotamian deity. The Sumerian rulers were the gods' representatives on earth and the stewards of their earthly treasure. The rulers and priests directed all communal activities, including canal construction, crop collection, and food distribution. The development of agriculture to the point where only a portion of the population had to produce food made possible such an organization of the labor force. Some members of the community could thus specialize in other activities, including manufacturing, trade, and administration. Such labor specialization is the hallmark of the first complex urban societies. In the city-states of ancient Sumer, activities that once had been individually initiated became institutionalized for the first time. The community, rather than the family, assumed functions such as defense against enemies and against the caprices of nature. Whether ruled by a single person or a council chosen from among the leading families, these communities gained permanent identities as discrete cities. The city-state was one of the great Sumerian inventions.

CITY PLANNING AND RELIGION The Sumerian city plan reflected the central role of the local god in the daily life of the city-state's occupants. The god's temple formed the city's monumental nucleus. It was not only the focus of local religious practice but also an administrative and economic center. It was indeed the domain of the god, whom the Sumerians regarded as a great and rich holder of lands and herds, as well as the protector of the city-state. The vast temple complex, a kind of city within a city, thus had both religious and secular functions. A temple staff of priests and scribes carried on official business, looking after both the god's and the ruler's possessions.

URUK'S WHITE TEMPLE The outstanding preserved example of early Sumerian temple architecture is the 5,000-year-old White

Temple (FIG. **2-1**) at Uruk, the home of Gilgamesh (see "The Invention of Writing," above). Usually only the foundations of early Mesopotamian temples can still be recognized. The White Temple is a rare exception. Sumerian builders did not have access to stone quarries and instead formed mud bricks for the superstructures of their temples and other buildings. Almost all these structures have eroded over the course of time. The fragile nature of the building materials did not, however, prevent the Sumerians from erecting towering works, such as the Uruk temple, several centuries before the Egyptians built their stone pyramids (see Chapter 3). This says a great deal about the Sumerians' desire to provide monumental settings for the worship of their deities.

Enough of the Uruk complex remains to permit a fairly reliable reconstruction drawing (FIG. **2-2**). The temple (whose white-washed walls lend it its modern nickname) stands on top of a high platform, or *ziggurat,* 40 feet above street level in the city center. A stairway on the far side, not shown, leads to the top but does not end in front of any of the temple doorways, necessitating two or three angular changes in direction. This "bent-axis" approach is the standard arrangement for Sumerian temples, a striking contrast to the linear approach the Egyptians preferred for their temples and tombs (see Chapter 3).

Like other Sumerian temples, the corners of the White Temple are oriented to the cardinal points of the compass. The building, probably dedicated to Anu, the sky god (see "The Gods and Goddesses of Mesopotamia," page 35), is of modest proportions

2-2 Reconstruction drawing of the White Temple and ziggurat, Uruk (modern Warka), Iraq, ca. 3200–3000 BCE (after S. E. Piggott).

(61 × 16 feet). By design, it did not accommodate large throngs of worshipers but only a select few, the priests and perhaps the leading community members. The temple has several chambers. The central hall, or *cella,* was set aside for the divinity and housed a stepped altar. The Sumerians referred to their temples as "waiting rooms," a reflection of their belief that the deity would descend from the heavens to appear before the priests in the cella. How or if the Uruk temple was roofed is uncertain.

The Sumerian idea that the gods reside above the world of humans is central to most of the world's religions. Moses ascended Mount Sinai to receive the Ten Commandments from the Hebrew God, and the Greeks placed the home of their gods and goddesses on Mount Olympus. The elevated placement of Mesopotamian temples on giant platforms reaching toward the sky is consistent with this widespread religious concept. Eroded ziggurats still dominate most of the ruined cities of Sumer. The loftiness of the great temple platforms made a profound impression on the peoples of the ancient Near East. The tallest ziggurat of all, at Babylon, was about 270 feet high. Known to the Hebrews as the Tower of Babel, it became the centerpiece of a biblical story about the insolent pride of humans (see "Babylon: City of Wonders," page 49).

A MARBLE-AND-GOLD INANNA? The White Temple at Uruk towers over all other vestiges of that ancient city, but a fragmentary white marble female head (FIG. **2-3**) is also an extraordinary achievement at so early a date. The lustrous hard stone had to be imported at great cost. The head is actually only a face with a flat back. It has drilled holes for attachment to a head and body, possibly of wood. Although found in the sacred precinct of the goddess Inanna, the subject is unknown. Many

have suggested that the face is an image of Inanna, but a mortal woman, perhaps a priestess, may be portrayed.

Often the present condition of an artwork can be very misleading, and the Uruk head is a dramatic example. Its original appearance would have been much more vibrant than the pure white fragment archaeologists uncovered. Colored shell or stone filled the deep recesses for the eyebrows and the large eyes. The deep groove at the top of the head anchored a wig, probably made of gold leaf. The hair strands engraved in the metal fell in waves over the forehead and sides of the face. The bright coloration of the eyes, brows, and hair likely overshadowed the soft modeling of the cheeks and mouth. The missing body was probably clothed in expensive fabrics and bedecked with jewels.

GIFTS FOR A GODDESS The Sumerians, pioneers in so many areas, also may have been the first to use pictures to tell coherent stories. Sumerian narrative art goes far beyond the Stone Age artists' tentative efforts at storytelling. The so-called *Warka Vase* (FIG. **2-4**) from Uruk (modern Warka) is the first great work of

2-3 Female head (Inanna?), from Uruk (modern Warka), Iraq, ca. 3200–3000 BCE. Marble, approx. 8″ high. Iraq Museum, Baghdad.

2-4 Presentation of offerings to Inanna *(Warka Vase),* from Uruk (modern Warka), Iraq, ca. 3200–3000 BCE. Alabaster, 3′ $\frac{1}{4}$″ high. Iraq Museum, Baghdad.

The Gods and Goddesses of Mesopotamia

The Sumerians and their successors in the ancient Near East worshiped numerous deities, mostly nature gods. The Mesopotamian gods and goddesses discussed in this chapter are listed here.

Anu, the chief deity of the Sumerians, was the god of the sky and of the city of Uruk. One of the earliest Sumerian temples (FIGS. 2-1 and 2-2) may have been dedicated to his worship.

Enlil, Anu's son, was the lord of the winds and the earth. He eventually replaced his father as king of the gods.

Inanna was the Sumerian goddess of love and war. Later known as *Ishtar,* she is the most important female deity in all periods of Mesopotamian history. At a very early date, the Sumerians constructed a sanctuary to Inanna at Uruk. Amid the ruins, excavators uncovered fourth-millennium statues and reliefs (FIGS. 2-3 and 2-4) connected with her worship. Whether or not the goddess herself was represented in human form at that time is uncertain. Inanna/Ishtar is unmistakably depicted with her sacred lion in a mural painting in the 18th-century BCE palace of Zimri-Lim at Mari (FIG. 2-17).

Nanna, the moon god, also known as *Sin,* was the chief deity of Ur, where his most important shrine was located.

Utu, god of the sun, known later as *Shamash,* was especially revered at Sippar. On a Babylonian stele (FIG. 2-16) of ca. 1780 BCE, King Hammurabi presents his law code to Shamash, who is depicted with flames radiating from his shoulders.

Marduk was the chief god of the Babylonians. His son *Nabu* was the god of writing and wisdom. *Adad* was the Babylonian god of storms. Nabu's dragon and Adad's sacred bull are depicted on the sixth-century BCE Ishtar Gate at Babylon (FIG. 2-25).

Ningirsu was the local god of Lagash and Girsu. His name means "lord of Girsu." Eannatum, one of the early rulers of Lagash, defeated an enemy army with the god's assistance and commemorated Ningirsu's role in the victory on the so-called *Stele of the Vultures* (FIG. 2-7) of ca. 2600–2500 BCE. Gudea (FIG. 2-15), one of Eannatum's Neo-Sumerian successors, built a great temple about 2100 BCE in honor of Ningirsu after the god instructed him to do so in a dream.

Ashur, the local deity of Assur, the city that took his name, became the king of the Assyrian gods. He sometimes is identified with Enlil.

---

narrative relief sculpture known. Found within the Inanna temple complex, it depicts a religious festival in honor of the goddess.

The sculptor divided the vase's reliefs into three bands (also called *registers* or *friezes*), and the figures stand on a ground line (the horizontal base of the composition). This new kind of composition marks a significant break with the haphazard figure placement found in earlier art. The register format for telling a story was to have a very long future. In fact, artists still employ registers today in modified form in comic books.

The lowest band on the *Warka Vase* shows ewes and rams—in strict profile, consistent with an approach to representing animals that was then some 20,000 years old—above crops and a wavy line representing water. These and the alternating male and female animals were the staple commodities of the Sumerian economy, but they were also associated with fertility. They underscore that Inanna had blessed Uruk's inhabitants with good crops and increased herds.

A procession of naked men fills the central band. The men carry baskets and jars overflowing with earth's abundance. They will present their bounty to the goddess as a *votive offering* (gift of gratitude to a deity usually made in fulfillment of a vow) and will deposit it in her temple. The spacing of each figure involves no overlapping. The Uruk men, like the prehistoric deer hunters at Çatal Höyük (see FIG. 1-17), are a composite of frontal and profile views, with large staring frontal eyes in profile heads. The artist indicated those human body parts necessary to communicate the human form and avoided positions, attitudes, or views that would conceal the characterizing parts. For example, if the figures were in strict profile, an arm and perhaps a leg would be hidden. The body would appear to have only half its breadth. And the eye would not "read" as an eye at all, because it would not have its distinctive flat oval shape. Art historians call this characteristic early approach to representation *conceptual,* as opposed to

optical, because artists who used it did not record the immediate, fleeting aspect of figures. Instead, they rendered the human body's distinguishing and fixed properties. The fundamental forms of figures, not their accidental appearance, dictated the artist's selection of the composite view as the best way to represent the human body.

In the uppermost (and tallest) band is a female figure with a tall horned headdress. Whether she is Inanna or her priestess is not known. A nude male figure brings a large vessel brimming with offerings to be deposited in the goddess's shrine. At the far right and barely visible in our illustration is an only partially preserved clothed man who is usually, if ambiguously, referred to as a "priest-king" because similar figures appear in other Sumerian artworks as leaders in both religious and secular contexts. The greater height of the priest-king and Inanna compared to the offering bearers indicates their greater importance, a convention called hierarchy of scale. Some scholars interpret the scene as a symbolic marriage between the priest-king and the goddess, ensuring her continued goodwill—and reaffirming the leader's exalted position in society.

ESHNUNNA'S PERPETUAL WORSHIPERS Further insight into Sumerian religious beliefs and rituals comes from a cache of sculptures reverently buried beneath the floor of a temple at Eshnunna (modern Tell Asmar) when the structure was remodeled. Carved of soft gypsum and inlaid with shell and black limestone, the statuettes range in size from well under a foot to about 30 inches tall. The two largest figures are shown in FIG. 2-5. All of the statuettes represent mortals, rather than deities, with their hands folded in front of their chests in a gesture of prayer, usually holding the small beakers the Sumerians used in religious rites. Hundreds of such goblets have been found in the temple complex at Eshnunna. The men wear belts and fringed

2-5 Statuettes of two worshipers, from the Square Temple at Eshnunna (modern Tell Asmar), Iraq, ca. 2700 BCE. Gypsum inlaid with shell and black limestone, male figure approx. 2′ 6″ high. Iraq Museum, Baghdad.

skirts. Most have beards and shoulder-length hair. The women wear long robes, with the right shoulder bare. Similar figurines from other sites bear inscriptions giving such information as the name of the donor and the god or even specific prayers to the deity on the owner's behalf. With their heads tilted upward, they wait in the Sumerian "waiting room" for the divinity to appear.

The sculptors of the Eshnunna statuettes employed simple forms, primarily cones and cylinders, for the figures. The statuettes are not portraits in the strict sense of the word, but the sculptors did distinguish physical types. At least one child was portrayed—next to the woman in FIG. 2-5 are the remains of two small legs. Most striking is the disproportionate relationship between the inlaid oversized eyes and the tiny hands. Scholars have explained the exaggeration of the eye size in various ways. But because the purpose of these votive figures was to offer constant prayers to the gods on their donors' behalf, the open-eyed stares most likely symbolize the eternal wakefulness necessary to fulfill their duty.

THE EUNUCH OF MARI Another group of Sumerian votive statuettes comes from the Temple of Ishtar at Mari. Of particular interest is the figure of Urnanshe (FIG. **2-6**), identified by an inscription. His eyes—inlaid with shell and lapis lazuli (a rich azure-blue stone imported from Afghanistan)—are unwavering in their intense gaze. Like the other figures in the group, Urnanshe

is bare chested, wears a tufted fleece skirt, and holds his arms (now broken) in front of his chest in a gesture of prayer. But he sits on a cushion with legs crossed, and he is beardless, with long straight hair that reaches to the waist, suggesting that he was a eunuch (castrated male). Urnanshe was neither priest nor ruler but the official singer at the Mari court. Another, very fragmentary, statuette portrays Urnanshe with a stringed instrument, that is, in his role as musician and singer at religious ceremonies. His statuettes attest that he stands ever ready to serve the goddess as well as his ruler.

VICTORY AND VULTURES The city-states of ancient Sumer were often at war with one another, and warfare is the theme of the so-called *Stele of the Vultures* (FIG. **2-7**) from Girsu. A *stele* is a carved stone slab erected to commemorate a historical event or, in some other cultures, to mark a grave (see FIG. 5-55). The Girsu stele presents a labeled historical narrative. (It is not, however, the first historical representation in the history of art. That honor belongs—at the moment—to an Egyptian relief [FIG. 3-2] carved more than three centuries earlier.) Although the *Stele of the Vultures* is fragmentary, cuneiform inscriptions almost everywhere on the monument reveal that it celebrates the victory of Eannatum, the *ensi* (ruler; king?) of Lagash, over the neighboring city-state of Umma. The stele has reliefs on both sides and takes its

2-6 Seated statuette of Urnanshe, from the Temple of Ishtar at Mari (modern Tell Hariri), Syria, ca. 2600–2500 BCE. Gypsum inlaid with shell and lapis lazuli, 10¼″ high. National Museum, Damascus.

2-7 Fragment of the victory stele of Eannatum (*Stele of the Vultures*), from Girsu (modern Telloh), Syria, ca. 2600–2500 BCE. Limestone, full stele approx. 5′ 11″ high. Louvre, Paris.

nickname from a fragment with a gruesome scene of vultures carrying off the severed heads and arms of the defeated enemy soldiers. Another fragment shows the giant figure of the local god Ningirsu holding tiny enemies in a net and beating one of them on the head with a mace.

The fragment in FIG. 2-7 depicts Eannatum leading an infantry battalion into battle (above) and attacking from a war chariot (below). The foot soldiers are protected behind a wall of shields and trample naked enemies as they advance. (The fragment that shows vultures devouring corpses belongs just to the right in the same register.) Both on foot and in a chariot, Eannatum is larger than anyone else, except Ningirsu on the other side of the stele. He is shown as the fearless general who paves the way for his army. Lives were lost, however, and Eannatum himself was wounded in the campaign. But the outcome was never in doubt, because Ningirsu fought with the men of Lagash.

Despite its fragmentary state, the *Stele of the Vultures* is an extraordinary document, not only as a very early effort to record historical events in relief but also for the insight it yields about Sumerian society. Through both words and pictures, it provides information about warfare techniques and the special nature of the Sumerian ruler. Eannatum was greater in stature than other men, and Ningirsu watched over him. According to the text, the ensi was born from the god Enlil's semen, which Ningirsu implanted in the womb. When Eannatum was wounded in battle, it says, the god shed tears for him. He was a divinely chosen ruler who presided over all aspects of his city-state, both in war and in peace. This also seems to have been the role of the ensi in the other Sumerian city-states.

WAR AND PEACE The spoils of war as well as success in farming and trade brought considerable wealth to some of the city-states of ancient Sumer. Nowhere is this clearer than in the so-called Royal Cemetery at Ur, the city that was home to the biblical Abraham. In the third millennium BCE, the leading families of Ur buried their dead in vaulted chambers beneath the earth. Scholars still debate whether these deceased were true kings and queens or simply aristocrats and priests, but they were laid to rest in regal fashion. Archaeologists exploring the Ur cemetery uncovered gold helmets and daggers with handles of lapis lazuli, golden beakers and bowls, jewelry of gold and lapis, musical instruments, chariots, and other luxurious items. Dozens of bodies were also found in the richest tombs. A retinue of musicians, servants, charioteers, and soldiers was sacrificed in order to accompany the "kings and queens" into the afterlife. Comparable rituals are documented in other societies, for example, in ancient America (see Chapter 14).

Not the costliest object found in the "royal" graves, but probably the most significant from the viewpoint of the history of art, is the so-called *Standard of Ur* (FIG. **2-8**). This rectangular box of uncertain function has sloping sides inlaid with shell, lapis lazuli, and red limestone. The excavator, Leonard Woolley, thought the object was originally mounted on a pole, and he considered it a kind of military standard—hence its nickname. Art historians usually refer to the two long sides of the box as the "war side" and "peace side," but the two sides may represent the first and second parts of a single narrative. The artist divided each into three horizontal bands. The narrative reads from left to right and bottom to top.

On the war side, four ass-drawn four-wheeled war chariots mow down enemies, whose bodies appear on the ground in front of and beneath the animals. The gait of the asses accelerates along the band from left to right. Above, foot soldiers gather up and lead away captured foes. In the uppermost register, soldiers present bound captives (who have been stripped naked to degrade them) to a king-like figure, who has stepped out of his chariot. His central place in

2-8 War side *(top)* and peace side *(bottom)* of the *Standard of Ur*, from Tomb 779, Royal Cemetery, Ur (modern Tell Muqayyar), Iraq, ca. 2600 BCE. Wood inlaid with shell, lapis lazuli, and red limestone, approx. 8″ × 1′ 7″. British Museum, London.

the composition and his greater stature (his head breaks through the border at the top) set him apart from all the other figures.

In the lowest band on the peace side, men carry provisions, possibly war booty, on their backs. Above, attendants bring animals, perhaps also spoils of war, and fish for the great banquet depicted in the uppermost register. There, seated dignitaries and a larger-than-life "king" (third from the left) feast, while a lyre player and singer (at the far right, with long straight hair—like Urnanshe, FIG. 2-6) entertain the group. Art historians have interpreted the scene both as a victory celebration and as a banquet in connection with cult ritual. The two are not necessarily incompatible. The absence of an inscription prevents connecting the scenes with a specific event or person, but the *Standard of Ur* undoubtedly is another early example of historical narrative.

ANIMAL ACTORS From the "King's Grave" at Ur comes a splendid lyre (FIG. 2-9) that, in its restored state, resembles the instrument depicted in the feast scene on the *Standard of Ur*. A magnificent bull's head caps the instrument's sound box. It is fashioned of gold leaf over a wooden core. The hair, beard, and details are of lapis lazuli. The sound box (FIG. 2-10) also features bearded—but here human-headed—bulls in the uppermost of its four inlaid panels. Such imaginary composite creatures are commonplace in the art of the ancient Near East and Egypt. On the Ur lyre, a heroic figure embraces the two man-bulls in a *heraldic composition* (symmetrical on either side of a central figure). His body and that of the scorpion-man in the lowest panel are in composite view. The animals are, equally characteristically, solely in profile: the dog wearing a dagger and carrying a laden

2-9 Bull-headed lyre (restored) from Tomb 789 ("King's Grave"), Royal Cemetery, Ur (modern Tell Muqayyar), Iraq, ca. 2600 BCE. Gold leaf and lapis lazuli over a wooden core, approx. 5' 5" high. University Museum, University of Pennsylvania, Philadelphia.

2-10 Soundbox of the lyre from Tomb 789 ("King's Grave"), Royal Cemetery, Ur (modern Tell Muqayyar), Iraq, ca. 2600 BCE. Wood with inlaid gold, lapis lazuli, and shell, approx. 1' 7" high. University Museum, University of Pennsylvania, Philadelphia.

table, the lion bringing in the beverage service, the ass playing the lyre, the jackal playing the zither, the bear steadying the lyre (or perhaps dancing), and the gazelle bearing goblets. The banquet animals almost seem to be burlesquing the kind of regal feast reproduced on the peace side of the *Standard of Ur*. The meaning of the sound box scenes is unclear. Some scholars have suggested, for example, that the creatures inhabit the land of the dead and that the narrative has a funerary significance. In any event, the sound box is a very early specimen of the recurring theme in both literature and art of animals acting as people. Later examples include Aesop's fables in ancient Greece, medieval bestiaries, and Walt Disney's cartoon animal actors.

SUMERIAN ART IN MINIATURE A banquet is also the subject of a *cylinder seal* (FIG. 2-11) found in the tomb of "Queen" Pu-abi and inscribed with her name. (Many historians prefer to designate her more conservatively and ambiguously as "Lady" Pu-abi.) The seal is typical of the period, consisting of a cylindrical piece of stone engraved to produce a raised impression when rolled over clay (see "Mesopotamian Seals," page 40). In the upper zone, a man and a woman, probably Pu-abi, sit and drink from beakers, attended by servants. Below, male attendants serve two more seated men. Even in miniature and in a medium very different from that of the *Standard of Ur*, the Sumerian artist employed the same figure types and followed the same compositional rules.

2-11 Banquet scene, cylinder seal *(left)* and its modern impression *(right),* from the Tomb of Pu-abi (Tomb 800), Royal Cemetery, Ur (modern Tell Muqayyar), Iraq, ca. 2600 BCE. Lapis lazuli, approx. 2" high. British Museum, London.

Mesopotamian Seals

Seals have been unearthed in great numbers at sites throughout Mesopotamia. Generally made of stone—the favorite materials were carnelian, jasper, lapis lazuli, and agate—seals of ivory, glass, and other materials also survive. The seals take two forms: flat *stamp seals* and *cylinder seals.* The latter have a hole drilled lengthwise through the center of the cylinder so that they could be strung and worn around the neck or suspended from the wrist. Cylinder seals were prized possessions, signifying high positions in society, and they frequently were buried with the dead.

The primary function of cylinder seals, however, like the earlier stamp seals, was not to serve as items of adornment. The Sumerians (and other peoples of the Near East) used both stamp and cylinder seals to identify their documents and protect storage jars and doors against unauthorized opening. The oldest seals predate the invention of writing and conveyed their messages with pictographs that ratified ownership. Later seals (FIG. 2-11) often bear long cuneiform inscriptions and record the names and titles of rulers, bureaucrats, and deities. Although sealing is increasingly rare, the tradition lives on today whenever a letter is sealed with a lump of wax and then stamped with a monogram or other identifying mark. Customs officials often still seal packages and sacks with official stamps when goods cross national borders.

In the ancient Near East, artists decorated both stamp and cylinder seals with incised designs, producing a raised pattern when the seal was pressed into soft clay. (Cylinder seals largely displaced stamp seals because they could be rolled over the clay and thus cover a greater area more quickly.) We illustrate a cylinder seal from the Royal Cemetery at Ur and a modern impression made from it (FIG. 2-11). Note how cracks in the stone cylinder become raised lines in the impression and how the engraved figures, chairs, and cuneiform characters appear in relief. Continuous rolling of the seal over a clay strip results in a repeating design, as our illustration also demonstrates at the edges.

The miniature reliefs the seals produce are a priceless source of information about Mesopotamian religion and society. Without them, archaeologists would know much less about how Mesopotamians dressed and dined; what their shrines looked like; how they depicted their gods, rulers, and mythological figures; how they fought wars; and what role women played in ancient Near Eastern society. Clay seal impressions excavated in architectural contexts shed a welcome light on the administration and organization of Mesopotamian city-states. Mesopotamian seals are also an invaluable resource for art historians, providing them with thousands of examples of relief sculpture that span roughly 3,000 years.

All the figures are in composite views with large frontal eyes in profile heads, and the seated dignitaries are once again larger in scale to underscore their elevated position in the social hierarchy.

AKKADIAN, NEO-SUMERIAN, BABYLONIAN, AND HITTITE ART

THE FIRST NEAR EASTERN KINGS In 2334 BCE, the loosely linked group of cities known as Sumer came under the domination of a great ruler, Sargon of Akkad. Archaeologists have yet to locate the specific site of the city of Akkad, but it was in the vicinity of Babylon. The Akkadians were Semitic in origin—that is, they were a Near Eastern people who spoke a language related to Hebrew and Arabic. Their language, Akkadian, was entirely different from the language of Sumer, but they used the Sumerians' cuneiform characters for their written documents. Under Sargon (whose name means "true king") and his followers, the Akkadians introduced a new concept of royal power based on unswerving loyalty to the king rather than to the city-state. During the rule of Sargon's grandson, Naram-Sin (r. 2254–2218 BCE), governors of cities were considered mere servants of the king, who, in turn, called himself "King of the Four Quarters"—in effect, ruler of the earth, akin to a god.

IMPERIAL MAJESTY VANDALIZED A magnificent copper head of an Akkadian king (FIG. **2-12**) found at Nineveh embodies this new concept of absolute monarchy. The head is all that survives of a statue that was knocked over in antiquity, perhaps when the Medes sacked Nineveh in 612 BCE. But the damage to the portrait was not due solely to the statue's toppling. There are also signs of deliberate mutilation. To make a political statement,

the enemy gouged out the eyes (once inlaid with precious or semiprecious stones), broke off the lower part of the beard, and slashed the ears of the royal portrait. Nonetheless, the king's majestic serenity, dignity, and authority are evident. So, too, is the

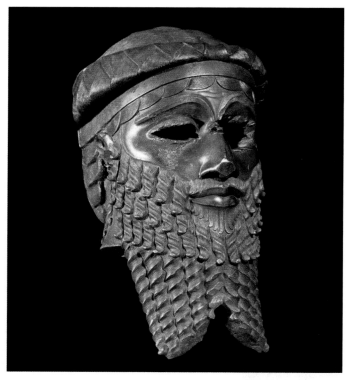

2-12 Head of an Akkadian ruler, from Nineveh (modern Kuyunjik), Iraq, ca. 2250–2200 BCE. Copper, 1′ 2⅜″ high. Iraq Museum, Baghdad.

masterful way the sculptor balanced naturalism and abstract patterning. The artist carefully observed and recorded the man's distinctive features—the profile of the nose and the long, curly beard. The sculptor brilliantly communicated the differing textures of flesh and hair—even the contrasting textures of the mustache, beard, and braided hair on the top of the head. The coiffure's triangles, lozenges, and overlapping disks of hair and the great arching eyebrows that give such character to the portrait reveal that the artist was also sensitive to formal pattern.

No less remarkable is the fact this is a life-size, hollow-cast metal sculpture (see "Hollow-Casting Life-Size Bronze Statues," Chapter 5, page 131), one of the earliest known. The head demonstrates the artisan's sophisticated skill in casting and polishing copper and in engraving the details. The portrait is the earliest known great monumental work of hollow-cast sculpture.

A GOD-KING CRUSHES AN ENEMY The godlike sovereignty the kings of Akkad claimed is also evident in the victory stele (FIG. **2-13**) Naram-Sin set up at Sippar. The stele commemorates his defeat of the Lullubi, a people of the Iranian mountains to the east. It is inscribed twice, once in honor of Naram-Sin and once by an Elamite king who had captured Sippar in 1157 BCE and taken the stele as booty back to Susa, where it was found. On the stele, the grandson of Sargon leads his victorious army up the slopes of a wooded mountain. His routed enemies fall, flee, die, or beg for mercy. The king stands alone, far taller than his men, treading on the bodies of two of the fallen Lullubi. He wears the horned helmet signifying divinity—the first time a king appears as a god in Mesopotamian art. At least three favorable stars (the stele is damaged at the top) shine on his triumph.

By storming the mountain, Naram-Sin seems also to be scaling the ladder to the heavens, the same conceit that lies behind the great ziggurat towers of the ancient Near East. His troops march up the mountain behind him in orderly files, suggesting the discipline and organization of the king's forces. The enemy, by contrast, is in disarray, depicted in a great variety of postures—one falls headlong down the mountainside. The sculptor adhered to older conventions in many details, especially by portraying the king and his soldiers in composite views and by placing a frontal two-horned helmet on Naram-Sin's profile head. But in other respects this work shows daring innovation. Here, the sculptor created the first landscape in Near Eastern art since the Çatal Höyük mural (see FIG. 1-18) and set the figures on successive tiers within that landscape. This was a bold rejection of the standard means of telling a story in a series of horizontal registers, the compositional formula that was the rule not only in earlier Mesopotamian art but also in Egyptian art.

2-13 Victory stele of Naram-Sin, from Susa, Iran, 2254–2218 BCE. Pink sandstone, approx. 6′ 7″ high. Louvre, Paris.

THE RESURGENCE OF SUMER Around 2150 BCE, a mountain people, the Gutians, brought Akkadian power to an end. The cities of Sumer, however, soon united in response to the alien presence, drove the Gutians out of Mesopotamia, and established a Neo-Sumerian state ruled by the kings of Ur. This age, which historians call the Third Dynasty of Ur, saw the construction of the ziggurat at Ur (FIG. **2-14**), one of the largest in Mesopotamia.

2-14 Ziggurat (northeastern facade with restored stairs), Ur (modern Tell Muqayyar), Iraq, ca. 2100 BCE.

The Piety of Gudea

One of the central figures of the Neo-Sumerian age was Gudea, ensi of Lagash ca. 2100 BCE. Nearly two dozen portraits of him survive. All stood in temples where they could render perpetual service to the gods and intercede with the divine powers on his behalf. Although a powerful ruler, Gudea rejected the regal trappings of Sargon of Akkad and his successors in favor of a return to the Sumerian votive tradition of the statuettes from Eshnunna and Mari (FIGS. 2-5 and 2-6). Like the earlier examples, some of Gudea's statues are inscribed with messages to the gods of Sumer. One from Girsu says, "I am the shepherd loved by my king [Ningirsu, the god of Girsu]; may my life be prolonged." Another, also from Girsu, as if in answer to the first, says, "Gudea, the builder of the temple, has been given life."

In fact, Gudea built or rebuilt, at great cost, all the temples where he placed his statues. One characteristic portrait (FIG. 2-15) depicts the pious ruler of Lagash seated with his hands clasped in front of him in a gesture of prayer. The head is unfortunately lost, but the statue is of unique interest because Gudea has a temple plan drawn on a tablet on his lap. The ruler buried accounts of his building enterprises in the temple foundations. The surviving texts describe how the Neo-Sumerians prepared and purified the sites, obtained the materials, and dedicated the completed temples. They also record Gudea's dreams of the gods asking him to erect temples in their honor, promising him prosperity if he fulfilled his duty. In one of these dreams, Ningirsu addresses Gudea:

> When, O faithful shepherd Gudea, thou shalt have started work for me on Erinnu, my royal abode [Ningirsu's new temple], I will call up in heaven a humid wind. It shall bring the abundance from on high. . . . All the great fields will bear for thee; dykes and canals will swell for thee; . . . good weight of wool will be given in thy time.[1]

In our statue, Gudea presents Ningirsu with his plan for the god's new temple. When the structure was completed and his people enjoyed good harvests and plentiful flocks, they knew it was the result of Gudea's piety.

[1] Thorkild Jacobsen, trans., *The Art and Architecture of the Ancient Orient*, by Henri Frankfort, 5th ed. (New Haven: Yale University Press, 1996), 98.

The Ur ziggurat was built about a millennium later than that at Uruk (FIGS. 2-1 and 2-2) and is much grander. The base is a solid mass of mud brick 50 feet high. The builders used baked bricks laid in bitumen, an asphaltlike substance, for the facing of the entire monument. Three ramplike stairways of a hundred steps each converge on a tower-flanked gateway. From there another flight of steps probably led to the temple proper, which does not survive.

GUDEA'S DIORITE PORTRAITS The most conspicuous preserved sculptural monuments of the Neo-Sumerian age portray Gudea of Lagash (see "The Piety of Gudea," above). His statues show him seated or standing, hands tightly clasped, head shaven, sometimes wearing a woolen brimmed hat, and always dressed in a long garment that leaves one shoulder and arm exposed (FIG. 2-15). Gudea was zealous in granting the gods their due, and the numerous statues he commissioned are an enduring testimony to his piety—and to his wealth and pride. All his portraits are of polished diorite, a rare and costly dark stone that had to be imported. Diorite is also extremely hard and difficult to carve. The prestige of the material—which in turn lent prestige to Gudea's portraits—is evident from an inscription on one of Gudea's statues: "This statue has not been made from silver nor from lapis lazuli, nor from copper nor from lead, nor yet from bronze; it is made of diorite."

HAMMURABI OF BABYLON The resurgence of Sumer was short-lived. The last of the kings of the Third Dynasty of Ur fell at the hands of the Elamites, who ruled the territory east of the Tigris River. The following two centuries witnessed the reemergence of the traditional Mesopotamian political pattern of several independent city-states existing side by side. Until Babylon's most powerful king, Hammurabi (r. 1792–1750 BCE), reestablished a centralized government that ruled southern Mesopotamia, Babylon was one of these city-states. Perhaps the most renowned king in Mesopo-

2-15 Seated statue of Gudea holding temple plan, from Girsu (modern Telloh), Iraq, ca. 2100 BCE. Diorite, approx. 2′ 5″ high. Louvre, Paris.

Hammurabi's Law Code

In the early 18th century BCE, King Hammurabi of Babylon formulated a comprehensive law code for his people. At the time, parts of Europe were still in the Stone Age (see FIG. 1-19). Even in Greece, it was not until more than 1,000 years later that Draco provided Athens with its first written set of laws. Hammurabi was following the tradition his Sumerian predecessors established. Two similar earlier law codes survive in part, but Hammurabi's laws are the only ones known in great detail, thanks to the chance survival of a tall and narrow stele (FIG. 2-16) depicting the god Shamash extending to Hammurabi the rod and ring that symbolize authority. The symbols derive from builders' tools—measuring rods and coiled rope—and connote the ruler's capacity to build the social order and to measure people's lives, that is, to render judgments. The sculptor thus informed viewers that Hammurabi had the god-given authority to enforce the laws spelled out on the stele. The judicial code, written in Akkadian, was inscribed in 3,500 lines of cuneiform characters. Hammurabi's laws governed all aspects of Babylonian life, from commerce and property to murder and theft to marital fidelity, inheritances, and the treatment of slaves.

We list only a small sample of the infractions described and the penalties imposed (which vary with the person's standing in society).

- If a man puts out the eye of another man, his eye shall be put out.
- If he kills a man's slave, he shall pay one-third of a *mina*.
- If someone steals property from a temple, he will be put to death, as will the person who receives the stolen goods.
- If a man rents a boat and the boat is wrecked, the renter shall replace the boat with another.
- If a married woman dies before bearing any sons, her dowry shall be repaid to her father, but if she gave birth to sons, the dowry shall belong to them.
- If a man's wife is caught in bed with another man, both will be tied up and thrown in the water.

tamian history, Hammurabi was famous for his conquests. But he is best known today for his law code, which prescribed penalties for everything from adultery and murder to the cutting down of a neighbor's trees (see "Hammurabi's Law Code," above).

The code is inscribed on a tall black-basalt stele (FIG. 2-16) that was carried off as booty to Susa in 1157 BCE, together with the Naram-Sin stele (FIG. 2-13). At the top is a relief depicting Hammurabi in the presence of the flame-shouldered sun god, Shamash. The king raises his hand in respect. The god bestows on Hammurabi the authority to rule and to enforce the laws.

The sculptor depicted Shamash in the familiar convention of combined front and side views, but with two important exceptions. His great headdress with its four pairs of horns is in true profile so that only four, not all eight, of the horns are visible. And the artist seems to have tentatively explored the notion of *foreshortening*—a device for suggesting depth by representing a figure or object at an angle, rather than frontally or in profile. The god's beard is a series of diagonal rather than horizontal lines, suggesting its recession from the picture plane.

ZIMRI-LIM AND ISHTAR While Hammurabi ruled Babylon, King Zimri-Lim (r. 1779–1757 BCE) controlled the Neo-Sumerian city-state of Mari. Zimri-Lim constructed a huge palace complex at Mari, but in 1757 BCE Hammurabi led an army into the city and destroyed the royal residence. The mud-brick palace walls were adorned with paintings on plaster. Fortunately, despite their extreme fragility, some of the paintings survive. They provide a rare opportunity to study the art of mural painting in Mesopotamia.

The painting we reproduce (FIG. 2-17) covered one wall of the palace's main courtyard near the entrance to the throne room suite. At the center, the painter represented the *investiture* of Zimri-Lim, the granting of his right to rule, by the goddess Ishtar. The king approaches Ishtar with his right arm raised in greeting and respect, just as Hammurabi appeared before Shamash

2-16 Stele with law code of Hammurabi, from Susa, Iran, ca. 1780 BCE. Basalt, approx. 7′ 4″ high. Louvre, Paris.

2-17 Investiture of Zimri-Lim, mural painting from Court 106 of the palace at Mari (modern Tell Hariri), Syria, ca. 1775–1760 BCE. Louvre, Paris.

(FIG. 2-16). The goddess has one foot on her sacred lion and offers Zimri-Lim the emblems of power, the rod and ring. A god and two other goddesses witness the ceremony. Below, two more goddesses display vases from which plants grow and streams of life-giving water flow. Fish swim freely in the current. The general theme is a venerable one. The gods grant royal authority to their chosen kings and prosperity to their people.

As on Hammurabi's stele, the horned crowns the deities wear are in profile, although the painter showed no interest in foreshortening. In fact, such experiments are very uncommon. Innovations in representational modes like this one and the bold abandonment of the register format in favor of a tiered landscape on the Naram-Sin stele (FIG. 2-13) were exceptional in early eras

of the history of art. These occasional departures from the norm testify to the creativity of some ancient Near Eastern artists.

THE HITTITES' FORTIFIED CAPITAL The Babylonian Empire toppled in the face of an onslaught by the Hittites, an Anatolian people who conquered and sacked Babylon around 1595 BCE. They then retired to their homeland, leaving Babylon in the hands of the Kassites. Remains of the strongly fortified capital city of the Hittites still may be seen near Boghazköy, Turkey. Constructed of large blocks of heavy stone—a striking contrast to the brick architecture of Mesopotamia—the walls and towers of the Hittites effectively protected them from attack. Symbolically guarding the gateway (FIG. **2-18**) to the Boghazköy

2-18 Lion Gate, Boghazköy, Turkey, ca. 1400 BCE. Limestone, lions approx. 7′ high.

citadel are two huge (seven-foot-high) lions. Their simply carved forequarters project from massive stone blocks on either side of the entrance. These Hittite guardian beasts are early examples of a theme that was to be echoed on many Near Eastern gates. Notable are those of Assyria (FIG. 2-21), one of the greatest empires of the ancient world, and of the reborn Babylon (FIG. 2-25) in the first millennium BCE. But the idea of protecting a city, palace, temple, or tomb from evil by placing wild beasts or fantastic monsters before an entranceway was not unique to the Near Eastern world. Examples abound in Egypt, Greece, Italy, and elsewhere.

MIDDLE ELAMITE AND ASSYRIAN ART

ELAM AT ITS HEIGHT To the east of Sumer, Akkad, and Babylon, the Elamites and their ancestors had occupied southwestern Iran since the fourth millennium BCE. Elam appears in the Bible as early as Genesis 10:22, and Proto-Elamite and Elamite records are among the earliest written documents known (see "The Invention of Writing," page 33). During the second half of the second millennium BCE, Elam reached the height of its political and military power. At this time the Elamites were strong enough to plunder Babylonia and to carry off the stelae of Naram-Sin and Hammurabi (FIGS. 2-13 and 2-16) and reerect them at their capital city, Susa. The Assyrian king Ashurbanipal finally destroyed the empire of Elam in 641 BCE when he sacked Susa. The city would rise again to great importance under the Achaemenid Persian Empire.

NAPIR-ASU'S IMMOVABLE PORTRAIT In the ruins of Susa, archaeologists discovered a life-size bronze-and-copper statue of Queen Napir-Asu (FIG. **2-19**), wife of one of the most powerful Elamite kings, Untash-Napirisha. The statue weighs 3,760 pounds even in its fragmentary and mutilated state, because the sculptor, incredibly, cast the statue with a solid bronze core inside a hollow-cast copper shell. The bronze core increased the cost of the statue enormously, but the queen wished her portrait to be a permanent, immovable votive offering in the temple where it was found. In fact, the Elamite inscription on the queen's skirt explicitly asks the gods to protect the statue:

> He who would seize my statue, who would smash it, who would destroy its inscription, who would erase my name, may he be smitten by the curse of [the gods], that his name shall become extinct, that his offspring be barren. . . . This is Napir-Asu's offering.[1]

The statue thus falls within the votive tradition going back to the third millennium BCE and the figurines from Eshnunna and Mari (FIGS. 2-5 and 2-6). In the Elamite statue of Queen Napir-Asu, the Mesopotamian instinct for cylindrical volume is again evident. The portrait's tight silhouette, strict frontality, and firmly crossed hands held close to the body are all enduring characteristics common to the Sumerian statuettes. Yet within these rigid conventions of form and pose, the Elamite artist managed to create refinements that must have come from close observation. The sculptor conveyed the feminine softness of arm and bust, the grace and elegance of the long-fingered hands, the supple and quiet bend of the wrist, the ring and bracelets, and the gown's patterned fabric. The loss of the head is especially unfortunate. The figure presents a portrait of the ideal queen. The hands crossed over the belly may allude to fertility and the queen's role in assuring peaceful dynastic succession.

ASSYRIAN FORTRESS-PALACES During the first half of the first millennium BCE, the fearsome Assyrians vanquished the various warfaring peoples that succeeded the Babylonians and Hittites. The Assyrians took their name from Assur, the city on the Tigris River in northern Iraq named for the god Ashur. At the height of their power, the Assyrians ruled an empire that extended from the Tigris to the Nile Rivers and from the Persian Gulf to Asia Minor. Their palaces have been excavated in large part, yielding not only their plans but also statues, mural paintings, and the most extensive series of narrative reliefs in the ancient Near East.

2-19 Statue of Queen Napir-Asu, from Susa, Iran, ca. 1350–1300 BCE. Bronze and copper, 4′ 2¾″ high. Louvre, Paris.

2-20 Reconstruction drawing of the citadel of Sargon II, Dur Sharrukin (modern Khorsabad), Iraq, ca. 720–705 BCE (after Charles Altman).

The unfinished royal citadel of Sargon II (r. 721–705 BCE) at Dur Sharrukin (FIG. **2-20**) reveals in its ambitious layout the confidence of the Assyrian kings in their all-conquering might. Its strong defensive walls also reflect a society ever fearful of attack during a period of almost constant warfare. The city measures about a square mile in area. The palace, elevated on a mound 50 feet high, covered some 25 acres and had more than 200 courtyards and rooms. As our reconstruction drawing shows, although the palace complex layout had a basic symmetry, the plan is rambling. Timber-roofed rectangular rooms and halls are grouped around square and rectangular courts. Behind the main courtyard, whose sides each measured 300 feet, were the residential quarters of the king, who received foreign emissaries in the long, high, brightly painted throne room. All visitors entered from another large courtyard, where giant figures of the king and his courtiers lined the walls.

Sargon II regarded his city and palace as an expression of his grandeur. The Assyrians cultivated an image of themselves as merciless to anyone who dared oppose them, although they were forgiving to those who submitted to their will. Sargon, for example, wrote in an inscription, "I built a city with [the labors of] the peoples subdued by my hand, whom Ashur, Nabu, and Marduk had caused to lay themselves at my feet and bear my yoke." And in another text, he proclaimed, "Sargon, King of the World, has built a city. Dur Sharrukin he has named it. A peerless palace he has built within it."

In addition to the complex of courtyards, throne room, state chambers, service quarters, and guard rooms that made up the palace, the citadel included a great ziggurat and six sanctuaries for six different gods. The ziggurat at Dur Sharrukin may have had as many as seven stories. Four remain, each 18 feet high and painted a different color. A continuous ramp spiraled around the building from its base to the temple at its summit. Here, the legacy of the Sumerian bent-axis approach may be seen more than two millennia after the erection of the White Temple on the ziggurat at Uruk (FIG. 2-1).

2-21 Lamassu (winged, human-headed bull), from the citadel of Sargon II, Dur Sharrukin (modern Khorsabad), Iraq, ca. 720–705 BCE. Limestone, approx. 13′ 10″ high. Louvre, Paris.

2-22 Assyrian archers pursuing enemies, relief from the Northwest Palace of Ashurnasirpal II, Kalhu (modern Nimrud), Iraq, ca. 875–860 BCE. Gypsum, 2′ 10$\frac{5}{8}$″ high. British Museum, London.

MONSTROUS GUARDIANS Guarding the gate to Sargon's palace were colossal limestone monsters (FIG. 2-21), which the Assyrians probably called *lamassu*. These winged, man-headed bulls served to ward off the king's enemies. The task of moving and installing such immense stone sculptures was so daunting that several reliefs in the palace of Sargon's successor celebrate the feat, showing scores of men dragging lamassu figures with the aid of ropes and sledges.

The Assyrian lamassu sculptures are partly in the round, but the sculptor nonetheless conceived them as high reliefs on adjacent sides of a corner. They combine the front view of the animal at rest with the side view of it in motion. Seeking to present a complete picture of the lamassu from both the front and the side, the sculptor gave the monster five legs (two seen from the front, four seen from the side). The three-quarter view the modern photographer chose would not have been favored in antiquity. This sculpture, then, is yet another case of early artists' providing a *conceptual picture* of an animal or person and of all its important parts, as opposed to an *optical view* of the lamassu as it actually would stand in space.

CHRONICLES OF GREAT DEEDS For their palace walls the Assyrian kings commissioned extensive series of narrative reliefs exalting royal power and piety. The sculptures record not only battlefield victories but also the slaying of wild animals. (The Assyrians, like many other societies before and after, regarded prowess in hunting as a manly virtue on a par with success in warfare.) These narrative reliefs have precedents in Egypt, but in a very different format (see Chapter 3). The degree of documentary detail in the Assyrian reliefs is without parallel in the ancient Near East, even in such narratives as those on the *Stele of the Vultures* (FIG. 2-7) and the *Standard of Ur* (FIG. 2-8). Archaeologists have found nothing else comparable made before the Roman Empire (see Chapter 10).

One of the most extensive—and earliest—examples of a cycle of historical narrative reliefs comes from the palace of Ashurnasirpal II (r. 883–859 BCE) at Kalhu. (The Assyrian kings frequently incorporated Ashur's name into their own.) Throughout

the palace, painted gypsum reliefs sheathed the lower parts of the mud-brick walls below brightly colored plaster. Rich textiles on the floors contributed to the luxurious ambience. Every relief celebrated the king and bore an inscription naming Ashurnasirpal and describing his accomplishments.

The example we illustrate (FIG. 2-22) probably depicts an episode that occurred in 878 BCE when Ashurnasirpal drove his enemy's forces into the Euphrates River. In the relief, two Assyrian archers shoot arrows at the fleeing foe. Three enemy soldiers are in the water. One swims with an arrow in his back. The other two attempt to float to safety by inflating animal skins. Their destination is a fort where their compatriots await them. The artist showed the fort as if it were in the middle of the river, but it must, of course, have been on land, perhaps at some distance from where the escapees entered the water. The artist's purpose was to tell the story clearly and economically. In art, distances can be compressed and the human actors enlarged so that they stand out from their environment. (Literally interpreted, the defenders of the fort are too tall to walk through its archway.) The sculptor also combined different viewpoints in the same frame, just as the figures are composites of frontal and profile views. Viewers see the river from above while observing the men, trees, and fort from the side. The artist also made other adjustments for clarity. So as not to hide the archers' faces, the sculptor depicted their bowstrings in front of their bodies but behind their heads. The men will snare their own heads in their bows when they launch their arrows! All these liberties with optical reality result, however, in a vivid and easily legible retelling of a decisive moment in the king's victorious campaign. This was the artist's primary goal.

ASSYRIAN PAINTING The Assyrian palace reliefs frequently portrayed the king and his retinue in ceremonial roles or paying homage to the gods. The same subjects occupied the court painters. Unfortunately, Assyrian paintings, because of their fragile nature, are much rarer today than stone reliefs. A fine example of the painter's art is the *glazed brick* (painted and then kiln fired to fuse the color with the baked clay) from

NOBLE ANIMAL ADVERSARIES Two centuries later, sculptors carved hunting reliefs for the Nineveh palace of the conqueror of Elamite Susa, Ashurbanipal (r. 668–627 BCE). The hunt did not take place in the wild but in a controlled environment, ensuring the king's safety and success. In the relief illustrated here (FIG. **2-24**), lions released from cages in a large enclosed arena charge the king, who, in his chariot and with his attendants, thrusts a spear into a savage lion. The animal leaps at the king even though it already has two arrows in its body. All around the royal chariot is a pathetic trail of dead and dying animals, pierced by what appear to be far more arrows than needed to kill them. Blood streams from some of the lions, but they refuse to die. The artist brilliantly depicted the straining muscles, the swelling veins, the muzzles' wrinkled skin, and the flattened ears of the powerful and defiant beasts. Modern sympathies make this scene of carnage a kind of heroic tragedy, with the lions as protagonists. It is unlikely, however, that the king's artists had any intention other than to glorify their ruler by showing the king of men pitting himself against and repeatedly conquering the king of beasts. Portraying Ashurbanipal's beastly foes as possessing not merely strength but courage and nobility served to make the king's accomplishments that much grander.

NEO-BABYLONIAN AND ACHAEMENID PERSIAN ART

The Assyrian Empire was never very secure, and most of its kings had to fight revolts in large sections of the Near East. Assyria's conquest of Elam in the seventh century BCE and frequent rebellions in Babylonia apparently overextended its resources. During the last years of Ashurbanipal's reign, the empire began to disintegrate. Under his successors, it collapsed from the simultaneous onslaught of the Medes from the east and the resurgent Babylonians from the south. Neo-Babylonian kings held sway over the former Assyrian Empire until the Persian conquest.

WONDROUS BABYLON The most renowned of the Neo-Babylonian kings was Nebuchadnezzar II (r. 604–562 BCE), whose exploits the biblical Book of Daniel recounts. Nebuchadnezzar restored Babylon to its rank as one of the great cities of antiquity. The city's famous hanging gardens were counted among the Seven Wonders of the ancient world, and its enormous ziggurat was

2-23 Ashurnasirpal II with attendants and soldier, from his palace at Kalhu, Iraq, ca. 875–860 BCE. Glazed brick, 11¾″ high. British Museum, London.

Ashurnasirpal II's Kalhu palace (FIG. **2-23**). It shows the king, taller than everyone else as befits his rank, delicately holding a cup. With it, he will make a *libation* (ritual pouring of liquid) in honor of the protective gods. The artist rendered the figures in outline, lavishing much attention on the patterns of the rich fabrics they wear. The king and the attendant behind him are in consistent profile view, but the rule of showing the eye from the front in a profile head still held. Painted scenes such as this hint at what the Assyrian stone reliefs might have looked like with their original paint intact.

2-24 Ashurbanipal hunting lions, relief from the North Palace of Ashurbanipal, Nineveh (modern Kuyunjik), Iraq, ca. 645–640 BCE. Gypsum, 5′ 4″ high. British Museum, London.

Babylon: City of Wonders

The uncontested list of the Seven Wonders of the ancient world was not codified until the 16th century. But already in the 2nd century BCE, Antipater of Sidon, a Greek poet, compiled a roster of seven must-see monuments, including six of the seven later Wonders. All of the Wonders were of colossal size and constructed at great expense. Three of them were of great antiquity: the pyramids of Gizeh (see FIG. 3-8), which Antipater described as "man-made mountains," and the "hanging gardens" and "walls of impregnable Babylon."

Babylon was the only site on Antipater's list that could boast two Wonders. Later list makers preferred to distribute the Seven Wonders among seven different cities. Most of these Wonders date to Greek times—the Temple of Artemis at Ephesus, with its 60-foot-tall columns; Phidias's colossal gold-and-ivory statue of Zeus at Olympia; the grandiose tomb of Mausolus (the "Mausoleum") at Halikarnassos; the Colossus of Rhodes, a bronze statue of the sun god 110 feet tall; and the lighthouse at Alexandria, perhaps the tallest building in the ancient world. The pyramids are the oldest and the Babylonian gardens the only Wonder in the category of "landscape architecture."

Several ancient texts describe Babylon's gardens. We quote part of the account Quintus Curtius Rufus wrote in the mid-first century CE:

On the top of the citadel are the hanging gardens, a wonder celebrated in the tales of the Greeks. . . . Columns of stone were set up to sustain the whole work, and on these was laid a floor of squared blocks, strong enough to hold the earth which is thrown upon it to a great depth, as well as the water with which they irrigate the soil; and the structure supports trees of such great size that the thickness of their trunks equals a measure of eight cubits [about twelve feet].

They tower to a height of fifty feet, and they yield as much fruit as if they were growing in their native soil. . . . To those who look upon [the trees] from a distance, real woods seem to be overhanging their native mountains.[1]

Not qualifying as a Wonder, but in some ways no less impressive, was Babylon's Marduk ziggurat, the biblical Tower of Babel. According to the Bible, humankind's arrogant desire to build a tower to Heaven angered God. The Lord put an end to it by causing the workers to speak different languages, preventing them from communicating with one another. The fifth-century BCE Greek historian Herodotus described the Babylonian temple complex:

In the middle of the sanctuary [of Marduk] has been built a solid tower . . . which supports another tower, which in turn supports another, and so on: there are eight towers in all. A stairway has been constructed to wind its way up the outside of all the towers; halfway up the stairway there is a shelter with benches to rest on, where people making the ascent can sit and catch their breath. In the last tower there is a huge temple. The temple contains a large couch, which is adorned with fine coverings and has a golden table standing beside it, but there are no statues at all standing there. . . . [The Babylonians] say that the god comes in person to the temple [compare the Sumerian notion of the temple as a "waiting room"] and rests on the couch; I do not believe this story myself.[2]

[1] John C. Rolfe, trans., *Quintus Curtius I* (Cambridge: Harvard University Press, 1971), 337–39.
[2] Robin Waterfield, trans., *Herodotus: The Histories* (New York: Oxford University Press, 1998), 79–80.

---

immortalized in the Bible as the Tower of Babel (see "Babylon: City of Wonders," above).

Nebuchadnezzar's Babylon was a mud-brick city, but dazzling blue-glazed bricks faced the most important monuments. Some of the buildings, such as the Ishtar Gate (FIG. **2-25**), with its imposing arched opening flanked by towers, featured glazed bricks with molded reliefs of animals, real and imaginary. Glazed bricks had been used earlier (FIG. 2-23), but the surface of the bricks, even of those with figures, was flat. Each Babylonian brick was molded and glazed separately, then set in proper sequence on the wall. On Ishtar's Gate, profile figures of Marduk's dragon and Adad's bull alternate. Lining the processional way leading up to the gate were reliefs of Ishtar's sacred lion, glazed in yellow, brown, and red against a blue ground.

THE TRIUMPH OF PERSIA Although Nebuchadnezzar, "King of Kings" of the biblical Daniel, had boasted that he "caused a mighty wall to circumscribe Babylon . . . so that the enemy who would do evil would not threaten," Cyrus of Persia (r. 559–529BCE) captured the city in the sixth century. Cyrus, who may have been descended from an Elamite line, was the founder of the Achaemenid dynasty and traced his ancestry back to a mythical King Achaemenes. Babylon was but one of the Persians' conquests. Egypt fell to them in 525 BCE, and by 480 BCE the Persian Empire

2-25 Ishtar Gate (restored), Babylon, Iraq, ca. 575 BCE. Glazed brick. Staatliche Museen, Berlin.

2-26 Persepolis (royal audience hall in the background), Iran, ca. 521–465 BCE.

was the largest the world had yet known, extending from the Indus River in South Asia to the Danube River in northeastern Europe. Only the successful Greek resistance in the fifth century BCE prevented Persia from embracing southeastern Europe as well (see Chapter 5). The Achaemenid line ended with the death of Darius III in 330 BCE, after his defeat at the hands of Alexander the Great (see FIG. 5-69).

IMPERIAL PERSEPOLIS The most important source of knowledge about Persian art and architecture is the ceremonial and administrative complex on the citadel at Persepolis (FIG. 2-26), which the successors of Cyrus, Darius I (r. 522–486 BCE) and Xerxes (r. 486–465 BCE), built between 521 and 465 BCE. Situated on a high plateau, the heavily fortified complex of royal buildings stood on a wide platform overlooking the plain. Alexander the Great razed the site in a gesture symbolizing the destruction of Persian imperial power. Some said it was an act of revenge for the Persian sack of the Athenian Acropolis in the early fifth century BCE (see Chapter 5). But even in ruins, the Persepolis citadel is impressive.

The approach to the citadel led through a monumental gateway called the Gate of All Lands, a reference to the harmony among the peoples of the vast Persian empire. Assyrian-inspired colossal man-headed winged bulls flanked the great entrance. Broad ceremonial stairways provided access to the platform and the royal audience hall, or *apadana,* a huge hall 60 feet high and 217 feet square, containing 36 colossal columns. An audience of thousands could have stood within the hall.

The reliefs (FIG. 2-27) decorating the walls of the terrace and staircases leading to the apadana represent processions of royal guards, Persian nobles and dignitaries, and representatives from 23 subject nations bringing the king tribute. Every one of the emissaries wears his national costume and carries a typical regional gift for the conqueror. The carving of the Persepolis reliefs is technically superb, with subtly modeled surfaces and crisply chiseled details. Traces of color prove that the reliefs were painted, and the original effect must have been even more striking than it is today. Although the Persepolis sculptures may have been inspired by those in Assyrian palaces, they are different in style. The forms are more rounded, and they project more from the background. Some of the details, notably the treatment of drapery folds, echo forms characteristic of Archaic Greek sculpture, and Greek influence seems to be one of the many ingredients of Achaemenid style. Persian art testifies to the active exchange of ideas and artists among Mediterranean and Near Eastern civilizations at this date. A building inscription at Susa, for example, names Ionian Greeks, Medes (who occupied the land north of Persia), Egyptians, and Babylonians among those who built and decorated the palace. Under the single-minded direction of its Persian masters, this heterogeneous workforce, with a widely varied cultural and artistic background, created a new and coherent style that perfectly suited the expression of Persian imperial ambitions.

SASANIAN ART

THE NEW PERSIAN EMPIRE Alexander the Great's conquest of Persia in 330 BCE marked the beginning of a long period of first Greek and then Roman rule of large parts of the ancient Near East, beginning with one of Alexander's former generals, Seleucus I (r. 312–281 BCE), founder of the Seleucid dynasty. In the third century CE, however, a new power rose up in Persia that challenged the Romans and sought to force them out of Asia. The new rulers called themselves Sasanians. They traced their lineage to a legendary figure named Sasan, said to be a direct descendant of the Achaemenid kings. Their New Persian Empire was founded in 224 CE, when the first Sasanian king, Artaxerxes I (r. 211–241), defeated the Parthians (another of Rome's eastern enemies). It endured more than 400 years, until the Arabs drove the Sasanians out of Mesopotamia in 636, just four years after the death of Muhammad, the prophet and founder of Islam (see Chapter 13).

SHAPUR AND CTESIPHON The son and successor of Artaxerxes, Shapur I (r. 241–272), succeeded in further extending

Sasanian territory. He also erected a great palace (FIG. **2-28**) at Ctesiphon, the capital his father had established near modern Baghdad in Iraq. The central feature of Shapur's palace was the monumental *iwan,* or brick audience hall, covered by a *barrel vault* (in effect, a deep *arch* over an oblong space) that came almost to a point some 900 feet above the ground. The facade to the left and right of the iwan was divided into a series of horizontal bands made up of *blind arcades,* a series of arches without actual openings, applied as wall decoration. A thousand years later, Islamic architects looked at Shapur's palace and especially its soaring iwan and established it as the standard for judging their own engineering feats (see Chapter 13).

2-28 Palace of Shapur I, Ctesiphon, Iraq, ca. 250 CE.

2-29 Head of a Sasanian king (Shapur II?), ca. 350 CE. Silver with mercury gilding, 1' 3¾" high. Metropolitan Museum of Art, New York.

SASANIAN SPLENDOR A silver head (FIG. 2-29), possibly a portrait of Shapur II (r. 310–379), suggests the splendor of Sasanian court life. It testifies not only to the wealth of the Sasanian dynasty but also to the superb skills of its court artists. The head is slightly under life-size. The sculptor employed the *repoussé* technique, that is, hammered the shape from a single sheet of metal and pushed the features out from behind. The artist then engraved the details into the silver surface to give form and texture to the hair and beard and to lend the eyes an almost hypnotic stare. Selected portions of the portrait have mercury gilding to give the metal an even richer look and to add color. In this work, an unknown sculptor captured the essence of imperial majesty.

A REVERSAL OF FORTUNES So powerful was the Sasanian army that in 260 CE Shapur I even succeeded in capturing the Roman emperor Valerian near Edessa (in modern Turkey). His victory over Valerian was so significant an event that Shapur commemorated it in a series of rock-cut reliefs in the cliffs of Bishapur in Iran, far from the site of his triumph. We illustrate a detail (FIG. 2-30) of one of the Bishapur reliefs. Shapur appears larger than life, riding in from the left and wearing the same distinctive tall Sasanian crown worn by the king in the silver portrait (FIG. 2-29). The crown breaks through the relief's border

2-30 Triumph of Shapur I over Valerian, rock-cut relief, Bishapur, Iran, ca. 260 CE.

and draws attention to the king. The crumpled body of a Roman soldier lies between the legs of the Sasanian's horse — a time-honored motif (compare the *Standard of Ur,* FIG. 2-8). Here the sculptor probably meant to personify the entire Roman army. At the right, attendants lead in Valerian, who kneels before Shapur and begs for mercy. Above, a *putto*-like (cherub or childlike) figure borrowed from the repertory of Greco-Roman art hovers above the king and brings him a victory garland. Similar scenes of kneeling enemies before triumphant generals are commonplace in Roman art — but at Bishapur the roles are reversed. This appropriation of Roman compositional patterns and motifs in a relief celebrating the Sasanian defeat of the Romans adds another, ironic, level of meaning to the political message in stone.

CONCLUSION

The birth of civilization — urban life — and the invention of writing both occurred in Mesopotamia in the fourth millennium BCE. There, the Sumerians built the first monumental temples and filled their religious precincts and tombs with statues, reliefs, and objects of gold, lapis lazuli, and other costly materials. Their successors — the Akkadians, Babylonians, Assyrians, Persians, and others — continued the tradition of monumental art and architecture, erecting ruler portraits, stelae recording victories and law codes, and great palaces decorated with painted narrative reliefs. At times challenging both the Greeks and the Romans for supremacy in the Mediterranean, the empires of the ancient Near East finally succumbed to the Arabs in the seventh century CE. Thereafter, the greatest artists and architects of Mesopotamia worked in the service of Islam.

URUK			3500 BCE
JAMDAT NASR			3100 BCE

DEVELOPMENT OF WRITING AND THE BEGINNINGS OF RECORDED HISTORY

FLOWERING OF INDEPENDENT CITY-STATES

2900 BCE

1 BURIALS IN THE ROYAL CEMETERY, UR

1 Standard of Ur, ca. 2600 BCE

2300 BCE

SARGON OF AKKAD, CA. 2300 BCE

NARAM-SIN, R. CA. 2254–2218 BCE

2150 BCE

GUTIAN INVASION, CA. 2150 BCE

GUDEA OF LAGASH, CA. 2100 BCE

2000 BCE

1800 BCE

2 HAMMURABI, R. CA. 1792–1750 BCE

1600 BCE

SACK OF BABYLON BY HITTITES, CA. 1595 BCE

2 Stele of Hammurabi, ca. 1780 BCE

1000 BCE

900 BCE

ASHURNASIRPAL II, R. 883–859 BCE

SARGON II, R. 721–705 BCE

ASHURNASIRPAL, R. 668–627 BCE

612 BCE

3 NEBUCHADNEZZAR II, R. 604–562 BCE

3 Ishtar Gate, Babylon, ca. 575 BCE

538 BCE

DARIUS I, R. 522–486 BCE

XERXES, R. 486–465 BCE

BATTLE OF ISSUS, 333 BCE

330 BCE

DEATH OF ALEXANDER THE GREAT, 323 BCE

SELEUCUS I, R. 312–281 BCE

224 CE

DEFEAT OF VALERIAN BY SHAPUR I, 260 CE

4 SHAPUR II, R. 310–379 CE

4 Head of Shapur II(?), ca. 350 CE

636 CE

FINAL DEFEAT OF PERSIANS BY THE ARABS, 641 CE

Left margin vertical labels (top to bottom):

URUK
JAMDAT NASR
EARLY DYNASTIC (SUMERIAN)
AKKADIAN DYNASTY
THIRD DYNASTY OF UR (NEO-SUMERIAN)
OLD BABYLONIAN
KASSITES AND MITANNI (MESOPOTAMIA)
HITTITES (ANATOLIA)
MIDDLE ELAMITE PERIOD (IRAN)
ASSYRIAN EMPIRE
NEO-BABYLONIAN AND MEDIAN EMPIRES
ACHAEMENID PERSIAN EMPIRE
SELEUCID, PARTHIAN, AND ROMAN
SASANIAN DYNASTY

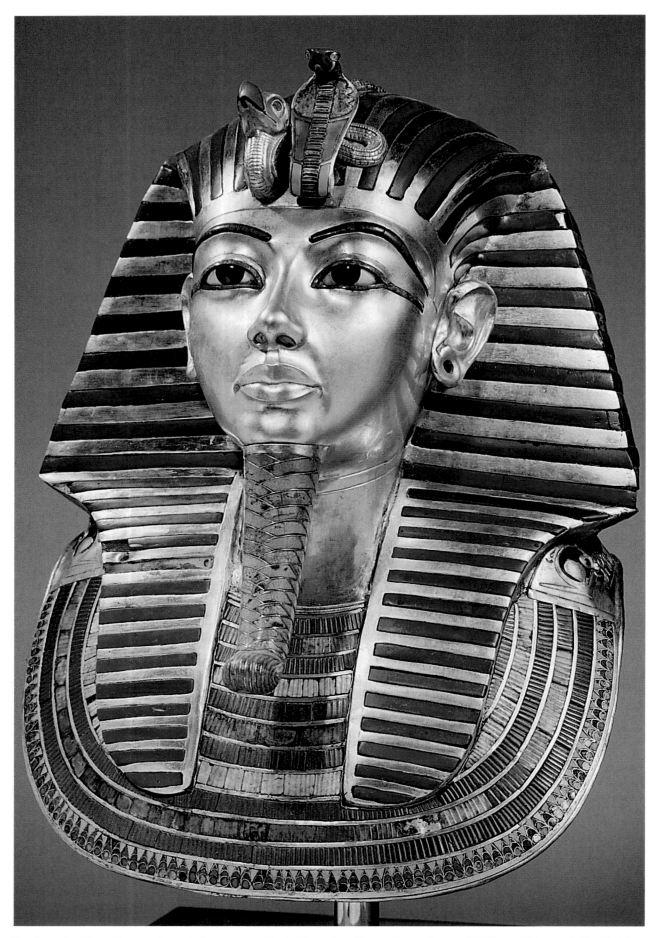

Death mask of Tutankhamen, from the innermost coffin in his tomb at Thebes, Egypt, Dynasty XVIII, ca. 1323 BCE. Gold with inlay of semiprecious stones, 1′ 9¼″ high. Egyptian Museum, Cairo.

3

PHARAOHS AND THE AFTERLIFE

THE ART OF ANCIENT EGYPT

Nearly 2,500 years ago, the Greek historian Herodotus wrote, "Concerning Egypt itself I shall extend my remarks to a great length, because there is no country that possesses so many wonders, nor any that has such a number of works that defy description."[1] Even today, many would agree with this assessment. The ancient Egyptians left to the world a profusion of spectacular monuments dating across three millennia. From the cliffs of the Libyan and Arabian Deserts they cut giant blocks of stone and erected grand temples to their immortal gods (see "The Gods and Goddesses of Egypt," page 57). From the same imperishable material that symbolized the timelessness of their world, the Egyptians set up countless statues of their equally immortal god-kings and built thousands of tombs to serve as eternal houses of the dead. The solemn and ageless art of the Egyptians expresses the unchanging order that, for them, was divinely established.

The backbone of Egypt was, and still is, the Nile River, whose annual floods supported all life in that ancient land (MAP 3-1). Even more than the Tigris and the Euphrates Rivers of Mesopotamia, the Nile defined the cultures that developed along its banks. Originating deep in Africa, the world's longest river flows through regions that may not receive a single drop of rainfall in a decade. Yet crops thrive from the rich soil that the Nile brings thousands of miles from the African hills. In the time of the *pharaohs,* the ancient Egyptian kings, the land bordering the Nile consisted of marshes dotted with island ridges. Amphibious animals swarmed in the marshes and were hunted through tall forests of *papyrus* and rushes (FIGS. 3-16 and 3-30). Egypt's fertility was famous. When Egypt became a province of the Roman Empire after Queen Cleopatra's death (r. 51–30 BCE), it served as the granary of the Mediterranean world.

THE BIRTH OF EGYPTOLOGY Even in the Middle Ages, Egypt's reputation as an ancient land of wonders and mystery lived on. Until the late 18th century, people regarded its undeciphered writing and exotic monuments as treasures of occult wisdom, locked away from any but those initiated in the mystic arts. Scholars knew something of Egypt's history from references in the Old Testament, from Herodotus

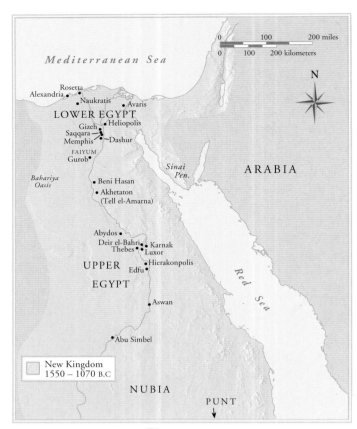

MAP 3-1 Ancient Egypt.

absolute dates of the pharaohs are still debated. The chronologies scholars have proposed for the earliest Egyptian dynasties can vary by as much as two centuries. Exact years cannot be assigned to the reigns of individual pharaohs until 664 BCE (Dynasty XXVI).[2]

At the end of the 18th century, when Europeans rediscovered Egypt, the land of the Nile became the first subject of archaeological exploration. In 1799, Napoleon Bonaparte, on a military expedition to Egypt, took with him a small troop of scholars, linguists, antiquarians, and artists. The chance discovery of the famed *Rosetta Stone,* now in the British Museum, gave the eager scholars a key to deciphering Egyptian *hieroglyphic* writing. The stone bears an inscription in three sections: one in Greek, which was easily read; one in *demotic* (Late Egyptian); and one in formal hieroglyphic. Scholars at once suspected that the text was the same in all three sections and that, using Greek as the key, they could decipher the other two sections. But progress was slow. Eventually, a young linguist, Jean-François Champollion, deduced that the hieroglyphs were not simply pictographs. He proposed that they were the signs of a once-spoken language whose traces survived in Coptic, the later language of Christian Egypt. Champollion's feat established him as a giant in the new field of *Egyptology.*

THE PREDYNASTIC AND EARLY DYNASTIC PERIODS

Painting and Sculpture

THE OLDEST EGYPTIAN ART The Predynastic, or prehistoric, beginnings of Egyptian civilization are chronologically vague. But tantalizing remains of tombs, paintings, pottery, and other artifacts from around 3500 BCE attest to the existence of a sophisticated culture on the banks of the Nile. A wall painting (FIG. 3-1) from the late Predynastic period, found in a tomb at

and other Greco-Roman authors, and from preserved portions of a history of Egypt written in Greek in the third century BCE by an Egyptian high priest named Manetho. Manetho described the succession of pharaohs, dividing them into the still-useful groups called *dynasties,* but his chronology was inaccurate, and the

3-1 People, boats, and animals, detail of a watercolor copy of a wall painting from Tomb 100 at Hierakonpolis, Egypt, Predynastic, ca. 3500–3200 BCE. Paint on plaster, entire painting approx. 16′ 3″ long. Egyptian Museum, Cairo.

The Gods and Goddesses of Egypt

The worldview of the Egyptians was distinct from those of their neighbors in the ancient Mediterranean and Near Eastern worlds. Egyptians believed that before the beginning of time the primeval waters, called *Nun*, existed alone in the darkness. At the moment of creation, a mound rose out of the limitless waters—just as muddy mounds emerge from the Nile after the annual flood recedes. On this mound the creator god appeared and brought light to the world. In later times, the mound was formalized as a pyramidal stone called the *ben-ben* supporting the supreme god, *Amen*, the god of the sun *(Re)*.

The supreme god also created the first of the other gods and goddesses of Egypt. According to one version of the myth, the creator masturbated and produced *Shu* and *Tefnut*, the primary male and female forces in the universe. They coupled to give birth to *Geb* (Earth) and *Nut* (Sky), who bore Osiris, Seth, Isis, and Nephthys. The eldest, *Osiris* (FIG. 3-39), was the god of order and was revered as the king who brought civilization to Egypt. His brother, *Seth*, was his evil opposite, the god of chaos. Seth murdered Osiris and cut him into pieces, which he scattered across Egypt. *Isis* (FIG. 3-39), the sister and consort of Osiris, with the help of *Nephthys* (FIG. 3-39), Seth's wife, succeeded in collecting Osiris's body parts, and with her powerful magic brought him

back to life. The resurrected Osiris fathered a son with Isis—*Horus*, who avenged his father's death and displaced Seth as king of Egypt. Osiris then became the lord of the underworld. Horus is represented in art either as a falcon, considered the noblest bird of the sky, or as a falcon-headed man (FIGS. 3-2, 3-12, 3-28, and 3-39). All Egyptian pharaohs were identified with Horus while alive and with Osiris after they died.

Other Egyptian deities included *Mut*, the consort of the sun god Amen, and *Khonsu*, the moon god, who was their son. *Thoth*, another lunar deity and the god of knowledge and writing, appears in art as an ibis, a baboon, or an ibis-headed man crowned with the crescent moon and the moon disk (FIG. 3-39). When Seth tore out Horus's falcon-eye *(wedjat)*, Thoth restored it. He, too, was associated with rebirth and the afterlife. *Hathor*, daughter of Re, was a divine mother of the pharaoh, nourishing him with her milk. She appears in Egyptian art as a cow-headed woman or as a woman with a cow's horns (FIGS. 3-2 and 3-28). *Anubis*, a jackal or jackal-headed deity, was the god of mummification and the weigher of hearts in the underworld (FIG. 3-39). *Maat*, another daughter of Re, was the goddess of truth and justice. Her feather was used to measure the weight of the deceased's heart to determine if the *ka* (life force) would be blessed in the afterlife.

Hierakonpolis, represents what seems to be, at least in part, a funerary scene with people, animals, and large boats. The painting is in the form of a frieze running around three adjacent walls of the tomb. The stick figures and their apparently random arrangement recall the Neolithic painted hunters of Çatal Höyük (see FIG. 1-17). One black and five white boats, symbolic of the journey down the river of life and death, carry cargo of uncertain significance. The figures include a heraldic grouping of two animals flanking a human figure (at the lower left) and a man striking three prisoners with a mace (lower left corner). The heraldic group, a compositional type usually associated with Mesopotamian art (see FIG. 2-10), suggests that influences from Mesopotamia not only had reached Egypt by this time but also already had made the thousand-mile journey up the Nile. The second group, however, is characteristically Egyptian, and the motif was to have a long history in Egyptian painting and sculpture alike.

THE UNIFICATION OF EGYPT In Predynastic times, Egypt was divided geographically and politically into Upper Egypt (the southern, upstream part of the Nile Valley), a narrow tract of grassland that encouraged hunting, and Lower (northern) Egypt, where the rich soil of the Nile Delta islands encouraged agriculture and animal husbandry (MAP 3-1). The ancient Egyptians began the history of their kingdom with the unification of the two lands. Until recently, this was thought to have occurred during the rule of the First Dynasty pharaoh Menes, identified by many scholars with King Narmer. Narmer's image and name appear on both sides of a ceremonial *palette* (stone slab with a circular depression) found at Hierakonpolis. The palette (FIG. **3-2**) is one of the earliest historical (versus prehistorical) artworks preserved. Although it is no longer regarded as commemorating the

foundation of the first of Egypt's 31 dynasties around 2920 BCE (the last ended in 332 BCE), it does record the unification of Upper and Lower Egypt at the very end of the Predynastic period. Although scholars now believe this unification occurred over several centuries, the *Palette of King Narmer* reflects the ancient Egyptian belief that the creation of the "Kingdom of the Two Lands" was a single great event.

The palette is an elaborate, formalized version of a utilitarian object commonly used in the Predynastic period to prepare eye makeup. (Egyptians used makeup to protect their eyes against irritation and the glare of the sun.) Narmer's palette is important not only as a document marking the transition from the prehistorical to the historical period in ancient Egypt but also as a kind of early blueprint of the formula for figure representation that characterized most Egyptian art for 3,000 years. At the top of each side of the palette are two heads of the goddess Hathor, represented as a cow with a woman's face. Between the Hathor heads is a hieroglyph giving Narmer's name within a frame representing the royal palace, making Narmer's palette the earliest existing labeled work of historical art.

On the back of the palette, the king, wearing the high, white, bowling-pin–shaped crown of Upper Egypt and accompanied by an official who carries his sandals, is shown slaying an enemy. The motif closely resembles the group at the lower left of the Hierakonpolis mural (FIG. 3-1) and became the standard pictorial formula signifying the inevitable triumph of the Egyptian god-kings over their enemies. Above and to the right, the falcon with human arms is Horus, the king's protector. The falcon-god takes captive a man-headed hieroglyph with a papyrus plant growing from it that stands for the land of Lower Egypt. Below the king are two fallen enemies.

On the front of the palette, the elongated necks of two felines form the circular depression that would have held eye makeup in

3-2 *Palette of King Narmer* (*left,* back; *right,* front), from Hierakonpolis, Egypt, Predynastic, ca. 3000–2920 BCE. Slate, approx. 2′ 1″ high. Egyptian Museum, Cairo.

an ordinary palette not made for display. The intertwined necks of the animals may be another pictorial reference to Egypt's unification. In the uppermost register, Narmer, wearing the red crown of Lower Egypt, reviews the beheaded bodies of the enemy. The dead are seen from above, like the bison lying on the ground on the ceiling of the Altamira cave (see FIG. 1-9). The artist depicted each body with its severed head neatly placed between its legs. By virtue of his superior rank, the king, on both sides of the palette, performs his ritual task alone and towers over his own men and the enemy. The king's superhuman strength is symbolized in the lowest band by a great bull knocking down a rebellious city whose fortress walls also are seen in an "aerial view." Specific historical narrative is not the artist's goal in this work. What is important is the characterization of the king as supreme, isolated from and larger than all ordinary men and solely responsible for the triumph over the enemy. Here, at the very beginning of Egyptian history, is evidence of the Egyptian convention of thought, of art, and of state policy that established the pharaoh as a divine ruler.

PORTRAYING THE HUMAN FIGURE The artist's portrayal of Narmer on both sides of his palette combines profile views of his head, legs, and arms with front views of his eye and torso. As noted in Chapters 1 and 2, this composite view of the human figure also characterized Mesopotamian art and even some Stone Age paintings. Although the proportions of the human figure changed, the method of its representation became standard. The *Palette of King Narmer* established the basic laws that governed

most Egyptian art for millennia. In the Hierakonpolis painting (FIG. 3-1), the artist scattered the figures across the wall more or less haphazardly. On Narmer's palette, the sculptor subdivided the surface into registers and inserted the pictorial elements into their organized setting in a neat and orderly way. The horizontal lines separating the narratives also define the ground supporting the figures. This was also the preferred mode for narrative art in the ancient Near East (see Chapter 2). Egyptian artists who departed from this compositional scheme did so deliberately, usually to express the absence of order, as in a chaotic battle scene (FIG. 3-38).

Architecture

TOMBS AND THE AFTERLIFE Narmer's palette is exceptional among surviving Egyptian artworks because it is commemorative rather than funerary in nature. Far more typical is the Predynastic mural from Hierakonpolis (FIG. 3-1). In fact, Egyptian tombs provide the principal, if not the exclusive, evidence for the historical reconstruction of Egyptian civilization. The overriding concern in this life was to ensure safety and happiness in the next life. The majority of monuments the Egyptians left behind were dedicated to this preoccupation (see "Mummification and the Afterlife," page 59).

The standard tomb type in early Egypt was the *mastaba* (FIG. **3-3**). The mastaba (Arabic for "bench") was a rectangular brick or stone structure with sloping sides erected over an

Mummification and the Afterlife

The Egyptians did not make the sharp distinction between body and soul that is basic to many religions. Rather, they believed that from birth a person was accompanied by a kind of other self, the *ka* or life force, which, on the death of the body, could inhabit the corpse and live on. For the ka to live securely, however, the body had to remain as nearly intact as possible. To ensure that it did, the Egyptians developed the technique of embalming *(mummification)* to a high art. Although the Egyptians believed that the god Anubis invented embalming to preserve the body of the murdered Osiris (see "The Gods and Goddesses of Egypt," page 57), they did not practice mummification systematically until the Fourth Dynasty.

The first step in the 10-week process was the surgical removal of the lungs, liver, stomach, and intestines through an incision in the left flank. The Egyptians thought these organs were most subject to decay. The organs were individually wrapped and placed in four containers known as *canopic jars* for eventual deposit in the burial chamber with the corpse. (The jars take their name from the Egyptian port of Canopus, where human-headed jars were worshiped as personifications of Osiris. These jars were not, however, used in embalming.) The brain was extracted through the nostrils and discarded. The Egyptians did not attach any special significance to the brain. But they left in place the heart, necessary for life and regarded as the seat of intelligence.

Next, the body was treated for 40 days with *natron*, a naturally occurring salt compound that dehydrated the body. Then the corpse was filled with resin-soaked linens, and the embalming incision was closed and covered with a representation of the wedjat eye of Horus, a powerful *amulet* (a device to ward off evil and promote rebirth). Finally, the body was treated with lotions and resins and then wrapped tightly with hundreds of yards of linen bandages to maintain its shape. The Egyptians often placed other amulets within the bandages or on the corpse. The most important were heart *scarabs* (gems in the shape of beetles). Spells written on them ensured that the heart would be returned to its owner if it were ever lost. A scroll copy of the *Book of the Dead* (FIG. 3-39) frequently was placed between the legs of the deceased. It contained some 200 spells intended to protect the mummy and the ka in the afterlife. The mummies of the wealthy had their faces covered with funerary masks (FIG. 3-37).

The Egyptian practice of mummification endured for thousands of years, even when Egypt was ruled by Greek kings and later by Roman emperors. Roman mummies with painted portraits (see FIG. 10-63) have long been known. Their number has recently been greatly expanded by the discovery in 1996 of a cemetery at Bahariya Oasis in the desert southwest of Cairo. The site—at least four square miles in size—has come to be called the Valley of the Golden Mummies. The largest tomb found to date contained 32 mummies, but another held 43—some stacked on top of others because the tomb was used for generations and space ran out.

The care with which the dead were laid to rest in the Bahariya cemetery varied markedly with the social position and wealth of the deceased. The bodies of the poorer members of the community were carelessly wrapped in linen and have almost completely decayed. The 60 most elaborate mummies, probably those of successful merchants and their families, have gilded stucco masks. Some also have gilded chest plates with reliefs depicting Egyptian deities, including Thoth holding Maat's feather (compare the weighing scene in FIG. 3-39). Others have painted decoration, and some have eyes of white marble with black obsidian irises and copper eyelashes. The excavators believe the cemetery was still in use as late as the fourth or fifth century CE.

Preserving the deceased's body by mummification was only the first requirement for immortality in ancient Egypt. Food and drink also had to be provided, as did clothing, utensils, and furniture. Nothing that had been enjoyed on earth was to be lacking. Statuettes called *ushabtis* (answerers) also were placed in the tomb. These figurines performed any labor required of the deceased in the afterlife, answering whenever his or her name was called.

Beginning in the Old Kingdom, images of the dead, sculpted in the round and placed in shallow recesses, were also set up in the tomb. They were meant to guarantee the permanence of the person's identity by providing substitute dwelling places for the ka in case the mummy disintegrated. Wall paintings and reliefs recorded the recurring round of human activities. The Egyptians hoped and expected that the images and inventory of life, collected and set up within the protective stone walls of the tomb, would ensure immortality.

1. Chapel   2. False door   3. Shaft into burial chamber   4. Serdab (chamber for statue of deceased)   5. Burial chamber

3-3 Section *(left)*, plan *(center)*, and restored view *(right)* of typical Egyptian mastaba tombs.

3-4 IMHOTEP, Stepped Pyramid and mortuary precinct of Djoser, Saqqara, Egypt, Dynasty III, ca. 2630–2611 BCE.

underground burial chamber. A shaft connected this chamber with the outside, providing the ka with access to the tomb. The form probably was developed from earth or stone mounds that had covered even earlier tombs. Although mastabas originally housed single burials, as in our example, during the latter part of the Old Kingdom they were used for multiple family burials and became increasingly complex. The central underground chamber was surrounded by storage rooms and compartments whose number and size increased with time until the area covered far surpassed that of the tomb chamber. Built into the superstructure, or sometimes attached to the outside, was a chapel housing a statue of the deceased in a small concealed chamber called the *serdab*. The chapel's interior walls and the ancillary rooms were decorated with colored relief carvings and paintings of scenes from daily life intended magically to provide the deceased with food and entertainment.

THE FIRST PYRAMID One of the most renowned figures in Egyptian history is IMHOTEP, the royal builder for King Djoser (r. 2630–2611 BCE) of the Third Dynasty. Imhotep was a man of legendary talent who served also as the pharaoh's chancellor and high priest of the sun god. After his death, the Egyptians revered Imhotep as a god and in time may have inflated the list of his achievements. Nonetheless, his is the first known name of an artist in recorded history.

The historian Manetho states that Imhotep designed the Stepped Pyramid (FIG. **3-4**) of Djoser at Saqqara, the ancient *necropolis* (Greek for "city of the dead") for Memphis, Egypt's capital at the time. Built before 2600 BCE, the pyramid is one of the oldest stone structures in Egypt and, in its final form, the first truly grandiose royal tomb. Begun as a large mastaba with each of its faces oriented toward one of the cardinal points of the compass, the tomb was enlarged at least twice before taking on its ultimate shape. About 200 feet high, the Stepped Pyramid seems to be composed of a series of mastabas of diminishing size, stacked one on top of another to form a structure that resembles the great ziggurats of Mesopotamia (see FIG. 2-14). Unlike the ziggurats, however, Djoser's pyramid is a tomb, not a temple platform, and its dual function was to protect the mummified king and his possessions and to symbolize, by its gigantic presence, his absolute and godlike power. Beneath the pyramid was a network of underground galleries resembling a palace. It was to be Djoser's new home in the afterlife.

Befitting the god-king's majesty, Djoser's pyramid stands near the center of an immense (37-acre) rectangular enclosure (FIG. **3-5**) surrounded by a monumental (34-foot-high and 5,400-foot-long) wall of white limestone. The huge precinct, with its protective walls and tightly regulated access, stands in sharp contrast to the roughly contemporary Sumerian Royal Cemetery at Ur, where no barriers kept people away from the burial area. Nor did the Mesopotamian cemetery have a temple for the worship of the deified dead. At Saqqara, a funerary temple stands against the northern face of Djoser's pyramid (no. 2 on the plan). Priests performed daily rituals at the temple in celebration of the divine pharaoh.

FROM PLANT TO STONE Djoser's funerary temple was but one of many buildings arranged around several courts. Most of the others were dummy structures (no. 6 on the plan) with stone walls enclosing fills of rubble, sand, or gravel. The buildings imitated in stone masonry various types of temporary structures made of plant stems and mats erected in Upper and Lower Egypt to celebrate the Jubilee Festival. This event perpetually reaffirmed the royal existence in the hereafter.

The translation into stone of structural forms previously made out of plants may be seen in the long entrance corridor

1. Stepped pyramid derived from square-plan mastaba
2. Funerary temple of Djoser
3. Court with serdab
4. Large court with altar and two B-shaped stones
5. Entrance portico
6. Heb-Sed court flanked by sham chapels
7. Small temple
8. Court before North Palace
9. North Palace
10. Court before South Palace
11. South Palace
12. South tomb
13. Royal Pavilion
14. Magazines

3-5 Plan *(top)* and restored view *(bottom)* of the mortuary precinct of Djoser, Saqqara, Egypt, Dynasty III, ca. 2630–2611 BCE.

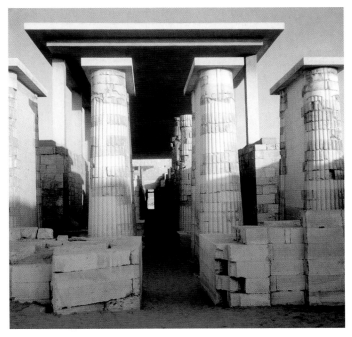

3-6 Columnar entrance corridor to the mortuary precinct of Djoser, Saqqara, Egypt, Dynasty III, ca. 2630–2611 BCE.

(FIG. **3-6**) to Djoser's funerary precinct. There, *columns* that resemble bundles of reeds project from short spur walls on either side of the once-roofed and dark passageway. A person walking through it would have emerged suddenly into a large courtyard and the brilliant light of the Egyptian sun. To the right, the visitor would have seen the gleaming focus of the entire complex, Djoser's pyramid.

The columns flanking the pathway into Djoser's precinct resemble later Greek columns. Architectural historians have little doubt today that the buildings of ancient Egypt had a profound impact on the designers of the first Greek stone columnar temples (see Chapter 5). The upper parts of the Saqqara entrance portico columns are not preserved, but those of Djoser's North Palace (FIG. **3-7**; no. 9 in FIG. 3-5) still stand. They end in *capitals* ("heads") that take the form of the papyrus blossoms of Lower Egypt. The column shafts resemble papyrus stalks. The later Greek columns also terminate in capitals, although the Greek capitals differ markedly in form. Greek column shafts are also generally freestanding, whereas all the columns in the Saqqara complex are *engaged* (attached) to walls. Still, this is the first appearance of stone columns in the history of architecture.

3-7 Facade of the North Palace of the mortuary precinct of Djoser, Saqqara, Egypt, Dynasty III, ca. 2630–2611 BCE.

THE OLD KINGDOM

The Old Kingdom is the first of the three great periods of Egyptian history, called the Old, Middle, and New Kingdoms, respectively. Many Egyptologists now begin the Old Kingdom with the first pharaoh of the Fourth Dynasty, Sneferu (r. 2575–2551 BCE), although the traditional division of kingdoms places Djoser and the Third Dynasty in the Old Kingdom. It ended with the demise of the Eighth Dynasty around 2134 BCE.

Architecture

PYRAMIDS AND THE SUN GOD At Gizeh, across the Nile from modern Cairo, stand the three Great Pyramids (FIG. **3-8;** see "Building the Great Pyramids," page 63), the oldest of the Seven Wonders of the ancient world (see "Babylon: City of Wonders," Chapter 2, page 49). The prerequisites for membership in this elite club were colossal size and enormous cost, and the Gizeh pyramids testify to the wealth and pretensions of the Fourth Dynasty pharaohs Khufu (r. 2551–2528 BCE), Khafre (r. 2520–2494 BCE), and Menkaure (r. 2490–2472 BCE).

The three pyramids, built in the course of about 75 years, represent the culmination of an architectural evolution that began with the mastaba. The pyramid form did not evolve out of necessity, and the Egyptian kings could have gone on indefinitely stacking mastabas to make their weighty tombs. The new tomb shape probably reflects the influence of Heliopolis, the seat of the powerful cult of Re, whose emblem was a pyramidal stone, the *ben-ben* (see "The Gods and Goddesses of Egypt," page 57). The Great Pyramids are symbols of the sun. The Pyramid Texts, inscribed on the burial chamber walls of many royal tombs beginning with the Fifth Dynasty Pyramid of Unas (r. 2356–2323 BCE), refer to the sun's rays as the ramp the pharaoh uses to ascend to the heavens.

3-8 Great Pyramids, Gizeh, Egypt, Dynasty IV. *From left:* Pyramids of Menkaure, ca. 2490–2472 BCE; Khafre, ca. 2520–2494 BCE; and Khufu, ca. 2551–2528 BCE.

Building the Great Pyramids

The three Great Pyramids of Khufu, Khafre, and Menkaure at Gizeh (FIG. 3-8) attest to Egyptian builders' mastery of stone masonry and to their ability to mobilize, direct, house, and feed a huge workforce engaged in one of the most labor-intensive enterprises ever undertaken. Like all building projects of this type, the process of erecting the pyramids began with the quarrying of stone, in this case primarily the limestone of the Gizeh plateau itself. Teams of skilled workers had to cut into the rock and remove large blocks of roughly equal size using stone or copper chisels and wooden mallets and wedges. Often, the artisans had to cut deep tunnels to find high-quality stone free of cracks and other flaws. To remove a block, the workers cut channels on all sides and partly underneath. Then they pried the stones free from the bedrock with wooden levers.

After workers liberated the stones, the rough blocks had to be transported to the building site and *dressed* (shaped to the exact dimensions required, with smooth faces for a perfect fit). Small blocks could be carried on a man's shoulders or on the back of a donkey, but the massive blocks used to construct the Great Pyramids were moved using wooden rollers and sleds. The artisans dressed the blocks by chiseling and pounding the surfaces and, in the last stage, by rubbing and grinding the surfaces with fine polishing stones. This kind of construction, in which carefully cut and regularly shaped blocks of stone are piled in successive rows, or *courses*, is called *ashlar masonry*.

To set the ashlar blocks in place, workers erected great rubble ramps against the core of the pyramid. Their size and slope were adjusted as work progressed and the tomb grew in height. Scholars still debate whether the Egyptians used simple linear ramps inclined at a right angle to one face of the pyramid or zigzag or spiral ramps akin to staircases. Linear ramps would have had the advantage of simplicity and would have left three sides of the pyramid unobstructed. But zigzag ramps placed against one side of the structure or spiral ramps winding around the pyramid would have greatly reduced the slope of the incline and would have made the dragging of the blocks easier. Some scholars also have suggested a combination of straight and spiral ramps.

Ropes, pulleys, and levers were used both to lift and to lower the stones, guiding each block into its designated place. Finally, the pyramid was surfaced with a casing of white limestone, cut so precisely that the eye could scarcely detect the joints. A few casing stones still can be seen in the cap that covers the Pyramid of Khafre (FIGS. 3-8, *center*, and 3-11, *left*). They are all that remain after many centuries of stripping the pyramids to supply limestone for the Islamic builders of Cairo.

Djoser's Stepped Pyramid (FIG. 3-4) may also have been conceived as a giant stairway. The pyramids were where Egyptian kings were reborn in the afterlife, just as the sun is reborn each day at dawn.

Of the three Fourth Dynasty pyramids at Gizeh, the tomb of Khufu (FIG. 3-9) is the oldest and largest. Except for the galleries and burial chamber, it is an almost solid mass of limestone

1. Silhouette with original facing stone
2. Thieves' tunnels
3. Entrance
4. Grand gallery
5. King's chamber
6. So-called Queen's chamber
7. False tomb chamber
8. Relieving blocks
9. Airshafts(?)

3-9 Section of the Pyramid of Khufu, Gizeh, Egypt.

masonry—a stone mountain built on the same principle as the earlier Stepped Pyramid at Saqqara. When its original stone facing (no. 1 in FIG. 3-9) was intact, the sunlight it reflected would have been dazzling, underscoring the pyramid's role as a solar symbol.

The immensity of the Gizeh pyramids and that of Khufu in particular is indicated by some dimensions. At the base, the length of one side of Khufu's tomb is approximately 775 feet, and its area is some 13 acres. Its present height is about 450 feet (originally 480 feet). The structure contains roughly 2.3 million blocks of stone, each weighing an average of 2.5 tons. Napoleon's scholars calculated that the blocks in the three Great Pyramids were sufficient to build a wall 1 foot wide and 10 feet high around France.

As with Djoser's Stepped Pyramid, the four sides of each of the Great Pyramids are oriented to the cardinal points of the compass. But the funerary temples associated with the three Gizeh pyramids are not placed on the north side, facing the stars of the northern sky, as was Djoser's temple. The temples sit on the east side, facing the rising sun and underscoring their connection with Re.

KHAFRE AND THE SPHINX From the remains surrounding the Pyramid of Khafre at Gizeh, archaeologists have been able to reconstruct an entire funerary complex (FIG. 3-10). The complex included the pyramid itself with the pharaoh's burial chamber; the *mortuary temple* adjoining the pyramid on the east side, where offerings were made to the dead king, ceremonies performed, and cloth, food, and ceremonial vessels stored; the covered *causeway*, or raised corridor, whose walls were decorated with painted reliefs; and the *valley temple* at the edge of the floodplain. According to one theory, the complex served not only as the king's tomb and temple but also as his palace in the afterlife.

3-10 Model of the pyramid complex, Gizeh, Egypt. Cambridge, Massachusetts, Harvard University Semitic Museum. 1) Pyramid of Menkaure, 2) Pyramid of Khafre, 3) Mortuary temple of Khafre, 4) Causeway, 5) Great Sphinx, 6) Valley temple of Khafre, 7) Pyramid of Khufu, 8) Pyramids of the royal family and mastabas of nobles

3-11 Great Sphinx (with Pyramid of Khafre in the background at left), Gizeh, Egypt, Dynasty IV, ca. 2520–2494 BCE. Sandstone, approx. 65′ high, 240′ long.

Beside the causeway and dominating the valley temple of Khafre rises the Great Sphinx (FIG. **3-11**). Carved from a spur of rock in an ancient quarry, the colossal statue—the largest in the ancient Near East—is probably an image of Khafre, although some scholars believe it portrays Khufu and was carved before construction of Khafre's complex began. Whoever it portrays, the *sphinx*— a lion with a human head—was associated with the sun god and therefore an appropriate image for a pharaoh. The composite form suggests that the pharaoh combines human intelligence with the awesome strength and authority of the king of beasts.

Sculpture

STATUES FOR ETERNITY As already noted, statues fulfilled an important function in Egyptian tombs. Sculptors created images of the deceased to serve as abodes for the ka should the mummies be destroyed. Although wood, clay, and other materials were used, mostly for images of those not of the royal or noble classes, the primary material for funerary statuary was stone.

The seated statue of Khafre (FIG. **3-12**) is one of a series of similar statues carved for the pharaoh's valley temple (FIG. 3-10, no. 6) near the Great Sphinx. The stone is diorite, an exceptionally hard dark stone brought some 400 miles down the Nile from royal quarries in the south. (The Neo-Sumerian ruler Gudea [see FIG. 2-15] so admired diorite that he imported it to faraway Girsu.) Khafre wears a simple kilt and sits rigidly upright on a throne formed of two stylized lions' bodies. Intertwined lotus and papyrus plants—symbol of the united Egypt—are carved between the throne's legs. The falcon-god Horus extends his protective wings to shelter the pharaoh's head. Khafre has the royal false beard fastened to his chin and wears the royal linen *nemes* headdress with the *uraeus* cobra of kingship on the front. The headdress covers his forehead and falls in pleated folds over his shoulders. (The head of the Great Sphinx is similarly attired.) As befitting a divine ruler, Khafre is shown with a well-developed, flawless body and a perfect face, regardless of his actual age and appearance. The Egyptians considered ideal proportions appropriate for representing imposing majesty, and artists used them quite independently of reality. This and all other generalized representations of the pharaohs are not true portraits and were not intended to be. Their purpose was not to record individual features or the distinctive shapes of bodies, but rather to proclaim the godlike nature of Egyptian kingship.

The seated king radiates serenity. The sculptor created this effect, common to Egyptian royal statues, in part by giving the figure great compactness and solidity, with few projecting, breakable parts. The form manifests the purpose: to last for eternity. Khafre's body is attached to the unarticulated slab that forms the back of the king's throne. His arms are held close to the torso and thighs, and his legs are close together and connected to the chair by the stone the artist chose not to remove. The pose is frontal, rigid, and *bilaterally symmetrical* (the same on either side of an axis, in this case the vertical axis). The sculptor suppressed all movement and with it the notion of time, creating an eternal stillness.

To produce the statue, the artist first drew the front, back, and two profile views of the pharaoh on the four vertical faces of the stone block. Next, apprentices chiseled away the excess stone on each side, working inward until the planes met at right angles. Finally, the master sculpted the parts of Khafre's body, the falcon, and so forth. The finishing was done by *abrasion* (rubbing or grinding the surface). This subtractive method of creating the

3-12 Khafre, from Gizeh, Egypt, Dynasty IV, ca. 2520–2494 BCE. Diorite, approx. 5′ 6″ high. Egyptian Museum, Cairo.

pharaoh's portrait accounts in large part for the blocklike look of the standard Egyptian statue. Nevertheless, other sculptors, both ancient and modern, with different aims, have transformed stone blocks into dynamic, twisting human forms (see, for example, FIG. 5-85).

AN EMOTIONLESS EMBRACE The seated statue is one of only a small number of basic formulaic types the sculptors of the Old Kingdom employed to represent the human figure. Another is the image of a person or deity standing, either alone or in a group. A superb example of the standing type is the double portrait statue of Menkaure and one of his wives, probably the queen Khamerernebty (FIG. **3-13**). The portraits once stood in the valley temple of Menkaure's pyramid complex at Gizeh. Here, too, the figures remain wedded to the stone block from which they were carved, and the sculptor used conventional postures to suggest the timeless nature of these eternal substitute homes for the ka. Menkaure's pose, which is duplicated in countless other Egyptian statues, is rigidly frontal with the arms hanging straight down and close to his well-built body. His hands are clenched into

3-13 Menkaure and Khamerernebty(?), from Gizeh, Egypt, Dynasty IV, ca. 2490–2472 BCE. Graywacke, approx. 4' 6½" high. Museum of Fine Arts, Boston.

fists with the thumbs forward. His left leg is slightly advanced, but no shift occurs in the angle of the hips to correspond to the uneven distribution of weight. Khamerernebty stands in a similar position. Her right arm, however, circles around the king's waist, and her left hand gently rests on his left arm. This frozen stereotypical gesture indicates their marital status. The husband and wife show no other sign of affection or emotion and look not at each other but out into space.

EGYPTIAN REALISM Traces of paint remain on the portraits of Menkaure and Khamerernebty. Most Egyptian statues were painted, although sometimes the stone was left its natural color, enhancing the sense of abstraction and timelessness. A striking example of painted statuary is the portrait of a Fifth Dynasty seated scribe sometimes identified as Kay (FIG. 3-14). Despite the stiff

3-14 Seated scribe (Kay?), from his mastaba at Saqqara, Egypt, Dynasty V, ca. 2450–2350 BCE. Painted limestone, approx. 1' 9" high. Louvre, Paris.

upright posture and the frontality of head and body, the color lends a lifelike quality to the statue. The head displays an extraordinary sensitivity. The sculptor conveyed the personality of a sharply intelligent and alert individual with a penetration and sympathy seldom achieved at such an early date. The scribe sits directly on the ground, not on a throne nor even on a chair. Although he occupied a position of honor in a largely illiterate society, the scribe was a much lower figure in the Egyptian hierarchy than the pharaoh, whose divinity made him superhuman. In the history of art, especially portraiture, it is almost a rule that as a human subject's importance decreases, formality is relaxed and realism is increased. It is telling that the scribe is shown with sagging chest muscles and a protruding belly. Such signs of age would have been disrespectful and wholly inappropriate in a depiction of an Egyptian god-king. But the statue of the scribe is not a true portrait either. Rather, it is a composite of conventional types. In fact, the scribe's sunken cheeks are difficult to reconcile with his flabby body.

A PORTRAIT IN WOOD A second portrait illustrating this rule of relaxed formality and increased realism is the Fifth Dynasty wooden statue of an official named Ka-Aper (FIG. 3-15). Like the statue of the seated scribe, Ka-Aper's portrait comes from the deceased's simple brick mastaba at Saqqara. Ka-Aper's face is also startlingly alive, even though the paint does not survive. The eyes of rock crystal are intact, however, and heighten the effect. The figure stands erect in the conventional frontal pose used for pharaonic portraits, with the left leg advanced. He is shown with the badges of his rank—a tall walking stick in his left hand and a baton (missing) in his right. Ka-Aper's paunchy physique contrasts even more sharply than the scribe's with the idealized proportions used to portray Khafre and Menkaure. Obesity characterizes many nonroyal Old Kingdom portraits, perhaps because it attested to the comfortable life of the person represented and his relatively high position in society. Ka-Aper's statue somewhat retains the shape of the tree trunk from which the sculptor fashioned it (the arms were carved separately and pegged onto the body). Because the statue has no back slab, it seems to stand more freely than the stone images of Menkaure and Khamerernebty. The artist, however, had no more interest in portraying motion than had the sculptor of those royal images in stone.

HUNTING IN THE AFTERLIFE In Egyptian tombs, the deceased were not represented exclusively in freestanding statuary. Artists also depicted many individuals in relief sculpture and in mural painting, sometimes alone—as on the wooden panel of Hesire discussed in the Introduction (FIG. Intro-14)—and sometimes in a narrative context. The scenes in painted limestone relief that decorate the walls of the mastaba of Ti at Saqqara typify the subjects Old Kingdom patrons favored for the adornment of their final resting places. Ti was an official of the Fifth Dynasty. Depictions of agriculture and hunting fill his tomb. These activities were associated with the provisioning of the ka in the hereafter, but they also had powerful symbolic overtones. In ancient Egypt, success in the hunt, for example, was a metaphor for triumph over the forces of evil.

On one wall (FIG. **3-16**), Ti, his men, and his boats move slowly through the marshes, hunting hippopotami and birds in a dense growth of towering papyrus. The reedy stems of the plants are

3-15 Ka-Aper, from his mastaba at Saqqara, Egypt, Dynasty V, ca. 2450–2350 BCE. Wood, approx. 3′ 7″ high. Egyptian Museum, Cairo.

3-16 Ti watching a hippopotamus hunt, relief in the mastaba of Ti, Saqqara, Egypt, Dynasty V, ca. 2450–2350 BCE. Painted limestone, hunting scene approx. 4′ high.

3-17 Goats treading seed and cattle fording a canal, reliefs in the mastaba of Ti, Saqqara, Egypt, Dynasty V, ca. 2450–2350 BCE. Painted limestone.

delineated with repeated fine grooves that fan out gracefully at the top into a commotion of frightened birds and stalking foxes. The water beneath the boats, signified by a pattern of wavy lines, is crowded with hippopotami and fish. Ti's men seem frantically busy with their spears, while Ti, depicted twice their size, stands aloof. The basic conventions of Egyptian figure representation used half a millennium earlier in the *Palette of King Narmer* (FIG. 3-2) are seen again here. As on the Predynastic palette and the portrait relief of Hesire (see FIG. Intro-14), the artist used the *conceptual* rather than the *optical* approach, representing what was known to be true of the subject, instead of a random view of it, and showing its most characteristic parts at right angles to the line of vision. This conceptual approach expressed a feeling for the constant and changeless aspect of things and was well suited for Egyptian funerary art. Ti's outsize proportions bespeak his rank. His conventional pose contrasts with the realistically rendered activities of his tiny servants and with the naturalistically carved and painted birds and animals among the papyrus buds. Ti's immobility suggests that he is not an actor in the hunt. He does not *do* anything. He simply *is,* a figure apart from time and an impassive observer of life, like his ka.

THE EGYPTIAN CANON The idealized and stiff image of Ti is typical of Egyptian relief sculpture. Egyptian artists regularly ignored the endless variations in body types of real human beings. Painters and sculptors did not sketch their subjects from life but applied a strict *canon,* or system of proportions, to the human figure. They first drew a grid on the wall. Then they placed various human body parts at specific points on the network of squares. The height of a figure, for example, was a fixed number of squares, and the head, shoulders, waist, knees, and other parts of the body also had a predetermined size and place within the scheme. This approach to design lasted for thousands of years. Specific proportions might vary from workshop to workshop and change over time, but the principle of the canon persisted.

FORDING THE NILE On another wall of Ti's mastaba, the artist represented goats treading in seeds and cattle fording a canal

in the Nile in two registers (FIG. **3-17**). Ti is absent, and all the men and animals participate in the narrative. Despite the sculptor's repeated use of similar poses for most of the human and animal figures, the reliefs are full of anecdotal details. Especially charming is the group at the lower right of our illustration. A youth, depicted in a complex unconventional posture, carries a calf on his back. The animal, not a little afraid, turns its head back a full 180 degrees (compare the Paleolithic bison in FIG. 1-8) to seek reassurance from its mother, who returns the calf's gaze. Scenes such as this demonstrate that Egyptian artists could be close observers of daily life. The absence of the anecdotal (that is, of the time-bound) from their representations of the deceased both in relief and in the round was a deliberate choice. Their primary purpose was to suggest the deceased's eternal existence in the afterlife, not to portray nature. Once again, the scenes may be interpreted on a symbolic, as well as a literal, level. The fording of the Nile was a metaphor for the deceased's passage from life to the hereafter.

THE MIDDLE KINGDOM

About 2150 BCE, the Egyptians challenged the pharaohs' power, and for more than a century the land was in a state of civil unrest and near anarchy. But in 2040 BCE, the pharaoh of Upper Egypt, Mentuhotep II (r. 2050–1998 BCE), managed to unite Egypt again under the rule of a single king and established the so-called Middle Kingdom (Dynasties XI–XIV).

Sculpture

A BROODING PHARAOH One of Mentuhotep II's successors was Senusret III (r. 1878–1859 BCE), who fought four brutal military campaigns in Nubia. Although Egyptian armies devastated the land and poisoned the wells, Senusret III never fully achieved secure control over the Nubians. In Egypt itself, he attempted, with greater success, to establish a more powerful central government.

His portraits are of special interest because they represent a sharp break from Old Kingdom practice. Although the king's preserved statues have idealized bodies, the sculptors brought a stunning and unprecedented realism to the rendition of Senusret III's features (FIG. 3-18). His pessimistic expression reflects the dominant mood of the time and is echoed in Middle Kingdom literature. The strong mouth, the drooping lines about the nose and eyes, and the shadowy brows show a determined ruler who had also shared in the cares of the world, sunk in brooding meditation. The portrait is different in kind from the typically impassive faces of the Old Kingdom. It is personal, almost intimate, in its revelation of the mark of anxiety that a troubled age might leave on the soul of a king.

Architecture

MOUNTAIN TOMBS Senusret III's tomb, at Dashur, is a mudbrick pyramid, but the most characteristic burials of the Middle Kingdom are rock-cut tombs, like those at Beni Hasan (FIG. 3-19). Such tombs also existed during the Old Kingdom, but the best preserved date to the later period. One of those is the 12th Dynasty tomb of Khnumhotep, who boasted in an inscription of its elaborateness, saying that its doors were of cedar 7 cubits (about 12 feet) high. Expressing the characteristic Egyptian attitude toward the last resting place, he added:

> My chief nobility was I executed a cliff-tomb, for a man should imitate that which his father does. My father made for himself a house of the ka in the town of Menofret, of good stone of Ayan, in order to perpetuate his name forever and establish it eternally.

3-18 Fragmentary head of Senusret III, Dynasty XII, ca. 1860 BCE. Red quartzite, approx. $6\frac{1}{2}''$ high. Metropolitan Museum of Art, New York.

3-19 Rock-cut tombs BH 3–5, Beni Hasan, Egypt, Dynasty XII, ca. 1950–1900 BCE.

3-20 Interior hall of the rock-cut tomb of Amenemhet (BH 2), Beni Hasan, Egypt, Dynasty XII, ca. 1950–1900 BCE.

The rock-cut tombs of the Middle Kingdom largely replaced the Old Kingdom mastabas. Hollowed out of the cliffs, these tombs often were fronted by a shallow columnar vestibule (porch), which led into a columned hall and then into a burial chamber. In the hall of the 12th Dynasty tomb of Amenemhet (FIG. **3-20**), the columns serve no supporting function because, like the porch columns, they are continuous parts of the rock fabric. (Note the broken column in the rear suspended from the ceiling like a stalactite.) The column shafts are *fluted* with vertical channels in a manner similar to later Greek columns. Archaeologists believe fluting derived from the dressing of softwood trunks with the rounded cutting edge of the adze. Fluted stone columns are yet another case of Egyptian builders' translating perishable natural forms into permanent architecture. Artists decorated the tomb walls with paintings and painted reliefs, as in former times, and placed statues of the deceased in niches. The statue in Amenemhet's tomb depicts him, his wife, and his mother.

THE NEW KINGDOM

EGYPT AT ITS HEIGHT Like its predecessor, the Middle Kingdom disintegrated, and power passed to the Hyksos, or shepherd kings, who descended on Egypt from the Syrian and Mesopotamian uplands. They brought with them a new and influential culture and that practical animal, the horse. Their innovations in weaponry and war techniques ironically contributed to their own overthrow by native Egyptian kings of the 17th Dynasty around 1600–1550 BCE. Ahmose I (r. 1550–1525 BCE), final conqueror of the Hyksos and first king of the 18th Dynasty, ushered in the New Kingdom, the most brilliant period in Egypt's long history.

At this time, Egypt extended its borders by conquest from the Euphrates River in the east deep into Nubia (the Sudan) to the south (MAP 3-1). A new capital—Thebes, in Upper Egypt, south of the Predynastic royal cemetery at Abydos—became a great and luxurious metropolis with magnificent palaces, tombs, and temples along both banks of the Nile. Visiting embassies and new

and profitable trade with Asia and the Aegean Islands widened foreign contact (see "Minoan Paintings Discovered in Egypt," Chapter 4, page 91).

Architecture

HATSHEPSUT'S TEMPLE If the most impressive monuments of the Old Kingdom are its pyramids, those of the New Kingdom are its grandiose temples, often built to honor pharaohs and queens, as well as gods. Great pharaonic mortuary temples arose along the Nile near Thebes. These shrines provided the rulers with a place for worshiping their patron gods during their lifetimes and then served as temples in their own honor after their death. The temples were elaborate and luxuriously decorated, befitting both the pharaohs and the gods.

The most majestic of these royal mortuary temples, at Deir el-Bahri (FIG. **3-21**), was constructed for the female pharaoh Hatshepsut, one of the most remarkable women of the ancient world (see "Hatshepsut: The Woman Who Would Be King," page 71). Some have attributed the temple to SENMUT, Hatshepsut's chancellor and possible lover, who is described in two inscriptions as royal architect. His association with this project is uncertain, however. Modeled in part on the neighboring Middle Kingdom temple of Mentuhotep II (at the far left in FIG. 3-21), Hatshepsut's temple rises from the valley floor in three colonnaded terraces connected by ramps. It is remarkable how visually well suited the structure is to its natural setting. The long horizontals and verticals of the *colonnades* and their rhythm of light and dark repeat the pattern of the limestone cliffs above. The colonnade *pillars*, which are either simply rectangular or *chamfered* (beveled, or flattened at the edges) into 16 sides, are well proportioned and rhythmically spaced.

In Hatshepsut's day, the terraces were not the barren places they are now but gardens with frankincense trees and rare plants the pharaoh brought from the faraway "land of Punt" on the Red Sea. Her expedition to Punt figures prominently in the poorly preserved but once brightly painted low reliefs that cover many walls of the complex. In addition to representing great deeds, the

Hatshepsut: The Woman Who Would Be King

In 1479 BCE, Thutmose II, the fourth pharaoh of the 18th Dynasty (r. 1492–1479 BCE), died. His principal wife (and half sister), Queen Hatshepsut (r. 1473–1458 BCE), had not given birth to any sons who survived, so the title of king went to the 12-year-old Thutmose III, son of Thutmose II by a minor wife. (Egyptian pharaohs had extensive harems.) Hatshepsut was named regent for the boy king. Within a few years, however, the queen proclaimed herself pharaoh and insisted that her father Thutmose I had actually chosen her as his successor during his lifetime. Underscoring her claim, one of the reliefs decorating Hatshepsut's enormous funerary complex (FIG. 3-21) depicts Thutmose I crowning his daughter as king in the presence of the Egyptian gods.

Hatshepsut is the first great female monarch whose name has been recorded. (In the 12th Dynasty, Sobekneferu was crowned king of Egypt, but she reigned as pharaoh for only a few years.)

Hatshepsut boasted of having made the "Two Lands to labor with bowed back" for her, and for two decades she ruled what was then the most powerful and prosperous empire in the world.

Hatshepsut commissioned numerous building projects, and sculptors produced portraits of the female pharaoh in great numbers for display in those complexes. Many of Hatshepsut's portraits were destroyed after her death at the order of the resentful Thutmose III (r. 1458–1425 BCE), whose elevation to sole kingship was delayed for two decades when his stepmother declared herself pharaoh. In her surviving portraits, Hatshepsut uniformly wears the costume of the male pharaohs, with royal headdress and kilt, and in some cases even a false ceremonial beard (FIG. 3-22). Many inscriptions refer to Hatshepsut as "*His* Majesty"! In other statues, however, Hatshepsut has delicate features, a slender frame, and breasts, leaving no doubt that artists also represented her as a woman.

reliefs also show Hatshepsut's coronation and divine birth. She was said to be the daughter of the god Amen-Re, whose sanctuary was situated on the temple's uppermost level. The painted reliefs of Hatshepsut's mortuary temple constituted the first great tribute to a woman's achievements in the history of art. Their defacement after her death by the jealous and resentful Thutmose III is therefore especially unfortunate.

A WOMAN PORTRAYED AS A MAN As many as 200 statues in the round depicting Hatshepsut in various guises complemented

3-21 Mortuary temple of Hatshepsut (with the Middle Kingdom mortuary temple of Mentuhotep II at left), Deir el-Bahri, Egypt, Dynasty XVIII, ca. 1473–1458 BCE.

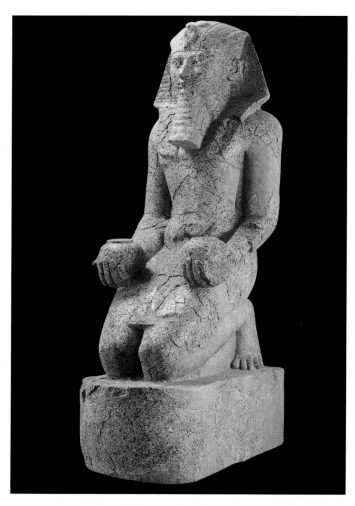

3-22 Hatshepsut with offering jars, from the upper court of her mortuary temple, Deir el-Bahri, Egypt, Dynasty XVIII, ca. 1473–1458 BCE. Red granite, approx. 8′ 6″ high. Metropolitan Museum of Art, New York.

the extensive relief program. Thutmose III removed or shattered them when he became pharaoh. On the lowest terrace, to either side of the processional way, Hatshepsut was repeatedly portrayed as a sphinx. On the uppermost level, the female pharaoh was represented standing, seated, and in the form of a mummy. At least eight colossal kneeling statues in red granite lined the way to the entrance of the Amen-Re sanctuary.

Our example (FIG. **3-22**) suffered the same fate as most of Hatshepsut's portraits. After it was smashed, the pieces were thrown in a dump. The statue has been skillfully reassembled from the recovered fragments. Hatshepsut holds a globular offering jar in each hand as she takes part in a ritual in honor of the sun god. (A king kneeled only before a god, never a mortal.) She wears the royal male nemes headdress (compare FIGS. 3-11 to 3-13) and the pharaoh's ceremonial beard. The agents of Thutmose III hacked off the uraeus cobra that once adorned the front of the headdress. The figure is also anatomically male, although other surviving portraits of Hatshepsut represent her with a woman's breasts. The male imagery is, however, consistent with the queen's formal assumption of the title of king and with the many inscriptions that address her as a man.

COLOSSI IN A CLIFF Hatshepsut's mortuary temple never fails to impress visitors by its sheer size, and this is no less true of the immense rock-cut temple of Ramses II (r. 1290–1224 BCE) at Abu Simbel (FIG. **3-23**). In 1968 the temple was moved nearly 700 feet—an impressive feat in its own right—to its present location to save it from submersion in the Aswan High Dam reservoir. Ramses was Egypt's last great warrior pharaoh, and he ruled for two-thirds of a century, an extraordinary accomplishment in an era when life expectancy was far less than it is today. The pharaoh, proud of his many campaigns to restore the empire, proclaimed his greatness by placing four colossal images of himself on the temple *facade*. The portraits are almost eight times as large as Hatshepsut's kneeling statues and almost a dozen times

3-23 Temple of Ramses II, Abu Simbel, Egypt, Dynasty XIX, ca. 1290–1224 BCE. Sandstone, colossi approx. 65′ high.

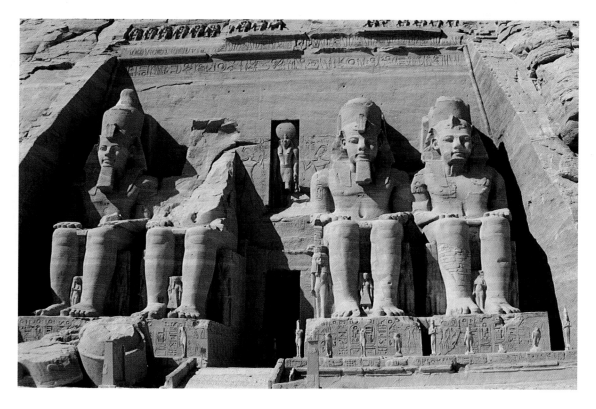

The Tomb of the Sons of Ramses II

In 1825, James Burton, a British explorer, uncovered the entrance and a few chambers of a royal tomb in the Valley of the Kings at Thebes. (The narrow valley across the Nile from Karnak and Luxor was so named because the tombs of numerous New Kingdom pharaohs are located there.) In an age when archaeological excavation was little more than treasure hunting, archaeologists never fully investigated the tomb (KV5) because no precious objects were found when it was opened. Almost a century later, in 1902, Howard Carter, who later discovered Tutankhamen's tomb, made a probe into KV5, but he, too, concluded that the site was unpromising, and abandoned work there. Later archaeologists ignored the tomb, and its location was forgotten until 1987, when an American team led by Kent R. Weeks found KV5 anew. It wasn't until 1995, however, that the tomb's immense size and unique character were revealed.

KV5 is the largest tomb ever found in the Valley of the Kings and may have been the largest in Egypt. No other Theban tomb has more than 30 chambers—a half dozen is typical—but this tomb has scores of rooms, and it is still only partially excavated. The chambers open onto several long corridors leading out of a central hall, 50 meters square, filled with 16 stone pillars. Inscriptions inside the tomb leave no doubt that this was the burial place of the sons of the great 19th Dynasty pharaoh Ramses II. Paintings and reliefs depicting Ramses and his royal sons with the major deities of Egypt—Osiris, Hathor, Horus, Thoth, and Isis—decorate the tomb walls.

KV5, unfortunately, was robbed within a half century of its construction. The culprit was identified—a workman named Kenena, son of Ruta. But the excavators found a statue of Osiris, god of the afterlife, in a niche at the end of a long corridor. The thief could not remove it because it was fixed to the wall. Weeks's team also discovered a number of small mummy-shaped statuettes called *ushabtis,* which served as servants of the royal sons for eternity. What they have not found are the royal burials themselves. The excavators have postulated that dozens more rooms—the actual burial chambers—may yet be discovered on a lower level. No one knows if Kenena or other thieves removed the presumed treasures buried with the pharaoh's sons or whether they remain to be uncovered. Work by Weeks and his colleagues is likely to continue for decades.

3-24 Interior of the temple of Ramses II, Abu Simbel, Egypt, Dynasty XIX, ca. 1290–1224 BCE. Sandstone, pillar statues approx. 32′ high.

the height of an ancient Egyptian, even though the pharaoh is seated. Spectacular as they are, the rock-cut statues nonetheless lack the refinement of earlier periods, because much was sacrificed to overwhelming size. This is a characteristic of colossal statuary of every period and every place.

PILLAR STATUES The grand scale was carried out in the interior (FIG. 3-24) also, where giant (32-foot-tall) figures of the king in the guise of Osiris, carved as one with the pillars, face each other across the narrow corridor. The pillars, carved from the cliff like the pharaoh's facade portraits, have no load-bearing function. In this respect, they resemble the columns in the tombs at Beni Hasan (FIG. 3-20). The statue-column, in its male *(atlantid)* or female *(caryatid)* variants, reappears throughout the history of art. Often, as here, the human figure is attached to a column or pier (for example, FIGS. 18-6 and 18-16). At other times the figure replaces the architectural member and forms the sole source of support (see FIG. 5-52).

THE FAMILY OF RAMSES Ramses, like other pharaohs, had many wives, and he fathered scores of sons. The most important members of his family were honored with immense monuments of their own. At Thebes, for example, north of his own mortuary temple, Ramses ordered the construction of a grand temple for his principal wife, Nefertari. Huge rock-cut statues—four standing images of the king and two of the queen—dominated the temple's facade. For his sons, Ramses constructed a huge underground tomb. The rediscovery of that subterranean complex was one of the major archaeological finds of the 20th century (see "The Tomb of the Sons of Ramses II," above).

IMMENSE PYLON TEMPLES Distinct from the pharaonic mortuary temples are the edifices built to honor one or more of the gods. Successive kings often added to them until they reached

3-25 Restored view of the temple of Amen-Re, Karnak, Egypt, begun 15th century BCE (Jean-Claude Golvin).

gigantic size. The temple of Amen-Re at Karnak (FIG. **3-25**), for example, was largely the work of the 18th-Dynasty pharaohs, including Thutmose I and III and Hatshepsut, but Ramses II (19th Dynasty) and others also contributed sections. Chapels were added to the complex as late as the 26th Dynasty. The artificial sacred lake within the precinct of the Karnak temple is a reference to the primeval waters before creation. The temple rises from the earth as the original sacred mound rose from the waters at the beginning of time.

The New Kingdom *pylon temples* all had similar plans. (The name derives from the simple and massive gateways, or pylons, with sloping walls, as in FIG. 3-28.) A typical pylon temple is bilaterally symmetrical along a single axis that runs from an approaching avenue through a colonnaded court and hall into a dimly lit sanctuary. This Egyptian temple plan evolved from ritualistic requirements. Only the pharaohs and the priests could enter the sanctuary. A chosen few were admitted to the great columnar hall. The majority of the people were allowed only as far as the open court, and a high wall shut off the site from the outside world. The central feature of the New Kingdom pylon temple plan—a narrow axial passageway through the complex—is characteristic of much of Egyptian architecture. Axial corridors are also the approaches to the Old Kingdom pyramids of Gizeh (FIG. 3-10) and to the multi-level mortuary temple of Hatshepsut at Deir el-Bahri (FIG. 3-21).

HYPOSTYLE HALLS The dominating feature of the statuary-lined approach to a New Kingdom temple was the monumental facade of the pylon, which was routinely covered with reliefs glorifying Egypt's rulers. Inside was an open court with columns on two or more sides, followed by a hall between the court and sanctuary, its long axis placed at right angles to the corridor of the entire building complex. This *hypostyle hall* (one where columns support the roof) was crowded with massive columns and roofed

by stone slabs carried on lintels. The lintels rested on cubical blocks that in turn rested on giant capitals. In the hypostyle hall at Karnak (FIGS. **3-26** and **3-27**), the central columns are 66 feet high, and the capitals are 22 feet in diameter at the top, large enough to hold a hundred people. The Egyptians, who used no cement, depended on precise cutting of the joints and the weight of the huge stone blocks to hold the columns in place.

In the Amen-Re temple at Karnak and in many other Egyptian hypostyle halls, the builders made the central rows of columns higher than those at the sides. Raising the roof's central section created a *clerestory*. Openings in the clerestory permitted sunlight to filter into the interior, although the stone grilles (FIG. 3-26) would have blocked much of the light. This method of construction appeared in primitive form as early as the Old Kingdom in the valley temple of the Pyramid of Khafre. The clerestory is evidently an Egyptian innovation, and its significance hardly can be overstated. Before the invention of the electric light bulb, illuminating a building's interior was always a challenge for architects. The clerestory played a key role, for example, in Roman *basilica* and medieval church design and has remained an important architectural feature up to the present.

SUNKEN RELIEFS ON COLUMNS In the hypostyle hall at Karnak, the columns are indispensable structurally, unlike the rock-cut columns of the tombs at Beni Hasan (FIGS. 3-19 and 3-20) and Abu Simbel (FIG. 3-24). But their function as vertical supports is almost hidden by horizontal bands of painted *sunken relief* sculpture. To create such reliefs, the New Kingdom sculptors chiseled deep outlines below the stone's surface, rather than cut back the stone around the figures to make the figures project from the surface. Sunken reliefs preserve the contours of the columns they adorn. Otherwise, the Karnak columns would have had an irregular, wavy profile. But despite this effort to maintain sharp architectural lines, the overwhelming of the surfaces with reliefs indicates that the architects'

3-27 Model of hypostyle hall, temple of Amen-Re, Karnak, Egypt, Dynasty XIX, ca. 1290–1224 BCE. Metropolitan Museum of Art, New York.

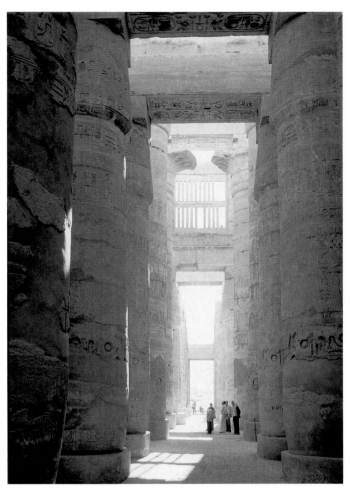

3-26 Hypostyle hall, temple of Amen-Re, Karnak, Egypt, Dynasty XIX, ca. 1290–1224 BCE.

intention was not to emphasize the functional role of the columns. Instead, they used columns as image- and message-bearing surfaces.

Egyptian columns seem to have originated from an early building technique that used firmly bound sheaves of reeds and swamp plants as roof supports in adobe structures. Egyptian masons first translated such early and relatively impermanent building methods into stone in Djoser's funerary precinct at Saqqara (FIGS. 3-6 and 3-7). Evidence of their swamp-plant origin is still seen in the columns at Karnak, which have bud-cluster or bell-shaped capitals resembling lotus or papyrus (the plants of Upper and Lower Egypt).

ARCHITECTURE AFTER ALEXANDER Once formulated, Egyptian traditions tended to have very long lives, in architecture as in the other arts. The pylon temple of Horus at Edfu (FIG. 3-28), built during the third, second, and first centuries BCE, after

3-28 Temple of Horus, Edfu, Egypt, ca. 237–47 BCE.

Alexander the Great's conquest of Egypt, still follows the basic scheme architects worked out more than a thousand years before. The great entrance pylon at Edfu is especially impressive. The broad surface of its massive facade, with its sloping walls, is broken only by the doorway with its overshadowing cornice, moldings at the top and sides, deep channels to hold great flagstaffs, and sunken reliefs. The reliefs depict Horus and Hathor witnessing an oversized King Ptolemy XIII (r. 51–47 bce) smiting undersized enemies. It is a striking monument to the persistence of Egyptian architectural and sculptural types, despite many variations over the millennia.

Sculpture and Painting

SENMUT AND NEFRUA Extremely popular during the Middle and New Kingdoms were *block statues*. In these works the idea that the ka could find an eternal home in the cubic stone image of the deceased was expressed in an even more radical simplification of form than was common in Old Kingdom statuary. An example of this genre is the block statue of Senmut and Princess Nefrua

3-29 Senmut with Princess Nefrua, from Thebes, Egypt, Dynasty XVIII, ca. 1470–1460 bce. Granite, approx. 3′ ½″ high. Ägyptisches Museum, Berlin.

(FIG. **3-29**). Hatshepsut's chancellor holds the pharaoh's daughter by Thutmose II in his "lap" and envelops the girl in his cloak. The streamlined design concentrates attention on the heads and treats the two bodies as a single cubic block, given over to inscriptions. The polished stone shape has its own simple beauty, with the surfaces turning subtly about smoothly rounded corners. The work—one of many surviving statues depicting Senmut with Hatshepsut's daughter—is also a reflection of the power of Egypt's female ruler. The frequent depiction of Senmut with Nefrua was meant to enhance Senmut's stature through his association with the princess (he was her tutor) and, by implication, with Hatshepsut herself. Toward the end of her reign, however, Hatshepsut believed Senmut had become too powerful, and she had him removed.

PAINTING AT THEBES The art of adorning tomb walls with paintings, attested already in the Predynastic period (FIG. 3-1), flourished in the New Kingdom. In the 18th-Dynasty Theban tomb of Nebamun, the deceased nobleman, whose official titles were "scribe and counter of grain," is shown standing in his boat, flushing birds from a papyrus swamp (FIG. **3-30**). The hieroglyphic text beneath his left arm says that Nebamun is enjoying recreation in his eternal afterlife. (Here, as elsewhere in Egyptian art, the accompanying text amplifies the message of the picture—and vice versa.) In contrast to the static pose of Ti watching others hunt hippopotami (FIG. 3-16), Nebamun is shown striding forward and vigorously swinging his throwing stick. In his right hand, he holds three birds he has caught. A wild cat, impossibly perched on a papyrus stem just in front of and below him, has caught two more in its claws and is holding the wings of a third in its teeth. Nebamun's wife and daughter accompany him on this hunt. They hold the lotuses they have gathered. The artist scaled down their figures in proportion to their rank, as did Old Kingdom artists. And, as in Ti's tomb, the Thebes animals show a naturalism based on careful observation.

3-30 Fowling scene, from the tomb of Nebamun, Thebes, Egypt, Dynasty XVIII, ca. 1400–1350 bce. Fresco on dry plaster, approx. 2′ 8″ high. British Museum, London.

3-31 Musicians and dancers, detail of a fresco from the tomb of Nebamun, Thebes, Egypt, Dynasty XVIII, ca. 1400–1350 BCE. Fragment approx. 1′ × 2′ 3″. British Museum, London.

The painting technique, also employed in earlier Egyptian tombs, is *fresco secco* (dry fresco), whereby artists let the plaster dry before painting on it. This procedure, in contrast to true fresco painting on wet plaster (see "Fresco Painting," Chapter 19, page 530), permitted slower and more meticulous work than painting on wet plaster, which had to be completed before the plaster dried. Fresco secco, however, is not as durable as true fresco painting, because the colors do not fuse with the wall surface.

A FEAST FOR THE DEAD Another fresco fragment from Nebamun's tomb shows four noblewomen watching and apparently participating in a musicale and dance where two nimble and almost nude dancing girls perform at a banquet (FIG. **3-31**). When Nebamun was buried, his family must have eaten the customary ceremonial meal at his tomb. They would have returned one day each year to partake in a commemorative banquet for the living to commune with the dead. This fresco represents just such a funerary feast, with an ample supply of wine jars at the right. It also shows that New Kingdom artists did not always adhere to the old standards for figural representation. The overlapping of the dancers' figures, their facing in opposite directions, and their rather complicated gyrations were carefully and accurately observed and executed, and the result is also a pleasing intertwined motif. The profile view of the dancers is consistent with their lower stature in the Egyptian hierarchy. The composite view is still reserved for Nebamun and his family. Of the four seated women, the artist represented the two at the left conventionally, but the other two face the observer in what is a rarely attempted frontal pose. They clap and beat time to the dance, while one of them plays the reeds. The artist took careful note of the soles of their feet as they sat cross-legged and suggested the movement of the women's heads by the loose arrangement of their hair strands. This informality constituted a relaxation of the Old Kingdom's stiff representational rules.

The frescoes in Nebamun's tomb testify to the luxurious life of the Egyptian nobility, filled with good food and drink, fine musicians, lithe dancers, and leisure time to hunt and fish in the marshes. But, as in the earlier tomb of Ti, the scenes should be read both literally and allegorically. Although Nebamun is shown enjoying himself in the afterlife, the artist symbolically asked viewers to recall how he got there. Hunting scenes reminded Egyptians of Horus, the son of Osiris, hunting down his father's murderer, Seth, the god of disorder, thus ensuring a happy existence for Nebamun. And music and dance were sacred to Hathor, who aided the dead in their passage to the other world. The sensual women at the banquet are a reference to fertility, rebirth, and regeneration—the conquest of death that made the afterlife possible.

Akhenaton and the Amarna Period

RELIGIOUS UPHEAVAL Not long after Nebamun was laid to rest in his tomb at Thebes, a revolution occurred in Egyptian society and religion. In the mid-14th century BCE, the pharaoh Amenhotep IV, later known as Akhenaton (r. 1353–1335 BCE), abandoned the worship of most of the Egyptian gods in favor of Aton, whom he declared to be the universal and only god, identified with the sun disk. He blotted out the name of Amen from all inscriptions and even from his own name and that of his father, Amenhotep III. He emptied the great temples, enraged the priests, and moved his capital downriver from Thebes to a site he named Akhetaton (after his new god), where he built his own city and shrines. It is now called Tell el-Amarna. The pharaoh claimed to be both the son and sole prophet of Aton. To him alone could the god make revelation. Moreover, in stark contrast to earlier practice, Akhenaton's god was represented neither in animal nor in human form but simply as the sun disk emitting life-giving rays. The pharaohs who followed Akhenaton reestablished the cult and priesthood of Amen and restored the temples and the inscriptions. The gigantic temple complex at Karnak (FIG. 3-25), for example, was dedicated to the renewed worship of the Theban god Amen. Akhenaton's brief religious revolution was soon undone, and his new city was largely abandoned.

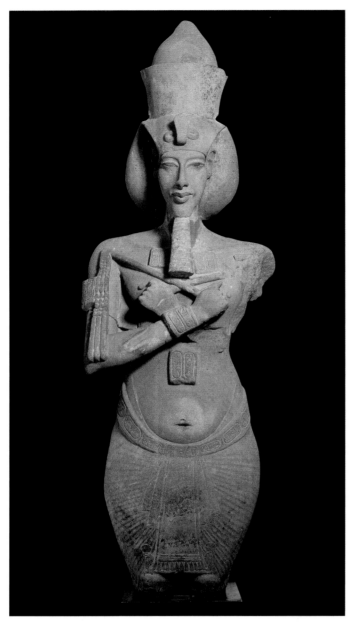

3-32 Akhenaton, from the temple of Aton, Karnak, Egypt, Dynasty XVIII, ca. 1353–1335 BCE. Sandstone, approx. 13′ high. Egyptian Museum, Cairo.

ARTISTIC REVOLUTION During the brief heretical episode of Akhenaton, however, profound changes occurred in Egyptian art. A colossal statue of Akhenaton (FIG. 3-32) from Karnak, toppled and buried after his death, retains the standard frontal pose of canonical pharaonic portraits. But the effeminate body, with its curving contours, and the long face with full lips and heavy-lidded eyes are a far cry indeed from the heroically proportioned figures of the pharaoh's predecessors (compare FIG. 3-13). Akhenaton's body is curiously misshapen, with weak arms, a narrow waist, protruding belly, wide hips, and fatty thighs. Modern doctors have tried to explain his physique by attributing a variety of illnesses to the pharaoh. They cannot agree on a diagnosis, and their premise—that the statue is an accurate depiction of a physical deformity—is probably faulty. Some art historians think that Akhenaton's portrait is a deliberate artistic reaction against the established style, paralleling the suppression of traditional religion. They argue that Akhenaton's artists tried to formulate a new

androgynous image of the pharaoh as the manifestation of Aton, the sexless sun disk. But no consensus exists other than that the style was revolutionary and short-lived.

NEFERTITI AND TIYE A painted limestone bust (FIG. 3-33) of Akhenaton's queen, Nefertiti (her name means "The Beautiful One Is Here"), exhibits a similar expression of entranced musing and an almost mannered sensitivity and delicacy of curving contour. The piece was found in the workshop of the sculptor THUTMOSE and is a deliberately unfinished model very likely by the master's own hand. The left eye socket still lacks the inlaid eyeball, making the portrait a kind of before-and-after demonstration piece. With this elegant bust, Thutmose may have been alluding to a heavy flower on its slender stalk by exaggerating the weight of the crowned head and the length of the almost serpentine neck. The Tell el-Amarna sculptor seems to have adjusted the actual likeness of his subject to meet the era's standard of spiritual beauty.

A moving portrait of old age is preserved in the miniature head of Queen Tiye (FIG. 3-34), mother of Akhenaton. Although the daughter of a chariot officer and not of royal birth, Tiye became the chief wife of Amenhotep III. Her portrait, of dark yew wood, probably to match her complexion, was found at Gurob with other objects connected with the funerary cult of

3-33 THUTMOSE, Nefertiti, from Tell el-Amarna, Egypt, Dynasty XVIII, ca. 1353–1335 BCE. Painted limestone, approx. 1′ 8″ high. Ägyptisches Museum, Berlin.

Amenhotep III. The work was probably remodeled during her son's reign to eliminate all reference to deities of the old religion. That is when the head acquired the present wig of plaster and linen with small blue beads. Tiye is shown as an older woman with lines and furrows, consistent with the new relaxation of artistic rules in the Amarna age. Her heavy-lidded slanting eyes are inlaid with alabaster and ebony, the lips are painted red, and the earrings (one is hidden by the later wig) are of gold and lapis lazuli. The wig covers what was originally a silver-foil headdress. A gold band still adorns the forehead. Such luxurious materials were common for royal portraits.

Both Nefertiti and Tiye figured prominently in the art and life of the Amarna age. Tiye, for example, regularly appeared in art beside her husband during his reign, and she apparently played an important role in his administration as well as her son's. Letters survive from foreign rulers advising the young Akhenaton to seek his mother's counsel in the conduct of international affairs. Nefertiti too was an influential woman. She frequently appears in the decoration of the Aton temple at Karnak, and she not only equals her husband in size but also sometimes wears pharaonic headgear.

ROYAL INTIMACY A sunken relief stele (FIG. **3-35**), perhaps from a private shrine, provides a rare look at this royal family. The style is familiar from the colossus of Akhenaton (FIG. 3-32) and the portrait head of Nefertiti (FIG. 3-33). Undulating curves replace rigid lines, and the figures possess the prominent bellies that characterize figures of the Amarna school. The pharaoh, his wife, and their three daughters bask in the life-giving rays of Aton, the sun disk. The mood is informal and anecdotal. Akhenaton lifts one of his daughters in order to kiss her. Another daughter sits on Nefertiti's lap and gestures toward her father while the youngest

3-34 Tiye, from Gurob, Egypt, Dynasty XVIII, ca. 1353–1335 BCE. Wood, with gold, silver, alabaster, and lapis lazuli, approx. $3\frac{3}{4}''$ high. Ägyptisches Museum, Berlin.

3-35 Akhenaton, Nefertiti, and three daughters, from Tell el-Amarna, Egypt, Dynasty XVIII, ca. 1353–1335 BCE. Limestone, approx. $12\frac{1}{4}''$ high. Ägyptisches Museum, Berlin.

daughter reaches out to touch a pendant on her mother's crown. Such an intimate portrayal of the pharaoh and his family is unprecedented in Egyptian art. The political and religious revolution under Akhenaton was matched by an equally radical upheaval in art.

The Tomb of Tutankhamen and the Post-Amarna Period

TREASURES OF A BOY KING The legacy of the Amarna style may be seen in the fabulously rich art and artifacts found in the largely unplundered tomb of Tutankhamen (r. 1333–1323 BCE), who was probably Akhenaton's son by a minor wife. Tutankhamen ruled for a decade and died at age 18. The treasures of his tomb, which include sculpture, furniture, jewelry, and accessories of all sorts, were uncovered in 1922. The adventure of their discovery gained world renown not only for their excavator, Howard Carter, but also for the boy king. Tutankhamen was a very minor figure in Egyptian history. The public remembers him today solely because of the chance survival of his tomb's furnishings.

The principal monument in the collection is the enshrined body of the pharaoh himself. The royal mummy reposed in the innermost of three coffins, nested one within the other. The

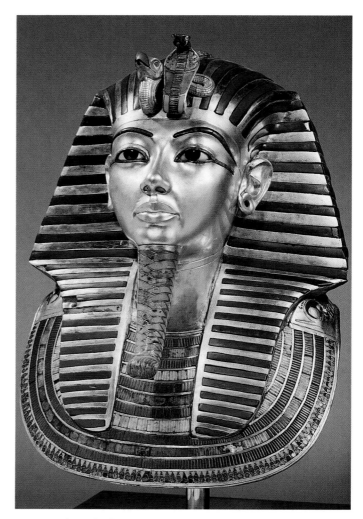

3-37 Death mask of Tutankhamen, from the innermost coffin in his tomb at Thebes, Egypt, Dynasty XVIII, ca. 1323 BCE. Gold with inlay of semiprecious stones, 1′ 9¼″ high. Egyptian Museum, Cairo.

innermost coffin (FIG. **3-36**) was the most luxurious of the three. Made of beaten gold (about a quarter ton of it) and inlaid with such semiprecious stones as lapis lazuli, turquoise, and carnelian, it is a supreme monument to the sculptor's and goldsmith's crafts. The portrait mask (FIG. **3-37**), which covered the king's face, is also made of gold with inlaid semiprecious stones. It is a sensitive portrayal of the serene adolescent king dressed in his official regalia, including the nemes headdress and false beard. The general effect of the mask and of the tomb treasures as a whole is of grandeur and richness expressive of Egyptian power, pride, and affluence.

TUTANKHAMEN THE CONQUEROR Although Tutankhamen probably was considered too young to fight, his position as king required that he be represented as a conqueror. He is shown as such in the panels of a painted chest (FIG. **3-38**) deposited in his tomb. The lid panel shows the king as a successful hunter pursuing droves of fleeing animals in the desert, and the side panel shows him as a great warrior. Together, the two panels are a double advertisement of royal power comparable to the later reliefs adorning Assyrian palaces (see FIGS. 2-22 and 2-24). From a war chariot pulled by spirited, plumed horses, Tutankhamen, shown larger than all other figures on the chest, draws his bow against a cluster of bearded Asian enemies, who fall in confusion before him. (The absence of a ground line in an Egyptian painting or relief implies chaos and death.) Tutankhamen slays the enemy, like game, in

3-36 Innermost coffin of Tutankhamen, from his tomb at Thebes, Egypt, Dynasty XVIII, ca. 1323 BCE. Gold with inlay of enamel and semiprecious stones, approx. 6′ 1″ long. Egyptian Museum, Cairo.

3-38 Painted chest, from the Tomb of Tutankhamen, Thebes, Egypt, Dynasty XVIII, ca. 1333–1323 BCE. Wood, approx. 1′ 8″ long. Egyptian Museum, Cairo.

great numbers. Behind him are three tiers of undersized war chariots, which serve to magnify the king's figure and to increase the count of his warriors. The themes are traditional, but the fluid, curvilinear forms are features reminiscent of the Amarna style.

THE *BOOK OF THE DEAD* Tutankhamen's mummy case (FIG. 3-36) shows the boy king in the guise of Osiris, god of the dead and king of the underworld, as well as giver of eternal life. The ritual of the cult of Osiris is recorded in the so-called *Book of the Dead*, a collection of spells and prayers. Illustrated papyrus scrolls, some as long as 70 feet, containing these texts were the essential equipment of the tombs of well-to-do persons.

The scroll of Hu-Nefer, the royal scribe and steward of the pharaoh Seti I, was found in his tomb in the Theban necropolis. Our illustration (FIG. 3-39) represents the final judgment of the deceased. At the left, Anubis, the jackal-headed god of embalming,

3-39 Last judgment of Hu-Nefer, from his tomb at Thebes, Egypt, Dynasty XIX, ca. 1290–1280 BCE. Painted papyrus scroll, approx. 1′ 6″ high. British Museum, London.

3-40 Mentuemhet, from Karnak, Egypt, Dynasty XXVI, ca. 650 BCE. Granite, approx. 4′ 5″ high. Egyptian Museum, Cairo.

Hu-Nefer kneels in adoration before them. Having been justified by the scales, Hu-Nefer is brought by Osiris's son, the falcon-headed Horus, into the presence of the green-faced Osiris and his sisters Isis and Nephthys to receive the award of eternal life.

In Hu-Nefer's scroll, the figures have all the formality of stance, shape, and attitude of traditional Egyptian art. Abstract figures and hieroglyphs alike are aligned rigidly. Nothing here was painted in the flexible, curvilinear style suggestive of movement that was evident in the art of Amarna and Tutankhamen. The return to conservatism is unmistakable.

THE LATE PERIOD

EGYPT IN DECLINE During the last millennium BCE, Egypt lost the commanding role it once had played in the ancient Near East. The empire dwindled away, and foreign powers invaded, occupied, and ruled the land, until it was taken over by Alexander the Great of Macedon and his Greek successors and, eventually, by the emperors of Rome.

A portrait statue of Mentuemhet (FIG. **3-40**), a rich and powerful man who was Mayor of Thebes and Fourth Priest of Amen during the 26th Dynasty in the seventh century BCE, exemplifies Egyptian sculpture at about the time the Greeks first encountered the art of the Nile Valley (see Chapter 5). The double wig, characteristic of the New Kingdom, and the realism of the head, with its rough and almost brutal characterization, differentiate Mentuemhet's portrait from earlier works. But the rigidity of the stance, the frontality, and the spareness of silhouette with arms at the side and left leg advanced still recall Old Kingdom statuary (FIG. 3-13).

CONCLUSION

In the Predynastic period, Egyptian sculptors and painters began to formulate the patterns for representing figures and narrating stories that endured for thousands of years. Although there were many divergences from the traditional means of representation, the exceptional longevity of formal traditions in Egypt is one of the marvels of the history of art. It is perhaps the most eloquent testimony of all to the greatness of Egyptian figural art. In architecture too, the Egyptian achievement was extraordinary. From the time of Imhotep, the first master of building in stone, to the architects of the Late Period, the tombs and temples of the Egyptians have expressed the grandeur and permanence of the Kingdom of the Nile. Even after Egypt became a province of the Roman Empire, its prestige remained high. Today, visitors to Rome who enter the city from the airport are greeted by the tomb of a Roman nobleman who died around 12 BCE. His memorial takes the form of a pyramid—2,500 years after the Old Kingdom pharaohs erected the great pyramids of Gizeh, the oldest of the Seven Wonders of the ancient world.

leads Hu-Nefer into the hall of judgment. The god then adjusts the scales to weigh the dead man's heart against the feather of the goddess Maat, protectress of truth and right. A hybrid monster, Ammit, half hippopotamus and half lion, the devourer of the sinful, awaits the decision of the scales. If the weighing had been unfavorable to the deceased, the monster would have eaten his heart. The ibis-headed god Thoth records the proceedings. Above, the gods of the Egyptian pantheon are arranged as witnesses, while

PREDYNASTIC

■ UNION OF UPPER AND LOWER EGYPT, CA. 3000–2920 BCE

2920 BCE

EARLY DYNASTIC (DYNASTIES I–III)

■ IMHOTEP, FIRST RECORDED NAME OF AN ARTIST, CA. 2625 BCE

2575 BCE

OLD KINGDOM (DYNASTIES IV–VIII)

■ SNEFERU, FIRST PHARAOH OF THE OLD KINGDOM, R. 2575–2551 BCE

2 ■ KHUFU, KHAFRE, AND MENKAURE, BUILDERS OF THE GREAT PYRAMIDS, CA. 2551–2472 BCE

1 Palette of King Narmer, ca. 3000–2920 BCE

2134 BCE

■ FIRST INTERMEDIATE PERIOD, 2134–2040 BCE

2040 BCE

MIDDLE KINGDOM (DYNASTIES XI–XIV)

■ REUNIFICATION OF EGYPT UNDER MENTUHOTEP II, 2040 BCE

2 Great Sphinx, Gizeh, ca. 2520–2494 BCE

1640 BCE

■ SECOND INTERMEDIATE PERIOD, 1640–1550 BCE

1550 BCE

NEW KINGDOM (DYNASTIES XVII–XX)

■ AHMOSE I DEFEATS THE HYKSOS, 1550 BCE

■ HATSHEPSUT, R. 1473–1458 BCE

■ AKHENATON AND THE AMARNA PERIOD, 1353–1335 BCE

3 ■ TUTANKHAMEN, R. 1333–1323 BCE

■ RAMSES II, R. 1290–1224 BCE

1070 BCE

■ THIRD INTERMEDIATE PERIOD, 1070–712 BCE

3 Death mask of Tutankhamen, ca. 1323 BCE

712 BCE

LATE PERIOD (DYNASTIES XXV–XXXI)

■ PERSIA CONQUERS EGYPT, 525 BCE

332 BCE

GREEK (PTOLEMAIC)

■ ALEXANDER THE GREAT CONQUERS PERSIA AND EGYPT, 332 BCE

■ PTOLEMY I, R. 304–284 BCE

4

4 Temple of Horus, Edfu, ca. 237–47 BCE

30 BCE

ROMAN

■ EGYPT BECOMES A ROMAN PROVINCE, 30 BCE

Male lyre player, from Keros (Cyclades), Greece, ca. 2700–2500 BCE. Marble, approx. 9″ high. National Archaeological Museum, Athens.

4

MINOS AND THE HEROES OF HOMER

THE ART OF THE PREHISTORIC AEGEAN

In the *Iliad,* Homer describes the might and splendor of the Greek armies poised before the walls of Troy.

> Clan after clan poured out from the ships and huts onto the plain . . . innumerable as the leaves and blossoms in their season . . . the Athenians . . . the men of Argos and Tiryns of the Great Walls . . . troops from the great stronghold of Mycenae, from wealthy Corinth . . . from Knossos . . . Phaistos . . . and the other troops that had their homes in Crete of the Hundred Towns.[1]

The Greeks had come from far and wide, from the mainland and the islands (MAP **4-1**), to seek revenge against Paris, the Trojan prince who had abducted Helen, wife of King Menelaus of Sparta. Many consider the *Iliad* to be the finest epic poem ever written. Composed around 750 BCE, it is unquestionably the first great work of Greek literature. In fact, until about 1870 Homer's tale was generally regarded as pure fiction. Scholars discounted the bard as a historian, attributing the profusion of names and places in his writings to the rich abundance of his imagination. The prehistory of Greece in the Bronze Age (the successor of the Stone Age) remained shadowy and lost in an impenetrable world of myth.

SCHLIEMANN, TROY, AND MYCENAE In the late 1800s, however, a wealthy German businessman turned archaeologist proved that scholars had done less than justice to the truth of Homer's account. Between 1870 and his death 20 years later, Heinrich Schliemann (whose methods have sometimes been harshly criticized) uncovered some of the very cities Homer named. In 1870, he began work at Hissarlik on the northwestern coast of Turkey, which a British archaeologist, Frank Calvert, had postulated was the site of Homer's Troy. Schliemann dug into a vast mound and found a number of fortified cities built on the remains of one another. One of them had been destroyed by fire in the 13th century BCE. This, scholars now generally agree, was the Troy of King Priam and his son Paris, the city Homer celebrated some 500 years later.

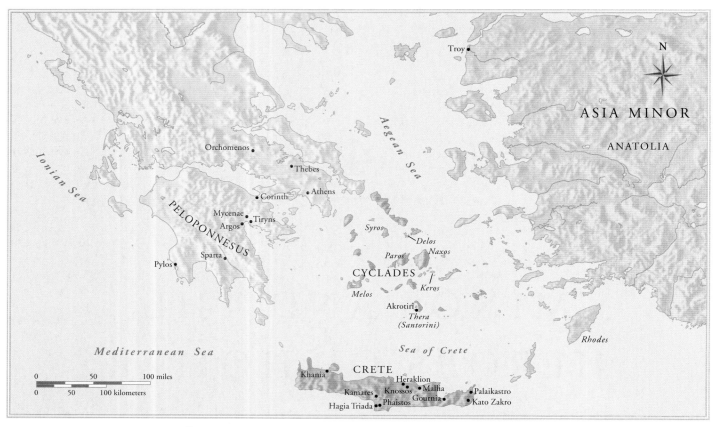

MAP 4-1 The prehistoric Aegean.

Schliemann continued his excavations at Mycenae on the Greek mainland, where, he believed, King Agamemnon, Menelaus's brother, had once ruled. Here his finds were even more startling. A massive fortress-palace (FIG. 4-20); elaborate tombs (FIGS. 4-21 and 4-22); quantities of gold jewelry, masks (FIG. 4-23), and cups; and inlaid weapons (FIG. 4-24) revealed a magnificent civilization far older than the famous vestiges of classical Greece that had remained visible in Athens and elsewhere. Further discoveries proved that Mycenae had not been the only center of this fabulous civilization.

KING MINOS AND CRETE The lesson of Schliemann's success in uncovering Homeric sites was not lost on his successors. Another legendary figure was King Minos of Knossos on the island of Crete. He was said to have exacted from Athens a tribute of youths and maidens to be fed to the Minotaur, a creature half bull and half man housed in a vast labyrinth. Might this story, too, be based on fact? In 1900, an Englishman, Arthur Evans, began work at Knossos. A short time later he uncovered a palace (FIGS. 4-3 and 4-4) that did indeed resemble a maze. Evans named the people who had erected it the Minoans, after their mythological king. His initial findings were soon augmented by additional excavations at Phaistos, Hagia Triada, and other sites, including Gournia, which Harriet Boyd Hawes, an American archaeologist (and one of the first women of any nationality to direct a major excavation), explored between 1901 and 1904.

More recently, important Minoan remains have been excavated at many other locations on Crete, and contemporary sites have been discovered on other islands in the Aegean, most notably on Santorini (ancient Thera). Art historians now have an array of buildings, paintings, and, to a lesser extent, sculptures that attests to the wealth and sophistication of the people who lived in that once obscure heroic age celebrated in later Greek mythology.

AEGEAN ARCHAEOLOGY TODAY Less glamorous than the palaces and art objects, but arguably more important for the understanding of Aegean society, are the many documents archaeologists have found written in scripts dubbed Linear A and Linear B. The progress made during the past several decades in deciphering these texts has provided a welcome corrective to the romanticism that characterized the work of Schliemann and Evans. Linear B can now be read, and scholars have begun to reconstruct Aegean civilization by referring to contemporary records and not just to Homer's heroic account.

Historians now also know that humans inhabited Greece as far back as the Lower Paleolithic period and that village life was firmly established in Greece in Neolithic times. But the heyday of the ancient Aegean was not until the second millennium BCE, well after the emergence of the river valley civilizations of Egypt, Mesopotamia, and South Asia (see Chapters 2, 3, and 6).

AEGEAN GEOGRAPHY The sea-dominated geography of the Aegean contrasts sharply with that of the Near East (MAP 2-1), as does its temperate climate. The situation of Crete and the Aegean Islands at the commercial crossroads of the ancient Mediterranean had a major effect on their prosperity. The sea also provided a natural defense against the frequent and often disruptive invasions that checker the histories of land-bound civilizations such as those of Mesopotamia.

Historians, art historians, and archaeologists alike divide the prehistoric Aegean into three geographic areas. Each has a distinctive artistic identity. Cycladic art is the art of the Cycladic Islands (so named because they *circle* around Delos), as well as of the adjacent islands in the Aegean, excluding Crete. Minoan art encompasses the art of Crete. Helladic art is the art of the Greek mainland (*Hellas* in Greek). Scholars subdivide each area chronologically into early, middle, and late periods, with the art of the Late Helladic period designated Mycenaean after Agamemnon's great citadel of Mycenae.

CYCLADIC ART

"MODERN" SCULPTURE CA. 2500 BCE Marble was abundantly available in the superb quarries of the Aegean Islands, especially on Naxos and Paros. These same quarries later supplied the master sculptors of classical Greece and Rome with fine marble blocks for monumental statues. But nothing surviving from the classical era is quite like the marble statuettes (FIGS. 4-1 and 4-2) that date from the Early Cycladic period. These sculptures are much revered today (see "Archaeology, Art History, and the Art Market," page 88) because of their striking abstract forms, which call to mind the simple and sleek shapes of some 20th-century statues (see FIGS. 33-16 and 33-71).

Most of the Cycladic sculptures, like many of their Stone Age predecessors in the Aegean, the Near East, and western Europe

(see FIG. 1-4), represent nude women with their arms folded across their abdomens. They vary in height from a few inches to almost life-size. Our example (FIG. 4-1) is about a foot and a half tall and comes from a grave on the island of Syros. The statuette typifies many of these figures. It is almost flat, and the human body is rendered in a highly schematized manner. Large simple triangles dominate the form—the head, the body itself (which tapers from exceptionally broad shoulders to tiny feet), and the incised triangular pubis. The feet are too fragile to support the figurine. If these sculptures were primarily funerary offerings, as archaeologists believe they were, they must have been placed on their backs in the graves—lying down, like the deceased themselves. Whether they represent those buried with the statuettes or fertility figures or goddesses is still debated. As is true of all such images, the sculptor took pains to emphasize the breasts as well as the pubic area. In the Syros statuette, a slight swelling of the belly may suggest pregnancy.

Traces of paint found on some of the Cycladic figurines indicate that at least parts of these sculptures were colored. The now almost featureless faces would have had painted eyes and mouths in addition to the sculpted noses. Red and blue necklaces and bracelets, as well as painted dots on the cheeks, characterize a number of the surviving figurines.

MUSIC FOR ETERNITY Male figures also occur in the Cycladic repertoire. The most elaborate of these take the form of seated musicians, such as the lyre player from Keros (FIG. 4-2). Wedged between the echoing shapes of chair and instrument, he may be playing for the deceased in the afterlife, although, again, the meaning of these statuettes remains elusive. The harpist

4-1 Figurine of a woman, from Syros (Cyclades), Greece, ca. 2500–2300 BCE. Marble, approx. 1′ 6″ high. National Archaeological Museum, Athens.

4-2 Male lyre player, from Keros (Cyclades), Greece, ca. 2700–2500 BCE. Marble, approx. 9″ high. National Archaeological Museum, Athens.

Archaeology, Art History, and the Art Market

One way the ancient world is fundamentally different from the world today is that ancient art is largely anonymous and undated. No equivalent exists in antiquity for the systematic signing and dating of artworks commonplace in the contemporary world. That is why the role of archaeology in the study of ancient art is so important. Only the scientific excavation of ancient monuments can establish their context. Exquisite and strikingly "modern" sculptures such as the marble Cycladic figurines we illustrate (FIGS. 4-1 and 4-2) may be appreciated as masterpieces when displayed in splendid isolation in glass cases in museums or private homes. But to understand the role these or any other artworks played in ancient society—in many cases, even to determine the date and place of origin of an object—the art historian must know where the piece was uncovered. Only when the context of an artwork is known can one go beyond an appreciation of its formal qualities and begin to analyze its place in art history—and in the society that produced it.

The extraordinary popularity of Cycladic figurines in recent decades has had unfortunate consequences. Clandestine treasure hunters, anxious to meet the insatiable demands of modern collectors, have plundered many sites and smuggled their finds out of Greece to sell to the highest bidder on the international art market. Entire prehistoric cemeteries and towns have been destroyed because of the high esteem in which these sculptures are now held. Two British scholars have calculated that only about 10 percent of the known Cycladic marble statuettes come from secure archaeological contexts. Many of the rest are probably forgeries, produced mostly after World War II when developments in modern art fostered a new appreciation of these abstract renditions of human anatomy and created a boom in demand for "Cycladica" among collectors. For some categories of Cycladic sculptures—those of unusual type or size—not a single piece with a documented provenance exists. Those groups may be 20th-century inventions designed to fetch even higher prices due to their rarity. Consequently, most of the conclusions art historians have drawn about chronology, attribution to different workshops, range of types, and how the figurines were used are purely speculative. The importance of the information the original contexts would have provided cannot be overestimated. That information is, however, probably never recoverable.

reflects the same preference for simple geometric shapes and large flat planes as the female figures. Still, the artist showed a keen interest in recording the elegant shape of what must have been a prized possession: the harp with a duck-bill or swan-head ornament at the apex of its sound box. (Animal-headed instruments are well documented in contemporary Mesopotamia [see FIGS. 2-8 *bottom*, 2-9, and 2-10] and Egypt.)

In one instance, figurines of both a musician and a reclining woman were placed in a woman's grave. This suggests that the lyre players are not images of dead men, but it does not prove that the female figurines represent dead women. The man might be entertaining the deceased herself, not her image. Given the absence of written documents in Greece at this date, as everywhere else in prehistoric times, art historians cannot be sure of the meaning of most artworks. Some Cycladic figurines have been found in settlements rather than cemeteries, and it is likely, in fact, that the same form took on different meanings in different contexts.

MINOAN ART

Architecture

A PALACE CULTURE EMERGES During the third millennium BCE, both on the Aegean Islands and on the Greek mainland, most settlements were small and consisted only of simple buildings. Only rarely were the dead buried with costly offerings such as the Cycladic statuettes just examined. In contrast, the opening centuries of the second millennium (the Middle Minoan period on Crete) are marked by the construction of large palaces. This first, or Old Palace, period came to an abrupt end around 1700 BCE, when these grand structures were destroyed, probably by an earthquake. Rebuilding began sometime after 1700 BCE, and the ensuing New Palace (Late Minoan) period is the golden age of Crete, an era when the first great Western civilization emerged.

The rebuilt palaces were large, comfortable, and handsome, with ample staircases and courtyards for pageants, ceremonies, and games. They also had storerooms, offices, and shrines that permitted these huge complexes to serve as the key administrative, commercial, and religious centers of Minoan life. The principal palace sites on Crete are at Knossos, Phaistos, Mallia, Kato Zakro, and Khania. All of the complexes were laid out along similar lines. Their size and number, as well as the rich finds they have yielded, attest to the power and prosperity of the Minoans.

THE MINOTAUR'S LABYRINTH The largest of the palaces, at Knossos (FIGS. **4-3** and **4-4**), was the legendary home of King Minos. Here, the hero Theseus was said to have battled with the bullman Minotaur. According to the myth, after defeating the monster, Theseus found his way out of the mazelike complex only with the aid of the king's daughter, Ariadne. She had given Theseus a spindle of thread to mark his path through the labyrinth and then safely out again. In fact, the English word *labyrinth* derives from the intricate plan and scores of rooms of the Knossos palace. *Labrys* means "double ax," and it is a recurring motif in the Minoan palace, referring to sacrificial slaughter. The *labyrinth* was the "House of the Double Axes."

Our aerial view (FIG. 4-3) reveals that the Knossos palace was a rambling structure built against the upper slopes and across the top of a low hill that rises from a fertile plain. All around the palace proper were mansions and villas of the Minoan elite. The great rectangular court (no. 4 in FIG. 4-4), with the palace units grouped around it, had been leveled in the time of the old palace. The new layout suggests that the later palace was carefully planned, with the court serving as the major organizing element.

A secondary organization of the palace plan involves two long corridors. On the west side of the court, a north-south corridor (no. 6) separates official and ceremonial rooms from the magazines (no. 8), where wine, grain, oil, and honey were stored in large jars. On the east side of the court, a smaller east-west corridor (no. 14)

4-3 Aerial view (looking northeast) of the palace at Knossos (Crete), Greece, ca. 1700–1400 BCE.

Reconstruction

Earlier { — Existing
structures { ···· Reconstruction

1. West porch
2. Corridor of the procession
3. South propylon
4. Central court
5. "Theater area"
6. North-south corridor
7. Pillar hall
8. Magazines
9. Throne room
10. Palace shrine and lower verandas
11. Stepped porch
12. Grand staircase
13. Light well
14. East-west corridor
15. Hall of the Double Axes
    (principal reception room)
16. "Queen's Megaron"

0   25   50   75   100
                      FEET
0   10   20   30
                 METERS

4-4 Plan of the palace at Knossos (Crete), Greece, ca. 1700–1400 BCE.

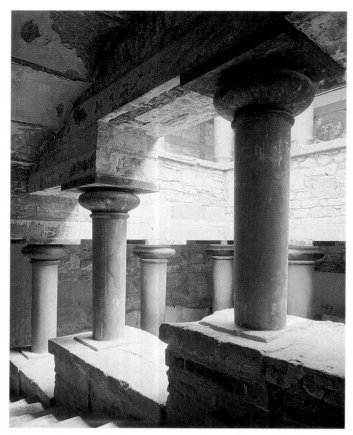

4-5 Stairwell in the residential quarter of the palace at Knossos (Crete), Greece, ca. 1700–1400 BCE.

separates the living quarters and reception rooms (to the south) from the workers' and servants' quarters (to the north). At the northwest corner of the palace is a theater-like area (no. 5) with steps on two sides that may have served as seats. This form is a possible forerunner of the later Greek theater (see FIG. 5-70). Its purpose is unknown, but it is a feature paralleled in the Phaistos palace.

The Cretan palaces were well constructed, with thick walls composed of rough, unshaped fieldstones embedded in clay. Ashlar masonry was used at building corners and around door and window openings. The Minoans also gave thought to such questions as drainage of rainwater. At Knossos, a remarkably efficient system of terracotta pipes underlies the enormous building.

The Knossos palace was complex not only in plan but also in elevation. It had as many as three stories around the central court and even more on the south and east sides where the terrain sloped off sharply. Interior staircases built around light and air wells (FIG. 4-5) provided necessary illumination and ventilation. Painted Minoan columns, originally fashioned of wood but which Evans restored in stone, are characterized by their bulbous, cushionlike capitals and distinctive shafts. The capitals resemble those of the later Greek Doric order (see "Doric and Ionic Temples," Chapter 5, page 116), but the shafts taper from a wide top to a narrower base—the opposite of both Egyptian and later Greek columns.

Painting

MINOAN PALACE FRESCOES Mural paintings liberally adorn the palace at Knossos, constituting one of its most striking aspects. The brightly painted walls and the red shafts and black capitals of the wooden columns provided an extraordinarily rich

effect. The paintings depict many aspects of Minoan life (bull-leaping, processions, and ceremonies) and of nature (birds, animals, flowers, and marine life).

From a ceremonial scene of uncertain significance comes the fragment (FIG. 4-6) dubbed *La Parisienne (The Parisian Woman)* on its discovery because of the elegant dress, elaborate coiffure, and full rouged lips of the young woman (perhaps a priestess or even a goddess) depicted. Although the representation is still convention-bound (note especially the oversized frontal eye in the profile head), the charm and freshness of the mural are undeniable. The painting method used is appropriate to the lively spirit of the Minoans. Unlike the Egyptians, who painted in fresco secco (dry fresco), the Minoans coated the rough fabric of their rubble walls with a fine white lime plaster and used a true (wet) fresco method (see "Fresco Painting," Chapter 19, page 530). The Minoan frescoes required rapid execution and great skill in achieving quick, almost impressionistic effects. The simple, light delicacy of the *Parisienne* painter's technique matches the vivacity of the subject.

BULL-LEAPING AT KNOSSOS Liveliness and spontaneity also characterize a fresco (FIG. 4-7) from the palace at Knossos depicting the Minoan ceremony of bull-leaping (see "Minoan Paintings Discovered in Egypt," page 91). Here, too, only fragments of the full composition have been recovered (the dark patches are original; the rest is a modern restoration). The Minoan artist painted the

4-6 Minoan woman or goddess *(La Parisienne),* from the palace at Knossos (Crete), Greece, ca. 1450–1400 BCE. Fragment of a fresco, approx. 10″ high. Archaeological Museum, Herakleion.

Minoan Paintings Discovered in Egypt

Knowledge of ancient art and architecture grows daily as archaeologists uncover new paintings, sculptures, pots, and other objects, as well as remains of previously unknown buildings. Although excavators infrequently make a truly astounding discovery, that is what happened when, in the 1980s, an Austrian expedition to Tell el-Daba in the eastern Nile Delta explored a huge palace of the 16th century BCE.

Tell el-Daba, ancient Avaris (see MAP 3-1), was the capital city of the Hyksos. Until Ahmose, founder of the New Kingdom, drove them out around 1530 BCE, the Hyksos ruled the land of the Nile. The palatial complex the Austrians discovered was either built by Ahmose at the beginning of the 18th Dynasty, or built under the last Hyksos pharaoh and destroyed by Ahmose. The archaeologists uncovered the unexpected: pumice from the eruption of the Theran volcano (see "A Volcano Erupts," page 94) and thousands of fragments of Aegean-style wall paintings.

The most impressive of the Avaris murals depicts bull-leapers seen against a maze background that many believe is a topographical reference to the Minoan palace at Knossos. Not only is the subject of the painting Aegean but also the technique (primarily true fresco on lime plaster) and most aspects of style and iconography. Few doubt that Aegean rather than Egyptian artists decorated the palace, although there is little agreement as to why the Egyptians employed foreign painters or chose an Aegean subject.

Whatever the final answer to this archaeological and historical riddle, the excavations at Tell el-Daba have demonstrated that contacts between Egypt and the Aegean world were not confined to trade and politics. In fact, painted walls and floors of Aegean style, technique, and subject also have been discovered in recent years in a Canaanite palace at Tel Kabri in northern Israel. Similar finds had been made much earlier at Alalakh in Syria (see MAP 2-1 for both sites). Together these startling discoveries provide evidence for a rich international exchange of artists and ideas in the Mediterranean world at the middle of the second millennium BCE. Art historians can no longer study the great civilizations of Egypt, the Near East, and the Aegean in isolation.

---

young women (with fair skin) and the youth (with dark skin) according to the widely accepted ancient convention for distinguishing male and female. The young man is shown in the air, having, it seems, grasped the bull's horns and vaulted over its back in a perilous and extremely difficult acrobatic maneuver. The painter brilliantly suggested the powerful charge of the bull by elongating the animal's shape and using sweeping lines to form a funnel of energy, beginning at the very narrow hindquarters of the bull and culminating in its large, sharp horns and galloping forelegs. The human figures also have stylized shapes, with typically Minoan pinched waists, and are highly animated. Although the profile pose with the full-view eye was a familiar convention in Egypt and Mesopotamia, the elegance of the Cretan figures, with their long, curly hair and proud and self-confident bearing, distinguishes them from all

4-7 Bull-leaping, from the palace at Knossos (Crete), Greece, ca. 1450–1400 BCE. Fresco, approx. 2′ 8″ high, including border. Archaeological Museum, Herakleion.

A Volcano Erupts, and the History of Art Is Revised

Today, ships bound for the beautiful Greek island of San-torini, with its picture-postcard white houses, churches, shops, and restaurants, weigh anchor in a bay beneath steep, crescent-shaped cliffs. Until about 20,000 BCE, however, ancient Thera had a roughly circular shape and gentler slopes. Then, sud-denly, a volcanic eruption blew out the center of the island, leav-ing behind the moon-shaped main island and several lesser is-lands grouped around a bay that roughly corresponds to the shape of the gigantic ancient volcano. The volcano erupted again, thousands of years later, during the zenith of Aegean civilization.

Then, the site of Akrotiri, which Greek excavators gradually are uncovering, was buried by a pumice layer more than a yard deep in some areas and by an even larger volume of volcanic ash *(tephra)* that often exceeds five yards in depth, even after nearly 37 centuries of erosion. Tephra filled whole rooms, and boulders the volcano spewed forth pelted the walls of some houses. Closer to the volcano's cone, the tephra is almost 60 yards deep in places. In fact, the force of the eruption was so powerful that sea currents carried the pumice and wind blew the ash throughout the ancient Mediterranean, not only to Crete, Rhodes, and Cyprus but also as far away as Anatolia, Egypt (see "Minoan Paintings Discovered in Egypt," page 91), Syria, and Israel.

Until recently, most scholars embraced the theory formulated decades ago by Spyridon Marinatos, an eminent Greek archae-ologist, that the otherwise unexplained demise of Minoan

civilization on Crete around 1500 BCE was the by-product of the volcanic eruption on Thera. According to Marinatos, devastating famine followed the rain of ash that fell on Crete. But archaeolo-gists now know that after the eruption, life went on in Crete, if not on Thera. At one Cretan site, the Minoans collected Theran pumice and deposited it in conical cups on a monumental stair-way, possibly as a votive offering.

Teams of researchers, working closely in an impressive and most welcome interdisciplinary effort, have pinpointed 1628 BCE as the date of a major climatic event. They have studied tree rings at sites in Europe and in North America for evidence of retarded growth and have examined ice cores in Greenland for peak acid-ity layers. Both kinds of evidence testify to a significant disruption in weather patterns in that year. Today, most—but not all—scholars believe the cause of this disruption to be the cataclysmic volcanic eruption on Thera.

The revised date of the Theran eruption has profound conse-quences for the chronology of Aegean art. The Akrotiri frescoes (FIGS. 4-8 and 4-9) are now thought to be at least 150 years older than they were considered not long ago. They predate by many decades the paintings from the Knossos palace (FIGS. 4-6 and 4-7). The discovery has implications for the dating of art objects from other areas as well because of the important interconnec-tions between the Aegean, Egypt, and the Near East during the second millennium BCE.

other early figure styles. The angularity of the figures seen in Egyp-tian wall paintings is modified by the curving Minoan line that sug-gests the elasticity of the living and moving being.

BURIED BY A VOLCANO Much better preserved than the Knossos frescoes are those uncovered much more recently in the excavations of Akrotiri on the volcanic island of Santorini (an-cient Thera) in the Cyclades, some 60 miles north of Crete. In the Late Cycladic period, Thera was artistically, and possibly also po-litically, within the Minoan orbit. The mural paintings from Akrotiri are invaluable additions to the fragmentary and fre-quently misrestored frescoes from Crete. The excellent condition of the Theran paintings is due to an enormous seismic explosion

on Santorini that buried Akrotiri in volcanic pumice and ash, making it a kind of Pompeii of the prehistoric Aegean (see "A Vol-cano Erupts, and the History of Art Is Revised," above). The Akrotiri frescoes decorated the walls of houses, not the walls of a great palace such as that at Knossos, and therefore the number of painted walls from the site is especially impressive.

SEAFARING IN THE CYCLADES One especially interesting Theran fresco is filled with dozens of figures, ships, and buildings. This *Miniature Ships Fresco,* as it has been called, formed a frieze about 17 inches high at the top of at least three walls of a room in the so-called West House at Akrotiri. In our detail of the fresco (FIG. **4-8**), a great fleet sails from one Aegean port headed for

4-8 Flotilla, detail of *Miniature Ships Fresco,* from Room 5, West House, Akrotiri, Thera (Cyclades), Greece, ca. 1650 BCE. Fresco, approx. 1′ 5″ high. National Archaeological Museum, Athens.

4-9 Landscape with swallows (*Spring Fresco*), from Room Delta 2, Akrotiri, Thera (Cyclades), Greece, ca. 1650 BCE. Fresco, approx. 7′ 6″ high. National Archaeological Museum, Athens.

another (not visible in the illustration), perhaps taking part in a sea festival or perhaps engaged in a naval campaign that calls to mind Homer's much later catalog of ships in the *Iliad*. Such a detailed representation of the movement of ships and people from port to port does not appear again until the Column of the Roman emperor Trajan (see FIG. 10-42) almost two millennia later. The details of ship design and sailing are carefully observed in the fresco, as if it were painted by one who knew ships well. Just as closely studied are the placement and poses of sailors, rowers, and passengers.

Little of the conventional stereotyping and repetition that appear in such representations throughout the history of art is evident in the Akrotiri fresco. Instead, the arrangement of figures and poses varies significantly according to each person's role—steering, tending to the sail, rowing, or simply sitting and conversing. Dolphins frolic about the ships, and on the left shore a lion pursues fleeing deer. The port—encircled by a river represented as arching above it—has quays, houses, and streets filled with men attentive to the coming and going of the ships. The whole composition has an openness and lightness that suggest the freedom of movement of a people born to the sea.

CELEBRATING NATURE The almost perfectly preserved mural paintings of another room from Akrotiri capture especially well the freshness and vitality of this vision of the Aegean world. In *Spring Fresco* (FIG. 4-9), nature itself is the sole subject, although the artist's aim was not to render the rocky island terrain realistically but, rather, to capture the landscape's essence and to express joy in the splendid surroundings. The irrationally undulating and vividly colored rocks, the graceful lilies swaying in the cool island breezes, and the darting swallows express the vigor of growth, the delicacy of flowering, and the lightness of birdsong and flight. In the lyrical language of curving line, the artist celebrated the rhythms of spring. This is the first known example of a pure landscape painting, one that not only has no humans but also has no narrative element (compare FIG. 1-18). The Theran *Spring Fresco* represents the polar opposite of the first efforts at mural painting in the caves of Paleolithic Europe, where animals (and occasionally humans) appeared as isolated figures without any indication of setting.

SEA LIFE ON POTTERY The love of nature manifested itself in Crete on the surfaces of painted vases even before the period of the new palaces. During the Middle Minoan period, Cretan potters fashioned sophisticated shapes using newly introduced potters' wheels, and decorated their vases in a distinctive and fully polychromatic style. These Kamares Ware vessels, named for the cave on the slope of Mount Ida where they were first discovered, have been found in quantity at Phaistos and Knossos. On our example (FIG. 4-10), as on other Kamares vases, creamy white and reddish-brown

4-10 Kamares Ware jar, from Phaistos (Crete), Greece, ca. 1800–1700 BCE. Approx. 1′ 8″ high. Archaeological Museum, Herakleion.

decoration is set against a rich black ground. The central motif is a great leaping fish—a forerunner of the diving dolphins of Late Minoan and Late Cycladic murals—and perhaps a fishnet surrounded by a host of curvilinear abstract patterns including waves and spirals. The swirling lines evoke life in the sea, and both the abstract and the natural forms beautifully complement the shape of the vessel.

The sea and the creatures that inhabit it also inspired the Late Minoan Marine Style octopus jar (FIG. **4-11**) from Palaikastro, which is contemporary with the new palaces at Knossos and elsewhere. The tentacles of the octopus reach out over the curving surfaces of the vessel, embracing the piece and emphasizing its volume. This is a masterful realization of the relationship between the vessel's decoration and its shape, always a problem for the ceramist. This later vase differs markedly from its Kamares Ware predecessor in color. Not only is the octopus jar more muted in tone, but the Late Minoan artist also reversed the earlier scheme and placed dark silhouettes on a light ground. This remained the norm for about a millennium in Greece, until about 530 BCE when, albeit in a very different form, light figures on a dark ground emerged once again as the preferred manner (see FIG. 5-20).

MINOAN FUNERARY RITUALS Midway in size and complexity between the decorated clay vessels and the monumental frescoes of Crete and Thera are the paintings on a Late Minoan limestone *sarcophagus* (FIG. **4-12**) found at Hagia Triada on the southern coast of Crete. The paintings are closely related in technique, color scheme, and figure style to contemporary palace frescoes, but the subject is foreign to the palace repertoire. Befitting the function of the sarcophagus as a burial container, the paintings illustrate the funerary rites in honor of the dead. They provide welcome information about Minoan religion, which still remains obscure despite more than a century of excavation on Crete. At the right, the dead man appears upright in front of his own tomb, like the New Testament's raised Lazarus in medieval

4-11 Marine Style octopus jar, from Palaikastro (Crete), Greece, ca. 1500 BCE. Approx. 11″ high. Archaeological Museum, Herakleion.

art, and watches as three men (note their dark flesh tone) bring offerings to him. At the left, two light-skinned women carry vessels and pour a libation to the deceased while a male musician plays a lyre. The musician immediately brings to mind the Early Cycladic statuettes of lyre players (FIG. 4-2) deposited in tombs, which may indicate some continuity in funerary customs and beliefs from the Early to the Late Bronze Age in the Aegean.

4-12 Sarcophagus, from Hagia Triada (Crete), Greece, ca. 1450–1400 BCE. Painted limestone, approx. 4′ 6″ long. Archaeological Museum, Herakleion.

Sculpture

JOYFUL FARMERS Also from Hagia Triada is the so-called *Harvester Vase* (FIG. **4-13**), probably the finest surviving example of Minoan relief sculpture. Only the upper half of the egg-shaped body and neck of the vessel are preserved. Missing are the lower parts of the harvesters (or, as some think, sowers) and the ground on which they stand. Formulaic scenes of sowing and harvesting were staples of Egyptian funerary art (see FIG. 3-17), but the Minoan artist shunned static repetition in favor of a composition that bursts with the energy of its individually characterized figures. The relief shows a riotous crowd singing and shouting as they go to or return from the fields. The artist vividly captured the forward movement and lusty exuberance of the youths.

Although most of the figures conform to the age-old convention of combined profile and frontal views, one figure (at the center of our illustration) is singled out from his companions. He shakes a rattle to beat time, and the artist depicted him in full profile with his lungs so inflated with air that his ribs show. This is one of the first instances in the history of art of a sculptor showing a keen interest in the underlying muscular and skeletal structure of the human body. The artist's painstaking study of human anatomy is a remarkable achievement, especially given the size of the *Harvester Vase*, barely five inches at its greatest diameter. Equally noteworthy is how the sculptor recorded the tension and relaxation of facial muscles with astonishing exactitude. This degree of animation of the human face is without precedent in ancient art.

GODDESS OR PRIESTESS? In contrast to Mesopotamia and Egypt, no temples or monumental statues of gods, kings, or monsters have been found in Minoan Crete. Large wooden images may once have existed, but what remains of Minoan sculpture in the round is small in scale, such as the *faience* (glazed earthenware) statuette known as the *Snake Goddess* (FIG. **4-14**), from the palace at Knossos. It is one of several similar figurines that some scholars believe may represent mortal attendants rather than a deity, although the prominently exposed breasts suggest that these figurines stand in the long line of prehistoric fertility images usually considered divinities. (The woman depicted in the Knossos statuette not only holds snakes in her hands but also supports a leopardlike feline peacefully on her head. This implied power over the animal world also seems appropriate for a deity.) The frontality of the figure is reminiscent of Egyptian and Near Eastern statuary, but the costume, with its open bodice and flounced skirt, is distinctly Minoan. If the statuette represents a goddess, as seems likely, then it is yet another example of how human beings fashion their gods in their own image.

SCULPTURE IN GOLD AND IVORY British excavations at Palaikastro between 1987 and 1990 yielded fragments of one of the

4-13 *Harvester Vase,* from Hagia Triada (Crete), Greece, ca. 1500 BCE. Steatite, greatest diameter approx. 5″. Archaeological Museum, Herakleion.

4-14 *Snake Goddess,* from the palace at Knossos (Crete), Greece, ca. 1600 BCE. Faience, approx. 1′ 1½″ high. Archaeological Museum, Herakleion.

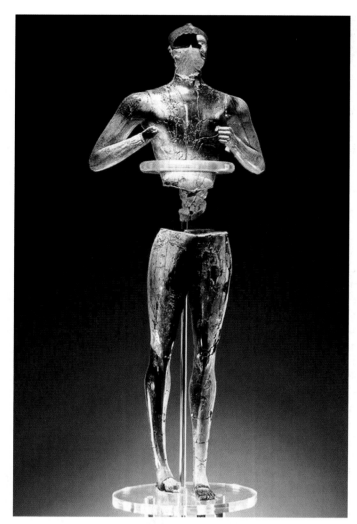

4-15 Young god(?), from Palaikastro (Crete), Greece, ca. 1500–1475 BCE. Ivory, gold, serpentine, and rock crystal, original height approx. 1′ 7½″. Archaeological Museum, Siteia.

most remarkable objects ever found on Crete. It is a statuette (FIG. **4-15**) nearly 20 inches tall, fashioned from hippopotamus tusk ivory, gold, serpentine, and rock crystal. The figurine is a very early example of *chryselephantine* (gold and ivory) sculpture, a technique that the Greeks would later use for their largest and costliest cult images (see FIG. 5-44). The ivory and gold were probably imported from Egypt, the source also of the pose with left foot advanced (see FIGS. 3-13 and 3-15), but the style and iconography are unmistakably Cretan. The work is the creation of a sculptor of extraordinary ability who delighted in rendering minute details of muscles and veins (compare FIG. 4-13). The Palaikastro youth (his coiffure, with shaved head save for a central braid, indicates his age) was displayed alone in a shrine and therefore seems to have been a god rather than a mortal. The statuette's blackened state is the result of fire. The scattered fragments the archaeologists retrieved suggest an act of vandalism in the 15th century BCE.

MINOAN DECLINE Scholars dispute the circumstances ending the Minoan civilization, although they now widely believe that Mycenaeans had already moved onto Crete and established themselves at Knossos at the end of the New Palace period. From the palace at Knossos, these intruders appear to have ruled the is-

land for at least half a century, perhaps much longer. Parts of the palace continued to be occupied until its final destruction around 1200 BCE, but its importance as a cultural center faded soon after 1400 BCE, as the focus of Aegean civilization shifted to the Greek mainland.

MYCENAEAN ART

HOMER'S MYCENAEANS The origins of the Mycenaean culture are still debated. The only certainty is the presence of these forerunners of the Greeks on the mainland about the time the old palaces were built on Crete — that is, about the beginning of the second millennium BCE. Doubtless Cretan civilization influenced these people even then, and some believe that the mainland was a Minoan economic dependency for a long time. In any case, Mycenaean power developed on the mainland in the days of the new palaces on Crete, and by 1500 BCE a distinctive Mycenaean culture was flourishing in Greece. Several centuries later, Homer described Mycenae as "rich in gold." The dramatic discoveries of Schliemann and his successors have fully justified this characterization, even if today's archaeologists no longer view the Mycenaeans solely through the heroic eyes of Homer.

Architecture

CITADELS GIANTS BUILT The destruction of the Cretan palaces left the mainland culture supreme. Although this Late Helladic civilization has come to be called Mycenaean, Mycenae was but one of several large citadels. Archaeologists have also unearthed Mycenaean remains at Tiryns, Orchomenos, Pylos, and elsewhere, and Mycenaean fortification walls have even been found on the Acropolis of Athens. The best-preserved and most impressive Mycenaean remains are those of the fortified palaces at Tiryns and Mycenae. Both were built beginning about 1400 BCE and burned (along with all the others) between 1250 and 1200 BCE, when the Mycenaeans seem to have been overrun by northern invaders or to have fallen victim to internal warfare.

Homer knew the citadel of Tiryns (FIG. **4-16**), located about 10 miles from Mycenae, as Tiryns of the Great Walls. In the second century CE, when Pausanias, author of an invaluable guidebook to Greece, visited the site, he marveled at the towering fortifications and considered the walls of Tiryns as spectacular as the pyramids of Egypt. Indeed, the Greeks of the historical age believed mere humans could not have erected such edifices and instead attributed the construction of the great Mycenaean citadels to the mythical *Cyclopes,* a race of one-eyed giants. Historians still refer to the huge, roughly cut stone blocks forming the massive fortification walls of Tiryns and other Mycenaean sites as *Cyclopean masonry.*

The heavy walls of Tiryns and other Mycenaean palaces contrast sharply with the open Cretan palaces (FIG. 4-3) and clearly reveal their defensive character. Those of Tiryns average about 20 feet in thickness, and in one section they house a long gallery (FIG. **4-17**) covered by a *corbeled vault* (FIG. **4-18***b*). Here the builders piled the large, irregular Cyclopean blocks in horizontal courses and then cantilevered them inward until the two walls met in a pointed arch. No mortar was used, and the vault is held in place only by the weight of the blocks (often several tons each), by the smaller stones used as wedges, and by the clay that fills some of the empty spaces. This primitive but effective vaulting

4-16 Aerial view of the citadel at Tiryns, Greece, ca. 1400–1200 BCE.

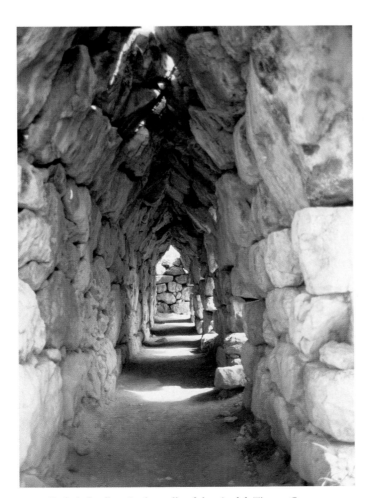

4-17 Corbeled gallery in the walls of the citadel, Tiryns, Greece, ca. 1400–1200 BCE.

a

b

c

4-18 Three methods of spanning a passageway: *(a)* post and lintel, *(b)* corbeled arch, *(c)* arch.

scheme possesses an earthy monumentality. It is easy to see how a later age came to believe that the uncouth Cyclopes were responsible for these massive but unsophisticated fortifications.

THE KING'S HALL Would-be attackers at Tiryns were compelled to approach the palace (FIG. 4-19) within the walls via a long ramp that forced the (usually right-handed) soldiers to expose their unshielded sides to the Mycenaean defenders above. Then — if they got that far — they had to pass through a series of narrow gates that also could be defended easily. Inside, at Tiryns as elsewhere, the most important element in the palace plan was the *megaron,* or reception hall, of the king. The main room of the megaron had a throne against the right wall and a central hearth bordered by four Minoan-style wooden columns serving as supports for the roof. A vestibule with a columnar facade preceded the throne room. A variation of this plan later formed the core of some of the earliest Greek temple plans (see FIG. 5-5). This fact suggests some architectural continuity during the so-called Dark Ages that followed the collapse of Mycenaean civilization.

MYCENAE'S LION GATE The severity of these fortress-palaces was relieved by frescoes, as in the Cretan palaces, and, at Agamemnon's Mycenae at least, by monumental architectural sculpture. The Lion Gate (FIG. 4-20) is the outer gateway of the stronghold at Mycenae. It is protected on the left by a wall built on a natural rock outcropping and on the right by a projecting bastion of large blocks. Any approaching enemies would have had to enter this 20-foot-wide channel and face Mycenaean defenders above them on both sides. The gate itself is formed of two great monoliths capped with a huge lintel (FIG. 4-18*a*). Above the lintel, the masonry courses form a *corbeled arch* (FIG. 4-18*b*), leaving an opening that lightens the weight the lintel carries. This *relieving triangle* is filled with a great limestone slab where two lions carved in high relief stand on the sides of a Minoan-type column. The whole design admirably fills its triangular space, harmonizing in dignity, strength, and scale with the massive stones that form the walls and gate. Similar groups appear in miniature on Cretan

4-19 Plan of the palace and southern part of the citadel, Tiryns, Greece, ca. 1400–1200 BCE.

seals, but the idea of placing monstrous guardian figures at the entrances to palaces, tombs, and sacred places has its origin in Egypt and the Near East (compare, for example, the Great Sphinx of Gizeh, FIG. 3-11, and the later lion and lamassu gates of Assyria, FIGS. 2-18 and 2-21). At Mycenae the animals' heads were

4-20 Lion Gate, Mycenae, Greece, ca. 1300–1250 BCE. Limestone, relief panel approx. 9′ 6″ high.

4-21 Treasury of Atreus, Mycenae, Greece, ca. 1300–1250 BCE.

fashioned separately and are lost. Some scholars have suggested that the "lions" were actually composite beasts in the Eastern tradition, possibly sphinxes.

BEEHIVE TOMBS The Lion Gate at Mycenae and the towering fortification wall circuit of which it formed a part were constructed a few generations before the presumed date of the Trojan War. At that time, wealthy Mycenaeans were laid to rest outside the citadel walls in beehive-shaped tombs covered by enormous earthen mounds. The best preserved of these *tholos tombs* is the so-called Treasury of Atreus (FIG. 4-21), which already in antiquity was mistakenly believed to be the repository of the treasure of Atreus, father of Agamemnon and Menelaus. Approached by a long passageway *(dromos),* the tomb chamber was entered through a doorway surmounted by a relieving triangle similar to that employed in the roughly contemporary Lion Gate. The tholos (FIG. 4-22) is composed of a series of stone corbeled courses laid on a circular base and ending in a lofty dome. The builders probably constructed the vault using rough-hewn blocks. After they set the stones in place, the masons had to finish the surfaces with great precision to make them conform to both the horizontal and vertical curves of the wall. The principle involved is no different from that of the corbeled gallery of Tiryns (FIG. 4-17). But the problem of constructing a complete dome is much more complicated, and the execution of the vault in the Treasury of Atreus is much more sophisticated than that of the vaulted gallery at Tiryns. About 43 feet high, this is the largest known vaulted space without interior supports that had ever been built. The achievement was not surpassed until the Romans constructed the Pantheon (see FIG. 10-50) almost 1,500 years later using a new technology—concrete construction—unknown to the Mycenaeans.

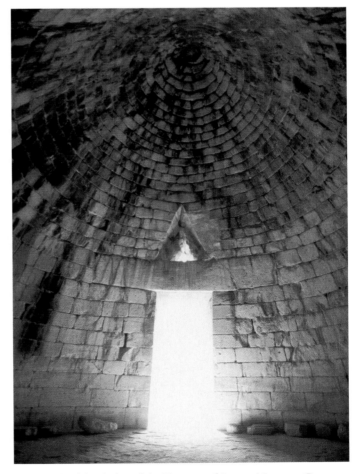

4-22 Vault of the tholos of the Treasury of Atreus, Mycenae, Greece, ca. 1300–1250 BCE. Approx. 43′ high.

Metalwork, Sculpture, and Painting

TREASURES OF REVERED KINGS The Treasury of Atreus had been thoroughly looted long before its modern rediscovery, but excavators have found spectacular grave goods elsewhere at Mycenae. Just inside the Lion Gate, Schliemann uncovered what archaeologists now designate as Grave Circle A. It predates the Lion Gate and the walls of Mycenae by some three centuries. Grave Circle A encloses six deep shafts that had served as tombs for kings and their families. The Mycenaeans laid their dead to rest on the floors of these shaft graves with masks covering their faces, recalling the Egyptian funerary practice. They buried women with their jewelry and men with their weapons and golden cups.

Among the most spectacular of Schliemann's finds is a beaten (repoussé) gold mask (FIG. **4-23**), one of several from the royal burial complex. It often has been compared to the fabulous gold mummy mask of Tutankhamen (see FIG. 3-37). The treatment of the human face is, of course, more primitive in the Mycenaean mask. But this was one of the first known attempts in Greece to render the human face at life-size, whereas Tutankhamen's mask stands in a long line of monumental Egyptian sculptures going back more than a millennium. It is not known whether the Mycenaean masks were intended as portraits, but the goldsmiths recorded different physical types with care. They portrayed youthful faces as well as mature ones. Our example, with its full beard, must depict a mature man, perhaps a king—although not Agamemnon, as Schliemann wished. If Agamemnon was a real king, he lived some 300 years after this mask was fashioned. Clearly the Mycenaeans were "rich in gold" long before Homer's heroes fought at Troy.

Also found in Grave Circle A were several magnificent bronze dagger blades inlaid with gold, silver, and niello (a black metallic alloy), again attesting to the wealth of the Mycenaean kings, as well as to their warlike nature. The largest and most elaborate of the group (FIG. **4-24**) is decorated on one side with a scene of four hunters attacking a lion that has struck down a fifth hunter, while two other lions flee. The other side shows lions attacking deer. The slim-waisted, long-haired figures are Minoan in style, but the artist borrowed the subject from the repertoire of the ancient Near East. It is likely that a Minoan metalworker made the dagger for a Mycenaean patron who admired Minoan art but had different tastes in subject matter than his Cretan counterparts.

MONUMENTAL SCULPTURE Large-scale figural art is very rare on the Greek mainland, as on Crete, other than the Minoan-style paintings that once adorned the walls of Mycenaean palaces.

4-23 Funerary mask, from Grave Circle A, Mycenae, Greece, ca. 1600–1500 BCE. Beaten gold, approx. 1' high. National Archaeological Museum, Athens.

4-24 Inlaid dagger blade with lion hunt, from Grave Circle A, Mycenae, Greece, ca. 1600–1500 BCE. Bronze, inlaid with gold, silver, and niello, approx. 9″ long. National Archaeological Museum, Athens.

The triangular relief of the Lion Gate at Mycenae is exceptional, as is the painted plaster head (FIG. **4-25**) of a woman, goddess, or, perhaps, sphinx found at Mycenae. The white flesh tone indicates that the head is female. The hair and eyes are dark blue, almost black, and the lips, ears, and headband are red. The artist decorated the cheeks and chin with red circles surrounded by a ring of red dots, recalling the facial paint or tattoos recorded on Early Cycladic figurines of women. Although the large star-ing eyes give the face a menacing, if not terrifying, expression appropriate for a guardian figure such as a sphinx, the closest parallels to this work are terracotta images of goddesses from Mycenaean shrines. This head may therefore be a very early example of a monumental cult statue in Greece.

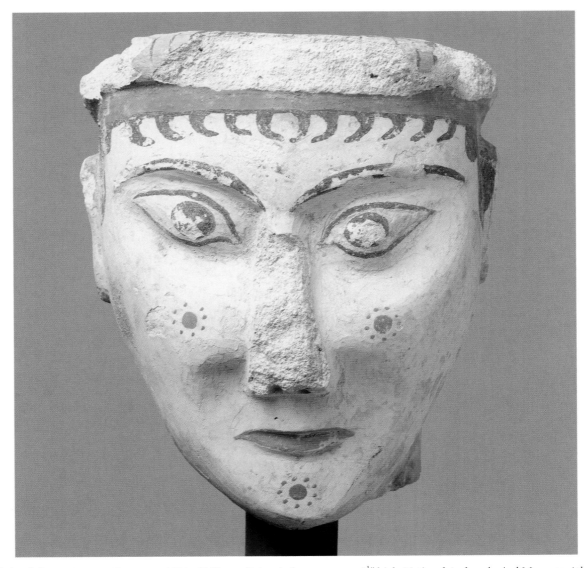

4-25 Female head, from Mycenae, Greece, ca. 1300–1250 BCE. Painted plaster, approx. $6\frac{1}{2}$″ high. National Archaeological Museum, Athens.

4-26 *Warrior Vase*, from Mycenae, Greece, ca. 1200 BCE. Approx. 1′ 4″ high. National Archaeological Museum, Athens.

Were it not for this plaster head and a few other exceptional pieces, art historians might have concluded, wrongly, that the Mycenaeans had no monumental freestanding statuary—a reminder that it is always dangerous to generalize from the fragmentary remains of an ancient civilization. Nonetheless, life-size Aegean statuary must have been rare. After the collapse of Mycenaean civilization and for the next several hundred years, no attempts at monumental statuary are evident until, after the waning of the Dark Ages, Greek sculptors were exposed to the great sculptural tradition of Egypt.

WARRIORS MARCH TO BATTLE An art form that did continue throughout the period after the downfall of the Mycenaean palaces was vase painting. One of the latest examples of Bronze Age painting is the *krater* (bowl for mixing wine and water) from Mycenae commonly called the *Warrior Vase* (FIG. 4-26) after its prominent frieze of soldiers marching off to war. At the left a woman bids farewell to the column of heavily armed warriors moving away from her. The painting on this vase has no indication of setting and lacks the landscape elements that characterized earlier Minoan and Mycenaean art. All the soldiers also repeat the same pattern, a far cry from the variety and anecdotal detail of the lively procession of the Minoan *Harvester Vase* (FIG. 4-13).

This simplification of narrative is paralleled in other painted vases by the increasingly schematic and abstract treatment of marine life. The octopus, for example, eventually became a stylized motif composed of concentric circles and spirals that are almost unrecognizable as a sea creature. By the end of the so-called Sub-Mycenaean period, three centuries after the fall of Mycenae, the art of figure painting had been forgotten.

CONCLUSION

In Homer's time (eighth century BCE), the heyday of Aegean civilization was but a distant memory. The men and women of Crete and Mycenae—Minos and Ariadne, Agamemnon and Helen—had assumed the stature of heroes from a lost golden age. Since the late 19th century, however, archaeologists have been uncovering the remains of that heroic era. The ruins of Cretan palaces, with their open access and mural paintings of palace life and nature itself, attest to the prosperity—and security—of the Minoans. The citadels of Mycenae and Tiryns, with their fortified "Cyclopean" walls, paint a very different picture of Mycenaean society—constantly at war, whether against Troy, northern invaders, or each other. With the destruction of the Mycenaean palaces around 1200 BCE, Greece was plunged into a "Dark Age," when the arts of painting, carving, building, and even writing almost disappeared. The historical Greeks looked back on the achievements of their Minoan and Mycenaean predecessors with awe, but in time they would surpass them and put their stamp on Western civilization and Western art forever.

CYCLADES	CRETE	MAINLAND GREECE
EARLY CYCLADIC	EARLY MINOAN	EARLY HELLADIC
MIDDLE CYCLADIC	MIDDLE MINOAN	MIDDLE HELLADIC
LATE CYCLADIC	LATE MINOAN	LATE HELLADIC (MYCENAEAN)
	SUB-MINOAN	SUB-MYCENAEAN

3000 BCE

2000 BCE

▮ OLD PALACE PERIOD ON CRETE, CA. 2000–1700 BCE

1 Cycladic lyre player, Keros,
ca. 2700–2500 BCE

1700 BCE

▮ LINEAR A SCRIPT DEVELOPED, CA. 1700–1600 BCE
▮ NEW PALACE PERIOD ON CRETE, CA. 1700–1400 BCE

1600 BCE

▮ THERAN ERUPTION, CA. 1628 BCE

2 Gold funerary mask, Mycenae,
ca. 1600–1500 BCE

1500 BCE

▮ MYCENAEANS AT KNOSSOS, CA. 1450–1400 BCE

1400 BCE

▮ LINEAR B SCRIPT DEVELOPED, CA. 1400–1300 BCE
▮ POST-PALATIAL PERIOD ON CRETE, CA. 1400–1200 BCE

3 Bull-leaping fresco, Knossos,
ca. 1450–1400 BCE

1300 BCE

1200 BCE

▮ DESTRUCTION OF MYCENAEAN PALACES, CA. 1200 BCE

4 Citadel, Tiryns, ca. 1400–1200 BCE

Euthymides, Three revelers (Attic red-figure amphora), from Vulci, Italy, ca. 510 bce. Approx. 2′ high. Staatliche Antiken-sammlungen, Munich.

5

GODS, HEROES, AND ATHLETES
THE ART OF ANCIENT GREECE

"For we are lovers of the beautiful, yet simple in our tastes, and we cultivate the mind without loss of manliness. . . . [We are] the school of Hellas."[1] In the fifth century BCE, the golden age of Athens, the historian Thucydides quoted Pericles, the leader of the Athenians, making this assertion in praise of his fellow citizens. Pericles was comparing the Athenians' open, democratic society with the closed barracks state of their rivals, the Spartans. But Pericles might have been speaking in general of Greek culture and its ideal of humanistic education and life.

GREEK HUMANISM

For the Greeks, humanity was what mattered, and humans were, in the words of the philosopher Protagoras, the "measure of all things." This humanistic worldview led the Greeks to create the concept of democracy (rule by the *demos*, the people) and to make seminal contributions in the fields of art, literature, and science. The Greek exaltation of humanity and honoring of the individual are so completely part of modern Western habits of mind that most people are scarcely aware that these ideas originated in the minds of the Greeks.

GODS AND HUMANS Even the gods of the Greeks (see "The Gods and Goddesses of Mount Olympus," page 107), in marked contrast to the divinities of the Near East, assumed human forms whose grandeur and nobility were not free from human frailty. Indeed, unlike the Egyptian and Mesopotamian gods, the Greek deities differed from human beings only in that they were immortal. It has been said that the Greeks made their gods into humans and their humans into gods. Humans, becoming the measure of all things, in turn must represent, if all things in their perfection are beautiful, the unchanging standard of the best. The perfect individual became the Greek ideal.

MAP 5-1 The Greek world.

GREEK ORIGINS The Greeks, or *Hellenes,* as they called themselves, appear to have been the product of an intermingling of Aegean peoples and Indo-European invaders. They never formed a single nation but instead established independent city-states or *poleis* (singular, *polis*). The Dorians of the north, who many believe brought an end to Mycenaean civilization, settled in the Peloponnesos (MAP **5-1**). Across the Aegean, the Ionians settled the western coast of Asia Minor (modern Turkey). The origin of the Ionians is disputed. Some say the northern invaders forced the Ionians out of Greece and that they then sailed from Athens to Asia Minor. Others hold that the Ionians developed in Asia Minor itself between the 11th and 8th centuries BCE out of a mixed stock of settlers. Whatever the origins of the various regional populations, political development differed from polis to polis, although a pattern emerged. Rule was first by kings, then by nobles, and then by tyrants who seized personal power. At last, in Athens, 2,500 years ago, the tyrants were overthrown, and democracy was established.

OLYMPIA AND HELLAS In 776 BCE, the separate Greek-speaking states held their first ceremonial games in common at Olympia. The later Greeks calculated their chronology from these first Olympic Games—the first *Olympiad.* From then on, despite their differences and rivalries, the Greeks regarded themselves as citizens of *Hellas,* distinct from the surrounding "barbarians" who did not speak Greek. The enterprising Hellenes, greatly aided by their indented coasts and stepping-stone islands, became a trading and colonizing people who enlarged the geographic and cultural boundaries of Hellas. In fact, today the best preserved of all the grand temples the Greeks erected are found not in Greece proper but in their western colonies in Italy.

ATHENS AND GREEK CULTURE Nonetheless, Athens, the capital of Greece today, has justifiably become the symbol of ancient Greek culture. Many of the finest products of Greek civilization were created there. Athens is where the great plays of Aeschylus, Sophocles, and Euripides were first performed. And there, in the city's marketplace *(agora),* covered colonnades *(stoas),* and gymnasiums *(palaestras),* Socrates engaged his fellow citizens in philosophical argument, and Plato formulated his prescription for the ideal form of government in the *Republic.* Complementing the rich intellectual life of ancient Athens was a strong interest in physical exercise, which played a large role in education, as well as in daily life. The Athenian aim of achieving a balance of intellectual and physical discipline, an ideal of humanistic education, is well expressed in the familiar phrase "a sound mind in a sound body."

The distinctiveness and originality of Greek contributions to art, science, and politics should not, however, obscure the enormous debt Greek civilization owed to the earlier great cultures of Egypt and the Near East. Scholars today increasingly recognize this debt, and the ancient Greeks themselves readily acknowledged borrowing ideas, motifs, conventions, and skills from these older civilizations.

REASSESSING GREEK CIVILIZATION Nor should a high estimation of Greek art and culture blind historians to the realities of Hellenic life and society. The uncritical admiration in the 18th and 19th centuries of anything Greek has undergone sharp revision in our time. Many modern artists have rejected Greek standards (the late-19th-century French painter Paul Gauguin called Greek art "a lie"). Even Athenian "democracy" was a political reality for only one segment of the demos. Slavery was regarded as

The Gods and Goddesses of Mount Olympus

The names of scores of Greek gods and goddesses were recorded as early as the eighth century BCE in Homer's epic tales of the war against Troy *(Iliad)* and of the adventures of the Greek hero Odysseus on his long and tortuous journey home *(Odyssey)*. Even more are enumerated in the poems of Hesiod, especially his *Theogony (Genealogy of the Gods)* composed around 700 BCE.

The Greek deities most often represented in art are all ultimately the offspring of the two key elements of the Greek universe, Earth *(Gaia/Ge;* we give the names in Greek/Latin form) and Heaven *(Ouranos/Uranus).* Earth and Heaven mated to produce 12 Titans, including Ocean *(Okeanos/Oceanus)* and his youngest brother *Kronos (Saturn).* Kronos castrated his father in order to rule in his place, married his sister *Rhea,* and then swallowed all his children as they were born, lest one of them seek in turn to usurp him (see FIG. 28-44). When *Zeus (Jupiter)* was born, Rhea deceived Kronos by feeding him a stone wrapped in clothes in place of the infant. After growing to manhood, Zeus forced Kronos to vomit up Zeus's siblings. Together they overthrew their father and the other Titans and ruled the world from their home on Mount Olympus, Greece's highest peak.

This cruel and bloody tale of the origin of the Greek gods has parallels in Near Eastern mythology and is clearly pre-Greek in origin, one of many Greek borrowings from the East. The Greek version of the creation myth, however, appears infrequently in painting and sculpture. Instead, the later 12 Olympian gods and goddesses, the chief deities of Greece, figure most prominently in art—not only in Greek, Etruscan, and Roman times but also in the Middle Ages, the Renaissance, and up to the present.

THE OLYMPIAN GODS (AND THEIR ROMAN EQUIVALENTS)

ZEUS (JUPITER) King of the gods, Zeus (see FIGS. 5-36 and 29-43) ruled the sky and allotted the sea to his brother Poseidon and the Underworld to his other brother Hades. His weapon was the thunderbolt, and with it he led the other gods to victory over the Giants (FIGS. 5-17 and 5-79), who had challenged the Olympians for control of the world.

HERA (JUNO) Wife and sister of Zeus, Hera was the goddess of marriage, and Zeus's many love affairs often angered her. Her favorite cities were Mycenae, Sparta, and Argos, and she aided the Greeks in their war against the Trojans.

POSEIDON (NEPTUNE) Poseidon (see FIGS. 10-22 and 23-16) was one of the three sons of Kronos and Rhea and was lord of the sea. He controlled waves, storms, and earthquakes with his three-pronged pitchfork *(trident).*

HESTIA (VESTA) Daughter of Kronos and Rhea and sister of Zeus, Poseidon, and Hera, Hestia was goddess of the hearth. In Rome, Vesta had an ancient shrine with a sacred fire in the Roman Forum. Her six Vestal Virgins were the most important priestesses of the state, drawn only from aristocratic families.

DEMETER (CERES) Third sister of Zeus, Demeter was the goddess of grain and agriculture. She taught humans how to sow and plow. The English word *cereal* derives from *Ceres.*

ARES (MARS) God of war, Ares was the son of Zeus and Hera and the lover of Aphrodite. In the *Iliad* he took the side of the Trojans. Mars, father of the twin founders of Rome, *Romulus* and *Remus* (see FIG. 9-10), looms much larger in Roman mythology and religion than Ares does in Greek.

ATHENA (MINERVA) Goddess of wisdom and warfare, Athena (FIGS. 5-32, 5-44, and 5-79) was a virgin *(parthenos* in Greek), born not from a woman's womb but from the head of her father, Zeus. Her city was Athens, and her greatest temple was the Parthenon (FIG. 5-42).

HEPHAISTOS (VULCAN) God of fire and of metalworking, Hephaistos fashioned the armor Achilles wore in battle against Troy. He also provided Zeus his scepter and Poseidon his trident, and was the "surgeon" who split open Zeus's head when Athena was born. In some accounts, Hephaistos is the son of Hera without a male partner. In others, he is the son of Hera and Zeus. He was born lame and, uncharacteristically for a god, ugly. His wife Aphrodite was unfaithful to him.

APOLLO (APOLLO) God of light and music, and a great archer, Apollo (see FIGS. 5-3, 5-57, and 24-70) was the son of Zeus with *Leto/Latona,* daughter of one of the Titans. His epithet *Phoibos* means "radiant," and the young, beautiful Apollo is sometimes identified with the sun *(Helios/Sol).*

ARTEMIS (DIANA) Sister of Apollo, Artemis (see FIGS. 5-57 and 22-47) was goddess of the hunt and of wild animals. As Apollo's twin, she was occasionally regarded as the moon *(Selene/Luna).*

APHRODITE (VENUS) Daughter of Zeus and *Dione* (daughter of Okeanos and one of the *nymphs*—the goddesses of springs, caves, and woods), Aphrodite (FIGS. 5-60 and 5-83) was the goddess of love and beauty. In one version of her myth, she was born from the foam *(aphros* in Greek) of the sea (see FIG. 21-27). She was the mother of Eros by Ares and of the Trojan hero *Aeneas* by *Anchises.* Julius Caesar and Augustus traced their lineage to Venus through Aeneas.

HERMES (MERCURY) Son of Zeus and another nymph, Hermes (FIGS. 5-58 and 5-62) was the fleet-footed messenger of the gods and possessed winged sandals. He was also the guide of travelers, including the dead journeying to the Underworld. He carried the *caduceus,* a magical herald's rod, and wore a traveler's hat, often also shown with wings.

Equal in stature to the Olympians was *Hades (Pluto),* one of the children of Kronos who fought with his brothers against the Titans but who never resided on Mount Olympus. Hades was the lord of the Underworld and god of the dead.

Other important Greek gods and goddesses were *Dionysos (Bacchus,* see FIGS. 10-15 and 22-37), the god of wine and the son of Zeus and a mortal woman; *Eros (Amor* or *Cupid)* (see FIGS. 5-48, 5-84, 22-43, and 28-5), the winged child god of love and the son of Aphrodite and Ares; and *Asklepios (Aesculapius),* son of Apollo and a mortal woman, the Greek god of healing, whose serpent-entwined staff is the emblem of modern medicine.

natural, even beneficial, and was a universal institution among the Greeks. Aristotle, the eminent philosopher who tutored Alexander the Great, declared at the beginning of his *Politics:* "It is clear that some are free by nature, and others are slaves."[2] And Greek women were in no way the equals of Greek men. Women normally remained secluded in their homes, emerging usually only for weddings, funerals, and religious festivals. They played little part in public or political life. Despite the fame of the poet Sappho, only a handful of female artists' names are known, and none of their works survive. The existence of slavery and the exclusion of women from public life are both reflected in Greek art. On many occasions freeborn men and women appear with their slaves in monumental sculpture. The symposium (attended only by men and prostitutes) is a popular subject on painted vases.

Although the Greeks invented and passed on to future generations the concept and practice of democracy, most Greek states, even those constituted as democracies, were dominated by well-born white males, and the most admired virtues were not wisdom and justice but statecraft and military valor. Greek men were educated in the values of Homer's heroes and in the athletic exercises of the palaestra. War among the city-states was chronic and often atrocious. Fighting among themselves, the Greeks eventually fell victim to Macedon's autocracy and Rome's imperialism.

THE GEOMETRIC AND ORIENTALIZING PERIODS

OUT OF THE DARK AGE Disintegration of the Bronze Age social order accompanied the destruction of the Mycenaean palaces. The disappearance of powerful kings and their retinues led to the loss of the knowledge of how to cut masonry, to construct citadels and tombs, to paint frescoes, and to sculpt in stone. Even the arts of reading and writing were forgotten. Depopulation, poverty, and an almost total loss of contact with the outside world characterized the succeeding centuries, sometimes called the Dark Age of Greece.

Only in the eighth century BCE did economic conditions improve and the population begin to grow again. This era was in its own way a heroic age, a time when the poleis of Classical Greece took shape; when the Greeks broke out of their isolation and once again began to trade with cities both in the east and the west; when Homer's epic poems, formerly memorized and passed down from bard to bard, were recorded in written form; and when the Olympic Games were established.

Geometric Art

FIGURE PAINTING REVIVED Also during the eighth century the human figure returned to Greek art — not, of course, in monumental statuary, which was exceedingly rare even in Bronze Age Greece, but painted on the surfaces of ceramic pots, which continued to be manufactured after the fall of Mycenae and even throughout the Dark Age. One of the earliest examples is a huge krater (FIG. **5-1**), or mixing bowl, that marked the grave of an Athenian man buried around 740 BCE. At well over three feet tall, this remarkable vase is a considerable technical achievement and testifies both to the potter's skill and to the wealth and position of the deceased's family in the community. The bottom of the great vessel is open, perhaps to permit visitors to the grave to pour

5-1 Geometric krater, from the Dipylon cemetery, Athens, Greece, ca. 740 BCE. Approx. 3′ 4½″ high. Metropolitan Museum of Art, New York.

libations in honor of the dead, perhaps simply to provide a drain for rainwater, or both. The artist covered much of the surface with precisely painted abstract angular motifs in horizontal bands. Especially prominent is the *meander,* or key, pattern around the rim of the krater. Most early Greek vases were decorated exclusively with abstract motifs. The nature of the ornament has led art historians to designate this formative period of Greek art as *Geometric.* The earliest examples of the Geometric style date to the ninth century BCE.

On our krater, the artist reserved the widest part of the vase for two bands of human figures and horse-drawn chariots, rather than for geometric ornament. Befitting the vase's function as a grave marker, the scenes depict the mourning for a man laid out on his bier and the grand chariot procession in his honor. In the upper band, the shroud, raised to reveal the corpse, is an abstract checkerboard-like backdrop, and the funerary couch has only two legs because the artist had no interest in suggesting depth or representing space. The human figures and the furniture are as two-dimensional as the geometric shapes elsewhere on the vessel. The painter filled every empty surface with circles and M-shaped ornaments, further negating any sense that the mourners inhabit open space. The figures are silhouettes constructed of triangular (frontal) torsos with attached profile arms, legs, and heads (with a single large frontal eye in the center!), following the age-old convention. To distinguish male from female, the painter added a penis growing out of one of the deceased's thighs. The mourning women, who tear their hair out in grief,

Herakles, Greatest of Greek Heroes

Greek heroes were a class of mortals intermediate between ordinary humans and the immortal gods. Most often the children of gods, some were great warriors, such as those who fought at Troy and were celebrated in Homer's epic poems. Others went from one fabulous adventure to another, ridding the world of monsters and generally benefiting humankind. Many heroes were worshiped after their deaths, and the greatest of them were honored with shrines, especially in the cities most closely associated with them. For example, the bones of Theseus, king of Athens and victor over the Minotaur who inhabited the labyrinthine palace at Knossos (see FIGS. 4-3 to 4-5), were transferred to Athens around 475 BCE from Skyros, where Theseus had been killed, and deposited in his sanctuary near the city center.

The greatest of all the Greek heroes was *Herakles* (the Roman *Hercules*), born in Thebes and the son of Zeus and Alkmene, a mortal woman. Zeus's wife Hera hated Herakles and sent two serpents to attack him in his cradle, but the infant strangled them. Later, Hera caused the hero to go mad and to kill his wife and children. As punishment he was condemned to perform 12 great labors. In the first, he defeated the legendary lion of Nemea and ever after wore its pelt. The lion's skin and his weapon, a club, are Herakles' distinctive attributes (FIGS. 5-63 and 5-66). His last task was to obtain the golden apples Gaia gave to Hera at her marriage (FIG. 5-32). They grew from a tree in the garden of the Hesperides at the farthest western edge of the ocean, and a dragon guarded them. After completion of the 12 seemingly impossible tasks, Herakles was awarded immortality. Athena, who had watched over him carefully throughout his life and assisted him in performing the labors, introduced him into the realm of the gods on Mount Olympus. According to legend, it was Herakles who established the Olympic Games.

have breasts emerging beneath their armpits. In both cases the artist was concerned with specifying gender, not with anatomical accuracy. Below are warriors, drawn as though they are walking shields, and several chariots. In the old conceptual manner, both wheels are shown. The horses have the correct number of heads and legs but seem to share a common body, negating any sense of depth. Despite its highly stylized and conventional manner of representation, this vessel marks a significant turning point in the history of Greek art. Not only was the human figure reintroduced into the painter's repertoire, but the art of storytelling also was revived.

HERO VERSUS MONSTER Similar schematic figures also appeared in the round at this date, but only at very small scale. One of the most impressive surviving Geometric sculptures is a small solid-cast bronze group (FIG. 5-2) of a hero, probably Herakles (see "Herakles, Greatest of Greek Heroes," above), battling a *centaur* (a mythological beast that was part man, part horse), possibly Nessos, the centaur who had volunteered to carry the hero's bride across a river and then assaulted her. Whether or not the hero is Herakles and the centaur is Nessos, the mythological nature of the group is certain. The repertoire of the Geometric artist was not limited to scenes inspired by daily life (and death).

Composite monsters were enormously popular in the ancient Near East and Egypt (see Chapters 2 and 3), and renewed contact with foreign cultures may have inspired such figures in Geometric Greece. The centaur is, however, a purely Greek invention — and one that posed a problem for the artist, who had, of course, never seen such a creature. The Geometric centaur was conceived as a man in front and a horse in back, a rather unhappy and unconvincing configuration that results in the forelegs belonging to a different species than the hind legs. In our example, the sculptor rendered the figure of the hero and the human part of the centaur in a similar fashion. Both are bearded and wear helmets, but (contradictory to nature) the man is larger than the horse, probably to suggest that he will be the victor. Like other Geometric male figures, both painted and sculpted, this hero is nude, in contrast to the Near Eastern statuettes that might have inspired such

5-2 Hero and centaur (Herakles and Nessos?), ca. 750–730 BCE. Bronze, approx. $4\frac{1}{2}''$ high. Metropolitan Museum of Art, New York (gift of J. Pierpont).

Greek works. Here, at the very beginning of Greek figural art, one can recognize the Hellenic instinct for the natural beauty of the human figure. In fact, Greek athletes exercised without their clothes and even competed nude in the Olympic Games from very early times.

Orientalizing Art

AN OFFERING TO APOLLO One of the masterworks of the early seventh century BCE is the *Mantiklos Apollo* (FIG. 5-3), a small bronze statuette dedicated to Apollo at Thebes by an otherwise unknown man named Mantiklos. With characteristic pride in the ability to write, the sculptor (or another) scratched into the thighs of the figure a message from the dedicator to the deity: "Mantiklos dedicated me as a tithe to the far-shooting Lord of the Silver Bow; you, Phoibos [Apollo], might give some pleasing favor in return." Because the Greeks conceived their gods in human form, one cannot be sure whether the figure was meant to represent the youthful Apollo or Mantiklos (or neither). But if the left hand at one time held a bow, then the statuette is certainly an image of the deity. In any case, the purpose of the votive offering is clear. Equally apparent is the increased interest Greek artists at this time had in reproducing details of human anatomy, such as the long hair framing the unnaturally elongated neck, and the pectoral and abdominal muscles, which define the stylized triangular torso. The triangular face has eye sockets that were once inlaid, and the head may have had a separately fashioned helmet on it.

THE GREEKS LOOK EASTWARD The *Mantiklos Apollo* was created when the pace and scope of Greek trade and colonization had accelerated and when Greek artists were exposed more than ever before to Eastern artworks, especially small portable objects such as Syrian ivory carvings. The closer contact had a profound effect on the development of Greek art. Indeed, so many motifs borrowed from or inspired by Egyptian and Near Eastern art entered the Greek pictorial vocabulary at this time that historians have dubbed the seventh century BCE the *Orientalizing* period.

An elaborate Corinthian *amphora* (FIG. **5-4**), or two-handled storage jar, typifies the new Greek fascination with the Orient. In a series of bands recalling the organization of Geometric painted vases, animals such as the native boar appear beside exotic lions and panthers and composite creatures inspired by Eastern monsters such as the sphinx and lamassu—in this instance the *siren* (part bird, part woman) prominently displayed on the amphora's neck.

5-3 *Mantiklos Apollo,* statuette of a youth dedicated by Mantiklos to Apollo, from Thebes, Greece, ca. 700–680 BCE. Bronze, approx. 8″ high. Museum of Fine Arts, Boston.

5-4 Corinthian black-figure amphora with animal friezes, from Rhodes, Greece, ca. 625–600 BCE. Approx. 1′ 2″ high. British Museum, London.

BLACK-FIGURE PAINTING The appeal of such vases was not due solely to their Orientalizing animal friezes but also to a new ceramic technique the Corinthians invented, which art historians call *black-figure painting*. The black-figure painter first put down black silhouettes on the clay surface, as in Geometric times, but then used a sharp pointed instrument to incise linear details within the forms, usually adding highlights in purplish red or white over the black figures before firing the vessel. The combination of the weighty black silhouettes with the delicate detailing and the bright polychrome overlay proved to be irresistible, and Athenian painters soon copied the technique from the Corinthians.

GREECE'S FIRST STONE TEMPLES The foundation of the Greek trading colony of Naukratis in Egypt (see MAP 3-1) before 630 BCE brought the Greeks into direct contact with the monumental stone architecture of the Egyptians. Not long after that, the first stone buildings since the fall of the Mycenaean kingdoms began to be constructed in Greece. At Prinias on Crete, for example, a stone temple, called Temple A (FIG. 5-5), was built around 625 BCE to honor an unknown deity. Although the inspiration for the structure came from the East, the form resembles that of a typical Mycenaean megaron, such as that at Tiryns (see FIG. 4-19), with two interior columns flanking a hearth or sacrificial pit. The facade consisted of three great piers; the roof was probably flat.

5-5 Plan of Temple A, Prinias, Greece, ca. 625 BCE.

Above the doorway of the Prinias temple was a huge limestone lintel (FIG. 5-6) supporting confronting statues of seated women, probably goddesses, wearing tall headdresses and capes. Two other similarly dressed, but standing, goddesses are carved in relief on the underside of the block, visible to those entering the temple. On the face of the lintel is a frieze of Orientalizing panthers with frontal heads—the same motif as that on the contemporary Corinthian black-figure amphora (FIG. 5-4). Temple A at Prinias is the earliest known example of a Greek temple with sculptured decoration.

GODDESS OR WOMAN? Somewhat earlier and probably also originally from Crete is a limestone statuette of a goddess or maiden (*kore*; plural, *korai*) popularly known as the *Lady of Auxerre* (FIG. 5-7) after the French town that is her oldest recorded location. As with the figure dedicated by Mantiklos, it is uncertain whether the young woman is a mortal or a deity. She wears a long skirt and a cape, as do the women of the Prinias temple, but the Auxerre maiden has no headdress, and the right hand placed across the chest is probably a gesture of prayer, indicating that this is a kore. The style is, however, comparable. Characteristic is the triangular flat-topped head framed by long strands of hair that form complementary triangles to that of the face. Also typical are the small, belted waist and a fondness for pattern. Note the almost Geometric treatment of the long skirt with its incised concentric squares, once brightly painted. Despite its monumental quality, the statue is only a little more than two feet tall—smaller than the seated goddesses of the Prinias lintel but much larger than the bronze statuettes of the era.

DAEDALUS, MASTER OF ALL ARTS The *Lady of Auxerre* is the masterpiece of a style usually referred to as *Daedalic*, after the legendary artist DAEDALUS, whose name means "the skillful one." In addition to having been a great sculptor, Daedalus was said to have built the labyrinth in Crete to house the Minotaur and also to have designed a temple at Memphis in Egypt (see MAP 3-1). The historical Greeks attributed to him almost all the great achievements in early sculpture and architecture before the names of artists and architects were recorded. The story that Daedalus worked in Egypt reflects the enormous impact of Egyptian art and architecture on the Greeks of the aptly named Orientalizing age, as well as on their offspring in the succeeding Archaic period.

5-6 Lintel of Temple A, Prinias, Greece, ca. 625 BCE. Limestone, approx. 2′ 9″ high. Archaeological Museum, Herakleion.

5-7 *Lady of Auxerre,* statue of a goddess or kore, ca. 650–625 BCE. Limestone, approx. 2′ 1½″ high. Louvre, Paris.

THE ARCHAIC PERIOD

Statuary

GREEK KOUROI AND EGYPT According to one Greek writer, Daedalus used the same compositional patterns for his statues as the Egyptians used for their own, and the first truly monumental stone statues of the Greeks follow very closely the canonical Egyptian format. A life-size marble *kouros* ("youth"; plural, *kouroi*) now in New York (FIG. **5-8**) emulates the stance of Egyptian statues—for example, the portrait of Mentuemhet (see FIG. 3-40) carved only a half century before the Greek statue. In both cases the figure is rigidly frontal with the left foot advanced

slightly. The arms are held beside the body, and the fists are clenched with the thumbs forward. This kouros even served a funerary purpose. It stood over a grave in the countryside somewhere near Athens. Such statues replaced the huge vases (FIG. 5-1) of Geometric times as the preferred form of grave marker in the sixth century BCE. They also were used as votive offerings in sanctuaries. The kouros type, because of its generic quality, could be employed in several different contexts.

Despite the adherence to Egyptian prototypes, Greek kouros statues differ from their models in two important ways. First, they were liberated from their original stone block. The Egyptian obsession with permanence was alien to the Greeks, who were preoccupied with finding ways to represent motion rather than stability in their sculpted figures. Second, the kouroi are nude, and if

5-8 Kouros, ca. 600 BCE. Marble, approx. 6′ ½″ high. Metropolitan Museum of Art, New York.

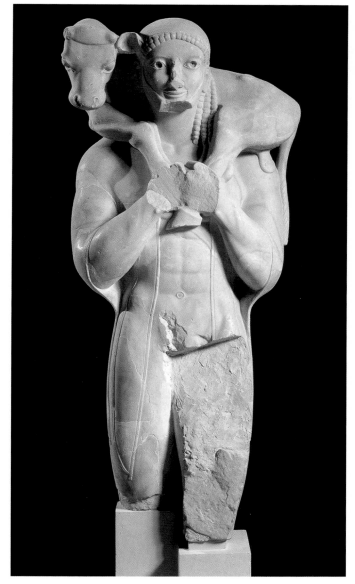

5-9 Calf Bearer, dedicated by Rhonbos on the Acropolis, Athens, Greece, ca. 560 BCE. Marble, restored height approx. 5′ 5″. Acropolis Museum, Athens.

5-10 Kroisos, from Anavysos, Greece, ca. 530 BCE. Marble, approx. 6′ 4″ high. National Archaeological Museum, Athens.

the monumental marble statues lack identifying attributes, they, like the tiny bronze dedicated by Mantiklos (FIG. 5-3), are formally indistinguishable from Greek images of deities with their perfect bodies exposed for all to see.

The New York kouros shares many traits with Greek Orientalizing works such as the *Mantiklos Apollo* and the *Lady of Auxerre,* especially the triangular shape of head and hair and the flatness of the face—the hallmarks of the Daedalic style. Eyes, nose, and mouth all sit on the front of the head, ears were placed on the sides, and the long hair forms a flat backdrop behind the head. In every instance, one sees the result of the sculptor's having drawn these features on four independent sides of the marble block, following the same workshop procedure used in Egypt for millennia. The New York kouros also has the slim waist of earlier Greek statues, and exhibits the same love of pattern. The pointed arch of the rib cage, for example, echoes the V-shaped ridge of the hips, which suggests but does not accurately reproduce the rounded flesh and muscle of the human body.

A SMILING CALF BEARER A generation later than the New York kouros is the statue of a *moschophoros,* or calf bearer (FIG. 5-9), found in fragments on the Athenian Acropolis. Its inscribed base (not visible in our photograph) states that a man whose name has been reconstructed as Rhonbos dedicated the statue. Rhonbos is almost certainly the calf bearer himself, bringing an offering to Athena in thanksgiving for his prosperity. He stands in the left-foot-forward manner of the kouroi, but he is bearded and therefore no longer a youth. He wears a thin cloak (once painted to set it off from the otherwise nude body). No one dressed in such a manner in ancient Athens. The sculptor adhered to the artistic convention of male nudity and attributed to the calf bearer the noble perfection such nudity suggests while also indicating that this mature gentleman is clothed, as any respectable citizen would be in such a context. The Archaic sculptor's love of pattern may be seen once again in the handling of the difficult problem of representing man and animal together. The calf's legs and the moschophoros's arms form a bold X that unites the two bodies both physically and formally.

The calf bearer's face differs markedly from those of earlier Greek statues (and those of Egypt and the Near East) in one notable way. The man smiles—or at least seems to. From this time on, Archaic Greek statues always smile, even in the most inappropriate contexts (see, for example, FIG. 5-27, where a dying warrior with an arrow in his chest grins broadly at the spectator!). This so-called *Archaic smile* has been variously interpreted, but it is not to be taken literally. Rather, the smile seems to be the Archaic sculptor's way of indicating that the person portrayed is alive. By adopting such a convention, the Greek artist signaled a very different intention from any Egyptian counterpart.

THE GRAVE OF KROISOS Sometime around 530 BCE a young man named Kroisos died a hero's death in battle, and his grave at Anavysos, not far from Athens, was marked by a kouros statue (FIG. **5-10**). The inscribed base invites visitors to "stay and mourn at the tomb of dead Kroisos, whom raging Ares destroyed one day as he fought in the foremost ranks." The statue, with its distinctive Archaic smile, is no more a portrait of a specific youth than is the New York kouros. But two generations later, without rejecting the Egyptian stance, the Greek sculptor rendered the human body in a far more naturalistic manner. The head is no longer too large for the body, and the face is more rounded, with swelling cheeks replacing the flat planes of the earlier work. The long hair does not form a stiff backdrop to the head but falls naturally over the back. Rounded hips replace the V-shaped ridges of the New York kouros.

Some of the original paint survives on the Kroisos statue, enhancing the sense of life. All Greek stone statues were painted. The modern notion that classical statuary was pure white is mistaken. The Greeks did not, however, color their statues garishly. The flesh was left in the natural color of the stone, which was waxed and polished, while eyes, lips, hair, and drapery were painted in *encaustic* (see "Iaia of Cyzicus and the Art of Encaustic Painting," Chapter 10, page 288). In this technique, the painter mixed the pigment with wax and applied it to the statue while hot.

BROKEN AND BURIED KORAI A stylistic "sister" to the Anavysos kouros is the statue of a kore wearing a *peplos* (FIG. **5-11**), a simple, long, woolen belted garment, which gives the female figure a columnar appearance. Traces of paint are preserved here also. As was true of the Kroisos statue, the *Peplos Kore*, as she is known, was buried for more than two millennia, protecting the painted surface from the destructive effects of exposure to the atmosphere and to bad weather. The kore—along with the calf bearer (FIG. 5-9) and many other statues—had been knocked over by the Persians during their sack of the Acropolis in 480 BCE (discussed later). Shortly thereafter, the Athenians buried all the damaged Archaic sculptures. Before that time, they stood as votive offerings in Athena's sanctuary.

The *Peplos Kore*'s missing left arm was extended, a break from the frontal compression of the arms at the sides in Egyptian statues. She once held in her hand an attribute that would identify the

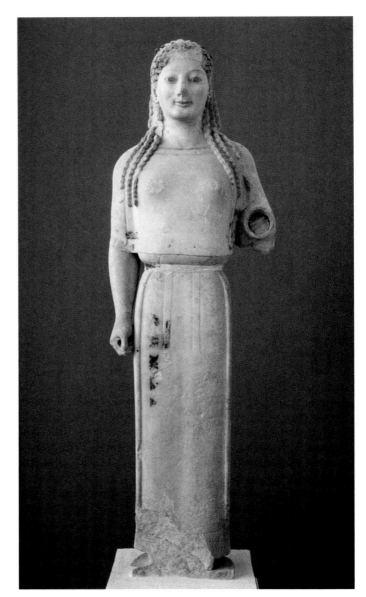

5-11 *Peplos Kore,* from the Acropolis, Athens, Greece, ca. 530 BCE. Marble, approx. 4′ high. Acropolis Museum, Athens.

figure as a maiden or, as some have suggested, a goddess, perhaps Athena herself. Whatever her identity, the contrast with the *Lady of Auxerre* (FIG. 5-7) is striking. Although in both cases the drapery conceals the entire body save for head, arms, and feet, the sixth-century sculptor rendered the soft female form much more naturally. This softer treatment of the flesh also sharply differentiates later korai from contemporary kouroi, which have hard, muscular bodies.

The *Peplos Kore* is one of the latest peplos-clad dedications on the Acropolis. By the later sixth century, the light linen Ionian *chiton,* worn in conjunction with a heavier *himation* (mantle), was the garment of choice for fashionable women. Archaic sculptors delighted in rendering the intricate patterns created by the cascading folds of thin, soft material, as may be seen in another kore (FIG. 5-12) the Athenians buried after the Persian destruction of the Acropolis. In this statue the asymmetry of the folds greatly relieves the stiff frontality of the body and makes the figure appear much more lifelike than contemporary kouroi. The sculptor

5-12 Kore, from the Acropolis, Athens, Greece, ca. 520–510 BCE. Marble, approx. 1' 9½" high. Acropolis Museum, Athens.

achieved added variety by showing the kore grasping part of her chiton in her left hand (unfortunately broken off) to lift it off the ground in order to take a step forward. This is the equivalent of the advanced left foot of the kouroi and became standard for statues of korai. Despite the varied surface treatment of brightly colored garments on the korai, the kore postures are as fixed as those of their male counterparts.

Architecture and Architectural Sculpture

HOUSES FOR THE GODS Many of the earliest Greek temples do not survive because they were made of wood and mud brick. Pausanias, who wrote an invaluable guidebook to Greece in the second century CE, noted that in the even-then-ancient Temple of Hera at Olympia, one oak column was still in place. The others had been replaced by stone columns. Archaic and later Greek temples were, however, built of more permanent materials—

limestone, in many cases, and, where it was available, marble, which was more impressive and durable (and more expensive). In Greece proper, if not in its western colonies, marble was readily at hand. Bluish white marble came from Hymettus, just east of Athens. Glittering white marble particularly adapted for carving was brought from Pentelicus, northeast of the city, and from the Aegean Islands, especially Paros (MAP 5-1).

Already in the Orientalizing seventh century BCE, at Prinias, the Greeks had built a stone temple embellished with stone sculptures (FIGS. 5-5 and 5-6). But despite the contemporary Daedalic style of its statues and reliefs, the Cretan temple resembled the megaron of a Mycenaean palace more than anything Greek traders had seen in their travels overseas. In the Archaic age of the sixth century, with the model of Egyptian columnar halls such as that at Karnak (see FIG. 3-25) before them, Greek architects began to build the columnar stone temples that have been more influential on the later history of architecture in the Western world than any other building type ever devised.

Greek temples differed in function from most later religious shrines. The altar lay outside the temple—at the east end, facing the rising sun—and the Greeks gathered outside, not inside, the building to worship. The temple proper housed the so-called *cult statue* of the deity, the grandest of all votive offerings. Both in its early and mature manifestations, the Greek temple was the house of the god or goddess, not of his or her followers.

Figural sculpture played a major role in the exterior program of the Greek temple from early times, partly to embellish the god's shrine, partly to tell something about the deity symbolized within, and partly to serve as a votive offering. But the building itself, with its finely carved capitals and moldings, also was conceived as sculpture, abstract in form and possessing the power of sculpture to evoke human responses. The commanding importance of the sculptured temple, its inspiring function in public life, was emphasized in its elevated site, often on a hill above the city (*acropolis* means "high city"). As Aristotle stipulated: "The site should be a spot seen far and wide, which gives due elevation to virtue and towers over the neighborhood."[3]

PLAN AND PROPORTION In basic plan, the Greek temple (see "Doric and Ionic Temples," pages 116–117) still discloses a close affinity with the Mycenaean megaron (see FIG. 4-19), and, even in its most elaborate form, it retains the latter structure's basic simplicity. In all cases, the remarkable order, compactness, and symmetry of the Greek scheme strike the eye first, reflecting the Greeks' sense of proportion and their effort to achieve ideal forms in terms of regular numerical relationships and geometric rules. Whether the plan is simple or more complex, no fundamental change occurs in the nature of the units or of their grouping. Classical Greek architecture, like classical music, has a simple core theme with a series of complex, but always quite intelligible, variations developed from it.

The Greeks' insistence on proportional order guided their experiments with the proportions of temple plans. The earliest temples tended to be long and narrow, with the proportion of the ends to the sides roughly expressible as 1:3. From the sixth century on, plans approached but rarely had a proportion of exactly 1:2. Classical temples tended to be a little longer than twice their width. To the Greek mind, proportion in architecture and sculpture was much the same as harmony in music, reflecting and embodying the cosmic order (see "Polykleitos's Prescription for the Perfect Statue," page 133).

Doric and Ionic Temples

The plan and elevation of Greek temples varied with date, geography, and the requirements of individual projects, but all but the earliest Greek temples have common defining elements that set them apart from both the religious edifices of other civilizations and other kinds of Greek buildings.

PLAN The temple core was the *naos,* or *cella,* a room with no windows that usually housed the cult statue of the deity. It was preceded by a *pronaos,* or porch, often with two columns between the *antae,* or extended walls (columns *in antis*). A smaller second room might be placed behind the cella, but in its classical form, the Greek temple had a porch at the rear *(opisthodomos)* set against the blank back wall of the cella. The purpose was not functional but decorative, satisfying the Greek passion for balance and symmetry. A colonnade could be placed across the front of the temple *(prostyle;* FIG. 5-50), across both front and back *(amphiprostyle;* FIG. 5-53), or, more commonly, all around the cella and its porch(es) to form a *peristyle,* as in our diagram (compare FIGS. 5-13 and 5-14). Single *(peripteral)* colonnades were the norm, but double *(dipteral)* colonnades were features of especially elaborate temples (FIG. 5-74).

ELEVATION The elevation of a Greek temple is described in terms of the platform, the colonnade, and the superstructure

(entablature). In the Archaic period, two basic systems evolved for articulating the three units. These are the so-called *orders* of Greek architecture. The orders are differentiated both in the nature of the details and in the relative proportions of the parts. The names of the orders are derived from the Greek regions where they were most commonly employed. The *Doric* was formulated on the mainland and remained the preferred manner there and in the western colonies of the Greeks. The *Ionic* was the order of choice in the Aegean Islands and on the western coast of Asia Minor. The geographical distinctions are by no means absolute. The Ionic order was, for example, often used in Athens (where, according to some, the Athenians were considered Ionians who never migrated).

In both orders, the columns rest on the *stylobate,* the uppermost course of the platform. Metal clamps held together the stone blocks in each horizontal course, and metal dowels joined vertically the blocks of different courses. The columns have two or three parts, depending on the order: the *shaft,* which is marked with vertical channels *(flutes);* the *capital;* and, in the Ionic order, the *base.* Greek column shafts, in contrast to their Minoan and Mycenaean forebears, taper gradually from bottom to top. They usually are composed of separate *drums* joined by metal dowels to prevent turning as well as shifting, although instances of *monolithic* (single-piece) columns are known. In the Doric order, the top of the shaft is marked with one or several horizontal lines *(necking)* that furnish the transition to the capital. The capital has two elements. The lower part (the *echinus*) varies with the order. In the Doric, it is convex and cushionlike, similar to the echinus of Minoan (see FIG. 4-5) and Mycenaean (see FIG. 4-20) capitals. In the Ionic, it is small and supports a bolster ending in scroll-like spirals (the *volutes*). The upper element, present in both orders, is a flat, square block (the *abacus*) that provides the immediate support for the entablature.

The entablature has three parts: the *architrave* or *epistyle,* the main weight-bearing and weight-distributing element; the *frieze;*

ORNAMENT AND COLOR Sculptural ornament was concentrated on the upper part of the building, in the frieze and pediments. Architectural sculpture, like freestanding statuary, was painted and usually was placed only in the building parts that had no structural function. This is true particularly of the Doric order, where decorative sculpture appears only in the metope and pediment "voids." Ionic builders, less severe in this respect as well, were willing to decorate the entire frieze and sometimes even the lower column drums. Occasionally, they replaced their columns with female figures (caryatids; FIGS. 5-16 and 5-52). Capitals, decorative moldings, and other architectural elements were also painted. By painting parts of the building, the designer could bring out more clearly the relationships of the structural parts and soften the stone's glitter at specific points, as well as provide a background to set off the figures.

Although color was used for emphasis and to relieve what might have seemed too bare a simplicity, Greek architecture primarily depended on clarity and balance. To the Greeks, it was

unthinkable to use surfaces in the way the Egyptians used their gigantic columns—as fields for complicated ornamentation (see FIG. 3-25). The history of Greek temple architecture is the history of Greek architects' unflagging efforts to find the most satisfactory (that is, what they believed were perfect) proportions for each part of the building and for the structure as a whole.

EARLY DORIC IN ITALY The prime example of early Greek efforts at Doric temple design is not in Greece but in Italy, south of Naples, at Paestum (Greek Poseidonia). The huge (80 × 170 feet) Archaic temple (FIG. **5-13**) erected there around 550 BCE retains its entire peripteral colonnade, but most of the entablature, including the frieze, pediment, and all of the roof, has vanished. Called the Basilica after the Roman columnar hall building type that early investigators felt it resembled, the structure is now known to be a temple dedicated to Hera. Scholars refer to it as the Temple of Hera I to distinguish it from the later Temple of Hera II (FIG. 5-29), which stands nearby.

and the *cornice,* a molded horizontal projection that together with two sloping *(raking)* cornices forms a triangle that enframes the *pediment.* In the Ionic order, the architrave is usually subdivided into three horizontal bands *(fasciae).* In the Doric order, the frieze is subdivided into *triglyphs* and *metopes,* whereas in the Ionic the frieze is left open to provide a continuous field for relief sculpture.

Many of the Doric components seem to be translations into stone of an earlier timber architecture. The frieze division into triglyphs and metopes, for example, can be explained best as a stone version of what was originally carpentry. The triglyphs most likely are derived from the ends of crossbeams that rested on the main horizontal support, the architrave. The metopes then would correspond to the voids between the beam ends in the original wooden structure.

The Doric order is massive in appearance, its sturdy columns firmly planted on the stylobate. Compared with the weighty and severe Doric, the Ionic order seems light, airy, and much more decorative. Its columns are more slender and rise from molded bases. The Doric flutes meet in sharp ridges *(arrises),* but the Ionic ridges are flat *(fillets).* The most obvious differences between the two orders are, of course, in the capitals—the Doric, severely plain, and the Ionic, highly ornamental.

5-13 Temple of Hera I ("Basilica"), Paestum, Italy, ca. 550 BCE.

5-14 Plan of the Temple of Hera I, Paestum, Italy, ca. 550 BCE. 🖭

The misnomer is partly due to the building's plan (FIG. **5-14**), which differs from that of most other Greek temples. The unusual feature, found only in early Archaic temples, is the central row of columns that divides the cella into two aisles. Placing columns underneath the *ridgepole* (the timber beam running the length of the building below the peak of the gabled roof) might seem the logical way to provide interior support for the roof structure. But it resulted in several disadvantages. Among these was that this interior arrangement allowed no place for a central statue of the deity to whom the temple was dedicated. Also, the peripteral colonnade, in order to correspond with the interior, had to have an odd number of columns (nine in this case) across the building's facade. At Paestum, three columns were also set in antis instead of the standard two, which in turn ruled out a central doorway for viewing the statue. However, a simple 1:2 ratio of facade and flank columns was achieved by erecting 18 columns on each side of the temple.

The temple's elevation is characterized by heavy, closely spaced columns with a pronounced swelling *(entasis)* at the middle of the shafts, giving the columns a profile akin to that of a cigar. The shafts are topped by large, bulky, pancakelike Doric capitals, which seem compressed by the overbearing weight of the entablature. If the temple's immense roof were preserved, these columns would seem even more compressed, squatting beneath what must have been a high and massive entablature. The columns and capitals thus express in a vivid manner their weight-bearing function. One structural reason, perhaps, for the heaviness of the design and the narrowness of the spans between the columns might be that the Archaic builders were afraid thinner and more widely spaced

columns would result in the superstructure's collapse. In later Doric temples, the columns were placed farther apart, and the forms were gradually refined. The shafts became more slender, the entasis subtler, the capitals smaller, and the entablature lighter. Greek architects sought the ideal proportional relationship among the parts of their buildings. The sculptors of Archaic kouroi and korai grappled with similar problems. Architecture and sculpture developed in a parallel manner in the sixth century.

THE PEDIMENT PROBLEM Architects and sculptors were also frequently called on to work together, as at Corfu (ancient Corcyra), where a great Doric temple dedicated to Artemis was constructed early in the sixth century BCE. Corfu is an island off the western coast of Greece and was an important stop on the trade route between the mainland and the Greek settlements in Italy (MAP 5-1). Prosperity made possible the erection of one of the earliest stone peripteral temples in Greece, one also lavishly embellished with sculpture. The metopes were decorated with reliefs (unfortunately very fragmentary today), and both pediments were filled with huge sculptures (more than nine feet high at the center). The pediments on both ends of the temple appear to have been decorated in an identical manner. The west pediment (FIG. **5-15**) is better preserved.

Designing figural decoration for a pediment was never an easy task for the Greek sculptor because of the pediment's awkward triangular shape. The central figures had to be of great size. By contrast, as the pediment tapered toward the corners, the available area became increasingly cramped. At the center of the Corfu pediment is the *gorgon* Medusa, a demon with a woman's body and bird wings. Medusa also had a hideous face and snake hair, and anyone who gazed at her was turned into stone. She is shown in the conventional Archaic bent-leg, bent-arm, pinwheel-like posture that signifies running or, for a winged creature, flying. To her left and right are two great felines. Together they serve as temple guardians, repulsing all enemies from the sanctuary of the goddess. Similar panthers stand sentinel on the lintel of the seventh-century temple at Prinias (FIG. 5-6). The Corfu felines are in the tradition of the guardian lions of the citadel gate at Mycenae (see FIG. 4-20) and the lamassu that stood guard at the entrances to Near Eastern palaces (see FIGS. 2-18 and 2-21). The triad of Medusa and the felines recalls as well Mesopotamian heraldic human-beast compositions (see FIG. 2-10). The Corfu figures are, in short, still further examples of the Orientalizing manner in early Greek sculpture.

Between Medusa and the great beasts are two small figures—the human Chrysaor at her left and the winged horse Pegasus at her right (only the rear legs are preserved). Chrysaor and Pegasus

5-15 West pediment from the Temple of Artemis, Corfu, Greece, ca. 600–580 BCE. Limestone, greatest height approx. 9′ 4″. Archaeological Museum, Corfu.

were Medusa's children. According to legend, they sprang from her head when the Greek hero Perseus severed it with his sword. Their presence here on either side of the living Medusa is therefore a chronological impossibility. The Archaic artist was not interested in telling a coherent story but in identifying the central figure by depicting her offspring.

Narration was, however, the purpose of the much smaller groups situated in the pediment corners. To the viewer's right is Zeus, brandishing his thunderbolt and slaying a kneeling giant. In the extreme corner was a dead giant. The *gigantomachy* (battle of gods and giants) was a popular theme in Greek art from Archaic through Hellenistic times and was a metaphor for the triumph of reason and order over chaos. In the pediment's left corner is one of the Trojan War's climactic events: Achilles' son Neoptolemos kills the enthroned King Priam. The fallen figure to the left of this group may be a dead Trojan.

The master responsible for the Corfu pediments was a pioneer, and the composition shows all the signs of experimentation. The lack of narrative unity in the Corfu pediment and the extraordinary scale diversity of the figures eventually gave way to pedimental designs with figures all acting out a single event and appearing the same size. But the Corfu designer already had shown the way. That sculptor realized, for example, that the area beneath the raking cornice could be filled with gods and heroes of similar size if a combination of standing, leaning, kneeling, seated, and prostrate figures were employed in the composition. And the Corfu master discovered that animals could be very useful space fillers because, unlike humans, they have one end taller than the other.

CARYATIDS AND GIANTS The sixth century BCE also saw the erection of grandiose Ionic temples on the Aegean Islands and the west coast of Asia Minor. The gem of Archaic Ionic architecture and architectural sculpture is, however, not a temple but a treasury (FIG. 5-16) erected by the city of Siphnos in the Sanctuary of Apollo at Delphi. Greek *treasuries* were small buildings set up for the safe storage of votive offerings. At Delphi many poleis expressed their civic pride by erecting these templelike, but nonperipteral, structures. Athens built one with Doric columns in the porch and sculptured metopes in the frieze. The Siphnians equally characteristically employed the Ionic order for their

5-16 Reconstruction drawing of the Siphnian Treasury, Delphi, Greece, ca. 530 BCE.

Delphic treasury. Wealth from the island's gold and silver mines made the luxurious building possible. In the porch, where one would expect to find fluted Ionic columns, far more elaborate caryatids were employed instead. Caryatids are rare, even in Ionic architecture, but they are unknown in Doric architecture, where they would have been discordant elements in that much more severe order. The Siphnian statue-columns resemble contemporary korai dressed in Ionian chitons and himations (FIG. 5-12).

Another Ionic feature of the Siphnian Treasury is the continuous sculptured frieze on all four sides of the building. The north frieze represents the popular theme of the gigantomachy, but it is a much more detailed rendition than that in the corner of the Corfu pediment. In the section reproduced here (FIG. 5-17), Apollo and Artemis pursue a fleeing giant at the right, while behind them one of the lions pulling a goddess's chariot attacks a giant and bites into his midsection. Paint originally enlivened the crowded composition, and painted labels identified the various protagonists. Some figures had metal weapons. The effect must have been dazzling. On one of the shields the sculptor inscribed his name (unfortunately lost), a clear indication of pride in accomplishment.

5-17 Gigantomachy, detail of the north frieze of the Siphnian Treasury, Delphi, Greece, ca. 530 BCE. Marble, approx. 2′ 1″ high. Archaeological Museum, Delphi.

Vase Painting

ARTISTS' SIGNATURES Labeled figures and artists' signatures also appear on Archaic painted vases (see "Greek Vase Painting," page 121). The masterpiece of early black-figure painting is the *François Vase* (FIG. **5-18**), named for the excavator who uncovered it (in an enormous number of fragments) in an Etruscan tomb at Chiusi in Italy (see MAP 9-1), where it had been imported from Athens. This is in itself a testimony to the esteem in which Athenian potters and painters were held at this time. In fact, having learned the black-figure technique from the Corinthians (FIG. 5-4), the Athenians had by the mid-sixth century BCE taken over the export market for fine painted ceramics.

The *François Vase* (a new kind of krater with volute-shaped handles probably inspired by costly metal prototypes) is signed by both its painter ("KLEITIAS painted me") and potter ("ERGOTIMOS made me"). In fact, each signed twice! The krater has more than 200 figures in six registers. Labels abound, naming humans and animals alike, even some inanimate objects. Only one of the bands was given over to the Orientalizing repertoire of animals and sphinxes. The rest constitute a selective encyclopedia of Greek mythology, focusing on the exploits of Peleus and his son Achilles, the great hero of Homer's *Iliad*, and of Theseus, the legendary king of Athens.

In the detail shown here, Lapiths (a northern Greek tribe) and centaurs battle *(centauromachy)* after a wedding celebration where the man-beasts, who were invited guests, got drunk and attempted to abduct the Lapith maidens and young boys. Theseus, also on the guest list, was prominent among the centaurs' Greek adversaries. Kleitias did not fill the space between his figures with decorative ornament, as did his Geometric predecessors (FIG. 5-1). But his heroes conform to the age-old composite type (profile heads with frontal eyes, frontal torsos, and profile legs and arms). His centaurs are much more believable than their Geometric counterparts (FIG. 5-2). The man-horse combination is top/bottom rather than front/back. The lower (horse) portion

5-18 KLEITIAS and ERGOTIMOS, *François Vase* (Attic black-figure volute krater), from Chiusi, Italy, ca. 570 BCE. General view *(top)* and detail of centauromachy on other side of vase *(bottom)*. Approx. 2′ 2″ high. Museo Archeologico, Florence.

Greek Vase Painting

The techniques Greek ceramists used to shape and decorate fine vases required a great deal of skill, acquired over many years as apprentices in the workshops of master potters. During the Archaic and Classical periods, when the art of vase painting was at its zenith in Greece, both potters and painters frequently signed their work. These signatures reveal the pride of the artists. They also might have functioned as "brand names" for a large export market. The products of the workshops in Corinth and Athens in particular were much prized and have been found all over the Mediterranean world. The Corinthian amphora we illustrate (FIG. 5-4) was found on Rhodes, an island at the opposite side of the Aegean from mainland Corinth (MAP 5-1). Athenian (Attic) vases were staples in Etruscan tombs in Italy, and all but one of our examples (FIGS. 5-18 to 5-23, 5-57, and 5-58) came from an Etruscan site (see MAP 9-1). Other painted Attic pots have been found as far away as France, Russia, and the Sudan.

The first step in manufacturing a Greek vase was to remove any impurities found in the natural clay and then to knead it, like dough, to remove air bubbles and make it flexible. The Greeks used dozens of different kinds and shapes of pots, and most were fashioned in several parts. The vessel's body was formed by placing the clay on a rotating horizontal wheel. While an apprentice turned the wheel by hand, the potter pulled up the clay with the fingers until the desired shape was achieved. The handles were shaped separately and attached to the vase body by applying *slip* (liquefied clay) to the joints.

Then a specialist, the painter, was called in, although many potters decorated their own work. (Today most people tend to regard painters as more elevated artists than potters, but in Greece the potters owned the shops and employed the painters.) The "pigment" the painter applied to the clay surface is customarily referred to as *glaze*, but the black areas on Greek pots are neither pigment nor glaze but a slip of finely sifted clay that originally was of the same rich red orange color as the clay of the pot. In the three-phase firing process Greek potters used, the first *(oxidizing)* phase turned both pot and slip red. During the second *(reducing)* phase, the oxygen supply into the kiln was shut off, and both pot and slip turned black. In the final *(reoxidizing)* phase, the pot's coarser material reabsorbed oxygen and became red again, while the smoother, silica-laden slip did not and remained black. After long experiment, Greek potters developed a velvety jet-black "glaze" of this kind, produced in kilns heated to temperatures as high as 950° Celsius (about 1,742° Fahrenheit). The firing process was the same whether the painter worked in black-figure or in red-figure. In fact, sometimes both manners were used on the same vase (FIG. 5-20).

---

has four legs of uniform type, and the upper part of the monster is fully human. In characteristic fashion, the animal section of the centaur is shown in strict profile, while the human head and torso are a composite of frontal and profile views. (Kleitias used a consistent profile for the more adventurous detail of the collapsed centaur at the right.)

EXEKIAS, BLACK-FIGURE MASTER The acknowledged master of the black-figure technique was an Athenian named EXEKIAS, whose vases were not only widely exported but copied as well. Perhaps his greatest work is an amphora (FIG. **5-19**), found in an Etruscan tomb at Vulci, that Exekias signed as both painter and potter. He did not divide the surface into a series of horizontal

5-19 EXEKIAS, Achilles and Ajax playing a dice game (detail from an Attic black-figure amphora), from Vulci, Italy, ca. 540–530 BCE. Whole vessel approx. 2′ high. Vatican Museums, Rome.

bands. Instead, he placed figures of monumental stature in a single large framed panel. At the left is Achilles, fully armed. He plays a dice game with his comrade Ajax. Out of the lips of Achilles comes the word *tesara* (four); Ajax calls out *tria* (three). Ajax has taken off his helmet, but both men hold their spears. Their shields are nearby, and each man is ready for action at a moment's notice. It is a classic case of "the calm before the storm." The moment Exekias chose to depict is the antithesis of the Archaic preference for dramatic action. The gravity and tension that will characterize much Classical Greek art of the next century, but are absent in Archaic art, already may be seen here.

Exekias had no equal as a black-figure painter. This may be seen in such details as the extraordinarily intricate engraving of the patterns on the heroes' cloaks (highlighted with delicate touches of white) and in the brilliant composition. The arch formed by the backs of the two warriors echoes the shape of the rounded shoulders of the amphora. The shape of the vessel (compare FIG. 5-4) is echoed again in the void between the heads and spears of Achilles and Ajax. Exekias also used the spears to lead the viewer's eyes toward the thrown dice, where the heroes' eyes are fixed. Of course, those eyes do not really look down at the table but stare out from the profile heads in the old manner. For all his brilliance, Exekias was still wedded to many of the old conventions. Real innovation in figure drawing would have to await the invention of a new ceramic painting technique of greater versatility than black-figure, with its dark silhouettes and incised details.

"BILINGUAL" PAINTING The birth of this new technique came around 530 BCE, and the person responsible is known as the ANDOKIDES PAINTER, that is, the anonymous painter who decorated the vases signed by the potter ANDOKIDES. The differences between the two techniques can best be studied on a series of experimental vases with the same composition painted on both sides, once in black-figure and once in the new technique, *red-figure*. Such vases, nicknamed *bilingual vases,* were produced for only a short time. An especially interesting example is an amphora (FIG. 5-20) by the Andokides Painter that features copies of the Achilles and Ajax panel by Exekias, his teacher.

In neither black-figure nor red-figure did the Andokides Painter capture the intensity of the model, and the treatment of details is decidedly inferior. Yet the new red-figure technique had obvious advantages over the old black-figure manner. Red-figure is the opposite of black-figure. What was previously black became red, and vice versa. The artist still employed the same black glaze. But instead of using the glaze to create the silhouettes of figures, the painter outlined the figures and then colored the background black. The red clay was reserved for the figures themselves. Interior details were then drawn with the soft brush in place of the stiff metal graver. The artist could vary the glaze thickness, building it up to give relief to hair curls or diluting it to create brown shades, thereby expanding the chromatic range of the Greek vase painter's craft. The Andokides Painter—many think he was the potter Andokides himself—did not yet appreciate the full potential of

5-20 ANDOKIDES PAINTER, Achilles and Ajax playing a dice game (Attic bilingual amphora), from Orvieto, Italy, ca. 525–520 BCE. Black-figure side *(left)* and red-figure side *(right)*. Approx. 1′ 9″ high. Museum of Fine Arts, Boston.

his own invention. But he created a technique that, in the hands of other, more skilled artists, helped revolutionize the art of drawing.

EUPHRONIOS AND RED-FIGURE One of these younger and more adventurous painters was EUPHRONIOS, whose krater depicting the struggle between Herakles and Antaios (FIG. **5-21**) reveals the exciting possibilities of the new red-figure technique. Antaios was a Libyan giant, a son of Earth, and he derived his power from contact with the ground. To defeat him, Herakles had to lift him up into the air and strangle him while no part of the giant's body touched the earth. But Euphronios did not represent the moment of Herakles' triumph. The two wrestle on the ground, and Antaios still possesses enormous strength. Nonetheless, Herakles has the upper hand. The giant's face is a mask of pain. His eyes roll and his teeth are bared. His right arm is paralyzed, with the fingers limp. Euphronios used diluted glaze to show Antaios's unkempt golden brown hair—intentionally contrasted with the neat coiffure and carefully trimmed beard of the emotionless Greek hero.

The artist also used thinned glaze to delineate the muscles of both figures. But Euphronios was interested in more than rendering human anatomy convincingly. He also wished to show that his figures occupy space. Euphronios deliberately rejected the conventional composite posture for the human figure, which communicates so well the specific parts of the human body, and attempted to reproduce how a particular human body is *seen*. He presented, for example, not only Antaios's torso but also his right thigh from the front. The lower leg disappears behind the giant, and one glimpses only part of the right foot. The viewer must mentally make the connection between the upper leg and the foot. The red-figure painter did not create a two-dimensional panel filled with figures in stereotypical postures, as his Archaic and pre-Greek predecessors always did. His panel is a window onto a mythological world with protagonists occupying three-dimensional space—a revolutionary new conception of what a picture was supposed to be.

RIVALS OF EUPHRONIOS A preoccupation with the art of drawing per se may be seen in a remarkable amphora (FIG. **5-22**) painted by EUTHYMIDES, a contemporary and competitor of Euphronios. The subject is appropriate for a wine storage jar—three tipsy revelers. But the theme was little more than an excuse for the artist to experiment with the representation of unusual positions of the human form. It is no coincidence that the bodies do not overlap, for each is an independent figure study. Euthymides cast aside the conventional frontal and profile composite views. Instead, he painted torsos that are not two-dimensional surface patterns but are *foreshortened*, that is, drawn in a three-quarter view. Most noteworthy is the central figure, who is shown from the rear with a twisting spinal column and buttocks in three-quarter view. Earlier artists had no interest in attempting such postures because they not only are incomplete but also do not show the "main" side of the human body. But for Euthymides the challenge of drawing the figure from such an unusual viewpoint was a reward in itself. With understandable pride he proclaimed his achievement by adding to the formulaic signature "Euthymides painted me" the phrase "as never Euphronios [could do]"!

5-21 EUPHRONIOS, Herakles wrestling Antaios (detail of an Attic red-figure calyx krater), from Cerveteri, Italy, ca. 510 BCE. Whole vessel approx. 1′ 7″ high. Louvre, Paris.

5-22 EUTHYMIDES, Three revelers (Attic red-figure amphora), from Vulci, Italy, ca. 510 BCE. Approx. 2′ high. Staatliche Antikensammlungen, Munich.

5-23 ONESIMOS, Girl preparing to bathe (interior of an Attic red-figure kylix), from Chiusi, Italy, ca. 490 BCE. Tondo approx. 6″ in diameter. Musées Royaux, Brussels.

THE FEMALE NUDE Interest in the foreshortening of the human figure soon extended to studies of nude women, as on the interior (FIG. 5-23) of a *kylix* (drinking cup) by ONESIMOS. The representation is unusual not only for the successful foreshortening of the girl's torso and breasts, seen in three-quarter view, but also for its subject. This is neither mythology nor a scene of wealthy noblemen partying. This is a servant girl, not the lady of the house, who has removed her clothes to bathe. Such a genre scene, not to mention female nudity, would never have been portrayed publicly in monumental painting or sculpture of this time. Only in the private sphere was such a subject acceptable.

Aegina and the Transition to the Classical Period

EVOLUTION AND REVOLUTION The years just before and after 500 BCE were also a time of dynamic transition in architecture and architectural sculpture. Some of the changes were evolutionary in nature, others revolutionary. Both kinds are evident in

the Temple at Aegina dedicated to Aphaia, a local goddess. The temple (FIG. 5-24) sits on a prominent ridge with dramatic views out to the sea. The colonnade is 45 × 95 feet and consists of 6 Doric columns on the facade and 12 on the flanks. This is a much more compact structure than the impressive but ungainly Archaic Temple of Hera I at Paestum (FIG. 5-13), even though the ratio of width to length is similar. Doric architects had learned a great deal in the half century that elapsed between construction of the two temples. The columns of the Aegina temple are more widely spaced and more slender. The capitals create a smooth transition from the vertical shafts below to the horizontal architrave above. Gone are the Archaic flattened echinuses and bulging shafts of the Paestum columns.

The Aegina architect also refined the temple plan and internal elevation (FIG. 5-25). In place of a single row of columns down the center of the cella is a double colonnade — and each row has two stories. This arrangement allowed a statue to be placed on the central axis and also gave those gathered in front of the building an unobstructed view through the pair of columns in the pronaos.

Both pediments were filled with life-size statuary (FIG. 5-26) depicting the same subject and using a similar composition. The theme was the battle of Greeks and Trojans, with Athena at the center of the bloody combat. She is larger than all the other figures because she is superhuman, but the sculptors carved all the mortal heroes at the same scale, regardless of the statue's position in the pediment. Unlike the experimental design at Corfu (FIG. 5-15), the Aegina pediments feature a unified theme and consistent size. The latter was achieved by using the whole range of body postures from upright (Athena) to leaning, falling, kneeling, and lying (Greeks and Trojans).

ARCHAISM TO CLASSICISM The sculptures of the Aegina pediments were set in place when the temple was completed

5-24 Temple of Aphaia, Aegina, Greece, ca. 500–490 BCE.

around 490 BCE. But the pedimental statues at the eastern end were damaged and replaced with a new group a decade or two later. It is very instructive to compare the earlier and later figures. The west pediment's dying warrior (FIG. **5-27**) was still conceived in the Archaic mode. His torso is rigidly frontal, and he looks out directly at the spectator. In fact, he smiles at us, in spite of the bronze arrow that punctures his chest. He is like a mannequin in a store window whose arms and legs have been arranged by someone else for effective display. The viewer has no sense whatsoever of a thinking and feeling human being.

5-25 Plan *(left)* and restored cutaway view *(right)* of the Temple of Aphaia, Aegina, Greece, ca. 500–490 BCE.

5-26 West pediment of the Temple of Aphaia, Aegina, Greece, ca. 500-490 BCE. Marble, approx. 5′ 8″ high at center. Glyptothek, Munich. 💿

5-27 Dying warrior, from the west pediment of the Temple of Aphaia, Aegina, Greece, ca. 500–490 BCE. Marble, approx. 5′ 2½″ long. Glyptothek, Munich. 💿

5-28 Dying warrior, from the east pediment of the Temple of Aphaia, Aegina, Greece, ca. 490–480 BCE. Marble, approx. 6′ 1″ long. Glyptothek, Munich. 💿

The comparable figure (FIG. **5-28**) in the later east pediment is radically different. His posture is more natural and more complex, with the torso placed at an angle to the viewer. (He is on a par with the painted figures of Euphronios, FIG. 5-21.) Moreover, he reacts to his wound as a flesh-and-blood human would. He knows that death is inevitable, but he still struggles to rise once again, using his shield for support. And he does not look out at the spectator. He is concerned with his pain, not with the spectator. Only a decade, perhaps two, separates the two statues, but they belong to different eras. The later warrior is not a creation of the Archaic world, when sculptors imposed anatomical patterns (and smiles) on statues from without. This statue belongs to the Classical world, where statues move as humans move and possess the self-consciousness of real men and women. This was a radical change in the conception of what a statue was meant to be. In sculpture, as in painting, the Classical revolution had occurred.

THE EARLY AND HIGH CLASSICAL PERIODS

THE AFTERMATH OF WAR Art historians reckon the beginning of the Classical* age from a historical event, the defeat of the Persian invaders of Greece by the allied Hellenic city-states. Shortly after Athens was occupied and sacked in 480 BCE, the Greeks won a decisive naval victory over the Persians at Salamis. It had been a difficult war, and at times it had seemed as though

---

*Note: In *Art through the Ages* the adjective "Classical," with uppercase *C*, refers specifically to the Classical period of ancient Greece, 480–323 BCE. Lowercase "classical" refers to Greco-Roman antiquity in general, that is, the period treated in Chapters 5, 9, and 10.

Asia would swallow up Greece, and the Persian king Xerxes (see Chapter 2) would rule over all. When the Persians destroyed the Greek city Miletos in 494 BCE, they killed the male inhabitants and sold the women and children into slavery. The close escape of the Greeks from domination by Asian "barbarians" nurtured a sense of Hellenic identity so strong that from then on the history of European civilization would be distinct from the civilization of Asia, even though they continued to interact.

Typical of the time were the views of the great dramatist Aeschylus, who celebrated, in his *Oresteia*, the triumph of reason and law over barbarous crimes, blood feuds, and mad vengeance. Himself a veteran of the epic battle of Marathon, Aeschylus repudiated in majestic verse all the slavish and inhuman traits of nature that the Greeks at that time of crisis associated with the Persians.

The decades following the removal of the Persian threat are universally considered the high point of Greek civilization. This is the era of the dramatists Sophocles and Euripides, as well as Aeschylus, the historian Herodotus, the statesman Pericles, the philosopher Socrates, and many of the most famous Greek architects, sculptors, and painters.

Architecture and Architectural Sculpture

ZEUS'S OLYMPIAN TEMPLE The first great monument of Classical art and architecture is the Temple of Zeus at Olympia,

site of the Olympic Games. The temple was begun about 470 BCE and was probably completed by 457 BCE. The architect was LIBON OF ELIS. Today the structure is in ruins, its picturesque tumbled column drums an eloquent reminder of the effect of the passage of time on even the grandest monuments humans have built. One can get a good idea of its original appearance, however, by looking at a slightly later Doric temple modeled closely on the Olympian shrine of Zeus—the second Temple of Hera at Paestum (FIG. 5-29). The plans and elevations of both temples follow the pattern of the Temple of Aphaia at Aegina (FIG. 5-25): an even number of columns (six) on the short ends, two columns in antis, and two rows of columns in two stories inside the cella. But the Temple of Zeus was more lavishly decorated than even the Aphaia temple. Statues filled both pediments, and the six metopes over the doorway in the pronaos and the matching six of the opisthodomos were adorned with reliefs.

TREACHERY AND A CURSE The subject of the Temple of Zeus's east pediment (FIG. 5-30) had deep local significance: the chariot race between Pelops (from whom the Peloponnesos takes its name) and King Oinomaos. The story is a sinister one. Oinomaos had one daughter, Hippodameia, and it was foretold that he would die if she married. Consequently, Oinomaos challenged any suitor who wished to make Hippodameia his bride to a chariot race from Olympia to Corinth. If the suitor won, he also won the hand of the king's daughter. But if he lost, he was killed. The

5-30 East pediment from the Temple of Zeus, Olympia, Greece, ca. 470–456 BCE. Marble, approx. 87' wide. Archaeological Museum, Olympia.

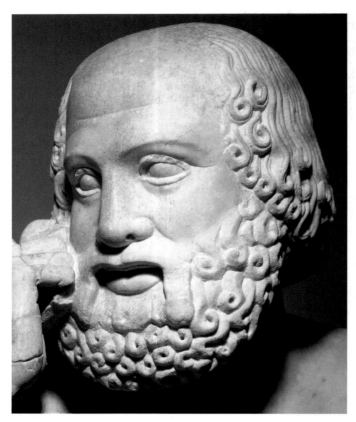

5-31 Seer, from the east pediment of the Temple of Zeus, Olympia, Greece, ca. 470–456 BCE. Marble, full figure approx. 4′ 6″ high. Archaeological Museum, Olympia.

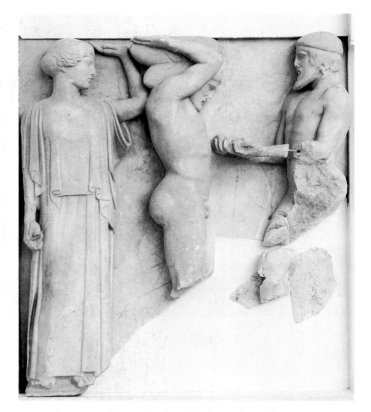

5-32 Athena, Herakles, and Atlas with the apples of the Hesperides, metope from the Temple of Zeus, Olympia, Greece, ca. 470–456 BCE. Marble, approx. 5′ 3″ high. Archaeological Museum, Olympia.

outcome of each race was predetermined, because Oinomaos possessed divine horses his father Ares gave him. To ensure his victory when all others had failed, Pelops resorted to bribing the king's groom, Myrtilos, to rig the royal chariot so that it would collapse during the race. Oinomaos was killed and Pelops won his bride, but he drowned Myrtilos rather than pay his debt to him. Before he died, Myrtilos brought a curse on Pelops and his descendants. This curse led to the murder of Pelops's son Atreus and to events that figure prominently in some of the greatest Greek tragedies of the classical era, Aeschylus's three plays known collectively as the *Oresteia:* the sacrifice by Atreus's son Agamemnon of his daughter Iphigeneia; the slaying of Agamemnon by Aegisthus, lover of Agamemnon's wife Clytaemnestra; and the murder of Aegisthus and Clytaemnestra by Orestes, the son of Agamemnon and Clytaemnestra.

The pedimental statues (which faced toward the starting point of all Olympic chariot races) are, in fact, posed like actors on a stage—Zeus in the center, Oinomaos and his wife on one side, Pelops and Hippodameia on the other, and their respective chariots to each side. All are quiet; the horrible events known to every spectator have yet to occur. Only one man reacts—a seer (FIG. 5-31) who knows the future. He is a remarkable figure. Unlike the gods, heroes, and noble youths and maidens who are the almost exclusive subjects of Archaic and Classical Greek statuary, this seer is a rare depiction of old age. He has a balding, wrinkled head and sagging musculature—and a shocked expression on his face. This is a true show of emotion, unlike the stereotypical "Archaic smile," without precedent in earlier Greek sculpture and not a regular feature of Greek art until the Hellenistic age.

THE LABORS OF HERAKLES The metopes of the Zeus temple are also thematically connected with the site, for they depict the 12 labors of Herakles (see "Herakles," page 109), the legendary founder of the Olympic Games. In the metope illustrated here (FIG. 5-32), Herakles holds up the sky (with the aid of the goddess Athena—and a cushion) in place of Atlas, who had undertaken the dangerous journey to fetch the golden apples of the Hesperides for the hero. The load soon will be transferred back to Atlas, but now each of the very high relief figures in the metope stands quietly with the same serene dignity as the statues in the Olympia pediment.

In both attitude and dress (simple Doric peplos for the women), all the Olympia figures display a severity that contrasts sharply with the smiling and elaborately clad figures of the Late Archaic period. Many art historians call this Early Classical phase of Greek art the "Severe Style."

Statuary

A NEW WAY TO STAND Early Classical sculptors were also the first to break away from the rigid and unnatural Egyptian-inspired pose of the Archaic kouroi. This change may be seen in the postures of the Olympia figures and in a somewhat earlier statue from the Athenian Acropolis that, although it is well under life-size, is one of the most important works of Greek sculpture. It is known as the *Kritios Boy* (FIG. 5-33) because it was once thought to have been carved by the sculptor Kritios. Never before had a sculptor been concerned with portraying how a human being (as opposed to a stone image) actually stands. Real people do not stand in the stiff-legged pose of the kouroi and korai or their Egyptian predecessors. Humans shift their weight and the position of the main body parts around the vertical, but flexible, axis of the spine. When

5-33 *Kritios Boy,* from the Acropolis, Athens, Greece, ca. 480 BCE. Marble, approx. 2′ 10″ high. Acropolis Museum, Athens.

humans move, the body's elastic musculoskeletal structure dictates a harmonious, smooth motion of all its elements. The sculptor of the *Kritios Boy* was among the first to grasp this fact and to represent it in statuary. The youth has a slight dip to the right hip, indicating the shifting of weight onto his left leg. His right leg is bent, at ease. The head also turns slightly to the right and tilts, breaking the unwritten rule of frontality dictating the form of virtually all earlier statues. This weight shift, which art historians describe as *contrapposto* (counterbalance), separates Classical from Archaic Greek statuary. Its reappearance, after a long absence, is one of the hallmarks of the renewed interest in Classical art during the later Middle Ages and Renaissance.

5-34 Warrior, from the sea off Riace, Italy, ca. 460–450 BCE. Bronze, approx. 6′ 6″ high. Archaeological Museum, Reggio Calabria.

RESCUED FROM THE SEA The innovations of the *Kritios Boy* were carried even further in the bronze statue of a warrior (FIG. **5-34**) found in the sea near Riace at the "toe" of the Italian "boot." It is one of a pair of statues a diver accidentally discovered in the cargo of a ship that sank in antiquity on its way from Greece probably to Rome, where Greek sculpture was much admired. Known as the Riace Bronzes, they had to undergo several years of cleaning and restoration after nearly two millennia of submersion in salt water, but they are nearly intact. The statue shown here lacks only its shield, spear, and helmet. It is a masterpiece of hollow-casting (see "Hollow-Casting Life-Size Bronze Statues," page 131), with inlaid eyes, silver teeth and eyelashes, and copper lips and nipples (see FIG. Intro-17). The weight shift is more pronounced than in the *Kritios Boy.* The warrior's head turns more forcefully to the right, his shoulders tilt, his hips swing more markedly, and his arms have been freed from the body. Natural motion in space has replaced Archaic frontality and rigidity.

VICTORY AT DELPHI The high technical quality of the Riace warrior is equaled in another bronze statue set up a decade or two earlier to commemorate the victory of the tyrant Polyzalos of

5-35 Charioteer, from a group dedicated by Polyzalos of Gela in the Sanctuary of Apollo, Delphi, Greece, ca. 470 BCE. Bronze, approx. 5′ 11″ high. Archaeological Museum, Delphi.

5-36 Zeus (or Poseidon?), from the sea off Cape Artemision, Greece, ca. 460–450 BCE. Bronze, approx. 6′ 10″ high. National Archaeological Museum, Athens.

the head and confines the hair. The eyes are made of glass paste and shaded by delicate bronze lashes.

ZEUS THE THUNDERER The male human form in motion is, in contrast, the subject of another Early Classical bronze statue (FIG. 5-36), which, like the Riace warrior, divers found in an ancient shipwreck, this time off the coast of Greece itself at Cape Artemision. The bearded god once hurled a weapon held in his right hand, probably a thunderbolt, in which case he is Zeus. A less likely suggestion is that this is Poseidon with his trident. The pose could be employed equally well for a javelin thrower. Both arms are boldly extended, and the right heel is raised off the ground, underscoring the lightness and stability of hollow-cast monumental statues.

GREEK STATUES IN ROMAN COPIES A bronze statue similar to the Artemision Zeus was the renowned *Diskobolos (Discus Thrower)* by MYRON, which is known only through marble copies (FIG. 5-37) made in Roman times. Even when the original was removed from Greece, as were the Riace and Artemision bronzes, only one community or individual could own it. Demand so far exceeded the supply that a veritable industry was born to meet the Roman call for Greek statuary to display in public places and private villas alike. The copies usually were made in less costly marble. The change in medium resulted in a different surface appearance. In most cases, the copyist also had to add an intrusive tree trunk to support the great weight of the stone statue and struts between arms and body to strengthen weak points. The

Gela (Sicily) in a chariot race at Delphi. The statue (FIG. 5-35) is almost all that remains of an enormous group composed of Polyzalos's driver, the chariot, the team of horses, and a young groom. The charioteer stands in an almost Archaic pose, but the turn of the head and feet in opposite directions as well as a slight twist at the waist are in keeping with the Severe Style. The moment chosen for depiction is not during the frenetic race but after, when the driver quietly and modestly holds his horses still in the winner's circle. He grasps the reins in his outstretched right hand (the lower left arm, cast separately, is missing), and he wears the standard charioteer's garment, girdled high and held in at the shoulders and the back to keep it from flapping. The folds emphasize both the verticality and calm of the figure and recall the flutes of a Greek column. A band inlaid with silver is tied around

Hollow-Casting Life-Size Bronze Statues

Monumental bronze statues such as the Riace warrior (FIG. 5-34), the Delphi charioteer (FIG. 5-35), and the Artemision god (FIG. 5-36) required great technical skill to produce. They could not be manufactured using a single simple mold, as were small-scale Geometric and Archaic figures (FIGS. 5-2 and 5-3). Weight, cost, and the tendency of large masses of bronze to distort when cooling made life-size castings in solid bronze impractical, if not impossible. Instead, large statues were hollow-cast by the *cire perdue* (lost-wax) method. The lost-wax process entailed several steps and had to be repeated many times, because monumental statues were typically cast in parts—head, arms, hands, torso, and so forth.

First, the sculptor fashioned a full-size clay model of the intended statue. Then a clay master mold was made around the model and removed in sections. When dry, the various pieces of the master mold were put back together for each separate body part. Next, a layer of beeswax was applied to the inside of each mold. When the wax cooled, the mold was removed, and the sculptor was left with a hollow wax model in the shape of the original clay model. The artist could then correct or refine details—for example, engrave fingernails on the wax hands or individual locks of hair on the head.

In the next stage, a final clay mold (*investment*) was applied to the exterior of the wax model, and a liquid clay core was poured inside the hollow wax. Metal pins (*chaplets*) then were driven through the new mold to connect the investment with the clay core *(a)*. Now the wax was melted out ("lost") and molten bronze poured into the mold in its place *(b)*. When the bronze hardened and assumed the shape of the wax model, the investment and as

much of the core as possible were removed, and the casting process was complete. Finally, the individually cast pieces were fitted together and soldered, surface imperfections and joins smoothed, eyes inlaid, teeth and eyelashes added, attributes such as spears and wreaths provided, and so forth. Such statues were costly to make and much prized.

Two stages of the lost-wax method of bronze casting (after S. A. Hemingway[1]): *(a)* clay mold (investment), wax model, and clay core connected by chaplets; *(b)* wax melted out and molten bronze poured into the mold.

[1] Sean A. Hemingway, *How Bronze Statues Were Made in Classical Antiquity* (Cambridge: Harvard University Art Museums, 1996), 4.

copies rarely approach the quality of the originals, and the Roman sculptors sometimes took liberties with their models to conform to their own tastes and needs. Occasionally, for example, a mirror image of the original was created for a specific setting. Nevertheless, the copies are indispensable today. Without them it would be impossible to reconstruct the history of Greek sculpture after the Archaic period.

Myron's *Discus Thrower* is a vigorous action statue, like the Artemision Zeus, but it is composed in an almost Archaic manner, with profile limbs and a nearly frontal chest, suggesting the tension of a coiled spring. Like the arm of a pendulum clock, the right arm of the *Diskobolos* has reached the apex of its arc but has not yet begun to swing down again. Myron froze the action and arranged the body and limbs to form two intersecting arcs, creating the impression of a tightly stretched bow a moment before the string is released. This tension is not, however, mirrored in the athlete's face, which remains expressionless. Once again, as in the later of the two warrior statues from the Aegina pediments (FIG. 5-28), the head is turned away from the spectator. In contrast to Archaic athlete statues, the Classical *Diskobolos* does not perform for the spectator but concentrates on the task at hand.

THE QUEST FOR IDEAL FORM One of the most frequently copied Greek statues was the *Doryphoros (Spear Bearer)* by POLY-KLEITOS, a work that epitomizes the intellectual rigor of Classical statuary design. The original is lost. We illustrate a marble copy that stood in a palaestra at Pompeii, where it served as a model for

5-37 MYRON, *Diskobolos (Discus Thrower).* Roman copy after a bronze original of ca. 450 BCE, 5′ 1″ high. Museo Nazionale Romano—Palazzo Massimo alle Terme, Rome.

5-38 POLYKLEITOS, *Doryphoros (Spear Bearer)*. Roman copy from Pompeii, Italy, after a bronze original of ca. 450–440 BCE, 6′ 11″ high. Museo Nazionale, Naples.

Roman athletes (FIG. **5-38**). The *Doryphoros* is the embodiment of Polykleitos's vision of the ideal statue of a nude male athlete or warrior. In fact, it was made as a demonstration piece to accompany a treatise on the subject. *Spear Bearer* is but a modern descriptive epithet for the statue. The name Polykleitos assigned to it was *Canon* (see "Polykleitos's Prescription for the Perfect Statue," page 133).

The *Doryphoros* is the culmination of the evolution in Greek statuary from the Archaic kouros to the *Kritios Boy* to the Riace warrior. The contrapposto is more pronounced than ever before in a standing statue, but Polykleitos was not content with simply rendering a figure that stands naturally. His aim was to impose order on human movement, to make it "beautiful," to "perfect" it. He achieved this through a system of *chiastic,* or cross, balance. What appears at first to be a casually natural pose is, in fact, the result of an extremely complex and subtle organization of the figure's various parts. Note, for instance, how the rigid supporting leg is echoed by the straight-hanging arm, providing the figure's

right side with the columnar stability needed to anchor the left side's dynamically flexed limbs. If read anatomically, however, the tensed and relaxed limbs may be seen to oppose each other diagonally—the right arm and the left leg are relaxed, and the tensed supporting leg opposes the flexed arm, which held a spear. In like manner, the head turns to the right while the hips twist slightly to the left. And although the *Doryphoros* seems to take a step forward, he does not move. This dynamic asymmetrical balance, this motion while at rest, and the resulting harmony of opposites are the essence of the Polykleitan style.

The Athenian Acropolis

ALLIANCE AND TYRANNY While Polykleitos was formulating his *Canon* in Argos, the Athenians, under the leadership of Pericles, were at work on one of the most ambitious building projects ever undertaken, the reconstruction of the Acropolis after the Persian sack of 480 BCE. Athens, despite the damage it suffered at the hands of the army of Xerxes, emerged from the war with enormous power and prestige. The Athenian commander Themistocles had decisively defeated the Persian navy off the island of Salamis, southwest of Athens, and forced it to retreat to Asia.

In 478 BCE, in the aftermath of the Persians' expulsion from the Aegean, the Greeks formed an alliance for mutual protection against any renewed threat from the east. The new confederacy came to be known as the Delian League, because its headquarters were on the sacred island of Delos, midway between the Greek mainland and the coast of Asia Minor. Although at the outset each league member had an equal vote, Athens was "first among equals," providing the allied fleet commander and determining which cities were to furnish ships and which were instead to pay an annual tribute to the treasury at Delos. Continued fighting against the Persians kept the alliance intact, but Athens gradually assumed a dominant role. In 454 BCE the Delian treasury was transferred to Athens, ostensibly for security reasons. Pericles, who was only in his teens when the Persians laid waste to the Acropolis, was by midcentury the recognized leader of the Athenians, and he succeeded in converting the alliance into an Athenian empire. Tribute continued to be paid, but the surplus reserves were not expended for the common good of the allied Greek states. Instead, they were expropriated to pay the enormous cost of executing Pericles' grand plan to embellish the Acropolis of Athens.

The reaction of the allies—in reality the subjects of Athens—was predictable. Plutarch, who wrote a biography of Pericles in the early second century CE, indicated the wrath the Greek victims of Athenian tyranny felt by recording the protest voiced against Pericles' decision even in the Athenian assembly. Greece, Pericles' enemies said, had been dealt "a terrible, wanton insult" when Athens used the funds contributed out of necessity for a common war effort to "gild and embellish itself with images and extravagant temples, like some pretentious woman decked out with precious stones."[4] This is important to keep in mind when examining those great and universally admired buildings erected on the Acropolis in accordance with Pericles' vision of his polis reborn from the ashes of the Persian sack. They are *not,* as some would wish people to believe, the glorious fruits of Athenian democracy but are instead the by-products of tyranny and the abuse of power. Too often art and architectural historians do not ask how a monument was financed. The answer can be very revealing—and very embarrassing.

THE "OLYMPIAN PERICLES" A number of Roman copies are preserved of a famous bronze portrait statue of Pericles fashioned

Polykleitos's Prescription for the Perfect Statue

One of the most influential philosophers of the ancient world was Pythagoras of Samos, who lived during the latter part of the sixth century BCE. A famous geometric theorem still bears his name. Pythagoras also is said to have discovered that harmonic chords in music are produced on the strings of a lyre at regular intervals that may be expressed as ratios of whole numbers—2:1, 3:2, 4:3. He and his followers, the Pythagoreans, believed more generally that underlying harmonic proportions could be found in all of nature, determining the form of the cosmos as well as of things on earth, and that beauty resided in harmonious numerical ratios.

By this reasoning, a perfect statue would be one constructed according to an all-encompassing mathematical formula. In the mid-fifth century BCE, the sculptor Polykleitos of Argos set out to make just such a statue (FIG. 5-38). He recorded the principles he followed and the proportions he used in a treatise titled the *Canon*. His treatise is unfortunately lost, but Galen, a physician who lived during the second century CE, summarized the sculptor's philosophy as follows:

[Beauty arises from] the commensurability *[symmetria]* of the parts, such as that of finger to finger, and of all the fingers to the palm and the wrist, and of these to the forearm, and of the forearm to the upper arm, and, in fact, of everything to everything else, just as it is written in the *Canon* of Polykleitos.... Polykleitos supported

his treatise [by making] a statue according to the tenets of his treatise, and called the statue, like the work, the *Canon.*"[1]

This is why Pliny the Elder, writing in the first century CE, maintained that Polykleitos "alone of men is deemed to have rendered art itself [that is, the theoretical basis of art] in a work of art."[2]

Polykleitos's belief that a successful statue resulted from the precise application of abstract principles is reflected in an anecdote (probably a later invention) told by the Roman historian Aelian:

Polykleitos made two statues at the same time, one which would be pleasing to the crowd and the other according to the principles of his art. In accordance with the opinion of each person who came into his workshop, he altered something and changed its form, submitting to the advice of each. Then he put both statues on display. The one was marvelled at by everyone, and the other was laughed at. Thereupon Polykleitos said, "But the one that you find fault with, you made yourselves; while the one that you marvel at, I made."[3]

[1] Galen, *De placitis Hippocratis et Platonis*, 5. Translated by J. J. Pollitt, *The Art of Ancient Greece: Sources and Documents* (New York: Cambridge University Press, 1990), 76.

[2] Pliny the Elder, *Natural History*, 34.55. Translated by Pollitt, 75.

[3] Aelian, *Varia historia*, 14.8. Translated by Pollitt, 79.

5-39 KRESILAS, Pericles. Roman herm copy after a bronze original of ca. 429 BCE, approx. 6' high. Vatican Museums, Rome.

by KRESILAS, who was born on Crete but who worked in Athens. The portrait was set up on the Acropolis, probably immediately after the leader's death in 429 BCE, and depicted Pericles in heroic nudity. The statue must have resembled the Riace warrior (FIG. 5-34). The copies, in marble, reproduce the head only. Ours (FIG. 5-39) is a *herm* (a bust on a square pillar), a popular format in Roman times for abbreviated copies of famous statues. The herm is inscribed "Pericles, son of Xanthippos, the Athenian," leaving no doubt as to the identification. Pericles wears the helmet of a *strategos* (general), the position he was elected to 15 times. The Athenian leader was said to have had an abnormally elongated skull, and Kresilas recorded this feature (while also concealing it) by providing a glimpse through the helmet's eye slots of the hair at the top of the head. This, together with the unblemished features of Pericles' Classically aloof face and, no doubt, his body's perfect physique, led Pliny to assert that Kresilas had the ability to make noble men appear even more noble in their portraits. This is because this is not a portrait at all in the modern sense of a record of actual features. Pliny refers to Kresilas's "portrait" as "the Olympian Pericles," for in this image Pericles appeared almost godlike.[5]

PERICLES' ACROPOLIS The centerpiece of Pericles' great building program on the Acropolis (FIG. 5-40) was the Parthenon (FIG. 5-41, no. 1), or the Temple of Athena Parthenos, erected in the remarkably short period between 447 and 438 BCE. (Work on the great temple's ambitious sculptural ornamentation continued until 432 BCE.) As soon as the Parthenon was completed, construction commenced on a grand new gateway to the Acropolis from the west (the only accessible side of the natural plateau), the Propylaia (FIG. 5-41, no. 2). Begun in 437 BCE, it was left

5-40 Aerial view of the Acropolis, Athens, Greece.

unfinished in 431 at the outbreak of the Peloponnesian War between Athens and Sparta. Two later temples, the Erechtheion (FIG. 5-41, no. 3) and the Temple of Athena Nike (FIG. 5-41, no. 4), built after Pericles' death, were probably also part of the original design. The greatest Athenian architects and sculptors of the Classical period focused their attention on the construction and decoration of these four buildings. More human creative genius concentrated on the Periclean Acropolis than at any other place or time in the history of Western civilization.

5-41 Model of the Acropolis, Athens, Greece. Acropolis Museum, Athens. 1) Parthenon, 2) Propylaia, 3) Erechtheion, 4) Temple of Athena Nike.

THE ACROPOLIS TODAY That these buildings exist at all today is something of a miracle. In the Middle Ages, the Parthenon, for example, was converted into a Byzantine and later a Roman Catholic church and then, after the Ottoman conquest of Greece, into a mosque. Each time the building was remodeled for a different religion, it was modified structurally. The Christians early on removed the colossal statue of Athena inside. The churches had a great curved *apse* at the east end housing the altar, and the mosque had a *minaret* (tower used to call Muslims to prayer). In 1687, the Venetians besieged the Acropolis, which at that time was in Turkish hands. One of their rockets scored a direct hit on the ammunition depot the Turks had installed in part of the Parthenon. The resultant explosion blew out the building's center. To make matters worse, the Venetians subsequently tried to remove some of the statues from the Parthenon's pediments. In more than one case, statues were dropped and smashed on the ground. Today, a uniquely modern blight threatens the Parthenon and the other buildings of the Periclean age. The corrosive emissions of factories and automobiles are decomposing the ancient marbles. A great campaign has been under way for some time to protect the columns and walls from further deterioration. What little original sculpture remained *in situ* when modern restoration began was transferred to the Acropolis Museum's climate-controlled rooms.

PARTHENON: IDEAL TEMPLE Despite the ravages of time and humanity, most of the Parthenon's peripteral colonnade (FIG. **5-42**) is still standing (or has been reerected), and art historians know a great deal about the building and its sculptural program. The architects were IKTINOS and KALLIKRATES. The statue of Athena (FIG. 5-44) was the work of PHIDIAS, who was also the overseer of the temple's sculptural decoration. In fact, Plutarch

5-42 Iktinos and Kallikrates, Parthenon, the Temple of Athena Parthenos (view from the northwest), Acropolis, Athens, Greece, 447–438 BCE.

claims that Phidias was in charge of the entire Periclean Acropolis project.

Just as the contemporary *Doryphoros* by Polykleitos may be seen as the culmination of nearly two centuries of searching for the ideal proportions of the various human body parts, so, too, the Parthenon may be viewed as the ideal solution to the Greek architect's quest for perfect proportions in Doric temple design. Its well-spaced columns, with their slender shafts, and the capitals, with their straight-sided conical echinuses, are the ultimate refinement of the bulging and squat Doric columns and compressed capitals of the Archaic Hera temple at Paestum (FIG. 5-13).

MATHEMATICS AND OPTICS The Parthenon architects and the *Doryphoros* sculptor were kindred spirits in their belief that beautiful proportions resulted from strict adherence to harmonious numerical ratios, whether they were designing a temple more than 200 feet long or a life-size statue of a nude man. For the Parthenon, the controlling ratio for the *symmetria* of the parts may be expressed algebraically as $x = 2y + 1$. Thus, for example, the temple's short ends have 8 columns and the long sides have 17: $17 = (2 \times 8) + 1$. The stylobate's ratio of length to width is 9:4 ($9 = [2 \times 4] + 1$), and this ratio also characterizes the cella's proportion of length to width, the distance between the centers of two adjacent column drums (the *interaxial*) in proportion to the columns' diameter, and so forth.

The Parthenon's harmonious design and the mathematical precision of the sizes of its constituent elements tend to obscure the fact that this temple, as actually constructed, is quite irregular in shape. Throughout the building are pronounced deviations from the strictly horizontal and vertical lines assumed to be the basis of all Greek post-and-lintel structures. The stylobate, for example, curves upward at the center on both the sides and the facade, forming a kind of shallow dome, and this curvature is carried up

into the entablature. Moreover, the peristyle columns lean inward slightly. Those at the corners have a diagonal inclination and are also about two inches thicker than the rest. If their lines were continued, they would meet about 1.5 miles above the temple. These deviations from the norm meant that virtually every Parthenon block and drum had to be carved according to the special set of specifications dictated by its unique place in the structure.

This was obviously a daunting task, and a reason must have existed for these so-called refinements in the Parthenon. Some modern observers note, for example, how the curving of horizontal lines and the tilting of vertical ones create a dynamic balance in the building—a kind of architectural contrapposto—and give it a greater sense of life. The oldest recorded explanation, however, may also be correct. Vitruvius, a Roman architect of the late first century BCE who claims to have had access to the treatise on the Parthenon written by Iktinos—again note the kinship with the *Canon* of Polykleitos—maintains that these adjustments were made to compensate for optical illusions. Vitruvius states, for example, that if a stylobate is laid out on a level surface, it will appear to sag at the center and that the corner columns of a building should be thicker because they are surrounded by light and would otherwise appear thinner than their neighbors.

MIXING DORIC AND IONIC The Parthenon is "irregular" in other ways as well. One of the ironies of this most famous of all Doric temples is that it is "contaminated" by Ionic elements (FIG. 5-43). Although the cella had a two-story Doric colonnade around Phidias's Athena statue (FIG. 5-44), the back room (which housed the goddess's treasury and the tribute collected from the Delian League) had four tall and slender Ionic columns as sole supports for the superstructure. And whereas the temple's exterior had a canonical Doric frieze, the inner frieze that ran around the top of the cella wall was Ionic. Perhaps this fusion of Doric

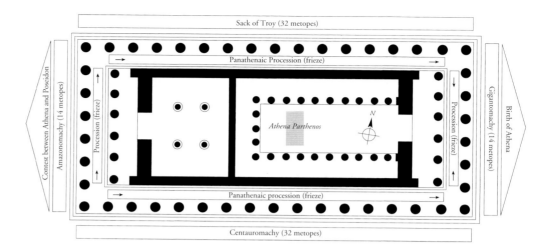

5-43 Plan of the Parthenon, Acropolis, Athens, Greece, with diagram of sculptural program (after A. Stewart), 447–432 BCE.

Sack of Troy (32 metopes)

Panathenaic Procession (frieze)

Contest between Athena and Poseidon

Amazonomachy (14 metopes)

Procession (frieze)

Athena Parthenos

N

Procession (frieze)

Gigantomachy (14 metopes)

Birth of Athena

Panathenaic procession (frieze)

Centauromachy (32 metopes)

and Ionic elements reflects the Athenians' belief that the Ionians of the Cycladic Islands and Asia Minor were descended from Athenian settlers and were therefore their kin. Or it may be Pericles and Iktinos's way of suggesting that Athens was the leader of *all* the Greeks. In any case, a mix of Doric and Ionic features characterizes the fifth-century buildings of the Acropolis as a whole.

LORD ELGIN'S MARBLES The costly decision to incorporate two sculptured friezes in the Parthenon's design is symptomatic. This Pentelic-marble temple was more lavishly decorated than any Greek temple before it, Doric or Ionic (FIG. 5-43). Every one of the

5-44 PHIDIAS, *Athena Parthenos*, in the cella of the Parthenon, Acropolis, Athens, Greece, ca. 438 BCE. Model of the lost statue, which was approx. 38′ tall. Royal Ontario Museum, Toronto.

92 Doric metopes was decorated with relief sculpture. So, too, was every inch of the 524-foot-long Ionic frieze. The pediments were filled with dozens of larger-than-life-size statues. Most of the Parthenon's reliefs and statues are today exhibited in a special gallery in the British Museum in London, where they are known popularly as the Elgin Marbles. Between 1801 and 1803, while Greece was still under Turkish rule, Lord Elgin, the British ambassador to the Ottoman court at Istanbul, was permitted to dismantle many of the Parthenon sculptures and to ship the best-preserved ones to England. He eventually sold them to the British government at a great financial loss to himself. Although he often has been accused of "stealing" Greece's cultural heritage (the Greek government has long sought the return of the Elgin Marbles to Athens), Lord Elgin must be credited with saving the sculptures from almost certain ruin if they had been left at the site.

PHIDIAS'S ATHENA One statue that even Elgin could not recover was Phidias's *Athena Parthenos,* the Virgin, which had been destroyed long before the 19th century. Art historians know a great deal about it, however, from descriptions by Greek and Latin authors and from Roman copies. A model (FIG. **5-44**) gives a good idea of its appearance and setting. It was a chryselephantine statue, that is, fashioned of gold and ivory, the latter used for Athena's exposed flesh. Phidias's statue stood 38 feet tall, and to a large extent the Parthenon was designed around it. To accommodate its huge size, the cella had to be wider than usual. This, in turn, dictated the width of the facade—eight columns at a time when six columns were the norm, as at Aegina (FIGS. 5-24 and 5-25).

Athena was fully armed with shield, spear, and helmet, and she held Nike (the winged female personification of Victory) in her extended right hand. No one doubts that this Nike referred to the victory of 479 BCE. The memory of the Persian sack of the Acropolis was still vivid, and the Athenians were intensely conscious that by driving back the Persians, they were saving their civilization from the eastern "barbarians" who had committed atrocities at Miletos. In fact, the *Athena Parthenos* had multiple allusions to the Persian defeat. On the thick soles of Athena's sandals was a representation of a centauromachy. The exterior of her shield was emblazoned with high reliefs depicting the battle of Greeks and Amazons (*Amazonomachy*), in which Theseus drove the Amazons out of Athens. And Phidias painted a gigantomachy on the shield's interior. Each of these mythological contests was a metaphor for the triumph of order over chaos, of civilization over barbarism, and of Athens over Persia.

5-45 Lapith versus centaur, metope from the south side of the Parthenon, Acropolis, Athens, Greece, ca. 447–438 BCE. Marble, approx. 4′ 8″ high. British Museum, London.

CENTAURS AND PERSIANS These same themes were taken up again in the Parthenon's Doric metopes (FIG. 5-43). The best-preserved metopes—although the paint on these and all the other Parthenon marbles long ago disappeared—are those of the south side, which depicted the battle of Lapiths and centaurs, a combat in which Theseus of Athens played a major role. On one extraordinary slab (FIG. **5-45**), a triumphant centaur rises up on its hind legs, exulting over the crumpled body of the Greek it has defeated. The relief is so high that parts are fully in the round; some have broken off. The sculptor knew how to distinguish the vibrant, powerful form of the living beast from the lifeless corpse on the ground. In other metopes the Greeks have the upper hand, but the full set suggests that the battle was a difficult one against a dangerous enemy and that losses as well as victories occurred. The same was true of the war against the Persians.

THE BIRTH OF ATHENA The subjects of the two pediments were especially appropriate for a temple that celebrated not only Athena but also the Athenians. The east pediment depicted the birth of Athena. At the west was the contest between Athena and Poseidon to determine which one would become the city's patron deity. Athena won, giving her name to the polis and its citizens. It is significant that in the story and in the pediment the Athenians are the judges of the relative merits of the two gods. Here one sees the same arrogance that led to the use of Delian League funds to adorn the Acropolis.

The center of the east pediment was damaged when the apse was added to the Parthenon at the time of its conversion into a church. What remains are the spectators to the left and the right who witnessed Athena's birth on Mount Olympus. At the far left are the head and arms of Helios (the Sun) and his chariot horses rising from the pediment floor (FIG. **5-46**). Next to them is a powerful male figure usually identified as Dionysos or possibly Herakles, who entered the realm of the gods on completion of his 12 labors. At the right are three goddesses, probably Hestia, Dione, and Aphrodite (FIG. **5-47**), and either Selene (the Moon) or Nyx (Night) and more horses, this time sinking below the pediment's floor. Here, Phidias,

5-46 Helios and his horses, and Dionysos (Herakles?), from the east pediment of the Parthenon, Acropolis, Athens, Greece, ca. 438–432 BCE. Marble, great-est height approx. 4′ 3″. British Museum, London.

5-47 Three goddesses (Hestia, Dione, and Aphrodite?), from the east pediment of the Parthenon, Acropolis, Athens, Greece, ca. 438–432 BCE. Marble, greatest height approx. 4′ 5″. British Museum, London.

who designed the composition even if his assistants executed it, discovered an entirely new way to deal with the awkward triangular frame of the pediment. Its bottom line is the horizon line, and charioteers and their horses move through it effortlessly. The individual figures, even the animals, are brilliantly characterized. The horses of the Sun, at the beginning of the day, are energetic. Those of the Moon or Night, having labored until dawn, are weary.

The reclining figures fill the space beneath the raking cornice beautifully. Dionysos/Herakles and Aphrodite in the lap of her mother Dione are monumental Olympian presences yet totally relaxed organic forms. The sculptors fully understood not only the surface appearance of human anatomy, both male and female, but also the mechanics of how muscles and bones make the body move. The Phidian school also mastered the rendition of clothed forms. In the Dione-Aphrodite group, the thin and heavy folds of the garments alternately reveal and conceal the main and lesser body masses while swirling in a compositional tide that subtly unifies the two figures. The articulation and integration of the bodies produce a wonderful variation of surface and play of light and shade.

ATHENIANS ON THE PARTHENON In many ways the most remarkable part of the Parthenon's sculptural program is the inner Ionic frieze (FIG. 5-48). Scholars still debate the subject of the frieze, but most agree that what is represented is the Panathenaic

5-48 Details of the Panathenaic Festival procession frieze, from the Parthenon, Acropolis, Athens, Greece, ca. 447–438 BCE. Marble, approx. 3′ 6″ high. Horsemen of north frieze *(top)*, British Museum, London; seated gods and goddesses (Poseidon, Apollo, Artemis, Aphrodite, and Eros) of east frieze *(center)*, Acropolis Museum, Athens; and elders and maidens of east frieze *(bottom)*, Louvre, Paris.

Festival procession that took place every four years in Athens. If this identification is correct, the Athenians judged themselves fit for inclusion in the temple's sculptural decoration. It is another example of the extraordinarily high opinion the Athenians had of their own worth.

The procession began at the Dipylon Gate, passed through the agora (marketplace), and ended on the Acropolis, where a new peplos was placed on an ancient wooden statue of Athena. That statue (probably similar in general appearance to the *Lady of Auxerre*, FIG. 5-7) was housed in the Archaic temple razed by the Persians. The statue had been removed from the Acropolis before the Persian attack for security reasons, and eventually it was installed in the Erechtheion (FIG. 5-51, no. 1). On the Parthenon frieze the procession begins on the west, that is, at the temple's rear, the side facing the gateway to the Acropolis. It then proceeds in parallel lines down the long north and south sides of the building and ends at the center of the east frieze, over the doorway to the cella housing Phidias's statue. It is noteworthy that the upper part of the relief is higher than the lower part so that the more distant and more shaded upper zone is as legible from the ground as the lower part of the frieze. This is another instance of the architects' taking optical effects into consideration.

The frieze vividly communicates the procession's acceleration and deceleration. At the outset, on the west side, marshals gather and youths mount their horses. On the north (FIG. 5-48, *top*) and south, the momentum picks up as the cavalcade moves from the lower town to the Acropolis, accompanied by chariots, musicians, jar carriers, and animals destined for sacrifice. On the east, seated gods and goddesses (FIG. 5-48, *center*), the invited guests, watch the procession slow almost to a halt (FIG. 5-48, *bottom*) as it nears its goal at the shrine of Athena's ancient wooden idol. Most remarkable of all is the role assigned to the Olympian deities. They do not take part in the festival or determine its outcome but are merely spectators. Aphrodite, in fact, extends her left arm to draw her son Eros's attention to the Athenians, just as today a parent at a parade would point out important people to a child. And the Athenian

people *were* important—self-important one might say. They were the masters of an empire, and in Pericles' famous funeral oration he painted a picture of Athens that elevated its citizens almost to the stature of gods. The Parthenon celebrated the greatness of Athens and the Athenians as much as it honored Athena.

PROPYLAIA: ACROPOLIS GATEWAY Even before all the sculpture was in place on the Parthenon, work began on a new monumental entrance to the Acropolis, the Propylaia (FIG. 5-49). The architect entrusted with this important commission was MNESIKLES. The site was a difficult one, on a steep slope, but Mnesikles succeeded in disguising the change in ground level by splitting the building into eastern and western sections (FIG. 5-41, no. 2), each one resembling a Doric temple facade. Practical considerations dictated that the space between the central pair of columns on each side be enlarged. This was the path the chariots and animals of the Panathenaic Festival procession took, and they required a wide ramped causeway. To either side of the central ramp were stairs for pedestrian traffic. Inside, tall, slender Ionic columns supported the split-level roof. Once again an Athenian architect mixed the two orders on the Acropolis. But as with the Parthenon, the Doric order was used for the stately exterior and the Ionic only for the interior. It would have been considered unseemly at this date to combine different kinds of columns on one facade. Later Greek architects were not as reticent (FIG. 5-77).

Mnesikles' full plan for the Propylaia was never executed because of a change in the fortunes of Athens after the outbreak of the Peloponnesian War in 431 BCE. Of the side wings that were part of the original project, only the northwest one was completed. That wing is of special importance in the history of art. In Roman times it housed a *pinakotheke* (picture gallery). In it were displayed paintings on wooden panels by some of the major artists of the fifth century BCE. It is uncertain whether or not this was the wing's original function. But if it was, the Propylaia's pinakotheke is the first recorded structure built for the specific purpose of displaying paintings, and it is the forerunner of modern museums.

5-49 MNESIKLES, Propylaia (view from the northeast), Acropolis, Athens, Greece, 437–432 BCE.

5-50 Erechtheion (view from the southeast), Acropolis, Athens, Greece, ca. 421–405 BCE.

ERECHTHEION: MULTIPLE SHRINE In 421 BCE work finally began on the temple that was to replace the Archaic Athena temple the Persians had razed. The new structure, the Erechtheion (FIGS. 5-50 and 5-51), built to the north of the old temple's remains, was, however, to be a multiple shrine. It honored Athena and housed the ancient wooden image of the goddess that was the goal of the Panathenaic Festival procession. But it also incorporated shrines to a host of other gods and demigods who loomed large in the city's legendary past. Among these were Erechtheus, an early king of Athens, during whose reign the ancient wooden idol of Athena was said to have fallen from the heavens, and Kekrops, another

0   25   50 FEET
0   5   10   15 METERS

1. Shrine housing wooden image of Athena
2. Athena's olive tree
3. Poseidon's trident mark
4. Ruins of Archaic temple

N

5-51 Plan of the Erechtheion, Acropolis, Athens, Greece, ca. 421–405 BCE.

king of Athens, who served as judge of the contest between Athena and Poseidon. In fact, the site chosen for the new temple was the very spot where that contest occurred. Poseidon had staked his claim to Athens by striking the Acropolis rock with his trident and producing a salt-water spring. The imprint of his trident remained for Athenians of the historical period to see. Nearby, Athena had miraculously caused an olive tree to grow. This tree still stood as a constant reminder of her victory over Poseidon.

The asymmetrical plan (FIG. 5-51) of the Ionic Erechtheion is unique for a Greek temple and the antithesis of the simple and harmoniously balanced plan of the Doric Parthenon across the way. Its irregular form reflected the need to incorporate the tomb of Kekrops and other preexisting shrines, the trident mark, and the olive tree into a single complex. The unknown architect responsible for the building also had to struggle with the problem of uneven terrain. The area could not be made level by terracing because that would disturb the ancient sacred sites. As a result, the Erechtheion not only has four sides of very different character, but each side also rests on a different ground level.

Perhaps to compensate for the awkward character of the building as a whole, the architect took great care with the Erechtheion's decorative details. The frieze, for example, was given special treatment. The stone chosen was the dark-blue limestone of Eleusis to contrast with the white Pentelic marble of the walls and columns. Marble relief figures were attached to this dark ground.

CLASSICAL CARYATIDS The temple's most striking and famous feature is its south porch, where caryatids (FIGS. 5-50 and 5-52) replaced Ionic columns, as they did a century earlier on the Ionic Siphnian Treasury at Delphi (FIG. 5-16). The Delphi caryatids resemble Archaic korai, and their Classical counterparts equally characteristically look like Phidian-era statues. Although they exhibit the weight shift that was standard for the fifth century, the role of the caryatids as architectural supports for the unusual flat roof is underscored by the vertical flutelike drapery folds concealing their stiff, weight-bearing legs. The Classical

5-52 Caryatid from the south porch of the Erechtheion, Acropolis, Athens, Greece, ca. 421–405 BCE. Marble, 7′ 7″ high. British Museum, London.

5-53 KALLIKRATES, Temple of Athena Nike (view from the northeast), Acropolis, Athens, Greece, ca. 427–424 BCE.

5-54 Nike adjusting her sandal, from the south side of the parapet of the Temple of Athena Nike, Acropolis, Athens, Greece, ca. 410 BCE. Marble, approx. 3′ 6″ high. Acropolis Museum, Athens.

architect-sculptor successfully balanced the dual and contradictory functions of these female statue-columns. The figures have enough rigidity to suggest the structural column and just the degree of flexibility needed to suggest the living body.

ATHENA, BRINGER OF VICTORY Another Ionic building on the Athenian Acropolis is the little Temple of Athena Nike (FIG. **5-53**), designed by Kallikrates, who worked with Iktinos on the Parthenon (and perhaps was responsible for the Ionic elements of that Doric temple). The temple is amphiprostyle with four columns on both the east and west facades. It stands on what used to be a Mycenaean bastion near the Propylaia and greets all visitors entering Athena's great sanctuary. As on the Parthenon, reference was made here to the victory over the Persians—and not just in the temple's name. Part of its frieze was devoted to a representation of the decisive battle at Marathon that turned the tide against the Persians—a human event, as in the Parthenon's Panathenaic Festival procession frieze. But now the sculptors chronicled a specific occasion, not a recurring event acted out by anonymous citizens.

Around the building, at the bastion's edge, a *parapet* was built about 410 BCE and decorated with exquisite reliefs. The theme of the balustrade matched that of the temple proper—Nike (Victory). Her image was repeated dozens of times, always in different attitudes, sometimes erecting trophies bedecked with Persian spoils and sometimes bringing forward sacrificial bulls to Athena. The most beautiful of the reliefs shows Nike adjusting her sandal (FIG. **5-54**)—an awkward posture rendered elegant and graceful

A Greek Woman in Her Father's Home: The Hegeso Stele

In Geometric times, huge amphoras and kraters (FIG. 5-1) marked the graves of wealthy Athenians. In the Archaic period, kouroi (FIGS. 5-8 and 5-10) and, to a lesser extent, korai were placed over Greek burials, as were grave stelae ornamented with relief depictions of the deceased. The grave stele of Hegeso (FIG. 5-55) is in this tradition. It was erected at the end of the fifth or beginning of the fourth century BCE to commemorate the death of Hegeso, daughter of Proxenos. Both names are inscribed on the cornice of the pediment that crowns the stele. Antae at left and right complete the architectural framework.

Hegeso is the well-dressed woman seated on an elegant chair (with footstool). She examines a piece of jewelry (once rendered in paint, not now visible) selected from a box a servant girl brings to her. The maid's simple ungirt chiton contrasts sharply with the more elaborate attire of her mistress. The garments of both women reveal the body forms beneath them. The faces are serene, without a trace of sadness. Indeed, both mistress and maid are shown in a characteristic shared moment out of daily life. Only the epitaph reveals that Hegeso is the one who has departed.

The simplicity of the scene on the Hegeso stele is deceptive, however. This is not merely a bittersweet scene of tranquil domestic life before an untimely death. The setting itself is significant—the secluded women's quarters of a Greek house, from which Hegeso rarely would have emerged. Contemporary grave stelae of men regularly show them in the public domain, as warriors. And the servant girl is not so much the faithful companion of the deceased in life as she is Hegeso's possession, like the jewelry box. The slave girl may look solicitously at her mistress, but Hegeso has eyes only for her ornaments. Both slave and jewelry attest to the wealth of Hegeso's father, unseen but prominently cited in the epitaph. (It is noteworthy that the mother's name is not mentioned.) Indeed, even the jewelry box carries a deeper significance, for it probably represents the dowry Proxenos would have provided to his daughter's husband when she left her father's home to enter her husband's home. In the patriarchal society of ancient Greece, the dominant position of men is manifest even when only women are depicted.

5-55 Grave stele of Hegeso, from the Dipylon cemetery, Athens, Greece, ca. 400 BCE. Marble, 5′ 2″ high. National Archaeological Museum, Athens.

by an anonymous master sculptor. The artist carried the style of the Parthenon pediments (FIG. 5-47) even further and created a figure whose garments cling so tightly to the body that they seem almost transparent, as if drenched with water. The sculptor was, however, interested in much more than revealing the supple beauty of the young female body. The drapery folds form intricate linear patterns unrelated to the body's anatomical structure and have a life of their own as abstract designs. Deep carving produced pockets of shade to contrast with the polished marble surface and enhance the ornamental beauty of the design.

REMEMBERING THE DEAD Although the decoration for the great building projects on the Acropolis must have occupied most of the finest sculptors of Athens in the second half of the fifth century BCE, other commissions were available in the city, notably in the Dipylon cemetery. There, around 400 BCE, a beautiful and touching grave stele (FIG. **5-55**) in the style of the Temple of Athena Nike parapet reliefs was set up in memory of a woman named Hegeso. Its subject—a young woman in her home, attended by her maid (see "A Greek Woman in Her Father's Home," above)—and its composition have close parallels in contemporary vase painting.

Painting

POLYCHROMY IN VASE PAINTING Art historians know from ancient accounts that in the Classical period some of the most renowned artists were the painters of monumental wooden panels displayed in public buildings, both secular and religious. Such works are by nature perishable, and all of the great panels of the masters are unfortunately lost. Nonetheless, one can get some idea of the polychrome nature of those panel paintings by studying Greek vases such as the *lekythos* (plural *lekythoi;* flasks containing perfumed oil) painted by the so-called ACHILLES PAINTER

5-56 ACHILLES PAINTER, *Warrior taking leave of his wife* (Attic white-ground lekythos), from Eretria, Greece, ca. 440 BCE. Approx. 1′ 5″ high. National Archaeological Museum, Athens.

of white-ground painting were explored almost exclusively on lekythoi, which were commonly placed in Greek graves as offerings to the deceased. For such vessels designed for short-term use, the fragile nature of the white-ground technique was of little concern.

The Achilles Painter's lekythos is decorated with a scene appropriate for its funerary purpose. A youthful warrior takes leave of his wife. The red scarf, mirror, and jug hanging on the wall behind the woman indicate that the setting is the interior of their home. The motif of the seated woman is strikingly similar to that of Hegeso on her grave stele (FIG. 5-55), but here the woman is the survivor. It is her husband, preparing to go to war with helmet, shield, and spear, who will depart, never to return. On his shield is a large painted eye, roughly life-size. Greek shields often were decorated with devices such as the horrific face of Medusa, intended to ward off evil spirits and frighten the enemy. This eye undoubtedly was meant to recall this tradition, but it was little more than an excuse for the Achilles Painter to display superior drawing skills. Since the late sixth century BCE, Greek painters had abandoned the Archaic habit of placing frontal eyes on profile faces and attempted to render the eyes in profile. The Achilles Painter's mastery of this difficult problem in foreshortening is on exhibit here.

POLYGNOTOS'S REVOLUTION The leading painter of the first half of the fifth century BCE was POLYGNOTOS OF THASOS, whose works adorned important buildings both in Athens and Delphi. One of these was the pinakotheke of Mnesikles' Propylaia, but the most famous was a portico in the Athenian marketplace that came to be called the Stoa Poikile (Painted Stoa). Descriptions of Polygnotos's paintings make clear that he introduced a revolutionary compositional style, rejecting the scheme used on all the Greek vases examined thus far. Before Polygnotos, figures stood on a common ground line at the bottom of the picture plane, whether they appeared in horizontal bands or single panels. Polygnotos placed his figures on different levels, staggered in tiers in the manner of Ashurbanipal's lion hunt relief (see FIG. 2-24) of two centuries before. He also incorporated landscape elements into his paintings, making his pictures true "windows onto the world" and not simply surface designs peopled with foreshortened figures. The abandonment of a single ground line by Polygnotos and his followers was as momentous a break from the past as the rejection of frontality in statuary by Early Classical Greek sculptors.

HUBRIS AND MASSACRE One can visualize Polygnotos's compositions by looking at a red-figure krater (FIG. 5-57) painted around the middle of the fifth century BCE by the NIOBID PAINTER. The painter, whose vases are unsigned, was given this modern nickname from this krater, where one side is devoted to the massacre of the Niobids, the children of Niobe. Niobe, who had at least a dozen children, had boasted that she was superior to the goddess Leto, who had only two offspring, Apollo and Artemis. To punish her *hubris* (arrogance) and teach the lesson that no mortal could be superior to a god or goddess, Leto sent her two children to slay all of Niobe's many sons and daughters. On the Niobid Painter's krater, the influence of Polygnotos is clear. The horrible slaughter occurs in a schematic landscape setting of rocks and trees. The figures are disposed on several levels, and they actively interact with their setting. One slain son, for example, not only has fallen upon a rocky outcropping but is partially hidden by it. The Niobid Painter also drew his face in a three-quarter view, something that even Euphronios and Euthymides had not attempted.

(FIG. **5-56**) about 440 BCE. The artist here employed the *white-ground* technique, which takes its name from the chalky-white slip used to provide a background for the painted figures. Experiments with white-ground painting date back to the Andokides Painter, but the method became popular only toward the middle of the fifth century BCE.

White-ground is essentially a variation of the red-figure technique. First the painter covered the pot with a slip of very fine white clay, then applied black glaze to outline the figures, and diluted brown, purple, red, and white to color them. Other colors—for example, the yellow chosen for the garments of both figures on our lekythos—also could be employed, but these had to be applied after firing because the Greeks did not know how to make them withstand the heat of the kiln. Despite the obvious attractions of the white-ground technique, the impermanence of the expanded range of colors discouraged its use for everyday vessels, such as drinking cups and kraters. In fact, the full polychrome possibilities

5-57 Niobid Painter, *Artemis and Apollo slaying the children of Niobe* (Attic red-figure calyx krater), from Orvieto, Italy, ca. 450 BCE. Approx. 1′ 9″ high. Louvre, Paris.

5-58 Phiale Painter, *Hermes bringing the infant Dionysos to Papposilenos* (Attic white-ground calyx krater), from Vulci, Italy, ca. 440–435 BCE. Approx. 1′ 2″ high. Vatican Museums, Rome.

WHITE-GROUND LANDSCAPES Further insight into the appearance of monumental panel painting of the fifth century BCE comes from a white-ground krater (FIG. **5-58**) by the so-called Phiale Painter. The subject is Hermes handing over his half brother, the infant Dionysos, to Papposilenos ("grandpa-satyr"). The other figures represent the nymphs in the shady glens of Nysa, where Zeus had sent Dionysos, one of his numerous natural sons, to be raised, safe from the possible wrath of his wife Hera. Unlike the decorators of funerary lekythoi, the Phiale Painter used for this krater only colors that could survive the heat of a Greek kiln— reds, brown, purple, and a special snowy white reserved for the flesh of the nymphs and for such details as the hair, beard, and shaggy body of Papposilenos. The use of diluted brown wash to color and shade the rocks may reflect the coloration of Polygnotos's landscapes. This vase and the Niobid krater together provide art

historians with a shadowy idea of the character and magnificence of Polygnotos's great paintings.

A PLUNGE INTO THE NETHERWORLD Although all of the panel paintings of the masters were lost long ago, some Greek mural paintings are preserved today. An early example is in the so-called Tomb of the Diver at Paestum in southern Italy. The four walls of this small, coffinlike tomb are decorated with banquet scenes such as appear regularly on Greek vases. On the tomb's ceiling (FIG. **5-59**), a youth dives from a stone platform into a body of water. The scene most likely symbolizes the plunge from this life into the next. Trees resembling those of the Niobid krater are included within the decorative frame. The theme has no parallels on extant Greek vases, but it appears on an Etruscan tomb wall of the late sixth century BCE (see FIG. 9-9). The Greek

5-59 Youth diving, painted ceiling of the Tomb of the Diver, Paestum, Italy, ca. 480 BCE. Approx. 3′ 4″ high. Museo Archeologico Nazionale, Paestum.

painter of the Tomb of the Diver seems to have been as aware of developments in Etruscan painting in Italy as of the work of contemporaries in mainland Greece.

THE LATE CLASSICAL PERIOD

THE RISE OF MACEDON The Peloponnesian War, which began in 431 BCE, ended in 404 BCE with the complete defeat of a plague-weakened Athens, and left Greece drained of its strength. The victor, Sparta, and then Thebes undertook the leadership of Greece, both unsuccessfully. In the middle of the fourth century, a threat from without caused the rival Greek states to put aside their animosities and unite for their common defense, as they had earlier against the Persians. But at the battle of Chaeronea in 338 BCE, the Greek cities suffered a devastating loss and had to relinquish their independence to Philip II, king of Macedon. Philip was assassinated in 336, and his son, Alexander III, better known simply as Alexander the Great, succeeded him. In the decade before his death in 323 BCE, Alexander led a powerful army on an extraordinary campaign that overthrew the Persian Empire (the ultimate revenge for the Persian invasion of Greece in the early fifth century), wrested control of Egypt, and even reached India.

NEW DIRECTIONS IN ART The fourth century BCE was thus a time of political upheaval in Greece, and the chaos had a profound impact on the psyche of the Greeks and on the art they produced. In the fifth century BCE, Greeks had generally believed that rational human beings could impose order on their environment, create "perfect" statues such as the *Canon* of Polykleitos, and discover the "correct" mathematical formulas for constructing temples such as the Parthenon. The Parthenon frieze celebrated the Athenians as a community of citizens with shared values. The Peloponnesian War and the unceasing strife of the fourth century BCE brought an end to the serene idealism of the fifth century. Disillusionment and alienation followed. Greek thought and Greek art began to focus more on the individual and on the real world of appearances rather than on the community and the ideal world of perfect beings and perfect buildings.

Sculpture

HUMANIZING THE GODS The new approach to art is immediately apparent in the work of PRAXITELES, one of the great masters of the fourth century BCE. Praxiteles did not reject the themes favored by the sculptors of the High Classical period. His Olympian gods and goddesses retained their superhuman beauty, but in his hands they lost some of their solemn grandeur and took on a worldly sensuousness.

Nowhere is this new humanizing spirit plainer than in the statue of Aphrodite (FIG. **5-60**) that Praxiteles sold to the Knidians after another city had rejected it. The lost original, carved from Parian marble, is known only through copies of Roman date, but Pliny considered it "superior to all the works, not only of Praxiteles, but indeed in the whole world." It made Knidos famous, and many people sailed there just to see the statue in its round temple (compare FIG. 5-71), where "it was possible to view the image of the goddess from every side." According to Pliny, some visitors were "overcome with love for the statue."[6]

The *Aphrodite of Knidos* caused such a sensation in its time because Praxiteles took the unprecedented step of representing the

5-60 PRAXITELES, *Aphrodite of Knidos*. Roman copy after an original of ca. 350–340 BCE. Approx. 6′ 8″ high. Vatican Museums, Rome.

goddess of love completely nude. Female nudity was rare in earlier Greek art and had been confined almost exclusively to paintings on vases designed for household use, such as the kylix of Onesimos (FIG. 5-23) discussed earlier. The women so depicted also tended to be courtesans or slave girls, not noblewomen or goddesses, and no one had dared fashion for a temple a statue of a goddess without her clothes. Moreover, Praxiteles' Aphrodite is not a cold and remote image. In fact, the goddess engages in a trivial act out of everyday life. She has removed her garment, draped it over a large *hydria* (water pitcher), and is about to step into the bath. The motif is strikingly similar to the one Onesimos painted.

DEWY EYES Although shocking in its day, the *Aphrodite of Knidos* is not openly erotic (the goddess modestly shields her pelvis with her right hand), but she is quite sensuous. Lucian, writing in the second century CE, noted that she has a "welcoming look" and a "slight smile" and that Praxiteles was renowned for his ability to transform marble into soft and radiant flesh. Lucian mentions, for example, the "dewy quality of Aphrodite's eyes."[7] Unfortunately, the rather mechanical Roman copies do not

5-61 Head of a woman, from Chios, Greece, ca. 320–300 BCE. Marble, approx. 1′ 2″ high. Museum of Fine Arts, Boston.

5-62 PRAXITELES, Hermes and the infant Dionysos, from the Temple of Hera, Olympia, Greece. Copy after an original of ca. 340 BCE, approx. 7′ 1″ high. Archaeological Museum, Olympia.

capture the quality of Praxiteles' modeling of the stone, but one can imagine the "look" of the *Aphrodite of Knidos* from original works by sculptors who emulated the master's manner.

One of the finest of these is the head of a woman from Chios (FIG. **5-61**) that was once set into a draped statue. This sculptor wielded the chisel in the Praxitelean manner, suggesting the softness of the young girl's face and the "dewy" gaze of the eyes. The sharp outlining of precisely measured body parts that characterized the work of Polykleitos and his contemporaries gave way to a smooth flow of flesh from forehead to chin, and to a very human sensuousness. In the statues of Praxiteles and his followers, the deities of Mount Olympus still possess a beauty mortals can aspire to, although not achieve, but they are no longer awesome and remote. Praxiteles' gods have stepped off their fifth-century pedestals and entered the fourth-century world of human experience.

SENSUOUS LANGUOR The Praxitelean manner also may be seen in a statue once thought to be by the hand of the master himself but now generally considered a copy of the highest quality. The statue of Hermes and the infant Dionysos (FIG. **5-62**) found in the Temple of Hera at Olympia brings to the realm of monumental statuary the theme the Phiale Painter had chosen for a white-ground krater (FIG. **5-58**) a century earlier. Hermes has stopped to rest in a forest on his journey to Nysa to entrust the upbringing of Dionysos to Papposilenos and the nymphs. Hermes leans on a tree trunk (here it is an integral part of the composition and not the copyist's addition), and his slender body forms a sinuous, shallow S-curve that is the hallmark of many of Praxiteles' statues. He looks off dreamily into space while he dangles a bunch of grapes (now missing) as a temptation for the

infant, who is to become the Greek god of the vine. This is the kind of tender and very human interaction between an adult and a child that one encounters frequently in real life but that had been absent from Greek statuary before the fourth century.

The superb quality of the carving appears to be faithful to the Praxitelean original. The modeling is deliberately smooth and subtle, producing soft shadows that follow the planes as they flow almost imperceptibly one into another. The delicacy of the marble facial features stands in sharp contrast to the metallic precision of Polykleitos's bronze *Doryphoros* (FIG. 5-38). Even the *Spear Bearer*'s locks of hair were subjected to the fifth-century sculptor's laws of symmetry and do not violate the skull's perfect curve. One need only compare these two statues to see how broad a change in artistic attitude and intent took place from the mid-fifth to the mid-fourth century BCE. Sensuous languor and an order of beauty that appeals more to the eye than to the mind replaced majestic strength and rationalizing design.

THE PASSION OF SKOPAS In the Archaic period and throughout most of the Early and High Classical periods, Greek sculptors generally shared common goals, but in the Late Classical period of the fourth century BCE, distinctive individual styles emerged. The dreamy, beautiful divinities of Praxiteles had enormous appeal, and, as the head of the woman from Chios (FIG. 5-61) attests, the master had many followers. But other sculptors pursued very different interests. One of these was SKOPAS OF PAROS, and although his work reflects the general trend toward the humanization of the Greek gods and heroes, his hallmark is intense emotionalism.

Skopas was an architect as well as a sculptor. He designed the Temple of Athena Alea at Tegea. Fragments of the pedimental statues from that temple are preserved, and they epitomize Skopas's approach to sculpture, even if they are not by his own hand. One of the heads (FIG. **5-63**) portrays a hero wearing a lion-skin headdress. It must be either Herakles or his son Telephos, whose battle with Achilles was the subject of the west pediment. The head, like others from the Tegea pediments, is highly dramatic. The hero turns abruptly, and his facial expression shows great psychological tension. His large eyes are set deeply into his head. Fleshy overhanging brows create deep shadows. His lips are slightly parted. The passionate face reveals an anguished soul within. Skopas's work broke with the Classical tradition of benign, serene features and prefigured later Hellenistic depictions of unbridled emotion.

DEATH AND IRONY An unprecedented psychological intensity also may be seen in a grave stele (FIG. **5-64**) found near the Ilissos River in Athens. The stele was originally set into an architectural frame similar to that of the earlier Hegeso stele (FIG. 5-55). A comparison between the two works is very telling. In the Ilissos stele the relief is much higher, with parts of the figures carved fully in the round. But the major difference is the pronounced change in mood, which reflects the innovations of Skopas. The later work makes a clear distinction between the living and the dead, and depicts overt mourning. The deceased is a young hunter whose features recall those of Skopas's Tegean heroes. At his feet a small boy, either his servant or perhaps a younger brother, sobs openly. The hunter's dog also droops its head in sorrow. Beside the youth an old man, undoubtedly his father, leans on a walking stick and, in a gesture reminiscent of that of the Olympia seer (FIG. 5-31), ponders the irony of fate that has taken the life of his powerful son and preserved him in his frail old age. Most remarkable of all, the hunter himself looks out at the viewer, inviting sympathy and creating an emotional bridge between the spectator and the artwork that was inconceivable in the art of the High Classical period.

LYSIPPOS AND A NEW CANON The third great Late Classical sculptor, LYSIPPOS of Sikyon, was so renowned that Alexander the Great selected him to create his official portrait. (Alexander could afford to employ the best. The Macedonian kingdom enjoyed vast wealth. King Philip hired the leading thinker of his age, Aristotle, as the young Alexander's tutor!)

Lysippos introduced a new canon of proportions in which the bodies were more slender than those of Polykleitos—whose own canon continued to exert enormous influence—and the heads roughly one-eighth the height of the body rather than one-seventh, as in the previous century. The new proportions may be seen in one of Lysippos's most famous works, a bronze statue of an *apoxyomenos* (an athlete scraping oil from his body after exercising),

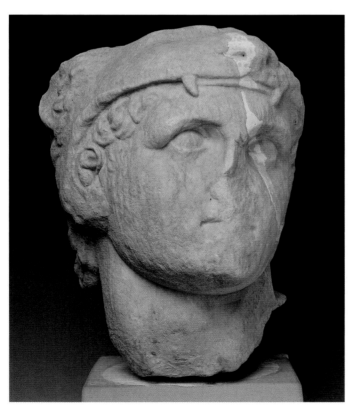

5-63 Head of Herakles or Telephos, from the west pediment of the Temple of Athena Alea, Tegea, Greece, ca. 340 BCE. Marble, approx. 1′ $\frac{1}{2}$″ high. (Stolen from) Archaeological Museum, Tegea.

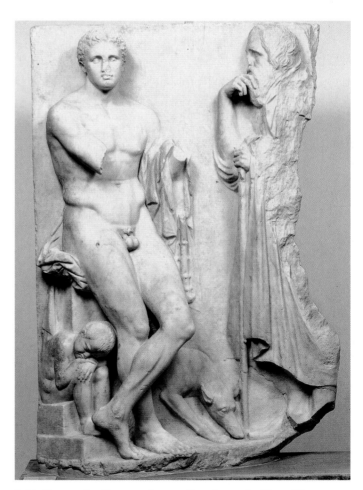

5-64 Grave stele of a young hunter, found near the Ilissos River, Athens, Greece, ca. 340–330 BCE. Marble, approx. 5′ 6″ high. National Archaeological Museum, Athens.

known, as usual, only from Roman copies in marble (FIG. 5-65). A comparison with Polykleitos's *Doryphoros* (FIG. 5-38) reveals more than a change in physique. A nervous energy runs through Lysippos's *Apoxyomenos* that one seeks in vain in the balanced form of the *Doryphoros*. The strigil (scraper) is about to reach the end of the right arm, and at any moment the athlete will switch it to the other hand so that he can scrape his left arm. At the same time, he will shift his weight and reverse the positions of his legs. Lysippos also began to break down the dominance of the frontal view in statuary and encouraged the observer to look at his athlete from multiple angles. Because Lysippos represented the apoxyomenos with his right arm boldly thrust forward, the figure breaks out of the shallow rectangular box that defined the boundaries of earlier statues. To comprehend the action, the observer must move to the side and view Lysippos's work at a three-quarter angle or in full profile.

COLOSSAL FATIGUE To grasp the full meaning of another work of Lysippos, a colossal statue (FIG. 5-66) depicting a weary Herakles, the viewer must walk around it. Once again, the original

is lost. The most impressive of the surviving marble copies is nearly twice life-size and was exhibited in the Baths of Caracalla in Rome (see FIGS. 10-67 and 10-68). Like the marble copy of Polykleitos's *Doryphoros* (FIG. 5-38) from the Roman palaestra at Pompeii, Lysippos's muscle-bound Greek hero provided inspiration for Romans who came to the baths to exercise. (The statue is signed by the copyist, GLYKON OF ATHENS. Lysippos's name is not mentioned. The educated Roman public did not need a label to identify the famous work.) In the hands of Lysippos, however, the exaggerated muscular development of Herakles is poignantly ironic, for the sculptor depicted the strongman as so weary that he must lean on his club for support. Without that prop Herakles would topple over. Lysippos and other fourth-century BCE artists rejected stability and balance as worthy goals for statuary.

Herakles holds the golden apples of the Hesperides in his right hand behind his back—unseen unless one walks around the statue. Lysippos's subject is thus the same as that of the metope (FIG. 5-32) of the Early Classical Temple of Zeus at Olympia, but the fourth-century BCE Herakles is no longer

5-65 LYSIPPOS, *Apoxyomenos (Scraper)*. Roman copy after a bronze original of ca. 330 BCE, approx. 6′ 9″ high. Vatican Museums, Rome.

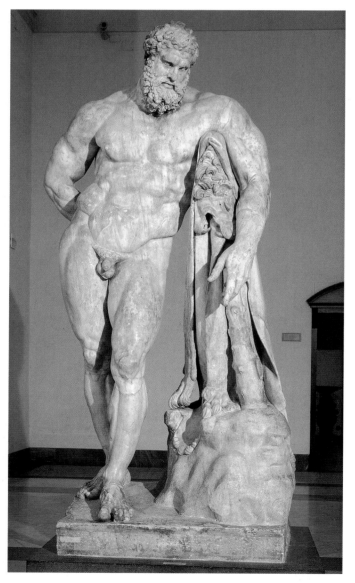

5-66 LYSIPPOS, Weary Herakles (*Farnese Herakles*). Roman copy from Rome, Italy, signed by GLYKON OF ATHENS, after a bronze original of ca. 320 BCE. Approx. 10′ 5″ high. Museo Nazionale, Naples.

serene. Instead of expressing joy, or at least satisfaction, at having completed one of the impossible 12 labors (see "Herakles," page 109), he is almost dejected. Exhausted by his physical efforts, he can think only of his pain and weariness, not of the reward of immortality that awaits him. Lysippos's portrayal of Herakles in this statue is perhaps the most eloquent testimony yet to Late Classical sculptors' interest in humanizing the great gods and heroes of the Greeks. In this respect, despite their divergent styles, Praxiteles, Skopas, and Lysippos followed a common path.

Alexander the Great and Macedonian Court Art

ALEXANDER AS EPIC HERO Alexander the Great's favorite book was the *Iliad,* and his own life was very much like an epic saga, full of heroic battles, exotic places, and unceasing drama. Alexander was a man of singular character, an inspired leader with boundless energy and an almost foolhardy courage. He personally led his army into battle on the back of Bucephalus, the wild and mighty steed only he could tame and ride.

Ancient sources reveal that Alexander believed that only Lysippos had captured his essence in a portrait, and that is why only he was authorized to sculpt the king's image. Lysippos's most famous portrait of the Macedonian king was a full-length heroically nude bronze statue of Alexander holding a lance and turning his head toward the sky. Plutarch reported that an epigram was inscribed on the base stating that the statue depicted Alexander gazing at Zeus and proclaiming, "I place the earth under my sway; you, O Zeus, keep Olympus." Plutarch further stated that the portrait was characterized by "leonine" hair and a "melting glance."[8]

The Lysippan original is lost, and because Alexander was portrayed so many times for centuries after his death, it is very difficult to determine which of the many surviving images is most faithful to the fourth-century BCE portrait. A leading candidate is a second-century BCE marble head (FIG. **5-67**) from Pella, the capital of Macedonia and Alexander's birthplace. It has the sharp turn of the head and thick mane of hair that were key ingredients of Lysippos's portrait. The sculptor's treatment of the features also is consistent with the style of the later fourth century. The deep-set eyes and parted lips recall the manner of Skopas, and the delicate handling of the flesh brings to mind the faces of Praxitelean statues. Although not a copy, this head very likely approximates the young king's official portrait and provides insight into Alexander's personality as well as the art of Lysippos.

MACEDONIAN OPULENCE Alexander's palace has not been excavated, but one can form an idea of the sumptuousness of life at the Macedonian court from the costly objects found in Macedonian graves and from the abundance of mosaics (see "Mosaics," Chapter 11, page 315) uncovered at Pella in the homes of the wealthy. The Pella mosaics are *pebble mosaics*. The floors are formed of small stones of various colors collected from beaches and riverbanks and set into a thick coat of cement. The finest pebble mosaic yet to come to light has a stag hunt (FIG. **5-68**) as its *emblema* (central framed panel), bordered in turn by an intricate floral pattern and a stylized wave motif (not shown in our detail). The artist signed his work in the same manner as proud Greek vase painters and potters did: "Gnosis made it." This is the earliest mosaicist's signature known, and its prominence in the design undoubtedly attests to the artist's reputation. The house owner wanted guests to know that Gnosis himself, and not an imitator, had laid this floor.

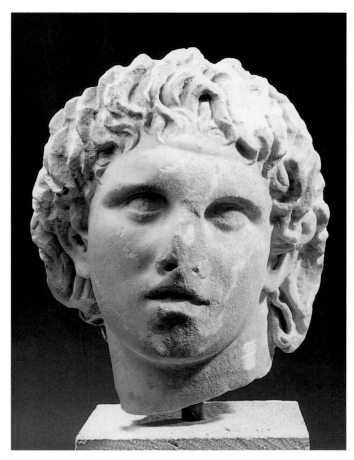

5-67 Head of Alexander the Great, from Pella, Greece, ca. 200–150 BCE. Marble, approx. 1′ high. Archaeological Museum, Pella.

5-68 GNOSIS, Stag hunt, from Pella, Greece, ca. 300 BCE. Pebble mosaic, figural panel 10′ 2″ high. Archaeological Museum, Pella.

The Pella stag hunt, with its light figures against a dark ground, has much in common with red-figure painting. In the pebble mosaic, however, thin strips of lead or terracotta define most of the contour lines and some of the interior details. Subtle gradations of yellow, brown, and red, as well as black, white, and gray pebbles suggest the interior volumes. The musculature of the hunters, and even their billowing cloaks and the animals' bodies, are modeled by shading. Such use of light and dark to suggest volume is rarely seen on Greek painted vases, although examples do exist. Monumental painters, however, commonly used shading. The Greek term for shading was *skiagraphia* (literally, "shadow painting"), and it was said to have been invented by an Athenian painter of the fifth century BCE named APOLLODOROS. Gnosis's emblema, with its sparse landscape setting, probably reflects contemporary panel painting.

ALEXANDER HUMILIATES DARIUS A mosaic that decorated the floor of one room of a lavishly appointed Roman house at Pompeii gives an even better idea of monumental painting during Alexander's time. In the *Alexander Mosaic* (FIG. **5-69**), the mosaicist employed *tesserae* (tiny stones or pieces of glass cut to the desired size and shape) instead of pebbles (see "Mosaics," Chapter 11, page 315). The subject is a great battle between the armies of Alexander the Great and the Persian king Darius III, probably the battle of Issus in southeastern Turkey, when Darius fled the battlefield in his chariot in humiliating defeat. The mosaic dates to the late second or early first century BCE. It is widely believed to be a reasonably faithful copy of *Battle of Issus,* a famous panel painting of ca. 310 BCE made by PHILOXENOS OF ERETRIA for King Cassander, one of Alexander's successors.

Philoxenos's painting is notable for its technical mastery of problems that had long fascinated Greek painters. Even Euthymides would have marveled at the fourth-century painter's depiction of the rearing horse seen in a three-quarter rear view below Darius. The subtle modulation of the horse's rump through shading in browns and yellows is precisely what Gnosis was striving to imitate in his pebble mosaic. Other details are even more impressive. The Persian to the right of the rearing horse has fallen to the ground and raises, backwards, a dropped Macedonian shield to protect himself from being trampled. Philoxenos recorded the reflection of the man's terrified face on the polished surface of the shield. Everywhere in the scene, men, animals, and weapons cast shadows on the ground. Philoxenos and other Classical painters' interest in the reflection of insubstantial light on a shiny surface, and in the absence of light (shadows), was far removed from earlier painters' preoccupation with the clear presentation of weighty figures seen against a blank background. The Greek painter here truly opened a window into a world filled not only with figures, trees, and sky but also with light. This Classical Greek notion of what a painting should be characterizes most of the history of art in the Western world from the Renaissance on.

Most impressive about *Battle of Issus,* however, is not the virtuoso details but the psychological intensity of the drama unfolding before the viewer's eyes. Alexander is on horseback leading his army into battle, recklessly one might say, without even a helmet to protect him. He drives his spear through one of Darius's trusted "Immortals," who were sworn to guard the king's life, while the Persian's horse collapses beneath him. The Macedonian king is only a few yards away from Darius, and Alexander directs his gaze at the Persian king, not at the man impaled on his now-useless spear. Darius has called for retreat. In fact, his charioteer is already whipping the horses and speeding the king to safety. Before he escapes, Darius looks back at Alexander and in a pathetic gesture reaches out toward his brash foe. But the victory has

5-69 PHILOXENOS OF ERETRIA, *Battle of Issus,* ca. 310 BCE. Roman copy *(Alexander Mosaic)* from the House of the Faun, Pompeii, Italy, late second or early first century BCE. Tessera mosaic, approx. 8′ 10″ × 16′ 9″. Museo Nazionale, Naples.

slipped out of his hands. Pliny says Philoxenos's painting of the battle between Alexander and Darius was "inferior to none."[9] It is easy to see how he reached that conclusion.

Architecture

A WONDROUS MAUSOLEUM Five of the Seven Wonders of the ancient world were Greek (see "Babylon: City of Wonders," Chapter 2, page 49), but only one Greek Wonder was a tomb. The tomb built at Halikarnassos for Mausolos, the ruler of Caria in Asia Minor from 377 to 353 BCE, was the only funerary monument the ancients considered worthy of comparison with the pyramids of Egypt (see FIG. 3-8), the solitary Egyptian Wonder. Mausolos's wife, Artemisia, erected the tomb and employed some of the leading sculptors of the day, Skopas among them, to decorate it.

Mausolos's tomb was dismantled long ago, but ancient descriptions have encouraged numerous scholars to attempt a reconstruction. None has won wide acceptance. Nonetheless, the building can be visualized in general terms. It was a multistory structure consisting of a high stepped podium, an Ionic colonnade, and a pyramidal roof capped by a colossal marble group of Mausolos in a four-horse chariot. The height of the tomb, including the chariot, was 140 feet. The fame of the Halikarnassos Wonder was so great that already in Roman times *mausoleum* had become a generic term for any grandiose funerary monument. But the tomb, famous as it was, was only one of the triumphs of Greek architects in the fourth century BCE.

GREEK THEATERS In ancient Greece, plays were not performed repeatedly over months or years as they are today, but only once, during sacred festivals. Greek drama was closely associated with religious rites and was not pure entertainment. At Athens in the fifth century BCE, for example, the great tragedies of Aeschylus, Sophocles, and Euripides were performed at the Dionysos festival in the theater dedicated to the god on the southern slope of the Acropolis (FIG. 5-40, far right). The finest theater in Greece, however, is at Epidauros (FIG. 5-70). It was constructed shortly after Alexander the Great was born. The architect was POLYKLEITOS THE YOUNGER, possibly a nephew of the great fifth-century sculptor. His theater is still used for performances of ancient Greek dramas.

The precursor of the formal Greek theater was a place where ancient rites, songs, and dances were performed. This circular piece of earth with a hard and level surface later became the orchestra of the theater. *Orchestra* literally means "dancing place." The actors and the chorus performed there, and at Epidauros an altar to Dionysos stood at the center of the circle. The spectators sat on a slope overlooking the orchestra—the *theatron,* or "place for seeing." When the Greek theater took architectural shape, the auditorium (*cavea,* Latin for "hollow place, cavity") was always situated on a hillside. The cavea at Epidauros, composed of wedge-shaped sections (*cunei,* singular *cuneus*) of stone benches separated by stairs, is somewhat greater than a semicircle in plan. The auditorium is 387 feet in diameter, and its 55 rows of seats accommodated about 12,000 spectators. They entered the theater via a passageway between the seating area and the scene building *(skene),* which housed dressing rooms for the actors and also formed a backdrop for the plays. The design is simple but perfectly suited to its function. Even in antiquity the Epidauros theater was renowned for the harmony of its proportions. Although spectators sitting in some of the seats would have had a poor view of the skene, all had unobstructed views of the orchestra. Because of the open-air cavea's excellent acoustics, everyone could hear the actors and chorus.

CORINTHIAN CAPITALS The theater at Epidauros is situated some 500 yards southeast of the sanctuary of Asklepios, and Polykleitos the Younger worked there as well. He was the architect

5-70 POLYKLEITOS THE YOUNGER, Theater, Epidauros, Greece, ca. 350 BCE.

The Corinthian Capital

The Corinthian capital (FIG. 5-72) is more ornate than either the Doric or Ionic (see "Doric and Ionic Temples," pages 116–117). It consists of a double row of acanthus leaves, from which tendrils and flowers emerge, wrapped around a bell-shaped echinus. Although this capital often is cited as the distinguishing feature of the Corinthian order, strictly speaking no Corinthian order exists. The new capital type was simply substituted for the volute capital in the Ionic order.

The sculptor KALLIMACHOS invented the Corinthian capital during the second half of the fifth century BCE. Vitruvius recorded the circumstances that supposedly led to its creation:

> A maiden who was a citizen of Corinth . . . died. After her funeral, her nurse collected the goblets in which the maiden had taken delight while she was alive, and after putting them together in a basket, she took them to the grave monument and put them on top of it. In order that they should remain in place for a long time, she covered them with a tile. Now it happened that this basket was placed over the root of an acanthus. As time went on the acanthus root, pressed down in the middle by the weight, sent forth, when it was about springtime, leaves and stalks; its stalks growing up along the sides of the basket and being pressed out from the angles because of the weight of the tile, were forced to form volute-like curves at their extremities. At this point, Kallimachos happened to be going by and noticed the basket with this gentle growth of leaves around it. Delighted with the order and the novelty of the form, he made columns using it as his model and established a canon of proportions for it.[1]

Kallimachos worked on the Acropolis. He made the golden lamp that stood beside the ancient wooden statue of Athena in the Erechtheion. Many scholars believe that a Corinthian column supported the outstretched right hand of the Phidian *Athena Parthenos* (FIG. 5-44) because some of the Roman copies of the lost statue have such a column. In any case, the earliest preserved Corinthian capital dates to the time of Kallimachos. The new type was, however, rarely used before the mid-fourth century BCE and did not become popular until Hellenistic and especially Roman times. Later architects favored the Corinthian capital because of its ornate character and because it eliminated certain problems of both the Doric and Ionic orders.

The Ionic capital, unlike the Doric, has two distinct profiles— the front and back (with the volutes) and the sides. The volutes always faced outward on a Greek temple, but architects met with a vexing problem at the corners of their buildings, which had two adjacent "fronts." They solved the problem by placing volutes on both outer faces of the corner capitals (as on the Erechtheion, FIG. 5-50, and the Temple of Athena Nike, FIG. 5-53), but the solution was an awkward one.

Doric design rules also presented problems for Greek architects at the corners of buildings. The Doric frieze was organized according to three supposedly inflexible rules: (1) A triglyph must be exactly over the center of each column; (2) a triglyph must be over the center of each *intercolumniation* (the space between two columns); and (3) triglyphs at the corners of the frieze must meet so that no space is left over. But the rules are contradictory. If the corner triglyphs must meet, then they cannot be placed over the center of the corner column (see, for example, the Doric temples at Aegina and Paestum and the Parthenon in Athens, FIGS. 5-24, 5-29, and 5-42).

The Corinthian capital eliminated both problems. Because the capital's four sides have a similar appearance, corner Corinthian capitals do not have to be modified, as do corner Ionic capitals. And because the Ionic frieze is used for the Corinthian "order," architects do not have to contend with metopes or triglyphs.

[1] Vitruvius, *De architectura*, 4.1.8–10. Translated by J. J. Pollitt, *The Art of Ancient Greece: Sources and Documents* (New York: Cambridge University Press, 1990), 193–94.

5-71 THEODOROS OF PHOKAIA, Tholos, Delphi, Greece, ca. 375 BCE.

of the *tholos,* the circular shrine that probably housed the sacred snakes of the healing god. That building lies in ruins today, its architectural fragments removed to the local museum, but one can get an approximate idea of its original appearance by looking at the somewhat earlier and partially reconstructed tholos at Delphi (FIG. 5-71) that THEODOROS OF PHOKAIA designed. Both tholoi had an exterior colonnade of Doric columns. Inside, however, both the Delphi and Epidauros columns (FIG. 5-72) were crowned by *Corinthian capitals* (see "The Corinthian Capital," above), an innovation of the second half of the fifth century BCE.

Consistent with the extremely conservative nature of Greek temple design, architects did not readily embrace the Corinthian capital. Until the second century BCE, Corinthian capitals were employed, as at Delphi and Epidauros, only for the interiors of sacred buildings. The earliest instance of a Corinthian capital on the exterior of a Greek building is the Choragic Monument of Lysikrates (FIG. 5-73), which is not really a building at all. Lysikrates had sponsored a chorus in a theatrical contest in 334, and, after he won, he erected a monument to commemorate his

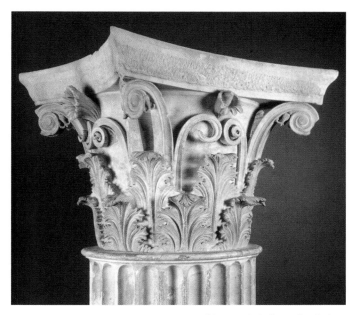

5-72 POLYKLEITOS THE YOUNGER, Corinthian capital, from the tholos, Epidauros, Greece, ca. 350 BCE. Archaeological Museum, Epidauros.

5-73 Choragic Monument of Lysikrates, Athens, Greece, 334 BCE.

victory. The monument consists of a cylindrical drum resembling a tholos on a rectangular base. Engaged Corinthian columns adorn the drum of Lysikrates' monument, and a huge Corinthian capital sits on top of the roof. The freestanding capital once supported the victor's prize, a bronze tripod.

THE HELLENISTIC PERIOD

AFTER ALEXANDER Alexander the Great's conquest of the Near East and Egypt (where the Macedonian king was buried) ushered in a new cultural age that historians and art historians alike call *Hellenistic*. The Hellenistic period is traditionally reckoned from the death of Alexander in 323 BCE, and lasted nearly three centuries, until 31 BCE, when Queen Cleopatra of Egypt and her Roman consort Mark Antony were decisively defeated at the battle of Actium by Antony's rival Augustus. A year later, Augustus made Egypt a province of the Roman Empire. It is said that when Alexander was on his deathbed, his generals, greedy for the lands their young leader had conquered, asked, "To which one of us do you leave your empire?" He supposedly answered, "To the strongest."[10] Although probably a later invention, this exchange points out the near inevitability of what followed—the division of Alexander's far-flung empire among his Greek generals and their subsequent naturalization among those they subjugated.

The cultural centers of the Hellenistic period were the court cities of the Greek kings—Antioch in Syria, Alexandria in Egypt, Pergamon in Asia Minor, and others (MAP 5-1). An international culture united the Hellenistic world, and its language was Greek. Hellenistic kings became enormously rich on the spoils of the East, priding themselves on their libraries, art collections, scientific enterprises, and skills as critics and connoisseurs, as well as on the learned men they could assemble at their courts. The world of the small, austere, and heroic city-state passed away, as did the power and prestige of its center, Athens. A cosmopolitan ("citizen of the world," in Greek) civilization, much like today's, replaced it.

Architecture

BREAKING OLD RULES The greater variety, complexity, and sophistication of Hellenistic culture called for an architecture on an imperial scale and of wide diversity, something far beyond the requirements of the Classical polis, even beyond that of Athens at the height of its power. Building activity shifted from the old centers on the Greek mainland to the opulent cities of the Hellenistic monarchs in Asia Minor—sites more central to the Hellenistic world.

Great scale, a theatrical element of surprise, and a willingness to break the rules of canonical temple design characterize one of the most ambitious temple projects of the Hellenistic period, the Temple of Apollo at Didyma. The Hellenistic temple was built to replace the Archaic temple at the site the Persians had burned down in 494 BCE when they sacked nearby Miletos. Construction began in 313 BCE according to the design of two architects who were natives of the area, PAIONIOS OF EPHESOS and DAPHNIS OF MILETOS. So vast was the undertaking, however, that work on the temple continued off and on for more than 500 years—and still the project was never completed.

5-74 PAIONIOS OF EPHESOS and DAPHNIS OF MILETOS, Temple of Apollo, Didyma, Turkey, begun 313 BCE. Plan *(left)* and aerial view *(right)*.

The temple was dipteral in plan (FIG. **5-74,** *left*) and had an unusually broad facade of 10 huge Ionic columns almost 65 feet tall. The sides had 21 columns, consistent with the Classical formula for perfect proportions used for the Parthenon—21 = (2 × 10) + 1—but nothing else about the design is Classical. One anomaly immediately apparent to anyone who approached the building was that it had no pediment and no roof—it was *hypaethral,* or open to the sky. And the grand doorway to what should be the temple's cella was elevated nearly five feet off the ground so that it could not be entered. The explanation for these peculiarities is that the doorway served rather as a kind of stage where the oracle of Apollo could be announced to those assembled in front of the temple. The unroofed dipteral colonnade was really only an elaborate frame for a central courtyard (FIG. **5-74,** *right*) that housed a small prostyle shrine that protected a statue of Apollo. Entrance to the interior court was through two smaller doorways to the left and right of the great portal and down two narrow vaulted tunnels that could accommodate only a single file of people. From these dark and mysterious lateral passageways worshipers emerged into the clear light of the courtyard, which contained a sacred spring and was planted with laurel trees in honor of Apollo. Opposite Apollo's inner temple, a stairway some 50 feet wide rose majestically toward three portals leading into the oracular room that also opened onto the front of the temple. This complex spatial planning marked a sharp departure from Classical Greek architecture, which stressed a building's exterior almost as a work of sculpture and left its interior relatively undeveloped.

THE IDEAL CITY When the Persians were finally expelled from Asia Minor in 479 BCE, the Greek cities there were in near ruin. Reconstruction of Miletos began after 466 BCE, according to a plan laid out by HIPPODAMOS OF MILETOS, whom Aristotle

singled out as the father of rational city planning. Hippodamos imposed a strict grid plan on the site, regardless of the terrain, so that all streets met at right angles. Such *orthogonal* planning actually predates Hippodamos, not only in Archaic Greece but also in the ancient Near East and Egypt. But Hippodamos was so famous that his name has ever since been synonymous with such urban plans. The so-called *Hippodamian plan* also designated separate quarters for public, private, and religious functions. A "Hippodamian city" was logically as well as regularly planned. This desire to impose order on nature and to assign a proper place in the whole to each of the city's constituent parts was very much in keeping with the philosophical tenets of the fifth century BCE. Hippodamos's formula for the ideal city was another manifestation of the same outlook that produced Polykleitos's *Canon* for the human body and Iktinos's treatise on the Parthenon.

Hippodamian planning was still the norm in Late Classical and Hellenistic Greece. The city of Priene (FIG. **5-75**), also in Asia Minor, was laid out during the fourth century BCE. It had fewer than 5,000 inhabitants (Hippodamos thought 10,000 was the ideal number). Situated on sloping ground, many of its narrow north-south streets were little more than long stairways. Uniformly sized city blocks, the standard planning unit, were nonetheless imposed on the irregular terrain. The central agora (marketplace) was allotted six blocks. More than one unit also was reserved for major structures such as the Temple of Athena and the theater.

LIFE IN A GREEK HOME As in any city, ancient or modern, houses rather than civic or religious buildings occupied most of the area within Priene's walls. Information about the homes of ordinary citizens is scanty, in part because archaeologists have been more interested in uncovering grand edifices, such as

5-75 Model of the city of Priene, Turkey, fourth century BCE and later. Staatliche Museen, Berlin.

temples and theaters, and in part because ancient authors usually described only exceptional buildings, not common dwellings. The unpretentious Priene houses (for example, FIG. **5-76**) were typical of later Greek times. They were rectangular in plan and fit neatly into the Hippodamian grid, but internally they were not laid out symmetrically. A single entrance from the street led to a modest central court, the largest room in the house, surrounded by several smaller roofed units. In the wealthiest homes, the courtyard was framed by a peristyle and paved with a pebble mosaic. The house illustrated here has columns (of differing dimensions) on only two sides of the court. Exterior windows were rare, because most houses shared walls with their neighbors, and the court provided welcome light and air to the interior. These

5-76 Plan of House XXXII, Priene, Turkey, fourth century BCE. ⊙

courtyards also allowed the collection of rainwater, stored in underground cisterns and used for drinking, cooking, and washing. In most houses a dining room *(andron)* opened onto the court (or onto an anteroom that in turn opened onto the court, as in our example). It was furnished with couches so that the man of the house and his male guests could recline while eating. A kitchen would not be far away. Bedrooms also might open onto the court, but, when a second floor existed, they were normally located upstairs.

PHILOSOPHERS AND STOAS The heart of Priene was its agora, bordered by *stoas*. These covered colonnades, or *porticos*, which often housed shops and civic offices, were ideal vehicles for shaping urban spaces, and they were staples of Hellenistic cities. Even the agora of Athens, an ancient city notable for its haphazard, unplanned development, was eventually framed to the east and south by stoas placed at right angles to one another. These new porticos joined the famous Painted Stoa (see page 143), where the Hellenistic philosopher Zeno and his successors taught. The *Stoic* school of Greek philosophy took its name from that building.

The finest of the new Athenian stoas was the Stoa of Attalos II (FIG. **5-77**), a gift to the city by a grateful alumnus, the king of Pergamon, who had studied at Athens in his youth. The stoa was meticulously reconstructed under the direction of the American School of Classical Studies at Athens and today has a second life as a museum housing more than seven decades of finds from the Athenian agora, as well as the offices of the American excavation team. The stoa has two stories, each with 21 shops opening onto the colonnade. The facade columns are Doric on the ground level and Ionic on the second story. Such mixing of the two orders on a single facade had occurred even in the Late Classical period. But it became increasingly common in the Hellenistic period, when

5-77 Stoa of Attalos II, Agora, Athens, Greece, ca. 150 BCE (Acropolis in the background).

respect for the old rules of Greek architecture was greatly diminished and a desire for variety and decorative effects often prevailed. Practical considerations also governed the form of the Stoa of Attalos. The columns are far more widely spaced than in Greek temple architecture, to allow for easy access. And the builders left the lower third of every Doric column shaft unfluted to guard against damage from constant traffic.

Pergamon

A HELLENISTIC ACROPOLIS Pergamon, the kingdom of Attalos II (r. 159–138 BCE), was one of those born in the early third century BCE after the breakup of Alexander's empire. Founded by Philetairos, the Pergamene kingdom embraced almost all of western and southern Asia Minor. Upon the death in 133 BCE of its last king, Attalos III (r. 138–133 BCE), Pergamon was

bequeathed to Rome, which by then was the greatest power in the Mediterranean world. The Attalids enjoyed immense wealth, and much of it was expended on embellishing their capital city, especially its acropolis. Located there were the royal palace, an arsenal and barracks, a great library and theater, an agora, and the sacred precincts of Athena and Zeus. The Altar of Zeus, erected about 175 BCE, is the most famous of all Hellenistic sculptural ensembles. The monument's west front (FIG. 5-78) has been reconstructed in Berlin. The altar proper was on an elevated platform and framed by an Ionic stoalike colonnade with projecting wings on either side of a broad central staircase.

A GIGANTIC STRUGGLE All around the altar platform was a sculpted frieze almost 400 feet long, populated by about a hundred larger-than-life-size figures. The subject is the battle of Zeus and the gods against the giants. It is the most extensive representation Greek artists ever attempted of that epic conflict for

5-78 Reconstructed west front of the Altar of Zeus, from Pergamon, Turkey, ca. 175 BCE. Staatliche Museen, Berlin.

5-79 Athena battling Alkyoneos, detail of the gigantomachy frieze, from the Altar of Zeus, Pergamon, Turkey, ca. 175 BCE. Marble, approx. 7′ 6″ high. Staatliche Museen, Berlin.

control of the world. A similar subject appeared on the shield of Phidias's *Athena Parthenos* and on some of the Parthenon metopes, where the Athenians wished to draw a parallel between the defeat of the giants and the defeat of the Persians. In the third century, King Attalos I (r. 241–197 BCE) had successfully turned back an invasion by the Gauls in Asia Minor. The gigantomachy of the Altar of Zeus alluded to the Pergamene victory over those barbarians.

A deliberate connection was also made with Athens, whose earlier defeat of the Persians was by then legendary, and with the Parthenon, which already was recognized as a Classical monument—in both senses of the word. The figure of Athena, for example, who grabs the hair of the giant Alkyoneos as Nike flies in to crown her (FIG. **5-79**), is a quotation of the Athena from the Parthenon's east pediment. Zeus himself (not illustrated) was based on the Poseidon of the west pediment. But the Pergamene frieze is not a dry series of borrowed motifs. On the contrary, its tumultuous narrative has an emotional intensity that has no parallel in earlier monuments. The battle rages everywhere, even up and down the very steps one must ascend to reach Zeus's altar (FIG. 5-78). Violent movement, swirling draperies, and vivid depictions of death and suffering are the norm. Wounded figures writhe in pain, and their faces reveal their anguish. When Zeus hurls his thunderbolt, one can almost hear the thunderclap. Deep carving creates dark shadows. The figures project from the background like bursts of light. These features have been justly termed "baroque" and reappear in 17th-century European sculpture (see

Chapter 24). One can hardly imagine a greater contrast than between the Pergamene gigantomachy frieze and that of the Archaic Siphnian Treasury at Delphi (FIG. 5-17).

NOBILITY IN DEFEAT On the Altar of Zeus, the victory of Attalos I over the Gauls was presented in mythological disguise. An earlier statuary group set up on Pergamon's acropolis explicitly represented the defeat of the barbarians. Roman copies of some of these figures survive. The sculptor carefully studied and reproduced the distinctive features of the foreign Gauls, most notably their long, bushy hair and mustaches and the *torques* (neck bands) they frequently wore. The Pergamene victors were apparently not included in the group. The viewer saw only their foes and their noble and moving response to defeat.

In what was probably the centerpiece of the Attalid group, a heroic Gallic chieftain (FIG. **5-80**) defiantly drives a sword into his own chest just below the collarbone, preferring suicide to surrender. He already has taken the life of his wife, who, if captured, would have been sold as a slave. In the best Lysippan tradition, the group can be fully appreciated only by walking around it. From one side, the observer sees the Gaul's intensely expressive face, from another his powerful body, and from a third the woman's limp and almost lifeless body. The man's twisting posture, the almost theatrical gestures, and the emotional intensity of the suicidal act are hallmarks of the Pergamene baroque style and were closely paralleled in the later frieze of Zeus's altar.

The third Gaul from this group is a trumpeter (FIG. **5-81**) who collapses upon his large oval shield as blood pours out of the gash in his chest. He stares at the ground with a pained expression on his face. The Hellenistic figure is reminiscent of the dying warrior from the east pediment of the Temple of Aphaia at Aegina (FIG. 5-28), but the pathos and drama of the suffering Gaul are far more pronounced. As in the suicide group and the gigantomachy frieze, the sculptor rendered the male musculature in an exaggerated manner. Note the tautness of the chest and the bulging veins of the left leg—implying that the unseen Attalid hero who has struck down this noble and savage foe must have been an extraordinary man. If this figure is the *tubicen* (trumpeter) Pliny mentioned as the work of the Pergamene master EPIGONOS, then Epigonos may be the sculptor of the entire group and the creator of the dynamic Hellenistic baroque style.

Sculpture

VICTORY IN A FOUNTAIN One of the masterpieces of the Hellenistic baroque style was not created for the Attalid kings but was set up in the Sanctuary of the Great Gods on the island of Samothrace. The *Nike of Samothrace* (FIG. **5-82**) has just alighted on the prow of a Greek warship. Her missing right arm was once raised high to crown the naval victor. (Compare Nike placing a wreath on Athena on the Altar of Zeus, FIG. 5-79). But the Pergamene relief figure seems calm by comparison. The Samothracian Nike's wings still beat, and the wind sweeps her drapery. Her himation bunches in thick folds around her right leg, and her chiton is pulled tightly across her abdomen and left leg. The statue's setting amplified its theatrical effect. The war galley was displayed in the upper basin of a two-tiered fountain. In the lower basin were large boulders. The fountain's flowing water created the illusion of rushing waves dashing up against the prow of the ship. The statue's reflection in the shimmering water below accentuated the sense of lightness and movement. The sound of splashing water added an aural dimension to the visual drama. Art and nature were here combined in one of

5-80 EPIGONOS(?), Gallic chieftain killing himself and his wife. Roman copy after a bronze original from Pergamon, Turkey, ca. 230–220 BCE, approx. 6′ 11″ high. Museo Nazionale Romano— Palazzo Altemps, Rome.

5-81 EPIGONOS(?), Dying Gaul. Roman copy after a bronze original from Pergamon, Turkey, ca. 230–220 BCE, approx. 3′ $\frac{1}{2}$″ high. Museo Capitolino, Rome.

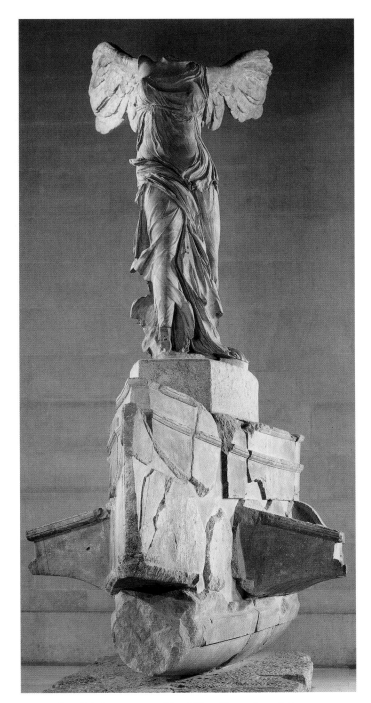

5-82 Nike alighting on a warship *(Nike of Samothrace)*, from Samothrace, Greece, ca. 190 BCE. Marble, figure approx. 8′ 1″ high. Louvre, Paris.

5-83 ALEXANDROS OF ANTIOCH-ON-THE-MEANDER, Aphrodite *(Venus de Milo)*, from Melos, Greece, ca. 150–125 BCE. Marble, approx. 6′ 7″ high. Louvre, Paris.

the most successful sculptures ever fashioned. In the *Nike of Samothrace* and other works in the Hellenistic baroque manner, sculptors resoundingly rejected the Polykleitan conception of a statue as an ideally proportioned, self-contained entity on a bare pedestal. The Hellenistic statues interact with their environment and appear as living, breathing, and intensely emotive human (or divine) presences.

HELLENISTIC EROTICISM In different ways, Praxiteles, Skopas, and Lysippos had already taken bold steps in redefining the nature of Greek statuary. Their distinctive styles continued to influence sculptors throughout the Hellenistic period. The undressing of Aphrodite, for example, became the norm, but Hellenistic sculptors went beyond Praxiteles and openly explored the eroticism of the

nude female form. The famous *Venus de Milo* (FIG. **5-83**) is a larger-than-life-size marble statue of Aphrodite found on Melos together with its inscribed base (now lost) signed by the sculptor, ALEXANDROS OF ANTIOCH-ON-THE-MEANDER. In this statue, the goddess of love is more modestly draped than the *Aphrodite of Knidos* (FIG. 5-60) but more overtly sexual. Her left hand (separately preserved) holds the apple Paris awarded her when he judged her as the most beautiful goddess of all. Her right hand may have lightly grasped the edge of her drapery near the left hip in a halfhearted attempt to keep it from slipping farther down her body. The sculptor intentionally designed the work to tease the spectator. By so doing he imbued his partially draped Aphrodite with a sexuality that is not present in Praxiteles' entirely nude image of the goddess.

5-84 Aphrodite, Eros, and Pan, from Delos, Greece, ca. 100 BCE. Marble, 4′ 4″ high. National Archaeological Museum, Athens.

5-85 Sleeping satyr (Barberini Faun), from Rome, Italy, ca. 230–200 BCE. Marble, approx. 7′ 1″ high. Glyptothek, Munich.

APHRODITE ATTACKED The *Aphrodite of Knidos* was directly quoted in an even more playful and irreverent statue of the goddess (FIG. **5-84**) found on Delos. Here, Aphrodite resists the lecherous advances of the semihuman, semigoat Pan, the Greek god of the woods. She defends herself with one of her sandals, while her loyal son Eros flies in to grab one of Pan's horns in an attempt to protect his mother from an unspeakable fate. One may wonder about the taste of Dionysios of Berytos (Beirut), who paid to have this statue erected in a businessmen's clubhouse—especially since both Aphrodite and Eros are portrayed as almost laughing—but such groups were commonplace in Hellenistic times. The combination of eroticism and parody of earlier Greek masterpieces was apparently irresistible. These Hellenistic groups are a far cry from the solemn depictions of the deities of Mount Olympus produced during Classical times.

Also different from earlier periods is the way Eros was represented. In the Hellenistic age he was shown as the pudgy infant Cupid as portrayed in innumerable later artworks, whereas in earlier Greek art he was depicted as an adolescent (FIG. 5-48, *center*). In the history of art, babies are all too frequently rendered as miniature adults—often with adult personalities to match their mature bodies. Hellenistic sculptors knew how to reproduce the soft forms of infants and how to portray the spirit of young children in memorable statues.

SLEEP AND INTOXICATION Archaic statues smile at their viewers, and even when Classical statues look away from the viewer they are always awake and alert. Hellenistic sculptors often portrayed sleep. The suspension of consciousness and the entrance into the fantasy world of dreams—the antithesis of the Classical ideals of rationality and discipline—had great appeal for them. This newfound interest can be seen in a statue of a drunken, restlessly sleeping *satyr* (a semihuman follower of Dionysos) known as the *Barberini Faun* (FIG. **5-85**). The statue was found in Rome in the 17th century and restored (not entirely accurately) by Gianlorenzo Bernini, the great Italian Baroque sculptor (see Chapter 24). Bernini no doubt felt that this dynamic statue in the Pergamene manner was the work of a kindred spirit. The satyr has consumed too much wine and has thrown down his panther skin on a convenient rock and then fallen into a disturbed, intoxicated sleep. His brows are furrowed, and one can almost hear him snore.

Eroticism also comes to the fore in this statue. Although men had been represented naked in Greek art for hundreds of years, Archaic kouroi and Classical athletes and gods do not exude sexuality. Sensuality surfaced in the works of Praxiteles in the fourth century BCE. But the dreamy and supremely beautiful Hermes playfully dangling grapes before the infant Dionysos (FIG. 5-62) has nothing of the blatant sexuality of the *Barberini Faun*, whose wantonly spread legs focus attention on his genitals. Homosexuality was common in the man's world of ancient Greece. (In Plato's *Symposium*, Alcibiades refers to Socrates' almost superhuman ability to resist seduction.) It is not surprising that when Hellenistic sculptors began to explore the sexuality of the human body, they turned their attention to both men and women.

A BATTERED BOXER Although Hellenistic sculptors tackled an expanded range of subjects, they did not abandon such traditional themes as the Greek athlete. But they often rendered the old subjects in novel ways. This is certainly true of the magnificent bronze statue of a seated boxer (FIG. **5-86**), a Hellenistic original

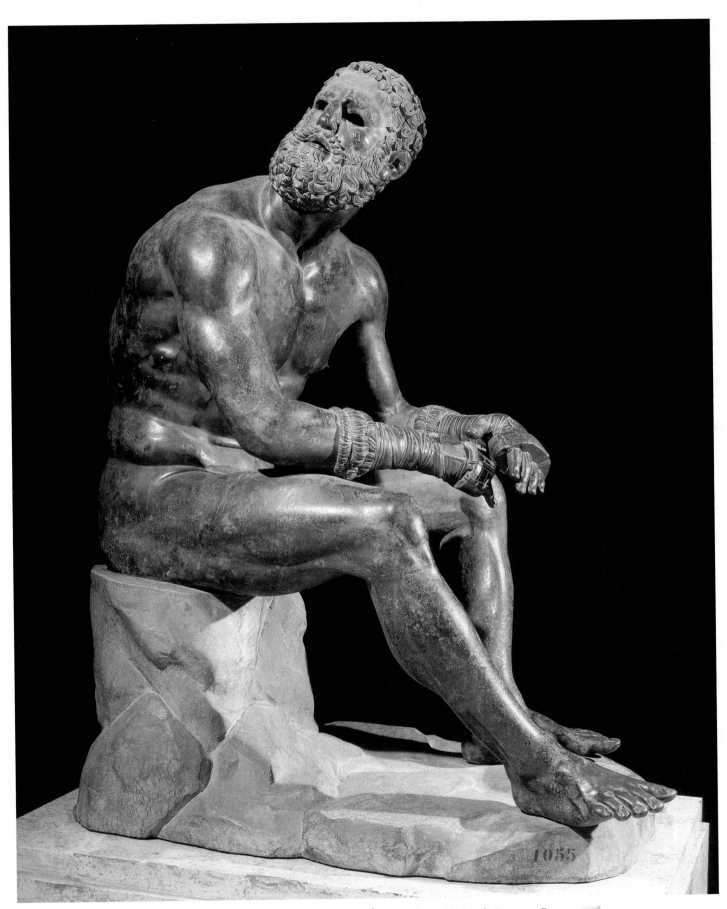

5-86 Seated boxer, from Rome, Italy, ca. 100–50 BCE. Bronze, approx. 4′ 2½″ high. Museo Nazionale Romano, Rome.

found in Rome and perhaps at one time part of a group. The boxer is not a victorious young athlete with a perfect face and body but a heavily battered, defeated veteran whose upward gaze may have been directed at the man who had just beaten him. Too many punches from powerful hands wrapped in leather thongs — Greek boxers did not use the modern sport's cushioned gloves — have distorted the boxer's face. His nose is broken, as are his teeth. He has smashed "cauliflower" ears. Inlaid copper blood drips from the cuts on his forehead, nose, and cheeks. How different is this rendition of a powerful bearded man from that of the noble warrior from Riace (see FIGS. 5-34 and Intro-17) of the Early Classical period! The Hellenistic sculptor appealed not to the intellect but to the emotions when striving to evoke compassion for the pounded hulk of a once-mighty fighter.

THE AGED AND THE UGLY The realistic bent of much of Hellenistic sculpture — the very opposite of the Classical period's idealism — is evident above all in a series of statues of old men and women from the lowest rungs of the social order. Shepherds, fishermen, and drunken beggars are common — the kinds of people who were pictured earlier on red-figure vases but never before were thought worthy of monumental statuary. One of the finest preserved statues of this type (FIG. **5-87**) depicts a haggard old woman bringing chickens and a basket of fruits and vegetables to sell in the market. Her face is wrinkled, her body bent with age,

and her spirit broken by a lifetime of poverty. She carries on because she must, not because she derives any pleasure from life. No one knows the purpose of such statues, but they attest to an interest in social realism absent in earlier Greek statuary.

Statues of the aged and the ugly are, of course, the polar opposites of the images of the young and the beautiful that dominated Greek art until the Hellenistic age, but they are consistent with the period's changed character. The Hellenistic world was a cosmopolitan place, and the highborn could not help but encounter the poor and a growing number of foreigners (non-Greek "barbarians") on a daily basis. Hellenistic art reflects this different social climate in the depiction of a much wider variety

5-88 POLYEUKTOS, Demosthenes. Roman copy after a bronze original of ca. 280 BCE. 6′ 7½″ high. Ny Carlsberg Glyptotek, Copenhagen.

5-87 Old market woman, ca. 150–100 BCE. Marble, approx. 4′ ½″ high. Metropolitan Museum of Art, New York.

of physical types, including different ethnic types. The sensitive portrayal of Gallic warriors with their shaggy hair, strange mustaches, and golden torques (FIGS. 5-80 and 5-81) has already been noted. Africans, Scythians, and others, formerly only the occasional subject of vase painters, also entered the realm of monumental sculpture in Hellenistic art.

STRONG SPIRIT, WEAK BODY These sculptures of foreigners and the urban poor, however realistic, are not portraits. Rather, they are sensitive studies of physical types. But the growing interest in the individual beginning in the Late Classical period did lead in the Hellenistic era to the production of true likenesses of specific persons. In fact, one of the great achievements of Hellenistic artists was the redefinition of portraiture. In the Classical period, Kresilas was admired for having made the noble Pericles appear even nobler in his portrait (FIG. 5-39). But in Hellenistic times sculptors sought not only to record the actual appearance of their subjects in bronze and stone but also to capture the essence of their personalities in likenesses that were at once accurate and moving.

One of the earliest of these, perhaps the finest of the Hellenistic age and frequently copied in Roman times, was a bronze portrait statue of Demosthenes (FIG. 5-88) by POLYEUKTOS. The original was set up in the Athenian agora in 280 BCE, 42 years after the great orator's death. Demosthenes was a frail man and in his youth even suffered from a speech impediment, but he had enormous courage and great moral conviction. A veteran of the disastrous battle against Philip II at Chaeronea, he repeatedly tried to rally opposition to Macedonian imperialism, both before and after Alexander's death. In the end, when it was clear the Macedonians would capture him, he took his own life by drinking poison.

Polyeuktos rejected Kresilas's and Lysippos's notions of the purpose of portraiture and did not attempt to portray a supremely confident leader with a magnificent physique. His Demosthenes has an aged and slightly stooped body. Demosthenes clasps his hands nervously in front of him as he looks downward, deep in thought. His face is lined, his hair is receding, and his expression is one of great sadness. Whatever physical discomfort Demosthenes felt is here joined by an inner pain, his deep sorrow over the tragic demise of democracy at the hands of the Macedonian conquerors.

Hellenistic Art under Roman Patronage

ROME IN GREECE In the opening years of the second century BCE, the Roman general Flamininus defeated the Macedonian army and declared the old poleis of Classical Greece as free once again. They never regained their former glory, however. Greece became a Roman province in 146 BCE. When, 60 years later, Athens sided with King Mithridates VI of Pontus (r. 120–63 BCE) in his war against Rome, the general Sulla crushed the Athenians. Thereafter, Athens retained some of its earlier prestige as a center of culture and learning, but politically Athens was just another city in the ever-expanding Roman Empire. Nonetheless, Greek artists continued to be in great demand, both to furnish the Romans with an endless stream of copies of Classical and Hellenistic masterpieces and to create new statues *à la grecque* for Roman patrons.

LAOCOÖN'S AGONY One such work is the famous group of the Trojan priest Laocoön and his sons (FIG. 5-89), which was unearthed in Rome in 1506 in the presence of the great Italian

5-89 ATHANADOROS, HAGESANDROS, and POLYDOROS OF RHODES, Laocoön and his sons, from Rome, Italy, early first century CE. Marble, approx. 7′ 10½″ high. Vatican Museums, Rome.

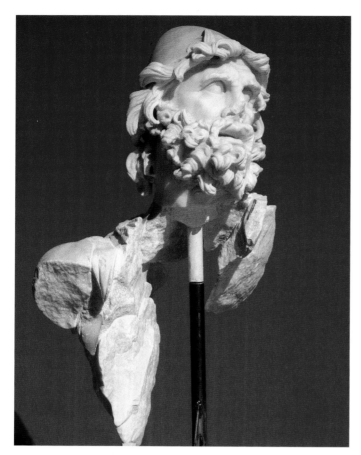

5-90 Athanadoros, Hagesandros, and Polydoros of Rhodes, Odysseus, from Sperlonga, Italy, early first century CE. Marble, full figure approx. 7' high. Museo Archeologico, Sperlonga.

Pergamon, and Laocoön himself is strikingly similar to Alkyoneos (FIG. 5-79), Athena's opponent. In fact, many scholars believe that a Pergamene statuary group of the second century BCE was the inspiration for the three Rhodian sculptors.

HOMER AT SPERLONGA That the work seen by Pliny and displayed in the Vatican Museums today was made for Romans rather than Greeks was confirmed in 1957 by the discovery of fragments of several Hellenistic-style groups illustrating scenes from Homer's *Odyssey*. These fragments were found in a grotto that served as the picturesque summer banquet hall of the seaside villa of the Roman emperor Tiberius (r. 14–37 CE) at Sperlonga, some 60 miles south of Rome. One of these groups—depicting the monster Scylla attacking Odysseus's ship—is signed by the same three sculptors Pliny cited as the creators of the Laocoön group. Another of the groups, installed around a central pool in the grotto, depicted the blinding of the Cyclops Polyphemos by Odysseus and his comrades, an incident also set in a cave in the Homeric epic. The figure of Odysseus (FIG. **5-90**) from this theatrical group is one of the finest sculptures of antiquity. The hero's cap can barely contain his swirling locks of hair. Even Odysseus's beard seems to be swept up in the emotional intensity of the moment. The parted lips and the deep shadows produced by sharp undercutting add drama to the head, which was attached to an agitated body. At Tiberius's villa in Sperlonga and in Titus's palace in Rome, the baroque school of Hellenistic sculpture lived on long after Greece ceased to be a political force.

CONCLUSION

The earliest monumental art and architecture in Greece appeared shortly after the founding of a Greek trading post in the Nile delta, and Egypt provided models for the Greeks' earliest stone sculptures and columnar temples. But in time, the Greeks rejected the Egyptian-inspired Archaic style and revolutionized the history of art.

Greek painters formulated a new way of depicting human figures in space, and Greek sculptors introduced contrapposto into their statues. In the mid-fifth century BCE, Polykleitos developed his *Canon*, a formula for the perfect statue, in the belief that harmonious proportions produced beauty. Similarly, Iktinos and Kallikrates applied numerical ratios to the parts of buildings and constructed their ideal temple, the Parthenon.

In the aftermath of the Peloponnesian War, however, while still adhering to the philosophy that humanity was the "measure of all things," Greek artists began to focus more on the real world of appearances than on the ideal world of perfect beings. Late Classical and Hellenistic sculptors humanized the gods of Mount Olympus and expanded the range of subjects for monumental art to encompass the old, ugly, and foreign, as well as the young, beautiful, and Greek.

By the second century BCE, Greece had come under the sway of the Romans, and when Rome inherited the Pergamene kingdom from the last of the Attalids in 133 BCE, it also became heir to the Greek artistic legacy. What Rome adopted from Greece it passed on to the medieval and modern worlds. If Greece was peculiarly the inventor of the European spirit, Rome was its propagator and amplifier.

Renaissance artist Michelangelo. The marble group, long believed an original of the second century BCE, was found in the remains of the palace of the emperor Titus (r. 79–81 CE), exactly where Pliny had seen it more than 14 centuries before. Pliny attributed the statue to three sculptors—ATHANADOROS, HAGESANDROS, and POLYDOROS OF RHODES—who are now generally thought to have worked in the early first century CE. They probably based their group on a Hellenistic masterpiece depicting Laocoön and only one son. Their variation on the original added the son at Laocoön's left (note the greater compositional integration of the two other figures) to conform with the Roman poet Vergil's account in the *Aeneid*. Vergil vividly described the strangling of Laocoön and his *two* sons by sea serpents while sacrificing at an altar. The gods who favored the Greeks in the war against Troy had sent the serpents to punish Laocoön, who had tried to warn his compatriots about the danger of bringing the Greeks' wooden horse within the walls of their city.

In Vergil's graphic account, Laocoön suffered in terrible agony, and the torment of the priest and his sons is communicated in a spectacular fashion in the marble group. The three Trojans writhe in pain as they struggle to free themselves from the death grip of the serpents. One bites into Laocoön's left hip as the priest lets out a ferocious cry. The serpent-entwined figures recall the suffering giants of the great frieze of the Altar of Zeus at

900 BCE

GEOMETRIC

First Olympic Games, 776 BCE

Homer, active ca. 750–700 BCE

[1]

700 BCE

ORIENTALIZING

Greek trading post established at Naukratis, Egypt, ca. 650–630 BCE

Draco formulates first written law code for Athens, 621 BCE

[1] Dipylon krater, Athens, ca. 740 BCE

600 BCE

ARCHAIC

Sappho, active ca. 600 BCE

Aeschylus, 525–456 BCE

Democratic reforms of Kleisthenes, 507 BCE

[2] Persian Wars, 490–479 BCE

Sophocles, 496–406 BCE

Pericles, 490–429 BCE

Herodotus, ca. 485–425 BCE

Euripides, 485–406 BCE

480 BCE

EARLY CLASSICAL (SEVERE)

Persians sack Athenian Acropolis, 480 BCE

Socrates, 469–399 BCE

Delian League treasury transferred to Athens, 454 BCE

[2] Kroisos, kouros from Anavysos, ca. 530 BCE

450 BCE

HIGH CLASSICAL

[3] Peloponnesian War, 431–404 BCE

Plato, 429–347 BCE

400 BCE

LATE CLASSICAL

Aristotle, 384–322 BCE

Alexander the Great, r. 336–323 BCE

Battle of Issus, 333 BCE

[3] Parthenon, Acropolis, Athens, 447–438 BCE

323 BCE

HELLENISTIC

Greece becomes a Roman province, 146 BCE

[4] Attalos III wills Pergamene kingdom to Rome, 133 BCE

Sulla sacks Athens, 86 BCE

31 BCE

Battle of Actium, 31 BCE

[4] Altar of Zeus, Pergamon, ca. 175 BCE

Interior of chaitya hall, Karle, India, ca. 100 CE.

6

PATHS TO ENLIGHTENMENT

THE ART OF SOUTH AND SOUTHEAST ASIA BEFORE 1200

South and Southeast Asia is a vast geographic area comprising, among others, the modern nations of India, Pakistan, Sri Lanka, Thailand, Vietnam, Cambodia, Bangladesh, and Indonesia (MAP 6-1). Not surprisingly, the region's inhabitants display tremendous cultural and religious diversity. The people of India alone speak more than 20 different major languages. Those spoken in the north belong to the Indo-European language family, whereas those in the south form a completely separate linguistic family called Dravidian. The art of South and Southeast Asia is equally diverse—and very ancient. When Alexander the Great and his army reached India in 326 BCE, the civilization they encountered was already more than two millennia old. The remains of the first cities in the Indus Valley predate the palaces of Homer's Trojan War heroes (see FIGS. 4-16 and 4-20) by a millennium. This chapter discusses the art and architecture of South and Southeast Asia from their beginnings almost five millennia ago through the 12th century. Chapter 25 treats the later art of the region up to the present day.

INDIA AND PAKISTAN

Indus Civilization

URBAN SOPHISTICATION In the third millennium BCE, the Sumerians were burying their dead in the Royal Cemetery at Ur (see FIGS. 2-8 to 2-11), the Egyptians were erecting the Great Pyramids at Gizeh (see FIG. 3-8), and Aegean sculptors in the Cyclades were carving abstract marble statuettes of women and musicians (see FIGS. 4-1 and 4-2). At the same time, a great civilization arose over a wide geographic area along the Indus River in present-day Pakistan and extended into India as far south as Gujarat and east beyond Delhi. Archaeologists have uncovered impressive remains of this Indus Civilization, as it has come to be called, as well as evidence for active trade between the peoples of the ancient Near East and the Indus Valley.

MAP 6-1 Early sites in South and Southeast Asia.

The most important excavated Indus sites are Harappa and Mohenjo-daro. These early fully developed cities featured streets oriented to compass points, and multistoried houses built of carefully formed and precisely laid kiln-baked bricks. The Indus cities also boasted one of the world's first sophisticated systems of water supply and sewage. In Mohenjo-daro, hundreds of wells throughout the city provided fresh water to homes that featured some of the oldest recorded private bathing areas and toilet facilities, with drainage into public sewers. In the heart of the city stood the so-called Great Bath, a complex of rooms centered on a sunken brick pool (FIG. 6-1) 39 feet long, 23 feet wide, and 8 feet deep. The builders made the pool watertight by sealing the joints between the bricks with bitumen, an asphaltlike material also used in

Mesopotamia. The bath was unlikely to have been a purely recreational facility. Rather, most scholars believe it was designed for ritual bathing of the kind still practiced in the region today.

One intriguing characteristic of the Indus Civilization is that no surviving structures have yet been identified as either temples or palaces. This marks a sharp contrast to the contemporaneous civilizations of Mesopotamia and Egypt.

ELITE SCULPTURE Excavators have discovered surprisingly little art from the long-lived Indus Civilization, and all of the objects found are small. The most impressive is a robed male figure (FIG. 6-2) found at Mohenjo-daro. This steatite (a soft local soapstone) sculpture depicts a figure with half-closed eyes and a closely trimmed beard with shaved upper lip. He wears a headband with a central circular emblem, matched by a similar armband. Holes on each side of his neck suggest that he also wore a necklace of precious metal. *Trefoils* (cloverlike designs with three stylized leaves) decorate his elegant robe. They, as well as the circles of the head- and armbands, originally held red paste and shell inlays, as did the eyes. Scholars often compare the Mohenjo-daro statuette to Sumerian sculptures, where the trefoil motif appears in sacred contexts, and refer to the person portrayed as a "priest-king," the ambiguous term used for some Sumerian leaders. The identity and rank of the Mohenjo-daro figure are, however, uncertain. Nonetheless, the elaborate costume and precious materials make clear that he too was an elite individual.

INDUS SEALS The most common Indus art objects are steatite seals with incised designs. They are similar in many ways to the stamp seals found at contemporaneous sites in Mesopotamia (see "Mesopotamian Seals," Chapter 2, page 40). Most of the Indus

6-1 Great Bath, Mohenjo-daro, Pakistan, ca. 2600–1900 BCE.

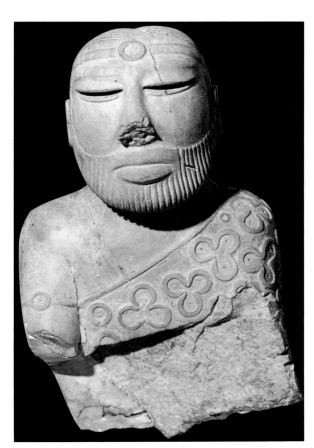

6-2 Robed male figure, from Mohenjo-daro, Pakistan, ca. 2000–1900 BCE. Steatite, $6\frac{7}{8}''$ high. National Museum of Pakistan, Karachi.

6-3 Seal with seated figure in yogic posture, from Mohenjo-daro, Pakistan, ca. 2600–1900 BCE. Steatite coated with alkali and baked, approx. $1\frac{3}{8}'' \times 1\frac{3}{8}''$. National Museum, New Delhi.

examples have an animal or tiny narrative carved on the face, along with an as yet untranslated script. On the back, a *boss* (circular knob) with a hole permitted insertion of a string so that the seal could be worn or hung on a wall. As in the ancient Near East, the Indus peoples sometimes used the seals to make impressions on clay, apparently for securing trade goods wrapped in textiles. The animals most frequently represented include the humped bull, elephant, rhinoceros, and tiger. Each is portrayed in strict profile. Some of the narrative seals appear to show that the Indus peoples considered trees sacred, as both Buddhists and Hindus later did. Many scholars have suggested that religious and ritual continuities existed between the Indus Civilization and later Indian culture.

One of the most elaborate seals (FIG. 6-3) depicts a male figure with a horned headdress and, perhaps, three faces, seated (with erect penis) among the profile animals that regularly appear alone on other seals. The figure's folded legs with heels pressed together and his arms resting on the knees suggest a yogic posture (compare FIG. 6-11). *Yoga* (literally "to yoke") is a method for controlling the body and relaxing the mind used in later Indian religions to yoke, or unite, the practitioner to the divine. Although most scholars reject the identification of this figure as a prototype of the multiheaded Hindu god Shiva (FIG. 6-17) as Lord of Beasts, the yogic posture argues that this important Indian meditative practice began as early as the Indus Civilization.

Vedic and Upanishadic Periods

THE NOBLE ONES By 1700 BCE, the urban phase of the Indus Civilization had ended in most areas. The production of sculptures, seals, and script gradually ceased, and village life replaced urban culture. Very little art survives from the next thousand years, but the religious foundations laid during this period, based on the oral hymns the Aryans brought to India from Central Asia, helped define most later South and Southeast Asian art. The Aryans were a mobile herding people who occupied the Punjab, an area of northwestern India, in the second millennium BCE. They called themselves *Aryas* (Noble Ones) and spoke Sanskrit, the earliest language yet identified in South Asia.

VEDAS AND BRAHMINS Around 1500 BCE, the Aryans composed the first of four *Vedas*. These compilations of religious learning (veda means "knowledge"), written in Sanskrit, included hymns intended for priests (called *Brahmins*) to chant or sing. The Aryan priests headed a social hierarchy that has come to be called the *caste system*, which still forms the basis of Indian society today. Below the priests were the warriors, traders, and manual laborers (including artists and architects), respectively. The Aryan religion centered on sacrifice, the ritual enactment of often highly intricate and lengthy ceremonies in which the Brahmin priests placed materials, such as milk and *soma* (the sacrificial brew), into a fire that took the sacrifices to the gods in the heavens. It was believed that if the priests performed these rituals accurately, the gods would fulfill the prayers of those who sponsored the sacrifices. These gods, primarily male, included Indra, Varuna, Surya, and Agni, gods associated, respectively, with the rains, the ocean, the sun, and fire. It appears that the Aryans did not make images of these deities.

SAMSARA, KARMA, AND MOKSHA The next phase of South Asian urban civilization developed east of the Indus heartland, in the Ganges River Valley. Here, from 800 to 500 BCE, religious thinkers composed a variety of texts called the *Upanishads*. Among the innovative ideas of the Upanishads were *samsara*, *karma*, and *moksha* (or *nirvana*). Samsara is the belief that individuals are born again after death in an almost endless round of rebirths. The type of rebirth can vary. One can be reborn as a human being, an animal, or even a god. An individual's past actions (karma), either good or bad, determine the nature of future rebirths. The ultimate goal of a person's religious life is to escape from the cycle of birth and death by merging the individual self into the vital force of the universe. This escape is called either moksha (liberation, for Hindus) or nirvana (cessation, for Buddhists).

HINDUISM AND BUDDHISM Hinduism and Buddhism, the two major modern religions originating in Asia, developed in the late centuries BCE and the early centuries CE. Hinduism, the dominant religion in India today, discussed in more detail later (see page 178), has its origins in Aryan religion. Buddhism was founded by the Buddha, a historical figure who advocated the path of *asceticism,* or self-discipline and self-denial, as the means to free oneself from attachments to people and possessions, thus ending rebirth (see "Buddhism and Buddhist Iconography," page 171). Unlike their predecessors in South Asia, both Hindus and Buddhists use images of gods and holy persons in religious rituals. Buddhists have the older artistic tradition. Their earliest monuments date to the Maurya period.

Maurya Dynasty

CHANDRAGUPTA AND THE GREEKS When Alexander the Great reached the Indus River in 326 BCE, his troops refused to go further. Reluctantly, Alexander abandoned his dream of conquering India and headed home. After Alexander's death three years later, his generals divided his empire among themselves (see Chapter 5). One of them, Seleucus Nicator, re-invaded India, but Chandragupta Maurya (r. 323–298 BCE), founder of the Maurya dynasty, defeated him in 305 BCE and eventually consolidated almost all of present-day India under his domain. Chandragupta's capital was Pataliputra (modern Patna) in northeastern India, far from the center of the Indus Civilization. Megasthenes, Seleucus's ambassador to the Maurya court, described Pataliputra in his book on India as a large and wealthy city enclosed within mighty wooden walls so extensive that the circuit had 64 gates and 570 towers.

ASHOKA'S PILLARS The greatest Maurya ruler was Ashoka (r. 272–231 BCE), who left his imprint on history by converting to Buddhism and spreading the Buddha's teaching throughout and beyond India (see "Ashoka's Conversion to Buddhism," page 173). Ashoka formulated a legal code based on the Buddha's dharma and inscribed his laws on enormous monolithic (one-piece) stone columns erected throughout his kingdom. Ashoka's pillars reached 30 to 40 feet high and are the first monumental stone artworks in India. The pillars penetrated deep into the ground, connecting earth and sky, forming an "axis of the universe," a pre-Buddhist concept that became an important motif in Buddhist architecture. The columns stood along pilgrimage routes to sites associated with the Buddha and on the roads leading to Pataliputra. Capping Ashoka's pillars were elaborate capitals, also carved from a single block of stone. The finest of these is the seven-foot lion capital (FIG. 6-4) at Sarnath, where the Buddha gave his first sermon and set the Wheel of the Law into motion (see "Buddhism," page 171). Stylistically, Ashoka's capital owes much to the ancient Near East, especially the Achaemenid art of Persepolis (see FIG. 2-26), but its iconography is Buddhist. Two pairs of back-to-back lions stand on a round abacus decorated with four wheels and four animals symbolizing the four quarters of the world. The lions once carried a large stone wheel on their backs.

6-4 Lion capital of column erected by Ashoka at Sarnath, India, ca. 250 BCE. Polished sandstone, approx. 7′ high. Archaeological Museum, Sarnath.

The wheel (chakra) referred to the Wheel of the Law but also indicated Ashoka's stature as a *chakravartin* ("holder of the wheel"), a universal king imbued with divine authority.

Shunga, Andhra, and Kushan Dynasties

The Maurya Dynasty came to an abrupt end when its last ruler was assassinated by one of his generals, who founded a new dynasty in his own name. The Shungas, however, never ruled an empire as extensive as that of the Mauryas. Their realm was confined to central India. They were succeeded by the Andhras, who also controlled the Deccan plateau to the south. By the middle of the first century CE, an even greater empire, the Kushan, rose in northern India. Its most celebrated king was Kanishka (r. 78–144 CE), whose capital was at Peshawar in Gandhara, a region largely in Pakistan today, close to the Afghanistan border. The Kushans grew rich on trade between China and the west along one of the main caravan routes bringing the luxuries of the Orient to the Roman Empire (see "Silk and the Silk Road," Chapter 7, page 201). Kanishka even struck coins modeled on the imperial coinage of Rome (see Chapter 10), some featuring Greco-Roman deities, but Kanishka's coins also carried portraits of himself and images of the Buddha and various Hindu deities.

Buddhism and Buddhist Iconography

THE BUDDHA AND THE EIGHTFOLD PATH

The Buddha (Enlightened One) was born around 563 BCE as Prince Siddhartha Gautama, the eldest son of the king of the Shakya Clan. A prophecy foretold that he would grow up to be either a world conqueror or a great religious leader. His father preferred the secular role for young Siddhartha and groomed him for kingship by shielding the boy from the hardships of the world. When he was 29, however, the prince rode out of the palace, abandoned his wife and family, and encountered firsthand the pain of old age, sickness, and death. Siddhartha responded to the suffering he witnessed by renouncing his opulent life and becoming a wandering ascetic searching for knowledge through meditation. Six years later, he achieved complete enlightenment, or buddhahood, while meditating beneath a pipal tree (the Bodhi tree) at Bodh Gaya ("place of enlightenment") in eastern India. Known from that day on as Shakyamuni (Wise Man of the Shakya Clan), the Buddha preached his first sermon in the Deer Park at Sarnath. There he set in motion the Wheel (*chakra*) of the Law (*dharma*) and expounded the Four Noble Truths that are the core insights of Buddhism: (1) life is suffering; (2) the cause of suffering is desire; (3) one can overcome and extinguish desire; (4) the way to conquer desire and end suffering is to follow the Buddha's Eightfold Path of right understanding, right thought, right speech, right action, right livelihood, right effort, right mindfulness, and right concentration. The Buddha's path leads to nirvana, the cessation of the endless cycle of painful life, death, and rebirth. The Buddha continued to preach until his death at 80 at Kushinagara. His disciples carried on his teaching and established monasteries where others could follow the Buddha's path to enlightenment and nirvana.

THE SPREAD OF BUDDHISM

This earliest form of Buddhism is called *Theravada* (the Path of the Elders) Buddhism. The new religion developed and changed over time as the Buddha's teachings spread from India throughout Asia. The second major school of Buddhist thought, *Mahayana* (Great Path) Buddhism, emerged around the beginning of the Common era. Mahayana Buddhists refer to Theravada Buddhism as *Hinayana* (Lesser Path) Buddhism and believe in a larger goal than nirvana for an individual—namely, buddhahood for all. Mahayana Buddhists also revere *bodhisattvas* ("Buddhas-to-be"), exemplars of compassion who, holding back at the threshold of nirvana, aid others in earning merit and achieving buddhahood (see FIGS. 6-14, 7-12, 8-7, and 8-8). Theravada Buddhism became the dominant sect in southern India, Sri Lanka, and mainland Southeast Asia, whereas Mahayana Buddhism took root in northern India and spread to China, Korea, Japan, and Nepal.

A third important Buddhist sect, especially popular in East Asia, venerates the *Amitabha* Buddha (*Amida* in Japanese), the Buddha of Infinite Light and Life. The devotees of this Buddha hope to be reborn in the Pure Land Paradise of the West (see FIG. 7-13), where the Amitabha resides and can grant them salvation. Pure Land teachings maintain that people have no possibility of attaining enlightenment on their own, but can achieve paradise by faith alone.

THE BUDDHA IN ART

When artists began depicting the Buddha in human form, probably in the first century CE, it was as a robed monk. They distinguished the Enlightened One from monks and bodhisattvas by *lakshanas,* body attributes or characteristics indicating the Buddha's superhuman nature. These distinguishing marks include an *urna,* or curl of hair between the eyebrows, shown as a dot; an *ushnisha,* a cranial bump shown as hair on the earliest images (FIGS. 6-9 to 6-11) but later as an actual part of the head (see FIG. 6-12); and, less frequently, palms of hands and soles of feet imprinted with a wheel (FIG. 6-11). The Buddha is also recognizable by his elongated ears, the result of wearing heavy royal jewelry in his youth, but the enlightened Shakyamuni is rarely bejeweled, as are many bodhisattvas. Sometimes the Buddha appears with a halo, or sun disk, behind his head (FIGS. 6-9, 6-11, and 6-12).

Representations of the Buddha also feature a repertory of *mudras,* or hand gestures, conveying fixed meanings. These include the *dhyana* (meditation) mudra, with hands overlapping in the lap, palms upward (FIGS. 6-9 and 25-11); the *bhumisparsha* (earth touching) mudra, right hand down reaching to the ground, calling the earth to witness the Buddha's enlightenment (FIGS. 6-10*b*, and 7-27); the *dharmachakra* (Wheel of the Law, or teaching) mudra, a two-handed gesture with right thumb and index finger forming a circle (FIGS. 6-12 and 8-8); and the *abhaya* (do not fear) mudra, right hand up, palm outward, a gesture of protection or blessing (FIGS. 6-10*c*, 6-11, and 8-7).

Episodes from the Buddha's life are among the most popular subjects in all Buddhist artistic traditions. No single text provides the complete or authoritative narrative of his life and death. Thus, numerous versions and variations exist, allowing for a rich artistic repertory. Four of the most important events are his birth at Lumbini from the side of his mother, Queen Maya (FIG. 6-10*a*) the achievement of buddhahood while meditating beneath the Bodhi tree at Bodh Gaya (FIGS. 6-10*b* and 7-27); the Buddha's first sermon at Sarnath (FIGS. 6-10*c* and 6-12); and his attainment of nirvana when he died (*parinirvana*) at Kushinagara (FIGS. 6-10*d* and 6-25). Buddhists erected monasteries and monuments at the four sites where these key events occurred. Monks and lay pilgrims from throughout the world continue to visit these places today.

THE GREAT STUPA AT SANCHI In the world of art and architecture, the unifying characteristic of this age of regional dynasties in South Asia was the patronage of Buddhism. One of the most important Buddhist monasteries, founded during Ashoka's reign and in use for more than a thousand years, is at Sanchi in central India. It consists of many buildings constructed over the centuries, including *viharas* (celled structures where monks live), large *stupas* (see "The Stupa," page 172), *chaitya halls* (halls with rounded, or *apsidal,* ends for housing smaller stupas), and temples for sheltering images.

The Great Stupa at Sanchi dates originally to Ashoka's reign, but its present form, with its tall stone fence and four gates, dates

The Stupa

An essential element of Buddhist sanctuaries is the *stupa,* a grand circular mound modeled on earlier South Asian burial mounds of a type familiar in many other ancient cultures (see FIGS. 4-21 and 9-5). The stupa was not a tomb, however, but a monument housing relics of the Buddha. When the Buddha died, his cremated remains were placed in eight *reliquaries,* or containers, similar in function to the later reliquaries housed in medieval churches at pilgrimage sites throughout the Christian world (see "Pilgrimages and the Cult of Relics," Chapter 17, page 449). Unlike their Western equivalents, which were meant to be viewed, the Buddha's relics were buried in solid earthen mounds (stupas) that could not be entered. In the mid-third century BCE, Ashoka opened the original eight stupas and spread the Buddha's relics among thousands of stupas in all corners of his realm. Buddhists venerated the Buddha's remains by *circumambulation,* walking around the stupa in a clockwise direction, following the path of the sun, bringing the devotee into harmony with the cosmos. Stupas come in many sizes, from tiny handheld objects to huge structures, such as the Great Stupa at Sanchi (FIG. 6-5) that Ashoka constructed in the third century BCE and later kings enlarged.

The monumental stupas are three-dimensional *mandalas,* or sacred diagrams of the universe. The domed stupa itself represents the world mountain, with the cardinal points marked by *toranas,* or gateways (FIGS. 6-5 and 6-6). The *harmika,* positioned atop the stupa dome, is a stone fence or railing that encloses a square area symbolizing the sacred domain of the gods. At the harmika's center, a *yasti,* or pole, corresponds to the axis of the universe, a motif already present in Ashoka's pillars. Three *chatras,* or stone disks, assigned various meanings, crown the yasti. The yasti rises from the mountain-dome and passes through the harmika, thus uniting this world with the heavenly paradise. A stone fence often encloses the entire structure, clearly separating the sacred space containing the Buddha's relics from the profane world outside.

6-5 Great Stupa, Sanchi, India, third century BCE to first century CE (view from the east).

6-6 Exterior diagram of Great Stupa, Sanchi, India, third century BCE to first century CE.

Ashoka's Conversion to Buddhism

The reign of the Maurya king Ashoka marks both the beginning of monumental stone art and architecture in India (FIG. 6-4) and the first official sponsorship of Buddhism. The impact of Ashoka's conversion to Buddhism on the later history of art and religion in Asia cannot be overstated. An edict carved into a rock at Dhauli in the ancient region of Kalinga (roughly equivalent to the modern state of Orissa on the Bay of Bengal) records Ashoka's embrace of nonviolence and of the teachings of the Buddha after an especially bloody conquest that claimed more than 100,000 lives. The inscription also captures Ashoka's missionary zeal, which spread Buddhism far beyond the boundaries of his kingdom.

> The Beloved of the Gods [Ashoka], conqueror of the Kalingas, is moved to remorse now. For he has felt profound sorrow and regret because the conquest of a people previously unconquered involves slaughter, death, and deportation. . . . [King Ashoka] now thinks that even a person who wrongs him must be forgiven . . .

[and he] considers moral conquest [conquest by dharma] the most important conquest. He has achieved this moral conquest repeatedly both here and among the peoples living beyond the borders of his kingdom. . . . Even in countries which [King Ashoka's] envoys have not reached, people have heard about dharma and about [the king's] ordinances and instructions in dharma. . . . This edict on dharma has been inscribed so that my sons and great-grandsons who may come after me should not think new conquests worth achieving. . . . Let them consider moral conquest the only true conquest.[1]

The story of Ashoka at Kalinga and his renunciation of violence still resonates today. It inspired one of the most important 20th-century Indian sculptors to take up the theme and imbue it with contemporary meaning (see FIG. 25-14).

[1] Rock Edict XIII. Translated by N. A. Nikam and Richard McKeon, *The Edicts of Asoka* (Chicago: The University of Chicago Press, 1959), 27–30.

---

from ca. 50 BCE to 50 CE (FIGS. **6-5** and **6-6**). The dome, solid and filled with earth and rubble, stands 50 feet high. Worshipers enter through one of the gateways, walk on the lower circumambulation path, then climb the stairs on the south side to circumambulate at the second level. Carved onto the different parts of the Great Stupa are more than 600 brief inscriptions showing that the donations of hundreds of individuals (more than a third of them

6-7 Yakshi, detail of eastern gateway, Great Stupa, Sanchi, India, mid-first century BCE to early first century CE.

women) made the monument's construction possible. Veneration of the Buddha was open to all, not just the monks, and most of the dedications are by common laypeople, who hoped to accrue merit for future rebirths with their gifts.

THE BUDDHA'S PAST LIVES The reliefs on the four toranas at Sanchi (FIGS. 6-5 and 6-6) depict not only the Buddha's life story but also the stories of his past lives *(jatakas)*. In Buddhist belief, everyone has had innumerable past lives, including Siddhartha. During Siddhartha's former lives, as recorded in the jatakas, he accumulated sufficient merit to achieve enlightenment and become the Buddha. In the life stories recounted in the Great Stupa reliefs, however, the Buddha never appears as a human being. Instead, the artists indicated his presence by using symbols, for example, footprints, a parasol, or an empty seat. Some scholars regard these symbols as markers of where the Buddha once was, so others can follow in his footsteps.

YAKSHI AND FLOWERING TREE Also carved on the eastern gateway is a scantily clad, sensuous woman called a *yakshi* (FIG. 6-7). These goddesses, worshiped throughout India, personified fertility and vegetation. The Sanchi yakshi reaches up to hold on to a mango tree branch while pressing her left foot against the trunk, an action that has brought the tree to flower. Buddhists later adopted this pose, with its rich associations of procreation and abundance, for representing the Buddha's mother, Maya, giving birth (FIG. 6-10a). Thus, the Buddhists adopted pan-Indian symbolism, such as the woman under the tree, when creating their own Buddhist iconography.

ROCK-CUT MONASTIC HALLS The best early example of a chaitya hall is the one carved out of the living rock at Karle (FIG. **6-8**), datable around 100 CE. The Karle hall has pillared

6-8 Interior *(left)*, section *(top right)*, and plan *(bottom right)* of chaitya hall, Karle, India, ca. 100 CE.

ambulatories (walking paths) that allow worshipers to circumambulate the stupa placed at the back of the sacred cave. The hall is nearly 45 feet high and 125 feet long. It surpasses in size even the rock-cut chamber of the temple of the Egyptian pharaoh Ramses II (see FIG. 3-24). Elaborate capitals atop the rock-cut pillars depict men and women riding on elephants. Outside, amorous couples *(mithunas)* flank the entrance. Like the yakshis at Sanchi, these auspicious figures symbolize the creative life force. The Sanchi and Karle figures are early examples of what will become a long tradition of eroticism in Indian religious art (compare FIG. 6-23).

FIRST BUDDHAS IN HUMAN FORM The first anthropomorphic representations of the Buddha probably appeared in the first century CE. Scholars still debate what brought about this momentous shift in Buddhist iconography, but one factor may be the changing perception of the Buddha himself. Originally revered as an enlightened mortal, the Buddha increasingly became regarded as a divinity. Consequently, the Buddha's followers desired images of him to worship.

Many of the early portrayals of the Buddha in human form come from the Gandhara region and from Mathura, a city about 90 miles south of Delhi. Both were part of the Kushan Empire during the first three centuries CE.

GANDHARA AND GRECO-ROMAN ART In Gandhara, sculptors fashioned representations of the Buddha both in freestanding statuary and narrative reliefs. A second-century CE statue (FIG. 6-9) carved in gray schist, the local stone, shows the Buddha, with ushnisha and urna, dressed in a monk's robe, seated in a cross-legged yogic posture similar to that of the ancient figure on the Indus seal discussed earlier (FIG. 6-3). His hands overlap, palms upward, in the dhyana mudra, the gesture of meditation (see "Buddhism," page 171). Gandhara was part of a widespread region of Hellenized culture and art that stretched across reaches of modern Iran, Russia, Afghanistan, and Pakistan, a legacy of Alexander's incursions in these regions. Gandharan sculpture owes much to Greco-Roman art, both in the treatment of body forms, such as the sharp, arching brows and continuous profile of forehead and nose (see, for example, FIG. 5-39), and in the draping of the togalike garment (see FIG. 10-72).

LIFE AND DEATH OF THE BUDDHA One of the earliest pictorial narrative cycles in which the Buddha appears in human form also comes from Gandhara. The schist frieze (FIG. **6-10**) depicts, in chronological order from left to right, the Buddha's birth at Lumbini, the enlightenment at Bodh Gaya, the first sermon at Sarnath, and the Buddha's death at Kushinagara. At the left, Queen Maya, in a posture derived from that of earlier South Asian

6-9 Meditating Buddha, from Gandhara, Pakistan, second century CE. Gray schist, 3′ 7½″ high. Royal Museum, National Museums of Scotland, Edinburgh.

yakshis (FIG. 6-7), gives birth to Prince Siddhartha, who emerges from her right hip, already with his attributes of ushnisha, urna, and halo. Receiving him is the god Indra. Elegantly dressed ladies, one with a fan of peacock feathers, suggest the opulent court life the Buddha left behind. In the next scene, the Buddha sits beneath the Bodhi tree while the soldiers and demons of the evil Mara attempt to distract him from his quest for knowledge. They are unsuccessful, and the Buddha reaches down to touch the earth (bhumisparsha mudra) as witness to his enlightenment. Next, the Buddha preaches the Eightfold Path to nirvana in the Deer Park at Sarnath. The sculptor has set the scene by placing two deer and the Wheel of the Law beneath the figure of the Buddha, who raises his right hand (abhaya mudra) to bless the monks and other devotees who have come to hear his first sermon. In the final section of the frieze, the parinirvana, the Buddha lies dying among his devotees, some of whom wail in grief, while one monk, who realizes that the Buddha has been permanently released from suffering, remains tranquil in meditation.

Although the iconography of the frieze is Buddhist, Roman reliefs must have served as stylistic models for the sculptor. For example, the distribution of standing and equestrian figures over the relief ground, with those behind the first row seemingly suspended in the air, is familiar in Roman art of the second and third centuries CE (see FIGS. 10-66 and 10-71). The figure of the Buddha on his deathbed finds parallels in the reclining figures on the lids of Roman sarcophagi (see FIG. 10-62). The type of hierarchical composition placing a large seated central figure between balanced tiers of smaller onlookers can be seen on the later Arch of the Roman emperor Constantine (see FIG. 10-77), which has precedents in earlier Roman art.

a

b

c

d

6-10 The life and death of the Buddha, frieze from Gandhara, Pakistan, second century CE. Schist, 2′ 2⅜″ × 9′ 6⅛″. Freer Gallery of Art, Washington, D.C. a) birth at Lumbini, b) enlightenment at Badh Gaya, c) first sermon at Sarnath, d) death at Kushinagara.

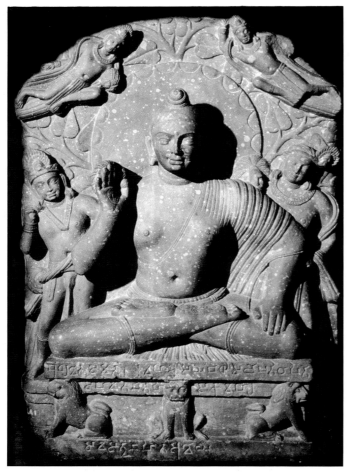

6-11 Buddha seated on lion throne, from Mathura, India, second century CE. Red sandstone, 2′ 3½″ high. Archaeological Museum, Muttra.

6-12 Seated Buddha preaching first sermon, from Sarnath, India, second half of fifth century. Tan sandstone, 5′ 3″ high. Archaeological Museum, Sarnath.

BUDDHIST IMAGERY IN MATHURA Contemporary to the Gandharan sculptures, but stylistically distinct from them, are the Buddha images of Mathura (FIG. **6-11**). The Mathura statues are more closely linked to the Indian portrayals of *yakshas,* the male equivalents of the yakshis. Indian artists represented yakshas as robust, powerful males with broad shoulders and open, staring eyes. Mathura Buddhas, carved from red sandstone, retain these characteristics but wear a monk's robe (with right shoulder bare) and lack the jewelry and other signs of wealth of the yakshas. The robe appears almost transparent, revealing the full, fleshy body beneath. In our example, the Buddha sits in a yogic posture on a lion throne under the Bodhi tree, attended by fly-whisk bearers. He raises his right hand palm-out in the abhaya gesture, indicating to worshipers that they need have no fear. His hands and feet bear the mark of the dharma Wheel.

The Gupta and Post-Gupta Periods

Around 320* a new empire arose in north central India. The Gupta emperors chose Pataliputra as their capital, deliberately associating themselves with the prestige of the former Maurya Empire. The heyday of this dynasty was under Chandragupta II

(r. 375–415), whose very name recalled the first Maurya emperor. The Guptas were great patrons of art and literature.

THE CLASSICAL BUDDHA STATUE Under the Guptas, artists formulated what became the canonical image of the Buddha, combining the Gandharan monastic robe covering both shoulders with the soft, full-bodied Buddha figures with clinging garments of Mathuran sculpture. These disparate styles beautifully merge in a fifth-century Buddha from Sarnath (FIG. **6-12**), whose smooth, unadorned surfaces conform to the Indian notion of perfect body form and emphasize the figure's spirituality. The Buddha's eyes are downcast in meditation, and he holds his hands in front of his body in the Wheel-turning gesture, preaching his first sermon, indicated by the tiny Wheel of the Law seen on its edge below the figure. Flanking the Wheel, two now partially broken deer symbolize the Deer Park at Sarnath. Buddha images such as this one became so popular that temples housing Buddha statues seem largely to have displaced the stupa as the norm in Buddhist sacred architecture.

THE CAVES OF AJANTA The new popularity of Buddha imagery may be seen in the interior of a chaitya hall (FIG. **6-13**) carved out of the mountainside at Ajanta, northeast of Bombay,

---

* From this point on, all dates in this chapter are CE unless otherwise stated.

The Painted Caves of Ajanta

Art historians assume India had a rich painting tradition in ancient times, but because early Indian artists often used perishable materials, such as palm leaf and wood, and because of the tropical climate in much of India, nearly all early Indian painting has been lost. At Ajanta in the Deccan, however, paintings cover the walls, pillars, and ceilings of several caves datable to the second half of the fifth century. FIG. 6-14 reproduces a detail of one of the Ajanta murals.

To create these paintings, the artists first applied two layers of clay mixed with straw and other materials to the walls. They then added a third layer of fine white lime plaster. Unlike true fresco painting (see "Fresco," Chapter 19, page 530), in which the painters apply colors to the wet plaster, the Indian painters waited for the lime to dry. This method produces less durable results, and the Ajanta murals have suffered water damage over the centuries. The painters next outlined the figures in dark red and then painted in the details of faces, costumes, and jewelry. The colors used were water soluble and mostly produced from local minerals, including red and yellow ocher. Blue, used sparingly, came from costly lapis lazuli imported from Afghanistan. The last step was to polish the painted surface with a smooth stone.

The Ajanta caves provide a tantalizing glimpse of early Indian painting. Significant later examples of paintings in India are rare before the 13th century (see Chapter 25).

at about the same time a Gupta sculptor created the classic Sarnath seated Buddha. Ajanta had been the site of a small Buddhist monastery for centuries, but royal patrons of the local Vakataka dynasty, allied to the Guptas by marriage, added more than 20 new caves in the second half of the fifth century. The typological similarity of the fifth-century Ajanta chaitya halls to the earlier example at Karle (FIG. 6-8) is immediately evident and consistent with the conservative nature of religious architecture in all cultures. At Ajanta, however, sculptors carved a standing Buddha flanked by columns into the front of the stupa.

PAINTED BODHISATTVAS Ajanta is renowned above all because the caves retain much of their painted wall and ceiling decoration (see "The Painted Caves of Ajanta," above). We illustrate a detail of one of the restored painted walls in cave 1 depicting the bodhisattva Padmapani (FIG. 6-14) among a crowd of devotees, both princes and commoners. With long, dark hair hanging down below a jeweled crown, he stands holding his attribute, a blue lotus flower, in his right hand. The bodhisattva's face shows great compassion as he gazes downward at the actual worshipers passing through the shrine entrance on their way to

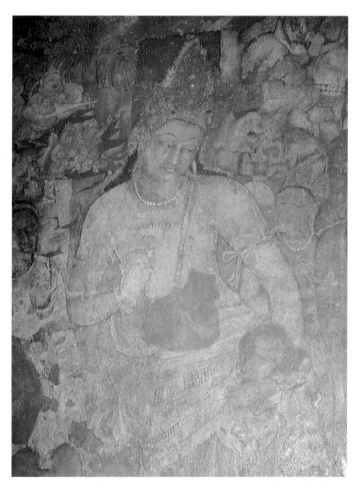

6-13 Interior of cave 19, Ajanta, India, second half of fifth century.

6-14 Bodhisattva Padmapani, wall painting in cave 1, Ajanta, India, second half of fifth century.

Hinduism and Hindu Iconography

Unlike Buddhism (and Christianity, Islam, and other religions), Hinduism recognizes no founder or great prophet. Hinduism also has no simple definition, but means "the religion of the Indians." Both "India" and "Hindu" have a common root in the name of the Indus River. The actual practices and beliefs of Hindus vary tremendously, but the literary origins of Hinduism can be traced to the Vedic period, and some aspects of Hindu practice seem already to have been present in the Indus Civilization of the third millennium BCE. Ritual sacrifice by Brahmin priests is central to Hinduism, as it was to the Aryans. The goal of sacrifice is to please a deity in order to achieve release (*moksha*, liberation) from the endless cycle of birth, death, and rebirth (*samsara*) and become one with the universal spirit.

Not only is Hinduism a religion of many gods, but the Hindu deities have various natures and take many forms. This multiplicity suggests the all-pervasive nature of the Hindu gods. The three most important deities are the gods Shiva and Vishnu and the goddess Devi. Each of the three major sects of Hinduism today considers one of these three to be supreme—Shiva in Shaivism, Vishnu in Vaishnavism, and Devi in Shaktism. (*Shakti* is the female creative force.)

Shiva (FIGS. 6-16, 6-17, and 6-24) is the Destroyer, but, consistent with the multiplicity of Hindu belief, he is also a regenerative force and, in the latter role, can be represented in the form of a *linga* (a phallus or cosmic pillar). When Shiva appears in human form in Hindu art, he frequently has multiple limbs and heads, signs of his superhuman nature. He often has matted locks piled on top of his head, crowned by a crescent moon. Sometimes he wears a serpent scarf and has a third eye on his forehead (the emblem of his all-seeing nature). Shiva rides the bull *Nandi* (FIG. 6-16) and often carries a trident. His son is the elephant-headed *Ganesha* (FIG. 6-16).

Vishnu (FIGS. 6-19 and 6-28) is the Preserver of the Universe. Artists frequently portray him with four arms holding various attributes, including a conch-shell trumpet and discus. He sometimes reclines on a serpent floating on the waters of the cosmic sea. When the evil forces of the universe become too strong, he descends to earth to restore balance and assumes different forms (*avatars*, or incarnations), including a boar (FIG. 6-15), fish, and tortoise, as well as *Krishna*, the divine lover (FIG. 25-6), and even the Buddha himself.

Devi is the Great Goddess who takes many forms and has many names. Hindus worship her alone or as a consort of male gods (*Parvati* or *Uma*, wife of Shiva; *Lakshmi*, wife of Vishnu), as well as *Radha*, lover of Krishna (FIG. 25-6). She has both benign and horrific forms; she both creates and destroys. In one manifestation, she is *Durga*, a multiarmed goddess who rides or is accompanied by a lion.

The stationary images of deities in Hindu temples are often made of stone. Hindus periodically remove portable images of their gods, often of bronze (for example, FIG. 6-24), from the temple, particularly during festivals to enable many worshipers to take *darshan* (seeing the deity and being seen by the deity) at one time. In temples dedicated to Shiva, the stationary form is the linga.

---

the monumental rock-cut Buddha image housed in a cell at the back of the cave. The painter has rendered with finesse the sensuous form of the richly attired bodhisattva, gently modeling the figure with gradations of color and delicate highlights and shadows, especially evident in the face and neck.

BUDDHIST AND HINDU COEXISTENCE Buddhists and Hindus (and adherents of other faiths) practiced their religions side by side in India, often at the same site. The Hindu Vakataka king Harishena (r. 462–481) and members of his court were the sponsors of the new caves at the Buddhist monastery at Ajanta. Buddhism and Hinduism are not monotheistic religions, such as Judaism, Christianity, and Islam. Instead, Buddhists and Hindus approach the spiritual through many gods and varying paths, which permits mutually tolerated differences. In fact, in Hinduism, the Buddha was one of the 10 incarnations of Vishnu, one of the three principal Hindu deities (see "Hinduism and Hindu Iconography," above). More early Buddhist than Hindu art has survived in India, because the Buddhists constructed large monastic institutions with durable materials such as stone and brick. In the Gupta period, Hindu stone sculpture and architecture began to rival the great Buddhist monuments of South Asia.

VISHNU RESCUES THE EARTH The earliest Hindu cave temples are at Udayagiri, near Sanchi. They date to the early fifth century, some 600 years after the first Buddhist examples. Although the Udayagiri temples are architecturally simple and small, the site boasts monumental relief sculptures showing an already fully developed religious iconography. One of these reliefs (FIG. **6-15**), carved in a shallow niche of rock, shows a 13-foot-tall Vishnu in his incarnation as the boar Varaha (see "Hinduism," above). The avatar has a human body and a boar's head. Vishnu assumed this form when he rescued the earth—personified as the goddess Bhudevi clinging to the boar's tusk—from being carried off to the bottom of the ocean. Vishnu stands with one foot resting on the coils of a snake king (identified by the multiple hoods behind his human head), who represents the conquered demon that attempted to abduct the earth. Rows of gods and sages form lines to witness the event.

The relief served a political as well as a religious purpose. The patron of the relief was a local king who honored the great Gupta king Chandragupta II in a nearby inscription dated to the year 401. Many scholars believe that the local king wanted viewers to see Chandragupta (he is known to have visited the site) as saving his kingdom by ridding it of its enemies in much the same way Varaha saved the earth. Thus, the Udayagiri sculptors, acting on their patron's wishes, clothed contemporary events in mythological guise, as the Greeks frequently did (see Chapter 5).

DANCING MANY-ARMED SHIVA During the sixth century, the Huns brought down the Gupta empire, and various regional dynasties rose to power. In the Deccan, a plateau area in central India, the Chalukya kings ruled from their capital at Badami. There, Chalukya sculptors carved a series of reliefs in the walls of halls cut into the cliff above the city. One relief (FIG. **6-16**), datable to the late sixth century, shows Shiva, the second major Hindu male deity (see "Hinduism," page 178) dancing the cosmic dance, his 18 arms swinging rhythmically in an arc. Some of the hands hold objects, and others form prescribed mudras. At the right, a drummer (not visible in FIG. 6-16) accompanies the dance, while Shiva's son, the elephant-headed Ganesha, tentatively mimics his father. Nandi, Shiva's bull mount, stands at the left.

Artists often represented Hindu deities as part human and part animal (FIG. 6-15) or, as in the Badami relief, as figures with

multiple body parts. Such composite and multilimbed forms indicate that the subjects are not human but more-than-human gods with supernatural powers.

SHIVA WITH THREE FACES Another portrayal of Shiva as a superhuman being is found at a third Hindu cave site, on Elephanta, an island in Bombay's harbor named by early Portuguese colonizers who found a life-size stone elephant sculpture there. A king of the Kalachuri dynasty that took control of Elephanta in the sixth century may have commissioned the largest of the island's cave temples. Just inside the cave's west entrance is a shrine housing Shiva's linga, the god's emblem. Deep within the temple, in a niche once closed off with wooden doors, is a nearly 18-foot-high image of Shiva as Mahadeva (FIG. **6-17**), the "Great God" or Lord of Lords. Mahadeva appears to emerge out of the depths of the cave as worshipers' eyes become accustomed to the darkness. This image of Shiva has three faces, each showing a different aspect of the deity. (A fourth, unseen at the back, is implied, the god has not emerged fully from the rock.) The central face expresses Shiva's quiet, balanced demeanor. The clean planes of the face contrast with the richness of the piled hair encrusted with jewels. The two side faces differ significantly. That on the right is female, with framing hair curls. The left face is a grimacing male with a curling mustache who wears a cobra as an earring. The female (Uma) indicates the creative aspect of Shiva. The fierce male (Bhairava) represents Shiva's destructive side. Shiva holds these two opposing forces in check, and the central face expresses their balance. The cyclic destruction and creation of the universe, which the side faces also symbolize, are part of Indian notions of time, matched by the cyclic pattern of death and rebirth (samsara).

VISHNU'S TOWER AT DEOGARH The excavated cave shrines just considered are characteristic of early Hindu religious architecture, but temples constructed using quarried stone became more important as Hinduism evolved over the centuries (see "Hindu Temples," page 180). As they did with the cave temples, the Hindus initially built rather small and simple temples but decorated them with narrative reliefs displaying a fully developed

6-16 Dancing Shiva, rock-cut relief in cave temple, Badami, India, late sixth century.

Hindu Temples

The Hindu temple is the home of the gods on earth and the place where they make themselves visible to humans. At the core of all Hindu temples is the *garbha griha,* the "womb chamber," which houses images or symbols of the deity, for example Shiva's linga (see "Hinduism," page 178). Only the Brahmin priests can enter this inner sanctuary to make offerings to the gods. The worshipers can only stand at the threshold and behold the deity as manifest by its image. In the elaborate multiroomed temples of later Hindu architecture, the worshipers and priests progress through a series of ever more sacred spaces, usually on an east-west axis. Hindu priests and architects attached great importance to each temple's plan and sought to make it conform to the sacred geometric diagram *(mandala)* of the universe.

Architectural historians, following ancient Indian texts, divide Hindu temples into two major typological groups tied to geography. The most important distinguishing feature of the *northern,* or *Nagara,* style of temple (FIG. 6-22) is its beehivelike tower or *shikhara* ("mountain peak"), capped by an *amalaka,* a ribbed cushionlike form, derived from the shape of the amala fruit (believed to have medicinal powers). Amalakas appear on the corners of the lower levels of the shikhara too. Northern temples also have smaller towerlike roofs over the halls *(mandapas)* leading to the garbha griha.

Southern, or *Dravida,* temples (FIG. 6-21) can easily be recognized by the flat roofs of their pillared mandapas and by their shorter towered shrines, called *vimanas,* which lack the curved profile of their Nagara counterparts and resemble multilevel pyramids.

iconography. The Vishnu Temple at Deogarh (FIG. **6-18**) in north central India, erected in the early sixth century, is among the first Hindu temples constructed with stone blocks. A simple square building on a stone *plinth* (base), it has an elaborately decorated doorway at the front and a relief in a niche on each of the other three sides. Sculpted guardians and mithuna couples protect the doorway at Deogarh, because it is the transition point between the dangerous outside and the sacred interior, the garbha griha. A small shrine once stood at each corner of the plinth. The temple culminates in a tower (poorly preserved).

THE CREATION OF THE UNIVERSE The reliefs in the three niches of the Deogarh temple depict important episodes in the saga of Vishnu. The one we reproduce (FIG. **6-19**) shows Vishnu asleep on the coils of the giant serpent Ananta, whose multiple heads form a kind of umbrella around the god's face. While Lakshmi massages her husband's legs (he has cramps as he gives birth), the four-armed Vishnu dreams the universe into reality. A lotus plant (said

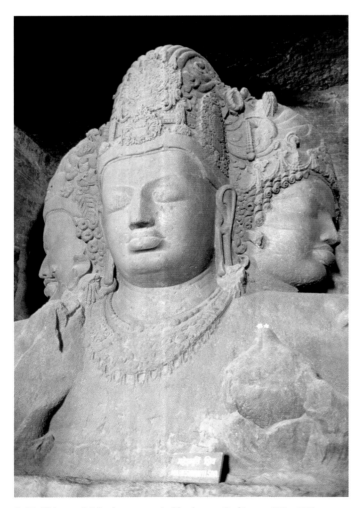

6-17 Shiva as Mahadeva, cave 1, Elephanta, India, ca. 550–575. Basalt, Shiva 17′ 10″ high.

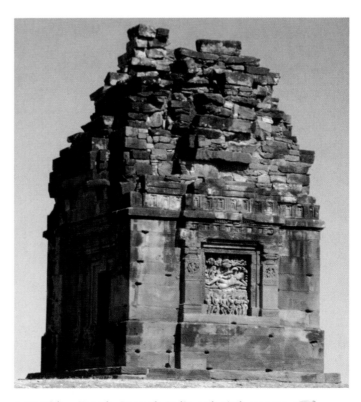

6-18 Vishnu Temple, Deogarh, India, early sixth century.

to have grown out of Vishnu's navel) supports the four-headed Hindu god of creation, Brahma. Flanking him are other important Hindu divinities, including Shiva on his bull. Below are six figures. The four at the right are personifications of Vishnu's various powers. They will defeat the two armed demons at the left. The sculptor carved all the figures in the classic Gupta style, with smooth bodies and clinging garments (compare FIG. 6-12).

Early Medieval Period

During the several centuries corresponding to the early medieval period in western Europe (see Chapter 16), the early Islamic period in the Near East (see Chapter 13), the Tang and Song dynasties in China (see Chapter 7), and the Hakuho, Nara, and Heian periods in Japan (see Chapter 8), regional dynasties ruled parts of India. Among the most important of these kingdoms were the Palas and Chandellas in northern India and the Pallavas and Cholas in the south. Whereas Buddhism spread rapidly throughout eastern Asia, in medieval India it gradually declined, and the various local kings vied with one another to erect glorious shrines to the Hindu gods.

TEMPLES CARVED FROM BOULDERS In addition to cave temples and masonry temples, Indian architects created a third type of monument: freestanding temples carved out of rocky outcroppings. Such sculpted temples are rare. Some of the earliest and most impressive of these monolithic temples (FIG. 6-20) are

6-19 Vishnu asleep on the serpent Ananta, detail of facade of the Vishnu Temple, Deogarh, India, early sixth century.

6-20 Rock-cut temples, Mamallapuram, India, second half of seventh century. From *left* to *right*: Dharmaraja, Bhima, Arjuna, and Draupadi rathas.

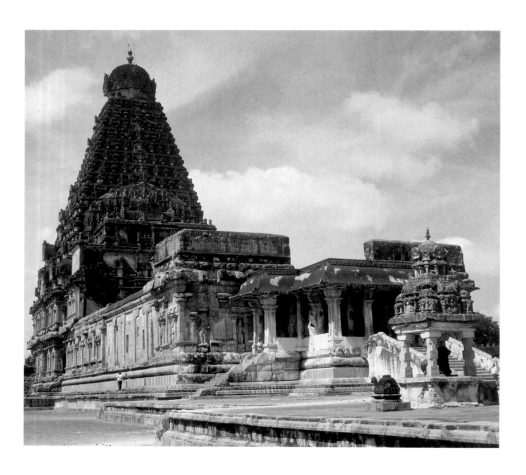

6-21 Rajarajeshvara Temple, Thanjavur, India, ca. 1010.

at Mamallapuram, south of Madras on the Bay of Bengal, where they are called *rathas,* or "chariots" (that is, vehicles of the gods). In the late seventh century, the Pallava dynasty had five rathas carved out of a single huge granite boulder jutting out from the sand. The group is of special interest because it illustrates the variety of temple forms at this period, based on earlier wooden structures, before a standard masonry type of temple became the rule in southern India. The largest Mamallapuram ratha, the Dharmaraja (in the foreground), dedicated to Shiva, is an early example of the typical southern-style temple with stepped-pyramid vimana (see "Hindu Temples," page 180). The tower ascends in pronounced tiers of cornices decorated with miniature shrines. The lower walls include carved columns and figures of deities inside niches. The Bhima ratha to the right, dedicated to Vishnu, has a rectangular plan and a rounded roof; the next ratha, the Arjuna, is a smaller example of the southern Indian type. At the end of the row sits the very small Draupadi ratha, which was modeled on a thatched hut and is dedicated to Durga, a form of the goddess Devi. The two largest temples were never finished.

THE APOGEE OF THE SOUTHERN TEMPLE Under the Cholas, whose territories extended into part of Sri Lanka and even Java, architects constructed temples of unprecedented size and grandeur in the southern Indian tradition. The Rajarajeshvara Temple at Thanjavur (FIG. **6-21**), dedicated in 1010 to Shiva as the lord of Rajaraja, was the largest and tallest temple (210 feet high) in India at its time. The temple stands inside a walled precinct. It consists of a stairway leading to two flat-roofed mandapas, the larger one having 36 pillars, and to the garbha griha in the base of the enormous pyramidal vimana that is as much an emblem of the Cholas' secular power as of their devotion to Shiva. On the exterior walls of the lower stories are numerous reliefs in niches depicting the god in his various forms.

THE HINDU TEMPLE AS MOUNTAIN At the same time the Cholas were building the Rajarajeshvara Temple at Thanjavur in the south, the Chandella dynasty was constructing temples—in northern style—at Khajuraho. The Vishvanatha Temple (FIG. **6-22**) is one of more than 20 large and elaborate temples at that site. Vishvanatha ("Lord of the Universe") is another of the many names for Shiva. Dedicated in 1002, the structure has three towers over the mandapas, each rising higher than the preceding one, leading to the tallest tower at the rear, in much the same way the foothills of the Himalayas, Shiva's home, rise to meet their highest peak. The mountain symbolism applies to the interior of the Vishvanatha Temple as well. Under the tallest of the towers, the shikhara, is the garbha griha, the small and dark inner sanctuary chamber, like a cave, which houses the image of the deity. Thus, temples such as the Vishvanatha symbolize constructed mountains with caves, comparable to the actual cave temples at Elephanta and other Indian sites. In all cases, the deity manifests himself or herself within the cave and takes various forms in sculptures. The temple mountains, however, are not intended to appear natural but rather are perfect mountains designed using ideal mathematical proportions.

THE MITHUNAS OF KHAJURAHO The reliefs of the Rajarajeshvara Temple at Thanjavur (FIG. 6-21) are typical of southern temple decoration, which is generally limited to images of deities. The exterior walls of Khajuraho's Vishvanatha Temple are equally typical of northern temples in the profusion of sculptures depicting not only gods but mortals, especially pairs of men and women (mithunas) embracing or engaged in sexual intercourse in an extraordinary range of positions (FIG. **6-23**). The use of seminude yakshis and amorous couples as motifs on religious buildings in India has a very long history, going back to the earliest architectural traditions, both Hindu and Buddhist (Sanchi, FIG. 6-7, and

Shikhara   Plinth

Doorway   Stairs

Great
mandapa

Mandapa   Porch

Garbha
griha

N

6-22 Vishvanatha Temple, Khajuraho, India, ca. 1000. (View looking northwest and plan).

Karle). As in the earlier examples already discussed, the erotic sculptures of Khajuraho suggest fertility and the propagation of life and serve as auspicious protectors of the sacred precinct.

A PORTABLE BRONZE SHIVA We conclude our survey of early Indian art with an object quite different in function from anything considered thus far. The statuette of Shiva (FIG. **6-24**) in the Naltunai Ishvaram Temple in Punjai, cast in solid bronze around 1000, recalls the sixth-century relief in the Badami cave (FIG. 6-16). It is one of many examples of portable images of deities created under the Chola kings, the builders of the towering Rajarajeshvara Temple at Thanjavur (FIG. 6-21). Here, Shiva dances as Nataraja ("Lord of the Dance") by balancing on one leg atop a dwarf representing ignorance, which the god stamps out as he dances. Shiva extends all four arms, two of them touching the flaming *nimbus* (light of glory) encircling him. These two upper

hands also hold a small drum (at right) and a flame (at left). Shiva creates the universe to the drumbeat's rhythm, while the small fire represents destruction. His lower left hand points to his upraised foot, indicating the foot as the place where devotees can find refuge and enlightenment. Shiva's lower right hand, raised in the fear-not gesture, tells worshipers to come forward without fear. As Shiva spins, his matted hair comes loose and spreads like a fan on both sides of his head.

This Shiva Nataraja is a movable image (the holes on the base held poles for carrying the statuette), but even when stationary, it would not appear as it does in an art history book. Rather, when Hindus worship the Shiva Nataraja, they dress the image, cover it with jewels, and garland it with flowers. The only bronze part visible is the face, marked with colored powders and scented pastes. Considered the embodiment of the deity, the image is not a symbol of the god but the god itself. All must treat the god/image as a

6-23 Sculptures on temple wall, Vishvanatha Temple, Khajuraho, India, ca. 1000.

6-24 Shiva as Nataraja, bronze in the Naltunai Ishvaram Temple, Punjai, India, ca. 1000.

living being. Worship of the deity involves taking care of him as if he were an honored person. Bathed, clothed, given foods to eat, and taken for outings, the image also receives such gifts as songs, lights (lit oil lamps), good smells (incense), and flowers—all things he can enjoy through the senses. The food given to the god is particularly important, as he eats the "essence," leaving the remainder for the worshiper. The food is then *prasada* (grace), sacred because it came in contact with the divine. In an especially religious household, the deity resides as an image and receives the food for each meal before the family eats. When the god resides in a temple, it is then the duty of the priests to feed, clothe, and take care of him.

The Chola dynasty ended in the 13th century, a time of political, religious, and cultural change in South Asia. At this point, Buddhism survived in only some areas of India. It soon died out completely there, although the late form of northern Indian Buddhism continued in Tibet and Nepal. At the same time, Islam, which had arrived in India as early as the eighth century, became a potent political force with the establishment of the Delhi Sultanate in 1206. Hindu and Islamic art assumed preeminent roles in India in the 13th century (see Chapter 25).

SOUTHEAST ASIA

For scholars of earlier generations, much of the art of Southeast Asia was merely an extension of Indian civilization. Because the Indian character of many Southeast Asian monuments was readily apparent, some researchers hypothesized that Indian artists had constructed and decorated them and that Indians had colonized Southeast Asia. Today, historians have concluded that such colonization did not occur. The cultural transfer during the first millennium CE was peaceful and nonimperialistic. It appears to have developed almost as a by-product of trade.

In the early centuries CE, extensive trade took place among Rome, India, and China, their ships passing Southeast Asia on the monsoon winds. The tribal chieftains of Southeast Asia quickly saw an opportunity to participate, mainly with their own forest products, such as aromatic woods, bird feathers, and spices. Accompanying the trade goods from India were Sanskrit, Buddhism, and Hinduism—and Buddhist and Hindu art. The Southeast Asian chiefs initially used the transferred elements as a sort of "cultural vocabulary" to compete with one another and to participate in an Indian world. But the Southeast Asian peoples soon modified the Indian cultural material, including the art, to make it their own. Art historians now recognize Southeast Asian art and architecture as a distinctive and important tradition.

Sri Lanka

Sri Lanka (formerly Ceylon) is an island located at the very tip of the Indian subcontinent. Theravada Buddhism, the oldest form of Buddhism, stressing worship of the historical Buddha, Shakyamuni Buddha (see "Buddhism," page 171), arrived in Sri Lanka as early as the third century BCE. From there it spread to other parts of Southeast Asia. With the demise of Buddhism in India in about the 13th century, Sri Lanka now has the longest-lived Buddhist tradition in the world.

GAL VIHARA'S GIANT BUDDHA One of the largest sculptures in Southeast Asia is the 46-foot-long recumbent Buddha (FIG. **6-25**) carved out of a rocky outcropping at Gal Vihara in the 11th or 12th century. To the left of the Buddha, much smaller in scale, stands his cousin and chief disciple, Ananda, arms crossed, mourning Shakyamuni's death. Although more than half a millennium later in date, the Sri Lankan representation of the Buddha's parinirvana reveals its sculptor's debt to the classic Gupta sculptures of India, with their clinging garments, rounded faces, and distinctive renditions of hair (compare FIG. 6-12). Other Southeast Asian monuments, in contrast, exhibit a marked independence from Indian models.

Java

BOROBUDUR, COSMIC MOUNTAIN On the island of Java, part of the modern nation of Indonesia, the period from the 8th to the 10th centuries witnessed the erection of both Hindu and Buddhist monuments. Borobudur (FIG. **6-26**), a Buddhist monument unique in both form and meaning, is the most impressive. Colossal in size, Borobudur measures about 400 feet per side at the base and about 98 feet tall. Built over a small hill on nine terraces accessed by four stairways aligned with the cardinal points, the structure contains literally millions of blocks of volcanic stone. Visitors ascending the massive monument on their way to the summit encounter more than 500 life-size Buddha images, at least 1,000 relief panels, and some 1,500 stupas of various sizes.

Scholars debate the intended meaning of Borobudur. Most think the structure is a constructed cosmic mountain, a three-dimensional mandala where worshipers pass through various realms on their way to ultimate enlightenment. As they

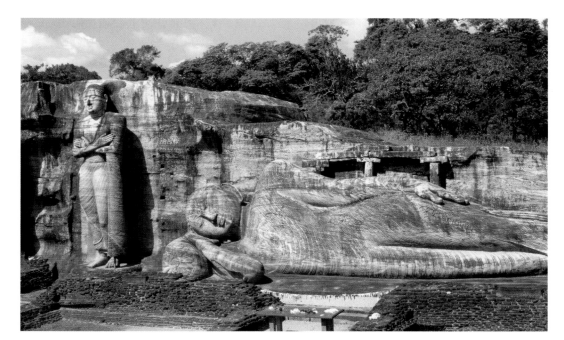

6-25 Death of the Buddha (Parinirvana), Gal Vihara, near Polonnaruwa, Sri Lanka, 11th to 12th century. Granulite, Buddha approx. 46′ long.

6-26 Borobudur, Java, Indonesia, ca. 800.

circumambulate Borobudur, pilgrims first see reliefs illustrating the karmic effects of various kinds of human behavior, then reliefs depicting jatakas of the Buddha's earlier lives, and, further up, events from the life of Shakyamuni. On the circular terraces near the summit, each stupa is hollow and houses a statue of the seated Buddha, who has achieved spiritual enlightenment and preaches using the wheel-turning mudra. At the very top is the largest, sealed stupa. It may once have contained another Buddha image, but some think it was left empty to symbolize the formlessness of true enlightenment. Although scholars have interpreted the iconographic program in different ways, all agree on two essential points: the dependence of Borobudur on Indian art, literature, and religion, and the fact that nothing comparable exists in India itself. Borobudur's sophistication, complexity, and originality underline how completely Southeast Asians had absorbed, rethought, and reformulated Indian religion and art by 800.

Cambodia

In 802, at about the same time the Javanese built Borobudur, the Khmer King Jayavarman II (r. 802–850) founded the Angkor dynasty, which ruled Cambodia for the next 400 years and sponsored the construction of hundreds of monuments. For at least two centuries before the founding of Angkor, the Khmer (the predominant ethnic group in Cambodia) produced Indian-related sculpture of exceptional quality. Images of Vishnu were particularly important during the pre-Angkorian period.

HARIHARA: SHIVA-VISHNU A statue (FIG. **6-27**) from Prasat Andet shows Vishnu in his manifestation as Harihara (Shiva-Vishnu). To represent Harihara, the sculptor divided the statue vertically, with Shiva on the god's right side, Vishnu on his left. The tall headgear reflects the division most clearly. The Shiva half, embellished with the winding locks of an ascetic, contrasts with the kingly Vishnu's plain miter. Attributes (now lost) held in the four hands also helped differentiate the two sides. Stylistically, the Cambodian statue, like the Sri Lankan parinirvana group (FIG. 6-25), derives from Indian sculptures of Gupta style (FIG. 6-12). But unlike almost all stone sculpture in India, carved in relief on slabs or steles, this Khmer image is in the round. The Harihara's broken arms and ankles vividly attest to the vulnerability of this format. The Khmer sculptors, however, wanted viewers to see their statues from all sides in the center of the garbha grihas of brick temples.

VISHNU ON THE COSMIC OCEAN The Khmer kings were exceedingly powerful and possessed enormous wealth. A now fragmentary statue portraying Vishnu lying on the cosmic ocean (FIG. **6-28**) testifies to both the luxurious nature of much Khmer art and to the mastery of Khmer bronze casters. The surviving portion is about 8 feet long. In complete form, at well over 20 feet long, the Vishnu statue was among the largest bronzes of the ancient and medieval worlds, surpassed only by such lost wonders as the statue of Athena in the Parthenon (FIG. 5-44) and the 120-foot-tall colossus of the Roman emperor Nero (see "An Imperial Pleasure Palace," Chapter 10, page 270). Originally, gold and silver inlays and jewels embellished the image, and the god wore a separate miter on his head. The subject of the gigantic statue is the same as that carved in stone on the early Vishnu temple at Deogarh (FIG. 6-19). Vishnu lies asleep on the cosmic ocean at the moment of the creation of the universe. In the myth, a lotus stem grows from Vishnu's navel, its flower supporting Brahma, the creator god. In this statue, Vishnu had a waterspout emerging from his navel, indicating his ability not only to protect the earth and create Brahma but also to create the waters. In fact, the statue was displayed in an island temple in the western *baray* (reservoir) of Angkor.

6-28 Vishnu lying on the cosmic ocean, from Mebon temple on island in western baray, Angkor, Cambodia, 11th century. Bronze, approx. 8′ long.

6-27 Harihara, from Prasat Andet, Cambodia, early seventh century. Stone, 6′ 3″ high. National Museum, Phnom Penh.

KHMER KINGSHIP For more than four centuries, successive kings worked on the construction of the site of Angkor. Founded by Indravarman (r. 877–889), Angkor is an engineering marvel, a grand complex of temples and palaces within a rectangular grid of canals and reservoirs fed by local rivers. Each of the Khmer kings built a temple mountain at Angkor and installed his personal god—Shiva, Vishnu, or the Buddha—on top. He named the image/god with part of his own royal name, implying that the king was a part or manifestation of the deity. When the king died, the Khmer believed that the god reabsorbed him, because he had been the earthly portion of the deity during his lifetime, so they worshiped the king's image posthumously as the god. This concept of kingship approaches an actual deification of the human ruler, familiar in many other societies, such as ancient Egypt (see Chapter 3).

SURYAVARMAN II AND ANGKOR WAT Of all the monuments the Khmer kings erected, Angkor Wat (FIG. **6-29**) is the most spectacular. Built by Suryavarman II (r. 1113–1150), it is the largest of the many Khmer temple complexes. Angkor Wat rises from a huge rectangle of land delineated by a moat measuring about 5,000 × 4,000 feet. Like the other Khmer temples, its purpose was to associate the king with his personal god, in this case Vishnu. The centerpiece of the complex is a tall stepped tower surrounded by four smaller towers connected by covered galleries. The five towers symbolize the five peaks of Mount Meru, the sacred mountain at the center of the universe. Two more circuit walls with galleries, towers, and gates enclose the central block. Thus, as one progresses inward through the complex, the towers rise ever higher, like the towers of the Vishvanatha Temple at Khajuraho (FIG. 6- 22), but in a more complex sequence and on a much grander scale.

Throughout Angkor Wat, stone reliefs glorify both Vishnu in his various avatars and Suryavarman II. The example we illustrate (FIG. **6-30**), on the inner wall of the lowest gallery, shows the king holding court. Suryavarman II sits on an elaborate wooden throne, its

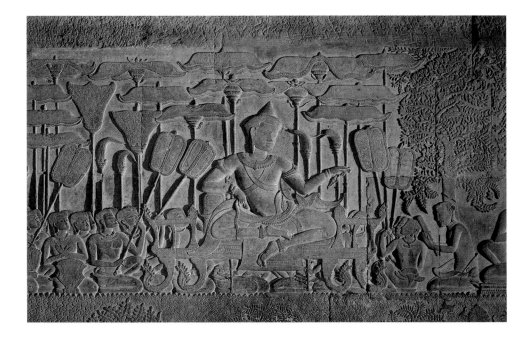

6-30 King Suryavarman II holding court, lowest gallery, south side, Angkor Wat, Angkor, Cambodia, first half of 12th century. Stone.

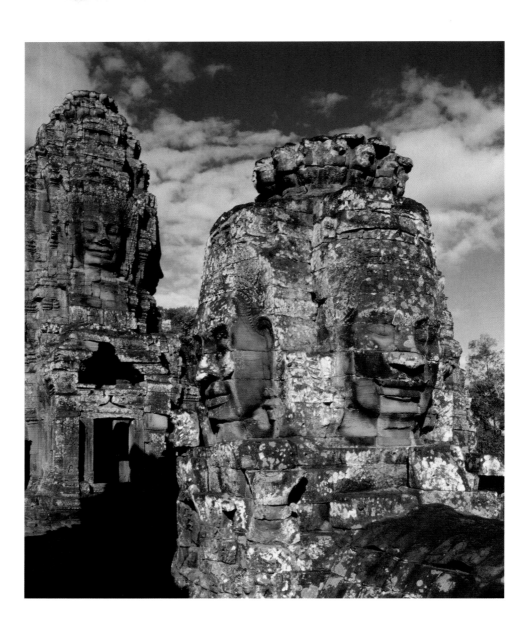

6-31 Bayon, Angkor Thom, Cambodia, ca. 1200.

CONCLUSION

bronze legs rising as cobra heads. Kneeling retainers, smaller than the king because they are lesser figures in the Khmer hierarchy, hold a forest of umbrellas and fans, emblems of Suryavarman's exalted rank. In the reliefs of Angkor Wat, religion and politics are united.

JAYAVARMAN VII AND THE BAYON Jayavarman VII (r. 1181–1219), Suryavarman II's son, ruled over much of mainland Southeast Asia and built more during his reign than all the Khmer kings preceding him combined. His most important temple, the Bayon, is a complicated monument constructed with unique circular terraces surmounted by towers carved with giant faces (FIG. **6-31**). Jayavarman turned to Buddhism from the Hinduism embraced by the earlier Khmer rulers, but adapted Buddhism so that the Buddha and the bodhisattva Lokeshvara ("Lord of the World") were seen as divine prototypes of the king, in the Khmer tradition. The faces on the Bayon towers perhaps portray Lokeshvara, intended to indicate the watchful compassion emanating in all directions from the capital. Other researchers have proposed that the faces depict Jayavarman himself. Jayavarman's great experiment in religion and art was short-lived, but it also marked the point of change in Southeast Asia when Theravada Buddhism began to dominate most of the mainland.

The Indian subcontinent was the birthplace of Buddhism and Hinduism as well as one of the world's earliest civilizations. Third-millennium BCE sites in the Indus Valley feature monumental architecture and sophisticated water supply and sewage systems. Surviving art objects are few and small, however. The first large-scale sculpture and the first temples in South Asia appeared in connection with the spread of Buddhism at the end of the first millennium BCE. Hindu art and architecture emerged in the mid-first millennium CE. Hindu temples, with their distinctive beehive or pyramidal towers, often covered with elaborate relief sculptures, were built throughout the subcontinent. From India, Buddhist and Hindu art and architecture were exported throughout Southeast Asia.

During the first to fourth centuries, Buddhism also traveled to other parts of Asia—to China, Korea, and Japan. Although the artistic traditions in these countries differ greatly from one another, they share, along with Southeast Asia, a tradition of Buddhist art and an ultimate tie with India. Chapters 7 and 8 trace the changes Buddhist art underwent in East Asia, along with the region's other rich artistic traditions.

INDIA AND PAKISTAN	SOUTHEAST ASIA		

INDUS CIVILIZATION

2600 BCE

1500 BCE

VEDIC AND UPANISHADIC PERIODS

| ARYANS COMPILE FIRST OF FOUR *Vedas*, CA. 1500 BCE
| *Upanishads* COMPOSED, CA. 800–500 BCE
| SIDDHARTHA GAUTAMA, SHAKYAMUNI BUDDHA, CA. 563–483 BCE
| ALEXANDER THE GREAT REACHES INDUS RIVER, 326 BCE

1 Robed male figure, Mohenjo-daro, Pakistan, ca. 2600–1900 BCE

323 BCE

MAURYA DYNASTY

| CHANDRAGUPTA MAURYA, R. 323–298 BCE
| 2 | ASHOKA, MAURYA KING, R. 272–231 BCE

185 BCE

SHUNGA, ANDHRA, AND KUSHAN DYNASTIES

| SHUNGA DYNASTY, CENTRAL INDIA, 185–72 BCE
| ANDHRA DYNASTY, SOUTHERN INDIA, CA. 50–320 CE
| KUSHAN DYNASTY, NORTHERN INDIA, CA. 50–320 CE
| KANISHKA, KUSHAN KING, R. 78–144 CE

2 Lion capital of Ashoka, Sarnath, India, ca. 250 BCE

320 CE

GUPTA AND POST-GUPTA PERIODS

| CHANDRAGUPTA II, GUPTA KING, R. 375–415
| 3 | HARISHENA, VAKATAKA KING, R. 462–481
| CHALUKYA DYNASTY, CENTRAL INDIA, 543–743 AND CA. 975–1189
| PALLAVA DYNASTY, SOUTHERN INDIA, CA. 550–728

647

| PALA AND SENA DYNASTIES, NORTHERN INDIA, CA. 700–1200
| CHANDELLA DYNASTY, NORTHERN INDIA, 800–1308

802

MEDIEVAL PERIOD

ANGKOR DYNASTY, CAMBODIA

| JAYAVARMAN II, ANGKOR KING, R. 802–850
| INDRAVARMAN, ANGKOR KING, R. 877–889
| 4 | CHOLA DYNASTY, SOUTHERN INDIA, CA. 907–1279
| SURYAVARMAN II, ANGKOR KING, R. 1113–1150

3 Bodhisattva Padmapani, Ajanta, India, second half of fifth century

1200

| MUSLIM SULTANATE, DELHI, 1206

4 Vishvanatha Temple, Khajuraho, India, ca. 1000

Army of the First Emperor of Qin in pits next to his burial mound, Lintong, China, Qin dynasty, ca. 210 BCE. Painted terracotta, average figure 5′ $10\frac{7}{8}$″ high.

7

THE SILK ROAD
AND BEYOND

THE ART OF EARLY CHINA AND KOREA

East Asia is a vast area, varied both topographically and climatically. Dominated by the huge land mass of China, the region also encompasses the peninsula of Korea and the islands of Japan. In this chapter, we examine the early arts of China and Korea. Early Japanese art and architecture are treated in Chapter 8. Later developments in China and Korea and in Japan are discussed in Chapters 26 and 27.

CHINA

China's landscape includes sandy plains, mighty rivers, towering mountains, and fertile farmlands (MAP **7-1**). Its political and cultural boundaries have varied over the millennia and at times have grown to about twice the area of the United States, encompassing Tibet, Chinese Turkestan (Xinjiang), Mongolia, Manchuria, and parts of Korea. China boasts the world's largest population and is ethnically diverse. The spoken language varies so much that speakers of different dialects do not understand one another. However, the written language, which employs *characters* (signs that record meaning rather than sounds), has permitted different peoples living thousands of miles apart to share literary, philosophic, and religious traditions.

Neolithic China

China is the only continuing civilization that originated in the ancient world. The Chinese archaeological record, extraordinarily rich, goes back to Neolithic times. Discoveries in recent years have expanded the early record enormously. They have provided evidence of settled village life as far back as the seventh or early sixth millennium BCE. Excavators have uncovered sites with large multifamily houses constructed of wood, bamboo, wattle, daub, and mud plaster, and equipped with hearths. These early villages also had pens for domesticated animals, kilns for pottery production, pits

MAP 7-1 Early sites in China and Korea.

for storage and refuse, and cemeteries for the dead. Chinese Neo-lithic artisans produced impressive artworks, especially from jade and clay.

YANGSHAO POTTERY Mastery of the art of pottery occurred at a very early date in China. The potters of the Yangshao Culture, which arose along the Yellow River in northeastern China, produced fine decorated *earthenware* bowls (see "Chinese Earthenwares and Stonewares," page 193) even before the invention of the potter's wheel in the fourth millennium BCE. In the third millennium, the Yangshao potters of Gansu Province manufactured painted vessels (FIG. 7-1) of astonishing sophistication. The multiplicity of shapes suggests that the vessels served a wide variety of functions in daily life, but most of the finds come from graves. Decoration is in red and brownish black on a cream-colored ground. Some pots and bowls have stylized animal motifs, but most feature abstract designs. The painters reveal a highly refined aesthetic sensibility, effectively integrating a variety of angular and curvilinear geometric motifs, including stripes, zigzags, lozenges, circles, spirals, and waves.

Shang Dynasty

During the past century, China's earliest royal dynasties, long thought to have been mythical, have begun to be confirmed archaeologically. Most recently, excavators have found what they believe to be traces of the Xia (ca. 2000–1600 BCE), China's oldest dynasty. Much better documented, however, is the Shang dynasty (ca. 1600–1050 BCE), the first great Chinese dynasty of the

7-1 Yangshao Culture vases, from Gansu Province, China, mid-third millennium BCE. Earthenware.

Chinese Earthenwares and Stonewares

China has no rival in the combined length and richness of its ceramic history. Beginning with the makers of the earliest pots in prehistoric villages, ancient Chinese potters showed a flair for shaping carefully prepared and kneaded clay into diverse, often dramatic and elegant vessel forms.

Until Chinese potters developed true *porcelains* (extremely fine, hard white ceramics; see "Chinese Porcelain," Chapter 26, page 767) in about 1300 CE, they produced only two types of clay vessels or objects—earthenwares and stonewares. For both types, potters used clays colored by mineral impurities, especially iron compounds ranging from yellow to brownish black.

The clay bodies of *earthenwares* (FIG. 7-1), fired at low temperatures in open pits or simple kilns, remain soft and porous, thus allowing liquids to seep through. Chinese artists also used the low-fire technique to produce terracotta sculptures, even life-size figures of humans and animals (FIG. 7-5). Over time, Chinese potters developed kilns allowing them to fire their clay vessels at much higher temperatures—more than 2000° Fahrenheit. Such temperatures produce *stonewares,* named for their stonelike hardness and density.

Potters in China excelled at the various techniques commonly used to decorate earthenwares and stonewares. Most of these decorative methods depend on changes occurring in the kiln to chemical compounds found in clay as natural impurities. When fired, many compounds change color dramatically, depending on the conditions in the kiln. For example, if little oxygen remains in a hot kiln, iron oxide (rust) turns either gray or brownish black, whereas an abundance of oxygen produces a reddish hue.

Chinese potters also decorated vessels simply by painting their surfaces. In one of the oldest decorative techniques, the potters applied *slip* (a mixture of clay and water like a fine, thin mud)—by painting, pouring, or dipping—to a clay body not yet fully dry. The natural variety of clay colors produced a broad, if not bright, palette, as seen in Neolithic vessels (FIG. 7-1). But Chinese potters often also added compounds such as iron oxide to the slip to change or intensify the colors. After the vessels had partially dried, the potters could incise lines through the slip down to the clay body to produce designs such as those often seen in later Chinese stonewares (FIG. 7-20).

The slip technique compares with that used by Archaic Greek black-figure painters (see FIGS. 5-4, 5-18, and 5-19). Chinese artists sometimes inlaid designs, too, carving them into plain vessel surfaces and then filling them with slip or soft clay of a contrasting color. Such techniques spread throughout East Asia (FIG. 7-28).

To produce a hard, glassy surface after firing, potters coated plain or decorated vessels with a *glaze,* a finely ground mixture of minerals. Clear or highly translucent glazes best reveal decorated surfaces. More opaque, richly colored glazes (FIG. 7-17) serve as primary decoration.

Bronze Age. The Shang kings ruled from a series of royal capitals in the Yellow River valley and vied for power and territory with the rulers of neighboring states.

ROYAL BURIALS AT ANYANG In 1928, excavations at Anyang (ancient Yin) brought to light the last Shang capital. There, archaeologists found a large number of objects—turtle shells, animal bones, and bronze containers—inscribed in the earliest form of the Chinese language. These fragmentary records and the other finds at Anyang provide important information about the Shang kings and their affairs. They reveal a warlike, highly stratified society. Walls of pounded earth protected Shang cities. Servants, captives, and even teams of charioteers with chariots and horses accompanied Shang kings to their tombs, a practice noted earlier with regard to the Royal Cemetery at Ur (see Chapter 2). The excavated tomb furnishings include weapons and a great wealth of objects in jade, ivory, lacquer, and bronze. Not only the kings received lavish burials. The tomb of Fu Hao, the wife of Wu Ding (r. ca. 1215–1190 BCE), for example, contained more than a thousand bronze and jade objects, as well as an ivory beaker inlaid with turquoise.

SHANG BRONZES Shang artists perfected the casting of elaborate bronze vessels in piece molds (see "Shang Bronze-Casting," page 194). Many of these vessels were used in sacrifices to ancestors and in funerary ceremonies. Shang bronzes held wine, water, grain, or meat for sacrificial rites. Each vessel's shape matched its intended purpose. One of the most dramatic Shang vessel forms is the *guang* (FIG. **7-2**), a libation vessel shaped like a covered gravy boat. Preserved examples display the characteristic Shang decorative vocabulary of abstract and animal motifs. These range from

7-2 Guang, probably from Anyang, China, Shang dynasty, 12th or 11th century BCE. Bronze, $6\frac{1}{2}''$ high. Asian Art Museum of San Francisco, San Francisco (Avery Brundage Collection).

Shang Bronze-Casting

Among the finest bronzes of the second millennium BCE are those that Shang artists created using piece molds (FIG. 7-2). The Shang bronzeworkers began the process by producing a solid clay model of the desired object and allowing it to dry to durable hardness. Then they pressed damp clay around it to form a mold that hardened but remained somewhat flexible. At that point, they carefully cut the mold in pieces, removed the pieces from the model, and baked the pieces in a kiln to form hard earthenware sections. Sculptors then carved the intricate details of the relief decoration into the inner surfaces of the piece molds. Next, the artists shaved the model to reduce its size to form a core for the piece mold. They then reassembled the mold around the model using bronze spacers to preserve a void between the model and the mold—a space equivalent to the layer of wax used in the lost-wax method (see "Hollow-Casting Life-Size Bronze Statues," Chapter 5, page 131). The Shang bronze casters then added a final clay layer on the outside to hold everything together, leaving open ducts for pouring molten bronze into the space between the model and the mold and to permit gases to escape. Once the mold cooled, they broke it apart, removed the new bronze vessel, and cleaned and polished it.

Shang bronzes show a skill in casting rivaling that of any other ancient civilization and indicating a long developmental period for achieving such mastery. The great numbers of cast-bronze vessels strongly suggest well-organized workshops, but no records provide a clear picture of such matters or of the place the artists held in their society. Bronze-casting may have been a hereditary occupation.

mere suggestions of animal forms emerging out of linear patterns to identifiable representations of specific creatures. Often, distinct motifs stand out against a background of round or squared spirals ending in hooks. Sometimes the same motifs also cover the figures.

In the Shang guang we illustrate (FIG. 7-2), the multiple designs and their fields of background spirals integrate so closely with the form of the vessel that they are not merely an external embellishment but an integral part of the sculptural whole. Some motifs on the vessel's side may represent the eyes of a tiger and the horns of a ram. A horned animal forms the front of the lid, and at the rear is a horned head with a bird's beak. Another horned head appears on the handle. Fish, birds, elephants, rabbits, and more abstract composite creatures swarm over the surface against a background of spirals. The fabulous animal forms, real and imaginary, are unlikely to have been purely decorative. They are probably connected with the world of spirits addressed in the rituals.

SURPRISING SANXINGDUI Recent excavations in other regions of China have greatly expanded historical understanding of the Bronze Age. They suggest that at the same time Anyang flourished under its Shang rulers in northern China, so did other major centers with distinct aesthetic traditions. For example, in 1986, pits at Sanxingdui, near Chengdu in southwestern China, yielded a treasure of elephant tusks and objects in gold, bronze, jade, and clay of types never before discovered. They attest to an independent kingdom of enormous wealth contemporary with the better-known Shang dynasty.

The most dramatic find, a bronze statue (FIG. **7-3**) more than eight feet tall, matches anything from Anyang in masterful casting technique. Very different in subject and style from the Shang bronzes, it initially shocked art historians who had formed their ideas about Bronze Age Chinese aesthetics based on Shang material. This figure—of unknown identity—is highly stylized, with elongated proportions and large, staring eyes. It stands on a thin platform supported by four legs formed of fantastic animal heads with horns and trunklike snouts. These, in turn, rest on a thick, heavy square base. The statue as a whole tapers gently as it rises, and the figure gradually becomes rounder. Just below the neck, great arms branch dramatically outward, ending in oversized hands that once held an object, perhaps an attribute revealing its

7-3 Standing figure, from Sanxingdui, China, ca. 1200-1050 BCE. Bronze, 8′ 5″ high, including base. Museum, Sanxingdui.

Chinese Jade

The Chinese first used jade, or more precisely, nephrite, for art-works and ritual objects in the Neolithic period. Nephrite polishes to a more lustrous, slightly buttery finish than jadeite (the stone Chinese sculptors preferred from the 18th century on), which is quite glassy. Both stones come in colors other than the well-known green and are tough, hard, and heavy, as well as beautiful. In China, such qualities became metaphors for the fortitude and moral perfection of superior persons. Jade was also believed to have magical qualities that could protect the dead. Archaeologists have found the tomb of a prince and princess of the Han dynasty (206 BCE–220 CE), each of whom was laid to rest in a suit composed of more than 2,000 jade tablets sewn together with gold wire.

Because of its extreme hardness, jade could not be carved with the Neolithic sculptor's stone tools. Researchers can only speculate on how these early artists were able to cut, shape, and incise the nephrite objects discovered at many Neolithic Chinese sites. The sculptors probably used cords embedded with sand to incise lines into the surfaces. Sand placed in a bamboo tube drill could perforate the hard stone, but the process would have been long and arduous, requiring great patience as well as superior skill. Even after the invention of bronze tools, Chinese sculptors still had to rely on grinding and abrasion rather than simple drilling and chiseling to produce the intricately shaped, pierced, and engraved works such as the *bi* illustrated in FIG. 7-4.

---

identity. Representations of the human figure on this scale in this period are otherwise unknown. Surface decoration of squared spirals and hook-pointed curves is all that links this gigantic statue with the intricate piece-mold bronze vessels of the Shang (FIG. 7-2). Archaeology will probably continue to produce such surprises and cause art historians to revise once again their picture of Chinese art in the second half of the second millennium BCE.

Zhou Dynasty

Around 1050 BCE, the Zhou, former vassals of the Shang, captured Anyang and overthrew their Shang overlords. The Zhou dynasty proved to be the longest lasting in China's history—so long that historians divide the Zhou era into two great periods: Western Zhou (ca. 1050–771 BCE) and Eastern Zhou (770–256 BCE). The dividing event is the transfer of the Zhou capital from Chang'an (modern Xi'an) in the west to Luoyang in the east. The closing centuries of Zhou rule include a long period of warfare among competing states (Warring States Period, ca. 475–221 BCE). The Zhou fell to one of these states, the Qin, in 256 BCE. By 221 BCE the Qin had defeated all their other rivals.

Under the Zhou, the decline of old ceremonial rules and the development of markets, together with bronze coinage and the rise of freelance artists, supported a taste for lavish products, such as bronzes inlaid with gold and silver. Late Zhou bronzes featured scenes of hunting, religious rites, and magic practices. These may relate to the subjects and compositions of lost paintings mentioned in Zhou literature. Other materials favored in the late Zhou period were jade (see "Chinese Jade," above) and *lacquer*, a varnishlike substance made from the sap of the Asiatic sumac, used to decorate wood furniture and other objects (see "Lacquered Wood," Chapter 26, page 769).

JADE DRAGONS The carving of jade objects for burial with the dead, beginning in Neolithic times, reached a peak of technical perfection during the Zhou dynasty. Among the most common finds in tombs of the period are *bi* disks—thin, flat circular pieces of jade with a hole in the center, which may have symbolized the circle of Heaven. Our example (FIG. 7-4) probably came

from a royal Eastern Zhou tomb at Jincun, near Luoyang in north central China. Rows of raised spirals, created by laborious grinding and polishing, decorate the disk itself. Within the inner circle and around the outer edge of the bi are elegant dragons, which required long hours of work to pierce through the hard jade. The bi testifies to the Zhou sculptor's mastery of this difficult material. The Chinese thought dragons inhabited the water and flew between Heaven and Earth, bringing rain, so these animals long have been symbols of good fortune in East Asia. They also symbolized the rulers' power to mediate between Heaven and Earth.

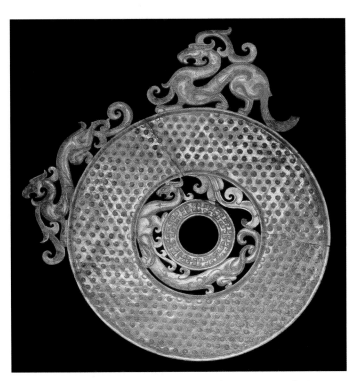

7-4 *Bi* disk with dragons, from Jincun(?), China, Eastern Zhou dynasty, fourth to third century BCE. Nephrite, $6\frac{1}{2}''$ in diameter. Nelson-Atkins Museum of Art, Kansas City.

Daoism and Confucianism

Daoism and Confucianism are both philosophies and religions native to China. Both schools of thought attracted wide followings during the Warring States Period (ca. 475–221 BCE), when political turbulence led to social unrest.

Daoism emerged out of the metaphysical teachings attributed to Laozi (604?–531? BCE) and Zhuangzi (370?–301? BCE). It takes its name from Laozi's treatise *Daodejing (The Way and Its Power)*. Daoist philosophy stresses an intuitive awareness, nurtured by harmonious contact with nature, and eschews everything artificial. Daoists seek to follow the universal path, or principle, called the Dao, whose features cannot be described but only suggested through analogies. For example, the Dao is said to be like water, always yielding but eventually wearing away the hard stone that does not yield. For Daoists, strength comes from flexibility and inaction. Historically, Daoist principles encouraged retreat from society in favor of personal cultivation.

Confucius (551–479 BCE) was born in the state of Lu (roughly modern Shandong Province) to an aristocratic family that had fallen on hard times. From an early age, he showed a strong interest in the rites and ceremonies that helped unite people into an orderly society. As he grew older, he developed a deep concern for the suffering caused by the civil conflict of his day. Thus, he adopted a philosophy he hoped would lead to order and stability.

The ideal social order Confucius sought is personified by the *junzi* ("superior person" or "gentleman"), who possesses *ren* ("human-heartedness"). Although the term junzi originally assumed noble birth, in Confucian thought anyone can become a junzi by cultivating the virtues Confucius espoused, especially empathy for suffering, pursuit of morality and justice, respect for ancient ceremonies, and adherence to traditional social relationships, such as those between parent and child, elder and younger sibling, husband and wife, and ruler and subject.

Confucius's disciple Mencius (or Mengzi, 371?–289? BCE), developed the master's ideas further, stressing that the deference to age and rank that is at the heart of the Confucian social order brings a reciprocal responsibility. For example, a king's legitimacy depends on the good will of his people. A ruler should share his joys with his subjects, and will know his laws are unjust if they bring suffering to the people.

Confucius spent much of his adult life trying to find rulers willing to apply his teachings, but he died in disappointment. However, he and Mencius had a profound impact on Chinese thought and social practice. Chinese traditions of venerating deceased ancestors and outstanding leaders encouraged the development of Confucianism as a religion as well as a philosophic tradition. Eventually, Emperor Wu Di (r. 140–87 BCE) of the Han dynasty established Confucianism as the state's official doctrine. Thereafter, it became the primary subject of the civil service exams required for admission into and advancement within government service.

"Confucian" and "Daoist" are broad, imprecise terms scholars often use to distinguish aspects of Chinese culture stressing social responsibility and order (Confucian) from those emphasizing cultivation of individuals, often in reclusion (Daoist). But both philosophies share the idea that anyone can cultivate wisdom or ability, regardless of birth.

Qin Dynasty

THE FIRST EMPEROR During the Warring States Period, China endured more than two centuries of political and social turmoil. This was also a time of intellectual and artistic upheaval, when conflicting schools of philosophy, including Legalism, Daoism, and Confucianism, emerged (see "Daoism and Confucianism," above). Order was finally restored when the powerful armies of the ruler of the state of Qin (from which the modern name "China" derives) conquered all rival states. Qin's ruler took the name Zheng, but he is known to history by his title, Qin Shi Huangdi, the First Emperor of Qin. Between 221 and 210 BCE he controlled an area equal to about half of modern China, much larger than the territories of any of the dynasties before him. During his reign, he ordered the linkage of active fortifications along the northern border of his realm to form the famous Great Wall. The wall defended China against the fierce nomadic peoples of the north, especially the Huns, who eventually made their way to eastern Europe. By sometimes brutal methods, Shi Huangdi consolidated rule through a centralized bureaucracy and adopted standardized written language, weights and measures, and coinage. He also repressed schools of thought other than Legalism, which espoused absolute obedience to the state's authority and advocated strict laws and punishments. Chinese historians long have condemned China's First Emperor, but the bureaucratic system he put in place had a long-lasting impact. Its success was due in large part to Shi Huangdi's decision to replace the feudal lords with talented salaried administrators and to reward merit rather than favor high birth.

THE EMPEROR'S ARMY In 1974, excavations started at the site of the immense burial mound of the First Emperor of Qin at Lintong. For its construction, the ruler conscripted many thousands of laborers and had the tomb filled with treasure—a task that continued after his death. The mound itself remains unexcavated, but researchers believe it contains a vast underground funerary palace designed to match the fabulous palace the emperor occupied in life. The historian Sima Qian (136–85 BCE) described both palaces, but scholars did not take his account seriously until the discovery of pits around the tomb filled with more than 6,000 life-size painted terracotta figures of soldiers and horses (FIG. 7-5), as well as bronze horses and chariots. Replicating the emperor's invincible hosts, they served as the immortal imperial bodyguard deployed in trenches outside the First Emperor's tomb.

The terracotta army, comprised of cavalry, chariots, archers, lancers, and hand-to-hand fighters, was one of the 20th century's greatest archaeological discoveries. Lesser versions of Shi Huangdi's army have since been uncovered at other Chinese sites, suggesting that the First Emperor's tomb became the model for many others. The huge assemblage at Lintong testifies to a very high degree of

7-5 Army of the First Emperor of Qin in pits next to his burial mound, Lintong, China, Qin dynasty, ca. 210 BCE. Painted terracotta, average figure 5′ 10⅞″ high.

organization in the Qin imperial workshop. Manufacturing this army of statues required a veritable army of sculptors and painters as well as a large number of huge kilns. The First Emperor's artisans could have opted to use the same molds over and over again to produce thousands of identical soldiers standing in strict formation. In fact, they did employ the same molds repeatedly for different parts of the statues, but assembled the parts in many different combinations. Consequently, the stances, arm positions, garment folds, equipment, coiffures, and facial features vary, sometimes slightly, sometimes markedly, from statue to statue. Additional hand modeling of the cast body parts before firing permitted the sculptors to differentiate the figures even more. The Qin painters undoubtedly added further variations to the appearance of the terracotta army. The result of these efforts was a brilliant balance of uniformity and individuality.

Han Dynasty

Soon after Qin Shi Huangdi's death, the people who had suffered under his reign revolted, assassinated his son, and founded the Han dynasty in 206 BCE. The Han ruled China for four centuries and extended its southern and western boundaries. Chinese armies penetrated far into Central Asia (modern Xinjiang) and even began to trade indirectly with distant Rome via the fabled Silk Road (see "Silk and the Silk Road," page 201).

7-6 Funeral banner, from tomb 1 (tomb of Dai), Mawangdui, China, Han dynasty, ca. 168 BCE. Painted silk, 6′ 8¾″ × 3′ ¼″. Hunan Provincial Museum, Changsha.

PAINTING ON SILK In 1972, archaeologists excavated the tomb of the wife of the Marquis of Dai at Mawangdui in Hunan Province. The tomb contained a rich array of burial goods used during the funerary ceremonies and to accompany the deceased into the afterlife. Among the many finds were decorated lacquer utensils, various textiles, and an astonishingly well-preserved corpse in the innermost of four nested sarcophagi. Most remarkable of all, however, was the discovery of a painted T-shaped silk banner (FIG. 7-6) draped over the woman's coffin. Scholars generally agree that

7-7 The archer Yi(?) and a reception in a mansion, Wu family shrine, Jiaxiang, China, Han dynasty, 147–168 CE. Rubbing of a stone relief, approx. 3′ × 5′.

the area within the cross at the top of the T represents Heaven. Most of the vertical section below is the human realm. At the very bottom is the Underworld. In the heavenly realm, dragons and immortal beings appear between and below two orbs—the red sun and its symbol, the raven, on the right, and the silvery moon and its symbol, the toad, on the left. Below, the standing figure on the first white platform near the center of the vertical section is probably the Marquise of Dai herself—one of the first portraits in Chinese art. The Marquise awaits her ascent to Heaven, where she can attain immortality. Nearer the bottom, the artist depicted the wealthy woman's funeral. Between these two sections is a form resembling a bi disk with two intertwining dragons (compare FIG. 7-4). Their tails reach down to the Underworld and their heads point to Heaven, unifying the whole composition.

HAN ANCESTRAL SHRINES Even more extensive Han pictorial narratives were carved into the stone walls of the Wu family shrines at Jiaxiang in Shandong Province between 147 and 168 CE. The shrines document the emergence of private, nonaristocratic families as patrons of religious and mythological art with political overtones. Dedicated to deceased male family members, the Wu shrines consist of three low walls covered by a pitched roof. On the interior surfaces, images of flat polished stone stand out against an equally flat, though roughly textured, ground. The historical scenes include a representation of the attempt to assassinate the tyrannical First Emperor of Qin by the celebrated third-century BCE hero Jing Ke. On the slab shown here (FIG. 7-7, a rubbing taken from the stone relief) the archer at the upper left is probably the hero Yi, saving the Earth from scorching by shooting down the nine extra suns, represented as crows in the Fusang tree. (The small orbs below the sun on the Mawangdui banner probably allude to the same story.) The lowest zone shows a procession of umbrella-carriages moving to the left. Above, underneath the overhanging eaves of a two-story mansion, robed men bearing

gifts pay homage to a central figure of uncertain identity, who is represented as larger and therefore more important. Two men kneel before the larger figure. Women occupy the upper story. Again, one figure is singled out as the most important; she faces forward. Whatever the identities of the individual figures (interpretations vary widely), these scenes of homage and loyalty are consistent with the Confucian ideals of Han society (see "Daoism and Confucianism," page 196).

HAN HOUSES AND PALACES No actual remains of Han buildings survive, but ceramic models of houses deposited in Han tombs, together with representations such as those in the Wu family shrines, provide a good idea of Chinese architecture during the early centuries CE. An especially large painted earthenware model (FIG. 7-8) reproduces a Han house with sharply projecting tiled roofs resting on a framework of timber posts, lintels, and brackets. This construction method, in which the walls do not bear the weight of the roof but serve only as screens separating inside from outside and room from room, typifies much Chinese architecture even today (see "Chinese Wooden Construction Methods and Principles," page 200). Descriptions of Han palaces suggest that they were grandiose versions of the type of house reproduced in this model, but with more luxurious decoration, including walls of lacquered wood and mural paintings.

Period of Disunity

BUDDHISM REACHES CHINA For three and a half centuries, from 220 to 589,* civil strife divided China into competing states. Scholars variously refer to this era as the Period of Disunity or the

---

* From this point on, all dates in this chapter are CE unless otherwise stated.

els in the flat, relief-like handling of the robe's heavy concentric folds, the ushnisha (cranial bump) on the head, and the cross-legged position. So new were the icon and its meaning, however, that the Chinese sculptor misrepresented the canonical dhyana mudra, or meditation gesture. Here, the Buddha clasps his hands across his stomach. In South Asian art, they are turned palms upward, with thumbs barely touching in front of the torso.

PAINTING MATERIALS AND FORMATS Secular arts also flourished in the Period of Disunity. Rulers sought calligraphers and painters to lend prestige to their courts. Several distinctive materials and formats characterize early Chinese painting. The basic requirements for paintings not on walls are the same as for writing—a round tapered brush, soot-based ink, and either silk or paper. The Chinese were masters of the brush. Sometimes they employed modulated lines that elastically thicken and thin to convey not only outline but depth and mass as well. In other works, they used *iron-wire lines* (thin, unmodulated lines with a suggestion of tensile strength) to define the figures. Chinese painters also used richly colored minerals as pigments, finely ground and suspended in a gluey medium, and watery washes of mineral and vegetable dyes.

The formats of Chinese paintings (other than mural paintings) tend to be personal and intimate. Some pictures were mounted on scrolls for vertical display (unrolled) on appropriate occasions. Others were attached to long, narrow scrolls that the viewer unrolled horizontally, section by section. Stiff round or arched folding fans were also popular painting formats. Artists also painted small panels on paper leaves, which were collected in albums. Although some Chinese paintings are monumental in size, most are intimate in scale and best viewed by only one or two people at a time.

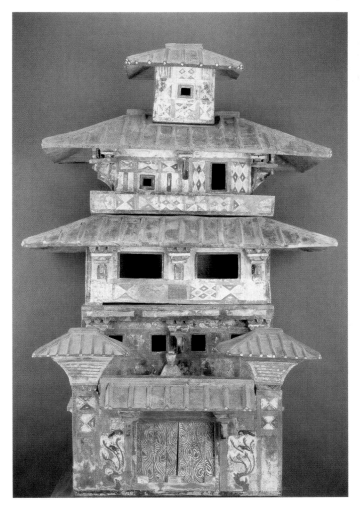

7-8 Model of a house, Han dynasty, first century CE. Painted earthenware, 4' 4" high. Nelson-Atkins Museum of Art, Kansas City.

period of the Six Dynasties or of the Northern and Southern Dynasties. The history of this era is extremely complex, but one development deserves special mention—the occupation of the north by peoples who were not ethnically Han Chinese and who spoke non-Chinese languages. It was in the northern states, connected to India by the desert caravan routes of the Silk Road (see "Silk and the Silk Road," page 201), that Buddhism first took root in China during the Han dynasty (see "Buddhism," Chapter 6, page 171). Certain practices shared with Daoism, such as withdrawal from ordinary society, helped Buddhism gain an initial foothold in the north. But Buddhism's promise of hope beyond the troubles of this world earned it an ever broader audience during the upheavals of the Period of Disunity. In addition, the fully developed Buddhist system of thought attracted intellectuals. Buddhism never fully displaced Confucianism and Daoism, but it did prosper throughout China for centuries and had a profound effect on the further development of the religious forms of those two native traditions.

The earliest extant precisely datable Chinese Buddhist image is a gilded bronze statuette (FIG. **7-9**) of Shakyamuni Buddha, the historical Buddha, dated by inscription to the year 338. The oldest Chinese Buddhist texts describe the Buddha as golden and radiating light. This no doubt accounts for the choice of gilded bronze as the sculptor's medium. In both style and iconography, this early Buddha resembles the prototype conceived and developed at Gandhara (see FIG. 6-9). The Chinese figure recalls its presumed South Asian mod-

7-9 Shakyamuni Buddha, Zhao dynasty, Period of Disunity, 338. Gilded bronze, 1' 3½" high. Asian Art Museum of San Francisco, San Francisco (Avery Brundage Collection).

Chinese Wooden Construction Methods and Principles

Although the basic unit of Chinese architecture, the rectangular hall with columns supporting a roof, was common in many ancient civilizations, Chinese buildings are distinguished from Egyptian hypostyle halls (see FIG. 3-27) and Greco-Roman temples (see "Doric and Ionic Temples," Chapter 5, pages 116–117) by the curving silhouettes of their roofs and by their method of construction.

The Chinese, like other ancient peoples, used wood to construct their earliest buildings. Although those structures do not survive, scholars believe that many of the features giving East Asian architecture its specific character may go back to Zhou times. Even the simple buildings reproduced on Han stone carvings (FIG. 7-7) or in clay models (FIG. 7-8) reveal a style and a method of construction long basic to China.

The typical Chinese hall has a pitched roof with projecting eaves. Wooden columns, lintels, and brackets provide the support. The walls serve no weight-bearing function but act only as screens. The colors of Chinese buildings, predominantly red, black, yellow, and white, are also distinctive. Chinese timber architecture is customarily multicolored throughout, save for certain parts left in natural color, such as railings made of white marble. The builders usually painted the screen walls and the columns red. Chinese designers often chose dazzling combinations of colors and elaborate patterns for the beams, brackets, eaves, rafters, and ceilings. The builders painted or lacquered the surfaces to protect the timber from rot and wood parasites, as well as to produce an arresting aesthetic effect.

Our diagram shows the basic construction method of Chinese architecture, with the major components of a Chinese building labeled. The builders laid *beams* (no. 1) between columns, decreasing the length of the beams as the structure rose. The beams supported vertical *struts* (no. 2), which in turn supported higher beams and eventually the *purlins* (no. 3) running the length of the building and carrying the roof's sloping *rafters* (no. 4). Unlike the rigid elements of the triangular trussed timber roof common in the West, which produce flat sloping rooflines, the varying lengths of the Chinese structure's cross beams and the variously placed purlins can create curved profiles. Early Chinese roofs have flat profiles (FIGS. 7-7 and 7-8), but curving rafters later became the norm, not only in China but throughout East Asia (FIGS. 7-14, 7-21, 7-22, 8-6, 8-10, and 8-12). In addition, the interlocking clusters of brackets could cantilever (support with brackets) the roof to allow for broad overhang of the *eaves* (no. 5), another typical feature of Chinese architecture. Multiplication of the *bays* (spaces between the columns) could extend the building's length to any dimension desired, although each bay could be no wider or longer than the length of a single tree trunk. The proportions of the structural elements could be fixed into modules, allowing for standardization of parts. This enabled rapid construction of a building. The workers fit the parts together without using any adhesive substance, such as mortar or glue. Delicately joined as the parts were, they still could easily carry the heavy tiled roofs of Chinese buildings (FIGS. 7-8, 7-14, 7-21, and 26-5).

1. Beam
2. Strut
3. Purlin
4. Rafter
5. Eaves

Chinese raised beam construction (after L. Liu).

Silk and the Silk Road

Silk is the finest natural fabric ever produced. It comes from the cocoons of caterpillars called silkworms. The manufacture of silk was a well-established industry in China by the second millennium BCE. The basic procedures probably have not changed much since then. Farmers today still raise silkworms from eggs, which they place in trays. The farmers also must grow mulberry trees or purchase mulberry leaves, the silkworms' only food source. Eventually, the silkworms form cocoons out of very fine filaments they extrude as liquid from their bodies. The filaments soon solidify with exposure to air. Before the transformed caterpillars emerge as moths and badly damage the silk, the farmers kill them with steam or high heat. They soften the cocoons in hot water and unwind the filaments onto a reel. The filaments are so fine that workers generally unwind those from 5 to 10 cocoons together to bond into a single strand while the filaments are still soft and sticky. Later, the silkworkers twist several strands together to form a thicker yarn and then weave the yarn on a loom to produce silk cloth. Both the yarn and the cloth can be dyed, and the silk fabric can be decorated by weaving threads of different colors together in special patterns *(brocades)* or by stitching in threads of different colors *(embroidery)*. Many Chinese artists painted directly on plain silk (FIGS. 7-6, 7-10, 7-15, 7-18, 7-19, 7-23, 7-24, 26-9, and 26-14).

Greatly admired throughout most of Asia, Chinese silk and the secrets of its production gradually spread throughout the ancient world. The Romans knew of silk as early as the second century BCE and treasured it for garments and hangings. Silk came to the Romans along the ancient fabled Silk Road, actually a network of caravan tracts across Central Asia linking China and the Mediterranean world. The western part, between the Mediterranean region and India, developed first, due largely to the difficult geographic conditions to India's northeast. In Central Asia, the caravans had to skirt the Taklamakan Desert, one of the most inhospitable environments on earth, as well as climb high, dangerous mountain passes.

Very few traders actually traveled the entire route. Along the way, goods usually passed through the hands of people from many lands, who often only dimly understood the ultimate origins and destinations of what they traded. The Roman passion for silk ultimately led to the modern name for the caravan tracts, but silk was far from the only product traded along the way. Gold, ivory, gems, glass, lacquer, incense, furs, spices, cotton, linens, exotic animals, and other merchandise precious enough to warrant the risks passed along the Silk Road.

Ideas moved along these trade routes as well. Most important perhaps, travelers on the Silk Road brought Buddhism to China from India in the first century CE, opening up a significant new chapter in both the history of religion and the history of art in China.

LADY FENG'S HEROISM The most famous early Chinese painter with whom extant works can be associated was GU KAIZHI (ca. 344–406). Gu was a friend of important members of the Eastern Jin dynasty (317–420) and was renowned as a calligrapher, a painter of court portraits, and a pioneer of landscape painting. A horizontal scroll now in the British Museum, although attributed to Gu Kaizhi in the 11th century, is not actually by his hand, but it provides a good idea of the key elements of his art. Called *Admonitions of the Instructress to the Court Ladies,* the scroll contains painted scenes and accompanying explanatory text. Like all Chinese *handscrolls,* this one was unrolled and read from right to left, with only a small section exposed for viewing at one time. The section we illustrate (FIG. 7-10) records a well-known act of heroism, the Lady Feng saving her emperor's life by

7-10 GU KAIZHI, Lady Feng and the Bear, detail of *Admonitions of the Instructress to the Court Ladies,* Period of Disunity, late fourth century. Handscroll, ink and colors on silk, $9\frac{3}{4}'' \times 11' \, 4\frac{1}{2}''$. British Museum, London.

Xie He's Six Canons

China has a long and rich history of scholarship on painting, preserved today in copies of texts from as far back as the fourth century and in citations to even earlier sources. Few of the first texts on painting survive, but later authors often quoted them, preserving the texts for posterity. Thus, educated Chinese painters and their clients could steep themselves in a rich art historical tradition. Perhaps the most famous subject of later commentary is a set of six "canons" or "laws" of painting formulated in the early sixth century by Xie He. The canons, as translated by James Cahill,[1] are as follows:

1. Engender a sense of movement through spirit consonance.
2. Use the brush with the bone method.
3. Responding to things, depict their forms.
4. According to kind, describe appearances [with color].
5. Dividing and planning, positioning and arranging.
6. Transmitting and conveying earlier models through copying and transcribing.

Several variant translations have also been proposed, and scholars actively debate the precise meaning of these succinct (Xie He employed only four characters for each) and cryptic laws. Interpreting the canons in connection with actual paintings is often difficult, but nonetheless offers valuable insights into what the Chinese valued in painting.

The simplest canons to understand are the third, fourth, and fifth, because they show painters' concern for accuracy in rendering forms and colors and for care in composition, concerns common in many cultures. However, separating form and color into different laws gives written expression to a distinctive feature of early Chinese painting. Painters such as Gu Kaizhi (FIG. 7-10) and Yan Liben (FIG. 7-15) used an outline-and-color technique. Their brushed-ink outline drawings employ flat applications of color. To suggest volume, they used ink shading along edges, such as drapery folds.

Also noteworthy is the order of the laws, suggesting Chinese painters' primary concern: to convey the vital spirit of their subjects and their own sensitivity to that spirit. Next in importance was the handling of the brush and the careful placement of strokes, especially of ink. The sixth canon also speaks to a standard Chinese painting practice: copying. Chinese painters, like painters in other cultures throughout history, trained by copying the works of their teachers and other painters. In addition, artists often copied famous paintings as sources of forms and ideas for their own works and to preserve great works created using fragile materials (FIG. 7-10). In China, as elsewhere, change and individual development occurred in constant reference to the past, the artists always preserving some elements of it.

---

[1] James Cahill, "The Six Laws and How to Read Them," *Ars Orientalis* 4 (1961), 372–81.

---

placing herself between him and an attacking bear—a perfect model of Confucian behavior. As in many early Chinese paintings, the figures are set against a blank background with only a minimal setting for the scene, although in other works Gu provided landscape settings for his narratives. The figures' poses and fluttering drapery ribbons, in concert with individualized facial expressions, convey a clear quality of animation. This style accords well with painting ideals expressed in texts of the time, when representing inner vitality and spirit took precedence over reproducing surface appearances (see "Xie He's Six Canons," above).

THE MEETING OF TWO BUDDHAS A gilded bronze statuette (FIG. **7-11**) shows how the sculptors of the Northern Wei dynasty (386–534) had transformed the Gandhara-derived style of earlier Buddhist art in China (FIG. 7-9). Dated 518, the piece was probably made for private devotion in a domestic setting or as a votive offering in a temple. It represents the meeting of Shakyamuni Buddha (at the viewer's right) and Prabhutaratna, the Buddha who had achieved nirvana in the remote past, as recounted in the *Lotus Sutra,* an encyclopedic collection of Buddhist thought and poetry. When Shakyamuni was preaching on Vulture Peak, Prabhutaratna's stupa miraculously appeared in the sky. Shakyamuni opened it and revealed Prabhutaratna himself, who had promised to be present whenever the Lotus Law was preached. Shakyamuni sat beside him and continued to expound the Law. The meeting of the two Buddhas symbolized the continuity of Buddhist thought across the ages.

7-11 Shakyamuni and Prabhutaratna, Northern Wei dynasty, 518. Gilded bronze, 10¼″ high. Musée Guimet, Paris.

Behind each Buddha is a flamelike nimbus (*mandorla*). Both figures sit in the *lalitasana* pose—one leg folded and the other hanging down. This standard pose, which indicates relaxation, underscores the ease of communication between the two Buddhas. Their bodies have elongated proportions, and their smiling faces have sharp noses and almond eyes. The folds of the garments drop like a waterfall from their shoulders to their knees and spill over onto the pedestal, where they form sharp ridges resembling the teeth of a saw. The rhythmic sweep and linear elegance of the folds recall the brushwork of contemporary painting.

Tang Dynasty

The emperors of the short-lived Sui dynasty (581–618) succeeded in reuniting China and prepared the way for the brilliant Tang dynasty (618–906). Under the Tang emperors, China entered a period of unequaled magnificence (MAP 7-1). Chinese armies marched across Central Asia, prompting an influx of foreign peoples, wealth, and ideas into China. Traders, missionaries, and other travelers journeyed to the cosmopolitan Tang capital at Chang'an, and the Chinese, in turn, ventured westward.

WU ZETIAN'S COSMIC BUDDHA In its first century, the new dynasty continued to support Buddhism and to sponsor great monuments for Buddhist worshipers. Cave complexes decorated with reliefs and paintings, modeled on those of India (see Chapter 6), were especially popular. One of the most spectacular Tang Buddhist sculptures is carved into the face of a cliff in the great Longmen Cave complex near Luoyang in north central China. Work at Longmen had begun almost two centuries earlier, during the Period of Disunity, under the Northern Wei dynasty (386–534). The site's 1,352 caves, 97,000 statues, 3,600 inscriptions, and 785 carved niches attest to its importance as a Buddhist center.

The colossal relief (FIG. 7-12) that dominates the Longmen complex features a central figure of the Buddha that is 44 feet tall—seated. An inscription records that the project was completed in 675 when Gaozong (r. 649–683) was the Tang emperor and that in 672 the empress Wu Zetian underwrote a substantial portion of the considerable cost with her private funds. Wu Zetian was an exceptional woman by any standard, and when Gaozong died in 683, she declared herself emperor and ruled until 705, when she was forced to abdicate at age 82 (compare "Hatshepsut," Chapter 3, page 71).

Wu Zetian's Buddha is the Vairocana Buddha, not the historical Buddha of FIGS. 7-9 and 7-11 but the Mahayana Cosmic Buddha, the Buddha of Boundless Space and Time (see "Buddhism," Chapter 6, page 171). Flanking him are two of his monks, attendant bodhisattvas, and guardian figures—all smaller than the Buddha but still of colossal size. (FIG. 7-12, which includes two visitors to the site, underscores the scale of the work.) The sculptors represented the Buddha in serene majesty. An almost geometric regularity of contour and smoothness of planes emphasize the volume of the massive figure. The folds of his robes fall in a few concentric arcs. The artists suppressed surface detail in the interest of monumental simplicity and dignity.

THE DUNHUANG GROTTOES The westward expansion of the Tang Empire increased the importance of Dunhuang, the westernmost gateway to China on the Silk Road. Dunhuang long had been a wealthy, cosmopolitan trade center, a Buddhist pilgrimage destination, and home to thriving communities of Buddhist monks and nuns of varied ethnicity, as well as to adherents of other religions. In the course of several centuries, hundreds of sanctuaries with painted murals were cut into the soft rock of the cliffs near Dunhuang. Known today as the Mogao Grottoes and in antiquity as the Caves of a Thousand Buddhas, the caves also contain images of painted unfired clay and stucco. The earliest recorded cave at Dunhuang was dedicated in 366, but the oldest extant caves date to the late fifth century.

The Dunhuang caves are especially important because in 845 the emperor Wuzong instituted a major persecution, destroying 4,600 Buddhist temples and 40,000 shrines and forcing the return of 260,500 monks and nuns to lay life. Wuzong's policies did not affect Dunhuang, then under Tibetan rule, so the site preserves much of the type of art lost elsewhere.

7-12 Vairocana Buddha, disciples, and bodhisattvas, Longmen Caves, Luoyang, China, Tang dynasty, completed 675. Buddha, approx. 44′ high.

7-13 Paradise of Amitabha, cave 172, Dunhuang, China, Tang dynasty, mid-eighth century. Wall painting, approx. 10′ high.

Paradise of Amitabha (FIG. **7-13**), on the wall of one of the Dunhuang caves, shows how the splendor of the Tang era and religious teachings could come together in a powerful image. Buddhist Pure Land sects, especially those centered on Amitabha, Buddha of the West, had captured the popular imagination in the Period of Disunity under the Six Dynasties and continued to flourish during the Tang dynasty. Pure Land teachings asserted that individuals had no hope of attaining enlightenment through their own power because of the waning of the Buddha's Law. Instead, they could obtain rebirth in a realm free from spiritual corruption simply through faith in Amitabha's promise of salvation. Richly detailed, brilliantly colored pictures steeped in the opulence of the Tang dynasty, such as this one, greatly aided worshipers in gaining faith by visualizing the wonders of such a paradise. Amitabha sits in the center of a raised platform, his principal bodhisattvas and lesser divine attendants surrounding him. Before them a celestial dance takes place. Bodhisattvas had strong appeal in East Asia as compassionate beings ready to achieve buddhahood but dedicated to humanity's salvation. Some received direct worship and became the main subjects of sculpture and painting.

TANG TEMPLES In the Dunhuang mural, Amitabha appears against a backdrop of ornate buildings characteristic of the Tang era. The Tang rulers embellished their empire with extravagant wooden structures, colorfully painted and of colossal size, possessing furnishings of great luxury and elaborate gold, silver, and bronze ornaments. Unfortunately, few Tang buildings survive. Among them is the Foguang Si (Buddha Radiance Temple), one of the oldest surviving Buddhist temples in China. It lacks the costly embellishment of imperial structures in the capital, but its east main hall (FIG. **7-14**) displays the distinctive curved roofline

of later Chinese architecture, which was not present in the Han examples (FIGS. 7-7 and 7-8) discussed earlier. A complex grid of beams and purlins, and a thicket of interlocking brackets, support the overhang of the eaves—some 14 feet out from the column faces—as well as the timbered and tiled roof.

COURT PAINTING Chang'an, the Tang capital captured from the Sui, was laid out on a grid scheme and occupied more than 30 square miles. It was the greatest city in the world during the seventh and eighth centuries. The Tang emperors also fostered a brilliant tradition of painting. Although few examples are preserved, many art historians regard the early Tang dynasty as the golden age of Chinese figure painting.

In perfect accord with the glowing descriptions of Tang painting style by Chinese poets and critics are the unrestored portions

7-14 Schematic cross-section and perspective drawing of east main hall, Foguang Si (Buddha Radiance Temple), Mount Wutai, China, Tang dynasty, ca. 857 (after L. Liu).

of *The Thirteen Emperors* (FIG. **7-15**), a masterpiece of line drawing and colored washes. The painting has long been attributed to YAN LIBEN (d. 673). Born into an aristocratic family and the son of a famous artist, Yan Liben was prime minister under the emperor Gaozong as well as a celebrated painter. This handscroll depicts 13 Chinese rulers from the Han to the Sui dynasties. Its purpose was to portray these historical figures as exemplars of moral and political virtue, in keeping with the Confucian ideal of learning from the past. Each emperor stands or sits in an undefined space, his eminence clearly indicated by his great size relative to his attendants. Simple shading in the faces and the robes gives the figures an added semblance of volume and presence. Our detail represents the emperor Xuan of the Chen dynasty (557–589) seated among his attendants, two of whom carry the ceremonial fans that signify his imperial status. The poses of the attendants vary sharply from figure to figure, lending vitality to the composition. Xuan stands out easily from the others not only because of his size and central position but also because of his dark robes and majestic serenity.

A PRINCESS'S PAINTED TOMB Wall paintings in the tomb of the Tang princess Yongtai (684–701) at Qianxian, near Chang'an, permit an analysis of court painting styles unobscured by problems of authenticity and reconstruction. When she was 17 years old, Yongtai was either murdered or forced to commit suicide by Wu Zetian. Her underground tomb dates to 706, however, because her formal burial had to await Wu Zetian's own death. The detail illustrated here (FIG. **7-16**) depicts palace ladies and their attendants, images of pleasant court life to accompany the princess into her afterlife. The figures appear as if on a shallow stage. The artist did not provide any indications of background or setting, but intervals between the two rows and the figures' grouping in an oval suggest a consistent ground plane. The women assume a variety of poses, seen in full-face and in three-quarter views, from the front or the back. The device of paired figures facing into and out of the space of the picture appears often in paintings of this period and effectively creates depth. Thick, even contour lines describe full-volumed faces

and suggest solid forms beneath the drapery, all with the utmost economy. This simplicity of form and line, along with the measured cadence of the poses, results in an air of monumental dignity.

By the eighth century, China had become an international cultural center, integrating concepts and artistic forms from farther west and affecting developments to the south and east. In particular, Tang artists and craftspeople taught visitors from Korea and Japan, and some even traveled abroad. Thus, fair approximations of the Tang artists' elegant approach to figurative painting, dominated by sweeping brush lines, began to appear elsewhere in East Asia (see FIG. 8-9). They cannot, however, make up for the loss of famous works, including those by the greatest Tang figure painter, Wu Daozi (active ca. 710–760).

7-16 Palace ladies, detail of a wall painting in the tomb of Princess Yongtai, Qianxian, China, Tang dynasty, 706. Approx. 5' 10" × 6' 6".

GLAZED EARTHENWARE SCULPTURE Tang ceramists also achieved renown. They produced thousands of earthenware figures of people, domesticated animals, and fantastic creatures for burial in tombs. These statuettes attest to a demand for such objects by a much wider group of patrons than ever before, but terracotta funerary sculpture has a long history in China. The most spectacular example is the ceramic army of the First Emperor of Qin (FIG. 7-5). The subjects of the Tang figurines are also much more diverse than in earlier periods. The depiction of a broad range of foreigners, including Semitic traders and Central Asian musicians on camels, accurately reflects the cosmopolitanism of Tang China.

The artists painted some figurines with colored slips and decorated others, such as the spirited, handsomely adorned neighing horse in FIG. **7-17**, with colorful lead glazes that ran in dramatic streams down the objects' sides when fired. The popularity of the horse as a subject of Chinese art reflects the importance the emperors placed on the quality of their stables. The breed represented here is powerful in build. Its beautifully arched neck terminates in a small, elegant head. Richly harnessed and saddled, the horse testifies to its rider's nobility. During the period of Tang power, representing horses in painting and ceramics was a special genre, on equal footing with figural composition and landscape.

7-17 Neighing Horse, Tang dynasty, eighth to ninth century. Glazed earthenware, 1′ 8″ high. Victoria & Albert Museum, London.

Song Dynasty

The last century of Tang rule witnessed many popular uprisings and the empire's gradual disintegration. After an interim of internal strife known as the Five Dynasties period (906–960), General Zhao Kuangyin succeeded in consolidating the country once again. He established himself as the first emperor (r. 960–976) of the Song dynasty (960–1279), which ruled China from a capital in the north at Bianliang (modern Kaifeng) during the Northern Song period (960–1127). Under the Song emperors, many of the hereditary privileges of the elite class were curtailed. Political appointments were made on the basis of scores on civil service examinations, and education came to be a more important prerequisite for Song officials than high birth.

The three centuries of Song rule, including the Southern Song period (1127–1279) when the capital was at Lin'an (modern Hangzhou) in southern China, were also a time of extraordinary technological innovation. Under the Song emperors, the Chinese invented the magnetic compass for sea navigation, printing with movable clay type, paper money, and gunpowder. Song China was the most technologically advanced society in the world in the early second millennium.

FAN KUAN'S LANDSCAPES For many observers, the Song dynasty also marks the apogee of Chinese landscape painting, which first emerged as a major subject during the Period of Disunity. Although many of the great Northern Song masters worked for the imperial court, FAN KUAN (ca. 960–1030) was a Daoist recluse (see "Daoism and Confucianism," page 196) who shunned the cosmopolitan life of Bianliang. He believed that nature was a better teacher than other artists, and he spent long days in the mountains studying not only configurations of rocks and trees but also the effect of sunlight and moonlight on natural forms. Just as centuries later in Italy, Giorgio Vasari would credit his contemporaries with the conquest of naturalism (see Chapter 21), so did Song critics laud Fan Kuan and other leading painters of the day as the first masters of the recording of light, shade, distance, and texture.

In *Travelers among Mountains and Streams* (FIG. **7-18**), painted in the early 11th century, Fan Kuan presents a vertical landscape of massive mountains rising from the distance. The overwhelming natural forms dwarf the few human and animal figures (for example, the mule train in the lower right corner), which the artist reduced to minute proportions. The nearly seven-foot-long silk hanging scroll cannot contain nature's grandeur, and the landscape continues in all directions beyond its borders. The painter depicted some elements from level ground (for example, the great boulder in the foreground), and others obliquely from the top (the shrubbery on the highest cliff). The shifting perspectives lead viewers on a journey through the mountains. To appreciate such landscapes fully, viewers must focus not only on the larger composition but also on intricate details and on the character of each brush stroke. Numerous "texture strokes" help model massive forms and convey a sense of tactile surfaces. For the face of the mountain, for example, Fan Kuan employed small, pale brush marks, the kind of texture stroke the Chinese call "raindrop strokes."

HUIZONG, EMPEROR AND PAINTER A century after Fan Kuan painted in the mountains of Shanxi, the emperor HUIZONG (1082–1135; r. 1101–1125) assumed the Song throne at Bianliang. Less interested in governing than in the arts, he brought the country to near bankruptcy and lost much of China's territory to the armies of the Tartar Jin dynasty (1115–1234), who captured the Song capital in 1126 and took Huizong as a prisoner. He died in their hands several years later. Himself an accomplished poet, calligrapher, and painter, Huizong reorganized the imperial painting academy and required the study of poetry and calligraphy as part of the official training of court painters. *Calligraphy,* or the art of writing, was highly esteemed in China throughout its history, and prominent inscriptions are frequent elements of Chinese paintings (see "Calligraphy and Inscriptions on Chinese Paintings," Chapter 26, page 766). Huizong also promoted the careful study both of

7-18 FAN KUAN, *Travelers among Mountains and Streams,* Northern Song period, early 11th century. Hanging scroll, ink and colors on silk, 6′ 7¼″ × 3′ 4¼″. National Palace Museum, Taibei.

7-19 Attributed to HUIZONG, *Auspicious Cranes,* Northern Song period, 1112. Section of a handscroll, ink and colors on silk, 1′ 8⅛″ × 4′ 6⅜″. Liaoning Provincial Museum, Shenyang.

nature and of the classical art of earlier periods, and was an avid art collector as well as the sponsor of a comprehensive catalogue of the vast imperial art holdings.

A short handscroll (FIG. **7-19**) usually attributed to Huizong is more likely the work of court painters under his direction, but it displays the emperor's style as both calligrapher and painter. Huizong's characters represent one of many styles of Chinese calligraphy. They are made up of thin strokes, and each character is meticulously aligned with its neighbors to form neat vertical rows. The painting depicts cranes flying over the roofs of Bianliang. It is a masterful combination of elegant composition and realistic observation. The black and red feathers of the white cranes are carefully recorded, and the birds are depicted from a variety of viewpoints to suggest that they were circling around the roof. Huizong did not, however, choose this subject because of his interest in the anatomy and flight patterns of birds. The painting was a propaganda piece commemorating the appearance of 20 white cranes at the palace gates during a festival in 1112. The cranes were regarded as an auspicious sign, proof that Heaven had blessed Huizong's rule. Although few would ever have viewed the handscroll, the cranes were also displayed on painted banners on special occasions, where they could be seen by a larger public.

CIZHOU POTTERY Song artists also produced superb ceramics. Some reflect their patrons' interests in antiquities and imitate the powerful forms of the Shang and Zhou bronzes. However, Song ceramics more commonly had elegant shapes with fluid silhouettes. Many featured monochrome glazes, such as the famous celadon wares, also produced in Korea (FIG. **7-28**), but a quite different kind of pottery, loosely classed as Cizhou, emerged in northern China. The example shown (FIG. **7-20**) is a vase of the high-shouldered shape known as *meiping.* Chinese potters developed the subtle techniques of *sgraffitto* (incising the design through a colored slip) during the Northern Song period. They achieved the intricate black-and-white design here by cutting through a black slip (see "Chinese Earthenwares and Stonewares,"

7-20 Meiping vase, from Xiuwi, China, Northern Song period, 12th century. Stoneware, Cizhou type, with sgraffito decoration, 1′ 7½″ high. Asian Art Museum of San Francisco, San Francisco (Avery Brundage Collection).

7-21 Foguang Si Pagoda, Yingxian, China, Liao dynasty, 1056.

page 193). The tightly twining vine and flower petal motifs on this vase closely embrace the vessel in a perfect accommodation of surface design to vase shape.

CHINESE PAGODAS For two centuries during the Northern Song period, the Liao dynasty (907–1125) ruled part of northern China. In 1056, the Liao rulers built the Foguang Si Pagoda (FIGS. **7-21** and **7-22**), the tallest wooden building in the world, at Yingxian in Shanxi Province. The *pagoda*, or tower, the building type most often associated with Buddhism in China and other parts of East Asia, is the most eye-catching feature of a Buddhist temple complex. It somewhat resembles the tall towers of Indian temples (see "Hindu Temples," Chapter 6, page 180) and their distant ancestor, the Indian stupa (see "The Stupa," Chapter 6, page 172). Like stupas, many early pagodas housed relics and provided a focus for devotion to the Buddha. Later pagodas served other functions, such as housing sacred images and texts. The Chinese and Koreans built both stone and brick pagodas, but wooden pagodas were also common and became the standard in Japan.

The nine-story octagonal pagoda at Yingxian is 216 feet tall and made entirely of wood (see "Chinese Wooden Construction," page 200). Sixty giant four-tiered bracket clusters carry the floor beams and projecting eaves of the five main stories. They rest on two concentric rings of columns at each level. Alternating main stories and windowless mezzanines with cantilevered balconies, set back further on each story as the tower rises, form an elevation of nine stories altogether. Along with the open veranda on the ground level and the soaring pinnacle, the balconies visually lighten the building's mass. Our cross-section (FIG. 7-22) shows the symmetrical placement of statues of the Buddha inside, the colossal scale of the ground-floor statue, and the intricacy of the beam-and-bracket system at its most ingenious.

7-22 Plan and cross-section of Foguang Si Pagoda, Yingxian, China, Liao dynasty, 1056 (after L. Liu).

Southern Song Period

When the Jin captured Bianliang and the emperor Huizong in 1126 and took control of northern China, Gaozong (r. 1127–1162), Huizong's sixth son, escaped and eventually established a new Song capital in the south at Lin'an (present-day Hangzhou). From there, he and his successors during the Southern Song period ruled their reduced empire until 1279.

EMPERORS, POETS, AND PAINTERS Court sponsorship of painting continued in the new capital and, as in the Northern Song period, some of the emperors were directly involved with the painters of the imperial painting academy. During the reign of Ningzong (r. 1194–1224), members of the court, including Ningzong himself and the empress Yang, frequently added brief poems to the paintings created under their direction. Some of the painters belonged to families that had worked for the Song emperors for several generations. The most famous of these was the Ma family, which began working for the Song dynasty during the Northern Song period.

MA YUAN (ca. 1160–1225) painted *On a Mountain Path in Spring* (FIG. **7-23**), a small silk album leaf, for Ningzong in the early 13th century. In his composition, in striking contrast to Fan Kuan's much larger *Travelers among Mountains and Streams* (FIG. 7-18), the landscape is reduced to a few elements and confined to the foreground and left side of the page. A large, solitary figure gazes out into the infinite distance. Framing him are the carefully placed diagonals of willow branches. Near the upper right corner

a bird flies toward the couplet that Ningzong added in ink, demonstrating his mastery of both poetry and calligraphy (see "Calligraphy and Inscriptions," Chapter 26, page 766):

> *Brushed by his sleeves, wild flowers dance in the wind;*
> *Fleeing from him, hidden birds cut short their songs.*

Some scholars have suggested that the author of the two-line poem is actually the empress Yang, but the inscription is in the emperor's hand. In any case, landscape paintings such as this one are perfect embodiments of the Chinese ideals of peace and unity with nature.

TWO SPHERES OF BEING Religious painting also flourished under the Southern Song emperors. Neo-Confucianism, a blend of traditional Chinese thought and selected Buddhist concepts, became the leading philosophy, but Buddhist themes were still the subject of many painters. ZHOU JICHANG (ca. 1130–1190) painted *Arhats Giving Alms to Beggars* (FIG. **7-24**) in 1184 as part of a series of 100 scrolls produced at the southern coastal city of Ningbo for an abbot who invited individual donors to pay for the paintings as offerings in the nearby Buddhist temple. *Arhats* are enlightened disciples of the Buddha who have achieved freedom from rebirth (nirvana) by suppression of all desire for earthly things. They were charged with protecting the Buddhist Law until the arrival of the Buddha of the Future.

In the scroll we illustrate (FIG. 7-24), Zhou Jichang arranged the foreground, middle ground, and background vertically to clarify the arhats' positions relative to one another and to the

7-23 MA YUAN, *On a Mountain Path in Spring*, Southern Song period, early 13th century. Album leaf, ink and colors on silk, $10\frac{3}{4}'' \times 17''$. National Palace Museum, Taibei.

7-24 ZHOU JICHANG, *Arhats Giving Alms to Beggars,* Southern Song period, 1184. Ink and colors on silk, 3′ 8″ × 1′ 9″. Museum of Fine Arts, Boston.

beggars. The arhats move with slow dignity in a plane above the ragged wretches who scramble miserably for the alms their serene benefactors throw down. The extreme difference in deportment between the two groups distinguishes their status, as do their contrasting features. The arhats' vividly colored attire, flowing draperies, and quiet gestures set them off from the dirt-colored and jagged shapes of the people physically and spiritually beneath them. The composition of the landscape—the cloudy platform and lofty peaks of the arhats and the desertlike setting of the beggars—also sharply distinguishes the two spheres of being.

7-25 LIANG KAI, *Sixth Chan Patriarch Chopping Bamboo,* Southern Song period, early 13th century. Hanging scroll, ink on paper, 2′ 5¼″ high. Tokyo National Museum, Tokyo.

LIANG KAI AND CHAN Chan Buddhism (see "Chan Buddhism," page 212), which stressed the quest for personal enlightenment through meditation, flourished under the Song dynasty. LIANG KAI (active early 13th century) was a master of an abbreviated, expressive style of ink painting that found great favor among Chan monks in China, Korea, and Japan. He served in the painting academy of the imperial court in Hangzhou, and his early works include poetic landscapes typical of the Southern Song. Later in life, he left the court and concentrated on figure painting, including Chan subjects.

Surviving works attributed to him include an ink painting (FIG. 7-25) of the Sixth Chan Patriarch, Huineng, crouching as he chops bamboo. In Chan thought, the performance of even such mundane tasks had the potential to become a spiritual exercise. More specifically, this scene represents the patriarch's "Chan moment," when the sound of the blade striking the bamboo resonates within his spiritually attuned mind to propel him through the final doorway to enlightenment. The scruffy, caricature-like representation of the revered figure suggests that Huineng's mind is not burdened by worldly matters, such as physical appearance or signs of social status. Liang Kai utilized a variety of brushstrokes in the execution of this deceptively

Chan Buddhism

Under the Song emperors (960–1279), the new school of *Chan* Buddhism gradually gained importance, until it was second only to Neo-Confucianism. The Chan school traced its origins through a series of patriarchs (the founder and early leaders, joined in a master–pupil lineage). The First Chan Patriarch was Bodhidharma, a semilegendary sixth-century Indian missionary. By the time of the Sixth Chan Patriarch, Huineng (638–713; FIG. 7-25) in the early Tang period, the religious forms and practices of the school were already well established.

Although Chan monks adapted many of the rituals and ceremonies of other schools over the course of time, they focused on the cultivation of the mind or spirit of the individual in order to break through the illusions of ordinary reality, especially by means of meditation. In Chan thought, the means of enlightenment

lie within the individual, and direct personal experience with some ultimate reality is the necessary step to its achievement. Meditation is a critical practice. In fact, the word "Chan" is a translation of the Sanskrit word for meditation. Bodhidharma is said to have meditated so long in a cave that his arms and legs withered away. The "Northern School" of Chan holds that enlightenment comes only gradually after long meditation, but the "Southern School" believes that the breakthrough to enlightenment can be sudden and spontaneous.

These beliefs influenced art and aesthetics as they developed in China and spread to Korea and Japan. In Japan, Chan (Japanese *Zen*) had an especially extensive, long-term impact on the arts and remains an important school of Buddhism there today (see "Zen and Zen-Inspired Art," Chapter 27, page 781).

simple picture. Most are pale and wet, ranging from the fine lines of Huineng's beard to the broad texture strokes of the tree. A few darker strokes, which define the vine growing around the tree and the patriarch's clothing, offer visual accents in the painting. This kind of quick and seemingly casual execution of paintings has traditionally been interpreted as a sign of a painter's ability to produce compelling pictures spontaneously as a result of superior training and character, or, in the Chan setting, progress toward enlightenment.

KOREA

Korea is a northeast Asian peninsula that shares borders with China and Russia, and faces the islands of Japan (MAP 7-1). Korea's pivotal location is a key factor in understanding the relationship of its art to that of China and the influence of its art on that of Japan. Ethnically, the Koreans are related to the peoples of eastern Siberia and Mongolia, as well as to the Japanese. In the early centuries, the Koreans used Chinese characters to write Korean words, but later they invented their own phonetic alphabet. Korean art, although frequently based on Chinese models, is not merely derivative but has, like Korean civilization, a distinct identity.

Three Kingdoms Period

CHINA AND THE THREE KINGDOMS Pottery-producing cultures appeared on the Korean peninsula in the Neolithic period no later than 6000 BCE, and the Korean Bronze Age dates from ca. 1000 BCE. Bronze technology was introduced from the area that is today northeastern China (formerly known as Manchuria). About 100 BCE, during the Han dynasty, the Chinese established outposts in Korea. The most important was Lelang, which became a prosperous commercial center. By the middle of the century, however, three native kingdoms—Koguryo, Paekche, and Silla—controlled most of the Korean peninsula and reigned for more than seven centuries until Silla completed its

conquest of its neighbors in 668. During this era, known as the Three Kingdoms period (ca. 57 BCE–688 CE), Korea remained in continuous contact with both China and Japan. Buddhism was introduced into Korea from China in the fourth century CE. The Koreans in turn transmitted it from the peninsula to Japan in the sixth century.

GOLD CROWNS IN SILLA TOMBS Tombs of the Silla kingdom have yielded spectacular artifacts representative of the wealth and power of its rulers. Finds in the region of Kyongju justify the city's ancient name—Kumsong ("City of Gold"). The gold-and-jade crown (FIG. 7-26) from a tomb at Hwangnam-dong, near Kyongju, dated to the fifth or sixth century, also attests to the high quality of artisanship among Silla artists. The crown's major elements, the band and the uprights, as well as the myriad spangles adorning them, were cut from sheet gold and embossed along the edges. Gold rivets and wires secure the whole, as do the comma-shaped pieces of jade further embellishing the crown. Archaeologists interpret the uprights as stylized tree and antler forms believed to symbolize life and supernatural power. The Hwangnamdong crown has no counterpart in China, although the technique of working sheet gold may have come to Korea from northeast China.

Unified Silla Kingdom

Aided by China's emperor, the Silla Kingdom conquered the Koguryo and Paekche kingdoms and unified Korea in 668. The era of the Unified Silla Kingdom (688–935) is roughly contemporary with the Tang dynasty's brilliant culture in China, and many consider it to be Korea's golden age.

BUDDHIST SOKKURAM The Silla rulers embraced Buddhism both as a source of religious enlightenment and as a protective force. They considered the magnificent Buddhist temples they constructed in and around their capital of Kyongju to be not only places of worship but also a supernatural defense against external

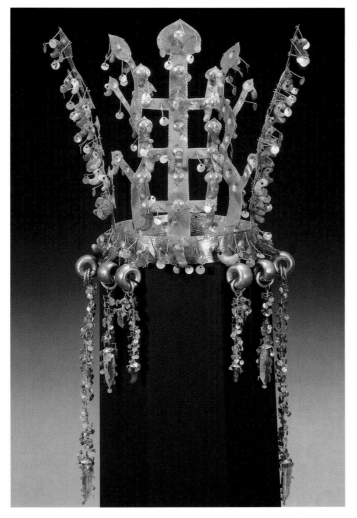

7-26 Crown, from north mound of tomb 98 at Hwangnamdong, near Kyongju, Korea, Silla kingdom, fifth to sixth century. Gold, $10\frac{3}{4}''$ high. Kyongju National Museum, Kyongju.

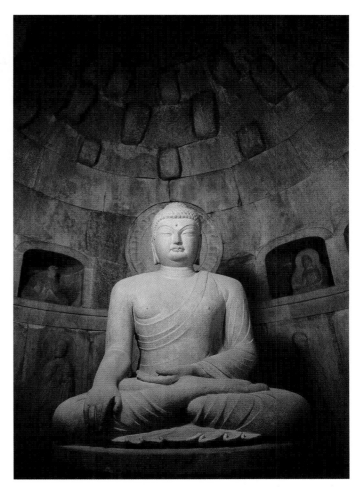

7-27 Shakyamuni Buddha, at entrance to cave temple, Sokkuram, Korea, Great Silla, 751–774. Granite, approx. 11′ high.

threats. Unfortunately, none of these temples survived Korea's turbulent history. However, at Sokkuram, near the summit of Mount Toham, northeast of the city, a splendid granite Buddhist monument is preserved. Scant surviving records suggest that it was built under the supervision of Kim Tae-song, a member of the royal family who served as prime minister. He initiated construction in 742 to honor his parents in his previous life. Certainly the intimate scale of Sokkuram and the quality of its reliefs and freestanding figures support the idea that it was a private chapel for royalty.

The main *rotunda* (circular area under a dome; FIG. **7-27**) measures about 21 feet in diameter. Despite its modest size, the Sokkuram project required substantial resources. Unlike the Chinese Buddhist caves at Longmen (FIG. 7-12), the interior wall surfaces and sculpture were not cut from the rock in the process of excavation. Instead, workers assembled hundreds of granite pieces of various shapes and sizes, attaching them with stone rivets instead of mortar. Sculpted images of bodhisattvas, arhats, and guardians line the lower zone of the wall. Above, 10 niches contain miniature statues of seated bodhisattvas and believers.

All these figures face inward toward the 11-foot-tall statue of Shakyamuni, the historical Buddha, which dominates the cham-

ber as it sits slightly back from center and faces the entrance. Carved from a single block of granite, the image represents the Buddha as he touched the earth to call it to witness the realization of his enlightenment at Bodh Gaya (see FIG. 6-10*b*). Although remote in time and place from the Sarnath Buddha in India (see FIG. 6-12), this majestic image remains faithful to its iconographic prototype. More immediately, the Korean statue draws on the robust, round-faced figures of Tang China (FIG. 7-12), and its drapery is a more schematic version of the fluid type found in Tang sculpture. However, the figure has a distinctly broad-shouldered dignity combined with harmonious proportions that are without close precedents. It is regarded as one of the finest images of the Buddha in East Asia.

Koryo Dynasty

Although Buddhism was the established religion of Korea, Confucianism, introduced from China during the Silla era, increasingly shaped social and political conventions. In the ninth century, the three old kingdoms began to reemerge as distinct political entities, but by 935 the Koryo (from Koguryo) had taken control, and they dominated for the next three centuries. The Unified Silla and Koryo kingdoms overlap slightly (the period

7-28 Maebyong vase, Koryo period, ca. 918–1000. Celadon with inlaid decoration, 1′ 4½″ tall. Kansong Art Museum, Seoul.

glazes, fired in an oxygen-deprived kiln to become gray, pale blue, pale green, or brownish olive. Incised or engraved designs in the vessel alter the thickness of the glaze to produce elegant tonal variations.

A vase in the shape known as *maebyong* in Korean (FIG. **7-28**; *meiping* in Chinese, FIG. 7-20) probably dates to early in the Koryo period (ca. 918–1000). It is decorated using the inlay technique for which Koryo potters were famous. On our vase, the artist incised delicate motifs of flying cranes—some flying down and others, in *roundels* (circular frames), flying up—into the clay's surface and then filled the grooves with white and colored slip. Next, the potter covered the incised areas with the celadon green glaze. Variation in the spacing of the motifs shows the potter's sure sense of the dynamic relationship between ornamentation and ceramic volume.

CONCLUSION

Chinese culture has its roots long before recorded history, and China has often been in the vanguard of technological innovation. The Chinese invented, for example, the magnetic compass, movable type, paper money, and gunpowder, and Chinese silk was treasured in the West.

The Chinese also excelled in the fields of art and architecture. The bronzes of the Shang dynasty are among the finest produced anywhere during the Bronze Age, and Chinese artists were masters in working jade, ivory, and lacquer. Although Chinese artworks of monumental scale, such as the Qin terracotta army, are world renowned, many of the most famous Chinese artists worked on a much more intimate scale, painting landscapes and other subjects in handscrolls and displaying their expertise in recording light, shade, distance, and texture. The Chinese method of bracketed wooden construction, in which walls do not bear weight but serve as screens, was emulated throughout Asia.

China's achievements in virtually every field spread beyond even the boundaries of the vast empires it sometimes controlled. Although Buddhism began in India, the Chinese adaptations and transformations of its teachings, religious practice, and artistic forms were those that spread farther east. The cultural debt of China's neighbors to China is immense. But it was Korea that was the crucial artistic, cultural, and religious link between the mainland and the islands of Japan.

ca. 918–935) because both kingdoms existed as these shifts in power occurred. In 1231, the Mongols, who had invaded China, pushed into Korea, beginning a war lasting 30 years. In the end, the Koryo had to submit to forming an alliance with the Mongols, who eventually conquered all of China (see Chapter 26).

CELADON WARE Koryo potters in the 12th century produced the famous Korean *celadon* wares, admired worldwide. Celadon wares are characterized by highly translucent iron-pigmented

CHINA	KOREA		

LATE NEOLITHIC

5000 BCE

2000 BCE

XIA

1600 BCE

SHANG

■ 1

1050 BCE

ZHOU (WARRING STATES, 475–221 BCE)

| LAOZI, DAOIST PHILOSOPHER, CA. 604–531 BCE

| XIE HE, *Six Laws of Painting*, EARLY SIXTH CENTURY BCE

| SHAKYAMUNI BUDDHA, CA. 563–483 BCE

| CONFUCIUS, 551–479 BCE

| MENCIUS, CONFUCIAN PHILOSOPHER, CA. 371–289 BCE

| ZHUANGZI, DAOIST PHILOSOPHER, CA. 370–301 BCE

221 BCE

QIN

■2 | THE FIRST EMPEROR OF QIN, R. 221–210 BCE

206 BCE

HAN

220 CE

PERIOD OF DISUNITY

THREE KINGDOMS PERIOD (57 BCE–668 CE)

| BUDDHISM INTRODUCED TO KOREA, 372

589

SUI

| BODHIDHARMA, FIRST CHAN BUDDHIST PATRIARCH, SIXTH CENTURY

618

TANG

UNIFIED SILLA KINGDOM (TO 935)

■3 | BUDDHIST PERSECUTION BY WUZONG, 845

906

FIVE DYNASTIES

960

NORTHERN SONG

■4 | JIN CAPTURE BIANLIANG FROM SONG, 1126

1127

SOUTHERN SONG

KORYO (TO 1392)

| MONGOLS INVADE KOREA, 1231

1279

■1 Guang, from Anyang, 12th or 11th century BCE

■2 Army of the First Emperor of Qin, Lintong, ca. 210 BCE

■3 Yan Liben, *The Thirteen Emperors*, ca. 650

■4 Foguang Si Pagoda, Yingxian, China, Liao Dynasty, 1056

Taizokai (Womb World) of Ryokai Mandara, Kyoogokokuji (Toji), Kyoto, Japan, Early Heian period, second half of ninth century. Hanging scroll, color on silk, $6' \times 5' \frac{5}{8}''$.

8

SHRINES, STATUES, AND SCROLLS

THE ART OF EARLY JAPAN

The Japanese archipelago (MAP 8-1) consists of four main islands—Hokkaido, Honshu, Shikoku, and Kyushu—and hundreds of smaller ones, a surprising number of them inhabited. Two distinct population groups lived on the islands by earliest historical times, and the great majority of Japan's inhabitants trace their ancestry to one of these two early groups. The history of Japanese art and culture is a history of change and adaptation. Over the centuries, the Japanese have demonstrated a remarkable ability to surmount challenges, such as a mountainous island terrain that made travel and communication difficult. Japanese culture also reveals a responsiveness to imported ideas, such as Buddhism and Chinese writing systems, filtering in from continental eastern Asia. To acknowledge this responsiveness to mainland influences is not to suggest that Japan simply absorbed these imported ideas and practices. Indeed, over the centuries, Japan has developed a truly distinct culture, characterized by wide variety. There are strong regional variations, not just in art but in dialect, cuisine, and local customs—differences that persist to some degree even today. Ultimately, Japan's close proximity to the continent has promoted extensive exchange with mainland cultures, while the sea has helped protect it from outright invasions and allowed it to develop an individual and unique character.

JAPAN BEFORE BUDDHISM

Jomon Period (ca. 10,500–300 BCE)

CORD-MARKED POTTERY Japan's earliest distinct culture is the Jomon. The term *jomon*, meaning "cord markings," refers to the technique that this culture used to decorate earthenware vessels. The Jomon people were hunter-gatherers, but in contrast to most hunter-gatherer societies, which were nomadic, the Jomon enjoyed surprisingly

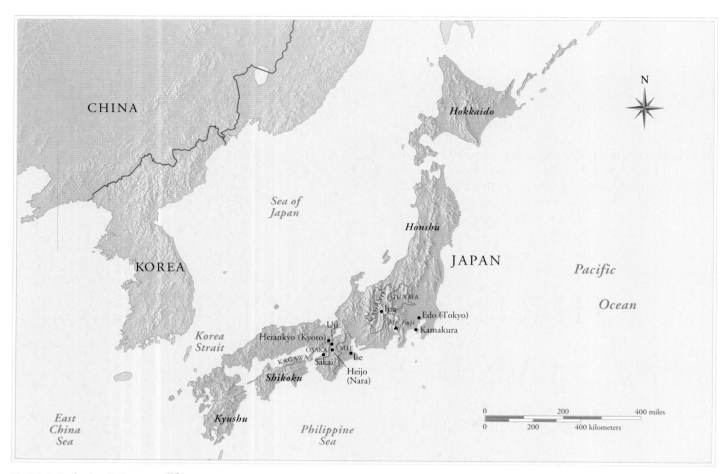

MAP 8-1 Early sites in Japan.

settled lives. Their villages consisted of pit dwellings—shallow round excavations with raised earthen rims and thatched roofs. Their settled existence permitted the Jomon people to develop distinctive ceramic technology, even before their development of agriculture. In fact, archaeologists have dated some ceramic sherds found in Japan to before 10,000 BCE—older than the sherds from any other area of the world.

In addition to rope markings, incised lines and applied coils of clay adorned Jomon pottery surfaces. The most impressive examples come from the Middle Jomon period (2500–1500 BCE). Much of the population then lived in the mountainous inland region, where local variations in ceramic form and surface treatment flourished. However, all Jomon potters shared a highly developed feeling for modeled, rather than painted, ceramic ornament. Jomon pottery displays such a wealth of applied clay coils, striped incisions, and sometimes quasi-figural motifs that the sculptural treatment in certain instances even jeopardizes the basic functionality of the vessel. Jomon vessels served a wide variety of purposes, from storage to cooking to bone burial. Some of the most elaborate pots may have served ceremonial functions.

A dramatic example (FIG. 8-1) from Miyanomae in Nagano Prefecture (a prefecture is a district with a governor) shows a characteristic, intricately modeled surface and a partially sculpted rim. Jomon pottery contrasts strikingly with China's most celebrated Neolithic earthenwares (see FIG. 7-1) in that the Japanese vessels are extremely thick and heavy. The harder, thinner, and lighter Neolithic Chinese earthenware emphasizes basic ceramic form and painted decoration.

8-1 Vessel, from Miyanomae, Nagano Prefecture, Japan, Middle Jomon period, 2500–1500 BCE. Earthenware, $1' 11\frac{2}{3}'' \times 1' 1\frac{1}{4}''$. Tokyo National Museum, Tokyo.

Yayoi (ca. 300 BCE – 300 CE) and Kofun (ca. 330 – 552 CE) Periods

Jomon culture gradually gave way to Yayoi beginning around 300 BCE in Kyushu, the southernmost of the main Japanese islands. Increased interaction with both China and Korea and immigration from Korea brought dramatic social and technological transformations. People continued to live in pit dwellings, but their villages grew in size, and they developed fortifications, indicating a perceived need for defense. Toward the end of this period, near 300 CE*, Chinese visitors noted that Japan had walled towns, many small kingdoms, and a highly stratified social structure. Wet-rice agriculture provided the social and economic foundations for such development.

BANDED BRONZE BELLS The Yayoi period was a time of tremendous change in Japanese material culture as well. The Yayoi produced pottery that was less sculptural and sometimes polychrome, a departure from the modeled Jomon ceramic vessels. In addition, they developed bronze casting and loom weaving. Among the most intriguing objects Yayoi artisans produced are the *dotaku*, or bells, based on Han Chinese bell forms. However, the Yayoi eventually abandoned the Chinese use of dotaku as musical instruments, and the bells evolved into treasured ceremonial bronzes. Cast in clay molds, these bronzes generally featured raised geometric decoration presented in bands or blocks. On a few, including one from Kagawa Prefecture (FIG. **8-2**), the ornament consists of simple line drawings of people and animals. Scholars have reached no consensus on the meaning of these images. Whatever their meaning, the dotaku engravings are the earliest surviving examples of pictorial art in Japan.

TREASURE-FILLED BURIAL MOUNDS Historians named the succeeding Kofun period (*ko* means "old"; *fun* means "tomb") after the great *tumuli* (pit graves covered by sometimes enormous mounds) that had begun to appear in the third century. These burial mounds were most likely initially built by a horse-riding people

8-2 *Dotaku* (bell) with incised figural motifs, from Kagawa Prefecture, Japan, late Yayoi period, 100 – 300. Bronze, 1′ 4⅞″ high. Tokyo National Museum, Tokyo.

from the Korean peninsula. The tumuli recall earlier Jomon practices of placing the dead on sacred mountains. The mounds grew dramatically in number and scale in the fourth century. The largest tumulus in Japan (FIG. **8-3**) is believed by scholars to be the tomb of Emperor Nintoku. The central mound, which takes the "keyhole"

---

* From this point on, all dates in this chapter are CE unless otherwise stated.

8-3 Tomb of Emperor Nintoku. Sakai, Osaka Prefecture, Japan, Kofun period, late fourth to early fifth century.

form standard for tumuli during the Kofun period, is approximately 1,600 feet long and rises to a height of 90 feet. Surrounded by three moats, the entire site covers 458 acres. Numerous objects were placed with the coffin in the pit-shaft burial chamber to assist in the transition to the next life. For exalted individuals like Emperor Nintoku, objects buried included important symbolic items and imperial regalia—mirrors, swords, and comma-shaped jewels. Numerous bronze mirrors came from China, but the form of the tombs themselves and many of the buried goods suggest even closer connections with Korea. For example, the comma-shaped jewels closely resemble those found on Korean Silla crowns (see FIG. 7-26), whose simpler gilt bronze counterparts lay in the Japanese tombs.

CYLINDER-STATUES FOR THE DEAD Burial practices at Japanese tumuli also included the placement of unglazed ceramic sculptures called *haniwa* on and around the pit grave mounds. These sculptures, such as one from Gunma Prefecture (FIG. **8-4**), are distinctly Japanese. Compared to the terracotta soldiers and horses buried with the Qin emperor at Lintong, China (see FIG. 7-5), these statues appear deceptively whimsical as variations on a cylindrical theme (*hani* means "clay," *wa* means "circle").

8-4 *Haniwa* (cylindrical) warrior figure, from Gunma Prefecture, Japan, late Kofun period, fifth to mid-sixth century. Low-fired clay, 4' 1¼" high. Aikawa Archaeological Museum, Aikawa.

Yet haniwa sculptors skillfully adapted the basic clay cylinder into a host of forms, from abstract shapes to objects, animals (for example, deer, bears, horses, and monkeys), and human figures, such as warriors and female shamans. These artists altered the shapes of the cylinders, emblazoned them with applied ornaments, excised or built up forms, and then painted the haniwa. The variety of figure types suggests that haniwa functioned not as military guards but as a spiritual barrier protecting both the living and the dead from contamination. The Japanese of the Kofun period set these sculptures, usually several feet in height, both in curving rows and in tableaux, or scenes, around a haniwa house placed directly over the deceased buried in the mound. Presumably, the number of sculptures reflected the status of the deceased; scholars estimate that Emperor Nintoku's tumulus included 20,000 haniwa placed around the mound.

AMATERASU'S ANCIENT SHRINE The shrine of the sun goddess, Amaterasu (FIG. **8-5**), at Ise in Mie Prefecture, is the greatest of all monuments associated with the religious system that came to be known as Shinto (see "Pre-Buddhist Beliefs and Rituals in Japan," page 221). The location, use, and ritual reconstruction of this shrine every 20 years (with occasional interruptions) reflect the primary characteristics of Shinto—sacred space, ritual renewal, and purification. The Ise shrine is traditionally dated to the Kofun period. Recent scholarship, however, suggests a later date, but the shrine still serves as a representative example of sacred architecture in ancient Japan. The imperial clan traced its origins to Amaterasu, which reinforced her position as the dominant *kami*, or spiritual being. Although shrine architecture varies tremendously in Japan, scholars believe that the Ise shrine preserves some of the very earliest design elements. Yet the Ise shrine is unique; because of its connection to the Japanese imperial family, no other shrines may be constructed with this same design. The original source of the main sanctuary's form appears to be early granaries, sometimes represented on bronze mirrors or as clay haniwa. This is certainly appropriate, given that granaries were among the most important buildings in Japan's early agrarian society. Although not every aspect of the Ise shrine is equally ancient, the three main structures of the inner shrine convey some sense of Japanese architecture before the introduction of Buddhism and before the development of more elaborately constructed and adorned buildings.

Aside from the thatched roofs and some metallic decorations, the sole construction material at Ise is wood, fitted together in a *mortise-and-tenon* system, in which the wallboards were slipped into slots in the pillars. Two massive freestanding posts (once great cypress trunks), one at each end of the main sanctuary, support most of the weight of the *ridgepole*, the beam at the crest of the roof. The golden-hued cypress columns and planks contrast in color and texture with the white gravel covering the sacred grounds. The roof was originally constructed of thatch, which was smoked, sewn into bundles, and then laid in layers. The smooth shearing of the entire surface produced a gently changing contour. Today, cypress bark covers the roof. Decorative elements enhance the roofline, and include *chigi*, or ridge billets, which were originally extensions of the gable rafters at each end of the roof, and cylindrical wooden weights placed at right angles across the ridgepole. These decorative touches originally had a structural function. This shrine highlights the connection, central to Shinto, between nature and spirit. Not only are the materials derived from the natural world, but the shrine is sited in a specific location at which a kami is believed to have taken up residence.

Pre-Buddhist Beliefs and Rituals in Japan

The early beliefs and practices of pre-Buddhist Japan, which form a part of the belief system later called *Shinto* ("Way of the Gods"), did not derive from the teachings of any individual founding figure or distinct leader. Formal scriptures, in the strict sense, do not exist for these beliefs and practices either. Shinto developed in Japan in conjunction with the advent of agriculture during the Yayoi period. Shinto thus originally focused on the needs of this agrarian society, and included agricultural rites surrounding planting and harvesting. Villagers venerated and prayed to a multitude of local, sometimes specialized, deities or spirits called *kami*. The early Japanese believed kami existed in mountains, waterfalls, trees, and other features of nature, as well as in charismatic people, and they venerated not only the kami themselves but also the places the kami occupy, which are considered sacred.

Each clan (a local group claiming a common ancestor, and the basic societal unit during the Kofun period) had its own protector kami, to whom members offered prayers in the spring for successful planting and in the fall for good harvests. Clan members built shrines made up of several buildings, such as the one at Ise (FIG. 8-5), for kami. Priests made offerings of grains and fruits at these shrines and prayed on behalf of the clans. Rituals of divination, water purification, and ceremonial purification at the shrines proliferated. Visitors to the shrine area had to wash before entering in a ritual of spiritual and physical cleansing.

Purity was such a critical aspect of Japanese religious beliefs that people would abandon buildings and even settlements if negative events, such as poor harvests, suggested spiritual defilement. Even the early imperial court moved several times to newly built towns to escape impurity and the trouble it caused. Such purification concepts are also the basis for the cyclical rebuilding of the sanctuaries at grand shrines. The actual buildings of the inner shrine at Ise, for example, have been rebuilt every 20 years—at least 60 times—with few interruptions. Such rebuilding rids the sacred site of physical and spiritual impurities that otherwise might accumulate. During rebuilding, the old structure remains standing until the carpenters erect an exact duplicate next to it. In this way, the Japanese have preserved ancient forms with great precision.

When Buddhism arrived in Japan from the mainland in the sixth century, Shinto practices changed under its influence. For example, until the introduction of Buddhism, painted or carved images of Shinto deities did not exist. Yet despite the eventual predominance of Buddhism in Japan, Shinto continues to exist as a vital religion for many Japanese.

8-5 Main hall, Ise shrine, Ise, Mie Prefecture, Japan, as rebuilt in 1993.

BUDDHIST JAPAN

Asuka (552–645), Early Nara (Hakuho; 645–710), and Nara (710–784) Periods

ESTABLISHING BUDDHISM IN JAPAN In 552, according to traditional interpretation, the ruler of Paekche, one of Korea's Three Kingdoms (see Chapter 7), sent Japan's ruler a gilded bronze statue of the Buddha along with *sutras* (Buddhist scriptures) translated into Chinese, at the time the written language of eastern Asia. This event marked the beginning of the Asuka period, when Japan's ruling elite embraced major elements of continental culture that had been gradually filtering into Japan. These cultural components became firmly established in Japan and included Chinese writing, Confucianism (see "Daoism and Confucianism," Chapter 7, page 196), and Buddhism (see "Buddhism and Buddhist Iconography," Chapter 6, page 171). The Japanese court, ruling from a series of capitals south of modern Kyoto, increasingly adopted the forms and rites of the Chinese court. In 710, the Japanese finally established what they intended as a permanent capital at Heijo (present-day Nara). City planners laid out the new capital on a symmetrical grid closely modeled on the plan of the Chinese capital of Chang'an. However, Nara remained the capital only until 784; after a transitional period, Heiankyo became the capital in 794.

For half a century after 552, Buddhism met with opposition, but by the end of that time, the new religion was established firmly in Japan. Older beliefs and practices (those that came to be known as Shinto) continued to have significance (and do to the present day), especially as agricultural rituals and imperial court rites. As time passed, Shinto deities even gained new identities as local manifestations of Buddhist deities.

In the arts associated with Buddhist practices, Japan followed Korean and Chinese prototypes very closely, especially during the Asuka, Early Nara (Hakuho), and Nara periods. In fact, early Buddhist architecture in Japan adhered so closely to mainland standards (although generally with a considerable time lag) that surviving Japanese temples have helped greatly in the reconstruction of what was almost completely lost on the continent. Buddhist temples served as monasteries as well and were actually building complexes rather than individual structures.

A GOLDEN HALL FOR WORSHIP The main building in a Japanese Buddhist temple complex, the image hall, housed the major sculptural icons and provided a site of worship and prayer. At Horyuji, an important surviving early temple complex located outside Nara, the image hall (FIG. 8-6) is known as the *kondo* (Golden Hall) and dates from around 680. Although periodically repaired and somewhat altered (the covered porch is an eighth-century addition; the upper railing dates to the 17th century), the structure retains its graceful but sturdy forms beneath the modifications. The main pillars (not visible in our illustration due to the porch addition) decrease in diameter from bottom to top, as in classical architecture. The tapering provides an effective transition between the more delicate brackets above and the columns' stout forms. Also somewhat masked by the added porch is the harmonious reduction in scale from the first to the second story. Following Chinese models, the builders used ceramic tiles as roofing material. Other buildings at the site include a five-story pagoda that serves as a reliquary.

A BRONZE BUDDHA TRIAD Although wood later became the primary material of Buddhist sculpture through much of Japanese history, bronze was not uncommon. Among the earliest extant examples of Japanese Buddhist sculpture is a bronze *Buddha triad* (Buddha flanked by two bodhisattvas; FIG. 8-7). Rescued from Horyuji's predecessor, which was destroyed by fire in the seventh century, it became one of the main images in the Horyuji kondo. The central figure in the triad is Shaka (the Indian/Chinese Sakyamuni), the historical Buddha. Despite this identification, this depiction is not, properly speaking, a portrait (in the Western sense of the term). Rather, Shaka is presented in a transhistorical guise, having achieved a higher state of being. Behind the main

8-6 Horyuji *kondo* (Golden Hall), Nara, Japan, Early Nara (Hakuho) period, ca. 680.

image, a flaming mandorla (a lotus-petal-shaped nimbus) bears small figures of other Buddhas. The sculptor, TORI BUSSHI (*busshi* means "maker of Buddhist images"), was a descendant of a Chinese immigrant. Tori's Buddha triad dates to 623 but reflects the style of the early to mid-sixth century in China and Korea. He elongated the heads and gave greater attention to the drapery's elegantly stylized folds than to a naturalistic modeling of the physical substance of the bodies or their garments.

MANDORLA-FRAMED STATUES Within little more than half a century, however, Japan began to move beyond the style of the Asuka period in favor of new ideas and forms coming out of Tang China and Korea. More direct relations with China also narrowed the time lag between developments there and their transfer to Japan. In the triad of Yakushi (Bhaisajyaguru, the Buddha of Healing who presides over the Eastern Pure Land; FIG. 8-8) in the kondo at the Yakushiji temple of the late seventh century in Nara, the sculptor favored greater anatomical definition and shape-revealing drapery over the dramatic stylizations of the Horyuji statues. The attendant bodhisattvas, especially, reveal the long stylistic trail back through China (see FIG. 7-12) to the sensuous fleshiness of Indian sculpture (see FIG. 6-12). The sculpture's original gilding was destroyed by fire.

THE PAINTED WALLS OF HORIYUJI Until a disastrous fire in 1949, the interior walls of the Golden Hall at Horyuji preserved some of the finest examples of Buddhist wall painting in eastern Asia, executed around 710, the beginning of the Nara period. Now the only record of them consists of color photographs. The most important paintings depicted the Buddhas of the four directions. Like the other three, Amida (Amitabha), the Buddha of immeasurable light and infinite life, ruler of the Western Pure

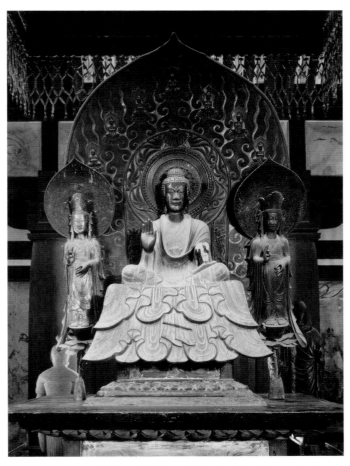

8-7 TORI BUSSHI, Shaka triad, Horyuji kondo, Nara, Japan, Asuka period, 623. Bronze, 5′ 9½″ high.

8-8 Yakushi triad, Yakushiji kondo, Nara, Japan, Early Nara (Hakuho) period, late seventh or early eighth century. Bronze, central figure 8′ 4″ high.

8-9 Amida triad, wall painting (damaged), from Horyuji kondo, Nara, Japan, Early Nara (Hakuho) period, ca. 710. Ink and colors, 10′ 3″ × 8′ 6″. Horyuji Treasure House, Nara.

Land (FIG. 8-9), sits enthroned in his paradisical land, attended by bodhisattvas. The exclusive worship of Amida later became a major trend in Japanese Buddhism, and much grander depictions of his paradise appeared, resembling those at Dunhuang in China (see FIG. 7-13). Here, however, the representation is simple and iconic. Although executed on a dry wall, the painting process involved techniques similar to fresco, such as transferring designs from paper to wall by piercing holes in the paper and pushing colored powder through the perforations. As with the Buddha triad at Yakushiji, the mature Tang style, with its echoes of Indian sensuality, surfaces in this work. The smooth brush lines, thoroughly East Asian, give the figures their substance and life. Such lines belong to a particular type, often seen in Buddhist painting, called iron-wire lines because they are thin and even with a suggestion of tensile strength. Also, as in many other Buddhist paintings, the lines are red instead of black. The identity of the painters of these pictures is unknown, but some scholars have suggested they were Chinese or Korean rather than Japanese.

THE GREAT BUDDHA During the Nara period, the imperial court sponsored the construction in Nara of a temple complex, the Golden Hall (FIG. 8-10) at the Todaiji temple. Later destroyed, it was rebuilt in the early 18th century. Also known as the Great Buddha Hall *(Daibutsuden),* it housed a 53-foot bronze image of the Cosmic Buddha, Roshana (Vairocana), inspired by colossal stone statues of this type in China (see FIG. 7-12). The commissioning of Todaiji and its Great Buddha *(Daibutsu)* by Emperor Shomu in

743 was historically important as part of an imperial attempt to unify and strengthen the country by utilizing religious authority to reinforce imperial power. The temple served as the administrative center of a network of branch temples built in every province. Thus, the consolidation of imperial authority and thorough penetration of Buddhism throughout the country went hand in hand. The dissemination of a common religion contributed to the eventual disruption of the clan system and the unification of disparate political groups. So important was the construction of both the building and the Daibutsu that court and government officials as well as Buddhist dignitaries from China and India were present at the opening ceremonies in 752. Sadly, the current building does not match the original—it is significantly smaller (the current building has 7 bays; the original had 11). Yet it still radiates enormous presence. Even in its diminished size, the Daibutsuden is still the largest wooden building in the world. The treasures that Todaiji houses serve today as almost a museum of eighth-century pan-Asian culture. Many of the temple's sculptures were inspired by the finest Tang Chinese art forms.

Heian Period (794–1185)

In 784, possibly to escape the power of the Buddhist priests in Nara, the imperial house moved its capital north, eventually relocating in 794 in what became its home until modern times. Originally called Heiankyo ("capital of peace and tranquility"), it is known today as Kyoto. In the early Heian period, Japan maintained fairly close ties with China, but from the middle of the ninth century on, relations between Japan and China deteriorated so rapidly that, by that century's end, court-sponsored contacts had ceased. Japanese culture, especially at court, became much more self-directed than it had been in the preceding few centuries.

ESOTERIC BUDDHISM Among the major developments during the early Heian period was the introduction of Esoteric Buddhism to Japan from China. Esoteric, or secret, Buddhism is so named because of the secret transmission of its teachings. Two Esoteric sects made their appearance in Japan during the early Heian period: Tendai in 805 and Shingon in 806. The teachings of Tendai were based on the *Myohorenge kyo,* the *Lotus Sutra,* one of the Buddhist scriptural narratives. Tendai was brought to Japan by a Buddhist priest who traveled to China specifically to study Tendai Buddhism. He believed that all individuals possessed buddha nature and could become enlightened to this reality through such acts as meditation and careful living.

The introduction of Shingon (True Word) Buddhism had a wider impact. Conveyed by a Japanese student-priest, after a trip to the Chinese capital of Chang'an, Shingon is based on the various sutras. Shingon followers believe that anyone can achieve enlightenment through contemplation and rituals. To aid focus during meditation, Shingon disciples use special hand gestures (mudras; see FIG. 6-12) and recite particular words or syllables (mantras in Sanskrit, shingon in Japanese). Shingon became the primary form of Buddhism in Japan through the mid-10th century.

Because of the emphasis on ritual and meditation in Shingon, the arts flourished during the early Heian period. Both paintings and sculptures provided followers with visualizations of specific Buddhist deities and allowed them to contemplate the transcendental concepts central to the religion. Of particular importance in Shingon meditation was the mandala *(mandara* in Japanese), a diagram of the cosmic universe. Among the most famous mandalas is the Womb World (Taizokai), which was usually hung on

8-10 Daibutsuden, Todaiji, Japan, Nara period, eighth century, rebuilt ca. 1700.

the wall of a Shingon kondo. The Womb World is composed of 12 zones, each representing one of the various dimensions of buddha nature (for example, universal knowledge, wisdom, achievement, and purity). The mandala we illustrate here (FIG. **8-11**) is among the best preserved in Japan, and is located at Kyoogokokuji (Toji), the Shingon teaching center established in 823.

SUGGESTING CELESTIAL ARCHITECTURE During the middle and later Heian period, belief in the vow of Amida, the Buddha of the Western Pure Land, to save believers through rebirth in his realm gained great prominence among the Japanese aristocracy. Eventually, the simple message of Pure Land Buddhism—universal salvation—facilitated the spread of Buddhism to all classes of Japanese. The most important surviving monument in Japan related to Pure Land beliefs is the so-called Phoenix Hall of the Byodoin (FIG. **8-12**), a temple built by Fujiwara Yorimichi (r. 990–1074) in memory of his father Michinaga on the grounds of Michinaga's summer villa at Uji. Dedicated in 1053, the Phoenix Hall houses a wooden statue of Amida carved from multiple joined blocks, the predominant wooden sculpture technique by this time. The building's elaborate winged form evokes images of the Buddha's palace in his Pure Land, as depicted in East Asian paintings (see FIG. 7-13) based on the design of great Chinese palaces. By placing only light pillars on the exterior, elevating the wings, and situating the whole on a reflective pond, the Phoenix Hall builders suggested the floating weightlessness of a celestial architecture. The building's name derives

8-11 Taizokai (Womb World) of Ryokai Mandara, Kyoogokokuji (Toji), Kyoto, Japan, Early Heian period, second half of ninth century. Hanging scroll, color on silk, $6' \times 5' \frac{5}{8}''$.

Japanese Literature and Court Culture

During the Nara and Heian periods (710–1185), the Japanese imperial court developed as the center of an elite culture. Both men and women produced literature, paintings, calligraphy, and decorative arts that critics generally consider "classical" today. Heian court members, especially those from the great Fujiwara clan that dominated the court for a century and a half, compiled the first great anthologies of Japanese poetry and wrote Japan's most influential secular prose.

Japanese poetry and related painting and decorative art emphasize human sentiments intertwined with responses to nature, seasonality, and a body of standard metaphors and symbols. For example, the full moon, flying geese, crying deer, and certain plants symbolize autumn, which in turn evokes somber emotions, fading love, and dying. Such concrete but evocative images frequently appear in paintings. Exchanging poems was a common Japanese social practice and a frequent preoccupation of lovers.

A lady-in-waiting to an empress of the early 11th century wrote the best-known and longest-admired work of literature in Japan, *Tale of Genji*. Known as Lady Murasaki, the author is one of many important Heian women writers, including especially diarists and poets. Generally considered the world's first lengthy novel, *Tale of Genji* tells of the life and loves of Prince Genji and, after his death, of his heirs. The novel and much of Japanese literature consistently display a sensitivity to the sadness in the world caused by the transience of love and life. Illustrated scrolls of *Tale of Genji* (FIG. 8-13) rely on key poetic motifs and careful compositions to convey such feelings.

---

from its overall birdlike shape and from two bronze phoenixes decorating the ridgepole ends. In eastern Asia, these birds were believed to alight on lands properly ruled. Here, they represented imperial might, sometimes associated especially with the empress. The authority of the Fujiwara family derived primarily from the marriage of daughters to the imperial line.

A TALE OF LOVE AND INTRIGUE Japan's most admired literary classic is *Tale of Genji* (see "Japanese Literature and Court Culture," above), written around 1000 by Murasaki Shikubu (usually referred to as Lady Murasaki), a lady-in-waiting at the court. Recounting the lives and loves of Prince Genji and his descendants, *Tale of Genji* provides readers with a view of Heian court culture. The oldest extant examples of illustrated copies are fragments from a deluxe set of early-12th-century handscrolls. From textual and physical evidence, scholars have suggested that the set originally consisted of about 10 handscrolls produced by about five teams of artisans. Each team consisted of a nobleman talented in calligraphy, a chief painter, and assistants. The script is primarily *hiragana*, a sound-based writing system developed in Japan from Chinese characters. Hiragana originally served the needs of women (who were not taught Chinese) and became the primary script for Japanese court poetry. In these handscrolls, pictures alternate with text, as in Gu Kaizhi's *Admonitions* scrolls (see FIG. 7-10). However, the Japanese work focuses on emotionally charged moments in personal relationships, rather than on lessons in exemplary behavior. In the scene illustrated here (FIG. **8-13**), for example, Genji meets with his greatest love near the time of her death. The bush-clover in the garden identifies the season as autumn, the season associated with the fading of life and love.

Here, a radically upturned ground plane and strong diagonal lines suggest three-dimensional space rather than depict it illusionistically. Further, these features convey an elevated viewpoint; the painter omitted roofs and ceilings to allow a privileged view of the emotionally charged moments typically represented in the interiors. Flat fields of unshaded color emphasize the painting's two-

8-12 Phoenix Hall, Byodoin, Uji, Japan, Heian period, 1053. 🔘

dimensional character, but rich patterns in the textiles and architectural ornament give a feeling of sumptuousness. The human figures appear constructed of stiff layers of contrasting fabrics, and the artist simplified and generalized the aristocratic faces, using a technique called "line for eye and hook for nose." This lack of individualization may reflect societal restrictions on looking directly at exalted persons, or it may have served to ease viewers' identification with a character in the story. Several formal features of the *Genji* illustrations—native subjects, bright mineral pigments, lack of emphasis on strong brushwork, and general flatness—were later considered typical of *yamato-e* (native-style painting; the term *yamato* means "Japan" and is used to describe anything that is characteristically Japanese). In the early Heian period before this example was made, however, *yamato-e* probably referred only to Japanese subject matter.

PAINTINGS OF BUDDHIST TALES Painted during the late 12th century, at the end of the Heian period, *The Legends of Mount Shigi* (FIG. **8-14**) represents a different facet of narrative

8-13 Scene from Minori chapter, *Tale of Genji*, Late Heian period, first half of 12th century. Handscroll, ink and color on paper, $8\frac{5}{8}''$ high. Goto Art Museum, Tokyo.

8-14 Detail of the Flying Storehouse, from *The Legends of Mount Shigi*, Late Heian period, late 12th century. Handscroll, ink and colors on paper, $1'\frac{1}{2}''$ high. Chogosonshiji, Nara.

handscroll painting. The stories belong to a genre of pious Buddhist tales devoted to miraculous events involving virtuous individuals. Unlike the *Genji* scrolls, short segments of text and pictures do not alternate. Instead, the painters took advantage of the scroll format to present several scenes in a long, unbroken stretch. For example, the first scroll shows the same travelers at several stages of their journey through a continuous landscape.

The *Mount Shigi* scrolls illustrate three miracles associated with a Buddhist monk named Myoren and his mountaintop temple. The first relates the story of the flying storehouse and depicts Myoren's begging bowl lifting the rice-filled storehouse of a wealthy landowner and carrying it off to the monk's hut in the mountains (FIG. 8-14). The painter depicted the astonished landowner, his attendants, and several onlookers in various poses—some grimacing, others gesticulating wildly and scurrying about in frantic amazement. The artist exaggerated each feature of the painted figures, in striking contrast to the *Genji* scroll figures.

Kamakura Period (1185–1332)

In the late 12th century, a series of civil wars between rival warrior families led to the end of the Japanese imperial court as a major political and social force. The victors, headed by the Minamoto family, established their *shogunate* (military government) at Kamakura in eastern Japan. The imperial court remained in Kyoto as the theoretical source of political authority but without actual power. During the Kamakura period, more frequent and positive contact with China brought with it an appreciation for more recent cultural developments there, ranging from new architectural styles to Zen Buddhism.

A PRIESTLY PORTRAIT Rebuilding in Nara presented an early opportunity for architectural experimentation. A leading figure in planning and directing the reconstruction efforts was the priest Shunjobo Chogen (1121–1206), who is reputed to have made three trips to China between 1166 and 1176. After learning about contemporary Chinese architecture, he oversaw the rebuilding of Todaiji, among other projects. His portrait statue (FIG. 8-15) is one of the most striking examples of the high level of naturalism prevalent in the early Kamakura period. Characterized by finely painted details, a powerful rendering of the signs of aging, and the inclusion of such personal attributes as prayer beads, the statue of Chogen exhibits the carving skill and style of the Kei school of sculptors (see "Japanese Artists, Workshops, and Patrons," page 229). The Kei school traced its lineage to Jocho, a famous sculptor of the mid-11th century. Its works display fine Heian carving

8-15 Detail of the priest Shunjobo Chogen, Todaiji, Nara, Japan, Kamakura period, early 13th century. Painted cypress wood, 2′ 8⅜″ high.

Japanese Artists, Workshops, and Patrons

For much of early Japanese history, art production was largely dependent on commissions. Until the Late Heian period (1086–1185), major commissions came almost exclusively from the imperial court or the great temples. As warrior families gained wealth and power, they too extended great commissions—in many cases closely following the aristocrats' precedents in subject and style.

Artists, for the most part, did not work independently, but rather were affiliated with workshops. Indeed, until recently, hierarchically organized male workshops produced most Japanese art. Membership in these workshops was often based on familial relationships. Each workshop was dominated by a master, and many of his main assistants and apprentices were relatives. Outsiders of considerable skill sometimes joined workshops, often through marriage or adoption. The eldest son usually inherited the master's position, after rigorous training in the necessary skills from a very young age. Therefore, one meaning of the term "school of art" in Japan is a network of workshops tracing their origins back to the same master, a kind of artistic clan. Inside the workshops, the master and senior assistants handled the most important production stages, but artists of lower rank helped with the more routine work. The portrait statue of Chogen (FIG. 8-15), for example, was created by a workshop based on familial ties.

Artistic cooperation also surfaced in court bureaus, an alternative to family workshops. These official bureaus, located at the imperial palace, had emerged by the Heian period. The painting bureau accrued particular fame; teams of court painters, led by the bureau director, produced pictures such as the scenes in the *Tale of Genji* handscrolls (FIG. 8-13). This system remained vital into the Kamakura period and well beyond. Under the direction of a patron or the patron's representative, the master painter laid out the composition by brushing in the initial outlines and contours. Under his supervision, junior painters applied the colors. The master then completed the work by brushing in fresh contours and details such as facial features. Very junior assistants and apprentices assisted in the process by preparing paper, ink, and pigments. Unlike mastership in hereditarily run workshops, competition among several families determined control of the Court Painting Bureau during the Heian and Kamakura periods.

Not all art was controlled by the bureaus or family workshops. Priest-artists were trained in temple workshops; these artists produced Buddhist art objects for public viewing as well as images for private priestly meditation. Amateur painting was common among aristocrats of all ranks. As they did for poetry composition and calligraphy, aristocrats frequently held elegant competitions in painting. Both women and men participated in such activities. In fact, court ladies probably played a significant role in developing the painting style seen in the *Genji* scrolls, and a few participated in public projects.

techniques combined with an increased concern for natural volume and detail learned from studying, among other sources, surviving Nara period works and works imported from Song China. Enhancing the natural quality of Japanese portrait statues is the use of inlaid rock crystal for the eyes, a technique found only in Japan.

MOUNTED WARRIORS ON A HANDSCROLL All the painting types flourishing in the Heian period continued to prosper in the Kamakura period. A striking example of narrative handscroll painting is *The Burning of the Sanjo Palace* (FIG. **8-16**), a fragment of a work illustrating some of the battles in the civil wars at the end of the Heian period. Here, the viewer sees the drama unfold in swift and violent staccato brushwork and vivid flashes of color. At the beginning of the scroll (read from right to left), the eye focuses first on a mass of figures rushing toward a blazing building (not shown here)—the painting's crescendo—and then moves at a slowed pace through swarms of soldiers, horses, and bullock

8-16 Detail of *The Burning of the Sanjo Palace,* Kamakura period, 13th century. Handscroll, ink and colors on paper, 1′ 4¼″ high; complete scroll, 22′ 10″ long. Museum of Fine Arts, Boston (Fenollosa-Weld Collection).

8-17 *Amida Descending over the Mountains*, Kamakura period, 13th century. Hanging scroll, ink and colors on silk, 4′ 3⅛″ × 3′ 10½″. Zenrinji, Kyoto.

carts. Finally, a warrior on a rearing horse arrests the viewer's gaze. The horse and rider, however, serve as a *deceptive cadence* (false ending). They are merely a prelude to the single figure of an archer, who picks up and completes the soldiers' mass movement, drawing the turbulent narrative to a quiet close.

THE SAVING POWER OF AMIDA Buddhism and Buddhist painting remained vital in the Kamakura period. Evangelical monks spread Pure Land beliefs throughout Japan to people from all levels of society, and new Pure Land sects emerged that the lower ranks of society, including peasants, found especially appealing. But elite patrons continued to commission major Pure Land artworks. Pure Land Buddhism in Japan stressed the saving power of Amida, who, if called on, hastened to believers at the moment of death and conveyed them to his Pure Land. Pictures of this scene often hung in the presence of a dying person, who recited Amida's name to ensure salvation.

In *Amida Descending over the Mountains* (FIG. **8-17**), a gigantic Amida appears to move directly toward the viewer. His two main attendant bodhisattvas have already made the passage. The grand frontal presentation of Amida gives the painting an iconic quality even as the bodhisattvas' movement continues his descent. Particularly striking in this painting is the way in which Amida's halo resembles a rising moon, an image long admired in Japan for its spiritual beauty.

CONCLUSION

Striking transformations mark the long history of Japanese art as the country's population received, responded to, and developed new forms and ideas from continental eastern Asia. Early metalwork, Buddhist architecture, and the basic painting formats and media, to name only a few examples, readily reveal Japan's close ties to the continent. However, from earliest times, Japan maintained distinctive aesthetic ideals and preferences. For instance, the dynamic forms of Jomon pottery and haniwa figures suggest that the early Japanese derived a deep pleasure from allowing the colors and textures of their raw materials to remain prominent in the final objects. This tendency may not have been exclusive to Japanese art and certainly did not dominate in later centuries, but it did remain a vital part of Japan's aesthetic heritage, helping determine what people accepted from the continent and how they adapted it. In the end, however, the most distinctive feature of Japanese art is its great variety. This reflects the people's capacity to embrace radically different aesthetics simultaneously, appreciating their separate contributions to a richly diverse material culture. Chapter 27 shows how this cultural flexibility continued after several decades of upheaval, the Kamakura rulers' downfall in the early 14th century (1332), and the establishment of a new shogunate by the end of the century.

JOMON	**10,500 BCE**
	▮ HUNTING AND FISHING
MIDDLE JOMON	**2500 BCE**
	1500 BCE
	300 BCE
	▮ RICE GROWING AND METALWORKING
YAYOI	**100 CE**
	300
KOFUN	▮ EMERGENCE OF IMPERIAL FAMILY
	552
ASUKA	▮ BUDDHISM OFFICIALLY INTRODUCED, 552
	645
EARLY NARA (HAKUHO)	**710**
NARA	▮ TRANSFER OF CAPITAL TO NARA, 710
	794
HEIAN	▮ TRANSFER OF CAPITAL TO HEIANKYO (KYOTO), 794
	▮ NEW SECTS OF ESOTERIC BUDDHISM INTRODUCED, CA. 805
	▮ SUSPENSION OF DIPLOMATIC RELATIONS WITH CHINA, 894
	▮ PURE LAND BUDDHISM TEACHINGS GAIN IMPORTANCE, FROM 10TH CENTURY
	▮ WARRIOR CLANS RISE IN POWER, 12TH CENTURY
	1185
KAMAKURA	▮ KAMAKURA SHOGUNATE ESTABLISHED, 1185
	▮ POPULAR PURE LAND SECTS EMERGE, 13TH CENTURY
	1332

1 Vessel, 2500–1500 BCE

2 Dotaku, 100–300

3 Haniwa warrior figure, fifth to mid-sixth century

4 *Amida Descending over the Mountains,* 13th century

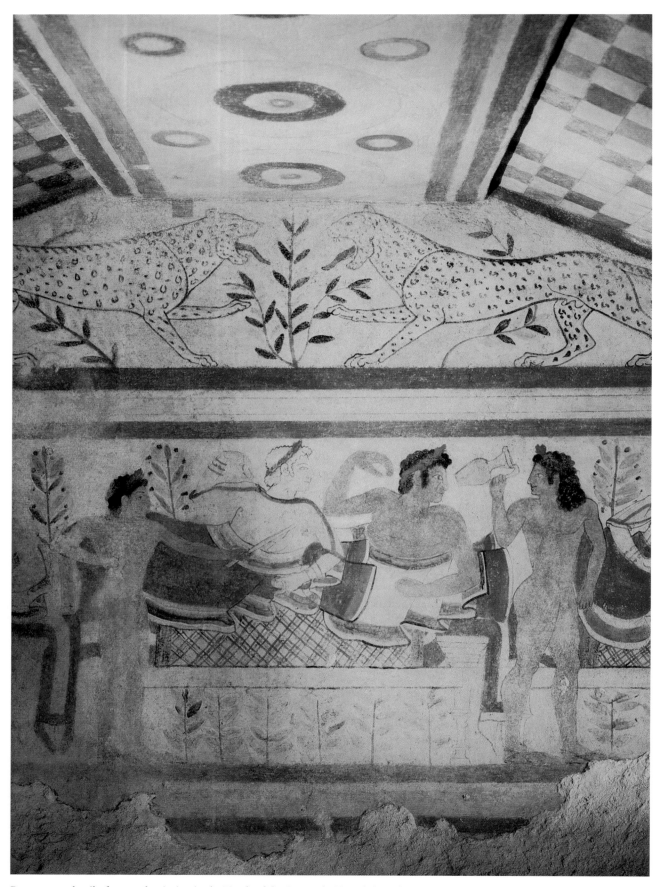

Banqueters, detail of a mural painting in the Tomb of the Leopards, Tarquinia, Italy, ca. 480–470 BCE.

9

ITALY BEFORE
THE ROMANS

THE ART OF THE ETRUSCANS

"The Etruscans, as everyone knows, were the people who occupied the middle of Italy in early Roman days, and whom the Romans, in their usual neighbourly fashion, wiped out entirely." So opens D. H. Lawrence's witty and sensitive *Etruscan Places* (1929), one of the earliest modern essays that highly values Etruscan art and treats it as much more than a debased form of the art of the contemporary city-states of Greece and southern Italy. ("Most people despise everything B.C. that isn't Greek, for the good reason that it ought to be Greek if it isn't," Lawrence goes on to say!) Today it is no longer necessary to argue the importance and originality of Etruscan art. Deeply influenced by, yet different from, Greek art, Etruscan sculpture, painting, and architecture not only provided the models for early Roman art and architecture but also had an impact on the art of the Greek colonies in Italy.

ETRUSCAN ORIGINS The heartland of the Etruscans was the territory between the Arno and Tiber rivers of central Italy (MAP **9-1**). The lush green hills still bear their name — Tuscany, the land of the people the Romans called *Tusci,* the region centered on Florence, birthplace of Renaissance art. So do the blue waters that splash up against the western coastline of the Italian peninsula, for the Greeks referred to the Etruscans as *Tyrrhenians* and gave their name to the sea off Tuscany. The origin of the Tusci people — the enduring "mystery of the Etruscans" — is, however, not clear at all. Their language, although written in a Greek-derived script and extant in inscriptions that are still in large part obscure, is unrelated to the Indo-European linguistic family. Ancient authors, as fascinated by the puzzle as modern scholars are, generally felt that the Etruscans emigrated from the east. Herodotus, the fifth-century BCE Greek historian, specifically declared that they came from Lydia in Asia Minor and were led by King Tyrsenos — hence their Greek name. But Dionysius of Halicarnassus, writing at the end of the first century BCE, maintained that the Tusci were native Italians. And some modern researchers have theorized that the Etruscans came into Italy from the north.

All these theories are current today, and no doubt some truth exists in each of them. The Etruscan people of historical times were very likely the result of a gradual

MAP 9-1 Italy in Etruscan times.

9-1 Fibula with Orientalizing lions, from the Regolini-Galassi Tomb, Cerveteri, Italy, ca. 650–640 BCE. Gold, approx. $1' \frac{1}{2}''$ high. Vatican Museums, Rome.

fusion of native and immigrant populations. This mixing of peoples occurred between the end of the Bronze Age and the so-called Villanovan era (named after an important northern Italian site, and contemporary with the Geometric period in Greece). At that time the Etruscans emerged as a people with a culture related to but distinct from those of other Italic peoples and from the civilizations of Greece and the Orient.

THE CITIES OF ETRURIA During the eighth and seventh centuries BCE, the Etruscans, as highly skilled seafarers, enriched themselves through trade abroad. By the sixth century, they controlled most of northern and central Italy from such strongholds as Tarquinia (ancient Tarquinii), Cerveteri (Caere), Vulci, and Veii. But these cities never united to form a state, so it is improper to speak of an Etruscan "nation" or "kingdom," only of *Etruria,* the territory occupied by the Etruscans. The cities coexisted, flourishing or fading independently. Any semblance of unity among them was based primarily on common linguistic ties and religious beliefs and practices. This lack of political cohesion eventually made the Etruscans relatively easy prey for Lawrence's Roman aggressors.

EARLY ETRUSCAN ART

Orientalizing Art

ETRUSCAN WEALTH Iron, tin, copper, and silver were all successfully mined in Etruria. This great mineral wealth transformed Etruscan society during the seventh century BCE. The modest Villanovan villages and their agriculturally based economies gave way to prosperous cities engaged in international commerce. Such cities as Cerveteri, blessed with rich mines, could acquire foreign goods, and Etruscan aristocrats quickly developed a taste for luxury objects incorporating Eastern motifs. To satisfy the demand, local artisans, inspired by imported goods, produced magnificent objects for both homes and tombs. As is true of Greece at the same time, art historians speak of an Orientalizing period of Etruscan art followed by an Archaic period. And, as in Greece, the local products cannot be mistaken for the foreign models.

GOLD JEWELRY About the middle of the seventh century BCE, a wealthy Etruscan family stocked the so-called Regolini-Galassi Tomb (named for its excavators) at Cerveteri with bronze cauldrons and gold jewelry of Etruscan manufacture and Orientalizing style. The most spectacular of the many luxurious objects in the family tomb is a golden *fibula* (clasp or safety pin; FIG. 9-1) of unique shape used to fasten a woman's gown at the shoulder. The giant fibula is in the Italic tradition, but the five lions that walk across the gold surface were borrowed from the Orient. The technique, also emulating Eastern imports, is masterful, combining hammered relief *(repoussé)* and *granulation* (the fusing of tiny metal balls, or granules, to a metal surface). The Regolini-Galassi fibula equals or exceeds in quality anything that might have served as a model.

The jewelry from the Regolini-Galassi Tomb also includes a golden *pectoral* that covered a deceased woman's chest, and two gold circlets that may be earrings, although they are large enough to be bracelets. Such a taste for ostentatious display is frequently the hallmark of newly acquired wealth, and this was certainly the case in seventh-century BCE Etruria.

Etruscan Counterparts of Greco-Roman Gods and Heroes

ETRUSCAN	GREEK	ROMAN
Tinia	Zeus	Jupiter
Uni	Hera	Juno
Menrva	Athena	Minerva
Apulu	Apollo	Apollo
Artumes	Artemis	Diana
Hercle	Herakles	Hercules

Archaic Art and Architecture

ETRUSCAN TEMPLES Etruscan artists looking eastward for inspiration were also greatly impressed by the art and architecture of Greece. But however eager they may have been to emulate Greek works, the distinctive Etruscan temperament always manifested itself. The vast majority of Archaic Etruscan artworks depart markedly from their prototypes. This is especially true of religious architecture. The design of Etruscan temples superficially owes much to Greece, but the differences far outweigh the similarities. Because of the materials Etruscan architects employed, usually only the foundations of Etruscan temples have survived. These are nonetheless sufficient to reveal the plans of the edifices. Supplementing the archaeological record is the Roman architect Vitruvius's treatise on architecture written near the end of the first century BCE. In it, Vitruvius provided an invaluable chapter on Etruscan temple design.

Archaeologists have constructed a model (FIG. **9-2**) of a typical Archaic Etruscan temple based on Vitruvius's account. The sixth-century Etruscan temple resembled contemporary Greek stone gable-roofed temples (see "Doric and Ionic Temples," Chapter 5, pages 116–117), but it had wooden columns and a wooden roof, and its walls were of sun-dried brick. Entrance was possible only via a narrow staircase at the center of the front of the temple, which sat on a high podium, the only part of the building made of stone. Columns also were restricted to the front of the building, creating a deep porch that occupied roughly half the podium and setting off one side of the structure as the main side. In contrast, the front and rear of Greek temples were indistinguishable, and steps and columns were placed on all sides. The Etruscan temple was not meant to be seen as a sculptural mass from the outside and from all directions, as Greek temples were. Instead it functioned primarily as an ornate home for grand statues of Etruscan gods. It was a place of shelter, protected by the wide overhang of its roof.

Etruscan temples differed in other ways from those of Greece. Etruscan (or *Tuscan*) columns resembled Greek Doric columns, but they were made of wood, were unfluted, and had bases. Because of the lightness of the superstructure they had to support, Etruscan columns were, as a rule, much more widely spaced than Greek columns. Unlike their Greek counterparts, Etruscan temples frequently had three cellas—one for each of their chief gods, Tinia, Uni, and Menrva (see "Etruscan Counterparts of Greco-Roman Gods and Heroes," above). And pedimental statuary was exceedingly rare in Etruria. The Etruscans normally placed narrative statuary—in terracotta instead of stone—on the peaks of their temple roofs.

9-2 Model of a typical Etruscan temple of the sixth century BCE, as described by Vitruvius. Istituto di Etruscologia e di Antichità Italiche, Università di Roma, Rome.

Etruscan Artists in Rome

In 616 BCE, according to the traditional chronology, Tarquinius Priscus of Tarquinia became Rome's first Etruscan king. He ruled for almost 40 years. His grandson, Tarquinius Superbus ("the Arrogant"), was Rome's last king. Outraged by his tyrannical behavior, the Romans drove him out in 509 BCE. Before his expulsion, however, Tarquinius Superbus embarked on a grand program to embellish the modest city of huts Romulus had founded two centuries before.

The king's most ambitious undertaking was the erection of a magnificent temple (see FIG. 10-1, no. 4) on the Capitoline Hill for the joint worship of Jupiter, Juno, and Minerva. For this great commission, he summoned architects, sculptors, and workers from all over Etruria. Rome's first great religious shrine was Etruscan in patronage, in manufacture, and in form. The architect's name is unknown, but several sources preserve the identity of the Etruscan sculptor brought in to adorn the temple. His name was Vulca of Veii. Pliny the Elder describes his works as "the finest images of deities of that era ... more admired than gold."[1] The Romans entrusted Vulca with making the statue of Jupiter that stood in the central of the Capitoline temple's three cellas. He also fashioned the enormous terracotta statuary group of Jupiter in a four-horse chariot, which was placed on the roof at the highest point directly over the center of the temple facade. The fame of Vulca's red-faced (painted terracotta) portrayal of Jupiter was so great that Roman generals would paint their faces red in emulation of his Jupiter when they paraded in triumph through Rome after a battlefield victory. (One can get an approximate idea of the appearance of this early Jupiter temple and of Vulca's roof statue from the model reproduced in FIG. 9-2.)

One story told about Vulca's chariot group underscores both its tremendous size and the reverent awe in which it was held by later generations. Terracotta statuary normally condenses and contracts in the furnace as the clay's moisture evaporates in the heating process. Vulca's statue swelled instead and could be removed from the furnace only by dismantling its walls and lifting off its roof.[2]

Vulca is the only Etruscan artist named by any ancient writer, but the signatures of other Etruscan artists appear on surviving artworks. One of these is Novios Plautios (FIG. 9-12), who also worked in Rome, although a few centuries later. By then the Etruscan kings of Rome were a distant memory, and the Romans had captured Veii and annexed its territory.

[1] Pliny, *Natural History,* 35.157.

[2] Plutarch, *Life of Poplicola,* 13.

AN EPIC ROOFTOP CONTEST The finest of these rooftop statues to survive today is the life-size image of Apulu (FIG. **9-3**), which displays the energy and excitement that characterize Archaic Etruscan art in general. The statue comes from a temple in the Portonaccio sanctuary at Veii. It is but one of a group of at least four painted terracotta figures that adorned the top of the temple roof. The god confronts Hercle for possession of the Ceryneian hind, a wondrous beast with golden horns that was sacred to Apulu's sister Artumes. The bright paint and the rippling folds of Apulu's garment call to mind the Ionian korai of the Acropolis (see FIG. 5-12). But this vital figure's extraordinary force, huge swelling contours, plunging motion, gesticulating arms, fanlike calf muscles, and animated face are distinctly Etruscan. Some scholars have attributed the Apulu to VULCA OF VEII, the most famous Etruscan sculptor of the time (see "Etruscan Artists in Rome," above). The statue's discovery in 1916 was instrumental in prompting a reevaluation of the originality of Etruscan art.

DINING IN THE AFTERLIFE Although life-size terracotta statuary was known in Greece, this medium was especially favored in Etruria. Another Archaic Etruscan terracotta masterwork is the sarcophagus in the form of a husband and wife reclining on a banqueting couch (FIG. **9-4**), from a tomb in the Cerveteri necropolis. The sarcophagus was cast in four sections and is of monumental size, but it contained only the ashes of the deceased. Cremation was the most common means of disposing of the dead in Italy at this time. This kind of funerary monument had no parallel at this date in Greece, where there were no monumental tombs that could house such sarcophagi. The Greeks buried their dead in simple graves marked by a stele or a statue. Moreover, although banquets were commonly depicted on Greek vases (which, by the late sixth century BCE, the Etruscans

9-3 Apulu (Apollo), from the roof of the Portonaccio Temple, Veii, Italy, ca. 510–500 BCE. Painted terracotta, approx. 5′ 11″ high. Museo Nazionale di Villa Giulia, Rome.

The "Audacity" of Etruscan Women

At the instigation of the emperor Augustus at the end of the first century BCE, Titus Livy wrote a history of Rome from its legendary founding in 753 BCE to his own day. In the first book of his great work, Livy recounted the tale of Tullia, daughter of Servius Tullius, an Etruscan king of Rome in the sixth century. The princess had married the less ambitious of two brothers of the royal Tarquinius family, while her sister had married the bolder of the two princes. Together, Tullia and her brother-in-law, Tarquinius Superbus, arranged for the murder of their spouses. They then married each other and plotted the overthrow and death of Tullia's father. After the king's murder, Tullia ostentatiously drove her carriage over her father's corpse, spraying herself with his blood. (The Roman road where the evil deed occurred is still called the Street of Infamy.) Livy, though condemning Tullia's actions, placed them in the context of the famous "audacity" of Etruscan women.

The independent spirit and relative freedom women enjoyed in Etruscan society similarly horrified (and threatened) other Greco-Roman male authors. The stories the fourth-century BCE Greek historian Theopompus heard about the debauchery of Etruscan women appalled him. Etruscan women epitomized immorality for Theopompus, but much of what he reported is untrue. Etruscan women did not, for example, exercise naked alongside Etruscan men. But archaeological evidence confirms the accuracy of at least one of his "slurs": Etruscan women did attend banquets and recline with their husbands on a common couch (FIGS. 9-4 and 9-8). Aristotle also remarked on this custom. It was so foreign to the Greeks that it both shocked and frightened them. Only men, boys, slave girls, and prostitutes attended Greek symposia. The wives remained at home, excluded from most aspects of public life. In Etruscan Italy, in striking contrast to contemporary Greece, women also regularly attended sporting events with men. This, too, is well documented in Etruscan paintings and reliefs.

Etruscan inscriptions also reflect the higher status of women in Etruria as compared to Greece. They often give the names of both the father and mother of the person commemorated (for example, the inscribed portrait of Aule Metele, FIG. 9-15), a practice unheard of in Greece (witness the grave stele of "Hegeso, daughter of Proxenos," FIG. 5-55). Etruscan women, moreover, retained their own names and could legally own property independently of their husbands. The frequent use of inscriptions on Etruscan mirrors and other toilet items (FIG. 9-12) buried with women seems to attest to a high degree of female literacy as well.

imported in great quantities and regularly deposited in their tombs), only men dined at Greek symposia. The image of a husband and wife sharing the same banqueting couch is uniquely Etruscan (see "The 'Audacity' of Etruscan Women," above).

The man and woman on the Cerveteri sarcophagus are as animated as the Apulu of Veii (FIG. 9-3), even though they are at rest. They are the antithesis of the stiff and formal figures encountered in Egyptian tomb sculptures (compare the portraits of Menkaure and Khamerernebty[?] from Gizeh, FIG. 3-13). Also typically Etruscan, and in striking contrast to contemporary Greek statues with their emphasis on proportion and balance, is the manner in which the Cerveteri sculptor rendered the upper and lower parts of each body. The legs were only summarily modeled, and the transition to the torso at the waist is unnatural. The Etruscan artist's interest focused on the upper half of the figures, especially on the vibrant faces and gesticulating arms. Gestures are still an important ingredient of Italian conversation today, and the Cerveteri banqueters and the Veii Apulu speak to viewers in a way that Greek statues of similar date, with their closed contours and calm demeanor, never do.

9-4 Sarcophagus with reclining couple, from Cerveteri, Italy, ca. 520 BCE. Painted terracotta, approx. 3′ 9½″ × 6′ 7″. Museo Nazionale di Villa Giulia, Rome.

HOUSES FOR THE DEAD The exact findspot of the Cerveteri sarcophagus is not known, but the kind of tomb that housed such sarcophagi is well documented. The typical tomb at Cerveteri (FIG. 9-5) took the form of a mound, or *tumulus* (plural *tumuli*), not unlike the Mycenaean Treasury of Atreus (see FIG. 4-21). But whereas the Mycenaean tholos tomb was constructed of masonry blocks and then covered by an earthen mound, each Etruscan tumulus covered one or more subterranean multichambered tombs cut out of the dark local limestone called tufa. These burial mounds sometimes reached colossal size, with diameters in excess of 130 feet. They were arranged in cemeteries in an orderly manner along a network of streets, producing the effect of veritable cities of the dead (which is the literal meaning of the Greek word *necropolis*), and were always located some distance from the cities of the living.

The underground tomb chambers cut into the rock resembled the houses of the living. In the plan of the sixth-century BCE Tomb of the Shields and Chairs at Cerveteri (FIG. 9-6), for example, the central entrance and the smaller chambers opening onto a large central space mirror the axial sequence of rooms in actual Etruscan houses of the time. The effect of a domestic interior was enhanced by the beds and grand armchairs with curved backs and footstools (clearly visible on the plan), as well as the ceiling beams, framed doorways, and even windows that were cut out of the rock. The technique recalls that of the rock-cut Egyptian tombs at Beni Hasan (see FIG. 3-20). One cannot help but notice the very different values of the Etruscans and the Greeks. The Etruscans' temples no longer stand because they were constructed of wood and mud brick, but their grand subterranean tombs are as permanent as the bedrock itself. The Greeks employed stone for the shrines of their gods but only rarely built monumental tombs for their dead.

The most elaborate of the Cerveteri underground tombs, in decoration if not in plan, is the so-called Tomb of the Reliefs (FIG. 9-7). Like the much earlier Tomb of the Shields and Chairs, it accommodated several generations of a single family. The walls and

0   5   10   15
FEET

0   1   2   3   4   5
METERS

9-6 Plan of the Tomb of the Shields and Chairs, Cerveteri, Italy, second half of the sixth century BCE.

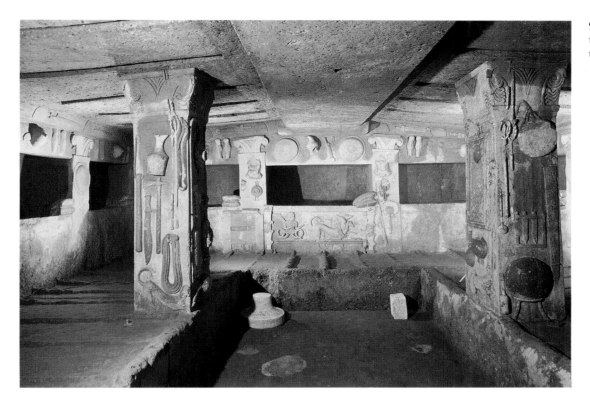

9-7 Interior of the Tomb of the Reliefs, Cerveteri, Italy, third century BCE.

piers of this tomb were, as usual, gouged out of the tufa bedrock, but in this instance brightly painted stucco reliefs covered the stone. The stools, mirrors, drinking cups, pitchers, and knives effectively suggest a domestic context, underscoring the connection between Etruscan houses of the dead and those of the living.

TARQUINIA'S PAINTED TOMBS Large underground burial chambers hewn out of the natural rock were also the norm at Tarquinia. But tumuli do not cover the Tarquinian tombs, and the interiors do not have carvings imitating the appearance of Etruscan houses. In some cases, however, paintings decorate the tomb chamber walls. Painted tombs are statistically rare, the privilege of only the wealthiest Etruscan families. Nevertheless, archaeologists have discovered many at Tarquinia by using periscopes to explore tomb contents from the surface before considering time-consuming and costly excavation. Consequently, art historians have an almost unbroken record of monumental painting in Etruria from Archaic to Hellenistic times.

LEOPARDS AND A FEAST A characteristic example dating to the early fifth century BCE is the Tomb of the Leopards (FIG. **9-8**), named for the beasts that guard the interior of the painted

9-8 Leopards, banqueters, and musicians, mural paintings in the Tomb of the Leopards, Tarquinia, Italy, ca. 480–470 BCE.

9-9 Diving and fishing, mural painting in the Tomb of Hunting and Fishing, Tarquinia, Italy, ca. 530–520 BCE.

chamber from their perch within the rear wall pediment. They are reminiscent of the panthers on each side of Medusa in the pediment of the Archaic Greek Temple of Artemis at Corfu (see FIG. 5-15). But mythological figures, whether Greek or Etruscan, are uncommon in Tarquinian murals, and the Tomb of the Leopards has none. Instead, banqueting couples (the men with dark skin, the women with light skin, in conformity with the age-old convention) adorn the walls—painted versions of the terracotta sarcophagus from Cerveteri (FIG. 9-4). Pitcher- and cupbearers serve them, and musicians entertain them. The banquet takes place in the open air or perhaps in a tent set up for the occasion. In characteristic Etruscan fashion, the banqueters, servants, and entertainers all make exaggerated gestures with unnaturally enlarged hands. The man on the couch at the far right on the rear wall holds up an egg, the symbol of regeneration. The tone is joyful. The painting is a celebration of life, food, wine, music, and dance, rather than a somber contemplation of death.

ETRUSCAN LANDSCAPES In stylistic terms, the Etruscan figures are comparable to those on sixth-century Greek vases before Late Archaic painters became preoccupied with the problem of foreshortening. Etruscan painters may be considered somewhat backward in this respect, but in other ways they seem to have outpaced their counterparts in Greece, especially in their interest in

rendering nature. In the Tomb of the Leopards, the landscape is but a few trees and shrubs placed between the entertainers (and leopards) and behind the banqueting couches. But elsewhere the natural environment was the chief interest of Tarquinian painters.

Scenes of Etruscans enjoying the pleasures of nature decorate all the walls of the main chamber of the aptly named Tomb of Hunting and Fishing at Tarquinia. In our detail (FIG. **9-9**), a youth dives off a rocky promontory, while others fish from a boat and birds fill the sky all around. On another wall, youthful hunters aim their slingshots at the brightly painted birds. The scenes of hunting and fishing recall the painted reliefs in the Old Kingdom Egyptian Tomb of Ti (see FIG. 3-16) and the mural paintings from the New Kingdom Tomb of Nebamun (see FIG. 3-30), and may indicate knowledge of this Egyptian funerary tradition. The multicolored rocks may be compared to those of the Aegean *Spring Fresco* from Thera (see FIG. 4-9), but art historians know of nothing similar in contemporary Greek art save the Tomb of the Diver at Paestum (see FIG. 5-59). The latter is, however, exceptional and is from a Greek tomb in Italy about a half century *later* than the Tarquinian tomb. In fact, it is likely that the Paestum composition emulated older Etruscan designs, undermining the now outdated art historical judgment that Etruscan art was merely derivative and that Etruscan artists never set the standard for Greek artists.

LATER ETRUSCAN ART

The fifth century BCE was a golden age in Greece but not in Etruria. In 509 BCE, the Romans expelled the last of their Etruscan kings, Tarquinius Superbus (see "Etruscan Artists in Rome," page 236), replacing the monarchy with a republican form of government. In 474 BCE, an alliance of Cumaean Greeks and Hieron I of Syracuse (Sicily) defeated the Etruscan fleet off Cumae, effectively ending Etruscan dominance of the seas, and with it Etruscan prosperity. These events had important consequences in the world of art and architecture. The number of Etruscan tombs, for example, decreased sharply, and the quality of the furnishings declined markedly. No longer were tombs filled with golden jewelry and imported Greek vases or decorated with mural paintings of the first rank. But Etruscan art did not cease. Indeed, in the areas in which Etruscan artists excelled, especially the casting of statues in bronze and terracotta, they continued to produce impressive works, even though fewer in number.

Classical Art

ROME'S ETRUSCAN WOLF The best-known of these later Etruscan statues—one of the most memorable portrayals of an animal in the history of world art—is the *Capitoline Wolf* (FIG. 9-10). The statue is a somewhat larger than life-size hollow-cast bronze portrayal of the she-wolf that, according to legend, nursed Romulus and Remus after they were abandoned as infants. When the twins grew to adulthood, they quarreled, and Romulus killed his brother. On April 21, 753 BCE, Romulus founded Rome on the Palatine Hill and became the city's king. The statue of the she-wolf seems to have been made, however, for the new Roman Republic after the expulsion of Tarquinius Superbus. It became the new government's totem. The appropriately defiant image has remained the emblem of Rome to this day.

The *Capitoline Wolf* is not, however, a work of Roman art, which had not yet developed a distinct identity, but the product of an Etruscan workshop. (The suckling infants are additions by the Italian Renaissance sculptor Antonio Pollaiuolo.) The vitality noted in the human figure in Etruscan art is here concentrated in the tense, watchful animal body of the she-wolf, with her spare flanks, gaunt ribs, and taut, powerful legs. The lowered neck and head, alert ears, glaring eyes, and ferocious muzzle capture the psychic intensity of the fierce and protective beast as danger approaches. Not even the great animal reliefs of Assyria (see FIG. 2-24) match, much less surpass, this profound rendering of animal temper.

AREZZO'S BRONZE CHIMERA Another masterpiece of Etruscan bronze-casting, found in 1553 and greatly admired during the Renaissance, is the *Chimera of Arezzo* (FIG. 9-11), which dates about a century later than the *Capitoline Wolf*. The *chimera* is a monster of Greek invention with a lion's head and body and a serpent's tail. A second head, that of a goat, grows out of the lion's left side. The goat's neck bears the wound the Greek hero Beller-ophon inflicted when he hunted and slew the composite beast. As rendered by the Etruscan sculptor, the chimera, although injured and bleeding, is nowhere near defeated. Like the earlier she-wolf statue, the bronze chimera has muscles that are stretched tightly over its rib cage. It prepares to

9-10 *Capitoline Wolf,* from Rome, Italy, ca. 500–480 BCE. Bronze, approx. 2′ 7½″ high. Palazzo dei Conservatori, Rome.

9-11 *Chimera of Arezzo,* from Arezzo, Italy, first half of fourth century BCE. Bronze, approx. 2′ 7½″ high. Museo Archeologico Nazionale, Florence.

9-12 NOVIOS PLAUTIOS, *Ficoroni Cista,* from Palestrina, Italy, late fourth century BCE. Bronze, approx. 2′ 6″ high. Museo Nazionale di Villa Giulia, Rome.

attack, and a ferocious cry emanates from its open jaws. Some scholars have postulated that the statue was part of a group that originally included Bellerophon, but the chimera could have just as well stood alone. The menacing gaze upward toward an unseen adversary need not have been answered. In this respect, too, the chimera is in the tradition of the guardian nurse of Romulus and Remus.

Etruscan Art and the Rise of Rome

ROME OVERWHELMS ETRURIA At about the time the *Chimera of Arezzo* was fashioned, Rome began to appropriate Etruscan territory. Veii fell to the Romans in 396 BCE, after a terrible 10-year siege. Peace was concluded with Tarquinia in 351, but by the beginning of the next century, Tarquinia, too, was annexed by Rome, and Cerveteri was conquered in 273 BCE. Rome's growing power in central Italy is indicated indirectly by the engraved inscription on the *Ficoroni Cista* (FIG. **9-12**). Etruscan artists produced such *cistae* (cylindrical containers for a woman's toilet articles), made of sheet bronze with cast handles and feet and elaborately engraved bodies, in large numbers from the fourth century BCE forward. Along with engraved bronze mirrors, they were popular gifts for both the living and the dead. The Etruscan bronze cista industry centered in Palestrina (ancient Praeneste), where the *Ficoroni Cista* was found. The inscription on the cista's handle states that Dindia Macolnia, a local noblewoman, gave the bronze container to her daughter and that the artist was one NOVIOS PLAUTIOS. According to the inscription, his workshop was not in Palestrina but in Rome, which by this date was becoming an important Italian cultural, as well as political, center.

The engraved frieze of the *Ficoroni Cista* depicts an episode from the Greek story of the expedition of the Argonauts in search of the Golden Fleece. Scholars generally agree that the composition is an adaptation of a lost Greek panel painting, perhaps one on display in Rome—another testimony to the burgeoning

wealth and prestige of the city once ruled by Etruscan kings. The Greek source for Novios Plautios's engraving is evident in the figures seen entirely from behind or in three-quarter view, and in the placement of the protagonists on several levels in the Polygnotan manner (see FIG. 5-57).

THE GATE OF MARS In the third century BCE, the Etruscan city of Perugia (ancient Perusia) formed an alliance with Rome and was spared the destruction suffered by Veii, Cerveteri, and other Etruscan towns. Portions of Perugia's ancient walls are still standing, as are some of its gates. One of these, the so-called Porta Marzia (Gate of Mars), was dismantled by the Renaissance architect Antonio da Sangallo, but the upper part of the gate is preserved, embedded in a later wall (FIG. **9-13**). The archway is formed by a series of trapezoidal stone *voussoirs* held in place by being pressed against each other (see FIG. 4-18*c*). Such arches were built earlier in Greece as well as in Mesopotamia (see FIG. 2-25), but Italy, first under the Etruscans and later under the Romans, is where *arcuated* (arch-shaped) gateways and freestanding ("triumphal") arches became a major architectural type.

The use of Hellenic-inspired pilasters to frame the rounded opening of the Porta Marzia typifies the Etruscan adaptation of Greek motifs. Arches bracketed by engaged columns or pilasters have a long and distinguished history in Roman and later times. In the Porta Marzia, sculpted half-figures of Jupiter and his sons Castor and Pollux and their steeds look out from between the fluted pilasters. The divine twins had appeared miraculously on a battlefield in 484 BCE to turn the tide in favor of the Romans. The presence of these three deities at the apex of the Porta Marzia may reflect the new Roman practice of erecting triumphal arches crowned by gilded bronze statues.

TORMENT IN THE UNDERWORLD In Hellenistic Etruria, the descendants of the magnificent Archaic terracotta sarcophagus from Cerveteri (FIG. 9-4) were made of local stone. The leading production center was Tarquinia, and that is where the sar-

cophagus of Lars Pulena (FIG. **9-14**) was fashioned early in the second century BCE and placed in his family's tomb. The deceased is shown in a reclining position, but he is not at a festive banquet, and his wife is not present. His expression is somber, a far cry from the smiling, confident faces of the Archaic era when Etruria enjoyed its greatest prosperity. Similar heads—realistic but generic types, not true portraits—are found on all later Etruscan sarcophagi and in tomb paintings. They are symptomatic of the economic and political decline of the once-mighty Etruscan city-states.

9-14 Sarcophagus of Lars Pulena, from Tarquinia, Italy, early second century BCE. Tufa, approx. 6′ 6″ long. Museo Archeologico Nazionale, Tarquinia.

9-15 Aule Metele *(Arringatore)*, from Cortona, near Lake Trasimeno, Italy, early first century BCE. Bronze, approx. 5′ 7″ high. Museo Archeologico Nazionale, Florence.

Also attesting to a gloomy assessment of the future is the theme chosen for the coffin proper. The deceased is shown in the underworld, attacked by two *Charuns* (Etruscan death demons) swinging lethal hammers. Above, on the lid, Lars Pulena exhibits a partially unfurled scroll inscribed with the record of his life's accomplishments. Lacking confidence in a happy afterlife, he dwells instead on the past.

ETRUSCAN OR ROMAN? In striking contrast, the portrait of Aule Metele (FIG. 9-15) is a supremely self-confident image. He is portrayed as a magistrate raising his arm to address an assembly— hence his modern nickname *Arringatore* (Orator). This life-size bronze statue was discovered in 1566 near Lake Trasimeno and is yet another Etruscan masterpiece known to Italian Renaissance sculptors. The statue of the orator proves that Etruscan artists continued to be experts at bronze-casting long after the heyday of Etruscan prosperity.

The *Arringatore* was most likely produced at about the time that Roman hegemony over the Etruscans became total. The so-called Social War of the early first century BCE ended in 89 BCE with the conferring of Roman citizenship on all of Italy's inhabitants. In fact, Aule Metele—his Etruscan name and his father's and mother's names are inscribed on the hem of his garment—wears the short toga and high laced boots of a Roman magistrate. His head, with its close-cropped hair and signs of age in the face, resembles portraits produced in Rome at the time. This orator is Etruscan in name only.

CONCLUSION

In the Archaic period, the Etruscans dominated the Italian peninsula. Although they imported Greek objects, especially painted vases, in great numbers, their art, while influenced by that of Greece, was distinctive and innovative. No Greek parallels exist for Etruscan tombs with mural paintings, temples with rooftop statuary, or sarcophagi depicting married couples.

By the first century BCE, however, Etruria had been incorporated into the ever-expanding empire of Rome. The portrait of Aule Metele (FIG. 9-15), for example, is indistinguishable from contemporary Roman portraits. If the origin of the Etruscans remains debatable, the question of their demise has a ready answer. Aule Metele and his compatriots became Romans, and Etruscan art became Roman art.

900 BCE

VILLANOVAN

| Greek colonization of southern Italy and Sicily begins, mid-eighth century BCE

| Founding of Rome, 753 BCE

700 BCE

ORIENTALIZING

| Tarquinius Priscus, first Etruscan king of Rome, (R. 616–578 BCE)

1 Regolini-Galassi fibula, Cerveteri, ca. 650–640 BCE

600 BCE

ARCHAIC

| Expulsion of Etruscan kings from Rome, 509 BCE

2 Tomb of the Leopards, Tarquinia, ca. 480–470 BCE

480 BCE

| Greeks defeat the Etruscan navy at Cumae, 474 BCE

| Romans destroy Veii, 396 BCE

| Peace between Rome and Tarquinia, 351 BCE

CLASSICAL

323 BCE

| Roman conquest of Cerveteri, 273 BCE

3 Ficoroni Cista, late fourth century

HELLENISTIC

89 BCE

| End of Social War and completion of Romanization of Italy, 89 BCE

4 Porta Marzia, Perugia, second century BCE

Interior of the Pantheon, Rome, Italy, 118–125 CE.

10

FROM SEVEN HILLS TO THREE CONTINENTS

THE ART OF ANCIENT ROME

With the rise and triumph of Rome, a single government ruled, for the first time in human history, from the Tigris and Euphrates to the Thames and beyond, from the Nile to the Rhine and Danube (MAP **10-1**). Within the Roman Empire's borders lived people of numerous races, religions, tongues, traditions, and cultures: Britons and Gauls, Greeks and Egyptians, Africans and Syrians, Jews and Christians, to name but a few. Of all the ancient civilizations, only the Roman approximates today's world in its multicultural character.

Roman monuments of art and architecture, spread throughout the vast territory the Romans governed, are the most conspicuous and numerous of all the remains of ancient civilization. Many, converted to other uses, are part of the fabric of modern life, not merely ruins that spark the curiosity of tourists, students, and scholars. Even in North America, where no Roman remains exist save for imported statues, paintings, and mosaics, modern versions of Roman buildings such as the Pantheon (FIG. 10-48) may be found in cities and on college campuses.

FROM VILLAGE TO WORLD CAPITAL The far-flung Roman Empire centered on the city on the Tiber River that, according to legend, Romulus founded as a modest village of huts on April 21, 753 BCE. Nine centuries later, Rome was the capital of the greatest empire the world had ever known. The imperial city (FIG. **10-1**) awed foreign kings and even later Roman rulers. The historian Ammianus Marcellinus reported that when the emperor Constantius visited Rome in 357 CE and entered the Forum of Trajan (FIG. 10-41), constructed 250 years earlier, he "stopped in his tracks, astonished" and marveled at the Forum's opulence and size, "which cannot be described by words and could never again be attempted by mortal men."[1]

REPUBLIC

KINGS, SENATORS, AND CONSULS Our story, however, begins long before Roman art and architecture embodied the imperial ideal of the Roman state, at a time when that "state" encompassed no territory beyond one of its famous seven hills. The

MAP 10-1 The Roman world.

ART AND SOCIETY

An Outline of Roman History

MONARCHY (753–509 BCE)

Latin and Etruscan kings ruled Rome from the city's foundation by Romulus until the revolt against Tarquinius Superbus (exact dates of rule unreliable).

REPUBLIC (509–27 BCE)

The Republic lasted from the expulsion of Tarquinius Superbus until the bestowing of the title of Augustus on Octavian, the grandnephew of Julius Caesar and victor over Mark Antony in the Civil War that ended the Republic. Some major figures were:

- Marcellus, b. 268(?), d. 208 BCE, consul
- Marius, b. 157, d. 86 BCE, consul
- Sulla, b. 138, d. 79 BCE, consul and dictator
- Pompey, b. 106, d. 48 BCE, consul
- Julius Caesar, b. 100, d. 44 BCE, consul and dictator
- Mark Antony, b. 83, d. 30 BCE, consul

EARLY EMPIRE (27 BCE–96 CE)

The Early Empire began with the rule of Augustus and his Julio-Claudian successors and continued until the end of the Flavian dynasty. Selected emperors and their dates of rule (with names of the most influential empresses in parentheses) were:

- Augustus (Livia), r. 27 BCE–14 CE
- Tiberius, r. 14–37
- Caligula, r. 37–41
- Claudius (Agrippina the Younger), r. 41–54
- Nero, r. 54–68
- Vespasian, r. 69–79

- Titus, r. 79–81
- Domitian, r. 81–96

HIGH EMPIRE (96–192 CE)

The High Empire began with the rule of Nerva and the Spanish emperors, Trajan and Hadrian, and ended with the last emperor of the Antonine dynasty. The emperors (and empresses) of this period were:

- Nerva, r. 96–98
- Trajan (Plotina), r. 98–117
- Hadrian (Sabina), r. 117–138
- Antoninus Pius (Faustina the Elder), r. 138–161
- Marcus Aurelius (Faustina the Younger), r. 161–180
- Lucius Verus, co-emperor, r. 161–169
- Commodus, r. 180–192

LATE EMPIRE (192–337 CE)

The Late Empire began with the Severan dynasty and included the so-called soldier emperors of the third century, the tetrarchs, and Constantine, the first Christian emperor. Selected emperors (and empresses) were:

- Septimius Severus (Julia Domna), r. 193–211
- Caracalla (Plautilla), r. 211–217
- Severus Alexander, r. 222–235
- Trajan Decius, r. 249–251
- Trebonianus Gallus, r. 251–253
- Diocletian, r. 284–305
- Constantine I, r. 306–337

10-1 Model of the city of Rome during the early fourth century CE. Museo della Civiltà Romana, Rome. 1) Temple of Fortuna Virilis, 2) Circus Maximus, 3) Palatine Hill, 4) Temple of Jupiter Capitolinus, 5) Pantheon 6) Column of Trajan, 7) Forum of Trajan, 8) Markets of Trajan, 9) Forum of Julius Caesar, 10) Forum of Augustus, 11) Forum Romanum, 12) Basilica Nova, 13) Arch of Titus, 14) Temple of Venus and Roma, 15) Arch of Constantine, 16) Colossus of Nero, 17) Colosseum.

Rome of Romulus in the eighth century BCE comprised only small huts of wood, wattle, and daub, clustered together on the Palatine Hill (FIG. 10-1, no. 3) overlooking what was then uninhabited marshland. In the Archaic period, Rome was essentially an Etruscan city, both politically and culturally. Its greatest shrine, the Temple of Jupiter Optimus Maximus (Best and Greatest) on the Capitoline Hill, was built by an Etruscan king, designed by an Etruscan architect, made of wood and mud brick in the Etruscan manner, and decorated with terracotta statuary by an Etruscan sculptor (see "Etruscan Artists in Rome," Chapter 9, page 236).

In 509 BCE, the Romans threw out Tarquinius Superbus, the last of Rome's Etruscan kings, and established a constitutional government (see "An Outline of Roman History," page 248) The new Roman Republic vested power mainly in a *senate* (literally, "a council of elders," *senior* citizens) and in two elected *consuls.* Under extraordinary circumstances a *dictator* could be appointed for a specified time and a specific purpose, such as commanding the army during a crisis. All leaders came originally from among the wealthy landowners, or *patricians,* but later also from the *plebeian* class of small farmers, merchants, and freed slaves.

Before long, the descendants of Romulus conquered Rome's neighbors one by one: the Etruscans and the Gauls to the north, the Samnites and the Greek colonists to the south. Even the Carthaginians of North Africa, who under Hannibal's dynamic leadership had annihilated some of Rome's legions and almost brought down the Republic, fell before the might of Roman armies.

THE CRAZE FOR GREEK ART The year 211 BCE was a turning point both for Rome and for Roman art. Breaking with precedent, Marcellus, conqueror of the fabulously wealthy Sicilian Greek city of Syracuse, brought back to Rome not only the usual spoils of war—captured arms and armor, gold and silver coins, and the like—but also the city's artistic patrimony. Thus began, in the words of the historian Livy, "the craze for works of Greek art."[2] According to the biographer Plutarch, the Romans, "who had hitherto been accustomed only to fighting or farming," now began "affecting urbane opinions about the arts and about artists, even to the point of wasting the better part of a day on such things."[3] Ships filled with plundered Greek statues and paintings became a frequent sight in the harbor of Ostia at the mouth of the Tiber River.

Exposure to Greek sculpture and painting and to the splendid marble temples of the Greek gods increased as the Romans expanded their conquests beyond Italy. Greece became a Roman province in 146 BCE, and in 133 BCE the last Attalid king of Pergamon willed his kingdom to Rome (see Chapter 5). Nevertheless, although the Romans developed a virtually insatiable taste for Greek "antiques," their own monuments were not slavish imitations of Greek masterpieces. The Etruscan basis of Roman art and architecture was never forgotten, and the statues and buildings of the Roman Republic are highly eclectic, drawing on both Greek and Etruscan traditions. The resultant mix, however, is distinctly Roman.

The Roman Architectural Revolution
Concrete Construction

The history of Roman architecture would be very different if the Romans had been content to use the same building materials the Greeks, Etruscans, and other ancient peoples did. Instead, the Romans developed concrete construction, which revolutionized architectural design. Roman *concrete* was made from a changing recipe of lime mortar, volcanic sand, water, and small stones (*caementa,* from which the English word *cement* is derived). Builders placed the mixture in wooden frames and left it to dry and to bond with a brick or stone facing. When the concrete dried completely, the wooden molds were removed, leaving behind a solid mass of great strength, though rough in appearance. The Romans often covered the rough concrete with stucco or with marble *revetment* (facing). Despite this lengthy procedure, concrete walls were much less costly to construct than walls of imported Greek marble or even local tufa and travertine.

The advantages of concrete go well beyond cost, however. It is possible to fashion concrete shapes that masonry construction cannot achieve, especially huge vaulted and domed rooms without internal supports. The Romans came to prefer these over the Greek and Etruscan post-and-lintel structures. Concrete enabled Roman builders to think of architecture in radical new ways. Roman concrete architecture became an architecture of space rather than of sheer mass.

To cover and give shape to these new "spatial envelopes," the Romans employed a variety of vaulting systems. The following were the most common types:

BARREL VAULTS Also called the *tunnel vault,* the *barrel vault* is an extension of a simple arch, creating a semicylindrical ceiling over parallel walls. Pre-Roman builders constructed barrel vaults using traditional ashlar masonry (see FIG. 2-25), but those earlier vaults and all later stone vaults (see, for example, FIG. 17-6) are less stable than concrete barrel vaults. If any of the blocks of a cut-stone vaults comes loose, the whole may collapse. Also, masonry barrel vaults can be illuminated only by light entering at either end of the tunnel. In contrast, windows can be placed at any point in concrete barrel vaults, because once the concrete hardens, it forms a seamless sheet of "artificial stone" that may be punctured

almost at will. Whether made of stone or concrete, barrel vaults require *buttressing* (lateral support) of the walls below the vaults to counteract their downward and outward *thrust.*

GROIN VAULTS A *groin* or *cross vault* is formed by the intersection at right angles of two barrel vaults of equal size. Besides appearing lighter than the barrel vault, the groin vault needs less buttressing. The barrel vault's thrust is concentrated along the entire length of the supporting wall. The groin vault's thrust, however, is concentrated along the groins, and buttressing is needed only at the points where the groins meet the vault's vertical supports, usually *piers.* The system leaves the area between the supports open, permitting light to enter. Groin vaults, like barrel vaults, can be built using stone blocks—but with the same structural limitations when compared to concrete vaulting.

When a series of groin vaults covers an interior hall, as in our diagram and in FIGS. 10-44, 10-68, and 10-79, the open lateral arches of the vaults form the equivalent of a *clerestory* of a traditional timber-roofed structure (for example, see FIG. 11-8). Such a *fenestrated* (with openings or windows) sequence of groin vaults has a major advantage over wooden clerestories. Concrete vaults are relatively fireproof, always an important consideration given that fires were common occurrences (see "Timber Roofs and Stone Vaults," Chapter 17, page 451).

HEMISPHERICAL DOMES The largest domed space in the ancient world for more than a millennium was the corbeled, beehive-shaped tholos of the Treasury of Atreus at Mycenae (see FIG. 4-22). The Romans were able to surpass the Mycenaeans by using concrete to construct hemispherical *domes,* which usually rested on concrete cylindrical *drums.* If a barrel vault is described as a round arch extended in a line, then a hemispherical dome may be described as a round arch rotated around the full circumference of a circle. Masonry domes (compare FIG. 10-73), like masonry vaults, cannot accommodate windows without threatening their stability. Concrete domes can be opened up even at their apex with a circular "eye" (*oculus*), as in our diagram and FIGS. 10-33, 10-49, and 10-50, allowing much-needed light to reach the vast spaces beneath.

Barrel vault

Groin vault

Fenestrated sequence of groin vaults

Hemispherical dome with oculus

10-2 Temple of "Fortuna Virilis" (Temple of Portunus), Rome, Italy, ca. 75 BCE.

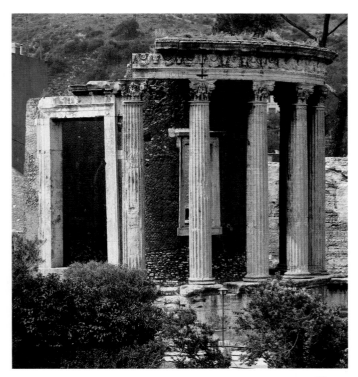

10-3 Temple of Vesta(?), Tivoli, Italy, early first century BCE.

Architecture

ECLECTICISM ON THE TIBER Eclecticism is the primary characteristic of the Republican temple on the east bank of the Tiber known as the Temple of "Fortuna Virilis" (FIGS. **10-2** and 10-1, no. 1), actually the Temple of Portunus, the Roman god of harbors. In plan it follows the Etruscan pattern. The high podium is accessible only at the front, with its wide flight of steps. Freestanding columns are confined to the deep porch. But the structure is built of stone (local tufa and travertine), overlaid originally with stucco in imitation of the gleaming white marble temples of the Greeks. The columns are not Tuscan but Ionic, complete with flutes and bases, and a matching Ionic frieze. Moreover, in an effort to approximate a peripteral Greek temple while maintaining the basic Etruscan plan, the architect added a series of engaged Ionic half-columns on the sides and back of the cella. The result was a *pseudoperipteral* temple. Although the design combines Etruscan and Greek elements, it is uniquely Roman.

TIVOLI'S TEMPLE ON A CLIFF The Romans' admiration for the Greek temples they encountered in their conquests also led to the importation into Republican Italy of a temple type unknown in Etruscan architecture—the round, or tholos, temple. At Tivoli (ancient Tibur), on a dramatic site overlooking a deep gorge, a Republican architect erected such a Greek-inspired temple early in the first century BCE. Usually called the Temple of Vesta (FIG. **10-3**), it is circular in plan and has travertine Corinthian columns. The frieze is carved with garlands held up by oxen heads, also in emulation of Greek models. But the high podium can be reached only via a narrow stairway leading to the cella door. This arrangement introduced an axial alignment not found in Greek tholoi (see FIG. 5-71), where, as in Greek rectangular temples, steps continue all around the structure. Also in contrast with the Greeks, the Roman builders did not construct the cella wall using masonry blocks but a new material of recent invention: concrete (see "The Roman Architectural Revolution: Concrete Construction," page 250).

CONCRETE TRANSFORMS A HILLSIDE The most impressive and innovative use of concrete during the Republic was in the Sanctuary of Fortuna Primigenia (FIG. **10-4**), the goddess of good fortune, at Palestrina (ancient Praeneste, formerly an Etruscan city). The great complex was constructed in the late second century BCE. Spread out over several terraces leading up the hillside

10-4 Reconstruction drawing of the Sanctuary of Fortuna Primigenia, Palestrina, Italy, late second century BCE.

10-5 Funerary relief with portraits of the Gessii, from Rome(?), Italy, ca. 30 BCE. Marble, approx. 2′ 1½″ high. Museum of Fine Arts, Boston.

to a tholos at the peak of an ascending triangle, the layout reflects the Republican taste for colossal Hellenistic designs. The means of construction, however, was distinctly Roman.

The builder used concrete barrel vaults of enormous strength to support the imposing terraces and to cover the great ramps leading to the grand central staircase, as well as to give shape to the shops aligned on two consecutive levels. In this way, the unknown architect transformed the entire hillside into a grandiose complex symbolic of Roman power. This subjection of nature to human will and rational order was the first full-blown manifestation of the Roman imperial spirit. It contrasts with the more restrained Greek practice of simply crowning a hill with sacred buildings, as opposed to converting the hill itself into architecture.

Sculpture

PORTRAITS AND SOCIETY The patrons of the Roman Republic's great temples and sanctuaries were in almost all cases men from old and distinguished families, often victorious generals who used the spoils of war to finance public works. These aristocratic patricians were fiercely proud of their lineage. They kept likenesses (*imagines*) of their ancestors in wooden cupboards in their homes and paraded them at the funerals of prominent relatives. Marius, a renowned Republican general who lacked a long and distinguished genealogy, was ridiculed by his patrician colleagues as a man who had no ancestral portraits in his home. Slaves and former slaves could not possess *any* family portraits, because, under Roman law, their parents and grandparents were not people but property. Freed slaves often ordered portrait reliefs (FIGS. **10-5** and **10-6**) for their tombs to commemorate their new status as Roman citizens (see "Art for Former Slaves," page 253).

REPUBLICAN VERISM The surviving portraits of prominent Roman Republican figures, which appear to be literal reproductions of individual faces, must be seen in this context. Although their style derives to some degree from Hellenistic and Etruscan, and perhaps even Ptolemaic Egyptian, portraits, Republican portraits are one way the patrician class celebrated its elevated position in society. The subjects of these portraits were almost exclusively men (and to a lesser extent women) of advanced age, for generally only elders held power in the Republic. These patricians did not ask sculptors to make them appear nobler than they were, as Kresilas portrayed Pericles (see FIG. 5-39). Instead, they requested

10-6 Relief with funerary procession, from Amiternum, Italy, second half of first century BCE. Limestone, approx. 2′ 2″ high. Museo Nazionale d'Abruzzo, L'Aquila.

Art for Former Slaves

Historians and art historians alike tend to focus on the lives and monuments of famous individuals, but some of the most interesting remains of ancient Roman civilization are the artworks commissioned by ordinary people, especially former slaves, or *freedmen* and *freedwomen*. Slavery was common in the Roman world. It is estimated that Italy at the end of the Republic had some two million slaves, or roughly one slave for every three citizens. The very rich might own hundreds of slaves, but slaves could be found in all but the poorest households. The practice was so much a part of Roman society that even slaves often became slave owners when their former masters freed them. Some gained freedom in return for meritorious service. Others were only freed in their masters' wills. Most slaves died as slaves in service to their original or new owners.

The most noteworthy of all the artworks commissioned by Roman freedmen and freedwomen are the stone reliefs that regularly adorned their tomb facades. One of these reliefs (FIG. 10-5) depicts three people, all named Gessius. At the left is Gessia Fausta and at the right Gessius Primus. Both are the freed slaves of Publius Gessius, the freeborn citizen in the center, shown wearing a general's *cuirass* (breastplate) and portrayed in the standard Republican superrealistic fashion (FIGS. 10-7 to 10-9). As slaves this couple had no legal standing; they were the property of Publius Gessius. After they were freed, however, in the eyes of the law the ex-slaves became people. These stern frontal portraits proclaim their new status as legal members of Roman society—and their gratitude to Publius Gessius for granting them that status.

As was the custom, the two ex-slaves bear their patron's name, but whether they are sister and brother, wife and husband, or unrelated is unclear. The inscriptions on the relief explicitly state that the monument was paid for with funds provided by the will of Gessius Primus and that the work was directed by Gessia Fausta, the only survivor of the three. The relief thus depicts the living and the dead side by side, indistinguishable except by the accompanying message. This theme is common in Roman art (compare FIGS. 10-46 and 10-57) and proclaims that death does not break bonds formed in life.

More rarely, freed slaves commissioned tomb reliefs that were narrative in character. A relief from Amiternum (FIG. 10-6) depicts the cortege in honor of the deceased, complete with musicians, professional female mourners who pull their hair in a display of feigned grief, and the deceased's wife and children. The deceased is laid out on a bier with a canopy as a backdrop, much like the figures on Greek Geometric vases (see FIG. 5-1). Here, however, the dead man surprisingly props himself up as if still alive, surveying his own funeral. This may be an effigy, like the reclining figures on the lids of Etruscan sarcophagi (see FIGS. 9-4 and 9-14), rather than the deceased himself.

Compositionally, the relief is also not what one would expect. Mourners and musicians stand on floating ground lines, as if on flying carpets. They are not to be viewed as suspended in space, however, but as situated behind the front row of pallbearers and musicians. This sculptor, in striking contrast to the (usually Greek) artists employed by the patrician aristocracy, had little regard for the rules of classical art. The Amiternum artist studiously avoided overlapping and placed the figures wherever they fit, so long as they were clearly visible. This approach to making pictures was characteristic of preclassical art, but it had been out of favor for several centuries. One looks in vain for similar compositions in the art commissioned by the consuls and senators of the Roman Republic. In ancient Rome's cosmopolitan world, as today, stylistic tastes often were tied to a person's political and social status.

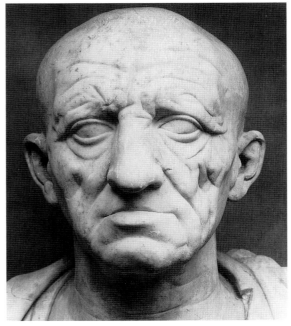

10-7 Head of a Roman patrician, from Otricoli, Italy, ca. 75–50 BCE. Marble, approx. 1′ 2″ high. Museo Torlonia, Rome.

brutally realistic images of distinctive features, in the tradition of the treasured household imagines.

One of the most striking of these so-called *veristic* (superrealistic) portraits is the head of an unidentified patrician (FIG. **10-7**) found near Otricoli. The sculptor painstakingly recorded each rise and fall, each bulge and fold, of the facial surface, like a mapmaker who did not want to miss the slightest detail of surface change. Scholars debate whether such portraits were truly blunt records of actual features or exaggerated types designed to make a statement about personality: serious, experienced, determined, loyal to family and state—virtues that were much admired during the Republic.

OLD HEADS ON YOUNG BODIES The portrait from Otricoli is in bust form. The Romans believed that the head alone was enough to constitute a portrait. The Greeks, in contrast, believed that head and body were inseparable parts of an integral whole, so their portraits were always full length (see FIG. 5-88). In fact, in Republican portraiture veristic heads were often, although incongruently, placed on bodies to which they could not possibly belong.

Such is the case in the curious and discordant portrait of a general (FIG. **10-8**) found at Tivoli. The cuirass at his side, which acts as a prop for the heavy marble statue, is the emblem of his

10-9 Denarius with portrait of Julius Caesar, 44 BCE. Silver, diameter approx. $\frac{3}{4}''$. American Numismatic Society, New York.

10-8 Portrait of a Roman general, from the Sanctuary of Hercules, Tivoli, Italy, ca. 75–50 BCE. Marble, approx. 6′ 2″ high. Museo Nazionale Romano-Palazzo Massimo alle Terme, Rome.

rank. But the general does not appear as he would in life. Although he has a typically stern and lined Republican head, it sits atop a powerful, youthful, almost nude body. The sculptor modeled the portrait on the statues of Greek athletes and heroes the Romans admired so much and often copied (see Chapter 5). The incorporation of references to Greek art in these portrait statues evoked the notion of patrician cultural superiority as well as heroicized the person portrayed. In the Tivoli statue, however, the patron's modesty dictated that a mantle shield the genitals.

CAESAR BREAKS THE RULES Beginning early in the first century BCE, the Roman desire to advertise distinguished ancestry led to the placement of portraits of illustrious forebears on Republican coins. These ancestral portraits supplanted the earlier Roman tradition (based on Greek convention) of using images of divinities on coins. No Roman, however, dared to place his own likeness on a coin until 44 BCE, when Julius Caesar, shortly before his assassination on the Ides of March, issued coins featuring his portrait and his newly acquired title, *dictator perpetuus* (dictator for life). The *denarius* (the standard Roman silver coin, from which the word *penny* ultimately derives) illustrated here (FIG. **10-9**) records Caesar's aging face and receding hairline in conformity with the Republican veristic tradition. But placing the likeness of a living person on a coin violated all the norms of

Republican propriety. Henceforth, Roman coins, which circulated throughout the vast territories under Roman control, would be used to mold public opinion in favor of the ruler by announcing his achievements—both real and fictional.

POMPEII AND THE CITIES OF VESUVIUS

BURIED BY A VOLCANO On August 24, 79 CE, Mount Vesuvius, a long-dormant volcano whose fertile slopes were covered with vineyards during the Late Republic and Early Empire, suddenly erupted (see "An Eyewitness Account of the Eruption of Mount Vesuvius," page 255). Many prosperous towns around the Bay of Naples (the ancient Greek city of Neapolis), among them Pompeii, were buried in a single day. This catastrophe for the inhabitants of the Vesuvian cities has, however, been a boon for archaeologists and art historians. When researchers first explored the buried cities in the 18th century, the ruins had been undisturbed for nearly 1,700 years (see "Rising from the Ashes: The Excavation of Herculaneum and Pompeii," Chapter 28, page 815). The Vesuvian sites are still being excavated, but the remains already uncovered permit a reconstruction of the art and life of Roman towns of the Late Republic and Early Empire with a completeness far beyond that possible anywhere else.

OSCANS, SAMNITES, AND ROMANS The Oscans, one of the many Italic tribes that occupied Italy during the heyday of the Etruscans, were the first to settle at Pompeii. Toward the end of the fifth century BCE, the Samnites, another Italic people, took over the town. Under the influence of their Greek neighbors, the Samnites greatly expanded the original settlement and gave monumental shape to the city center. Pompeii fought with other Italian cities on the losing side against Rome in the Social War, and in 80 BCE Sulla founded a new Roman colony on the site, with Latin as its official language. The colony's population had grown to between 10,000 and 20,000 when, in February 62 CE, an earthquake shook the city, causing extensive damage. When Mount Vesuvius erupted 17 years later, repairs were still in progress.

AN ARCHAEOLOGICAL PARK Walking through Pompeii today is an experience that cannot be approximated at any other site.

An Eyewitness Account of the Eruption of Mount Vesuvius

Pliny the Elder, whose *Natural History* is one of the most important sources for the history of Greek art, was among those who tried to rescue others from danger when Mount Vesuvius erupted. He was overcome by fumes the volcano spewed forth, and died. His nephew, Pliny the Younger, a government official under the emperor Trajan, left an account of the eruption and his uncle's demise:

[The volcanic cloud's] general appearance can best be expressed as being like a pine . . . for it rose to a great height on a sort of trunk and then split off into branches. . . . Sometimes it looked white, sometimes blotched and dirty, according to the amount of soil and ashes it carried with it. . . . The buildings were now shaking with violent shocks, and seemed to be swaying to and fro as if they were torn from their foundations. Outside, on the other hand, there was the danger of falling pumice-stones, even though these were light and porous. . . . Elsewhere there was daylight, [but around Vesuvius, people] were still in darkness, blacker and denser than any night that ever was. . . . When daylight returned on the 26th—two days after the last day [my uncle] had been seen—his body was found intact and uninjured, still fully clothed and looking more like sleep than death.[1]

[1] Betty Radice, trans., *Pliny the Younger: Letters and Panegyricus*, vol. 1 (Cambridge, Mass.: Harvard University Press, 1969), 427–33.

The streets, with their heavy flagstone pavements and sidewalks, are still there, as are the stepping stones that enabled pedestrians to cross the streets without having to step in puddles. Ingeniously, the city planners placed these stones in such a way that vehicle wheels could straddle them, enabling supplies to be brought directly to the shops, taverns, and bakeries. Tourists still can visit the impressive concrete-vaulted rooms of Pompeii's public baths and sit in the seats of its open-air theater and indoor concert hall, even walk among the tombs outside the city walls. The sights include private homes with magnificently painted walls and pleasant gardens. Some still have their kitchen utensils in place. Pompeii has been called the living city of the dead for good reason.

Architecture

THE HEART OF POMPEII The center of civic life in any Roman town was its *forum,* or public square, usually located at the city's geographic center at the intersection of the main north-south street, the *cardo,* and the main east-west avenue, the *decumanus* (FIG. 10-40). The forum, however, generally was closed to all but pedestrian traffic. Pompeii's forum (FIG. **10-10**) lies in the southwest corner of the expanded Roman city but at the heart of the original town. The forum took on monumental form in the second century BCE when the Samnites, inspired by Hellenistic architecture, erected two-story colonnades on three sides of the long and narrow plaza. At the north end they constructed a Temple of Jupiter (FIG. 10-10, no. 2). When Pompeii became a Roman colony in 80 BCE, the Romans converted the temple into a *Capitolium*—a triple shrine of Jupiter, Juno, and Minerva (see "The Gods and Goddesses of Mount Olympus," Chapter 5, page 107). The temple is of standard Republican type, constructed of tufa covered with fine white stucco and combining an Etruscan plan with Corinthian columns. It faces into the civic square, dominating the area. This is very different from the siting of Greek temples (see FIGS. 5-40 and 5-41), which stood in isolation and could be approached and viewed from all sides, like colossal statues on giant stepped pedestals. The Roman forum, like the Etrusco-Roman temple, has a chief side, a focus of attention.

The area within the porticos of the forum at Pompeii was empty, except for statues commemorating local dignitaries and, later, Roman emperors. This is where the citizens conducted daily commerce and held festivities. All around the square, behind the colonnades, were secular and religious structures, including the town's administrative offices. Most noteworthy is the *basilica* (FIG. 10-10, no. 3) at the southwest corner, the earliest well-preserved building of its kind. Constructed during the late second century BCE, the basilica housed the law court of Pompeii and also was used for other official purposes. In plan it resembles the forum itself: long and narrow, with two stories of internal columns dividing the space into a central *nave* and flanking *aisles.* This scheme had a long afterlife in architectural history and will be familiar to anyone who has ever entered a Christian church.

GLADIATORS AND WILD ANIMALS The forum was an oasis in the heart of Pompeii—an open, airy plaza. Throughout the rest of the city, every square foot of land was developed. Shortly after the Romans took control of Pompeii, two of the town's wealthiest officials, Quinctius Valgus and Marcus Porcius, used their own

10-10 Aerial view of the forum (1), with Temple of Jupiter (Capitolium, 2) and Basilica (3), Pompeii, Italy, second century BCE and later.

10-11 Aerial view of the amphitheater, Pompeii, Italy, ca. 70 BCE.

10-12 Brawl in the Pompeii amphitheater, wall painting from House I,3,23, Pompeii, Italy, ca. 60–79 CE. Approx. 5′ 7″ × 6′ 1″. Museo Nazionale, Naples.

funds to erect a large amphitheater (FIG. **10-11**) at the southeastern end of town. It is the earliest such structure known and could seat some 20,000 spectators—more than the entire population of the town even a century and a half after it was built! The donors would have had choice reserved seats in the new entertainment center. In fact, seating was assigned by rank, both civic and military, so that the Roman social hierarchy was on display at every event.

The word *amphitheater* means "double theater," and the Roman structures closely resemble two Greek theaters put together, although the Greeks never built amphitheaters. Greek theaters were situated on natural hillsides (see FIGS. 5-40 and 5-70), but supporting an amphitheater's continuous elliptical *cavea* (seating area) required building an artificial mountain. Only concrete, unknown to the Greeks, was capable of such a job. In the Pompeii amphitheater, a series of radially disposed concrete barrel vaults forms a giant retaining wall that holds up the earthen mound and stone seats. Barrel vaults also form the tunnels leading to the *arena*, the central area where bloody gladiatorial combats and wild animal hunts occurred. (*Arena* is Latin for "sand," which soaked up the blood of the wounded and killed.) The Roman amphitheater stands in sharp contrast, both architecturally and functionally, to the Greek theater, home of refined performances of comedies and tragedies.

A painting (FIG. **10-12**) on the wall of a Pompeian house records an unfortunate incident that occurred in the amphitheater. A brawl broke out between the Pompeians and their neighbors, the Nucerians, during a gladiatorial contest in 59 CE. The fighting left many seriously wounded and led to the closing of the amphitheater for a decade. The painting shows the cloth awning (*velarium*) that could be rolled down from the top of the cavea to shield spectators from sun and rain. It also features the distinctive external double staircases (not visible in FIG. 10-11) that enabled large numbers of people to enter and exit the cavea in an orderly fashion.

TOWNHOUSES FOR THE WEALTHY At Pompeii, as in modern cities and towns, private homes occupied most of the area outside the civic center. The evidence from Pompeii regarding Roman domestic architecture (see "The Roman House," page 257) is unparalleled anywhere else and is the most precious

by-product of the catastrophic volcanic eruption of 79 CE. One of the best preserved houses at Pompeii, partially rebuilt and an obligatory stop on every tourist's itinerary today, is the House of the Vettii, an old Pompeian house remodeled and repainted after the earthquake of 62 CE. Our photograph (FIG. **10-13**) was taken

10-13 Atrium of the House of the Vettii, Pompeii, Italy, second century BCE, rebuilt 62–79 CE.

The Roman House

The Roman house was more than just a place to live. It played an important role in Roman societal rituals. In the Roman world, individuals were frequently bound to others in a patron-client relationship whereby a wealthier, better-educated, and more powerful *patronus* would protect the interests of a *cliens,* sometimes large numbers of them. The standing of a patron in Roman society often was measured by clientele size. Being seen in public accompanied by a crowd of clients was a badge of honor. In this system, a plebeian might be bound to a patrician, a freed slave to a former owner, or even one patrician to another. Regardless of rank, all clients were obligated to support their patron in political campaigns and to perform specific services on request, as well as to call on and salute the patron at the patron's home.

A client calling on a patron would enter the typical Roman *domus* (private house) through a narrow foyer (*fauces,* the "throat" of the house), which led to a large central reception area, the *atrium.* The rooms flanking the fauces could open inward, as in our diagram, or outward, in which case they were rented out as shops. The roof over the atrium was partially open to the sky, not only to admit light but also to channel rainwater into a basin *(impluvium)* below. The water could be stored in cisterns for household use. Opening onto the atrium was a series of small bedrooms called *cubicula* (cubicles). At the back were the patron's *tablinum* or "home office," a dining room *(triclinium),* a kitchen, and sometimes a small garden.

Endless variations of the same basic plan exist, dictated by the owners' personal tastes and means, the nature of the land plot, and so forth, but all Roman houses of this type were inward-looking in nature. The design shut off the street's noise and dust, and all internal activity focused on the brightly illuminated atrium at the center of the residence. This basic module (only the front half of the typical house in our diagram) resembles the plan of the typical Etruscan house as reflected in the Tomb of the Shields and Chairs (see FIG. 9-6) and other tombs at Cerveteri. Thus, few doubt that the early Roman house, like the early Roman temple, grew out of the Etruscan tradition.

During the second century BCE, when Roman architects were beginning to construct stone temples with Greek columns, the Roman house also took on Greek airs. Builders added a peristyle garden behind the Etruscan-style house, providing a second internal illumination source as well as a pleasant setting for meals served in a summer triclinium. The axial symmetry of the plan meant that on entering the fauces of the house, a visitor could be greeted by a vista through the atrium directly into the peristyle garden (as in FIG. 10-13), which often boasted a fountain or pool, marble statuary, mural paintings, and mosaic floors.

Such houses were not, of course, the norm. While they were typical of Pompeii and other towns, they were very rare in large cities such as Rome, where the masses lived instead in multistory apartment houses (FIG. 10-53).

1. Fauces
2. Atrium
3. Impluvium
4. Cubiculum
5. Tablinum
6. Peristyle
7. Triclinium

in the *fauces.* It shows the *impluvium* in the center of the *atrium,* the opening in the roof above, and, in the background, the *peristyle* garden with its marble tables and splendid mural paintings dating to the last years of the Vesuvian city. At that time, two brothers, Aulus Vettius Restitutus and Aulus Vettius Conviva, probably freedmen who had made their fortune as merchants, owned the house. Their wealth enabled them to purchase and furnish the kind of fashionable townhouse that in an earlier era only patricians could have acquired.

One such house, a luxurious Pompeian mansion of the second century BCE, the so-called House of the Faun, epitomizes Livy's Republican "craze for things Greek." The house takes its nickname from the Hellenistic-style bronze statue that stood in one of its two atriums. The mansion, which occupied an entire city block, also had two huge peristyle gardens. First Style murals (see page 258) of Greek type covered most of the walls, and mosaics decorated the floors of many rooms. The most spectacular mosaic panel found in the house depicts Alexander the Great battling Darius of Persia (see FIG. 5-69) and is a copy of a fourth-century BCE Greek panel painting.

Painting

PAINTED WALLS EVERYWHERE The houses and villas around Mount Vesuvius have yielded a treasure trove of mural paintings, the most complete record of the changing fashions in interior decoration found anywhere in the ancient world. The sheer quantity of these paintings tells a great deal about both the prosperity and the tastes of the times. How many homes today, even of the very wealthy, have custom-painted murals in nearly every room? Roman wall paintings were true frescoes (see "Fresco Painting," Chapter 19, page 530), with the colors applied while the plaster was still damp. The process was a painstaking one. First the painter had to prepare the wall by applying the plaster (mixed with marble dust if the patron could afford it) in several layers with a smooth trowel. Only then could painting begin. Finally, when the surface dried, the painter polished the wall to achieve a marblelike finish.

In the early years of exploration at Pompeii and nearby Herculaneum, excavators focused almost exclusively on the figural panels that formed part of the overall mural designs, especially those depicting Greek heroes and famous myths. These were cut out of the walls and transferred to the Naples Archaeological Museum. (The painting of the brawl in the amphitheater, FIG. 10-12, suffered this fate.) In time, more enlightened archaeologists put an end to the practice of cutting pieces out of the walls, and gave serious attention finally to the mural designs as a whole. Toward the end of the 19th century, August Mau, a German art historian, divided the various mural painting schemes into four so-called Pompeian Styles, numbered in the order they were introduced. Mau's classification system, although later refined and modified in detail, still serves as the basis for the study of Roman painting.

THE FIRST STYLE AND GREECE The *First Style* also has been called the Masonry Style because the decorator's aim was to imitate costly marble panels using painted stucco relief. (For walls faced with real marble slabs, see FIGS. 10-50 and 17-18.) In the fauces (FIG. **10-14**) of the Samnite House at Herculaneum, the visitor is greeted at the doorway by a stunning illusion of walls constructed, or at least faced, with marbles imported from quarries all over the Mediterranean. This approach to wall decoration is comparable to the modern practice, employed in private libraries and corporate meeting rooms alike, of using cheaper manufactured materials to approximate the look and shape of genuine wood paneling. The practice is not, however, uniquely Pompeian or Roman. First Style walls are well documented in the Greek world from the late fourth century BCE on. The use of the First Style in Republican houses is yet another example of the Hellenization of Roman architecture.

SECOND STYLE ILLUSIONISM The First Style never went completely out of fashion, but after 80 BCE a new approach to mural design became more popular. The *Second Style* is in most respects the antithesis of the First Style. Some scholars have argued that the Second Style also has precedents in Greece, but most believe it is a Roman invention. Certainly, the Second Style evolved in Italy and was popular until around 15 BCE, when Roman painters introduced the Third Style. Second Style painters aimed not to create the illusion of an elegant marble wall, as First Style painters sought to do. Rather, they wanted to dissolve a room's confining walls and replace them with the illusion of an imaginary three-dimensional world. They did this purely pictorially. The First Style's modeled stucco panels gave way to the Second Style's flat wall surfaces.

DIONYSIAC MYSTERIES AT POMPEII An early example of the new style is the room (FIG. **10-15**) that gives its name to the Villa of the Mysteries at Pompeii. Many scholars believe that this chamber was used to celebrate, in private, the rites of the Greek god Dionysos (Roman Bacchus). Dionysos was the focus of an unofficial mystery religion popular among women in Italy at this time. The precise nature of the Dionysiac rites is unknown, but the figural cycle in the Villa of the Mysteries, illustrating mortals (all female save for one boy) interacting with mythological figures, probably provides some evidence for the cult's initiation rites. In these rites young women, emulating Ariadne, daughter of King Minos (see Chapter 4), were united in marriage with Dionysos.

10-14 First Style wall painting in the fauces of the Samnite House, Herculaneum, Italy, late second century BCE.

The backdrop for the nearly life-size figures is a series of painted panels imitating marble revetment, just as in the First Style but without the modeling in relief. In front of this marble wall (but actually on the same two-dimensional surface), the painter created the illusion of a shallow ledge on which the human and divine actors move around the room. Especially striking is the way some of the figures interact across the corners of the room. For example, a seminude winged woman at the far right of the rear wall lashes out with her whip across the space of the room at a kneeling woman with a bare back (the initiate and bride-to-be of Dionysos) on the left end of the right wall. Nothing comparable to this room existed in Hellenistic Greece. Despite the presence of Dionysos, satyrs, and other figures from Greek mythology, this is a Roman design.

PERSPECTIVE PAINTING In the early Second Style Dionysiac mystery frieze, the spatial illusionism is confined to the painted platform that projects into the room. But in mature Second Style designs, painters created a three-dimensional setting that also extends beyond the wall. An example is a cubiculum (FIG. **10-16**) from the Villa of Publius Fannius Synistor at Boscoreale, near

10-15 Dionysiac mystery frieze, Second Style wall paintings in Room 5 of the Villa of the Mysteries, Pompeii, Italy, ca. 60–50 BCE. Frieze approx. 5′ 4″ high.

10-16 Second Style wall paintings (general view, *left*, and detail of tholos, *right*) from Cubiculum M of the Villa of Publius Fannius Synistor, Boscoreale, Italy, ca. 50–40 BCE. Approx. 8′ 9″ high. Metropolitan Museum of Art, New York.

10-17 Gardenscape, Second Style wall painting, from the Villa of Livia, Primaporta, Italy, ca. 30–20 BCE. Approx. 6' 7" high. Museo Nazionale Romano-Palazzo Massimo alle Terme, Rome.

Pompeii, decorated between 50 and 40 BCE. The frescoes were removed soon after their discovery, and today they are part of a reconstructed Roman bedroom in the Metropolitan Museum of Art. All around the room the Second Style painter opened up the walls with vistas of Italian towns, marble temples, and colonnaded courtyards. Painted doors and gates invite the viewer to walk through the wall into the magnificent world the painter created.

Although the Boscoreale painter was inconsistent in applying it, this Roman artist, like many others in the towns Vesuvius buried, demonstrated a knowledge of single-point *linear perspective,* often incorrectly said to be an innovation of Italian Renaissance artists (see "Depicting Objects in Space," Chapter 21, page 578). In this kind of perspective, all the receding lines in a composition converge on a single point along the painting's central axis to show depth and distance. Ancient writers state that Greek painters of the fifth century BCE first used linear perspective for the design of Athenian stage sets (hence its Greek name, *skenographia,* "scene painting"). In the Boscoreale cubiculum the device is most successfully employed in the far corners, where a low gate leads to a peristyle framing a tholos temple (FIG. 10-16, detail). Roman painters used one-point linear perspective more consistently and on an even grander scale in the somewhat later Room of the Masks in what was probably the house of the emperor Augustus on the Palatine Hill in Rome. Linear perspective was a favored tool of Second Style painters seeking to transform the usually windowless walls of Roman houses into "picture-window" vistas that expanded the apparent space of the rooms.

AN EMPRESS'S PAINTED GARDEN The ultimate example of a Second Style picture-window wall (FIG. **10-17**) was found in the Villa of Livia, wife of the emperor Augustus, at Primaporta, just north of Rome. There, imperial painters decorated a vaulted, partly underground room on all sides with lush gardenscapes. The only architectural element is the flimsy fence of the garden itself. To suggest recession, the painter mastered another kind of perspective, *atmospheric perspective,* indicating depth by the increasingly blurred appearance of objects in the distance. At Livia's villa, the fence, trees, and birds in the foreground are precisely painted, while the details of the dense foliage in the background are indistinct. Among the wall paintings examined so far, only the landscape

fresco from Thera (see FIG. 4-9) offers a similar wraparound view of nature. But the Aegean fresco's white sky and red, yellow, and blue rock formations do not create a successful illusion of a world filled with air and light just a few steps away.

THIRD STYLE ELEGANCE The open, verdant Primaporta gardenscape is the polar opposite of First Style designs, which reinforce, rather than deny, the heavy presence of confining walls. But tastes changed rapidly in the Roman world, as in society today. Not long after Livia had her villa painted, Roman patrons began to favor mural designs that reasserted the primacy of the wall surface. In the *Third Style* of Pompeian painting, artists no longer attempted to replace the walls with three-dimensional worlds of their own creation. Nor did they seek to imitate the appearance of the marble walls of Hellenistic kings. Instead they decorated walls with delicate linear fantasies sketched on predominantly monochromatic (one-color) backgrounds.

One of the earliest examples of the new style is a room (FIG. **10-18**) in the Villa of Agrippa Postumus at Boscotrecase, near Pompeii, also a property owned by the imperial family. The villa was probably painted just before 10 BCE. Nowhere did the artist use illusionistic painting to penetrate the wall. In place of the stately columns of the Second Style are insubstantial and impossibly thin *colonnettes* supporting featherweight canopies barely reminiscent of pediments. In the center of this delicate and elegant architectural frame is a tiny floating landscape painted directly on the jet-black ground. It is hard to imagine a sharper contrast with the panoramic gardenscape at Livia's villa. On other Third Style walls, landscapes and mythological scenes appear in frames, like modern canvas paintings hung on walls. Never could these framed panels be mistaken for windows opening onto a world beyond the room.

ROMAN PAINTING AND LATIN POETRY Despite the differences in style, the landscapes of the Primaporta and Boscotrecase villas reveal a love of country life and idealization of nature that also appear in the pastoral poetry of Vergil, a contemporary of Livia and Augustus. Horace, another renowned Augustan poet, also proclaimed in one of his odes the satisfaction afforded the city dweller by a villa in the countryside, where life is beautiful, simple, and natural, in contrast with the urban greed for gold and

The Roman Illustrated Book

The hundreds of paintings uncovered in the cities buried by the eruption of Mount Vesuvius give the false impression that the history of Roman painting is well documented and that art historians can trace its development decade by decade. But Pompeii, Herculaneum, and the other towns around the Bay of Naples have yielded only frescoes. As in Greece, no Roman paintings on wooden panels have been discovered, save for the special case of Roman Egypt (FIGS. 10-63 and 10-64). Nor has anyone found any of the grand tableaux of battles and besieged cities that were exhibited in Roman triumphal processions and then displayed in public buildings to perpetuate the memory of a general's great achievements on the state's behalf.

Also apparently lost are virtually all illustrated Roman books, although art historians know they once existed in great numbers. The oldest preserved painted manuscript, itself very incomplete, is the *Vatican Vergil,* which dates from the early fifth century CE. It originally contained more than 200 pictures illustrating all of Vergil's works. Today only 50 painted *folios* (pages) of the *Aeneid* and *Georgics* survive.

The page illustrated here (FIG. 10-19) includes a section of text from the *Georgics* at the top and a framed illustration below. Vergil recounts his visit to a modest farm near Tarentum (Taranto, in southern Italy) belonging to an old man from Corycus in Asia Minor. In the illustration, the old farmer is seated at the left. His rustic farmhouse is in the background, rendered in a three-quarter view. The farmer speaks about the pleasures of the simple life in the country and on his methods of gardening. His audience is two laborers and, at the far right, Vergil himself in the guise of a farmhand. The style is reminiscent of Pompeian landscapes, with quick touches that suggest space and atmosphere. In fact, the heavy, dark frame has close parallels in the late Pompeian styles of mural painting (FIG. 10-20).

power. A fifth-century CE illustrated manuscript (FIG. **10-19**) containing some of Vergil's pastoral poems also provides invaluable evidence about the nature of Roman illustrated books (see "The Roman Illustrated Book," above).

NERO AND THE FOURTH STYLE In the *Fourth Style,* a taste for illusionism returned once again. This style became popular around the time of the Pompeian earthquake of 62 CE, and it was the preferred manner of mural decoration when the town was buried in volcanic ash in 79. The earliest examples, such as

10-18 Detail of a Third Style wall painting, from Cubiculum 15 of the Villa of Agrippa Postumus, Boscotrecase, Italy, ca. 10 BCE. Approx. 7′ 8″ high. Metropolitan Museum of Art, New York.

10-19 The old farmer of Corycus, folio 7 verso of the *Vatican Vergil,* ca. 400–420 CE. Tempera on parchment, approx. 1′ $\frac{1}{2}$″ × 1′. Biblioteca Apostolica Vaticana, Rome.

10-20 Fourth Style wall paintings in Room 78 of the Domus Aurea (Golden House) of Nero, Rome, Italy, 64–68 CE.

Room 78 (FIG. **10-20**) in the emperor Nero's fabulous Domus Aurea, or Golden House, in Rome (see "An Imperial Pleasure Palace: The Golden House of Nero," page 270), display a kinship with the Third Style. All the walls are an austere creamy white. In some areas the artist painted sea creatures, birds, and other motifs directly on the monochromatic background, much like the landscape in the Boscotrecase villa (FIG. 10-18). Landscapes appear here also—as framed paintings in the center of each large white subdivision of the wall. But views through the wall are also part of the design, although the Fourth Style architectural vistas are irrational fantasies. The viewer looks out not on cityscapes or round temples set in peristyles but at fragments of buildings—columns supporting half-pediments, double stories of columns supporting nothing at all—painted on the same white ground as the rest of the wall. In the Fourth Style, architecture became just another motif in the painter's ornamental repertoire.

PAINTING BEFORE THE ERUPTION In the latest Fourth Style designs, Pompeian painters rejected the quiet elegance of the Third Style and early Fourth Style in favor of crowded and confused compositions and sometimes garish color combinations. The Ixion Room (FIG. **10-21**) of the House of the Vettii at Pompeii was decorated in this manner just before the eruption of Mount Vesuvius. The room served as a triclinium in the house the Vettius brothers remodeled after the earthquake. It opened onto the peristyle seen in the background of FIG. 10-13.

The decor of the dining room is a kind of résumé of all the previous styles, another instance of the eclecticism noted earlier as characteristic of Roman art in general. The lowest zone, for example, is one of the most successful imitations anywhere of costly multicolored imported marbles, despite the fact that the illusion

is created without recourse to relief, as in the First Style. The large white panels in the corners of the room, with their delicate floral frames and floating central motifs, would fit naturally into the most elegant Third Style design. Unmistakably Fourth Style, however, are the fragmentary architectural vistas of the central and upper zones of the Ixion Room walls. They are unrelated to one another, do not constitute a unified cityscape beyond the wall, and are peopled with figures that would tumble into the room if they took a single step forward.

GREEK MYTHS ON ROMAN WALLS The Ixion Room takes its nickname from the mythological panel painting at the center of the rear wall (FIG. 10-21). Ixion had attempted to seduce Hera, and Zeus punished him by binding him to a perpetually spinning wheel. The panels on the two side walls also have Greek myths as subjects. The Ixion Room may be likened to a small private art gallery with paintings decorating the walls, as in many modern homes. Scholars long have believed that these and the many other mythological paintings on Third and Fourth Style walls were based on lost Greek panels. They attest to the Romans' continuing admiration for Greek artworks three centuries after Marcellus brought the treasures of Syracuse to Rome. But few, if any, of these mythological paintings can be described as true copies of "Old Masters," as are the many Roman replicas of famous Greek statues that have been found throughout the Roman world, including Pompeii (see FIG. 5-38).

Mythological figures were on occasion also the subject of Roman mosaics. In the ancient world, mosaics were usually confined to floors (as was the *Battle of Issus,* FIG. 5-69), where the tesserae formed a durable as well as decorative surface. In Roman times, however, mosaics also decorated walls and even ceilings, foreshadowing the extensive use of wall and vault mosaics in the Middle Ages

10-21 Fourth Style wall paintings in the Ixion Room (Triclinium P) of the House of the Vettii, Pompeii, Italy, ca. 70–79 CE.

10-22 Neptune and Amphitrite, wall mosaic in the summer triclinium of the House of Neptune and Amphitrite, Herculaneum, Italy, ca. 62–79 CE.

10-23 Portrait of a husband and wife, wall painting from House VII,2,6, Pompeii, Italy, ca. 70–79 CE. Approx. 1′ 11″ × 1′ 8½″. Museo Nazionale, Naples.

(see "Mosaics," Chapter 11, page 315). The mosaic shown in FIG. **10-22** adorns a wall in the House of Neptune and Amphitrite at Herculaneum. The sea god and his wife preside over the running water of the fountain in the courtyard in front of them where the house's owners and guests enjoyed outdoor dining in warm weather.

PRETENTIOUS PRIVATE PORTRAITS The subjects chosen for Roman wall paintings and mosaics were diverse. Although mythological themes were immensely popular, Romans commissioned a vast range of other subjects. As noted, landscape paintings frequently appear on Second, Third, and Fourth Style walls. Paintings and mosaics depicting scenes from history include the *Battle of Issus* mosaic and the mural painting of the brawl in the amphitheater of Pompeii (FIG. 10-12). Given the Roman custom of keeping *imagines* of illustrious ancestors in atriums, it is not surprising that painted portraits also appear in Pompeian houses. The portrait of a husband and wife illustrated here (FIG. **10-23**) originally formed part of a Fourth Style wall of an *exedra* (recessed area) opening onto the atrium of a Pompeian house. The man holds a scroll and the woman a stylus (writing instrument) and a wax writing tablet, standard attributes in Roman marriage portraits. They suggest the fine education of those depicted—even if, as was sometimes true, the individuals were uneducated or even illiterate. Such portraits were thus the Roman equivalent of modern wedding photographs of the bride and groom posing in rented formal garments never worn by them before or afterward. In contrast, the heads are not standard types but sensitive studies of the man and woman's individual faces. This is another instance of a realistic portrait placed on a conventional figure type, a recurring phenomenon in Roman portraiture (see "Role Playing in Roman Portraiture," page 265), first seen here in the statue of the Republican general found at Tivoli (FIG. 10-8).

PAINTING THE INANIMATE The Roman interest in recording individual appearance extended to everyday objects. This explains the frequent inclusion of still-life paintings in the mural schemes of the Second, Third, and Fourth Styles. A still life with peaches and a carafe (FIG. **10-24**), a detail of a painted wall from Herculaneum, demonstrates that Roman painters sought to create illusionistic effects when depicting small objects, as well as buildings and landscapes. The artist paid scrupulous attention to shad-

ows and highlights, working directly from an arrangement made specifically for this painting. The fruit, the stem and leaves, and the glass jar were set out on shelves to give the illusion of the casual, almost accidental, relationship of objects in a cupboard. Art historians have not found evidence of anything like these Roman studies of food and other inanimate objects until the Dutch still lifes of the 17th and 18th centuries (see FIGS. 24-55 and 24-56). The

10-24 Still life with peaches, detail of a Fourth Style wall painting, from Herculaneum, Italy, ca. 62–79 CE. Approx. 1′ 2″ × 1′ 1½″. Museo Nazionale, Naples.

Role Playing in Roman Portraiture

In every town throughout the vast Roman Empire, portraits of the emperors and empresses and their families were on display—in forums, basilicas, baths, and markets; in front of temples; atop triumphal arches—anywhere a statue could be placed. The rulers' heads varied little from Britain to Syria. All were replicas of official images, either imported or scrupulously copied by local artists. But the portrait heads were placed on many types of bodies. The type chosen depended on the position the person held in Roman society or the various fictitious guises assumed by imperial family members. Portraits of Augustus, for example, show him not only as armed general (FIG. 10-25) but also as recipient of the civic crown for saving the lives of fellow citizens (see FIG. Intro-9), veiled priest, toga-clad magistrate, traveling commander on horseback, heroically nude warrior, and various Roman gods, including Jupiter, Apollo, and Mercury.

Such role playing was not confined to emperors and princes but extended to their wives, daughters, sisters, and mothers.

Statues of Livia (FIG. 10-26) portray her as many goddesses, including Ceres, Juno, Venus, and Vesta. She also appears as the personification of Health, Justice, and Piety. In fact, it was common for imperial women to appear on Roman coins not only as goddesses but also as embodiments of feminine virtue. Faustina the Younger, for example, the wife of Marcus Aurelius and mother of 13 children, appears as Venus and Fecundity, among many other roles. Julia Domna (FIG. 10-64), Septimius Severus's wife, is Juno, Venus, Peace, or Victory in some portraits.

Ordinary citizens also engaged in role playing. Some assumed literary pretensions, as did a husband and wife (FIG. 10-23) in their Pompeian home. Others equated themselves with Greek heroes (FIG. 10-61) or Roman deities (FIG. 10-62) on their coffins. The common people followed the lead of the emperors and empresses.

Roman murals are not as exact in drawing, perspective, or rendering of light and shade as the Dutch canvases. Still, the ancient painter understood that the look of things is a function of light. The goal was to paint light as one would strive to paint the touchable object that reflects and absorbs it.

EARLY EMPIRE

ANTONY AND CLEOPATRA The murder of Julius Caesar on the Ides of March, 44 BCE, plunged the Roman world into a bloody civil war. The fighting lasted 13 years and ended only when Octavian (better known as Augustus), Caesar's grandnephew and adopted son, crushed the naval forces of Mark Antony and Queen Cleopatra of Egypt at Actium in northwestern Greece. Antony and Cleopatra committed suicide, and in 30 BCE, Egypt, once the wealthiest and most powerful kingdom of the ancient world, became another province in the ever-expanding Roman Empire.

Historians reckon the passage from the old Roman Republic to the new Roman Empire from the day in 27 BCE when the Senate conferred the majestic title of Augustus (r. 27 BCE–14 CE) on Octavian. The Empire was ostensibly a continuation of the Republic, with the same constitutional offices, but in fact Augustus, who was recognized as *princeps* (first citizen), occupied all the key positions. He was consul and *imperator* (commander in chief; root of the word *emperor*) and even, after 12 BCE, *pontifex maximus* (chief priest of the state religion). These offices gave Augustus control of all aspects of Roman public life.

THE PAX ROMANA With powerful armies keeping order on the Empire's frontiers and no opposition at home, Augustus brought peace and prosperity to a war-weary Mediterranean world. Known in his own day as the *Pax Augusta* (Augustan Peace), the peace Augustus established prevailed for two centuries. It came to be called simply the *Pax Romana*. During this time the emperors commissioned a huge number of public works throughout the Empire: roads, bridges, forums, temples, basilicas, theaters, amphitheaters, market halls, and bathing complexes, all

on an unprecedented scale. And the erection of imperial portraits and arches covered with reliefs recounting the emperor's great deeds reminded people everywhere of the source of this beneficence. These portraits and reliefs often presented a picture of the emperor and his achievements that bore little resemblance to historical fact. Their purpose, however, was not to provide an objective record but to mold public opinion. The Roman emperors and the artists they employed have had few equals in the effective use of art and architecture for propagandistic ends.

Augustus and the Julio-Claudians (27 BCE–68 CE)

AUGUSTUS, SON OF A GOD When Octavian inherited Caesar's fortune in 44 BCE, he was not yet 19 years old. When he vanquished Antony and Cleopatra at Actium in 31 BCE and became undisputed master of the Mediterranean world, he had not reached his 32nd birthday. The rule by elders that had characterized the Roman Republic for nearly half a millennium came to an abrupt end. Suddenly, Roman portraitists were called on to produce images of a *youthful* head of state. But Augustus was more than young. Caesar had been made a god after his death, and Augustus, though never claiming to be a god himself, widely advertised himself as the son of a god. His portraits—produced in great numbers by anonymous artists paid by the state—were designed to present the image of a godlike leader, a superior being who, miraculously, never aged. Although Augustus lived until 14 CE, even official portraits made near the end of his life continued to show him as a handsome youth (see FIG. Intro-9). Such a notion may seem ridiculous today, when television, the Internet, magazines, and newspapers portray world leaders as they truly appear, but in antiquity few people had actually seen the emperor. His official image was all most knew. It therefore could be manipulated at will.

The models for Augustus's idealized portraits cannot be found in the veristic likenesses of the Roman Republic. Rather, Classical Greek art inspired the emperor's sculptors. The portrait

10-25 Portrait of Augustus as general, from Primaporta, Italy, early first century CE copy of a bronze original of ca. 20 BCE. Marble, 6′ 8″ high. Vatican Museums, Rome.

10-26 Portrait bust of Livia, from Faiyum, Egypt, early first century CE. Marble, approx. 1′ 1½″ high. Ny Carlsberg Glyptotek, Copenhagen.

statue of Augustus (FIG. **10-25**) found at his wife Livia's villa at Primaporta (FIG. 10-17) depicts the emperor as general. (Others portray him in different roles. See "Role Playing in Roman Portraiture," page 265.) It is based closely on Polykleitos's *Doryphoros* (see FIG. 5-38). Here, however, the emperor addresses his troops with his right arm extended in the manner of the orator Aule Metele (see FIG. 9-15). Although the head is that of an individual and not a nameless athlete, its overall shape, the sharp ridges of the brows, and the tight cap of layered hair emulate the Polykleitan style. The reliefs on the emperor's cuirass advertise an important diplomatic victory—the return of the Roman military standards the Parthians had captured from a Republican general. The Cupid at Augustus's feet proclaims his divine descent. Caesar's family, the Julians, traced their ancestry back to Venus. Cupid was the goddess's son. Thus, the sculptor designed every facet of the Primaporta statue to carry a political message.

LIVIA, NEVER-AGING EMPRESS A marble portrait of Livia (FIG. **10-26**) shows that the imperial women of the Augustan age shared the emperor's eternal youthfulness. Although she sports the latest Roman coiffure, with the hair rolled over the forehead and knotted at the nape of the neck, Livia's blemish-free skin and sharply defined features derive from images of Classical Greek goddesses. Livia outlived Augustus by 15 years, dying at age 87. In her portraits, the coiffure changed with the introduction of each

new fashion, but her face remained ever young, as befitted her exalted position in the Roman state.

A SHRINE TO PEACE On Livia's birthday in 9 BCE, Augustus dedicated the Ara Pacis Augustae (Altar of Augustan Peace), the monument celebrating his most important achievement, the establishment of peace. The altar (FIG. **10-27**) was reconstructed during the Fascist era in Italy in connection with the 2,000th anniversary of Augustus's birth, when Mussolini was seeking to build a modern Roman Empire. Figural reliefs and acanthus tendrils adorn the altar's marble precinct walls. Four panels on the east and west ends depict carefully selected mythological subjects, including (at the right in FIG. 10-27) a relief of Aeneas making a sacrifice. Aeneas was the son of Venus and one of Augustus's forefathers. The connection between the emperor and Aeneas was a key element of Augustus's political ideology for his new Golden Age. It is no coincidence that the *Aeneid* was written during the rule of Augustus. Vergil's epic poem glorified the young emperor by celebrating the founder of the Julian line.

A second panel (FIG. **10-28**), on the other end of the altar enclosure, depicts a seated matron with two lively babies on her lap. Her identity is uncertain. She is usually called Tellus (Mother Earth), although some have named her Pax (Peace), Ceres (goddess of grain), or even Venus. Whoever she is, she epitomizes the fruits of the Pax Augusta. All around her the bountiful earth is in bloom, and animals of different species live peacefully side by side. Personifications of refreshing breezes (note their windblown drapery) flank her. One rides a bird, the other a sea creature. Earth, sky, and water are all elements of this picture of peace and fertility in the Augustan cosmos.

Processions of the imperial family and other important dignitaries appear on the long north and south sides of the Ara Pacis (FIG. **10-29**). These parallel friezes were clearly inspired to some

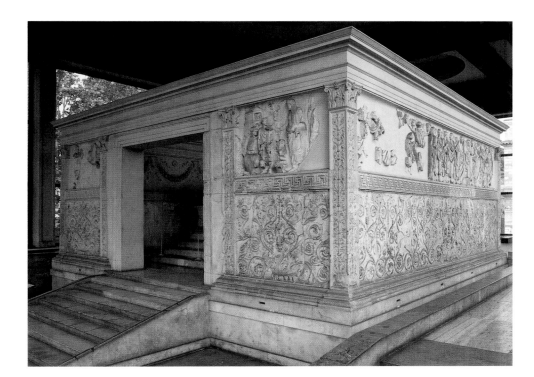

10-27 Ara Pacis Augustae (Altar of Augustan Peace), view from the south-west, Rome, Italy, 13–9 BCE.

10-28 Female personification (Tellus?), panel from the east facade of the Ara Pacis Augustae, Rome, Italy, 13–9 BCE. Marble, approx. 5′ 3″ high.

10-29 Procession of the imperial family, detail of the south frieze of the Ara Pacis Augustae, Rome, Italy, 13–9 BCE. Marble, approx. 5′ 3″ high.

degree by the Panathenaic procession frieze of the Parthenon (see FIG. 5-48, *bottom*). Augustus sought to present his new order as a Golden Age equaling that of Athens under Pericles in the middle of the fifth century BCE. The emulation of Classical models thus made a political statement, as well as an artistic one.

Even so, the Roman procession is very different in character from the Greek. On the Parthenon, anonymous figures act out an event that recurred every four years. The frieze stands for *all* Panathenaic Festival processions. The Ara Pacis depicts a specific event—probably the inaugural ceremony of 13 BCE when work on the altar began—and recognizable contemporary figures. Among those portrayed are children, who restlessly tug on their elders' garments and talk to one another when they should be quiet on a solemn occasion—in short, children who act like children and not like miniature adults, as they frequently do in the history of art. Their presence lends a great deal of charm to the procession, but that is not why children were included on the Ara Pacis when they had never before appeared on any Greek or Roman state monument. Augustus was concerned about a decline in the birthrate among the Roman nobility, and he enacted a series of laws designed to promote marriage, marital fidelity, and raising children. The portrayal of men with their families on the Altar of Peace was intended as a moral exemplar. Once again, the emperor used art to further his own political and social agendas.

ROME, THE MARBLE CITY Augustus's most ambitious project in the capital was the construction of a new forum (FIG. 10-1, no. 10) next to Julius Caesar's forum (FIG. 10-1, no. 9), which Augustus completed. Both forums were made of white marble from Carrara (ancient Luna), the same source used by the great sculptors of the Italian Renaissance. Prior to the opening of these quarries in the second half of the first century BCE, marble had to be imported at great cost from abroad, and it was used sparingly. The ready availability of Italian marble under Augustus made

possible the emperor's famous boast that he had found Rome a city of brick and transformed it into a city of marble.

The extensive use of Carrara marble for public monuments (including the Ara Pacis) must be seen as part of Augustus's larger program to make his city the equal of Periclean Athens. In fact, the Forum of Augustus incorporated several explicit references to Classical Athens and to the Acropolis in particular, most notably copies of the caryatids of the Erechtheion (see FIG. 5-52) in the upper story of the porticos. Roman history also was evoked. The porticos contained dozens of portrait statues, including images of all the major figures of the Julian family going back to Aeneas. Augustus's forum became a kind of public atrium filled with imagines. His family history thus became part of the Roman state's official history. The Forum of Augustus and those of his successors did serve a practical function by providing alternative areas to the old and overcrowded Republican Forum Romanum for the conduct of state business. Yet they also gave the emperors the opportunity to present their own version of history to the Roman people.

ROME IN FRANCE The Forum of Augustus is in ruins today, but the conservative neoclassical Augustan style it epitomizes may be seen in an exceptionally well preserved temple at Nîmes (ancient Nemausus) in southern France (ancient Gaul). The so-called Maison Carrée (FIG. **10-30**) dates to the opening years of the first century CE. Larger than the Temple of "Fortuna Virilis" in Rome (FIG. 10-2), this Corinthian pseudoperipteral temple was patterned on the Temple of Mars in the Forum of Augustus. In fact, many scholars believe that some of the artisans who worked on the Roman temple went immediately afterward to Nîmes to work on the Maison Carrée.

Vitruvius, whose treatise, *The Ten Books of Architecture*, dedicated to Augustus, became the bible of Renaissance architects, preferred the classicizing architectural style of the Maison Carrée and

10-30 Maison Carrée, Nîmes, France, ca. 1–10 CE.

10-31 Pont-du-Gard, Nîmes, France, ca. 16 BCE.

the Forum of Augustus to the newer Roman vaulted concrete technology. (Another admirer of classical architecture was Thomas Jefferson, U.S. president and architect. He modeled his design for the State Capitol in Richmond, Virginia, on the Nîmes temple.)

An earlier Augustan project at Nîmes was the construction of the great aqueduct-bridge known today as the Pont-du-Gard (FIG. **10-31**). Beginning in the fourth century BCE, the Romans built aqueducts to carry water from mountain sources to their city on the Tiber River. As Rome's power spread through the Mediterranean world, its architects constructed aqueducts, roads, and bridges to serve colonies throughout the far-flung empire. The Pont-du-Gard demonstrates the skill of Rome's engineers. The aqueduct provided about 100 gallons of water a day for each inhabitant of Nîmes from a source some 30 miles away. The water was carried over the considerable distance by gravity flow, which required channels built with a continuous gradual decline over the entire route from source to city. The three-story bridge at Nîmes was erected to maintain the height of the water channel where the water crossed the Gard River. Each large arch spans some 82 feet and is constructed of blocks weighing up to two tons each. The bridge's uppermost level consists of a row of smaller arches, three above each of the large openings below. They carry the water channel itself. Their quickened rhythm and the harmonious proportional relationship between the larger and smaller arches reveal that the Roman engineer had a keen aesthetic, as well as practical, sense.

CLAUDIAN RUSTICATION Many aqueducts were required to meet the demand for water in the capital. Under the emperor Claudius (r. 41–54 CE), a grandiose gate, the Porta Maggiore (FIG. **10-32**), was constructed at the point where two of Rome's water lines (and two intercity trunk roads) converged. Its huge *attic* (uppermost story) bears a wordy dedicatory inscription that conceals the conduits of both aqueducts, one above the other. The gate is the outstanding example of the Roman *rusticated* (rough) masonry

style. Instead of using the precisely shaped blocks favored by Greek and Augustan architects, the designer of the Porta Maggiore combined smooth and rusticated surfaces. These created an exciting, if eccentric, facade with crisply carved pediments resting on engaged columns composed of rusticated drums.

NERO'S GOLDEN HOUSE In 64 CE, when Nero (r. 54–68 CE), stepson and successor of Claudius, was emperor, a great fire destroyed large sections of Rome. Rebuilding was carried out in accordance with a new code that required greater fireproofing, resulting in the widespread use of concrete, which was both cheap and fire resistant. Increased use of concrete gave Roman architects

10-32 Porta Maggiore, Rome, Italy, ca. 50 CE.

An Imperial Pleasure Palace: The Golden House of Nero

Nero's Domus Aurea, or Golden House, was a vast and notoriously extravagant country villa in the heart of Rome. The second-century CE Roman biographer Suetonius described it vividly:

> The entrance-hall was large enough to contain a huge statue [of Nero in the guise of Sol, the sun god; FIG. 10-1, no. 16], 120 feet high; and the pillared arcade ran for a whole mile. An enormous pool, like a sea, was surrounded by buildings made to resemble cities, and by a landscape garden consisting of ploughed fields, vineyards, pastures, and woodlands–where every variety of domestic and wild animal roamed about. Parts of the house were overlaid with gold and studded with precious stones and mother-of-pearl. All the dining-rooms had ceilings of fretted ivory, the panels of which could slide back and let a rain of flowers, or of perfume from hidden sprinklers, shower upon [Nero's] guests. The main dining-room was circular, and its roof revolved, day and night, in time with the sky. Sea water, or sulphur water, was always on tap in the baths. When the palace had been decorated throughout in this lavish style, Nero dedicated it, and condescended to remark: "Good, now I can at last begin to live like a human being!"[1]

Suetonius's description is a welcome reminder that the Roman ruins tourists flock to see are but a dim reflection of the magnificence of the original structures. Only in rare instances, such as the Pantheon, with its marble-faced walls and floors (FIG. 10-50), can visitors experience anything approaching the architects' intended effects. Even there, much of the marble paneling is of later date, and the gilding is missing from the dome.

[1] Suetonius, *Nero*, 31. Translated by Robert Graves, *Suetonius: The Twelve Caesars* (New York: Penguin, 1957; illustrated edition, 1980), 197–98.

---

the opportunity to explore the possibilities opened up by the still relatively new material.

After the great fire, Nero asked SEVERUS and CELER, two brilliant architect-engineers, to build a grand new palace for him on a huge confiscated plot of fire-ravaged land near the Forum Romanum (see "An Imperial Pleasure Palace: The Golden House of Nero," above). Nero's Domus Aurea has been excavated only in part, but traces of rich decorations, with marble paneling and painted and gilded stucco, have been found in some rooms, while others are adorned with frescoes (FIG. 10-20) in the latest style. Structurally, most of these chambers, although built of concrete, are unremarkable. One octagonal hall (FIG. **10-33**), however, stands apart from the rest and testifies to Severus and Celer's entirely new approach to architectural design.

The ceiling of the octagonal room is a dome that modulates from an eight-sided to a hemispherical form as it rises toward the oculus—the circular opening that admitted light to the room. Radiating outward from the five inner sides (the other three, directly or indirectly, face the outside) are smaller, rectangular rooms, covered by concrete vaults. Decorative recesses enlivened these satellite rooms. The middle one contained a waterfall. The architects ingeniously lit the rooms by leaving spaces between their vaulted ceilings and the central dome's exterior. But the most significant aspect of the design is that here, for the first time, the architects appear to have thought of the walls and vaults not as limiting space but as shaping it.

Today, the octagonal hall is deprived of its stucco decoration and marble *incrustation* (veneer). The concrete shell stands bare, but this serves to focus the visitor's attention on the design's spatial complexity. When one walks through the rooms, one sees that the central domed octagon is defined not by walls but by eight angled piers. The wide square openings between the piers are so large that the rooms beyond look like extensions of the central hall. The grouping of spatial units of different sizes and proportions under a variety of vaults creates a dynamic three-dimensional composition that is both complex and unified. Nero's architects were not

10-33 SEVERUS and CELER, plan *(above)* and section *(below)* of the octagonal hall of the Domus Aurea (Golden House) of Nero, Rome, Italy, 64–68 CE.

only inventive but also progressive in their recognition of the malleable nature of concrete, a material not limited to the rectilinear forms of traditional post-and-lintel construction.

The Flavians (69 – 96 CE)

Because of his outrageous behavior, Nero was forced to commit suicide in 68 CE, bringing the Julio-Claudian dynasty to an end. A year of renewed civil strife followed. The man who emerged triumphant in this brief but bloody conflict was Vespasian (r. 69 – 79 CE), a general who had served under Claudius and Nero. Vespasian, whose family name was Flavius, had two sons, Titus (r. 79 – 81 CE) and Domitian (r. 81 – 96 CE). The Flavian dynasty ruled Rome for more than a quarter century.

COLOSSUS AND COLOSSEUM The Flavians left their mark on the capital in many ways, not the least being the construction of the Colosseum (FIGS. **10-34** and 10-1, no. 17), the monument

that, for most people, still represents Rome more than any other building. In the past it was identified so closely with Rome and its empire that in the early Middle Ages there was a saying, "While stands the Colosseum, Rome shall stand; when falls the Colosseum, Rome shall fall; and when Rome falls — the World."[4] The Flavian Amphitheater, as it was known in its own day, was one of Vespasian's first undertakings after becoming emperor. The decision to build the Colosseum was very shrewd politically. The site chosen was the artificial lake on the grounds of Nero's Domus Aurea, which was drained for the purpose. By building the new amphitheater there, Vespasian reclaimed for the public the land Nero had confiscated for his private pleasure and provided Romans with the largest arena for gladiatorial combats and other lavish spectacles that had ever been constructed. The Colosseum takes its name, however, not from its size — it could hold more than 50,000 spectators — but from its location beside the Colossus of Nero (FIG. 10-1, no. 16), the huge statue of the emperor portrayed as the sun god, at the entrance to his urban villa.

Vespasian, who died in 79 CE, did not live to see the Colosseum in use. Titus completed and formally dedicated the amphitheater in 80. To mark the opening, games were held for 100 days, at extravagant cost but to the people's delight. The highlight was the flooding of the arena to stage a complete naval battle with more than 3,000 participants. Later emperors would compete to see who could put on the most elaborate spectacles, and over the years many thousands of lives were lost in the gladiatorial and animal combats staged in the amphitheater. Many of those who died were Christians, and the Colosseum has never quite outlived its infamy in this respect.

AN ENGINEERING MARVEL The Colosseum, like the much earlier amphitheater at Pompeii (FIG. 10-11), could not have been built without concrete. A complex system of barrel-vaulted corridors holds up the enormous oval seating area. This concrete "skeleton" reveals itself today to anyone who enters the amphitheater. In the centuries following the fall of Rome, the Colosseum served as a convenient quarry for ready-made building materials. Almost all its marble seats were hauled away, exposing the network of vaults below. Hidden in antiquity but visible today are the arena substructures, which housed waiting rooms for the gladiators, animal cages, and machinery for raising and lowering stage sets as well as animals and humans. Cleverly designed lifting devices brought beasts from their dark dens into the arena's bright light. Above the seats a great velarium, as at Pompeii (FIG. 10-12), once shielded the spectators. Poles affixed to the Colosseum's facade held up the giant awning.

10-34 Aerial view (top) and facade (bottom) of the Colosseum (Flavian Amphitheater), Rome, Italy, ca. 70 – 80 CE.

The exterior travertine shell is approximately 160 feet high, the height of a modern 16-story building. Numbered entrances led to the cavea, where the spectators sat according to their place in the social hierarchy. The relationship of the 76 gateways to the tiers of seats within was carefully thought out and resembles that seen in modern sports stadiums. The decor of the exterior, however, had nothing to do with function. The facade is divided into four bands, with large arched openings piercing the lower three. Ornamental Greek orders frame the arches in the standard Roman sequence for multistoried buildings: from the ground up, Tuscan Doric, Ionic, and then Corinthian. This sequence is based on the proportions of the orders, with the Tuscan viewed as capable of supporting the heaviest load. The uppermost story is circled with Corinthian pilasters (and between them the brackets for the wooden poles that held up the velarium).

The use of engaged columns and a lintel to frame the openings in the Colosseum's facade is a variation of the scheme used on the Etruscan Porta Marzia at Perugia (see FIG. 9-13). The Romans commonly used this scheme from Late Republican times on. Like the pseudoperipteral temple, which is an eclectic mix of Greek orders and Etruscan plan, this way of decorating a building's facade combined Greek orders with an architectural form foreign to Greek post-and-lintel architecture, namely the arch. Revived in the Italian Renaissance, the motif had a long, illustrious history in classical architecture. The Roman practice of framing an arch with an applied Greek order had no structural purpose, but it added variety to the surface. It also unified a multistoried facade by casting a net of verticals and horizontals over it.

THE REVIVAL OF VERISM Vespasian was an unpretentious career army officer who desired to distance himself from Nero's extravagant misrule. His portraits (FIG. **10-35**) reflect his much simpler tastes. They also made an important political statement. Breaking with the tradition Augustus established of depicting the Roman emperor as an eternally youthful god on earth, Vespasian's sculptors resuscitated the veristic tradition of the Republic, possibly at his specific direction. Although not as brutally descriptive as many Republican likenesses, Vespasian's portraits frankly recorded his receding hairline and aging, leathery skin—proclaiming his traditional Republican values in contrast to Nero's.

AN ELEGANT FLAVIAN WOMAN Portraits of people of all ages survive from the Flavian period, in contrast to the Republic, when only elders were deemed worthy of depiction. A portrait bust of a young woman (FIG. **10-36**), probably a Flavian princess, is a case in point. Its purpose was not to project Republican virtues but rather idealized beauty—through contemporary fashion rather than by reference to images of Greek goddesses. The portrait is notable for its elegance and delicacy and for the virtuoso way the sculptor rendered the differing textures of hair

10-35 Portrait of Vespasian, ca. 75-79 CE. Marble, approx. 1′ 4″ high. Ny Carlsberg Glyptotek, Copenhagen.

10-36 Portrait bust of a Flavian woman, from Rome, Italy, ca. 90 CE. Marble, approx. 2′ 1″ high. Museo Capitolino, Rome.

10-37 Arch of Titus, Rome, Italy, after 81 CE.

art and architecture, beginning in the second century BCE and continuing even into the era of Christian Roman emperors. The term is something of a misnomer, however, because Roman arches celebrated more than just military victories. Such free-standing arches, usually crowned by gilded bronze statues, commemorated a wide variety of events, ranging from victories abroad to the building of roads and bridges at home.

The Arch of Titus is typical of the early triumphal arch and consists of one passageway only. As on the Colosseum, engaged columns frame the arcuated opening, but their capitals are the *Composite* type, an ornate combination of Ionic volutes and Corinthian acanthus leaves that became popular at about the same time as the Fourth Style in Roman painting. Reliefs depicting personified Victories (winged women, as in Greek art) fill the *spandrels* (the area between the arch's curve and the framing columns and entablature). A dedicatory inscription stating that the arch was set up to honor the god Titus, son of the god Vespasian, dominates the attic. Roman emperors normally were proclaimed gods after they died, unless they ran afoul of the Senate and were damned. The statues of those who suffered *damnatio memoriae* were torn down, and their names were erased from public inscriptions. This was Nero's fate.

THE SPOILS OF JERUSALEM Inside the passageway of the Arch of Titus are two great relief panels. They represent the triumphal parade of Titus down the Sacred Way after his return from the conquest of Judaea at the end of the Jewish Wars in 70 CE. One of the reliefs (FIG. **10-38**) depicts Roman soldiers carrying the spoils—including the sacred seven-branched candelabrum, the *menorah*—from the Temple in Jerusalem. Despite considerable damage to the relief, the illusion of movement is convincing. The parade moves forward from the left background into the center foreground and disappears through the obliquely placed arch in the right background. The energy and swing of the column of soldiers suggest a rapid march. The sculptor rejected the classicizing low relief of the Ara Pacis (FIG. 10-29) in favor of extremely deep carving, which produces strong shadows. The heads of the forward figures have broken off because they stood free from the block. Their high relief emphasized their different placement in space compared to the heads in low relief, which are intact. The play of light and shade across the protruding foreground and receding background figures enhances the sense of movement.

and flesh. The elaborate Flavian coiffure, with its corkscrew curls punched out by skilled hands using a drill instead of a chisel, creates a dense mass of light and shadow set off boldly from the softly modeled and highly polished skin of the face and swanlike neck. The drill played an increasing role in Roman sculpture in succeeding periods and in time was used even for portraits of men, when much longer hair and full beards were fashionable.

A NEW ARCH FOR A NEW GOD When Titus died in 81 CE, only two years after becoming emperor, his younger brother, Domitian, succeeded him. Domitian erected an arch (FIGS. **10-37** and 10-1, no. 13) in Titus's honor on the Sacred Way leading into the Republican Forum Romanum (FIG. 10-1, no. 11). This type of arch, the so-called *triumphal arch,* has a long history in Roman

10-38 Spoils of Jerusalem, relief panel in the passageway of the Arch of Titus, Rome, Italy, after 81 CE. Marble, approx. 7′ 10″ high.

TITUS IN TRIUMPH The panel on the other side of the passageway shows Titus in his triumphal chariot (FIG. **10-39**). The seeming historical accuracy of the spoils panel (FIG. 10-38)—it closely corresponds to the contemporary description of Titus's triumph by the Jewish historian Josephus—gave way in this panel to allegory. Victory rides with Titus in the four-horse chariot and places a wreath on his head. Below her is a bare-chested youth who is probably a personification of Honor *(Honos)*. A female personification of Valor *(Virtus)* leads the horses. These allegorical figures transform the relief from a record of Titus's battlefield success into a celebration of imperial virtues. Such an intermingling of divine and human figures occurs on the Republican Villa of the Mysteries frieze at Pompeii (FIG. 10-15), but the Arch of Titus panel is the first known instance of divine beings interacting with humans on an official Roman historical relief. (On the Ara Pacis, FIG. 10-27, Aeneas and "Tellus" appear in separate framed panels and were carefully segregated from the procession of living Romans.) The Arch of Titus was erected after the emperor's death, and its reliefs were carved when Titus was already a god. Soon afterward, however, this kind of interaction between mortals and immortals became a staple of Roman narrative relief sculpture, even on monuments honoring a living emperor.

HIGH EMPIRE

THE ROMAN EMPIRE AT ITS PEAK In the second century CE, under Trajan, Hadrian, and the Antonines, the Roman Empire reached its greatest geographic extent (MAP 10-1) and the height of its power. Rome's might was unchallenged in the Western world, although the Germanic peoples in Europe, the Berbers in Africa, and the Parthians and Persians in the Near East constantly applied pressure. Within the empire's secure boundaries, the Pax Romana meant unprecedented prosperity for all who came under Roman rule.

Trajan (98–117 CE)

THE FIRST SPANISH EMPEROR Domitian's extravagant lifestyle and ego resembled Nero's. He demanded to be addressed as *dominus et deus* (lord and god), and so angered the senators that he was assassinated in 96 CE. The Senate chose the elderly

Nerva, one of its own, as emperor. Nerva ruled for only 16 months, but before he died he established a pattern of succession by adoption that lasted for almost a century. Nerva picked Trajan, a capable and popular general born in Italica (Spain), as the next emperor. Trajan was the first non-Italian to rule Rome. Under Trajan, imperial armies brought Roman rule to ever more distant areas, and the imperial government took on ever greater responsibility for its people's welfare by instituting a number of far-sighted social programs. Trajan was so popular that he was granted the title *Optimus* (the Best), an epithet he shared with Jupiter (who was said to have instructed Nerva to choose Trajan as his successor). In late antiquity, Augustus, the founder of the Roman Empire, and Trajan became the yardsticks for success. The goal of new emperors was to be *felicior Augusto, melior Traiano* (luckier than Augustus, better than Trajan).

A NEW COLONY IN AFRICA In 100 CE, Trajan founded a new colony for army veterans at Timgad, ancient Thamugadi (FIG. **10-40**), in what is today Algeria. Timgad was built along a major road about 100 miles from the sea. Like other colonies, it became the physical embodiment of Roman authority and civilization for the local population and served as a key to the Romanization of the provinces. The town was planned with great precision, its design resembling that of a Roman military encampment or *castrum*. (Scholars still debate which came first. The castrum may have been based on the layout of Roman colonies.) Unlike the sprawling unplanned cities of Rome and Pompeii, Timgad is a square divided into equal quarters by its two main streets, the cardo and the decumanus. They cross at right angles and are bordered by colonnades. Monumental gates in the colony's original walls mark the ends of the two avenues. The forum is located at the point where the streets intersect. The quarters are subdivided into square blocks, and the forum and public buildings, such as the theater and baths, occupy areas sized as multiples of these blocks. The Roman plan is a modification of the Hippodamian plan of Greek cities (see FIG. 5-75), though more rigidly ordered.

The fact that most of these colonial settlements were laid out in the same manner, regardless of whether they were in North Africa, Mesopotamia, or England, expresses concretely the unity and centralized power of the Roman Empire at its height. But even the Romans could not regulate human behavior completely. As the population of Timgad grew sevenfold and burst through

1. Forum
2. Theater
3. Library
4. East bath
5. North bath
6. Small baths
7. Temple of Ceres

10-40 Plan of Timgad (Thamugadi), Algeria, founded 100 CE.

the Trajanic settlement walls, rational planning was ignored, and the city and its streets branched out haphazardly.

ROME'S GREATEST FORUM Trajan's major building project in Rome was a huge new forum (FIGS. **10-41** and 10-1, no. 7), roughly twice the size of the forum Augustus built (FIG. 10-1, no. 10) a century before—even if the enormous market complex next to the forum is excluded. The new forum glorified Trajan's victories in his two wars against the Dacians (who lived in what is now Romania) and was paid for with the spoils of those campaigns. The architect was APOLLODORUS OF DAMASCUS, Trajan's chief military engineer during the Dacian wars, who had constructed a world-famous bridge across the Danube River. Apollodorus's plan incorporated the main features of most early forums (FIG. 10-10), except that a huge basilica, not a temple, dominated the colonnaded open square. The temple (completed after the emperor's death and dedicated to the newest god in the Roman pantheon, Trajan himself) was set instead behind the basilica. It stood at the rear end of the forum in its own courtyard, with two libraries and a giant commemorative column, the Column of Trajan (FIGS. 10-41, no. 2, and 10-42).

One entered Trajan's forum through an impressive gateway resembling a triumphal arch. Inside the forum were other reminders of Trajan's military prowess. A larger-than-life-size gilded-bronze equestrian statue of the emperor stood at the center of the great court in front of the basilica. Statues of captive Dacians stood above the columns of the forum porticos.

The Basilica Ulpia (Trajan's family name was Ulpius) was a much larger and far more ornate version of the basilica in the

10-41 APOLLODORUS OF DAMASCUS, Forum of Trajan, Rome, Italy, dedicated 112 CE. Reconstruction by James E. Packer and John Burge.
1) Temple of Trajan, 2) Column of Trajan, 3) Libraries, 4) Basilica Ulpia, 5) Forum, 6) Equestrian statue of Trajan.

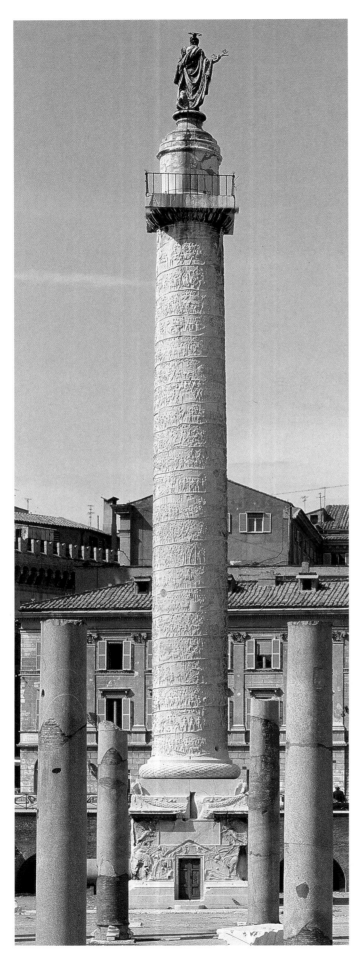

10-42 Column of Trajan, Forum of Trajan, Rome, Italy, dedicated 112 CE.

forum of Pompeii (FIG. 10-10, no. 3). As shown in FIG. 10-41, no. 4, it had *apses,* or semicircular recesses, on each short end. Two aisles flanked the nave on each side. In contrast to the Pompeian basilica and later Christian churches, the entrances were on the long side facing the forum. The building was vast: about 400 feet long (without the apses) and 200 feet wide. Light entered through clerestory windows, made possible by elevating the timber-roofed nave above the colonnaded aisles. In the Republican basilica at Pompeii, light reached the nave only indirectly through aisle windows. The clerestory (used millennia before at Karnak in Egypt, see FIGS. 3-25 and 3-26) was a much better solution. Early Christian architects embraced this feature of the Basilica Ulpia for the design of the first churches (see FIGS. 11-8 and 11-16).

TRAJAN'S COLUMNAR TOMB The Column of Trajan (FIG. 10-42) was probably also the brainchild of Apollodorus of Damascus. The idea of covering the shaft of a colossal freestanding column with a continuous spiral narrative frieze seems to have been invented here, but it was often copied. As late as the 19th century, a column inspired by the Column of Trajan was erected in the Place Vendôme in Paris in commemoration of the victories of Napoleon. The type even appeared in Christian settings with reliefs illustrating the life of Christ (see FIG. 16-25).

Trajan's Column is 128 feet high. Coins indicate that it was once topped by a heroically nude statue of the emperor. Trajan's portrait was lost in the Middle Ages, and in the 16th century a statue of Saint Peter replaced it. The square base, decorated with captured Dacian arms and armor, served as Trajan's tomb. His ashes and those of his wife, Plotina, were placed inside it in golden urns.

The 625-foot band that winds around the column has been likened to an illustrated scroll of the type housed in the neighboring libraries (and that Lars Pulena holds on his sarcophagus, see FIG. 9-14). The reliefs depict Trajan's two successful campaigns against the Dacians. The story is told in more than 150 episodes in which some 2,500 figures appear. The band increases in width as it winds to the top of the column, so that it is easier to see the upper portions. Throughout, the relief is very low so as not to distort the contours of the shaft. Legibility was enhanced in antiquity by paint, but it still would have been very difficult for anyone to follow the narrative from beginning to end.

Much of the spiral frieze is given over to easily recognizable compositions like those found on coin reverses and on historical relief panels: Trajan addressing his troops, sacrificing to the gods, and so on. The narrative is not a reliable chronological account of the Dacian Wars, as was once thought. The sculptors nonetheless accurately recorded the general character of the campaigns. Notably, battle scenes take up only about a quarter of the frieze. As is true of modern military operations, the Romans spent more time constructing forts, transporting men and equipment, and preparing for battle than fighting. The focus is always on the emperor, who appears again and again in the frieze, but the enemy is not belittled. The Romans won because of their superior organization and more powerful army, not because they were inherently superior beings.

SHOPPING IN IMPERIAL ROME On the Quirinal Hill overlooking the forum, Apollodorus built the Markets of Trajan (FIGS. 10-43 and 10-1, no. 8) to house both shops and administrative offices. As earlier at Palestrina (FIG. 10-4), the transformation of a natural slope into a multilevel complex was possible here only by using concrete. Trajan's architect was a master of this modern

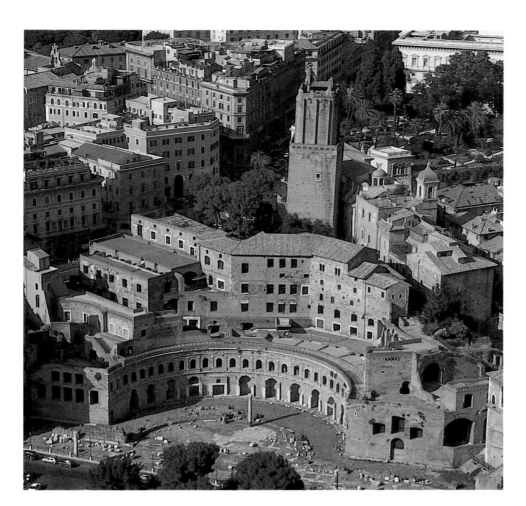

medium as well as of the traditional stone-and-timber post-and-lintel architecture of the forum below.

The basic unit was the *taberna,* a single-room shop covered by a barrel vault. Each taberna had a wide doorway, usually with a window above it that allowed light to enter a wooden inner attic used for storage. The shops were on several levels. They opened either onto a hemispherical facade winding around one of the great exedras of Trajan's forum, onto a paved street farther up the hill, or onto a great indoor market hall (FIG. **10-44**) resembling a modern shopping mall. The hall housed two floors of shops, with

10-44 APOLLODORUS OF DAMASCUS, interior of the great hall, Markets of Trajan, Rome, Italy, ca. 100–112 CE.

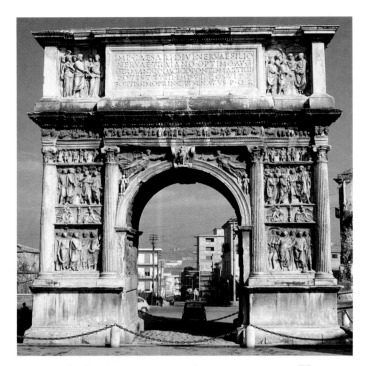

10-45 Arch of Trajan, Benevento, Italy, ca. 114–118 CE.

founder of colonies for army veterans and as the builder of a new port at Ostia, Rome's harbor at the mouth of the Tiber. The reliefs present Trajan as the guarantor of peace and security in the Empire, the benefactor of the poor, and the patron of soldiers and merchants alike. In short, the emperor was "all things to all people."

In several of the panels, Trajan freely intermingles with divinities, and on the arch's attic (which may have been completed after his death and deification) Jupiter hands his thunderbolt to the emperor, awarding him dominion over the earth. Such scenes, depicting the "first citizen" of Rome as a divinely sanctioned ruler in the company of the gods, henceforth became the norm, not the exception, in official Roman art.

RACING IN THE CIRCUS MAXIMUS One of Trajan's other benefactions to the Roman people was the restoration of the Circus Maximus (FIG. 10-1, no. 2), where the world's best horse teams competed in chariot races. A relief (FIG. **10-46**) that once decorated a circus official's tomb gives a partial view of the refurbished racecourse. The relief is not a product of one of the emperor's official sculptural workshops. It illustrates once again how different the art produced for Rome's huge working class was from the art commissioned by the state and old aristocratic families.

The relief shows the Circus Maximus in distorted perspective. Only one team of horses races around the central island, but the charioteer is shown twice, once driving the horses and a second time holding the palm branch of victory. Art historians refer to such representations as *continuous narration;* that is, the same figure appears more than once in the same space at different stages of a story. This is not the first instance of continuous narration, but few earlier examples exist, and only much later did this way of telling a story in pictures become common. (The emperor's appearance in different settings in the Column of Trajan's frieze is not an example of continuous narration.)

In fact, the charioteer may appear a third time within the same relief, for he may be, later in life, the toga-clad official who appears at the panel's left end. There the recently deceased official clasps hands with his wife. (The handshake between man and woman is a symbol of marriage in Roman art.) She is of smaller stature—and less important than her husband in this context, for it is *his* career in the circus commemorated on *his* tomb—and

the upper shops set back on each side and lit by skylights. Light from the same sources reached the ground-floor shops through arches beneath the great umbrella-like groin vaults covering the hall (see "The Roman Architectural Revolution," page 250).

TRIUMPHAL ARCH BILLBOARDS In 109 CE, Trajan opened a new road, the Via Traiana, in southern Italy. Several years later a great arch (FIG. **10-45**) honoring Trajan was built at the point where the road entered Benevento (ancient Beneventum). Architecturally, the Arch of Trajan at Benevento is almost identical to Titus's arch (FIG. 10-37) on the Sacred Way in Rome, but relief panels cover both facades of the Trajanic arch, giving it a billboardlike function. Every inch of the surface was used to advertise the emperor's achievements. In one panel, he enters Rome after a successful military campaign. In another, he distributes largess to needy children. In still others, he was portrayed as the

10-46 Funerary relief of a circus official, from Ostia, Italy, ca. 110–130 CE. Marble, approx. 1′ 8″ high. Vatican Museums, Rome.

she is shown standing on a base. The base indicates that she is not a living person but a statue. The handshake between man and statue is the plebeian artist's shorthand way of saying the wife died before the husband, that her death had not broken their marriage bond, and that, because the husband has now died, the two will be reunited in the afterlife. The rules of classical design, which still guided the artists employed by the Roman state, were ignored here, as in the funerary relief from Amiternum (FIG. 10-6), also made for a non-elite patron. Later in the century, however, some of these nonclassical elements appeared in official art as well.

Hadrian (117–138 CE)

HADRIAN AND GREECE Hadrian, Trajan's chosen successor and fellow Spaniard, was a connoisseur and lover of all the arts, as well as an author and architect. He greatly admired Greek culture and traveled widely as emperor, often in the Greek East. Everywhere he went, statues and arches were set up in his honor. More portraits of Hadrian exist today than of any other emperor except Augustus. Hadrian, who was 41 years old at the time of Trajan's death and who ruled for more than two decades, is always depicted in his portraits as a mature adult who never ages.

A rare bronze portrait of Hadrian is the fragmentary statue (FIG. **10-47**) of the emperor wearing a cuirass found at Tel Shalem, Israel, several miles south of the ancient city of Scythopolis. The portrait probably was erected toward the end of Hadrian's lifetime, when Rome put down a second Jewish revolt and Judaea was reorganized as a new province called Syria Palaestina. Hadrian's portraits more closely resemble Kresilas's portrait of Pericles (see FIG. 5-39) than those of any Roman emperor before him, and no one doubts that Classical Greek statuary inspired his likenesses. Fifth-century BCE statues also provided the prototypes for the idealizing official portraits of Augustus, but the Augustan models were Greek images of young athletes. The models for Hadrian's artists were statues of mature Greek men. Hadrian himself wore a beard—a habit that, in its Roman context, must be viewed as a Greek affectation. Beards then became the norm for all subsequent Roman emperors for more than a century and a half.

THE TEMPLE OF ALL GODS Soon after Hadrian became emperor, work began on the Pantheon (FIGS. **10-48** and 10-1, no. 5), the temple of all the gods, one of the best-preserved buildings of antiquity. It also has been one of the most influential designs in architectural history. The Pantheon reveals the full potential of concrete, both as a building material and as a means for shaping architectural space. The temple originally was approached from a columnar courtyard and, like temples in Roman forums, stood at one narrow end of the enclosure. Its facade of eight Corinthian columns—almost all that could be seen from ground level in antiquity—was a bow to tradition. Everything else about the Pantheon was revolutionary. Behind the columnar porch is an immense concrete cylinder covered by a huge hemispherical dome 142 feet in diameter. The dome's top is also 142 feet from the floor (FIG. **10-49**). The design is thus based on the intersection of two circles (one horizontal, the other vertical) so that the interior space can be imagined as the orb of the earth and the dome as the vault of the heavens.

10-47 Portrait bust of Hadrian as general, from Tel Shalem, Israel, ca. 130–138 CE. Bronze, approx. 2′ 11″ high. Israel Museum, Jerusalem.

10-48 Aerial view of the Pantheon, Rome, Italy, 118–125 CE.

10-49 Longitudinal and lateral sections of the Pantheon, Rome, Italy, 118–125 CE.

If the Pantheon's design is simplicity itself, executing that design took all the ingenuity of Hadrian's engineers. The cylindrical drum was built up level by level using concrete of varied composition. Extremely hard and durable basalt was employed in the mix for the foundations, and the "recipe" was gradually modified until, at the top, featherweight pumice replaced stones to lighten the load. The dome's thickness also decreases as it nears the oculus, the

10-50 Interior of the Pantheon, Rome, Italy, 118–125 CE.

circular opening 30 feet in diameter that is the only light source for the interior (FIG. 10-50). The dome's weight was lessened, without weakening its structure, through the use of *coffers* (sunken decorative panels). These further reduced the dome's mass and also provided a handsome pattern of squares within the vast circle. Renaissance drawings suggest that each coffer once had a glistening gilded-bronze rosette at its center, enhancing the symbolism of the dome as the starry heavens.

Below the dome, much of the original marble veneer of the walls, niches, and floor has survived (FIG. 10-50). In the Pantheon, visitors can get a sense, as almost nowhere else, of how magnificent the interiors of Roman concrete buildings could be. But despite the luxurious skin of the Pantheon's interior, on first entering the structure one senses not the weight of the enclosing walls but the space they enclose. In pre-Roman architecture, the form of the enclosed space was determined by the placement of the solids, which did not so much shape space as interrupt it. Roman architects were the first to conceive of architecture in terms of units of space that could be shaped by the enclosures. The Pantheon's interior is a single unified, self-sufficient whole, uninterrupted by supporting solids. It encloses visitors without imprisoning them, opening through the oculus to the drifting clouds, the blue sky, the sun, and the gods. In this space, the architect used light not just to illuminate the darkness but to create drama and underscore the symbolism of the interior shape. On a sunny day, the light that passes through the oculus forms a circular beam, a disk of light that moves across the coffered dome in the course of the day as the sun moves across the sky itself. Escaping from the noise and torrid heat of a Roman summer day into the Pantheon's cool, calm, and mystical immensity is an experience almost impossible to describe and one that should not be missed.

HADRIAN'S COUNTRY RETREAT Although some have suggested that Hadrian himself was the architect of the Pantheon, the amateur builder does not deserve credit for the design. Hadrian was, however, deeply involved with the construction of his own country villa at Tivoli, where building activity seems never to have ceased until the emperor's death.

One of his projects was the construction of a pool and an artificial grotto, called the Canopus and Serapeum (FIG. **10-51**), respectively. Canopus was an Egyptian city connected to Alexandria by a canal. Its most famous temple was dedicated to the god

Hadrian: Emperor and Architect

Dio Cassius, a third-century CE senator who wrote a history of Rome from its foundation to his own day, recounted a revealing anecdote about Hadrian and Apollodorus of Damascus, architect of the Forum of Trajan (FIG. 10-41):

> Hadrian first drove into exile and then put to death the architect Apollodorus who had carried out several of Trajan's building projects. . . . When Trajan was at one time consulting with Apollodorus about a certain problem connected with his buildings, the architect said to Hadrian, who had interrupted them with some advice, "Go away and draw your pumpkins. You know nothing about these problems." For it so happened that Hadrian was at that time priding himself on some sort of drawing. When he became emperor he remembered this insult and refused to put up with Apollodorus's outspokenness. He sent him [his own] plan for the temple of Venus and Roma [FIG. 10-1, no. 14], in order to demonstrate that it was possible for a great work to be conceived without his [Apollodorus's] help, and asked him if he thought the building was well designed. Apollodorus sent a [very critical] reply. . . . [The emperor did not] attempt to restrain his anger or hide his pain; on the contrary, he had the man slain.[1]

The story says a great deal both about the absolute power Roman emperors wielded and about how seriously Hadrian took his architectural designs. But perhaps the most interesting detail is the description of Hadrian's drawings of "pumpkins." These must have been drawings of concrete domes like the one in the Serapeum (FIG. 10-51) at Hadrian's Tivoli villa. Such vaults were too adventurous for Apollodorus, or at least for a public building in Trajanic Rome, and Hadrian had to try them out later at home at his own expense.

[1] Dio Cassius, *Roman History*, 69.4.1–5. Translated by J. J. Pollitt, *The Art of Rome, c. 753 B.C.–A.D. 337: Sources and Documents* (New York: Cambridge University Press, 1983), 175–76.

Serapis. Nothing about the Tivoli design, however, derives from Egyptian architecture. The grotto at the end of the pool is made of concrete and has an unusual pumpkin-shaped dome that Hadrian probably designed himself (see "Hadrian: Emperor and Architect," above). Yet, in keeping with the persistent eclecticism of Roman art and architecture, Greek columns and marble copies of famous Greek statues lined the pool, as one would expect from a lover of Greek art. The Corinthian colonnade at the curved end of the pool is, however, of a type unknown in Classical Greek architecture. The colonnade not only lacks a superstructure but has arcuated (curved or arched) lintels, as opposed to traditional Greek horizontal lintels, between alternating pairs of columns. This simultaneous respect for Greek architecture and willingness to break Greek design rules typifies much Roman architecture of the High and Late Empire.

A BAROQUE TOMB IN A MOUNTAIN An even more extreme example of what many have called Roman "baroque" architecture (because of the striking parallels with 17th-century Italian buildings) is the second-century CE tomb nicknamed

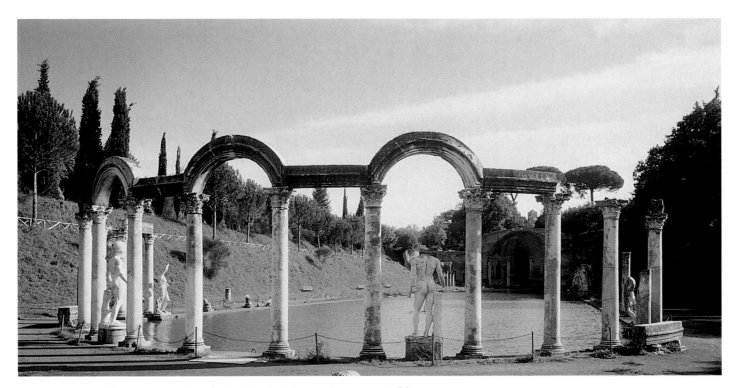

10-51 Canopus and Serapeum, Hadrian's Villa, Tivoli, Italy, ca. 125–128 CE.

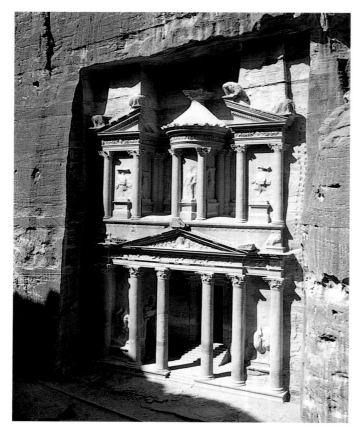

10-52 Al-Khazneh ("Treasury"), Petra, Jordan, second century CE.

the rhythmic alternation of deep projection and indentation creates dynamic patterns of light and shade. At Petra, as at Tivoli, the vocabulary of Greek architecture was maintained, but the syntax is new and distinctively Roman. In fact, the design recalls some of the architectural fantasies painted on the walls of Roman houses—for example, the tholos seen through columns surmounted by a broken pediment (FIG. 10-16, detail) in the Second Style cubiculum from Boscoreale.

Ostia

THE CROWDED LIFE OF THE CITY The average Roman, of course, did not own a luxurious country villa and was not buried in a grand tomb. About 90 percent of Rome's population of close to one million lived in multistory apartment blocks (*insulae*). After the great fire of 64 CE, these were built of brick-faced concrete. The rents were not cheap, as the law of supply and demand in real estate was just as valid in antiquity as it is today. Juvenal, a Roman satirist of the early second century CE, commented that people willing to give up chariot races and the other diversions Rome had to offer could purchase a fine home in the countryside "for a year's rent in a dark hovel" in a city so noisy that "the sick die mostly from lack of sleep."[5]

Al-Khazneh, the "Treasury" (FIG. **10-52**), at Petra, Jordan. It is one of the most elaborate of many tomb facades cut into the sheer rock faces of the local rose-colored mountains. As at Hadrian's villa, classical architectural elements are used here in a purely ornamental fashion and with a studied disregard for classical rules.

The Treasury's facade is more than 130 feet high and consists of two stories. The lower story resembles a temple facade with six columns, but the columns are unevenly spaced and the pediment is only wide enough to cover the four central columns. On the upper level, a temple-within-a-temple is set on top of the lower temple. Here the facade and roof split in half to make room for a central tholoslike cylinder, which contrasts sharply with the rectangles and triangles of the rest of the design. On both levels,

Conditions were much the same for the inhabitants of Ostia, Rome's harbor city. After its new port opened under Trajan, Ostia's prosperity increased dramatically and so did its population. A burst of building activity began under Trajan and continued under Hadrian and throughout the second century CE. Many multistory second-century insulae (FIG. **10-53**) have been preserved at Ostia. Shops occupied the ground floors. Above were up to four floors of apartments. Although many of the insula apartments were large, they had neither the space nor the light of the typical Pompeian private domus (see "The Roman House," page 257). In place of peristyles, the insulae of Ostia and Rome had only narrow light wells or small courtyards. Consequently, instead of looking inward, large numbers of glass windows faced the city's noisy streets. Only deluxe apartments had private toilets. Others shared latrines, often on a different floor from the apartment. Still, these insulae were quite similar to modern apartment houses, which also sometimes have shops on the ground floor.

Another strikingly modern feature of these multifamily residences is their brick facades, which were not concealed by stucco

10-53 Model of an insula, Ostia, Italy, second century CE. Museo della Civiltà Romana, Rome.

or marble veneers. When a classical motif was desired, brick pilasters or engaged columns could be added, but the brick was always left exposed. Ostia and Rome have many examples of apartment houses, warehouses, and tombs with intricate moldings and contrasting colors of brick. In the second century CE, brick came to be appreciated as attractive in its own right.

FRESCOED WALLS AND VAULTS Although the decoration of Ostian insulae tended to be more modest than that of the private houses of Pompeii, the finer apartments had mosaic floors and painted walls and ceilings. The frescoed groin vaults of Ostia are of special interest, because few painted ceilings are preserved in the cities buried by the eruption of Mount Vesuvius, and they are rarely of the vaulted type. Room IV (FIG. **10-54**) in the aptly named Insula of the Painted Vaults is typical of painted ceiling design of the second and third centuries CE. Such designs appear both in urban buildings and in the underground Christian catacombs (see FIG. 11-3). The painter treated the groin vault as if it were a dome, with a central oculus-like medallion surrounded by eight wedge-shaped segments resembling wheel spokes. In each segment is a white lunette with delicate paintings of birds and flowers, motifs also common earlier at Pompeii.

NEPTUNE'S MOSAICS The most popular choice for elegant pavements at Ostia in both private and public edifices was the black-and-white mosaic. One of the largest and best preserved examples is in the so-called Baths of Neptune, named for the grand mosaic floor (FIG. **10-55**) showing four seahorses pulling the Roman god of the sea across the waves. Neptune needs no chariot to support him as he speeds along, his mantle blowing in the strong wind. All about the god are other sea denizens, positioned so that wherever a visitor enters the room, some figures appear right side up. The artist rejected the complex polychrome modeling of figures seen in Pompeian mosaics such as the *Battle of Issus* (see FIG. 5-69) and used simple black silhouettes enlivened by white interior lines. Roman black-and-white mosaics were conceived as surface decorations and not as three-dimensional windows and thus were especially appropriate for floors.

WORKERS' TOMBS Ostian tombs of the second century CE were usually constructed of brick-faced concrete, and the facades of these houses of the dead resembled those of the contemporary insulae of the living. These were normally communal tombs, not the final resting places of the very wealthy. Many of them were adorned with small painted terracotta plaques immortalizing the activities of middle-class merchants and professional people.

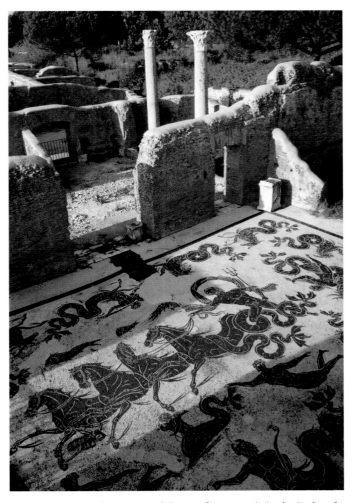

10-55 Neptune and creatures of the sea, floor mosaic in the Baths of Neptune, Ostia, Italy, ca. 140 CE.

10-56 Funerary reliefs of a vegetable vendor *(left)* and a midwife *(right)*, from Ostia, Italy, second half of second century CE. Painted terracotta, approx. 1′ 5″ and 11″ high, respectively. Museo Ostiense, Ostia.

We illustrate two of these plaques (FIG. **10-56**). One depicts a vegetable seller behind a counter (which has been tilted forward so that the observer can see the produce clearly). The other shows a midwife delivering a baby. Because she looks out at the viewer rather than at what she is doing and because almost all these reliefs focus on the livelihoods of the deceased, it is likely that the relief commemorates the midwife rather than the mother. Scenes of daily life such as these appeared on Roman funerary reliefs all over western Europe. Centuries later they may have served as the models for some medieval illustrations of the "labors of the months." They were as much a part of the classical legacy to the later history of art as the monuments commissioned by Roman emperors, which until recently were the exclusive interest of art historians.

The Antonines (138–192 CE)

SUCCESSION BY ADOPTION Early in 138 CE, Hadrian adopted the 51-year-old Antoninus Pius (r. 138–161 CE). At the same time, he required that Antoninus adopt Marcus Aurelius (r. 161–180 CE) and Lucius Verus (r. 161–169 CE), thereby assuring a peaceful succession for at least another generation. When Hadrian died later in the year, he was proclaimed a god, and Antoninus Pius became emperor. Antoninus ruled the Roman world with distinction for 23 years. After his death and deification, Marcus Aurelius and Lucius Verus became the Roman Empire's first coemperors.

CLASSICAL AND NONCLASSICAL Shortly after Antoninus Pius's death, Marcus and Lucius erected a memorial column in his honor. Its pedestal has a dedicatory inscription on one side and a relief (FIG. **10-57**) illustrating the *apotheosis* (ascent to the heavens) of Antoninus and his wife Faustina the Elder on the opposite side. On the adjacent sides are two identical representations of the *decursio* (FIG. **10-58**), or ritual circling of the imperial funerary pyre.

The two figural compositions are very different. The apotheosis relief remains firmly in the classical tradition with its elegant, well-proportioned figures, personifications, and single ground line corresponding to the panel's lower edge. The Campus Martius (Field of Mars), personified as a youth holding the Egyptian obelisk that stood in that area of Rome, reclines at the lower left corner. Roma (Rome personified) leans on a shield decorated with the she-wolf suckling Romulus and Remus (compare FIG. 9-10). Roma bids farewell to the couple being lifted into the realm of the gods on the wings of a personification of uncertain identity. All this was familiar from earlier scenes of apotheosis. New to the imperial repertoire, however, was the fusion of time the joint apotheosis represents. Faustina had died 20 years before Antoninus Pius. By depicting the two as ascending together, the artist wished to suggest that Antoninus had been faithful to his wife for two decades and that now they would be reunited in the afterlife. This notion had been employed before in the funerary reliefs of freed slaves and the middle class (FIG. 10-46) but had never been used in an elite context.

The decursio reliefs break even more strongly with classical convention. The figures are much stockier than those in the apotheosis relief, and the panel was not conceived as a window onto the world. The ground is the whole surface of the relief, and marching soldiers and galloping horses alike are shown on floating patches of earth. This, too, had not occurred before in imperial art, only in plebeian art (FIG. 10-6). After centuries of following classical design rules, elite Roman artists and patrons finally became dissatisfied with them. When seeking a new direction, they adopted some of the nonclassical conventions of the art of the lower classes.

IMPERIAL MAJESTY ON HORSEBACK Another break with the past occurred in the official portraits of Marcus Aurelius, although the pompous trappings of imperial iconography were

10-57 Apotheosis of Antoninus Pius and Faustina, pedestal of the Column of Antoninus Pius, Rome, Italy, ca. 161 CE. Marble, approx. 8′ 1½″ high. Vatican Museums, Rome.

10-58 Decursio, pedestal of the Column of Antoninus Pius, Rome, Italy, ca. 161 CE. Marble, approx. 8′ 1½″ high. Vatican Museums, Rome.

retained. In a larger-than-life-size gilded-bronze equestrian statue (FIG. 10-59), the emperor possesses a superhuman grandeur and is much larger than any normal human would be in relation to his horse. Marcus stretches out his right arm in a gesture that is both a greeting and an offer of clemency. Some evidence suggests that beneath the horse's raised right foreleg an enemy once cowered, begging the emperor for mercy. The statue conveys the awesome power of the godlike Roman emperor as ruler of the whole world.

In the 16th century, Pope Paul III selected this statue as the centerpiece for Michelangelo's new design for the Capitoline Hill in Rome (see FIGS. 22-26 and 22-27). The statue inspired many Renaissance sculptors to portray their patrons on horseback (see FIGS. 21-29 and 21-30). Recently removed from its Renaissance site and painstakingly restored, Marcus's portrait owed its preservation throughout the Middle Ages to the fact that it was mistakenly thought to portray Constantine, the first Christian emperor of Rome. Most ancient bronze statues were melted down for their metal value, because they were regarded as impious images from the pagan world. Even today, after centuries of new finds, only a very few bronze equestrian statues are known. The type was, however, often used for imperial portraits—an equestrian statue of

10-59 Equestrian statue of Marcus Aurelius, from Rome, Italy, ca. 175 CE. Bronze, approx. 11′ 6″ high. Musei Capitolini, Rome.

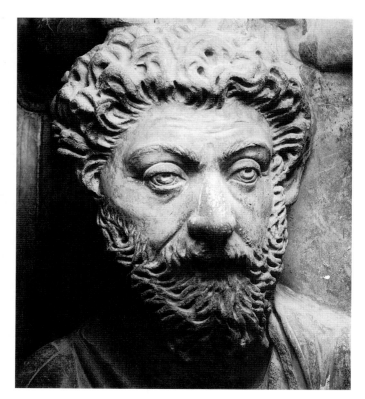

10-60 Portrait of Marcus Aurelius, detail of a relief from a lost arch, Rome, Italy, ca. 175–180 CE. Marble, approx. life-size. Palazzo dei Conservatori, Rome.

Trajan stood in the middle of his forum (FIG. 10-41). Perhaps more than any other statuary type, the equestrian portrait expresses the Roman emperor's majesty and authority.

DISQUIETING ANTONINE PORTRAITS This message of supreme confidence is not, however, conveyed by the portrait head of Marcus's equestrian statue or by the late portraits of the emperor in marble, such as the one illustrated here (FIG. **10-60**). The latter is a detail of a panel from a lost arch that probably resembled Trajan's arch at Benevento (FIG. 10-45). The emperor rides in a triumphal chariot, and, like Titus before him (FIG. 10-39), he is crowned by Victory. The Antonine sculptor, in keeping with contemporary practice, used a drill to render the emperor's long hair and beard and even to accentuate the pupils of his eyes, creating bold patterns of light and shadow across his face. A chisel was used to carve the lines in Marcus's forehead and the deep ridges running from his nostrils to the corners of his mouth.

Portraits of aged emperors were not new (FIG. 10-35), but Marcus's were the first ones in which a Roman emperor appears weary, saddened, and even worried. For the first time, the strain of constant warfare on the frontiers and the burden of ruling a worldwide empire show in the emperor's face. The Antonine sculptor ventured beyond Republican verism. The ruler's character, his thoughts, and his soul were exposed for all to see, as Marcus revealed them himself in his *Meditations,* a deeply moving philo-

sophical treatise setting forth the emperor's personal worldview. This was a major turning point in the history of ancient art, and, coming as it did when the classical style was being challenged in relief sculpture (FIG. 10-58), it marked the beginning of the end of classical art's domination in the Greco-Roman world.

FROM CREMATION TO BURIAL Other profound changes also were taking place in Roman art and society at this time. Beginning under Trajan and Hadrian and especially during the rule of the Antonines, Romans began to favor burial over cremation. This reversal of funerary practices may reflect the influence of Christianity and other Eastern religions, whose adherents believed in an afterlife for the human body. Although the emperors themselves continued to be cremated in the traditional Roman manner, many private citizens opted for burial. Thus they required larger containers for their remains than the ash urns that were the norm until the second century CE. This in turn led to a sudden demand for sarcophagi, which are more similar to modern coffins than any other ancient type of burial container.

ORESTES ON ROMAN SARCOPHAGI Greek mythology was one of the most popular subjects for the decoration of these sarcophagi. In many cases, especially in the late second and third centuries CE, the Greek heroes and heroines were given the portrait features of the deceased Roman men and women in the marble coffins. These private patrons were following the model of imperial portraiture, where emperors and empresses frequently masqueraded as gods and goddesses and heroes and heroines (see "Role Playing in Roman Portraiture," page 265). An early example of the type (although it lacks any portraits) is the sarcophagus (FIG. **10-61**) now in Cleveland, one of many decorated with the story of the tragic Greek hero Orestes. All the examples of this type

10-61 Sarcophagus with the myth of Orestes, ca. 140–150 CE. Marble, 2′ 7½″ high. Cleveland Museum of Art, Cleveland.

use the same basic composition. Orestes appears several times: slaying his mother Clytaemnestra and her lover Aegisthus to avenge their murder of his father Agamemnon, taking refuge at Apollo's sanctuary at Delphi (symbolized by the god's tripod at the right), and so forth.

The repetition of sarcophagus compositions indicates that sculptors had access to pattern books. In fact, sarcophagus production was a major industry during the High and Late Empire. Several important regional manufacturing centers existed. The sarcophagi produced in the Latin West, such as the Cleveland Orestes sarcophagus, differ in format from those made in the Greek-speaking East. Western sarcophagi have reliefs only on the front and sides, because they were placed in floor-level niches

inside Roman tombs. Eastern sarcophagi have reliefs on all four sides and stood in the center of the burial chamber. This contrast parallels the essential difference between the Etrusco-Roman and the Greek temple. The former was set against the wall of a forum or sanctuary and approached from the front, whereas the latter could be reached (and viewed) from every side.

A MORTAL VENUS'S COFFIN An elaborate example (FIG. 10-62) of a sarcophagus of the Eastern type comes from Rapolla, near Melfi in southern Italy. It was manufactured, however, in Asia Minor and attests to the vibrant export market for such luxury items in Antonine times. The decoration of all four sides of the marble box with statuesque images of Greek gods and heroes in

10-62 Asiatic sarcophagus with *kline* portrait of a woman, from Rapolla, near Melfi, Italy, ca. 165–170 CE. Marble, approx. 5′ 7″ high. Museo Nazionale Archeologico del Melfese, Melfi.

Iaia of Cyzicus and the Art of Encaustic Painting

The names of very few Roman artists are known. Those that are tend to be names of artists and architects who directed major imperial building projects (Severus and Celer, Domus Aurea; Apollodorus of Damascus, Forum of Trajan), worked on a gigantic scale (Zenodorus, Colossus of Nero), or made precious objects for famous patrons (Dioscurides, gem cutter for Augustus).

An interesting exception to this rule is Iaia of Cyzicus. Pliny the Elder, who died in the eruption of Mount Vesuvius (see "An Eyewitness Account," page 255), reported the following about this renowned painter from Asia Minor who worked in Italy during the Republic:

> Iaia of Cyzicus, who remained a virgin all her life, painted at Rome during the time when M. Varro [116–27 BCE] was a youth, both with a brush and with a cestrum on ivory, specializing mainly in portraits of women; she also painted a large panel in Naples representing an old woman and a portrait of herself done with a mirror. Her hand was quicker than that of any other painter, and her artistry was of such high quality that she commanded much higher prices than the most celebrated painters of the same period.[1]

The *cestrum* Pliny mentioned is a small spatula used in *encaustic* painting, a technique of mixing colors with hot wax and then applying them to the surface. Pliny knew of encaustic paintings of considerable antiquity, including those of Polygnotos of Thasos, a famous fifth-century BCE Greek painter (see Chapter 5, page 143). The best evidence of the technique comes, however, from Roman Egypt, where mummies were routinely furnished with portraits painted with encaustic on wooden panels (FIG. 10-63).

Artists applied encaustic to marble as well as to wood. According to Pliny, when Praxiteles was asked which one of his statues he preferred, the fourth-century BCE Greek artist, perhaps the ancient world's greatest marble sculptor, replied: "Those that Nikias painted."[2] This anecdote underscores the importance of coloration in ancient statuary.

[1] Pliny the Elder, *Natural History,* 35.147–148. Translated by J. J. Pollitt, *The Art of Rome, c. 753 B.C.–A.D. 337: Sources and Documents* (New York: Cambridge University Press, 1983), 87.

[2] Pliny the Elder, *Natural History,* 35.133.

---

architectural frames is distinctively Asiatic. But the lid portrait, which carries on the tradition of Etruscan sarcophagi (see FIGS. 9-4 and 9-14), is also a feature of the most expensive Western Roman coffins. Here the deceased, a woman, reclines on a *kline* (bed). With her are her faithful little dog (only its forepaws remain at the left end of the lid) and Cupid (at the right). The winged infant god mournfully holds a downturned torch, a reference to the death of a woman whose beauty rivaled that of his mother, Venus (who appears in one of the niches on the back of the sarcophagus).

ROMAN MUMMY PORTRAITS In Egypt, burial had been practiced for millennia. Even after the Kingdom of the Nile was reduced to a Roman province in 30 BCE, Egyptians continued to bury their dead in mummy cases. Recent excavations at the Bahariya Oasis have dramatically demonstrated the persistence of these burial customs. In Roman times, however, painted portraits on wood often replaced the traditional stylized portrait masks (see "Iaia of Cyzicus and the Art of Encaustic Painting," above). Hundreds of Roman mummy portraits have been preserved in the cemeteries of the Faiyum district. One of them (FIG. **10-63**) depicts a man who, following the lead of Marcus Aurelius, has long, curly hair and a full beard. Such portraits, which mostly date to the second and third centuries CE, were probably painted while the subjects were still alive. Art historians use them to trace the evolution of portrait painting after Mount Vesuvius erupted in 79 CE (compare FIG. 10-23). Our example exhibits the painter's refined use of the brush and spatula, mastery of the depiction of varied textures and of the play of light over the soft and delicately modeled face, and sensitive portrayal of the deceased's calm demeanor.

The Western and Eastern Roman sarcophagi and the mummy cases of Roman Egypt all served the same purpose, despite their differing shape and character. In an empire as vast as Rome's, regional differences are to be expected. As will be discussed later, geography also played a major role in the Middle Ages, when Western and Eastern Christian art differed sharply.

10-63 Mummy portrait of a man, from Faiyum, Egypt, ca. 160–170 CE. Encaustic on wood, approx. 1′ 2″ high. Albright-Knox Art Gallery, Buffalo.

LATE EMPIRE

A CIVILIZATION IN TRANSITION By the time of Marcus Aurelius, two centuries after Augustus established the Pax Romana, Roman power was beginning to erode. It was more and more difficult to keep order on the frontiers, and even within the Empire the authority of Rome was being challenged. Marcus's son Commodus (r. 180–192 CE), who succeeded his father, was assassinated, bringing the Antonine dynasty to an end. The economy was in decline, and the efficient imperial bureaucracy was disintegrating. Even the official state religion was losing ground to Eastern cults, Christianity among them, which were beginning to gain large numbers of converts. The Late Empire was a pivotal era in world history during which the pagan ancient world was gradually transformed into the Christian Middle Ages.

The Severans (193–235 CE)

AN AFRICAN RULES THE EMPIRE Civil conflict followed Commodus's death. When it ended, an African-born general named Septimius Severus (r. 193–211 CE) was master of the Roman world. The new emperor, anxious to establish his legitimacy, adopted himself into the Antonine dynasty, proclaiming himself as Marcus Aurelius's son. It is not surprising, then, that official portraits of Septimius Severus depict him with the long hair and beard of his Antonine "father"—whatever his actual appearance may have been. Many portraits in marble and bronze exist today of the African emperor and of his wife, Julia Domna, the daughter of a Syrian priest, and their two sons, Caracalla and Geta. But only one painted portrait of the family has been found. In fact, the portrait (FIG. **10-64**), discovered in Egypt and painted in *tempera* (pigments in egg yolk) on wood (as were many of the mummy portraits from Faiyum), is the only surviving painted likeness of any Roman emperor. Such portraits, however, must have been quite common all over the empire. Their perishable nature explains their almost total loss.

The Severan family portrait is of special interest for two reasons beyond its mere survival. The emperor's hair is tinged with gray, suggesting that his marble portraits—which, like all marble sculptures in antiquity, were painted—also may have revealed his advancing age in this way. (The same was very likely true of the marble likenesses of the old and tired Marcus Aurelius, FIG. 10-60.) The group portrait is also notable because the face of the emperor's younger son, Geta, was erased. When Caracalla (r. 211–217 CE) succeeded his father as emperor, he had his brother murdered and his memory damned. (Caracalla also ordered the death of his own wife, Plautilla.) The painted *tondo* (circular format) portrait from Egypt is an eloquent testimony to that damnatio memoriae and to the long arm of Roman authority. This kind of defacement of a political rival's portrait is not new. As noted earlier, for example, Thutmose III of Egypt destroyed the portraits of Hatshepsut after her death (see FIG. 3-22). But the Romans employed damnatio memoriae as a political tool more often and more systematically than any other civilization.

PORTRAYING A RUTHLESS EMPEROR One of the finest marble portraits of the ruthless Caracalla is illustrated in FIG. **10-65**. The sculptor brilliantly suggested the texture of the emperor's short hair and close-cropped beard through deft handling of the chisel and incisions into the marble surface. More remarkable, however, is the moving characterization of Caracalla's suspicious nature, a further development from the groundbreaking introspection of the portraits of Marcus Aurelius. Caracalla's brow is knotted, and he abruptly turns his head over his left shoulder, as if he suspects danger from behind. The emperor had reason to be fearful. He was felled by an assassin's dagger in the sixth year of his rule. Assassination would be the fate of many Roman emperors during the turbulent third century CE.

10-64 Painted portrait of Septimius Severus and his family, from Egypt, ca. 200 CE. Tempera on wood, approx. 1′ 2″ diameter. Staatliche Museen, Berlin.

10-65 Portrait of Caracalla, ca. 211–217 CE. Marble, approx. 1′ 2″ high. Metropolitan Museum of Art, New York.

10-66 Chariot procession of Septimius Severus, relief from the Arch of Septimius Severus, Lepcis Magna, Libya, 203 CE. Marble, approx. 5′ 6″ high. Castle Museum, Tripoli.

THE NONCLASSICAL STYLE TAKES ROOT The hometown of the Severans was Lepcis Magna, on the coast of what is now Libya. In the late second and early third centuries CE, imperial funds were used to construct a modern harbor there, as well as a new forum, basilica, arch, and other monuments. The Arch of Septimius Severus, erected in 203 at the intersection of two major streets, lay in ruins for centuries but has recently been rebuilt. It has friezes on the attic on all four sides. One of these (FIG. **10-66**) shows the chariot procession of Septimius and his two sons. Unlike the triumph panel (FIG. 10-39) from the Arch of Titus in Rome, this relief gives no sense of rushing motion. Rather, it has a stately stillness. The chariot and the horsemen behind it are moving forward, but the emperor and his sons are detached from the procession and facing the viewer. Also different is the way the figures in the second row have no connection with the ground and are elevated above the heads of those in the first row so that they can be seen more clearly.

Both the frontality and the floating figures were new to official Roman art in Antonine and Severan times, but both appeared long before in the private art of freed slaves (compare FIGS. 10-5 and 10-6). Once sculptors in the emperor's employ embraced these nonclassical elements, they had a long afterlife, appearing

in medieval art in frontal images of Christ and the saints. As is often true in the history of art, the emergence of a new aesthetic was a by-product of a period of social, political, and economic upheaval. Art historians call this new non-naturalistic, more abstract style the Late Antique style.

CARACALLA'S GIGANTIC BATHS The Severans were also active builders in the capital. The Baths of Caracalla in Rome (FIG. **10-67**) were the greatest in a long line of bathing and recreational complexes erected with imperial funds to win the public's favor. Made of brick-faced concrete and covered by enormous vaults springing from thick walls up to 140 feet high, Caracalla's baths covered an area of almost 50 acres. They dwarfed the typical baths of cities and towns such as Ostia and Pompeii and even Rome itself. The design was symmetrical along a central axis, facilitating the Roman custom of taking sequential plunges in cold-, warm-, and hot-water baths in, respectively, the *frigidarium, tepidarium,* and *caldarium.*

The caldarium (FIG. 10-67, no. 4) of Caracalla's baths was a circular chamber so large that until recently it seated hundreds of spectators at open-air performances of Italian operas. Its dome was almost as large as the Pantheon's (FIG. 10-50), and the

10-67 Plan of the central section of the Baths of Caracalla, Rome, Italy, 212–216 CE. 1) Natatio, 2) Frigidarium, 3) Tepidarium, 4) Caldarium, 5) Palaestra. The bathing, swimming, and exercise areas were surrounded by landscaped gardens, lecture halls, and other rooms, all enclosed within a great concrete perimeter wall.

1. Natatio
2. Frigidarium
3. Tepidarium
4. Caldarium
5. Palaestra

10-68 Reconstruction drawing of the central hall (*frigidarium*) of the Baths of Caracalla, Rome, Italy, 212–216 CE.

concrete drum that supported it was much taller. Our reconstruction of the frigidarium (FIG. **10-68**), which was also the central hall of the baths, shows not only the scale of the architecture and the way light entered through fenestrated groin vaults but also how lavishly the rooms were decorated. Stuccoed vaults, mosaic floors (both black-and-white and polychrome), marble-faced walls, and colossal statuary were found throughout the complex. Although the vaults themselves collapsed long ago, many of the mosaics and statues are preserved. Among these is the 10-foot-tall copy of Lysippos's Herakles (see FIG. 5-66), whose muscular body must have inspired Romans to exercise vigorously.

Caracalla's baths also had landscaped gardens, lecture halls, libraries, colonnaded exercise courts (*palaestras*), and a giant swimming pool (*natatio*). Archaeologists estimate that up to 1,600 bathers at a time could enjoy this Roman equivalent of a modern health spa. A branch of one of the city's major aqueducts supplied water, and furnaces circulated hot air through hollow floors and walls throughout the complex.

The Soldier Emperors (235–284 CE)

A STORMY HALF CENTURY The Severan dynasty ended when Severus Alexander (r. 222–235 CE) was murdered. The next half century was one of almost continuous civil war. One general after another was declared emperor by his troops, only to be murdered by another general a few years or even a few months later. (In the year 238, two coemperors the Senate chose were dragged from the imperial palace and murdered in public after only three months in office.) In these unstable times, no emperor could begin ambitious architectural projects. The only significant building activity in Rome during the "soldier emperors" era occurred under Aurelian (r. 270–275 CE). He constructed a new defensive

wall circuit for the capital—a military necessity and a poignant commentary on the decay of Roman power.

IMPERIAL SOUL PORTRAITS If architects went hungry in third-century Rome, sculptors and engravers had much to do. Great quantities of coins (in debased metal) were produced so that the troops could be paid with money stamped with the current emperor's portrait and not with that of his predecessor or rival. Each new ruler set up portrait statues and busts everywhere to assert his authority.

The sculpted portraits of the third century CE are among the most moving ever produced. Following the lead of the sculptors of the Marcus Aurelius and Caracalla portraits, artists fashioned likenesses of the soldier emperors that are as notable for their emotional content as they are for their technical virtuosity. Trajan Decius (r. 249–251), for example, whose brief reign is best known for persecution of Christians, was portrayed as an old man with bags under his eyes and a sad expression (FIG. **10-69**). In his eyes, which glance away nervously rather than engage the viewer directly, is the anxiety of a man who knows he can do little to restore order to an out-of-control world. The sculptor modeled the marble as if it were pliant clay, compressing the sides of the head at the level of the eyes, etching the hair and beard into the stone, and chiseling deep lines in the forehead and around the mouth. The portrait reveals the anguished soul of the man—and of the times.

10-69 Portrait bust of Trajan Decius, 249–251 CE. Marble, full bust approx. 2′ 7″ high. Museo Capitolino, Rome.

Decius's successor was Trebonianus Gallus (r. 251–253 CE), another short-lived emperor. In a larger-than-life-size bronze portrait (FIG. **10-70**), Trebonianus appears in heroic nudity, as had so many emperors and generals before him. His physique is not, however, that of the strong but graceful Greek athletes Augustus and his successors admired so much. Instead, his is a wrestler's body with massive legs and a swollen trunk. The heavy-set body dwarfs his head, with its nervous expression. In this portrait, the Greek ideal of the keen mind in the harmoniously proportioned body gave way to an image of brute force, an image well suited to the era of the soldier emperors.

BARBARIANS AND MITHRAS By the third century, burial of the dead had become so widespread that even the imperial family was practicing it in place of cremation. Sarcophagi were more popular than ever. An unusually large sarcophagus (FIG. **10-71**), discovered in Rome in 1621 and purchased by Cardinal Ludovisi, is decorated on the front with a chaotic scene of battle between Romans and one of their northern foes, probably the Goths. The sculptor spread the writhing and highly emotive figures evenly across the entire relief, with no illusion of space behind them. This piling of figures is an even more extreme rejection of classical perspective than was the use of floating ground lines on the pedestal of the Column of Antoninus Pius (FIG. 10-58). It underscores the increasing dissatisfaction Late Roman artists felt with the classical style.

Within this dense mass of intertwined bodies, the central horseman stands out vividly. He wears no helmet, and thrusts out his open right hand to demonstrate that he holds no weapon. Several scholars have identified him as one of the sons of Trajan Decius. In an age when the Roman army was far from invincible and Roman emperors were constantly felled by other Romans, the young general on the *Ludovisi Battle Sarcophagus* is boasting that he is a fearless commander assured of victory. His self-assurance may stem from his having embraced one of the increasingly popular Oriental mystery religions. On the youth's forehead is carved the emblem of Mithras, the Persian god of light, truth, and victory

10-70 Heroic portrait of Trebonianus Gallus, from Rome, Italy, 251–253 CE. Bronze, approx. 7′ 11″ high. Metropolitan Museum of Art, New York.

10-71 Battle of Romans and barbarians *(Ludovisi Battle Sarcophagus)*, from Rome, Italy, ca. 250–260 CE. Marble, approx. 5′ high. Museo Nazionale Romano-Palazzo Altemps, Rome.

10-72 Sarcophagus of a philosopher, ca. 270–280 CE. Marble, approx. 4′ 11″ high. Vatican Museums, Rome.

over death. Many shrines to Mithras dating to this period have been found at Rome and Ostia.

PHILOSOPHERS AND STUDENTS The insecurity of the times led many Romans to seek solace in philosophy. On many third-century sarcophagi, the deceased assumes the role of the learned intellectual. (Others continued to masquerade as Greek heroes or Roman generals.) One especially large example (FIG. 10-72) depicts a seated Roman philosopher holding a scroll. Two standing women (also with portrait features) look to him for wisdom. In the background are other philosophers, students of the central deceased teacher. This type of sarcophagus became very popular for Christian burials, where the wise-man motif was used not only to portray the deceased (see FIG. 11-4) but also Christ flanked by his apostles (see FIG. 11-5). Compositions with a central frontal figure and subordinate flanking figures, such as on this sarcophagus and on the Severan arch at Lepcis Magna (FIG. 10-66), are also quite common in Early Christian art (see FIGS. 11-5 and 11-17).

A CRITIQUE OF THE PANTHEON The decline in respect for classical art also can be seen in architecture. At Baalbek (ancient Heliopolis) in modern Lebanon, the architect of the Temple of Venus (FIG. 10-73), following in the "baroque" tradition of the Treasury at Petra (FIG. 10-52), ignored almost every rule of classical design. Although made of stone, the third-century building, with its circular domed cella set behind a gabled columnar facade, was in many ways a critique of the concrete Pantheon (FIG. 10-48), which by then had achieved the status of a "classic." Many features of the Baalbek temple intentionally depart from the norm. The platform, for example, is scalloped all around the cella. The columns—the only known instance of *five*-sided Corinthian capitals with corresponding pentagonal bases—support a matching scalloped entablature (which serves to buttress the shallow stone dome). These concave forms and those of the niches in the cella walls play off against the cella's convex shape. Even the "traditional" facade of the Baalbek temple is eccentric. The unknown architect inserted an arch within the triangular pediment.

10-73 Restored view (*top*) and plan (*bottom*) of the Temple of Venus, Baalbek, Lebanon, third century CE.

Diocletian and the Tetrarchy (284–306 CE)

POWER SHARED, ORDER RESTORED In an attempt to re-store order to the Roman Empire, Diocletian (r. 284–305 CE), whose troops proclaimed him emperor, decided to share power with his potential rivals. In 293, he established the *tetrarchy* (rule by four) and adopted the title of Augustus of the East. The other three tetrarchs were a corresponding Augustus of the West, and Eastern and Western Caesars (whose allegiance to the two Augusti was cemented by marriage to their daughters). Together, the four emperors ruled without strife until Diocletian retired in 305. Without his leadership, the new tetrarchs began fighting among themselves, and the tetrarchic form of government collapsed. The division of the Roman Empire into eastern and western spheres survived, however. It persisted throughout the Middle Ages, setting the Latin West apart from the Byzantine East.

INDIVIDUALITY LOST The four tetrarchs often were por-trayed together, both on coins and in the round. Artists did not try to capture their individual appearances and personalities but sought instead to represent the nature of the tetrarchy itself—that is, to portray four equal partners in power. In the two pairs of porphyry (purple marble) portraits of the tetrarchs we illustrate (FIG. 10-74), it is impossible to name the rulers. Each of the four emperors has lost his identity as an individual and been sub-sumed into the larger entity of the tetrarchy. All the tetrarchs are identically clad in cuirass and cloak. Each grasps a sheathed sword in the left hand. With their right arms they embrace one another in an overt display of concord. The figures, like those on the de-cursio relief (FIG. 10-58) of the Column of Antoninus Pius, have large cubical heads on squat bodies. The drapery is schematic and the bodies are shapeless. The faces are emotionless masks, distin-guished only by the beard on two of the figures (probably the older Augusti, distinguishing them from the younger Caesars). Nonetheless, each pair is as alike as freehand carving can achieve. In this group portrait, carved eight centuries after Greek sculp-tors first freed the human form from the formal rigidity of the Egyptian-inspired kouros stance, the human figure was once again conceived in iconic terms. Idealism, naturalism, individual-ity, and personality now belonged to the past.

DIOCLETIAN'S FORTRESS-PALACE When Diocletian abdi-cated in 305, he returned to Dalmatia (roughly the area of the

10-74 Portraits of the four tetrarchs, from Constantinople, ca. 305 CE. Porphyry, approx. 4′ 3″ high. Saint Mark's, Venice.

former Yugoslavia), where he was born. There he built a palace (FIG. 10-75) for himself at Split, near ancient Salona on the Adri-atic coast in Croatia. Just as Aurelian had felt it necessary to girdle Rome with fortress walls, Diocletian instructed his architects to provide him with a well-fortified suburban palace. The complex, which covers about 10 acres, was laid out like a Roman castrum, complete with watchtowers flanking the gates. It gave the em-peror a sense of security in the most insecure of times.

Within the high walls, two avenues (comparable to the cardo and decumanus in a provincial colony such as Timgad, FIG. 10-40)

10-75 Model of the Palace of Diocletian, Split, Croatia, ca. 300–305 CE. Museo della Civiltà Romana, Rome.

intersected at the palace's center. Where a city's forum would have been situated, Diocletian's palace had a colonnaded court leading to the entrance to the imperial residence. If admitted to the emperor's private quarters, a visitor passed through a templelike facade with an arch within its pediment, as in the Temple of Venus at Baalbek (FIG. 10-73). The formal purpose of this motif was undoubtedly to emphasize the design's central axis, but symbolically it became the "gable of glorification" under which Diocletian appeared before those who gathered in the court to pay homage to him. On one side of the court was a Temple of Jupiter; on the other side, Diocletian's mausoleum (left rear in FIG. 10-75), which towered above all the other structures in the complex. The emperor's huge domed tomb was a type that would become very popular in Early Christian times not only for mausoleums but eventually also for churches, especially in the Byzantine East. It is, in fact, used as a church today.

Constantine (306–337 CE)

CONSTANTINE AND CHRISTIANITY The short-lived concord among the tetrarchs that ended with Diocletian's abdication was followed by an all-too-familiar period of conflict. This latest civil war among rival Roman armies lasted two decades. The eventual victor was Constantine I ("the Great"), son of Constantius Chlorus, Diocletian's Caesar of the West. After the death of his father, Constantine invaded Italy in 312. At the battle of the Milvian Bridge, the gateway to Rome, he defeated and killed Maxentius and took control of the capital. Constantine attributed his victory to the aid of the Christian god. In 313, he and Licinius, Constantine's coemperor in the East, issued the Edict of Milan, ending the persecution of Christians.

In time, Constantine and Licinius became foes, and in 324 Constantine defeated and executed Licinius near Byzantium (modern Istanbul, Turkey). Constantine was now unchallenged ruler of the whole Roman Empire. Shortly after the death of Licinius, he founded a "New Rome" on the site of Byzantium and named it Constantinople ("City of Constantine"). A year later, in 325, at the Council of Nicaea, Christianity became the de facto official religion of the Roman Empire. From this point on, paganism declined rapidly. Constantinople was dedicated on May 11, 330, "by the commandment of God." In succeeding decades, many Christian churches were erected there. Constantine himself was baptized on his deathbed in 337. For many scholars, the transfer of the seat of power from Rome to Constantinople and the recognition of Christianity mark the beginning of the Middle Ages.

Constantinian art is a mirror of this transition from the classical to the medieval world. In Rome, for example, Constantine was a builder in the grand tradition of the emperors of the first, second, and early third centuries, erecting public baths, a basilica on the Sacred Way leading into the Roman Forum, and a triumphal arch. But he was also the patron of the city's first churches, including Saint Peter's (see FIG. 11-7).

A NEW ARCH WITH OLD RELIEFS After his decisive victory at the Milvian Bridge, Constantine erected a great triple-passageway arch (FIG. 10-76 and 10-1, no. 15) in the shadow of the Colosseum to commemorate his defeat of Maxentius. The arch was the largest erected in Rome since the end of the Severan dynasty nearly a century before. Much of the sculptural decoration, however, was taken from earlier monuments of Trajan, Hadrian, and Marcus Aurelius. The columns also date to an earlier era. Sculptors refashioned the second-century reliefs to honor Constantine by recutting the heads of the earlier emperors with the features of the new ruler. They also added labels to the old reliefs, such as *Fundator Quietus* (bringer of peace) and *Liberator Urbis* (liberator of the city), references to the downfall of Maxentius and the end of civil war.

The reuse of statues and reliefs on the Arch of Constantine has often been cited as evidence of a decline in creativity and technical skill in the waning years of the pagan Roman Empire. Although such a judgment is in large part deserved, it ignores the fact that the reused sculptures were carefully selected to associate Constantine with the "good emperors" of the second century. That message is underscored in one of the new Constantinian reliefs above the arch's lateral passageways. It shows Constantine on the speaker's platform in the Roman Forum, flanked by statues of Hadrian and Marcus Aurelius.

10-76 Arch of Constantine (south side), Rome, Italy, 312–315 CE.

10-77 Distribution of largess, detail of the north frieze of the Arch of Constantine, Rome, Italy, 312–315 CE. Marble, approx. 3′ 4″ high.

In another Constantinian relief (FIG. **10-77**), the emperor is shown with attendants, distributing largess to grateful citizens who approach him from right and left. Constantine is a frontal and majestic presence, elevated on a throne above the recipients of his munificence. The figures are squat in proportion, like the tetrarchs (FIG. 10-74). They do not move according to any classical principle of naturalistic movement but, rather, with the mechanical and repeated stances and gestures of puppets. The relief is very shallow, the forms were not fully modeled, and the details were incised. The heads were not distinguished from one another. The sculptor depicted a crowd, not a group of individuals. (Constantine's head, which was carved separately and set into the relief, has been lost.) The frieze is less a narrative of action than a picture of actors frozen in time so that the viewer can distinguish instantly the all-important imperial donor (at the center on a throne) from his attendants (to the left and right above) and the recipients of the largess (below and of smaller stature).

This approach to pictorial narrative was once characterized as a "decline of form," and when judged by classical art standards, it was. But the composition's rigid formality, determined by the rank of those portrayed, was consistent with a new set of values. It soon became the preferred mode, supplanting the classical notion that a picture is a window onto a world of anecdotal action. Comparing this Constantinian relief with a Byzantine icon (see FIG. 12-16) reveals that the new compositional principles of the Late Antique style are those of the Middle Ages. They were very different from, but not necessarily "better" or "worse" than, those of classical antiquity. The Arch of Constantine was the quintessential monument of its era, exhibiting a respect for the classical past in its reuse of second-century sculptures while rejecting the norms of classical design in its frieze, paving the way for the iconic art of the Middle Ages.

CONSTANTINE'S COLOSSUS After Constantine's victory over Maxentius, his official portraits broke with tetrarchic tradition as well as with the style of the soldier emperors, and resuscitated the Augustan image of an eternally youthful head of state. The most impressive by far of Constantine's preserved portraits is an eight-and-one-half-foot-tall head (FIG. **10-78**), one of several marble fragments of a colossal enthroned statue of the emperor that was composed of a brick core, a wooden torso covered with bronze, and a head and limbs of marble. Constantine's artist modeled the semi-nude seated portrait on Roman images of Jupiter. The emperor held an orb (possibly surmounted by the cross of Christ), the

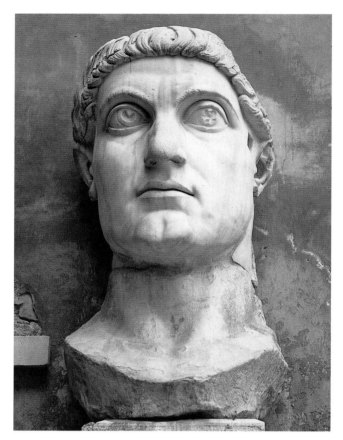

10-78 Portrait of Constantine, from the Basilica Nova, Rome, Italy, ca. 315–330 CE. Marble, approx. 8′ 6″ high. Palazzo dei Conservatori, Rome.

symbol of global power, in his extended left hand. The nervous glance of third-century portraits is absent, replaced by a frontal mask with enormous eyes set into the broad and simple planes of the head. The emperor's personality is lost in this immense image of eternal authority. The colossal size, the likening of the emperor to Jupiter, the eyes directed at no person or thing of this world—all combine to produce a formula of overwhelming power appropriate to Constantine's exalted position as absolute ruler.

ROME'S NEW BASILICA Constantine's gigantic portrait sat in the western apse of the Basilica Nova ("New Basilica") in Rome (FIGS. **10-79** and 10-1, no. 12), a project Maxentius had begun on a site not far from the Arch of Titus. Constantine completed the building after his rival's death. From its position in the apse, the emperor's image dominated the interior of the basilica in much the same way that enthroned statues of Greco-Roman divinities loomed over awestruck mortals who entered the cellas of pagan temples.

The Basilica Nova ruins never fail to impress tourists with their size and mass. The original structure was 300 feet long and 215 feet wide. Brick-faced concrete walls 20 feet thick supported coffered barrel vaults in the aisles. These vaults also buttressed the groin vaults of the nave, which was 115 feet high. The walls and floors were richly marbled and stuccoed, and could be readily admired by those who came to the basilica to conduct business, because the groin vaults permitted ample light to enter the nave directly. Our reconstruction effectively suggests the immensity of the interior, where the great vaults dwarf not only humans but also even the emperor's colossal portrait. The drawing also clearly reveals the fenestration of the groin vaults, a lighting system akin to the clerestory of a traditional stone-and-timber basilica. The

10-79 Reconstruction drawing of the Basilica Nova (Basilica of Constantine), Rome, Italy, ca. 306–312 CE.

lessons learned in the design and construction of buildings such as Trajan's great market hall (FIG. 10-43) and the Baths of Caracalla (FIG. 10-68) were applied here to the Roman basilica.

Although one could argue that the Basilica Nova was the ideal solution to the problem of basilica design with its spacious, well-lit interior and economical, fire-resistant concrete frame, it became the exception rather than the rule. The traditional basilica form exemplified by Trajan's Basilica Ulpia (FIG. 10-41) remained the norm for centuries.

CONSTANTINE IN GERMANY At Trier (ancient Augusta Treverorum) on the Moselle River in Germany, the imperial seat of Constantius Chlorus as Caesar of the West, Constantine built a new palace complex. It included a basilica-like audience hall, the Aula Palatina (FIG. **10-80**), of traditional form and materials. The Aula Palatina measures about 190 feet long and 95 feet wide. Its austere brick exterior characterized much later Roman—and Early Christian—architecture. The verticality of the building's boldly projecting buttresses originally was lessened by horizontal timber galleries, which permitted the servicing of the windows. The brick wall was stuccoed in grayish white. The use of lead-framed panes of glass for the windows enabled Late Roman builders to give life and movement to blank exterior surfaces.

Inside (FIG. **10-81**), the audience hall was also very simple. Its flat, wooden, coffered ceiling is some 95 feet above the floor. The interior has no aisles, just a wide space with two stories of large windows that provide ample light. At the narrow north end, the main hall is divided from the semicircular apse (which also has a flat ceiling) by a so-called *triumphal arch*. The Aula Palatina's interior is quite severe, although the arch and apse originally were covered with marble veneer and mosaics to provide a magnificent environment for the enthroned emperor. The design of both the interior and exterior was closely paralleled in many Early Christian basilicas (for example, see FIG. 11-8). The Aula Palatina itself was later converted into a Christian church.

10-80 Aula Palatina (exterior), Trier, Germany, early fourth century CE.

10-81 Aula Palatina (interior), Trier, Germany, early fourth century CE.

10-82 Coins with portraits of Constantine. Nummus *(top)*, 307 CE. Billon, diameter approx. 1″. American Numismatic Society, New York. Medallion *(bottom)*, ca. 315 CE. Silver, diameter approx. 1″. Staatliche Münzsammlung, Munich.

TWO FACES OF CONSTANTINE We close our survey of ancient Roman art with two portraits of Constantine stamped on Roman coins. These images reveal both the essential character of Roman imperial portraiture and the special nature of Constantinian art. The first (FIG. **10-82,** *top*) was struck shortly after the death of Constantine's father, when Constantine was in his early 20s and his position was still insecure. Here, in his official portrait, he appears considerably older, because he adopted the imagery of the tetrarchs. Indeed, were it not for the accompanying label identifying this Caesar as Constantine, it would be impossible to know who was portrayed.

Eight years later, after the defeat of Maxentius and the issuance of the Edict of Milan, Constantine's portrait (FIG. 10-82, *bottom*) was transformed. Clean-shaven and looking his actual 30 years of age, the unchallenged Augustus of the West rejected the mature tetrarchic "look" in favor of youth. Eternal youthfulness henceforth characterized all the emperor's portraits (compare FIG. 10-78) until his death more than two decades later. These two coins should dispel any uncertainty about the often fictive nature of imperial portraiture and the ability of Roman emperors to choose any official image that suited their needs. In Roman art, "portrait" is often not synonymous with "likeness."

CLASSICAL AND MEDIEVAL The later coin is also an eloquent testimony to the dual nature of Constantinian rule. The emperor appears in his important role as imperator (general), dressed in armor, wearing an ornate helmet, and carrying a shield bearing the enduring emblem of the Roman state — the she-wolf nursing Romulus and Remus (compare FIG. 9-10 and Roma's shield in FIG. 10-57). Yet he does not carry the scepter of the pagan Roman emperor. Rather, he holds a cross crowned by an orb. And at the crest of his helmet, at the front, just below the grand plume, is a disk containing the *Christogram,* the monogram made up of *chi* (X), *rho* (P), and *iota* (I), the initial letters of Christ's name in Greek (compare the shield one of the soldiers holds in FIG. 12-10).

Constantine was at once portrayed as Roman emperor and as a soldier in the army of the Lord. The coin, like Constantinian art in general, belongs both to the classical and to the medieval world.

CONCLUSION

In Europe, the Middle East, and Africa today, the remains of Roman civilization are everywhere. Roman temples and basilicas have an afterlife as churches. The powerful concrete vaults of ancient Roman buildings form the cores of modern houses, stores, restaurants, factories, and museums. Bullfights, sports events, operas, and rock concerts are staged in Roman amphitheaters. Roman aqueducts continue to supply water to some modern towns. Ships dock in what were once Roman ports, and western Europe's highway system still closely follows the routes of Roman roads.

Roman civilization also lives on in law and government, in languages, in the calendar — even in the coins used daily. Roman art speaks in a language almost everyone can readily understand. Its diversity and eclecticism foreshadowed the modern world. The Roman use of art, especially portraits and historical relief sculptures, to manipulate public opinion is similar to the carefully crafted imagery of contemporary political campaigns. And the Roman mastery of concrete construction began an architectural revolution still felt today. Indeed, the Roman Empire is the bridge — in politics, the arts, and religion — between the ancient and the medieval and modern Western worlds.

753 BCE

KINGS

▌ FOUNDATION OF ROME BY ROMULUS, 753 BCE

509 BCE

REPUBLIC

▌ EXPULSION OF ETRUSCAN KINGS FROM ROME, 509 BCE

▌ MARCELLUS BRINGS SPOILS OF SYRACUSE TO ROME, 211 BCE

▌ ROMAN CONQUEST OF GREECE, 146 BCE

▌ ROME INHERITS KINGDOM OF PERGAMON, 133 BCE

▌ FOUNDATION OF ROMAN COLONY AT POMPEII, 80 BCE

1 ▌ ASSASSINATION OF JULIUS CAESAR, 44 BCE

▌ BATTLE OF ACTIUM, 31 BCE

1 House of the Vettii, Pompeii, second century BCE

27 BCE

EARLY EMPIRE

2 ▌ AUGUSTUS, R. 27 BCE–14 CE

▌ VITRUVIUS, *The Ten Books of Architecture*, CA. 25 BCE

▌ VERGIL, 70–19 BCE

▌ JULIO-CLAUDIANS, R. 14–68 CE

▌ FLAVIANS, R. 69–96

▌ ERUPTION OF MOUNT VESUVIUS, 79

2 Portrait of Augustus, from Primaporta, ca. 20 BCE

96 CE

HIGH EMPIRE

▌ TRAJAN, R. 98–117

3 ▌ HADRIAN, R. 117–138

▌ ANTONINES, R. 138–192

192

LATE EMPIRE

▌ SEVERANS, R. 193–235

▌ SOLDIER EMPERORS, R. 235–284

▌ DIOCLETIAN, R. 284–305

▌ CONSTANTINE, R. 306–337

▌ DEDICATION OF CONSTANTINOPLE, 330

3 Pantheon, Rome, 118–125

4

337

4 Arch of Constantine, Rome, 312–315

Rebecca and Eliezer at the well, folio 7 recto of the *Vienna Genesis,* early sixth century. Tempera, gold, and silver on purple vellum, approx. $1'\frac{1}{4}'' \times 9\frac{1}{4}''$. Österreichische Nationalbibliothek, Vienna.

11

PAGANS, CHRISTIANS, AND JEWS

THE ART OF LATE ANTIQUITY

The Roman Empire was home to an extraordinarily diverse population. In Rome alone on any given day, someone walking through the city's various quarters would have encountered people of an astonishing range of social, ethnic, racial, linguistic, and religious backgrounds. And the multicultural character of Roman society became only more pronounced as the empire grew. The previous chapter focused on the rich legacy of art and architecture bequeathed by the pagan Roman world. But during the third and fourth centuries a rapidly growing number of people rejected the emperors' polytheism (belief in multiple gods) in favor of monotheism (the worship of a single all-powerful god). This chapter addresses the Jewish and Christian art produced under Roman rule. These Late Antique sculptures, paintings, mosaics, and buildings occupy a special place in our account of art through the ages because they formed the foundation of the art and architecture of the Middle Ages.

DURA-EUROPOS The powerful religious crosscurrents of late antiquity may be seen in microcosm in a distant outpost of the Roman Empire on a promontory overlooking the Euphrates River in Syria (MAP **11-1**). Called Europos by the Greeks and Dura by the Romans, the town probably was founded shortly after the death of Alexander the Great by one of his successors. By the end of the second century BCE, Dura-Europos was in the hands of the Parthians. The Roman emperor Trajan captured the city in 115 CE, but Dura reverted to Parthian control shortly thereafter.* In 165, under Marcus Aurelius, the Romans retook the city and placed a permanent garrison there. Dura-Europos fell in 256 to Rome's new enemy in the East, the Sasanians, heirs to the Parthian Empire (see Chapter 2). The Sasanian victory at Dura is an important fixed point in the chronology of late antiquity because the fortified town's population was evacuated and its buildings left largely intact. This "Pompeii of the desert" has revealed the remains of more than a dozen different cult buildings, including many shrines of the polytheistic religions of the Mediterranean and Near East. But the excavators also discovered worship places for the monotheistic creeds of Judaism and Christianity, even though neither was an approved religion in the Roman state.

---

* From this point on, all dates in this chapter are CE unless otherwise stated.

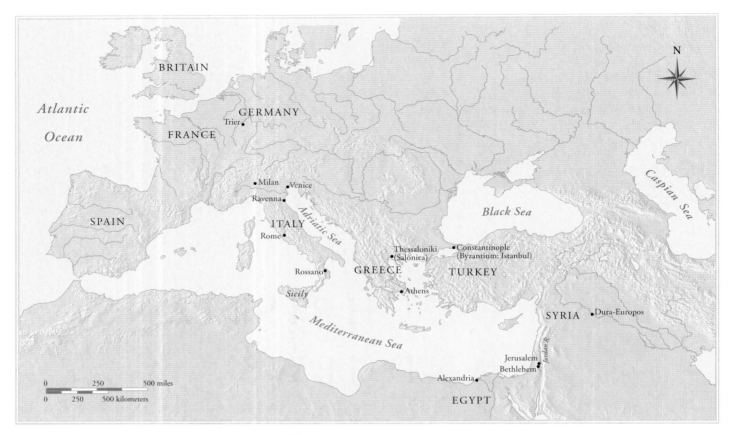

MAP 11-1 Europe and the Near East in late antiquity.

SYNAGOGUE PAINTINGS The synagogue at Dura-Europos is remarkable not only for its very existence in a Roman garrison town but also for its extensive cycle of mural paintings (FIG. **11-1**) depicting biblical themes. The building, originally a private house with a central courtyard, was converted into a synagogue during the latter part of the second century. The paintings surprised scholars when they were first reported, because they seem to defy the Bible's Second Commandment prohibiting the making of graven images. It is now apparent that although the Jews of the Roman Empire did not worship idols as did their pagan contemporaries, biblical stories appeared on the painted walls of synagogues and probably also in painted manuscripts, although no illustrated Bible of this period survives. God (YHWH, or Yahweh in the Old Testament), however, never appears in the Dura paintings, except as a hand emerging from the top of the framed panels.

The Dura murals are mostly devoid of action, even when the subject is a narrative theme. The artists tell the stories through stylized gestures, and the figures, which have expressionless features and lack both volume and shadow, tend to stand in frontal rows. This Late Antique style, discussed in Chapter 10, is characteristic of much pagan art during the third and fourth centuries, including the friezes of the Arch of Septimius Severus at Lepcis Magna (see FIG. 10-66) and the Arch of Constantine in Rome (FIG. 10-77). The style of the Dura synagogue paintings is thus consistent with a major artistic trend in pagan, Jewish, and Christian art alike during the Late Roman Empire.

The Dura painting of Samuel anointing David (FIG. 11-1, center) exemplifies the Late Antique style. The episode is depicted just to the right of the niche that housed the sacred Jewish *Torah* (the scroll containing the *Pentateuch,* the first five books of the Hebrew Scriptures). The prophet anoints the future king of Israel, while David's six older brothers look on. The painter drew attention to

Samuel by depicting him larger than all the rest, a familiar convention of Late Antique art. David and his brothers are emotionless and almost disembodied spiritual presences. Their bodies do not even have enough feet! David, however, is distinguished from his brothers by the purple toga he wears. Purple was the color associated with the Roman emperor. The Dura artist borrowed the imperial toga to signify David's royalty.

BAPTISM IN AN OLD HOUSE The Christian community house (FIG. **11-2**) at Dura-Europos was also a remodeled private residence with a central courtyard. Its meeting hall (created by breaking down the partition between two rooms on the court's south side) could accommodate no more than about 70 people at a time. It had a raised platform at one end where the congregation leader sat or stood. Another room, on the opposite side of the courtyard, had a canopy-covered font for baptismal rites, the all-important ceremony initiating a new convert into the Christian community. Upstairs a communal dining room may have existed for the celebration of the *Eucharist,* when the faithful partook of the bread and wine symbolic of the body and blood of Christ (see "The Life of Jesus in Art," pages 308–309).

Although the baptistery had mural paintings (poorly preserved), the place where Christians gathered to worship at Dura, as elsewhere in the Roman Empire, was a modest secondhand house, in striking contrast to the grand temples of the Roman gods. Without the approval of the state, Christian communities remained small in number and often attracted the most impoverished classes of society. They found the promise of an afterlife where rich and poor were judged on equal terms especially appealing. Nonetheless, the emperor Diocletian was so concerned by the growing popularity of Christianity in the Roman army ranks that he ordered a fresh round of persecutions in 303 to 305, a half

11-1 Interior of the synagogue at Dura-Europos, Syria, with wall paintings of Old Testament themes, ca. 245–256. Tempera on plaster. Reconstruction in National Museum, Damascus.

0 10 20 30 40 50 FEET
0 5 10 15 METERS

1. Courtyard of private house converted into Christian community house
2. Meeting hall
3. Baptistery

11-2 Reconstruction of the Christian community house at Dura-Europos, Syria, ca. 240–256.

century after the last great persecutions under Trajan Decius. The Romans hated the Christians because of their alien beliefs—that their god had been incarnated in the body of a man and that the death and Resurrection of the god-man Christ made possible the salvation and redemption of all. But they also hated them because they refused to pay even token homage to the Roman state's official gods (which included deified emperors as well as the traditional pantheon of classical gods and goddesses). As Christianity's appeal grew, so too did the Roman state's fear of weakening imperial authority. Persecution ended only when Constantine, after defeating Maxentius at the Milvian Bridge in Rome in 312, came to believe that the Christian god was the source of his power rather than a threat to it. A year after that victory, the Edict of Milan brought an end to the official mistreatment of Christians.

THE CATACOMBS
AND FUNERARY ART

THE "HOLLOWS" OF ROME Very little is known about the art of the first Christians. When we speak of "Early Christian art," we mean the earliest preserved works with Christian subjects, not the art of Christians at the time of Jesus. Most Early Christian art in Rome dates to the third and fourth centuries and is found in the *catacombs*—vast subterranean networks of galleries (passageways) and chambers designed as cemeteries for burying the Christian dead, many of them sainted martyrs. To a much lesser extent, the catacombs also housed the graves of Jews and others. The builders tunneled the catacombs out of the tufa bedrock, much as the Etruscans created the underground tomb chambers in the necropolis at Cerveteri (see FIG. 9-7). The catacombs are less elaborate than the Etruscan tombs, but much more extensive. The name derives from the Latin *ad catacumbas,* which means "in the hollows." The catacombs in Rome (others exist elsewhere) comprise galleries estimated to run for 60 to 90 miles—and additional catacombs may be discovered yet. From the second through the fourth centuries, these catacombs were in constant use, housing as many as four million bodies.

In accordance with Roman custom, Christians had to be buried outside a city's walls on private property, usually purchased by a *confraternity,* or association, of Christian families pooling funds. Each of the catacombs was initially of modest extent. First, the builders dug a gallery three to four feet wide around the perimeter of the burial ground at a convenient level below the surface. In the walls of these galleries, they cut openings to receive the bodies of the dead. These openings, called *loculi,* were placed one above another, like shelves. Often, the Christians carved small rooms out of the rock, called *cubicula* (as in Roman houses of the living), to serve as mortuary chapels. Once the original perimeter galleries were full of loculi and cubicula, they cut other galleries at right angles to them. This process continued as long as lateral space permitted. They then dug lower levels connected by staircases. Some catacomb systems extended as deep as five levels. When adjacent burial areas belonged to members of the same Christian confraternity, or by gift or purchase fell into the same hands, the owners opened passageways between the respective cemeteries. The galleries thus spread laterally and gradually acquired a vast extent. After Christianity received official approval, churches rose on the land above the catacombs so that the pious could worship openly at the grave sites of some of the earliest Christian martyrs.

Painting

JONAH AND JESUS The frescoes that decorated many cubicula were Roman in style but Christian in subject. The ceiling (FIG. 11-3) of a cubiculum in the Catacomb of Saints Peter and Marcellinus in Rome, for example, is similar to the second-century frescoed vault (see FIG. 10-54) in the Insula of the Painted Vaults at Ostia. In the catacomb, the polygonal frame of the Ostian spoked-wheel design became a large circle with the symbol of the Christian faith, the cross, at its center. The arms of the cross terminate in four *lunettes* (semicircular frames), which also find parallels in the Ostian composition.

The lunettes contain the key episodes from the Old Testament story of Jonah. The sailors throw him from his ship on the left. He emerges on the right from the "whale" (the Greek word is *ketos,* or sea dragon, and that is how the artist represented the monstrous marine creature that swallowed Jonah). And, safe on land at the bottom, Jonah contemplates the miracle of his salvation and the mercy of God. Jonah was a popular figure in Early Christian painting and sculpture, especially in funerary contexts. The Christians honored him as a *prefiguration* (prophetic forerunner) of Christ, who rose from death as Jonah had been delivered from the belly of the ketos, also after three days. Old Testament miracles prefiguring

11-3 The Good Shepherd, the story of Jonah, and orants, painted ceiling of a cubiculum in the Catacomb of Saints Peter and Marcellinus, Rome, Italy, early fourth century.

Jewish Subjects in Christian Art

From the beginning, the Old Testament played an important role in Christian life and Christian art, in part because Jesus was a Jew and so many of the first Christians were converted Jews, but also because Christians came to view many of the persons and events of the Old Testament as prefigurations of New Testament persons and events. Christ himself established the pattern for this kind of biblical interpretation when he compared Jonah's spending three days in the belly of the sea monster (usually translated as "whale" in English) to the comparable time he would be entombed in the earth before his Resurrection (Matt. 12:40). In the fourth century, Saint Augustine (354–430) confirmed the validity of this approach to the Old Testament when he stated that "the New Testament is hidden in the Old; the Old is clarified by the New."[1]

Thus the Old Testament figured prominently in Early Christian art in all media. Biblical tales of Jewish faith and salvation were especially common in funerary contexts but appeared also in churches and on household objects. The Old Testament stories depicted in paintings, sculptures, and mosaics discussed in Chapters 11 and 12 are listed here.

JONAH (FIGS. 11-3 and 11-4) Jonah, an Old Testament prophet, had disobeyed God's command. In his wrath, the Lord caused a storm while Jonah was at sea. Jonah asked the sailors to throw him overboard, and the storm subsided. A sea dragon then swallowed Jonah, but God answered his prayers, and the monster spat out Jonah after three days and nights, foretelling Christ's Resurrection.

ABRAHAM AND THE THREE ANGELS (see FIGS. 12-8, upper right, and 12-34) Sarah, wife of Abraham, the father of the Hebrew nation, was 90 years old and childless when three angels visited Abraham. They announced that Sarah would bear a son, and she later miraculously gave birth to Isaac. Christians believe the Old Testament angels symbolized the Holy Trinity.

SACRIFICE OF ISAAC (FIGS. 11-5 and 12-8, upper right) God instructed Abraham to sacrifice Isaac, his only son, as proof of his faith. When it became clear that Abraham would obey, the Lord sent an angel to restrain him and provided a ram for sacrifice in Isaac's place. Christians view this episode as a prefiguration of the sacrifice of God's only son, Jesus.

DANIEL (FIG. 11-5) Daniel, one of the most important Jewish prophets, violated a Persian decree against prayer, and the Persians threw him into a den of lions. God sent an angel to shut the lions' mouths, and Daniel emerged unharmed. Like Jonah's story, this is an Old Testament salvation tale, a precursor of Christ's triumph over death.

ADAM AND EVE (FIG. 11-5) Eve, the first woman, tempted by a serpent, ate the forbidden fruit of the tree of knowledge. She also fed some to Adam, the first man. As punishment, God expelled Adam and Eve from Paradise. This "Original Sin" ultimately led to Christ's sacrifice on the cross so that all humankind could be saved. Christian theologians often consider Christ the new Adam and his mother, Mary, the new Eve.

[1] Augustine, *City of God*, 16.26.

Christ's Resurrection abound in the catacombs and in Early Christian art in general (see "Jewish Subjects in Christian Art," above).

CHRIST AND HIS SHEEP A man, a woman, and at least one child occupy the compartments between the Jonah lunettes. They are *orants* (praying figures), raising their arms in the ancient attitude of prayer. Together they make up a cross-section of the Christian family seeking a heavenly afterlife. The cross's central medallion shows Christ as the Good Shepherd, whose powers of salvation are underscored by his juxtaposition with Jonah's story. The motif can be traced back to Archaic Greek art (see FIG. 5-9), but there the pagan calf bearer offered his sheep in sacrifice to Athena. In Early Christian art, Christ is the youthful and loyal protector of the Christian flock, who said to his disciples, "I am the good shepherd; the good shepherd gives his life for the sheep" (John 10:11). In the Christian motif, the sheep on Christ's shoulders is one of the lost sheep he has retrieved, symbolizing a sinner who has strayed and been rescued.

Prior to the fourth century, artists almost invariably represented Christ either as the Good Shepherd or as a teacher. Only after Christianity became the Roman Empire's official religion did Christ take on in art such imperial attributes as the halo, the purple robe, and the throne, which denoted rulership. Eventually artists depicted Christ with the beard of a mature adult, which has been the standard form for centuries, supplanting the youthful imagery of most Early Christian portrayals of Christ.

Sculpture

COFFINS FOR THE FAITHFUL All Christians rejected cremation, and the wealthiest Christian faithful, like their pagan contemporaries, favored impressive marble sarcophagi. Many of these coffins have survived in the catacombs and elsewhere. As one would expect, the most common themes painted on the walls and vaults of the Roman subterranean cemeteries were also the subjects that appeared on Early Christian sarcophagi. Often, the decoration of the marble coffins was a collection of significant Christian themes, just as on the painted ceiling in the Catacomb of Saints Peter and Marcellinus (FIG. 11-3).

On the front of a sarcophagus (FIG. **11-4**) in Santa Maria Antiqua in Rome, the story of Jonah takes up the left third. At the center are an orant and a seated philosopher, the latter a motif borrowed directly from contemporary pagan sarcophagi (see FIG. 10-72). The heads of both the praying woman and the seated man reading from a scroll are unfinished. Roman workshops often produced sarcophagi before knowing who would purchase them. The sculptors added the portraits at the time of burial, if they added them at all. This practice underscores the universal appeal of the themes chosen. At the right are two different, yet linked, representations of Jesus—as the Good Shepherd and as a child receiving baptism in the Jordan River, though he really was baptized at age 30 (see "The Life of Jesus in Art," pages 308–309). The sculptor suggested the future

11-4 Sarcophagus with philosopher, orant, and Old and New Testament scenes, Santa Maria Antiqua, Rome, Italy, ca. 270. Marble, 1' 11$\frac{1}{4}$" × 7' 2".

ministry of the baptized Jesus by turning the child's head toward the Good Shepherd and by placing his right hand on one of the sheep. In the early centuries of Christianity, baptism was usually delayed almost to the moment of death because it cleansed the Christian of all sin. One of those who was baptized on his deathbed was the emperor Constantine (see Chapter 10).

A CONVERT'S SARCOPHAGUS Another pagan convert to Christianity was the city prefect of Rome, Junius Bassus, who, according to the inscription on his sarcophagus (FIG. **11-5**), was baptized just before he died in 359. The sarcophagus, decorated only on

three sides in the western Roman manner (see Chapter 10), is, however, divided into two registers of five compartments, each framed by columns in the tradition of Asiatic sarcophagi (see FIG. 10-62). In contrast to the Santa Maria Antiqua sarcophagus, the deceased does not appear on the body of the coffin. Instead, stories from the Old and New Testaments fill the 10 niches. Christ has pride of place and appears in the central compartment of each register: as a teacher enthroned between his chief apostles, Saints Peter and Paul (above), and triumphantly entering Jerusalem on a donkey (below). Appropriately, the scene of Christ's heavenly triumph is situated above that of his earthly triumph. Both compositions owe a great deal to

11-5 Sarcophagus of Junius Bassus, from Rome, Italy, ca. 359. Marble, 3' 10$\frac{1}{2}$" × 8'. Museo Storico del Tesoro della Basilica di San Pietro, Rome.

11-6 Christ seated, from Civita Latina, Italy, ca. 350–375. Marble, approx. 2′ 4½″ high. Museo Nazionale Romano — Palazzo Massimo alle Terme, Rome.

Bassus and other Christians, whether they were converts from paganism or from Judaism, hoped for a similar salvation.

AN "IDOL" OF CHRIST Apart from the reliefs on privately commissioned sarcophagi, monumental sculpture became increasingly uncommon in the fourth century. Portrait statues of Roman emperors and other officials continued to be erected, and statues of pagan gods and mythological figures were still made, but their numbers decreased sharply. In his *Apologia,* Justin Martyr, a second-century philosopher who converted to Christianity and was mindful of the Second Commandment's admonition to shun graven images, accused the pagans of worshiping statues as gods. Christians tended to suspect the freestanding statue, linking it with the false gods of the pagans, so Early Christian houses of worship had no "cult statues." Nor did the first churches have any equivalent of the pedimental statues and relief friezes of Greco-Roman temples.

The Greco-Roman experience, however, was still a living part of the Mediterranean mentality, and many Christians like Junius Bassus were recent converts from paganism who retained some of their classical values. This may account for those rare instances of Early Christian "idols," such as the marble statuette of the seated Christ shown here (FIG. **11-6**). Less than three feet tall, the sculpture is a freestanding version of the Christ between Saints Peter and Paul on the Junius Bassus sarcophagus (FIG. 11-5). As on the relief, Christ's head is that of a long-haired Apollo-like youth, but the statuary type was one employed for bearded Roman philosophers of advanced age. Like those learned men, Christ wears the Roman tunic, toga, and sandals, and holds an unopened scroll in his left hand. The piece is unique and, unfortunately, of unknown provenance, so art historians only can speculate about its original context and function. Several third- and fourth-century marble statuettes of Christ as the Good Shepherd and of Jonah also survive, but they too are exceptional. Monumental sculpture of Christian character was not significant in the history of art until the 12th century (see Chapter 17).

ARCHITECTURE AND MOSAICS

IMPERIAL PATRONAGE Although some Christian ceremonies were held in the catacombs, regular services took place in private community houses of the type found at Dura-Europos (FIG. 11-2). Once Christianity achieved imperial sponsorship under Constantine, an urgent need suddenly arose to construct churches. The new buildings had to meet the requirements of Christian liturgy, provide a suitably monumental setting for the celebration of the Christian faith, and accommodate the rapidly growing numbers of worshipers.

Constantine was convinced that the Christian god had guided him to victory over Maxentius, and in lifelong gratitude he protected and advanced Christianity throughout the empire, as well as in the obstinately pagan capital city of Rome. As emperor, he was, of course, obliged to safeguard the ancient Roman religion, traditions, and monuments, and, as noted in Chapter 10, he was (for his time) a builder on a grand scale in the heart of the city. But eager to provide buildings to house the Christian rituals and venerated burial places, especially the memorials of founding saints, Constantine also was the first major patron of Christian architecture. He constructed elaborate basilicas, memorials, and mausoleums not only in Rome but also in Constantinople, his "New Rome" in the East, and at sites sacred to Christianity, most notably Bethlehem, the birthplace of Jesus, and Jerusalem, the site of his crucifixion.

pagan Roman art. In the upper zone, Christ, like an enthroned Roman emperor, sits above a personification of the sky god holding a billowing mantle over his head, indicating that Christ is ruler of the universe. The scene below derives in part from portrayals of Roman emperors entering cities on horseback, but Christ's steed and the absence of imperial attributes contrast sharply with the imperial models the sculptor used as compositional sources.

The Old Testament scenes on the Junius Bassus sarcophagus were chosen for their significance in the early Christian Church. Adam and Eve, for example, are in the second niche from the left on the lower level. Their Original Sin of eating the apple in the Garden of Eden ultimately necessitated Christ's sacrifice for the salvation of humankind. To the right of the entry into Jerusalem is Daniel, unscathed by flanking lions, saved by his faith. At the upper left, Abraham is about to sacrifice Isaac. Christians believe that this Old Testament story was a prefiguration of God's sacrifice of his own son, Jesus.

The Crucifixion itself, however, does not appear on the Junius Bassus sarcophagus. Indeed, the subject was very rare in Early Christian art, and unknown prior to the fifth century. Artists emphasized Christ's divinity and exemplary life as teacher and miracle worker, not his suffering and death at the hands of the Romans. This sculptor, however, alluded to the Crucifixion in the scenes in the two compartments at the upper right depicting Jesus being led before Pontius Pilate for judgment. The Romans condemned Jesus to death, but he triumphantly overcame it. Junius

The Life of Jesus in Art

Christians believe that Jesus of Nazareth is the son of God, the *Messiah* (Savior, *Christ*) of the Jews prophesied in the Old Testament. His life—his miraculous birth from the womb of a virgin mother, his preaching and miracle working, his execution by the Romans and subsequent ascent to heaven—has been the subject of countless artworks from Roman times through the present day. The primary literary sources for these representations are the Gospels of the New Testament attributed to the Four Evangelists, Saints Matthew, Mark, Luke, and John (see "The Four Evangelists," Chapter 16, page 426); later apocryphal works; and commentaries on these texts by medieval theologians.

The life of Jesus dominated the subject matter of Christian art to a far greater extent than Greco-Roman religion and mythology ever did classical art. Whereas images of athletes, portraits of statesmen and philosophers, narratives of war and peace, genre scenes, and other secular subjects were staples of the classical tradition, Christian iconography held a near monopoly in the art of the Western world in the Middle Ages.

Although many of the events of Jesus' life were rarely or never depicted during certain periods, the cycle as a whole has been one of the most frequent subjects of Western art, even after the revival of classical and secular themes in the Renaissance. Thus it is useful to summarize the entire cycle here in one place, giving selected references to illustrations of the various episodes, from late antiquity to the 17th century. We describe the events as they usually appear in the artworks.

INCARNATION AND CHILDHOOD

The first "cycle" of the life of Jesus consists of the events of his conception, birth, infancy, and childhood.

ANNUNCIATION TO MARY (see FIGS. 12-33, 19-12, and 21-36) The archangel Gabriel announces to the Virgin Mary that she will miraculously conceive and give birth to God's son Jesus. God's presence at the *Incarnation* is sometimes indicated by a dove, the symbol of the Holy Spirit, the third "person" of the Trinity with God the Father and Jesus.

VISITATION (see FIG. 18-22) The pregnant Mary visits Elizabeth, her older cousin, who is pregnant with the future Saint John the Baptist. Elizabeth is the first to recognize that the baby Mary is bearing is the Son of God, and they rejoice.

NATIVITY (see FIGS. 13-30, 19-3, and 19-4), **ANNUNCIATION TO THE SHEPHERDS** (see FIG. 16-28), and **ADORATION OF THE SHEPHERDS** (see FIG. 24-64) Jesus is born at night in Bethlehem and placed in a basket. Mary and her husband Joseph marvel at the newborn in a stable or, in Byzantine art, in a cave. An angel announces the birth of the Savior to shepherds in the field, who rush to Bethlehem to adore the child.

ADORATION OF THE MAGI (see FIG. 21-9) A bright star alerts three wise men *(magi)* in the East that the King of the Jews has been born. They travel 12 days to find the Holy Family and present precious gifts to the infant Jesus.

PRESENTATION IN THE TEMPLE (see FIG. 13-30) In accordance with Jewish tradition, Mary and Joseph bring their firstborn son to the temple in Jerusalem, where the aged Simeon, who God said would not die until he had seen the Messiah, recognizes Jesus as the prophesied Savior of humankind.

MASSACRE OF THE INNOCENTS and **FLIGHT INTO EGYPT** King Herod, fearful that a rival king has been born, orders the massacre of all infants in Bethlehem, but an angel warns the Holy Family and they escape to Egypt.

DISPUTE IN THE TEMPLE Joseph and Mary travel to Jerusalem for the feast of Passover (the celebration of the release of the Jews from bondage to the pharaohs of Egypt). Jesus, only 12 years old at the time, engages in learned debate with astonished Jewish scholars in the temple, foretelling his ministry.

PUBLIC MINISTRY

The public ministry cycle comprises the teachings of Jesus and the miracles he performed.

BAPTISM (FIG. 11-4) The beginning of Jesus' public ministry is marked by his baptism at age 30 by John the Baptist in the Jordan River, where the dove of the Holy Spirit appears and God's voice is heard proclaiming Jesus as his son.

CALLING OF MATTHEW (see FIG. 24-19) Jesus summons Matthew, a tax collector, to follow him, and Matthew becomes one of his 12 disciples, or *apostles* (from the Greek for "messenger"), and later the author of one of the four Gospels.

MIRACLES In the course of his teaching and travels, Jesus performs many miracles, revealing his divine nature. These include acts of healing and the raising of the dead, the turning of water into wine, walking on water and calming storms, and the creation of wondrous quantities of food. In the miracle of loaves and fishes (FIG. 11-17), for example, Jesus transforms a few loaves of bread and a handful of fishes into enough food to feed several thousand people.

DELIVERY OF THE KEYS TO PETER (see FIG. 21-40) The fisherman Peter was one of the first Jesus summoned as a disciple. Jesus chooses Peter (whose name means "rock") as his successor. He declares that Peter is the rock on which his church will be built, and symbolically delivers to Peter the keys to the Kingdom of Heaven.

TRANSFIGURATION (see FIG. 12-13) Jesus scales a high mountain and, in the presence of Peter and two other disciples, James and John the Evangelist, is transformed into radiant light. God, speaking from a cloud, discloses that Jesus is his son.

CLEANSING OF THE TEMPLE Jesus returns to Jerusalem, where he finds money changers and merchants conducting business in the temple. He rebukes them and drives them out of the sacred precinct.

The Life of Jesus in Art (continued)

PASSION

The Passion (from Latin *passio,* "suffering") cycle includes the episodes leading to Jesus' death, Resurrection, and ascent to heaven.

ENTRY INTO JERUSALEM (FIGS. 11-5 and 13-30) On the Sunday before his Crucifixion (Palm Sunday), Jesus rides triumphantly into Jerusalem on a donkey, accompanied by disciples. Crowds of people enthusiastically greet Jesus and place palm fronds in his path.

LAST SUPPER (see FIGS. 20-9, 21-37, 22-3, 22-52, and 23-4) and *WASHING OF THE DISCIPLES' FEET* In Jerusalem, Jesus celebrates Passover with his disciples. During this Last Supper, Jesus foretells his imminent betrayal, arrest, and death and invites the disciples to remember him when they eat bread (symbol of his body) and drink wine (his blood). This ritual became the celebration of *Mass (Eucharist)* in the Christian Church. At the same meal, Jesus sets an example of humility for his apostles by washing their feet.

AGONY IN THE GARDEN Jesus goes to the Mount of Olives in the Garden of Gethsemane, where he struggles to overcome his human fear of death by praying for divine strength. The apostles who accompanied him there fall asleep despite his request that they stay awake with him while he prays.

BETRAYAL and *ARREST* (see FIG. 19-11) One of the disciples, Judas Iscariot, agrees to betray Jesus to the Jewish authorities in return for 30 pieces of silver. Judas identifies Jesus to the soldiers by kissing him, and Jesus is arrested. Later, a remorseful Judas hangs himself from a tree (FIG. 11-21).

TRIALS OF JESUS (FIGS. 11-5 and 11-20) and *DENIAL OF PETER* Jesus is brought before Caiaphas, the Jewish high priest, and is interrogated about his claim to be the Messiah. Meanwhile, the disciple Peter thrice denies knowing Jesus, as Jesus predicted he would. Jesus is then brought before the Roman governor of Judaea, Pontius Pilate, on the charge of treason because he had proclaimed himself as King of the Jews. Pilate asks the crowd to choose between freeing Jesus or Barabbas, a murderer. The people choose Barabbas, and the judge condemns Jesus to death. Pilate washes his hands, symbolically relieving himself of responsibility for the mob's decision.

FLAGELLATION and *MOCKING* The Roman soldiers who hold Jesus captive whip (flagellate) him and mock him by dressing him as King of the Jews and placing a crown of thorns on his head.

CARRYING OF THE CROSS, RAISING OF THE CROSS (see FIG. 24-34), and *CRUCIFIXION* (see FIGS. 11-21, 12-22, 16-15, and 16-26) The Romans force Jesus to carry the cross on which he will be cruci-

fied from Jerusalem to Mount Calvary (Golgotha, the "place of the skull," where Adam was buried). He falls three times and gets stripped along the way. Soldiers erect the cross and nail his hands and feet to it. Jesus' mother, John the Evangelist, and Mary Magdalene mourn at the foot of the cross, while soldiers torment Jesus. One of them (the centurion Longinus) stabs his side with a spear. After suffering great pain, Jesus dies. The Crucifixion occurred on a Friday, and Christians celebrate the day each year as Good Friday.

DEPOSITION (see FIGS. 20-7 and 22-42), *LAMENTATION* (see FIGS. 12-27 and 19-9), and *ENTOMBMENT* (see FIG. 17-33) Two disciples, Joseph of Arimathea and Nicodemus, remove Jesus' body from the cross (the Deposition); sometimes those present at the Crucifixion look on. They take Jesus to the tomb Joseph had purchased for himself, and Joseph, Nicodemus, the Virgin Mary, Saint John the Evangelist, and Mary Magdalene mourn over the dead Jesus (the Lamentation). (When in art the isolated figure of the Virgin Mary cradles her dead son in her lap, it is called a *Pietà* [Italian for "pity"; see FIG. 18-51].) In portrayals of the Entombment, his followers lower Jesus into a sarcophagus in the tomb.

DESCENT INTO LIMBO (see FIG. 12-31) During the three days he spends in the tomb, Jesus (after death, Christ) descends into Hell, or Limbo, and triumphantly frees the souls of the righteous, including Adam, Eve, Moses, David, Solomon, and John the Baptist. In Byzantine art, this episode is often labeled *Anastasis* (Greek, *resurrection*), although it refers to events preceding Christ's emergence from the tomb and reappearance on earth.

RESURRECTION and *THREE MARYS AT THE TOMB* On the third day (Easter Sunday), Christ rises from the dead and leaves the tomb while the guards outside are sleeping. The Virgin Mary, Mary Magdalene, and Mary, the mother of James, visit the tomb, find it empty, and learn from an angel that Christ has been resurrected.

NOLI ME TANGERE, SUPPER AT EMMAUS, and *DOUBTING OF THOMAS* During the 40 days between Christ's Resurrection and his ascent to heaven, he appears on several occasions to his followers. Christ warns Mary Magdalene, weeping at his tomb, with the words "Don't touch me" (*Noli me tangere* in Latin), but he tells her to inform the apostles of his return. At Emmaus he eats supper with two of his astonished disciples. Later, Thomas, who cannot believe that Christ has risen, is invited to touch the wound in his side that he received at his Crucifixion.

ASCENSION (see FIGS. 12-15 and 17-26) On the 40th day, on the Mount of Olives, with his mother and apostles as witnesses, Christ gloriously ascends to heaven in a cloud.

Rome

CONSTANTINE AND PETER Constantine's dual role as both Roman emperor and champion of the Christian faith was reflected in his decision to locate the new churches of Rome on the city's outskirts to avoid any confrontation between Christian and pagan ideologies. The greatest of Constantine's churches in Rome was Old Saint Peter's (FIG. **11-7**), probably begun as early as 319. The present-day church (see FIG. 24-4), one of the masterpieces of Italian Renaissance and Baroque architecture, is a replacement for the Constantinian structure. Old Saint Peter's stood on the western side of the Tiber River on the spot where Constantine and Pope Sylvester believed Peter, the first apostle and founder of the Christian community in Rome, had been buried (see "Constantine and Old Saint Peter's," page 311). Excavations in the Roman cemetery beneath the church have in fact revealed a second-century memorial erected in honor of the Christian martyr at his reputed grave. The great Constantinian church, capable of housing 3,000 to 4,000 worshipers at one time, was raised, at immense cost, upon a terrace over the ancient cemetery on the irregular slope of the Vatican Hill. It enshrined one of the most hallowed sites in Christendom, second only to the Holy Sepulcher in Jerusalem, the site of Christ's Resurrection. The project also fulfilled the figurative words of Christ himself, when he said, "Thou art Peter, and upon this rock I will build my church" (Matt. 16:18). Peter was Rome's first bishop and also the head of the long line of popes that extends to the present.

BASILICA TO CHURCH The plan and elevation of Old Saint Peter's resemble those of Roman basilicas and audience halls, such as the Basilica Ulpia in the Forum of Trajan (FIG. 10-41) and the Aula Palatina at Trier (see FIGS. 10-80 and 10-81), rather than the design of any Greco-Roman temple. The Christians, understandably, did not want their houses of worship to mimic the form of pagan shrines, but practical considerations also contributed to their shunning the pagan temple type. The Greco-Roman temple housed only the cult statue of the deity. All rituals took place outside at open-air altars. The classical temple, therefore, could have been adapted only with great difficulty as a building that could accommodate large numbers of people within it. The Roman basilica, in contrast, was ideally suited as a place for congregation.

Like Roman basilicas, Old Saint Peter's (FIG. 11-7) had a wide central *nave* (300 feet long) with flanking *aisles* and an *apse* at the

1. Nave   4. Transept
2. Aisles   5. Narthex
3. Apse   6. Atrium

11-7 Restored view *(a)*, plan *(b)*, and section *(c)* of Old Saint Peter's, Rome, Italy, begun ca. 320. (The restoration of the forecourt is conjectural.)

Constantine and Old Saint Peter's

Constantine the Great was the first emperor to sponsor the construction of churches in Rome. His generosity went well beyond providing land and erecting edifices. It extended to outfitting the interiors with costly altars, chandeliers, candlesticks, pitchers, goblets, and plates fashioned of gold and silver and sometimes embellished with jewels and pearls. The *Liber pontificalis,* or *Book of the Pontiffs (Popes),* compiled by an anonymous sixth-century author, provides a vivid picture of the emperor's involvement with the building of Old Saint Peter's (FIG. 11-7) and of his gifts to the new basilica, as well as a list of the income from imperial properties in cities in various parts of the Empire that was donated as an endowment for the new church. The information is contained in the life of Pope Sylvester, 34th bishop of Rome (r. 314–335).

> The emperor Constantine built a basilica to St. Peter the Apostle . . . where he buried the tomb with St. Peter's body. . . . He sealed [the tomb] on all sides with copper. . . . Above he decorated it with porphyry and other vine-scroll columns which he brought from Greece. He also built the basilica's apse-vault of shining gold-foil; and over St. Peter's body . . . he provided a cross of finest gold weighing 150 lb. . . . He also provided 4 brass candelabra, 10 ft in size, finished in silver . . . , each weighing 300 lb; 3 gold chalices with . . . jewels . . . ; 20 silver chalices . . . ; a gold paten . . . adorned with . . . jewels and with pearls, 215 in number . . . ; 5 silver patens; . . . a gold crown . . . , which is a chandelier, with 50 dolphins . . . ; 32 silver lights in the centre of the basilica, with dolphins . . . ; on the right of the basilica, 30 silver lights . . . ; the altar itself, of silver chased with gold, weighing 350 lb, decorated on all sides with . . . jewels and pearls, the jewels 400 in number; [and] a censer of finest gold, decorated on all sides with jewels, 60 in number.[1]

[1] Raymond Davis, trans., *The Book of Pontiffs* (Liverpool: Liverpool University Press, 1989), 18–19.

end. Preceding it was an open colonnaded courtyard, very much like the forum proper in the Forum of Trajan but called an *atrium,* like the central room in a private house. Worshipers entered the basilica through a *narthex,* or vestibule. When they emerged in the nave, they had an unobstructed view of the altar in the apse, framed by the so-called *triumphal arch* dividing the nave from the transept. The *transept,* or transverse aisle, an area perpendicular to the nave between the nave and apse, was a special feature of the Constantinian church. It housed the relics of Saint Peter that hordes of pilgrims came to see. (*Relics* are the body parts, clothing, or objects associated with a saint or Christ himself; see "Pilgrimages and the Cult of Relics," Chapter 17, page 449.) The transept became a standard element of church design in the West only much later, when it also took on, with the nave and apse, the symbolism of the Christian cross.

INSIDE AN EARLY CHURCH Unlike pagan temples, Old Saint Peter's was not adorned with lavish exterior sculptures. Its brick walls were as austere as those of the Aula Palatina at Trier (see FIG. 10-80). Inside, however, were frescoes and mosaics, marble columns (taken from pagan buildings, as was customary at the time), grandiose chandeliers, and gold and silver vessels on jeweled altar cloths for use in the Mass. A huge marble *baldacchino* (domical canopy over an altar), supported by four spiral columns, marked the spot of Saint Peter's tomb.

One can get some idea of the character of the timber-roofed interior of Old Saint Peter's by comparing our section drawing (FIG. 11-7c) with the photograph of the interior (FIG. **11-8**) of Santa Sabina in Rome. Santa Sabina, built a century later, is a basilican church of much more modest proportions, but it still retains its Early Christian character. The Corinthian columns of Santa

11-8 Interior of Santa Sabina, Rome, Italy, 422–432.

11-9 Interior of Santa Costanza, Rome, Italy, ca. 337–351.

Sabina's nave produce a steady rhythm that focuses all attention on the apse, which frames the altar. In Santa Sabina, as in Old Saint Peter's, the nave is drenched with light from the *clerestory* windows piercing the thin upper wall beneath the timber roof. The same light would have illuminated the frescoes and mosaics that commonly adorned the nave and apse of Early Christian churches. Outside, Santa Sabina has plain brick walls. They closely resemble the exterior of Trier's Aula Palatina (FIG. 10-80).

THE CENTRAL PLAN The rectangular basilican church design was long the favorite of the Western Christian world, but Early Christian architects also adopted another classical architectural type: the *central-plan* building. The type is so named because the building's parts are of equal or almost equal dimensions around the center. Roman central-plan buildings were usually round or polygonal domed structures. Byzantine architects developed this form to monumental proportions and amplified its theme in numerous ingenious variations. In the West, the central plan was used generally for structures adjacent to the main basilicas, such as mausoleums, baptisteries, and private chapels, rather than for actual churches, as in the East (see Chapter 12).

A highly refined example of the central-plan design is Santa Costanza in Rome (FIGS. 11-9 and 11-10), built in the mid-fourth century, possibly as the mausoleum for Constantina, the emperor Constantine's daughter. Recent excavations have called the traditional identification into question, but Constantina's monumental porphyry sarcophagus was placed in the building, even if the structure was not built as her tomb. The mausoleum, later converted into a church, stood next to the basilican church of Saint Agnes, whose tomb was in a nearby catacomb. Santa Costanza has antecedents that can be traced back to the beehive tombs of the Mycenaeans (see FIGS. 4-21 and 4-22), but its immediate predecessors were the domed structures of the Romans, such as the Pantheon (see FIGS. 10-48 to 10-50) and especially imperial mausolea such as Diocletian's at Split (see FIG. 10-75). At Santa Costanza, the interior design of the Roman buildings was modified to accommodate an

11-10 Longitudinal section *(top)* and plan *(bottom)* of Santa Costanza, Rome, Italy, ca. 337–351.

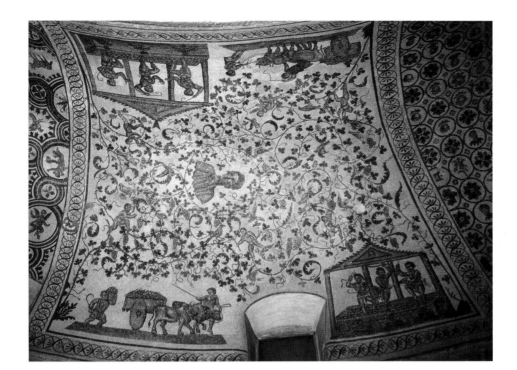

11-11 Detail of vault mosaic in the ambulatory of Santa Costanza, Rome, Italy, ca. 337–351.

ambulatory, a ringlike barrel-vaulted corridor separated from the central domed cylinder by a dozen pairs of columns. It is as if the nave of the Early Christian basilica with its clerestory wall were bent around a circle, the ambulatory corresponding to the basilican aisles.

A MOSAIC VINEYARD Like Early Christian basilicas, Santa Costanza has a severe brick exterior. Its interior was once richly adorned with mosaics, although most are lost. Old and New Testament themes appeared side by side, as in the catacombs and on Early Christian sarcophagi. The Santa Costanza mosaic program, however, also included pagan subjects, although they were susceptible to a Christian interpretation. In our detail (FIG. **11-11**) of a mosaic in the ambulatory vault, a portrait bust is at the center of a rich vine scroll. There is a second bust in another section of the mosaic vault, but both are heavily restored, and the identification of the pair as Constantina and her husband is uncertain. Scenes of putti harvesting grapes and producing wine, echoing the decoration of Constantina's sarcophagus (not shown), surround the portraits. In the Roman world, wine was primarily associated with Bacchus, but for a Christian, the imagery of the Santa Costanza mosaics brought to mind the wine of the Eucharist and the blood of Christ.

Mosaic decoration played an important role in the interiors of Early Christian buildings (see "Mosaics," page 315). When, under Constantine, Christianity suddenly became a public and official religion in Rome, not only were new buildings required in order to house the faithful, but wholesale decoration programs for the churches also became necessary. To advertise the new faith in all its diverse aspects—its dogma, scriptural narrative, and symbolism—and to instruct and edify believers, acres of walls in dozens of new churches had to be filled in the style and medium that would carry the message most effectively.

CHRIST AS SUN GOD The earliest known mosaic of explicitly Christian content is the late-third-century vault mosaic (FIG. **11-12**) in a small Christian mausoleum not far from Saint Peter's tomb in the Roman cemetery beneath Old Saint Peter's. It depicts Christ in the guise of a familiar pagan deity, Sol Invictus (in Greek, Helios), the Invincible Sun, driving the sun chariot through the golden heavens. All about Christ are vines, as in Santa

Costanza (FIG. 11-11). He holds an orb in his left hand, characterizing him as ruler of the universe, another borrowing from the repertory of pagan Roman art. But viewers could easily distinguish the Christian charioteer from Sol by the halo around his head. The halo's rays suggest the pattern of a cross. This is a far more grandiose conception of Christ than the role of Good Shepherd, and a fitting theme for the vaulted ceiling above the deceased. Christ does appear, however, as the caretaker of the Christian flock below, on the west wall of the tomb. On the east wall, in typical Early Christian fashion, is the story of Jonah.

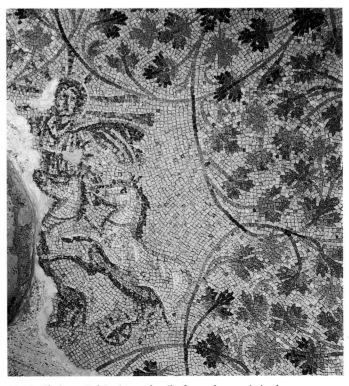

11-12 Christ as Sol Invictus, detail of a vault mosaic in the Mausoleum of the Julii, Rome, Italy, late third century.

11-13 The parting of Lot and Abraham, mosaic in the nave of Santa Maria Maggiore, Rome, Italy, 432–440.

ABRAHAM AND LOT Old Testament themes are the focus of the extensive fifth-century mosaic cycle in the nave of the basilican church of Santa Maria Maggiore in Rome, the first major church in the West dedicated to the Virgin Mary. The church was begun in 432, the year after Mary had been officially designated as the Mother of God (*Theotokos,* "bearer of god" in Greek) at the Council of Ephesus. A characteristic panel (FIG. **11-13**) of great dramatic power represents the parting of Abraham and his nephew Lot, as set forth in Genesis, the Bible's opening book. Agreeing to disagree, Lot leads his family and followers to the right, toward the city of Sodom, while Abraham heads for Canaan, moving toward a building (perhaps symbolizing the Christian Church) on the left. Lot's is the evil choice, and the instruments of the evil (his two daughters) are in front of him. The figure of the yet unborn Isaac, the instrument of good (and, as noted earlier, a prefiguration of Christ), stands before his father, Abraham.

The cleavage of the two groups is emphatic, and each group was represented by a shorthand device that could be called a "head cluster," which had precedents in antiquity and had a long history in Christian art. The figures turn from each other in a sharp dialogue of glance and gesture. The wide eyes, turned in their sockets; the broad gestures of enlarged hands; and the opposed movements of the groups all may remind viewers of a silent, expressive chorus that comments on the drama's action only with hands and bodies. Such simplified motion, characteristic of Late Antique narrative art of both pagan and Christian subject matter, has great power to communicate without ambiguity.

The heritage of classical art is, however, still apparent in the Santa Maria Maggiore mosaics. In the Abraham and Lot mosaic, for example, the background town and building would not be out of place in the spiral frieze of Trajan's Column (see FIG. 10-42).

The figures themselves also still loom with massive solidity. They cast shadows and were modeled in dark and light to give them their three-dimensional appearance. Another century had to pass before Western Christian mosaicists portrayed figures entirely as flat images, rather than as plastic bodies, finally rejecting the norms of classical art in favor of a style better suited for a focus on the spiritual instead of the natural world.

Ravenna

A CRUMBLING EMPIRE In the decades following the foundation in 324 of Constantinople, the New Rome in the East, and the death of Constantine in 337, the pace of Christianization of the Roman Empire quickened. In 380 the emperor Theodosius I issued an edict finally establishing Christianity as the state religion. In 391 he enacted a ban against pagan worship. In 394 the Olympic Games, the enduring symbol of the classical world and its values, were abolished. Theodosius died in 395, and imperial power passed to his two sons, Arcadius, who became Emperor of the East, and Honorius, Emperor of the West. The problems that plagued the last pagan emperors, most notably the threat of invasion from the north, did not, however, disappear with the conversion to Christianity.

In 404, when the Visigoths, under their king, Alaric, threatened to overrun Italy from the northwest, Honorius moved the capital of his crumbling empire from Milan to Ravenna, an ancient Roman city (perhaps founded by the Etruscans) near Italy's Adriatic coast, some 80 miles south of Venice. There, in a city surrounded by swamps and thus easily defended, his imperial authority survived the fall of Rome to Alaric in 410. Honorius died in 423, and the reins of government were taken by his half sister,

Mosaics

As an art form, mosaic had a rather simple and utilitarian beginning, seemingly invented primarily to provide an inexpensive and durable flooring. Originally, small beach pebbles were set, unaltered from their natural form and color, into a thick coat of cement. Artisans soon discovered, however, that the stones could be arranged in decorative patterns. At first, these *pebble mosaics* were uncomplicated and were confined to geometric shapes. Generally, the artists used only black and white stones. Examples of this type, dating back to the eighth century BCE, have been found at Gordion in Asia Minor. Eventually, artists arranged the stones to form more complex pictorial designs, and by the fourth century BCE the technique had developed to a high level of sophistication. Mosaicists depicted elaborate figural scenes using a broad range of colors—yellow, brown, and red in addition to black, white, and gray—and shaded the figures, clothing, and setting to suggest volume. Thin strips of lead provided linear definition (see FIG. 5-68).

By the middle of the third century BCE, artists had invented a new kind of mosaic that permitted the best mosaicists to create designs that more closely approximated true paintings. The new technique employed *tesserae* (Latin for "cubes" or "dice"). These tiny cut stones gave the artist much greater flexibility because their size and shape could be adjusted at will, eliminating the need for lead strips to indicate contours and interior details. Much more gradual gradations of color also became possible, and mosaicists finally could aspire to rival the achievements of panel painters (see FIG. 5-69).

In Early Christian mosaics, the tesserae are usually made of glass, which reflects light and makes the surfaces sparkle. Glass tesserae were occasionally used in ancient mosaics, but the Romans preferred opaque marble pieces. Mosaics quickly became the standard means of decorating walls and vaults in Early Christian buildings, although mural paintings were also used. The mosaics caught the light flooding through the windows in vibrant reflection, producing sharp contrasts and concentrations of color that could focus attention on a composition's central, most relevant features. Mosaics worked in the Early Christian manner were not meant to incorporate the subtle tonal changes a naturalistic painter's approach would require. Color was *placed*, not blended. Bright, hard, glittering texture, set within a rigorously simplified pattern, became the rule. For mosaics situated high in an apse or ambulatory vault or over the nave colonnade, far above the observer's head, the painstaking use of tiny tesserae seen in Roman floor mosaics would be meaningless. Early Christian mosaics, designed to be seen from a distance, employed larger tesserae. The pieces were also set unevenly so that their surfaces could catch and reflect the light. Artists favored simple designs for optimal legibility. For several centuries, mosaic, in the service of Christian theology, was the medium of some of the supreme masterpieces of medieval art.

Galla Placidia, whom the Visigoths had captured in Rome in 410. Galla Placidia had married a Visigothic chieftain before returning to Ravenna and the Romans after the chieftain's death six years later. In 476 Ravenna fell to Odoacer, the first Germanic king of Italy, who was overthrown in turn by Theodoric, king of the Ostrogoths, who established his capital at Ravenna in 493. The subsequent history of the city belongs with that of the Byzantine Empire (see Chapter 12).

MOSAICS FOR A MARTYR The so-called Mausoleum of Galla Placidia (FIG. **11-14**) in Ravenna is a rather small *cruciform* (cross-shaped) structure with barrel-vaulted arms and a tower at the crossing. Built shortly after 425, almost a quarter century before Galla Placidia's death in 450, it was probably intended as a chapel to the martyred Saint Lawrence. The building was, however, once thought to be Galla Placidia's tomb, hence its name today. Originally the building adjoined the narthex of the now greatly altered palace-church of Santa Croce (Holy Cross), which was also cruciform in plan. Although the chapel's plan is that of a Latin cross, the cross arms are very short and appear as little more than apselike extensions of a square. The emphasis is on the tall *crossing tower* with its vault resembling a dome. The chapel is in essence a central-plan structure. Yet this small, unassuming building also represents one of the earliest successful fusions of the two basic Late Antique plans, the *longitudinal,* used for basilican churches, and the *central,* used primarily for baptisteries and mausoleums. It introduced, on a small scale, a building type that was to have a long history in church architecture: the basilican plan with a vaulted or domed crossing.

The chapel's unadorned brick shell encloses one of the richest mosaic ensembles in Early Christian art. Mosaics cover every square inch of the interior surfaces above the marble-faced walls. Garlands and decorative medallions resembling snowflakes on a dark blue ground adorn the barrel vaults of the nave and

11-14 Mausoleum of Galla Placidia, Ravenna, Italy, ca. 425.

11-15 Christ as the Good Shepherd, mosaic from the entrance wall of the Mausoleum of Galla Placidia, Ravenna, Italy, ca. 425.

cross arms. The tower has a large golden cross set against a star-studded sky. Representations of saints and apostles cover the other surfaces.

Christ as Good Shepherd is the subject of the lunette (FIG. **11-15**) above the entrance. No earlier version of the Good Shepherd is as regal as this one. Instead of carrying a lamb on his shoulders, Jesus sits among his flock, haloed and robed in gold and purple. To his left and right, the sheep are distributed evenly in groups of three. But their arrangement is rather loose and informal, and they occupy a carefully described landscape that extends from foreground to background beneath a blue sky. All the forms have three-dimensional bulk and cast shadows. In short, the panel is full of Greco-Roman illusionistic devices. The mosaicist was still deeply rooted in the classical tradition. Some 50 years later, this artist's successors in Ravenna worked in a much more abstract and formal manner.

THEODORIC'S PALACE-CHURCH Around 504, soon after Theodoric settled in Ravenna, he ordered the construction of his own palace-church, a three-aisled basilica dedicated to the Savior. In the ninth century, the relics of Saint Apollinaris were transferred to this church. The building was rededicated and has been known since that time as Sant'Apollinare Nuovo. The rich mosaic decorations of the interior nave walls (FIG. **11-16**) are divided into three zones. Only the upper two date from Theodoric's time. Old Testament patriarchs and prophets stand between the clerestory windows. Above them, scenes from Christ's life alternate with decorative panels.

The mosaic depicting the miracle of the loaves and fishes (FIG. **11-17**) illustrates well the stylistic change that had occurred since the decoration of the Mausoleum of Galla Placidia. Jesus, beardless, in the imperial dress of gold and purple, and now distinguished by the cross-inscribed *nimbus* (halo) that signifies his divinity, faces directly toward the viewer. With extended arms he directs his disciples to distribute to the great crowd the miraculously increased supply of bread and fish he has produced. The artist made no attempt to supply details of the event. The emphasis is instead on the holy character of it, the spiritual fact that Jesus is performing a miracle by the power of his divinity. The fact of the miracle takes it out of the world of time and of incident. The presence of almighty power, not anecdotal narrative, is the important aspect of this scene. The mosaicist told the story with the least number of figures necessary to make its meaning explicit. The artist aligned the figures laterally, moved them close to the foreground, and placed them in a shallow picture box cut off by a golden screen close behind their backs. The landscape setting, which the artist who worked for Galla Placidia so explicitly described, is here merely a few rocks and bushes that enclose the figure group like parentheses. The blue sky of the physical world has given way to the otherworldly splendor of heavenly gold, the standard background color for mosaics from this point on. Remnants of Roman illusionism appear only in the handling of the individual figures, which still cast shadows and retain some of their former volume. But the shadows of the drapery folds already are only narrow bars. Soon afterward, they disappeared in Christian art.

11-16 Interior of Sant'Apollinare Nuovo, Ravenna, Italy, dedicated 504.

11-17 Miracle of the loaves and fishes, mosaic from the top register of the nave wall (above the clerestory windows) of Sant'Apollinare Nuovo, Ravenna, Italy, ca. 504.

11-18 Saints Onesiphorus and Porphyrius, detail of the dome mosaic, Church of Saint George, Thessaloniki, Greece, ca. 390–450.

A CITY NOT OF THIS WORLD In the eastern Roman Empire, the pace of stylistic change was even more rapid. Many of the features of the Sant'Apollinare Nuovo mosaic may be seen, in more advanced form and created perhaps as much as a century earlier, in the mosaics of the dome of the Church of Saint George at Thessaloniki (Salonica) in northern Greece. The church, of the central-plan type, was originally built around 300 as the mausoleum of Galerius, the tetrarchic Caesar of the East under Diocletian. It was converted into a church sometime between 390 and 450.

Only part of the mosaic decoration of the Church of Saint George is preserved. The detail we illustrate here (FIG. **11-18**) comes from the lower of two bands of mosaics, which had eight panels. Seven are fairly well preserved. In each one, two saints with their arms raised in prayer stand before two-story architectural fantasies that resemble Roman mural paintings (see FIG. 10-16) and the facades of the rock-cut tombs of Petra (see FIG. 10-52). In this respect, the Thessaloniki mosaics are more closely tied to the classical past than are those of Sant'Apollinare Nuovo. Yet figures and architecture alike have lost almost all substance, and it is increasingly difficult to imagine, for example, rounded torsos and limbs beneath the flat, curtainlike garments the saints wear. A new aesthetic is on exhibit here, one quite foreign to classical art, with its worldly themes, naturalism, perspective illusionism, modeling in light and shade, and proportionality. The formality of the poses and the solemn, priestly demeanor of the Thessaloniki figures, as well as the ethereal golden background,

became prominent features of Byzantine art (see Chapter 12). The Saint George dome mosaic seems to have completed the change from the naturalistic images of the pagan floor mosaic, which are literally under the feet and of this world, to the floating images of a celestial world high above the Christian's wondering gaze.

LUXURY ARTS

Illuminated Manuscripts

THE FIRST ILLUSTRATED BIBLES Although few examples survive, illustrated books were popular in the ancient world. The long tradition of placing pictures in manuscripts began in pharaonic Egypt (see FIG. 3-39). The oldest well-preserved painted manuscript containing biblical scenes is the early sixth-century *Vienna Genesis,* so called because of its present location. The book is sumptuous. The pages are fine calfskin dyed with rich purple, the same dye used to give imperial cloth its distinctive color, and the Greek text is written in silver ink (see "Medieval Manuscript Illumination," page 319).

The page we reproduce (FIG. **11-19**) illustrates the story of Rebecca and Eliezer in the Book of Genesis (24:15–61). When Isaac, Abraham's son, was 40 years old, his parents sent their servant Eliezer to find a wife for him. Eliezer chose Rebecca because

Medieval Manuscript Illumination

Rare as medieval books are, they are far more numerous than their ancient predecessors (see "The Roman Illustrated Book," Chapter 10, page 261). The dissemination of manuscripts, as well as their preservation, was aided greatly by an important invention of the Early Empire period, the codex. The *codex* is much like a modern book, composed of separate leaves (*folios*) enclosed within a cover and bound together at one side. The new format superseded the long manuscript scroll (*rotulus*) used by the Egyptians, Greeks, Etruscans, and Romans. (The Etruscan magistrate Lars Pulena, FIG. 9-14; the philosophers on Roman and Early Christian sarcophagi, FIGS. 10-72 and 11-4; and Christ himself in his role as teacher, FIGS. 11-5 and 11-6, all hold rotuli in their hands.) Much more durable *vellum* (calfskin) and *parchment* (lambskin), which provided better surfaces for painting, also replaced the comparatively brittle papyrus used for ancient scrolls. As a result, luxuriousness of ornament became more and more typical of sacred books in the Middle Ages, and at times the material beauty of the pages and their illustrations overwhelm or usurp the spiritual beauty of the text. Art historians refer to the luxurious painted books produced before the invention of the printing press as *illuminated manuscripts,* from the Latin *illuminare,* meaning "to adorn, ornament, or brighten."

Such books were costly to produce and involved many steps. Numerous artisans performed very specialized tasks, beginning with the curing and cutting (and sometimes the dyeing) of the animal skin, followed by the sketching of lines to guide the scribe and to set aside spaces for illumination, the lettering of the text, the addition of paintings, and finally the binding of the pages and attachment of covers, buckles, and clasps. The covers could be even more sumptuous than the book itself. Many covers survive that are fashioned of gold and decorated with jewels, ivory carvings, and repoussé reliefs (see FIG. 16-15).

when he stopped at a well, she was the first woman to draw water for him and his camels. The *Vienna Genesis* illustration presents two episodes of the story within a single frame. In the first episode, at the left, Rebecca leaves the city of Nahor to fetch water from the well. In the second episode, she gives water to Eliezer and his 10 camels, while one of them already laps water from the well.

The artist painted Nahor as a walled city seen from above, in the manner of the cityscapes on the Santa Maria Maggiore mosaics (FIG. 11-13), which maintained Roman pictorial conventions in widespread use in painting, mosaic, and relief sculpture. Rebecca walks to the well along the colonnaded avenue of a Roman city. A seminude female personification of a spring is the source of the well water. These are further reminders of the persistence of classical motifs and stylistic modes in Early Christian art. The painter presented the action with all possible simplicity but included convincing touches, such as the drinking camel and Rebecca bracing herself with her raised left foot on the rim of the well as she tips up her jug for Eliezer. The figures appear as silhouetted against a blank landscape except for the miniature city and the road to the well. Everything necessary for bare narrative is present and nothing else.

JESUS BEFORE PILATE Closely related to the *Vienna Genesis* is another early-sixth-century Greek manuscript, the *Rossano Gospels,* the earliest preserved illuminated book that contains illustrations of the New Testament. By this time a canon of New Testament iconography had been fairly well established. Like that of the *Vienna Genesis,* the text of the *Rossano Gospels* is in silver on purple vellum. The Rossano artist, however, attempted with considerable success to harmonize the colors with the purple background.

The subject of our illustration (FIG. **11-20**) is the appearance of Jesus before Pilate, who asks the Jews to choose between Jesus and Barabbas (Matt. 27:2–26). In the fashion of the continuous narrative of the *Vienna Genesis,* the separate episodes of the story appear in the same frame, but in this case without repeating any of the protagonists. The vividly gesturing figures are on two levels separated by a simple ground line. In the upper level, Pilate presides over the tribunal. He sits on an elevated dais, following a long-established pattern in Roman art (compare Constantine in the distribution-of-largess frieze on the Arch of Constantine,

11-19 Rebecca and Eliezer at the well, folio 7 recto of the *Vienna Genesis,* early sixth century. Tempera, gold, and silver on purple vellum, approx. $1' \frac{1}{4}'' \times 9\frac{1}{4}''$. Österreichische Nationalbibliothek, Vienna.

11-20 Christ before Pilate, folio 8 verso of the *Rossano Gospels*, early sixth century. Tempera on purple vellum, approx. 11″ × 10¼″. Museo Diocesano d'Arte Sacra, Rossano.

FIG. 10-77). The people form an arch around Pilate (the artist may have based the composition on a painting in an apse) and demand the death of Jesus, while a court scribe records the proceedings. Jesus (here a bearded adult, as soon became the norm for medieval and later depictions of Christ) and the bound Barabbas appear in the lower level. The painter explicitly labeled Barabbas to avoid any possible confusion so that the picture would be as readable as the text. The haloed Christ and Pilate on his magistrate's dais, flanked by painted imperial portraits, needed no further identification.

Ivory Carving

CHRIST'S PASSION IN IVORY A century before the pages of the *Rossano Gospels* were illuminated with scenes from the Passion cycle, a Roman or northern Italian sculptor produced a series of panels for an ivory box dramatically recounting the suffering and triumph of Christ. Ivory carving (see "Ivory Carving in Antiquity and the Early Middle Ages," page 321) was another luxury art much admired in the Early Christian period, and these plaques, now in the British Museum, are among the finest known. The narrative on the box begins with Pilate washing his hands, Jesus carrying the cross on

the road to Calvary, and the denial of Peter, all compressed into a single panel. The plaque we illustrate (FIG. **11-21**) is the next in the sequence and shows, at the left, Judas hanging from a tree with his open bag of silver dumped on the ground beneath his feet. The Crucifixion is at the right. The Virgin Mary and Joseph of Arimathea are to the left of the cross. On the other side Longinus thrusts his spear into the side of the "King of the Jews" (*REX IVD* is inscribed above Jesus' head). The two remaining panels show two Marys and two soldiers at the open doors of a tomb with an empty coffin within and the doubting Thomas touching the wound of the risen Christ. The series is one of the oldest cycles of Passion scenes preserved today. The artist who fashioned the ivory box helped establish the iconographical types for medieval narratives of Christ's life.

On the London ivories, Jesus appears once again as a beardless youth. In the Crucifixion (FIG. 11-21), the earliest known rendition of the subject in the history of art, he exhibits a superhuman imperviousness to pain. The Savior is a muscular, nearly nude, heroic figure who appears virtually weightless. He does not *hang* from the cross; he is *displayed* on it, a divine being with open eyes who has conquered death. The striking contrast between the powerful frontal unsuffering Jesus on the cross and the limp hanging body of his betrayer with his snapped neck is very effective, both visually and symbolically.

Ivory Carving in Antiquity and the Early Middle Ages

Ivory has been prized since the earliest times, when the tusks of Ice Age European mammoths were fashioned into pendants, beads, and other items for bodily adornment, and, occasionally, statuettes (see FIG. 1-3). The primary ivory sources in the historical period are the elephants of India and especially Africa, where the species is larger than the Asian counterpart and the tusks longer, heavier, and of finer grain. African elephant tusks 5 to 6 feet in length and weighing 10 pounds are common, but tusks of male elephants can be 10 feet long or more and weigh well over 100 pounds. Carved ivories are familiar, if precious, finds at Mesopotamian and Egyptian sites, and ivory objects were manufactured and coveted in the prehistoric Aegean and throughout the classical world. Most frequently employed then for household objects, small votive offerings, and gifts to the deceased, ivory also could be used for grandiose statues such as Phidias's *Athena Parthenos* (see FIG. 5-44).

In the Greco-Roman world, people admired ivory both for its beauty and because of its exotic origin. Elephant tusks were costly imports, and Roman generals proudly displayed them in triumphal processions when they paraded the spoils of war before the people. (In FIG. 12-1, a barbarian brings tribute to a Byzantine emperor in the form of an ivory tusk.) Adding to the expense of the material itself was the fact that only highly skilled artisans were capable of working in ivory. The tusks were very hard and of irregular shape, and the ivory workers needed a full toolbox of saws, chisels, knives, files, and gravers close at hand to cut the tusks into blocks for statuettes or thin plaques decorated with relief figures and ornament.

In late antiquity and the early medieval period, ivory was employed most frequently for book covers, boxes and chests (FIG. 11-21), and diptychs (FIGS. 11-22 and 12-2). A *diptych* is a pair of hinged tablets, usually of wood, with a wax layer on the inner sides for writing letters and other documents. (The court scribe recording Jesus' trial in the *Rossano Gospels*, FIG. 11-20, and the woman in a painted portrait from Pompeii, FIG. 10-23, both hold wooden diptychs.) Diptychs fashioned out of ivory generally were created for ceremonial and official purposes—for example, to announce the election of a consul or a marriage between two wealthy families or to commemorate the death of an elevated member of society.

11-21 Suicide of Judas and Crucifixion of Christ, plaque from a box, ca. 420. Ivory, $3'' \times 3\frac{7}{8}''$. British Museum, London.

temples and banned all pagan cults in 391. An ivory plaque (FIG. 11-22), probably produced in Rome around 400, strikingly exhibits the endurance of pagan themes and patrons and of the classical style. The ivory, one of a pair of leaves of a diptych, may commemorate either the marriage of members of two powerful Roman families of the senatorial class, the Nicomachi and the Symmachi, or the passing within a decade of two prominent male members of the two families. Whether or not the diptych was connected with any specific event(s), the Nicomachi and the Symmachi here ostentatiously reaffirmed their faith in the old pagan gods. Certainly, they favored the aesthetic ideals of the classical past, as exemplified by such works as the stately processional friezes of the Greek Parthenon (see FIG. 5-48) and the Roman Ara Pacis (see FIG. 10-29).

The leaf we reproduce, inscribed "of the Symmachi," represents a woman sacrificing at an altar in front of a tree. She wears ivy in her hair and seems to be celebrating the rites of Bacchus, although scholars dispute the identity of the divinity honored. The other diptych panel, inscribed "of the Nicomachi," also shows a woman at an open-air altar. On both panels, the precise yet fluent and graceful line; the easy, gliding poses; and the mood of spiritual serenity reveal an artist who practiced within a still-vital classical tradition that idealized human beauty as its central focus.

The great senatorial magnates of Rome, who resisted the empirewide imposition of the Christian faith at the end of the fourth century, probably deliberately sustained the classical tradition. Despite the great changes that had occurred in art during the later third and fourth centuries, classical values lived on. Many artists had turned away from Greco-Roman naturalism to something archaic, abstract, and bluntly expressive—as seen even in official imperial commissions such as the portraits of the tetrarchs (see FIG. 10-74) and the frieze of the Arch of Constantine (see FIG. 10-77). But for other artists and patrons, classical art was still the standard for measuring success. The classical tradition was never fully extinguished in the Middle Ages. It survived in intermittent revivals, renovations, and restorations side by side and in contrast with the opposing nonclassicizing medieval styles. The rise of classical art to dominance in the Renaissance would be one of the signs of the end of the medieval world.

CONCLUSION

Under Constantine, Christianity became an imperially sponsored religion, and Christian themes have ever since been the subjects of many of the greatest works of Western art. Although Old Testament themes were popular because they were frequently interpreted as prefigurations of events in the New Testament, Early Christian artists established much of the iconography of the life of Jesus in art. In architecture, too, Early Christian basilican churches stand at the head of a long line of shrines of similar plan extending to the present day.

The conversion of the pagan world to Christianity was accompanied by the rejection of the classical style in sculpture and painting and the emergence of a new non-naturalistic, hieratic aesthetic featuring wafer-thin, frontal figures and gold backgrounds. This Late Antique style was ideally suited to a focus on the spiritual world rather than the natural one, and became the norm in Byzantine art (see Chapter 12).

11-22 Woman sacrificing at an altar, right leaf of the Diptych of the Nicomachi and the Symmachi, ca. 400. Ivory, $11\frac{3}{4}'' \times 5\frac{1}{2}''$. Victoria & Albert Museum, London.

THE ENDURING PAGAN GODS It is important to remember that although after Constantine all the most important architectural projects in Italy were Christian in character, not everyone converted to the new religion, even after Theodosius closed all

29

PRE-CONSTANTINIAN

- Crucifixion of Christ, 29
- Persecution of the Christians under Trajan Decius, 249–251
- Persecution of the Christians under Diocletian, 303–305

1 Mausoleum of the Julii, Rome, late third century

306

CONSTANTINE

2 Constantine, r. 306–337
- Edict of Milan, 313
- Pope Sylvester, r. 314–335
- Foundation of Constantinople, 324

337

SUCCESSORS OF CONSTANTINE

- Theodosius I, r. 379–395
3 Christianity proclaimed state religion of Roman Empire, 380
- Theodosius prohibits pagan worship, 391
- Honorius, r. 395–423
- Honorius moves capital to Ravenna, 404
- Fall of Rome to Alaric, 410
- Mary declared *Theotokos* at Council of Ephesus, 431
- Romulus Augustulus, last Roman emperor, r. 475–476

2 Catacomb of Saints Peter and Marcellinus, Rome, early fourth century

476

ODOACER

- Fall of Ravenna to Odoacer, 476

3 Sarcophagus of Junius Bassus, ca. 359

493

THEODORIC

- Theodoric at Ravenna, 493–526

4

526

4 Sant'Apollinare Nuovo, Ravenna, 504

Christ as Savior of Souls, icon from the church of Saint Clement, Ohrid, Macedonia, early 14th century. Tempera, linen, and silver on wood, $3'\ \frac{1}{4}'' \times 2'\ 2\frac{1}{2}''$. Icon Gallery of Saint Clement, Ohrid.

12

ROME IN THE EAST

THE ART OF BYZANTIUM

When Constantine I founded a "New Rome" in the East in 324 on the site of the ancient Greek city of Byzantium and called it Constantinople in honor of himself, he legitimately could claim to be ruler of a united Roman Empire. In the fifth century, however, that empire, by then officially a Christian state, fell apart. After the sack of Rome in 410, an Emperor of the West ruled first from Milan and then from Ravenna, and an Emperor of the East ruled from Constantinople. Though not formally codified, the division of the Roman Empire became permanent. Centralized government disintegrated in the western half and was replaced by warring kingdoms that, during the Middle Ages, formed the foundations of the modern Western European nations (MAP 12-1). The eastern half of the Roman Empire, only loosely connected by religion to the west and with only minor territorial holdings there, had a long and complex history of its own. Centered at New Rome, the Eastern Christian Empire remained a cultural and political entity for a millennium, until the last of a long line of Eastern Roman emperors, ironically named Constantine XI, died at Constantinople in 1453, defending it in vain against the Ottoman Turks.

Historians call that Eastern Christian Roman Empire "Byzantium," employing Constantinople's original name, and use the term *Byzantine* to identify whatever pertains to Byzantium—its territory, its history, and its culture. The Byzantine emperors, however, did not use these terms to define themselves. They called their empire "Rome" *(Romania)* and themselves "Romans" *(Romaioi).* Though they spoke Greek and not Latin, the Eastern Roman emperors never relinquished their claim as the legitimate successors to the ancient Roman emperors. Nevertheless, *Byzantium* and *Byzantine,* though inexact terms, have become in modern times the accepted designations for the Eastern Roman Empire, and we shall use them here.

Byzantium preserved its identity throughout alternating periods of good rule and misrule, stability and instability, expansion and contraction, victory and defeat. When its shrinking borders reduced it to a mere fragment of the once mighty Byzantine Empire, when it became only a small medieval Greek kingdom, an enclave around the city of Constantinople, it still was stubbornly "Rome." As such, it had resisted successive

MAP 12-1 Europe and the Byzantine Empire ca. 1000.

assaults of Sasanian Persians, Arabs, Russians, Serbs, Normans, Franks, Venetians, and others, until Ottoman armies finally captured Constantinople. During the long course of its history, Byzantium was the Christian buffer against the expansion of Islam into central and northern Europe, and its cultural influence was felt repeatedly in Europe throughout the Middle Ages. Byzantium Christianized the Slavic peoples of the Balkans and of Russia, giving them its Orthodox religion and alphabet, its literary culture, and its art and architecture. Byzantium's collapse in 1453 brought the Ottoman Empire into Europe as far as the Danube River, but the effect of Constantinople's fall was felt even further to the west. The westward flight of Byzantine scholars from the Rome of the East introduced the study of classical Greek to Italy and helped inspire there the new consciousness of antiquity that historians call the Renaissance.

CHURCH AND STATE UNITED Constantine recognized Christianity at the beginning of the fourth century, Theodosius established it as the Roman Empire's official religion at the end of the fourth century, and Justinian, in the sixth century, proclaimed it New Rome's only *lawful* religion. By that time it was not simply the Christian religion but the *Orthodox* Christian doctrine that the Byzantine emperor asserted as the only permissible faith for his subjects. This Orthodox Christianity was *trinitarian*. Its central article of faith was the equality of the three aspects of the Trinity of Father, Son, and Holy Spirit (as stated in Roman Catholic, Protestant, and Eastern Orthodox creeds today). All other versions of Christianity were called heresies, especially the *Arian*, which asserted that Christ had a human nature and was

therefore not equal to God but only one of his creations, and the *Monophysite*, which insisted that Christ had only one nature, which was divine. Justinian considered it his first duty not only to stamp out the few surviving pagan cults but also to crush all those who professed any Christian doctrine other than the Orthodox.

The Byzantine emperors considered themselves the earthly vicars of Jesus Christ. Their will was God's will. They exercised the ultimate spiritual as well as temporal authority. As sole executives for church and state, the emperors shared power with neither senate nor church council. They reigned supreme, combining the functions of both pope and caesar, which the Western Christian world would keep strictly separate. The Byzantine emperors' exalted position made them quasidivine. The imperial court, with its hierarchy of lesser and greater functionaries converging upward to the throne, was an image of the Kingdom of Heaven.

In practice, the Byzantine emperors' attempt to make real the ideal of absolute political and religious unity was a failure. They ruled over peoples of great ethnic, religious, cultural, and linguistic diversity, with varying histories and institutions—Armenians, Syrians, Egyptians, Jews, and Arabs, as well as Greeks, Italians, Germans, Slavs, and many others. Many of these were heretical Christians, and Byzantine efforts to force Orthodoxy on them in the interest of political and doctrinal unity led to bitter resistance, especially in Monophysite Egypt and Syria. When Islam made its way into the Byzantine Empire in the seventh century, the disaffected peoples of these provinces gave it ready support. Religious intolerance lost the great Eastern provinces. The same rigid Orthodoxy also eventually severed its last ties to the Latin Christianity of the West.

The Emperors of New Rome

Byzantine art is generally, and properly, considered to belong to the Middle Ages rather than to the ancient world, but the emperors of Byzantium, New Rome, considered themselves the direct successors of the emperors of Old Rome. Although the official state religion was Christianity and all pagan cults were suppressed, the political imagery of Byzantine art displays a striking continuity between ancient Rome and medieval Byzantium. Artists continued to portray emperors sitting on thrones holding the orb of the earth in their hands, battling foes while riding on mighty horses, and receiving tribute from defeated enemies. In the Early Byzantine period, official portraits continued to be set up in great numbers throughout the territories Byzantium controlled. But, as was true of the classical world, much of imperial Byzantine statuary is forever lost. Nonetheless, some of the lost portraits of the Byzantine emperors can be visualized from miniature versions of them on ivory reliefs such as the *Barberini Ivory* (FIG. 12-1) and from descriptions in surviving texts.

One especially impressive portrait in the Roman imperial tradition, melted down long ago, depicted the emperor Justinian on horseback atop a grandiose column. Cast in glittering bronze, like the equestrian statue of Marcus Aurelius (see FIG. 10-59) set up nearly 400 years earlier, it attested to the continuity between the art of Old and New Rome, where pompous imperial images were commonly displayed at the apex of freestanding columns. (Compare FIG. 10-42, where a statue of Saint Peter has replaced a lost statue of the emperor Trajan.) Procopius, the sixth-century historian who chronicled Justinian's wars and who wrote, at the emperor's behest, a treatise on his ambitious building program, described the equestrian portrait:

> Finest bronze, cast into panels and wreaths, encompasses the stones [of the column] on all sides, both binding them securely together and covering them with adornment. . . . This bronze is in color softer than pure gold, while in value it does not fall much short of an equal weight of silver. At the summit of the column stands a huge bronze horse turned towards the east, a most noteworthy sight. . . . Upon this horse is mounted a bronze image of the Emperor like a colossus. . . . He wears a cuirass in heroic fashion and his head is covered with a helmet . . . and a kind of radiance flashes forth from there. . . . He gazes towards the rising sun, steering his course, I suppose, against the Persians. In his left hand he holds a globe, by which the sculptor has signified that the whole earth and sea were subject to him, yet he carries neither sword nor spear nor any other weapon, but a cross surmounts his globe, by virtue of which alone he has won the kingship and victory in war. Stretching forth his right hand towards the regions of the East and spreading out his fingers, he commands the barbarians that dwell there to remain at home and not to advance any further.[1]

Statues such as this are the missing links in an imperial tradition that never really died and that lived on also in the Holy Roman Empire of the Western medieval world (see FIG. 16-11) and in the Renaissance (see FIGS. 21-29 and 21-30).

[1] Cyril Mango, trans., *The Art of the Byzantine Empire, 312–1453: Sources and Documents* (Upper Saddle River, NJ: Prentice Hall, 1972), 110–11.

A THRICE GLORIOUS EMPIRE The Byzantine Empire's unity, fragmented from invasions by hostile peoples and hostile creeds, also was regularly disrupted by events at home: palace intrigues, conspiracies and betrayals, bureaucratic corruption, violent religious controversy, civil commotion, rebellions, and assassinations. Yet with characteristic resilience, Byzantium, in three periods of revived energy, recovered from dismal defeats, disunity, and stagnation. At those times intelligent, able, and successful rulers in war and peace guided the state. Under them Byzantium prospered and its culture flourished. These were the periods when the unique stylistic features of Byzantine art and architecture were shaped and refined.

Art historians divide the history of Byzantine art into the three periods of its greatest glory, sometimes referred to as "golden ages." The first, *Early Byzantine*, extends from the age of the emperor Justinian (r. 527–565) to the onset of *Iconoclasm* (the destruction of images used in religious worship) under Leo III in 726. The *Middle Byzantine* period begins with the renunciation of Iconoclasm in 843 and ends with the western Crusaders' occupation of Constantinople in 1204. *Late Byzantine* corresponds to a third golden age in the 14th and early 15th centuries after the Byzantines recaptured Constantinople in 1261 until its final loss in 1453 to the Ottoman Turks and the conversion of many churches to mosques (see Chapter 13).

EARLY BYZANTINE ART (527–726)

THE GOLDEN AGE OF JUSTINIAN The reign of Justinian and his politically astute consort, the Empress Theodora, marks the end of the Late Roman Empire and the beginning of the Byzantine Empire. At this time Byzantine art emerged as a recognizably novel and distinctive style, leaving behind the uncertainties and hesitations of Early Christian artistic experiment. Though still revealing its sources in Late Antique art, it definitively expressed, with a new independence and power of invention, the unique character of the Eastern Christian culture centered at Constantinople.

Justinian briefly restored the Roman Empire's power and extent. His generals, Belisarius and Narses, drove the Ostrogoths out of Italy, expelled the Vandals from the African provinces, beat back the Bulgars on the northern frontier, and held the Sasanians at bay on the eastern borders. At home, the emperor put down a dangerous rebellion of political and religious factions in the city, and Orthodoxy triumphed over the Monophysite heresy. In Constantinople alone Justinian built or restored more than 30 churches of the Orthodox faith, and his activities as builder extended throughout the Byzantine Empire. The historian of his reign, Procopius, declared that the emperor's ambitious building program was an obsession that cost his subjects dearly in taxation. But his grand monuments defined the Byzantine style in architecture forever after. Justinian also supervised the codification of Roman law in a great work known as the *Corpus juris civilis (Code of Civil Law)*, which became the foundation of the law systems of many modern European nations. Justinian could claim, with considerable justification, to have revived the glory of "Old Rome" in New Rome (see "The Emperors of New Rome," above).

Luxury Arts

JUSTINIAN THE CONQUEROR The triumphant image of Justinian's New Rome was set forth for all to see on an ivory plaque known today as the *Barberini Ivory* (FIG. **12-1**). Carved in five parts (one is lost), the *Barberini Ivory* shows at the center an emperor, usually identified as Justinian, riding triumphantly on a rearing horse, while a startled, half-hidden barbarian recoils in fear behind him. The dynamic twisting postures of both horse and rider and the motif of the spear-thrusting equestrian emperor are survivals of the pagan Roman Empire, as are the personifications of bountiful Earth (below the horse) and palm-bearing Victory (flying in to crown the conqueror). Also borrowed from pagan art are the barbarians at the bottom of the plaque bearing tribute and seeking clemency. They are juxtaposed with a lion, elephant, and tiger—exotic animals native to Africa and Asia, sites of Justinianic conquest. At the left, a Roman soldier carries a statuette of another Victory, reinforcing the central panel's message.

The source of the emperor's strength, however, comes not from his earthly armies but from God. The uppermost panel depicts two angels holding aloft a youthful image of Christ carrying a cross in his left hand. Christ blesses Justinian with a gesture of his right hand, indicating approval of Justinian's rule. Still conceived in the language of classical art, the *Barberini Ivory* announced Byzantium's theocratic state.

VICTORY BECOMES AN ARCHANGEL Another ivory panel (FIG. **12-2**), created somewhat earlier than the *Barberini Ivory* and likewise carved in the Eastern Christian Empire, perhaps in Constantinople, offers further evidence of the persistence of classical art. The panel, the largest extant Byzantine ivory, is all that is preserved of what was once a hinged diptych in the Early Christian tradition. It depicts Saint Michael the Archangel, patron of the imperial church of Hagia Sophia (FIGS. 12-3 to 12-5), and is inscribed "Receive these gifts." The dedication is perhaps a reference to the cross-surmounted orb of power that the archangel once offered to a Byzantine emperor depicted on the missing diptych leaf. The prototype of Michael must have been a pagan winged Victory, although Victory was personified as a woman in Greco-Roman art and usually carried the palm branch of victory, as does the Victory on the *Barberini Ivory*.

The archangel's flowing drapery, which reveals the body's shape, the delicately incised wings, and the facial type and coiffure are other indications that the artist who carved this ivory was still working in the tradition of classical art. Nonetheless, the Byzantine ivory carver had little concern for the rules of naturalistic representation. The archangel dwarfs the architectural setting. Michael's feet, for example, rest on three steps at once, and his upper body, wings, and arms are in front of the column shafts while his lower body is behind the column bases at the top of the reced-

12-1 Justinian as world conqueror *(Barberini Ivory)*, mid-sixth century. Ivory, 1′ 1½″ × 10½″. Louvre, Paris.

12-2 Saint Michael the Archangel, right leaf of a diptych, early sixth century. Ivory, approx. 1′ 5″ × 5½″. British Museum, London.

ing staircase. These spatial ambiguities, of course, do not detract from the figure's striking beauty, but they do signify the emergence of a new aesthetic that characterized Byzantine art for centuries. Here, the sculptor has rejected the goal of most classical artists: to render the three-dimensional world in convincing and consistent fashion and to people that world with fully modeled figures firmly rooted on the ground. Michael seems more to float in front of the architecture than to stand in it.

Architecture and Mosaics

BYZANTIUM'S GREATEST CHURCH The most important monument of early Byzantine art is Hagia Sophia (FIG. 12-3), the church of Holy Wisdom, in Constantinople. ANTHEMIUS OF TRALLES and ISIDORUS OF MILETUS—a mathematician and a physicist rather than architects in the modern sense of the word—designed and built the church for Justinian between 532 and 537. It is Byzantium's grandest building and one of the supreme accomplishments of world architecture. Its dimensions are formidable for any structure not made of steel. In plan (FIG. 12-4), it is about 270 feet long and 240 feet wide. The dome is 108 feet in diameter, and its crown rises some 180 feet above the pavement. (The first dome collapsed in 558 and was replaced. It required repair again in the 9th and 14th centuries. The present dome is greater in height and more stable than the original.) In scale, Hagia Sophia rivals the architectural wonders of Rome: the Pantheon, the Baths of Caracalla, and the Basilica of Constantine. In exterior view, the great dome dominates the structure, but the building's present external aspects are much changed from their original appearance. Huge buttresses were added to the Justinianic design, and four towering Turkish minarets were constructed after the Ottoman conquest of 1453, when Hagia Sophia became a mosque. The building was secularized in the 20th century and is now a museum.

The characteristic Byzantine plainness and unpretentiousness of the exterior (which, in this case, also disguise the great scale) scarcely prepare visitors for the building's interior (FIG. 12-5), which was once richly appointed. A poet and member of Justinian's court, Paul the Silentiary, recorded his impressions of Hagia Sophia. His words allow readers to visualize the original magnificence of the interior, whose walls and floors were clad with colored stones from all over the known world:

> Who . . . shall sing the marble meadows gathered upon the mighty walls and spreading pavement. . . . [There is stone] from the green flanks of Carystus [and] the speckled Phrygian stone, sometimes rosy mixed with white, sometimes gleaming with purple and silver flowers. There is a wealth of porphyry stone, too, besprinkled with little bright stars. . . . You may see the bright green stone of Laconia and the glittering marble with wavy veins found in the deep gullies of the Iasian peaks, exhibiting slanting streaks of blood-red and livid white; the pale yellow with swirling red from the Lydian headland; the glittering crocus-like golden stone [of Libya]; . . . glittering [Celtic] black [with] here and there an abundance of milk; the pale onyx with glint of precious metal; and [Thessalian marble] in parts vivid green not unlike emerald. . . . It has spots resembling snow next to flashes of black so that in one stone various beauties mingle.[1]

THE MYSTICISM OF LIGHT What distinguishes Hagia Sophia from the equally lavishly revetted and paved interiors of Roman buildings such as the Pantheon (see FIG. 10-50) is the special mystical quality of the light that floods the interior (FIG. 12-5). The soaring canopy-like dome that dominates the inside as well as the outside of the church rides on a halo of light from windows in the dome's base. Visitors to Hagia Sophia from Justinian's time to today have been struck by the light within the church and its effect on the human spirit. The 40 windows at the base of the dome create the illusion that the dome is resting on the light that pours through them. The historian Procopius observed that the dome looked as if it were suspended by "a golden chain from Heaven." Said he: "You might say that the space is not illuminated

12-3 ANTHEMIUS OF TRALLES and ISIDORUS OF MILETUS, Hagia Sophia (view facing north), Constantinople (Istanbul), Turkey, 532–537.

12-4 ANTHEMIUS OF TRALLES and ISIDORUS OF MILETUS, longitudinal section *(left)* and plan *(right)* of Hagia Sophia, Constantinople (Istanbul), Turkey, 532–537 (after drawings by Van Nice and Antoniades). 🔵

```
0    25   50   75   100   FEET
0    10    20    30    METERS
```

12-5 ANTHEMIUS OF TRALLES and ISIDORUS OF MILETUS, interior of Hagia Sophia (view facing southwest), Constantinople (Istanbul), Turkey, 532–537. 🔵

by the sun from the outside, but that the radiance is generated within, so great an abundance of light bathes this shrine all around."[2]

Paul the Silentiary compared the dome to "the firmament which rests on air" and described the vaulting as covered with "gilded tesserae from which a glittering stream of golden rays pours abundantly and strikes men's eyes with irresistible force. It is as if one were gazing at the midday sun in spring."[3] Thus, Hagia Sophia has a vastness of space shot through with light,

and a central dome that appears to be supported by the light it admits. Light is the mystic element—light that glitters in the mosaics, shines forth from the marbles, and pervades and defines spaces that, in themselves, seem to escape definition. Light seems to dissolve material substance and transform it into an abstract spiritual vision. Pseudo-Dionysius, perhaps the most influential mystic philosopher of the age, wrote in *The Divine Names:* "Light comes from the Good and . . . light is the visual image of God."[4]

Pendentives and Squinches

Perhaps the most characteristic feature of Byzantine architecture is the placement of a dome, which is circular at its base, over a square, as in the Justinianic church of Hagia Sophia (FIGS. 12-3 to 12-5) and countless later structures (for example, FIGS. 12-20 and 12-23). Two structural devices that are the hallmark of Byzantine engineering made this feat possible: *pendentives* and *squinches.*

In pendentive construction (from the Latin *pendere,* "to hang") a dome rests on what is, in effect, a second, larger dome. The top portion and four segments around the rim of the larger dome are omitted so that four curved triangles, or pendentives, are formed. The pendentives join to form a ring and four arches whose planes bound a square. The weight of the dome is thus transferred through the pendentives and arches to the four piers from which the arches spring, instead of to the walls. The first use of pendentives on a monumental scale was in Hagia Sophia in the mid-sixth century, although Near Eastern architects had experimented with them earlier. In Roman and Early Christian central-plan buildings, such as the Pantheon (see FIG. 10-50) and Santa Costanza (see FIGS. 11-9 and 11-10), the domes spring directly from the circular top of a cylinder (see "The Roman Architectural Revolution," Chapter 10, page 250).

The pendentive system is a dynamic solution to the problem of setting a round dome over a square or rectangular space, making possible a union of centralized and longitudinal or basilican structures. A similar effect can be achieved using squinches—arches, corbels, or lintels—that bridge the corners of the supporting walls and form an octagon inscribed within a square. To achieve even greater height, a builder can rest a dome on a cylindrical drum that in turn rests on either pendentives or squinches, but the principle of supporting a dome over a square is the same.

■ Pendentives   ▨ Squinches

Domes on pendentives *(left)* and squinches *(right)*

PENDENTIVES How was this illusion of a floating "dome of Heaven" achieved? Justinian's architects used *pendentives* (see "Pendentives and Squinches," above) to transfer the weight from the great dome to the piers beneath, rather than to the walls. With pendentives, not only could the space beneath the dome be unobstructed but scores of windows could puncture the walls themselves. This created the impression of a dome suspended above, not held up by, walls. Experts today can explain the technical virtuosity of Anthemius and Isidorus, but it remained a mystery to their contemporaries. Procopius communicated the sense of wonderment experienced by those who entered Justinian's great church: "No matter how much they concentrate their attention on this and that, and examine everything with contracted eyebrows, they are unable to understand the craftsmanship and always depart from there amazed by the perplexing spectacle."[5]

THE DOMED BASILICA By placing a hemispherical dome on a square base instead of on a circular base, as in the Pantheon, Anthemius and Isidorus succeeded in fusing two previously independent and seemingly mutually exclusive architectural traditions: the vertically oriented central-plan building and the longitudinally oriented basilica. Hagia Sophia is, in essence, a domed basilica (FIGS. 12-4 and 12-5)—a uniquely successful conclusion to several centuries of experimentation in Christian church architecture. However, the thrusts of the pendentive construction at Hagia Sophia made external buttresses necessary, as well as huge internal northern and southern wall piers and eastern and western half-domes. The semidomes' thrusts descend, in turn, into still smaller half-domes surmounting columned exedrae that give a curving flow to the design.

The diverse vistas and screenlike ornamented surfaces mask the structural lines. The columnar *arcades* of the nave and galleries have no real structural function. Like the walls they pierce, they are only part of a fragile "fill" between the huge piers. Structurally, although Hagia Sophia may seem Roman in its great scale and majesty, it does not have Roman organization of its masses. The very fact that the "walls" in Hagia Sophia are actually concealed (and barely adequate) piers indicates that the architects sought Roman monumentality as an *effect* and did not design the building according to Roman principles. Using brick in place of concrete marked a further departure from Roman practice and characterizes Byzantine architecture as a distinctive structural style. Hagia Sophia's eight great supporting piers are ashlar masonry, but the screen walls are brick, as are the vaults of the aisles and galleries and the dome and semicircular half-domes known as *conches.*

BYZANTINE LITURGY The ingenious design of Hagia Sophia provided the illumination and the setting for the solemn liturgy of the Orthodox faith. The large windows along the rim of the great dome poured light down upon the interior's jeweled splendor, where priests staged the sacred spectacle. Sung by clerical choirs, the Orthodox equivalent of the Latin Mass celebrated the sacrament of the Eucharist at the altar in the apsidal sanctuary, in spiritual reenactment of Jesus' Crucifixion. Processions of chanting priests, accompanying the *patriarch* (archbishop) of Constantinople, moved slowly to and from the sanctuary and the vast nave. The gorgeous array of their vestments (compare FIG. 12-35) rivaled the interior's polychrome marbles, metals, and mosaics, all glowing in shafts of light from the dome.

The nave of Hagia Sophia was reserved for the clergy, not the congregation. The laity, segregated by sex, were confined to the shadows of the aisles and galleries, restrained in most places by marble parapets. The complex spatial arrangement allowed only partial views of the brilliant ceremony. The emperor was the only lay person privileged to enter the sanctuary. When he participated with the patriarch in the liturgical drama, standing at the pulpit beneath the great dome, his rule was again sanctified and his person exalted. Church and state were symbolically made one, as in fact they were. The church building was then the earthly image of the court of Heaven, its light the image of God and God's holy wisdom.

At Hagia Sophia, the intricate logic of Greek theology, the ambitious scale of Rome, the vaulting tradition of the Near East, and the mysticism of Eastern Christianity combined to create a monument that is at once a summation of antiquity and a positive assertion of the triumph of Christian faith.

RAVENNA, SACRED FORTRESS In 493, Theodoric, the Ostrogoths' greatest king, chose the Italian city of Ravenna as the capital of his kingdom, which encompassed much of the Balkans and all of Italy (see Chapter 11). During the short history of Theodoric's unfortunate successors, the importance of the city declined. But in 539, Justinian's general Belisarius captured Ravenna, initiating the third and most important stage of the city's history. Reunited with the Eastern Empire, Ravenna remained the "sacred fortress" of Byzantium, a Byzantine foothold in Italy for two centuries, until the Lombards and then the Franks overtook it.

Ravenna enjoyed its greatest cultural and economic prosperity during Justinian's reign, at a time when repeated sieges, conquests, and sackings threatened the "eternal city" of Rome with complete extinction. As the seat of Byzantine dominion in Italy,

ruled by Byzantine *exarchs* (governors), Ravenna and its culture became an extension of Constantinople. Its art, even more than that of the Byzantine capital (where relatively little outside of architecture has survived), clearly reveals the transition from the Early Christian to the Byzantine style.

SAN VITALE, MARTYR'S SHRINE San Vitale (FIGS. **12-6** and **12-7**), dedicated by Bishop Maximianus in 547 in honor of Saint Vitalis, who was martyred at Ravenna in the second century, is the most spectacular building in Ravenna. The church is an unforgettable experience for all who have entered it and marveled at its intricate design and magnificent golden mosaics. Construction of San Vitale began under Bishop Ecclesius shortly after Theodoric's death in 526. Julianus Argentarius (Julian the Banker) provided the enormous sum of 26,000 gold *solidi* (weighing in excess of 350 pounds) required to proceed with the work. The church is unlike any of the other sixth-century churches of Ravenna (see FIG. 11-16). Indeed, it is unlike any other church in Italy. Although it has a traditional plain exterior and a polygonal apse, San Vitale is not a basilica. It is centrally planned, like Justinian's churches in Constantinople, and it seems, in fact, to have been loosely modeled on the earlier Church of Saints Sergius and Bacchus there.

The design features two concentric octagons. The dome-covered inner octagon rises above the surrounding octagon to provide the interior with clerestory lighting. The central space is defined by eight large piers that alternate with curved, columned exedrae, pushing outward into the surrounding two-story ambulatory and creating, on the plan, an intricate eight-leafed design. The exedrae closely integrate the inner and outer spaces that otherwise would have existed simply side by side as independent units. A cross-vaulted *choir* preceding the apse interrupts the ambulatory and gives the plan some axial stability. This effect is weakened, however, by the off-axis placement of the narthex, whose odd angle never has been explained fully. (The atrium, which no longer exists, may have paralleled a street that ran in the same direction as the angle of the narthex.)

12-6 Aerial view of San Vitale (view facing northwest), Ravenna, Italy, 526–547. 🔊

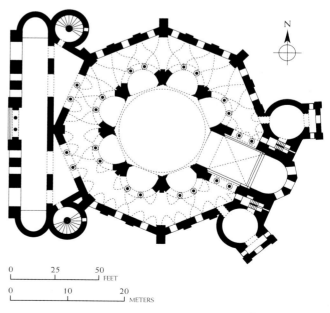

0   25   50
└────┴────┘ FEET

0   10   20
└────┴────┘ METERS

12-7 Plan of San Vitale, Ravenna, Italy, 526–547. 🔊

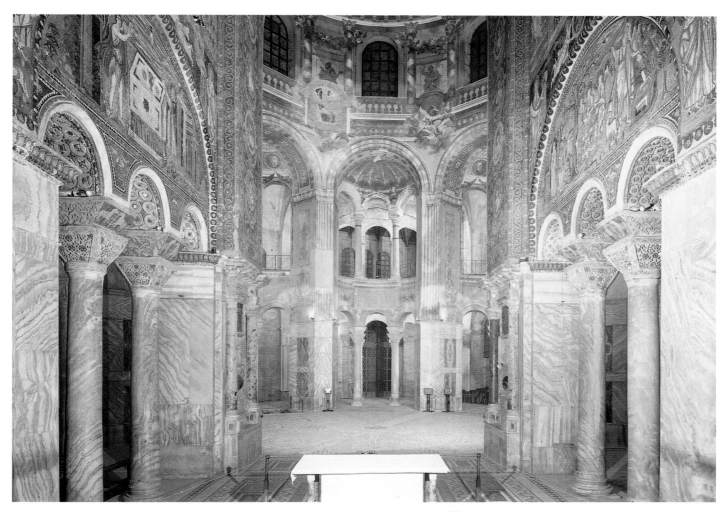

12-8 Interior of San Vitale (view from the apse into the choir), Ravenna, Italy, 526–547.

San Vitale's intricate plan and elevation combine to produce an effect of great complexity. The exterior's octagonal regularity is not readily apparent inside. A rich diversity of ever-changing perspectives greets visitors walking through the building (FIG. 12-8). Arches looping over arches, curving and flattened spaces, and wall and vault shapes seem to change constantly with the viewer's position. Light filtered through alabaster-paned windows plays over the glittering mosaics and glowing marbles that cover the building's complex surfaces, producing a sumptuous effect.

THE SECOND COMING The mosaics that decorate San Vitale's choir and apse (FIG. 12-9), like the building itself, must be regarded as one of the climactic achievements of Byzantine art. Completed less than a decade after the Ostrogoths surrendered Ravenna, the apse and choir decorations form a unified composition, whose theme is the holy ratification of Justinian's right to rule.

In the apse vault, Christ, youthful in the Early Christian tradition, holds a scroll with seven seals (Rev. 5:1) and sits on the orb of the world at the time of his Second Coming. The four rivers of Paradise flow beneath him, and rainbow-hued clouds float above. Christ extends the golden martyr's wreath to Vitalis, the patron saint of the church, introduced here by an angel. At Christ's left, another angel introduces Bishop Ecclesius, in whose time the church foundations were laid. Ecclesius offers a model of San Vitale to Christ. The arrangement recalls Christ's prophecy of the last days of the world: "And then shall they see the Son of Man

coming in the clouds with great power and glory. And then shall he send his angels, and shall gather together his elect from the four winds, from the uttermost part of Heaven" (Mark 13:26–27).

Images and symbols covering the entire sanctuary express the single idea of Christ's redemption of humanity and the reenactment of it in the Eucharist. Below the apse mosaic (at the right in FIG. 12-8), for example, the lunette mosaic over the two columns of the choir depicts Abraham and the three angels and the sacrifice of Isaac, prefigurations of the Trinity and of the Crucifixion, respectively (see "Jewish Subjects in Christian Art," Chapter 11, page 305).

JUSTINIAN AND MAXIMIANUS On the choir wall to the left of the apse mosaic appears Justinian (FIG. 12-10). He stands on the Savior's right side. The two are united visually and symbolically by the imperial purple they wear and by their haloes. Justinian is also accompanied by a dozen attendants, paralleling Christ's Twelve Apostles. Thus, the mosaic program underscores the dual political and religious roles of the Byzantine emperor. The laws of the Eastern Church and the laws of the state, united in the laws of God, were manifest in the person of the emperor, whose right to rule was God-given.

The positions of the figures are all-important. They express the formulas of precedence and rank. Justinian is at the center, distinguished from the other dignitaries by his purple robe and halo. At his left (at right in the mosaic) is Bishop Maximianus, the man responsible for San Vitale's completion. The mosaicist stressed the bishop's importance by labeling his figure with the

12-9 Choir and apse of San Vitale with mosaic of Christ between two angels, Saint Vitalis, and Bishop Ecclesius, Ravenna, Italy, 526–547.

12-10 Justinian, Bishop Maximianus, and attendants, mosaic from the north wall of the apse, San Vitale, Ravenna, Italy, ca. 547.

12-11 Theodora and attendants, mosaic from the south wall of the apse, San Vitale, Ravenna, Italy, ca. 547.

Theodora: A Most Unusual Empress

Theodora (FIG. 12-11), wife of Justinian and empress of Byzantium, was not born into an aristocratic family. Her father, who died when she was a child, was the "keeper of bears" for one of the circus *factions* (teams, distinguished by color) at Constantinople. His responsibility was to prepare these animals for bear fights, bear hunts, and acrobatic performances involving bears in a long tradition rooted in ancient Rome. Theodora's mother was an actress, and after the death of her father the young Theodora took up the same career. Acting was not a profession the highborn held in esteem. At Byzantium, actresses often doubled as prostitutes, and the beautiful Theodora was no exception. In fact, actresses were so low on the Byzantine social ladder that the law prohibited senators from marrying them.

Justinian met Theodora when he was about 40 years old, she only 25. She became his mistress, but before they could wed, as they did in 525, ignoring all the social norms of the day, Justinian's uncle, the emperor Justin, first had to rewrite the law against senatorial marriages to actresses to permit wedlock with an *ex-actress*. When Justin died in April 527, Justinian was crowned emperor by the patriarch of Constantinople, and Theodora became empress of Byzantium, capping what can be fairly described as one of the most remarkable and improbable "success stories" of any age. By all accounts, even of those openly hostile to the imperial couple, Justinian and Theodora remained faithful to each other for the rest of their lives.

It was not Theodora's beauty alone that attracted Justinian. John the Lydian, a civil servant at Constantinople at the time, described her as "surpassing in intelligence all men who ever lived." As her husband's trusted adviser, she repaid him for elevating her from poverty and disgrace to riches and prestige. During the Nika revolt in Constantinople in 532, when all of her husband's ministers counseled flight from the city, Theodora, by the sheer force of her personality, persuaded Justinian and his generals to hold their ground. The revolt was suppressed.

---

only identifying inscription in the composition. Some have identified the figure behind and between Justinian and Maximianus as Julius Argentarius, the church's benefactor.

The artist divided the figures into three groups: the emperor and his staff; the clergy; and the imperial guard, bearing a shield with the *chi-rho-iota* monogram of Christ. Each group has a leader whose feet precede (by one foot overlapping) the feet of those who follow. The positions of Justinian and Maximianus are curiously ambiguous. Although the emperor appears to be slightly behind the bishop, the golden *paten* (large bowl holding the Eucharist bread) he carries overlaps the bishop's arm. Thus, symbolized by place and gesture, the imperial and churchly powers are in balance. Justinian's paten, Maximianus's cross, and the attendant clerics' book and censer produce a slow forward movement that strikingly modifies the scene's rigid formality. No background is indicated. The artist wished the observer to understand the procession as taking place in this very sanctuary. Thus, the emperor appears forever as a participant in the sacred rites and as the proprietor of this royal church, the very symbol of his rule of the Western Empire.

THE NEW BYZANTINE AESTHETIC The procession at San Vitale recalls but contrasts with that of Augustus and his entourage on the Ara Pacis (see FIG. 10-29), erected more than half a millennium earlier in Rome. There the fully modeled marble figures have their feet planted firmly on the ground. The Romans talk among themselves, unaware of the viewer's presence. All is anecdote, all very human and of this world, even if the figures themselves conform to a classical ideal of beauty that cannot be achieved in reality. The frontal figures of the Byzantine mosaic, however, hover before viewers, weightless and speechless. Their positions in space are as uncertain as that of Saint Michael on the ivory diptych examined earlier (FIG. 12-2). Tall, spare, angular, and elegant, the figures have lost the rather squat proportions characteristic of much Early Christian work. The garments fall straight, stiff, and thin from the narrow shoulders. The organic body has dematerialized, and, except for the heads, some of which seem to be true portraits, viewers see a procession of solemn spirits gliding silently in the presence of the sacrament. This mosaic reveals the Byzantine world's new aesthetic, one very different from that of the classical world but equally compelling. Blue sky has given way to heavenly gold, and matter and material values are disparaged. Byzantine art is an art without solid bodies or cast shadows, with blank golden spaces, and with the perspective of Paradise, which is nowhere and everywhere.

THEODORA AT SAN VITALE Justinian's counterpart on the opposite wall of the apse is his empress, Theodora (FIG. **12-11**), one of the most remarkable women of the Middle Ages (see "Theodora: A Most Unusual Empress," above). She too is accompanied by her retinue. Both processions move into the apse, Justinian proceeding from left to right and Theodora from right to left, in order to take part in the Eucharist. Justinian carries the paten containing the bread and Theodora the golden cup with the wine. The portraits in the Theodora mosaic exhibit the same stylistic traits as those in the Justinian mosaic, but the women are represented within a definite architecture, perhaps the atrium of San Vitale. The empress stands in state beneath an imperial canopy, waiting to follow the emperor's procession. An attendant beckons her to pass through the curtained doorway. The fact that she is outside the sanctuary in a courtyard with a fountain and only about to enter attests that, in the ceremonial protocol, her rank was not quite equal to her consort's. But the very presence of Theodora at San Vitale is significant. Neither she nor Justinian ever visited Ravenna. Their participation in the liturgy at San Vitale is pictorial fiction. The mosaics are proxies for the absent sovereigns. Justinian was represented because he was the head of the Byzantine state, and by his presence he exerted his authority over his territories in Italy. But Theodora's portrayal is more surprising and testifies to her unique position in Justinian's court. Theodora's prominent role in the mosaic program of San Vitale is proof of the power she wielded at Constantinople and, by extension, at Ravenna. In fact, the representation of the Three Magi on the border of her robe suggests that she belongs in the elevated company of the three monarchs who approached the newborn Jesus bearing gifts.

12-12 Saint Apollinaris amid sheep, apse mosaic, Sant'Apollinare in Classe, Ravenna, Italy, ca. 533–549.

SAINT APOLLINARIS Until the ninth century, the Church of Sant'Apollinare in Classe housed the body of Saint Apollinaris, who suffered his martyrdom in Classe, Ravenna's port. The building itself is Early Christian in type, a basilica with a nave and flanking aisles, like Theodoric's palace-church dedicated to the same saint in Ravenna (see FIG. 11-16). As in the earlier church, the Justinianic building's outside is plain and unadorned, but the interior is decorated with sumptuous mosaics, although in this case they are confined to the apse (FIG. **12-12**).

The mosaic decorating the semivault above the apse probably was completed by 549, when the church was dedicated. (The mosaics of the framing arch were added later.) Against a gold ground, a large medallion with a jeweled cross (symbol of the transfigured Christ) dominates the composition. This may represent the cross Constantine erected on the hill of Calvary to commemorate the martyrdom of Jesus. Visible just above the cross is the hand of God. On either side of the medallion, in the clouds, are Moses and Elijah, who appeared before Christ during his Transfiguration. Below these two figures are three sheep, the three disciples who accompanied Christ to the foot of the Mount of the Transfiguration. Beneath, amid green fields with trees, flowers, and birds, stands the church's patron saint, Apollinaris. He is portrayed in the Early Christian manner as an orant with uplifted arms. Accompanying him are 12 sheep, perhaps representing the Christian congregation under the protection of Saint Apollinaris, and forming, as they march in regular file across the apse, a wonderfully decorative base.

BYZANTINE ART AND DOGMA Comparison of the Early Byzantine Sant'Apollinare in Classe mosaic with the Galla Placidia mosaic (see FIG. 11-15) from the Early Christian period at Ravenna shows how the style and artists' approach to the subject changed during the course of a century. Both mosaics portray a human figure and some sheep in a landscape. But in Classe, in the mid-sixth century, the artist did not try to re-create a segment of the physical world, telling the story instead in terms of flat symbols, lined up side by side. The mosaicist carefully avoided overlapping in what must have been an intentional effort to omit all reference to the three-dimensional space of the material world and physical reality. Shapes have lost the volume seen in the earlier mosaic and instead are flat silhouettes with linear details. The effect is that of an extremely rich, flat tapestry without illusionistic devices. This new Byzantine style became the ideal vehicle for conveying the extremely complex symbolism of the fully developed Christian dogma.

The Sant'Apollinare in Classe apse mosaic, for example, has much more meaning than first meets the eye. The Transfiguration of Christ—here, into the cross—symbolizes not only his own death, with its redeeming consequences, but also the death of his martyrs (in this case, Saint Apollinaris). The lamb, also a symbol of martyrdom, appropriately represents the martyred apostles. The whole scene expands above the altar, where the priests celebrated the sacrament of the Eucharist—the miraculous recurrence of the supreme redemptive act. The very altars of Christian churches were, from early times, sanctified by the bones and relics of martyrs (see "Pilgrimages and the Cult of Relics," Chapter 17, page 449). Thus, the mystery and the martyrdom were joined in one concept. The death of the martyr, in imitation of Christ, is a triumph over death that leads to eternal life. The images above the altar present an inspiring vision to the eyes of believers. The way of the martyr is open to them, and the reward of eternal life is within their reach. The organization of the symbolism and the images is *hieratic,* and the graphic message must have been delivered to the faithful with overwhelming force. Looming above their eyes is the apparition of a great mystery, ordered to make perfectly simple and clear that humankind's duty is to seek salvation. The anonymous artist, working under the direction of the priests, made sure that the devout could read the pictorial message as easily as an inscription—more easily, in fact, for many of the faithful were illiterate.

MONASTICISM IN EGYPT During Justinian's reign, almost continuous building took place, not only in Constantinople and Ravenna but all over the Byzantine Empire. At about the time mosaicists in Ravenna were completing their work at San Vitale and Sant'Apollinare in Classe, Justinian's builders were rebuilding an important early monastery at Mount Sinai in Egypt where Moses received the Ten Commandments from God. Now called Saint Catherine's, the monastery marked the spot at the foot of the mountain where the Bible says God first spoke to the Hebrew prophet from a burning bush.

The monastic movement began in Egypt in the third century and spread rapidly to Palestine and Syria in the east and as far as Ireland in the west. It began as a migration to the wilderness by those who sought a more spiritual way of life, far from the burdens, distractions, and temptations of town and city. In desert places these refuge seekers lived austerely as hermits, in contemplative isolation, cultivating the soul's perfection. So many thousands fled the cities that the authorities became alarmed—noting the effect on the tax base, military recruitment, and business in general.

The origins of organized monasticism are associated with Saint Anthony and Saint Pachomius in Egypt in the fourth century. By the fifth century, regulations governing monastic life began to be codified. Individual monks were brought together to live according to a rule within a common enclosure, a community under the direction of an abbot (see "Medieval Monasteries and Benedictine Rule," Chapter 16, page 434). The monks typically lived in a walled monastery, an architectural complex that included the monks' residence (an alignment of single cells), a *refectory* (dining hall), a kitchen, storage and service quarters, a guest house for pilgrims, and, of course, an *oratory* or monastery church (see FIG. 16-19).

TRANSFIGURATION AT MOUNT SINAI Justinian rebuilt the monastery at Mount Sinai between 548 and 565 and enclosed it within protective walls. The site had been an important pilgrimage destination since the fourth century, and Justinian's fortress was intended to protect not only the hermit-monks but also the lay pilgrims during their visits. The Mount Sinai church was dedicated to the Virgin Mary, whom the Orthodox Church had officially recognized in the mid-fifth century as the Mother of God (*Theotokos*, "bearer of God" in Greek), putting to rest a controversy about the divine nature of Christ. The church's apse mosaic (FIG. **12-13**) depicts the Transfiguration. Jesus appears in a deep-blue almond-shaped *mandorla* (aureole of light). Flanking him are the Old Testament prophets Elijah and Moses. (Other mosaics in the church depict Moses receiving the Law and standing before the burning bush.) At Christ's feet are the disciples John, Peter, and James. Portrait busts of saints and prophets in medallions frame the whole scene. The artist stressed the intense whiteness of Jesus' transfigured, spiritualized form, from which rays stream down on the disciples. The stately figures of Elijah and Moses and the static frontality of Jesus set off the frantic terror and astonishment of the gesticulating disciples. This effectively contrasts the eternal composure of heavenly beings with the distraught responses of the earthbound.

In this apse the mosaicist swept away all traces of landscape and architectural setting for a depthless field of gold, fixing the

12-13 Transfiguration of Jesus, apse mosaic, Church of the Virgin, monastery of Saint Catherine, Mount Sinai, Egypt, ca. 548–565.

figures and their labels in isolation from one another. A rainbow band of colors graduating from yellow to blue bounds the golden field at its base. The figures are ambiguously related to this multicolor ground line. Sometimes they are placed behind it; sometimes they overlap it. The bodies cast no shadows, even though supernatural light streams over them. This is a world of mystical vision, where the artist subtracted all substance that might suggest the passage of time or motion through physical space so that the devout can contemplate the eternal and motionless world of religious truth.

Painting

ANICIA JULIANA AND THE ARTS The physical world was, however, the focus of one of the rare secular books to survive from the early Middle Ages, either in Byzantium or the West. In the mid-first century, a Greek physician named Dioskorides compiled an encyclopedia of medicinal herbs called *De materia medica*. An early-sixth-century copy of this medical manual, nearly a thousand pages in length, is in the Austrian National Library. The *Vienna Dioskorides* (FIG. **12-14**), as it is called, was a gift from the people of Honoratai, near Constantinople, to Anicia Juliana, daughter of the short-lived Emperor of the West, Anicias Olybrias (r. 472). Anicia Juliana was a leading patron of the arts in and around Constantinople. She had built a church dedicated to the Virgin Mary at Honoratai in 512. She also provided the funds to erect Saint Polyeuktos in Constantinople between 524 and 527.

The excavated ruins of that church indicate that it was a domed basilica—an important forerunner of the pioneering design of Justinian's Hagia Sophia (FIGS. 12-3 to 12-5).

The *Vienna Dioskorides* contains 498 illustrations, almost all images of plants rendered with a scientific fidelity to nature that stands in stark contrast to contemporary Byzantine paintings and mosaics of religious subjects. It is likely that the *Vienna Dioskorides* painters copied the illustrations as well as the text of a classical manuscript. One page, however, cannot be a copy—the dedication page (FIG. 12-14) featuring a portrait of Anicia Juliana in an eight-pointed star and circle frame. She is enthroned between personifications of Magnanimity and Prudence, with a kneeling figure labeled Gratitude of the Arts at her feet. The shading and modeling of the figures, the heads seen at oblique angles, the perspectival rendering of the throne's footstool, and the use of personifications establish that the painter still worked in the classical tradition that most other Byzantine artists had rejected.

MARY AT THE ASCENSION One of the essential Christian beliefs is that following his Crucifixion and entombment, Christ rose from the dead after three days and, on the 40th day, ascended from the Mount of Olives to Heaven. The Ascension is the subject of a full-page painting (FIG. **12-15**) in a manuscript known as the *Rabbula Gospels*. Written in Syriac by the monk Rabbula at the monastery of Saint John the Evangelist at Zagba in Syria, it dates to the year 586. The composition shows Christ, bearded and in a mandorla, as in the Mount Sinai Transfiguration (FIG. 12-13), but the mandorla is here borne aloft by angels. Below, Mary, other

12-14 Anicia Juliana between Magnanimity and Prudence, folio 6 verso of the *Vienna Dioskorides,* from Honoratai, near Constantinople (Istanbul), Turkey, ca. 512. Tempera on parchment, approx. 1′3″ × 1′11″. Österreichische Nationalbibliothek, Vienna.

12-15 Ascension of Christ, folio 13 verso of the *Rabbula Gospels,* from Zagba, Syria, 586. Approx. 1′ 1″ × 10½″. Biblioteca Medicea-Laurenziana, Florence.

12-16 Virgin (Theotokos) and Child between Saints Theodore and George, icon, sixth or early seventh century. Encaustic on wood, 2′ 3″ × 1′ 7⅜″. Monastery of Saint Catherine, Mount Sinai, Egypt.

ICONS FOR THE DEVOUT Gospel books such as the *Rabbula Gospels* played an important role in monastic religious life. So, too, did *icons,* which also figured prominently in private devotion. Unfortunately, few early icons survive because of the wholesale destruction of images *(iconoclasm)* that occurred in the eighth century (see "Icons and Iconoclasm," page 341). Some of the finest early examples come from Saint Catherine's monastery at Mount Sinai. The one we illustrate (FIG. **12-16**) was painted in encaustic on wood, continuing a tradition of panel painting in Egypt that, like so much else in the Byzantine world, goes back to the Roman Empire (see FIG. 10-63).

In a composition reminiscent of the portrait of Anicia Juliana in the *Vienna Dioskorides* (FIG. 12-14), the Sinai icon painter represented the enthroned Theotokos and Child with Saints Theodore and George. The two guardian saints intercede with the Virgin on the viewer's behalf. Behind them, two angels look upward to a shaft of light where the hand of God appears. The foreground figures are strictly frontal and have a solemn demeanor. Background details are few and suppressed. The forward plane of the picture dominates. Space is squeezed out. It is a perfect example of Byzantine hieratic style. Traces of the Greco-Roman illusionism noted in the Anicia Juliana portrait remain in the Virgin's rather personalized features, in her sideways glance, and in the posing of the angels' heads. But the painter rendered the saints in the new Byzantine manner.

ICONOCLASM (726–843)

BYZANTIUM IN CRISIS The preservation of the Early Byzantine icons at the Mount Sinai monastery is fortuitous but ironic, for opposition to icon worship was especially prominent in the Monophysite provinces of Syria and Egypt. And there, in the seventh century, a series of calamities erupted, indirectly causing the imperial ban on images. The Sasanians (see Chapter 2), chronically at war with Rome, swept into the eastern provinces early in the seventh century. Between 611 and 617 they captured the great cities of Antioch, Jerusalem, and Alexandria. Hardly had the Byzantine emperor Heraclius (r. 610–641) pressed them back and defeated them in 627 when a new and overwhelming power appeared unexpectedly on the stage of history. The Arabs, under the banner of the new Islamic religion, conquered not only Byzantium's eastern provinces but also Persia itself, replacing the Sasanians in the age-old balance of power with the Christian West (see Chapter 13). In a few years the Arabs were launching attacks on Constantinople, and Byzantium was fighting for its life.

These were catastrophic years for the Eastern Roman Empire. They terminated once and for all the long story of imperial Rome, closed the Early Byzantine period, and inaugurated the medieval era of Byzantine history. Almost two-thirds of the Byzantine Empire's territory was lost—many cities and much of its population, wealth, and material resources. The shock of these events persuaded the emperor Leo III (r. 717–741) that God had punished the Christian Roman Empire for its idolatrous worship of icons by setting upon it the merciless armies of the infidel. In 726 he formally prohibited the use of images, and for more than a century Byzantine artists produced little new religious figurative art. In place of images, the iconoclasts used symbolic forms already familiar in Early Christian art—the cross (FIG. 12-12), the vacant Throne of Heaven, the cabinet with the scriptural scrolls, and so forth. Stylized floral, animal, and architectural motifs provided decorative fill.

angels, and various apostles look on. The artist set the figures into a mosaic-like frame (compare FIGS. 12-10 and 12-11), and many think the manuscript page was modeled after a mural painting or mosaic in a Byzantine church somewhere in the Eastern Empire.

The account of Christ's Ascension is not part of the accompanying text of the *Rabbula Gospels* but is borrowed from the Book of Acts. And even Acts omits mention of the Virgin's presence at the miraculous event. Here, however, the Theotokos occupies a very prominent position, central and directly beneath Christ. It is an early example of the prominent role the Mother of God played in later medieval art, both in the East and in the West. Frontal, with a nimbus, and posed as an orant, Mary stands apart from the commotion all about her and looks out at the viewer. Other details also depart from the Gospel texts. Christ, for example, does not rise in a cloud. Rather, as in the vision of Ezekiel in the book of Revelation, he ascends in a mandorla above a fiery winged chariot. The chariot carries the symbols of the Four Evangelists—the man, lion, ox, and eagle (see "The Four Evangelists," Chapter 16, page 426). This page is not therefore an *illustration* of the Gospels but an independent *illumination* presenting one of the central tenets of Christian faith. Similar compositions appear on pilgrims' flasks from Palestine that were souvenir items reproducing important monuments visited. They reinforce the theory that the *Rabbula Gospels* Ascension was based on a lost painting or mosaic in a major church.

Icons and Iconoclasm

*I*cons ("images" in Greek) are small portable paintings depicting Christ, the Virgin, or saints (or a combination of all three, as in FIG. 12-16). Icons survive from as early as the fourth century. From the sixth century on, they became enormously popular in Byzantine worship, both public and private. Eastern Christians considered icons a personal, intimate, and indispensable medium for spiritual transaction with holy figures. Some icons (for example, FIG. 12-29) came to be regarded as wonder-working, and believers ascribed miracles and healing powers to them.

Icons, however, were by no means universally accepted. From the beginning, many Christians were deeply suspicious of the practice of imaging the divine, whether on portable panels, on the walls of churches, or especially as statues that reminded them of pagan idols. The opponents of Christian figural art had in mind the Old Testament prohibition of images the Lord dictated to Moses in the Second Commandment: "Thou shalt not make unto thee any graven image or any likeness of anything that is in heaven above, or that is in the earth beneath, or that is in the water under the earth. Thou shalt not bow down thyself to them, nor serve them" (Exod. 20:4, 5).

When, early in the fourth century, Constantia, sister of the emperor Constantine, requested an image of Christ from Eusebius, the first great historian of the Christian Church, he rebuked her, referring to the Second Commandment:

> Can it be that you have forgotten that passage in which God lays down the law that no likeness should be made of what is in heaven or in the earth beneath? . . . Are not such things banished and excluded from churches all over the world, and is it not common knowledge that such practices are not permitted to us . . . lest we appear, like idol worshipers, to carry our God around in an image?[1]

Opposition to icons became especially strong in the eighth century, when the faithful often burned incense and knelt before them in prayer to seek protection or a cure for illness. Although icons were intended only to evoke the presence of the holy figures addressed in prayer, in the minds of many, icons became identified with the personages represented. Icon veneration became confused with idol worship, and this brought about an imperial ban on *all* sacred images. The term for this destruction of holy pictures is *iconoclasm*. The *iconoclasts* (breakers of images) and the *iconophiles* (lovers of images) became bitter and irreconcilable enemies. The anguish of the latter can be read in a graphic description of the deeds of the iconoclasts, written in about 754:

> In every village and town one could witness the weeping and lamentation of the pious, whereas, on the part of the impious, [one saw] sacred things trodden upon, [liturgical] vessels turned to other use, churches scraped down and smeared with ashes because they contained holy images. And wherever there were venerable images of Christ or the Mother of God or the saints, these were consigned to the flames or were gouged out or smeared over.[2]

The consequences of iconoclasm for the history of Byzantine art are difficult to overstate. For more than a century not only did the portrayal of Christ, the Virgin, and the saints cease, but the iconoclasts also systematically destroyed countless works from the early centuries of Christendom. Knowledge of Byzantine art before the revival of image making in the ninth century is therefore very fragmentary. Writing a history of Early Byzantine art presents a great challenge to art historians.

[1] Cyril Mango, trans., *The Art of the Byzantine Empire, 312–1453: Sources and Documents* (Upper Saddle River, N.J.: Prentice Hall, 1972), 17–18.
[2] Ibid., 152.

MIDDLE BYZANTINE ART (843–1204)

THE IMAGE MAKERS RETURN In the ninth century, a powerful reaction against iconoclasm set in. The destruction of images was condemned as a heresy, and restoration of the images began in 843. Shortly thereafter, under a new line of emperors, the Macedonian dynasty, art, literature, and learning sprang to life once again. In this great renovation, as historians have called it, Byzantine culture recovered something of its ancient Hellenistic sources and accommodated them to the forms inherited from the Justinianic age.

Basil I (r. 867–886), head of the new dynasty, thought of himself as the restorer of the Roman Empire. He denounced as usurpers the Frankish Carolingian monarchs of the West (see Chapter 16) who, since 800, had claimed the title "Roman Empire" for their realm. Basil bluntly reminded their emissary that the only true emperor of Rome reigned in Constantinople. They were not Roman emperors but merely "kings of the Germans." Iconoclasm had forced Byzantine artists westward, where doubtless they found employment at the courts of these Germanic kings. They strongly influenced the character of Western European art. But under Basil and his successors, mural painters, mosaicists, book illuminators, ivory carvers, and metalworkers once again received commissions aplenty.

Architecture and Mosaics

UNDOING ICONOCLASM Basil I and his successors undertook the laborious and costly task of refurbishing the churches the iconoclasts defaced and neglected, Hagia Sophia first among them. There, in 867, the Macedonian dynasty dedicated a new mosaic (FIG. 12-17) in the apse depicting the enthroned Virgin with the Christ Child in her lap. In the vast space beneath the dome of the great church, the figures look undersized, but the seated Theotokos is actually more than 16 feet tall. An accompanying inscription, now fragmentary, announced that "pious emperors" (the Macedonians) had commissioned the mosaic to replace one the "impostors" (the iconoclasts) had destroyed.

The original mosaic's subject is uncertain, but the ninth-century work echoes the style and composition of the Early Byzantine Mount Sinai icon (FIG. 12-16) of the Theotokos, Christ, and saints. Here, the strict frontality of Mother and (much older) Child is alleviated by the angular placement of the throne and footstool. The mosaicist rendered the furnishings in a perspective that, although imperfect, recalls once more the Greco-Roman roots of Byzantine art. The treatment of the folds of Christ's robes is, by contrast, even more schematic and flatter than in earlier mosaics. These seemingly contradictory stylistic features are not uncommon in Byzantine paintings and mosaics. Most significant about the images in the Hagia Sophia apse is their very existence. The iconophiles had triumphed over the iconoclasts.

NEW CHURCHES FOR THE OLD FAITH Although the new emperors did not wait very long to redecorate the churches of their predecessors, they undertook little new church construction in the decades following the renunciation of iconoclasm in 843. But in the 10th century and through the 12th, a number of monastic churches arose that are the flowers of Middle Byzantine architecture. They feature a brilliant series of variations on the domed central plan. From the exterior, the typical later Byzantine church building is a domed cube, with the dome rising above the square on a kind of cylinder or drum. The churches are small, vertical, high shouldered, and, unlike earlier Byzantine buildings, have exterior wall surfaces with vivid decorative patterns, probably reflecting the impact of Islamic architecture.

VISUAL DRAMA AT HOSIOS LOUKAS The monastery Church of the Theotokos (FIGS. **12-18**, *right*, and **12-19**, *top*) at Hosios Loukas (Saint Luke) in Greece, near ancient Delphi, dates

12-17 Virgin (Theotokos) and Child enthroned, apse mosaic, Hagia Sophia, Constantinople (Istanbul), Turkey, dedicated 867.

12-18 Monastery churches at Hosios Loukas, Greece (view from the east). Katholikon *(left),* first quarter of 11th century, and Church of the Theotokos *(right),* second half of 10th century.

0	10	20	30	FEET	

0	2	4	6	8	10 METERS

to the second half of the 10th century. One of two churches at the site, it exemplifies church design during this second golden age of Byzantine art and architecture. Light stones framed by dark red bricks—the so-called *cloisonné* technique, a term borrowed from enamel work (see FIG. 16-2)—make up the walls. The interplay of arcuated windows, projecting apses, and varying roof lines further enhances this surface dynamism. The plan (FIG. 12-19) shows the form of a domed cross in square with four equal-length, vaulted cross arms (the Greek cross). The dome rests on pendentives. Around this unit, and by the duplication of it, Byzantine architects developed dynamic intersecting spaces.

In the adjacent, larger Katholikon (FIGS. 12-18, *left,* and 12-19, *bottom),* built in the early 11th century, the architect placed a dome over an octagon inscribed within a square. The octagon was formed by squinches, which, as noted earlier (see "Pendentives and Squinches," page 331), play the same role as pendentives in making the transition from a square base to a round dome but create a different visual effect on the interior (FIG. **12-20**). This arrangement departs from the older designs, such as Santa Costanza's circular plan (see FIG. 11-10), San Vitale's octagonal plan (FIG. 12-7), and Hagia Sophia's dome on pendentives rising from a square (FIG. 12-4). The Katholikon's complex core lies within two rectangles, the outermost one forming the exterior walls. Thus, in plan from the center out, a circle-octagon-square-oblong series exhibits an intricate interrelationship that is at once complex and unified.

The interior elevation of the Katholikon reflects its involved plan. Like earlier Byzantine buildings, the church creates a mystery out of space, surface, light, and dark. High and narrow, it forces one's gaze to rise and revolve. The eye is drawn upward toward the dome, but much can distract it in the interplay of flat walls and concave recesses; wide and narrow openings; groin and barrel vaults; single, double, and triple windows; and illuminated and dark spaces. Middle Byzantine architects seem to have aimed for the creation of complex interior spaces with dramatically shifting perspectives.

12-20 Interior of Katholikon (view facing east), Hosios Loukas, Greece, first quarter of 11th century.

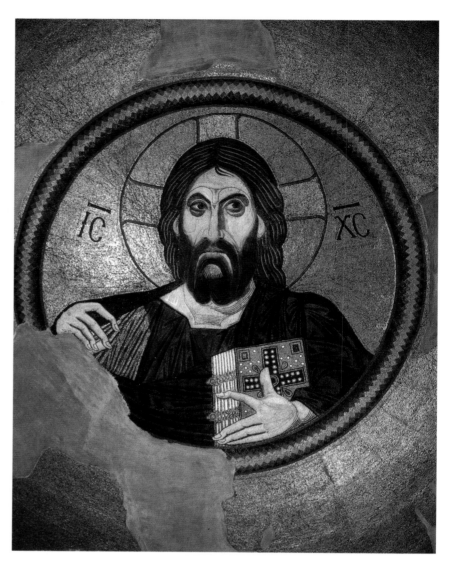

CHRIST, PANTOKRATOR Much of the original mosaic decoration of the Hosios Loukas Katholikon does not survive, but at Daphni, near Athens, the mosaics produced during Byzantium's second golden age fared much better. In the monastery Church of the Dormition (from the Latin for "sleep," referring to the ascension of the Virgin Mary to Heaven at the moment of her death), the main elements of the late-11th-century pictorial program are intact, although the mosaics were restored in the 19th century. Gazing down from on high in the central dome (FIG. **12-21**) is the fearsome image of Christ as *Pantokrator* (literally "ruler of all" in Greek but usually applied to Christ in his role as Last Judge of humankind). The dome mosaic is the climax of an elaborate hierarchical pictorial program including several New Testament episodes below. The Daphni Pantokrator is like a gigantic icon hovering dramatically in space. The mosaic serves to connect the awestruck worshiper in the church below with heaven through Christ. The Pantokrator theme was a common one in churches throughout the Byzantine Empire. There was also a mosaic of the Pantokrator in the dome of the Hosios Loukas Katholikon. Today a painting replaces it. The most famous Pantokrator of all was the work of Eulalios, who decorated the dome of the Church of the Holy Apostles in Constantinople (see "Eulalios: Painter of Christ," page 345).

On one of the walls below the Daphni dome, beneath the barrel vault of one arm of the Greek cross, an unknown artist depicted Christ's Crucifixion (FIG. **12-22**) in a pictorial style characteristic of the post-Iconoclastic Middle Byzantine period. Like the Pantokrator mosaic in the dome, the Daphni Crucifixion is a subtle blend of the painterly, Hellenistic style and the later more abstract and formalistic Byzantine style. The Byzantine artist fully assimilated classicism's simplicity, dignity, and grace into a perfect synthesis with Byzantine piety and pathos. The figures have regained the classical organic structure to a surprising degree, particularly compared to figures from the Justinianic period (compare FIGS. 12-9 and 12-10). The style is a masterful adaptation of classical statuesque qualities to the linear Byzantine manner.

In quiet sorrow and resignation, the Virgin and Saint John flank the crucified Christ. A skull at the foot of the cross indicates Golgotha, the "place of the skulls." Nothing else was needed to set the scene. Symmetry and closed space combine to produce an effect of the motionless and unchanging aspect of the deepest mystery of the Christian religion. The timeless presence is, as it were, beheld in unbroken silence. The picture is not a narrative of the historical event of the Crucifixion, the approach taken by the carver of the Early Christian ivory panel (see FIG. 11-21) examined in the previous chapter. Nor is Christ a triumphant, beardless youth, oblivious to pain and defiant of the laws of gravity. Rather, he has a tilted head and sagging body, and blood spurts from the wound Longinus inflicted on him, although he is not overtly in pain. The Virgin and John point to the figure on the cross as if to a devotional object. They act as intercessors between the viewer below and Christ, who, in the dome, appears as the Last Judge of all humans.

Eulalios: Painter of Christ

Most of the art of Byzantium, and of the Middle Ages in general, is anonymous. The names of the builders of Justinian's great sixth-century church of Hagia Sophia in Constantinople (FIG. 12-3) are known. But the mosaicist who adorned its apse (FIG. 12-17) in the ninth century is nameless, even though the homily the patriarch Photius delivered for the building's dedication in 867 survives. The scribe Rabbula signed the *Gospels* he wrote in Syriac in 586, but the identity of the painter of its full-page miniatures (FIG. 12-15) is unknown.

Medieval authors did, however, record the name of Eulalios, a painter who worked in the 12th century. So great was his fame that more than one writer notes his name and describes his paintings. Eulalios's most important commission was the decoration of the dome of the Church of the Holy Apostles in Constantinople with an image of Christ as Pantokrator. Nicephorus Callistus, an early-14th-century poet, historian, and author of saints' lives, was so struck by Eulalios's portrayal of Christ that he speculated that the painter had actually seen the Pantokrator:

> Either Christ himself came down from heaven and showed the exact traits of his face to [the painter] or else the famous Eulalios mounted up to the very skies to paint with his skilled hand Christ's exact appearance.[1]

Nicholas Mesarites, who visited the Church of the Holy Apostles around the year 1200, left a more precise description of Eulalios's Christ:

[The dome] exhibits an image of the God-man Christ looking down, as it were, from the rim of heaven towards the floor of the church and everything that is in it. . . . His head is in proportion to his body that is represented down to the navel, his eyes are joyful and welcoming to those who are not reproached by their conscience, but to those who are condemned by their own judgment, they are wrathful and hostile. . . . The right hand blesses those who walk a straight path, while it admonishes those who do not and, as it were, checks them and turns them back from their disorderly course. The left hand, with its fingers spread as far apart as possible, supports the Gospel.[2]

It is easy to visualize Eulalios's Pantokrator by comparing Nicholas Mesarites' description with surviving representations of the same theme: for example, the mosaic dome of the Church of the Dormition at Daphni (FIG. 12-21), or even the apse of the Cathedral at Monreale (FIG. 12-24) in faraway Sicily. Both conform to the same basic iconographic type—an image of the stern but benevolent judge of human worth who can strike fear into sinners who come before him but who can reward the blessed.

---

[1] Cyril Mango, trans., *The Art of the Byzantine Empire, 312–1453: Sources and Documents* (Upper Saddle River, N.J.: Prentice Hall, 1972), 231–32.

[2] Ibid., 232.

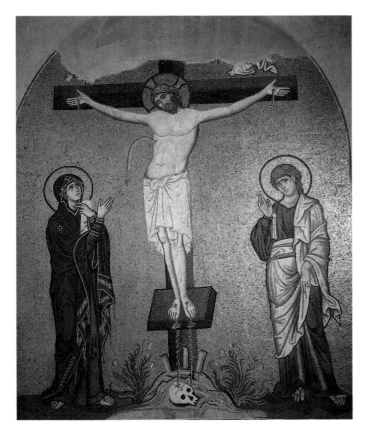

12-22 Crucifixion, mosaic in the Church of the Dormition, Daphni, Greece, ca. 1090–1100.

VENICE AND BYZANTIUM The revival on a grand scale of church building, featuring vast stretches of mosaic-covered walls, was not confined to the Greek-speaking Byzantine East in the 10th to 12th centuries. A resurgence of religious architecture and of the mosaicist's art also occurred in areas of the former Western Roman Empire where the ties with Constantinople were the strongest. In the Early Byzantine period, Venice, about 80 miles north of Ravenna on the eastern coast of Italy, was a dependency of that Byzantine stronghold. In 751, Ravenna fell to the Lombards, and they wrested control of most of northern Italy from Constantinople. Venice, however, became an independent power. Its *doges* (dukes) enriched themselves and the city through seaborn commerce, serving as the crucial link between Byzantium and the West.

Venice had obtained the relics of Saint Mark from Alexandria in Egypt in 829, and the doges constructed the first Venetian shrine dedicated to the evangelist—a palace chapel and martyrium—shortly thereafter. Fire destroyed the ninth-century chapel in 976. The Venetians then built a second shrine on the site, but a grandiose new church begun in 1063 by Doge Domenico Contarini replaced it. This building was modeled on the Church of the Holy Apostles at Constantinople, built in Justinian's time. The Constantinopolitan church no longer exists, but its key elements were a cruciform plan with a central dome over the crossing and four other domes over the four equal arms of the Greek cross, as at Saint Mark's. Because of its importance to the city, the doges repeatedly remodeled the 11th-century structure, in time disguising its lower levels with Romanesque and Gothic additions. In 1807 St. Mark's was consecrated as the Cathedral of Venice.

12-23 Interior of Saint Mark's (view facing east), Venice, Italy, begun 1063.

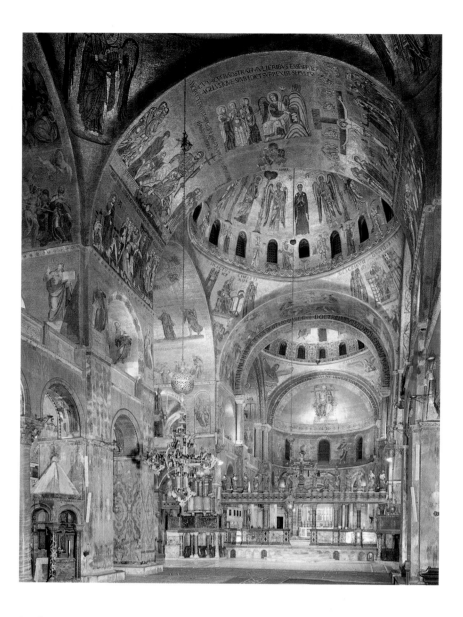

SAINT MARK'S MOSAICS The interior (FIG. **12-23**) of Saint Mark's is, like its plan, Byzantine in effect. Light enters through a row of windows at the bases of all five domes, vividly illuminating a rich cycle of mosaics. Both Byzantine and local artists worked on Saint Mark's mosaics over the course of several centuries. Most of the mosaics date to the 12th and 13th centuries. Cleaning and restoration on a grand scale have returned the mosaics to their original splendor, enabling visitors to experience the full radiance of mosaic (some 40,000 square feet of it) as it covers, like a gold-brocaded and figured fabric, all the walls, arches, vaults, and domes.

In the vast central dome, 80 feet above the floor and 42 feet in diameter, Christ ascends to heaven in the presence of the Virgin Mary and the Twelve Apostles. The great arch framing the church crossing bears a narrative of the Crucifixion and Resurrection of Christ and of his liberation from death (Anastasis) of Adam and Eve, Saint John the Baptist, and other biblical figures. The mosaics have explanatory labels in both Latin and Greek, reflecting Venice's position as the key link between eastern and western Christendom in the later Middle Ages. The insubstantial figures on the walls, vaults, and domes appear weightless, and they project no farther from their flat field than do the elegant Latin and Greek letters above them. Nothing here reflects on the world of matter, of solids, of light and shade, of perspective space. Rather, the mosaics reveal the mysteries of the Christian faith.

A ROYAL CHURCH IN SICILY Venetian success was matched in the western Mediterranean by the Normans, who, having driven the Arabs from Sicily, set up a powerful kingdom there, whose resources equaled those of Venice. Though they were the enemies of Byzantium, the Normans, like the Venetians, assimilated Byzantine culture and even employed Byzantine artisans. The mosaics of the great basilican church of Monreale, not far from Palermo, are striking evidence of Byzantium's presence in Sicily. They rival those of Saint Mark's in both quality and extent. One scholar has estimated that more than 100 million glass and stone tesserae were required for the Monreale mosaics.

The Norman king William II paid for the mosaics, and he is portrayed twice, continuing the theme of royal presence and patronage of the much earlier Ravenna portraits of Justinian and Theodora at San Vitale (FIGS. 12-10 and 12-11). In one panel, William, clearly labeled, unlike Justinian or his consort, stands next to the enthroned Christ, who places his hand on William's crown. In the second, the king kneels before the Virgin and presents her with a model of the Monreale church, a role that at San Vitale was played by Bishop Ecclesius (FIG. 12-9) rather than by the emperor or empress. As in the Ravenna church, the mosaic program commemorates both the piety and power of the ruler who reigns with divine authority.

12-24 Pantokrator, Theotokos and Child, angels, and saints, apse mosaic in the cathedral at Monreale, Italy, ca. 1180–1190.

The apse mosaics (FIG. **12-24**) are especially impressive. The image of Christ as Pantokrator, as ruler and judge of heaven and earth, looms menacingly in the vault, a colossal allusion to William's kingly power and a challenge to all who would dispute the royal right. In Byzantium proper, the Pantokrator's image usually appears in the main dome of centralized churches such as those at Hosios Loukas (FIG. 12-20) and Daphni (FIG. 12-21), but the Greek churches are monastic churches and were not built for the glorification of monarchs. Monreale, moreover, is a basilica—longitudinally planned in the Western tradition. The semidome of the apse, the only vault in the building and its architectural focus, was the most conspicuous place for the vast image with its political overtones. Below the Pantokrator in rank and dignity, the enthroned Theotokos is flanked by archangels and the Twelve Apostles symmetrically arranged in balanced groups. Lower on the wall (and less elevated in the hierarchy) are popes, bishops, and other saints. The artists observed the stern formalities of style characteristic of Byzantine hieraticism here, far from Constantinople. The Monreale mosaics, like those at Saint Mark's in Venice (FIG. 12-23), testify to the stature of Byzantium and of Byzantine art in medieval Italy.

AN EMPRESS AT SAINT MARK'S The wealth and pretensions of the Venetian dukes and the Norman kings of Sicily are revealed not only by their ambitious building programs with their acres of mosaic-covered walls, vaults, and domes but also by the sometimes extravagant furnishings of their churches. In 976, the Venetian doge Pietro Orseolo ordered from Constantinople a set of gold-and-enamel plaques nailed on wood for the second church of Saint Mark in Venice. In 1105, under Doge Ordelafo Falier, the plaques were refashioned into a *pala* (altarpiece, or panel placed behind and over the altar) that was again augmented in 1209 with booty from the Crusaders' sack of Constantinople. The altarpiece was modified once more in 1345. In its final form the Venetian *Pala d'Oro (Golden Pala)* reflects contemporaneous (Gothic) taste in Italy and unites plaques of several different periods featuring narrative scenes from Christ's life and dozens of saints, angels, prophets, and temporal rulers in golden niches surrounded by jewels of many different hues.

Among the figures added in 1105 were Doge Falier and probably also the Byzantine Emperor Alexius I Comnenus (r. 1081–1118), although the latter's portrait does not survive. Preserved, however, is the portrait of his wife, the Empress Irene (FIG. **12-25**). The regally attired and haloed gold-and-enamel Irene is a frontal, wafer-thin, weightless figure, a stylistic cousin to the mosaic saints and apostles of Monreale, despite the enormous differences in scale and technique. The portrayal of the empress (and the emperor?) suggests that the *Pala d'Oro* in its 1105 form was an imperial gift to the Venetian church. The inclusion of Irene's haloed

12-25 Empress Irene, detail of the *Pala d'Oro*, Saint Mark's, Venice, Italy, ca. 1105. Gold cloisonné inlaid with precious stones, detail approx. $7'' \times 4\frac{1}{2}''$.

12-26 Christ enthroned with saints *(Harbaville Triptych)*, ca. 950. Ivory, central panel $9\frac{1}{2}'' \times 5\frac{1}{2}''$. Louvre, Paris.

portrait in the pictorial program of Saint Mark's carried on a tradition that goes back to the sixth-century mosaic of Theodora (FIG. 12-11) at Ravenna. The *Pala d'Oro* Irene once again testifies to the important role the Byzantine empresses played in both life and art, as well as to continuing commercial, political, and artistic exchanges between Italy and Byzantium.

DIPTYCH TO TRIPTYCH Costly carved ivories also were produced in large numbers in the Middle Byzantine period, but after iconoclasm the three-part *triptych* replaced the earlier diptych as the standard format for ivory panels. One example of this type is the *Harbaville Triptych* (FIG. 12-26), a portable shrine with hinged wings that was used for private devotion. Such triptychs were very popular—among those who could afford such luxurious items—and they often replaced icons for use in personal prayer. Carved on the wings of the *Harbaville Triptych*, both inside and out, are four pairs of full-length figures and two pairs of medallions depicting saints. A cross dominates the central panel on the back of the triptych (not illustrated). On the inside is a scene of *Deësis* (supplication). Saint John the Baptist and the Theotokos appear as intercessors, praying on behalf of the viewer to the enthroned Savior. Below them are five apostles.

The hieratic formality and solemnity associated with Byzantine art, visible in the mosaics of Ravenna and Monreale and in the *Pala d'Oro* enamel plaques, yielded here to a softer, more fluid technique. The figures may lack true classical contrapposto, but the looser stances (most stand on bases, like freestanding statues) and three-quarter views of many of the heads relieve the hard austerity of the customary frontal pose. This more natural, classicizing spirit was a second, equally important, stylistic current of the Middle Byzantine period. It also surfaced in mural painting and book illumination.

Painting

BYZANTIUM IN THE BALKANS When the emperors lifted the ban against religious images and again encouraged religious painting at Constantinople, the impact was felt far and wide. The style varied from region to region, but a renewed enthusiasm for picturing the key New Testament figures and events was universal.

In 1164, at Nerezi in Macedonia, Byzantine painters embellished the church of Saint Pantaleimon with murals of great emotional power. One of these represents the Lamentation over the dead Christ (FIG. 12-27). It is an image of passionate grief. The artist captured Christ's followers in attitudes, expressions, and gestures of quite human bereavement. Joseph of Arimathea and the disciple Nicodemus kneel at his feet, while Mary presses her cheek against her dead son's face and Saint John clings to Christ's left hand. In the Gospels, neither Mary nor John was present at the entombment of Christ. Their presence here, as elsewhere in Middle Byzantine art, was designed to intensify for the viewer the emotional impact of Christ's death. Such representations parallel the development of liturgical hymns recounting the Virgin's lamenting her son's death on the Cross.

At Nerezi, the scene is set in a hilly landscape below a blue sky—a striking contrast to the abstract golden world of the mosaics favored for church walls elsewhere in the Byzantine Empire. The artist strove to make utterly convincing an emotionally charged realization of the theme by staging the Lamentation in a more natural setting and peopling it with fully modeled actors. This alternate representational mode is no less Byzantine than the hieratic style of Ravenna or the poignant melancholy of Daphni.

DAVID AS GREEK HARPIST Another example of this classicizing style is a page from a book of the Psalms of David. The

12-27 Lamentation, wall painting, Saint Pantaleimon, Nerezi, Macedonia, 1164.

so-called *Paris Psalter* (FIG. **12-28**) reasserts the artistic values of the Greco-Roman past with astonishing authority. Art historians believe the manuscript dates from the mid-10th century—the so-called Macedonian Renaissance, a time of enthusiastic and careful study of the language and literature of ancient Greece, and of humanistic reverence for the classical past. It was only natural that artists would once again draw inspiration from the Hellenistic naturalism of the pre-Christian Mediterranean world.

David, the psalmist, surrounded by sheep, goats, and his faithful dog, plays his harp in a rocky landscape with a town in the background. Similar settings appeared frequently in Pompeian murals. Befitting an ancient depiction of Orpheus, the Greek hero who could charm even inanimate objects with his music, allegorical figures accompany the Old Testament harpist. Melody looks over his shoulder, and Echo peers from behind a column. A reclining male figure points to a Greek inscription that identifies him as representing the mountain of Bethlehem. These allegorical figures do not appear in the Bible. They are the stock population of Greco-Roman painting. Apparently, the artist had seen a work from late antiquity or perhaps earlier and partly translated it into a Byzantine pictorial idiom. In works such as this, Byzantine artists kept the classical style alive in the Middle Ages.

A MIRACLE-WORKING ICON Nothing in Middle Byzantine art better demonstrates the rejection of the iconoclastic viewpoint than the painted icon's return to prominence. After the restoration of images, such icons multiplied by the thousands to meet public and private demand. In the 11th century, the clergy began to display icons in hieratic order (Christ, the Theotokos, John the Baptist, and then other saints, as on the *Harbaville Triptych*) in tiers on the *templon,* the low columnar screen separating the sanctuary from the main body of a Byzantine church.

12-28 David composing the Psalms, folio 1 verso of the *Paris Psalter,* ca. 950–970. Tempera on vellum, 1' $2\frac{1}{8}$" × $10\frac{1}{4}$". Bibliothèque Nationale, Paris.

12-29 Virgin (Theotokos) and Child, icon *(Vladimir Virgin)*, late 11th to early 12th century. Tempera on wood, original panel approx. 2' 6½" × 1' 9". Tretyakov Gallery, Moscow.

Our example, the renowned *Vladimir Virgin* (FIG. **12-29**), is a masterpiece of its kind. Descended from works such as the Mount Sinai icon (FIG. 12-16), the *Vladimir Virgin* clearly reveals the stylized abstraction resulting from centuries of working and reworking the conventional image. Probably painted by a Constantinopolitan artist, the characteristic traits of the Byzantine icon of the Virgin and Child are all present: the Virgin's long, straight nose and small mouth; the golden rays in the infant's drapery; the decorative sweep of the unbroken contour that encloses the two figures; and the flat silhouette against the golden ground. But this is a much more tender and personalized image of the Virgin than that in the Mount Sinai icon. Here Mary is depicted as the Virgin of Compassion, who presses her cheek against her son's in an intimate portrayal of Mother and Child. The image is also infused with a deep pathos as Mary contemplates the future sacrifice of her son. (The back of the icon bears images of the instruments of Christ's Passion.)

The icon of Vladimir, like most icons, has seen hard service. Placed before or above altars in churches or private chapels, the icon was blackened by the incense and smoke from candles that burned before or below it. It was frequently repainted, often by inferior artists, and only the faces show the original surface. First painted in the late 11th or early 12th century, it was taken to Kiev (Ukraine) in 1131, then to Vladimir (Russia) in 1155 (hence its

name), and in 1395, as a wonder-working image, to Moscow to protect that city from the Mongols. The Russians believed that the sacred picture saved the city of Kazan from later Tartar invasions and all of Russia from the Poles in the 17th century. The *Vladimir Virgin* is a historical symbol of Byzantium's religious and cultural mission to the Slavic world.

LATE BYZANTINE ART (1204–1453)

THE SACK OF CONSTANTINOPLE When rule passed from the Macedonian to the Comnenian dynasty in the later 11th and the 12th centuries, three events of fateful significance changed Byzantium's fortunes for the worse. The Seljuk Turks conquered most of Anatolia. The Byzantine Orthodox Church broke finally with the Church of Rome. And the Crusades brought the Latins (a generic term for the peoples of the West) into Byzantine lands on their way to fight for the Cross against the Saracens (Muslims) in the Holy Land (see "The Crusades," Chapter 17, page 466).

Crusaders had passed through Constantinople many times en route to "smite the infidel" and had marveled at its wealth and magnificence. Envy, greed, religious fanaticism (the Latins called the Greeks "heretics"), and even ethnic enmity motivated the Crusaders when, during the Fourth Crusade in 1203 and 1204, the Venetians persuaded them to divert their expedition against the Muslims in Palestine and to attack Constantinople instead. They took the city and sacked it. Nicetas Choniates, a contemporaneous historian, expressed the feelings of the Byzantines toward the Crusaders: "The accursed Latins would plunder our wealth and wipe out our race. . . . Between us there can be only an unbridgeable gulf of hatred. . . . They bear the Cross of Christ on their shoulders, but even the Saracens are kinder."[6]

The Latins set up kingdoms within Byzantium, notably in Constantinople itself. What remained of Byzantium was split into three small states. The Palaeologans ruled one of these, the kingdom of Nicaea. In 1261, Michael VIII Palaeologus (r. 1259–1282) succeeded in recapturing Constantinople. But his empire was no more than a fragment, and even that disintegrated during the next two centuries. Isolated from the Christian West by Muslim conquests in the Balkans and besieged by Muslim Turks to the east, Byzantium sought help from the West. It was not forthcoming. In 1453, the Ottoman Turks, then a formidable power, took Constantinople and brought to an end the long history of Byzantium (see Chapter 13). But despite the state's grim political condition under the Palaeologan dynasty, the arts flourished well into the 14th century.

Architecture

A MULTIPLICATION OF DOMES Late Byzantine architecture did not depart radically from the characteristic plans and elevations of Middle Byzantine architecture. But the number of domes and drums increased, and their groupings became more and more dramatic. Elevations became narrower and steeper. Wall and drum arcades were more deeply cut back into overlapping arches. The eaves curved rhythmically and varied brick patterns ornamented the external walls.

The church of Saint Catherine (FIG. **12-30**) in Thessaloniki, second city to Constantinople in rank, shows all these Palaeologan variations on the grand stylistic theme of Middle Byzantine architecture. The plan is an inscribed cross with a central dome

12-30 Church of Saint Catherine, Thessaloniki, Greece, ca. 1280.

and four additional domes at the corners. On the exterior these appear as *cupolas,* drums with shallow caps, the central drum rising a level above the others. Thus the church has a vertical gradation from a rectilinear base to the superstructure's cylindrical volumes, culminating in the dominant central unit. Wall and drum

arcades are grouped rhythmically in alternating pairs and triads. Lively patternings face and punctuate the enframements of arches and niches and the scalloped eaves. The intricate harmonizing by alternation and repetition of walls and openings and of verticals, half-circles, and cylinders produces a lively rhythm.

Painting

RESURRECTION AND REDEMPTION A new burst of creative energy also enlivened Late Byzantine painting. Artists produced masterpieces of mural and icon painting rivaling those of the earlier periods. A fresco (FIG. **12-31**) in the apse of the *parekklesion* (side chapel, in this instance a funerary chapel) of the Church of Christ in Chora (now the Kariye Museum, formerly the Kariye Camii mosque) in Constantinople depicts the Anastasis. One of many subsidiary subjects making up the complex mosaic program of Saint Mark's in Venice (FIG. 12-23), the Anastasis is here central to a cycle of pictures portraying the themes of human mortality and redemption by Christ and of the intercession of the Virgin, both appropriate for a funerary chapel.

In the Kariye fresco, Christ, trampling Satan and all the locks and keys of his prison house of Hell, raises Adam and Eve from their tombs. Looking on are John the Baptist, King David, and King Solomon on the left, and various martyr saints on the right. Christ, central and in a luminous mandorla, reaches out equally to Adam and Eve. The action is swift and smooth, the supple

12-31 Anastasis, apse fresco in the *parekklesion* of the Church of Christ in Chora (now the Kariye Museum), Constantinople (Istanbul), Turkey, ca. 1310–1320.

motions executed with the grace of a ballet. The figures float in a spiritual atmosphere, spaceless and without material mass or shadow-casting volume. This same smoothness and lightness can be seen in the modeling of the figures and the subtly nuanced coloration. The jagged abstractions of drapery found in many earlier Byzantine frescoes and mosaics are gone in a return to the fluid delineation of drapery characteristic of the long tradition of classical illusionism.

Throughout the centuries, Byzantine artists looked back to Greco-Roman illusionism. But unlike classical artists, Byzantine painters and mosaicists were not concerned with the systematic observation of material nature as the source of their representations of the eternal. They drew their images from a persistent and conventionalized vision of a spiritual world unsusceptible to change. That consistent vision is what unites works as distant in date as the sixth-century apse mosaic at Mount Sinai (FIG. 12-13) and the 14th-century Kariye fresco.

ICONS AND ICONOSTASIS Byzantine spirituality was perhaps most intensely revealed in icon painting. In the Late Byzantine period, the Early Byzantine templon developed into an *iconostasis* (icon stand), a high screen with doors. As its name implies, the iconostasis supported tiers of painted devotional images, which began to be produced again in large numbers, both in Constantinople and throughout the diminished Byzantine Empire.

Our example (FIG. **12-32**), notable for the lavish use of finely etched silver foil to frame the tempera figure of Christ as Savior of Souls, dates to the beginning of the 14th century. It comes from the church of Saint Clement at Ohrid in Macedonia, where many Late Byzantine icons imported from the capital have been preserved. The painter of the Ohrid Christ, in a manner consistent with Byzantine art's conservative nature, adhered to an iconographical and stylistic tradition that went back to the earliest icons from the monastery at Mount Sinai. As elsewhere (for example, FIG. 12-21), the Savior holds a bejeweled Bible in his left hand while he blesses the faithful with his right hand. The style is typical of Byzantine eclecticism. Note especially the juxtaposition of Christ's fully modeled head and neck, which reveal the Byzantine painter's Greco-Roman heritage, with the schematic linear folds of Christ's garment, which do not envelop the figure but rather seem to be placed in front of it.

A PARADE OF ICONS In the Late Byzantine period, icons often were painted on two sides because they were intended to be carried in processions. When they were deposited in the church, they were not mounted on the iconostasis but were exhibited on stands so they could be viewed from both sides. The Ohrid icon of Christ has a painting of the Crucifixion on its reverse. Another double icon from Saint Clement's, also imported from Constantinople, represents the Virgin on the front as Christ's counterpart as Savior of Souls. The Annunciation (FIG. **12-33**) is the subject of

12-32 Christ as Savior of Souls, icon from the church of Saint Clement, Ohrid, Macedonia, early 14th century. Tempera, linen, and silver on wood, 3′ $\frac{1}{4}$″ × 2′ 2$\frac{1}{2}$″. Icon Gallery of Saint Clement, Ohrid.

12-33 Annunciation, reverse of two-sided icon from the church of Saint Clement, Ohrid, Macedonia, early 14th century. Tempera and linen on wood, 3′ $\frac{1}{4}$″ × 2′ 2$\frac{3}{4}$″. Icon gallery of Saint Clement, Ohrid.

the reverse. With a commanding gesture of heavenly authority, the angel Gabriel announces to Mary that she is to be the Mother of God. She responds with a simple gesture conveying both astonishment and acceptance. The gestures and attitudes of the figures are again conventional, as are the highly simplified architectural props. The latter are rendered in inconsistent perspective derived from classical prototypes, but the sturdy three-dimensional forms have been set against an otherworldly gold sky, suggesting the sacred space in which the narrative unfolds. This icon also exemplifies the eclecticism that characterizes Byzantine art throughout its long history.

RUSSIAN ICON PAINTING In Russia, icon painting flourished for centuries, extending the life of the Byzantine painting style well beyond the collapse of the Byzantine Empire in 1453. Russian paintings usually had strong patterns, firm lines, and intense contrasting colors. All served to heighten the legibility of the icons in the wavering candlelight and clouds of incense that worshipers encountered in church interiors. For many art historians, Russian painting reached a climax in the work of ANDREI RUBLYEV (ca. 1370–1430). His rendition of the three Old Testament angels who appeared to Abraham (FIG. 12-34) is a work of great spiritual power, as well as an unsurpassed example of subtle line in union with intensely vivid color. The angels sit about a table, each framed with a halo and sweeping wings, three nearly identical figures dis-

tinguished only by their garment colors. The light linear play of the draperies sets off the tranquil demeanor of the figures. Color defines the forms and becomes more intense by the juxtaposition of complementary hues. The intense blue and green folds of the central figure's cloak, for example, stand out starkly against the deep-red robe and the gilded orange of the wings. In the figure on the left, the highlights of the orange cloak are an opalescent blue green. The unmodulated saturation, brilliance, and purity of the color harmonies are the hallmark of Rublyev's style.

Luxury Arts

PRIESTLY ROBES In Byzantium, other arts also played an indispensable part in the ensemble of a church interior — the carvings and rich metalwork of the iconostasis, serving to frame icons that themselves often were ornamented with precious metals and jewels; the finely wrought, gleaming candlesticks and candelabra; the illuminated books bound in gold or ivory and inlaid with jewels and enamels; and the crosses, croziers, sacred vessels, and processional banners. Each, with its great richness of texture and color, contributed to the total ambience of the Byzantine church. And amid these opulent inanimate treasures, the solemn clergy celebrated the liturgy of the Orthodox faith in magnificent embroidered and bejeweled robes.

12-35 Large sakkos of Photius, ca. 1417. Satin embroidered with gold and silver thread and silk with pearl ornament, approx. 4' 5" long. Kremlin Armory, Moscow.

Fortunately some of these vestments have been reverently preserved through centuries of political and social upheaval in Russia. One of them is the so-called large *sakkos* (a magnificent "small sakkos" also exists) or tunic (FIG. **12-35**) of Photius, the early-15th-century Metropolitan (Orthodox archbishop) of Russia. It can represent here this whole branch of the "minor arts" and remind readers of how incomplete the story of art through the ages would be if the narrative were confined to monumental works of painting, sculpture, and architecture.

Photius's satin sakkos is embroidered with gold and silver thread and colored silks outlined with pearls. Dozens of religious and secular figures appear in a dazzling array of rectilinear, L-shaped, cruciform, and circular frames. The Crucifixion dominates the center of the front, and below is the Anastasis. All around are various Orthodox Church feasts and figures of saints, as well as Old Testament scenes, including the sacrifice of Abraham, linked with the Crucifixion. Also portrayed are the Grand Prince of Moscow, Vasily Dimitrievich, and his wife Sophia Vitovtovna (labeled in Russian), as well as the future emperor John VIII Palaeologus (r. 1425–1448) and his wife Anna Vasilyevna (named in Greek). Beside John is Photius, "Metropolitan of Kiev and all Russia." Needleworkers most likely embroidered the sakkos between the time of John's marriage in 1416 and Anna Vasilyevna's death in 1418. The couple probably sent the sakkos to Photius as a gift. In 15th-century Russia, as in sixth-century Ravenna, the rulers of Byzantium, as the vicars of God on earth, joined the clergy in celebration of the liturgy of the Christian Church.

THE THIRD ROME A third of a century after Photius first donned his sakkos, Constantinople fell to the Ottoman Turks,

never to be recovered. With the passing of Byzantium, Russia became its self-appointed heir, defending Christendom against the infidel. The court of the tsar (derived from the word *caesar*) declared: "Because the Old Rome has fallen, and because the Second Rome, which is Constantinople, is now in the hands of the godless Turks, thy kingdom, O pious Tsar, is the Third Rome. . . . Two Romes have fallen, but the Third stands, and there shall be no more."[7] Rome, Byzantium, Russia—Old Rome, New Rome, and Third Rome—were a continuum, where artistic change was slow and the old ways never really died.

CONCLUSION

In the centuries following the foundation of Constantinople (Byzantium) in 330, the Christian world became divided into the Latin West, centered in Rome, and the Greek Orthodox East, with its capital at Constantinople. Under Justinian, Byzantine art reached an early pinnacle, setting the pattern for much of later Byzantine art. Justinianic mosaicists carried on and codified the formal, hieratic style of late antiquity. Justinian's architects also pioneered the distinctive form of Byzantine churches. Mirroring the schism in Christianity, Byzantine churches are centrally planned, dome-covered structures, in contrast to the longitudinal basilicas favored in the West. The New Rome of the East lasted for more than a millennium until its final defeat at the hands of the Muslims in 1453. By then, however, Byzantine artists had already made a major impact on the art of the West (see Chapter 19).

527

EARLY BYZANTINE

1 | JUSTINIAN, R. 527–565
| NIKA RIOTS IN CONSTANTINOPLE, 532
| BELISARIUS CAPTURES RAVENNA, 539
| HERACLIUS DEFEATS PERSIANS, 627
| ARABS BESIEGE CONSTANTINOPLE, 717–718

1 Hagia Sophia, Constantinople, 532–537

726

ICONOCLASM

| LEO III PROHIBITS IMAGE MAKING, 726
| RAVENNA FALLS TO THE LOMBARDS, 751

843

MIDDLE BYZANTINE

| RESTORATION OF IMAGES, 843
| BASIL I, R. 867–886, FOUNDER OF MACEDONIAN DYNASTY
2 | BASIL II, R. 980–1001, REVIVAL OF BYZANTINE POWER
| SCHISM BETWEEN BYZANTINE AND ROMAN CHURCHES, 1054
| NORMAN CONQUEST OF SICILY, 1060–1092
| SELJUK TURKS CAPTURE BYZANTINE ASIA MINOR, 1073
3 | FIRST CRUSADE, 1095–1099
| FOURTH CRUSADE AND THE FRANKISH CONQUEST, 1202–1204

2 *Paris Psalter,* ca. 950–970

1204

LATE BYZANTINE

| MICHAEL VIII PALAEOLOGUS RECAPTURES CONSTANTINOPLE
FROM THE FRANKS, 1261

3 Vladimir Virgin, late
11th–early 12th century

4

1453

| OTTOMAN TURKS CAPTURE CONSTANTINOPLE;
END OF BYZANTINE EMPIRE, 1453

4 Church of Christ in Chora,
Constantinople, ca. 1310–1320

Dome in front of the mihrab of the Great Mosque, Córdoba, Spain, 961–965.

13

IN PRAISE OF ALLAH

THE ART OF THE ISLAMIC WORLD

The religion of *Islam* (an Arabic word meaning "submission to God") arose among the peoples of the Arabian peninsula early in the seventh century (see "Muhammad and Islam," page 359). The Arabs were nomadic herders and caravan merchants traversing, from ancient times, the wastes and oases of the vast Arabian desert and settling and controlling its coasts. When Islam arose, the Arabs were peripheral to the Byzantine and Persian empires. Yet within little more than a century, the Mediterranean, once ringed and ruled by Byzantium, had become an Islamic lake, and the armies of Islam had subdued the Middle East, long the seat of Persian dominance and influence.

The swiftness of the Islamic advance is among the wonders of world history. By 640, Muslims ruled Syria, Palestine, and Iraq in the name of Allah. In 642, the Byzantine army abandoned Alexandria, marking the Muslim conquest of Lower (northern) Egypt. In 651, the successors of Muhammad brought more than 400 years of Sasanian rule in Iran to an end (see Chapter 2). By 710, all of North Africa was under Muslim control. A victory at Jerez de la Frontera in southern Spain in 711 seemed to open all of western Europe to the Muslims. By 732, they had advanced north to Poitiers in France. There, however, an army of Franks under Charles Martel, the grandfather of Charlemagne, opposed them successfully (see Chapter 16). Although Islamic forces continued to conduct raids in France, they could not extend their control beyond the Pyrenees along the French-Spanish border. But in Spain, the Muslim rulers of Córdoba flourished until 1031, and not until 1492 did Islamic influence and power in the Iberian Peninsula end. That year the caliphs of Granada fell to King Ferdinand and Queen Isabella, the sponsors of Columbus's voyage to the New World. In the East, the Muslims reached the Indus River by 751, and only in Anatolia could stubborn Byzantine resistance slow their advance. Relentless Muslim pressure against the shrinking Byzantine Empire eventually caused its collapse in 1453, when the Ottoman Turks entered Constantinople (see Chapter 12).

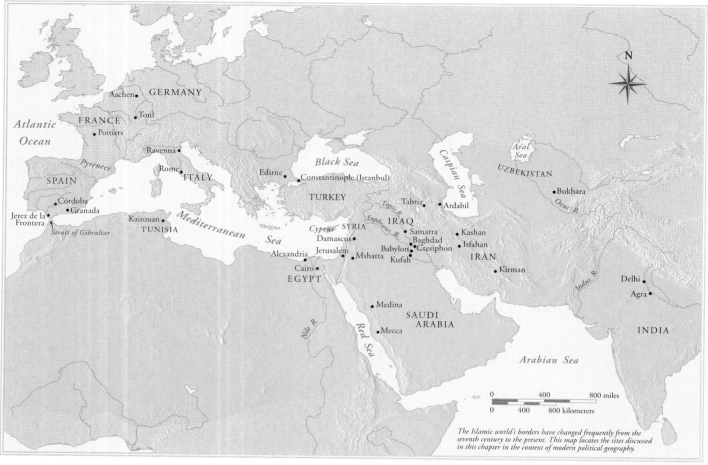

MAP 13-1 The Islamic world.

The Islamic world's borders have changed frequently from the seventh century to the present. This map locates the sites discussed in this chapter in the context of modern political geography.

THE IMPACT OF ISLAM The irresistible and far-ranging sweep of Islam from Arabia to India to North Africa and Spain (MAP **13-1**) was not due to military might alone. That the initial victories had effects that endured for centuries can be explained only by the nature of Islamic faith and its appeal to millions of converts. Islam remains today one of the world's great religions, with adherents on all continents. And the sophistication of its culture has had a profound impact around the globe. Christian scholars in the West during the 12th and 13th centuries eagerly studied Arabic translations of Aristotle and other Greek writers of antiquity (see Chapter 18). Arabic love lyrics and poetic descriptions of nature inspired the early French troubadours. Arab scholars laid the foundations of arithmetic and algebra, and their contributions to astronomy, medicine, and the natural sciences have made a lasting impression in the Western world.

The triumph of Islam also brought a new and compelling tradition to the history of world art and architecture. Like Islam itself, Islamic art spread quickly both eastward and westward from the land once inhabited by the peoples of the ancient Near East and their Sasanian successors (see MAP 2-1). In the Middle East and North Africa, Islamic art largely replaced Late Antique art. And from a foothold in the Iberian peninsula, Islamic art made an impact on Western medieval art, although Islamic art stands in sharp contrast both to the figural art of Europe and the Mediterranean and to the Western architectural vocabulary. Islamic artists and architects also brought their distinctive style to South Asia, where a Muslim sultanate was established at Delhi in India in the early 13th century (see Chapter 25). In fact, perhaps the most famous building in Asia, the Taj Mahal (see FIG. 25-5) at Agra, is an Islamic mausoleum.

EARLY ISLAMIC ART

During the early centuries of Islamic history, the Muslim world's political and cultural center was the Fertile Crescent of ancient Mesopotamia. This crescent-shaped area of cultivable land was strewn with impressive ruins of earlier cultures, from the Sumerians to the Sasanians (see Chapter 2). The caliphs of Damascus (capital of modern Syria) and Baghdad (capital of Iraq) appointed provincial governors to rule the vast territories they controlled. These governors eventually gained relative independence by setting up dynasties in various territories and provinces: the Umayyads in Syria (661–749) and in Spain (756–1031), the Abbasids in Iraq (750–1258, largely nominal after 945), the Fatimids in Egypt (909–1171), and so on. Like other potentates before and after, the Islamic rulers were builders on a grand scale.

Architecture

TRIUMPH IN JERUSALEM The first great achievement of Islamic architecture is the Dome of the Rock (FIG. **13-1**) in Jerusalem. The Muslims had taken the city from the Byzantines in 638, and the Umayyad caliph Abd al-Malik (r. 685–705) erected the monumental sanctuary between 687 and 692 as an architectural tribute to the triumph of Islam. The Dome of the Rock marked the coming of the new religion to the city that had been, and still is, sacred to both Jews and Christians. The structure rises from a huge platform known as the Noble Enclosure. Even today it dominates the skyline of the holy city. The sanctuary was erected

Muhammad and Islam

Muhammad, founder of Islam and revered as its Final Prophet, was a native of Mecca on the west coast of Arabia. Born around 570 into a family of merchants in the great Arabian caravan trade, Muhammad was inspired to prophecy. Critical of the polytheistic religion of his fellow Arabs, he preached a religion of the one and only God (*Allah* in Arabic), whose revelations Muhammad received beginning in 610 and for the rest of his life. Opposition to Muhammad's message among the Arabs was strong enough to prompt the Prophet and his growing number of followers to flee from Mecca to a desert oasis eventually called Medina ("City of the Prophet"). Islam dates its beginnings from this flight in 622, known as the *Hijra* (emigration).[1] Barely eight years later, in 630, Muhammad returned to Mecca with 10,000 soldiers. He took control of the city, converted the population to Islam, and destroyed all the idols. But he preserved as the Islamic world's symbolic center the small cubical building that had housed the idols, the *Kaaba* (from the Arabic for "cube"). The Arabs associated the Kaaba with the era of Abraham and Ishmael, the common ancestors of Jews and Arabs. Muhammad died in Medina in 632.

The essential meaning of Islam is acceptance of and submission to Allah's will. Believers in Islam are called *Muslims* ("those who submit"). Islam requires living according to the rules laid down in the collected revelations communicated through Muhammad during his lifetime. These are recorded in the *Koran,* Islam's sacred book, codified by the Muslim ruler Uthman (r. 644–656). The word "Koran" means "recitations"—a reference to the archangel Gabriel's instructions to Muhammad in 610 to "recite in the name of Allah." The Koran is composed of 114 *surahs* (chapters) divided into verses.

The profession of faith in the one God, Allah, is the first of five obligations binding all Muslims. In addition, the faithful must worship five times daily, facing in Mecca's direction; give alms to the poor; fast during the month of Ramadan; and once in a lifetime—if possible—make a pilgrimage to Mecca. Muslims are guided not only by the revelations in the Koran but also by Muhammad's life. The Prophet's exemplary ways and customs, collected in the *Sunnah,* are supplemental to the Koran, offering guidance to the faithful on ethical problems of everyday life. The reward for the Muslim faithful is Paradise.

Islam has much in common with Judaism and Christianity. Its adherents think of it as a continuation, completion, and in some sense a reformation of those other great monotheisms. Islam incorporates many of the Old Testament teachings, with their sober ethical standards and hatred of idol worship, and those of the New Testament Gospels. Adam, Abraham, Moses, and Jesus are acknowledged as the prophetic predecessors of Muhammad, the final and greatest of the prophets. Muhammad did not claim to be divine, as did Jesus, and he did not perform miracles. Rather, he was God's messenger, the purifier and perfecter of the common faith of Jews, Christians, and Muslims in one God. Islam also differs from Judaism and Christianity in its simpler organization. Muslims worship God directly, without a hierarchy of rabbis, priests, or saints acting as intermediaries.

In Islam, as Muhammad defined it, religious and secular authority were united even more completely than in Byzantium. Muhammad established a new social order, replacing the Arabs' old decentralized tribal one. In this he was influenced, no doubt, by the examples of the emperors and kings reigning in the lands his people would occupy. He took complete charge of his community's temporal, as well as spiritual, affairs. After Muhammad's death, the *caliphs* (from the Arabic for "successor") continued this practice of uniting religious and political leadership in one ruler.

[1] Muslims date events beginning with the Hijra in the same way Christians reckon events from Christ's birth and the Romans before them began their calendar with Rome's founding by Romulus in 753 BCE. The Muslim year is, however, a 354-day year of 12 lunar months, and dates cannot be converted by simply adding 622 to Christian-era dates.

13-1 Dome of the Rock, Jerusalem, 687–692.

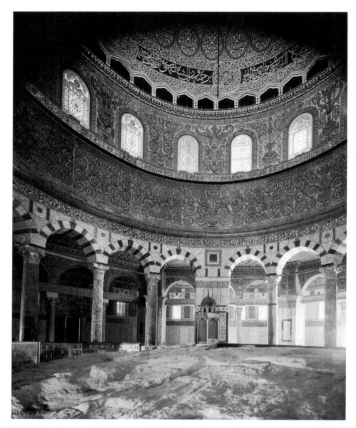

13-2 Interior of the Dome of the Rock, Jerusalem, 687–692.

design, construction, and ornamentation principles that had long been applied in, and were still current in, Byzantium and the Middle East. The Dome of the Rock is a domed octagon resembling San Vitale in Ravenna (see FIG. 12-6) in its basic design. In all likelihood, a neighboring Christian monument, Constantine the Great's Rotunda of the Holy Sepulchre, inspired the Dome of the Rock's designers. That fourth-century rotunda bore a family resemblance to the roughly contemporary Constantinian mausoleum (later rededicated as Santa Costanza) in Rome (see FIGS. 11-9 and 11-10). The Dome of the Rock is a member of the same extended family. Its double-shelled wooden dome, however, some 60 feet across and 75 feet high, so dominates the elevation as to reduce the octagon to function merely as its base. This soaring, majestic unit creates a decidedly more commanding effect than that of Late Roman and Byzantine domical structures (see, for example, FIGS. 11-10 and 12-3). The silhouettes of those domes are comparatively insignificant when seen from the outside.

The building's exterior has been much restored. Tiling from the 16th century and later has replaced the original mosaic. Yet the vivid, colorful patterning that wraps the walls like a textile is typical of Islamic ornamentation. It contrasts markedly with Byzantine brickwork and Greco-Roman sculptured profiling and carved decoration. The interior's rich mosaic ornament (FIG. 13-2) has been preserved. From it one can imagine how the exterior walls originally appeared. Islamic practice does not significantly distinguish interior and exterior decor. The splendor of infinitely various surfaces is given to public gaze both within and outside buildings.

NEW CAPITAL, NEW MOSQUE The Umayyads transferred their capital from Mecca to Damascus in 661. There, Abd al-Malik's son, the caliph al-Walid (r. 705–715), purchased a Byzantine church (formerly a Roman temple) and built an imposing new mosque for the expanding Muslim population (see "The Mosque," page 361). The Umayyads demolished the church, but they used the Roman precinct walls as a foundation for their own construction. Like the Dome of the Rock, the Great Mosque of Damascus (FIG. 13-3) owes much to the architecture of the

on the traditional site of Adam's burial, of Abraham's preparation for Isaac's sacrifice, and of the Temple of Solomon the Romans destroyed in 70. It houses the rock (FIG. **13-2**) from which Muslims later came to believe Muhammad ascended to Heaven.

As Islam took much of its teaching from Judaism and Christianity, so its architects and artists borrowed and transformed

13-3 Aerial view of the Great Mosque, Damascus, Syria, 706–715.

The Mosque

Islamic religious architecture is closely related to Muslim prayer, an obligation laid down in the Koran for all Muslims. In Islam, worshiping can be a private act. It requires neither prescribed ceremony nor a special locale. Only the *qibla*—the direction (toward Mecca) Muslims face while praying—is important. But worship also became a communal act when the first Muslim community established a simple ritual for it. To celebrate the Muslim sabbath, which occurs on Friday, the community convened each Friday at noon, probably in the Prophet's house in Medina. The main feature of Muhammad's house was a large square court with rows of palm trunks supporting thatched roofs along the north and south sides. The southern side was wider and had a double row of trunks. It faced Mecca. During these communal gatherings, the *imam,* or leader of collective worship, stood on a stepped pulpit, or *minbar,* set up in front of the southern (qibla) wall.

These features became standard in the Islamic house of worship, the *mosque* (from Arabic *masjid,* a place of prostration), where the faithful gathered for the five daily prayers. The *congregational mosque* (also called the *Friday mosque* or *great mosque*), was ideally large enough to accommodate a community's entire population for the Friday noonday prayer. A very important feature both of ordinary mosques and of congregational mosques is the *mihrab,* a semicircular niche usually set into the qibla wall (FIG. 13-8). Often a dome over the bay in front of it marked its position (FIGS. 13-3, 13-8, and 13-13). The niche was a familiar Greco-Roman architectural feature, generally enclosing a statue. But for Islamic architecture, its origin, purpose, and meaning are still debated. Some scholars believe the mihrab originally may have honored the place where the Prophet stood in his house at

Medina when he led communal worship. It thus would have been a revered religious memorial.

In some mosques, a *maqsura* precedes the mihrab. The maqsura is the area generally reserved for the ruler or his representative and can be quite elaborate in form (FIG. 13-12). Many mosques also have one or more *minarets* (FIGS. 13-3, 13-9, and 13-20), towers from which the faithful are called to worship. When buildings of other faiths were converted into mosques, the change was clearly signaled on the exterior by the erection of minarets (see FIG. 12-3). Early mosques are generally characterized by *hypostyle halls,* communal worship halls with roofs held up by a multitude of columns (FIGS. 13-8 and 13-11). Later variations of the early mosque formulation include mosques with four *iwans* (vaulted rectangular recesses), one on each side of the courtyard (FIG. 13-23), and *central-plan* mosques with a single large dome-covered interior space (FIGS. 13-20 to 13-22), as in Byzantine churches, some of which were later converted to mosques (see FIGS. 12-3 to 12-5).

The mosque's origin is still in dispute, although one prototype may well have been the Prophet's house in Medina. Once the Muslims had firmly established themselves in their acquired territories, they began to build on a large scale, impelled, perhaps, by a desire to create such visible evidence of their power as would surpass in size and splendor that of their non-Islamic predecessors. Today, mosques continue to be erected throughout the world. Despite many variations in design and detail and the employment of modern building techniques and materials unknown in Muhammad's day, the mosque's essential features are unchanged. All mosques, wherever they are built and whatever their plan, are oriented toward Mecca, and the faithful worship facing the qibla wall.

Greco-Roman and Early Christian East. It is constructed of masonry blocks, columns, and capitals salvaged from the Roman and Early Christian structures on the land al-Walid acquired for his mosque. The courtyard is bounded by pier arcades reminiscent of Roman aqueducts. The minarets, two at the southern corners and one at the northern side of the enclosure—the earliest in the Islamic world—are modifications of the preexisting Roman square towers. The grand prayer hall, taller than the rest of the complex, is on the south side of the courtyard (facing Mecca). Its main entrance is distinguished by a facade with a pediment and arches, recalling classical and Byzantine models, respectively. The facade faces into the courtyard, like a Roman forum temple (see FIG. 10-10), a plan maintained throughout the long history of mosque architecture. The Damascus mosque synthesizes elements received from other cultures into a novel architectural unity, which includes the distinctive Islamic elements of mihrab, mihrab dome, minbar, and minaret.

An extensive cycle of mosaics once covered the walls of the Great Mosque. In one of the surviving sections (FIG. **13-4**), a conch shell niche "supports" an arcaded pavilion with a flowering rooftop flanked by structures shown in classical perspective. Like the architectural design, the mosaics owe much to Roman, Early Christian, and Byzantine art (compare FIGS. 10-22 and 11-18). Indeed, some evidence indicates that the Great Mosque mosaics were the work of Byzantine mosaicists. Characteristically, tem-

13-4 Detail of a mosaic in the courtyard arcade of the Great Mosque, Damascus, Syria, 706–715.

ples, clusters of houses, trees, and rivers compose the pictorial fields, bounded by stylized vegetal design, familiar in Roman, Early Christian, and Byzantine ornament. No zoomorphic forms, human or animal, appear either in the pictorial or ornamental spaces. This is true of all the mosaics in the Great Mosque as well as the mosaics in the earlier Dome of the Rock (FIG. 13-2). Islamic tradition shuns the representation of fauna of any kind in sacred places. The world shown in the Damascus mosaics, suspended miragelike in a featureless field of gold, was explained in accompanying (but now lost) inscriptions as an image of Paradise. Many passages from the Koran describe the gorgeous places of Paradise awaiting the faithful—gardens, groves of trees, flowing streams, and "lofty chambers." Indeed, the abundant luxurious images and ornament, floating free of all human reference, create a vision of Paradise appealing to the spiritually oriented imagination, whatever its religion.

AN UMAYYAD DESERT PALACE The Umayyad rulers of Damascus constructed numerous palatial residences throughout the vast territories they governed. The urban palaces are lost, but some rural palaces survive. The latter were not merely idyllic residences removed from the congestion, noise, and disease of the cities. They seem to have served as nuclei for the agricultural development of acquired territories and possibly as hunting lodges. In addition, the Islamic palaces were symbols of authority over new lands, as well as expressions of their owners' wealth.

One of the most impressive Umayyad palaces, despite the fact that it was never completed, is at Mshatta in the Jordanian desert. Its plan (FIG. **13-5**) resembles that of Diocletian's palace at Split (see FIG. 10-75), which in turn reflects the layout of a Roman fortified camp. The high walls of the Mshatta palace incorporate 25 towers but lack parapet walkways for patrolling guards. The walls, nonetheless, offered safety from marauding nomadic tribes and provided privacy for the caliph and his entourage. Visitors entered the palace through a large portal on the south side. To the right was a mosque (the plan shows the mihrab niche in the qibla wall), in which the rulers and their guests could fulfill their obligation to pray five times a day. The mosque was separated from the palace's residential wing and official audience hall by a small ceremonial area and an immense open courtyard. Most Umayyad palaces also were provided with fairly elaborate bathing facilities that displayed technical features, such as heating systems, adopted from Roman baths. Just as under the Roman Empire, these baths probably served more than merely hygienic purposes. Indeed, in several Umayyad palaces, excavators have uncovered in the baths paintings and sculptures of hunting and other secular themes, including depictions of dancing women—themes traditionally associated with royalty in the Near East. Large halls frequently attached to many of these baths seem to have been used as places of entertainment, as was the case in Roman times. Thus, the bath-spa-social center, a characteristic amenity of Roman urban culture that died out in the Christian world, survived in Islamic culture.

The architectural ornamentation of many of the early Islamic palaces was confined to simply molded stucco and decorative brickwork, but at Mshatta the facade is enlivened by a richly carved stone frieze (FIG. **13-6**). The long band is more than 16 feet high and consists of a series of triangles framed by elaborately carved moldings. Each triangle contains a large rosette that

0   50   100   150   FEET
0   10   20   30   40   50   METERS

1. Entrance gate
2. Mosque
3. Small courtyard
4. Large courtyard
5. Audience hall

N

13-5 Plan of the Umayyad palace, Mshatta, Jordan, ca. 740–750 (after Alberto Berengo Gardin).

projects from a field densely covered with curvilinear, vegetal designs. No two triangles were treated the same way, and animal figures appear in some of them. Similar compositions of birds, felines, and vegetal scrolls can be found in Roman, Byzantine, and Sasanian art. The Mshatta frieze, however, has no animal figures to the right of the entrance portal—that is, on the part of the facade corresponding to the mosque's qibla wall.

THE ABBASID CITY OF PEACE In 750, after years of civil war, the Abbasids, who claimed descent from Abbas, an uncle of Muhammad, overthrew the Umayyad caliphs. The new rulers moved the capital from Damascus to a site in Iraq near the old Sasanian capital of Ctesiphon (see FIG. 2-28). There the caliph al-Mansur (r. 754–775) established a new capital, Baghdad, which he called Madina al-salam, the City of Peace. The city was laid out in 762 at a time astrologers determined as favorable. It was round in plan, about a mile and a half in diameter. The shape signified that the new capital was the center of the universe. At the city's center was the caliph's palace, oriented to the four compass points.

For almost 300 years Baghdad was the hub of Arab power and of a brilliant Islamic culture. The Abbasid caliphs were renowned throughout the world and even established diplomatic relations with Charlemagne at Aachen in Germany. The Abbasids lavished their wealth on art, literature, and science and were responsible for the translation of numerous Greek texts that otherwise would

13-6 Frieze of the Umayyad palace, Mshatta, Jordan, ca. 740–750. Limestone, 16′ 7″ high. Museum für Islamische Kunst, Staatliche Museen, Berlin.

have been lost. Many of these works were introduced to the medieval West through their Arabic versions.

KAIROUAN'S HYPOSTYLE MOSQUE Of all the variations in mosque plans, the hypostyle mosque most closely reflects the mosque's supposed origin, Muhammad's house in Medina (see "The Mosque," page 361). One of the finest hypostyle mosques, still in use today, is the mid-eighth-century Great Mosque at Kairouan (FIGS. **13-7** and **13-8**) in Abbasid Tunisia. It still houses its carved wooden minbar of 862, the oldest known. The precinct takes the form of a slightly askew parallelogram of huge scale, some 450 × 260 feet. Built of stone, its walls have sturdy buttresses, square in profile. A series of lateral entrances on the east and west lead to an arcaded forecourt (no. 7 on the plan), oriented north-south on axis with the mosque's impressive minaret

(no. 8) and the two domes (nos. 3 and 6) of the hypostyle prayer hall (no. 4). The first dome (no. 6) is over the entrance bay, the second (no. 3) over the bay that fronts the mihrab (no. 2) set into the qibla wall (no. 1). A raised nave connects the domed spaces and prolongs the north-south axis of the minaret and courtyard. Eight columned aisles flank the nave on either side, providing space for a large congregation.

SAMARRA'S SPIRAL MINARET The three-story minaret of the Kairouan mosque is square in plan and believed to be a near copy of a Roman lighthouse, but minarets can take a variety of forms. Perhaps the most striking and novel is that of the immense (more than 45,000 square yards) Great Mosque at Samarra, Iraq, the largest mosque in the world. The Abbasid caliph al-Mutawakkil (r. 847–861) erected it between 848 and

13-7 Aerial view of the Great Mosque, Kairouan, Tunisia, ca. 836–875.

1. Qibla wall	5. Nave
2. Mihrab	6. Entrance dome
3. Mihrab dome	7. Forecourt
4. Hypostyle prayer hall	8. Minaret

0   50   100   FEET

0   10   20   30   METERS

13-8 Plan of the Great Mosque, Kairouan, Tunisia, ca. 836–875.

13-9 *Malwiya* minaret of the Great Mosque, Samarra, Iraq, 848–852.

13-10 Mausoleum of the Samanids, Bukhara, Uzbekistan, early 10th century.

852. Known as the *Malwiya* ("snail shell" in Arabic) minaret (FIG. **13-9**) and more than 165 feet tall (note how it dwarfs the modern fence), it now stands alone, but originally a bridge linked it to the mosque. The brick tower is distinguished by its stepped spiral ramp, which increases in slope from bottom to top. Many have compared its form to the ziggurats of ancient Mesopotamia (see FIGS. 2-2 and 2-14), but those rectilinear stepped platforms bear very little resemblance to the Samarran minaret. Nonetheless, the minaret inspired some later European depictions of the biblical Tower of Babel (Babylon's ziggurat; see "Babylon: City of Wonders," Chapter 2, page 49). Too tall to have been used to call Muslims to prayer, the *Malwiya* minaret, visible from a considerable distance in the flat plain around Samarra, was probably intended to announce the presence of Islam in the Tigris Valley.

MEMORIALIZING THE DEAD The eastern realms of the Abbasid empire were overseen by dynasties of governors who exercised considerable independence while recognizing the ultimate authority of the Baghdad caliphs. One of these dynasties, the Samanids (r. 819–1005), presided over the eastern frontier beyond the Oxus River (Transoxiana) on the border with India. In the early 10th century, they erected an impressive domed brick mausoleum (FIG. **13-10**) at Bukhara in modern Uzbekistan. Monumental tombs were virtually unknown in the early Islamic period. Muhammad had been opposed to elaborate burials and instructed his followers to bury him in a simple unmarked grave. In time, however, the Prophet's resting place in Medina was enclosed by a wooden screen and covered by a dome. By the ninth century, Abbasid caliphs were laid to rest in dynastic mausoleums.

The Samanid mausoleum at Bukhara is one of the earliest preserved tombs in the Islamic world. It is constructed of baked bricks and takes the form of a cube with slightly sloping sides capped by a dome. With exceptional skill, the builders painstakingly shaped the bricks to create a vivid and varied surface pattern. Some of the bricks form engaged columns at the corners. A brick *blind arcade* (a series of arches in relief, with blocked openings) runs around all four sides. Inside, the walls are as elaborate as the exterior. The brick dome rests on arcuated brick squinches (see "Pendentives and Squinches," Chapter 12, page 331) framed by engaged colonnettes. The dome-on-cube form had a long and distinguished future in Islamic funerary architecture.

UMAYYAD CÓRDOBA At the opposite end of the Muslim world, Abd-al-Rahman I, the only Umayyad notable to escape the Abbasid massacre of his clan in Syria, fled to Spain in 750. There, the Arabs had overthrown the Christian kingdom of the Visigoths in 711. The Arab military governors of the peninsula accepted the fugitive as their overlord, and he founded the Spanish Umayyad dynasty, which lasted for almost three centuries. The capital of the Spanish Umayyads was Córdoba, which became the center of a brilliant culture rivaling that of the Abbasids at Baghdad and exerting major influence on the civilization of the Christian West.

The jewel of the capital at Córdoba was its Great Mosque, begun in 784 and enlarged several times during the 9th and 10th centuries. It eventually became one of the largest mosques in the Islamic West. The additions followed the original style and arrangement of columns and arches, and the builders maintained a striking stylistic unity for the entire building. The hypostyle prayer hall (FIG. **13-11**) has 36 piers and 514 columns topped by a unique system of double-tiered arches that carried a wooden roof (now replaced by vaults). The two-story system was the builders' response to the need to raise the roof to an acceptable height using short columns that had been employed earlier in other structures. The lower arches are horseshoe-shaped, a form perhaps adapted from earlier Near Eastern architecture or of Visigothic origin (see FIG. 16-10). In the West, the horseshoe arch quickly became closely associated with Muslim architecture. Visually, these arches seem to

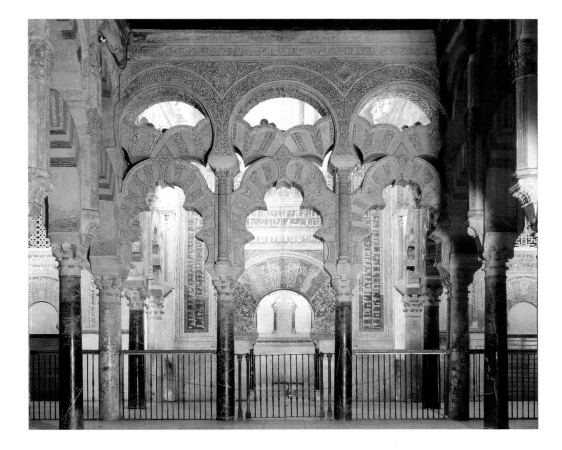

billow out like sails blown by the wind, and they contribute greatly to the light and airy effect of the Córdoba mosque's interior.

The caliph al-Hakam II (r. 961–976) undertook major renovations to the mosque. His builders expanded the prayer hall and added a series of domes. They also erected the elaborate maqsura (FIG. **13-12**), the area reserved for the caliph and connected to his palace by a corridor in the qibla wall. The Córdoba maqsura is a prime example of Islamic experimentation with highly decorative multilobed arches. The builders created rich and varied abstract patterns and further enhanced the magnificent effect of the complex arches by sheathing the walls with marbles and mosaics. The mosaicists and even the tesserae were brought to Spain from

13-12 Maqsura of the Great Mosque, Córdoba, Spain, 961–965.

13-13 Dome in front of the mihrab of the Great Mosque, Córdoba, Spain, 961–965.

Constantinople by al-Hakam II, who wished to emulate the great mosaic-clad monuments his Umayyad predecessors had erected in Jerusalem (FIG. 13-2) and Damascus (FIG. 13-4).

The same desire for decorative effect also inspired the design of the dome (FIG. **13-13**) that covers the area in front of the mihrab, one of the four domes built during the 10th century to emphasize the axis leading to the mihrab. The dome rests on an octagonal base of arcuated squinches and is crisscrossed by *ribs* that form an intricate pattern centered on two squares set at 45-degree angles to each other. The mosaics are the work of the same Byzantine artists responsible for the maqsura's decoration.

Luxury Arts

ARABESQUES In the mosaics at Córdoba, as elsewhere in the Islamic world, most of the design elements are based on plant motifs, which are sometimes intermingled with abstract geometric shapes and, in secular settings, with animal figures. Often the natural forms are so stylized that they are lost in the purely decorative tracery of the tendrils, leaves, and stalks. These *arabesque*s—so called because they are one of the most distinctive features of Islamic ("Arab") art—form abstract patterns of extraordinary beauty and complexity, usually covering an entire surface, whether that of a small utensil or the wall of a building. This ornamental system offers a potential for unlimited growth, as it

permits extension of the designs in any desired direction. Most characteristic, perhaps, is the arabesque's independence of its carrier. Neither its size (within limits) nor its forms are dictated by anything but the design itself.

ISLAMIC SILK Both arabesques and figural patterns appear frequently on movable furnishings, such as rugs and hangings. Wood is scarce in most of the Islamic world, and the kind of furniture used in the West—beds, tables, and chairs—is rarely found in Muslim structures. Architectural spaces, therefore, are not defined by the type of furniture placed in them. A room's function (eating or sleeping, for example) can change simply by rearranging the carpets and cushions.

Silk textiles and wool carpets are among the glories of Islamic art. Unfortunately, because of their fragile nature and the heavy wear carpets endure, early Islamic textiles are rare today and often fragmentary. Silk thread was also very expensive. Silk is produced by silkworms, which can flourish only in certain temperate regions. Silk textiles were manufactured first in China in the third millennium BCE. They were shipped over what came to be called the Silk Road through Asia to the Middle East and Europe (see "Silk and the Silk Road," Chapter 7, page 201).

One of the earliest Islamic silks (FIG. **13-14**) is found today in Nancy, France. Unfortunately, it is fragmentary, and its colors, once rich blues, greens, and oranges, faded long ago. The silk survives because it was associated with the relics of Saint Amon housed in Toul Cathedral. The precious fabric may have been used to wrap the treasures when they were transported to France in 820. It probably dates to the eighth century and is said to come from Zandana near Bukhara. The design consists of repeated medallions with confronting lions flanking a palm tree. Other animals scamper across the silk between the roundels. Such zoomorphic

13-14 Confronting lions and palm tree, fragment of a textile said to be from Zandana, near Bukhara, Uzbekistan, eighth century. Silk compound twill, 2′ 11″ × 2′ 9½″. Musée Historique de Lorraine, Nancy.

motifs are foreign to the decorative vocabulary of mosque architecture, but they could be found in Muslim households—even in Muhammad's in Medina. The Prophet, however, was said to have objected to curtains decorated with figures and permitted only cushions adorned with animals or birds.

A SIGNED ZOOMORPHIC EWER The furnishings of Islamic palaces and mosques reflected a love of sumptuous materials and rich decorative patterns. Metal, wood, glass, and ivory were artfully worked into a great variety of objects for the mosque or home. Colored glass was used with striking effect in mosque lamps. Ornate ceramics of high quality were produced in large numbers. Basins, ewers, jewel cases, writing boxes, and other decorative items were made of bronze or brass, engraved, and inlaid with silver.

One of the most striking examples of the metalworker's art is the cast brass ewer in the form of a bird (FIG. **13-15**) signed by SULAYMAN and dated 796. (The place of origin also was inscribed but is illegible today.) Some 15 inches tall, the ewer is nothing less than a freestanding statuette, although the holes between the eyes and beak function as a spout and betray its utilitarian purpose. The decoration on the body, which bears traces of silver and copper inlay, takes a variety of forms. In places, the incised lines seem

to suggest natural feathers, but the rosettes on the neck, the large medallions on the breast, and the inscribed collar have no basis in anatomy. Similar motifs can be found in Islamic textiles, pottery, and architectural tiles. The ready adaptability of motifs to various scales and to various techniques again illustrates both the flexibility of Islamic design and its relative independence from its carrier.

THE ART OF THE KORAN In the Islamic world, the art of *calligraphy,* ornamental writing, was more revered even than the art of textiles. The faithful wanted to reproduce the Koran's sacred words in as beautiful a script as human hands could contrive. And these words were displayed not only on the fragile pages of books but also on the walls of buildings. Quotations from the Koran appear, for example, in a mosaic band above the outer ring of columns inside the Dome of the Rock (FIG. 13-2). The practice of calligraphy was itself a holy task and required long and arduous training. The scribe had to possess exceptional spiritual refinement. An ancient Arabic proverb proclaims, "Purity of writing is purity of soul." Only in China does calligraphy hold so supreme a position among the arts (see "Calligraphy and Inscriptions on Chinese Paintings," Chapter 26, page 766).

Arabic script predates Islam. It is written from right to left with certain characters connected by a baseline. Although the chief Islamic book, the sacred Koran, was codified in the mid-seventh century, the earliest preserved Korans are datable to the ninth century. Koran pages were either bound into books or stored as loose sheets in boxes. Most of the early examples are written in the script form called *Kufic,* after the city of Kufah, one of the renowned centers of Arabic calligraphy. Kufic script is quite angular, with the uprights forming almost right angles with the baseline. As with Hebrew and other Semitic languages, the usual practice was to write in consonants only. But to facilitate recitation of the Koran, scribes often indicated vowels by red or yellow symbols above or below the line.

All of these features can be seen on a 9th- or early 10th-century page (FIG. **13-16**) in Dublin that carries the heading and opening lines of surah 18 of the Koran. Five text lines in black ink with red vowels appear below a decorative band incorporating the chapter title in gold and ending in a palm-tree *finial* (a crowning ornament). This approach to page design has parallels at the extreme northwestern corner of the then-known world—in the early medieval manuscripts of the British Isles, where text and ornament are similarly united (see FIG. 16-8). But the stylized human and animal forms that populate those Christian books never appear in Korans.

LATER ISLAMIC ART

Architecture

THE NASRIDS' RED FORTRESS In the early years of the 11th century, the Umayyad caliphs' power in Spain unraveled, and their palaces fell prey to Berber soldiers from North Africa. The Berbers ruled southern Spain for several generations but could not resist the pressure of Christian forces from the north. Córdoba fell to the Christians in 1236. From then until the final Christian triumph in 1492, the Nasrids, an Arab dynasty that had established its capital at Granada in 1230, ruled the remaining Muslim territories in Spain.

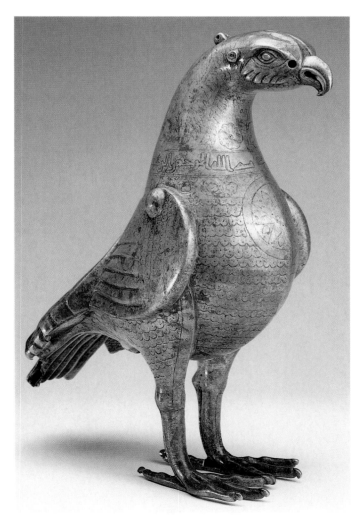

13-15 SULAYMAN, Ewer in the form of a bird, 796. Brass with silver and copper inlay, 1′ 3″ high. Hermitage, Saint Petersburg.

13-16 Koran page with beginning of surah 18, *al-Kahf (The Cave)*, 9th or early 10th century. Ink and gold on vellum, $7\frac{1}{4}'' \times 10\frac{1}{4}''$. Chester Beatty Library and Oriental Art Gallery, Dublin.

On a rocky spur at Granada, the Nasrids constructed a huge palace-fortress called the Alhambra ("the Red" in Arabic) because of the rose color of the stone used for its walls and 23 towers. By the end of the 14th century, the complex, a veritable city with a population of 40,000, included at least a half dozen royal residences. Only two of these fared well over the centuries. They present a vivid picture of court life in Islamic Spain before the Christian reconquest. Paradoxically, the two palaces owe their preservation to the Christian victors, who maintained a few of the buildings as trophies commemorating the expulsion of the Nasrids.

PARADISE AND HEAVEN One of those palaces is the Palace of the Lions, named for the courtyard fountain with marble lions carrying its water basin on their backs. It is an unusual instance of freestanding stone sculpture in the Islamic world. The palace was the residence of Muhammad V (r. 1354–1391), and its courtyards, lush gardens, and luxurious carpets and other furnishings were designed to conjure the image of Paradise. The complex is noteworthy also for its elaborate stucco ceilings and walls, which never fail to impress visitors.

We reproduce a view of the ceiling of the so-called Hall of the Two Sisters (FIG. **13-17**) in the Palace of the Lions. The dome of the square room rests on an octagonal drum supported by squinches and pierced by eight pairs of windows, but its structure is difficult to discern because of the intricately carved stucco decoration. The ceiling is covered with some 5,000 *muqarnas*—tier after tier of stalactite-like prismatic forms that seem aimed at denying the structure's solidity. The muqarnas ceiling was intended to catch and reflect sunlight as well as form beautiful abstract patterns. The lofty vault in this hall and others in the palace were meant to symbolize the dome of Heaven. The flickering light

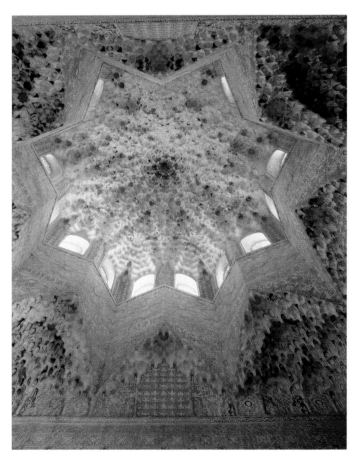

13-17 Muqarnas dome, Hall of the Two Sisters, Alhambra palace, Granada, Spain, 1354–1391.

and shadows create the effect of a starry sky as the sun's rays move from window to window during the day. To underscore the symbolism, the palace walls were inscribed with verses by the court poet Ibn Zamrak, who compared the Alhambra's lacelike muqarnas ceilings to "the heavenly spheres whose orbits revolve."

THE SLAVE SULTANS OF EGYPT In the mid-13th century, the Mongols from east-central Asia (see Chapter 26) conquered much of the eastern Islamic world. The center of Islamic power moved from Baghdad to Egypt. The lords of Egypt at the time were former Turkish slaves (*mamluks* in Arabic) who converted to Islam. The capital of the Mamluk *sultans* (rulers) was Cairo, which became the largest Muslim city of the late Middle Ages. The Mamluks were prolific builders, and Sultan Hasan, although not an important figure in Islamic history, was the most ambitious of all. He ruled briefly as a child and was deposed, but regained the sultanate from 1354 until 1361, when he was assassinated.

MADRASA AND MAUSOLEUM Hasan's major building project in Cairo was a huge madrasa complex (FIGS. **13-18** and **13-19**) on a plot of land about 8,000 square yards in area. A *madrasa* ("place of study" in Arabic) is a theological college devoted to the teaching of Islamic law. Hasan's complex was so large that it housed not only four such colleges for the study of the four major schools of Islamic law but also a mosque, mausoleum, orphanage, and hospital, as well as shops and baths. Like all Islamic building complexes incorporating religious, educational, and charitable functions, this one was supported by an endowment funded by rental properties. The income from these paid the salaries of attendants and faculty, provided furnishings and supplies such as oil for the lamps or free food for the poor, and supported scholarships for needy students.

The grandiose structure has a large central courtyard with a monumental fountain in the center and four iwans (rectangular vaulted recesses) opening onto it, a design used earlier for Iranian mosques (FIG. 13-23). In each corner of the main courtyard (FIG. 13-19), between the iwans, is a madrasa with its own courtyard and four or five stories of rooms for the students. The largest iwan in the complex, on the southern side, served as a mosque. Contemporaries believed the soaring vault that covered this iwan was taller than the arch of the Sasanian palace at Ctesiphon (see FIG. 2-28), which was then one of the most admired engineering feats in the world. Behind the qibla wall stands the sultan's mausoleum, a gigantic version of the type of tomb the Samanids erected at Bukhara (FIG. 13-10). The siting of the dome-covered cube south of the mosque was carefully calculated. The prayers of the faithful facing Mecca, therefore, were directed toward Hasan's tomb. (Only the sultan's two sons are actually buried there. Hasan's body was not returned when he was killed.)

A muqarnas cornice crowns the exterior walls of the complex, and marble plaques of several colors cover the mihrab in the mosque and the walls of Hasan's mausoleum. But the complex as a whole is relatively austere, characterized by its massiveness and geometric clarity. It presents a striking contrast to the filigreed elegance of the contemporary Alhambra, and testifies to the diversity of regional styles within the Islamic world, especially after the end of the Umayyad and Abbasid dynasties.

THE OTTOMANS COME TO POWER During the course of the 9th to 11th centuries, the Turkic people, of central Asian origin, largely converted to Islam. They moved into Iran and the Near East in the 11th century, and by 1055 the Seljuk Turkish dynasty had built an extensive, although short-lived, empire that stretched from India to western Anatolia. By the end of the 12th

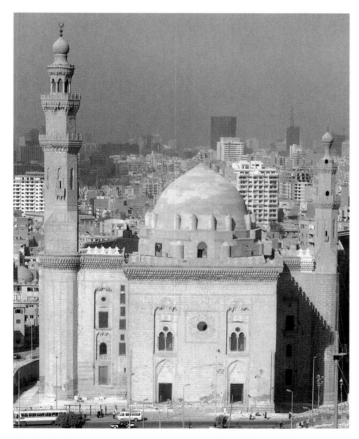

13-18 Madrasa-mosque-mausoleum complex of Sultan Hasan (view from the south with the mausoleum in the foreground), Cairo, Egypt, begun 1356.

1. Mausoleum
2. Mosque (southern iwan)
3. Iwans
4. Madrasas
5. Courtyard with fountain

13-19 Plan of the madrasa-mosque-mausoleum complex of Sultan Hasan, Cairo, Egypt, begun 1356.

century, this empire had broken up into regional states, and in the early 13th century it came under the sway of the Mongols, led by Genghis Khan (see Chapter 26). After the Seljuks fell, several local dynasties established themselves in Anatolia, among them the Ottomans, founded by Osman I (r. 1281–1326). Under Osman's successors, the Ottoman state expanded for a period of two and a half centuries throughout vast areas of Asia, Europe, and North Africa to become, by the middle of the 15th century, one of the great world powers.

The Ottoman emperors were lavish patrons of architecture. Ottoman builders developed a new type of mosque with a square prayer hall covered by a dome as its core. In fact, the dome-covered square, which had been a dominant form in Iran and was employed for the 10th-century mausoleum at Bukhara (FIG. 13-10), became the nucleus of all Ottoman architecture. The combination had an appealing geometric clarity. At first used singly, the domed units came to be used in multiples, a turning point in Ottoman architecture.

After the Ottoman Turks conquered Constantinople (Istanbul) in 1453, they firmly established their architectural code. The new lords of Constantinople were impressed by Hagia Sophia (see FIGS. 12-3 to 12-5), which, in some respects, conformed to their own ideals. They converted the Byzantine church into a mosque with minarets. But the longitudinal orientation of Hagia Sophia's interior never satisfied Ottoman builders, and Anatolian development moved instead toward the central-plan mosque.

SINAN THE GREAT The first examples of the central-plan mosque were built in the 1520s, eclipsed later only by the works of the most famous Ottoman architect, SINAN (ca. 1491–1588). A contemporary of the great Italian Renaissance sculptor, painter, and architect Michelangelo (see Chapter 22), and with equal aspirations to immortality, Sinan perfected the Ottoman architectural style. By his time, the basic domed unit was universally used. It could be multiplied, enlarged, or contracted as needed, and almost any number of units could be used together. Thus, the typical Ottoman building of Sinan's time was a creative assemblage of domical units and artfully juxtaposed geometric spaces. Builders usually erected domes with an extravagant margin of structural safety that has since served them well in earthquake-prone Istanbul and other Ottoman cities. (The sound construction of the Ottoman mosques was vividly demonstrated in August 1999 when a powerful earthquake centered 65 miles east of Istanbul toppled hundreds of modern buildings and killed thousands of people but caused no damage to the centuries-old mosques.) Working within this architectural tradition, Sinan searched for solutions to the problems of unifying the additive elements and of creating a monumental centralized space with harmonious proportions.

THE CENTRAL PLAN AT EDIRNE Sinan's efforts to overcome the limitations of a segmented interior found their ultimate expression in the Mosque of Selim II (FIGS. **13-20** to **13-22**) at Edirne, which had been the capital of the Ottoman Empire from 1367 to 1472 and where Selim II (r. 1566–1574) maintained a palace. There, Sinan created a structure that made it possible to see the mihrab from almost any spot in the mosque. The massive dome, effectively set off by four slender pencil-shaped minarets (each more than 200 feet high, among the tallest ever constructed), dominates the city's skyline (FIG. 13-20). Various dependent structures were placed around the mosque. Most important Ottoman mosques had numerous annexes, including libraries and schools, hospices, baths, soup kitchens for the poor,

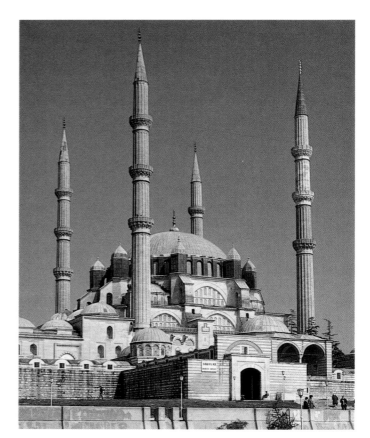

13-20 SINAN, Mosque of Selim II, Edirne, Turkey, 1568–1575.

1. Madrasa
2. Cemetery
3. Darül-Kurra (house for the readers of the Quran)
4. Mosque
5. Avlu (courtyard forming summer extension of mosque)
6. Arasta (covered market)

0   250   500 FEET
0   75   150 METERS

13-21 SINAN, plan of the Mosque of Selim II, Edirne, Turkey, 1568–1575.

Sinan the Great, the Mosque of Selim II, and Hagia Sophia

Sinan (ca. 1491–1588), called Sinan the Great, was in fact the greatest Ottoman architect. Born a Christian, he was recruited for service in the Ottoman government, converted to Islam, and was trained in engineering and the art of building while in the Ottoman army. His talent was quickly recognized, and he was entrusted with increasing responsibility until, in 1538, he was appointed the chief court architect for Suleyman the Magnificent (r. 1520–1566), a generous patron of art and architecture. Hundreds of building projects, both sacred and secular, have been attributed to Sinan, although he could not have been involved with all that bear his name.

The capstone of Sinan's distinguished career was the Edirne mosque (FIGS. 13-20 to 13-22) of Suleyman's son, Selim II, which Sinan designed when he was almost 80 years old. There, he sought to surpass the greatest achievements of Byzantine architects just as Sultan Hasan's builders in Cairo attempted to rival and exceed the Sasanian architects of antiquity. Sa'i Mustafa Çelebi, Sinan's biographer, recorded the architect's accomplishment in his own words:

Sultan Selim Khan ordered the erection of a mosque in Edirne. . . . His humble servant [I, Sinan] prepared for him a drawing depicting, on a dominating site in the city, four minarets on the four corners of a dome. . . . Those who consider themselves architects among Christians say that in the realm of Islam no dome can equal that of the Hagia Sophia; they claim that no Muslim architect would be able to build such a large dome. In this mosque, with the help of God and the support of Sultan Selim Khan, I erected a dome six cubits higher and four cubits wider than the dome of the Hagia Sophia.[1]

The Edirne dome is, in fact, higher than Hagia Sophia's (see FIG. 12-5) when measured from its base, but its crown is not as far above the pavement as that of the dome of Justinian's church. Nonetheless, Sinan's feat was universally acclaimed as a triumph, and the Mosque of Selim II was considered proof that the Ottomans finally had outshone the Christian emperors of Byzantium in the realm of architecture.

[1] Aptullah Kuran, *Sinan: The Grand Old Master of Ottoman Architecture* (Washington, D.C.: Institute of Turkish Studies, 1987), 168–69.

13-22 SINAN, interior of the Mosque of Selim II, Edirne, Turkey, 1568–1575.

markets, and hospitals, as well as a cemetery containing the mausoleum of the sultan responsible for building the mosque (compare Hasan's complex in Cairo, FIG. 13-19). These utilitarian buildings were grouped around the mosque and axially aligned with it if possible. More generally, they were adjusted to their natural site and linked with the central building by planted shrubs and trees.

The Edirne mosque is preceded by a rectangular court covering an area equal to that of the building (FIG. 13-21). Porticos formed by domed squares surround the courtyard. Behind it, the building rises majestically to its climactic dome, whose height surpasses that of Hagia Sophia (see "Sinan the Great, the Mosque of Selim II, and Hagia Sophia," above). But it is the organization of this mosque's interior space (FIG. 13-22) that reveals the genius of its builder. The mihrab is recessed into an apselike alcove deep enough to permit window illumination from three sides, making the brilliantly colored tile panels of its lower walls sparkle as if with their own glowing light. The plan of the main hall is an ingenious fusion of an octagon with the dome-covered square (FIG. 13-21). The octagon, formed by the eight massive dome supports, is pierced by the four half-dome-covered corners of the square. The result is a fluid interpenetration of several geometric volumes that represents the culminating solution to Sinan's lifelong search for a monumental unified interior space. Sinan's forms are clear and legible, like mathematical equations. Height, width, and masses are related to one another in a simple but effective ratio of 1:2. The building is generally regarded as the climax of Ottoman architecture. Sinan proudly proclaimed it his masterpiece.

ISFAHAN'S GREAT MOSQUE The Mosque of Selim II at Edirne was erected during a single building campaign under the direction of a single master architect, but many other major

13-23 Aerial view of the Great Mosque (looking southwest), Isfahan, Iran, 11th to 17th centuries.

Islamic architectural projects were built or remodeled over several centuries. A case in point is the Great Mosque at Isfahan (FIG. **13-23**) in Iran. The earliest mosque on the site, of the hypostyle type, was constructed in the eighth century during the caliphate of the Abbasids. But Sultan Malik Shah I (r. 1072–1092), whose capital was at Isfahan, transformed the structure in the 11th century. Later remodeling further altered the mosque's appearance. The present mosque, which retains its basic 11th-century plan, consists of a large courtyard bordered by a two-story arcade on each side. As in the 14th-century complex of Sultan Hasan (FIG. 13-19) in Cairo, four iwans open onto the courtyard, one at the center of each side. The southwestern iwan leads into a dome-covered room in front of the mihrab. It func-

tioned as a maqsura reserved for the sultan and his attendants. It is uncertain whether this plan, with four iwans and a dome before the mihrab, was employed for the first time in the Great Mosque at Isfahan, but it became standard in Iranian mosque design. In four-iwan mosques the qibla iwan is always the largest. Its size (and the dome that often accompanied it) immediately indicated to worshipers the proper direction for prayer.

IRANIAN TILEWORK The iwans of the Isfahan mosque feature soaring pointed arches framing tile-sheathed muqarnas vaults. The muqarnas ceilings probably were installed in the 14th century, and the ceramic-tile revetment on the walls and vaults is the work of the 17th-century Safavid rulers of Iran. The use of glazed

13-24 Winter prayer hall of the Shahi (Imam) Mosque, Isfahan, Iran, 1611–1638.

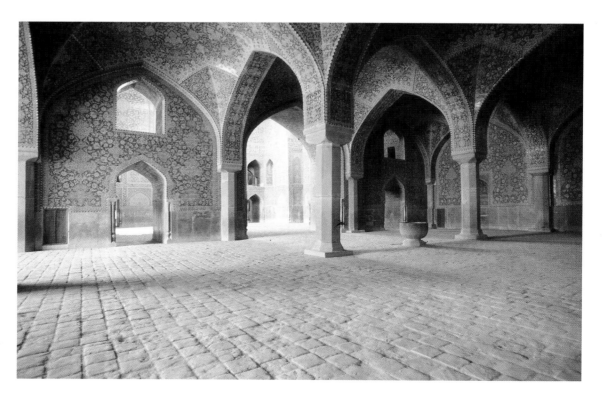

Islamic Tilework

From the Dome of the Rock (FIGS. 13-1 and 13-2), the earliest major Islamic building, to the present day, mosaics or ceramic tiles have been used to decorate the walls and vaults of mosques, madrasas, palaces, and tombs. The golden age of Islamic tilework was the 16th and 17th centuries. At that time, Islamic artists used two basic techniques to enliven building interiors with brightly colored tiled walls and to sheathe their exteriors with gleaming tiles that reflected the sun's rays.

In *mosaic tilework* (for example, FIG. 13-25), large ceramic panels of single colors are fired in the potter's kiln and then cut into smaller pieces and set in plaster in a manner similar to the laying of mosaic tesserae of stone or glass (see "Mosaics," Chapter 11, page 315).

Cuerda seca (dry cord) tilework was introduced in Umayyad Spain during the 10th century—hence its Spanish name even in Middle Eastern and Central Asian contexts. Cuerda seca tiles (for example, FIG. 13-24) are polychrome and can more easily bear complex arabesque patterns as well as Arabic script. They are more economical to use because vast surfaces can be covered with large tiles much more quickly than they can with thousands of smaller mosaic tiles. But when such tiles are used to sheathe curved surfaces, the ceramists must fire the tiles in the exact shape required. Polychrome tiles have other drawbacks. Because all the glazes are fired at the same temperature, cuerda seca tiles are not as brilliant in color as mosaic tiles and do not reflect light the way the more irregular surfaces of tile mosaics do. The preparation of the multicolored tiles also requires greater care. To prevent the colors from running together during firing, the potters outline the motifs on cuerda seca tiles with greased cords containing manganese, which leaves a matte black line between the colors after firing.

---

tiles has a long history in the Middle East. Even in ancient Mesopotamia, gates and walls were sometimes covered with colorful baked bricks (see FIGS. 2-23 and 2-25). In the Islamic world, the art of ceramic tilework reached its peak in the 16th and 17th centuries in Iran and Turkey (see "Islamic Tilework," above). Employed as a veneer over a brick core, tiles could sheathe entire buildings, including domes and minarets.

The Shahi (or Royal) Mosque in Isfahan, recently renamed the Imam Mosque, which dates from the early 17th century, is widely recognized as one of the masterpieces of Islamic tilework. Its dome is a prime example of tile mosaic, and its winter prayer hall (FIG. **13-24**) houses one of the finest ensembles of cuerda seca tiles in the world. Covering the walls, arches, and vaults of the prayer hall presented a special challenge to the Isfahan ceramists. They had to manufacture a wide variety of shapes with curved surfaces to sheathe the complex forms of the hall. The result was a technological triumph as well as a dazzling display of abstract ornament.

CERAMIC CALLIGRAPHY We noted earlier the Koran's central importance to the Islamic world and how its verses appeared in the mosaics of the earliest great Islamic building, the Dome of the Rock in Jerusalem (FIG. 13-2). Excerpts from the Koran appear on the walls of numerous other Islamic structures in a variety of media. Indeed, some of the masterworks of Arabic calligraphy are found not in manuscripts but on walls. A 14th-century mihrab (FIG. **13-25**) from the Madrasa Imami in Isfahan exemplifies the perfect aesthetic union between the calligrapher's art and arabesque ornament. The pointed arch that immediately enframes the mihrab niche bears an inscription from the Koran in Kufic, the stately rectilinear script employed for the early Koran page illustrated (FIG. 13-16). Many supple cursive styles also make up the repertoire of Islamic calligraphy. One of these styles, known as *Muhaqqaq,* fills the mihrab's outer rectangular frame. The mosaic tile ornament on the curving surface of the niche and the area above the pointed arch are composed of tighter and looser networks of geometric and abstract floral motifs. The mosaic technique is masterful. Every piece

13-25 Mihrab from the Madrasa Imami, Isfahan, Iran, ca. 1354. Glazed mosaic tilework, 11′ 3″ × 7′ 6″. Metropolitan Museum of Art, New York.

had to be chiseled and cut to fit its specific place in the mihrab—even the tile inscriptions. The framed inscription in the center of the niche—proclaiming that the mosque is the domicile of the pious believer—is smoothly integrated with the subtly varied patterns. The mihrab's outermost inscription—detailing the five pillars of Islamic faith—serves as a fringelike extension, as well as a boundary, for the entire design. The calligraphic and geometric elements are so completely unified that only the practiced eye can distinguish them. The artist transformed the architectural surface into a textile surface, the three-dimensional wall into a two-dimensional hanging, weaving the calligraphy into it as another cluster of motifs within the total pattern.

Luxury Arts

The tile-covered mosques of Isfahan, Sultan Hasan's madrasa complex in Cairo, and the architecture of Sinan the Great in Edirne are enduring testaments to the brilliant artistic culture of the Safavid, Mamluk, and Ottoman rulers of the Muslim world. But these are just some of the most conspicuous public manifestations of the greatness of later Islamic art and architecture (see Chapter 25 for the achievements of the Muslim rulers of India). In the smaller-scale, and often private, realm of the luxury arts, Muslim artists also excelled. From the vast array of manuscript paintings, ceramics, textiles, and metalwork, five masterpieces may serve to suggest both the range and the quality of the inappropriately dubbed Islamic "minor arts" of the 13th to 16th centuries.

MILLIONS OF KNOTS The first of these artworks (FIG. **13-26**) is by far the largest, one of a pair of carpets from Ardabil in Iran. They come from the funerary mosque of Shaykh Safi al-Din (1252–1334), the founder of the Safavid line, but were made in 1540, two centuries after the erection of the mosque, during the reign of Shah Tahmasp (r. 1524–1576). Tahmasp elevated carpet weaving to a national industry and set up royal factories at Isfahan, Kashan, Kirman, and Tabriz. The name of MAQSUD OF KASHAN is woven into the design of the carpet we illustrate. He must have been the designer who supplied the master pattern to two teams of royal weavers (one for each of the two carpets). The carpet, almost 35 × 18 feet, consists of roughly 25 million knots, some 340 to the square inch. (Its twin has even more knots.)

The design consists of a central sunburst medallion, representing the inside of a dome, surrounded by 16 pendants. Mosque lamps (appropriate motifs for the Ardabil funerary mosque) are suspended from two pendants on the long axis of the carpet. The lamps are of different sizes, and some scholars have suggested that this is an optical device to make the two appear equal in size when viewed from the end of the carpet at the room's threshold (the bottom end in our illustration). The rich blue background is covered with leaves and flowers attached to delicate stems that spread over the whole field. The entire composition presents the illusion of a heavenly dome with lamps reflected in a pool of water full of floating lotus blossoms. No human or animal figures appear, as befits a carpet intended for a mosque, although they can be found on other Islamic textiles used in secular contexts, both earlier (FIG. 13-14) and later.

THE BOOK OF KINGS Shah Tahmasp was also a great patron of books. Around 1525 he commissioned an ambitious decade-long project to produce an illustrated 742-page copy of the *Shahnama (Book of Kings)*. The *Shahnama* is the Persian national epic poem by Firdawsi (940–1025). It recounts the history of Iran from the Creation until the Muslim conquest. Tahmasp's *Shahnama*

contains 258 illustrations by many artists, including some of the most renowned painters of the day. It was eventually presented as a gift to Selim II, the Ottoman sultan who was the patron of Sinan's mosque at Edirne (FIGS. 13-20 to 13-22). The manuscript later entered a private collection in the West and ultimately was auctioned off as a series of individual pages, destroying its integrity—an unfortunate consequence of the esteem in which Islamic art is held throughout the world.

The page we reproduce (FIG. 13-27) is the work of SULTAN-MUHAMMAD and depicts Gayumars, the legendary first king of Iran, and his court. Gayumars was said to have ruled from a mountaintop when humans first learned to cook food and clothe themselves in leopard skins. In Sultan-Muhammad's representation of the story, Gayumars presides over his court (all the figures

13-26 MAQSUD OF KASHAN, carpet from the funerary mosque of Shaykh Safi al-Din, Ardabil, Iran, 1540. Knotted pile of wool and silk, 34′ 6″ × 17′ 7″. Victoria & Albert Museum, London.

13-27 SULTAN-MUHAMMAD, the court of Gayumars, detail of folio 20 verso of the *Shahnama* of Shah Tahmasp, from Tabriz, Iran, ca. 1525–1535. Ink, watercolor, and gold on paper, full page approx. 1′ 1″ × 9″. Prince Sadruddin Aga Khan Collection, Geneva.

13-28 Ottoman royal ceremonial caftan, from Istanbul, Turkey, ca. 1550. Polychrome silk and gilt-metal thread, 4′ 9″ high. Topkapi Palace Museum, Istanbul.

wear leopard skins) from his mountain throne. The king is surrounded by light amid a golden sky. His son and grandson are perched on multicolored rocky outcroppings to the viewer's left and right, respectively. The court encircles the ruler and his heirs. Dozens of human faces are portrayed within the rocks themselves. Many species of animals populate the lush landscape. According to the *Shahnama*, wild beasts became instantly tame in the presence of Gayumars. Sultan-Muhammad rendered the figures, animals, trees, rocks, and sky with an extraordinarily delicate touch. The sense of lightness and airiness that permeates the painting is enhanced by its placement on the page—floating, off center, on a speckled background of gold leaf. The painter gave his royal patron a singular vision of Iran's fabled past.

A ROYAL OTTOMAN CAFTAN When Tahmasp's *Shahnama* was presented to Selim II, the Ottoman sultan would have received the precious gift with due pomp and circumstance, perhaps wearing a majestic ceremonial caftan like the one illustrated here (FIG. **13-28**). It was woven of silk thread around 1550, perhaps for Suleyman the Magnificent's son Bayezid. More than a thousand such caftans are preserved in the Ottoman Topkapi Palace, now a museum. But this caftan was one of the most difficult to create on a loom because of its large number of colors and because of the complexity of its floral designs. This kind of

distinctive Ottoman design of sinuous curved leaves and complex blossoms is known as *saz*, a Turkish term recalling an enchanted forest. The saz design is never repeated on this garment, a remarkable feat. The designer, nonetheless, made sure the pattern matched across the front opening. Court protocol dictated that Ottoman rulers stood absolutely motionless in the presence of visitors. This explains why the caftan has no fastenings to prevent it from opening. The wearer's arms protruded through slits at the shoulders. The sleeves are ankle length; they served only for decoration and were draped over the back. The rich saz arabesque of the Ottoman robe presents a telling contrast with the Byzantine sakkos of Photius (see FIG. 12-35), which is covered with Jewish and Christian narratives, saints, and Russian royalty, as well as a portrait of Photius himself.

ISLAMIC ART FOR CHRISTIANS Figures and animals do adorn a brass basin (FIG. **13-29**) from Egypt inlaid with gold and silver and signed—six times—by the Mamluk artist MUHAMMAD IBN AL-ZAYN. The basin, used for washing hands at official ceremonies, must have been fashioned for a specific Mamluk patron. Some scholars think a court official named Salar ordered the piece as a gift for his sultan, but no inscription identifies him. The central band depicts Mamluk hunters and Mongol enemies. Running animals fill the friezes above and below. Arabesques of

13-29 MUHAMMAD IBN AL-ZAYN, basin (*Baptistère de Saint Louis*), from Egypt, ca. 1300. Brass, inlaid with gold and silver, $8\frac{3}{4}''$ high. Louvre, Paris.

Christian Patronage of Islamic Art

During the 11th, 12th, and 13th centuries, large numbers of Christians traveled to Islamic lands, especially to the Christian holy sites in Jerusalem and Bethlehem, either as pilgrims (see "Pilgrimages," Chapter 17, page 449) or as Crusaders (see "The Crusades," Chapter 17, page 466). Many returned with mementos of their journey, usually in the form of inexpensive mass-produced souvenirs. But some wealthy individuals commissioned local Islamic artists to produce custom-made pieces using costly materials.

A unique brass canteen (FIG. 13-30) inlaid with silver and decorated with scenes of the life of Christ appears to be the work of a 13th-century Ayyubid metalsmith in the employ of a Christian patron. The canteen is a luxurious version of the "pilgrim flasks" Christian visitors to the Holy Land often brought back to Europe. Four inscriptions in Arabic promise eternal glory, secure life, perfect prosperity, and increasing good luck to the canteen's owner, who is unfortunately not named. That the owner was a Christian is

suggested not only by the type of object but by the choice of scenes engraved into the canteen. The Madonna and Christ Child appear enthroned in the central medallion, and three panels depicting New Testament events (see "The Life of Jesus in Art," Chapter 11, pages 308–309) fill most of the band around the medallion. The narrative unfolds in a counterclockwise sequence (Arabic is read from right to left), beginning with the Nativity (at 2 o'clock) and continuing with the Presentation in the Temple (10 o'clock) and the Entry into Jerusalem (6 o'clock). The scenes may have been chosen because the patron had visited their locales (Bethlehem and Jerusalem). Most scholars believe that the artist used Syrian Christian manuscripts as the source for the canteen's Christian iconography. Many of the decorative details, however, are common in contemporary Islamic metalwork inscribed with the names of Muslim patrons. Whoever the owner was, the canteen testifies to the fruitful artistic interaction between Christians and Muslims in 13th-century Syria.

13-30 Canteen with episodes from the life of Christ, from Syria, ca. 1240–1250. Brass, inlaid with silver, 1' 2½" diameter. Freer Gallery of Art, Washington, D.C.

inlaid silver fill the background of all the bands and roundels. Figures and animals also decorate the inside and underside of the basin.

The basin has long been known as the *Baptistère de Saint Louis*, but the association with the famous French king (see "Louis IX: The Saintly King," Chapter 18, page 498) is a myth, for he died before the piece was made. Nonetheless, the *Baptistère*, brought to France long ago, was used in the baptismal rites of newborns of the French royal family as early as the 17th century. Like the Zandana silk in Toul Cathedral (FIG. 13-14) and a canteen (FIG. **13-30**) with scenes of the life of Christ (see "Christian Patronage of Islamic Art," above), Muhammad ibn al-Zayn's basin testifies to the prestige of Islamic art in western Europe.

CONCLUSION

The irresistible and far-ranging sweep of Islam from Arabia to India to North Africa and Spain brought a new and compelling tradition to the history of world art and architecture. Like Islam itself, Islamic art spread quickly. In the Middle East and North Africa, Islamic art largely replaced Late Antique art. And from a foothold in the Iberian peninsula, it made an impact on Western medieval art, although Islamic art stands in sharp contrast both to the figural art of Europe and the Mediterranean and to the Western architectural vocabulary. Islamic artists and architects also brought their distinctive style to South Asia, where a Muslim sultanate was established at Delhi in India in the early 13th century (see Chapter 25).

Region columns (vertical labels): SYRIA AND IRAQ · SPAIN · IRAN AND CENTRAL ASIA · EGYPT · TURKEY · INDIA

Dynasty labels (vertical): Umayyad Caliphate · Abbasid Caliphate · Umayyad Caliphate · Nasrid Dynasty · Samanid Dynasty · Seljuk Dynasty · Timurid Dynasty · Safavid Dynasty · Fatimid Dynasty · Ayyubid Dynasty · Mamluk Dynasty · Ottoman Empire · Delhi Sultanate · Mughal Dynasty

Timeline

Birth of Muhammad in Mecca, ca. 570

600

Muhammad's first revelation, 610

Muhammad's flight to Medina (Hijra), 622

Death of Muhammad in Medina, 632

Muslims capture Jerusalem, 638

Muslim conquest of Lower Egypt, 642

[1] Umayyad Caliphate established, 661

700

Muslim armies enter Spain, 711

Charles Martel defeats Muslims at Poitiers, 732

Abbasid caliphate established, 750

Umayyad caliphate established in Spain, 756

Abbasids found Baghdad, 762

800

Samanid dynasty established in Transoxiana, 819

900

[2] Fatimid dynasty established in Egypt, 909

Fatimids found Cairo, 969

1000

Fall of Umayyad caliphate in Spain, 1031

Seljuk dynasty established in Iran, 1038

[3] First Crusade captures Jerusalem, 1099

1100

Saladin founds Ayyubid dynasty in Egypt, 1171

Saladin captures Jerusalem from Crusaders, 1187

1200

Sultanate of Delhi established, 1206

Nasrid dynasty established at Granada, 1230

Mamluk dynasty established in Egypt, 1250

Mongols sack Baghdad, 1258

Ottoman Empire founded, 1281

1300

1400

Ottomans capture Constantinople, 1453

Fall of Granada to the Christians, 1492

1500

Safavid dynasty established in Iran, 1501

[4] Mughal dynasty established in India, 1526

Ottomans capture Baghdad, 1534

1600

[1] Dome of the Rock, Jerusalem, 687–692

[2] Koran page, Dublin, ca. 900

[3] Great Mosque, Isfahan, begun late 11th century

[4] Maqsud of Kashan, Ardabil carpet, 1540

Temple I (Temple of the Giant Jaguar), Maya, Tikal, Petén, Guatemala, ca. 732 CE.

14

FROM ALASKA
TO THE ANDES

NATIVE ARTS OF THE AMERICAS BEFORE 1300

The origins of the indigenous peoples of the Americas are still disputed. Sometime no later than 30,000 to 10,000 BCE these first Americans probably crossed the now submerged land bridge called Beringia, which connected the shores of the Bering Strait between Asia and North America (MAP **14-1**). Some scholars also have proposed that at least some migrants reached the Western Hemisphere via boats traveling along the Pacific coast of North America.

These Stone Age nomads were hunter-gatherers. They made tools only of bone, pressure-flaked stone, and wood. They had no knowledge of agriculture but possibly some of basketry. They could control fire and probably built simple shelters. For many centuries, they spread out until they occupied the two American continents. But they were always few in number. When the first Europeans arrived at the end of the 15th century (see Chapter 30), the total population of the Western Hemisphere may not have exceeded 40 million.

Between 8000 and 2000 BCE, a number of the migrants learned to fish, farm cotton, and domesticate such plants as squash and maize (corn). The nomads settled down in villages and learned to make clay pottery utensils and lively figurines. Metal technology, although extremely sophisticated when it existed, developed only in the Andean region of South America (eventually spreading north into modern-day Mexico) and generally met only the need for ornament, not for tools. With these skills as a base, many cultures rose and fell over long periods.

Several of the peoples of North, Central, and South America had already reached a high level of social complexity and technological achievement by the early centuries CE. Although most relied on stone tools, did not use the wheel (except for toys), and had no pack animals but the llama (in South America), the early Americans developed complex agricultural techniques and excelled in the engineering arts associated with the planning and construction of cities, civic and domestic buildings, roads and bridges, and irrigation and drainage systems. They carved monumental stone statues and reliefs, painted extensive murals, and mastered the arts of weaving, pottery, and metalwork. The Maya of Mesoamerica even had a highly developed writing system and knowledge of mathematical calculation that allowed them to keep precise

MAP 14-1 The Americas.

MAP 14-2 Early sites in Mesoamerica.

records and create a sophisticated calendar and a highly accurate astronomy.

DESTRUCTION AND RECONSTRUCTION These advanced civilizations abruptly collapsed, however, in the 16th century when Hernan Cortés, Francisco Pizarro, and their armies conquered the Aztec and Inka empires. Most of the once-glorious American cities were destroyed in the Spaniards' zeal to obliterate all traces of pagan beliefs. Other sites were abandoned to the forces of nature—erosion and the encroachment of tropical forests. But despite the ruined state of the pre-Hispanic cities today, archaeologists and art historians have been able to reconstruct much of the art and architectural history of ancient America. This chapter examines in turn the artistic achievements of the native peoples of Mesoamerica, South America, and North America before 1300. Chapter 30 treats the art and architecture of the Americas from 1300 to the present.

MESOAMERICA

GEOGRAPHY AND CLIMATE The term *Mesoamerica* names the region that comprises part of present-day Mexico, Guatemala, Belize, Honduras, and the Pacific coast of El Salvador (MAP **14-2**). Mesoamerica was the homeland of several of the great civilizations that flourished before the arrival of Christopher Columbus and the subsequent European invasion. The principal regions of *pre-Columbian* Mesoamerica are the Gulf Coast region (Olmec culture); the states of Jalisco, Colima, and Nayarit, collectively known as West Mexico; Chiapas, Yucatán, Quintana Roo, and Campeche states in Mexico and the Petén area of Guatemala (Maya culture); southwestern Mexico and the state of Oaxaca (Zapotec and Mixtec cultures); and the central plateau surrounding

modern-day Mexico City (Teotihuacán, Toltec, and Aztec cultures). These cultures were often influential over extensive areas.

The Mexican highlands are a volcanic and seismic region. In highland Mexico, great reaches of arid plateau land, fertile for maize and other crops wherever water is available, lie between heavily forested mountain slopes, which at some places rise to a perpetual snow level. The moist tropical rain forests of the coastal plains yield rich crops, when the land can be cleared. In Yucatán, a subsoil of limestone furnishes abundant material for both building and carving. This limestone tableland merges with the vast Petén region of Guatemala, which separates Mexico from Honduras. Yucatán and the Petén, where dense rain forest alternates with broad stretches of grassland, host some of the most spectacular Maya ruins. The great mountain chains of Mexico and Guatemala extend into Honduras and slope sharply down to tropical coasts. Highlands and mountain valleys, with their chill and temperate climates, alternate dramatically with the humid climate of tropical rain forest and coastlines.

LANGUAGE AND CHRONOLOGY The variegated landscape of Mesoamerica may have much to do with the diversity of languages its native populations speak. Numerous languages are distributed among no fewer than 14 linguistic families. Many of the languages spoken in the preconquest periods survive to this day. Various Mayan languages linger in Guatemala and southern Mexico. The Náhuatl of the Aztecs endures in the Mexican highlands. The Zapotec and Mixtec languages persist in Oaxaca and its environs. Diverse as the languages of these peoples were, their cultures otherwise had much in common. The Mesoamerican peoples shared maize cultivation, religious beliefs and rites, myths, social structures, customs, and arts.

Archaeologists, with ever-increasing refinement of technique, have been uncovering, describing, and classifying Mesoamerican monuments for more than a century. Since the 1950s, when linguists made important breakthroughs in deciphering the Maya hieroglyphic script, evidence for a detailed account of Maya history and art has emerged. Many Maya rulers now can be listed by name and the dates of their reigns fixed with precision. Other writing systems, such as that of the Zapotec, who began to record dates at a very early time, are less well understood, but researchers are making rapid progress in their interpretation. The general Mesoamerican chronology is now well established and widely accepted. The standard chronology, divided into three epochs, involves some overlapping of subperiods—the Preclassic (Formative) extends from 2000 BCE to about 300 CE; the Classic period runs from about 300 to 900; and the Postclassic begins ca. 900 and ends with the Spanish conquest of 1521.

Preclassic (ca. 2000 BCE–300 CE)

THE OLMEC The Olmec culture of the present-day states of Veracruz and Tabasco is often called the "mother culture" of Mesoamerica, because many distinctive Mesoamerican religious, social, and artistic traditions can be traced to it. Although little is known of Olmec origins, history, or language, the wide diffusion of Olmec institutional forms, monuments, arts, and artifacts reflects the culture's broad influence. Excavations in and around not only the principal Gulf Coast sites of Olmec culture—Tres Zapotes, San Lorenzo, and La Venta—but also in central Mexico and along the Pacific coast from the Mexican state of Guerrero to El Salvador indicate that Olmec influence was far more widespread than scholars once supposed.

Settling in the tropical lowlands of the Gulf of Mexico, the Olmec peoples cultivated a terrain of rain forest and alluvial lowland washed by numerous rivers flowing into the gulf. Here, between approximately 1500 and 400 BCE, social organization assumed the form that later Mesoamerican cultures adapted and developed. The mass of the population—food-producing farmers scattered in hinterland villages—provided the sustenance and labor that maintained a hereditary caste of rulers, hierarchies of priests, functionaries, and artisans. The nonfarming population presumably lived, arranged by rank, within precincts that served ceremonial, administrative, and residential functions, and perhaps also as marketplaces. At regular intervals, the whole community convened for ritual observances at the religious-civic centers of towns such as San Lorenzo and La Venta. These centers were the formative architectural expressions of the structure and ideals of Olmec society.

COLOSSAL RULER PORTRAITS At La Venta, low clay-and-earthen platforms and stone fences enclosed two great courtyards. At one end of the larger area was a mound almost 100 feet high. Although now very eroded, this early pyramid, built of earth and adorned with colored clays, may have been intended to mimic a mountain, held sacred by Mesoamerican peoples as both a life-giving source of water and a feared destructive force. (Volcanic eruptions and earthquakes still wreak havoc in this region.) The La Venta layout is an early form of the temple-pyramid and plaza complex aligned on a north-south axis that characterized later Mesoamerican ceremonial center design.

Four colossal basalt heads (FIG. **14-1**), weighing about 10 tons each and standing between 6 and 10 feet high, face out from the plaza. More than a dozen similar heads have been found at San Lorenzo and Tres Zapotes. Almost as much of an achievement as the carving of these huge stones with stone tools was their transportation across the 60 miles of swampland from the nearest known basalt source, the Tuxtla Mountains. Although the identities of the colossi are uncertain, their individualized features and distinctive headgear and ear ornaments, as well as the later Maya practice of carving monumental ruler portraits, suggest that the Olmec heads portray rulers rather than deities. The sheer size of the heads and their intensity of expression evoke great power, whether mortal or divine.

14-1 Colossal head, Olmec, La Venta, Mexico, 900–400 BCE. Basalt, 9′4″ high. Museo-Parque La Venta, Villahermosa.

14-3 *Drinker* (seated figure with raised arms), from Colima, Mexico, ca. 200 BCE–500 CE. Clay with orange and red slip, 1′ 1″ high. Los Angeles County Museum of Art (The Proctor Stafford Collection, purchased with funds provided by Mr. and Mrs. Allan C. Balch).

14-2 Ceremonial ax in the form of a jaguar-human, Olmec, from La Venta, Mexico, 900–400 BCE. Jadeite, 11½″ high. British Museum, London.

JADE CELTS The Olmec also carved sculptures in jade, an extremely hard dark green stone they acquired from unknown sources far from their homeland. All Mesoamerican peoples prized jade, as did the ancient Chinese (see "Chinese Jade," Chapter 7, page 195). Sometimes the Olmec carved it into ax-shaped polished forms called *celts,* which they then buried as votive offerings under their ceremonial courtyards or platforms. The celt shape could be modified into a figural form, combining relief carving with incising. Stone-tipped drills and abrasive materials, such as sand, were used to carve jade. Subjects represented include crying babies (of unknown significance) and figures combining human and animal features and postures (FIG. **14-2**). Although Olmec religious beliefs and practices are little known, such human-animal representations may refer to the belief that religious practitioners underwent dangerous transformations to wrest power from supernatural forces and harness it for the good of the community.

WEST MEXICAN SCULPTURE Far to the west of the tropical heartland of the Olmec are the Preclassic sites along Mexico's Pacific coast. The ancient peoples of the modern West Mexican states of Nayarit, Jalisco, and Colima were long thought to have existed at Mesoamerica's geographic and cultural fringes. Recent archaeological discoveries, however, have revealed that although the West Mexicans did not produce large-scale stone sculpture, they did build permanent structures. These included tiered platforms and ball courts (see "The Mesoamerican Ball Game," page 389), architectural features found in nearly all Mesoamerican

cultures. Yet West Mexico is best known for its rich tradition of clay sculpture.

The sculptures come from tombs consisting of shafts as deep as 50 feet with chambers at their base. Because scientific excavations began only recently, much of what is known about West Mexican tomb contents derives primarily from the artifacts found and sold by grave robbers. Researchers believe, however, that most of these tombs were built and filled with elaborate offerings during the late Preclassic period, the half millennium before 300 CE.

The large ceramic figures found in the Colima tombs are consistently a highly burnished red orange, in contrast with the distinctive polychrome surfaces of the majority of other West Mexican ceramics. The area also is noted for small-scale clay narrative scenes that include modeled houses and temples and numerous solid figurines shown in a variety of lively activities. These sculptures, which may provide informal glimpses of daily life, are not found in any other ancient Mesoamerican culture. Although their subjects are often described as anecdotal and secular rather than religious, the Mesoamerican belief system did not recognize such a division. Consequently, scholars are unsure whether the figure we illustrate (FIG. **14-3**) is a religious practitioner with a horn on his forehead (a common indigenous symbol of special powers) or a political leader wearing a shell ornament (often a Mesoamerican emblem of rulership)—or a person serving both roles.

Teotihuacán (ca. 100 BCE–750 CE)

THE PLACE OF THE GODS At Olmec sites, the characteristic later Mesoamerican temple-pyramid-plaza layout appeared in embryonic form. At Teotihuacán (FIG. **14-4**), northeast of modern Mexico City, the Preclassic scheme underwent a monumental

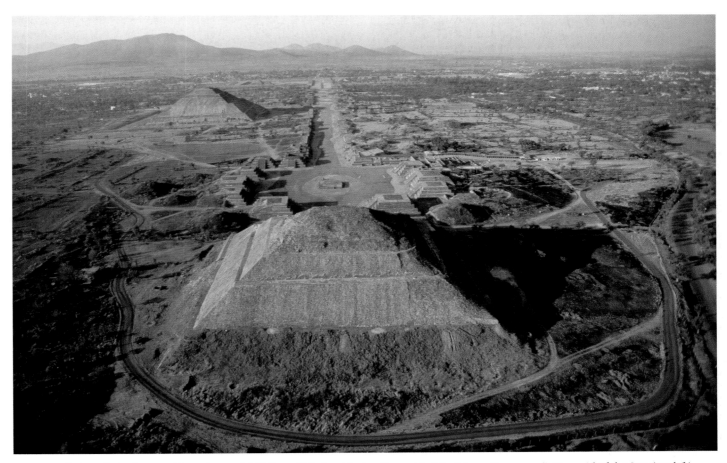

14-4 Aerial view of Teotihuacán (from the north), Valley of Mexico, Mexico. Pyramid of the Moon *(foreground)*, Pyramid of the Sun *(top left)*, and the Citadel *(background)*, all connected by the Avenue of the Dead; main structures ca. 50–200 CE; site ca. 100 BCE–750 CE.

expansion into a genuine city. Teotihuacán was a large, densely populated metropolis that fulfilled a central civic, economic, and religious role for the region and indeed for much of Mesoamerica. Built up during nearly a millennium, ca. 100 BCE to 750 CE, the site's major monuments were constructed between 50 and 250 CE, during the late Preclassic period. Teotihuacán covers nine square miles, laid out in a grid pattern with the axes oriented by sophisticated surveying. The city's orientation, as well as the placement of some of its key pyramids, also appear to have been related to astronomical phenomena.

At its peak, around 600 CE, Teotihuacán may have had as many as 125,000–200,000 residents, which would have made it the sixth largest city in the world at that time. Divided into numerous wardlike sectors, this metropolis must have had a uniquely cosmopolitan character, with Zapotec peoples located in the city's western wards, and merchants from Veracruz living in the eastern wards, importing their own pottery and building their houses and tombs in the style of their homelands. The city's urbanization did nothing to detract from its sacred nature. In fact, it vastly augmented Teotihuacán's importance as a religious center. The Aztecs, who visited Teotihuacán regularly and reverently long after it had been abandoned, gave it its current name, which means "the place of the gods." Because the city's inhabitants left only a handful of undeciphered hieroglyphs and linguists do not yet even know what language they spoke, the names of many major features of the site are unknown. The Avenue of the Dead and the Pyramids of the Sun and Moon are later Aztec designations that do not necessarily relate to the original names of these entities.

The grid plan is quartered by a north-south and an east-west axis, each four miles in length. The rational scheme recalls Hellenistic and Roman urban planning (compare FIGS. 5-75 and 10-40) and is very unusual in Mesoamerica before the Aztecs. The main north-south axis, the Avenue of the Dead (FIG. 14-4), is 130 feet wide and connects the Pyramid of the Moon complex with the Citadel and its Temple of Quetzalcoatl. This two-mile stretch is not a continuously flat street but is broken by sets of stairs, giving pedestrians a constantly changing view of the surrounding buildings and landscape.

TEOTIHUACÁN'S PYRAMIDS The Pyramid of the Sun (FIG. 14-4, *top left*), facing west on the east side of the Avenue of the Dead, was erected in the first century CE during the late Preclassic period. It is the city's centerpiece and its largest structure, rising to a height of more than 200 feet. The Pyramid of the Moon (FIG. 14-4, *foreground*) was built a century or more later, ca. 150–250 CE. The shapes of the monumental structures at Teotihuacán echo the surrounding mountains. Their imposing mass and scale surpass those of all other Mesoamerican sites. Rubble-filled and faced with the local volcanic stone, the pyramids consist of stacked squared platforms diminishing in perimeter from the base to the top, much like the Stepped Pyramid of Djoser in Egyptian Saqqara (see FIG. 3-4). Ramped stairways led to crowning temples constructed of perishable materials such as wood and thatch, no longer preserved.

The Teotihuacanos built the Pyramid of the Sun over a cave, which they reshaped and filled with ceramic offerings. The pyramid may have been constructed to honor a sacred spring within

14-5 Detail of Temple of Quetzal-coatl, the Citadel, Teotihuacán, Valley of Mexico, Mexico, third century CE.

the now-dry cave. The excavators found children buried at the four corners of each of the pyramid's tiers. The later Aztec sacrificed children to bring rainfall, and Teotihuacán art abounds with references to water, so the Teotihuacanos may have shared the Aztec preoccupation with rain and agricultural fertility. The city's inhabitants rebuilt the Pyramid of the Moon (currently being excavated) at least five times in Teotihuacán's early history. It may have been positioned to mimic the shape of Cerro Gordo, the volcanic mountain behind it, undoubtedly an important source of life-sustaining streams.

THE FEATHERED SERPENT At the south end of the Avenue of the Dead is the great quadrangle of the Citadel (FIG. 14-4, *background*). It encloses a smaller pyramidal shrine datable to the third century CE, the Temple of Quetzalcoatl (FIG. **14-5**). Quetzalcoatl, the "feathered serpent," was a major god in the Mesoamerican pantheon at the time of the Spanish conquest, hundreds of years after the fall of Teotihuacán. The later Aztecs associated him with wind, rain clouds, and life. Beneath the temple, archaeologists found a tomb looted in antiquity, perhaps that of a Teotihuacán ruler. The discovery has led them to speculate that like the Maya, the Teotihuacanos also buried their elite in or under pyramids. Surrounding the tomb both beneath and around the pyramid were the remains of at least a hundred sacrificial victims. Some were adorned with necklaces made of strings of human jaws, both real and sculpted from shell. Like most other Mesoamerican groups, the Teotihuacanos invoked and appeased their gods through human sacrifice. The presence of such a large number of victims also may reflect Teotihuacán's militaristic expansion — throughout Mesoamerica, the victors often sacrificed captured warriors.

The temple's sculptured panels, which feature projecting stone heads of Quetzalcoatl alternating with heads of a long-snouted scaly creature with rings on its forehead, decorate each of the temple's six terraces. This is the first unambiguous representation of the feathered serpent in Mesoamerica. The scaly creature's identity is unclear. Linking these alternating heads are low-relief carvings of feathered-serpent bodies and seashells. The latter reflect Teotihuacán contact with the peoples of the Mexican coasts and also symbolize water, an essential ingredient for the sustenance of an agricultural economy.

MURAL PAINTING Like those of most ancient Mesoamerican cities, Teotihuacán's buildings and streets were once stuccoed over and brightly painted. In a treatment unique to Teotihuacán during the Classic period, however, elaborate murals covered the walls of the rooms of its elite residential compounds. The paintings chiefly depict deities, ritual activities, and processions of priests, warriors, and even animals. Experimenting with a variety of surfaces, materials, and techniques over the centuries, Teotihuacán muralists finally settled on applying pigments to a smooth lime-plaster surface coated with clay. They then polished the surface to a high sheen. Although some Teotihuacán paintings have a restricted palette of varying tones of red (largely derived from the mineral hematite), creating subtle contrasts between figure and ground, most employ vivid hues arranged in flat, carefully outlined patterns. One mural (FIG. **14-6**) depicts an earth or nature goddess who some scholars think was the city's principal deity. Always shown frontally with her face covered by a jade mask, she is dwarfed by her large feathered headdress and reduced to a bust placed upon a stylized pyramid. She stretches her hands out to provide liquid streams filled with bounty (compare the Sumerian mural at Zimri-Lim's palace, FIG. 2-17), but the stylized human hearts that flank the frontal bird mask in her headdress reflect her dual nature. They remind viewers that the ancient Mesoamericans saw human sacrifice as essential to agricultural renewal.

The influence of Teotihuacán was all-pervasive in Mesoamerica. Colonies were established as far away as the southern borders of Maya civilization, in the highlands of Guatemala, some 800 miles from Teotihuacán.

14-6 Goddess, mural painting from Tetitla apartment complex at Teotihuacán, Valley of Mexico, Mexico, 650–750 CE. Pigments over clay and plaster.

Classic (ca. 300–900 CE)

THE MAYA Strong cultural influences stemming from the Olmec tradition and from Teotihuacán contributed to the development of Classic Maya culture. As was true of Teotihuacán, the foundations of Maya civilization were laid in the Preclassic period, perhaps by 600 BCE or even earlier. At that time, the Maya, who occupied the moist lowland areas of Belize, southern Mexico, Guatemala, and Honduras, seem to have abandoned their early somewhat egalitarian pattern of village life and adopted a hierarchical autocratic society. This system evolved into the typical Maya city-state governed by hereditary rulers and ranked nobility. How and why this happened is still uncertain.

Stupendous building projects signaled the change. Vast complexes of terraced temple-pyramids, palaces, plazas, ball courts (see "The Mesoamerican Ball Game," page 389), and residences of the governing elite dotted the Maya area. Unlike the Teotihuacán civilization, no one site ever achieved complete dominance as the single center of power. The new architecture, and the art embellishing it, advertised the power of the rulers, who appropriated cosmic symbolism and stressed their descent from gods to reinforce their claims to legitimate rulership. The unified institutions of religion and kingship were established so firmly, their hold on life and custom was so tenacious, and their meaning was so fixed in the symbolism and imagery of art that the rigidly conservative system of the Classic Maya lasted almost a thousand years. Maya civilization began to decline in the eighth century. By 900, it had vanished.

Although the causes of the beginning and end of Classic Maya civilization are obscure, researchers are gradually revealing its history, beliefs, ceremonies, conventions, and patterns of daily life. Long romanticized, the Maya now enter the world history stage as believably as the peoples of other great civilizations. No longer viewed as a peaceful, benign society under theocratic rule, the Maya are now seen as flesh-and-blood peoples who glorified their rulers and oppressed the lower classes, undertook (and broke) strategic political alliances, waged war, and practiced human sacrifice. This more accurate picture is the consequence of modern interdisciplinary scholarship. Archaeologists, epigraphers (scholars who decipher writing systems), art historians, and ethnographers (those who study contemporary societies) all have contributed to a clearer understanding of ancient Maya culture.

DECODING MAYAN SCRIPT Like the decipherment of Egyptian writing early in the 19th century (see Chapter 3), the decoding of the Mayan script has been an exciting intellectual adventure. By the end of the 19th century, numbers, dates, and some astronomical information could be read, but little else, leading scholars to conclude that the Maya were obsessed with time and religion and uninterested in recording the mundane events of human lives. Two important breakthroughs beginning in the 1950s radically altered the understanding of both Mayan writing and the Maya worldview. The first was the realization that the Maya depicted their rulers (rather than gods or anonymous priests) in their art and noted their rulers' achievements in their texts. The second was that Mayan writing is largely phonetic; that is, the hieroglyphs are made up of signs representing sounds in the Mayan language. Fortunately, the various Mayan languages were recorded in colonial texts and dictionaries, and most are still spoken today. Although perhaps only half of the ancient Mayan script can be translated accurately into spoken Mayan, today scholars can at least grasp the general meaning of many more hieroglyphs.

ASTRONOMY AND CALENDARS The Maya possessed a highly developed knowledge of arithmetic calculation and the ability to observe and record the movements of the sun, the moon, and numerous planets. They contrived an intricate but astonishingly accurate calendar, and although their calendric structuring of time was radically different in form from the Western calendar used today, it was just as precise and efficient. With their calendar, the Maya established the all-important genealogical lines of their rulers, which certified their claim to rule, and created the only true written history in ancient America. Although other ancient Mesoamerican societies, even in the Preclassic period, also possessed calendars, only the Maya calendar can be translated directly into today's calendrical system.

ARCHITECTURE AND RITUAL The most sacred and majestic buildings of Maya cities were raised in enclosed, centrally located precincts. The religious-civic transactions that guaranteed the order of the state and the cosmos occurred in these settings. The Maya held dramatic rituals within a sculptured and painted environment, where huge symbols and images proclaimed the nature and necessity of that order. Maya builders designed spacious plazas for vast audiences who were exposed to overwhelming propaganda. The programmers of that propaganda, the ruling families and troops of priests, nobles, and retainers, wore its symbolism in their costumes. In Maya paintings and sculptures, the Maya elite wear extravagant profusions of vividly colorful cotton textiles, feathers, jaguar skins, and jade, all emblematic of their rank and wealth. On the different levels of the painted and polished temple platforms, the ruling classes performed the offices of their rites in clouds of incense to the music of maracas, flutes, and drums. The Maya transformed the architectural complex at each city's center into a theater of religion and statecraft. In the stagelike layout of a characteristic Maya city well-preserved carved monuments than any other site in the Americas, it was one of the first Maya sites excavated. It also has proved one of the richest in the trove of architecture, sculpture, and artifacts recovered. Conspicuous plazas dominated the heart of the city. In Copán's Great Plaza, the Maya set up tall, sculpted stone stelae. Carved with the portraits of the rulers who erected them, these stelae also recorded their names, dates of reign, and notable achievements in glyphs on the front, sides, or back.

Stele D (FIG. 14-7), erected in 736 CE, represents one of the city's foremost rulers, Waxaklahun-Ubah-K'awil, known as 18-Rabbit (r. 695–738). In a dynastic succession of 16 rulers, 18-Rabbit was the 13th. During his long reign, Copán may have reached its greatest physical extent and range of political influence. On Stele D, 18-Rabbit wears an elaborate headdress and ornamented kilt and sandals. He holds across his chest a double-headed serpent bar, symbol of the sky and of his absolute power. His features have the quality of a portrait likeness, although highly idealized. The Maya elite, like the Egyptian pharaohs (see Chapter 3), tended to have themselves portrayed in a conventionalized manner and as eternally youthful. The dense, deeply carved ornamental details that frame the face and figure in florid profusion stand almost clear of the block and wrap around the sides of the stele. The high relief, originally painted, gives the impression of a freestanding statue, although a hieroglyphic text is carved on the flat back side of the stele. Although a powerful ruler who erected many stelae and buildings at Copán, including one of Mesoamerica's best-preserved (and carefully restored) ball courts (FIG. 14-8; see "The Mesoamerican Ball Game," page 389), 18-Rabbit eventually was captured and beheaded by the king of neighboring Quiriguá.

CLASSIC TIKAL Another great Maya site of the Classic period is Tikal in Guatemala, some 150 miles north of Copán. Tikal is one of the oldest and largest of the Maya cities. Together with its suburbs, Tikal originally covered some 75 square miles and served as the ceremonial center of a population of perhaps 75,000. The Maya did not lay out central Tikal on a grid plan as did the designers of contemporary Teotihuacán. Instead, causeways connected irregular groupings. Modern surveys have uncovered the remains of as many as 3,000 separate structures in an area of about six square miles. The site's nucleus, the Great Plaza, is studded with stelae and defined by numerous architectural complexes. The most prominent monuments are the two soaring

14-7 Stele D portraying the ruler 18-Rabbit, Maya, Great Plaza at Copán, Honduras, 736 CE. Stone, 11′ 9″ high.

center, its principal group, or "site core," was the religious and administrative nucleus for a population of dispersed farmers settled throughout a suburban area of many square miles.

COPÁN'S PORTRAIT STELAE Because Copán, on the western border of Honduras, has more hieroglyphic inscriptions and

14-8 Ball court (view looking north), Middle Plaza, Copán, Maya, Copán Valley, Honduras, 738 CE.

The Mesoamerican Ball Game

After witnessing the native ball game of Mexico soon after their arrival in the 16th century, the Spanish conquerors took Aztec ball players back to Europe to demonstrate the novel sport. Their chronicles remark on the athletes' great skill, the heavy wagering that accompanied the competition, and the ball itself, made of rubber, a substance the Spaniards had never seen before.

The game was played throughout Mesoamerica and into the southwestern United States, beginning at least 3,400 years ago, the date of the earliest known ball court. The Olmec were apparently avid players. Their very name—a modern invention in Nahuatl, the Aztec language—means "rubber people," after the latex-growing region they inhabited. Not only are ball players represented in Olmec art, but remnants of sunken earthen ball courts and even rubber balls have been found at Olmec sites.

The Olmec earthen playing field evolved in other Mesoamerican cultures into a plastered masonry surface, I- or T-shaped in plan, flanked by two parallel sloping or straight walls. Sometimes the walls were wide enough to support small structures on top, as at Copán (FIG. 14-8). At other sites, temples stood at either end of the ball court. These structures were common features of Mesoamerican cities. At Cantona, for example, archaeologists have uncovered 22 ball courts even though only a small portion of the site has been excavated. Teotihuacán (FIG. 14-4) is an exception. The excavators have not yet found a ball court there, but mural paintings at the site illustrate people playing the game with portable markers and sticks. Most ball courts were adjacent to the important civic structures of Mesoamerican cities, such as palaces and temple-pyramids, as at Copán.

Surprisingly little is known about the rules of the ball game itself—how many players were on the field, how goals were scored and tallied, and how competitions were arranged. Unlike a modern soccer field with its standard dimensions, Mesoamerican ball courts vary widely in size. The largest known—at Chichén Itzá—is nearly 500 feet long; Copán's is about 93 feet long. Some have stone rings, which a ball conceivably could have been tossed through, set high up on their walls at right angles to the ground, but many courts lack this feature. Alternatively, the ball may have been bounced against the walls and into the end zones. As in soccer, players could not touch the ball with their hands but used their heads, elbows, hips, and legs. They wore thick leather belts, and sometimes even helmets, and padded their knees and arms against the blows of the fast-moving solid rubber ball. Typically, the Maya portrayed ball players wearing heavy protective clothing and kneeling, poised to deflect the ball (FIG. 14-10).

Although widely enjoyed as a competitive spectator sport, the ball game did not serve solely for entertainment. The ball, for example, may have represented a celestial body such as the sun, its movements over the court imitating the sun's daily passage through the sky. Reliefs on the walls of ball courts at certain sites make clear that the game sometimes culminated in human sacrifice, probably of captives taken in battle and then forced to participate in a game they were predestined to lose.

Ball playing also had a role in Mesoamerican mythology. In the ancient Maya epic known as the *Popol Vuh (Council Book)*, first written down in Spanish in the colonial period, a legendary pair of twins is forced to play ball with the evil lords of the Underworld. The brothers lose and are sacrificed. The sons of one twin eventually travel to the Underworld and, after a series of trials including a ball game, outwit the lords and kill them. They revive their father, buried in the ball court after his earlier defeat at the hands of the Underworld gods. The younger twins rise to the heavens to become the sun and the moon, and the father becomes the god of maize, principal sustenance of all Mesoamerican peoples. The ball game and its aftermath, then, were a metaphor for the cycle of life, death, and regeneration that permeated Mesoamerican religion.

14-9 Temple I (Temple of the Giant Jaguar), Maya, Tikal, Petén, Guatemala, ca. 732 CE.

pyramids, taller than the surrounding rain forest, that face each other across an open square. The larger pyramid (FIG. **14-9**), Temple I (also called the Temple of the Giant Jaguar after a motif on one of its carved wooden lintels), reaches a height of about 150 feet. It is the temple-mausoleum of a great Tikal ruler, Hasaw Chan K'awil, who died in 732 CE. His body was placed in a vaulted chamber under the pyramid's base. The towering structure is made up of nine sharply inclining platforms, probably a reference to the nine levels of the Underworld. A narrow stairway leads up to a three-chambered temple. The temple is surmounted by an elaborately sculpted *roof comb,* a vertical architectural projection that once bore the ruler's giant portrait modeled in stucco. The entire structure exhibits most concisely the ancient Mesoamerican formula for the stepped temple-pyramid and the compelling aesthetic and psychological power of Maya architecture.

JAINA CLAY SCULPTURE The almost unlimited variety of figural attitude and gesture permitted in the modeling of clay explains the profusion of Maya ceramic figurines that, like their West Mexican predecessors (FIG. 14-3), may illustrate aspects of everyday life. Small-scale sculpture figures in the round, they are remarkably lifelike, carefully descriptive, and even comic at times.

They represent a wider range of human types and activities than is commonly depicted on Maya stelae. Ball players (FIG. **14-10**), women weaving, older men, dwarves, supernatural beings, and amorous couples, as well as elaborately attired rulers and warriors, make up the figurine repertory. Many of the hollow figurines are also whistles. They were made in ceramic workshops on the mainland, often with molds, but burials on the island cemetery of Jaina, off the western coast of Yucatán, yielded hundreds of such figures, including the ball player we illustrate. Traces of blue remain on the figure's belt, remnants of the vivid pigments that once covered many of these figurines. The Maya used "Maya blue," a combination of a particular kind of clay and indigo, a vegetable dye, to paint both ceramics and murals. This pigment has proven virtually indestructible, unlike the other colors that largely have disappeared over time. Like the larger terracotta figures of West Mexico, these figurines were made to accompany the dead on their inevitable voyage to the Underworld. The excavations at Jaina, however, have revealed nothing more that might clarify the meaning and function of the figures. Male figurines were not found exclusively in the burials of male individuals, for example.

HISTORY PAINTING AT BONAMPAK The vivacity of the Jaina figurines and their variety of pose, costume, and occupation were reinterpreted in two dimensions at Bonampak (Mayan for "painted walls") in southeastern Mexico. Three chambers in one Bonampak structure contain mural paintings that record important aspects of Maya court life. The example we reproduce (FIG. **14-11**) shows warriors surrounding captives on a terraced platform. The figures represented have naturalistic proportions and overlap, twist, turn, and gesture. The artists used fluid and calligraphic line to outline the figures, working with color to indicate both texture and

14-10 Ball player, Maya, from Jaina Island, Mexico, 700–900 CE. Painted clay, $6\frac{1}{4}''$ high. National Museum of Anthropology, Mexico City.

14-11 Presentation of captives to Lord Chan Muwan, Maya, room 2, structure 1, Bonampak, Mexico, ca. 790 CE. Mural, approx. $17' \times 15'$; watercolor copy by Antonio Tejeda. Peabody Museum, Harvard University, Cambridge.

volume. The Bonampak painters combined their pigments—both mineral and organic—with a mixture of water, crushed limestone, and vegetable gums and applied them to their stucco walls in a technique best described as a cross between fresco and tempera.

The Bonampak murals are filled with circumstantial detail. The information given is comprehensive, explicit, and presented with the fidelity of an eyewitness report. The royal personages are identifiable by both their physical features and their costumes, and accompanying inscriptions provide the precise day, month, and year for the events recorded. All the scenes at Bonampak relate the events and ceremonies that welcome a new royal heir (shown as a toddler in some scenes). They include presentations, preparations for a royal fete, dancing, battle, and the taking and sacrificing of prisoners. On all occasions of state, public bloodletting was an integral part of Maya ritual. The ruler, his consort, and certain members of the nobility drew blood from their own bodies and sought union with the supernatural world. The slaughter of captives taken in war regularly accompanied this ceremony. Indeed, Mesoamerican cultures undertook warfare largely to provide victims for sacrifice. The torture and eventual execution of prisoners served both to nourish the gods and to strike fear into enemies and the general populace.

The scene in structure 1, room 2, depicts the presentation of prisoners to Lord Chan Muwan (FIG. 14-11). The painter arranged the figures in registers that may represent a pyramid's steps. On the uppermost step, against a blue background, is a file of gorgeously appareled nobles wearing animal headgear. Conspicuous among them on the right are retainers clad in jaguar pelts and jaguar headdresses. Also present is Chan Muwan's wife (third from right). The ruler himself, in jaguar jerkin and high-backed sandals, stands at the center, facing a crouching victim who appears to beg for mercy. Naked captives, anticipating death, crowd the middle level. One of them, already dead, sprawls at the ruler's feet. Others dumbly contemplate the blood dripping from their mutilated hands. The lower zone, cut through by a doorway into the structure housing the murals, shows clusters of attendants who are doubtless of inferior rank to the lords of the upper zone. The stiff formality of the victors contrasts graphically with the supple imploring attitudes and gestures of the hapless victims. The Bonampak victory was short-lived. The murals were never finished, and shortly after the dates written on the walls the site seems to have been abandoned.

SHIELD JAGUAR AND LADY XOC A rare representation in monumental art of a woman playing an important role in Maya ritual appears on the painted lintels of a temple (structure 23) at Yaxchilán. Lintel 24 (FIG. 14-12) depicts the ruler Itzamna Balam II (r. 681–742 CE), known as Shield Jaguar, and his principal wife, Lady Xoc. Lady Xoc is magnificently outfitted in an elaborate woven garment, headdress, and jewels. She pierces her tongue with a barbed cord in a bloodletting ceremony that, according to accompanying inscriptions, celebrated the birth of a son to one of

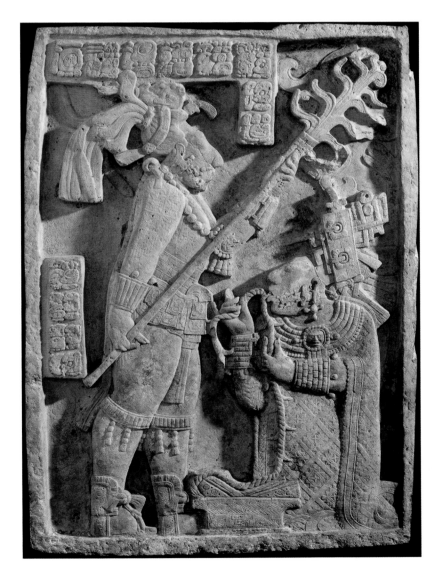

14-12 Shield Jaguar and Lady Xoc, Maya, lintel 24, temple 23, Yaxchilán, Mexico, ca. 725 CE. Limestone, $3' \ 7'' \times 2' \ 6\frac{1}{2}''$. British Museum, London.

14-13 Enthroned Maya lord and courtiers, cylinder vase (rollout view), Maya, from Motul de San José region, Guatemala, 672–830 CE. Ceramic with red, rose, orange, white, and black on cream slip, approx. 8″ high. Dumbarton Oaks Research Library and Collections, Washington, D.C.

the ruler's other wives as well as an alignment between the planets Saturn and Jupiter. The celebration must have taken place in a dark chamber or at night because Shield Jaguar provides illumination with a blazing torch. These ceremonies were intended to produce hallucinations. (Lintel 25 depicts Lady Xoc and her vision of an ancestor emerging from the mouth of a serpent.)

MAYA VASE PAINTING Vivid narratives also appear on the much smaller surfaces of painted cylinder vases. A rollout view of a typical vase design (FIG. **14-13**) shows a palace scene where an enthroned lord sits surrounded by courtiers and attendants. In this scene, at once regal and intimate, the participants gesture and talk. The elaborate costumes of the Copán stele, the Bonampak paintings, and the Yaxchilán lintel are absent. Instead, the figures wear simple loincloths, turbans of wrapped cloth and feathers, and black body paint. The red frame that surrounds the scene suggests an architectural setting. The painter provided a glimpse of the event through the open doorways of a palace.

The horizontal band of hieroglyphs at the top describes the vessel and names the artist. Although this particular name has not been completely deciphered, the names of a handful of Maya vase painters, all male, are now known. Some texts even list the contents of the vessel. One pot marked with the glyph for cacao, or chocolate, still contained remnants of the prestigious drink when it was discovered. In our example, the artist may have portrayed himself among the participants. He repeats his name in one of the vertical texts, which refer to both the figures and ritual events. Some artists even recorded their parentage, clearly stating they were of noble birth and high status. Vases such as this one may have been used as drinking and food vessels for noble Maya, but their final destination was the tomb, where they accompanied the deceased to the Underworld. They likely were commissioned by the deceased before his death or by his survivors and occasionally were sent from distant sites as funerary offerings. (The Maya intermarried with other powerful families to consolidate power between important cities, and both trade and gift exchanges were common.)

Terminal Classic and Early Postclassic (ca. 800–1250 CE)

Throughout Mesoamerica, the Classic period ended at different times with the disintegration of the great civilizations. Teotihuacán's political and cultural empire, for example, was disrupted

around 600, and its influence waned. About 650 the center of the great city was destroyed by fire, but the cause is still unknown. Within a century, however, Teotihuacán was deserted. Around 900, many of the great Maya sites were abandoned to the jungle, leaving a few northern Maya cities to flourish for another century or two before they, too, became depopulated. The Classic culture of the Zapotecs, centered at Monte Albán in the state of Oaxaca, came to an end around 700, and the neighboring Mixtec peoples assumed supremacy in this area during the Postclassic period. Classic El Tajín, later heir to the Olmec in the Veracruz plain, survived the general crisis that afflicted the others but was burned sometime in the 12th century. The war and confusion that followed the collapse of the Classic civilizations broke the great states up into small, local political entities isolated in fortified sites. The collapse encouraged even more warlike regimes and chronic aggression. The militant city-state of Chichén Itzá dominated Yucatán, while in central Mexico the Toltec and the later Aztec peoples, both ambitious migrants from the north, forged empires by force of arms.

CHICHÉN ITZÁ AND THE NORTH Yucatán, a flat, low limestone peninsula covered with scrub vegetation, lies north of the rolling and densely forested region of the Guatemalan Petén. During the Classic period, Mayan-speaking peoples sparsely inhabited this northern region. For reasons that are still the subject of debate, when the southern Classic Maya sites were abandoned after 900, the northern Maya continued to build many new temples in this area. They also experimented with building construction and materials to a much greater extent than their cousins farther south. Piers and columns appeared in doorways, and stone mosaics enlivened outer facades. The northern groups also invented a new type of construction, a solid core of coarse rubble faced inside and out with a veneer of square limestone plates.

CARACOL AND CASTILLO The design of the structure known as the Caracol ("snail" in Spanish) at Chichén Itzá (FIG. **14-14**, *foreground*) suggests that the northern Maya were as inventive of architectural form as they were experimental with construction and materials. A cylindrical tower rests on a broad terrace that is in turn supported by a larger rectangular platform measuring 169 × 232 feet. The tower, composed of two concentric walls, encloses a circular staircase that leads to a small chamber near the top of the structure. In plan, the building recalls the cross-section of a conch shell. The conch shell was an attribute of the feathered serpent, and round temples were dedicated to him in central Mexico.

14-14 The Caracol (*fore-ground*) and the Castillo (*background*), Maya, Chichén Itzá, Yucatán, Mexico, ca. 800–900 CE.

This building may therefore have been a temple to Kukulkan, the Maya equivalent of Quetzalcoatl. Windows along the Caracol's staircase and an opening at the summit probably were used for astronomical observation, which has given the building another nickname—the Observatory. Noted astronomers, the Maya tracked celestial events closely, both for practical reasons, such as determining when to plant and the date of the next eclipse, and to foretell and attempt to manipulate the future.

Behind the Caracol in our photograph (FIG. 14-14) is the Castillo ("Castle"), 98 feet high and 182 feet wide at the base. The monument is a temple dedicated to Kukulkan atop a great pyramid, the signature form of sacred architecture throughout Mesoamerica. Steps on four sides of the nine-tiered pyramid converge on the temple level. Painted reliefs throughout the structure relating to the cult of Quetzalcoatl are signatures of Central Mexican influence on the northern Maya of Yucatán.

TOLTEC GUARDIANS The name *Toltec,* which signifies "makers of things," generally refers to a powerful tribe of invaders from the north, whose arrival in central Mexico coincided with the great disturbances that must have contributed to the fall of the Classic civilizations. The Toltec capital at Tula flourished from about 900 to 1200. The Toltecs were great political organizers and military strategists, dominating large parts of north and central Mexico. They also were respected both as master artisans and farmers, and later peoples such as the Aztec looked back on them admiringly, proud to claim descent from them.

At Tula, four colossal *atlantids* (male statue-columns; FIG. **14-15**) portraying armed warriors reflect the grim, warlike regime of the Toltecs. These images of brutal authority stand eternally at attention, warding off all hostile threats. Built up of four stone drums each, the sculptures stand atop Pyramid B. They wear feathered headdresses and, as breastplates, stylized butterflies, heraldic symbols of the

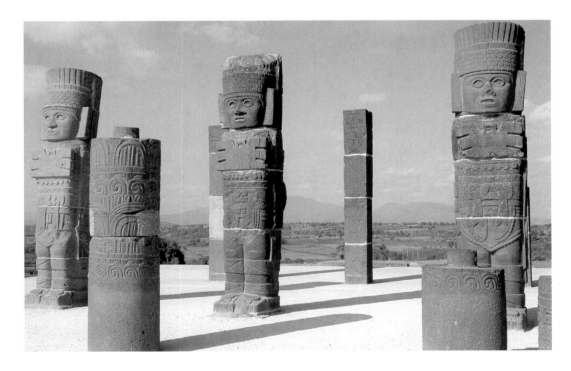

14-15 Colossal atlantids, Pyramid B, Toltec, Tula, Hidalgo, Mexico, ca. 900–1180 CE. Stone, each approx. 16′ high.

Toltec. In one hand they clutch a bundle of darts and in the other an *atlatl* (spear-thrower), typical weapons of highland Mexico. The figures originally supported a temple roof, now missing. Such an architectural function requires rigidity of pose, compactness, and strict simplicity of contour. The unity and regularity of architectural mass and silhouette here combine perfectly with abstraction of form.

By 1180, the last Toltec ruler abandoned Tula, followed by most of his people. Some years later, the city was catastrophically destroyed, its ceremonial buildings burned to their foundations, its walls thrown down, and the straggling remainder of its population scattered. The exact reasons for the Toltecs' departure and for their city's destruction are unknown. Although the stage was set for the rise of the last great civilization of Mesoamerica, the Aztecs (see Chapter 30), they did not reach the height of their power for another 300 years.

INTERMEDIATE AREA

Between the highly developed civilizations of Mesoamerica and the South American Andes (MAPS 14-2 and 14-3) lies a region archaeologists have dubbed the "Intermediate Area." Comprising parts of El Salvador, Honduras, Ecuador, and Venezuela, and all of Panama, Costa Rica, Nicaragua, and Colombia, at the time of the European invasion it was by no means a unified political territory but rather was occupied by many small rival chiefdoms. Although the people of the Intermediate Area did not produce monumental architecture on the scale of their neighbors to the north and south and, unlike the Mesoamericans, left no written records, they too were consummate artists. Potters in the Intermediate Area made some of the earliest ceramics of the Americas, and they continued to create an astonishing variety of terracotta vessels and figures until the time of the Spanish conquest. Among the other arts practiced in the Intermediate Area was stone sculpture, including large-scale figures and elaborately carved *metates* (ceremonial grinding stones, possibly used as thrones). The ancient Costa Ricans excelled at carving jade as well, particularly anthropomorphic and zoomorphic celts. Throughout the area, goldworking was prized, and the first Europeans to make contact here were astonished to see the inhabitants nearly naked but covered in gold jewelry. The legend of El Dorado, a Colombian chief who coated himself in gold as part of his accession rites, was largely responsible for the Spanish invaders' ruthless plunder of the region.

TAIRONA GOLD In northern Colombia, the Sierra Nevada de Santa Marta rises above the Caribbean. The topography of lofty mountains and river valleys allowed for considerable isolation and the independent development of various groups. Late inhabitants of this region (from about 1000 to contact with the Spanish conquerors, in the poorly documented chronology of the area) included a group known as the Tairona, whose metalwork is among the finest of all the ancient American goldworking styles.

Goldsmiths in Peru, Ecuador, and southern Colombia produced technologically advanced and aesthetically sophisticated work in gold mostly by cutting and hammering thin gold sheets. The Tairona smiths, however, who had to obtain gold by trade, used the lost-wax process (see "Hollow-Casting," Chapter 5, page 131) in part to preserve the scarce amount of the precious metal available to them. They cast small works of the highest quality in both fabrication and design.

Tairona pendants were not meant to be worn simply as rich accessories to costume but as amulets or talismans representing

14-16 Pendant in the form of a bat-faced man, Tairona, from northeastern Colombia, after 1000 CE. Gold, $5\frac{1}{4}''$ high. Metropolitan Museum of Art, New York (Jan Mitchell and Sons Collection).

powerful beings who gave the wearer protection and status. Our example (FIG. **14-16**) shows a bat-faced man—perhaps a masked man rather than a composite being, or a man in the process of spiritual transformation. In local mythology, the bat was the first animal to be created. This bat-man wears an immense headdress made up of two birds in the round, two great beaked heads, and a series of spirals crowned by two overarching stalks. The harmony of repeated curvilinear motifs, the rhythmic play of their contours, and the precise delineation of minute detail bespeak the anonymous artist's technical control and aesthetic sensitivity.

SOUTH AMERICA

As in Mesoamerica, the indigenous civilizations of Andean South America (MAP **14-3**) jarred against and stimulated one another, produced towering monuments and sophisticated paintings, sculptures, ceramics, and textiles, and were exterminated in violent confrontations with the Spanish conquistadors. Although less well studied than the ancient Mesoamerican cultures, those of South America are actually older, and in some ways they surpassed the accomplishments of their northern contemporaries. Andean peoples, for example, mastered metalworking much earlier, and their monumental architecture predates that of the earliest Mesoamerican culture, the Olmec, by more than a millennium. The peoples of northern Chile even began to mummify their dead at least 500 years before the Egyptians (see "Mummification," Chapter 3, page 59).

GEOGRAPHY The Central Andean region of South America lies between Ecuador and northern Chile, its western border the Pacific Ocean. It consists of three well-defined geographic zones, running north and south and roughly parallel to one another. The narrow western coastal plain is a hot desert crossed by rivers, creating habitable fertile valleys. Next, the high peaks of the great Cordillera of the Andes hem in plateaus of a temperate climate. The region's inland border, the eastern slopes of the Andes, is a hot and humid jungle.

CHRONOLOGY Andean civilizations flourished both in the highlands and on the coast. Highland cave dwellers fashioned the

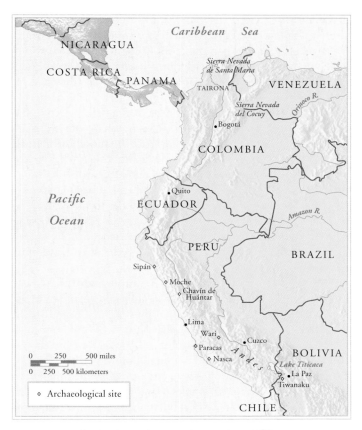

MAP 14-3 Early sites in Andean South America.

first rudimentary art objects by 8800 BCE. Sophisticated textiles started to be produced as early as 2500 BCE during the Preceramic period. The firing of clay began around 1800 BCE during the so-called Initial period. Beginning about 800 BCE, Andean chronology alternates between periods known as "horizons," when a single culture appears to have dominated a broad geographic area for a relatively long period, and "intermediate periods" characterized by more independent regional development. The first period, Early Horizon, is represented by the Chavín culture (ca. 800– 200 BCE); the Middle Horizon by the Tiwanaku and Wari cultures (ca. 600–1000 CE); and the Late Horizon by the Inka Empire (see Chapter 30). Among the many regional styles that flourished between these horizons, the most important are the Early Intermediate period (ca. 200 BCE–700 CE) Paracas and Nasca cultures of the south coast of Peru, and the Moche in the north.

Early Cultures (ca. 3000–800 BCE)

The discovery of complex ancient communities documented by radiocarbon dating is changing the picture of early South American cultures. Planned communities boasting organized labor systems and monumental architecture dot the narrow river valleys that drop from the Andes to the Pacific Ocean. In the Central Andes, these early sites began to develop around 3000 BCE, about a millennium before the invention of pottery there. Carved gourds and some fragmentary cotton textiles survive from this early period. They depict composite creatures, such as crabs turning into snakes, as well as doubled and then reversed images, both hallmarks of later Andean art.

CEREMONIAL ARCHITECTURE The architecture of the early coastal sites typically consists of large U-shaped flat-topped plat-

forms—some as high as a 10-story building—around sunken courtyards. Many had numerous small chambers on top. Construction materials included both uncut fieldstones and handmade *adobes* (sun-dried mud bricks) in the shape of cones, laid point to point in coarse mud plaster to form walls and platforms. These complexes almost always faced toward the Andes mountains, source of the life-giving rivers on which these communities depended for survival. Mountain worship, which continues in the Andean region to this day, was probably the focus of early religious practices as well. In the highlands, archaeologists also have discovered large ceremonial complexes. In place of the numerous interconnecting rooms found on top of many coastal mounds, the highland examples have a single small chamber at the top, often with a stone-lined firepit in the center. These pits probably played a role in ancient fire rituals. Burnt offerings, often of exotic objects such as marine shells and tropical bird feathers, have been found in the pits.

Chavín (ca. 800–200 BCE)

CHAVÍN DE HUÁNTAR Named after the ceremonial center of Chavín de Huántar, located in the northern highlands of Peru, the Chavín culture developed and spread throughout much of the coastal region and the highlands during the first millennium BCE. Once thought to be the "mother culture" of the Andean region, the Chavín horizon style is now seen as the culmination of developments that began some 2,000 years earlier elsewhere.

The main temple of Chavín de Huántar (FIG. 14-17) resembles some sacred complexes of the Preceramic and Initial periods. It is a U-shaped, stone-faced structure facing east between two rivers. Although at first glance its three stories appear to be a solid stepped platform, in fact a labyrinth of narrow passageways, small chambers, and stairways penetrate the temple. No windows, however, light the interior spaces. The few members of Chavín society with access to these rooms must have witnessed secret and sacred torch-lit ceremonies. The temple is fronted by sunken courts, an arrangement also adopted from earlier coastal sites. Modifications to the structure during the centuries have resulted in the asymmetrical shape seen today.

14-17 Reconstructed drawing of sacred center showing temple and associated sunken courtyards, Chavín de Huántar, Peru, first millennium BCE.

14-18 *Raimondi Stele,* from main temple, Chavín de Huántar, Peru, first millennium BCE. Incised green diorite, 6′ high. Instituto Nacional de Cultura, Lima.

The temple complex at Chavín de Huántar is famous for its extensive stone carvings. The most common subjects are composite creatures that combine feline, avian, reptilian, and human features. Consisting largely of low relief on panels, cornices, and columns, and some rarer instances of freestanding sculpture, Chavín carving is essentially shallow, linear incision. An immense oracular cult image stood in the center of the temple's oldest part. Other examples of sculpture in the round include heads of mythological creatures *tenoned* (attached by stone pegs) into the exterior walls.

A REVERSIBLE GOD The *Raimondi Stele* (FIG. **14-18**), named after its discoverer, represents a figure called the "staff god." He appears in various versions from Colombia to northern Bolivia but always holds staffs. Seldom, however, do the representations have the degree of elaboration found at Chavín. The Chavín god bares his teeth and gazes upward. His elaborate headdress dominates the upper two-thirds of the slab. Inverting the image reveals that the headdress is composed of a series of fanged jawless faces, each emerging from the mouth of the one above it. Snakes abound. They extend from the deity's belt, make up part of the staffs, serve as whiskers and hair for the deity and the headdress creatures, and form a braid at the apex of the composition. The *Raimondi Stele* clearly illustrates the Andean artistic tendency toward both multiplicity and dual readings. Upside down, the god's face turns into not one but two faces. The ability of gods to transform before the viewer's eyes is a core aspect of Andean religion.

Chavín iconography spread widely throughout the Andean region through portable media such as goldwork, textiles, and ceramics. For example, more than 300 miles from Chavín on the south coast of Peru, archaeologists have discovered cotton textiles with imagery recalling Chavín sculpture. Painted staff-bearing female deities, apparently local manifestations or consorts of the highland staff god, decorate these large cloths, which may have served as wall hangings in temples. Ceramic vessels found on the north coast of Peru also carry motifs much like those found on Chavín stone carvings.

Paracas (ca. 400 BCE–200 CE)

Several coastal traditions developed during the period between about 500 BCE and 600 CE. Together they exemplify the great variations within Peruvian art styles. The Paracas culture, which lasted about six centuries (ca. 400 BCE–200 CE), occupied a desert peninsula and a nearby river valley on the south coast of Peru.

FUNERARY MANTLES Outstanding among the Paracas arts are the funerary textiles used to wrap the bodies of the dead in multiple layers. The dry desert climate preserved the textiles, buried in shaft tombs beneath the sands. These textiles are among the enduring masterpieces of Andean art (see "Andean Weaving," page 397). Most are of woven cotton with designs embroidered onto the fabric in alpaca or vicuña wool imported from the highlands. The weavers used more than 150 vivid colors, the majority derived from plants.

Feline, bird, and serpent motifs appear on many of the textiles, but the human figure, real or mythological, predominates. A common theme on the grave mantles is humans dressed up as or changing into animals—consistent with the Andean transformation theme noted on the *Raimondi Stele* (FIG. 14-18). On the example we illustrate (FIG. **14-19**) is a figure with prominent eyes, who appears scores of times over the surface. The flowing hair and the slow kicking motion of the legs suggest airy, hovering movement. The flying or floating being carries what some have identified as batons and fans and others as knives and hallucinogenic mushrooms. On other mantles the figures carry the skulls or severed heads of enemies. Some scholars have interpreted the flying figures as Paracas religious practitioners dancing or flying during an ecstatic trance. Others believe they are images of the deceased. Despite endless repetitions of the figure, variations of detail occur throughout each textile, notably in the figures' positions and in subtle color changes.

Andean Weaving

When the Inka first encountered the Spanish conquistadors, they were puzzled by the Europeans' fixation on gold and silver. The Americans valued finely woven cloth just as highly as precious metal. Textiles and clothing dominated every aspect of their existence. Storing textiles in great warehouses, their leaders demanded cloth as tribute, gave it as gifts, exchanged it during diplomatic negotiations, and even burned it as a sacrificial offering. Although both men and women participated in cloth production, the Inka rulers selected the best women weavers from around the empire and sequestered them for life to produce textiles exclusively for the rulers.

The Andean weavers manufactured their textiles by spinning into yarn the cotton grown in five different shades on the warm coast and the fur sheared from highland llamas, alpacas, vicuñas, or guanacos, and then weaving the yarn into cloth. Rare tropical bird feathers and small plaques of gold and silver were sometimes sewn onto cloth destined for the nobility. Andean weavers mastered nearly every textile technique known today, many executed with a simple device known as a *backstrap loom.* Such looms are still in use in the Andes. The weavers stretch the long *warp* (vertical) threads between two wooden bars. The top one is tied to an upright. A belt or backstrap, attached to the bottom bar, encircles the waist of the seated weaver, who maintains the tension of the warp threads by leaning back. The weaver passes the *weft* (horizontal) threads over and under the warps and pushes them tightly against each other to produce the finished cloth. In ancient textiles, the sturdy cotton often formed the warp, and the wool, which can be dyed brighter colors, served to create complex designs in the weft. *Embroidery* (see

"Embroidery and Tapestry," Chapter 17, page 476), the sewing of threads onto a finished ground cloth to form contrasting designs, was the specialty of the Paracas culture (FIG. 14-19).

The dry deserts of coastal Peru have preserved not only numerous textiles from different periods but also hundreds of finely worked baskets containing spinning and weaving implements. These tools are invaluable sources of information about Andean textile production processes. The baskets found in documented contexts came from women's graves, attesting to the close identity between weaving and women, the reverence for the cloth-making process, and the Andean belief that textiles were necessary in the afterlife.

A special problem all weavers confront is that they must visualize the entire design in advance and cannot easily change it during the weaving process. No records exist of how Andean weavers learned, retained, and passed on the elaborate patterns they wove into cloth, but some painted ceramics depict weavers at work, apparently copying designs from finished models. However, the inventiveness of individual weavers is evident in the endless variety of colors and patterns in surviving Andean textiles. This creativity often led Andean artists to design textiles that are highly abstract and geometric. Paracas embroideries (FIG. 14-19), for example, may depict humans, down to the patterns on the tunics they wear, yet the figures are reduced to their essentials in order to focus on their otherworldly role. The culmination of this tendency toward abstraction may be seen in the Wari compositions (FIG. 14-25) in which figural motifs become stunning blocks of color that overwhelm the subject matter itself.

14-19 Embroidered funerary mantle, Paracas, from southern coast of Peru, first century CE. Plain weave camelid fiber with stem-stitch embroidery of camelid wool, 4′ 7$\frac{7}{8}$″ × 7′ 10$\frac{7}{8}$″. Museum of Fine Arts, Boston (William A. Paine Fund).

Nasca (ca. 200 BCE–600 CE)

NASCA PAINTED POTTERY The Nasca culture takes its name from the Nasca River Valley south of Paracas. The early centuries of the Nasca civilization are contemporary with the closing centuries of the Paracas culture, and Nasca style followed closely the Paracas flowing line and strong emphasis on color. The Nasca were renowned for their pottery. Thousands of their ceramic vessels survive. The vases usually have round bottoms, double spouts connected by bridges, and smoothly burnished polychrome surfaces. The subjects vary greatly, but plants, animals, and composite mythological creatures, partly human and partly animal, are most common. Nasca painters often represented ritual impersonators, some of whom, like the Paracas flying figures, hold trophy heads and weapons. In the example we illustrate (FIG. **14-20**), two such costumed figures fly around the vessel. The painter reduced their bodies and limbs to abstract appendages and focused on the heads. The figures wear a multicolored necklace, a whiskered gold mouthpiece, circular disks hanging from the ears, and a rayed crown on the forehead. Masks or heads with streaming hair, possibly more trophy heads, flow over the impersonators' backs, increasing the sense of motion.

EARTH DRAWINGS Nasca artists also depicted figures on a gigantic scale. Some 800 miles of lines drawn in complex networks on the dry surface of the Nasca Plain have long attracted world attention because of their colossal size, which defies human perception from the ground. Preserved today on the Nasca Plain are about three dozen images of birds, fish, and plants. Our illustration (FIG. **14-21**) shows a hummingbird several hundred feet long. The Nasca artists also drew geometric forms, such as trapezoids, spirals, and straight lines running for miles.

14-20 Bridge-spouted vessel with flying figures, Nasca, from Nasca River valley, Peru, ca. 50–200 CE. Painted ceramic, approx. $5\frac{1}{2}''$ high. Art Institute of Chicago, Chicago (Kate S. Buckingham Endowment).

These Nasca Lines, as the immense earth drawings are called, were produced when the artists selectively removed the dark top layer of stones to expose the light clay and calcite below. The lines were constructed quite easily from available materials and with

14-21 Hummingbird, Nasca Plain, Nasca, Peru, ca. 500 CE. Dark layer of pebbles scraped aside to reveal lighter clay and calcite beneath.

some rudimentary geometry. Small groups of workers have made modern reproductions of them with relative ease. The lines seem to be paths laid out using simple stone-and-string methods. Some lead in traceable directions across the deserts of the Nasca River drainage. Others are punctuated by many shrinelike nodes, like the knots on a cord. Some lines converge at central places usually situated close to water sources and seem to be associated with water supply and irrigation. They may have marked pilgrimage routes for those who journeyed to local or regional shrines on foot. Altogether, the vast arrangement of the Nasca Lines is a system—not a meaningless maze but a traversable map that plotted out the whole terrain of Nasca material and spiritual concerns. Remarkably, until quite recently similar ritual pathways were made and used in association with shrines in highland Bolivia, demonstrating the tenacity of the Andean indigenous belief systems.

Moche (ca. 1 – 700 CE)

MOCHE CERAMICS Among the most famous art objects the ancient Peruvians produced are the painted clay vessels of the Moche, who occupied a series of river valleys on the north coast of Peru around the same time the Nasca flourished to the south. Among ancient civilizations, only the Greeks and the Maya surpassed the Moche in the information recorded on their ceramics.

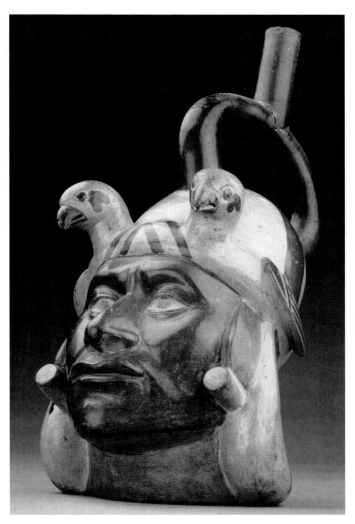

14-22 Vessel in the shape of a portrait head, Moche, from north coast Peru, fifth to sixth century CE. Painted clay, $1' \frac{1}{2}''$ high. Museu Arqueológico Rafael Larco Herrera, Lima.

Moche pots illustrate architecture, metallurgy, weaving, the brewing of *chicha* (fermented maize beer), human deformities and diseases, and even sexual acts. Moche vessels are predominantly flat-bottomed stirrup-spouted jars derived from Chavín prototypes. They are generally decorated with a bichrome (two-color) slip. Although the Moche made early vessels by hand without the aid of a potter's wheel, they fashioned later ones in two-piece molds. Thus, numerous near-duplicates survive. Moche potters continued to refine the stirrup spout, making it an elegant slender tube, much narrower than the Chavín examples. This refinement may be seen in the portrait vessel illustrated here (FIG. **14-22**), an elaborate example of a common Moche type. It may depict the face of a warrior, a ruler, or even a royal retainer whose image may have been buried with many other pots to accompany his dead master. The realistic rendering of the physiognomy is particularly striking.

THE LORD OF SIPÁN Elite men, along with retinues of sacrificial victims, appear to be the occupants of several rich Moche tombs excavated near the village of Sipán on the arid northwest coast of Peru. The Sipán burials have yielded a treasure of golden artifacts and more than a thousand ceramic vessels. The discovery of the tombs in the late 1980s made a great stir in the archaeological world, contributing significantly to the knowledge of Moche culture. Beneath a large adobe platform adjacent to two high but greatly eroded pyramids, excavators found several lavish burials, including the tomb of a man known today as the Lord of Sipán or the Warrior Priest. The splendor of the funeral trappings that adorned his body, the quantity and quality of the sumptuous accessories, and the bodies of the retainers buried with him indicate that he was a personage of the highest rank. Indeed, he may have been one of the warrior priests so often pictured on Moche ceramic wares and murals (and in this tomb on a golden pyramid-shaped rattle) assaulting his enemies and participating in sacrificial ceremonies.

An ear ornament (FIG. **14-23**) of turquoise and gold found in one Sipán tomb shows a warrior priest clad much like the Lord of Sipán. Two retainers appear in profile to the left and right of the

14-23 Ear ornament, from a tomb at Sipán, Moche, Peru, ca. 300 CE. Gold and turquoise, approx. $4\frac{4}{5}''$ diameter. Bruning Archaeological Museum, Lambayeque.

central figure. Represented frontally, he carries a war club and shield and wears a necklace of owl-head beads. The figure's blade-like crescent-shaped helmet is a replica of the large golden one buried with the Sipán lord. The war club and shield also match finds in the Warrior Priest's tomb. The ear ornament of the jewelry image is a simplified version of the piece itself. Other details also correspond to actual finds—for example, the removable nose ring that hangs down over the mouth. The value of the Sipán find is incalculable for what it reveals about elite Moche culture and for its confirmation of the accuracy of the iconography of Moche artworks.

Tiwanaku (ca. 100–1000 CE)

The bleak highland country of southeastern Peru and southwestern Bolivia contrasts markedly with the warm valleys of the coast. In the mountains, another culture developed beginning in the second century CE. Named Tiwanaku after its principal archaeological site on the southern shore of Lake Titicaca, the culture flourished for nearly a millennium, spreading to the adjacent coastal area as well as to other highland areas, eventually extending from southern Peru to northern Chile.

THE GATEWAY OF THE SUN Tiwanaku was an important ceremonial center. Its inhabitants constructed grand buildings using the region's fine sandstone, andesite, and diorite. Tiwanaku's imposing Gateway of the Sun (FIG. 14-24) is a huge monolithic block of andesite pierced by a single doorway. Moved in ancient times from its original location within the site, the gateway now forms part of an enormous walled platform. The gate is crowned with relief sculpture. The central figure is a Tiwanaku version of the Chavín staff god (FIG. 14-18). Larger than all the other figures and presented frontally, he dominates the composition and presides over the passageway. Rays project from his head. Many terminate in puma heads, representing the power of the highlands' fiercest predator. The staff god—possibly a sky and weather deity rather than the sun deity the rayed head suggests—appears in art throughout the Tiwanaku horizon, associated with smaller attendant figures. Those of the Gateway of the Sun are winged and have human or condor heads. Like the puma, the condor is an impressive carnivore, the largest raptor in the world. Sky and earth beings thus converge on the gate, which probably served as the doorway to a sacred area, a place of transformation. The reliefs were once colorfully painted. The figures' eyes were apparently also inlaid with turquoise, and the surfaces covered with gold, producing a dazzling effect.

14-24 Gateway of the Sun, Tiwanaku, Bolivia, ca. 375–700 CE. Stone, 9′ 10″ high.

Wari (ca. 500–800 CE)

The flat, abstract, and repetitive figures surrounding the central figure on the Gateway of the Sun recall woven textile designs. Indeed, the people of the Tiwanaku culture, like those of Paracas, were consummate weavers, although many fewer textiles survive from the damp highlands. However, from a contemporaneous Peruvian culture known as Wari, which dominated parts of the dry coast, many examples of weaving, especially tunics, have been recovered.

ABSTRACTION IN TAPESTRY Although Wari weavers fashioned cloth, like the earlier Paracas textiles (FIG. 14-19), from both wool and cotton fibers, the resemblance between the two textile styles ends there. Whereas Paracas motifs were embroidered onto the plain woven surface, Wari designs were woven directly into the fabric, the weft threads packed densely over the warp threads in a technique known as *tapestry* (see "Embroidery and Tapestry," Chapter 17, page 476). Some particularly fine pieces have more than 200 weft threads per inch. Furthermore, unlike the relatively naturalistic individual figures depicted on Paracas mantles, those appearing on Wari textiles are so closely connected and so abstract as to be nearly unrecognizable. In the tunic shown here, the so-called *Lima Tapestry* (FIG. 14-25), the Wari designer expanded or compressed each figure in a different way and placed them in vertical rows pressed between narrow red bands of plain cloth. Elegant tunics such as this must have been prestige garments made for the elite.

NORTH AMERICA

REGIONS AND PEOPLES In many parts of the United States and Canada, indigenous cultures have been discovered that reach back as far as 12,000 years ago. Most of the surviving art objects, however, come from the past 2,000 years. Scholars divide the vast and varied territory of North America (MAP 14-4) into cultural regions based on the relative homogeneity of language and social and artistic patterns. Native lifestyles varied widely over the continent, ranging from small bands of migratory hunters to settled—at times even urban—agriculturalists. Among the art-producing peoples who inhabited the continent before the arrival of Europeans are the Eskimos of Alaska and the Inuits of Canada, who hunted and fished across the Arctic from Greenland to Siberia, and the maize farmers of the American Southwest, who wrested water from their arid

14-25 *Lima Tapestry* (tunic), Wari, from Peru, ca. 500–800 CE. 3' 3⅜" × 2' 11⅜". National Museum of Archaeology, Anthropology, and History of Peru, Lima.

MAP 14-4 Early Native American sites in North America.

environment and built effective irrigation systems as well as roads and spectacular cliff dwellings. The vast, temperate Eastern Woodlands—ranging from eastern Canada to Florida and from the Atlantic to the Great Plains west of the Mississippi—also were home to farmers. Some of them left behind great earthen mounds that once functioned as their elite residences or burial places.

Eskimo

A MASK OF SEVERAL FACES The Eskimoan peoples originally migrated to North America across the Bering Strait. During the early first millennium CE, a community of Eskimo sea mammal hunters and tool makers occupied the Ipiutak site at Point Hope in Alaska during the Norton, or Old Bering Sea, culture that began around 500 BCE. Finds from the site include a variety of burial goods as well as tools. Of special interest is a burial mask (FIG. **14-26**) datable to ca. 100 CE, fashioned, like most Arctic artworks, out of walrus ivory because of the scarcity of wood in the region. The mask is composed of nine carefully shaped parts that are interrelated to produce several faces, both human and animal, echoing the transformation theme noted in other ancient American cultures. The confident, subtle composition in shallow relief is a tribute to the artist's imaginative control over the material. The mask's abstract circles and curved lines are common motifs on the decorated tools discovered at Point Hope. For centuries, the Eskimo also carved human and animal figures, always at small scale, reflecting a nomadic lifestyle that required the creation of portable objects.

14-26 Burial mask, Ipiutak, from Point Hope, Alaska, ca. 100 CE. Ivory, greatest width $9\frac{1}{2}''$. American Museum of Natural History, New York.

Woodlands

ADENA PIPES Early Native American artists also excelled in working stone into a variety of utilitarian and ceremonial objects. A pipe in the shape of a man (FIG. 14-27) is a product of the Adena culture of Ohio, documented at about 500 sites in the Central Woodlands. Carved between 500 BCE and the end of the millennium, the pipe is related in form and costume (note the prominent ear spools) to some Mesoamerican sculptures. The Adena buried their elite in great earthen mounds and often placed ceremonial pipes such as this one in the graves. Smoking was an important social and religious ritual in many Native American cultures, and pipes were treasured status symbols that men wanted to take with them into the afterlife. The standing figure on the illustrated pipe has naturalistic joint articulations and musculature, a lively flexed-leg pose, and an alert facial expression—all combining to suggest movement.

MISSISSIPPIAN MOUNDS The Adena were the first great mound builders of North America, but the Mississippian culture, which emerged around 800 CE and eventually encompassed much of the eastern United States, surpassed all earlier Woodlands peoples in the size and complexity of their communities. One Mississippian mound site, Cahokia in southern Illinois, was the largest city in North America in the early second millennium CE, with a population of at least 20,000 and an area of more than six square miles. There were approximately 120 mounds at Cahokia. The grandest, 100 feet tall and built in stages between ca. 900 and 1200 CE, was Monk's Mound. It is aligned with the position of the sun at the equinoxes and may have served as an astronomical observatory as well as the site of agricultural ceremonies. Each stage was topped by wooden structures that then were destroyed in preparation for the building of a new layer.

The Mississippians also constructed *effigy mounds* (mounds built in the form of animals or birds). One of the best preserved is Serpent Mound (FIG. 14-28), a twisting earthwork on a bluff overlooking a creek in Ohio. It measures nearly a quarter mile

14-27 Pipe, Adena, from a mound in Ohio, ca. 500–1 BCE. Stone, 8″ high. Ohio Historical Society, Columbus.

14-28 Serpent Mound, Mississippian, Ohio, ca. 1070 CE. 1200′ long, 20′ wide, 5′ high.

Serpent Mound

Serpent Mound (FIG. 14-28) is one of the largest and best known of the Woodlands effigy mounds, but it is the subject of considerable controversy. The mound was first excavated in the 1880s and represents one of the first efforts at preserving a Native American site from destruction at the hands of pot hunters and farmers. For a long time after its exploration, archaeologists attributed its construction to the Adena culture, which flourished in the Ohio area during the last several centuries BCE. New radiocarbon dates taken from the mound, however, indicate that it was built much later by the people known as Mississippians. Unlike most other ancient mounds, Serpent Mound contained no evidence of burials or temples. Serpents, however, were important in Mississippian iconography, appearing, for example, etched on shell gorgets similar to the one illustrated in FIG. 14-29. Snakes were strongly associated with the earth and the fertility of crops.

A stone figurine found at one site, for example, depicts a woman digging her hoe into the back of a large serpentine creature whose tail turns into a vine of gourds.

Another possible meaning for the construction of Serpent Mound, however, has been proposed recently. The new date suggested for it is 1070, not long after the brightest appearance in recorded history of Halley's Comet in 1066. Could Serpent Mound have been built in response to this important astronomical event? It even has been suggested that the serpentine form of the mound replicates the comet itself streaking across the night sky. Whatever its meaning, such a large and elaborate earthwork only could have been built by a large labor force under the firm direction of a powerful elite eager to leave its mark on the landscape forever.

from its open jaw (at the top right in our photograph), which seems to clasp an oval-shaped mound in its mouth, to its tightly coiled tail (at the far left). Both its date and meaning are controversial (see "Serpent Mound," above).

MISSISSIPPIAN GORGETS The Mississippian peoples, like their predecessors in North America, also manufactured small portable art objects. The shell *gorget*, or neck pendant, was a favorite item. Our example (FIG. 14-29) was found at a site in Tennessee and dates from ca. 1250 to 1300 CE. The incised gorget

depicts a running warrior, shown in the same kind of composite profile and frontal view with bent arms and legs used to suggest motion in other ancient cultures (compare, for example, FIG. 5-15). The Tennessee warrior wears an elaborate headdress incorporating an arrow. He carries a mace in his left hand and a severed human head in his right. On his face is the painted forked eye of a falcon. Most Mississippian gorgets come from burial and temple mounds and are thought to have been gifts to the dead to ensure their safe arrival and prosperity in the land of the spirits. Other art objects found in such contexts include fine mica

14-29 Incised shell gorget, Mississippian, from Sumner County, Tennessee, ca. 1250–1300 CE. 4″ wide. National Museum of the American Indian, Smithsonian Institution, Washington, D.C.

cutouts and embossed copper cutouts of hands, bodies, snakes, birds, and other presumably symbolic forms.

Southwest

MIMBRES POTTERY In the Southwest, Native Americans have been producing pottery since before the beginning of the Common Era. The most impressive examples of decorated pottery, however, date after 1000 CE. The Mimbres culture of southwestern New Mexico, which flourished between ca. 1000 and 1250 CE, is renowned for its black-on-white painted bowls. The one we illustrate (FIG. **14-30**) dates to ca. 1250 and features an animated graphic rendering of two black cranes on a white ground. The contrast between the bowl's abstract border designs and the birds creates a dynamic tension. Thousands of different compositions are known from Mimbres pottery. They range from lively and complex geometric patterns to abstract pictures of humans, animals, and composite mythological beings. Almost all are imaginative creations by artists who seem to have been bent on not repeating themselves. Their designs emphasize linear rhythms balanced and controlled within a clearly defined border. Because the potter's wheel was unknown in the Americas, the artists used the coiling method to build countless sophisticated shapes of varied size, always characterized by technical excellence. Although historians have no direct knowledge about the potters' identities, the fact that pottery making was usually women's work in the Southwest during the historic period (see "Gender Roles in Native American Art," Chapter 30, page 913) suggests that the Mimbres potters also may have been women.

Mimbres bowls have been found in burials under house floors, inverted over the head of the deceased and ritually "killed" by puncturing a small hole at the base, perhaps to allow the spirits of the deceased to join their ancestors in the sky (viewed as a dome by contemporary Southwestern peoples).

ANASAZI PUEBLOS The Anasazi (Navajo for "enemy ancestors"), northern neighbors of the Mimbres, emerged as an identifiable culture around 200 CE, but the culture did not reach its peak until about 1000. The Anasazi constructed architectural complexes that reflect masterful building skills. Many ruined Anasazi *pueblos* (urban settlements) are scattered throughout the Southwest. In Chaco Canyon, New Mexico, the Anasazi built a great semicircle of 800 rooms reaching to five stepped-back stories, the largest of several such sites in and around the canyon. Chaco Canyon was the center of a wide trade network extending as far as Mexico.

14-30 Bowl with two cranes and geometric forms, Mimbres, from New Mexico, ca. 1250 CE. Ceramic, black-on-white, approx. 1' $\frac{1}{2}$" diameter. Art Institute of Chicago, Chicago (Hugh L. and Mary T. Adams Fund).

14-31 Cliff Palace, Anasazi, Mesa Verde National Park, Colorado, ca. 1150–1300 CE.

Sometime in the late 12th century, a drought occurred, and the Anasazi largely abandoned their open canyon-floor dwelling sites to move farther north to the steep-sided canyons and lusher environment of Mesa Verde in southwestern Colorado. Cliff Palace (FIG. **14-31**) is wedged into a sheltered ledge above a valley floor. It contains about 200 rectangular rooms (mostly communal dwellings) of carefully laid stone and timber, once plastered inside and out with adobe. The location for Cliff Palace was not accidental. The Anasazi designed it to take advantage of the sun to heat the pueblo in winter and shade it during the hot summer months.

Scattered in the foreground of our Cliff Palace photograph are two dozen large circular semisubterranean structures, called *kivas,* which once were roofed over and entered with a ladder through a hole in the flat roof. These chambers were (and remain) the spiritual centers of native Southwest life, male council houses where ritual regalia are stored and private rituals and preparations for public ceremonies take place.

The Anasazi did not disappear but gradually evolved into the various Pueblo peoples who still live in Arizona, New Mexico, Colorado, and Utah. They continue to speak their native languages, practice deeply rooted rituals, and make pottery in the traditional manner. Their art is discussed in Chapter 30.

CONCLUSION

When Europeans first arrived in the Americas in the late 15th and early 16th centuries, they encountered native peoples whose artistic traditions were at least as ancient as those of classical Greece and Rome. In Mesoamerica, the Olmec erected great earthen pyramids and colossal stone portraits between ca. 900 and 400 BCE. At Teotihuacán, a great city featuring a grid plan and towering stone pyramids arose between 100 BCE and 750 CE. The Classic Maya (ca. 300–900 CE) built vast complexes of temple-pyramids, palaces, plazas, and ball courts, and decorated them with monumental sculptures and mural paintings. In Andean South America, the Chavín culture erected monumental ceremonial complexes with extensive stone carvings between 800 and 200 BCE. The Paracas, Nasca, Moche, and Wari cultures (ca. 400 BCE–800 CE) have left behind fabulous ceramics and textiles. In North America, the Mississippian culture constructed huge earthen mounds beginning around 900 CE. From an early date, the native peoples of the American Southwest lived in sophisticated urban communities and excelled in the art of pottery. The extraordinary diversity of American art and architecture before contact with Europeans reflects the enormous variety and vitality of the native cultures of the Western Hemisphere.

MESOAMERICA	SOUTH AMERICA	NORTH AMERICA

3000 BCE

2000 BCE

1200 BCE

■ OLMEC CULTURE, CA. 1200–400 BCE (M)

800 BCE

■ CHAVÍN CULTURE, CA. 800–200 BCE (S)

■ BEGINNINGS OF MAYA CIVILIZATION, CA. 600 BCE (M)

■ EARLIEST MESOAMERICAN WRITING, CA. 500 BCE (M)

■ ADENA CULTURE, CA. 500–1 BCE (N)

■ NORTON (OLD BERING SEA) CULTURE, 500 BCE–1000 CE (N)

■ PARACAS CULTURE, CA. 400 BCE–200 CE (S)

■ SHAFT-TOMB CULTURES OF WEST MEXICO, CA. 200 BCE–250 CE (M)

■ NASCA CULTURE, CA. 200 BCE–600 CE (S)

■ FOUNDATION OF TEOTIHUACÁN, CA. 100 BCE (M)

1 CE

■ MOCHE CULTURE, CA. 1–700 (S)

■ TIWANAKU CULTURE, CA. 100–1000 (S)

■ ANASAZI CULTURE, CA. 200–1400 (N)

300

400

■ WARI CULTURE, CA. 500–800 (S)

■ ITZAMNA BALAM II, YAXCHILÁN, R. 681–742 (M)

■ HASAW CHAN K'AWIL, TIKAL, R. 682–732 (M)

■ WAXAKLAHUN-UBAH-K'AWIL, COPÁN, R. 695–738 (M)

■ ABANDONMENT OF TEOTIHUACÁN, CA. 750 (M)

800

■ ASCENDANCE OF CHICHÉN ITZÁ, CA. 800 (M)

■ MISSISSIPPIAN CULTURE, CA. 800–1500 (N)

900

■ ABANDONMENT OF SOUTHERN MAYA SITES, CA. 900 (M)

■ TOLTEC DOMINATION AT TULA, CA. 900–1200 (M)

1000

■ MIMBRES CULTURE, CA. 1000–1250 (N)

1300

Vertical labels (left columns):
MESOAMERICA — PRECLASSIC (FORMATIVE) / CLASSIC / EARLY POSTCLASSIC
SOUTH AMERICA — PRECERAMIC / INITIAL PERIOD / EARLY HORIZON / EARLY INTERMEDIATE PERIOD / MIDDLE HORIZON / LATE INTERMEDIATE PERIOD
NORTH AMERICA — VARIOUS OVERLAPPING INDIGENOUS CULTURES (SEE LIST)

1 Olmec colossal head, La Venta, ca. 900–400 BCE

2 Embroidered funerary mantle, Paracas, first century CE

3 Temple I, Tikal, ca. 732

4 Serpent Mound, Ohio, ca. 1070

KEY: M = MESOAMERICA / N = NORTH AMERICA / S = SOUTH AMERICA

Ivory belt mask of a Queen Mother, from Benin, Nigeria, mid-16th century. Ivory and iron, $9\frac{3}{8}''$ high. Metropolitan Museum of Art, New York (The Michael C. Rockefeller Memorial Collection, gift of Nelson A. Rockefeller, 1972).

15

SOUTH FROM
THE SAHARA

EARLY AFRICAN ART

Africa (MAP **15-1**) is a vast continent comprising more than one-fifth of the world's land mass and many distinct topographical and ecological zones. Parched deserts occupy northern and southern regions, high mountains rise in the east, and three great rivers—the Niger, the Congo, and the Nile—and their lush valleys support agriculture and large settled populations. It is not yet possible to present a coherent, continent-wide history of early African art. A few areas have been fairly well surveyed archaeologically, but most of the continent remains little known in periods prior to European contact, which began along the seacoasts in the late 15th century. Many inland areas were virtually unknown to outsiders before 1850 or 1900.

Hundreds of distinct ethnic, cultural, and linguistic groups, often but inaccurately called "tribes," long have inhabited this enormous continent. Currently comprising more than 52 nations, such population groups historically have ranged in size from a few hundred, in hunting and gathering bands, to several million, in kingdoms and empires. Councils of elders often governed smaller groups, whereas larger populations sometimes have joined with other ethnic groups within a centralized state under a king. Kingdoms and empires headed by sacred rulers are known from several parts of Africa from about 1000 CE onward.

Within this great variety of African peoples are many shared core beliefs and practices. These include honoring ancestors and worshiping nature deities, often with blood sacrifice, and a tendency to elevate rulers to sacred status. Most peoples also consult diviners or fortune tellers. These beliefs have given rise to many richly expressive art traditions: rock engraving and painting, personal decoration, masquerades and other lavish festivals, the display of court arts and regalia, figural sculpture (often in shrines), elaborate architecture, and domestic arts, among other forms.

All the hundreds of ethnic groups in Africa, speaking as many mutually unintelligible languages, made visual arts that differ according to economy, lifestyle, ideology, and the materials available to them. Rock engravings and paintings in the Sahara and southern Africa, for example, depict thousands of animals as well as rituals held by the hunting and gathering or herding peoples who created most of the art. These nomadic and semi-nomadic peoples also excelled in the arts of personal adornment. Among farmers, in

MAP 15-1 Africa before 1800.

contrast, figural sculpture in terracotta, wood, and metal was often housed in shrines to legendary ancestors or nature deities held responsible for the health of crops and the well-being of the people. The regalia, art, and architecture of kings and their courts project ideas of wealth and power. Nearly all African peoples lavished artistic energy on the decoration of their own bodies to express their identity and status, and many communities mounted richly layered festivals, including masquerades, to celebrate harvests, the New Year, and the deaths of great people. In Africa, art helps define and create culture. It is integrated within African life and thought, and was not created solely for display until the final decades of the 20th century.

This chapter provides a chronological survey of sub-Saharan African art through the 18th century (see "Dating African Art and Identifying African Artists," page 411). Chapter 32 treats the past two centuries. The art and architecture of Egypt and of Roman and Islamic North Africa were examined in Chapters 3, 10, and 13 respectively.

PREHISTORIC AFRICAN ART

AFRICA'S EARLIEST ART Thousands of rock engravings and paintings found in hundreds of sites across the continent constitute the earliest known African art. Some painted animals from the Apollo 11 Cave in southwestern Africa (see FIG. 1-2) date to perhaps as long ago as 25,000 years, earlier than all but the oldest Paleolithic art of Europe (see Chapter 1). As humankind apparently originated in Africa, the world's earliest art may yet be discovered there as well. The greatest concentrations of rock art are in what are now dry desert regions—the Sahara to the north, the Horn in the east, and the Kalahari to the south—as well as in caves and on rock outcroppings in southern Africa. Probably because rock artists were more often hunter-gatherers or herders than farmers, these are precisely *not* the areas where most African sculpture is found. Accurately naturalistic renderings as well as stylized images on rock surfaces show animals and humans in many different positions and activities, singly or in groups, stationary or in motion. Most of these works date to within the past 4,000 to 6,000 years or slightly more, and they provide a rich record of the environment, human activities, and animal species.

The central Saharan painting shown here (FIG. **15-1**), for example, depicts a running woman with convincing animation and significant detail. The dotted marks on her shoulders, legs, and torso probably show body painting applied for a ritual. The white parallel patterns attached to her arms and waist appear to

Dating African Art and Identifying African Artists

Most African objects are unlabeled and unsigned and, consequently, insecurely dated. Early collectors did not bother to ask the names of artists or when the works were made. Organizing the vast array of African artworks into a firm chronology is therefore extremely difficult. Broad historical trends are reasonably clear, but more extensive archaeological work is needed in numerous parts of the continent before many artworks and even cultures can be firmly dated.

Some African peoples have left written documents that help date their artworks, even when their methods of measuring time differ from those used today. Other cultures, such as the Benin kingdom, preserve complex oral records of past events. Historians can check these against the accounts of Portuguese, German, and Dutch travelers and traders who visited the kingdom and recorded their observations.

The work of individual artists is now also being recognized, even if their names are often lost. Biographies have been compiled for some famous sculptors who worked in the late 19th or early 20th centuries. When artists are members of craft or occupational guilds—such as blacksmiths and brass casters in the Western Sudan—commissions go to the group chief, and the

specific artist who worked on the commission may never be known. Nevertheless, individual hands can be identified if their work is distinctive. Documentation now exists for several hundred individual artists.

Where documentation on authorship or dating is fragmentary or unavailable, art historians sometimes try to establish chronology from an object's style, determining what sorts of changes occurred over time to forms of a similar type. Scientific techniques such as *radiocarbon dating* (measuring the decay rate of carbon isotopes in organic matter to provide dates for wood, fiber, and ivory) and *thermoluminescence* (dating the amounts of radiation found in fired clay objects) have also proved useful. The history of African art is slowly being written, but there are still large gaps that need to be filled in. One of the major problems impeding compilation of an accurate African art history is illegal and uncontrolled excavation. By removing artworks from the ground, treasure hunters disturb or ruin their original contexts, and the possibility of establishing accurate chronologies is compromised or wholly lost. (This last problem is not unique to Africa; see "Archaeology, Art History, and the Art Market," Chapter 4, page 88.)

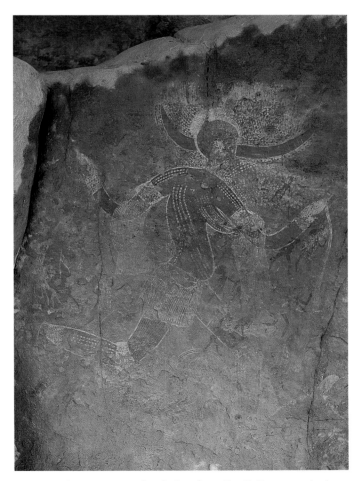

15-1 Running woman, rock painting, from Tassili (Inauouanrhat), Algeria, ca. 6000–4000 BCE.

represent flowing raffia decorations and her skirt, also probably raffia. Horns are part of her ceremonial attire. Notably, this detailed image was painted over a field of much smaller painted human beings, an indication of why it is often so difficult to date and interpret art on rock surfaces, as superimpositions are frequent.

Although both the precise dating and meaning are problematic for much rock art, a considerable literature exists that describes, analyzes, and interprets the varied human and animal activities shown, as well as the evidently symbolic, more abstract patterns. Overall meanings and uses probably coincide with those of the later arts—references to ideas and rituals about the origin, survival, health, and continuity of human populations. The human and humanlike renderings depict people and a host of spirits and other supernatural beings and gods.

AFRICAN ART, CA. 500 BCE–1000 CE

Nok Art (Central Sudan)

NOK TERRACOTTA HEADS Outside Egypt and neighboring Nubia, the earliest African sculptures in the round have been found at several sites in the Central Sudan, part of a broad band of grassland that spans the continent south of the Sahara. These dispersed sites are collectively designated the Nok culture, but there is no reason to believe that they were unified politically or socially. Named after the site where such sculptures were first discovered in 1928, Nok art dates between 500 BCE and 200 CE. Hundreds of Nok-style human and animal heads, body parts, and figures have been found accidentally during tin mining operations, as well as in archaeological excavations.

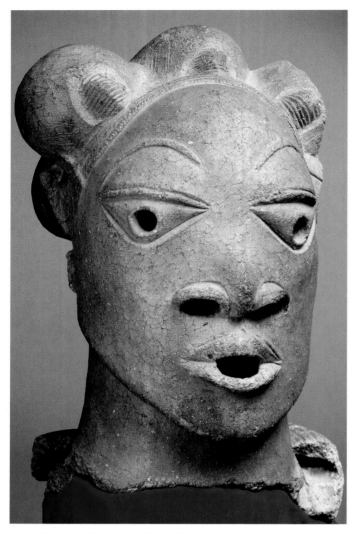

15-2 Nok head, from Rafin Kura, Nigeria, ca. 500 BCE–200 CE. Terracotta, 1′ 2 3/16″ high. National Museum, Lagos.

A representative Nok terracotta head (FIG. 15-2), a fragment of a full figure, depicts an expressive face with large alert eyes, flaring nostrils, and parted lips. The sculptor probably pierced the eyes, mouth, and ear holes—a characteristic of Nok style—to help equalize the heating of the hollow clay head during the firing process. The coiffure with incised grooves, the raised eyebrows, the deeply cut triangular eyes, and the sharp jaw line suggest that the sculptor carved some details of the head while modeling the rest. A probable earlier artistic tradition of woodcarving that has not survived may explain the lack of any known art tradition leading to the highly sophisticated Nok sculptures. The gender of Nok artists is unknown. Because the primary ceramists and clay sculptors across the continent are women, Nok sculptors may have been as well (see "Gender Roles in African Art Production," Chapter 32, page 955). Researchers are unclear about the function of these objects, but a ritual context is more likely than a simply decorative one.

Lydenburg Art (Southern Africa)

SCULPTURE IN SOUTH AFRICA Later in date than the Nok examples are the seven life-size (or nearly life-size) terracotta heads discovered outside the town of Lydenburg in present-day South Africa. They date to the later centuries of the first millennium of our era, although dating is controversial and still imprecise. The head shown here (FIG. 15-3), reconstructed from frag-

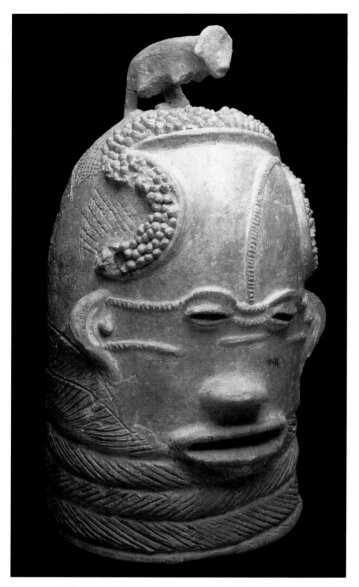

15-3 Head, from Lydenburg, South Africa, sixth to eighth century CE. Terracotta, 1′ 2 15/16″ high. IZIKO Museums of Cape Town, Cape Town.

ments, has a humanlike form, although its inverted pot shape differs markedly from the sculptural Nok heads. The artist created the eyes, ears, nose, and mouth, as well as the hairline, by applying thin clay fillets onto the head. The same method produced what are probably *scarification* marks (scars intentionally created to form patterns on the flesh) on the forehead, temples, and between the eyes. The horizontal neck bands, with their incised surfaces, resemble the ringed or banded necks that are considered signs of beauty in many parts of the continent. A small, unidentifiable animal sits atop the head. One can only guess at the uses and meanings of these heads, but a ritual function is again more likely than a purely secular one.

Igbo-Ukwu Art (Lower Niger Region)

EARLY BRONZE CASTING By the 9th or 10th century, a West African bronze-casting tradition of great sophistication had developed in the lower Niger area, just east of that great river. Dozens of refined, varied objects in an extremely intricate style were excavated in a family compound near the community of Igbo-Ukwu.

Art and Leadership in Africa

The relationships between leaders and art forms are strong, complex, and universal in Africa. Political, spiritual, and social leaders—kings, chiefs, titled people, and religious specialists—have the power and wealth to command the best artists and to require the richest, most durable materials to adorn themselves, furnish their homes, and make visible the cultural and religious organizations they lead. Leaders dispense art or the prerogative to use it. They use it instrumentally both to maintain existing patterns and to cause change. Thus the uses and meanings of leaders' arts are varied, whether overt or subtle, active or passive.

A number of formal or structural principles or trends characterize leaders' arts and thus set them off from the popular arts owned and used by ordinary people. Leaders' arts—for example, the sumptuous and layered regalia of chiefs and kings—tend to be durable and are often made of expensive materials, such as ivory, beads, copper alloys, and other rich metals. The art and architecture commissioned by African leaders also tend to be larger and more complex than those of other patrons. A palace, for example, is more extensive, with more rooms and finer decoration, than an ordinary dwelling. The arts often elevate leaders and draw attention to their superior status: stools or chairs, ornate clothing, and special weaponry serve these purposes. A leader's reach is often extended by handheld objects: staff, spear, or knife; pipe, fly whisk (FIG. 15-4), or scepter. Such forms also serve to magnify gestures. These and other objects, such as fans (see FIG. Intro-16), shields, umbrellas, and architectural forms, protect leaders physically or spiritually. Many of these forms have the effect of magnifying the apparent size and grandeur of the leader, further setting him or her off from the people at large. Sometimes a person is overloaded with regalia and implements to the point of virtual immobility, suggesting that the temporary holder of an office is less significant than the eternal office itself. Still, these arts render both the office and its holder visibly prominent and grand, thus contributing to the person's place at the center and top of the hierarchy.

Although it is easier to see leaders' arts in centralized, hierarchical societies (such as Benin, FIG. 15-11), leaders among less centralized peoples are no less conversant with the power of art to move people and effect change. Masquerades and religious cults, for example, are usually established and run by leaders who themselves may be less visible than the forms they commission and manipulate: shrines, altars, festivals, and rites of passage such as funerals, the last being especially elaborate and festive in many parts of Africa. Arts controlled by leaders thus help create pageantry, mystery, and spectacle, enriching and changing the lives of the people.

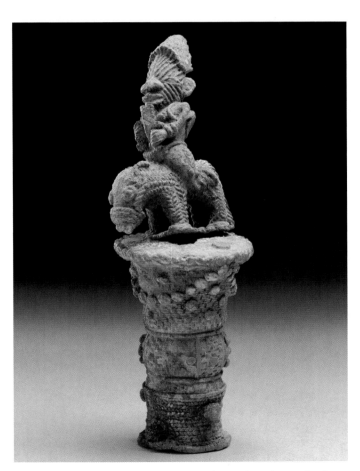

15-4 Equestrian figure on fly-whisk hilt, from Igbo-Ukwu, Nigeria, 9th to 10th century CE. Copper-alloy bronze, figure $6\frac{3}{16}$″ high. National Museum, Lagos.

The ceramic, copper, cast bronze, and iron artifacts included basins, bowls, altar stands, staffs, swords, scabbards, knives, and pendants. In one burial, the grave goods consisted of numerous prestige objects—copper anklets, armlets, spiral ornaments, a fan handle, and thousands of beads. The tomb also contained three elephant tusks, a beaded armlet, a crown, and a bronze leopard's skull. These items, doubtless the regalia of a leader (see "Art and Leadership in Africa, above), are the earliest metal castings known from regions south of the Sahara.

A lost-wax cast bronze (FIG. **15-4**), the earliest found in Africa, depicts an equestrian figure on a fly-whisk handle. The handle was made by a casting method similar to that used much earlier in the Mediterranean and Near East (see "Hollow-Casting," Chapter 5, page 131). The sculpture's upper section comprises a figure seated on a horselike animal, and the lower is an elaborately embellished handle with beaded and threadlike patterns. The facial stripes on the human figure probably represent marks of titled status, as can still be found among contemporary Igbo-speaking peoples in the same region today.

AFRICAN ART, CA. 1000–1800*

Inland Niger Delta Art (Western Sudan)

The inland floodplain of the Niger River in the Western Sudan was for the African continent a kind of "fertile crescent," analogous to that of ancient Mesopotamia (see Chapter 2). The metal-casting techniques used in Igbo-Ukwu, for example, may have come from this region. Although firm evidence for bronze casting

---

* From this point on, all dates in this chapter are CE unless otherwise stated.

Idealized Naturalism at Ile-Ife

When the German anthropologist Leo Frobenius first "discovered" the refined and naturalistic sculpture of Ile-Ife just after the turn of the 19th century in the Lower Niger River region, he could not believe that such works were locally made. Rather, he ascribed authorship to ancient Greece, where similarly lifelike art was well known. Other scholars traced such works to ancient Egypt, along with patterns of sacred kingship that were also believed to have been diffused several thousand miles from the Nile Valley to Yorubaland. Kings are known in numerous Yoruba city-states, all of which trace their origin to Ile-Ife, where Yoruba legends recount the world, its peoples, and sacred kingship began. Many careful archaeological excavations in and around the contemporary city of Ile-Ife, especially near the king's palace, moreover, confirm that the Yoruba ancestors of present-day residents were indeed the artists who made the extraordinary sculptures in stone, terracotta, and copper alloys ascribed to Ile-Ife. A number of these works were employed in the service of kingship, in ceremonies of installation, in funerals, and probably in annual festivals that reaffirmed the sacred power of the ruler and the allegiance of his people. Radiocarbon dates associated with several excavated Ife sites and with works of idealized naturalism place most of this art between the 11th or 12th and the 15th centuries.

Like the king figure we illustrate (FIG. 15-6), most Ife heads and figures are modeled with focused attention on naturalistic detail, apart from blemishes or signs of age, which are absent. Thus Ife style is lifelike but at the same time idealized, as if most of the people were portrayed as young adults in the prime of life and without any disfiguring warts or wrinkles. Some life-size heads, although still idealized, take naturalism to the point of descriptive, imitative portraiture. This is especially true of a group of about 30 heads cast in copper alloys. Many of these are sufficiently individualized that scholars are quite certain specific persons were being portrayed, although nearly all their names are lost. Among the most convincing portraits, however, is a mask of almost pure copper that has long carried the name of a famous early king, Obalufon. Until it became a holding of the Ife museum, the mask was apparently kept in the palace of the *oni* (king) from the time that it was made. Several very naturalistic heads have small holes above the forehead and around the lips and jaw, where black beads were found. These suggest that some heads were fitted with beaded veils, such as those known among Yoruba kings today, and perhaps human hair as well. Elaborate beadwork, a Yoruba royal prerogative, is also seen on the Ife king's image we illustrate (FIG. 15-6).

The hundreds of terracotta and copper-alloy heads, body parts and fragments, animals, and ritual vessels from Ile-Ife attest to a remarkable period in African art history, a period during which sensitive, meticulously rendered idealized naturalism prevailed. To this day, works in this style stand in contrast to the vast majority of African objects, which show the human figure in many different quite strongly conventionalized styles. Also clear is the distinction between the "perceptual naturalism" of most Ife works and the "conceptual naturalism" of most other African art. The latter suggests that for the most part, the representation of human forms conformed to local conventions passed down from one artist to another, whereas Ife style came about when artists actually perceived the human faces and bodies they portrayed.

---

in the Inland Delta has yet to be discovered, a copper industry is known to have flourished there from around 500, and sophisticated sculpture dates from around 1000.

JENNE TERRACOTTAS By about 800, a walled town, called Jenne-Jeno by archaeologists, had been built on high ground left dry during the flooding season. The archaeological evidence suggests the presence of several ethnic groups and many specialist workshops of blacksmiths, sculptors, potters, and others. Hundreds of accomplished, confidently modeled terracotta sculptures dating to between 1000 and 1500 have been found at numerous unmapped sites in the Jenne region. Unfortunately, as is true of the Nok terracottas, the vast majority of these sculptures were excavated illegally, and contextual information about them has been destroyed. The subject matter includes equestrians, male and female couples, emaciated and diseased people with lesions and swellings, and snake-entwined figures. There are seated, reclining, kneeling, and standing human figures. Some wear elaborate jewelry, but many are without adornment. The group we illustrate (FIG. 15-5) appears at first to be a mother and her children, but the "children" clambering up their "mother's" torso are in fact adults, easily discerned as such by their proportions. In some similar groups the "children" have beards. The woman therefore seems to be a metaphorical or legendary mother and the group is not a common family, although everyday genre scenes also occur among the preserved ceramic sculptures from the Inland Niger Delta.

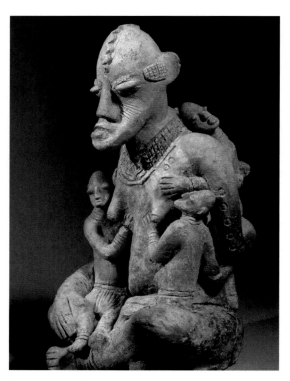

15-5 Mother with children(?), from the Inland Niger Delta, Mali, ca. 1000–1500. Terracotta, 1′ 1¾″ high. Private collection.

Ile-Ife Art (West of the Lower Niger)

By the 11th and 12th centuries, a very naturalistic style had appeared at Ile-Ife, about 200 miles west of Igbo Ukwu. Ile-Ife has long been considered the cradle of Yoruba civilization, the place where the gods created the universe. Origin stories also account for a line of divine Yoruba rulers extending from the legendary past until today.

SACRED KINGS An early work (FIG. **15-6**), cast in a zinc-brass alloy, undoubtedly represents a ruler. This finely rendered figure, unlike most later African wood sculpture, shows fleshlike modeling in the torso and the kind of idealized naturalism in facial features that approaches portraiture (see "Idealized Naturalism at Ile-Ife," page 414). Its proportions are less lifelike, however, than they are ideological. For modern Yoruba, the head is the locus of wisdom, destiny, and the essence of being. Such ideas probably developed at least 800 years ago. The sculptor accurately recorded the precise details of the heavily beaded costume, crown, and jewelry worn by both ancient and contemporary kings in Ile-Ife and other Yoruba city-states. The Ile-Ife figures and related works from the Yoruba kingdom of Owo to the southeast served mainly in rituals focused on sacred kingship. Many of these rituals have survived into the 21st century.

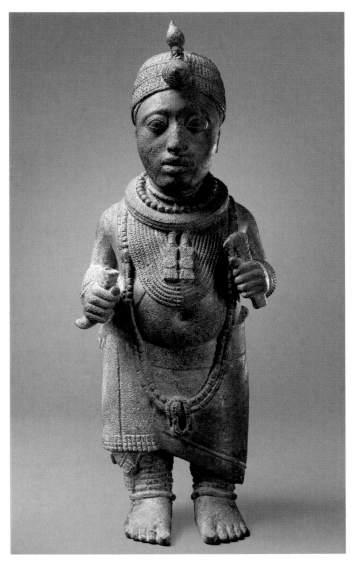

15-6 King, from Ife, Nigeria, 11th to 12th century. Zinc brass, 1′ 6½″ high. Ife Museum, Ife.

Great Zimbabwe Art (Southern Africa)

RUINS OF A LOST EMPIRE The most famous southern African site is a complex of stone ruins at the large southeastern political center called Great Zimbabwe. First occupied in the 11th century, the site features walled enclosures and towers that date from about the late 13th to the middle of the 15th century, when the Great Zimbabwe empire had a wide trade network. Finds of beads and pottery from Persia, the Near East, and China, along with copper and gold objects, underscore that Great Zimbabwe was a prosperous trade center well before Europeans began their coastal voyaging in the late 15th century. Most archaeologists and historians agree that the rulers at Great Zimbabwe and other nearby royal towns were ancestors of the area's present Shona-speaking peoples.

Using ethnographic information gathered from Portuguese accounts of the 16th to early 19th centuries and more recent studies of Shona culture, scholars have tried to interpret the meanings of the buildings and artifacts found at Great Zimbabwe. Most agree that the complex was a royal residence with special areas for the ruler (the royal hill complex), his wives, and nobles, including an open court for ceremonial gatherings. At the zenith of the empire's power, as many as 18,000 people may have lived in the surrounding area, with most of the commoners living outside the enclosed structures reserved for royalty. Although the actual habitations are gone, the remaining enclosures are unusual for their size and the excellence of their stonework. Some perimeter walls reach heights of 30 feet. One of these, known as the Great Enclosure (FIG. **15-7**), houses one large

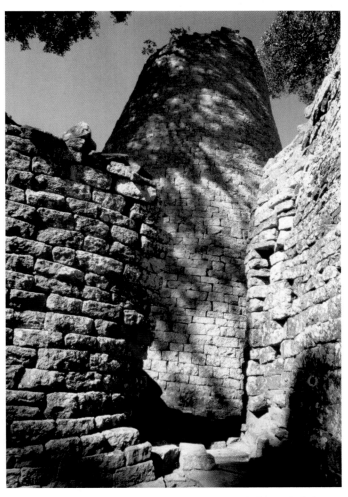

15-7 Walls and tower, Great Enclosure, Great Zimbabwe, Zimbabwe, 14th century.

and several small conical towerlike stone structures. Scholars have interpreted these symbolically as masculine (large) and feminine (small) forms, but their precise significance is unknown. The form of the largest tower suggests a granary. Such grain bins were symbols of royal power and generosity, as the ruler received tribute in grain and dispensed it to the people in times of need.

SOAPSTONE BIRDS Explorations at Great Zimbabwe have yielded eight soapstone monoliths. Seven came from the royal hill complex and probably were set up as part of shrines to ancestors. The eighth bird monolith (FIG. **15-8**), found in an area now considered the ancestral shrine of the ruler's first wife, stands several feet tall. Some have interpreted the bird as symbolizing the first wife's ancestors. (Ancestral spirits among the present-day Shona take the form of birds, especially eagles, believed to communicate between the sky and the earth.) The crocodile on the front of the monolith may represent the wife's elder male ancestors. The circles beneath the bird are called the "eyes of the crocodile" in Shona and may symbolically represent elder female ancestors. The double- and single-chevron motifs may represent young male and young female ancestors, respectively. The bird perhaps represents some form of bird of prey, such as an eagle, although this and other bird sculptures from the site have feet with five humanlike toes, rather than an eagle's three-toed talons. In fact, the species of the birds cannot be identified. Some researchers have speculated that the bird and crocodile symbolize previous rulers who would have acted as messengers between the living and the dead, as well as between the sky and the earth.

Lalibela Art and Architecture (Ethiopia)

CHRISTIAN ETHIOPIA The rugged highlands of present-day Ethiopia, where land travel is difficult, nevertheless played host to a Christian kingdom in the 13th to 15th centuries. Christianity had arrived in Ethiopia in the early fourth century, when the region was part of the indigenous Aksum Empire, where some fine stone monoliths were made. In the early 13th century, a ruler of the Zagwe dynasty, named Lalibela, commissioned a series of churches to be cut from living bedrock at his capital, today also called Lalibela. The largest of these rock-cut churches (FIG. **15-9**), Beta Medhane Alem ("House of the Savior of the World"), has a nave and

15-8 Bird with crocodile image on top of stone monolith, from Great Zimbabwe, Zimbabwe, 15th century. Soapstone, bird image 1′ 2½″ high. Great Zimbabwe Site Museum, Great Zimbabwe.

15-9 Beta Medhane Alem church, Lalibela, Ethiopia, 14th century.

four flanking aisles. The exterior takes the form of a colonnade of closely set square pillars, with a crowning pitched roof decorated with semicircular motifs in relief, one each above and between every column, reinforcing the rhythm of the pillars. The planning and skilled labor needed to carve from the bedrock a complex building such as this, with all its details, is truly astonishing. The bedrock tufa is soft and easily worked. Nonetheless, the entire design had to be visualized before the work began because there was no possibility of revision or correction. More amazing still is the fact that more than 1,500 such sculpted churches exist in Ethiopia. Churches are being "constructed" in this manner as acts of devotion even today.

Benin Art (Lower Niger)

The Benin kingdom was established just west of the lower reaches of the Niger River before 1400, most likely in the 13th century. It reached its greatest power and geographical extent in the 15th and 16th centuries. The kingdom's vicissitudes and slow decline thereafter culminated in the burning and sacking of the Benin palace and city by the British in 1897. Benin City thrives today, however, and the palace, where the Benin king continues to live, has been partially rebuilt. By observing current rituals and regalia and talking with elderly specialists who understand the significance of these cultural features, researchers continue to learn about earlier royal Benin art.

Benin artists have produced many complex, finely cast copper-alloy sculptures, as well as artworks in ivory, wood, ceramic, and wrought iron. Royalty commissioned (and sometimes still do) cast-metal pieces and ivory carvings from guilds of highly trained professional men. The hereditary *oba,* or sacred king, and his court still use and dispense art objects as royal favors to title holders and other chiefs (see "Art and Leadership," page 413). Benin kings to this day maintain ritual relationships with their Yoruba counterparts at Ile-Ife, and Benin oral tradition says that the first king of the new dynasty in the 14th century was the grandson of a Yoruba king. Other traditions, although contested, credit the Yoruba with the introduction of copper-alloy casting to Benin.

IVORY FOR A KING The ivory masquette we illustrate (FIG. **15-10**) was almost certainly worn by a Benin king at his waist. Probably this and the few other known naturalistic ivory carvings of human "masks" were commissioned by Oba Esigie (r. ca. 1504–1550), under whom, with the help of the Portuguese, the Benin kingdom flourished and expanded. Esigie's mother, Idia, helped him in warfare, and in return he created for her the title of Queen Mother, Iy'oba, and built her a separate palace and court. The mask probably represents Idia. Its sensitive naturalism places it in the 16th century. On its crown are alternating Portuguese heads and mudfish, respectively symbolic references to Benin's trade and diplomatic relationships with the Portuguese and to Olokun, god of the sea, wealth, and creativity. Another series of Portuguese heads also adorns the lower part of the carving. In the late 15th and 16th centuries, Benin people probably associated the Portuguese, with their large ships from across the sea, their powerful weapons, and their wealth in metals, cloth, and other goods, with Olokun, the deity they deem responsible for abundance and prosperity.

THE HAND AND ARM The centrality of the sacred oba in Benin culture is well demonstrated by his depiction twice on a cast-brass royal shrine called an *ikegobo* (FIG. **15-11**). It features symmetrical hierarchical compositions centered on the dominant king. Flanking and supporting him are smaller, lesser members of

15-10 Ivory belt mask of a Queen Mother, from Benin, Nigeria, mid-16th century. Ivory and iron, $9\frac{3}{8}''$ high. Metropolitan Museum of Art, New York (The Michael C. Rockefeller Memorial Collection, gift of Nelson A. Rockefeller, 1972).

15-11 Altar to the Hand and Arm *(ikegobo)*, from Benin, Nigeria, 17th to 18th century(?). Bronze, $1'\,5\frac{1}{2}''$ high. British Museum, London.

the court, and in front, a pair of leopards, animals sacrificed by the sacred king and symbolic of his power over all creatures. Similar compositions are common in Benin arts, as exemplified by the royal plaque from Benin discussed in the Introduction (see FIG. Intro-16). Notably, too, the proportions of the king are distorted to emphasize his head, the seat of his will and power. One of the king's praise names is "great head." The treatment of human faces on this altar is more conventionalized than on the ivory, attesting to its later manufacture (17th or 18th century).

At such personal altars, the king and other high-ranking officials made sacrifices to their own powers of success and accomplishment—symbolized by the hand and arm. The altar invokes power, both in the ritual's anticipated outcome and in the shrine's iconography. The inclusion of leopards on the top and around the base, along with ram and elephant heads and crocodiles (not all visible in FIG. 15-11), reiterates this power.

Sapi Art (West Atlantic Coast)

During the 15th and 16th centuries, the Sapi people on the Atlantic coast of Africa carved stone, wood, and ivory images for their own use. Between 1490 and 1540, however, Portuguese explorers and traders commissioned Sapi artists to create objects exclusively for export to Europe: delicate spoons, forks, and elaborate containers usually referred to as saltcellars, as well as boxes, hunting horns, and knife handles. All were meticulously carved from elephant tusk ivory with refined and even elegant detail and careful finish. Ivory was plentiful in those early days and was one of the coveted exports in early West and Central Africa trade with Europe. The Sapi export ivories are a fascinating hybrid art form. They are the earliest examples of African tourist art.

The saltcellar shown here (FIG. **15-12**), almost 17 inches high, has been attributed to the MASTER OF THE SYMBOLIC EXECUTION, one of the three major Sapi ivory carvers during the period 1500–1540. It is his name piece and depicts an extraordinary execution scene. A kneeling figure with a shield in one hand holds an axe in the other hand over another sitting figure about to lose his head. On the ground before the executioner, six severed heads (five visible here) grimly testify to the executioner's power. A double zigzag line separates the lid of the globular container from the rest of the vessel. This vessel rests in turn on a circular platform held up by slender rods adorned with crocodile images. Two male and two female figures sit between these rods, grasping them. The men wear European-style pants, and the women wear skirts, but the women have elaborate raised patterns, surely decorative scars, on their upper chests. The European components of this saltcellar are the overall design of a spherical container on a pedestal and some of the geometric patterning on the base and the sphere, as well as certain elements of dress such as the shirts and hats. What is distinctly African is the style of the human heads and figures and their proportions, the latter skewed here to emphasize the head, as so often seen in African art. Identical large noses with flaring nostrils, as well as the conventions for rendering eyes and lips, can be seen on Sapi stone figures from the same region and period. Scholars cannot be sure whether it was the African carver or the European patron who specified the subject matter and the configurations of various parts.

15-12 MASTER OF THE SYMBOLIC EXECUTION, saltcellar, Sapi-Portuguese, from Sierra Leone, 15th to 16th century. Ivory, 1′ 4$\frac{7}{8}$″ high. Museo Nazionale Preistorico e Etnografico Luigi Pigorini, Rome.

CONCLUSION

The art forms discussed in this chapter have survived for many centuries in large measure because they are made of durable materials such as terracotta, ivory, and cast metal (bronze or one of several copper alloys). It is clear that many of these art forms were used in elite contexts and were associated with kings and chieftains. Some of these traditions still continue in altered form. In Benin, for example, there is virtually no break between 16th- and 17th-century art forms and those that survive on kings' ancestral altars today. The same is true for Christian Ethiopia, where both painted icons and rock-cut churches are still being made. In the cases of Igbo Ukwu and Ile-Ife, recent forms are somewhat different from ancient ones, but the connections between the two eras are nevertheless clear. Some of the more recent versions of these art forms are examined in Chapter 32.

500 BCE

| First sub-Saharan ceramics, fifth century bce

1 | Nok culture, ca. 500 bce–200 ce

200 CE

| Christianity **introduced** to Ethiopia, fourth century

1 Nok head, Nigeria,
ca. 500 BCE–200 CE

500

| Islam spreads throughout North Africa, seventh century

800

| First bronze castings, 9th century

2 | Igbo-Ukwu culture, 9th–10th centuries

| Jenne culture, 9th–15th centuries

2 Igbo-Ukwu fly-whisk hilt,
Nigeria, 9th to 10th
century

1000

| Ile-Ife culture, 11th–12th centuries

| Great Zimbabwe culture, 11th–15th centuries

1200

| Benin kingdom, founded 13th century

3

3 Beta Medhane Alem church, Lalibela,
Ethiopia, 14th century

1400

| Sapi culture, 15th–16th centuries

1600

4

4 Altar of the Hand and Arm,
Benin, Nigeria, 17th to 18th
century

1800

Cross and carpet page, folio 26 verso of the *Lindisfarne Gospels*, from Northumbria, England, ca. 698–721. Tempera on vellum, 1′ $1\frac{1}{2}''$ × $9\frac{1}{4}''$. British Library, London.

16

EUROPE AFTER
THE FALL OF ROME

EARLY MEDIEVAL ART IN THE WEST

Historians once referred to the thousand years (roughly 400 to 1400) between the dying Roman Empire's adoption of Christianity as its official religion and the rebirth (Renaissance) of interest in classical antiquity as the Dark Ages. Scholars and laypersons alike thought this long "interval" — between the ancient and what was perceived as the beginning of the modern European world — was rough and uncivilized, and crude and primitive artistically. They viewed these centuries — dubbed the Middle Ages — as simply a blank between (in the middle of) two great civilizations.

This negative assessment, a legacy of the humanist scholars of Renaissance Italy, persists today in the retention of the noun *Middle Ages* and the adjective *medieval* to describe this period and its art. The force of tradition dictates that we continue to use those terms, even though modern scholars long ago ceased to see the art of medieval Europe as unsophisticated or inferior.

THE MEDIEVAL FUSION Art historians date the art of the early Middle Ages to the half millennium from about 500 to 1000. Early medieval civilization in western Europe represents a fusion of Christianity, the Greco-Roman heritage, and the cultures of the non-Roman peoples north of the Alps. Although the Romans called everyone who lived beyond the classical world's frontiers "barbarians," many northerners had risen to prominent positions within the Roman army and government during the later Roman Empire. Others established their own areas of rule, sometimes with Rome's approval, sometimes in opposition to imperial authority. In time, these non-Romans merged with the citizens of the former northwestern provinces of Rome and slowly developed political and social institutions that have continued into modern times. Over the centuries a new order gradually replaced what had been the Roman Empire, resulting eventually in the foundation of today's European nations (MAP **16-1**).

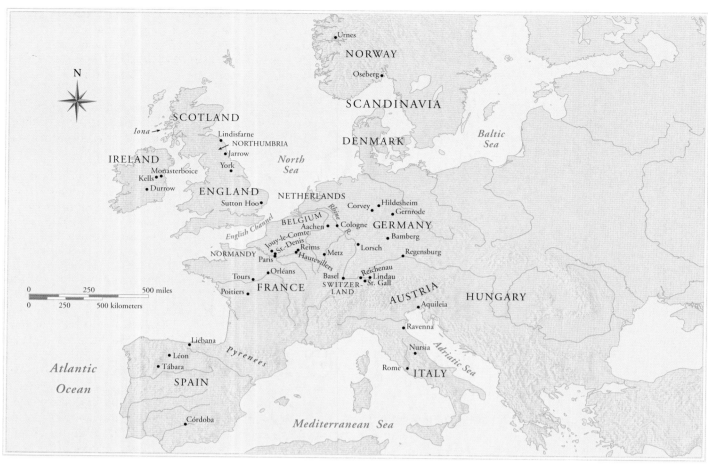

MAP 16-1 Early medieval sites in Europe.

THE ART OF THE WARRIOR LORDS

As Rome's power waned in late antiquity, armed conflicts and competition for political authority became commonplace among the non-Roman peoples of Europe—Huns, Vandals, Merovingians, Franks, Goths, and others. Once one group established itself in Italy or in one of Rome's European provinces, another often pressed in behind and compelled it to move on. The Visigoths, for example, who at one time controlled part of Italy and formed a kingdom in what is today southern France, were forced southward into Spain under pressure from the Franks, who had crossed the lower Rhine River and established themselves firmly in France, Switzerland, the Netherlands, and parts of Germany. The Ostrogoths moved from Pannonia (at the junction of modern Hungary, Austria, and the former Yugoslavia) to Italy. Under Theodoric, they established their kingdom there, only to have it fall less than a century later to the Lombards, the last of the early Germanic powers to occupy land within the limits of the old Roman Empire (see Chapter 12). In the North, Anglo-Saxons controlled what had been Roman Britain. Celts inhabited France and parts of the British Isles, including Ireland, the one area of western Europe the Romans never colonized. In Scandinavia the great seafaring Vikings held sway.

ART AND STATUS Art historians do not know the full range of art and architecture these non-Roman peoples produced. What has survived is not truly representative and consists almost exclusively of small "status symbols"—weapons and items of personal adornment such as bracelets, pendants, and belt buckles that archaeologists have discovered in lavish burials. Earlier scholars, who viewed medieval art through a Renaissance lens, ignored these "minor arts" because of their small scale, seeming utilitarian nature, and abstract ornament, and because the people who made them rejected the classical idea that the representation of organic nature should be the focus of artistic endeavor. In their own time, these objects, which often display a high degree of technical and stylistic sophistication, were regarded as treasures. They enhanced the prestige of those who owned them and testified to the stature of those who were buried with them. In the great early (possibly seventh-century) Anglo-Saxon epic *Beowulf*, the hero is cremated and his ashes placed in a huge tumulus overlooking the sea. As an everlasting tribute to Beowulf's greatness, his people "buried rings and brooches in the barrow, all those adornments that brave men had brought out from the hoard after Beowulf died. They bequeathed the gleaming gold, treasure of men, to the earth."[1]

MEROVINGIAN FIBULAE Most characteristic, perhaps, of the prestige adornments was the *fibula*, a decorative pin favored by the Romans (and the Etruscans before them; see FIG. 9-1). Fibulae were usually used to fasten the garments of men and women alike. Made of bronze, silver, or gold, they were often decorated profusely, sometimes with inlaid precious or semiprecious stones. The pair of fibulae we illustrate (FIG. **16-1**) was found in France with other Merovingian jewelry of the mid-sixth century. The pins once must have been the proud possession of a wealthy Merovingian woman and seem to have been buried with her. They resemble, in general form, the roughly contemporary but plain fibulae used to

16-1 Merovingian looped fibula, from Jouy-le-Comte, France, mid-sixth century. Silver gilt worked in filigree, with inlays of garnets and other stones, 4″ long. Musée des Antiquités Nationales, Saint-Germain-en-Laye.

fasten the outer garments of some of the attendants flanking the Byzantine emperor Justinian in the apse mosaic of San Vitale in Ravenna (see FIG. 12-10). (Note how much more elaborate is the emperor's clasp. In Rome, New Rome, and early medieval Europe alike, these fibulae were emblems of office and of prestige.)

Almost the entire surface of each of the Merovingian fibulae is covered with decorative patterns adjusted carefully to the basic shape of the object they adorn. They thus describe and amplify its form and structure, becoming an organic part of the object itself. Often zoomorphic elements were so successfully integrated into this type

of highly disciplined, abstract decorative design that they became almost unrecognizable. One must examine our examples carefully to discover that they contain animal forms. A fish may be discerned just below the center of each fibula. The looped forms around the edges are stylized eagles' heads with red garnets forming the eyes.

A KING'S FINAL VOYAGE The *Beowulf* saga also recounts the funeral of the warrior lord Scyld, who was laid to rest in a ship set adrift in the North Sea overflowing with arms and armor and costly adornments:

> They laid their dear lord, the giver of rings, deep within the ship by the mast in majesty; many treasures and adornments from far and wide were gathered there. I have never heard of a ship equipped more handsomely with weapons and war-gear, swords and corselets; on his breast lay countless treasures that were to travel far with him into the waves' domain.[2]

In 1939, a treasure-laden ship was discovered in a burial mound at Sutton Hoo in Suffolk, England. Although unique, it epitomizes the early medieval tradition of burying great lords with rich furnishings, as recorded in *Beowulf*. Among the many precious finds were a gold belt buckle, 10 silver bowls, a silver plate with the imperial stamp of the Byzantine emperor Anastasius I (r. 491–518), and 40 gold coins (perhaps to pay the 40 oarsmen who would row the deceased across the sea on his final voyage). Also placed in the ship were two silver spoons inscribed "Saulos" and "Paulos," Saint Paul's names in Greek before and after his baptism. They may allude to a conversion to Christianity. Some historians have associated the site with the East Anglian king Raedwald, who was baptized a Christian before his death in 625, but the identity of the king buried at Sutton Hoo is uncertain.

CLOISONNÉ Most extraordinary of all the Sutton Hoo finds is a purse cover (FIG. **16-2**) decorated with cloisonné-enamel plaques. The *cloisonné* technique is documented at least as early as the New Kingdom in Egypt, and was favored by early medieval

16-2 Purse cover, from the Sutton Hoo ship burial in Suffolk, England, ca. 625. Gold, glass, and enamel cloisonné with garnets and emeralds, $7\frac{1}{2}″$ long. British Museum, London.

"treasure givers." Metalworkers produced cloisonné jewelry by soldering small metal strips or *cloisons* (French for "partitions"), edge-up, to a metal background, and then filling the compartments with semiprecious stones, pieces of colored glass, or glass paste fired to resemble sparkling jewels. The edges of the cloisons are an important part of the design. Cloisonné is a cross between mosaic (see "Mosaics," Chapter 11, page 315) and stained glass (see "Stained-Glass Windows," Chapter 18, page 492), but was employed only on a miniature scale.

On the Sutton Hoo purse cover (FIG. 16-2), four symmetrically arranged groups of figures make up the lower row. The end groups consist of a man standing between two beasts. He faces front, and they appear in profile. This heraldic type of grouping has a venerable heritage in the ancient world (see FIG. 2-10), but must have delivered a powerful contemporary message. It is a pictorial parallel to the epic sagas of the era in which heroes like Beowulf battle and conquer horrific monsters. The two center groups represent eagles attacking ducks. The animal figures are cunningly composed. For example, the convex beaks of the eagles (compare the Merovingian fibulae, FIG. 16-1) fit against the concave beaks of the ducks. The two figures fit together so snugly that they seem at first to be a single dense abstract design. This is true also of the man-animals motif.

Above these figures are three geometric designs. The outer ones are clear and linear in style. In the central design, an interlace pattern, the interlacements turn into writhing animal figures. Elaborate interlace patterns are characteristic of many times and places, notably in the art of the Islamic world (see Chapter 13). But the combination of interlace with animal figures was uncommon outside the realm of the early medieval warlords. In fact, metalcraft with a vocabulary of interlace patterns and other motifs beautifully integrated with the animal form was, without doubt, *the* art of the early Middle Ages in the West. Interest in it was so great that the colorful effects of jewelry designs were imitated in the painted decorations of manuscripts, in stone sculpture, in the masonry of churches, and in sculpture in wood, an especially important medium of Viking art.

THE PIRATES OF THE NORTH In 793 the pagan traders and pirates known as Vikings (named after the *viks*—coves or "trading places"—of the Norwegian shoreline) set sail from Scandinavia and landed in the British Isles. They destroyed the Christian monastic community on Lindisfarne Island off the Northumbrian (northeastern) coast of England (see page 425). Shortly after, these *Norsemen* (North men) attacked the monastery at Jarrow in England as well as that on Iona Island, off the west coast of Scotland. From this time until the mid-11th century, the Vikings were the terror of western Europe. From their great ships they seasonally harried and plundered the coasts, harbors, and river settlements of the West. Their fast, seaworthy longboats took them on wide-ranging voyages, from Ireland eastward to Russia and westward to Iceland and Greenland and even, briefly, to Newfoundland in North America, long before Columbus arrived in the "New World."

The Vikings were not intent merely on a hit-and-run strategy of destruction but on colonizing the lands they occupied by conquest. Their exceptional talent for organization and administration, as well as for war, enabled them to take and govern large territories in Ireland, England, and France, as well as in the Baltic regions and Russia. For a while, in the early 11th century, the whole of England was part of a Danish empire. When Vikings settled in northern France in the early 10th century, their territory came to be called Normandy—home of the Norsemen who

16-3 Animal-head post, from the Viking ship burial, Oseberg, Norway, ca. 825. Wood, head approx. 5″ high. University Museum of National Antiquities, Oslo.

became *Normans.* (Later, a Norman duke, William the Conqueror, sailed across the English Channel and invaded and became the master of Anglo-Saxon England; see FIGS. 17-39 and 17-40.)

BURIAL IN A VIKING SHIP The art of the Viking sea rovers was early associated with their great wooden ships. Striking examples of Viking wood carving were found in a ship burial near Oseberg, Norway. The ship, which was covered by a mound like the earlier Sutton Hoo burial, was more than 70 feet long. When the vessel was found, it contained the remains of two women. The size of the burial alone and the lavishly carved wooden ornament of the sleek ship attest to the importance of those laid to rest there. The vessel also once must have carried many precious objects that robbers removed long before its modern discovery.

We illustrate a wooden animal-head post (FIG. **16-3**) from the Oseberg ship that, like the other animal forms in the carved bands that follow the prow's gracefully curving lines, expresses dynamic energy. This head combines in one composition the image of a roaring beast with protruding eyes and flaring nostrils and the deftly carved, controlled, and contained pattern of tightly interwoven animals that writhe, gripping and snapping, in serpentine fashion. The Oseberg animal head is a powerfully expressive example of the union of two fundamental motifs of the art of the warrior lords on the northern frontiers of the former Roman Empire—the animal form and the interlace pattern.

ANIMAL ART ON A CHURCH By the 11th century, much of Scandinavia had become Christian, but Viking artistic traditions persisted. Nowhere is this more evident than in the decoration of the portal (FIG. **16-4**) of the stave church (*staves* are wedge-shaped timbers placed vertically) at Urnes, Norway. The portal and a few staves are almost all that is preserved of a mid-11th-century church whose fragments were incorporated in the walls of a 12th-century church. Gracefully elongated animal forms intertwine with flexible plant stalks and tendrils in spiraling rhythm. The effect of natural growth is astonishing, yet it has been subjected to the designer's highly refined abstract sensibility. This intricate Urnes style was the culmination of three centuries (the 8th to the 11th) of Viking inventiveness.

Medieval Books

The central role books played in the medieval Christian Church led to the development of a large number of specialized types for priests, monks and nuns, and laypersons.

The primary sacred text came to be called the Bible ("the Book"), consisting of the Old Testament of the Jews, originally written in Hebrew, and the Christian New Testament, written in Greek. In the late fourth century, Saint Jerome produced the canonical Latin, or *Vulgate* (vulgar, or common tongue), version of the Bible, which incorporates 46 Old and 27 New Testament books. Before the invention of the printing press in the 15th century, all books were written by hand ("manuscripts," from the Latin *manu scriptus*). Bibles were extremely difficult to produce, and few early medieval monasteries possessed a complete Bible. Instead, several biblical books often were gathered in separate volumes.

The *Pentateuch* contains the first five books of the Old Testament, beginning with the Creation of Adam and Eve (Genesis). The *Gospels* ("good news") are the New Testament works of Saints Matthew, Mark, Luke, and John (see "The Four Evangelists," page 426) and tell the story of the life of Christ (see "The Life of Jesus in Art," Chapter 11, pages 308–309). Medieval Gospel books often contained *canon tables*—a concordance, or matching, of the corresponding passages of the four Gospels as compiled by Eusebius of Caesarea in the fourth century. *Psalters* contained the 150 psalms of King David, written in Hebrew and translated into both Greek and Latin.

Other types of books also were frequently employed in the Christian liturgy. The *lectionary* contains passages from the Gospels reordered to appear in the sequence they were read during the celebration of Mass throughout the liturgical year. *Breviaries* include the texts required for the daily recitations of monks. *Sacramentaries* were used by priests and incorporate the prayers they recited during Mass. *Benedictionals* contain bishops' blessings.

In the later Middle Ages, religious books were developed for the private devotions of the laity, patterned after monks' readers. The most popular was the *Book of Hours,* so called because it contains the prayers to be read at specified times of the day.

Many other types of books were written and copied in the Middle Ages—theological treatises, secular texts on history and science, and even some classics of Greco-Roman literature—but these were illustrated less frequently than the various sacred texts.

16-4 Wooden portal of the stave church at Urnes, Norway, ca. 1050–1070.

HIBERNO-SAXON ART

CHRISTIAN MISSIONARIES In 432 Saint Patrick established a church in Ireland and began the Christianization of the Celts. The new converts, although nominally subject to the popes of Rome, quickly developed a form of monastic organization that differed from the Church of Rome in its liturgical practices and even in its calendar of holidays. The relative independence of the Irish monasteries was due in part to their isolation. They often were situated in inaccessible and inhospitable places where the monks could carry on their duties far from worldly temptations and distractions.

Before long, Irish monks, filled with missionary zeal, set up monastic establishments in Britain and Scotland. In 563 Saint Columba founded an important monastery on the Scottish island of Iona, where he successfully converted the native Picts to Christianity. Iona monks established the monastery at Lindisfarne off the northern coast of Britain in 635. From these and other later foundations, which became great centers of learning for both Scotland and England, Irish and Anglo-Saxon missionaries journeyed through Europe, establishing great monasteries in Italy, Switzerland, Germany, the Low Countries, and France.

HIBERNO-SAXON BOOKS A style art historians designate as *Hiberno-Saxon* (Hibernia was the ancient name of Ireland), or sometimes as *Insular* to denote the Irish-English islands where it was produced, flourished within the monasteries of the British Isles. Its most distinctive products were the illuminated manuscripts of the Christian Church (see "Medieval Books," above). Liturgical books were the primary vehicles in the effort to Christianize the British Isles. They literally brought the Word of God to a predominantly illiterate population who regarded the monks' sumptuous volumes with awe. Books were scarce, jealously

The Four Evangelists

*E*vangelist derives from the Greek word for "one who announces good news," namely the Gospel of Christ. The authors of the Gospels, the first four books of the New Testament, are Saints Matthew, Mark, Luke, and John, collectively known as the Four Evangelists. The Gospel books provide the authoritative account of the life of Jesus, differing in some details, but together constituting the literary basis for the iconography of Christ throughout the long history of Christian art (see "The Life of Jesus in Art," Chapter 11, pages 308–309).

Matthew was a tax collector in Capernaum before Christ called him to become one of his apostles. Little else is known about him, and there are differing accounts as to how he became a martyr. Mark was the first bishop of Alexandria in Egypt, where he was martyred. He was a companion of both Saint Peter and Saint Paul. One tradition says that Peter dictated the Gospel to Mark, or at least inspired him to write it. Luke was a disciple of Saint Paul. Paul refers to him as a physician, but Luke is also said to have painted a portrait of the Virgin Mary and the Christ Child. In the later Middle Ages he was often chosen as the patron saint of painters' guilds. John was one of the most important of Christ's apostles. He sat next to Jesus at the Last Supper and was present at the Crucifixion, Lamentation, and Transfiguration.

John was also the author of the Apocalypse, the last book of the New Testament, which he wrote in exile on the Greek island of Patmos. The Apocalypse records John's visions of the end of the world, the Last Judgment, and the Second Coming.

Each of the Evangelists has a unique symbol derived from passages in Ezekiel (1:5–14) and the Apocalypse (4:6–8). Matthew's symbol is the winged man or angel, because his Gospel opens with a description of the human ancestry of Christ. Because Mark's Gospel begins with a voice crying in the wilderness, his symbol is the lion, the king of the desert. Luke's symbol is the ox, because his Gospel opens with a description of the priest Zacharias sacrificing an ox. John's symbol is the eagle, the soaring bird connected with his apocalyptic visions.

The Four Evangelists appear frequently in medieval art, especially in illuminated Gospel books where they regularly serve as frontispieces to their respective Gospels. Often they are represented as seated authors, with or without their symbols (see FIGS. Intro-7, 16-7, 16-12, and 16-13). In some instances, all Four Evangelists are shown together (see FIG. Intro-7). Frequently, both in painting and in sculpture, only the symbols are represented (see FIGS. 12-15, 16-5, 17-21, 17-23, 17-27, 17-32, and 18-5).

---

guarded treasures. Most of them were housed in the libraries and *scriptoria* (writing studios) of monasteries or major churches. Illuminated books are the most important extant monuments of the brilliant artistic culture that flourished in Ireland and Northumbria during the seventh and eighth centuries.

A CHECKERBOARD EVANGELIST Among the earliest Hiberno-Saxon illuminated manuscripts is the *Book of Durrow,* a Gospel book that may have been written and decorated in the monastic scriptorium at Iona, although its provenance is not documented. In the late Middle Ages it was housed in Durrow, Ireland—hence its modern nickname. The Durrow Gospels already display one of the most characteristic features of Insular book illumination: full pages devoted neither to text nor to illustration but to pure embellishment. Interspersed between the Durrow text pages are so-called *carpet pages,* resembling textiles, made up of decorative panels of abstract and zoomorphic forms. The *Book of Durrow* also contains pages where the initial letters of an important passage of sacred text are enormously enlarged and transformed into elaborate decorative patterns. Examples of Hiberno-Saxon carpet pages (FIG. 16-6) and initial pages (FIG. 16-8) will be examined later. It is important to note at the outset that this type of manuscript decoration had no precedent in classical art. It is one of many indications of the independence of Insular art from the classical tradition.

In the *Book of Durrow,* each of the four Gospel books has a carpet page facing a page dedicated to the symbol of the Evangelist who wrote that Gospel, framed by an elaborate interlace border. These pages served to highlight the major divisions of the text for liturgical use. The symbol of Saint Matthew (FIG. **16-5**) is a man (more commonly represented later as winged; see "The Four Evangelists," above), but the only human parts that the artist, a seventh-century

16-5 Man (symbol of Saint Matthew), folio 21 verso of the *Book of Durrow,* possibly from Iona, Scotland, ca. 660–680. Ink and tempera on parchment, $9\frac{5}{8}'' \times 6\frac{1}{8}''$. Trinity College Library, Dublin.

monk, chose to render are a schematic frontal head and two profile feet. The rest of the "body" is enveloped by a checkerboard cloak of yellow, red, and green squares filled with intricate abstract designs and outlined in dark brown or black. The cloak, as well as the prominent frame around the figure, resemble the cloisonné decoration of contemporary belt buckles, brooches, and purse ornaments. The *Book of Durrow* weds the abstraction of early medieval personal adornment with Early Christian pictorial imagery. The vehicle for the transmission of those Mediterranean forms was the illustrated book itself, brought to the North by Christian missionaries.

CARPETS AND CROSSES The marriage between Christian imagery and the animal-interlace style of the North may be seen in the cross-inscribed carpet page (FIG. **16-6**) of the *Lindisfarne Gospels*. The book, produced in the Northumbrian monastery on Lindisfarne Island, contains several ornamental pages and exemplifies Hiberno-Saxon art at its best. According to a later *colophon* (an inscription, usually on the last page, providing information regarding a book's manufacture), Eadfrith, Bishop of Lindisfarne between 698 and his death in 721, wrote the *Lindisfarne Gospels* "for God and Saint Cuthbert." Cuthbert's relics (see "Pilgrimages and the Cult of Relics," Chapter 17, page 449) recently had been deposited in the Lindisfarne church.

The patterning and detail of the Lindisfarne ornamental page are much more intricate and compact than those of the *Book of Durrow*. Serpentine interlacements of fantastic animals devour each other, curling over and returning on their writhing, elastic shapes. The rhythm of expanding and contracting forms produces a most vivid effect of motion and change. But it is held in check by the regularity of the design and by the dominating motif of the inscribed cross. The cross—the all-important symbol of the imported religion—stabilizes the rhythms of the serpentines and, perhaps by contrast with its heavy immobility, seems to heighten the effect of motion. The illuminator placed the motifs in detailed symmetries, with inversions, reversals, and repetitions that must be studied closely to appreciate not so much their variety as their mazelike complexity. The zoomorphic forms intermingle with clusters and knots of line, and the whole design vibrates with energy. The color is rich yet cool. The painter adroitly adjusted shape and color to achieve a smooth and perfectly even surface.

SAINT MATTHEW AT WORK All the works examined thus far, whether jeweled metalwork, wooden panels, or painted books, display the northern artists' preference for small, infinitely complex, and painstaking designs. Even the Matthew symbol in the *Book of Durrow* (FIG. 16-5) reveals that the illuminator's concern was abstract design, not the depiction of the natural world. But exceptions exist. In some Insular manuscripts it is clear that the northern artists based their compositions on classical pictures in imported Mediterranean books. Such is the case with the author portrait of Saint Matthew in the *Lindisfarne Gospels* (FIG. **16-7**). The Hiberno-Saxon illuminator's model must have been one of the illustrated Gospel books a Christian missionary brought from Italy to England. Author portraits were familiar features of Greek and Latin books, and similar representations of seated philosophers or poets writing or reading abound in ancient art (see FIGS. 10-72 and 11-4). Unlike the cross page of the same book, the Lindisfarne Evangelist portrait follows a long tradition of Mediterranean manuscript illumination.

16-6 Cross and carpet page, folio 26 verso of the *Lindisfarne Gospels*, from Northumbria, England, ca. 698–721. Tempera on vellum, $1' 1\frac{1}{2}'' \times 9\frac{1}{4}''$. British Library, London.

16-7 Saint Matthew, folio 25 verso of the *Lindisfarne Gospels*, from Northumbria, England, ca. 698–721. Tempera on vellum, $1' 1\frac{1}{2}'' \times 9\frac{1}{4}''$. British Library, London.

Matthew sits in his study composing his account of the life of Christ. A curtain sets the scene indoors, as in classical art (compare FIG. 5-56), and the Evangelist's seat is shown at an angle, which also suggests a Mediterranean model employing classical perspective. The painter (or the scribe) labeled Matthew in a curious combination of Greek (*O Agios*, saint—written in Roman rather than Greek characters) and Latin (*Mattheus*), perhaps to lend the prestige of two classical languages to the page. The former was the language of the New Testament, the latter that of the Church of Rome. Matthew is accompanied by his symbol, the winged man (labeled *imago hominis*, image of the man). The figure—actually just a disembodied head and shoulders—behind the curtain has been variously identified. He is probably Moses, holding the closed book of the Old Testament in contrast with the open book of Matthew's New Testament, a common juxtaposition in medieval Christian art and thought.

Although a southern manuscript inspired the Lindisfarne composition, the Northumbrian painter's goal was not to copy the model faithfully. Instead, uninterested in the emphasis on volume, shading, and perspective that are the hallmarks of the pictorial illusionism of classical and Late Antique painting, the Lindisfarne illuminator conceived his subject in terms of line and color exclusively. In the Hiberno-Saxon manuscript, the drapery folds are a series of sharp, regularly spaced, curving lines filled in with flat colors. The painter converted fully modeled forms bathed in light into the linear idiom of northern art. The result is not an inferior imitation of a Mediterranean prototype but a vivid new vision of the Evangelist.

ILLUMINATING THE WORD The greatest achievement of Hiberno-Saxon art in the eyes of almost all modern observers is the *Book of Kells* (FIG. **16-8**), the most elaborately decorated of the Insular Gospel books. Medieval commentators shared this high opinion, and one wrote in the *Annals of Ulster* for the year 1003 that this "great Gospel [is] the chief relic of the western world." The *Book of Kells* (named after the monastery in southern Ireland that owned it) was written and decorated either at Iona or a closely related Irish monastery. The manuscript probably was created for display on a church altar. From an early date it was housed in an elaborate metalwork box, befitting a greatly revered "relic." The *Book of Kells* boasts an unprecedented number of full-page illuminations, including carpet pages, evangelist symbols, portrayals of the Virgin Mary and of Christ, New Testament narrative scenes, canon tables, and several instances of monumentalized and embellished words from the Bible.

The page we reproduce (FIG. 16-8) opens the account of the nativity of Jesus in the Gospel of Saint Matthew. The initial letters of Christ in Greek (XPI, *chi-rho-iota*) occupy nearly the entire page, although two words—*autem* (abbreviated simply as *h*) and *generatio*—appear at the lower right. Together they read: "Now this is how the birth of Christ came about." The page corresponds to the opening of Matthew's Gospel, the passage read in church on Christmas Day. The illuminator transformed the holy words into extraordinarily intricate abstract designs that recall Celtic and Anglo-Saxon metalwork. But the cloisonné-like interlace is not purely abstract pattern. The letter *rho*, for example, ends in a male head, and animals are at its base to the left of *h generatio*. Half-figures of winged angels appear to the left of *chi*, accompanying the monogram as if accompanying Christ himself. Close observation reveals many other figures, human and animal.

When the priest Giraldus Cambrensis visited Ireland in 1185, he described a manuscript he saw that, if not the *Book of Kells* itself, must have been very much like it:

16-8 Chi-rho-iota page, folio 34 recto of the *Book of Kells,* probably from Iona, Scotland, late eighth or early ninth century. Tempera on vellum, 1′ 1″ × 9½″. Trinity College Library, Dublin.

Fine craftsmanship is all about you, but you might not notice it. Look more keenly at it and you . . . will make out intricacies, so delicate and subtle, so exact and compact, so full of knots and links, with colors so fresh and vivid, that you might say that all this was the work of an angel, and not of a man. For my part, the oftener I see the book, the more carefully I study it, the more I am lost in ever fresh amazement, and I see more and more wonders in the book.[3]

IRELAND'S HIGH CROSSES The preserved art of the early Middle Ages is, as has been noted, confined almost exclusively to small and portable works. The high crosses of Ireland, erected between the 8th and 10th centuries, are exceptional in their mass and scale. These majestic monuments, some more than 20 feet in height, preside over burial grounds adjoining the ruins of monasteries at sites widely distributed throughout the Irish countryside, and in some instances also in England. Freestanding and unattached to any architectural fabric, the high crosses have the imposing unity, weight, and presence of both building and statue—architecture and sculpture combined.

The *High Cross of Muiredach* (FIG. **16-9**) at Monasterboice, Ireland, is one of the largest and finest Irish crosses. An inscription on the bottom of the west face of the shaft asks a prayer for a man named Muiredach. Most scholars identify him as the influential Irish cleric of the same name who was abbot of Monasterboice and died in 923. The monastery he headed was one of Ireland's oldest, founded in the late fifth century. The cross probably marked the abbot's grave.

The concave arms of Muiredach's cross are looped by four arcs that form a circle. The arms expand into squared terminals sovereignty had brought new roads to the Iberian peninsula and new cities with Roman temples, forums, theaters, and aqueducts. But in the early fifth century, the Roman cities fell to Germanic invaders, most notably the Visigoths, who had converted to Christianity. The stone churches the Visigoths built in the sixth and seventh centuries were basilican in form and regularly incorporated horseshoe arches, a form usually associated with Islamic architecture (see FIG. 13-11), but which predates the Muslim conquest. Although the Islamic caliphs of Córdoba swept the Visigoths away, they never succeeded in gaining control of the northernmost parts of the peninsula. There, the Christian culture of Iberia, called *Mozarabic* (referring to Christians living in Arab territories), continued to flourish, centered in the monasteries of the various Christian kingdoms.

THE TÁBARA SCRIPTORIUM One northern Spanish monk, Beatus, abbot of San Martín at Liébana, wrote *Commentary on the Apocalypse* around 776. This influential work was widely copied and illustrated in the monastic scriptoria of medieval Europe. One such copy was produced at the monastery of San Salvador at Tábara in the Kingdom of Léon in 970. The colophon (FIG. **16-10**) to the illustrated *Commentary* presents the earliest known depiction of a medieval scriptorium. Because the artist provided a composite of exterior and interior views of the building, it is especially informative. At the left is a great bell tower with a monk on the ground floor ringing the bells. The painter carefully recorded the Islamic-style glazed-tile walls of the tower, its interior ladders, and its

16-9 *High Cross of Muiredach* (east face), Monasterboice, Ireland, 923. Sandstone, approx. 18′ high.

(compare FIG. 16-6). The circle intersecting the cross identifies the type as Celtic. The early high crosses bear abstract designs, especially the familiar interlace pattern. But the later ones, like Muiredach's, have figured panels, with scenes from the life of Christ or, occasionally, fantastic animals or events from the life of some Celtic saint. At the center of the west side of Muiredach's cross is a depiction of the Crucified Christ. On the east side (FIG. 16-9) the risen Christ stands as judge of the world, the hope of the dead. Below him the souls of the dead are being weighed on scales—a theme that sculptors of 12th-century church portals (see FIGS. Intro-6 and 17-25) took up with extraordinary force.

MOZARABIC ART

VISIGOTHS AND MUSLIMS When Muslim armies crossed into Spain from North Africa in 711 (see Chapter 13), they brought Islam to a land that the Romans had ruled for centuries. Roman

16-10 EMETERIUS, the tower and scriptorium of San Salvador de Tábara, colophon (folio 168) of the *Commentary on the Apocalypse* by Beatus, from Tábara, Spain, 970. Tempera on parchment, $1'2\frac{1}{8}'' \times 10''$. Archivo Histórico Nacional, Madrid.

elegant windows with their horseshoe arches, the legacy of the Visigoths. To the right, in the scriptorium proper, three monks are performing their respective specialized duties. The colophon identifies the two monks in the main room as the scribe Senior and the painter EMETERIUS. To the right, a third monk uses shears to cut sheets of parchment. The colophon also pays tribute to Magius, "the worthy master painter . . . May he deserve to be crowned with Christ,"[4] who died before he could complete his work on the book. His pupil Emeterius took his place and brought the project to fruition. He must be the painter of the colophon.

CAROLINGIAN ART

ROME RISES AGAIN On Christmas Day of the year 800, Pope Leo III crowned Charles the Great (Charlemagne), king of the Franks since 768, as emperor of Rome (r. 800–814). In time Charlemagne came to be seen as the first Holy (that is, Christian) Roman Emperor, a title his successors in the West did not formally adopt until the 12th century. The setting for Charlemagne's coronation, fittingly, was Saint Peter's basilica in Rome (see FIG. 11-7), built by Constantine, the first Roman emperor to embrace Christianity. Born in 742, when northern Europe was still in chaos, Charlemagne consolidated the Frankish kingdom his father and grandfather bequeathed him and defeated the Lombards in Italy. He thus united Europe and laid claim to reviving the glory of the ancient Roman Empire. He gave his name (Carolus Magnus in Latin) to an entire era, the *Carolingian* period.

Charlemagne's official seal bore the words *renovatio imperii Romani* (renewal of the Roman Empire). The "Carolingian Renaissance" was a remarkable historical phenomenon, an energetic, brilliant emulation of the art, culture, and political ideals of Early Christian Rome. Charlemagne's (Holy) Roman Empire, waxing and waning for a thousand years and with many hiatuses, existed in central Europe until Napoleon destroyed it in 1806.

IMPERIAL IMAGERY REVIVED When Charlemagne returned home from his coronation in Rome, he ordered the transfer of an equestrian statue of the Ostrogothic king Theodoric from Ravenna to the Carolingian palace complex at Aachen. That portrait is lost, as is the grand gilded bronze statue of the Byzantine emperor Justinian that once crowned a column in Constantinople (see "The Emperors of New Rome," Chapter 12, page 327). But in the early Middle Ages both statues stood as reminders of ancient Rome's glory and of the pretensions and aspirations of the medieval successors of Rome's Christian emperors. The portrait of Theodoric may have been the inspiration for a ninth-century bronze statuette (FIG. **16-11**) of a Carolingian emperor on horseback. Charlemagne greatly admired Theodoric, the first Germanic ruler of Rome. Many have identified the small bronze figure as Charlemagne himself, although others think it portrays his grandson, Charles the Bald (r. 840–877).

The ultimate model for the statuette was the equestrian portrait of Marcus Aurelius (see FIG. 10-59) in Rome. In the Middle Ages, it was mistakenly thought to represent Constantine, the first Christian emperor, another revered predecessor of Charlemagne and his Carolingian successors. The medieval sculptor portrayed the ninth-century emperor, like Marcus Aurelius, as overly large so that he, not the horse, is the center of attention. But unlike the Roman emperor, the Carolingian monarch sits rigidly upright. Quiet dignity replaced the torsion of Marcus Aurelius's body and the bold gesture of his right arm. Charlemagne (or Charles the Bald) is on parade, wearing imperial robes rather than a general's

16-11 Equestrian portrait of Charlemagne or Charles the Bald, from Metz, France, ninth century. Bronze, originally gilt, $9\frac{1}{2}''$ high. Louvre, Paris.

cloak, although his sheathed sword is visible. On his head is the imperial crown, and in his outstretched left hand he holds a globe, symbol of world dominion. The portrait proclaimed the *renovatio* of the Roman Empire's power and trappings.

The Art of the Book

CHARLEMAGNE'S BOOKS Charlemagne was a sincere admirer of learning, the arts, and classical culture (see "The Revival of Learning at Charlemagne's Court," page 431). He, his successors, and the scholars under their patronage placed a very high value on books, both sacred and secular, importing many and producing far more. One of these is the famous *Coronation Gospels* (also known as the *Gospel Book of Charlemagne*). An old (and probably inaccurate) legend says that the book was found on Charlemagne's knees when, in the year 1000, Otto III had the emperor's tomb opened. The text is written in handsome gold letters on purple vellum.

The major full-page illuminations show the four Gospel authors at work. The page we reproduce (FIG. 16-12) depicts Saint Matthew and may be compared to the portrait of the same Evangelist in the *Lindisfarne Gospels* (FIG. 16-7). The Carolingian painter's technique is markedly different from that of the Northumbrian painter. Deft, illusionistic brushwork defines the massive drapery folds wrapped around the body beneath. The illuminator used color and modulation of light and shade, not line, to create shapes. The cross-legged chair, the lectern, and the saint's toga are familiar Roman accessories. The landscape background is classicizing, and the frame is filled with the kind of

The Revival of Learning at Charlemagne's Court

To make his empire as splendid as Rome's, Charlemagne invited to his court at Aachen the best minds and the finest artisans of western Europe and the Byzantine East. Among them were Theodulf of Orléans, Paulinus of Aquileia, and Alcuin, master of the cathedral school at York, the center of Northumbrian learning. Alcuin brought Anglo-Saxon scholarship to the Carolingian court.

Charlemagne himself, according to Einhard, his biographer, could read and speak Latin fluently, in addition to Frankish, his native tongue. He also could understand Greek, and he studied rhetoric and mathematics with the learned men he gathered around him. But he never learned to write properly—that was a task best left to professional scribes. In fact, one of Charlemagne's

dearest projects was the recovery of the true text of the Bible, which, through centuries of errors in copying, had become quite corrupt. Various scholars undertook the great project at the emperor's behest, but Alcuin of York's revision of the Bible, prepared at the new monastery at Tours, became the most widely used.

Charlemagne's scribes also were responsible for the development of a new, more compact, and more easily written and legible version of Latin script called *Caroline minuscule.* The letters on this page are descended from the alphabet Carolingian scribes perfected. Later generations also owe to Charlemagne's patronage the restoration and copying of important classical texts. The earliest known manuscripts of many Greek and Roman authors are Carolingian in date.

acanthus leaves found in Roman temple capitals and friezes (see FIG. 10-30). Almost nothing is known in the Hiberno-Saxon or Frankish West that could have prepared the way for such a classicizing portrayal of Saint Matthew. If a Frank, rather than an Italian or a Byzantine, painted the Saint Matthew and the other Evangelist portraits of the *Coronation Gospels,* the northern artist had fully absorbed the classical manner. Classical painting style was one of the many components of Charlemagne's program to establish Aachen as the capital of a renewed Christian Roman Empire.

AN IMPASSIONED EVANGELIST The classicizing style evident in the *Coronation Gospels* was by no means the only one that appeared suddenly in the Carolingian world. Court schools and monasteries employed a wide variety of styles derived from Late Antique prototypes. Another Saint Matthew (FIG. **16-13**), in a Gospel book made for Archbishop Ebbo of Reims, France, may be an interpretation of an author portrait very similar to the one the *Coronation Gospels* master used as a model. It resembles it in pose and in brushwork technique, but there the resemblance stops. The *Ebbo Gospels* illuminator replaced the classical calm and

16-12 Saint Matthew, folio 15 recto of the *Coronation Gospels (Gospel Book of Charlemagne),* from Aachen, Germany, ca. 800–810. Ink and tempera on vellum, $1' \frac{3}{4}'' \times 10''$. Schatzkammer, Kunsthistorisches Museum, Vienna.

16-13 Saint Matthew, folio 18 verso of the *Ebbo Gospels (Gospel Book of Archbishop Ebbo of Reims),* from Hautvillers (near Reims), France, ca. 816–835. Ink and tempera on vellum, $10\frac{1}{4}'' \times 8\frac{3}{4}''$. Bibliothèque Municipale, Épernay.

solidity of the *Coronation Gospels* with an energy that amounts to frenzy, and the frail saint almost leaps under its impulse. Matthew (the winged man in the upper right corner identifies him) writes in frantic haste. His hair stands on end, his eyes open wide, the folds of his drapery writhe and vibrate, the landscape behind him rears up alive. The painter even set the page's leaf border in motion. Matthew's face, hands, inkhorn, pen, and book are the focus of the composition. This presentation contrasts strongly with the settled pose of the Saint Matthew of the *Coronation Gospels* with its even stress so that no part of the composition starts out at viewers to seize their attention. Just as the painter of the *Lindisfarne Gospels* Matthew (FIG. 16-7) transformed an imported model into something original, translating the classicizing manner of a southern manuscript into a Hiberno-Saxon idiom, so the *Ebbo Gospels* artist translated a classical prototype into a new Carolingian vernacular. This master painter brilliantly merged classical illusionism and the North's linear tradition.

ILLUSTRATING THE PSALMS One of the most extraordinary medieval manuscripts is the *Utrecht Psalter* (book of psalms). The text reproduces the Psalms of David in three columns of Latin capital letters emulating the script and page organization of ancient books. The artist illustrated each psalm with a pen-and-ink drawing stretching across the entire width of the page. Our example (FIG. 16-14) depicts figures acting out—literally and with a genius for anecdotal detail—Psalm 44 (Psalm 43 of the Vulgate text of the Carolingian era), in which the psalmist laments the plight of the oppressed Israelites. Where the text says, "we are counted as sheep for slaughter," the artist drew some slain sheep fallen to the ground in front of a walled city reminiscent of cities on the Column of Trajan in Rome (see FIG. 10-42) and in Early Christian mosaics and manuscripts (see FIG. 11-19). At the left, the faithful grovel on the ground before a temple because the psalm reads "our soul is bowed down to the dust; our belly cleaveth unto the earth." The artist's response to "Awake, why sleepest thou, O Lord" was to depict the Lord (as Christ instead of the Hebrew God, complete with cruciform halo), flanked by six pleading angels, reclining in a canopied bed overlooking the slaughter below.

The drawing shows a vivid animation of much the same kind as the Saint Matthew of the *Ebbo Gospels*, and the *Utrecht Psalter* may have been produced in the same "school of Reims." As in the *Ebbo Gospels*, even the earth heaves up around the figures. The bodies are tense, shoulders hunched, heads thrust forward. The rapid, sketchy techniques used to render the figures convey the same nervous vitality as the Evangelists in the *Ebbo Gospels*. Some scholars have argued that the costumes and other details indicate that the artist followed one or more manuscripts compiled 400 years before. Even if the *Utrecht Psalter* is not a copy, it certainly was designed to evoke earlier artworks and to appear "ancient."

BEJEWELED GOLDEN BOOKS The taste for sumptuously wrought and portable objects, shown previously in the art of the early medieval warrior lords, persisted under Charlemagne and his successors. They commissioned numerous works employing costly materials, including book covers made of gold and jewels, and sometimes also ivory or pearls. Gold and gems not only glorified the Word of God but also evoked the heavenly Jerusalem.

One of the most luxurious Carolingian book covers (FIG. 16-15) is the one later added to the *Lindau Gospels*. The gold cover was fashioned in one of the workshops of Charles the Bald's court and is monumental in conception. A youthful Christ in the Early Christian tradition is shown nailed to the cross, surrounded by pearls and jewels (raised on golden claw feet so that they can catch and reflect the light even more brilliantly and protect the delicate metal relief from denting). The statuesque open-eyed figure, rendered in *repoussé* (hammered or pressed relief), brings to mind the beardless unsuffering Christ of the fifth-century ivory casket from Italy in the British Museum (see FIG. 11-21). In contrast, the four angels and the personifications of the Moon and the Sun above and the crouching figures of the Virgin Mary and Saint John (and two other figures of uncertain identity) in the quadrants below display the vivacity and nervous energy of the *Utrecht Psalter* figures. This eclectic work highlights the stylistic diversity of early medieval art in Europe. Here, however, the translated figural style of the Mediterranean prevails, in keeping with the classical tastes and imperial aspirations of the Frankish "emperors of Rome."

16-14 Psalm 44, detail of folio 25 recto of the *Utrecht Psalter,* from Hautvillers (near Reims), France, ca. 820–835. Ink on vellum, full page, $1' \ 1'' \times 9\frac{7}{8}''$. University Library, Utrecht.

16-15 Crucifixion, front cover of the *Lindau Gospels,* from Saint Gall, Switzerland, ca. 870. Gold, precious stones, and pearls, $1' \, 1\frac{3}{8}'' \times 10\frac{3}{8}''$. Pierpont Morgan Library, New York.

Architecture

In his eagerness to reestablish the imperial past, Charlemagne also encouraged the use of Roman building techniques. In architecture, as in sculpture and painting, innovations made in the reinterpretation of earlier Roman Christian sources became fundamental to the subsequent development of northern European architecture. For his models, Charlemagne went to Rome and Ravenna. One was the former heart of the Roman Empire, which he wanted to

"renew." The other was the long-term western outpost of Byzantine might and splendor, which he wanted to emulate in his own capital at Aachen, a site chosen because of its renowned hot springs.

AACHEN AND RAVENNA Charlemagne often visited Ravenna, and, as already noted, he brought an equestrian statue of Theodoric from there to display in his palace complex at Aachen, where it served as a model for Carolingian equestrian portraits (FIG. 16-11). Charlemagne also imported porphyry (purple marble) columns from Ravenna to adorn his Palatine Chapel, and historians long have thought he chose one of Ravenna's churches as the model for the new structure. The plan (FIG. **16-16**) of the Aachen chapel resembles that of San Vitale (see FIG. 12-7), and a direct relationship very likely exists between the two.

A comparison between the northern building, the first vaulted structure of the Middle Ages in the West, and its southern counterpart is instructive. The Aachen plan is simpler. Omitted were San Vitale's apselike extensions reaching from the central octagon into the ambulatory. At Aachen, the two main units stand in greater independence of each other. This solution may lack the subtle sophistication of the Byzantine building, but the Palatine Chapel gains geometric clarity. A view of the interior of the Palatine Chapel (FIG. **16-17**) shows that the "floating" quality of San Vitale (see FIG. 12-8) was converted into massive geometric form.

The Carolingian conversion of a complex and subtle Byzantine prototype into a building that expresses robust strength and clear structural articulation foreshadows the architecture of the 11th and 12th centuries and the style called Romanesque (see Chapter 17). So, too, does the treatment of the Palatine Chapel's

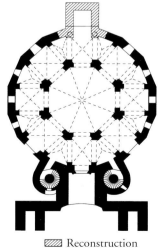

0 — 50 — 100 FEET
0 — 15 — 30 METERS
▨ Reconstruction

16-16 Restored plan of the Palatine Chapel of Charlemagne, Aachen, Germany, 792–805.

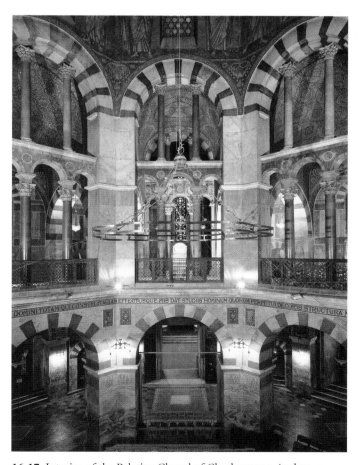

16-17 Interior of the Palatine Chapel of Charlemagne, Aachen, Germany, 792–805.

Medieval Monasteries and Benedictine Rule

Monastic foundations appeared in the West beginning in Early Christian times. The monks who established monasteries also made the rules that governed them. The most significant of these monks was Benedict of Nursia (Saint Benedict), who founded the Benedictine Order in 529. By the ninth century, the "Rule" Benedict wrote *(Regula Sancti Benedicti)* had become standard for all Western monastic establishments, in part because Charlemagne had encouraged its adoption throughout the Frankish territories.

Saint Benedict believed that the corruption of the clergy that accompanied the increasing worldliness of the Christian Church was rooted in the lack of firm organization and regulation. Neglect of the commandments of God and of the Church was due, as he saw it, to idleness and selfishness. The cure for this was communal association in an *abbey* under the absolute rule of an *abbot* the monks elected (or an *abbess* the nuns chose), who would see to it that each hour of the day was spent in useful work and in sacred reading. The emphasis was on work and study and not on meditation and austerity. This is of great historical significance. Since antiquity, manual labor had been considered disgraceful, the business of the lowborn or of slaves. Benedict raised it to the dignity of religion. The core idea of what many people today call the "work ethic" found early expression here as an essential feature of spiritual life. By thus exalting the virtue of manual labor, Benedict not only rescued it from its age-old association with slavery but also recognized it as the way to self-sufficiency for the entire religious community.

Whereas some of Saint Benedict's followers emphasized spiritual "work" over manual labor, others, most notably the Cistercians (see "Bernard of Clairvaux," Chapter 17, page 461), put his teachings about the value of physical work into practice. These monks reached into their surroundings and helped reduce the vast areas of daunting wilderness of early medieval Europe. They cleared dense forest teeming with wolves, bear, and wild boar; drained swamps; cultivated wastelands; and built roads, bridges, and dams, as well as monastic churches and their associated living and service quarters.

An ideal monastery (FIG. 16-19) provided all the facilities necessary for the conduct of daily life—a mill, bakery, infirmary, vegetable garden, and even a brewery—so that the monks felt no need to wander outside its protective walls. Such religious communities were centrally important to the revival of learning. The clergy, who were also often scribes and scholars, had a monopoly on the skills of reading and writing in an age of almost universal illiteracy. The monastic libraries and scriptoria (FIG. 16-10), where books were read, copied, illuminated, and bound with ornamented covers, became centers of study. These were almost the sole repositories of what remained of the literary culture of the Greco-Roman world and early Christianity. Saint Benedict's requirements of manual labor and sacred reading were expanded to include writing and copying books, studying music for chanting the day's offices, and—of great significance—teaching. The monasteries were the schools of the early Middle Ages, as well as self-sufficient communities and production centers.

---

exterior, where two cylindrical towers with spiral staircases flank the entrance portal (FIG. 16-16). This was a first step toward the great dual-tower facades of churches in the West from the 10th century to the present. Above the portal, Charlemagne could appear in a large framing arch and be seen by those gathered in the atrium in front of the chapel. (Only part of the atrium is included in our plan.) Directly behind that second-story arch was Charlemagne's marble throne. From there he could peer down at the altar in the apse. Charlemagne's imperial gallery followed the model of the imperial gallery at Hagia Sophia in Constantinople (see FIGS. 12-4 and 12-5). The Palatine Chapel was in every sense a royal chapel. Charlemagne's son, Louis the Pious (r. 814–840), was crowned there when he succeeded his father as emperor.

THE GATEWAY TO LORSCH The Carolingian evocation of the Roman past is illustrated by a remarkable survival from the ninth century, the Torhalle (FIG. **16-18**), or gatehouse, of the monastery at Lorsch, Germany. The gate is difficult to date because it is unique. Long thought to be from Charlemagne's time, it recently has been placed later in the century. Built as a freestanding structure in the atrium of the monastic church, the Lorsch Torhalle is a distant relative of the Arch of Constantine (see FIG. 10-76). But it follows more closely the design of Roman city gates, with its second-story windows and flanking towers (which also recall the arrangement of the Palatine Chapel's facade at Aachen). Also inspired by Roman architecture are the fairly close copies of Composite capitals and the framing of the arcuated passageways by engaged columns. The decorative treatment of the flat wall surfaces with colored inlays of cream and pink stone imitates

Roman *opus reticulatum,* a method of facing concrete walls with lozenge-shaped bricks or stones to achieve a netlike ornamental surface pattern. However, the columns support a decorative *stringcourse* (raised horizontal *molding,* or band) instead of a full entablature, and the second level has no parallel in classical

16-18 Torhalle (gatehouse), Lorsch, Germany, ninth century.

The figure contains the following labels:

Guest House School Abbot's House

Tower

Public Entrance

Tower

Choir Nave Choir Main Altar Presbytery Raised Gallery Transept

Infirmary

Convent of the Novices

Parlor

Storerooms

Cloister Court Beds

Hospital for the Poor

Kitchen

Cemetery

Apples Pears Figs Laurel Plums Chestnuts Medlars

Brew House Bake House Refectory Baths Latrine

Garden

Barns and Pens

Limekiln Mortars Mills Workrooms for Artisans Barn Poultry Pens

16-19 Schematic plan for a monastery at Saint Gall, Switzerland, ca. 819. (Redrawn after a ninth-century manuscript; original in red ink on parchment, $2' \, 4'' \times 3' \, 8\frac{1}{8}''$. Stiftsbibliothek, Saint Gall.)

architecture. Pseudo-Ionic pilasters carry a zigzag of ornamental moldings, and the opus reticulatum was converted into a decorative pattern of hexagons and triangles that form star shapes. Finally, the steeply pitched timber roof that shelters a chapel dedicated to Saint Michael unmistakably stamps this gatehouse as a northern building. Still, the source of inspiration is clear, and if the final product no longer closely resembles the original, it is due to the fact that it is not a copy but a free interpretation of its model.

THE IDEAL MONASTERY The Lorsch monastery itself is not preserved, but a fascinating contemporary document, the ideal plan (FIG. **16-19**) for a monastery at Saint Gall in Switzerland, provides precious information about the design of Carolingian monastic communities. About 819, a schematic plan for a Benedictine community (see "Medieval Monasteries and Benedictine Rule," page 434) was drawn for Haito, the abbot of Reichenau and bishop of Basel, and sent to the abbot of Saint Gall. The plan provided a coherent arrangement of all the buildings of a monastic community and was intended as a guide in the rebuilding of the Saint Gall monastery. The design's fundamental purpose was to separate the monks from the *laity,* or nonclergy, who also inhabited the community. Variations of the scheme may be seen in later monasteries all across western Europe.

Near the center, dominating everything, was the church with its *cloister,* a colonnaded courtyard (see FIG. 17-20) not unlike the Early Christian atrium (see FIG. 11-7) but situated to the side of the church rather than in front of its main portal. Reserved for the monks alone, the cloister provided the peace and quiet necessary for contemplation and was regarded as a kind of earthly paradise removed from the world at large. Around the cloister were grouped the most essential buildings: dormitory, refectory, kitchen, and storage rooms. Other structures, including an infirmary, school, guest house, bakery, brewery, and workshops, were grouped around this central core of church and cloister.

Haito invited the abbot of Saint Gall to adapt the plan as he saw fit, and the Saint Gall builders did not, in fact, follow the Reichenau model exactly. Nonetheless, if the abbot had wished, Haito's plan *could* have served as a practical guide for the Saint Gall masons because it was laid out using a *module* (standard unit) of two and a half feet. Parts or multiples of this module were employed consistently throughout the plan. For example, the nave's width, indicated on the plan as 40 feet, was equal to 16 modules; the length of each monk's bed to two and a half modules; and the width of paths in the vegetable garden to one and a quarter modules. This systematic building up of the plan from a prescribed module parallels the Carolingian invention of that most convenient device, the division of books into chapters and subchapters.

CAROLINGIAN BASILICAS The models that carried the greatest authority for Charlemagne and his builders were those from the Christian phase of the Late Roman Empire. The widespread adoption of the Early Christian basilica, at Saint Gall and elsewhere, rather than the domed central plan of Byzantine churches, was crucial to the subsequent development of Western church architecture. Unfortunately, no Carolingian basilica has survived in anything approaching its original form. Nevertheless, it is possible to reconstruct the appearance of some of them with fair accuracy. Several of these structures appear to have followed their Early Christian models quite closely. But in other instances Carolingian builders significantly modified the basilica plan, converting it into a much more complex form. The monastery church at Saint Gall (FIG. 16-19), for example, was essentially a traditional basilica, but it had features not found in any Early Christian church. Most obvious is the addition of a second apse on the west end of the building, perhaps to accommodate additional altars and relics (see "Pilgrimages and the Cult of Relics," Chapter 17, page 449). Whatever its purpose, this feature remained a characteristic regional element of German churches until the 11th century.

Not quite as evident but much more important to the subsequent development of church architecture in the North was the presence of a transept at Saint Gall, a very rare feature, but one that characterized the two greatest Early Christian basilicas in Rome, Saint Peter's (see FIG. 11-7) and Saint Paul's. The Saint Gall transept is as wide as the nave on the plan and was probably the same height. Early Christian builders had not been concerned with proportional relationships. They assembled the various portions of their buildings only in accordance with the dictates of liturgical needs. On the Saint Gall plan, however, the various parts of the building are related to one another by a geometric scheme that ties them together into a tight and cohesive unit. Equalizing the widths of nave and transept automatically makes the area where they cross (the *crossing*) a square. Most Carolingian churches shared this feature. But Haito's planner also used the *crossing square* as the unit of measurement for the remainder of the church plan. The transept arms are equal to one crossing square, the distance between transept and apse is one crossing square, and the nave is four and a half crossing squares long. The fact that the two aisles are half as wide as the nave integrates all parts of the church in a rational, lucid, and orderly plan.

TOWERS AND WESTWORKS The Saint Gall plan also reveals another important feature of many Carolingian basilicas: towers framing the end(s) of the church. Haito's plan shows only two towers, both cylindrical and on the west side of the church, as at the Palatine Chapel at Aachen (FIG. 16-16), but they stand apart from the church facade. If a tower existed above the crossing, the silhouette of Saint Gall would have shown three towers altering the horizontal profile of the traditional basilica and identifying the church even from afar.

Other Carolingian basilicas had towers that were incorporated in the fabric of the west end of the building, thereby creating a unified monumental facade that greeted all those who entered the church. Architectural historians call this feature of Carolingian and some later churches the *westwork* (German *Westwerck,* western entrance structure). In contemporary documents it is referred to as a *castellum* (Latin, castle or fortress) or *turris* (tower). The sole surviving example is the abbey church at Corvey (FIG. **16-20**). The uppermost parts are 12th-century additions (easily distinguishable from the

16-20 Westwork of the abbey church, Corvey, Germany, 873–885.

original westwork by the differing masonry technique). Stairs in each tower provided access to the upper stories of the westwork. On the second floor was a two-story chapel with an aisle and a gallery on three sides. As at Aachen, the chapel opened onto the nave, and from it, on occasion, the emperor and his entourage could watch and participate in the service below. Not all Carolingian westworks, however, served as seats for the visiting emperor. They also functioned as churches within churches, housing a second altar for special celebrations on major feast days. Boys' choirs stationed in the westwork chapel participated from above in the services conducted in the church's nave.

OTTONIAN ART

AFTER CHARLEMAGNE Charlemagne was buried in the Palatine Chapel at Aachen. His empire survived him by fewer than 30 years. When his son Louis the Pious died in 840, the Carolingian Empire was divided among Louis's sons, Charles the Bald, Lothair, and Louis the German. After bloody conflicts among the brothers, a treaty was signed in 843 partitioning the Frankish lands into western, central, and eastern areas, very roughly foreshadowing the later nations of France and Germany and a third realm corresponding to a long strip of land stretching from the Netherlands and Belgium to

Rome. Intensified Viking incursions in the West helped bring about the collapse of the Carolingians. The empire's breakup into weak kingdoms, ineffectual against the invasions, brought a time of confusion to Europe. The Viking scourge in the West was complemented by the invasions of the Magyars in the East and by the plundering and piracy of the Saracen (Muslim) corsairs in the Mediterranean.

Only in the mid-10th century did the eastern part of the former empire consolidate under the rule of a new Saxon line of German emperors called, after the names of the three most illustrious family members, the *Ottonians*. The first Otto (r. 936–973) was crowned emperor in Rome by the pope in 962, assuming the title Charlemagne's weak successors held during most of the previous century. The three Ottos made headway against the invaders from the East, remained free from Viking depredations, and not only preserved but also enriched the culture and tradition of the Carolingian period. The Christian Church, which had become corrupt and disorganized, recovered in the 10th century under the influence of a great monastic reform encouraged and sanctioned by the Ottonians, who also cemented ties with Italy and the papacy.

By the time the last of the Ottonian line, Henry II, died in the early 11th century, the pagan marauders had become Christianized and settled, and the monastic reforms had been highly successful.

Architecture

THE BASILICA TRANSFORMED Ottonian architects followed the course of their Carolingian predecessors, building basilican churches with towering spires and imposing westworks. The best preserved 10th-century Ottonian basilica is Saint Cyriakus at Gernrode. The church was the centerpiece of a convent that Margrave (military governor) Gero founded on the site in 961. Construction of the church began the same year. In the 12th century, a large apse replaced the western entrance, but the upper parts of the westwork, including the two cylindrical towers, were left intact. The interior (FIG. **16-21**), although heavily restored in the 19th century, retains its 10th-century character. Saint Cyriakus reveals how Ottonian architects enriched the form of the

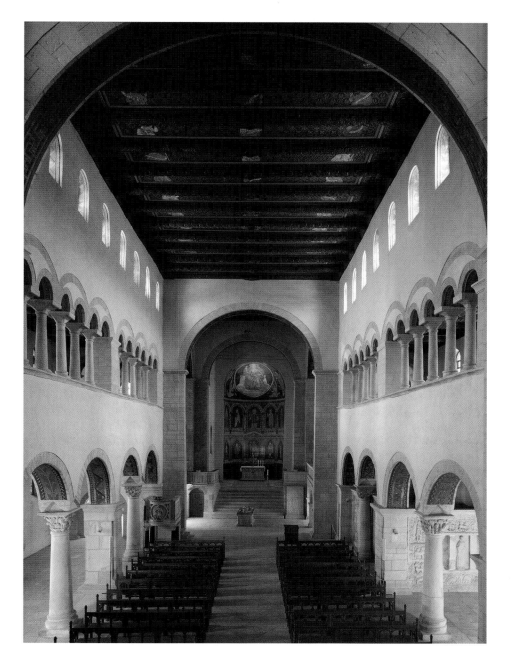

16-21 Nave of the church of Saint Cyriakus, Gernrode, Germany, 961–973.

16-22 Saint Michael's, Hildesheim, Germany, 1001–1031.

16-23 Longitudinal section *(top)* and plan *(bottom)* of the abbey church of Saint Michael's, Hildesheim, Germany, 1001–1031.

Early Christian basilica. The church has a transept at the east with a square choir in front of the apse. The nave is one of the first in the West to incorporate a gallery between the ground-floor arcade and the clerestory, a design that became very popular in the succeeding Romanesque era (see Chapter 17). Scholars have reached no consensus on the function of these galleries in Ottonian churches. They cannot have been reserved for women, as some think they were in Byzantium, because Saint Cyriakus is a nuns' church. One suggestion is that the galleries housed additional altars, as in the westwork at Corvey. They may also have been where the choirs sang.

The nave arcade itself was also transformed at Gernrode by the adoption of the *alternate-support system.* Heavy square piers alternate with columns, dividing the nave into vertical units and mitigating the tunnel-like horizontality of the Early Christian basilica. The division continues into the gallery level, breaking the smooth rhythm of an all-column arcade and leading the eye upward. Later architects would carry this "verticalization" of the basilican nave much further (see, for example, FIG. 18-17).

BISHOP BERNWARD One of the great patrons of Ottonian art and architecture was Bishop Bernward of Hildesheim, Germany. He was the tutor of Otto III (r. 983–1002) and builder of the abbey church of Saint Michael at Hildesheim (FIGS. **16-22** and **16-23**). Bernward, who made Hildesheim a center of learning, was an eager scholar, a lover of the arts, and, according to Thangmar of Heidelberg, his biographer, an expert craftsman and bronze caster. In 1001, he traveled to Rome as the guest of Otto III. During this stay, Bernward studied at first hand the monuments of the empire the Carolingian and Ottonian emperors revered.

Constructed between 1001 and 1031 (and rebuilt after being bombed during World War II), Bernward's Saint Michael's has a double-transept plan, tower groupings, and a westwork. The two transepts create eastern and western centers of gravity. The nave merely seems to be a hall that connects them. Lateral entrances leading into the aisles from the north and south (FIG. 16-23) additionally make for an almost complete loss of the traditional

basilican orientation toward the east. Some ancient Roman basilicas, such as the Basilica Ulpia in Trajan's Forum (see FIG. 10-41), also had two apses and were entered from the side, and Bernward probably was familiar with this variant basilican plan.

At Hildesheim, as in the plan of the monastery at Saint Gall (FIG. 16-19), the builders adopted a modular approach. The crossing squares, for example, were used as the basis for the nave's dimensions—three crossing squares long and one square wide. The three units were emphasized visually by the placement of heavy piers at the corners of each square. These piers alternate with pairs of columns as wall supports in a design similar to that of the earlier Ottonian church at Gernrode (FIG. 16-21).

Sculpture

COLOSSAL BRONZE DOORS In 1001, when Bishop Bernward was in Rome visiting the young Otto III, he resided in Otto's palace on the Aventine Hill in the neighborhood of Santa Sabina (see FIG. 11-8), an Early Christian church renowned for its carved wooden doors. Those doors, decorated with episodes from both the Old and New Testaments, may have inspired the remarkable bronze doors the bishop had cast for his new church in Germany. The colossal doors (FIG. **16-24**) for Saint Michael's, dated by inscription to 1015, are more than 16 feet tall. Each was cast in a single piece with the figural sculpture, a technological tour de force of lost-wax casting (see "Hollow-Casting," Chapter 5, page 131). Carolingian sculpture, like most sculpture since late antiquity, consisted primarily of small-scale art executed in ivory and precious metals, so the 16 individual panels of the Hildesheim doors may be compared to the covers of Carolingian (FIG. 16-15) and Ottonian books. Bernward's doors are more public than any book cover, but they were situated at the entrance to the church from the cloister, where only the monks could pass through them.

The panels of the left door illustrate highlights from the biblical Book of Genesis, beginning with the creation of Adam (at the

16-24 Doors with relief panels (Genesis, left door; life of Christ, right door), commissioned by Bishop Bernward for Saint Michael's, Hildesheim, Germany, 1015. Bronze, 16′ 6″ high. Dom-Museum, Hildesheim.

top) and ending with the murder of Adam and Eve's son Abel by his brother Cain (at the bottom). The right door recounts the life of Christ (reading from the bottom up), starting with the Annunciation and terminating with the appearance to Mary Magdalene of Christ after the Resurrection (see "The Life of Jesus in Art," Chapter 11, pages 308–309). Together, the doors tell the story of Original Sin and ultimate redemption, showing the expulsion from the Garden of Eden and the path back to Paradise through the Christian Church. As in Early Christian times, the Old Testament was interpreted as prefiguring the New Testament (see "Jewish Subjects in Christian Art," Chapter 11, page 305). The panel depicting the Fall of Adam and Eve, for example, is juxtaposed with the Crucifixion on the other door. Eve nursing the infant Cain is opposite Mary with the Christ Child in her lap.

The composition of many of the scenes on the doors derives from Carolingian manuscript illumination, and the style of the figures has an expressive strength that brings to mind the illustrations in the *Utrecht Psalter* (FIG. 16-14). For example, in the fourth panel from the top on the left door, God, portrayed as a man, accuses Adam and Eve after their fall from grace. As he lays on them the curse of mortality, the primal condemnation, he jabs his finger at them with the force of his whole body. The force is concentrated in the gesture, which becomes the psychic focus of the whole composition. The frightened pair crouch, not only to hide their shame but also to escape the lightning bolt of divine wrath. Each passes the blame—Adam pointing backward to Eve and Eve pointing downward to the deceitful serpent. The starkly flat setting throws into relief the gestures and attitudes of rage, accusation, guilt, and fear. The sculptor presented the story with simplicity, although with great emotional impact, as well as a flair for anecdotal detail. Adam and Eve both struggle to point with one arm while attempting to shield their bodies from sight with the other. With an instinct for expressive pose and gesture, the artist brilliantly communicated their newfound embarrassment at their nakedness and their unconvincing denials of wrongdoing.

CHRIST'S TRIUMPH The great doors of Saint Michael's were not the only large-scale examples of bronze-casting Bernward commissioned. Within the church stood a bronze spiral column (FIG. **16-25**) that is preserved intact, save for its later capital and missing surmounting cross. It probably was begun sometime after the doors were set in place and completed before the bishop's death in 1022. The seven spiral bands of relief tell the story of Jesus' life in 24 scenes, beginning with his baptism and concluding with his entry into Jerusalem. These are the missing episodes from the story told on the church's doors.

The narrative reads from bottom to top, exactly as on the Column of Trajan in Rome (see FIG. 10-42). That triumphal column was unmistakably the model for the Hildesheim column, even though the Ottonian narrative unfolds from right to left instead of from left to right. Once again, a monument in Rome provided the inspiration for the Ottonian artists working under Bernward's direction. Both the doors and the column of Saint Michael's lend credence to the Ottonian emperors' claim to be the heirs to Charlemagne's *renovatio imperii Romani*.

MONUMENTAL SUFFERING Nowhere was the revival of interest in monumental sculpture more evident than in the crucifix (FIG. **16-26**) Archbishop Gero commissioned and presented to Cologne Cathedral in 970. Carved in oak and then painted and gilded, the six-foot-tall image of Christ nailed to the cross is both statue and *reliquary* (a shrine for sacred relics; see "Pilgrimages

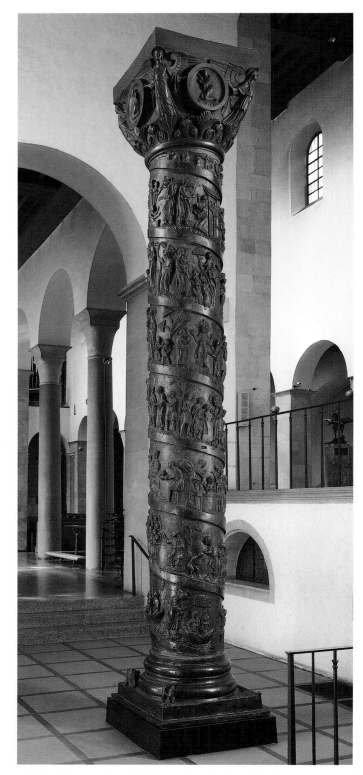

16-25 Column with reliefs illustrating the life of Christ, commissioned by Bishop Bernward for Saint Michael's, Hildesheim, Germany, ca. 1015–1022. Bronze, 12′ 6″ tall. Dom-Museum, Hildesheim.

and the Cult of Relics," Chapter 17, page 449). A compartment in the back of the head held the Host. A later story tells how a crack developed in the wood of Gero's crucifix but was miraculously healed. Similar tales of miracles are attached to many sacred Christian objects, for example, some Byzantine icons (see "Icons," Chapter 12, page 341).

The Gero crucifix presents a dramatically different conception of the Savior from that seen on the cover of the *Lindau Gospels*

16-26 Crucifix commissioned by Archbishop Gero for Cologne Cathedral, Cologne, Germany, ca. 970. Painted wood, height of figure 6′ 2″. Cathedral, Cologne.

(FIG. 16-15), with its Early Christian imagery of the youthful Christ triumphant over death. The bearded Christ of the Cologne crucifix is more akin to Byzantine representations of the suffering Jesus (see FIG. 12-22), but the emotional power of the Ottonian work is greater still. The sculptor depicted Christ as an all-too-human martyr. Blood streaks down his forehead from the (missing) crown of thorns. His eyelids are closed, and his face is contorted in pain. Christ's body sags under its own weight. The muscles are stretched to the limit—those of his right shoulder and chest seem almost to rip apart. The halo behind Christ's head may foretell his subsequent Resurrection, but all the worshiper can sense is his pain. Gero's crucifix is the most powerful characterization of intense agony of the early Middle Ages.

The Art of the Book

UTA AND THE VIRGIN Ottonian artists carried on the Carolingian tradition of producing sumptuous books for the clergy and royalty alike. One of the finest is the lectionary produced at Regensburg, Germany, for Uta, abbess of Niedermünster. The *Uta Codex* illustrates the important role that women could play both in religious life and as patrons of the arts during the early Middle Ages (see "Romanesque Countesses, Queens, and Nuns," Chapter 17, page 473). Uta was instrumental in bringing Benedictine reforms to the Niedermünster convent (see "Medieval Monasteries," page 434), whose nuns were usually the daughters of the local nobility. Uta herself was well known in Ottonian royal circles. Near the end of her life, she presented the nunnery with a luxurious codex containing many full-page illuminations interspersed with Gospel readings. The lectionary's gold, jewel, and enamel case also survives, underscoring the nature of medieval books as sacred objects to be venerated in their own right as well as embodiments of the eternal Word of God.

The dedicatory page (FIG. **16-27**) at the front of the *Uta Codex* depicts the Virgin Mary with the Christ Child in her lap in the central medallion. Labeled *Virgo Virginum*, Virgin of Virgins, Mary is the model for Uta and Niedermünster's nuns. Uta is, in fact, present. She is the full-length figure presenting a new book—*this* book—to the Virgin. An inscription accompanies

16-27 Abbess Uta dedicating her codex to the Virgin, folio 2 recto of the *Uta Codex,* from Regensburg, Germany, ca. 1025. Tempera on parchment, approx. $9\frac{5}{8}'' \times 5\frac{1}{8}''$. Bayerische Staatsbibliothek, Munich.

Theophanu: A Byzantine Princess in Ottonian Germany

Otto I was crowned king of the Saxons by the bishop of Mainz at Aachen in 936, but it was not until 962 that Pope John XII conferred the title of Emperor of Rome upon him in Saint Peter's basilica. Otto, known as the Great, had ambitions to restore the glory of Charlemagne's Christian Roman Empire and to enlarge the territory under his rule. In 951 he defeated a Roman noble who had taken prisoner Adelaide, the widow of the Lombard king Lothar. Otto then married Adelaide, assumed the title of King of the Lombards, and extended his power south of the Alps. Looking eastward, in 972 he arranged the marriage of his son, Otto II, to Theophanu (ca. 955–991), the daughter of the Byzantine emperor Romanos II. Otto II was 60, Theophanu 17. They wed in Saint Peter's, with Pope John XIII presiding. When Otto the Great died the next year, Otto II succeeded him. The second Otto died in Italy in 983 and was buried in the atrium of Saint Peter's. His son, Otto III, only three years old at the time, nominally became king, but it was his mother, Theophanu, co-regent with Adelaide until 985 and sole regent thereafter, who wielded power in the Ottonian Empire until her own death in 991. Adelaide then served as regent until Otto III was old enough to rule on his own. He was crowned Emperor of Rome in 996.

Theophanu brought the prestige of Byzantium to Germany, and also Byzantine culture and art. The Ottonian court emulated much of the splendor and pomp of Constantinople and imported Byzantine luxury goods in great quantities. One surviving ivory panel, carved in the West but of Byzantine style and labeled in Greek, depicts Christ simultaneously crowning Otto II and Theophanu. The impact of Byzantine art in Ottonian Germany can also be seen in manuscript illumination (FIG. 16-28).

---

the dedicatory image: "Virgin Mother of God, happy because of the divine Child, receive the votive offerings of your Uta of ready service."[5] The artist painted Uta last, superimposing her figure upon the design and carefully placing it so that Uta's head touches the Virgin's medallion but does not penetrate it, suggesting the interplay between, but also the separation of, the divine and human realms (FIG. 16-24).

A ROYAL LECTIONARY Uta presented her codex to the Niedermünster convent about the time the last Ottonian emperor, Henry II (r. 1002–1024), died. He also commissioned a book of Gospel readings for the Mass, the *Lectionary of Henry II*, a gift to Bamberg Cathedral. We reproduce the full-page illumination of the Annunciation of Christ's birth to the shepherds (FIG. **16-28**). The angel has just alighted on a hill, his wings still beating, and the wind of his landing agitates his draperies. Although the angel is a far cry from the dynamic marble *Nike of Samothrace* (see FIG. 5-82) of Hellenistic times, the framed panel still incorporates much that was at the heart of the classical tradition, including the rocky landscape setting with grazing animals, common also in Early Christian art (see FIG. 11-15). The golden background betrays, however, knowledge of Byzantine book illumination and mosaic decoration. (Otto II, r. 973–983, married a Byzantine princess; see "Theophanu: A Byzantine Princess in Ottonian Germany," above). The angel looms immense above the startled and terrified shepherds, filling the golden sky, and bends on them a fierce and menacing glance as he extends his hand in the gesture of authority and instruction. Emphasized more than the message itself are the power and majesty of God's authority. The artist portrayed it here with the same emotional impact as the electric force of God's violent pointing in the Hildesheim doors (FIG. 16-24).

THE IMPERIAL IDEAL Henry II's predecessor was his cousin, Otto III, son of Otto II and Theophanu. Of the three Ottos, the last dreamed the most of a revived Christian Roman Empire. Indeed, it was his life's obsession. Otto III was keenly aware of his descent from both German and Byzantine imperial lines. It is said that he was more proud of his Constantinopolitan than his German roots. He moved his court, with its Byzantine rituals, to Rome and there set up theatrically the symbols and trappings of Roman imperialism. Otto's romantic dream of imperial unity for Europe never materialized. He died prematurely, at age 21, and, at his own request, was buried beside Charlemagne at Aachen.

16-28 Annunciation to the Shepherds, folio in the *Lectionary of Henry II*, from Reichenau, Germany, 1002–1014. Tempera on vellum, approx. 1′ 5″ × 1′ 1″. Bayerische Staatsbibliothek, Munich.

16-29 Otto III enthroned, folio 24 recto of the *Gospel Book of Otto III*, from Reichenau, Germany, 997–1000. Tempera on vellum, 1' 1" × 9⅜". Bayerische Staatsbibliothek, Munich.

Otto III is portrayed in a Gospel book (FIG. **16-29**) that takes his name. The illuminator represented the emperor enthroned, holding the scepter and cross-inscribed orb that represent his universal authority, conforming to a Christian imperial iconographic tradition that went back to Constantine (see FIG. 10-82, *right*). At his sides are the clergy and the barons (the Christian Church and the state), both aligned in his support. On the facing page (not illustrated), classicizing female personifications of Slavinia, Germany, Gaul, and Rome—the provinces of the Ottonian Empire—bring tribute to the young emperor. Stylistically remote from Byzantine art, the picture still has a clear political resemblance to the Justinianic mosaic in San Vitale (see FIG. 12-10).

CONCLUSION

The last emperor of the Western Roman Empire died in 476. For centuries, western Europe, save for the Byzantine Empire's stronghold at Ravenna, was home to competing groups of non-Romans—Franks, Anglo-Saxons, and Vikings, among others. Constantly on the move, these peoples left behind monuments that are all of small scale, but often of costly materials, expert workmanship, and sophisticated design. The permanent centers

of artistic culture in the early Middle Ages were the monasteries that Christian missionaries established beyond the Alps and across the English Channel. There, master painters illuminated liturgical books in a distinctive style that fused the abstract and animal interlace forms of the native peoples with Christian iconography. When the Frankish Charlemagne was crowned Emperor of Rome in 800, imperial rule was reestablished in the former Roman provinces. With it came a revival of interest in the classical style and monumental architecture, a tradition carried on by Charlemagne's Carolingian and Ottonian successors.

The ideal of a Christian Roman Empire gave partial unity to western Europe in the 9th, 10th, and early 11th centuries. To this extent, ancient Rome lived on to the millennium, culminating in the frustrated ambition of Otto III. The Romanesque period that followed, however, denied the imperial spirit that had prevailed for centuries—but not the notion of Western Christendom. A new age was about to begin, and Rome—an august memory—ceased to be the deciding influence. Europe found unity, rather, in a common religious heritage and a missionary zeal. By the year 1000, even remote Iceland had adopted Christianity. The next task for the kings and church leaders of Europe was to take up the banner of Christ and attempt to wrest control of the Holy Land from the Muslims.

FRANCE AND GERMANY

NORTHERN EUROPE

MEROVINGIAN

CAROLINGIAN

OTTONIAN

HIBERNO-SAXON PERIOD IN THE BRITISH ISLES, VIKING PERIOD IN SCANDINAVIA

476

1 Sutton Hoo purse cover, ca. 625

| END OF WESTERN ROMAN EMPIRE, 476

| ANGLO-SAXONS TAKE OVER ROMAN BRITAIN, CA. 480

| MEROVINGIAN DYNASTY, 482–751

| SAINT BENEDICT ESTABLISHES BENEDICTINE RULE FOR MONASTERIES, 529

| MUSLIMS DEFEAT VISIGOTHS IN SPAIN, 711

| CHARLES MARTEL DEFEATS MUSLIMS AT POITIERS, 732

751

| BEATUS OF LIÉBANA, *Commentary on the Apocalypse*, CA. 776

| CHARLEMAGNE, R. 768–814, CROWNED EMPEROR IN ROME, 800

| VIKING RAIDS BEGIN IN BRITAIN, 793

| LOUIS THE PIOUS, R. 814–840

| CHARLES THE BALD, R. 840–875

| CLUNIAC ORDER FOUNDED, 910

2 Ebbo Gospels, ca. 816–835

936

| OTTO I, R. 936–973, CROWNED EMPEROR IN ROME, 962

| OTTO II, R. 973–983; MARRIES BYZANTINE PRINCESS THEOPHANU, 972

| OTTO III, R. 983–1002

| HUGH CAPET, KING OF FRANCE, R. 987–996

| BERNWARD, BISHOP OF HILDESHEIM, 993–1022

3 Gero Crucifix, ca. 970

1000

| HENRY II, R. 1002–1024, LAST OTTONIAN EMPEROR

| UTA, ABBESS OF NIEDERMÜNSTER, 1002–1025

1024

| EDWARD THE CONFESSOR, ANGLO-SAXON KING OF ENGLAND, R. 1042–1066

1050

4 Saint Michael's, Hildesheim, Germany, 1001–1031

South portal of Saint-Pierre, Moissac, France, ca. 1115–1135.

17

THE AGE OF PILGRIMAGES

ROMANESQUE ART

The Romanesque era is the first since Archaic and Classical Greece to take its name from an artistic style rather than from politics or geography. Unlike Carolingian and Ottonian art, named for emperors, or Hiberno-Saxon art, a regional term, Romanesque is a title art historians invented to describe an artistic phenomenon. *Romanesque* means "Romanlike" and was first applied in the early 19th century to describe European architecture of the 11th and 12th centuries. Scholars noted that certain architectural elements of this period, principally barrel and groin vaults based on the round arch, resembled those of ancient Roman architecture. Thus, the word distinguished most Romanesque buildings from earlier medieval timber-roofed structures, as well as from later Gothic churches with vaults resting on pointed arches. Scholars in other fields quickly borrowed the term. Today "Romanesque" broadly designates the history and culture of western Europe between about 1050 and 1200.

THE RISE OF TOWNS In the early Middle Ages, the focus of life was the *manor,* or estate, of a landholding *liege lord,* who might grant tenure of a portion of his land to *vassals.* The vassals swore allegiance to their liege and rendered him military service in return for the land and the promise of protection. But in the Romanesque period, a sharp increase in trade encouraged the growth of towns and cities, gradually displacing *feudalism* as the governing political, social, and economic system of late medieval Europe (MAP **17-1**). The new towns were granted independence from the feudal lords in the form of *charters,* which enumerated the communities' rights, privileges, immunities, and exemptions beyond the feudal obligations they owed the lords. Often located on navigable rivers, the new urban centers naturally became the nuclei of networks of maritime and overland commerce.

MONASTERIES AND CHURCHES Separated by design from the busy secular life of Romanesque towns were the monasteries (see "Medieval Monasteries," Chapter 16, page 434) and their churches. During the 11th and 12th centuries, thousands of ecclesiastical buildings were remodeled or newly constructed. This immense building

MAP 17-1 Europe about 1100.

enterprise reflected in part the rise of independent cities and the prosperity they enjoyed. But it also was an expression of the widely felt relief and thanksgiving that the conclusion of the first Christian millennium in the year 1000 had not brought an end to the world, as many had feared. In the Romanesque age, the construction of churches became almost an obsession. Raoul Glaber (ca. 985–ca. 1046), a monk who witnessed the coming of the new millennium, noted the beginning of it:

> [After the] year of the millennium, which is now about three years past, there occurred, throughout the world, especially in Italy and Gaul, a rebuilding of church basilicas. Notwithstanding, the greater number were already well established and not in the least in need, nevertheless each Christian people strove against the others to erect nobler ones. It was as if the whole earth, having cast off the old by shaking itself were clothing itself everywhere in the white robe of the church.[1]

PILGRIMAGES The enormous investment in ecclesiastical buildings and furnishings also reflected a significant increase in pilgrimage traffic in Romanesque Europe (see "Pilgrimages and the Cult of Relics," page 449). Pilgrims were important sources of funding for those monasteries that possessed the relics of venerated saints. The clergy of the various monasteries vied with one another to provide magnificent settings for the display of their relics. Justification for such heavy investment to attract donations could be found in the Bible itself, for example in Psalm 26:8, "Lord, I have loved the beauty of your house, and the place where your glory dwells." Traveling pilgrims fostered the growth of towns as well as monasteries. Pilgrimages were, in fact, the primary economic and conceptual catalyst for the art and architecture of the Romanesque period.

ARCHITECTURE

Although the widespread use of stone vaults in 11th- and 12th-century churches inspired the term "Romanesque," Romanesque architecture was, in fact, highly varied and not always vaulted. Some Romanesque churches, especially in Italy, retained the wooden roofs of their Early Christian predecessors long after stone vaulting had become commonplace elsewhere. Nonetheless, despite pronounced regional differences, almost all Romanesque buildings manifest a new, widely shared method of architectural thinking, a new logic of design and construction. To a certain extent, Romanesque architecture can be compared to the Romance languages of Europe, which vary regionally but have a common core in Latin, the language of the Romans.

France

WOOD AND STONE AT VIGNORY This regional diversity is evident even in the earliest Romanesque buildings. The church of Saint-Étienne (Saint Stephen) at Vignory (FIGS. **17-1** and **17-2**) in the Champagne region of central France exemplifies the northern style of French Romanesque architecture in which builders used large sawn blocks of stone to construct the walls of their buildings but roofed them with timber. Many elements of the Vignory church have strong ties to the past. Other features became widely adopted only in later Romanesque architecture. The interior (FIG. 17-1), for example, reveals a kinship with the three-story wooden-roofed churches of the Ottonian era (see FIG. 16-21). At Vignory, however, the second story is not a true *tribune* (upper

Pilgrimages and the Cult of Relics

The cult of relics was not new in the Romanesque era. For centuries, Christians had traveled to sacred shrines housing the body parts of, or objects associated with, the holy family or the saints. The faithful had long believed that such relics—bones, clothing, instruments of martyrdom, and the like—had the power to heal body and soul. The veneration of relics reached a high point in the 11th and 12th centuries.

In Romanesque times, pilgrimage was the most conspicuous feature of public devotion, proclaiming the pilgrim's faith in the power of saints and hope for their special favor. The major shrines—Saint Peter's and Saint Paul's in Rome and the Church of the Holy Sepulcher in Jerusalem—drew pilgrims from all over Europe. The visitors braved, for salvation's sake, bad roads and hostile wildernesses infested with robbers who preyed on innocent travelers. The journeys could take more than a year to complete—when they were successful. People often undertook pilgrimage as an act of repentance or as a last resort in their search for a cure for some physical disability. Hardship and austerity were means of increasing pilgrims' chances for the remission of sin or of disease. The distance and peril of the pilgrimage were measures of pilgrims' sincerity of repentance or of the reward they sought.

For those with less time or money than required for a pilgrimage to Rome or Jerusalem, holy destinations could be found closer to home. In France, for example, the church at Vézelay housed the bones of Mary Magdalene. Saint Foy's remains were enshrined at Conques, Lazarus's at Autun, Saint Martin's at Tours, and Saint Saturninus's at Toulouse. Each of these great shrines was also an important way station en route to the most venerated shrine in the West, the tomb of Saint James at Santiago de Compostela in northwestern Spain (MAP 17-1; see "A Pilgrim's Guide to Santiago de Compostela," page 450).

Hordes of pilgrims paying homage to saints placed a great burden on the churches that stored their relics, but they also provided significant revenues, making possible the erection of ever grander and more luxuriously appointed structures. The popularity of pilgrimages led to changes in church design, necessitating longer and wider naves and aisles, transepts and ambulatories with additional chapels (FIG. 17-5), and second-story galleries (FIG. 17-6). Pilgrim traffic also established the routes that later became the major avenues of European commerce and communication.

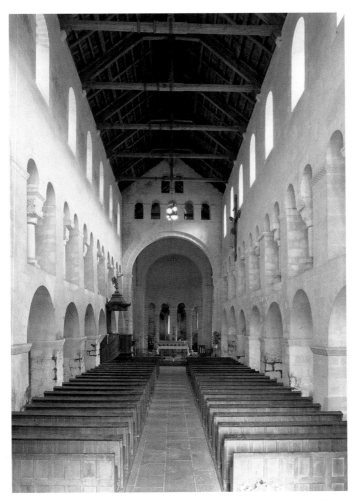

17-1 Interior of Saint-Étienne, Vignory, France, 1050–1057.

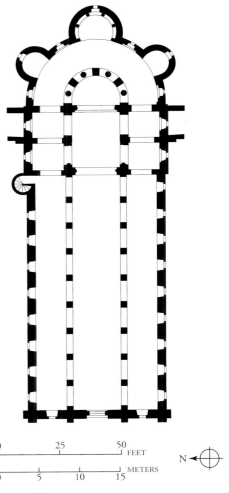

17-2 Plan of Saint-Étienne, Vignory, France, 1050–1057.

A Pilgrim's Guide to Santiago de Compostela

The volume of traffic along the major pilgrimage roads of western Europe gave rise to travel guides that, like modern guidebooks, provided pilgrims not only with information about saints and shrines but also with practical information about roads, accommodations, food, and drink. The most famous Romanesque guidebook described the four roads leading to the church of Saint James at Santiago de Compostela through Arles and Toulouse; Conques and Moissac; Vézelay and Périgueux; and Tours and Bordeaux (MAP 17-1). James was the symbol of Christian resistance to Muslim expansion in western Europe, and his relics, discovered in the ninth century, drew pilgrims from far and wide. The guidebook's anonymous 12th-century author, possibly Aimery Picaud, a Cluniac monk, was himself a well-traveled pilgrim. The text states that it was written "in Rome, in the lands of Jerusalem, in France, in Italy, in Germany, in Frisia and mainly in Cluny."[1]

Pilgrims reading the guidebook learned about the saints and their shrines at each stop along the way to Spain. Saint Saturninus of Toulouse, for example, endured a martyr's death at the hands of pagans when he "was tied to some furious and wild bulls and

then precipitated from the height of the citadel. . . . His head crushed, his brains knocked out, his whole body torn to pieces, he rendered his worthy soul to Christ. He is buried in an excellent location close to the city of Toulouse where a large basilica [FIGS. 17-4 to 17-6] was erected by the faithful in his honor."[2]

Given the competition among monasteries and cities for the possession of saints' relics, the *Pilgrim's Guide to Santiago de Compostela* also included comments on authenticity. About Saint James's tomb, the author stated: "May therefore the imitators from beyond the mountains blush who claim to possess some portion of him or even his entire relic. In fact, the body of the Apostle is here in its entirety, divinely lit by paradisiacal carbuncles, incessantly honored with immaculate and soft perfumes, decorated with dazzling celestial candles, and diligently worshipped by attentive angels."[3]

[1] William Melczer, *The Pilgrim's Guide to Santiago de Compostela* (New York: Italica Press, 1993), 133.

[2] Ibid., 103.

[3] Ibid., 127.

---

gallery over the aisle opening onto the nave) but rather a screen with alternating piers and columns opening onto very tall flanking aisles. The east end of the church, in contrast, has an innovative and influential plan (FIG. 17-2) with an ambulatory around the choir and three semicircular chapels opening onto it. These *radiating chapels* probably housed the church's relics, which the faithful could view without having to enter the choir where the main altar was situated.

Saint-Étienne is also an early example of the introduction of stone sculpture into Romanesque ecclesiastical architecture, one of the period's defining features. Here the sculptures were confined to relief decoration of the capitals of the ambulatory and false tribunes where abstract and vegetal ornament, lions, and other quadrupeds are the exclusive motifs. The earliest Romanesque sculptures appeared in Romanesque churches constructed with ashlar masonry, and the two traditions are closely allied.

VAULTING AT TOURNUS Further south, in southern France, Spain, and Lombardy, early Romanesque builders generally preferred to construct their edifices with brick or small bricklike blocks of stone and to cover the nave and aisles with vaults. The church of Saint-Philibert (FIG. **17-3**) at Tournus in Burgundy is an example of this southern tradition. Originally, Saint-Philibert, like Saint-Étienne, had a fire-prone timber roof (see "Timber Roofs and Stone Vaults," page 451). Around 1060, masonry vaults replaced the wooden roof. In the nave, cylindrical piers support barrel vaults that run perpendicular to the nave's axis, one in each bay, separated by *transverse arches*. This scheme made possible the opening of clerestory windows at the ends of the vaults, providing ample illumination to the nave. As at Vignory, the aisles are almost as tall as the nave, and they are covered by groin vaults that help buttress the barrel vaults.

TOULOUSE'S PILGRIMAGE CHURCH Around 1070, not long after Saint-Philibert was vaulted, the counts of Toulouse began construction of a great new church in honor of the city's first bishop, Saint Saturninus (Saint Sernin in French), who was

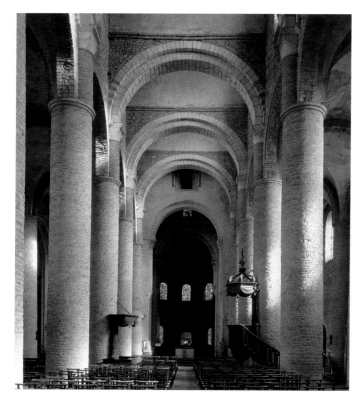

17-3 Interior of Saint-Philibert, Tournus, France. Nave vaults, ca. 1060.

Timber Roofs and Stone Vaults

The perils of wooden construction are well documented by the chroniclers of medieval ecclesiastical history. In some cases, churches burned over and over again in the course of a single century and repeatedly had to be extensively repaired or completely rebuilt. In September 1174, for example, Canterbury Cathedral, which had been dedicated only 44 years earlier, was accidentally set ablaze and destroyed. A vivid eyewitness account is preserved in the *Chronica* of Gervase of Canterbury (1141–1210), who entered the monastery at Canterbury in 1163 and wrote a history of the archbishopric from 1100 to 1199:

> During an extraordinarily violent south wind, a fire broke out before the gate of the church, and outside the walls of the monastery, by which three cottages were half destroyed. From thence, while the citizens were assembling and subduing the fire, cinders and sparks carried aloft by the high wind, were deposited upon the church, and being driven by the fury of the wind between the joints of the lead, remained there amongst the half-rotten planks, and shortly glowing with increased heat, set fire to the rotten rafters; from these the fire was communicated to the larger beams and their braces, no one yet perceiving or helping. For the well-painted ceiling below, and the sheet-lead covering above, concealed between them the fire that had arisen within. . . . But beams and braces burning, the flames arose to the slopes of the roof; and the sheets of lead yielded to the increasing heat and began to melt. Thus the raging wind, finding a freer entrance, increased the fury of the fire. . . . And now that the fire had loosened the beams from the pegs that bound them together, the half-burnt timbers fell into the choir below upon the seats of the monks; the seats, consisting of a great mass of woodwork, caught fire, and thus the mischief grew worse and worse. And it was marvellous, though sad, to behold how that glorious choir itself fed and assisted the fire that was destroying it. For the flames multiplied by this mass of timber, and extending upwards full fifteen cubits [about twenty-five feet], scorched and burnt the walls, and more especially injured the columns of the

church. . . . In this manner the house of God, hitherto delightful as a paradise of pleasures, was now made a despicable heap of ashes, reduced to a dreary wilderness.[1]

After the fire, the Canterbury monks summoned a master builder from Sens, a French city 75 miles southeast of Paris, to supervise the construction of their new church. Gervase reports that the first task William of Sens tackled was "the procuring of stone from beyond the sea."

A quest for fireproof structures, however, seems not to have been the primary rationale for stone vaulting. Although protection from devastating conflagrations was no doubt one of the attractions of building stone roofs in an age when candles provided interior illumination, other factors probably played a greater role in the decision to make the enormous investment that stone masonry required. A desire to provide a suitably majestic setting for the display of relics—and the competition for pilgrimage traffic and the donations pilgrims brought with them—as well as enhanced acoustics for the Christian liturgy and the music that accompanied it, probably better explain the rapid spread of stone vaulting throughout Romanesque Europe. Some contemporary texts, in fact, comment on the visual impact of costly stone vaults. For example, in 1150 at Angers in northwestern France, a church chronicler explained why the bishop replaced the timber roof of his cathedral with stone vaults:

> [He] took down the timber beams of the nave of the church, threatening to fall from sheer old age, and began to build stone vaults of wondrous effect.[2]

---

[1] Quoted in Elizabeth Gilmore Holt, *A Documentary History of Art*, 2nd ed. (Princeton, N.J.: Princeton University Press, 1981), 1: 52–54.

[2] Roger Stalley, *Early Medieval Architecture* (New York: Oxford University Press, 1999), 132.

---

martyred in the middle of the third century. Toulouse was an important stop on the pilgrimage road through southwestern France to Santiago de Compostela in northwestern Spain (see "A Pilgrim's Guide to Santiago de Compostela," page 450). Large congregations were common at the shrines along the great pilgrimage routes, and Saint-Sernin was designed to accommodate them. The grand scale of the building is highlighted in our aerial view (FIG. **17-4**), which includes automobiles, trucks, and nearly invisible pedestrians. The church's 12th-century exterior is still largely intact, although the two towers of the western facade (at the left in FIG. 17-4) were never completed, and the prominent crossing tower is largely Gothic and later.

Saint-Sernin's plan (FIG. **17-5**) closely resembles those of the churches of Saint James at Santiago de Compostela and Saint Martin at Tours, and exemplifies what has come to be called the "pilgrimage church" type. At Toulouse one clearly can see how the builders provided additional space for curious pilgrims, worshipers, and liturgical processions alike. They increased the length

of the nave, doubled the side aisles, and added a transept, ambulatory, and radiating chapels. Radiating chapels opening onto an ambulatory already were a feature of the abbey church at Vignory (FIG. 17-2), but at Toulouse the chapels are greater in number and are attached to the transept as well as the ambulatory, to accommodate the hordes of pilgrims who had journeyed from afar to view the church's relics.

GEOMETRY AND VAULTING The Saint-Sernin plan is extremely regular and geometrically precise. The crossing square, flanked by massive piers and marked off by heavy arches, served as the module for the entire church. Each nave bay, for example, measures exactly one-half of the crossing square, and each aisle bay measures exactly one-quarter. The builders employed similar simple ratios throughout the building. The first suggestion of such a planning scheme in medieval Europe was the Saint Gall monastery plan (see FIG. 16-19), almost three centuries earlier. The Toulouse solution was a crisply rational and highly refined

17-4 Aerial view of Saint-Sernin (from the southeast), Toulouse, France, ca. 1070–1120.

realization of an idea first seen in Carolingian architecture. This approach to design became increasingly common in the Romanesque period.

Saint-Sernin, unlike the more modestly sized churches at Vignory (FIG. 17-1) and Tournus (FIG. 17-3), has tribunes over the inner aisle and opening onto the nave (FIG. **17-6**), which housed overflow crowds on special occasions. The tribunes also played an important role in buttressing the continuous semicircular cut-stone barrel vault that covers Saint-Sernin's nave. Groin vaults (indicated by Xs on the plan, FIG. 17-5) in the tribunes as well as in the ground-floor aisles absorbed the pressure exerted by the barrel vault along the entire length of the nave. The groin vaults

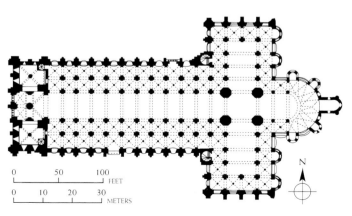

17-5 Plan of Saint-Sernin, Toulouse, France, ca. 1070–1120 (after Kenneth John Conant).

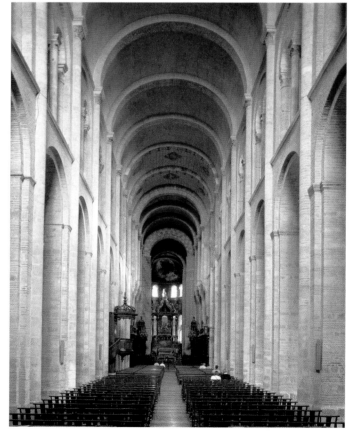

17-6 Interior of Saint-Sernin, Toulouse, France, ca. 1070–1120.

17-7 Model of the third abbey church ("Cluny III"), Cluny, France, 1088–1130. Musée du Farinier, Cluny.

served as buttresses for the barrel vault and transferred the main thrust to the thick outer walls.

The builders of Saint-Sernin were not content with just buttressing the massive nave vault. They also carefully coordinated the design of the vault with that of the nave arcade below and with the modular plan of the building as a whole. Our view of the interior (FIG. 17-6) shows that the geometric floor plan (FIG. 17-5) is fully reflected in the nave walls, where the piers marking the corners of the bays are embellished with engaged half-columns. Architectural historians refer to piers with columns or pilasters attached to their rectangular cores as *compound piers.* At Saint-Sernin the engaged columns rise from the bottom of the compound piers to the vault's *springing* (the lowest stone of an arch) and continue across the nave as transverse arches.

As a result, the Saint-Sernin nave seems to be composed of numerous identical vertical volumes of space placed one behind the other, marching down the building's length in orderly procession, an effect also characteristic of the Tournus nave (FIG. 17-3), although achieved by using transverse barrel vaults. Saint-Sernin's spatial organization corresponds to and renders visually the plan's geometric organization. The segmentation of the nave also is reflected in the building's exterior walls (FIG. 17-4), where buttresses frame each bay. This rationally integrated scheme, with repeated units decorated and separated by moldings, had a long future in later church architecture in the West.

EUROPE'S LARGEST CHURCH In 909 William, Duke of Aquitaine, donated land near Cluny to a community of reform-minded Benedictine monks under Berno of Baume's leadership. Because William waived his feudal rights to the land, the abbot of Cluny was subject only to the pope in Rome, a unique privilege. Berno founded a new order at Cluny according to the rules of Saint Benedict (see "Medieval Monasteries and Benedictine Rule," Chapter 16, page 434). Under Berno's successors, the Cluniac monks became famous for their scholarship, music, and art. Their influence and wealth grew rapidly, and they built a series of ever more elaborate monastic churches at Cluny.

The third church at Cluny was erected between 1088 and 1130, when Hugh of Semur was abbot. Called Cluny III by art historians,

the building is, unfortunately, largely destroyed today. It has, however, been reconstructed on paper and in models (FIG. **17-7**). At the time of its erection, Cluny III was the largest church in Europe, and it retained that distinction for almost 500 years until the new Saint Peter's in Rome was completed in the early 17th century (see FIGS. 24-2 to 24-4). Contemporaries considered Cluny III a place worthy for angels to dwell if they lived on earth. The church had an innovative and influential design, with a barrel-vaulted nave, four aisles, and radiating chapels, as at Saint-Sernin, but with a three-story nave elevation (arcade-tribune-clerestory) and slightly pointed nave vaults. With a nave more than 500 feet long and more than 100 feet high (both dimensions are about 50 percent greater than at Saint-Sernin), it epitomized the grandiose scale of the new stone-vaulted Romanesque churches and was a symbol of the power and prestige of the Cluniac order.

CISTERCIAN AUSTERITY Underlying Hugh of Semur's decision to make the huge expenditure that Cluny III required was the conviction that a magnificent setting for the Christian liturgy was a fitting tribute to the Lord. In the minds of many medieval monks, especially those of the Cluniac order, the construction of beautiful churches and the dedication of luxurious reliquaries were equated with piety. But one of the founding principles of monasticism was the rejection of worldly pleasures in favor of a life of contemplation. Some monks were appalled by the costly churches being erected all around them. One group founded a new order at Cîteaux in eastern France in 1098. The Cistercians (so called from the Latin name for Cîteaux) were Benedictine monks who split from the Cluniac order to return to the strict observance of the Rule of Saint Benedict, changing the color of their habits from Cluniac Benedictine black to unbleached white. These so-called White Monks emphasized productive manual labor, and their systematic farming techniques stimulated the agricultural transformation of Europe. The Cistercian movement expanded with astonishing rapidity. Within a half century, more than 500 Cistercian monasteries had been established.

The Cistercians' rejection of worldly extravagance and their emphasis on poverty, labor, and prayer are reflected in the austerity of their churches. The abbey at Cîteaux itself no longer

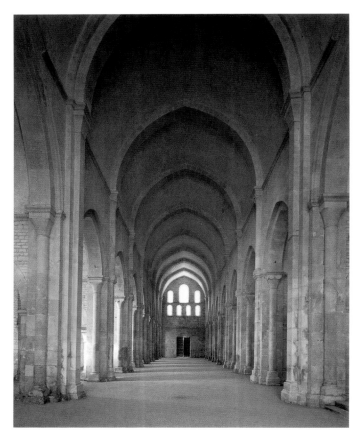

17-8 Interior of abbey church of Notre-Dame, Fontenay, France, 1139–1147.

stands, but the nearby church of Notre-Dame at Fontenay (FIG. 17-8) is representative of the Cistercian approach to architectural design. The church has a square east end, without an ambulatory or chapels. The walls are devoid of ornament, and the column capitals are plain. The nave has a single-story elevation with neither clerestory nor gallery. Light, however, reaches the nave through the large windows in the flat east wall and because the aisle bays have transverse barrel vaults like those in the Tournus nave (FIG. 17-3). Pointed arches—a feature of Cluny III—were used both in the nave arcade and in the barrel vault. This forward-looking structural device would permit later architects to increase the height of the nave dramatically. Pointed arches transfer the thrust of the vaults more directly downward to the piers and require less buttressing on the sides.

Germany and Lombardy

GROIN VAULTS IN NAVES The continuous barrel-vaulted naves of Cluny III, Saint-Sernin at Toulouse (FIG. 17-6), and Notre-Dame at Fontenay (FIG. 17-8) provided an impressive setting as well as excellent acoustics for church services, and were relatively fireproof. But the barrel vaults often failed in one critical requirement—lighting. Due to the great outward thrust the barrel vaults exerted along their full length, even when pointed instead of semicircular, a clerestory was difficult to construct. (The Toulouse and Fontenay designers did not even attempt to introduce a clerestory, although their counterparts at Cluny III succeeded.) A more complex and efficient type of vaulting was needed. Structurally, the central problem of Romanesque architecture was the need to develop a masonry vault system that admitted light and

was also aesthetically pleasing. The system used at Tournus (FIG. 17-3) met the first test but apparently failed the second, because the design was almost never adopted elsewhere.

Covering the nave with groin vaults instead of barrel vaults became the solution. Ancient Roman builders had used the groin vault widely, because they realized that its concentration of thrusts at four supporting points permitted clerestory windows (see "The Roman Architectural Revolution," Chapter 10, page 250, and FIGS. 10-68 and 10-79). The great Roman vaults were made possible by the use of concrete, which could be poured into forms, where it solidified into a homogeneous mass. But the technique of mixing concrete had not survived into the Middle Ages. The technical problems of building groin vaults of cut stone and heavy rubble, which had very little cohesive quality, at first limited their use to the covering of small areas, such as the individual bays of the aisles of Saint-Philibert (FIG. 17-3) and Saint-Sernin (FIG. 17-5). But during the 11th century, masons, using ashlar blocks joined by mortar, developed a groin vault of monumental dimensions.

THE SPEYER SOLUTION Speyer Cathedral (FIG. 17-9) in the German Rhineland is an early example of groin vaults used over a nave. The church was begun in 1030 and was the burial place of the Holy Roman Emperors until the beginning of the 12th century. Like all cathedrals, Speyer was also the seat (*cathedra* in Latin) of the powerful local bishop. In its earliest form, Speyer Cathedral was a timber-roofed structure. When the emperor Henry IV rebuilt it between 1082 and 1106, his masons replaced the old roof with stone groin vaults. The large clerestory windows above the nave arcade provided much light to the interior. Scholars disagree about where the first comprehensive use of groin vaulting occurred in

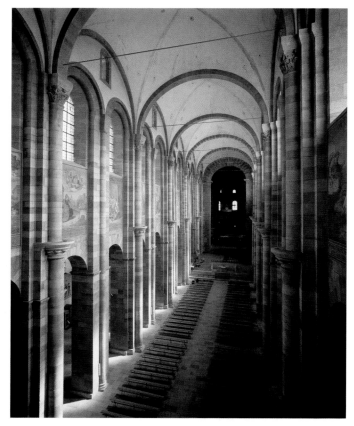

17-9 Interior of Speyer Cathedral, Speyer, Germany, begun 1030; nave vaults, ca. 1082–1106.

Romanesque times, and nationalistic concerns sometimes color the debate. We will not argue here for the precedence of any one region. But no one doubts that the large groin vaults covering the nave of Speyer Cathedral represent one of the most daring and successful engineering experiments of the time. The nave is 45 feet wide, and the crowns of the vaults are 107 feet high.

Also in contrast to Saint-Sernin, Speyer Cathedral employs an alternate-support system in the nave, as in the Ottonian church of Saint Cyriakus at Gernrode (see FIG. 16-21). At Speyer, however, the alternation continues all the way up into the vaults, with the nave's more richly molded compound piers marking the corners of the groin vaults. Speyer's interior shows the same striving for height and the same compartmentalized effect seen in Saint-Sernin (FIG. 17-6). By virtue of the alternate-support system, the rhythm of the Speyer nave is a little more complex. Because each compartment is individually vaulted, the effect of a sequence of vertical spatial blocks is even more convincing.

LOMBARD INNOVATION Ever since Charlemagne crushed the Lombards in 773, German kings held sway over Lombardy, and the Rhineland and northern Italy cross-fertilized each other artistically. No agreement exists as to which source of artistic influence was dominant in the Romanesque age, the northern or the southern. The question, no doubt, will remain the subject of controversy until the construction date of Sant'Ambrogio in Milan (FIGS. **17-10** and **17-11**) can be established unequivocally. The church, erected in honor of Saint Ambrose, Milan's first bishop (d. 397), is the central monument of Lombard Romanesque architecture.

Whether or not it was a prototype for Speyer Cathedral, Sant'Ambrogio remains a remarkable building. It has an atrium

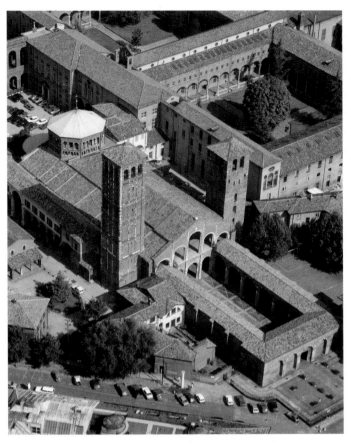

17-10 Aerial view of Sant'Ambrogio, Milan, Italy, late 11th to early 12th century.

17-11 Interior of Sant'Ambrogio, Milan, Italy, late 11th to early 12th century.

in the Early Christian tradition (one of the last to be built), a two-story narthex pierced by arches on both levels, two bell towers *(campaniles)* joined to the building, and, over the nave's east end, an octagonal tower that recalls the crossing towers of German churches. Of the facade bell towers, the shorter one dates back to the 10th century, and the taller north campanile is a 12th-century addition.

Sant'Ambrogio has a nave and two aisles, but no transept. Each bay consists of a full square in the nave flanked by two small squares in each aisle, all covered with groin vaults. The main vaults are slightly domical, rising higher than the transverse arches. An octagonal dome covers the last bay, its windows providing the major light source (the building lacks a clerestory) for the otherwise rather dark interior. The emphatic alternate-support system perfectly reflects the geometric regularity of the plan. The lightest pier moldings are interrupted at the gallery level, and the heavier ones rise to support the main vaults. At Sant'Ambrogio, the compound piers even continue into the ponderous vaults, which have supporting arches, or *ribs,* along their groins. This is one of the first instances of rib vaulting, a salient characteristic of mature Romanesque and of later Gothic architecture (see "The Gothic Rib Vault," Chapter 18, page 482).

The regional character of Romanesque architecture can be seen clearly by comparing the proportions of Sant'Ambrogio with those of both Speyer Cathedral (FIG. 17-9) and Saint-Sernin at Toulouse (FIGS. 17-4 and 17-6). The Milanese building does not aspire to the soaring height of the French and German churches. Save for the later of the two towers, Sant'Ambrogio's proportions are low and broad and remain close to those of Early Christian basilicas. Italian architects, with their firm roots in the venerable Early Christian style, never accepted the verticality found in northern architecture, not even during the Gothic period.

Normandy and England

After their conversion to Christianity in the early 10th century, the Vikings (see Chapter 16) settled on the northern coast of France in present-day Normandy. Almost at once, they proved themselves not only aggressive warriors but also skilled administrators and

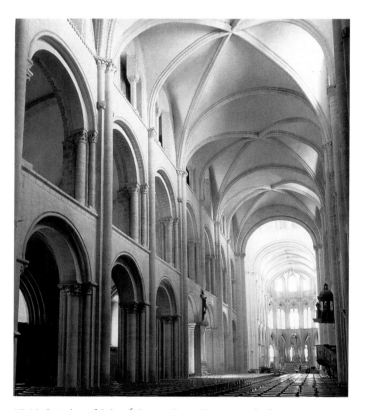

17-13 Interior of Saint-Étienne, Caen, France, vaulted ca. 1115–1120.

17-14 Plan of Saint-Étienne, Caen, France.

11th to early 12th century
13th century
14th century

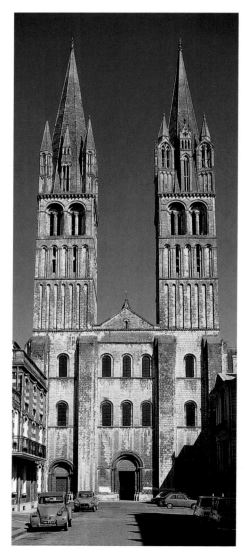

17-12 West facade of Saint-Étienne, Caen, France, begun 1067.

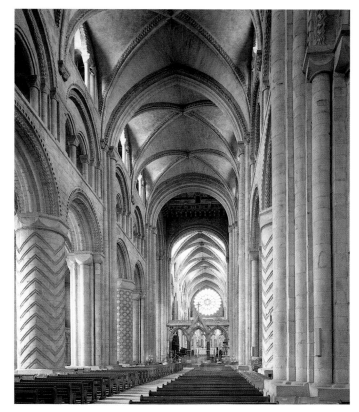

17-15 Interior of Durham Cathedral, Durham, England, begun ca. 1093.

Addition

17-16 Lateral section *(top)* and plan *(bottom)* of Durham Cathedral, Durham, England (after Kenneth John Conant).

builders, active in Sicily (see FIG. 12-24) as well as in northern Europe. The Normans quickly developed a distinctive Romanesque architectural style that became the major source of French Gothic architecture.

THE CONQUEROR'S CHURCH Most critics consider the abbey church of Saint-Étienne at Caen the masterpiece of Norman Romanesque architecture. It was begun by William of Normandy (William the Conqueror; see page 476) in 1067 and must have advanced rapidly, as he was buried there in 1087. Saint-Étienne's west facade (FIG. 17-12) is a striking design rooted in the tradition of Carolingian and Ottonian westworks, but it displays the increased rationalism of Romanesque architecture. Four large buttresses divide the facade into three bays that correspond to the nave and aisles. Above the buttresses, the towers also display a triple division and a progressively greater piercing of their walls from lower to upper stages. (The culminating spires are a Gothic addition.) The tripartite division is employed throughout the facade, both vertically and horizontally, organizing it into a close-knit, well-integrated design that reflects the careful and methodical planning of the entire structure.

The original design of Saint-Étienne called for a wooden roof, as originally at Speyer and Tournus. But the Caen nave (FIG. 17-13) has compound piers with simple engaged half-columns alternating with piers with half-columns attached to pilasters. When groin vaults were introduced around 1115, the varied nave piers proved an ideal match. The alternating compound piers soar all the way to the vaults' springing. Their branching ribs divide the large square-vault compartments into six sections, making a *sexpartite vault* (FIG. 17-14). These vaults rise high enough to provide room for an efficient clerestory. The resulting three-

story elevation, with its large arched openings, provides more light to the interior. It also makes the nave appear even taller than it actually is. As in the Milanese church of Sant'Ambrogio (FIG. 17-11), the Norman building has rib vaults. The diagonal and transverse ribs compose a structural skeleton that partially supports the still fairly massive paneling between them. But despite the heavy masonry, the large windows and reduced interior wall surface give Saint-Étienne's nave a light and airy quality that is unusual in the Romanesque period.

ENGLISH ROMANESQUE William of Normandy's conquest of Anglo-Saxon England in 1066 began a new epoch in English history. In architecture, it signaled the importation of French Romanesque building and design methods. Durham Cathedral (FIGS. **17-15** and **17-16**) sits majestically on a cliff overlooking the Wear River in northern England. It was begun around 1093, in the generation following the Norman conquest, and is the centerpiece of a monastery, cathedral, and fortified-castle complex near the border with Scotland.

Unlike Speyer Cathedral and Saint-Étienne, Durham Cathedral, which predates the remodeled Caen church, was conceived from the very beginning as a vaulted structure. Consequently, the pattern of the ribs of the nave's groin vaults is reflected in the design of the arcade below. Each seven-part nave vault covers two bays. Large, simple pillars ornamented with abstract designs (diamond, chevron, and cable patterns, all originally painted) alternate with compound piers that carry the transverse arches of the vaults. The pier-vault relationship scarcely could be more visible or the building's structural rationale better expressed.

The bold surface patterning of the Durham nave is a reminder that the raising of imposing stone edifices such as the Romanesque churches of England and Normandy required more than just the talents of master designers. A corps of expert masons had to transform rough stone blocks into the precise shapes necessary for their specific place in the church's fabric. Although thousands of simple quadrangular ashlar blocks make up the great walls of these buildings, much more complex shapes also needed to be produced in large numbers. To cover the nave and aisles, the stonecutters had to carve blocks with concave faces to conform to the curve of the vault. Also required were blocks with projecting moldings for the ribs, blocks with convex surfaces for the pillars or with multiple profiles for the compound piers, and so forth. It was an immense undertaking, and it is no wonder that medieval building campaigns often lasted for decades.

The plan (FIG. 17-16, *bottom*) of Durham Cathedral is typically English with its long, slender proportions. It does not employ the modular scheme with the same care and logic seen at Caen. But in other ways this English church is even more innovative than the French church. It is the earliest example known of a ribbed groin vault placed over a three-story nave. And in the nave's western parts, completed before 1130, rib vaults were combined with slightly pointed arches, bringing together for the first time two of the key elements that determined the structural evolution of Gothic architecture. Also of great significance is the way the nave vaults were buttressed. Our lateral section (FIG. 17-16,

top) reveals that simple *quadrant arches* (arches whose curve extends for one quarter of a circle's circumference) were used in place of groin vaults in the tribune. The structural descendants of the Durham quadrant arches are the flying buttresses that epitomize the mature Gothic solution to church construction (see "The Gothic Cathedral," Chapter 18, page 488).

Tuscany

South of the Lombard region, Italy retained its ancient traditions and, for the most part, produced Romanesque architecture that was structurally less experimental than that of Lombardy. The buildings of Tuscany, along with those of Rome itself, adhered closely to the traditions of the Early Christian basilica. They underscore that diversity is the rule, not the exception, in Romanesque Europe.

ROMANESQUE PISA The cathedral complex at Pisa (FIG. **17-17**) dramatically testifies to the prosperity the busy maritime city enjoyed. The cathedral, its freestanding bell tower, and the *baptistery,* where infants and converts were initiated into the Christian community, present a rare opportunity to study a coherent group of three Romanesque buildings. Save for the upper portion of the baptistery, with its remodeled Gothic exterior, the three structures are stylistically homogeneous.

Construction of Pisa Cathedral began first — in 1063, the same year work began on Saint Mark's (see FIG. 12-23) in Venice, another powerful maritime city. The Pisan project was funded by the spoils of a naval victory over the Muslims off Palermo in Sicily in 1062. The cathedral is large, with a nave and four aisles, and is one of the most impressive and majestic of all Romanesque churches. The Pisans, according to a document of the time, wanted their bishop's church not only to be a monument to the glory of God

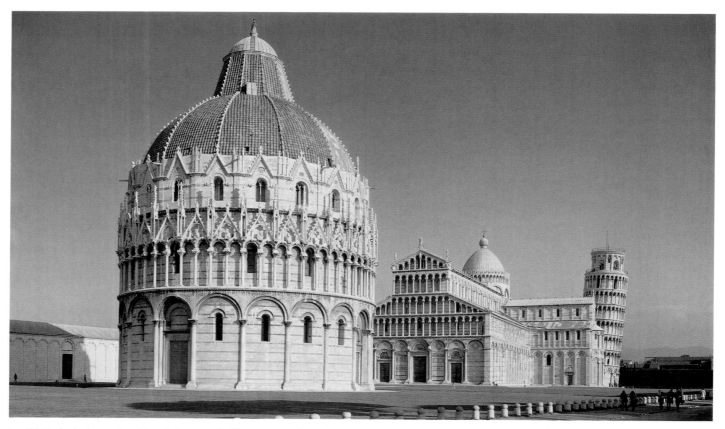

17-17 Cathedral complex, Pisa, Italy; cathedral begun 1063; baptistery begun 1153; campanile begun 1174.

but also to bring credit to the city. At first glance, Pisa Cathedral resembles an Early Christian basilica. But the broadly projecting transept, the crossing dome, and the facade's multiple arcaded galleries distinguish it as Romanesque. So too does the rich marble *incrustation* (wall decoration consisting of bright panels of different colors, as in the Pantheon's interior, FIG. 10-50).

The cathedral's campanile, detached in the standard Italian fashion, is the famous Leaning Tower of Pisa (FIG. 17-17, *right*). The tilted vertical axis is the result of a settling foundation. It began to "lean" even while under construction and now inclines some 21 perilous feet out of plumb at the top. Graceful arcaded galleries mark the tower's stages and repeat the cathedral's facade motif, effectively relating the round campanile to its mother building.

FLORENCE BAPTISTERY Florence is always associated with the Renaissance of the 15th and 16th centuries, but it was already an important independent city-state in the Romanesque period. The gem of Florentine Romanesque architecture is the baptistery of San Giovanni (FIG. **17-18**). Dedicated to Saint John, the city's patron saint, by Pope Nicholas II in 1059, it was constructed during the succeeding century. Like Pisa's baptistery (FIG. 17-17, *left*), which it predates, Florence's baptistery faces that city's great cathedral. These freestanding Italian baptisteries are unusual and reflect the great significance the Florentines and Pisans attached to baptisms. On the day of a newborn child's anointment, the citizenry gathered in the baptistery to welcome a new member into their community. The Tuscan baptisteries therefore were important civic, as well as religious, structures. Some of the most renowned artists of the late Middle Ages and the Renaissance were employed to provide the Florentine and Pisan baptisteries with pulpits (see FIG. 19-2), bronze doors (see FIGS. 21-1, 21-2, and 21-4), and mosaics.

The simple and serene classicism of San Giovanni's design recalls ancient Roman architecture. The baptistery stands in a direct line of descent from the Pantheon (see FIG. 10-48) and imperial mausoleums such as Diocletian's (see FIG. 10-75) to the Early Christian Santa Costanza (see FIG. 11-9), the Byzantine San Vitale (see FIG. 12-6), and other central-plan structures, pagan or Christian, including Charlemagne's Palatine Chapel at Aachen (see FIG. 16-17). The distinctive Tuscan Romanesque marble incrustation that patterns the walls stems ultimately from Roman wall designs (see FIGS. 10-14 and 10-50). The simple oblong and arcuated panels assert the building's structural lines and its elevation levels.

In plan, San Giovanni is a domed octagon, wrapped on the exterior by an elegant arcade, three arches to a bay. It has three entrances, one each on the north, south, and east sides. On the west side an oblong sanctuary replaces the original semicircular apse. The domical vault is some 90 feet in diameter, its construction a feat remarkable for its time.

THE BASILICAN TRADITION Contemporaneous with the baptistery and also featuring elaborate marble incrustation is the Benedictine abbey church of San Miniato al Monte (FIG. **17-19**). It sits, as its name implies, on a hillside overlooking the Arno River and the heart of Florence. The body of the church was completed by 1090, its facade not until the early 13th century. Even more than Pisa Cathedral, the structure recalls the Early Christian basilica, but *diaphragm arches* divide its nave into three equal compartments. The arches rise from compound piers and brace the rather high, thin walls. They also provide firebreaks beneath the wooden roof and compartmentalize the basilican interior in the manner so popular with most Romanesque builders. The compound piers alternate with pairs of simple columns with Roman-revival Composite capitals.

17-18 Baptistery of San Giovanni, Florence, Italy, dedicated 1059.

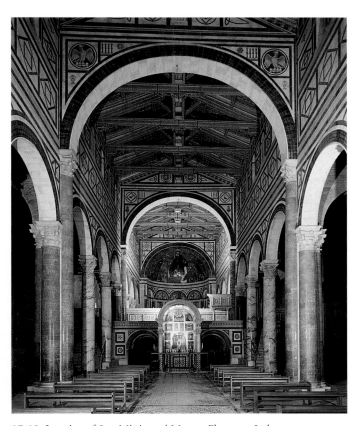

17-19 Interior of San Miniato al Monte, Florence, Italy, ca. 1062–1090.

SCULPTURE

Architectural Sculpture

STONE SCULPTURE REVIVED Stone sculpture, with some notable exceptions, such as the great crosses of the British Isles (see FIG. 16-9), had almost disappeared from the art of western Europe during the early Middle Ages. The revival of stonecarving is one of the hallmarks of the Romanesque age—and one of the reasons the period is aptly named. The inspiration for stone sculpture no doubt came, at least in part, from the abundant remains of ancient statues and reliefs throughout Rome's northwestern provinces. As one would expect, individual Romanesque sculptural motifs and compositions often originated in Carolingian and Ottonian ivory carving, metalwork, and manuscript illumination. But Roman sculptures throughout France, Italy, Germany, and Spain provided a powerful spur to the imaginations of Romanesque patrons and artists alike.

CLOISTER SCULPTURE The beginnings of a revived tradition of stonecarving can be seen in the carved capitals of northern Romanesque churches such as Saint-Étienne at Vignory (FIG. 17-1), and the practice of decorating capitals with reliefs continued in the 12th century. The most extensive preserved ensemble of sculptured early Romanesque capitals is found in the cloister (FIG. **17-20**) of Saint-Pierre at Moissac in southwestern France. The Moissac abbey had joined the Cluniac order in 1047 and was an important stop along the pilgrimage route to the tomb of Saint James at Santiago de Compostela. The monks, enriched by the gifts of pilgrims and noble benefactors, adorned their church with an elaborate series of relief sculptures.

Cloister (from the Latin word *claustrum,* an enclosed place) connotes being shut away from the world. Architecturally, the medieval church cloister expressed the seclusion of the spiritual life, the *vita contemplativa.* At Moissac, as elsewhere, the cloister provided the monks (and nuns) with a foretaste of Paradise. In its garden or the timber-roofed walkway supported by piers and columns that framed the garden, they could read their devotions, pray, and meditate in an atmosphere of calm serenity, each monk withdrawn into the private world where the soul communes only with God. The physical silence of the cloister was one with the silence that the more austere monastic communities required of their members. The monastery cloisters of the 12th century are monuments to the vitality, popularity, and influence of monasticism at its peak.

Moissac's cloister sculpture program consists of large figural reliefs on the piers as well as *historiated* (ornamented with figures) capitals on the columns. The pier reliefs portray the Twelve Apostles and the first Cluniac abbot of Moissac, Durandus (1047–1072), who was buried in the cloister. The 76 capitals alternately crown single and paired column shafts. They are variously decorated, some with abstract patterns, many with biblical scenes or the lives of saints, others with fantastic monsters of all sorts—basilisks, griffins, lizards, gargoyles, and more. Such *bestiaries* became very popular in the Romanesque age. The monstrous forms were reminders of the chaos and deformity of a world without God's order. Medieval artists delighted in inventing composite beasts with multiple heads and other fantastic creations. Historiated capitals were also a feature of Moissac's mother church, Cluny III, and were common in Cluniac monasteries. The Cistercians, not surprisingly, rejected such extravagances as distractions from their devotions. The most outspoken Cisterican critic of the new Romanesque sculptures was Abbot Bernard of Clairvaux (see "Bernard of Clairvaux on Cloister Sculpture," page 461).

ART AND THE LAITY The Romanesque period also witnessed the spread of sculpture to other areas of the church, both inside and out. Many art historians have noted that the reemergence of monumental stone sculpture in western Europe coincided with the introduction of stone vaulting in Romanesque churches. But stone-walled churches and monumental westworks had been built for centuries, even if the structures bore timber ceilings and roofs. The addition of stone vaults to basilican churches is not in itself an explanation for the resurgence of stonecarving in the Romanesque period. The earliest Romanesque sculptures, in fact, appear in

17-20 Cloister of Saint-Pierre, Moissac, France, ca. 1100–1115. Limestone with marble relief panels, piers approx. 6′ high.

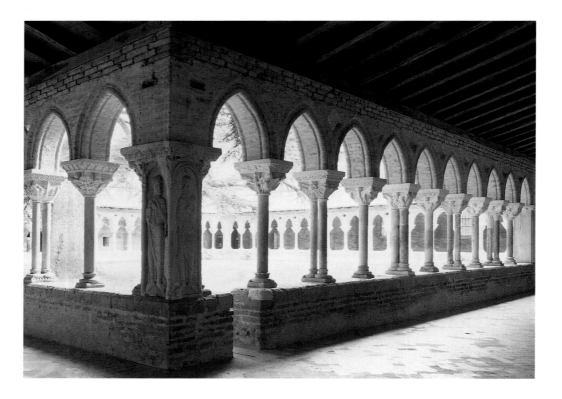

Bernard of Clairvaux on Cloister Sculpture

The most influential theologian of the Romanesque era was Bernard of Clairvaux (1090–1153). A Cistercian monk and abbot of the monastery he founded at Clairvaux in northern Burgundy, he embodied not only the reforming spirit of the Cistercian order but also the new religious fervor awakening in the West. Bernard's impassioned eloquence made him a European celebrity and drew him into the stormy politics of the Romanesque era. He intervened in high ecclesiastical and secular matters, defended and sheltered embattled popes, counseled kings, denounced heretics, and preached Crusades against the Muslims—all in defense of papal Christianity and spiritual values. He was declared a saint in 1174, barely two decades after his death.

In a letter Bernard wrote in 1127 to William, abbot of Saint-Thierry, he complained about the rich outfitting of non-Cistercian churches in general and the sculptural adornment of monastic cloisters in particular.

> I will overlook the immense heights of the places of prayer, their immoderate lengths, their superfluous widths, the costly refinements, and painstaking representations which deflect the attention . . . of those who pray and thus hinder their devotion. . . . But so be it, let these things be made for the honor of God . . . [But] in the cloisters, before the eyes of the brothers while they read—what . . . are the filthy apes doing there? The fierce lions? The monstrous centaurs? The creatures, part man and part beast? . . . You may see many bodies under one head, and conversely many heads on one body. On one side the tail of a serpent is seen on a quadruped, on the other side the head of a quadruped is on the body of a fish. Over there an animal has a horse for the front half and a goat for the back . . . Everywhere so plentiful and astonishing a variety of contradictory forms is seen that one would rather read in the marble than in books, and spend the whole day wondering at every single one of them than in meditating on the law of God. Good God! If one is not ashamed of the absurdity, why is one not at least troubled at the expense?[1]

[1] *Apologia* 12.28–29. Translated by Conrad Rudolph, *The "Things of Greater Importance": Bernard of Clairvaux's* Apologia *and the Medieval Attitude toward Art* (Philadelphia: University of Pennsylvania Press, 1990), 279, 283.

timber-roofed early Romanesque churches like Saint-Étienne at Vignory (FIG. 17-1). Stonecarving is, however, consistent with the widespread desire in the Romanesque period (the Cistercians were notable exceptions) to beautify the house of the Lord.

The proliferation of stone sculpture in the 12th century also reflects the changing role of many churches in Western Christendom. In the early Middle Ages, most churches served small monastic communities, and the worshipers were primarily or exclusively clergy. With the rise of towns in the Romanesque period, churches, especially those on the major pilgrimage routes, increasingly served the lay public. To reach this new, largely illiterate audience and to draw a wider population into their places of worship, church officials decided to display Christian symbols and stories throughout their churches, especially in portals. Stone, rather than painting or mosaic, was the most suitable durable medium for such exterior decorative programs.

SCULPTURE AT TOULOUSE One of the earliest precisely dated series of large Romanesque figure reliefs is a group of seven marble slabs, representing angels, apostles, and Christ, made for the great pilgrimage church of Saint-Sernin at Toulouse (FIGS. 17-4 to 17-6). An inscription states that the reliefs date to the year 1096 and that the artist was a certain BERNARDUS GELDUINUS. Today the plaques are affixed to the ambulatory wall. Their original location is uncertain. Some scholars have suggested that they once formed part of a shrine dedicated to Saint Saturninus that stood in the *crypt* of the grand structure. Others believe the reliefs once decorated a choir screen or an exterior portal.

We illustrate the centerpiece of the group, the figure of Christ in Majesty (FIG. **17-21**). Christ sits in a mandorla, his right hand raised in blessing, his left hand resting on an open book inscribed with the words *Pax vobis* ("peace be unto you"). The signs of the Four Evangelists (see "The Four Evangelists," Chapter 16, page 426) occupy the corners of the slab. Art historians debate the sources of Gelduinus's style, but one easily can imagine such a composition

used for a Carolingian or Ottonian work in metal or ivory, perhaps a book cover. The polished marble has the gloss of both materials, and the sharply incised lines and the ornamentation of Christ's aureole are characteristic of pre-Romanesque metalwork.

17-21 BERNARDUS GELDUINUS, Christ in Majesty, relief in the ambulatory of Saint-Sernin, Toulouse, France, ca. 1096. Marble, 4′ 2″ high.

17-22 WILIGELMO, creation and temptation of Adam and Eve, frieze on the west facade, Modena Cathedral, Modena, Italy, ca. 1110. Marble, approx. 3′ high.

GENESIS AT MODENA Some 15 years later, around 1110, another sculptor carved one of the first fully developed narrative reliefs in Romanesque art. The facade of Modena Cathedral in northern Italy has a marble frieze that extends on two levels across three of its bays. It represents scenes from Genesis set against an architectural backdrop of a type common on Late Roman and Early Christian sarcophagi, which were plentiful in the area. The segment shown (FIG. **17-22**) illustrates the creation and temptation of Adam and Eve (Gen. 2, 3:1–8), the theme employed almost exactly a century earlier on Bishop Bernward's bronze doors to Saint Michael's at Hildesheim (see FIG. 16-24). At Modena, as at Hildesheim, the faithful entered the house of the Lord with a reminder of Original Sin and the suggestion that the only path to salvation is through the Christian Church.

On the Modena frieze, Christ is at the far left, framed by a mandorla held up by angels—a variation on the motif of the Saint-Sernin ambulatory relief (FIG. 17-21). The creation of Adam, then Eve, and the serpent's temptation of Eve are to the right. The relief carving is high, and some parts are almost entirely in the round. The frieze is the work of a master craftsman whose name, WILIGELMO, is given in an inscription on another relief on the facade. There he boasts, "Among sculptors, your work shines forth, Wiligelmo." The inscription is also an indication of the pride of Wiligelmo's patrons in obtaining the services of such an accomplished sculptor for their city's cathedral.

THE SECOND COMING At Modena, the frieze recounts the beginning of the human race. Some 25 years later, the south portal (FIG. **17-23**) of Saint-Pierre at Moissac, facing the town square, announced its end. The portal's vast *tympanum* (see "The Romanesque Portal," page 463) depicts the Second Coming of Christ as King and Judge of the world in its last days. As befits his majesty, the enthroned Christ is at the center, reflecting a compositional rule followed since Early Christian times. The signs of the Four Evangelists flank him. To one side of each pair of signs is an attendant angel holding scrolls to record human deeds for judgment.

The figures of crowned musicians, which complete the design, are the Twenty-Four Elders who accompany Christ as the kings of this world and make music in his praise. Each turns to face him, much as would the courtiers of a Romanesque monarch in attendance on their lord. Two courses of wavy lines symbolizing the clouds of Heaven divide the Elders into three tiers.

17-23 South portal of Saint-Pierre, Moissac, France, ca. 1115–1135.

The Romanesque Portal

One of the most significant and distinctive features of Romanesque art is the revival of monumental sculpture in stone. Because of the Second Commandment's prohibition of graven images, large-scale carved Old and New Testament figures (and later saints) were almost unknown in Christian art before the Romanesque period. But in the late 11th and early 12th centuries, rich ensembles of figural reliefs began to appear again. Freestanding statuary, however, still associated with pagan idol worship, remained very rare.

Although sculpture in a variety of materials adorned different areas of Romanesque churches, it was most often found in the grand stone portals through which the faithful had to pass. Sculpture had been employed in church doorways before. For example, carved wooden doors greeted Early Christian worshipers as they entered Santa Sabina in Rome. And Ottonian bronze doors decorated with Old and New Testament scenes marked the entrance to Saint Michael's at Hildesheim (see FIG. 16-24). But these were exceptions. And in the Romanesque era (and during the Gothic period that followed), sculpture usually appeared in the area *around,* rather than *on,* the doors.

Our drawing shows the parts of church portals that Romanesque sculptors regularly decorated with figural reliefs:

- *Tympanum* (FIGS. 17-23 and 17-25 to 17-27), the prominent semicircular *lunette* above the doorway proper, comparable in importance to the triangular pediment of a Greco-Roman temple
- *Voussoirs* (FIG. 17-26), the wedge-shaped blocks that together form the *archivolts* of the arch framing the tympanum

- *Lintel* (FIG. 17-27), the horizontal beam above the doorway
- *Trumeau* (FIGS. 17-23 and 17-24), the center post supporting the lintel in the middle of the doorway
- *Jambs* (FIGS. 17-23 and 17-27), the side posts of the doorway

Many variations exist within the general style of Romanesque sculpture, as within Romanesque architecture. The figures of the Moissac tympanum contrast sharply with those of the reliefs previously examined. The extremely elongated bodies of the recording angels, the cross-legged dancing pose of Saint Matthew's angel, and the jerky, hinged movement of the Elders' heads are characteristic of the nameless Moissac master's style of representing the human figure. The zigzag and dovetail lines of the draperies, the bandlike folds of the torsos, the bending back of the hands against the body, and the wide cheekbones are also common features of this distinctive style. The animation of the individual figures, however, contrasts with the stately monumentality of the composition as a whole, producing a dynamic tension in the tympanum.

A PROPHET AT THE DOOR Below the tympanum are a richly decorated trumeau and elaborate door jambs with scalloped contours (FIG. 17-23), the latter a borrowing from Islamic architecture (see FIG. 13-12). On the trumeau's right face is a prophet (FIG. **17-24**) whom some identify as Jeremiah, others as Isaiah. Whoever the prophet is, he displays the scroll where his prophetic vision is written. His position below the apparition of Christ as the apocalyptic Judge is yet another instance of the pairing of Old and New Testament themes. This is in keeping with

an iconographic tradition established in Early Christian times (see "Jewish Subjects in Christian Art," Chapter 11, page 305).

The prophet's figure is very tall and thin, in the manner of the tympanum angels, and, like Matthew's angel, he executes a cross-legged step. The animation of the body reveals the passionate nature of the soul within. The flowing lines of the drapery folds ultimately derive from manuscript illumination and here play gracefully around the elegant figure. The long, serpentine locks of hair and beard frame an arresting image of the dreaming mystic. The prophet seems entranced by his vision of what is to come, the light of ordinary day unseen by his wide eyes.

Six roaring interlaced lions fill the trumeau's outer face (FIG. 17-23). The animal world was never far from the medieval mind. Kings and barons often were associated with animals thought to be the most fiercely courageous—for example, Richard the Lionheart, Henry the Lion, and Henry the Bear. Lions were the church's ideal protectors. In the Middle Ages, people believed lions slept with their eyes open. But the idea of placing fearsome images at the gateways to important places has a very ancient origin. The lions and composite monsters that guarded the palaces of Near Eastern and Mycenaean kings (see FIGS. 2-18, 2-21, and 4-20) and the panthers and leopards in Greek temple pediments (see FIG. 5-15) and Etruscan tombs (see FIG. 9-8) are the ancestors of the interlaced lions at Moissac.

JUDGMENT DAY AT AUTUN In 1132, the Cluniac bishop Étienne de Bage consecrated the Burgundian cathedral of Saint-Lazare (Saint Lazarus) at Autun. For its tympanum (FIG. **17-25**) he commissioned a dramatic vision of the Last Judgment, announced by four trumpet-blowing angels. In the tympanum's center, far larger than any other figure, is Christ, enthroned in a mandorla. He dispassionately presides over the separation of the Blessed from the Damned. At the left, an obliging angel boosts one of the Blessed into the heavenly city. Below, the souls of the dead line up to await their fate. Two of the men near the center of the lintel carry bags emblazoned with a cross and a shell. These are the symbols of pilgrims to Jerusalem and Santiago de Compostela. Those who had made the difficult journey would be judged favorably. To their right, three small figures beg an angel to intercede on their behalf. The angel responds by pointing to the Judge above. On the right side are those who will be condemned to Hell (see FIG. Intro-6). One poor soul is plucked from the earth by giant hands. Directly above, in the tympanum, is one of the most unforgettable renditions of the weighing of souls in the history of art. Angels and devils contest at the scales, each trying to manipulate the balance for or against a soul. Hideous demons guffaw and roar. Their gaunt, lined bodies, with legs ending in sharp claws, writhe and bend like long, loathsome insects. A devil, leaning from the dragon mouth of Hell, drags souls in, while, above him, a howling demon crams souls headfirst into a furnace. The resources of the Romanesque imagination, heated by a fearful faith, conjured up an appalling scene.

One can appreciate the terror the Autun tympanum must have inspired in the believers who passed beneath it as they entered the cathedral. Even those who could not read could, in the words of Bernard of Clairvaux, "read in the marble." For the literate, the Autun clergy composed explicit written warnings to reinforce the pictorial message, and had the words engraved in Latin on the tympanum. For example, beneath the weighing of souls, the inscription reads, "May this terror terrify those whom

17-24 Lions and Old Testament prophet (Jeremiah or Isaiah?), from the trumeau of the south portal of Saint-Pierre, Moissac, France, ca. 1115–1130. Marble, approx. life-size.

17-25 GISLEBERTUS, Last Judgment, west tympanum of Saint-Lazare, Autun, France, ca. 1120–1135. Marble, approx. 21′ wide at base.

earthly error binds, for the horror of these images here in this manner truly depicts what will be."[2] The admonition echoes the sentiment expressed in the colophon of a mid-10th-century illustrated copy of Beatus of Liébana's *Commentary on the Apocalypse*. There, the painter Magius (teacher of Emeterius; see FIG. 16-10) explained the purpose of his work: "I have painted a series of pictures for the wonderful words of [the Apocalypse's] stories, so that the wise may fear the coming of the future judgment of the world's end."[3]

A second prominent inscription on the Autun portal, directly beneath the feet of Christ, names GISLEBERTUS as the sculptor. It has been suggested that Gislebertus placed his signature on the tympanum not to advertise his own fame but as a kind of request to spectators to pray for his salvation on Judgment Day. Pride in individual accomplishment was nonetheless an important factor in the increasing number of artists' signatures in Romanesque times, as witnessed by Wiligelmo's boast at Modena.

VÉZELAY AND THE CRUSADES Another large tympanum (FIG. **17-26**), this one at the church of La Madeleine (Mary Magdalene) at Vézelay, not far from Autun, depicts the Ascension of Christ and the Mission of the Apostles. As related in Acts 1:4–9, Christ foretold that the Twelve Apostles would receive the power of the Holy Spirit and become the witnesses of the truth of the Gospels throughout the world. The light rays emanating from Christ's hands represent the instilling of the Holy Spirit in the apostles (Acts 2:1–42) at the Pentecost (the seventh Sunday after Easter). The apostles, holding the Gospel books, receive their spiritual assignment, to preach the Gospel to all nations. The Christ figure is a splendid essay in calligraphic theme and variation. The drapery lines shoot out in rays, break into quick zigzag rhythms, and spin into whorls, wonderfully conveying the spiritual light and energy that flow from Christ over and into the equally animated apostles. The overall composition, as well as the detailed treatment of the figures, contrasts with the much more sedate representation of the Second Coming at Moissac, where almost all the figures are contained within a grid of horizontal and vertical lines. The sharp differences between the two tympana once again highlight the regional diversity of Romanesque art.

The world's heathen, the objects of the apostles' mission, appear on the lintel below and in eight compartments around the tympanum. The portrayals of the yet-to-be-converted constitute a medieval anthropological encyclopedia. Present are the legendary giant-eared Panotii of India, Pygmies (who require ladders to mount horses), and a host of other races, some characterized by a dog's head, others by a pig's snout, and still others by flaming hair. The assembly of agitated figures also includes hunchbacks, mutes, blind men, and lame men. Humanity, still suffering, awaits the salvation to come. The whole world is electrified by the promise of the ascended Christ, who looms above human misery and deformity. Again, as at Autun, as worshipers entered the portal, the tympanum established God's omnipotence and presented the Church as the road to salvation.

The Mission of the Apostles theme was an ideal choice for the Vézelay tympanum. Vézelay is more closely associated with the Crusades (see "The Crusades," page 466) than any other church in Europe. Pope Urban II had intended to preach the launching of the First Crusade at Vézelay in 1095, a generation before the tympanum was carved. In 1147, Bernard of Clairvaux called for the Second Crusade at Vézelay, and King Louis VII of France took up the cross there. In 1190, it was from Vézelay that King Richard the Lionheart of England and King Philip Augustus of France set out on the Third Crusade. The spirit of the Crusades determined in part the iconography of the Vézelay tympanum. The Crusades were a kind of "second mission of the apostles" to convert the infidel.

17-26 Ascension of Christ and Mission of the Apostles, tympanum of the center portal of the narthex of La Madeleine, Vézelay, France, 1120–1132.

The Crusades

Between 1095, when Pope Urban II called for an assault on the Holy Land at the Council of Clermont, and 1190, Christians launched three great Crusades from France. The *Crusades* ("taking of the Cross") were mass armed pilgrimages, whose stated purpose was to wrest the Christian shrines of the Holy Land from Muslim control. Crusaders and pilgrims were bound by similar vows. They hoped not only to atone for sins and win salvation but also to glorify God and extend the power of the Christian Church. The joint action of the papacy and the barons—mostly French—in this type of holy war strengthened papal authority over the long run and created an image of Christian solidarity.

The joining of religious and secular forces in the Crusades was symbolically embodied in the Christian warrior, the fighting priest, or the priestly fighter. From the early medieval warrior evolved the Christian knight, who fought for the honor of God rather than in defense of his chieftain. The first and most typical of the crusading knights were the Knights Templar. After the Christian conquest of Jerusalem in 1099, they stationed themselves next to the Dome of the Rock (see FIG. 13-1), that is, on the site of Solomon's Temple, the source of their name. Their mission was to protect pilgrims visiting the recovered Christian shrines. Formally founded in 1118, the Knights Templar order was blessed by Bernard of Clairvaux, who gave them a rule of organization based on that of his own Cistercians. Bernard justified their militancy by declaring that "the knight of Christ" is "glorified in slaying the infidel . . . because thereby Christ is glorified," and the Christian knight then wins salvation. The Cistercian abbot saw the Crusades as part of the general reform of the Church and as the defense of the supremacy of Christendom. He himself preached the Second Crusade in 1147.

The Crusaders achieved little in the East. They established a few unstable kingdoms and princely states in Syria and the Holy Land, which the Muslims later overthrew and assimilated. But in western Europe, the Crusades' impact was much greater. They increased the power and prestige of the towns. Many communities purchased their charters from the barons when the barons needed to finance their campaigns in the Holy Land. A middle class of merchants and artisans arose to rival the power of the feudal lords and the great monasteries. Italian maritime towns such as Pisa (FIG. 17-17) thrived on the commercial opportunities presented by the transportation of Crusaders overseas. The Crusades, together with pilgrimages, contributed significantly to the growth of trade and the rise of cities in the Romanesque era.

PROVENCE AND ROME The core of what once was Roman Gaul is the French region of Provence ("the [Roman] Province"). It is rich in the remains of Roman art and architecture, and some of the ancient monuments directly inspired the articulation of Provençal church facades. One example is the mid-12th-century church of Saint-Trophîme (FIG. **17-27**) at Arles, a site described in the *Pilgrim's Guide to Santiago de Compostela* (see page 450).

Arles was an important Roman colony founded by Julius Caesar, and Saint Trophimus was an early bishop in Roman Gaul. The western entrance to the church has a projecting portal resembling a Roman arch "attached" to the building's otherwise simple facade. The frieze above the freestanding columns recalls the sculptured fronts of Late Antique sarcophagi. The figures in high relief between the columns emulate classical statuary.

17-27 Central portal, west facade, Saint-Trophîme, Arles, France, mid-12th century.

17-28 BENEDETTO ANTELAMI, King David, statue in a niche on the west facade of Fidenza Cathedral, Fidenza, Italy, ca. 1180–1190. Marble, approx. life-size.

church portals with jamb figures that approximated freestanding statuary (see FIGS. 18-5 and 18-6).

BENEDETTO ANTELAMI The reawakening of interest in stone sculpture in the round also may be seen in northern Italy, where the sculptor BENEDETTO ANTELAMI was active in the last quarter of the 12th century. Several reliefs by his hand exist, including Parma Cathedral's pulpit and the portals of that city's baptistery. But his most unusual works are the monumental marble statues of two Old Testament figures he carved for the west facade of Fidenza Cathedral. Antelami's King David (FIG. **17-28**) seems confined within his niche. His elbows are kept close to his body. Absent is the weight shift that is the hallmark of classical statuary. Yet the sculptor's conception of this prophet is undeniably rooted in Greco-Roman art. One need only compare the Fidenza David with the prophet on the Moissac trumeau (FIG. 17-24), who also displays an unfurled scroll, to see how much the Italian sculptor freed his figure from its architectural setting. Antelami's classical approach to portraying biblical figures in stone was not immediately emulated. But the idea of placing freestanding statues in niches would be taken up again in Italy by Early Renaissance sculptors (see FIG. 21-7).

Metalwork and Wood Sculpture

RAINER OF HUY Another Romanesque sculptor whose name is known is RAINER OF HUY, a bronzeworker from the Meuse River valley in Belgium, an area renowned for its metalwork. In 1118 he masterfully cast in a single piece the baptismal font (FIG. **17-29**) for Notre-Dame-des-Fonts in Liège. The bronze basin rests on the foreparts of a dozen oxen, a reference to the "molten sea . . . on twelve oxen" cast in bronze for King Solomon's temple (1 Kings 7 : 23 – 25). The Old Testament story was thought to prefigure Christ's baptism (the oxen were equated with the Twelve Apostles), which is the central scene on Rainer's font.

The subject matter is, however, strictly Christian and typically Romanesque. The tympanum shows Christ surrounded by the signs of the Four Evangelists. On the lintel, directly below him, the Twelve Apostles appear at the center of a continuous frieze depicting the Last Judgment. The outermost parts of the frieze represent the Saved (on Christ's right) and the Damned in the flames of Hell (on his left). Below, in the jambs and the front bays of the portals, stand grave figures of saints draped in classical garb. The sculptor gave pride of place to Saint Trophimus, the third figure from the left. Across the doorway is a depiction of the stoning of Saint Stephen, whose relics were housed at Arles. It is the only narrative relief on the facade's lower part.

The quiet stances of the saints of Saint-Trophîme contrast with the spinning, twisting, and dancing figures seen at Autun and Vézelay. The Arles draperies, modeled on ancient stone sculpture rather than medieval manuscripts and metalwork, are also less agitated and show nothing of the dexterous linear play of the earlier portals. But the statuesque treatment of the figures on the Arles jambs has parallels in French Gothic art. In fact, in the north of France, near Paris, sculptors already had begun to adorn

17-29 RAINER OF HUY, baptism of Christ, baptismal font from Notre-Dame-des-Fonts, Liège, Belgium, 1107–1118. Bronze, 2′ 1″ high. Saint-Barthélémy, Liège.

The style is classicizing. The figures are softly rounded, with idealized bodies and faces and heavy clinging drapery. One figure (at the left in our photo) is even shown in a three-quarter view from the rear, a popular motif in classical art. Some of Rainer's figures, including Christ himself, are naked. In Romanesque art, the classical spirit lived on both north and south of the Alps.

THE THRONE OF WISDOM Despite the widespread use of stone relief sculptures to adorn Romanesque church portals, resistance to the creation of statues in the round—in any material—continued. The avoidance of anything that might be construed as an idol was still the rule, in keeping with the Second Commandment. Two centuries after Archbishop Gero commissioned a monumental wooden image of the crucified Christ for Cologne Cathedral (see FIG. 16-26), freestanding statues of Christ, the Virgin Mary, and the saints were still quite rare. The veneration of relics, however, brought with it a demand for small-scale images of the holy family and saints to be placed on the chapel altars of churches along the pilgrimage roads. Reliquaries in the form of saints (or parts of saints), tabletop crucifixes, and small wooden devotional images began to be produced in great numbers.

One of the most popular types, a specialty of the workshops of Auvergne, France, was a wooden statuette depicting the Virgin Mary with the Christ Child in her lap. The *Morgan Madonna* (FIG. **17-30**), so named because it once belonged to the financier and collector J. Pierpont Morgan, is one example. The type—known as the Throne of Wisdom, *sedes sapientiae*—is a western European freestanding version of the Byzantine Theotokos theme popular in icons and mosaics (see FIGS. 12-16 and 12-17). Christ holds a Bible in his left hand and raises his right arm in blessing (both hands are broken off). He is the embodiment of the divine wisdom contained in the Holy Scriptures. His mother, seated on a wooden chair, is in turn the Throne of Wisdom because her lap is the Christ Child's throne. As in Byzantine art, familiar to many Romanesque painters and sculptors, both Mother and Child sit rigidly upright and are strictly frontal, emotionless figures. But the intimate scale, the gesture of benediction, the once-bright coloring of the garments, and the soft modeling of the Virgin's face make the group seem much less remote than its counterparts in Byzantium.

WIBALD'S SILVER RELIQUARY Far more costly, but also created for private devotional purposes, is the reliquary of Saint Alexander (FIG. **17-31**), made in 1145 for Abbot Wibald of Stavelot in Belgium to house the hallowed pope's relics. The idealized head, which resembles portraits of youthful Roman emperors such as Augustus (see FIG. Intro-9) and Constantine (see FIG. 10-78), is almost life-size and was fashioned in beaten (repoussé) silver with bronze gilding for the hair. The saint wears a collar of jewels and enamel plaques around his neck. Enamels and gems also adorn the box on which the head is mounted. The reliquary rests on four bronze dragons—mythical animals of the kind that populated Romanesque cloister capitals. Not surprisingly, Bernard of Clairvaux was as critical of lavish church furnishings like the Alexander reliquary as he was of Romanesque cloister sculpture:

> [Men's] eyes are fixed on relics covered with gold and purses are opened. The thoroughly beautiful image of some male or female saint is exhibited and that saint is believed to be the more holy the more highly colored the image is. People rush to kiss it, they are invited to donate, and they admire the beautiful more than they

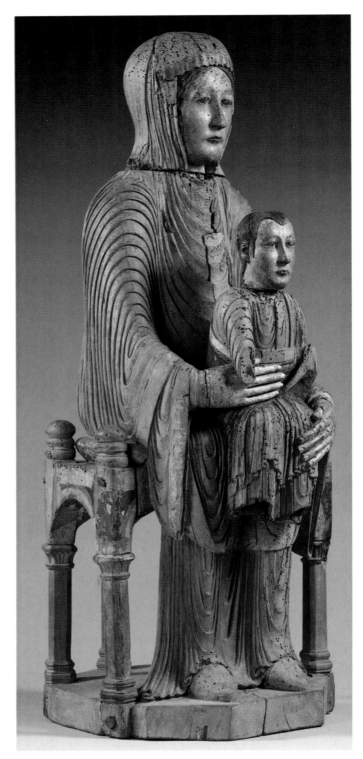

17-30 Virgin and Child *(Morgan Madonna),* from the Auvergne, France, second half of 12th century. Painted wood, 2′ 7″ high. Metropolitan Museum of Art, New York (gift of J. Pierpont Morgan, 1916).

venerate the sacred. . . . O vanity of vanities, but no more vain than insane! The Church . . . dresses its stones in gold and it abandons its children naked. It serves the eyes of the rich at the expense of the poor.[4]

The central plaque on the front of the Stavelot reliquary depicts Pope Alexander II (r. 1061–1073). Saints Eventius and Theodolus flank him. The nine plaques on the other three sides

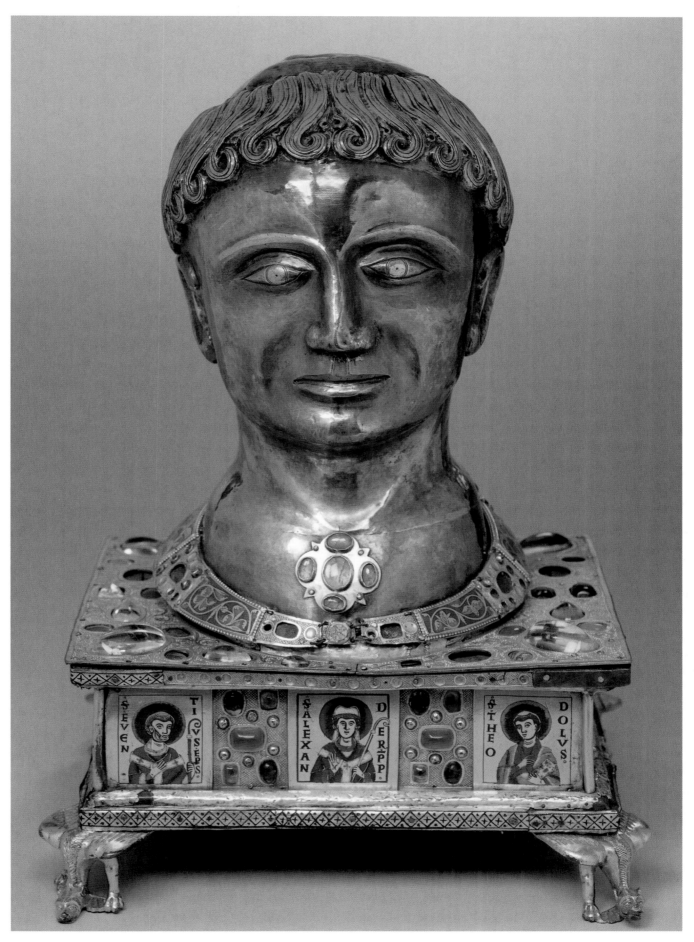

17-31 Head reliquary of Saint Alexander, from Stavelot Abbey, Belgium, 1145. Silver repoussé (partly gilt), gilt bronze, gems, pearls, and enamel, approx. 1′ 5½″ high. Musées Royaux d'Art et d'Histoire, Brussels.

represent female allegorical figures—Wisdom, Piety, and Humility among them. Although a local artist produced these enamels in the Meuse River region, the models were surely Byzantine (compare FIG. 12-25). Saint Alexander's reliquary underscores the multiple sources of Romanesque art, as well as its stylistic diversity. Not since antiquity had people journeyed as extensively as they did in the Romanesque period, and artists regularly saw works of wide geographic origin. Abbot Wibald himself epitomizes the well-traveled 12th-century clergyman. He was abbot of Montecassino in southern Italy, took part in the Second Crusade, and was sent by Frederick Barbarossa (Holy Roman Emperor, r. 1152–1190) to Constantinople to arrange Frederick's wedding to the niece of the Byzantine emperor Manuel Comnenus.

PAINTING

Unlike the practices of placing vaults over naves and aisles and decorating building facades with monumental stone reliefs, the art of painting did not need to be "revived" in the Romanesque period. Illuminated manuscripts had been produced in large numbers in the early Middle Ages, and even the Roman tradition of mural painting had never died, especially in Italy. But the quantity of preserved frescoes and illustrated books from the Romanesque era is unprecedented. As is true of Romanesque architecture and sculpture, painting of this period exhibits considerable regional and stylistic diversity. We discuss here a representative sample of Romanesque paintings from several regions in different media and formats.

Mural Painting

CHRISTIAN SPAIN In the eighth century, Muslim armies from North Africa defeated the Visigoths and occupied almost all of the Iberian Peninsula, bringing with them both Islam and Islamic art (see Chapter 13). But in northern Spain, the Muslim conquerors never completely controlled many areas, and Christianity and Christian art still flourished (see FIG. 16-10). In fact, Catalonia in northeastern Spain has more Romanesque mural paintings today than anywhere else.

One of the most impressive is the fresco (FIG. 17-32), now in Boston, that once filled the apse of Santa María de Mur, a monastery church not far from Lérida. The formality, symmetry, and placement of the figures are Byzantine—compare the 6th-century apse of Saint Catherine's at Mount Sinai in Egypt (see FIG. 12-13) and the late-12th-century apse of the basilica at Monreale (see FIG. 12-24). But the Spanish artist rejected Byzantine mosaic in favor of direct painting on plaster-coated walls. And the iconographic scheme in the semidome of the apse is more closely tied to those of the Romanesque church portals of France (FIGS. 17-23 and 17-27).

In the Santa María de Mur fresco, Christ in a star-strewn mandorla is flanked by the signs of the Four Evangelists—the Apocalypse theme that so fascinated the Romanesque imagination. Seven lamps between Christ and the Evangelist signs symbolize the seven Christian communities where Saint John addressed his revelation (the Apocalypse) at the beginning of his book (Rev. 1:4, 12, 20). Below stand apostles, paired off in formal frontality, much like the saints on the facade of Saint-Trophîme at Arles

17-32 Christ in Majesty, apse fresco from Santa María de Mur, near Lérida, Spain, mid-12th century. 24' × 22'. Museum of Fine Arts, Boston.

(FIG. 17-27), as well as in the apse at Monreale (see FIG. 12-24). The principal figures are rendered with partitioning of the drapery into volumes, here and there made tubular by local shading. The painter stiffened the irregular shapes of actual cloth into geometric patterns. The effect overall is one of simple, strong, and even blunt directness of statement, reinforced by harsh, bright color, appropriate for a powerful icon.

ITALY AND BYZANTIUM The tradition of decorating church apses with imposing images of Christ and saints is a venerable one, going back to Early Christian art. So, too, is the idea of illustrating episodes from the Old and New Testaments above the nave arcade of basilican churches, as at Santa Maria Maggiore (see FIG. 11-13) and Sant'Apollinare Nuovo (see FIG. 11-17). In the late 11th century, Romanesque artists used fresco rather than mosaic to create framed scenes from Christ's life along both sides of the nave of Sant'Angelo in Formis, near Capua in southern Italy.

Our detail (FIG. 17-33) shows the panel illustrating the entombment of Christ, with Mary cradling the head of her dead son as Joseph of Arimathea and Nicodemus lower him into his coffin. The weeping Saint John the Evangelist (with nimbus) watches. The fully modeled figures, the three-dimensional architectural setting, and the natural blue sky provide a sharp contrast with the Catalonian mural. But a comparison with the painted lamentation scene in Saint Pantaleimon in Macedonia (see FIG. 12-27) underscores that the Italian painters used Byzantine artworks as models. Sant'Angelo in Formis was constructed and decorated under the direction of Abbot Desiderius (later Pope Victor III) of Montecassino, the great monastery Saint Benedict founded in the sixth century. For the church at Montecassino, Desiderius imported artisans from Constantinople and instructed them to train his monks in mosaic and other arts. Sant'Angelo in Formis displays the work of these Italian pupils of Desiderius's Greek masters.

PAINTED VAULTS The Santa María de Mur and Sant'Angelo in Formis frescoes easily could be moved to an Early Christian basilica, where they would find ready homes in the apse and nave. But the murals of the Benedictine abbey church of Saint-Savin-sur-Gartempe (FIG. **17-34**) were inconceivable before the mastering of stone vaulting in the Romanesque period. Saint-Savin is a *hall church,* a church where the aisles are approximately the same height as the nave (as at Tournus, FIG. 17-3). The tall windows in the aisles provided more illumination to the nave than in churches that had low aisles and tribunes. This may explain why paintings (not true frescoes) decorate the nave's continuous barrel vault.

The subjects were all drawn from the Pentateuch, the opening five books of the Old Testament, in contrast to the New Testament themes of Sant'Angelo in Formis. They also bear little resemblance stylistically to the Byzantine-inspired murals of the Capuan and Catalonian churches. The elongated, agitated cross-legged figures of the Saint-Savin paintings are northern both in spirit and in form. They have stylistic affinities both to the reliefs of southern French portals and to some of the illuminated manuscripts discussed next.

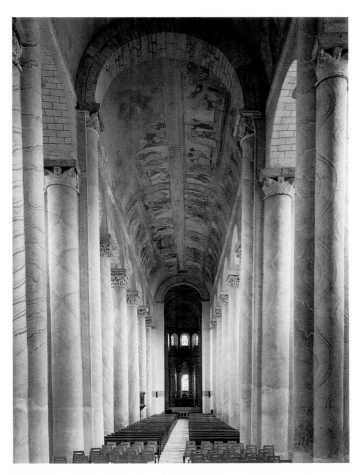

17-34 Nave of the abbey church, Saint-Savin-sur-Gartempe, France. Painted barrel vault, ca. 1100.

Manuscript Illumination

HILDEGARD'S VISIONS The number and variety of illuminated manuscripts dating to the Romanesque era attest to the great demand for illustrated religious tomes in the abbeys of western Europe and to the extraordinary productivity of the scribes and painters, almost exclusively monks and nuns, working in the scriptoria of these isolated religious communities. One manuscript, however, stands apart from all the rest: the *Scivias (Know the Ways [Scite vias] of God)* of Hildegard of Bingen. Hildegard was a German nun and eventually the abbess of the convent at Disibodenberg in the Rhineland (see "Romanesque Countesses, Queens, and Nuns," page 473). The manuscript, lost in 1945, is known today only through a facsimile. The original probably was written and illuminated at the monastery of Saint Matthias at Trier between 1150 and Hildegard's death in 1179, but it is possible the book was produced at Bingen under Hildegard's supervision. The *Scivias* contains a record of Hildegard's vision of the divine order of the cosmos and of humankind's place in it. The vision came to her as a fiery light that poured into her brain from the open vault of heaven.

On the opening page (FIG. **17-35**) of the Trier manuscript, Hildegard sits within the monastery walls, with her feet resting on a footstool, in much the same way the Evangelists of the *Coronation* and *Ebbo Gospels* (see FIGS. 16-12 and 16-13) were portrayed. This Romanesque page is a link in a chain of author portraits that goes back to classical antiquity. The painter showed Hildegard experiencing her divine vision by depicting five long tongues of fire emanating from above and entering her brain, just as she describes the experience in the accompanying text. Hildegard immediately sets down what has been revealed to her on a wax tablet resting on her left knee. Nearby, the monk Volmar, Hildegard's confessor, copies into a book all she has written. Here, in a singularly dramatic context, is a picture of the essential nature of ancient and medieval book manufacture—individual scribes copying and recopying texts by hand (compare FIG. 16-10).

KNIGHT VERSUS DRAGONS One of the major Romanesque scriptoria was at the abbey of Cîteaux, France, mother church of the Cistercian order. Just before Bernard joined the monastery in 1112, the monks completed work on an illuminated copy of Saint Gregory's *Moralia in Job*. It is an example of Cistercian illumination before Bernard's passionate opposition to figural art in monasteries led in 1134 to a Cistercian ban on elaborate paintings in manuscripts. After 1134, full-page illustrations were prohibited, and even initial letters had to be nonfigurative and of a single color.

The historiated initial we reproduce (FIG. **17-36**) clearly would have been in violation of Bernard's ban if it had not been painted before his prohibitions took effect. A knight, his squire, and two roaring dragons form an intricate letter *R*, the initial

17-35 The vision of Hildegard of Bingen, detail of a facsimile of a lost folio in the *Scivias* by Hildegard of Bingen, from Trier or Bingen, Germany, ca. 1150–1179. Formerly in Hessische Landesbibliothek, Wiesbaden.

17-36 Initial *R* with knight fighting a dragon, folio 4 verso of the *Moralia in Job*, from Cîteaux, France, ca. 1115–1125. Ink and tempera on vellum, 1′ 1¾″ × 9¼″. Bibliothèque Municipale, Dijon.

Romanesque Countesses, Queens, and Nuns

Romanesque Europe was still a man's world, but women could and did have power and influence. Countess Matilda of Canossa (1046–1115), who ruled Tuscany after 1069, was sole heiress of vast holdings in northern Italy. She was a key figure in the political struggle between the popes and the German emperors who controlled Lombardy. With unflagging resolution she defended Pope Gregory's reforms and at her death willed most of her lands to the papacy.

More famous and more powerful was Eleanor of Aquitaine (1122–1204), wife of Henry II of England. She married Henry after her marriage to Louis VII, king of France, was annulled. She was queen of France for 15 years and queen of England for 35 years. During that time she bore three daughters and five sons. Two became kings—Richard I (Lionheart) and John. She prompted her sons to rebel against their father, so Henry imprisoned her. Released at Henry's death, she lived on as dowager queen, managing England's government and King John's holdings in France.

Of quite different stamp was Hildegard of Bingen (1098–1179), the most prominent nun of the 12th century and one of the greatest religious figures of the Middle Ages. Hildegard was born into an aristocratic family that owned large estates in the German Rhineland. At a very early age she began to have visions. When she was eight, her parents placed her in the Benedictine *double monastery* (for monks *and* nuns) at Disibodenberg. She became a nun at 15. In 1141, God instructed Hildegard in a vision to disclose her visions to the world. Before then she had revealed them only to close confidants at the monastery. One of these was the monk Volmar, and Hildegard chose to dictate her visions to him (FIG. 17-35) for posterity. No less a figure than Bernard of Clairvaux certified in 1147 that her visions were authentic. Archbishop Heinrich of Mainz joined him in endorsing Hildegard. In 1148, the Cistercian pope Eugenius III formally authorized Hildegard "in the name of Christ and Saint Peter to publish all that she had learned from the Holy Spirit." At this time Hildegard became the abbess of a new convent built for her near Bingen. As reports of Hildegard's visions spread, kings, popes, barons, and prelates sought her counsel. All of them were attracted by her spiritual insight into the truth of the mysteries of the Christian faith.

In addition to her visionary works—the most important is the *Scivias* (FIG. 17-35)—Hildegard also wrote two scientific treatises. *Physica* is a study of the natural world, and *Causae et curae (Causes and Cures)* is a medical encyclopedia. Hildegard also composed the music and wrote the lyrics of 77 songs, which appeared under the title *Symphonia.*

Hildegard was the most famous of all Romanesque nuns, but she was by no means the only learned woman of her age. A younger contemporary, the abbess Herrad (d. 1195) of Hohenberg, Austria, was also the author of an important medieval encyclopedia. Herrad's *Hortus deliciarum (Garden of Delights)* is a history of the world intended for instructing the nuns under her supervision, but it was more widely read.

---

letter of the salutation *Reverentissimo.* This page is the opening of Gregory's letter to "the very reverent" Leandro, Bishop of Seville. The knight is a slender, regal figure who raises his shield and sword against the dragons while the squire, crouching beneath him, runs a lance through one of the monsters. Although the duel between knight and dragons was intended as an allegory of the spiritual struggle of monks, Bernard's opposition to this kind of illumination is clear from his condemnation of carvings of monstrous creatures and "fighting knights" on contemporary cloister capitals (see "Bernard of Clairvaux," page 461).

Ornamented initials go back to the Hiberno-Saxon period (see FIG. 16-8), but here the artist translated the theme into Romanesque terms. This page may be a reliable picture of a medieval baron's costume. The typically Romanesque banding of the torso and partitioning of the folds (especially the servant's skirts) are evident, but the master painter deftly avoided stiffness and angularity. The partitioning actually accentuates the knight's verticality and elegance and the thrusting action of his servant. The flowing sleeves add a spirited flourish to the swordsman's gesture. The knight, handsomely garbed, cavalierly wears no armor and aims a single stroke with proud disdain, unmoved by the ferocious dragons lunging at him.

MASTER HUGO The *Bury Bible,* produced at the Bury Saint Edmunds abbey in England around 1135, exemplifies the sumptuous illustration common to the large Bibles produced in wealthy Romanesque abbeys not subject to the Cistercian ban. Such costly books lent prestige to monasteries that could afford them (see "Medieval Books," Chapter 16, page 425).

The artist responsible for the *Bury Bible* is known: MASTER HUGO, who was also a sculptor and metalworker. He joins Bernardus Gelduinus (FIG. 17-21), Wiligelmo (FIG. 17-22), Gislebertus (FIG. 17-25), Benedetto Antelami (FIG. 17-28), and Rainer of Huy (FIG. 17-29) in the small but growing company of Romanesque artists who signed their works or whose names were recorded. In the 12th century, artists, illuminators as well as sculptors, increasingly began to identify themselves. Although most medieval artists remained anonymous, the contrast of the Romanesque period with the early Middle Ages is striking. Hugo seems to have been a secular artist, one of the emerging class of professional artists and artisans who depended for their livelihood on commissions from well-endowed monasteries. These artists resided in towns rather than within secluded abbey walls, and they traveled frequently to find work. They were the exception, however, and the typical Romanesque scribes and illuminators continued to be monks and nuns working anonymously in the service of God. The Benedictine Rule, for example, specified that "craftsmen in the monastery . . . should pursue their crafts with all humility after the abbot has given permission."

17-37 MASTER HUGO, *Moses expounding the Law,* folio 94 recto of the *Bury Bible,* from Bury Saint Edmunds, England, ca. 1135. Ink and tempera on vellum, approx. 1′ 8″ × 1′ 2″. Corpus Christi College, Cambridge.

Our page of the *Bury Bible* (FIG. **17-37**) shows two scenes from Deuteronomy framed by symmetrical leaf motifs in softly glowing harmonized colors. The upper register depicts Moses and Aaron proclaiming the law to the Israelites. Master Hugo represented Moses with horns, consistent with Saint Jerome's translation of the Hebrew word that also means "rays" (compare Michelangelo's similar conception of the Hebrew prophet, FIG. 22-10). The lower panel portrays Moses pointing out the clean and unclean beasts. The gestures are slow and gentle and have quiet dignity. The figures of Moses and Aaron seem to glide. This presentation is quite different from the abrupt emphasis and spastic movement seen in earlier Romanesque paintings. The movements of the figures appear more integrated and smooth. Yet patterning remains in the multiple divisions of the draped limbs, the lightly shaded volumes connected with sinuous lines and ladderlike folds. Hugo still thought of the drapery and body as somehow the same. The frame has a quite definite limiting function, and the painter carefully fit the figures within it.

THE PRINCE OF SCRIBES The *Eadwine Psalter* is the masterpiece of an English monk known as EADWINE THE SCRIBE. It contains 166 illustrations, and many are variations of those in

the Carolingian *Utrecht Psalter* (see FIG. 16-14). The last page (FIG. **17-38**), however, presents a rare picture of a Romanesque artist at work. The "portrait" of Eadwine—it is probably a generic type and not a specific likeness—also has models in the past. It is in the long tradition of author portraits in ancient and medieval manuscripts (see FIGS. 16-7, 16-12, 16-13, and 17-35), although the true author of the *Eadwine Psalter* is King David. Eadwine exaggerated his importance by likening his image to that of an Evangelist writing his gospel and by including an inscription within the inner frame that identifies him and proclaims that he is a "prince among scribes." He declares that, due to the excellence of his work, his fame will endure forever and that he can offer his book as an acceptable gift to God. Eadwine, like other Romanesque sculptors and painters who signed their works, may have been concerned for his fame, but these artists, whether monks or laity, were not yet aware of the concepts of fine art and fine artist. To them, their work existed not for its own sake but for God's.

The style of the Eadwine portrait is related to that of the *Bury Bible,* but, although the patterning is still firm (notably in the cowl and the thigh), the drapery falls more softly and follows the movements of the body beneath it. Here, the arbitrariness of many Romanesque painted and sculpted garments yielded slightly, but clearly, to the requirements of more naturalistic representation. The Romanesque artist's instinct for decorating the surface remained, as is apparent in the gown's whorls and spirals. But, significantly, these were painted in very lightly so that they would not conflict with the functional lines that contain them.

17-38 EADWINE THE SCRIBE(?), Eadwine the Scribe at work, folio 283 verso of the *Eadwine Psalter,* ca. 1160–1170. Ink and tempera on vellum. Trinity College, Cambridge.

THE CONQUEST OF ENGLAND This account of Romanesque painting concludes with a work that is *not* a painting. Nor is the so-called *Bayeux Tapestry* (FIGS. **17-39** and **17-40**) a woven tapestry. It is, instead, an embroidered fabric made of wool sewn on linen (see "Embroidery and Tapestry," page 476). But the *Bayeux Tapestry* is closely related to Romanesque manuscript illumination. Its borders are populated by the kinds of real and imaginary animals found in contemporaneous books, and an explanatory Latin text sewn in thread accompanies many of the pictures.

Some 20 inches high and about 230 feet long, the *Bayeux Tapestry* is a continuous, friezelike, pictorial narrative of a crucial moment in England's history and of the events that led up to it. The Norman defeat of the Anglo-Saxons at Hastings in 1066 brought England under the control of the Normans, uniting all of England and much of France under one rule. The dukes of Normandy became the kings of England. Commissioned by Bishop Odo, the half brother of the conquering Duke William, the embroidery may have been sewn by women at the Norman court. Many art historians, however, believe it was the work of English

17-39 Funeral procession to Westminster Abbey, detail of the *Bayeux Tapestry,* from Bayeux Cathedral, Bayeux, France, ca. 1070–1080. Embroidered wool on linen, 1′ 8″ high (entire length of fabric 229′ 8″). Centre Guillaume le Conquérant, Bayeux.

17-40 Battle of Hastings, detail of the *Bayeux Tapestry,* from Bayeux Cathedral, Bayeux, France, ca. 1070–1080. Embroidered wool on linen, 1′ 8″ high (entire length of fabric 229′ 8″). Centre Guillaume le Conquérant, Bayeux.

Embroidery and Tapestry

The most famous embroidery of the Middle Ages is, ironically, known as the *Bayeux Tapestry* (FIGS. 17-39 and 17-40). Embroidery and tapestry are related, but different, means of decorating textiles. *Tapestry* designs are woven on a loom as part of the fabric. *Embroidery* patterns are sewn with threads.

The needleworkers who fashioned the *Bayeux Tapestry* were either Norman or English women. They employed eight colors of dyed wool—two varieties of blue, three shades of green, yellow, buff, and terracotta red—and two kinds of stitches. In *stem stitching*, short overlapping strands of thread form jagged lines.

Laid-and-couched work creates solid blocks of color. In the latter technique, the needleworker first lays down a series of parallel and then a series of cross stitches. Finally, the stitcher tacks down the cross-hatched threads using couching (knotting). On the *Bayeux Tapestry*, the natural linen color was left exposed for the background, human flesh, building walls, and other "colorless" design elements. Stem stitches define the contours of figures and buildings and delineate interior details, such as facial features, body armor, and roof tiles. Laid-and-couched work was employed for clothing, animal bodies, and other solid areas.

stitchers in Kent, where Odo was earl after the Norman conquest. Odo donated the work to Bayeux Cathedral (hence its nickname), but it is uncertain whether it was originally intended for display in the church's nave, where the theme would have been a curious choice.

The circumstances leading to the Norman invasion of England are well documented. In 1066, Edward the Confessor, the Anglo-Saxon king of England, died. The Normans believed Edward had recognized William of Normandy as his rightful heir. But the crown went to Harold, earl of Wessex, the king's Anglo-Saxon brother-in-law, who had sworn an oath of allegiance to William. The betrayed Normans, descendants of the seafaring Vikings, boarded their ships, crossed the English Channel, and crushed Harold's forces.

We illustrate two episodes of the epic tale as represented in the *Bayeux Tapestry*. The first detail (FIG. 17-39) depicts King Edward's funeral procession. The hand of God points the way to the church where he was buried—Westminster Abbey, consecrated on December 28, 1065, just a few days before Edward's death. The church was one of the first Romanesque buildings erected in England, and the embroiderers took pains to record its main features, including the imposing crossing tower and the long nave with tribunes. Here William was crowned king of England on Christmas Day, 1066. (The coronation of every English monarch since then also has occurred in Westminster Abbey.)

The second detail (FIG. 17-40) shows the Battle of Hastings in progress. The Norman cavalry cuts down the English defenders. The lower border is filled with the dead and wounded, although the upper register continues the animal motifs of the rest of the embroidery. The Romanesque artist co-opted some of the characteristic motifs of Greco-Roman battle scenes. Note, for example, the horses with twisted necks and contorted bodies (compare FIG. 5-69). But the artists rendered the figures in the Romanesque manner. Linear patterning and flat color replaced classical three-dimensional volume and modeling in light and dark hues.

The *Bayeux Tapestry* is unique in Romanesque art in that it depicts an event in full detail at a time shortly after it occurred, recalling the historical narratives of ancient Roman art. The Norman embroidery often has been likened to the scroll-like frieze of the Column of Trajan (see FIG. 10-42). Like the Roman account, the story told on the *Bayeux Tapestry* is the conqueror's version of history, a proclamation of national pride. And as on Trajan's Column, the narrative is not confined to battlefield successes. It is a complete chronicle of events. Included are the preparations for war, with scenes depicting the felling and splitting of trees for ship construction; the loading of equipment onto the vessels; the cooking and serving of meals; and so forth. In this respect, the *Bayeux Tapestry* is the most *Roman*-esque of all Romanesque artworks.

CONCLUSION

With the death of the last Ottonian emperor in 1024, the greatest patrons of art and architecture in Europe became the monasteries, especially those along the pilgrimage routes leading to the tomb of Saint James at Santiago de Compostela in Spain. In the Romanesque age, immense churches with stone vaults rose throughout Europe, didactic relief sculptures adorned church portals and cloisters, and the relics of saints were housed in gold and silver and enamel reliquaries.

Not everyone embraced the new artistic trends. The Cistercians in particular shunned elaborate churches designed to accommodate multitudes of pilgrims, and banned figural adornment in their sacred books. Bernard of Clairvaux, the influential Cistercian abbot who was later beatified, protested as fervently against the decoration of monastic churches with sculpture as he preached Crusades to capture the Holy Land from the Muslims. But for most clergy and laity alike, the appeal of the new churches with their sculpted reliefs and glittering relics was irresistible. Each region had a characteristic style, but the revival of monumental architecture and sculpture was Europe-wide.

1000

- Hugh of Semur, 1024–1109, abbot of Cluny
- Countess Matilda of Canossa, 1046–1115

1050

- Final separation of Latin (Roman) Church from the Byzantine (Greek Orthodox) Church, 1054
- Norman conquest of southern Italy and Sicily, 1060–1101
- Norman conquest of England (Battle of Hastings), 1066

1 Bayeux Tapestry, ca. 1070–1080

1

1075

- Pope Gregory VII (1073–1085) asserts spiritual supremacy of papacy over kings and emperors, 1075
- Bernard of Clairvaux, ca. 1090–1153
- Pope Urban II preaches the First Crusade, 1095
- Hildegard of Bingen, 1098–1179
- Cistercian Order founded, 1098
- Crusaders capture Jerusalem, 1099

2 Durham Cathedral, begun ca. 1093

2

1100

- Foundation of the Knights Templar, 1118
- Eleanor of Aquitaine, 1122–1204
- King Louis VII of France, r. 1137–1180
- Gervase of Canterbury, 1141–1210
- Koran translated into Latin, 1143
- Second Crusade, 1147–1148

3 South Portal, Saint-Pierre, Moissac, ca. 1115–1135

1150

- Frederick Barbarossa, Holy Roman Emperor, r. 1152–1190
- King Henry II Plantagenet of England, r. 1154–1189
- King Philip Augustus of France, r. 1180–1223
- King Richard the Lionheart of England, r. 1189–1199
- Third Crusade, 1190–1192

4 Eadwine Psalter, ca. 1160–1170

1200

Blanche of Castile, Louis IX, and two monks, dedication page (folio 8 recto) of a moralized Bible, from Paris, France, 1226–1234. Ink, tempera, and gold leaf on vellum, 1′ 3″ × 10½″. Pierpont Morgan Library, New York.

18

THE AGE OF GREAT CATHEDRALS

GOTHIC ART

In the mid-16th century, Giorgio Vasari (1511–1574), the "father of art history," used "Gothic" as a term of ridicule to describe late medieval art and architecture. For him, Gothic art was "monstrous and barbarous," invented by the Goths.[1] With the publication of his famous treatise, Vasari codified for all time the notion already advanced by the early Renaissance artist Lorenzo Ghiberti (1378–1455), who, in his *Commentarii*, characterized the Middle Ages as a period of decline. The humanists of the Italian Renaissance, who placed Greco-Roman art on a pedestal, believed that the uncouth Goths were responsible not only for the downfall of Rome but also for the destruction of the classical style in art and architecture. They regarded "Gothic" art with contempt and considered it ugly and crude.

In the 13th and 14th centuries, however, when the Gothic style was the rage in most of Europe, especially north of the Alps, contemporary commentators considered Gothic buildings *opus modernum* (modern work) or *opus francigenum* (French work). They recognized that the great cathedrals towering over their towns displayed an exciting and new building and decoration style—and that the style originated in France. Clergy and the lay public alike regarded their new cathedrals not as distortions of the classical style but as images of the City of God, the Heavenly Jerusalem, which they were privileged to build on earth.

The Gothic style first appeared in northern France around 1140. In southern France (see FIG. 17-27) and elsewhere in Europe, the Romanesque style still flourished. But by the 13th century, the opus modernum of the region around Paris had spread throughout western Europe, and in the next century further still (MAP **18-1**). The Cathedral of Saint Vitus in Prague (Czech Republic), for example, begun in 1344, closely emulated French Gothic architecture.

Although it became an internationally acclaimed style, Gothic art was, nonetheless, a regional phenomenon. To the east and south of Europe, the Islamic and Byzantine styles still held sway. And many regional variants existed within European Gothic, just as distinct regional styles characterized the Romanesque period. Gothic began and ended at different dates in different places. When the banker Jacques

MAP 18-1 Europe about 1200.

Coeur built his home in Bourges (FIG. 18-28) in the Gothic style in the mid-15th century, classicism already reigned supreme in Italy. While the Gothic church of Saint-Maclou (FIG. 18-25) was under construction in Rouen in the early years of the 16th century, Michelangelo was painting the ceiling of the Sistine Chapel in Rome.

TURMOIL AND CHANGE The Gothic period was a time of great prosperity yet also one of turmoil in Europe. In 1337, the Hundred Years' War began, shattering the peace between France and England. In the 14th century, a great plague, the Black Death, swept over western Europe and killed at least a quarter of its people. From 1378 to 1417, opposing popes resided in Rome and in Avignon in southern France during the political-religious crisis known as the Great Schism (see Chapter 19).

Above all, the Gothic age was a time of profound change in European society. The focus of both intellectual and religious life shifted definitively from monasteries in the countryside and pilgrimage churches to rapidly expanding secular cities with great new cathedrals reaching to the sky. In these new Gothic urban centers, prosperous merchants made their homes, universities run by professional guilds of scholars formed, and minstrels sang of chivalrous knights and beautiful maidens at royal "courts of love." Although the papacy was at the height of its power and knights throughout Europe still gathered to wage Crusades against the Muslims, the independent secular nations of modern Europe were beginning to take shape. Foremost among them was France.

FRENCH GOTHIC

Architecture and Architectural Decoration

SUGER AND SAINT-DENIS On June 11, 1144, King Louis VII of France, Queen Eleanor of Aquitaine, royal court members, and a host of distinguished clergy, including five archbishops, converged on the Benedictine abbey church of Saint-Denis for the dedication of its new east end (FIGS. **18-1** and **18-2**). Saint Dionysius (Denis in French) was the apostle who brought Christianity to Gaul and who died a martyr's death there in the third century. The church, just a few miles north of Paris, housed the saint's tomb and those of the French kings, as well as the crimson military banner said to have belonged to Charlemagne. The Carolingian basilica was France's royal church, the very symbol of the monarchy (just as Speyer Cathedral [see FIG. 17-9] was the burial place of the German rulers of the Holy Roman Empire). But the old building was in disrepair and had become too small to accommodate the growing number of pilgrims. Its abbot, Suger, also believed it was of insufficient grandeur to serve as the official church of the French kings (see "Abbot Suger and the Rebuilding of Saint-Denis," page 481). Thus, Suger began to rebuild the church in 1135 by erecting a new west facade with sculptured portals. In 1140, work began on the east end. Suger died before he could remodel the nave, but he attended the 1144 dedication of the new choir, ambulatory, and radiating chapels.

Abbot Suger and the Rebuilding of Saint-Denis

Abbot Suger of Saint-Denis (1081–1151) rose from humble parentage to become the right-hand man of both Louis VI (r. 1108–1137) and Louis VII (r. 1137–1180). When the latter, accompanied by his queen, Eleanor of Aquitaine, left to join the Second Crusade (1147–1149), Suger served as regent of France. From his youth, Suger wrote, he had dreamed of the possibility of embellishing the church in which French monarchs had been buried since the ninth century. In 1122, he became abbot of Saint-Denis and within 15 years began rebuilding the monastery founded in the Merovingian age. In Suger's time, the power of the French kings, except for scattered holdings, extended over an area not much larger than the Île-de-France, the region centered on Paris. But the kings had pretensions to rule all of France. Suger aimed to increase the prestige both of his abbey and of the monarchy by rebuilding France's royal church in grand fashion.

Suger wrote three detailed treatises about his activities as abbot of Saint-Denis. He recorded that he summoned masons and artists from many regions to help design and construct his new church. And in one important passage he described the special qualities of the new east end (FIGS. 18-1 to 18-3) dedicated in 1144:

> [I]t was cunningly provided that—through the upper columns and central arches which were to be placed upon the lower ones built in the crypt—the central nave of the old [Carolingian church] should be equalized, by means of geometrical and arithmetical instruments, with the central nave of the new addition; and, likewise, that the dimensions of the old side-aisles should be equalized with the dimensions of the new side-aisles, except for that elegant and praiseworthy extension in [the form of] a circular string of chapels, by virtue of which the whole [church] would shine with the wonderful and uninterrupted light of most sacred windows, pervading the interior beauty.[1]

The abbot's brief discussion of Saint Denis's new ambulatory and chapels is key to the understanding of Early Gothic architecture. But he wrote at much greater length about his church's glorious golden and gem-studded furnishings. Here, for example, is Suger's description of the *altar frontal* (hanging in front of the altar) in the choir:

> Into this panel, which stands in front of [Saint Denis's] most sacred body, we have put . . . about forty-two marks of gold [and] a multifarious wealth of precious gems, hyacinths, rubies, sapphires, emeralds and topazes, and also an array of different large pearls.[2]

The costly furnishings and the light-filled space caused Suger to "delight in the beauty of the house of God" and "called [him] away from external cares." The new church made him feel as if he was "dwelling . . . in some strange region of the universe which neither exists entirely in the slime of the earth nor entirely in the purity of Heaven." In Suger's eyes, then, his splendid new church, permeated with light and outfitted with gold and precious gems, was a way station on the road to Paradise, which "transported [him] from this inferior to that higher world."[3] He regarded a lavish investment in art as a spiritual aid, not as an undesirable distraction for the pious monk, as did Bernard of Clairvaux (see "Bernard of Clairvaux," Chapter 17, page 461). Suger's forceful justification of art in the church set the stage for the proliferation of costly stained-glass windows and sculptures in the great cathedrals of the Gothic age.

[1] Erwin Panofsky, trans., *Abbot Suger on the Abbey Church of Saint-Denis and Its Art Treasures,* 2nd ed. (Princeton: Princeton University Press, 1979), 101.

[2] Ibid., 55.

[3] Ibid., 65.

18-1 Ambulatory and radiating chapels, abbey church, Saint-Denis, France, 1140–1144.

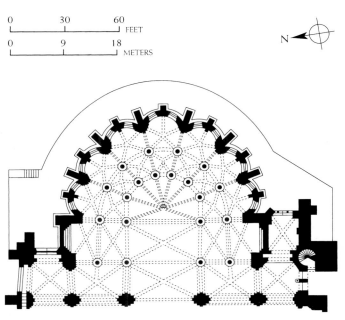

18-2 Plan of the east end, abbey church, Saint-Denis, France, 1140–1144 (after Sumner Crosby).

The Gothic Rib Vault

The ancestors of the Gothic *rib vault* are the Romanesque vaults found at Caen (see FIG. 17-13), Durham (see FIG. 17-15), and elsewhere. The rib vault's distinguishing feature is the crossed, or diagonal, arches under its groins, as seen in the Saint-Denis ambulatory and chapels (FIG. 18-3; compare FIG. 18-18). These arches form the *armature,* or skeletal framework, for constructing the vault. Gothic vaults generally have more thinly vaulted *webs* between the arches than Romanesque vaults have. But the chief difference between Romanesque and Gothic rib vaults is the *pointed arch,* an integral part of the Gothic skeletal armature. Pointed arches were first widely used in Sasanian architecture (see FIG. 2-28), and Islamic builders later adopted them. French Romanesque architects (see FIG. 17-8) borrowed the form from Muslim Spain and passed it to their Gothic successors. Pointed arches allowed Gothic builders to make the crowns of all the vault's arches approximately the same level, regardless of the space to be vaulted. The Romanesque architects could not achieve this with their semicircular arches.

Our diagrams illustrate this key difference. In diagram *a,* the rectangle *ABCD* is an oblong nave bay to be vaulted. *AC* and *DB* are the diagonal ribs; *AB* and *DC,* the transverse arches; and *AD* and *BC,* the nave arcade's arches. If the architect uses semicircular arches (*AFB,* *BJC,* and *DHC),* their radii and, therefore, their heights (*EF, IJ,* and *GH*) will be different, because the height of a semicircular arch is determined by its width. The result will be a vault (diagram *b*) with higher transverse arches (*DHC*) than the arcade's arches (*CJB*). The vault's crown (*F*) will be still higher. If the builder uses pointed arches, the transverse (*DLC*) and arcade (*BKC*) arches can have the same heights (*GL* and *IK* in diagram *a*). The result will be a Gothic rib vault (diagram *c*), where the points of the arches (*L* and *K*) are at the same level as the vault's crown (*F*).

A major advantage of the Gothic vault is its flexibility, which permits the vaulting of compartments of varying shapes, as may be seen at Saint-Denis (FIGS. 18-2 and 18-3). Pointed arches also channel the weight of the vaults more directly downward than do semicircular arches. The vaults, therefore, require less buttressing to hold them in place, in turn permitting the opening up of the walls with large windows beneath the arches. Because pointed arches also lead the eye upward, they make the vaults appear taller than they actually are. In our diagrams, the crown (*F*) of both the Romanesque (diagram *b*) and Gothic (diagram *c*) vaults is the same height from the pavement, but the Gothic vault seems taller. Both the physical and visual properties of rib vaults with pointed arches aided Gothic builders in their quest for soaring height in church interiors.

18-3 Vaults of the ambulatory and radiating chapels of the choir, abbey church, Saint-Denis, France, 1140–1144.

LUX NOVA Because the French considered the old church a relic in its own right, the new east end had to conform to the dimensions of the crypt below it. Nevertheless, the remodeled portion of Saint-Denis represented a sharp break from past practice. There, one can already see the basic features of the new Gothic style of architecture. Innovative rib vaults resting on *pointed arches* (see "The Gothic Rib Vault," page 482) cover the ambulatory and chapels (FIGS. 18-1 and **18-3**). These pioneering, exceptionally light vaults spring from slender columns in the ambulatory and from the thin masonry walls framing the chapels. The lightness of the vaults enabled the builders to eliminate the walls between the chapels and open up the outer walls and fill them with stained-glass windows (see "Stained-Glass Windows," page 492). Suger and his contemporaries marveled at the "wonderful and uninterrupted light" that poured in through the "most sacred windows." The abbot called the colored light *lux nova*, "new light." The multicolored rays coming through the windows shone on the walls and columns, almost dissolving them. Both the new type of vaulting and the use of stained glass became hallmarks of French Gothic architecture.

SCULPTURE AT SAINT-DENIS Saint-Denis is also the key monument of Early Gothic sculpture. Little of the sculpture that Suger commissioned for the west facade of the abbey church survived the French Revolution, but much of the mid-12th-century structure is intact. It consists of a double-tower westwork as at Saint-Étienne at Caen (see FIG. 17-12) and has massive walls in the Romanesque tradition. A restored large central *rose window*

(a circular stained-glass window), a new feature that became standard in French Gothic architecture, punctuates the facade's upper story. For the three portals, Suger imported sculptors to carry on the rich heritage of Romanesque Burgundy (see "The Romanesque Portal," Chapter 17, page 463). But at Saint-Denis, the sculptors introduced statues of Old Testament kings, queens, and prophets attached to columns, which screened the jambs of all three doorways.

THE ROYAL PORTAL This innovative treatment of the portals of Suger's church appeared immediately afterward at the Cathedral of Notre Dame ("Our Lady," that is, the Virgin Mary) at Chartres (FIG. **18-4**), also in the Île-de-France. Work on the west facade, the "Royal Portal" (FIG. **18-5**), began around 1145. (The Royal Portal is so named because of the statue-columns of kings and queens flanking its three doorways.) The lower parts of the massive west towers at Chartres and the portals between them are all that remain of a cathedral begun in 1134 and destroyed by fire in 1194 before it had been completed. Reconstruction of the cathedral began immediately, but in the High Gothic style (discussed later). The west portals, however, constitute the most complete and impressive surviving ensemble of Early Gothic sculpture. Thierry of Chartres, chancellor of the Cathedral School of Chartres (see "Paris: The Intellectual Capital of Gothic Europe," page 487) from 1141 until his death 10 years later, may have conceived the complex iconographical program. The archivolts of the right portal, for example, depict the seven female Liberal Arts and

18-5 Royal Portal, west facade, Chartres Cathedral, Chartres, France, ca. 1145–1155.

their male champions. The figures represent the core of medieval learning and symbolize human knowledge, which Thierry and others believed led to true faith.

CHRIST AND THE VIRGIN AT CHARTRES The sculptures of the west facade (FIG. 18-5) proclaim the majesty and power of Christ. To unite the three doorways iconographically and visually, the sculptors carved episodes from Christ's life on the capitals, which form a kind of frieze linking one entrance to the next. In the tympanum of the right portal, Christ appears in the lap of the Virgin Mary (Notre Dame). Scenes of his birth and early life fill the lintel below. The tympanum's theme and composition recall Byzantine representations of the Theotokos (see FIGS. 12-16 and 12-17), as well as the Romanesque Throne of Wisdom (see FIG. 17-30). But Mary's prominence on the Chartres facade has no parallel in the decoration of Romanesque church portals. At Chartres the designers gave her a central role in the sculptural program, a position she maintained throughout the Gothic period. The cult of the Virgin Mary reached a high point in the Gothic age. As the Mother of Christ, she stood compassionately between the Last Judge and the horrors of Hell, interceding for all her faithful. Worshipers in the later 12th and 13th centuries sang hymns to her, put her image everywhere, and dedicated great cathedrals to her. Soldiers carried the Virgin's image into battle on banners, and her name joined that of Saint Denis as part of the French king's battle cry. Mary became the spiritual lady of chivalry, and the Christian knight dedicated his life to her. The severity of Romanesque themes stressing the Last Judgment yielded to the gentleness of Gothic art, in which Mary is the kindly Queen of Heaven.

Christ's Ascension into Heaven appears in the tympanum of the left portal. All around, in the archivolts, are the signs of the

18-6 Old Testament kings and queen, jamb statues, central doorway of Royal Portal, Chartres Cathedral, Chartres, France, ca. 1145–1155.

18-7 West facade of Laon Cathedral, Laon, France, begun ca. 1190.

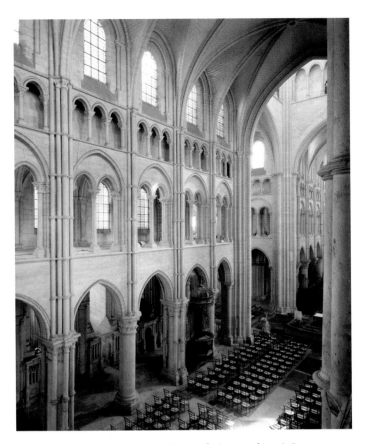

18-8 Interior of Laon Cathedral (view facing northeast), Laon, France, begun ca. 1190.

zodiac and scenes representing the various labors of the months of the year. They are symbols of the cosmic and earthly worlds. The Second Coming is the subject of the central tympanum. The signs of the Four Evangelists, the Twenty-Four Elders of the Apocalypse, and the Twelve Apostles appear around Christ or on the lintel. The Second Coming—in essence, the Last Judgment theme—was still of central importance, as it was in Romanesque portals. But at Early Gothic Chartres the theme became a symbol of salvation rather than damnation.

STATUE-COLUMNS Statues of Old Testament kings and queens (FIG. **18-6**) decorate the jambs flanking each doorway of the Royal Portal. They are the royal ancestors of Christ and, both figuratively and literally, support the New Testament figures above the doorways. They wear 12th-century clothes, and medieval observers also regarded them as images of the kings and queens of France, symbols of secular as well as of biblical authority. (This was the motivation for vandalizing the comparable figures at Saint-Denis during the French Revolution.)

Seen from a distance, the statue-columns appear to be little more than vertical decorative accents within the larger designs of the portals and facade (FIG. 18-5). The figures stand rigidly upright with their elbows held close against their hips. The linear folds of their garments—inherited from the Romanesque style, along with the elongated proportions—generally echo the vertical lines of the columns behind them. (In this respect, Gothic jamb statues differ significantly from classical caryatids; see FIG. 5-52. The Gothic figures are *attached* to columns. The classical statues *replaced* the columns.) And yet, within and despite this architectural straitjacket, the statues display the first signs of a new

naturalism. They stand out from the plane of the wall. The sculptors conceived and treated the statues as three-dimensional volumes, so the figures "move" into the space of observers. The new naturalism is noticeable particularly in the statues' heads, where kindly human faces replace the masklike features of most Romanesque figures. At Chartres, a personalization of appearance began that was transformed first into idealized portraits of the perfect Christian and finally, by 1400, into the portraiture of specific individuals. The sculptors of the Royal Portal statues initiated an era of artistic concern with personality and individuality.

EARLY GOTHIC AT LAON Both Chartres Cathedral and the abbey church of Saint-Denis had long building histories, and only small portions of the structures date to the Early Gothic period. Laon Cathedral (FIGS. **18-7** and **18-8**), however, begun about 1160 and finished shortly after 1200, provides a comprehensive picture of French church architecture of the second half of the 12th century. Although the Laon builders retained many Romanesque features in their design, they combined them with the rib vault resting on pointed arches, the essential element of Early Gothic architecture.

Among the plan's Romanesque features are the nave bays with their large sexpartite rib vaults, flanked by two small groin-vaulted squares in each aisle. The vaulting system (except for the pointed arches), as well as the vaulted gallery above the aisles, derived from Norman Romanesque churches such as Saint-Étienne at Caen (see FIG. 17-13), which enjoyed great prestige in northern France throughout the 12th century. A new feature found in the Laon interior, however, is the *triforium,* the band of arcades below the clerestory (FIG. 18-8). The triforium occupies the space

18-9 Nave elevations of four French Gothic cathedrals at the same scale (after Louis Grodecki).

0 10 20 30 FEET
0 5 10 METERS

a Laon | **b** Paris | **c** Chartres | **d** Amiens

corresponding to the exterior strip of wall covered by the sloping timber roof above the galleries. The insertion of the triforium into the Romanesque three-story nave-wall elevation reflected a growing desire to break up and eliminate all continuous wall surfaces. The new horizontal zone produced the characteristic four-story Early Gothic interior elevation: nave arcade, vaulted gallery, triforium, and clerestory with single *lancets* (tall, narrow windows ending in pointed arches). FIG. **18-9** compares the Laon nave elevation (FIG. 18-9*a*) with those of another four-story Early Gothic cathedral (FIG. 18-9*b*) and two three-story High Gothic cathedrals (FIGS. 18-9*c* and 18-9*d*).

The Laon architect also employed the alternate-support system of Caen and other Romanesque churches. In the nave arcade, compound piers alternate with simple piers. In the gallery and triforium, bundles of three and five shafts alternate in framing the aisle bays. The Laon designer moved away from the compartmentalized effect of Romanesque interiors, which tends to make visitors pause as they advance from unit to unit. Gothic architects aimed, even if rather timidly at Laon, to create a unified interior space that sweeps uninterruptedly from west to east. The level crowns of the successive nave vaults, made possible by pointed arches, enhance this longitudinal continuity (FIG. 18-8).

Laon Cathedral's west facade (FIG. 18-7) signals an even more pronounced departure from the Romanesque style still lingering at Saint-Denis and the Chartres Royal Portal. Typically Gothic are the huge central rose window, the deep porches in front of the doorways, and the open structure of the towers. A comparison of the facades of Laon Cathedral and Saint-Étienne at Caen (see

18-10 Notre-Dame (view from the south), Paris, France, begun 1163; nave and flying buttresses, ca. 1180–1200; remodeled after 1225.

Paris: The Intellectual Capital of Gothic Europe

A few years before the formal consecration of the altar of Notre-Dame in Paris (FIG. 18-10), Philip II (Philip Augustus, r. 1180–1223) succeeded to the throne. Philip brought the barons under his control and expanded the royal domains to include Normandy in the north and most of Languedoc in the south, laying the foundations for the modern nation of France. Renowned as "the maker of Paris," he gave the city its walls, paved its streets, and built the palace of the Louvre (now one of the world's great museums) to house the royal family. Although Rome remained the religious center of Western Christendom, Paris became its intellectual capital. The University of Paris attracted the best minds from all over Europe. Virtually every thinker of note in the Gothic world at some point studied or taught at Paris.

Even in the Romanesque period, Paris was a center of learning. Its Cathedral School professors were known as Schoolmen and the philosophy they developed as Scholasticism. The greatest of the early Schoolmen was Peter Abelard (1079–1142), a champion of logical reasoning. Abelard and his contemporaries had been introduced to the writings of the Greek philosopher Aristotle through the Arabic scholars of Islamic Spain. Abelard applied Aristotle's system of rational inquiry to the interpretation of religious belief. Until the 12th century, truth had been considered the exclusive property of divine revelation as given in the Holy Scriptures. But the Schoolmen, using Aristotle's method, sought to demonstrate that reason alone could lead to certain truths. Their goal was to prove the central articles of Christian faith by argument (*disputatio*). In Scholastic argument, a possibility is stated, an authoritative view is cited in objection, the positions are reconciled, and, finally, a reply is given to each of the rejected original arguments.

One of Abelard's greatest critics was Bernard of Clairvaux (see "Bernard of Clairvaux," Chapter 17, page 461), who believed Scholasticism was equivalent to questioning Christian dogma. Although Bernard succeeded in 1140 in having the Church officially condemn Abelard's doctrines, the Schoolmen's philosophy developed systematically until it became the dominant Western philosophy of the late Middle Ages. By the 13th century, the Schoolmen of Paris already had organized as a professional guild of master scholars, separate from the numerous Church schools overseen by the bishop of Paris. The structure of the Parisian guild served as the model for many other European universities.

The greatest exponent of Abelard's Scholasticism was Thomas Aquinas (1225–1274), an Italian monk who became a saint. Aquinas settled in Paris in 1244. There, the German theologian Albertus Magnus instructed him in Aristotelean philosophy. Aquinas went on to become an influential teacher at the University of Paris. His most famous work, the *Summa Theologica* (left unfinished at his death), is a model of the Scholastic approach to knowledge. Aquinas divided his treatise into books, the books into questions, the questions into articles, each article into objections with contradictions and responses, and, finally, answers to the objections. He set forth five ways to prove the existence of God by rational argument. Aquinas's work remains the foundation of contemporary Catholic teaching.

The earliest manifestations of the Gothic spirit in art and architecture—the sculptured portals and vaulted east end of Suger's Saint-Denis (FIGS. 18-1 to 18-3)—are contemporary with the first stages of Scholastic philosophy. Both also originated in Paris and its environs. Many art historians have noted the parallels between them, how the logical thrust and counterthrust of Gothic construction, the geometric relationships of building parts, and the systematic organization of the iconographical programs of Gothic church portals coincide with Scholastic principles and methods. Although no documents exist linking the scholars, builders, and sculptors, Gothic art and architecture shared with Scholasticism an insistence on systematic design and procedure. They both sought stable, coherent, consistent, and structurally intelligible solutions.

FIG. 17-12) reveals a much deeper penetration of the wall mass in the later building. At Laon, as in Gothic architecture generally, the operating principle was to reduce sheer mass and replace it with intricately framed voids.

PARIS AND NOTRE-DAME About 1130, Louis VI moved his official residence to Paris, spurring much commercial activity and a great building boom. Paris soon became the leading city of France, indeed of all northern Europe (see "Paris: The Intellectual Capital of Gothic Europe," above), making a new cathedral a necessity. Notre-Dame of Paris (FIG. **18-10**) occupies a picturesque site on an island in the Seine River called the Île-de-la-Cité. The Gothic church replaced a large Merovingian basilica and has a complicated building history. The choir and transept were completed by 1182; the nave, by ca. 1225; and the facade not until ca. 1250–1260. Sexpartite vaults covered the nave, as at Laon. The original elevation (the builders modified the design as work progressed) had four stories, but the scheme (FIG. 18-9b) differed from Laon's (FIG. 18-9a). In place of the triforium over the gallery, stained glass *oculi* (singular *oculus*, a small round window) opened up the wall below the clerestory lancets. As a result, two of the four stories were now filled by windows, further reducing the masonry area. (This four-story nave elevation can be seen in only one bay in FIG. 18-10, immediately to the right of the south transept and partially hidden by it.)

FLYING BUTTRESSES To hold the much thinner—and taller (compare FIGS. 18-9a and 18-9b)—walls of Notre-Dame in place, the unknown architect introduced *flying buttresses*, exterior arches that spring from the lower roofs over the aisles and ambulatory (FIG. 18-10) and counter the outward thrust of the nave vaults. Flying buttresses seem to have been employed as early as 1150 in a few smaller churches, but at Notre-Dame in Paris they circle a great urban cathedral. The internal quadrant arches beneath the aisle roofs at Durham (see FIG. 17-16, *top*), also employed at Laon, perform a similar function and may be regarded as precedents for exposed Gothic flying buttresses. The combination of precisely positioned flying buttresses and rib vaults with pointed arches was the ideal solution to the problem of constructing towering naves with huge windows filled with stained glass. The flying buttresses, like slender extended fingers holding up the walls, also are important elements contributing to the distinctive "look" of Gothic cathedrals (see "The Gothic Cathedral," page 488).

The Gothic Cathedral

The great cathedrals erected throughout Europe in the later 12th and 13th centuries are the enduring symbols of the Gothic age. These towering structures are eloquent testimonies to the extraordinary skill of the architects, engineers, carpenters, masons, sculptors, glassworkers, and metalsmiths who constructed and decorated the buildings.

Most of the architectural components of Gothic cathedrals appeared in earlier structures, but the way Gothic architects combined the elements made the buildings unique expressions of medieval faith. The key ingredients of the Gothic "recipe" were rib vaults with pointed arches, flying buttresses, and huge colored-glass windows (see "Stained-Glass Windows," page 492). Our "exploded" view of a typical Gothic cathedral illustrates how these and other important Gothic architectural devices worked together.

The Vocabulary of Gothic Architecture

1. *Pinnacle:* A sharply pointed ornament capping the piers or flying buttresses; also used on cathedral facades.

2. *Flying buttresses:* Masonry struts that transfer the thrust of the nave vaults across the roofs of the side aisles and ambulatory to a tall pier rising above the church's exterior wall. Compare the cross-section of Beauvais Cathedral (see FIG. Intro-18).

3. *Vaulting web:* The masonry blocks that fill the area between the ribs of a groin vault.

4. *Diagonal rib:* In plan, one of the ribs that form the X of a groin vault. In the diagrams of rib vaults on page 482, the diagonal ribs are the lines *AC* and *DB*.

5. *Transverse rib:* A rib that crosses the nave or aisle at a 90-degree angle (lines *AB* and *DC* in the diagrams on page 482).

6. *Springing:* The lowest stone of an arch; in Gothic vaulting, the lowest stone of a diagonal or transverse rib.

7. *Clerestory:* The windows below the vaults that form the nave elevation's uppermost level. By using flying buttresses and rib vaults on pointed arches, Gothic architects could build huge clerestory windows and fill them with *stained glass* held in place by ornamental stonework called *tracery*.

8. *Oculus:* A small round window.

9. *Lancet:* A tall, narrow window crowned by a pointed arch.

10. *Triforium:* The story in the nave elevation consisting of arcades, usually blind (FIGS. 18-9c and 18-12), but occasionally filled with stained glass (see FIG. Intro-2).

11. *Nave arcade:* The series of arches supported by piers separating the nave from the side aisles.

12. *Compound pier with shafts (responds):* Also called the *cluster pier,* a pier with a group, or cluster, of attached shafts, or *responds,* extending to the springing of the vaults.

1. Pinnacle
2. Flying Buttress
3. Vaulting Web
4. Diagonal Rib
5. Transverse Rib
6. Springing
7. Clerestory
8. Oculus
9. Lancet
10. Triforium
11. Nave Arcade
12. Compound Pier with Shafts (Responds)

FIRES AND FUNDRAISING Churches burned frequently in the Middle Ages (see "Timber Roofs," Chapter 17, page 451), and church officials often had to raise money suddenly for new building campaigns. In contrast to monastic churches, which usually were small and completed fairly quickly, the building histories of urban cathedrals often extended over decades and sometimes over centuries. Their financing depended largely on collections and public contributions (not always voluntary), and a lack of funds often interrupted building programs. Unforeseen events, such as wars, famines, or plagues, or friction between the town and cathedral authorities would often stop construction, which then might not resume for years. At Reims (FIG. 18-21), the clergy offered *indulgences* (pardons for sins committed) to those who helped underwrite the enormous cost of erecting the cathedral. The rebuilding of Chartres Cathedral after the devastating fire of 1194 took a relatively short 27 years, but at one point the townspeople revolted against the prospect of a heavier tax burden. They stormed the bishop's residence and drove him into exile for four years.

CHARTRES AFTER 1194 Chartres Cathedral's mid-12th-century west facade (FIGS. 18-4 and 18-5) and the masonry of the crypt to the east were all that were left standing after the 1194 conflagration. The crypt housed the most precious relic of Chartres—the mantle of the Virgin, which miraculously survived the fire. For piety and economy, the builders used the crypt for the foundation of the new structure. The incorporation of the old crypt and west facade in the new building determined the church's dimensions, but not its plan or elevation. Architectural historians usually consider the post-1194 Chartres Cathedral the first High Gothic building.

THE HIGH GOTHIC PLAN The Chartres plan (FIG. **18-11**) reveals a new kind of organization. Rectangular nave bays replaced the square bays with sexpartite vaults and the alternate-support system, still present in Early Gothic churches such as Laon Cathedral (FIG. 18-8). The new system, in which a rectangular unit in the nave, defined by its own vault, was flanked by a single square in each aisle rather than two, as before, became the High Gothic norm. A change in vault design and the abandonment of the alternate-support system usually accompanied this new bay arrangement. The High Gothic vault, which covered a relatively smaller area and therefore was braced more easily than its Early Gothic predecessor, had only four parts. The visual effect of these changes was to unify the interior (FIG. **18-12**). The High Gothic architect aligned identical units so that viewers saw them in too rapid a sequence to perceive them as individual volumes of space. The nave became a vast, continuous hall.

THE HIGH GOTHIC ELEVATION The 1194 Chartres Cathedral was also the first church to have been planned from the beginning with flying buttresses, another key High Gothic feature. The flying buttresses made it possible to eliminate the tribune

0 25 50 75 100
⊢———————————⊣ FEET
0   10   20   30
⊢————————⊣ METERS

18-11 Plan of Chartres Cathedral, Chartres, France, as rebuilt after 1194 (after Paul Frankl).

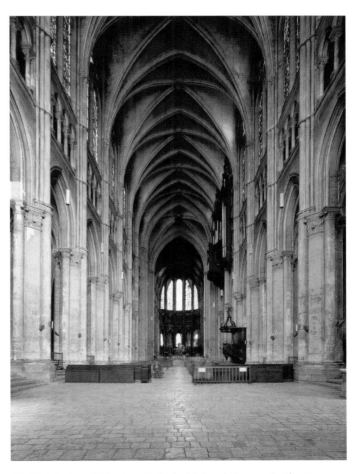

18-12 Interior of Chartres Cathedral (view facing east), Chartres, France, begun 1194.

above the aisle, which had partially braced Romanesque and Early Gothic naves (compare FIG. 18-9*c* with FIGS. 18-9*a* and 18-9*b*). The new High Gothic tripartite nave elevation consisted of arcade, triforium, and clerestory with greatly enlarged windows. The Chartres windows are almost as high as the main arcade and consist of double lancets crowned by a single oculus. The strategic placement of flying buttresses permitted the construction of nave walls with so many voids that heavy masonry played a minor role.

STAINED GLASS Despite the vastly increased size of the clerestory windows, the Chartres nave (FIG. 18-12) is relatively dark. The explanation for this seeming contradiction is that light-muffling colored glass fills the windows. These windows were not meant to illuminate the interior with bright sunlight but to transform natural light into Suger's mystical *lux nova* (see "Stained-Glass Windows," page 492). Chartres retains almost the full complement of its original stained glass, which, although it has a dimming effect, transforms the character of the interior in dramatic fashion. Gothic churches that have lost their original stained-glass windows give a false impression of what their designers intended.

THE VIRGIN'S WINDOW One Chartres window that survived the fire of 1194 and was subsequently reused in the High Gothic cathedral is the tall single lancet the French call *Notre Dame de la Belle Verrière* (Our Lady of the Beautiful Window, FIG. 18-13). The central section, depicting the Virgin Mary enthroned with the Christ Child in her lap, dates to ca. 1170 and has a red background. The framing angels seen against a blue ground were added when the window was reinstalled in the 13th-century choir. The artist represented Mary as the beautiful, young, rather worldly Queen of Heaven, haloed, crowned, and accompanied by the dove of the Holy Spirit. The frontal composition is traditional. Comparing this Virgin and Child with the Theotokos and Child of Hagia Sophia (see FIG. 12-17) highlights not only the greater severity and aloofness of the Byzantine image but also the sharp difference between the light-reflecting mosaic medium and Gothic light-filtering stained glass. Gothic and Byzantine builders used light to transform the material world into the spiritual, but in opposite ways. In Gothic architecture, light entered from outside the building through a screen of stone-set colored glass. In Byzantine architecture, light was reflected from myriad glass tesserae set into the thick masonry wall.

A QUEEN'S GIFT TO CHARTRES Chartres's 13th-century Gothic windows are even more spectacular than the *Belle Verrière* because they were designed from the outset to fill entire walls, thanks to the introduction of flying buttresses. The immense rose window (approximately 43 feet in diameter) and tall lancets of Chartres Cathedral's north transept (FIGS. 18-4 and **18-14**) were the gift of the Queen of France, Blanche of Castile, around 1220. The royal motifs of yellow castles on a red ground and yellow *fleurs-de-lis*—three-petaled iris flowers—on a blue ground fill the eight narrow windows in the rose's lower spandrels. The iconography is also fitting for a queen. The enthroned Virgin and Child appear in the roundel at the center of the rose, which resembles a gem-studded book cover or cloisonné brooch. Around her are four doves of the Holy Spirit and eight angels. Twelve square panels contain images of Old Testament kings, including David and Solomon (at the 12 and 1 o'clock

18-13 Virgin and Child and angels *(Notre Dame de la Belle Verrière)*, window in the choir of Chartres Cathedral, Chartres, France, ca. 1170, with 13th-century side panels. Stained glass, 16′ × 7′ × 8″.

positions respectively). These are the royal ancestors of Christ. Isaiah (11:1–3) had prophesied that the Messiah would come from the family of the patriarch Jesse, father of David. The genealogical "tree of Jesse" is a familiar motif in medieval art. Below, in the lancets, are Saint Anne and the baby Virgin flanked by four of Christ's Old Testament ancestors, Melchizedek, David, Solomon, and Aaron, echoing the royal genealogy of the rose, but at a larger scale. Many Gothic stained-glass windows also present narrative scenes, and their iconographical programs are sometimes as complex as those of the sculptured church portals.

The rose and lancets change in hue and intensity with the hours, turning solid architecture into a floating vision of the celestial heavens. Almost the entire mass of wall opens up into stained glass, which is held in place by an intricate stone armature of bar tracery. Here, the Gothic passion for luminous colored light led to a most daring and successful attempt to subtract all superfluous material bulk just short of destabilizing the structure. That this vast, complex fabric of stone-set glass has maintained its structural integrity for almost 800 years attests to the Gothic builders' engineering genius.

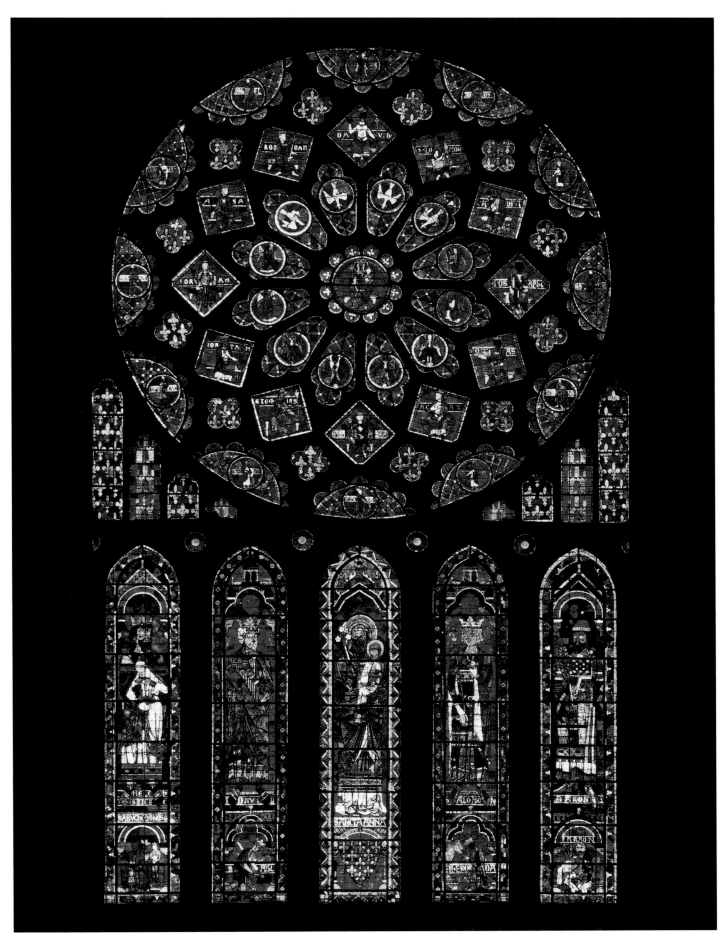

18-14 Rose window and lancets, north transept, Chartres Cathedral, Chartres, France, ca. 1220. Stained glass, rose window approx. 43′ in diameter.

Stained-Glass Windows

Stained glass is almost synonymous with Gothic architecture. No other age produced windows of such rich color and beauty. The art of making colored glass is, however, very old. Egyptian artists excelled at fashioning colorful glass vessels and other objects for both home and tomb. Archaeologists also have uncovered thousands of colored-glass artifacts at hundreds of sites throughout the classical world.

Although the technology of manufacturing colored glass was ancient, the way artists used stained glass in the Gothic period was new. Stained-glass windows were not just installed to introduce color and religious iconography into church interiors. That could have been done—and was done much earlier—with both mural paintings and mosaics, often with magnificent effect. But stained-glass windows differ from those earlier techniques in one all-important respect. They do not conceal walls; they replace them. And they transmit rather than reflect light, filtering and transforming the natural sunlight as it enters the building. Abbot Suger called this colored light "lux nova" (see "Abbot Suger," page 481). Hugh of Saint-Victor (1096–1142), a prominent Parisian theologian who died while Suger's Saint-Denis was under construction, also commented on the special mystical quality of stained-glass windows. "Stained-glass windows," he wrote, "are the Holy Scriptures . . . and since their brilliance lets the splendor of the True Light pass into the church, they enlighten those inside."[1] William Durandus, Bishop of Mende, expressed a similar sentiment at the end of the 13th century: "The glass windows in a church are Holy Scriptures, which expel the wind and the rain, that is, all things hurtful, but transmit the light of the True Sun, that is, God, into the hearts of the faithful."[2]

As early as the fourth century, architects used colored glass for church windows. Perfection of the technique came gradually. The stained-glass windows in the Saint-Denis ambulatory (FIG. 18-1) already show a high degree of skill. According to Suger, they were "painted by the exquisite hands of many masters from different regions," proving that the art was known widely at that time.[3]

The manufacture of stained-glass windows was costly and labor-intensive. The full process was recorded around 1100 in a treatise on the arts written by a Benedictine monk named Theophilus. First, the master designer drew the exact composition of the planned window on a wooden panel, indicating all the linear details and noting the colors for each section. Glassblowers provided flat sheets of glass of different colors to *glaziers* (glassworkers), who cut the windowpanes to the required size and shape with special iron shears. Glaziers produced an even greater range of colors by *flashing* (fusing one layer of colored glass to another). Purple, for example, resulted from the fusing of red and blue (compare the color triangle, FIG. Intro-10). Next, painters added details such as faces, hands, hair, and clothing in enamel by tracing the master design on the wood panel through the colored glass. Then they heated the painted glass to fuse the enamel to the surface. The glaziers then *leaded* the various fragments of glass; that is, they joined them by strips of lead called *cames*. The leading not only held the (usually quite small) pieces together but also separated the colors to heighten the effect of the design as a whole. The distinctive character of Gothic stained-glass windows is largely the result of this combination of fine linear details with broad flat expanses of color framed by black lead. Finally, the glassworkers strengthened the completed window with an armature of iron bands, which in the 12th century formed a grid over the whole design (FIG. 18-13). In the 13th century, the bands followed the outlines of the medallions and of the surrounding areas (FIGS. 18-14 and 18-23).

The form of the stone window frames into which the glass was set also evolved throughout the Gothic era. Early rose windows, such as the one on Chartres Cathedral's west facade (FIG. 18-4), have stained glass held in place by *plate tracery*. The glass fills only the "punched holes" in the heavy ornamental stonework. *Bar tracery* (FIG. 18-14), a later development, is much more slender. The stained-glass windows fill almost the entire opening, and the stonework is unobtrusive, more like delicate leading than masonry wall.

[1] Attributed to Hugh of Saint-Victor, *Speculum de mysteriis ecclesiae*, Sermon 2.

[2] William Durandus, *Rationale divinorum officiorum*, 1.1.24. Translated by John Mason Neale and Benjamin Webb, *The Symbolism of Churches and Church Ornaments* (Leeds, England: T. W. Green, 1843), 28.

[3] Erwin Panofsky, trans., *Abbot Suger on the Abbey Church of Saint-Denis and Its Art Treasures,* 2nd ed. (Princeton: Princeton University Press, 1979), 73.

PORCH OF THE CONFESSORS The sculptures adorning the portals of the two new Chartres transepts erected after the 1194 fire are also prime examples of the new High Gothic spirit. As at Laon (FIG. 18-7) and Paris (FIG. 18-10) Cathedrals, the Chartres transept portals project more forcefully from the church than do the Early Gothic portals of its west facade (compare FIGS. 18-4 and 18-5). Similarly, the statues of saints on the portal jambs are more independent from the architectural framework. Three figures from the Porch of the Confessors (FIG. **18-15**) in the south transept reveal the great changes Gothic sculpture underwent since the Royal Portal statues (FIG. 18-6) of the mid-12th century. These changes recall in many ways the revolutionary developments in ancient Greek sculpture during the transition from the Archaic to the Classical style (see Chapter 5). The Chartres transept statues we illustrate date from 1220 to 1230 and represent Saints Martin, Jerome, and Gregory. Although the figures are still attached to columns, the architectural setting does not determine their poses as much as it did on the west portals. The saints communicate quietly with one another, like waiting dignitaries. They turn slightly toward and away from each other, breaking the rigid vertical lines that, on the Royal Portal, fix the figures immovably. The drapery folds are not stiff and shallow vertical accents, as on the west facade. The fabric falls and laps over the bodies in soft, if still regular, folds.

The treatment of the faces is even more remarkable. The sculptor gave the figures individualized features and distinctive

18-15 Saints Martin, Jerome, and Gregory, jamb statues, Porch of the Confessors (right doorway), south transept, Chartres Cathedral, Chartres, France, ca. 1220–1230.

personalities and clothed them in the period's liturgical costumes. Saint Martin is a tall, intense priest with gaunt features (compare the spiritually moved but not particularized face of the Moissac prophet in FIG. 17-24). Saint Jerome appears as a kindly, practical administrator-scholar, holding his copy of the Scriptures. At the right, the introspective Saint Gregory seems lost in thought as he listens to the dove of the Holy Ghost on his shoulder. Thus, the sculptor did not contrast the three men simply in terms of their poses, gestures, and attributes but, most particularly and emphatically, as persons. Personality, revealed in human faces, makes the real difference.

THE IDEAL WARRIOR The south-transept figure of Saint Theodore (FIG. **18-16**), the martyred warrior on the Porch of the Martyrs, presents an even sharper contrast with Early Gothic jamb statues. The sculptor portrayed Theodore as the ideal Christian knight and clothed him in the cloak and chain-mail armor of Gothic Crusaders. The handsome, long-haired youth holds his spear firmly in his right hand and rests his left hand on his shield. He turns his head to the left and swings out his hip to the right. The body's resulting torsion and pronounced sway call to mind Classical Greek statuary, especially the contrapposto stance of Polykleitos's *Spear Bearer* (see FIG. 5-38). It is not inappropriate to speak of the changes that occurred in 13th-century Gothic sculpture as a second "Classical revolution."

18-16 Saint Theodore, jamb statue, Porch of the Martyrs (left doorway), south transept, Chartres Cathedral, Chartres, France, ca. 1230.

18-17 ROBERT DE LUZARCHES, THOMAS DE CORMONT, and RENAUD DE CORMONT, interior of Amiens Cathedral (view facing east), Amiens, France, begun 1220.

18-18 ROBERT DE LUZARCHES, THOMAS DE CORMONT, and RENAUD DE CORMONT, vaults, clerestory, and triforium of the choir of Amiens Cathedral, Amiens, France, begun 1220.

THE QUEST FOR HEIGHT Chartres Cathedral was one of the most influential buildings in the history of architecture. Its builders set a pattern that many other Gothic architects followed, even if they refined the details. Construction of Amiens Cathedral (FIGS. **18-17** to **18-19**) began in 1220, while work was still in progress at Chartres. The architects were ROBERT DE LUZARCHES, THOMAS DE CORMONT, and RENAUD DE CORMONT. The builders finished the nave by 1236 and the radiating chapels by 1247, but work on the choir continued until almost 1270. The Amiens elevation (FIGS. 18-9*d* and 18-17) derived from the High Gothic formula established at Chartres (FIGS. 18-9*c* and 18-12). But Amiens Cathedral's proportions are even more elegant, and the number and complexity of the lancet windows in both its clerestory and triforium are even greater. The whole design reflects the builders' confident use of the complete High Gothic structural vocabulary: the rectangular-bay system, the four-part rib vault, and a buttressing system that permitted almost complete dissolution of heavy masses and thick weight-bearing walls. At Amiens, the concept of a self-sustaining skeletal architecture reached full maturity. What remained as walls was stretched like a skin between the piers and seems to serve no purpose other than to provide a weather screen for the interior (FIG. 18-18).

Amiens Cathedral is one of the most impressive examples of the French Gothic obsession with constructing ever taller cathedrals. Using their new skeletal frames of stone, French builders attempted goals almost beyond limit, pushing to new heights with ever more slender supports. The nave vaults at Laon rise to a height of about 80 feet; at Paris, to 107 feet; and at Chartres, to 118 feet.

Those at Amiens are 144 feet above the floor (FIG. 18-9). The tense, strong lines of the Amiens vault ribs converge to the colonnettes and speed down the shell-like walls to the compound piers. Almost every part of the superstructure has its corresponding element below. The overall effect is of effortless strength, of a buoyant lightness one normally does not associate with stone architecture. Viewed directly from below, the choir vaults (FIG. 18-18) seem like a canopy, tentlike and suspended from bundled masts. The light flooding in from the clerestory makes the vaults seem even more insubstantial. The effect recalls another great building, one utterly different from Amiens but where light also plays a defining role: Hagia Sophia in Constantinople (see FIG. 12-5). Once again, the designers reduced the building's physical mass by structural ingenuity and daring, and light dematerializes further what remains. If Hagia Sophia is the perfect expression of Byzantine spirituality in architecture, Amiens, with its soaring vaults and giant windows admitting divine colored light, is its Gothic counterpart.

THE HIGH GOTHIC FACADE Work began on the Amiens west facade (FIG. 18-19) at the same time as the nave (1220). Its lower parts seem to reflect the influence of Laon Cathedral (FIG. 18-7) in the spacing of the funnel-like and gable-covered portals. But the Amiens builders punctured the upper parts of the facade to an even greater degree than did the Laon designer. The deep piercing of walls and towers at Amiens seems to have left few continuous surfaces for decoration, but the ones that remained were covered with a network of colonnettes, arches, pinnacles, rosettes, and other decorative stonework that visually screens and nearly dissolves the structure's solid core. Sculpture also extends to the

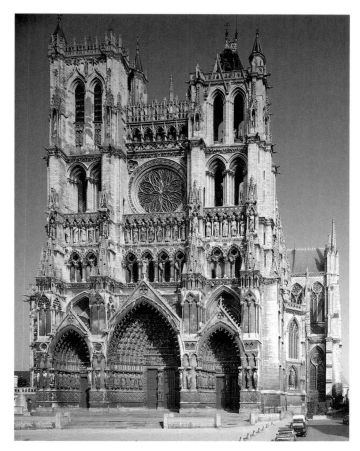

18-19 ROBERT DE LUZARCHES, THOMAS DE CORMONT, and RENAUD DE CORMONT, west facade of Amiens Cathedral, Amiens, France, begun 1220.

areas above the portals, especially the band of statues (the so-called kings' gallery) running the full width of the facade directly below the rose window (with 15th-century tracery). The uneven towers were later additions. The shorter one dates from the 14th century, the taller one from the 15th century.

THE BEAUTIFUL GOD The most prominent statue on the Amiens facade is of Christ (the *Beau Dieu*, or Beautiful God) on the central doorway's trumeau (FIG. **18-20**). The sculptor fully modeled Christ's figure, enveloping his body with massive drapery folds cascading from his waist. The statue stands freely and is as independent of its architectural setting as any Gothic facade statue ever was. Nonetheless, the sculptor still placed an architectural canopy over the figure's head. It is in the latest Gothic style, mimicking the east end of a 13th-century cathedral with a series of radiating chapels pierced by elegant lancet windows. Above the canopy is the great central tympanum with the representation of Christ as Last Judge. But the *Beau Dieu* is a handsome, kindly figure who does not strike terror into sinners. Instead he blesses those who enter the church and tramples a lion and a dragon symbolizing the evil forces in the world. This image of Christ gives humankind hope in salvation. The *Beau Dieu* epitomizes the bearded, benevolent image of Christ that replaced the youthful Early Christian Christ (see FIG. 11-6) and the stern Byzantine Pantocrator (see FIGS. 12-21 and 12-24) as the preferred representation of the Savior in later European art. The figure's quiet grace and grandeur also contrast sharply with the emotional intensity of the twisting Romanesque prophet carved in relief on the Moissac trumeau (see FIG. 17-24).

18-20 Christ *(Beau Dieu)*, trumeau statue of central doorway, west facade, Amiens Cathedral, Amiens, France, ca. 1220–1235.

18-21 West facade of Reims Cathedral, Reims, France, ca. 1225–1290.

GLASS REPLACES STONE Construction of Reims Cathedral (FIG. **18-21**) began only a few years after work commenced at Amiens. The Reims builders carried the High Gothic style of the Amiens west facade still further, both architecturally and sculpturally. The two facades, although similar, display some significant differences. The kings' gallery of statues at Reims is *above* the great rose window, and the figures stand in taller and more ornate frames. In fact, the designer "stretched" every detail of the facade. The openings in the towers and those to the left and right of the rose window are taller, narrower, and more intricately decorated, and they more closely resemble the elegant lancets of the clerestory within. A pointed arch also frames the rose window itself, and the pinnacles over the portals are taller and more elaborate than those at Amiens. Most striking, however, is the treatment of the tympanums over the doorways, where stained-glass windows replaced the stone relief sculpture of earlier facades. The contrast with Romanesque heavy masonry construction (see FIG. 17-12) is extreme. But the rapid transformation of the Gothic facade since the 12th-century designs of Saint-Denis and Chartres (FIG. 18-4) and even Laon (FIG. 18-7) is no less noteworthy.

STATUES BEGIN TO CONVERSE At Reims the fully ripened Gothic style also can be seen in sculpture. At first glance, the jamb statues of the west portals of Reims Cathedral (FIG. **18-22**)

18-22 Visitation, jamb statues of central doorway, west facade, Reims Cathedral, Reims, France, ca. 1230.

appear to be completely detached from their architectural background. The sculptors shrank the supporting columns into insignificance so that they in no way restrict the free and easy movements of the full-bodied figures. (Compare the Reims statue-columns with those of the Royal Portal of Chartres, FIG. 18-6, where the background columns occupy a volume equal to that of the figures.) The two Reims jamb statues we illustrate portray Saint Elizabeth visiting the Virgin Mary before the birth of Jesus. They are two of a series of statues celebrating Mary's life and are further testimony to the Virgin's central role in Gothic iconography.

The sculptor of the Visitation group reveals a classicizing bent startlingly unlike anything seen since Roman times. The artist probably studied actual classical statuary in France. Although art historians have been unable to pinpoint specific models, the heads of both women look like ancient Roman portraits. The youthful Mary, for example, resembles the women of the Antonine dynasty, especially Faustina the Younger, Marcus Aurelius's wife. Whatever the sculptor's source, the statues are astonishing approximations of the classical naturalistic style. The Reims master even incorporated the Greek contrapposto posture, going far beyond the stance of the Chartres Saint Theodore (FIG. 18-16). At Reims, the swaying of the hips is much more pronounced. The right legs bend, and the knees press through the rippling folds of the garments. The sculptor also set the figures' arms in motion. Mary and Elizabeth turn their faces toward each other and they converse through gestures. In the Reims Visitation group, the formerly isolated Gothic jamb statues became actors in a biblical narrative.

A RADIANT ROYAL CHAPEL The stained-glass windows inserted into the portal tympanums of Reims Cathedral exemplify the wall-dissolving High Gothic architectural style. The architect of Sainte-Chapelle (FIG. **18-23**) in Paris extended this style to an entire building. Louis IX built Sainte-Chapelle, joined to the royal palace, as a repository for the crown of thorns and other relics of Christ's Passion he had purchased in 1239 from his cousin Baldwin II, the Latin emperor of Constantinople. The chapel is a masterpiece of the so-called *Rayonnant* (radiant) style of the High Gothic age, which dominated the second half of the century. It was associated with the royal Parisian court of Saint Louis (see "Louis IX: The Saintly King," page 498). In Sainte-Chapelle, the dissolution of walls and the reduction of the bulk of the supports were carried to the point that some 6,450 square feet of stained glass make up more than three-quarters of the structure. The supporting elements were reduced so much that they are hardly more than large *mullions,* or vertical stone bars. The emphasis is on the extreme slenderness of the architectural forms and on linearity in general. Although the chapel was heavily restored in the 19th century (after damage during the French Revolution), it has retained most of its original 13th-century stained glass. Sainte-Chapelle's enormous windows filter the light and fill the interior with an unearthly rose-violet atmosphere. Approximately 49 feet high and 15 feet wide, they were the largest designed up to their time.

THE VIRGIN AS QUEEN The "court style" of Saint Louis was not confined to architecture. Indeed, the elegance and delicacy displayed in Sainte-Chapelle's design permeated the pictorial arts as well. By the early 14th century, a mannered elegance that marks Late Gothic art in general had replaced the monumental and

Louis IX: The Saintly King

The royal patron behind the Parisian "court style" of Gothic art and architecture was King Louis IX (1215–1270; r. 1226–1270), grandson of Philip Augustus. Louis inherited the throne when he was only 12 years old, so until he reached adulthood six years later, his mother, Blanche of Castile, granddaughter of Eleanor of Aquitaine (see "Romanesque Countesses, Queens, and Nuns," Chapter 17, page 473), served as France's regent.

The French regarded Louis as the ideal king, and in 1297, 27 years after Louis's death, Pope Boniface VIII declared him a saint. In his own time, Louis was revered for his piety, justice, truthfulness, and charity. His almsgiving and his donations to religious foundations were extravagant. He especially favored the *mendicant* (begging) orders, the Dominicans and Franciscans (see "Mendicant Orders and Confraternities," Chapter 19, page 524). He admired their poverty, piety, and self-sacrificing disregard of material things.

Louis launched two unsuccessful Crusades, the Seventh (1248–1254, when, in her son's absence, Blanche was again French regent) and the Eighth (1270). He died in Tunisia during the latter. As a crusading knight who lost his life in the service of the Church, Louis personified the chivalric virtues of courage, loyalty, and self-sacrifice. Saint Louis united in his person the best qualities of the Christian knight, the benevolent monarch, and the holy man. He became the model of medieval Christian kingship.

Louis's political accomplishments were also noteworthy. He subdued the unruly French barons, and between 1243 and 1314 no one seriously challenged the crown. He negotiated a treaty with Henry III, king of France's traditional enemy, England. Such was his reputation for integrity and just dealing that he served as arbiter in at least a dozen international disputes. So successful was he as peacekeeper that despite civil wars through most of the 13th century, international peace prevailed. Under Saint Louis, medieval France was at its most prosperous, and its art and architecture were admired and imitated throughout Europe.

18-23 Interior of the upper chapel, Sainte-Chapelle, Paris, France, 1243–1248.

18-24 Virgin and Child (*Virgin of Paris*), Notre-Dame, Paris, France, early 14th century.

solemn sculptural style of the High Gothic portals. Perhaps the best example of the late French court style in sculpture is the statue nicknamed the *Virgin of Paris* (FIG. **18-24**) because of its location in the Parisian Cathedral of Notre-Dame. The sculptor portrayed Mary as a worldly queen, decked out in royal garments and wearing a heavy gem-encrusted crown. The Christ Child is equally richly attired and is very much the infant prince in the arms of his young mother. The tender, anecdotal characterization of mother and son represents a further humanization of the portrayal of religious figures in Gothic sculpture.

The playful interaction of an adult and an infant in the *Virgin of Paris* may be compared with the similarly composed statuary group of Hermes and the infant Dionysos (see FIG. 5-62) by the Greek sculptor Praxiteles. Indeed, the exaggerated swaying S curve of the Virgin's body superficially resembles the shallow S curve Praxiteles introduced in the fourth century BCE. But unlike its Late Classical predecessor, the Late Gothic S curve was not organic (derived from within the figure), nor was it a rational, if pleasing, organization of human anatomical parts. Rather, the Gothic curve was an artificial form imposed on figures, a decorative device that produced the desired effect of elegance but that had nothing to do with body structure. In fact, in our example, the body is quite lost behind the heavy drapery, which, deeply cut and hollowed, almost denies the figure a solid existence. The ornamental line the sculptor created with the flexible fabric is analogous to the complex tracery of the Late Gothic style in architecture, which dominated northern Europe in the 14th and 15th centuries.

FLAMBOYANT ARCHITECTURE The change from Rayonnant architecture to the Late Gothic, or *Flamboyant,* style (named for the flamelike appearance of its pointed bar tracery), occurred in the 14th century. The style reached its florid maturity nearly a century later. This period was a difficult one for the French monarchy. Long wars against England and the duchy of Burgundy sapped its economic and cultural strength, and building projects in the royal domain either ceased or never began. Architects accepted the new style most enthusiastically in regions outside the Île-de-France.

Normandy is particularly rich in Flamboyant architecture, and the church of Saint-Maclou (FIG. **18-25**) in Rouen, its capital, is a masterpiece of the Flamboyant style. The church is tiny (only about 75 feet high and 180 feet long) compared to the great Gothic cathedrals. Its facade presents a sharp contrast with the High Gothic style of the 13th century (compare FIGS. 18-19 and 18-21). The five portals (two of them blind) bend outward in an arc. Ornate gables crown the doorways, pierced through and filled with wiry, "flickering" Flamboyant tracery made up of curves and countercurves that form brittle decorative webs and mask the building's structure. The transparency of the pinnacles over the doorways permits visitors to see the central rose window and the flying buttresses, even though they are set well back from the facade. The overlapping of all features, pierced as they are, confuses the structural lines and produces a bewildering complexity of views that is the hallmark of the Flamboyant style.

A DOUBLY FORTIFIED TOWN The Gothic age was truly the age of great cathedrals, but people, of course, also needed and built secular structures such as town halls, palaces, and private residences. In an age of frequent warfare, the feudal barons often constructed fortified castles in places enemies could not easily access. Sometimes thick defensive wall circuits or *ramparts* enclosed entire towns. In time, however, purely defensive wars became ob-

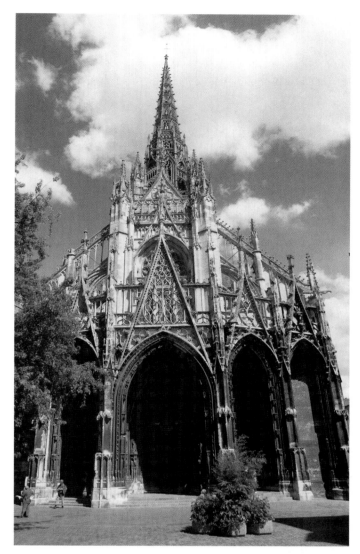

18-25 West facade of Saint-Maclou, Rouen, France, ca. 1500–1514.

solete due to the invention of artillery and improvements in siege craft. The fortress era gradually passed, and throughout Europe once-mighty ramparts fell into ruin.

One of the most famous Gothic fortified towns is Carcassonne (FIG. **18-26**) in Languedoc in southern France. It was the regional center of resistance to the northern forces of royal France. Built on a hill bounded by the Aude River, Carcassonne had been fortified since Roman times. It had Visigothic walls dating from the 6th century, but in the 12th century masons reinforced them. *Battlements* (low parapets) with *crenellations* (composed of alternating solid *merlons* and open *crenels*) protected guards patrolling the stone ring surrounding the town. Carcassonne might be forced to surrender but could not easily be taken by storm.

Within the town's double walls was a fortified castle (FIG. 18-26, *left*) with a massive attached *keep*, a secure tower that could serve as a place of last refuge. Balancing that center of secular power was the bishop's seat, the Cathedral of Saint-Nazaire (FIG. 18-26, *right*). The small church, built between 1269 and 1329, may have been the work of an architect brought in from northern France. In any case, Saint-Nazaire's builders were certainly familiar with the latest developments in architecture in the Île-de-France. Today, Carcassonne provides a rare glimpse of what was once a familiar sight in Gothic France: a tightly contained complex of castle, cathedral, and town within towered walls.

18-26 Aerial view of the fortified town of Carcassonne, France. Bastions and towers, 12th–13th centuries, restored by Eugène Viollet-le-Duc in the 19th century.

TOWERING GUILD HALLS One of the many signs of the growing secularization of urban life in the late Middle Ages was the erection of monumental meeting halls and warehouses for the increasing number of craft guilds that were being formed throughout Europe. An early example is the imposing guild hall and market (FIG. **18-27**) of the clothmakers of Bruges, begun in 1230. Situated in the city's major square, it was a forceful reminder of the important role of artisans and merchants in Gothic Europe. The design combines features of military (the corner "watchtowers" with their crenellations) and church (lancet windows with crowning oculi) architecture. The uppermost, octagonal portion of the tower with its flying buttresses and pinnacles dates to the 15th century, but even the original two-story tower is taller than the rest of the hall. Lofty towers were a common feature of late medieval guild and town halls and were intended to compete for attention and prestige with the towers of city cathedrals.

PROSPERITY AT HOME The fortunes of the new class of wealthy merchants that rose to prominence throughout Europe in the late Middle Ages may not have equaled those of the hereditary royalty, but their power and influence were still enormous. One such figure was the French trader and financier Jacques Coeur (1395–1456), whose astonishing career illustrates how wealth and power could be won and lost by enterprising private citizens. Coeur had banking houses in every city of France and many abroad. He employed more than 300 agents and competed with the great trading republics of Italy. His merchant ships filled the Mediterranean. With the papacy's permission, he traded widely with the Muslims of Egypt and the Middle East and gained concessions there that benefited French commerce for centuries. He was financial adviser to King Charles VII of France and a friend of Pope Nicholas V. The animosity of hundreds of his highborn debtors and competitors eventually led to Coeur's downfall. His enemies framed him on an absurd charge of having poisoned Agnes Sorel, the king's mistress, and he was imprisoned. His vast wealth and property were confiscated and distributed among the king's people. Coeur escaped from prison and made his way to Rome, where the pope warmly received him. He died of fever while leading a fleet of papal war galleys in the eastern Mediterranean.

Jacques Coeur's great town house (FIG. **18-28**), built between 1443 and 1451 in his native city of Bourges, still stands. It is the best-preserved example of Late Gothic domestic architecture.

18-27 Hall of the cloth guild, Bruges, Netherlands, begun 1230.

the production of fine books. The famous Florentine poet Dante Alighieri (1265–1321), in fact, referred to Paris in his *Divine Comedy* of ca. 1310–1320 as the city famed for the art of illumination.[2] Indeed, the Gothic period is when book manufacture shifted from monastic scriptoria shut off from the world to urban workshops staffed by laypersons. The owners of these new for-profit secular businesses sold their products to the royal family, scholars, and prosperous merchants. Concentrated in Paris, these Gothic shops were the forerunners of modern publishing houses.

THE ART OF GEOMETRY One of the most intriguing Parisian manuscripts preserved today was not, however, produced for sale. It is the personal sketchbook compiled by VILLARD DE HONNECOURT, an early 13th-century master mason. Its pages contain details of buildings, plans of choirs with radiating chapels, church towers, lifting devices, a sawmill, stained-glass windows, and other subjects of obvious interest to architects and masons. But also sprinkled liberally throughout the pages are drawings depicting religious and worldly figures, as well as animals, some realistic and others purely fantastic.

On the page we illustrate (FIG. **18-29**), Villard demonstrated the value of the *ars de geometria* (art of geometry) to artists. He showed that both natural forms and buildings are based on simple geometric shapes such as the square, circle, and triangle. Even where he

18-28 House of Jacques Coeur, Bourges, France, 1443–1451.

The house's plan is irregular, with the units arranged around an open courtyard. The service areas (maintenance shops and storage, servants' quarters, baths) occupy the ground level. The upper stories house the great hall and auxiliary rooms used for offices and family living rooms.

The focus of the broad facade is a tall central section with a very steep pyramidal roof, a spire-capped tower with Flamboyant tracery, a large pointed-arch stained-glass window, and two doorways (one for pedestrians and the larger one for horses and carriages). The elegant canopied niche beneath the great window once housed a royal equestrian statue. A comparable statue of Coeur on horseback dominated the facade opening onto the interior courtyard. An unusual feature of the external facade is the pair of false windows with life-size relief sculptures of a male and a female servant looking down upon passersby in the street. Jacques Coeur's house is both a splendid example of Late Gothic architecture and a monumental symbol of the period's new secular spirit—an expression of the triumph of city culture, of capital accumulation, and of the desire for worldly convenience and proud display.

Book Illumination and Luxury Arts

Paris's claim as the intellectual center of Gothic Europe (see "Paris," page 487) did not rest solely on the stature of its university faculty and on the reputation of its architects, masons, sculptors, and stained-glass makers. The city was also a renowned center for

18-29 VILLARD DE HONNECOURT, figures based on geometric shapes, folio 18 verso of a sketchbook, from Paris, France, ca. 1220–1235. Ink on vellum, $9\frac{1}{4}'' \times 6''$. Bibliothèque Nationale, Paris.

claimed to have drawn his animals from nature, he composed his figures around a skeleton not of bones but of abstract geometric forms. Geometry was, in Villard's words, "strong help in drawing figures."

But geometry played a symbolic as well as a practical role in Gothic art and architecture. Gothic artists, architects, and theologians alike thought the triangle, for example, embodied the idea of the Trinity of God the Father, Christ, and the Holy Spirit. The circle, which has neither a beginning nor an end, symbolized the eternity of the one God. When Gothic architects based their designs on the art of geometry, building their forms out of abstract shapes laden with symbolic meaning, they believed they were working according to the divinely established laws of nature.

GOD AS ARCHITECT A vivid illustration of this concept appears as the frontispiece (FIG. **18-30**) of a moralized Bible produced in Paris during the 1220s. *Moralized Bibles* are heavily illustrated, each page pairing paintings of Old and New Testament episodes with explanations of their moral significance. The page we show does not conform to this formula because it is the introduction to all that follows. Above the illustration, the scribe wrote (in French rather than Latin): "Here God creates heaven and earth, the sun and moon, and all the elements." God appears as the architect of the world, shaping the universe with the aid of a compass. Within

the perfect circle already created are the spherical sun and moon and the unformed matter that will become the earth once God applies the same geometric principles to it. In contrast to the biblical account of Creation, in which God created the sun, moon, and stars after the earth had been formed, and made the world by sheer force of will and a simple "Let there be . . ." command, the Gothic artist portrayed God as an industrious architect, creating the universe with some of the same tools used by mortal builders.

A BIBLE FIT FOR A QUEEN Not surprisingly, most of the finest Gothic books known today belonged to the French monarchy. Saint Louis in particular was an avid collector of both secular and religious books. The library he and his royal predecessors and successors formed was vast. It eventually became the core of France's national library, the Bibliothèque Nationale. One of the books the royal family commissioned is a moralized Bible now in the collection of New York's Pierpont Morgan Library. Louis's mother, Blanche of Castile, ordered the Bible during her regency (1226–1234) for her teenage son. The dedication page (FIG. **18-31**) has a costly gold background and depicts Blanche and Louis enthroned beneath triple-lobed arches and miniature cityscapes. The latter can be compared to the architectural canopies above the heads of contemporaneous French portal statues (FIG. 18-20). Below, in

18-30 God as architect of the world, folio 1 verso of a moralized Bible, from Paris, France, ca. 1220–1230. Ink, tempera, and gold leaf on vellum, $1' 1\frac{1}{2}'' \times 8\frac{1}{4}''$. Österreichische Nationalbibliothek, Vienna.

The preparation of the illuminated pages also involved several hands. Some artists, for example, specialized in painting borders or initials. Only the workshop head or one of the most advanced assistants would paint the main figural scenes. Given this division of labor and the assembly-line nature of Gothic book production, it is astonishing how uniform the style is on a single page, as well as from page to page, in most illuminated manuscripts.

SAINT LOUIS'S PSALTER The golden background of Blanche's Bible is unusual and has no parallel in Gothic windows. But the radiance of stained glass probably inspired the glowing color of other 13th-century Parisian illuminated manuscripts. In some cases, masters in the same urban workshop produced both glass and books. Many art historians believe that the *Psalter of Saint Louis* (FIG. **18-32**) is one of several books produced in Paris for Louis IX by artists associated with those who made the stained glass for his Sainte-Chapelle. Certainly, the painted architectural setting in Louis's psalter reflects the pierced screenlike lightness and transparency of royal buildings such as Sainte-Chapelle. The painted figures also express the same aristocratic elegance as the Rayonnant "court style" of architecture favored by royal Paris. The intense colors, especially the blues, emulate glass. The borders resemble glass partitioned by leading. And the gables, pierced by rose windows with bar tracery, are standard Rayonnant architectural features.

The page from the *Psalter of Saint Louis* shown here (FIG. 18-32) represents Abraham and the three angels. Christians believe that the Old Testament story prefigures the Christian Trinity (see "Jewish Subjects in Christian Art," Chapter 11, page 305). The subject was

18-31 Blanche of Castile, Louis IX, and two monks, dedication page (folio 8 recto) of a moralized Bible, from Paris, France, 1226–1234. Ink, tempera, and gold leaf on vellum, 1′ 3″ × 10½″. Pierpont Morgan Library, New York.

similar architectural frames, are a monk and a scribe. The older clergyman dictates a sacred text to his young apprentice. The scribe already has divided his page into two columns of four roundels each, a format often used for the paired illustrations of moralized Bibles. The inspirations for such designs were probably the roundels of Gothic stained-glass windows (compare the borders of the *Belle Verrière* window at Chartres, FIG. 18-13, and the windows of Louis's own, later, Sainte-Chapelle, FIG. 18-23).

The picture of Gothic book production on the dedication page of Blanche of Castile's moralized Bible is a very abbreviated one, as was the view of a monastic scriptorium discussed earlier (see FIG. 16-10). The manufacturing process used in the workshops of 13th-century Paris did not differ significantly from that of 10th-century Tábara. It involved many steps and numerous specialized artists, scribes, and assistants of varying skill levels. The Benedictine abbot Johannes Trithemius (1462–1516) described the way books were still made in his day in his treatise *In Praise of Scribes:*

> If you do not know how to write, you still can assist the scribes in various ways. One of you can correct what another has written. Another can add the rubrics [headings] to the corrected text. A third can add initials and signs of division. Still another can arrange the leaves and attach the binding. Another of you can prepare the covers, the leather, the buckles and clasps. All sorts of assistance can be offered the scribe to help him pursue his work without interruption. He needs many things which can be prepared by others: parchment cut, flattened and ruled for script, ready ink and pens. You will always find something with which to help the scribe.[3]

18-32 Abraham and the three angels, folio 7 verso of the *Psalter of Saint Louis,* from Paris, France, 1253–1270. Ink, tempera, and gold leaf on vellum, 5″ × 3½″. Bibliothèque Nationale, Paris.

upper panel, Samuel anoints the youthful David. Below, while King Saul looks on, David prepares to hurl his slingshot at his most famous opponent, the giant Goliath (who already touches the wound on his forehead!). And then, in a classic example of continuous narration, David slays Goliath with his sword.

Master Honoré's linear treatment of hair, his figures' delicate hands and gestures, and their elegant swaying postures are typical of Parisian painting of the time. But this painter was much more interested than most of his colleagues in giving his figures sculptural volume and showing the play of light on their bodies. Honoré was not concerned with locating his figures in space, however. The Goliath panel in the *Breviary of Philippe le Bel* has a textilelike decorative background, and the feet of Honoré's figures frequently overlap the border. Compared to his contemporaries, Master Honoré pioneered naturalism in figure painting. But he still approached the art of book illumination as a decorator of two-dimensional pages. He did not embrace the classical notion that a painting should be an illusionistic window into a three-dimensional world.

JEAN PUCELLE AND ITALY David and Saul also are the subjects of a miniature painting at the top left of an elaborately decorated text page in the *Belleville Breviary* (FIG. **18-34**). JEAN PUCELLE of Paris illuminated it around 1325. He went far beyond Honoré and other French artists by placing his fully modeled

18-33 MASTER HONORÉ, David anointed by Samuel and battle of David and Goliath, folio 7 verso of the *Breviary of Philippe le Bel,* from Paris, France, 1296. Ink and tempera on vellum, $7\frac{7}{8}'' \times 4\frac{7}{8}''$. Bibliothèque Nationale, Paris.

popular in Byzantine art (see FIGS. 12-8 and 12-34). The Gothic artist included two episodes on the same page, separated by the tree of Mamre mentioned in the Bible. At the left, Abraham greets the three angels. In the other scene, he entertains them while his wife Sarah peers at them from a tent. The figures' delicate features and the linear wavy strands of their hair have parallels in Blanche of Castile's moralized Bible, as well as in Parisian stained glass. The elegant proportions, facial expressions, theatrical gestures, and swaying poses are characteristic of the Parisian court style admired throughout Europe. A later example of this mannered style in sculpture, complete with the exaggerated contrapposto of the angel in the left foreground, is the *Virgin of Paris* (FIG. 18-24).

PRAYERS FOR A KING As in the Romanesque period, some Gothic manuscript illuminators signed their work. The names of others appear in royal accounts of payments made and similar official documents. One of the artists who produced books for the French court was MASTER HONORÉ, whose Parisian workshop was on the street known today as rue Boutebrie. Honoré illuminated a *breviary* (a book of selected prayers and psalms) for Philippe le Bel (Philip the Fair, r. 1285–1314) in 1296. The page we illustrate (FIG. **18-33**) features two Old Testament scenes involving David. In the

18-34 JEAN PUCELLE, David before Saul, folio 24 verso of the *Belleville Breviary,* from Paris, France, ca. 1325. Ink and tempera on vellum, $9\frac{1}{2}'' \times 6\frac{3}{4}''$. Bibliothèque Nationale, Paris.

figures in three-dimensional architectural settings rendered in convincing perspective. For example, Pucelle painted Saul as a weighty figure seated on a throne seen in a three-quarter view, and he meticulously depicted the receding coffers of the barrel vault over the young David's head. Such "stage sets" already had become commonplace in Italian painting, and Pucelle seems to have visited Italy and studied Duccio's work in Siena (see Chapter 19). Pucelle's (or one of his assistants') renditions of plants, a bird, butterflies, a dragonfly, a fish, a snail, and a monkey also reveal a keen interest in and close observation of the natural world. Nonetheless, in the *Belleville Breviary* the text still dominates the figures, and the artist (and his patron) delighted in ornamental flourishes, fancy initial letters, and abstract patterns. In that respect, comparisons to monumental panel paintings are inappropriate. Pucelle's breviary remains firmly in the tradition of book illumination.

The *Belleville Breviary* is of special interest because Pucelle's name and those of some of his assistants appear at the end of the book, in a memorandum recording the payment they received for their work. Inscriptions in other Gothic illuminated books regularly state the production costs—the prices paid for materials, especially gold, and for the execution of initials, figures, flowery script, and other embellishments. By this time, illuminators were professional guild members, and their personal reputation, like modern "brand names," guaranteed the quality of their work. Though the cost of materials was still the major factor determining a book's price, individual skill and reputation increasingly decided the value of the illuminator's services. The centuries-old monopoly of the Christian Church in book production had ended.

A VIRGIN FOR SAINT-DENIS The royal family also patronized goldsmiths, silversmiths, and other artists specializing in the production of luxury works in metal and enamel for churches, palaces, and private homes. Especially popular among the wealthy were statuettes of sacred figures, which were purchased either for private devotion or as gifts to churches. The Virgin Mary was a favored subject, reflecting her new prominence in the iconography of Gothic portal sculpture.

Perhaps the finest of these costly statuettes is the large silver-gilt figurine known as the *Virgin of Jeanne d'Evreux* (FIG. **18-35**). The queen, wife of Charles IV (r. 1322–1328), donated the image of the Virgin and Child to the royal abbey church of Saint-Denis in 1339. Mary stands on a rectangular base decorated with enamel scenes of Christ's Passion. (Some art historians think the enamels are Jean Pucelle's work.) But no hint of grief appears in the beautiful young Mary's face. The Christ Child, also without a care in the world, playfully reaches for his mother. The elegant proportions of the two figures, Mary's swaying posture, the heavy drapery folds, and the intimate human characterization of the holy figures are also features of the roughly contemporary *Virgin of Paris* (FIG. 18-24). The carver of large stone statues and the royal silversmith working at small scale approached the representation of the Virgin and Child in a similar fashion.

In the *Virgin of Jeanne d'Evreux,* as in the *Virgin of Paris,* Mary appears not only as the Mother of Christ but also as the Queen of Heaven. The Saint-Denis Mary also originally had a crown on her head, and the scepter she holds is in the form of the fleur-de-lis, the French monarchy's floral emblem. The statuette also served as a reliquary. The Virgin's scepter contained hairs believed to come from Mary's head.

THE CASTLE OF LOVE Gothic artists produced luxurious objects for secular, as well as religious, contexts. Sometimes they

18-35 *Virgin of Jeanne d'Evreux,* from the abbey church of Saint-Denis, France, 1339. Silver gilt and enamel, 2′ 3½″ high. Louvre, Paris.

decorated these costly pieces with stories of courtly love inspired by the romantic literature of the day, such as the famous story of Lancelot and Queen Guinevere, wife of King Arthur of Camelot. The French poet Chrétien de Troyes recorded their love affair in the late 12th century.

One of the most interesting objects of this type is a woman's jewelry box adorned with ivory relief panels. The theme of the panel illustrated here (FIG. **18-36**) is related to the *Romance of the Rose* by Guillaume de Lorris, written ca. 1225–1235 and completed by Jean de Meung between 1275 and 1280. At the left the sculptor carved the allegory of the siege of the Castle of Love. Gothic knights attempt to capture love's fortress by shooting flowers from their bows and hurling baskets of roses over the walls from catapults. Among the castle's defenders is Cupid, who aims his arrow at one of the knights while a comrade scales the walls on a ladder. The scene in the lid's two central sections shows two knights jousting on

18-36 The Castle of Love and knights jousting, lid of a jewelry casket, from Paris, France, ca. 1330–1350. Ivory and iron, $4\frac{1}{2}'' \times 9\frac{3}{4}''$. Walters Art Museum, Baltimore.

horseback. Several maidens look down on the contest from a balcony and cheer the knights on, as trumpets blare. A youth in the crowd holds a hunting falcon. The sport was a favorite pastime of the leisure class in the late Middle Ages. At the right, the victorious knight receives his prize (a bouquet of roses) from a chastely dressed maiden on horseback. The scenes on the casket's sides include the famous medieval allegory of female virtue, the legend of the unicorn, a white horse with a single ivory horn. Only a virgin could attract the rare animal, and any woman who could do so thereby also demonstrated her moral purity. Religious themes may have monopolized artistic production for churches in the Gothic age, but secular themes figured prominently in private contexts. Unfortunately, very few examples of the latter survive.

GOTHIC OUTSIDE OF FRANCE

OPERE FRANCIGENO In 1269, the prior (deputy abbot) of the church of Saint Peter at Wimpfen-im-Tal in the German Rhineland hired "a very experienced architect who had recently come from the city of Paris" to rebuild his monastery church.[4] The architect reconstructed the church *opere francigeno* (in the French manner)—that is, in the Gothic style of the Île-de-France. The spread of the Parisian Gothic style had begun even earlier, but in the second half of the 13th century the new style became dominant throughout western Europe. European architecture did not, however, turn Gothic all at once nor in a uniform way. Almost everywhere, patrons and builders modified the "court style" of the Île-de-France according to local preferences. Because the old Romanesque traditions lingered on in many places, each area, marrying its local Romanesque design to the new style, developed its own brand of Gothic architecture.

England

FRENCH TRANSLATED INTO ENGLISH Salisbury Cathedral (FIGS. **18-37** to **18-39**) embodies the essential characteristics of English Gothic architecture. Begun in 1220, the same year work started on Amiens Cathedral (FIGS. 18-17 to 18-19), Salisbury Cathedral was mostly completed in about 40 years. The two cathedrals are, therefore, almost exactly contemporary, and the differences between them are very instructive. Although Salisbury's facade has lancet windows and blind arcades with pointed arches, as well as statuary, it presents a striking contrast to French designs (compare Amiens, FIG. 18-19, and Reims, FIG. 18-21). The English facade is a squat screen in front of the nave, wider than the building behind it. The soaring height of the French facades is absent. The Salisbury facade also does not correspond to the three-part division of the interior (nave and two aisles). Different too is the emphasis on the great crossing tower (added ca. 1320–1330), which dominates the silhouette. Salisbury's height is modest compared with that of Amiens and Reims. And because height is not a decisive factor in the English building, the architect used the flying buttress sparingly and as a rigid prop, rather than as an integral part of the vaulting system within the church. In short, the English builders adopted some of the superficial motifs of French Gothic architecture but did not embrace its structural logic or emphasis on height.

Equally distinctive is the long rectilinear plan (FIG. 18-38), with its double transept and flat eastern end. The latter feature was characteristic of Cistercian churches (see FIG. 17-8) and had been favored in England since Romanesque times. The interior (FIG. 18-39), although Gothic in its three-story elevation, pointed arches, four-part rib vaults, and compound piers, conspicuously departs from the French Gothic style. The pier colonnettes stop at the springing of the nave arches and do not connect with the

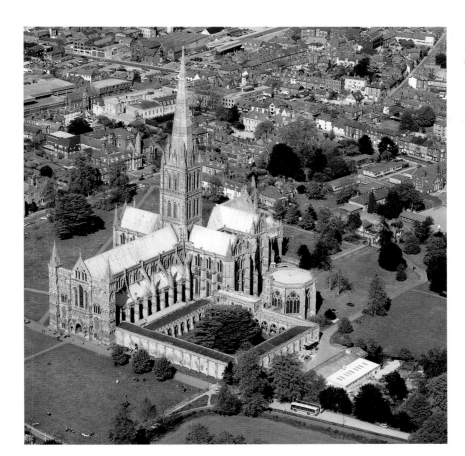

18-37 Aerial view of Salisbury Cathedral, Salisbury, England, 1220–1258; west facade completed 1265; spire ca. 1320–1330.

vault ribs (compare FIGS. 18-17 and 18-18). Instead, the vault ribs rise from corbels in the triforium, producing a strong horizontal emphasis. Underscoring this horizontality is the rich color contrast between the light stone of the walls and vaults and the dark Purbeck marble used for the triforium moldings and corbels, compound pier responds, and other details. Once again, however, the impact of the French Gothic style is clearly visible in the decorative details, especially the tracery of the triforium. Nonetheless, visitors to Salisbury could not mistake the English cathedral for a French one.

DECORATED AND PERPENDICULAR Early on, English architecture found its native language in the elaboration of architectural pattern for its own sake (for example, the decorative patterning of the Romanesque piers of Durham Cathedral; see FIG. 17-15). Structural logic, expressed in the building fabric, was secondary. The pier, wall, and vault elements, still relatively simple at Salisbury, became increasingly complex and decorative in

0 25 50 75 100
FEET

0 10 20 30
METERS

N

18-38 Plan of Salisbury Cathedral, Salisbury, England, 1220–1258.

18-39 Interior of Salisbury Cathedral (view facing east), Salisbury, England, 1220–1258.

18-40 Choir of Gloucester Cathedral (view facing east), Gloucester, England, 1332–1357.

18-41 ROBERT and WILLIAM VERTUE, Chapel of Henry VII, Westminster Abbey, London, England, 1503–1519.

the 14th century. Architectural historians usually call the English Gothic architectural style of that period the Decorated style. The choir of Gloucester Cathedral (FIG. **18-40**), remodeled about a century after Salisbury, illustrates the transition from the Decorated to the last English Gothic style, the Perpendicular style. The newer style took its name from the pronounced verticality of its decorative details, in contrast to the horizontal emphasis of Salisbury and early English Gothic.

A single enormous window divided into tiers of small windows of like shape and proportion fills the characteristically flat east end of Gloucester Cathedral. At the top, two slender lancets flank a wider central section that also ends in a pointed arch. The design has much in common with the screen facade of Salisbury, but the proportions are different. Vertical, as opposed to horizontal, lines dominate. In the choir wall, the architect also erased Salisbury's strong horizontal accents, as the vertical wall elements lift directly from the floor to the vaulting, unifying the walls with the vaults in the French manner. The vault ribs, which designers had begun to multiply soon after Salisbury, are at Gloucester a dense thicket of entirely ornamental strands that serve no structural purpose. The choir, in fact, is not covered by rib vaults at all but by a continuous Romanesque barrel vault with applied Gothic ornament. In the Gloucester choir, the taste for decorative surfaces triumphed over structural "honesty."

FAN VAULTS The decorative and structure-disguising qualities of the Perpendicular style became even more pronounced in its late phases. A primary example is the early 16th-century ceiling of the chapel of Henry VII (FIG. **18-41**) adjoining Westminster Abbey in London. In this chapel, the earlier linear play of ribs became a kind of architectural embroidery. The architect pulled the ribs into uniquely English *fan vault* shapes with large hanging *pendants* resembling stalactites. The vault looks like something organic that hardened in the process of melting. Intricate tracery recalling lace overwhelms the cones hanging from the ceiling. The chapel represents the dissolution of structural Gothic into decorative fancy. The architect released the Gothic style's original lines from their function and multiplied them into the uninhibited architectural virtuosity and theatrics of the Perpendicular style. A contemporaneous phenomenon in France was the Flamboyant style seen in such churches as Saint-Maclou at Rouen (FIG. 18-25).

ROYAL TOMBS Henry VII's chapel also houses the king's tomb in the form of a large stone coffin with sculpted portraits of Henry and his queen, Elizabeth of York, lying on their backs. This type of tomb is a familiar feature of the churches of Late Gothic England—indeed, of Late Gothic Europe. Though not strictly part of the architectural fabric, as are tombs set into niches in the church walls, freestanding tombs with recumbent images of the deceased are permanent and immovable units of church furniture. They preserve both the remains and the memory of the person entombed and testify to the deceased's piety as well as prominence.

Services for the dead were a vital part of the Christian liturgy. The Christian hope for salvation in the hereafter prompted the

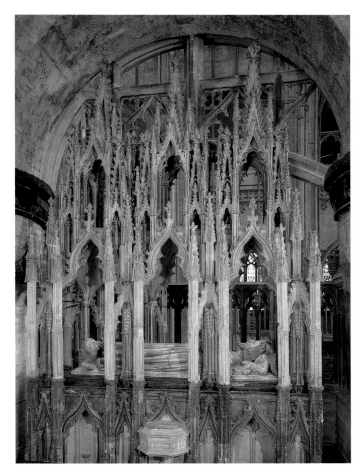

18-42 Tomb of Edward II, Gloucester Cathedral, Gloucester, England, ca. 1330–1335.

gables, buttresses, and pinnacles. A distinctive feature is the use of *ogee arches* (arches made up of two double-curved lines meeting at a point), a characteristic Late Gothic form. Art historians often have compared tombs like Edward's to reliquaries. Indeed, the shrinelike frame and the church setting transform the deceased into a kind of saintly relic worthy of veneration.

GOTHIC MAPS We conclude our survey of Gothic England with a monument of a very different kind—a large vellum map of the world (FIG. **18-43**) displayed in Hereford Cathedral. This *map-pamundi* ("cloth of the world" in Latin) is probably the work of RICHARD DE BELLO, a priest attached to Lincoln Cathedral from 1264 to 1283. It exemplifies the art of cartography (mapmaking) in the 13th century. Cartography had its roots in antiquity, especially in the imperially commissioned geographic surveys of the known world. In fact, at the bottom left of the Hereford map is a picture of the Roman emperor Augustus handing a document to three surveyors and instructing them to "Go into the whole world and report back to the Senate on each continent."

The orientation of the Hereford map and of many other medieval maps is unlike that of most modern maps. North is at the left and east at the top. The explanation is that Christians believed that on Judgment Day Christ would rise in the east, like the sun. At the gabled top of the Hereford map, Christ appears as the enthroned Last Judge of humankind. An angel leads the Saved to Paradise on the left (Christ's right), while grotesque demons pull the Damned into the mouth of Hell. This iconographical theme recalls the tympanum of the Romanesque church of Saint-Lazare at Autun (see FIGS. Intro-6 and 17-25). A distinctive Gothic element is the presence of the Virgin Mary below Christ, interceding with her son on behalf of those who prayed to her.

At the world's exact center is Jerusalem, not because medieval mapmakers believed the earth was a flat disk with Jerusalem at its

dying faithful to request masses sung, sometimes in perpetuity, for the eternal repose of their souls. Toward that end, the highborn and wealthy endowed whole chapels for the chanting of masses *(chantries),* and made rich bequests of treasure and property to the Church. Many also required that their tombs be placed as near as possible to the choir or at some other important location in the church, if not in a chapel especially designed and endowed to house it, such as Henry's chapel at Westminster Abbey. Freestanding tombs, accessible to church visitors, had a moral as well as a sepulchral and memorial purpose. The silent image of the deceased, cold and still, was a solemn reminder of human mortality, all the more effective because the remains of the person depicted were directly below the portrait. The tomb of an illustrious person could bring distinction, pilgrims, and patronage to the church in which it was placed, just as relics of saints attracted pilgrims from far and wide (see "Pilgrimages," Chapter 17, page 449).

EDWARD II AS RELIC A very elaborate example of a freestanding tomb (FIG. **18-42**) is that of Edward II (r. 1307–1327), installed in Gloucester Cathedral several years after the king's murder. Edward's successor, his son Edward III, paid for the memorial to his father, who reposes in regal robes with his crown on his head. The sculptor portrayed the dead king as an idealized Christlike figure (compare FIG. 18-20). On each side of Edward's head is an attentive angel tenderly touching his hair. At his feet is a guardian lion, emblem also of the king's strength and valor. An intricate Perpendicular Gothic canopy encases the coffin, forming a kind of miniature chapel protecting the deceased. It is a fine example of the English manner with its forest of delicate alabaster and Purbeck marble

18-43 RICHARD DE BELLO(?), *Mappa Mundi,* ca. 1300. Tempera on vellum, approx. 5′ 2″ × 4′ 4″. Hereford Cathedral, Hereford, England.

center but because of the central importance of the holy city in medieval thought. Jerusalem appears as a circular walled city accompanied by a picture of Christ on the cross. As was the norm, the Hereford artist characterized most of the world's famous places by their chief buildings. Crete's major feature, for example, is a circular maze, the legendary labyrinth of the Minoan palace at Knossos (see FIGS. 4-3 and 4-4). Babylon's Tower of Babel (see "Babylon: City of Wonders," Chapter 2, page 49) is a multistory fortress with crenellated battlements of the kind found at Carcassonne (FIG. 18-26). Alexandria's lighthouse, one of the Seven Wonders of the ancient world, stands at the mouth of the Nile River in Egypt. In some places, the mapmaker provided pictures of the monstrous races that were said to inhabit the far corners of the earth, just as the sculptor of the Vézelay tympanum (see FIG. 17-26) did in the previous century. The Gothic artist also answered the question of what a traveler would find beyond the oceans that bounded the continents—*MORS* (death).

Germany

COLOGNE'S SOARING VAULTS The architecture of Germany remained conservatively Romanesque well into the 13th century. In many German churches, the only Gothic feature was the rib vault, buttressed solely by the heavy masonry of the walls. By mid-century, though, the French Gothic style began to make a profound impact, as Cologne Cathedral (FIGS. **18-44** and **18-45**) demonstrates. Begun in 1248 under the direction of GERHARD OF COLOGNE, the cathedral was not completed until more than 600 years later, making it one of the longest building projects on record. Work halted entirely from the mid-16th to the mid-19th century, when the 14th-century design for the facade was unexpectedly found. Gothic Revival architects then completed the building according to the Gothic plans, adding the nave, towers, and facade to the east end that had stood alone for several centuries. The Gothic/Gothic Revival structure is the largest cathedral in northern Europe and boasts a giant (422-foot-long) nave with two aisles on each side.

The 150-foot-high 14th-century choir (FIG. 18-45) is a skillful variation of the Amiens Cathedral choir (FIGS. 18-17 and 18-18) design, with double lancets in the triforium and tall, slender single windows in the clerestory above and choir arcade below. Completed four decades after Gerhard's death, but according to his plans, the choir expresses the Gothic quest for height even more emphatically than many French Gothic buildings. Despite the cathedral's seeming lack of substance, the stability of the structure was proven during World War II, when the city of Cologne suffered from extremely heavy aerial bombardments.

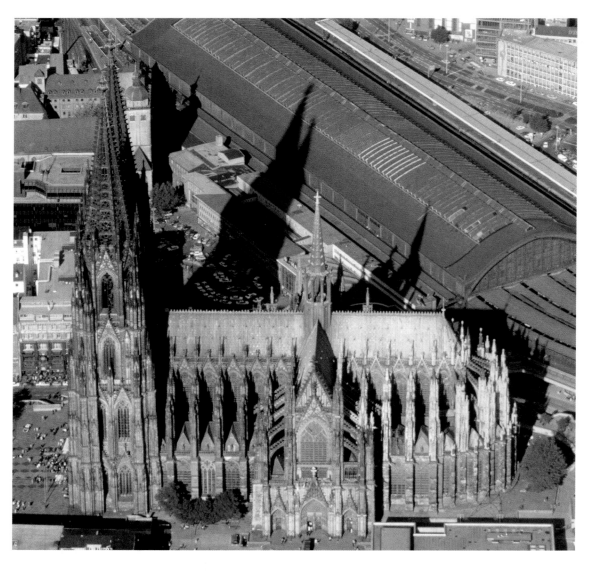

18-44 GERHARD OF COLOGNE, aerial view of Cologne Cathedral (from the south), Cologne, Germany, begun 1248; nave, facade, and towers completed 1880.

18-45 GERHARD OF COLOGNE, Choir of Cologne Cathedral (view facing east), Cologne, Germany, completed 1322.

The church survived the war by virtue of its Gothic skeletal design. Once the first few bomb blasts had blown out all of its windows, subsequent explosions had no adverse effects, and the skeleton remained intact and structurally sound.

MARBURG'S HALL CHURCH A different type of design, also probably of French origin (see FIG. 17-34) but developed especially in Germany, is the *Hallenkirche*, or hall church, in which the aisles are the same height as the nave. Hall churches, consequently, have no tribune, triforium, or clerestory. An early German example of this type is the church of Saint Elizabeth at Marburg (FIGS. **18-46** and **18-47**), built between 1235 and 1283. It incorporates French-inspired rib vaults with pointed arches and tall lancet windows. The facade has two spire-capped towers in the French manner but no tracery arcades or portal sculpture. Because the aisles provide much of the bracing for the nave vaults, the exterior of Saint Elizabeth is without the dramatic parade of flying buttresses that typically circles French Gothic churches. But the German interior, lighted by double rows of tall windows in the aisle walls, is more unified and free flowing, less narrow and divided, and more brightly illuminated than the interiors of French and English Gothic churches.

HIGH DRAMA AT STRASBOURG Like French Gothic architects, French sculptors also often set the standard for their counterparts abroad. In the German Rhineland, which the successors of the Carolingian and Ottonian emperors still ruled, work began in 1176 on a new cathedral for Strasbourg, today a French city. The apse, choir, and transepts were in place by around 1240. Stylistically, these sections of the new church are Romanesque. But the reliefs of the two south-transept portals are fully Gothic and reveal the impact of contemporary French sculpture, especially that of Reims.

18-46 Saint Elizabeth (view facing northwest), Marburg, Germany, 1235–1283.

18-47 Interior of Saint Elizabeth (view facing west), Marburg, Germany, 1235–1283.

18-48 Death of the Virgin, tympanum of left doorway, south transept, Strasbourg Cathedral, Strasbourg, France, ca. 1230.

We illustrate the left tympanum (FIG. **18-48**), where the theme is the death of the Virgin Mary. A comparison of the Strasbourg Mary on her deathbed with the Mary of the Reims Visitation group (FIG. 18-22) suggests that the German master had studied the recently installed French jamb statues. The Twelve Apostles gather around the Virgin, forming an arc of mourners well suited to the semicircular frame. At the center Christ receives his mother's soul (the doll-like figure he holds in his left hand). Mary Magdalene, wringing her hands in grief, crouches beside the deathbed. The sorrowing figures express emotion in varying degrees of intensity, from serene resignation to gesturing agitation. The sculptor organized the group by dramatic pose and gesture but also by the rippling flow of deeply incised drapery that passes among them like a rhythmic electric pulse. The sculptor's objective was to imbue the sacred figures with human emotions and to stir emotional responses in observers. In Gothic France, as already noted, art became increasingly humanized and natural. In Gothic Germany, artists carried this humanizing trend even further by emphasizing passionate drama.

DONOR "PORTRAITS" The Strasbourg style, with its feverish emotionalism, was particularly appropriate for narrating dramatic events in relief. The sculptor entrusted with the decoration of the west choir of Naumburg Cathedral faced a very different challenge. The task was to carve statues of the 12 benefactors of the original 11th-century church on the occasion of a new fundraising campaign. The vivid gestures and agitated faces in the Strasbourg tympanum contrast with the quiet solemnity of the Naumburg statues. Two of the figures stand out from the group because of their exceptional quality. They represent the margrave (German military governor) Ekkehard II of Meissen and his wife

Uta (FIG. **18-49**). The statues are attached to columns and stand beneath architectural canopies, following the pattern of French Gothic portal statuary. Their location indoors accounts for the preservation of much of the original paint. Ekkehard and Uta give an idea of how the facade and transept sculptures of Gothic cathedrals once looked.

The period costumes and the individualized features and personalities of the margrave and his wife give the impression that they sat for their own portraits, although the subjects lived well before the sculptor's time. Ekkehard, the intense and somewhat stout knight, contrasts with the beautiful and aloof Uta. With a wonderfully graceful gesture, she draws the collar of her gown partly across her face while she gathers up a soft fold of drapery with a jeweled, delicate hand. The sculptor understood that the drapery and the body it enfolds are distinct. The artist subtly revealed the shape of Uta's right arm beneath her cloak and rendered the fall of drapery folds with an accuracy that indicates the use of a model. The two statues are arresting images of real people, even if they bear the names of aristocrats the artist never met. By the mid-13th century, life-size images of secular personages had found their way into churches.

EQUESTRIAN STATUARY Somewhat earlier in date than the Naumburg "portraits" is the equestrian statue known as the *Bamberg Rider* (FIG. **18-50**). For centuries this statue has been mounted against a pier in Bamberg Cathedral beneath an architectural canopy that frames the rider's body but not his horse. Scholars debate whether the statue was made for this location or moved there, perhaps from the church's exterior. A similar equestrian statue of the same period stood in the market square of Magdeburg, Germany. Both statues revive the imagery of the

18-49 Ekkehard and Uta, statues in the west choir, Naumburg Cathedral, Naumburg, Germany, ca. 1249–1255. Painted limestone, approx. 6′ 2″ high.

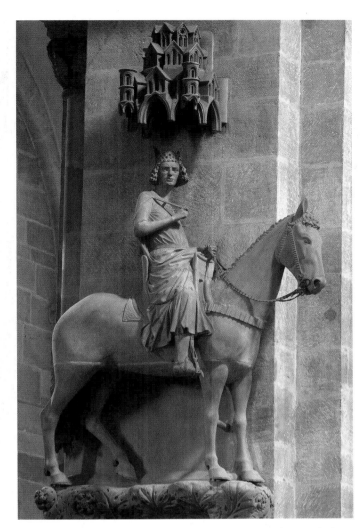

18-50 Equestrian portrait *(Bamberg Rider)*, statue in the east choir, Bamberg Cathedral, Germany, ca. 1235–1240. Sandstone, 7′ 9″ high.

Carolingian Empire (see FIG. 16-11), derived in turn from that of ancient Rome (see FIG. 10-59).

Like Ekkehard and Uta, the *Bamberg Rider* seems to be a true portrait. Some believe it represents a German emperor, perhaps Frederick II (r. 1220–1250), who was a benefactor of Bamberg Cathedral. The many other identifications include Saint George and one of the three magi, but a historical personality is most likely the subject. The presence of a Holy Roman Emperor in the

cathedral would have underscored the unity of church and state in 13th-century Germany. The artist carefully represented the rider's costume, the high saddle, and the horse's trappings. The proportions of horse and rider are correct, although the sculptor did not quite understand the animal's anatomy, so its shape is rather stiffly schematic. The rider turns toward the observer, as if presiding at a review of troops. The torsion of this figure seems to reflect the same impatience with subordination to architecture found in the Reims portal statues (FIG. 18-22).

MARY GRIEVES FOR CHRIST The confident 13th-century figures at Naumburg and Bamberg stand in marked contrast to a haunting 14th-century German image of the Virgin Mary holding the dead Christ in her lap (FIG. **18-51**). The widespread troubles of the 14th century—war, plague, famine, and social strife—brought on an ever more acute awareness of suffering. This found its way readily into religious art. The Dance of Death, Christ as the Man of Sorrow, and the Seven Sorrows of the Virgin Mary became favorite themes. A fevered and fearful piety sought comfort and reassurance in the reflection that Christ and the Virgin Mother shared humanity's woes. To represent this, artists emphasized the traits of human suffering in powerful, expressive exaggeration. In the illustrated carved and painted wood group (called a *Pietà,* "pity" or "compassion" in Italian), the sculptor portrayed

18-51 Virgin with the Dead Christ *(Röttgen Pietà),* from the Rhineland, Germany, ca. 1300–1325. Painted wood, 2′ 10½″ high. Rheinisches Landemuseum, Bonn.

Christ as a stunted, distorted human wreck, stiffened in death and covered with streams of blood gushing from a huge wound. The Virgin Mother, who cradles him like a child in her lap, is the very image of maternal anguish, her oversized face twisted in an expression of unbearable grief.

This statue expresses nothing of the serenity of Romanesque and earlier Gothic depictions of Mary (see FIGS. 17-30 and 18-5, right tympanum). Nor does the *Röttgen Pietà* (named after a collector) have anything in common with the aloof, iconic images of the Theotokos with the infant Jesus in her lap common in Byzantine art (see FIGS. 12-16 and 12-17). Here the artist forcibly confronts the devout with an appalling icon of agony, death, and sorrow that humanizes, almost to the point of heresy, the sacred personages. The work calls out to the horrified believer, "What is your suffering compared to this?"

The humanizing of religious themes and religious images accelerated steadily from the 12th century. By the 14th century, art addressed the private person (often in a private place) in a direct appeal to the emotions. The expression of feeling accompanied the representation of the human body in motion. As the figures of the church portals began to twist on their columns, then move within their niches, and then stand independently, their details became more outwardly related to the human audience as expressions of recognizable human emotions.

NICHOLAS OF VERDUN When Abbot Suger wanted to install a magnificent crucifix in the new Gothic choir of Saint-Denis, he selected artists from Germany's Meuse River Valley for the job. The Mosan region long had been famous for the quality of its metalworkers and enamelers (see FIGS. 17-29 and 17-31). The Saint-Denis crucifix is lost, but Suger described it in one of his treatises on the building and adorning of the royal abbey church. The cross stood on a sumptuous base decorated with 68 enamel

18-52 NICHOLAS OF VERDUN, the *Klosterneuburg Altar,* from the abbey church at Klosterneuburg, Austria, 1181. Gilded copper and enamel, 3′ 6¾″ high. Stiftsmuseum, Klosterneuburg.

scenes pairing Old and New Testament episodes. Costly furnishings such as this crucifix were key ingredients in Suger's plan to make his new church an earthly introduction to the splendors of Paradise (see "Abbot Suger," page 481).

The leading Mosan artist of the late 12th and early 13th centuries was NICHOLAS OF VERDUN. In 1181 he completed work on a gilded-copper and enamel *ambo* (a pulpit for biblical readings) for the Benedictine abbey church at Klosterneuburg, near Vienna in Austria. After a fire damaged the pulpit in 1330, the church hired artists to convert the pulpit into an altarpiece. The pulpit's sides became the wings of a triptych. The 14th-century artists also added 6 scenes to Nicholas's original 45.

We illustrate the *Klosterneuburg Altar* in its final form (FIG. 18-52), with its 51 enamels set into trefoil-arched niches framed by explanatory inscriptions. The central row of enamels depicts New Testament episodes, beginning with the Annunciation, and bears the label *sub gracia,* or the world "under grace," that is, after the coming of Christ. The upper and lower registers contain Old Testament scenes labeled, respectively, *ante legem,* "before the law" Moses received on Mount Sinai, and *sub lege,* "under the law" of the Ten Commandments. In this scheme, prophetic Old Testament events appear above and below the New Testament episodes they prefigure. This organization was unlikely to have been Nicholas's invention. Provost Wernher of Klosterneuburg or another church official probably formulated the iconographical program, consistent with a long tradition going back to the earliest Christian art (see "Jewish Subjects in Christian Art," Chapter 11, page 305).

On the *Klosterneuburg Altar,* the Annunciation to Mary of the coming birth of Jesus, for example, is framed above and below by enamels of angels announcing the births of Isaac and Samson. In the central section of the triptych, the Old Testament counterpart of Christ's Crucifixion is Abraham's sacrifice of Isaac (FIG. 18-53), a parallel already established in Early Christian times in both art (see FIG. 11-5) and literature. Nicholas of Verdun's gold figures stand out vividly from the blue enamel background. The biblical actors twist and turn, make emphatic gestures, and wear garments that are almost overwhelmed by the intricate linear patterns of their folds. In the Abraham and Isaac panel, the angel flies in at the very last moment to grab the blade of Abraham's sword

18-53 NICHOLAS OF VERDUN, Sacrifice of Isaac, detail of the *Klosterneuburg Altar,* from the abbey church at Klosterneuburg, Austria, 1181. Gilded copper and enamel, $5\frac{1}{2}''$ high. Stiftsmuseum, Klosterneuburg.

before he can kill the bound Isaac on the altar. The intense emotionalism of the representation and the linear complexity of the garments foreshadowed the tone and style of the Strasbourg tympanum depicting the death of the Virgin (FIG. 18-48).

THE MAGI'S RELICS Sculpted versions of the Klosterneuburg figures appear on the *Shrine of the Three Kings* (FIG. 18-54) in

18-54 NICHOLAS OF VERDUN, *Shrine of the Three Kings,* from Cologne Cathedral, Cologne, Germany, begun ca. 1190. Silver, bronze, enamel, and gemstones, $5'\ 8'' \times 6' \times 3'\ 8''$. Cathedral Treasury, Cologne.

Cologne Cathedral. Nicholas of Verdun probably began work on the huge reliquary (six feet long and almost as tall) in 1190. Philip von Heinsberg, archbishop of Cologne from 1167 to 1191, commissioned the shrine to contain relics of the three magi. The Holy Roman Emperor Frederick Barbarossa acquired them in the conquest of Milan in 1164 and donated them to the German cathedral. Possession of the magi's relics gave the Cologne archbishops the right to crown German kings. Nicholas's reliquary, made of silver and bronze with ornamentation in enamel and gemstones, is one of the most luxurious ever fashioned, especially considering its size. The shape resembles that of a basilican church. Repoussé figures of the Virgin Mary, the three magi, Old Testament prophets, and New Testament apostles in arcuated frames are variations of those on the Klosterneuburg pulpit. The deep channels and tight bunches of the drapery folds are hallmarks of Nicholas's style. A similar figural style appeared a half-century later in Strasbourg Cathedral's *Death of the Virgin* tympanum (FIG. 18-48).

Nicholas of Verdun's *Klosterneuburg Altar* and his *Shrine of the Three Kings,* together with Suger's treatises on the furnishings of Saint-Denis, are welcome reminders of how magnificently outfitted medieval church interiors were. The so-called minor arts played a defining role in creating a special otherworldly atmosphere for Christian ritual. These Gothic examples continued a tradition that dates back to the Roman emperor Constantine and the first imperial patronage of Christianity (see "Constantine and Old Saint Peter's," Chapter 11, page 311).

Italy

Nowhere is the regional diversity of Gothic architecture more evident than in Italy. In the Romanesque period, as already discussed, Italian architects stood apart from developments north of the Alps. Many Italian Romanesque churches more closely resemble Early Christian basilicas than contemporary buildings in France, Germany, or England. Similarly, few Italian architects accepted the northern Gothic style. Some architectural historians even have questioned whether it is proper to speak of late medieval Italian buildings as Gothic structures.

18-55 Lorenzo Maitani, west facade of Orvieto Cathedral, Orvieto, Italy, begun 1310.

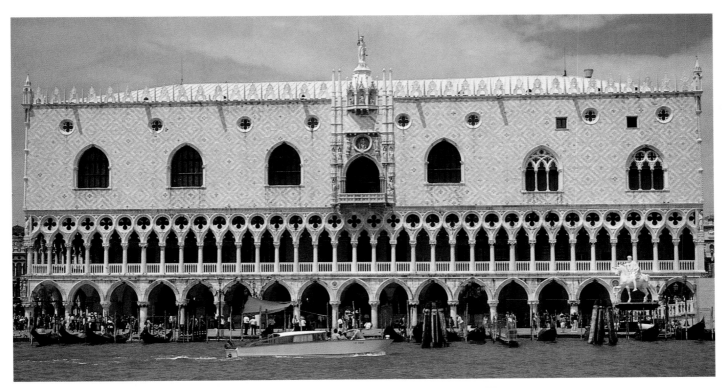

18-56 Doge's Palace, Venice, Italy, begun ca. 1340–1345; expanded and remodeled, 1424–1438.

ORVIETO CATHEDRAL The west facade of Orvieto Cathedral (FIG. **18-55**) is typical of late medieval architecture in Italy. Designed in the early 14th century by LORENZO MAITANI, an architect from nearby Siena, the Orvieto facade imitates some elements of the French Gothic architectural vocabulary. French influence is especially noticeable in the pointed gables over the three doorways, in the rose window in the upper zone framed by statues in niches, and in the four large pinnacles that divide the facade into three bays. The outer pinnacles serve as miniature substitutes for the big northern European west-front towers. Maitani's facade is, however, merely a Gothic overlay masking a marble-revetted basilican structure in the Tuscan Romanesque tradition, as our three-quarter view of the cathedral reveals. The Orvieto facade resembles a great altar screen, its single plane covered with carefully placed carved and painted ornament. In principle, Orvieto belongs with Pisa Cathedral (see FIG. 17-17) and other Italian buildings, rather than with Amiens (FIG. 18-19) or Reims (FIG. 18-21) Cathedrals. Inside, Orvieto Cathedral has a timber-roofed nave with a two-story elevation (columnar arcade and clerestory) in the Early Christian manner. Both the triumphal arch framing the apse and the nave arcade's arches are round as opposed to pointed.

A PALACE ON A LAGOON One of the wealthiest cities of late medieval Italy—and of Europe—was Venice, renowned for its streets of water. Situated on a lagoon on the northeastern coast of Italy, Venice was secure from land attack and could rely on a powerful navy for protection against invasion from the sea. Internally, Venice was a tight corporation of ruling families who, for centuries, provided stable rule and fostered economic growth. The Venetian republic's seat of government was the Doge's (Duke's) Palace (FIG. **18-56**). Begun around 1340–1345 and significantly

remodeled after 1424, it was the most ornate public building in medieval Italy. In a stately march, the first level's short and heavy columns support rather severe pointed arches that look strong enough to carry the weight of the upper structure. Their rhythm is doubled in the upper arcades, where more-slender columns carry ogee arches, which terminate in flamelike tips between medallions pierced with quatrefoils. Each story is taller than the one beneath it, the topmost as high as the two lower arcades combined. Yet the building does not look top-heavy. This is due in part to the complete absence of articulation in the top story and in part to the walls' delicate patterning, in cream- and rose-colored marbles, which makes them appear paper thin. The Doge's Palace is the monumental representative of a delightful and charming variant of Late Gothic architecture. Colorful, decorative, light and airy in appearance, and not overloaded, the Venetian Gothic is ideally suited to Venice, which floats between water and air.

MILAN'S ECLECTIC CATHEDRAL Since Romanesque times, northern European influences had been felt more strongly in Lombardy than in the rest of Italy. When Milan's citizens decided to build their own cathedral (FIG. 18-57) in 1386, they invited experts from France, Germany, and England, as well as from Italy. These masters argued among themselves and with the city council, and no single architect ever played a dominant role. The result of this attempt at "architecture by committee" was, not surprisingly, a compromise. The building's proportions, particularly the nave's, became Italian (that is, wide in relation to height), and the surface decorations and details remained Gothic. Clearly derived from France are the cathedral's multitude of pinnacles and the elaborate tracery on the facade, flank, and transept. But even before the building was half finished, the new classical style of the

Italian Renaissance had been well launched (see Chapter 21), and the Gothic design had become outdated. Thus, Milan Cathedral's elaborate facade represents a confused mixture of Late Gothic and classicizing Renaissance elements. With its pediment-capped rectilinear portals amid Gothic pinnacles, the cathedral stands as a symbol of the waning of the Gothic style.

CONCLUSION

The story of Gothic art and architecture begins in the Île-de-France around 1140. At Saint-Denis, Paris, Chartres, and elsewhere, French architects pioneered a new building style. Using rib vaults with pointed arches, flying buttresses, and stained-glass windows, French builders constructed towering cathedrals with statue-lined portals and interiors flooded with mystical multicolored light. Contemporaries regarded the new Gothic churches as images of the City of God on earth.

The French architectural style spread quickly throughout Europe, and with it the Parisian court style of book illumination and freestanding sculpture. As in the Romanesque period, however, regional diversity was the norm. In England, for example, Gothic architects embraced many of the characteristic motifs of contemporary French architecture, but not its structural logic or emphasis on height. South of the Alps, Italian builders adhered so tenaciously to the Early Christian basilican tradition that some scholars do not consider late medieval Italian architecture to be "Gothic" at all. But the Italians were pioneers in other fields, especially painting, and it was Italy, not France, that was shortly to become the birthplace of the new age known as the Renaissance.

EARLY GOTHIC

1140

- PETER ABELARD, 1079–1142
- SUGER, ABBOT OF SAINT-DENIS, 1122–1151
- KING LOUIS VII OF FRANCE, R. 1137–1180
- SECOND CRUSADE, 1147–1149
- FREDERICK BARBAROSSA, HOLY ROMAN EMPEROR, R. 1152–1190
- CHRÉTIEN DE TROYES, FL. CA. 1160–1190
- KING PHILIP AUGUSTUS OF FRANCE, R. 1180–1223
- SAINT FRANCIS OF ASSISI, 1182–1226

Royal Portal, Chartres Cathedral, France, ca. 1145–1155

HIGH GOTHIC

1194

- UNIVERSITY OF PARIS FOUNDED, CA. 1200
- CAPTURE OF CONSTANTINOPLE BY LATINS (FOURTH CRUSADE), 1204
- KING JOHN OF ENGLAND SIGNS MAGNA CARTA, 1215
- FREDERICK II, HOLY ROMAN EMPEROR, R. 1220–1250
- *Romance of the Rose,* PART I, CA. 1225–1235
- SAINT THOMAS AQUINAS, 1225–1274
- KING LOUIS IX (SAINT LOUIS) OF FRANCE, R. 1226–1270
- BLANCHE OF CASTILE, REGENT OF FRANCE, 1226–1234
- TREATY OF PARIS BETWEEN LOUIS IX AND HENRY III OF ENGLAND, 1259
- BYZANTINES RETAKE CONSTANTINOPLE, 1261
- DANTE ALIGHIERI, 1265–1321
- MARCO POLO IN CHINA, 1271–1292
- *Romance of the Rose,* PART II, CA. 1275–1280
- KING PHILIPPE LE BEL OF FRANCE, R. 1285–1314
- POPE BONIFACE VIII CANONIZES LOUIS IX, 1297

Amiens Cathedral, France, begun 1220

Psalter of St. Louis, 1253–1270

LATE GOTHIC

1300

- KING EDWARD II OF ENGLAND, R. 1307–1327
- KING CHARLES IV OF FRANCE, R. 1322–1328
- HUNDRED YEARS' WAR BETWEEN FRANCE AND ENGLAND, 1337–1453
- GEOFFREY CHAUCER, CA. 1343–1400
- BLACK DEATH FIRST SWEEPS OVER EUROPE, 1347–1350
- GREAT SCHISM, 1378–1417
- FALL OF CONSTANTINOPLE TO THE OTTOMAN TURKS, 1453
- KING HENRY VII OF ENGLAND, R. 1471–1509

1500

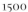

Chapel of Henry VII, London, England, 1503–1519

NOTES

Chapter 2

1. Translated by F. Tallon, in Prudence O. Harper et al., *The Royal City of Susa* (New York: Metropolitan Museum of Art, 1992), 132.

Chapter 3

1. Herodotus, *Histories,* 2.35.
2. We follow the chronology proposed by John Baines and Jaromír Malék in *Atlas of Ancient Egypt* (Oxford: Oxford University Press, 1980), 36–37, and the division of kingdoms favored by, among others, Mark Lehner, *The Complete Pyramids* (New York: Thames and Hudson, 1997), 8–9, and David P. Silverman, ed., *Ancient Egypt* (New York: Oxford University Press, 1997), 20–39.

Chapter 4

1. Homer, *Iliad,* 2.466–649.

Chapter 5

1. Thucydides, *Peloponnesian War,* 2.40–41.
2. Aristotle, *Politics,* 1.2.15.
3. Ibid., 7.11.1.
4. Plutarch, *Life of Pericles,* 12.
5. Pliny, *Natural History,* 34.74.
6. Ibid., 36.20.
7. Lucian, *Amores,* 13–14; *Imagines,* 6.
8. Plutarch, *Moralia,* 335A–B. Translated by J. J. Pollitt, *The Art of Ancient Greece: Sources and Documents* (New York: Cambridge University Press, 1990), 99.
9. Pliny, *Natural History,* 35.110.
10. Diodorus Siculus, *History,* 17.117.4.

Chapter 10

1. Ammianus Marcellinus, *History of Rome,* 16.10.15–16. Translated by J. J. Pollitt, *The Art of Rome, c. 753 B.C.–A.D. 337: Sources and Documents* (New York: Cambridge University Press, 1983), 170.
2. Livy, *History of Rome,* 25.40.1–3.
3. Plutarch, *Life of Marcellus,* 21. Translated by Pollitt, 32.
4. Recorded by the Venerable Bede, the great English scholar, monk, and saint, who died in 735; translated by Lord Byron in *Childe Harold's Pilgrimage* (1817), 4.145.
5. Juvenal, *Satires,* 3.225, 232.

Chapter 12

1. Translated by Cyril Mango, *The Art of the Byzantine Empire, 312–1453: Sources and Documents* (Upper Saddle River, N.J.: Prentice Hall, 1972), 85–86.

2. Ibid., 74.
3. Ibid., 83, 86.
4. Translated by Colm Luibheid, *Pseudo-Dionysius: The Complete Works* (New York: Paulist Press, 1987), 68ff.
5. Mango, 75.
6. Nina G. Garsoïan, "Later Byzantium," in John A. Garraty and Peter Gay, eds., *The Columbia History of the World* (New York: Harper and Row, 1972), 453.
7. Ibid., 460.

Chapter 16

1. *Beowulf,* translated by Kevin Crossley-Holland (New York: Farrar, Straus & Giroux, 1968), 119.
2. Ibid., 33.
3. Translated by Françoise Henry, *The Book of Kells* (New York: Alfred A. Knopf, 1974), 165.
4. Translated by John W. Williams, in *The Art of Medieval Spain A.D. 500–1200* (New York: Metropolitan Museum of Art, 1993), 156.
5. Translated by Adam S. Cohen, *The Uta Codex* (University Park: Pennsylvania State University Press, 2000), 11, 41.

Chapter 17

1. Quoted in Elizabeth G. Holt, *A Documentary History of Art* (Princeton, N.J.: Princeton University Press, 2nd ed., 1981), 1: 18.
2. Translated by Calvin B. Kendall, *The Allegory of the Church: Romanesque Portals and Their Verse Inscriptions* (Toronto: University of Toronto Press, 1998), 207.
3. John Williams, *A Spanish Apocalypse: The Morgan Beatus Manuscript* (New York: George Braziller, 1991), 223.
4. *Apologia,* 12.28. Translated by Conrad Rudolph, *The "Things of Greater Importance": Bernard of Clairvaux's* Apologia *and the Medieval Attitude toward Art* (Philadelphia: University of Pennsylvania Press, 1990), 281, 283.

Chapter 18

1. Giorgio Vasari, *Introduzione alle tre arti del disegno* (1550), ch. 3. Paul Frankl, *The Gothic: Literary Sources and Interpretations through Eight Centuries* (Princeton, N.J.: Princeton University Press, 1960), 290–91, 859–60.
2. Dante, *Divine Comedy,* Purgatory, 11.81.
3. Translated by Roland Behrendt, *Johannes Trithemius, In Praise of Scribes: De laude scriptorum* (Lawrence, Kans.: Coronado Press, 1974), 71.
4. Frankl, 55.

GLOSSARY

PRONUNCIATION KEY

ŭ abut, kitten   a cot, cart   ā bake   ă back   au out   ch chin

e less   ē easy   g gift   ĭ trip   ī life   j joke   k̲ kick

ⁿ French vin   ng sing   o flaw   ō boat   ö bi(r)d   oi coin

u foot   ū loot   ü few   y yoyo   zh vision

NOTE: The stress mark (′) goes before the stressed syllable (be-′for).

abacus—(ă-ba-′kŭs) The uppermost portion of the *capital* of a *column.*

abbess—The chief nun who presides over an *abbey*

abbey—A monastic community under the rule of an *abbott* or *abbess.*

abbot—The chief monk who presides over an *abbey.*

abrasion—The rubbing or grinding of stone or another material to produce a smooth finish.

acropolis—(a-′kra-pŭ-lŭs) Greek, "high city." In ancient Greece, usually the site of the city's most important temple(s).

additive light—The sum of all the wavelengths composing the visible spectrum; natural light, or sunlight.

additive sculpture—A kind of sculpture technique in which materials (for example, clay) are built up or "added" to create form.

adobe—(a-′dō-bē) The clay used to make a kind of sun-dried mud brick of the same name; a building made of such brick.

aerial perspective—See *perspective.*

agora—(a-go-′ra) An open square or space used for public meetings or business in ancient Greek cities.

aisle—The portion of a basilica flanking the *nave* and separated from it by a row of *columns* or *piers.*

altarpiece—A panel, painted or sculpted, situated above and behind an altar. See also *retable.*

alternate-support system—In church architecture, the use of alternating wall supports in the *nave,* usually *piers* and *columns* or *compound piers* of alternating form.

amalaka—(a-ma-′la-ka) In Hindu temple design, the large flat disk with ribbed edges surmounting the beehive-shaped tower.

Amazonomachy—(ă-mŭ-zon-′a-mŭ-kē) In Greek mythology, the legendary battle between the Greeks and Amazons.

ambo—A church pulpit for biblical readings.

ambulatory—(′ăm-byŭ-lŭ-to-rē) A covered walkway, outdoors (as in a church *cloister*) or indoors; especially the passageway around the *apse* and the *choir* of a church. In Buddhist architecture, the passageway leading around the *stupa* in a *chaitya* hall.

amphiprostyle—(ăm-fi-′pro-stīl) The style of Greek building in which the *colonnade* was placed across both the front and back, but not along the sides.

amphitheater—Greek, "double theater." A Roman building type resembling two Greek theaters put together. The Roman amphitheater featured a continuous elliptical *cavea* around a central *arena.*

amphora—(′ăm-fŏ-ra) A two-handled jar used for general storage purposes, usually to hold wine or oil.

amulet—(′ăm-yŭ-lŭt) An object worn to ward off evil or to aid the wearer.

anamorphic image—A distorted image that must be viewed by some special means (such as a mirror) or at an angle to be recognized.

andron—Dining room in a Greek house.

antae—(′ăn-tī) The molded projecting ends of the walls forming the *pronaos* or *opisthodomos* of an ancient Greek temple.

apadana—(ă-pa-′da-na) The great audience hall in ancient Persian palaces.

apotheosis—(ŭ-path-ē-′ō-sŭs) Elevated to the rank of gods, or the ascent to heaven.

apse—(ăps) A recess, usually semicircular, in the wall of a Roman *basilica* or at the east end of a church.

apsidal—Rounded; *apse* shaped.

arabesque—(ă-rŭ-′besk) "Arab-like." A flowing, intricate pattern derived from stylized organic motifs, usually floral; generally, an Islamic decorative motif.

arcade—A series of *arches* supported by *piers* or *columns.*

arch—A curved structural member that spans an opening and is generally composed of wedge-shaped blocks *(voussoirs)* that transmit the downward pressure laterally. See also *thrust.*

Archaic smile—In Archaic Greek sculpture, the smile sculptors represented on faces as a way of indicating that the person portrayed is alive.

architrave—(′ar-kŭ-trāv) The *lintel* or lowest division of the *entablature;* also called the epistyle.

archivolt—The continuous molding framing an *arch.* In *Romanesque* or *Gothic* architecture, one of the series of concentric bands framing the *tympanum.*

arcuated—*Arch* shaped.

arena—In a Roman *amphitheater,* the central area where bloody gladiatorial combats and other boisterous events took place.

arhat—(′ar-hat) A Buddhist holy person who has achieved enlightenment and *nirvana* by suppression of all desire for earthly things.

armature—(′ar-mŭ-chŭr) The crossed, or diagonal, *arches* that form the skeletal framework of a *Gothic rib vault.* In sculpture, the framework for a clay form.

arriccio—the first, rough layer of lime plaster in *fresco* painting.

arrises—(ŭ-′rēz-sŭz) In *Doric* columns, the raised edges of the *fluting.*

asceticism—Self-discipline and self-denial.

ashlar masonry—Carefully cut and regularly shaped blocks of stone used in construction, fitted together without mortar.

atlantid—(ăt-′lăn-tid) A male figure that functions as a supporting *column.* See also *caryatid.*

atlatl—(′ăt(-ŭ)-lăt(-ŭ)l) Spear-thrower, the typical weapon of the Toltecs of ancient Mexico.

atmospheric perspective—See *perspective.*

atrium—(′ā-trē-ŭm) The court of a Roman house that is partly open to the sky. Also the open, *colonnaded* court in front of and attached to a Christian *basilica.*

attic—The uppermost story of a building.

attribute—A unique characteristic that identifies a figure.

attribution—Assignment of a work to a maker or makers.

avatar—A manifestation of a deity incarnated in some visible form in which the deity performs a sacred function on earth. In Hinduism, an incarnation of a god.

axial plan—See *plan.*

backstrap loom—An Andean loom featuring a belt or backstrap encircling the waist of the seated weaver.

baldacchino—(bal-da-′kē-nō) A canopy on *columns,* frequently built over an altar. See also *ciborium.*

baptistery—(′băp-tus-trē) In Christian architecture, the building used for baptism, usually situated next to a church.

bar tracery—See *tracery.*

barays—The large reservoirs laid out around Cambodian *wats* that served as means of transportation as well as irrigation. The reservoirs were connected by a network of canals.

barrel vault—See *vault.*

base—In ancient Greek architecture, the lowest part of *Ionic* and *Corinthian columns.*

basilica—(bu-′sil-ŭ-kŭ) In Roman architecture, a building for legal and other civic proceedings, rectangular in plan with an entrance usually on a long side. In Christian architecture, a church somewhat resembling the Roman basilica, usually entered from one end and with an *apse* at the other.

bas-relief—(′ba rŭ-′lēf) See *relief.*

battlement—A low parapet at the top of a circuit wall in a fortification.

bay—The area between the *columns* or *piers* in the *nave* or *aisles* of a church.

beam—Horizontal wooden plank in Chinese buildings.

ben-ben—(′ben-ben) A pyramidal stone; a fetish of the Egyptian god Re.

bestiary—A collection of illustrations of real and imaginary animals.

bhakti—(′bŭk-tē) In Buddhist thought, the adoration of a personalized deity *(bodhisattva)* as a means of achieving unity with it; love felt by the devotee for the deity. In Hinduism, the devout, selfless direction of all tasks and activities of life to the service of one god.

bi—(bē) In ancient China, jade disks carved as ritual objects for burial with the dead. They were often decorated with piercework carving extending entirely through the object.

bilaterally symmetrical—A *composition* or *plan* in which the parts are the same on either side of an axis.

bilingual vases—Experimental Greek vases produced for a short time in the late sixth century BCE; one side featured *black-figure* decoration, the other *red-figure.*

black-figure painting—In early Greek pottery, the silhouetting of dark figures against a light background of natural, reddish clay, with linear details *incised* through the silhouettes.

blind arcade—An *arcade* having no actual openings, applied as decoration to a wall surface.

block statue—In ancient Egyptian sculpture, a cubic stone image with simplified body parts.

bodhisattva—(bod-hē-′sat-va) In Buddhist thought, one of the host of divinities provided to the Buddha to help him save humanity. A potential Buddha.

breviary—(′brē-vē-e-rē) A Christian religious book of selected daily prayers and psalms.

brocade—The weaving together of threads of different colors.

Buddha triad—A group consisting of the Buddha flanked on each side by a *bodhisattva.*

buon fresco—(bwan ′fres-kō) See *fresco.*

burin—(′byū-rin) A pointed tool used for *engraving* or *incising.*

buttress—(′bŭt-trŭs) An exterior masonry structure that opposes the lateral *thrust* of an *arch* or a *vault.* A pier buttress is a solid mass of masonry; a flying buttress consists typically of an inclined member carried on an arch or a series of arches and a solid buttress to which it transmits lateral *thrust.*

caduceus—(ka-′d(y)ū-sē-ŭs) In ancient Greek mythology, a magical rod entwined with serpents carried by Hermes (Roman, Mercury), the messenger of the gods.

caldarium—(kal-′dă-rē-ŭm) The hot-bath section of a Roman bathing establishment.

caliph(s)—(′kā-lef *or* ′kal-ŭf) *Muslim* rulers, regarded as successors of Muhammad.

calligraphy—Greek, "beautiful writing." Handwriting or penmanship, especially elegant writing as a decorative art.

cames—(kāms) The lead strips in *stained-glass* windows that join separate pieces of colored glass.

campanile—(kam-pa-′nē-lā) A bell tower of a church, usually, but not always, freestanding.

canon—A rule, for example, of proportion. The ancient Greeks considered beauty to be a matter of "correct" proportion and sought a canon of proportion, for the human figure and for buildings.

canopic jar—(kă-′nō-pik *jar*) In ancient Egypt, the container in which the organs of the deceased were placed for later burial with the mummy.

capital—The uppermost member of a *column*, serving as a transition from the *shaft* to the *lintel*. In classical architecture, the form of the capital varies with the *order*.

Capitolium—(kă-pi-′tō-lē-ŭm) An ancient Roman temple dedicated to the gods Jupiter, Juno, and Minerva.

cardo—(′kar-dō) The north-south street in a Roman town, intersecting the *decumanus* at right angles.

Caroline minuscule—The alphabet that *Carolingian* scribes perfected, from which our modern alphabet was developed.

Carolingian (adj.)—(kă-rō-′lin-jŭn) Pertaining to the empire of Charlemagne (Latin, Carolus Magnus) and his successors.

carpet pages—In early medieval manuscripts, decorative pages resembling textiles.

caryatid—(′kă-rē-ăt-id) A female figure that functions as a supporting *column*. See also *atlantid*.

casting—Pouring a fluid substance such as bronze into a *mold*.

castrum—(′kăs-trŭm) A Roman military encampment.

catacombs—(kăt-ŭ-kōmz) Subterranean networks of rock-cut galleries and chambers designed as cemeteries for the burial of the dead.

cathedral—A bishop's church.

cavea—(′kă-vē-ŭ) Latin, "hollow place or cavity." The seating area in ancient Greek and Roman theaters and *amphitheaters*.

celadon—(′sel-ŭ-dan) A Chinese-Korean pottery *glaze*, fired in an oxygen-deprived kiln to a characteristic gray-green or pale blue color.

cella—(′se-lŭ) The chamber at the center of an ancient temple; in a classical temple, the room (Greek, *naos*) in which the cult statue usually stood.

celt—(selt) In Olmec Mexico, an ax-shaped form made of polished jade; generally, a prehistoric metal or stone implement shaped like a chisel or ax head.

centaur—(′sen-tor) In ancient Greek mythology, a fantastical creature, with the front or top half of a human and the back or bottom half of a horse.

centauromachy—(sen-to-′ra-mŭ-kē) In ancient Greek mythology, the battle between the Greeks and *centaurs*.

central plan—See *plan*.

cestrum—(′kes-trŭm) A small spatula used in *encaustic* painting.

chaitya hall—(tshī-′tyŭ *hall*) An Indian rock-cut temple hall having a votive *stupa* at one end.

chakra—(′cha-kra) The Buddha's wheel, set in motion at Sarnath.

chakravartin—(cha-kra-′var-tīn) In India, the ideal king, the Universal Lord who rules through goodness.

chamfer—(′cham-fŭr) The surface formed by cutting off a corner of a board or post; a bevel.

Chan—See *Zen*.

chaplets—Metal pins driven through the *investment* to connect it to the clay core in the *lost-wax process* of *casting*.

character—In the Chinese language, a sign that records meaning rather than a sound, as for example, English letters do.

chatra—(′cha-tra) See *yasti*.

chevet—(shŭ-′va) The east, or *apsidal*, end of a *Gothic* church, including *choir*, *ambulatory*, and *radiating chapels*.

chigi—(chē-gē) The crosspiece at the gables of Japanese shrine architecture.

chimera—(kī-′mer-ŭ) A monster of Greek invention with the head and body of a lion and the tail of a serpent. A second head, that of a goat, grows out of one side of the body.

chiton—(′kī-tan) A Greek tunic, the essential (and often only) garment of both men and women, the other being the *himation*, or mantle.

choir—The space reserved for the clergy and singers in the church, usually east of the *transept* but, in some instances, extending into the *nave*.

Christogram—(′kris-tō-grăm) The three initial letters (chi-rho-iota) of Christ's name in Greek (XPI), which came to serve as a monogram for Christ.

chryselephantine—(kris-el-ŭ-′făn-tīn) Fashioned of gold and ivory.

ciborium—(su-′bor-ē-ŭm) A canopy, often freestanding and supported by four *columns*, erected over an altar; also, a covered cup used in the sacraments of the church. See *baldacchino*.

circumambulation—In Buddhist worship, walking around the *stupa* in a clockwise direction.

cire perdue—(sēr per-′dū) See *lost-wax process*.

cista (pl. **cistae**)—(′sis-tŭ/′sis-tī) An Etruscan cylindrical container made of sheet bronze with cast handles and feet, often with elaborately engraved bodies, used for women's toilet articles.

city-state—An independent, self-governing city.

clerestory—(′klēr-sto-rē) The *fenestrated* part of a building that rises above the roofs of the other parts. In Roman *basilicas* and medieval churches, the windows that form the *nave's* uppermost level below the timber ceiling or the *vaults*.

cloison—(′kloi-zŭn) A cell made of metal wire or a narrow metal strip soldered edge-up to a metal base to hold enamel or other decorative materials.

cloisonné—(′kloi-zŭ-nā) A process of enameling employing *cloisons*; also, decorative brickwork in later Byzantine architecture.

cloister—A monastery courtyard, usually with covered walks or *ambulatories* along its sides.

cluster pier—See *compound pier*.

codex (pl. **codices**)—(′kō-deks/′kō-dŭ-sēz) Separate pages of *vellum* or *parchment* bound together at one side; the predecessor of the modern book. The codex superseded the *rotulus*. In *Mesoamerica*, a painted and inscribed book on long sheets of bark paper or deerskin coated with fine white plaster and folded into accordion-like pleats.

coffer—A sunken panel, often ornamental, in a *vault* or a ceiling.

collage—(kō-′lazh) A composition made by combining on a flat surface various materials, such as newspaper, wallpaper, printed text and illustrations, photographs, and cloth.

colonnade—A series or row of *columns*, usually spanned by *lintels*.

colonnette—A thin *column*.

colophon—(′ka-lŭ-fan) An inscription, usually on the last page, giving information about a book's manufacture. In Chinese painting, written texts on attached pieces of paper or silk.

color—The value or tonality of a color is the degree of its lightness or darkness. The intensity or saturation of a color is its purity, its brightness or dullness. See also *primary*, *secondary*, and *complementary colors*.

column—A vertical, weight-carrying architectural member, circular in cross-*section* and consisting of a *base* (sometimes omitted), a *shaft*, and a *capital*.

complementary colors—Those pairs of colors, such as red and green, that together embrace the entire spectrum. The complement of one of the three *primary colors* is a mixture of the other two.

Composite capital—A capital combining *Ionic* volutes and *Corinthian* acanthus leaves, first used by the ancient Romans.

composite view—See *twisted perspective*.

composition—The way in which an artist organizes *forms* in an artwork, either by placing shapes on a flat surface or arranging forms in space.

compound pier—A *pier* with a group, or cluster, of attached *shafts*, or *responds*, especially characteristic of *Gothic* architecture.

conch—(kank) Half-dome.

concrete—A building material invented by the Romans and consisting of various proportions of lime mortar, volcanic sand, water, and small stones.

confraternity—(kon-frŭ-′tŭr-nŭ-tē) In late antiquity, an association of Christian families pooling funds to purchase property for burial. In late medieval Europe, an organization founded by laypersons who dedicated themselves to strict religious observances.

congregational mosque—A large *mosque* designed to accommodate a community's entire population for the Friday noonday prayer. Also called the Friday mosque or the great mosque.

connoisseur—An expert in assigning artworks to one artist rather than another.

continuous narration—In painting or sculpture, the convention of the same figure appearing more than once in the same space at different stages in a story.

contour line—In art, a continuous line defining the outer shape of an object.

contrapposto—(kon-trŭ-′pas-tō) The disposition of the human figure in which one part is turned in opposition to another part (usually hips and legs one way, shoulders and chest another), creating a counterpositioning of the body about its central axis. Sometimes called "weight shift" because the weight of the body tends to be thrown to one foot, creating tension on one side and relaxation on the other.

corbel—(′kor-bŭl) A projecting wall member used as a support for some element in the superstructure. Also, courses of stone or brick in which each course projects beyond the one beneath it. Two such walls, meeting at the topmost course, create a corbeled arch or *corbeled vault*.

corbeled arch—See *corbel*.

corbeled vault—A *vault* formed by the piling of stone blocks in horizontal courses, cantilevered inward until the two walls meet in an *arch*.

Corinthian capital—A more ornate form than *Doric* or *Ionic*; it consists of a double row of acanthus leaves from which tendrils and flowers grow, wrapped around a bell-shaped *echinus*. Although this *capital* form is often cited as the distinguishing feature of the Corinthian *order*, there is, strictly speaking, no Corinthian order, but only this style of capital used in the *Ionic* order.

cornice—The projecting, crowning member of the *entablature* framing the *pediment*; also, any crowning projection.

course—In masonry construction, a horizontal row of stone blocks.

crenel—See *crenellation*.

crenellation—(kren-ŭ-′lā-shŭn) Alternating solid merlons and open crenels in the notched tops of walls, as in *battlements*.

cromlech—(′krom-le̲k) A circle of *monoliths*. Also called henge.

cross-section—See *section*.

cross vault—See *vault*.

crossing—The space in a *cruciform* church formed by the intersection of the *nave* and the *transept*.

crossing square—The area in a church formed by the intersection (*crossing*) of a *nave* and a *transept* of equal width, often used as a standard *module* of interior proportion.

crossing tower—The tower over the *crossing* of a church.

cruciform—(′kru-sŭ-form) Cross shaped.

Crusades—In medieval Europe, armed pilgrimages aimed at recapturing the Holy Land from the *Muslims*.

crypt—A vaulted space under part of a building, wholly or partly underground; in churches, normally the portion under an *apse* or a *chevet*.

cubiculum (pl. **cubicula**)—(kŭ-′bik-yŭ-lŭm) A small cubicle or bedroom that opened onto the *atrium* of a Roman house. Also, a chamber in an Early Christian catacomb that served as a mortuary chapel.

cuerda seca—(′kwer-dŭ ′sā-kŭ) A type of polychrome tilework used in decorating Islamic buildings.

cuirass—(′kwēr-ăs) A military breastplate.

cult statue—The (usually over-life-size) statue placed in the *cella*, representing the deity to whom the temple is dedicated.

cuneiform—(kyŭ-′nā-ŭ-form) Latin, "wedge-shaped." A system of writing used in ancient Mesopotamia, in which wedge-shaped characters were produced by pressing a *stylus* into a soft clay tablet, which was then baked or otherwise allowed to harden.

cuneus (pl. **cunei**)—(′kŭ-nē-ŭs/′kŭ-nē-ī) In ancient Greek and Roman theaters and *amphitheaters*, wedge-shaped sections of stone benches separated by stairs.

cupola—(′kŭ-pō-lŭ) An exterior architectural feature composed of a *drum* with a shallow cap; a *dome*.

cutaway—An architectural drawing that combines an exterior view with an interior view of part of a building.

Cyclopean masonry—(sī-klō-′pē-ŭn *masonry*) A method of stone construction, named after the mythical one-eyed giant Cyclops, using massive, irregular blocks without mortar, characteristic of the Bronze Age fortifications of Tiryns and other Mycenaean sites.

cylinder seal—A cylindrical piece of stone usually about an inch or so in height, decorated with an *incised* design, so that a raised pattern was left when the seal was rolled over soft clay. In the ancient Near East, documents, storage jars, and other important possessions were signed, sealed, and identified in this way.

Daedalic—('de-dŭl-ĭk) Refers to a Greek *Orientalizing* style of the seventh century BCE named after the legendary Daedalus.

damnatio memoriae—(dam-'na-tē-ō mŭ-'mor-ĭ-ī) The Roman decree condemning those who ran afoul of the Senate. Those who suffered damnatio memoriae had their memorials demolished and their names erased from public inscriptions.

darshan—('dar-shan) In Hindu worship, seeing images of the divinity and being seen by the divinity.

deceptive cadence—In a horizontal scroll, the "false ending," which arrests the viewer's gaze by appearing to be the end of a narrative sequence, but which actually sets the stage for a culminating figure or scene.

decumanus—(de-cu-'ma-nŭs) The east-west street in a Roman town, intersecting the *cardo* at right angles.

decursio—(de-'cŏr-sĭ-ō) The ritual circling of a Roman funerary pyre.

demos—('dē-mas) The Greek word meaning "the people," from which the word *democracy* is derived.

demotic—(dē-'ma-tĭk) Late Egyptian writing.

denarius—(dĭ-'nar-ĭ-ŭs) The standard Roman silver coin from which the word *penny* ultimately derives.

dharma—('dar-mŭ) In Buddhism, moral law based on the Buddha's teaching.

diagonal rib—See *rib.*

diaphragm arch—A transverse, wall-bearing *arch* that divides a *vault* or a ceiling into compartments, providing a kind of firebreak.

dipteral—('dip-tŭr-ŭl) See *peristyle.*

diptych—('dip-tik) A two-paneled painting or *altarpiece;* also, an ancient Roman, Early Christian, or Byzantine hinged writing tablet, often of ivory and carved on the external sides.

dome—A hemispheric *vault;* theoretically, an *arch* rotated on its vertical axis.

domus—('dō-mŭs) A Roman private house.

donor portrait—A portrait of the individual who commissioned (donated) a religious work, for example, an *altarpiece,* as evidence of devotion.

Doric—('dor-ik) One of the two systems (or *orders*) evolved for articulating the three units of the elevation of an ancient Greek temple—the platform, the *colonnade,* and the superstructure (*entablature*). The Doric order is characterized by, among other features, *capitals* with funnel-shaped *echinuses, columns* without bases, and a frieze of *triglyphs* and *metopes.* See also *Ionic.*

dotaku—('do-ta-kū) Ancient Japanese bronze ceremonial bells, usually featuring raised decoration.

Dravida—Southern style of Hindu temple.

dressed masonry—Stone blocks shaped to the exact dimensions required, with smooth faces for a perfect fit.

dromos—('drŭ-mŭs) The passage leading to a *tholos tomb.*

drum—One of the stacked cylindrical stones that form the *shaft* of a *column;* the cylindrical wall that supports a *dome.*

dry fresco—See *fresco.*

earthenware—Pottery made of clay that is fired at low temperatures and is slightly porous.

eaves—The lower part of a roof that overhangs the wall.

echinus—(ŭ-'kīn-ŭs) In architecture, the convex element of a *capital* directly below the *abacus.*

effigy mounds—Ceremonial mounds built in the shape of animals or birds by native North American peoples.

elevation—In architecture, a head-on view of an external or internal wall, showing its features and often other elements that would be visible beyond or before the wall.

emblema—(em-'blā-mŭ) The central section or motif of a *mosaic.*

embrasure—A *splayed* opening in a wall that enframes a doorway or a window.

embroidery—The technique of sewing threads onto a finished ground to form contrasting designs.

encaustic—(en-'kos-tik) A painting technique in which pigment is mixed with wax and applied to the surface while hot.

engaged column—A half-round *column* attached to a wall. See also *pilaster.*

engraving—The process of *incising* a design in hard material, often a metal plate (usually copper); also, the print or impression made from such a plate.

entablature—(in-'tăb-lŭ-chŭr) The part of a building above the *columns* and below the roof. The entablature of a classical temple has three parts: *architrave* or *epistyle,* *frieze,* and *pediment.*

entasis—('en-tŭ-sŭs) The convex profile (an apparent swelling) in the *shaft* of a column.

epistyle—('ep-ŭ-stīl) See *architrave.*

Eucharist—('yū-ku-rist) In Christianity, the partaking of the bread and wine, which believers hold to be either Christ himself or symbolic of him.

exedra—(ek-'sē-drŭ) Recessed area, usually semicircular.

facade—(fŭ-'sad) Usually, the front of a building; also, the other sides when they are emphasized architecturally.

fan vault—See *vault.*

fasciae—('făsh-ē-ī) In the *Ionic order,* the three horizontal bands that make up the *architrave.*

fauces—('fo-sēz) Latin, "throat." In a Roman house, the narrow foyer leading to the *atrium.*

fenestrated—('fen-ŭ-strā-tŭd) Having windows.

fenestration—The arrangement of the windows of a building.

feudalism—The medieval political, social, and economic system held together by the relationship of a liege lord and vassal.

fibula—('fib-yū-lŭ) A decorative pin, usually used to fasten garments.

fillets—('fil-ŭts) In Ionic columns, the flat ridges of the *fluting.*

finial—A crowning ornament.

First Style mural—The earliest style of Roman mural painting. Also called the Masonry Style, because the aim of the artist was to imitate, using painted stucco relief, the appearance of costly marble panels.

Flamboyant style—A Late *Gothic* style of architecture superseding the *Rayonnant* style and named for the flamelike appearance of its pointed bar *tracery.*

flashing—In making *stained-glass* windows, fusing one layer of colored glass to another to produce a greater range of colors.

flute or **fluting**—Vertical channeling, roughly semicircular in cross-*section* and used principally on *columns* and *pilasters.*

flying buttress—See *buttress.*

folio—('fō-lĭ-ō) A page of a manuscript or book.

foreshortening—The use of *perspective* to represent in art the apparent visual contraction of an object that extends back in space at an angle to the perpendicular plane of sight.

form—In art, an object's shape and structure, either in two dimensions (for example, a figure painted on a surface) or in three dimensions (such as a statue).

formal analysis—The visual analysis of artistic form.

forum—The public square of an ancient Roman city.

Fourth Style mural—In Roman mural painting, the Fourth Style marks a return to architectural illusionism, but the architectural vistas of the Fourth Style are irrational fantasies.

freedmen, freedwomen—In ancient and medieval society, men and women who had been freed from servitude, as opposed to having been born free.

freestanding sculpture—See *sculpture in the round.*

fresco—('fres-kō) Painting on lime plaster, either dry (dry fresco or fresco secco) or wet (true or buon fresco). In the latter method, the pigments are mixed with water and become chemically bound to the freshly laid lime plaster. Also, a painting executed in either method.

fresco secco—('fres-kō 'sek-ō) See *fresco.*

fret or **meander**—An ornament, usually in bands but also covering broad surfaces, consisting of interlocking geometric motifs. An ornamental pattern of contiguous straight lines joined usually at right angles.

Friday mosque—See *congregational mosque.*

frieze—(frēz) The part of the *entablature* between the *architrave* and the *cornice;* also, any sculptured or painted band in a building. See *register.*

frigidarium—(fri-jŭ-'dă-rē-ŭm) The cold-bath section of a Roman bathing establishment.

garbha griha—('garb-ha 'grē-ha) Hindi, "womb chamber." In Hindu temples, the *cella,* the holy inner sanctum, for the cult image or symbol.

genre—('zhaⁿ-rŭ) A style or category of art; also, a kind of painting that realistically depicts scenes from everyday life.

gigantomachy—(jī-gŭn-'ta-mŭ-kē) In ancient Greek mythology, the battle between gods and giants.

giornata (pl. giornate)—Italian, "day." The section of plaster that a *fresco* painter expects to complete in one session.

glaze—A vitreous coating applied to pottery to seal and decorate the surface; it may be colored, transparent, or opaque, and glossy or *matte.* In oil painting, a thin, transparent, or semitransparent layer put over a color to alter it slightly.

glazed brick—Bricks painted and then kiln fired to fuse the color with the baked clay.

glazier—A glassworker.

gorget—('gor-jŭt) A neck pendant.

gorgon—In ancient Greek mythology, a hideous female demon with snake hair. Medusa, the most famous gorgon, was capable of turning anyone who gazed at her into stone.

Gospels—The four New Testament books that relate the life and teachings of Jesus.

Gothic—Originally a derogatory term named after the Goths, used to describe the history, culture, and art of western Europe in the 12th to 14th centuries.

granulation—A decorative technique in which tiny metal balls (granules) are fused to a metal surface.

graver—An *incising* tool used by engravers and sculptors.

groin—The edge formed by the intersection of two *vaults.*

groin vault—See *vault.*

ground line—In paintings and reliefs, a painted or carved baseline on which figures appear to stand.

guang—(gwŭng) In ancient China, covered vessels, often in animal forms, holding wine, water, grain, or meat for sacrificial rites.

hall church—See *Hallenkirche.*

Hallenkirche—('hal-ŭn-kēr-kŭ) German, "hall church"; a church design favored in Germany, but also used elsewhere, in which the *aisles* rise to the same height as the *nave.*

handscroll—In Asian art, a horizontal painted scroll that is unrolled to the left and often used to present illustrated religious texts or *landscapes.*

haniwa—(ha-nē-wa) Sculpted fired pottery cylinders, modeled in human, animal, or other forms and placed around early (archaic) Japanese burial mounds.

harmika—(har-'mē-ka) In Buddhist architecture, a stone fence or railing that encloses an area surmounting the dome of a *stupa* that represents one of the Buddhist heavens; from the center arises the *yasti.*

Hellenes (adj. **Hellenic**)—The name the ancient Greeks called themselves as the people of Hellas.

Hellenistic—The term given to the culture that developed after the death of Alexander the Great in 323 BCE and lasted almost three centuries, until the Roman conquest of Egypt in 31 BCE.

henge—See *cromlech.*

heraldic composition—A *composition* that is symmetrical on either side of a central figure.

herm—A bust on a quadrangular *pillar.*

Hiberno-Saxon—('hi-ber-no 'sak-sŭn) An art style that flourished in the monasteries of the British Isles in the early Middle Ages. Also called Insular.

hierarchy of scale—An artistic convention in which greater size indicates greater importance.

hieratic—(hī-ŭ-'ră-tik) A fixed, stylized method of representation, often determined by religious principles and ideas.

hieroglyphic—(hī-rō-ʹglif-ik) A system of writing using symbols or pictures.

high relief—See *relief.*

Hijra—(ʹhij-rŭ) The flight of Muhammad from Mecca to Medina in 622, the year from which Islam dates its beginnings.

himation—(hī-ʹmā-shŭn) An ancient Greek mantle worn by men and women over the *chiton* and draped in various ways.

Hippodamian plan—(hī-pō-ʹdā-mĭ-ŭn) A city plan devised by Hippodamos of Miletos ca. 466 BCE, in which a strict grid was imposed on a site, regardless of the terrain, so that all streets would meet at right angles.

hiragana—(hē-ra-ga-na) A sound-based writing system developed in Japan from Chinese characters; it came to be the primary script for Japanese court poetry.

historiated—Ornamented with representations, such as plants, animals, or human figures, that have a narrative—as distinct from a purely decorative—function.

hue—The name of a *color.* See *primary colors, secondary colors,* and *complementary colors.*

hydria—(ʹhī-drē-ŭ) An ancient Greek three-handled water pitcher.

hypaethral—(hīp-ʹēth-rŭl) A building having no pediment or roof, open to the sky.

hypostyle hall—(ʹhī-pŭ-stīl *hall*) A hall with a roof supported by *columns.*

icon—A portrait or image; especially in Byzantine art, a panel with a painting of sacred personages that are objects of veneration. In the visual arts, a painting, a piece of sculpture, or even a building regarded as an object of veneration.

iconoclasm—(ī-ʹkanŭ-klăz(-ŭ)m) The destruction of images. In Byzantium, the period from 726 to 843 when there was an imperial ban on images. The destroyers of images were known as iconoclasts. Those who opposed such a ban were known as iconophiles or iconodules.

iconodule—(ī-ʹkan-ŭ-dyül) See *iconoclasm.*

iconography—(ī-kŭn-ʹa-grŭ-fē) Greek, the "writing of images." The term refers both to the content, or subject, of an artwork and to the study of content in art. It also includes the study of the symbolic, often religious, meaning of objects, persons, or events depicted in works of art.

iconophile—See *iconoclasm.*

iconostasis—(ī-kŭ-ʹnas-tŭ-sŭs) In Byzantine churches, a screen or a partition, with doors and many tiers of *icons,* separating the sanctuary from the main body of the church.

ikegobo—(ʹē-kā-gō-bō) A Benin royal shrine.

illuminated manuscript—A luxurious handmade book with painted illustrations and decorations.

illumination—Decoration (usually in gold, silver, and bright colors), especially of medieval manuscript pages.

illusionistic—The depiction of the three-dimensional spatial world on a two-dimensional surface.

imagines—(i-ʹma-gi-nes) In ancient Rome, wax portraits of ancestors.

imam—(i-ʹmam or i-ʹmăm) In Islam, the leader of collective worship.

imperator—(im-pŭ-ʹra-tŭr) Latin, "commander in chief," from which the word *emperor* is derived.

impluvium—(im-ʹplū-vē-ŭm) In a Roman house, the basin located in the *atrium* that collected rainwater.

impost block—A stone with the shape of a truncated, inverted pyramid, placed between a *capital* and the *arch* that springs from it.

in antis—(in ʹăn-tĭs) In ancient Greek architecture, between the *antae.*

in situ—(in sŭ-ʹtŭ) In place; in the original position.

incise—(in-ʹsīz) To cut into a surface with a sharp instrument; also, a method of decoration, especially on metal and pottery.

incrustation—Wall decoration consisting of bright panels of different colors.

insula—(ʹin-sŭ-lŭ) In Roman architecture, a multistory apartment house, usually made of brick-faced *concrete;* also refers to an entire city block.

Insular—See *Hiberno-Saxon.*

interaxial—The distance between the center of the lowest *drum* of a *column* and the center of the next.

intonaco—The final, smooth layer of plaster in *fresco* painting.

investment—The final clay *mold* used in the *lost-wax process* of *casting.*

Ionic—(ī-ʹan-ik) One of the two systems (or *orders*) evolved for articulating the three units of the elevation of a Greek temple: the platform, the *colonnade,* and the superstructure *(entablature).* The Ionic order is characterized by, among other features, *volutes, capitals, columns* with *bases,* and an uninterrupted *frieze.*

iron-wire lines—In ancient Chinese painting, thin brush lines suggesting tensile strength.

iwan—(ʹē-wan) In Islamic architecture, a vaulted rectangular recess opening onto a courtyard.

jambs—(ʹjāms) In architecture, the side posts of a doorway.

jataka—(ʹjă-tă-kă) Tales of the past lives of the Buddha. See also *sutra.*

jomon—(jo-mon) Japanese, "cord markings." A type of Japanese decorative technique characterized by ropelike markings.

ka—(ka) In ancient Egypt, the immortal human life force.

Kaaba—(ʹka-ba) Arabic, "cube." A small cubical building in Mecca, the *Muslim* world's symbolic center.

kami—(ka-mī) Shinto deities or spirits, believed in Japan to exist in nature (mountains, waterfalls) and in charismatic people.

karma—(ʹkar-mŭ) In Vedic religions, the ethical consequences of a person's life, which determine his or her fate.

keep—A fortified tower in a castle that served as a place of last refuge.

key or **meander**—See *fret.*

keystone—See *voussoir.*

kiva—(ʹkē-vŭ) A large circular underground structure that is the spiritual and ceremonial center of Pueblo Indian life.

kondo—(kon-do) Japanese, "golden hall." In a Japanese Buddhist temple complex, the building housing the main sculptural icons.

Koran—(ko-ʹran) Islam's sacred book, composed of *surahs* (chapters) divided into verses.

kore (pl. **korai**)—(ʹkor-ā/ʹkor-ī) Greek, "young woman." An Archaic Greek statuary type depicting a young woman.

kouros (pl. **kouroi**)—(ʹkŭr-os/ʹkŭr-oi) Greek, "young man." An Archaic Greek statuary type depicting a young man.

krater—An ancient Greek wide-mouthed bowl for mixing wine and water.

Kufic—(ʹkŭ-fŭk) An early form of Arabic script, characterized by angularity, with the uprights forming almost right angles with the baseline.

kylix—(ʹkī-lĭks) An ancient Greek shallow drinking cup with two handles and a stem.

lacquer—(ʹlăk-ŭr) A varnishlike substance made from the sap of the Asiatic sumac, used to decorate wood and other organic materials. Often colored with mineral pigments, lacquer cures to great hardness and has a lustrous surface.

lakshana(s)—(laksh-ʹha-na) Distinguishing marks of the Buddha. They include the *urna* and *ushnisha.*

lalitasana—(la-ʹlē-ta-sa-na) In Buddhist iconography, the body pose with one leg folded and the other hanging down, indicating relaxation.

lamassu—(la-ʹma-sū) Assyrian guardian in the form of a man-headed winged bull.

lancet—(ʹlăn-sŭt) In *Gothic* architecture, a tall narrow window ending in a *pointed arch.*

landscape—A picture showing natural scenery, without narrative content.

lateral section—See *section.*

leading—In the manufacture of *stained-glass* windows, the joining of colored glass pieces using lead *cames.*

lectionary—(ʹlek-shŭn-er-ē) A book containing passages from the *Gospels,* arranged in the sequence that they are to be read during the celebration of religious services, including the *Mass,* throughout the year.

lekythos (pl. **lekythoi**)—(ʹlek-ē-thos/ʹlek-ē-thoi) A flask containing perfumed oil; lekythoi were often placed in Greek graves as offerings to the deceased.

linear perspective—See *perspective.*

linga—(ʹlin-ga) In Hindu art, the depiction of Shiva as a phallus or cosmic *pillar.*

lintel—(ʹlin-tŭl) A beam used to span an opening.

lithograph—A printmaking technique in which images are printed from a flat stone.

loculi—(ʹlak-yŭ-lē) Openings in the walls of *catacombs* to receive the dead.

longitudinal plan—See *plan.*

longitudinal section—See *section.*

lost-wax process (cire perdue)—A bronze-casting method in which a figure is modeled in wax and covered with clay; the whole is fired, melting away the wax and hardening the clay, which then becomes a mold for molten metal.

low relief—See *relief.*

lunette—(lū-ʹnet) A semicircular area (with the flat side down) in a wall over a door, niche, or window; also, a painting or *relief* with a semicircular frame.

madrasa—(mŭ-ʹdra-sŭ) An Islamic theological college adjoining and often containing a *mosque.*

maebyong—(mī-byŭng) A Korean vase similar to the Chinese *meiping.*

magi—(ʹmă-jī) The three wise men from the East who presented gifts to the infant Jesus.

mandala—(man-ʹda-la) Sacred diagram of the universe.

mandapa—(man-ʹda-pa) *Pillared* hall of a Hindu temple.

mandorla—(măn-ʹdor-lŭ) An almond-shaped *nimbus* surrounding the figure of Christ or other sacred figure.

maniera greca—Italian, "Greek style." The Italo-Byzantine style of painting of the 13th century.

maqsura—(mak-ʹsū-ra) In some *mosques,* a screened area in front of the *mihrab* reserved for a ruler.

Masonry Style—See *First Style mural.*

masquerade—Among some African groups, a ritualized drama performed by several masked dancers, embodying ancestors or nature spirits.

Mass—The Catholic and Orthodox ritual in which believers understand that Christ's redeeming sacrifice on the cross is repeated when the priest consecrates the bread and wine in the *Eucharist.*

mastaba—(ma-ʹsta-ba) Arabic, "bench." An ancient Egyptian rectangular brick or stone structure with sloping sides erected over a subterranean tomb chamber connected with the outside by a shaft.

matte (also **mat**)—(măt) In painting, pottery, and photography, a dull finish.

maulstick—A stick used to steady the hand while painting.

mausoleum—(mo-sō-ʹlē-ŭm) A monumental tomb. The name derives from the mid-fourth century BCE tomb of Mausolos at Halikarnassos, one of the Seven Wonders of the ancient world.

meander or **key**—See *fret.*

medium—The material (for example, marble, bronze, clay, fresco) in which an artist works; also, in painting, the vehicle (usually liquid) that carries the pigment.

megalith (adj., **megalithic**)—(ʹme-gŭ-lith/me-gŭ-ʹlith-ik) Greek, "great stone." A large, roughly hewn stone used in the construction of monumental prehistoric structures. See also *cromlech.*

megaron—(ʹmeg-ŭ-ron) The large reception hall in a Mycenaean palace, fronted by an open, two-*columned* porch.

meiping—(ʹmā-ping) A Chinese vase of a high-shouldered shape; the *sgrafitto* technique was used in decorating such vases.

mendicants—(ʹmen-di-cŭnts) In medieval Europe, friars belonging to the Franciscan and Dominican orders, who renounced all worldly goods, lived by contributions of laypersons (the word *mendicant* means "beggar"), and devoted themselves to preaching, teaching, and doing good works.

menorah—(mŭ-ʹno-rŭ) In antiquity, the Jewish sacred seven-branched candelabrum.

merlon—See *crenellation.*

Mesoamerica—The region that comprises Mexico, Guatemala, Belize, Honduras, and the Pacific coast of El Salvador.

Mesolithic—(mez-ō-ˈlith-ik) The "middle" Stone Age, between the *Paleolithic* and the *Neolithic* ages.

Messiah—(mǔ-ˈsi-ǔ) The savior of the Jews prophesied in the Old Testament. Christians believe that Jesus of Nazareth was the Messiah.

metate—(mǔ-ˈta-tā) A ceremonial grinding stone, perhaps used as a throne in northern South America and various Central American regions.

metope—(ˈmet-ǔ-pē) The panel between the *triglyphs* in a *Doric frieze*, often sculpted in *relief.*

mihrab—(mi-ˈrab) A semicircular niche set into the *qibla* wall of a *mosque.*

minaret—(ˈmin-ǔ-ret) A distinctive feature of *mosque* architecture, a tower from which the faithful are called to worship.

minbar—(ˈmin-bar) In a *mosque,* the pulpit on which the *imam* stands.

mithuna—Male and female couple embracing or engaged in sexual intercourse.

module—A basic unit of which the dimensions of the major parts of a work are multiples. The principle is used in sculpture and other art forms, but it is most often employed in architecture, where the module may be the dimensions of an important part of a building, such as the diameter of a *column.*

moksha—See *nirvana.*

mold—A hollow form for shaping a fluid substance.

molding—In architecture, a continuous, narrow surface (projecting or recessed, plain or ornamented) designed to break up a surface, to accent, or to decorate.

monolith—A *column* shaft that is all in one piece (not composed of *drums*); a large, single block or piece of stone used in *megalithic* structures.

moralized Bible—A heavily illustrated Bible, each page pairing paintings of Old and New Testament episodes with explanations of their moral significance.

mortise-and-tenon system—(ˈmor-tǔs- *and* -ˈten-ǔn) See *tenon.*

mosaic—(mō-ˈzā-ǔk) Patterns or pictures made by embedding small pieces *(tesserae)* of stone or glass in cement on surfaces such as walls and floors; also, the technique of making such works.

mosaic tilework—An Islamic decorative technique in which large ceramic panels are fired, cut into smaller pieces, and set in plaster.

mosque—(mask) The Islamic building for collective worship. From the Arabic word *masjid,* meaning a "place for bowing down."

mudra—(ˈmǔ-drǔ, *or* ˈmǔ-drǔ) In Buddhist and Hindu iconography, a stylized and symbolic hand gesture.

Muhaqqaq—(mǔ-ha-ˈkak) A cursive style of Islamic *calligraphy.*

mullion—(ˈmǔl-yǔn) A vertical member that divides a window or that separates one window from another.

mummification—A technique used by ancient Egyptians to preserve human bodies so that they may serve as the eternal home of the immortal *ka.*

muqarnas—(mǔ-ˈkar-nas) Stucco decorations of Islamic buildings in which stalactite-like forms break a structure's solidity.

mural—A wall painting.

Muslim—A believer in Islam.

Nagara—Northern style of Hindu temple.

naos—(ˈnā-os) See *cella.*

narthex—(ˈnar-theks) A porch or vestibule of a church, generally *colonnaded* or *arcaded* and preceding the *nave.*

natatio—(na-ˈta-tē-ō) The swimming pool in a Roman bathing establishment.

naturalism—The close observation of the natural world and the depiction in art of a perceptual reality.

nave—The central area of an ancient Roman *basilica* or of a church, demarcated from *aisles* by *piers* or *columns.*

nave arcade—In *basilica* architecture, the series of *arches* supported by *piers* or columns separating the *nave* from the *aisles.*

necking—A groove at the bottom of the ancient Greek *Doric capital* between the *echinus* and the *flutes* that masks the junction of *capital* and *shaft.*

necropolis—(nǔ-ˈkrop-ǔ-lǔs) Greek, "city of the dead"; a large burial area or cemetery.

nemes—(ˈne-mes) In ancient Egypt, the linen headdress worn by the pharaoh, with the uraeus cobra of kingship on the front.

Neolithic—(Nē-ō-ˈlith-ik) The "new" Stone Age.

nimbus—A halo or aureole appearing around the head of a holy figure to signify divinity.

nirvana—In Buddhism and Hinduism, a blissful state brought about by absorption of the individual soul or consciousness into the supreme spirit. Also called moksha.

nymphs—In classical mythology, female divinities of springs, caves, and woods.

oculus (pl. **oculi**)—(ˈa-kyǔ-lus/a-kyǔ-lē) Latin, "eye." The round central opening of a dome. Also, a small round window in a *Gothic cathedral.*

ogee arch—(ō-ˈjē) An *arch* made up of two double-curving lines meeting at a point.

oil paint—Pigment mixed with oil. Oil paint dries more slowly than *tempera,* allowing the painter to lay down the color in superimposed translucent layers. See *glaze.*

opisthodomos—(o-pis-ˈthad-ǔ-mǔs) In Greek architecture, a porch at the rear of a temple, set against the blank back wall of the *cella.*

opus reticulatum—(ˈō-pǔs rǔ-tik-ǔ-ˈlat-ǔm) An ancient Roman method of facing *concrete* walls with lozenge-shaped bricks or stones to achieve a netlike ornamental surface pattern.

orant—(ˈōr-ǎnt) In Early Christian art, a figure with both arms raised in the ancient gesture of prayer.

oratory—The church of a Christian monastery.

orchestra—Greek, "dancing place." In ancient Greek theaters, the circular piece of earth with a hard and level surface on which the performance took place.

order—In classical architecture, a style represented by a characteristic design of the *columns* and *entablature.* See also *superimposed orders.*

Orientalizing—The early phase of Archaic Greek art, so named because of the adoption of forms and motifs from the ancient Near East and Egypt.

orthogonal—(or-ˈthag-ǔn-ǔl) A line imagined to be behind and perpendicular to the picture plane; the orthogonals in a painting appear to recede toward a vanishing point on the horizon.

orthogonal plan—The imposition of a strict grid plan on a site, regardless of the terrain, so that all streets meet at right angles. See also *Hippodamian plan.*

Ottonian (adj.)—Pertaining to the empire of Otto I and his successors.

pagoda—(pǔ-ˈgō-dǔ) A Chinese tower, usually associated with a Buddhist temple, having a multiplicity of winged *eaves;* thought to be derived from the Indian *stupa.*

pala—(ˈpa-lǔ) In churches, an *altarpiece,* or panel placed behind and over the altar.

palaestra—(pǔ-ˈles-trǔ) An ancient Greek and Roman exercise area, usually framed by a *colonnade.*

Paleolithic—(pā-lē-ō-ˈlith-ik) The "old" Stone Age, during which humankind produced the first sculptures and paintings.

palette—In ancient Egypt, a slate slab used for preparing makeup. A thin board with a thumb hole at one end on which an artist lays and mixes colors; any surface so used. Also, the colors or kinds of colors characteristically used by an artist.

Pantocrator—(pan-ˈtak-rǔ-tǔr) Christ as ruler and judge of heaven and earth.

papyrus—(pǔ-ˈpī-rǔs) A plant native to Egypt and adjacent lands used to make paperlike writing material; also, the material or any writing on it.

parchment—Lambskin prepared as a surface for painting or writing.

parekklesion—(pǎ-rǔ-ˈklē-zǔ-an) The side chapel in a Byzantine church.

parapet—A low, protective wall along the edge of a balcony or roof.

parinirvana—(pǎ-ri-nör-ˈva-nǔ) Image of the reclining Buddha, often viewed as representing his death.

paten—A large bowl to hold the bread used in the Eucharist.

patricians—Roman freeborn landowners.

pebble mosaic—Mosaic made of irregularly shaped stones of various colors.

pectoral—An ornament worn on the chest.

pediment—In classical architecture, the triangular space (gable) at the end of a building, formed by the ends of the sloping roof above the *colonnade;* also, an ornamental feature having this shape.

pendant—The large hanging terminal element of a *Gothic* fan vault.

pendentive—A concave, triangular section of a hemisphere, four of which provide the transition from a square area to the circular base of a covering *dome.* Although pendentives appear to be hanging (pendant) from the dome, they in fact support it.

peplos—(ˈpep-los) A simple long woolen belted garment worn by ancient Greek women.

peripteral—(pǔ-ˈrip-tǔr-ǔl) See *peristyle.*

peristyle—(ˈper-rǔ-stīl) In ancient Greek architecture, a *colonnade* all around the *cella* and its porch(es). A peripteral colonnade consists of a single row of *columns* on all sides; a dipteral colonnade has a double row all around.

personification—An abstract idea represented in bodily form.

perspective—A method of presenting an illusion of the three-dimensional world on a two-dimensional surface. In linear perspective, the most common type, all parallel lines or surface edges converge on one, two, or three vanishing points located with reference to the eye level of the viewer (the horizon line of the picture), and associated objects are rendered smaller the farther from the viewer they are intended to seem. Atmospheric, or aerial, perspective creates the illusion of distance by the greater diminution of color intensity, the shift in color toward an almost neutral blue, and the blurring of contours as the intended distance between eye and object increases.

piazza—Italian, "plaza" or "square." An open-air public space.

pictograph—(ˈpik-tō-grǎf) A picture, usually stylized, that represents an idea; also, writing using such means; also painting on rock. See also *hieroglyphic.*

pier—A vertical, freestanding masonry support.

pier buttress—See *buttress.*

Pietà—(pē-a-ˈta) A painted or sculpted representation of the Virgin Mary mourning over the body of the dead Christ.

pilaster—A flat, rectangular, vertical member projecting from a wall of which it forms a part. It usually has a *base* and a *capital* and is often *fluted.*

pillar—Usually a weight-carrying member, such as a *pier* or a *column;* sometimes an isolated, freestanding structure used for commemorative purposes.

pinakotheke—(pin-a-kō-ˈthē-kē) Greek, "picture gallery;" a room or building for the exhibition of paintings on wooden panels.

pinnacle—In *Gothic* churches, a sharply pointed ornament capping the *piers* or flying *buttresses;* also used on church *facades.*

plan—The horizontal arrangement of the parts of a building or of the buildings and streets of a city or town, or a drawing or diagram showing such an arrangement. In an axial plan, the parts of a building are organized longitudinally, or along a given axis; in a central plan, the parts of the structure are of equal or almost equal dimensions around the center.

plane—A flat or two-dimensional surface.

plate tracery—See *tracery.*

plebeian—(pli-ˈbe-ǔn) The Roman social class that included small farmers, merchants, and freed slaves.

plinth—The square slab at the *base* of a *column.*

pointed arch—A narrow *arch* of pointed profile, in contrast to a semicircular arch.

polis (pl. **poleis**)—(ˈpa-lǔs/ˈpa-lās) An independent city-state in ancient Greece.

pontifex maximus—Latin, "chief priest." The high priest of the Roman state religion, often the emperor himself.

porcelain—(ˈpor-sǔ-lǔn) Extremely fine, hard, white ceramic. Unlike stoneware, porcelain is made from a fine white clay called kaolin mixed with ground petuntse, a type of feldspar. True porcelain is translucent and rings when struck.

portico—('por-tŭ-kō) A roofed *colonnade;* also an entrance porch.

post-and-lintel system—A system of construction in which two posts support a *lintel.*

prasada—(pra-'sa-dŭ) In Hindu worship, food that becomes sacred by first being given to a god.

pre-Columbian (adj.)—The cultures that flourished in the Western Hemisphere before the arrival of Christopher Columbus and the beginning of European contact and conquest.

prefiguration—In Early Christian art, the depiction of Old Testament persons and events as prophetic forerunners of Christ and New Testament events.

primary colors—Red, yellow, and blue—the colors from which all other colors may be derived.

print—An artwork on paper, usually produced in multiple impressions.

pronaos—('pro-nā-os) The space, or porch, in front of the *cella,* or *naos,* of an ancient Greek temple.

proscenium—the part of a theatrical stage in front of the curtain.

prostyle—('prō-stīl) A style of ancient Greek temple in which the *columns* are only in front of the *cella* and not on the sides or back.

provenance—('prō-vŭ-nan̄s) Origin or source; findspot.

psalter—('sol-tŭr) A book containing the Psalms.

pseudoperipteral—(sū-dō-pŭ-'rip-tŭr-ŭl) In Roman architecture, a pseudoperipteral temple has a series of engaged *columns* all around the sides and back of the *cella* to give the appearance of a *peripteral colonnade.*

pueblo—('pwe-blō) A communal multistoried dwelling made of stone or *adobe* brick by the Native Americans of the Southwest; with cap. also used to refer to various groups that occupied such dwellings.

purlins—('pŭr-lins) Horizontal beams in a roof structure, parallel to the *ridgepoles,* resting on the main rafters and giving support to the secondary rafters.

putto (pl. **putti**)—('pŭ-tō/'pŭ-ti) A cherubic young boy.

pylon—('pī-lan) A simple and massive gateway, with sloping walls.

pylon temple—The characteristic Egyptian New Kingdom type of temple, entered through a monumental *pylon.*

qibla—('kē-blŭ) The direction (toward Mecca) *Muslims* face when praying.

quadrant arch—An arch whose curve extends for one quarter of a circle's circumference.

radiating chapels—In medieval churches, chapels for the display of *relics* that opened directly onto the *ambulatory* and the *transept.*

radiocarbon dating—Method of measuring the decay rate of carbon isotopes in organic matter to provide dates for organic materials such as wood and fiber.

rafter—Sloping wooden planks in roofs of Chinese buildings.

raking cornice—The *cornice* on the sloping sides of a *pediment.*

ramparts—Defensive wall circuits.

ratha—('rat-ha) Small, freestanding Hindu temple carved from a huge boulder.

Rayonnant—(rā-yō-'naⁿ) The "radiant" style of *Gothic* architecture, dominant in the second half of the 13th century and associated with the French royal court of Louis IX at Paris.

red-figure painting—In later Greek pottery, the silhouetting of red figures against a black background, with painted linear details; the reverse of *black-figure painting.*

refectory—(rŭ-'fek-tŭ-rē) The dining hall of a Christian monastery.

register—One of a series of superimposed bands or *friezes* in a pictorial narrative, or the particular levels on which motifs are placed.

relics—The body parts, clothing, or objects associated with a holy figure, such as the Buddha or Christ or a Christian *saint.*

relief—In sculpture, figures projecting from a background of which they are part. The degree of relief is designated high, low *(bas),* or sunken. In the last, the artist cuts the design into the surface so that the highest projecting parts of the image are no higher than the surface itself. See also *repoussé.*

relieving triangle—In Mycenaean architecture, the triangular opening above the *lintel* that serves to lighten the weight to be carried by the lintel itself.

reliquary—('rel-ŭ-kwe-rē) A container for keeping *relics.*

repoussé—(rŭ-pū-'sā) Formed in *relief* by beating a metal plate from the back, leaving the impression on the face. The metal is hammered into a hollow mold of wood or some other pliable material and finished with a *graver.* See also *relief.*

respond—An engaged *column, pilaster,* or similar element that either projects from a *compound pier* or some other supporting device or is bonded to a wall and carries one end of an *arch.*

retable—(rē-'tā-bŭl) An architectural screen or wall above and behind an altar, usually containing painting, sculpture, carving, or other decorations. See also *altarpiece.*

revetment—(rŭ-'vet-mŭnt) In architecture, a wall covering or facing.

rib—A relatively slender, molded masonry *arch* that projects from a surface. In *Gothic* architecture, the ribs form the framework of the *vaulting.* A diagonal rib is one of the ribs that form the **X** of a *groin vault.* A transverse rib crosses the nave or aisle at a 90-degree angle.

rib vault—A *vault* in which the diagonal and transverse *ribs* compose a structural skeleton that partially supports the masonry *web* between them.

ridgepole—The beam running the length of a building below the peak of the gabled roof.

Romanesque—(rō-mŭ-'nesk) "Romanlike." A term used to describe the history, culture, and art of medieval western Europe from ca. 1050 to ca. 1200.

roof comb—The elaborately sculpted vertical projection surmounting a Maya temple-pyramid.

rose window—A circular *stained-glass* window.

rotulus—('rat-yū-lŭs) The manuscript scroll used by Egyptians, Greeks, Etruscans, and Romans; predecessor of the *codex.*

rotunda—(rō-'tŭnd-ŭ) The circular area under a *dome;* also a domed round building.

roundel—A circular painting or relief sculpture, also called a *tondo.*

rusticate—To give a rustic appearance by roughening the surfaces and beveling the edges of stone blocks to emphasize the joints between them. Rustication is a technique employed in ancient Roman architecture, and popular during the Renaissance, especially for stone courses at the ground-floor level.

rustication—Rough, unfinished masonry; see *rusticate.*

saint—From the Latin word *sanctus,* meaning "made holy by God." Persons who suffered and died for their Christian faith or who merited reverence for their Christian devotion while alive. In the Roman Catholic Church, a worthy deceased Catholic who is canonized by the pope.

samsara—(sŭm-'sa-rŭ) In Hindu belief, the rebirth of the soul into a succession of lives.

sarcophagus (pl. **sarcophagi**)—(sar-'kof-ŭ-gŭs/sar-'kof-ŭ-gī) Latin, "consumer of flesh." A coffin, usually of stone.

saturation—The brightness or dullness of a *hue.*

satyr—('săt-ŭr) A part-human, part-goat male follower of the ancient Greek god Dionysos.

saz—(săz) An Ottoman Turkish design of sinuous curved leaves and blossoms.

scarification—('scar-ŭ-fŭ-cā-zhŭn) Decorative markings made with scars on the human body.

school—A chronological and stylistic classification of works of art with a stipulation of place.

scriptorium (pl. **scriptoria**)—(skrip-'tor-ē-um/skrip-'tor-ē-ŭ) The writing studio of a monastery.

sculpture in the round—Freestanding figures, carved or modeled in three dimensions.

Second Style mural—The style of Roman mural painting in which the aim was to dissolve the confining walls of a room and replace them with the illusion of a three-dimensional world constructed in the artist's imagination.

secondary colors—Orange, green, and purple, obtained by mixing pairs of *primary colors* (red, yellow, blue).

section—In architecture, a diagram or representation of a part of a structure or building along an imaginary plane that passes through it vertically. Drawings showing a theoretical slice, or cross-section, across a structure's width are lateral sections. Those cutting through a building's length are longitudinal sections. See also *elevation* and *cutaway.*

senate—Latin, "council of elders." The legislative body in Roman constitutional government.

serdab—(sŭ(r)-'dab) A small concealed chamber in an Egyptian *mastaba* for the statue of the deceased.

sexpartite vault—(seks-'par-tīt *vault*) See *vault.*

sgrafitto—(skraf-'fē-tō) A Chinese ceramic technique in which the design is *incised* through a colored *slip.*

shaft—The tall, cylindrical part of a *column* between the *capital* and the *base.*

shakti—('shak-tē) In Hinduism, the female power of the deity Devi (or Goddess), which animates the matter of the cosmos.

shikara—The beehive-shaped tower of a Hindu temple.

shogun—('shō-gŭn) In 14th- through 19th-century Japan, a military governor who managed the country on behalf of a figurehead emperor.

sinopia—The burnt-orange pigment used in drawing on the *arriccio* in *fresco* painting.

siren—In ancient Greek mythology, a creature that was part bird, part woman.

skene—The scene building of a Greek theater.

skenographia—(skā-no-gra-'fē-u) Greek, "scene painting"; the Greek term for *perspective* painting.

skiagraphia—(skē-u-gra-'fē-u) Greek, "shadow painting"; the Greek term for shading, said to have been invented by Apollodoros, an Athenian painter of the fifth century BCE.

slip—A mixture of fine clay and water used in ceramic decoration.

spandrel—('spăn-drŭl) The roughly triangular space enclosed by the curves of adjacent *arches* and a horizontal member connecting their vertexes; also, the space enclosed by the curve of an *arch* and an enclosing right angle. The area between the arch proper and the framing *columns* and *entablature.*

spectrum—The full range of visible wavelengths of light.

sphinx—(sfengks) A mythical Egyptian beast with the body of a lion and the head of a human.

splayed—An opening (as in a wall) that is cut away diagonally so that the outer edges are farther apart than the inner edges. See also *embrasure.*

springing—The lowest stone of an *arch,* resting on the *impost block.* In *Gothic* vaulting, the lowest stone of a diagonal or transverse *rib.*

squinch—(skwinch) An architectural device used as a transition from a square to a polygonal or circular base for a *dome.* It may be composed of *lintels, corbels,* or *arches.*

stained glass—In *Gothic* architecture, the colored glass used for windows.

stave—A wedge-shaped timber; vertically placed staves embellish the architectural features of the building.

stele—('stē-lē) A carved stone slab used to mark graves or to commemorate historical events.

still life—A picture depicting an arrangement of objects.

stoa—('sto-ŭ) In ancient Greek architecture, an open building with a roof supported by a row of *columns* parallel to the back wall. A covered *colonnade* or *portico.*

stoneware—Pottery fired at high temperatures to produce a stonelike hardness and density.

stringcourse—A raised horizontal *molding,* or band in masonry, ornamental but usually reflecting interior structure.

strut—Vertical wooden support in Chinese buildings.

stupa—('stū-pŭ) A large, mound-shaped Buddhist shrine.

stylobate—('stī-lŭ-bāt) The uppermost course of the platform of a Greek temple, which supports the *columns.*

stylus—('stī-lŭs) A needlelike tool used in *engraving* and *incising;* also, an ancient writing instrument used to inscribe clay or wax tablets.

subtractive light—The light reflected from painting pigments and objects.

subtractive sculpture—A kind of sculpture technique in which materials are taken away from the original mass; carving.

sultan—A *Muslim* ruler.

sunken relief—See *relief.*

Sunnah—('su-nŭ) Collection of the Prophet Muhammad's moral sayings and descriptions of his deeds.

superimposed orders—*Orders* of architecture that are placed one above another in an *arcaded* or *colonnaded* building, usually in the following sequence: *Doric* (the first story), *Ionic,* and *Corinthian.* Superimposed orders are found in later Greek architecture and were used widely by Roman and Renaissance builders.

surahs—('su-rŭs) Chapters of the *Koran,* divided into verses.

sutra—('sū-trŭ) In Buddhism, an account of a sermon by or a dialogue involving the Buddha. A scriptural account of the Buddha. See also *jataka.*

symbol—In art, an image that stands for another image or encapsulates an idea.

symmetria—(sim-ŭ-'trē-ŭ) Greek, "commensurability of parts." Polykleitos's treatise on his *canon* of proportions incorporated the principle of symmetria.

taberna—(ta-'ber-na) In Roman architecture, a single-room shop usually covered by a barrel *vault.*

tablinum—('ta-bli-num) The study or office in a Roman house.

tapestry—A weaving technique in which the *weft* threads are packed densely over the *warp* threads so that the designs are woven directly into the fabric.

technique—The processes that artists employ to create *form,* as well as the distinctive, personal ways in which they handle their materials and tools.

tempera—('tem-pŭ-rŭ) A technique of painting using pigment mixed with egg yolk, glue, or casein; also the *medium* itself.

templon—('tem-plan) The columnar screen separating the sanctuary from the main body of a Byzantine church.

tenon—('te-nŭn) A projection on the end of a piece of wood that is inserted into a corresponding hole (mortise) in another piece of wood to form a joint.

tenoned—Attached by stone pegs.

tepidarium—(tep-ŭ-'dă-rē-ŭm) The warm-bath section of a Roman bathing establishment.

terracotta—(te-rŭ-'ko-tŭ) Hard-baked clay, used for sculpture and as a building material. It may be *glazed* or painted.

tesserae—('tes-ŭ-rē) Greek, "cubes." Tiny stones or pieces of glass cut to the desired shape and size to form a *mosaic.*

tetrarchy—(te-'trar-kē) Greek, "rule by four." A type of Roman government established in the late third century CE by Diocletian in an attempt to establish order by sharing power with potential rivals.

texture—The quality of a surface (rough, smooth, hard, soft, shiny, dull) as revealed by light. In represented texture, a painter depicts an object as having a certain texture even though the paint is the actual texture.

theatron—(thē-'ăt-ron) Greek, "place for seeing." In ancient Greek theaters, the slope overlooking the *orchestra* on which the spectators sat.

Theotokos—(thē-'ō-tō-kos) Greek, "bearer of God." The Virgin Mary, the mother of Jesus.

thermoluminescence—('thör-mō-lū-mū-'ne-sŭns) A method of dating amounts of radiation found within the clay of ceramic or sculptural forms, as well as in the clay cores from metal castings.

Third Style mural—In Roman mural painting, the style in which delicate linear fantasies were sketched on predominantly monochromatic backgrounds.

tholos (pl. **tholoi**)—('thō-los/'thō-loi) A temple with a circular plan.

tholos tomb—In Mycenean architecture, a beehive-shaped tomb with a circular plan.

thrust—The outward force exerted by an *arch* or a *vault* that must be counterbalanced by a *buttress.*

tondo—('ton-dō) See *roundel.*

Torah—('to-rŭ) The scroll containing the Pentateuch, the first five books of the Hebrew Scriptures.

torana—('to-ra-na) Gateway in the stone fence around a *stupa,* located at the cardinal points of the compass.

torque—(tork) The neck band worn by Gauls.

tracery—Ornamental stonework for holding *stained glass* in place, characteristic of *Gothic* cathedrals. In plate tracery the glass fills only the "punched holes" in the heavy ornamental stonework. In bar tracery the stained-glass windows fill almost the entire opening, and the stonework is unobtrusive.

transept—('trăn-sept) The part of a church with an axis that crosses the nave at a right angle.

transverse arch—An *arch* separating one vaulted *bay* from the next.

transverse rib—See *rib.*

treasury—In ancient Greece, a small building set up for the safe storage of *votive offerings.*

trefoil—('trē-foil) A cloverlike ornament or symbol with stylized leaves in groups of three.

tribune—In church architecture, a gallery over the inner *aisle* flanking the *nave.*

triclinium—(tri-'klin-ē-um) The dining room of a Roman house.

trident—The three-pronged pitchfork associated with the ancient Greek sea god Poseidon (Roman, Neptune).

triforium—(tri-'for-ē-ŭm) In a *Gothic* cathedral, the *blind arcaded* gallery below the *clerestory;* occasionally the arcades are filled with *stained glass.*

triglyph—('tri-glif) A triple projecting, grooved member of a *Doric frieze* that alternates with *metopes.*

trilithons—('tri-lith-onz) A pair of *monoliths* topped with a *lintel;* found in *megalithic* structures.

triptych—('trip-tik) A three-paneled painting or *altarpiece.*

triumphal arch—In Roman architecture, a freestanding *arch* commemorating an important event, such as a military victory or the opening of a new road. In Christian architecture, the arch framing the *apse* at the end of a church *nave.*

true fresco—See *fresco.*

trumeau—(trū-'mō) In church architecture, the *pillar* or center post supporting the *lintel* in the middle of the doorway.

tumulus (pl. **tumuli**)—('tū-myū-lus/'tū-myū-li) Burial mound; in Etruscan architecture, tumuli cover one or more subterranean multichambered tombs cut out of the local tufa (limestone). Also characteristic of the Japanese Kofun period of the third and fourth centuries.

tunnel vault—See *vault.*

Tuscan column—The standard type of Etruscan column. Resembles ancient Greek *Doric* columns, but is made of wood, is unfluted, and has a *base.*

twisted perspective—A convention of representation in which part of a figure is shown in profile and another part of the same figure is shown frontally; a composite view.

tympanum—('tim-pŭ-nŭm) The space enclosed by a *lintel* and an *arch* over a doorway.

uraeus—The rearing cobra, part of the royal headdress of Egyptian pharaohs.

urna—('ŭr-nŭ) A whorl of hair, represented as a dot, between the brows; one of the *lakshanas* of the Buddha.

ushabti/ushabtis—(ū-'shăb-te) Figurines placed in Egyptian tombs to perform labors for the deceased.

ushnisha—(ūsh-'nesh-ha) A knot of hair on the top of the head; one of the *lakshanas* of the Buddha.

value—The lightness or darkness of a *hue.*

vanishing point—The point on which all *orthogonal* lines converge in a composition employing one-point *perspective.*

vault—A masonry roof or ceiling constructed on the *arch* principle. A barrel or tunnel vault, semicylindrical in cross-*section,* is in effect a deep *arch* or an uninterrupted series of arches, one behind the other, over an oblong space. A quadrant vault is a half-barrel vault. A groin or cross vault is formed at the point at which two barrel vaults intersect at right angles. In a ribbed vault, there is a framework of *ribs* or arches under the intersections of the vaulting sections. A sexpartite vault is a vault whose ribs divide the vault into six compartments. A fan vault is a vault characteristic of English Perpendicular *Gothic,* in which radiating ribs form a fanlike pattern.

vaulting web—See *web.*

Veda—('vād-u) Sanskrit, "knowledge." An early South Asian compilations of religious learning.

velarium—(ve-'lar-ē-ŭm) In a Roman *amphitheater,* the cloth awning that could be rolled down from the top of the *cavea* to shield spectators from sun or rain.

vellum—Calfskin prepared as a surface for writing or painting.

veristic—(ver-'is-tik) True to natural appearance; superrealistic.

vihara—(vē-'ha-ra) A Buddhist monastery, often cut into a hill.

volute—(vŭ-'lūt) A spiral, scroll-like form characteristic of the ancient Greek *Ionic* and the Roman *Composite capital.*

votive offering—A gift of gratitude to a deity.

voussoir—(vū-'swar) A wedge-shaped block used in the construction of a true *arch.* The central voussoir, which sets the arch, is the keystone.

wall arcade—See *blind arcade.*

warp—The vertical threads of a loom or cloth.

wat—(wat) A Buddhist monastery in Cambodia.

web—In *Gothic* architecture, the masonry blocks that fill the area between the *ribs* of a groin *vault.*

weft—The horizontal threads of a loom or cloth.

westwork—The *facade* and towers at the western end of a medieval church, principally in Germany.

wet fresco—See *fresco.*

white-ground painting—An ancient Greek vase painting technique in which the pot was first covered with a *slip* of very fine white clay, over which black *glaze* was used to outline figures, and diluted brown, purple, red, and white were used to color them.

yaksha/yakshi—(yak-shŭ/yak-shē) Lesser local male and female Buddhist and Hindu divinities. Yakshis are goddesses associated with fertility and vegetation. Yakshas, the male equivalent of yakshis, are often represented as corpulent, powerful males.

yamato-e—(ya-ma-tō-ā) Also known as native-style painting, a purely Japanese style that often involved colorful, decorative representations of Japanese narratives or *landscapes.*

yasti—('yas-tē) In Buddhist architecture, the mast or pole that arises from the dome of the *stupa* and its *harmika* and symbolizes the axis of the universe; it is adorned with a series of chatras (stone disks).

Zen—A Japanese Buddhist sect and its doctrine, emphasizing enlightenment through intuition and introspection rather than the study of scripture. In Chinese, Chan.

ziggurat—('zig-ŭ-rot) In ancient Mesopotamian architecture, a monumental platform for a temple.

BIBLIOGRAPHY

This list of books is intended to be comprehensive enough to satisfy the reading interests of the beginning art history student and general reader, as well as those of more advanced readers who wish to become acquainted with fields other than their own. The resources listed range from works that are valuable primarily for their reproductions to those that are scholarly surveys of schools and periods. No entries for periodical articles appear, but some of the major periodicals that publish art-historical scholarship in English are noted.

SELECTED PERIODICALS

The following list is by no means exhaustive. Students wishing to pursue research in journals should contact their instructor, their college or university's reference librarian, or the online catalogue for additional titles.

African Arts
American Indian Art
American Journal of Archaeology
Archaeology
Archives of Asian Art
Ars Orientalis
The Art Bulletin
Art History
The Art Journal
The Burlington Magazine
Journal of the Society of Architectural Historians
Journal of the Warburg and Courtauld Institutes
Latin American Antiquity
Oxford Art Journal

GENERAL STUDIES

Arntzen, Etta, and Robert Rainwater. *Guide to the Literature of Art History.* Chicago: American Library Association, 1981.

Bator, Paul M. *The International Trade in Art.* Chicago: University of Chicago Press, 1988.

Baxandall, Michael. *Patterns of Intention: On the Historical Explanation of Pictures.* New Haven: Yale University Press, 1985.

Bindman, David, ed. *The Thames & Hudson Encyclopedia of British Art.* London: Thames & Hudson, 1988.

Broude, Norma, and Mary D. Garrard, eds. *The Expanding Discourse: Feminism and Art History.* New York: Harper Collins, 1992.

———. *Feminism and Art History: Questioning the Litany.* New York: Harper & Row, 1982.

Bryson, Norman. *Vision and Painting: The Logic of the Gaze.* New Haven: Yale University Press, 1983.

Bryson, Norman, Michael Ann Holly, and Keith Moxey. *Visual Theory: Painting and Interpretation.* New York: Cambridge University Press, 1991.

Cahn, Walter. *Masterpieces: Chapters on the History of an Idea.* Princeton, N.J.: Princeton University Press, 1979.

Chadwick, Whitney. *Women, Art, and Society.* New York: Thames & Hudson, 1990.

Cheetham, Mark A., Michael Ann Holly, and Keith Moxey, eds. *The Subjects of Art History: Historical Objects in Contemporary Perspective.* New York: Cambridge University Press, 1998.

Chilvers, Ian, and Harold Osborne, eds. *The Oxford Dictionary of Art.* Rev. ed. New York: Oxford University Press, 1997.

Cummings, P. *Dictionary of Contemporary American Artists.* 6th ed. New York: St. Martin's Press, 1994.

Deepwell, K., ed. *New Feminist Art.* Manchester: Manchester University Press, 1994.

Derrida, Jacques. *The Truth in Painting.* Chicago: University of Chicago Press, 1987.

Encyclopedia of World Art. 15 vols. New York: Publisher's Guild, 1959–1968. Supplementary vols. 16, 1983; 17, 1987.

Fielding, Mantle. *Dictionary of American Painters, Sculptors, and Engravers.* 2nd rev. and enl. ed. Poughkeepsie, N.Y.: Apollo, 1986.

Fleming, John, Hugh Honour, and Nikolaus Pevsner. *Penguin Dictionary of Architecture.* 4th ed. New York: Penguin, 1991.

Frazier, Nancy. *The Penguin Concise Dictionary of Art History.* New York: Penguin, 2000.

Freedberg, David. *The Power of Images: Studies in the History and Theory of Response.* Chicago: University of Chicago Press, 1989.

Giedion, Siegfried. *Space, Time and Architecture: The Growth of a New Tradition.* 5th ed. Cambridge, Mass.: Harvard University Press, 1982.

Gombrich, Ernst Hans Josef. *Art and Illusion.* 5th ed. London: Phaidon, 1977.

Haggar, Reginald G. *A Dictionary of Art Terms: Architecture, Sculpture, Painting, and the Graphic Arts.* Poole: New Orchard Editions, 1984.

Hall, James. *Dictionary of Subjects and Symbols in Art.* 2nd rev. ed. London: J. Murray, 1979.

Harris, Anne Sutherland, and Linda Nochlin. *Women Artists: 1550–1950.* Los Angeles: Los Angeles County Museum of Art; New York: Knopf, 1977.

Hauser, Arnold. *The Sociology of Art.* Chicago: University of Chicago Press, 1982.

Hind, Arthur M. *A History of Engraving and Etching from the Fifteenth Century to the Year 1914.* 3rd rev. ed. New York: Dover, 1963.

Holt, Elizabeth Gilmore, ed. *A Documentary History of Art.* 2nd ed. 2 vols. Princeton, N.J.: Princeton University Press, 1981.

Hults, Linda C. *The Print in the Western World: An Introductory History.* Madison: University of Wisconsin Press, 1996.

Kostof, Spiro. *A History of Architecture: Settings and Rituals.* 2nd ed. Oxford: Oxford University Press, 1995.

Kronenberger, Louis. *Atlantic Brief Lives: A Biographical Companion to the Arts.* Boston: Little, Brown, 1971.

Kultermann, Udo. *The History of Art History.* New York: Abaris, 1993.

Lucie-Smith, Edward. *The Thames & Hudson Dictionary of Art Terms.* London: Thames & Hudson, 1984.

Murray, Peter, and Linda Murray. *A Dictionary of Art and Artists.* 5th ed. New York: Penguin, 1988.

Myers, Bernard S., ed. *Encyclopedia of Painting: Painters and Painting of the World from Prehistoric Times to the Present Day.* 4th rev. ed. New York: Crown, 1979.

Myers, Bernard S., and Myers, Shirley D., eds. *Dictionary of 20th-Century Art.* New York: McGraw-Hill, 1974.

Nelson, Robert S., and Richard Shiff, eds. *Critical Terms for Art History.* Chicago: University of Chicago Press, 1996.

Osborne, Harold, ed. *The Oxford Companion to 20th Century Art.* New York: Oxford University Press, 1981.

Parker, Rozsika, and Griselda Pollock. *Old Mistresses: Women, Art, and Ideology.* London: Routledge & Kegan Paul, 1981.

Penny, Nicholas. *The Materials of Sculpture.* New Haven: Yale University Press, 1993.

Pevsner, Nikolaus. *A History of Building Types.* London: Thames & Hudson, 1987. Reprint of 1979 ed.

———. *An Outline of European Architecture.* 8th ed. Baltimore: Penguin, 1974.

———. *The Buildings of England.* 46 vols. Harmondsworth: Penguin, 1951–1974.

Pierce, James Smith. *From Abacus to Zeus: A Handbook of Art History.* 7th ed. Upper Saddle River, N.J.: Pearson Prentice Hall, 1998.

Placzek, Adolf K., ed. *Macmillan Encyclopedia of Architects.* 4 vols. New York: Macmillan, 1982.

Podro, Michael. *The Critical Historians of Art.* New Haven: Yale University Press, 1982.

Pollock, Griselda. *Vision and Difference: Femininity, Feminism and Histories of Art.* London: Routledge, 1988.

Preziosi, Donald, ed. *The Art of Art History: A Critical Anthology.* New York: Oxford University Press, 1998.

Reid, Jane D. *The Oxford Guide to Classical Mythology in the Arts 1300–1990s.* 2 vols. New York: Oxford University Press, 1993.

Rosenblum, Naomi. *A World History of Photography.* New York: Abbeville, 1984.

Roth, Leland M. *Understanding Architecture: Its Elements, History, and Meaning.* New York: Harper & Row, 1993.

Rubenstein, Charlotte Streifer. *American Women Artists from Early Indian Times to the Present.* Boston: G. K. Hall/Avon Books, 1982.

Slatkin, Wendy. *Women Artists in History: From Antiquity to the 20th Century.* 2nd ed. Upper Saddle River, N.J.: Prentice Hall, 1985.

Smith, Alistair, ed. *The Larousse Dictionary of Painters.* New York: Larousse, 1981.

Smith, G. E. Kidder. *The Architecture of the United States: An Illustrated Guide to Buildings Open to the Public.* 3 vols. Garden City, N.J.: Doubleday/Anchor, 1981.

Stangos, Nikos. *The Thames & Hudson Dictionary of Art and Artists.* Rev. ed. New York: Thames & Hudson, 1994.

Steer, John, and Antony White. *Atlas of Western Art History: Artists, Sites and Monuments from Ancient Greece to the Modern Age.* New York: Facts on File, 1994.

Stratton, Arthur. *The Orders of Architecture: Greek, Roman and Renaissance.* London: Studio, 1986.

Sutton, Ian. *Western Architecture: From Ancient Greece to the Present.* New York: Thames & Hudson, 1999.

Trachtenberg, Marvin, and Isabelle Hyman. *Architecture, from Prehistory to Post-Modernism.* New York: Abrams, 1986.

Tufts, Eleanor. *American Women Artists, Past and Present: A Selected Bibliographic Guide.* New York: Garland Publishers, 1984.

———. *Our Hidden Heritage: Five Centuries of Women Artists.* London: Paddington Press, 1974.

Turner, Jane, ed. *The Dictionary of Art.* 34 vols. New York: Grove Dictionaries, 1996.

Van Pelt, R., and Carroll William Westfall. *Architectural Principles in the Age of Historicism.* New Haven: Yale University Press, 1991.

Waterhouse, Ellis. *The Dictionary of British 18th Century Painters in Oils and Crayons.* Woodbridge, England: Antique Collectors' Club, 1981.

Wittkower, Rudolf. *Sculpture Processes and Principles.* New York: Harper & Row, 1977.

Wölfflin, Heinrich. *The Sense of Form in Art.* New York: Chelsea, 1958.

Young, William, ed. *A Dictionary of American Artists, Sculptors, and Engravers.* Cambridge, Mass.: W. Young, 1968.

ANCIENT ART, GENERAL

Aruz, Joan, and Ronald Wallenfels, eds. *Art of the First Cities: The Third Millennium B.C. from the Mediterranean to the Indus.* New York: Metropolitan Museum of Art, 2003.

Boardman, John, ed. *The Oxford History of Classical Art.* New York: Oxford University Press, 1997.

Clayton, Peter A., and Martin J. Price, eds. *The Seven Wonders of the Ancient World.* New York: Routledge, 1988.

Connolly, Peter, and Hazel Dodge. *The Ancient City: Life in Classical Athens and Rome.* New York: Oxford University Press, 1998.

Davies, W. Vivian, and Louise Schofield, eds. *Egypt, the Aegean and the Levant: Interconnections in the Second Millennium BC.* London: British Museum Press, 1995.

De Grummond, Nancy Thomson, ed. *An Encyclopedia of the History of Classical Archaeology.* 2 vols. Westport, Conn.: Greenwood, 1996.

Dunbabin, Katherine. *Mosaics of the Greek and Roman World.* New York: Cambridge University Press, 1999.

Kampen, Natalie B., ed. *Sexuality in Ancient Art.* New York: Cambridge University Press, 1996.

Lexicon Iconographicum Mythologiae Classicae. Zurich: Artemis, 1981.

Ling, Roger. *Ancient Mosaics.* Princeton, N.J.: Princeton University Press, 1998.

Lloyd, Seton, and Hans Wolfgang Muller. *Ancient Architecture: Mesopotamia, Egypt, Crete.* New York: Electa/Rizzoli, 1980.

Oliphant, Margaret. *The Atlas of the Ancient World: Charting the Great Civilizations of the Past.* New York: Simon & Schuster, 1992.

Onians, John. *Classical Art and the Cultures of Greece and Rome.* New Haven: Yale University Press, 1999.

Renfrew, Colin, and Paul G. Bahn. *Archaeology: Theories, Methods, and Practices.* London: Thames & Hudson, 1991.

Saggs, H.W.F. *Civilization before Greece and Rome.* New Haven: Yale University Press, 1989.

Stillwell, Richard, William L. MacDonald, and Marian H. McAllister, eds. *The Princeton Encyclopedia of Classical Sites.* Princeton, N.J.: Princeton University Press, 1976.

Ward-Perkins, John B. *Cities of Ancient Greece and Italy: Planning in Classical Antiquity.* Rev. ed. New York: Braziller, 1987.

White, Randall. *Prehistoric Art: The Symbolic Journey of Humankind.* New York: Abrams, 2003.

Wolf, Walther. *The Origins of Western Art: Egypt, Mesopotamia, the Aegean.* New York: Universe, 1989.

CHAPTER 1
THE BIRTH OF ART:
AFRICA, EUROPE, AND THE NEAR EAST
IN THE STONE AGE

Bahn, Paul G. *The Cambridge Illustrated History of Prehistoric Art.* New York: Cambridge University Press, 1998.

Bahn, Paul G., and Jean Vertut. *Journey through the Ice Age.* Berkeley: University of California Press, 1997.

Beltrán, Antonio, ed. *The Cave of Altamira.* New York: Abrams, 1999.

Burl, Aubrey. *Great Stone Circles.* New Haven: Yale University Press, 1999.

Chauvet, Jean-Marie, Eliette Brunel Deschamps, and Christian Hillaire. *Dawn of Art: The Chauvet Cave.* New York: Abrams, 1996.

Chippindale, Christopher. *Stonehenge Complete.* New York: Thames & Hudson, 1994.

Cunliffe, Barry, ed. *The Oxford Illustrated Prehistory of Europe.* Oxford: Oxford University Press, 1994.

Kenyon, Kathleen M. *Digging Up Jericho.* New York: Praeger, 1974.

Leroi-Gourhan, André. *The Dawn of European Art: An Introduction to Paleolithic Cave Painting.* Cambridge: Cambridge University Press, 1982.

———. *Treasures of Prehistoric Art.* New York: Abrams, 1967.

Marshack, Alexander. *The Roots of Civilization: The Cognitive Beginnings of Man's First Art, Symbol and Notation.* 2nd ed. Wakefield, R.I.: Moyer Bell, 1991.

Mellaart, James. *Çatal Hüyük: A Neolithic Town in Anatolia.* New York: McGraw-Hill, 1967.

———. *The Neolithic of the Near East.* New York: Scribner, 1975.

Pfeiffer, John E. *The Creative Explosion: An Inquiry into the Origins of Art and Religion.* New York: Harper & Row, 1982.

Piggott, Stuart. *Ancient Europe.* Chicago: Aldine, 1966.

Renfrew, Colin, ed. *British Prehistory: A New Outline.* London: Noyes Press, 1975.

Ruspoli, Mario. *The Cave of Lascaux: The Final Photographs.* New York: Abrams, 1987.

Scarre, Chris. *Exploring Prehistoric Europe.* New York: Oxford University Press, 1998.

Ucko, Peter J., and Andrée Rosenfeld. *Palaeolithic Cave Art.* New York: McGraw-Hill, 1967.

Wainwright, Geoffrey. *The Henge Monuments: Ceremony and Society in Prehistoric Britain.* London: Thames & Hudson, 1990.

White, Randall. *Prehistoric Art: The Symbolic Journey of Humankind.* New York: Abrams, 2003.

CHAPTER 2
THE RISE OF CIVILIZATION:
THE ART OF THE ANCIENT NEAR EAST

Akurgal, Ekrem. *Art of the Hittites.* New York: Abrams, 1962.

Amiet, Pierre. *Art of the Ancient Near East.* New York: Abrams, 1980.

Bienkowski, Piotr, and Alan Millard, eds. *Dictionary of the Ancient Near East.* Philadelphia: University of Pennsylvania Press, 2000.

Collon, Dominique. *Ancient Near Eastern Art.* Berkeley: University of California Press, 1995.

———. *First Impressions: Cylinder Seals in the Ancient Near East.* 2nd ed. London: British Museum, 1993.

———. *Near Eastern Seals.* Berkeley: University of California Press, 1990.

Crawford, Harriet. *Sumer and the Sumerians.* New York: Cambridge University Press, 1991.

Curtis, John E. *Ancient Persia.* Cambridge, Mass.: Harvard University Press, 1990.

Curtis, John E., and Julian E. Reade. *Art and Empire: Treasures from Assyria in the British Museum.* New York: Metropolitan Museum of Art, 1995.

Frankfort, Henri. *The Art and Architecture of the Ancient Orient.* 5th ed. New Haven: Yale University Press, 1996.

Ghirshman, Roman. *The Arts of Ancient Iran: From Its Origins to the Time of Alexander the Great.* New York: Golden Press, 1964.

———. *Persian Art: The Parthian and Sassanian Dynasties, 249 B.C.–A.D. 651.* New York: Golden Press, 1962.

Gunter, Ann C., ed. *Investigating Artistic Environments in the Ancient Near East.* Washington, D.C.: Arthur M. Sackler Gallery, 1990.

Harper, Prudence O., Joan Aruz, and Françoise Tallon, eds. *The Royal City of Susa: Ancient Near Eastern Treasures in the Louvre.* New York: Metropolitan Museum of Art, 1992.

Lloyd, Seton. *The Archaeology of Mesopotamia: From the Old Stone Age to the Persian Conquest.* London: Thames & Hudson, 1984.

Macqueen, James G. *The Hittites and Their Contemporaries in Asia Minor.* Rev. ed. New York: Thames & Hudson, 1986.

Meyers, Eric M., ed. *The Oxford Encyclopedia of Archaeology in the Near East.* New York: Oxford University Press, 1997.

Moortgat, Anton. *The Art of Ancient Mesopotamia.* New York: Phaidon, 1969.

Oates, Joan. *Babylon.* Rev. ed. London: Thames & Hudson, 1986.

Parrot, André. *The Arts of Assyria.* New York: Golden Press, 1961.

———. *Sumer: The Dawn of Art.* New York: Golden Press, 1961.

Porada, Edith. *Man and Images in the Ancient Near East.* Wakefield, R.I.: Moyer Bell, 1995.

Porada, Edith, and Robert H. Dyson. *The Art of Ancient Iran: Pre-Islamic Cultures.* Rev. ed. New York: Greystone, 1969.

Postgate, J. Nicholas. *Early Mesopotamia: Society and Economy at the Dawn of History.* London: Routledge, 1992.

Potts, Daniel T. *The Archaeology of Elam: Formation and Transformation of an Ancient Iranian State.* New York: Cambridge University Press, 1999.

Reade, Julian E. *Assyrian Sculpture.* Cambridge, Mass.: Harvard University Press, 1999.

———. *Mesopotamia.* Cambridge, Mass.: Harvard University Press, 1991.

Roaf, Michael. *Cultural Atlas of Mesopotamia and the Ancient Near East.* New York: Facts on File, 1990.

Russell, John M. *Sennacherib's Palace without Rival at Nineveh.* Chicago: University of Chicago Press, 1991.

Saggs, H.W.F. *Babylonians.* London: British Museum, 1995.

Sasson, Jack M., ed. *Civilizations of the Ancient Near East.* New York: Scribner, 1995.

Snell, Daniel C. *Life in the Ancient Near East: 3100–332 B.C.* New Haven: Yale University Press, 1997.

Strommenger, Eva, and Max Hirmer. *5000 Years of the Art of Mesopotamia.* New York: Abrams, 1964.

Zettler, Richard L., and Lee Horne. *Treasures from the Royal Tombs of Ur.* Philadelphia: University of Pennsylvania Museum of Archaeology and Anthropology, 1998.

CHAPTER 3
PHARAOHS AND THE AFTERLIFE:
THE ART OF ANCIENT EGYPT

Arnold, Dieter. *Building in Egypt: Pharaonic Stone Masonry.* New York: Oxford University Press, 1991.

Arnold, Dorothea. *The Royal Women of Amarna.* New York: Metropolitan Museum of Art, 1996.

———. *When the Pyramids Were Built: Egyptian Art of the Old Kingdom.* New York: Rizzoli, 1999.

Baines, John, and Jaromír Málek. *Atlas of Ancient Egypt.* New York: Facts on File, 1980.

Bard, Kathryn A., ed. *Encyclopedia of the Archaeology of Ancient Egypt.* London: Routledge, 1999.

Bianchi, Robert S. *Cleopatra's Egypt: Age of the Ptolemies.* Brooklyn: Brooklyn Museum, 1988.

———. *Splendors of Ancient Egypt from the Egyptian Museum, Cairo.* London: Booth-Clibborn, 1996.

Bietak, Manfred. *Avaris, the Capital of the Hyksos.* London: British Museum Press, 1996.

Capel, Anne K., and Glenn E. Markoe, eds. *Mistress of the House, Mistress of Heaven: Women in Ancient Egypt.* New York: Hudson Hills, 1996.

D'Auria, Sue, Peter Lacovara, and Catharine H. Roehrig. *Mummies and Magic: The Funerary Arts of Ancient Egypt.* Boston: Museum of Fine Arts, 1988.

Davis, Whitney. *The Canonical Tradition in Ancient Egyptian Art.* New York: Cambridge University Press, 1989.

Egyptian Art in the Age of the Pyramids. New York: Abrams, 1999.

Hawass, Zahi. *Valley of the Golden Mummies.* New York: Abrams, 2000.

Ikram, Salima, and Aidan Dodson. *The Mummy in Ancient Egypt: Equipping the Dead for Eternity.* New York: Thames & Hudson, 1998.

Kozloff, Arielle P., and Betsy M. Bryan. *Egypt's Dazzling Sun: Amenhotep III and His World.* Cleveland: Cleveland Museum of Art, 1992.

Lange, Kurt, and Max Hirmer. *Egypt: Architecture, Sculpture and Painting in Three Thousand Years.* 4th ed. London: Phaidon, 1968.

Lehner, Mark. *The Complete Pyramids: Solving the Ancient Mysteries.* New York: Thames & Hudson, 1997.

Mahdy, Christine, ed. *The World of the Pharaohs: A Complete Guide to Ancient Egypt.* London: Thames & Hudson, 1990.

Málek, Jaromír. *Egypt: 4000 Years of Art.* New York: Phaidon, 2003.

———. *Egyptian Art.* London: Phaidon, 1999.

———, ed. *Egypt: Ancient Culture, Modern Land.* Norman: University of Oklahoma Press, 1993.

Redford, Donald B. *Akhenaton, the Heretic King.* Princeton, N.J.: Princeton University Press, 1984.

———, ed. *The Oxford Encyclopedia of Ancient Egypt.* New York: Oxford University Press, 2001.

Reeves, C. Nicholas. *The Complete Tutankhamun: The King, the Tomb, the Royal Treasure.* London: Thames & Hudson, 1990.

Robins, Gay. *The Art of Ancient Egypt.* Cambridge, Mass.: Harvard University Press, 1997.

———. *Egyptian Painting and Relief.* Aylesbury: Shire Publications, 1986.

———. *Proportion and Style in Ancient Egyptian Art.* Austin: University of Texas Press, 1994.

———. *Women in Ancient Egypt.* London: British Museum, 1993.

Romer, John. *Valley of the Kings: Exploring the Tombs of the Pharaohs.* New York: Holt, 1994.

Russmann, Edna R. *Egyptian Sculpture: Cairo and Luxor.* Austin: University of Texas Press, 1989.

Schäfer, Heinrich. *Principles of Egyptian Art.* Rev. ed. Oxford: Clarendon, 1986.

Schulz, Regina, and Matthias Seidel, eds. *Egypt: The World of the Pharaohs.* Cologne: Könemann, 1999.

Shafer, Byron E., ed. *Temples of Ancient Egypt.* Ithaca, N.Y.: Cornell University Press, 1997.

Shaw, Ian, and Paul Nicholson. *The Dictionary of Ancient Egypt.* London: British Museum, 1995.

Silverman, David P., ed. *Ancient Egypt.* New York: Oxford University Press, 1997.

Smith, William Stevenson, and William Kelly Simpson. *The Art and Architecture of Ancient Egypt.* Rev. ed. New Haven: Yale University Press, 1998.

Trigger, Bruce G. *Ancient Egypt: A Social History.* Cambridge: Cambridge University Press, 1983.

Weeks, Kent R. *The Lost Tomb.* New York: William Morrow, 1998.

———, ed. *Valley of the Kings.* Vercelli: White Star, 2001.

Wildung, Dietrich. *Egypt: From Prehistory to the Romans.* Cologne: Taschen, 1997.

Chapter 4
Minos and the Heroes of Homer:
The Art of the Prehistoric Aegean

Barber, R.L.N. *The Cyclades in the Bronze Age.* Iowa City: University of Iowa Press, 1987.

Betancourt, Philip P. *A History of Minoan Pottery.* Princeton, N.J.: Princeton University Press, 1965.

Cadogan, Gerald. *Palaces of Minoan Crete.* London: Methuen, 1980.

Chadwick, John. *The Mycenaean World.* New York: Cambridge University Press, 1976.

Cullen, Tracey, ed. *Aegean Prehistory: A Review.* Boston: Archaeological Institute of America, 2001.

Demargne, Pierre. *The Birth of Greek Art.* New York: Golden Press, 1964.

Dickinson, Oliver P.T.K. *The Aegean Bronze Age.* New York: Cambridge University Press, 1994.

Doumas, Christos. *Thera, Pompeii of the Ancient Aegean: Excavations at Akrotiri, 1967–1979.* New York: Thames & Hudson, 1983.

———. *The Wall-Paintings of Thera.* Athens: Thera Foundation, 1992.

Fitton, J. Lesley. *Cycladic Art.* Cambridge, Mass.: Harvard University Press, 1989.

———. *The Discovery of the Greek Bronze Age.* London: British Museum, 1995.

Forsyth, Phyllis Young. *Thera in the Bronze Age.* New York: Peter Lang, 1997.

Getz-Preziosi, Patricia. *Sculptors of the Cyclades: Individual and Tradition in the Third Millennium B.C.* Ann Arbor: University of Michigan Press, 1987.

Graham, James W. *The Palaces of Crete.* Princeton, N.J.: Princeton University Press, 1987.

Hampe, Roland, and Erika Simon. *The Birth of Greek Art: From the Mycenaean to the Archaic Period.* New York: Oxford University Press, 1981.

Higgins, Reynold. *Minoan and Mycenaean Art.* Rev. ed. New York: Thames & Hudson, 1997.

Hood, Sinclair. *The Arts in Prehistoric Greece.* New Haven: Yale University Press, 1978.

Immerwahr, Sarah A. *Aegean Painting in the Bronze Age.* University Park: Pennsylvania State University Press, 1990.

MacGillivray, J. A. *Minotaur: Sir Arthur Evans and the Archaeology of the Minoan Myth.* New York: Hill and Wang, 2000.

Marinatos, Nanno. *Art and Religion in Thera: Reconstructing a Bronze Age Society.* Athens: Mathioulakis, 1984.

Marinatos, Spyridon, and Max Hirmer. *Crete and Mycenae.* London: Thames & Hudson, 1960.

McDonald, William A., and Carol G. Thomas. *Progress into the Past: The Rediscovery of Mycenaean Civilization.* 2nd ed. Bloomington: Indiana University Press, 1990.

Morgan, Lyvia. *The Miniature Wall Paintings of Thera: A Study in Aegean Culture and Iconography.* New York: Cambridge University Press, 1988.

Pendlebury, John. *The Archeology of Crete.* London: Methuen, 1967.

Preziosi, Donald, and Louise A. Hitchcock. *Aegean Art and Architecture.* New York: Oxford University Press, 1999.

Taylour, Lord William. *The Mycenaeans.* London: Thames & Hudson, 1990.

Vermeule, Emily. *Greece in the Bronze Age.* Chicago: University of Chicago Press, 1972.

Wace, Alan. *Mycenae: An Archeological History and Guide.* New York: Biblo & Tannen, 1964.

Warren, Peter. *The Aegean Civilisations from Ancient Crete to Mycenae.* 2nd ed. Oxford: Elsevier-Phaidon, 1989.

Chapter 5
Gods, Heroes, and Athletes:
The Art of Ancient Greece

Arias, Paolo. *A History of One Thousand Years of Greek Vase Painting.* New York: Abrams, 1962.

Ashmole, Bernard. *Architect and Sculptor in Classical Greece.* New York: New York University Press, 1972.

Berve, Helmut, Gottfried Gruben, and Max Hirmer. *Greek Temples, Theatres, and Shrines.* New York: Abrams, 1963.

Biers, William. *The Archaeology of Greece: An Introduction.* 2nd ed. Ithaca, N.Y.: Cornell University Press, 1996.

Boardman, John. *Athenian Black Figure Vases.* Rev. ed. New York: Thames & Hudson, 1985.

———. *Athenian Red Figure Vases: The Archaic Period.* New York: Thames & Hudson, 1988.

———. *Athenian Red Figure Vases: The Classical Period.* New York: Thames & Hudson, 1989.

———. *Early Greek Vase Painting, 11th–6th Centuries B.C.* New York: Thames & Hudson, 1998.

———. *Greek Sculpture: The Archaic Period.* Rev. ed. New York: Thames & Hudson, 1985.

———. *Greek Sculpture: The Classical Period.* New York: Thames & Hudson, 1987.

———. *Greek Sculpture: The Late Classical Period and Sculpture in Colonies and Overseas.* New York: Thames & Hudson, 1995.

———. *The Parthenon and Its Sculpture.* Austin: University of Texas Press, 1985.

Camp, John M. *The Archaeology of Athens.* New Haven: Yale University Press, 2001.

Carpenter, Thomas H. *Art and Myth in Ancient Greece.* New York: Thames & Hudson, 1991.

Charbonneaux, Jean, Roland Martin, and François Villard. *Archaic Greek Art.* New York: Braziller, 1971.

———. *Classical Greek Art.* New York: Braziller, 1972.

———. *Hellenistic Art.* New York: Braziller, 1973.

Coldstream, J. Nicholas. *Geometric Greece.* New York: St. Martin's, 1977.

Coulton, J. J. *Ancient Greek Architects at Work.* Ithaca, N.Y.: Cornell University Press, 1982.

Fullerton, Mark D. *Greek Art.* New York: Cambridge University Press, 2000.

Haynes, Denys E.L. *The Technique of Greek Bronze Statuary.* Mainz: von Zabern, 1992.

Houser, Caroline. *Greek Monumental Bronze Sculpture.* New York: Vendome, 1983.

Hurwit, Jeffrey M. *The Art and Culture of Early Greece, 1100–480 B.C.* Ithaca, N.Y.: Cornell University Press, 1985.

———. *The Athenian Acropolis: History, Mythology, and Archaeology from the Neolithic Era to the Present.* New York: Cambridge University Press, 1999.

Jenkins, Ian. *The Parthenon Frieze.* Austin: University of Texas Press, 1994.

Langlotz, Ernst, and Max Hirmer. *The Art of Magna Graecia: Greek Art in Southern Italy and Sicily.* New York: Abrams, 1965.

Lawrence, Arnold W., and R. A. Tomlinson. *Greek Architecture.* Rev. ed. New Haven: Yale University Press, 1996.

Martin, Roland. *Greek Architecture: Architecture of Crete, Greece, and the Greek World.* New York: Electa/Rizzoli, 1988.

Mattusch, Carol C. *Classical Bronzes: The Art and Craft of Greek and Roman Statuary.* Ithaca, N.Y.: Cornell University Press, 1996.

———. *Greek Bronze Statuary from the Beginnings through the Fifth Century B.C.* Ithaca, N.Y.: Cornell University Press, 1988.

Morris, Sarah P. *Daidalos and the Origins of Greek Art.* Princeton, N.J.: Princeton University Press, 1992.

Osborne, Robin. *Archaic and Classical Greek Art.* New York: Oxford University Press, 1998.

Palagia, Olga. *The Pediments of the Parthenon.* Leiden: E. J. Brill, 1993.

Palagia, Olga, and Jerome J. Pollitt, *Personal Styles in Greek Sculpture.* New York: Cambridge University Press, 1996.

Pedley, John Griffiths. *Greek Art and Archaeology.* 3rd ed. Upper Saddle River, N.J.: Prentice Hall, 2002.

Pollitt, Jerome J. *Art and Experience in Classical Greece.* New York: Cambridge University Press, 1972.

———. *Art in the Hellenistic Age.* New York: Cambridge University Press, 1986.

———. *The Art of Ancient Greece: Sources and Documents.* 2nd ed. New York: Cambridge University Press, 1990.

Pugliese Carratelli, G. *The Greek World: Art and Civilization in Magna Graecia and Sicily.* New York: Rizzoli, 1996.

Reeder, Ellen D., ed. *Pandora: Women in Classical Greece.* Baltimore: Walters Art Gallery, 1995.

Rhodes, Robin F. *Architecture and Meaning on the Athenian Acropolis.* New York: Cambridge University Press, 1995.

Richter, Gisela M. *The Portraits of the Greeks.* Rev. ed. by R.R.R. Smith. Ithaca, N.Y.: Cornell University Press, 1984.

Ridgway, Brunilde S. *The Archaic Style in Greek Sculpture.* 2nd ed. Chicago: Ares, 1993.

———. *Fifth Century Styles in Greek Sculpture.* Princeton, N.J.: Princeton University Press, 1981.

———. *Fourth-Century Styles in Greek Sculpture.* Madison: University of Wisconsin Press, 1997.

———. *Hellenistic Sculpture I: The Styles of ca. 331–200 B.C.* Madison: University of Wisconsin Press, 1990.

———. *Hellenistic Sculpture II: The Styles of ca. 200–100 B.C.* Madison: University of Wisconsin Press, 2000.

———. *Prayers in Stone: Greek Architectural Sculpture.* Berkeley: University of California Press, 1999.

———. *Roman Copies of Greek Sculpture: The Problem of the Originals.* Ann Arbor: University of Michigan Press, 1984.

———. *The Severe Style in Greek Sculpture.* Princeton, N.J.: Princeton University Press, 1970.

Robertson, Martin. *The Art of Vase-Painting in Classical Athens.* New York: Cambridge University Press, 1992.

———. *A History of Greek Art.* Rev. ed. 2 vols. New York: Cambridge University Press, 1986.

———. *A Shorter History of Greek Art.* New York: Cambridge University Press, 1981.

Rolley, Claude. *Greek Bronzes.* London: Sotheby's, 1986.

Shapiro, H. Alan. *Art and Cult in Athens under the Tyrants.* Mainz: von Zabern, 1989.

———. *Myth into Art: Poet and Painter in Classical Greece.* New York: Routledge, 1994.

Smith, R.R.R. *Hellenistic Sculpture.* New York: Thames & Hudson, 1991.

Spivey, Nigel. *Greek Art.* London: Phaidon, 1997.

Stansbury-O'Donnell, Mark D. *Pictorial Narrative in Ancient Greek Art.* New York: Cambridge University Press, 1999.

Stewart, Andrew. *Art, Desire, and the Body in Ancient Greece.* New York: Cambridge University Press, 1997.

———. *Greek Sculpture: An Exploration.* 2 vols. New Haven: Yale University Press, 1990.

Wycherley, Richard E. *How the Greeks Built Cities.* New York: Norton, 1976.

CHAPTER 6
PATHS TO ENLIGHTENMENT:
THE ART OF SOUTH AND SOUTHEAST ASIA
BEFORE 1200

Asher, Frederick M. *The Art of Eastern India, 300–800.* Minneapolis: University of Minnesota Press, 1980.

Blurton, T. Richard. *Hindu Art.* Cambridge, Mass.: Harvard University Press, 1993.

Chaturachinda, Gwyneth, Sunanda Krishnamurty, and Pauline W. Tabtiang. *Dictionary of South and Southeast Asian Art.* Chiang Mai, Thailand: Silkworm Books, 2000.

Chihara, Daigoro. *Hindu-Buddhist Architecture in Southeast Asia.* Leiden: E. J. Brill, 1996.

Craven, Roy C. *Indian Art: A Concise History.* Rev. ed. London: Thames & Hudson, 1997.

Dehejia, Vidya. *Early Buddhist Rock Temples.* Ithaca, N.Y.: Cornell University Press, 1972.

———. *Indian Art.* London: Phaidon, 1997.

Desai, Vishakha N., and Darielle Mason. *Gods, Guardians, and Lovers: Temple Sculptures from North India A.D. 700–1200.* New York: Asia Society Galleries, 1993.

Encyclopedia of Indian Temple Architecture. 8 vols. New Delhi: American Institute of Indian Studies. Philadelphia: University of Pennsylvania Press, 1983–1996.

Fisher, Robert E. *Buddhist Art and Architecture.* New York: Thames & Hudson, 1993.

Frederic, Louis. *Borobudur.* New York: Abbeville Press, 1996.

Gopinatha Rao, T. A. *Elements of Hindu Iconography.* 2nd ed. 4 vols. New York: Paragon, 1968.

Gray, Basil, ed. *The Arts of India.* Ithaca, N.Y.: Cornell University Press, 1981.

Harle, James C. *The Art and Architecture of the Indian Subcontinent.* 2nd ed. New Haven: Yale University Press, 1994.

Huntington, Susan L., and John C. Huntington. *The Art of Ancient India: Buddhist, Hindu, Jain.* New York: Weatherhill, 1985.

Jacques, Claude, and Michael Freeman. *Angkor: Cities and Temples.* Bangkok: River Books, 1997.

Jessup, Helen Ibbitson, and Thierry Zephir, eds. *Sculpture of Angkor and Ancient Cambodia: Millennium of Glory.* Washington, D.C.: National Gallery of Art, 1997.

McIntosh, Jane R. *A Peaceful Realm: The Rise and Fall of the Indus Civilization.* Boulder, Colo.: Westview Press, 2002.

Michell, George. *Hindu Art and Architecture.* New York: Thames & Hudson, 2000.

———. *The Hindu Temple: An Introduction to Its Meaning and Forms.* Chicago: University of Chicago Press, 1988.

Mitter, Partha. *Indian Art.* New York: Oxford University Press, 2001.

Rawson, Phillip. *The Art of Southeast Asia.* New York: Thames & Hudson, 1990.

Srinivasan, Doris Meth. *Many Heads, Arms and Eyes: Origin, Meaning and Form of Multiplicity in Indian Art.* Leiden: E. J. Brill, 1997.

Stierlin, Henri. *Hindu India from Khajuraho to the Temple City of Madurai.* Cologne: Taschen, 1998.

Williams, Joanna G. *The Art of Gupta India: Empire and Province.* Princeton, N.J.: Princeton University Press, 1982.

CHAPTER 7
THE SILK ROAD AND BEYOND:
THE ART OF EARLY CHINA AND KOREA

Bush, Susan, and Shio-yen Shih. *Early Chinese Texts on Painting.* Cambridge, Mass.: Harvard University Press, 1985.

Cahill, James. *Chinese Painting.* New York: Rizzoli, 1960.

———. *The Painter's Practice: How Artists Lived and Worked in Traditional China.* New York: Columbia University Press, 1994.

Clunas, Craig. *Art in China.* New York: Oxford University Press, 1997.

Fahr-Becker, Gabriele, ed. *The Art of East Asia.* Cologne: Könemann, 1999.

Fisher, Robert E. *Buddhist Art and Architecture.* New York: Thames & Hudson, 1993.

Fong, Wen C. *Beyond Representation: Chinese Painting and Calligraphy, 8th–14th Century.* New Haven: Yale University Press, 1992.

———. *The Great Bronze Age of China: An Exhibition from the People's Republic of China.* New York: Metropolitan Museum of Art, 1980.

Fong, Wen C., and James C. Y. Watt. *Preserving the Past: Treasures from the National Palace Museum, Taipei.* New York: Metropolitan Museum of Art, 1996.

Li, Chu-tsing, ed. *Artists and Patrons: Some Social and Economic Aspects of Chinese Painting.* Lawrence: Kress Department of Art History, in cooperation with Indiana University Press, 1989.

Little, Stephen, and Shawn Eichman. *Taoism and the Arts of China.* Chicago: Art Institute of Chicago, 2000.

Portal, Jane. *Korea: Art and Archaeology.* New York: Thames & Hudson, 2000.

Powers, Martin J. *Art and Political Expression in Early China.* New Haven: Yale University Press, 1991.

Rawson, Jessica. *Ancient China: Art and Archaeology.* New York: Harper & Row, 1980.

———, ed. *The British Museum Book of Chinese Art.* New York: Thames & Hudson, 1992.

Sickman, Laurence, and Alexander C. Soper. *The Art and Architecture of China.* 3rd ed. New Haven: Yale University Press, 1968.

Silbergeld, Jerome. *Chinese Painting Style: Media, Methods, and Principles of Form.* Seattle and London: University of Washington Press, 1982.

Steinhardt, Nancy S., ed. *Chinese Architecture.* New Haven: Yale University Press, 2002.

Sullivan, Michael. *The Arts of China.* 4th ed. Berkeley: University of California Press, 1999.

———. *The Birth of Landscape Painting.* Berkeley: University of California Press, 1962.

Thorp, Robert L. *Son of Heaven: Imperial Arts of China.* Seattle: Son of Heaven Press, 1988.

Thorp, Robert L., and Richard Ellis Vinograd. *Chinese Art and Culture.* New York: Abrams, 2001.

Vainker, S. J. *Chinese Pottery and Porcelain: From Prehistory to the Present.* New York: Braziller, 1991.

Watson, William. *The Arts of China to AD 900.* New Haven: Yale University Press, 1995.

———. *The Arts of China 900–1620.* New Haven: Yale University Press, 2000.

Weidner, Marsha, ed. *Flowering in the Shadows: Women in the History of Chinese and Japanese Painting.* Honolulu: University of Hawaii Press, 1990.

Whitfield, Roger, and Anne Farrer. *Caves of the Thousand Buddhas: Chinese Art of the Silk Route.* New York: Braziller, 1990.

Wu, Hung. *Monumentality in Early Chinese Art.* Stanford, Calif.: Stanford University Press, 1996.

———. *The Wu Liang Shrine: The Ideology of Early Chinese Pictorial Art.* Stanford, Calif.: Stanford University Press, 1989.

Xin, Yang, Nie Chongzheng, Lang Shaojun, Richard M. Barnhart, James Cahill, and Hung Wu. *Three Thousand Years of Chinese Painting.* New York: Yale University Press, 1997.

CHAPTER 8
SHRINES, STATUES, AND SCROLLS:
THE ART OF EARLY JAPAN

Aikens, C. Melvin, and Takayama Higuchi. *Prehistory of Japan.* New York: Academic Press, 1982.

Coaldrake, William H. *Architecture and Authority in Japan.* London: Routledge, 1996.

Elisseeff, Danielle, and Vadime Elisseeff. *Art of Japan.* Translated by I. Mark Paris. New York: Abrams, 1985.

Ienaga, Saburo. *Painting in the Yamato Style.* Translated by John M. Shields. New York: Weatherhill, 1973.

Kidder, J. Edward, Jr. *The Art of Japan.* New York: Park Lane, 1985.

Kurata, Bunsaku. *Horyu-ji: Temple of the Exalted Law.* Translated by W. Chie Ishibashi. New York: Japan Society, 1981.

Mason, Penelope. *History of Japanese Art.* New York: Abrams, 1993.

Nishi, Kazuo, and Kazuo Hozumi. *What Is Japanese Architecture?* Translated by H. Mack Horton. New York: Kodansha International, 1985.

Nishikawa, Kyotaro, and Emily Sano. *The Great Age of Japanese Buddhist Sculpture A.D. 600–1300.* Fort Worth, Tex.: Kimbell Art Museum, 1982.

Noma, Seiroku. *The Arts of Japan.* Translated and adapted by John Rosenfield and Glenn T. Webb. Tokyo: Kodansha International, 1966.

Okudaira, Hideo. *Narrative Picture Scrolls.* Adapted by Elizabeth ten Grotenhuis. New York: Weatherhill, 1973.

Pearson, Richard J. *Ancient Japan.* New York: Braziller, 1992.

Pearson, Richard J., Gina Lee Barnes, and Karl L. Hutterer, eds. *Windows on the Japanese Past.* Ann Arbor: Center for Japanese Studies, University of Michigan, 1986.

Rosenfield, John M. *Japanese Art of the Heian Period, 794–1185.* New York: Asia Society, 1967.

Rosenfield, John M., and Elizabeth ten Grotenhuis. *Journey of the Three Jewels.* New York: Asia Society, 1979.

Rosenfield, John M., and Shujiro Shimada. *Traditions of Japanese Art: Selections from the Kimiko and John Powers Collection.* Cambridge, Mass.: Fogg Art Museum, 1970.

Shimizu, Yoshiaki, ed. *The Shaping of Daimyo Culture 1185–1868.* Washington, D.C.: National Gallery of Art, 1988.

Stanley-Baker, Joan. *Japanese Art.* New York: Thames & Hudson, 1984.

Suzuki, Kakichi. *Early Buddhist Architecture in Japan.* Translated and adapted by Mary Neighbor Parent and Nancy Shatzman Steinhardt. New York: Kodansha International, 1980.

Swann, Peter C. *Concise History of Japanese Art.* New York: Kodansha International, 1979.

Weidner, Marsha, ed. *Flowering in the Shadows: Women in the History of Chinese and Japanese Painting.* Honolulu: University of Hawaii Press, 1990.

CHAPTER 9
ITALY BEFORE THE ROMANS:
THE ART OF THE ETRUSCANS

Banti, Luisa. *The Etruscan Cities and Their Culture.* Berkeley: University of California Press, 1973.

Barker, Graeme, and Tom Rasmussen. *The Etruscans.* Oxford: Blackwell, 1998.

Boethius, Axel. *Etruscan and Early Roman Architecture.* 2nd ed. New Haven: Yale University Press, 1978.

Bonfante, Larissa, ed. *Etruscan Life and Afterlife: A Handbook of Etruscan Studies.* Detroit: Wayne State University Press, 1986.

Brendel, Otto J. *Etruscan Art.* 2nd ed. New Haven: Yale University Press, 1995.

Cristofani, Mauro. *The Etruscans: A New Investigation.* London: Orbis, 1979.

Haynes, Sybille. *Etruscan Civilization: A Cultural History.* Los Angeles: J. Paul Getty Museum, 2000.

Heurgon, Jacques. *Daily Life of the Etruscans.* London: Weidenfeld & Nicolson, 1964.

Pallottino, Massimo. *Etruscan Painting.* Geneva: Skira, 1953.

———. *The Etruscans.* Harmondsworth: Penguin, 1978.

Richardson, Emeline. *The Etruscans: Their Art and Civilization.* Rev. ed. Chicago: University of Chicago Press, 1976.

Ridgway, David, and Francesca Ridgway, eds. *Italy before the Romans.* New York: Academic Press, 1979.

Spivey, Nigel. *Etruscan Art.* New York: Thames & Hudson, 1997.

Spivey, Nigel, and Simon Stoddart, *Etruscan Italy: An Archaeological History.* London: Batsford, 1990.

Sprenger, Maja, Gilda Bartoloni, and Max Hirmer. *The Etruscans: Their History, Art, and Architecture.* New York: Abrams, 1983.

Steingräber, Stephan, ed. *Etruscan Painting: Catalogue Raisonné of Etruscan Wall Paintings.* New York: Johnson, 1986.

Torelli, Mario, ed. *The Etruscans.* New York: Rizzoli, 2001.

CHAPTER 10
FROM SEVEN HILLS TO THREE CONTINENTS: THE ART OF ANCIENT ROME

Anderson, James C., Jr. *Roman Architecture and Society.* Baltimore: Johns Hopkins University Press, 1997.

Andreae, Bernard. *The Art of Rome.* New York: Abrams, 1977.

Bianchi Bandinelli, Ranuccio. *Rome: The Center of Power. Roman Art to A.D. 200.* New York: Braziller, 1970.

———. *Rome: The Late Empire. Roman Art A.D. 200–400.* New York: Braziller, 1971.

Brendel, Otto J. *Prolegomena to the Study of Roman Art.* New Haven: Yale University Press, 1979.

Claridge, Amanda. *Rome: An Oxford Archaeological Guide.* New York: Oxford University Press, 1998.

Clarke, John R. *The Houses of Roman Italy, 100 B.C.–A.D. 250.* Berkeley: University of California Press, 1991.

Cornell, Tim, and John Matthews. *Atlas of the Roman World.* New York: Facts on File, 1982.

D'Ambra, Eve. *Roman Art.* New York: Cambridge University Press, 1998.

———, ed. *Roman Art in Context.* Upper Saddle River, N.J.: Prentice Hall, 1994.

Elsner, Jaś. *Imperial Rome and Christian Triumph.* New York: Oxford University Press, 1998.

Gazda, Elaine K., ed. *Roman Art in the Private Sphere.* Ann Arbor: University of Michigan Press, 1991.

Grant, Michael. *Cities of Vesuvius: Pompeii and Herculaneum.* Harmondsworth: Penguin, 1976.

Hannestad, Niels. *Roman Art and Imperial Policy.* Aarhus: Aarhus University Press, 1986.

Henig, Martin, ed. *A Handbook of Roman Art.* Ithaca, N.Y.: Cornell University Press, 1983.

Kent, John P. C., and Max Hirmer. *Roman Coins.* New York: Abrams, 1978.

Kleiner, Diana E. E. *Roman Sculpture.* New Haven: Yale University Press, 1992.

Kleiner, Diana E. E., and Susan B. Matheson, eds. *I Claudia: Women in Ancient Rome.* New Haven: Yale University Art Gallery, 1996.

———. *I Claudia II: Women in Roman Art and Society.* Austin: University of Texas Press, 2000.

Kraus, Theodor. *Pompeii and Herculaneum: The Living Cities of the Dead.* New York: Abrams, 1975.

Ling, Roger. *Roman Painting.* New York: Cambridge University Press, 1991.

L'Orange, Hans Peter. *The Roman Empire: Art Forms and Civic Life.* New York: Rizzoli, 1985.

MacCormack, Sabine G. *Art and Ceremony in Late Antiquity.* Berkeley: University of California Press, 1981.

MacDonald, William L. *The Architecture of the Roman Empire I: An Introductory Study.* Rev. ed. New Haven: Yale University Press, 1982.

———. *The Architecture of the Roman Empire II: An Urban Appraisal.* New Haven: Yale University Press, 1986.

———. *The Pantheon: Design, Meaning, and Progeny.* Cambridge, Mass.: Harvard University Press, 1976.

McKay, Alexander G. *Houses, Villas, and Palaces in the Roman World.* Ithaca, N.Y.: Cornell University Press, 1975.

Nash, Ernest. *Pictorial Dictionary of Ancient Rome.* 2nd ed. 2 vols. New York: Praeger, 1962.

Pollitt, Jerome J. *The Art of Rome, 753 B.C.–A.D. 337: Sources and Documents.* Rev. ed. New York: Cambridge University Press, 1983.

Ramage, Nancy H., and Andrew Ramage. *Roman Art: Romulus to Constantine.* 3rd ed. Upper Saddle River, N.J.: Prentice Hall, 2000.

Richardson, Lawrence, Jr. *A New Topographical Dictionary of Ancient Rome.* Baltimore: Johns Hopkins University Press, 1992.

———. *Pompeii: An Architectural History.* Baltimore: Johns Hopkins University Press, 1988.

Sear, Frank. *Roman Architecture.* Rev. ed. Ithaca, N.Y.: Cornell University Press, 1989.

Stambaugh, John E. *The Ancient Roman City.* Baltimore: Johns Hopkins University Press, 1988.

Strong, Donald, and Roger Ling. *Roman Art.* 2nd ed. New Haven: Yale University Press, 1988.

Toynbee, Jocelyn M. C. *Death and Burial in the Roman World.* London: Thames & Hudson, 1971.

Wallace-Hadrill, Andrew. *Houses and Society in Pompeii and Herculaneum.* Princeton, N.J.: Princeton University Press, 1994.

Ward-Perkins, John B. *Roman Architecture.* New York: Electa/Rizzoli, 1988.

———. *Roman Imperial Architecture.* 2nd ed. New Haven: Yale University Press, 1981.

Wilson-Jones, Mark. *Principles of Roman Architecture.* New Haven: Yale University Press, 2000.

Wood, Susan. *Roman Portrait Sculpture A.D. 217–260.* Leiden: E. J. Brill, 1986.

Yegül, Fikret. *Baths and Bathing in Classical Antiquity.* Cambridge: MIT Press, 1992.

Zanker, Paul. *Pompeii: Public and Private Life.* Cambridge: Harvard University Press, 1998.

———. *The Power of Images in the Age of Augustus.* Ann Arbor: University of Michigan Press, 1988.

MEDIEVAL ART, GENERAL

Alexander, Jonathan J. G. *Medieval Illuminators and Their Methods of Work.* New Haven: Yale University Press, 1992.

Andrews, Francis B. *The Mediaeval Builders and Their Methods.* New York: Barnes & Noble, 1993.

The Art of Medieval Spain, A.D. 500–1200. New York: Metropolitan Museum of Art, 1993.

Ross, Leslie. *Medieval Art: A Topical Dictionary.* Westport, Conn.: Greenwood, 1996.

Benton, Janetta Rebold. *Art of the Middle Ages.* New York: Thames & Hudson, 2002.

Binski, Paul. *Painters (Medieval Craftsmen).* Toronto: University of Toronto Press, 1991.

Calkins, Robert G. *Illuminated Books of the Middle Ages.* Ithaca, N.Y.: Cornell University Press, 1983.

———. *Medieval Architecture in Western Europe: From A.D. 300 to 1500.* New York: Oxford University Press, 1998.

Coldstream, Nicola. *Masons and Sculptors (Medieval Craftsmen).* Toronto: University of Toronto Press, 1991.

———. *Medieval Architecture.* New York: Oxford University Press, 2002.

Cross, Frank L., and Livingstone, Elizabeth A., eds. *The Oxford Dictionary of the Christian Church.* 3rd ed. New York: Oxford University Press, 1997.

De Hamel, Christopher. *Scribes and Illuminators (Medieval Craftsmen).* Toronto: University of Toronto Press, 1992.

Lasko, Peter. *Ars Sacra, 800–1200.* 2nd ed. New Haven: Yale University Press, 1994.

Murray, Peter, and Linda Murray. *The Oxford Companion to Christian Art and Architecture.* New York: Oxford University Press, 1996.

Pelikan, Jaroslav. *Mary through the Centuries: Her Place in the History of Culture.* New Haven: Yale University Press, 1996.

Schiller, Gertrud. *Iconography of Christian Art.* 2 vols. Greenwich, Conn.: New York Graphic Society, 1971–1972.

Schütz, Bernard. *Great Cathedrals.* New York: Abrams, 2002.

Sekules, Veronica. *Medieval Art.* New York: Oxford University Press, 2001.

Snyder, James. *Medieval Art: Painting, Sculpture, Architecture, 4th–14th Century.* New York: Abrams, 1989.

Tasker, Edward G. *Encyclopedia of Medieval Church Art.* London: Batsford, 1993.

Webb, Geoffrey F. *Architecture in Britain: The Middle Ages.* Harmondsworth: Penguin, 1965.

CHAPTER 11
PAGANS, CHRISTIANS, AND JEWS: THE ART OF LATE ANTIQUITY

Bowersock, G. W., Peter Brown, and Oleg Grabar, eds. *Late Antiquity: A Guide to the Postclassical World.* Cambridge, Mass.: Harvard University Press, 1998.

Brown, Peter. *The World of Late Antiquity, A.D. 150–170.* London: Thames & Hudson, 1971.

Elsner, Jaś. *Art and the Roman Viewer: The Transformation of Art from the Pagan World to Christianity.* New York: Cambridge University Press, 1995.

———. *Imperial Rome and Christian Triumph.* New York: Oxford University Press, 1998.

Grabar, André. *The Beginnings of Christian Art, 200–395.* London: Thames & Hudson, 1967.

———. *Christian Iconography.* Princeton, N.J.: Princeton University Press, 1980.

Gutmann, Joseph. *Sacred Images: Studies in Jewish Art from Antiquity to the Middle Ages.* Northampton, Mass.: Variorum, 1989.

Hutter, Irmgard. *Early Christian and Byzantine Art.* London: Herbert, 1988.

Janes, Dominic. *God and Gold in Late Antiquity.* New York: Cambridge University Press, 1998.

Jensen, Robin Margaret. *Understanding Early Christian Art.* New York: Routledge, 2000.

Kitzinger, Ernst. *Byzantine Art in the Making.* Cambridge, Mass.: Harvard University Press, 1977.

———. *Early Medieval Art.* 3rd ed. London: British Museum, 1983.

Koch, Guntram. *Early Christian Art and Architecture.* London: SCM Press, 1996.

Krautheimer, Richard. *Rome, Profile of a City: 312–1308.* Princeton, N.J.: Princeton University Press, 1980.

Krautheimer, Richard, and Slobodan Curcić. *Early Christian and Byzantine Architecture.* 4th rev. ed. New Haven: Yale University Press, 1986.

Lowden, John. *Early Christian and Byzantine Art.* London: Phaidon, 1997.

Lowrie, Walter S. *Art in the Early Church.* New York: Norton, 1969.

Mathews, Thomas P. *The Clash of Gods: A Reinterpretation of Early Christian Art.* Rev. ed. Princeton, N.J.: Princeton University Press, 1999.

Milburn, Robert. *Early Christian Art and Architecture.* Berkeley: University of California Press, 1988.

Perkins, Ann Louise. *The Art of Dura-Europos.* Oxford: Clarendon, 1973.

Stevenson, James. *The Catacombs: Rediscovered Monuments of Early Christianity.* London: Thames & Hudson, 1978.

Volbach, Wolfgang. *Early Christian Mosaics, from the Fourth to the Seventh Centuries.* New York: Oxford University Press, 1946.

Volbach, Wolfgang, and Max Hirmer. *Early Christian Art.* New York: Abrams, 1962.

Webster, Leslie, and Michelle Brown, eds. *The Transformation of the Roman World, A.D. 400–900.* Berkeley: University of California Press, 1997.

Weitzmann, Kurt. *Ancient Book Illumination.* Cambridge, Mass.: Harvard University Press, 1959.

———. *Late Antique and Early Christian Book Illumination.* New York: Braziller, 1977.

———, ed. *Age of Spirituality: Late Antique and Early Christian Art, Third to Seventh Century.* New York: Metropolitan Museum of Art, 1979.

CHAPTER 12
ROME IN THE EAST:
THE ART OF BYZANTIUM

Borsook, Eve. *Messages in Mosaic: The Royal Programmes of Norman Sicily.* Oxford: Clarendon, 1990.

Cormack, Robin. *Byzantine Art.* New York: Oxford University Press, 2000.

———. *Painting the Soul: Icons, Death Masks, and Shrouds.* London: Reaktion, 1997.

———. *Writing in Gold: Byzantine Society and Its Icons.* New York: Oxford University Press, 1985.

Cutler, Anthony. *The Hand of the Master: Craftsmanship, Ivory, and Society in Byzantium (9th–11th Centuries).* Princeton, N.J.: Princeton University Press, 1994.

Demus, Otto. *Byzantine Art and the West.* New York: New York University Press, 1970.

———. *The Mosaic Decoration of San Marco, Venice.* Chicago: University of Chicago Press, 1990.

Evans, Helen C., and William D. Wixom, eds. *The Glory of Byzantium: Art and Culture of the Middle Byzantine Era A.D. 843–1261.* New York: Metropolitan Museum of Art, 1997.

Grabar, André. *Byzantine Painting.* New York: Rizzoli, 1979.

———. *The Golden Age of Justinian: From the Death of Theodosius to the Rise of Islam.* New York: Odyssey Press, 1967.

Grabar, André, and Manolis Chatzidakis. *Greek Mosaics of the Byzantine Period.* New York: New American Library, 1964.

Lowden, John. *Early Christian and Byzantine Art.* London: Phaidon, 1997.

Maguire, Henry. *Art and Eloquence in Byzantium.* Princeton, N.J.: Princeton University Press, 1981.

———. *The Icons of Their Bodies: Saints and Their Images in Byzantium.* Princeton, N.J.: Princeton University Press, 1996.

Mainstone, Rowland J. *Hagia Sophia: Architecture, Structure and Liturgy of Justinian's Great Church.* London: Thames & Hudson, 1988.

Mango, Cyril. *Art of the Byzantine Empire, 312–1453: Sources and Documents.* Toronto: University of Toronto Press, 1986. Reprint of 1972 ed.

———. *Byzantine Architecture.* New York: Electa/Rizzoli, 1985.

———. *Byzantium: The Empire of New Rome.* New York: Scribner's, 1980.

———. *Byzantium and Its Image: History and Culture of the Byzantine Empire and Its Heritage.* London: Variorum, 1984.

Mark, Robert, and Ahmet S. Cakmak, eds. *Hagia Sophia from the Age of Justinian to the Present.* New York: Cambridge University Press, 1992.

Mathews, Thomas F. *Byzantium: From Antiquity to the Renaissance.* New York: Abrams, 1998.

Ousterhout, Robert. *Master Builders of Byzantium.* Princeton, N.J.: Princeton University Press, 2000.

Pelikan, Jaroslav. *Imago Dei: The Byzantine Apologia for Icons.* Princeton, N.J.: Princeton University Press, 1990.

Rodley, Lyn. *Byzantine Art and Architecture: An Introduction.* New York: Cambridge University Press, 1994.

Von Simson, Otto G. *Sacred Fortress: Byzantine Art and Statecraft in Ravenna.* Princeton, N.J.: Princeton University Press, 1986.

Walter, Christopher. *Art and Ritual of the Byzantine Church.* London: Variorum, 1982.

Weitzmann, Kurt. *Ancient Book Illumination.* Cambridge, Mass.: Harvard University Press, 1959.

———. *Art in the Medieval West and Its Contacts with Byzantium.* London: Variorum, 1982.

———. *The Icon.* New York: Dorset, 1987.

———. *Illustrations in Roll and Codex.* Princeton, N.J.: Princeton University Press, 1970.

CHAPTER 13
IN PRAISE OF ALLAH:
THE ART OF THE ISLAMIC WORLD

Atil, Esin. *The Age of Sultan Suleyman the Magnificent.* Washington, D.C.: National Gallery of Art, 1987.

Baker, Patricia L. *Islamic Textiles.* London: British Museum, 1995.

Blair, Sheila S., and Jonathan Bloom. *The Art and Architecture of Islam 1250–1800.* New Haven: Yale University Press, 1994.

Bloom, Jonathan, and Sheila S. Blair. *Islamic Arts.* London: Phaidon, 1997.

Brend, Barbara. *Islamic Art.* Cambridge, Mass.: Harvard University Press, 1991.

Canby, Sheila. *Persian Painting.* London: British Museum, 1993.

Creswell, Keppel A. C. *A Short Account of Early Muslim Architecture.* Rev. ed. by James W. Allan. Aldershot: Scolar, 1989.

Dodds, Jerrilynn D., ed. *Al-Andalus: The Art of Islamic Spain.* New York: Metropolitan Museum of Art, 1992.

Ettinghausen, Richard. *From Byzantium to Sassanian Iran and the Islamic World.* Leiden: E. J. Brill, 1972.

Ettinghausen, Richard, Oleg Grabar, and Marilyn Jenkins-Madina. *The Art and Architecture of Islam, 650–1250.* Rev. ed. New Haven: Yale University Press, 2001.

Ferrier, Ronald W., ed. *The Arts of Persia.* New Haven: Yale University Press, 1989.

Frishman, Martin, and Hasan-Uddin Khan. *The Mosque: History, Architectural Development and Regional Diversity.* New York: Thames & Hudson, 1994.

Goodwin, Godfrey. *A History of Ottoman Architecture.* 2nd ed. New York: Thames & Hudson, 1987.

Grabar, Oleg. *The Alhambra.* Cambridge, Mass.: Harvard University Press, 1978.

———. *The Formation of Islamic Art.* Rev. ed. New Haven: Yale University Press, 1987.

Grube, Ernst J. *Architecture of the Islamic World: Its History and Social Meaning.* 2nd ed. New York: Thames & Hudson, 1984.

Hattstein, Markus, and Peter Delius, eds. *Islam: Art and Architecture.* Cologne: Könemann, 2000.

Hillenbrand, Robert. *Islamic Architecture: Form, Function, Meaning.* Edinburgh: Edinburgh University Press, 1994.

———. *Islamic Art and Architecture.* New York: Thames & Hudson, 1999.

Irwin, Robert. *Islamic Art in Context: Art, Architecture, and the Literary World.* New York: Abrams, 1997.

Lings, Martin. *The Qur'anic Art of Calligraphy and Illumination.* London: World of Islam Festival Trust, 1976.

Michell, George, ed. *Architecture of the Islamic World.* New York: Thames & Hudson, 1978.

Porter, Venetia. *Islamic Tiles.* London: British Museum, 1995.

Robinson, Frank. *Atlas of the Islamic World.* Oxford: Equinox, 1982.

Schimmel, Annemarie. *Calligraphy and Islamic Culture.* New York: New York University Press, 1984.

Stierlin, Henri. *Islam I: Early Architecture from Baghdad to Cordoba.* Cologne: Taschen, 1996.

———. *Islamic Art and Architecture from Isfahan to the Taj Mahal.* New York: Thames & Hudson, 2002.

Ward, Rachel M. *Islamic Metalwork.* New York: Thames & Hudson, 1993.

Welch, Anthony. *Calligraphy in the Arts of the Islamic World.* Austin: University of Texas Press, 1979.

CHAPTER 14
FROM ALASKA TO THE ANDES:
NATIVE ARTS OF THE AMERICAS BEFORE 1300

Alva, Walter, and Christopher Donnan. *Royal Tombs of Sipán.* Los Angeles: Fowler Museum of Cultural History, 1993.

Benson, Elizabeth P., and Beatriz de la Fuente, eds. *Olmec Art of Ancient Mexico.* Washington, D.C.: National Gallery of Art, 1996.

Berlo, Janet Catherine, ed. *Art, Ideology, and the City of Teotihuacan.* Washington, D.C.: Dumbarton Oaks, 1992.

Berlo, Janet Catherine, and Ruth B. Phillips. *Native North American Art.* New York: Oxford University Press, 1998.

Berrin, Kathleen, ed. *The Spirit of Ancient Peru: Treasures from the Museo Arqueologico Rafael Larco Herrera.* San Francisco: The Fine Arts Museums of San Francisco, 1997.

Berrin, Kathleen, and Esther Pasztory, eds. *Teotihuacan: Art from the City of the Gods.* San Francisco: Thames & Hudson/The Fine Arts Museums of San Francisco, 1993.

Boone, Elizabeth, ed. *Andean Art at Dumbarton Oaks.* 2 vols. Washington, D.C.: Dumbarton Oaks, 1996.

Brody, J. J., and Rina Swentzell. *To Touch the Past: The Painted Pottery of the Mimbres People.* New York: Hudson Hills, 1996.

Brose, David. *Ancient Art of the American Woodland Indians.* New York: Abrams, 1985.

Bruhns, Karen O. *Ancient South America.* New York: Cambridge University Press, 1994.

Burger, Richard. *Chavín and the Origins of Andean Civilization.* New York: Thames & Hudson, 1992.

Carrasco, David. *The Oxford Encyclopedia of Mesoamerican Cultures: The Civilizations of Mexico and Central America.* New York, Oxford University Press, 2001.

Clark, John E., and Mary E. Pye, eds. *Olmec Art and Archaeology in Mesoamerica.* Washington, D.C.: National Gallery of Art, 2000.

Coe, Michael D. *Mexico.* 4th ed. New York: Thames & Hudson, 1994.

———. *The Maya.* 6th ed. New York: Thames & Hudson, 1999.

Coe, Michael D., and Justin Kerr. *The Art of the Maya Scribe.* New York: Abrams, 1998.

Cordell, Linda S. *Ancient Pueblo Peoples.* Washington, D.C.: Smithsonian Institution Press, 1994.

Donnan, Christopher. *Ceramics of Ancient Peru.* Los Angeles: Fowler Museum of Cultural History, 1992.

Fagan, Brian. *Ancient North America: The Archaeology of a Continent.* 2nd ed. New York: Thames & Hudson, 1995.

Fash, William. *Scribes, Warriors, and Kings: The City of Copan and the Ancient Maya.* New York: Thames & Hudson, 1991.

Feest, Christian F. *Native Arts of North America.* 2nd ed. New York: Thames & Hudson, 1992.

Fitzhugh, William W., and Aron Crowell, eds. *Crossroads of Continents: Cultures of Siberia and Alaska.* Washington, D.C.: Smithsonian Institution Press, 1988.

Grube, Nikolai, ed. *Maya: Divine Kings of the Rain Forest.* Cologne: Könemann, 2000.

Hadingham, Evan. *Lines to the Mountain Gods: Nazca and the Mysteries of Peru.* Norman: University of Oklahoma Press, 1988.

Jones, Julie, ed. *The Art of Pre-Columbian Gold: The Jan Mitchell Collection.* New York: Metropolitan Museum of Art, 1985.

Kolata, Alan. *The Tiwanaku: Portrait of an Andean Civilization.* Cambridge: Blackwell, 1993.

Kubler, George. *The Art and Architecture of Ancient America: The Mexican, Maya, and Andean Peoples.* 3rd ed. New Haven: Yale University Press, 1992.

Mathews, Zena, and Aldona Jonaitis, eds. *Native North American Art History.* Palo Alto, Calif.: Peek Publications, 1982.

Miller, Mary Ellen. *The Art of Mesoamerica, from Olmec to Aztec.* 2nd ed. New York: Thames & Hudson, 1996.

———. *Maya Art and Architecture.* New York: Thames & Hudson, 1999.

Miller, Mary Ellen, and Karl Taube. *The Gods and Symbols of Ancient Mexico and the Maya: An Illustrated Dictionary of Mesoamerican Religion.* New York: Thames & Hudson, 1993.

Morris, Craig, and Adriana von Hagen. *The Inka Empire and Its Andean Origins.* New York: Abbeville, 1993.

Nabokov, Peter, and Robert Easton. *Native American Architecture.* New York: Oxford University Press, 1989.

O'Connor, Mallory M. *Lost Cities of the Ancient Southeast*. Gainesville: University Press of Florida, 1995.

Olmecs. Special edition of *Arqueología Mexicana*. Mexico City: Editorial Raíces, 1998.

Pang, Hilda. *Pre-Columbian Art: Investigations and Insights*. Norman: University of Oklahoma Press, 1992.

Pasztory, Esther. *Pre-Columbian Art*. New York: Cambridge University Press, 1998.

Paul, Anne. *Paracas Ritual Attire: Symbols of Authority in Ancient Peru*. Norman: University of Oklahoma Press, 1990.

Penney, David, and George C. Longfish. *Native American Art*. Hong Kong: Hugh Lauter Levin and Associates, 1994.

Schele, Linda, and Peter Mathews. *The Code of Kings: The Language of Seven Sacred Maya Temples and Tombs*. New York: Scribner, 1998.

Schele, Linda, and Mary E. Miller. *The Blood of Kings: Dynasty and Ritual in Maya Art*. Fort Worth, Tex.: Kimbell Art Museum, 1986.

Schmidt, Peter, Mercedes de la Garza, and Enrique Nalda, eds. *Maya*. New York: Rizzoli, 1998.

Stone-Miller, Rebecca. *Art of the Andes from Chavín to Inca*. New York: Thames & Hudson, 1996.

———, ed. *To Weave for the Sun: Andean Textiles in the Museum of Fine Arts, Boston*. Boston: Museum of Fine Arts, 1992.

Townsend, Richard F., ed. *Ancient West Mexico*. Chicago: Art Institute of Chicago, 1998.

———. *Art from Sacred Landscapes*. Chicago: Art Institute of Chicago, 1992.

Von Hagen, Adriana, and Craig Morris. *The Cities of the Ancient Andes*. New York: Thames & Hudson, 1998.

Wardwell, Allen. *Ancient Eskimo Ivories of the Bering Strait*. New York: Rizzoli, 1986.

Weaver, Muriel Porter. *The Aztecs, Mayas, and Their Predecessors*. 3rd ed. San Diego, Calif.: Academic Press, 1993.

Whiteford, Andrew H., Stewart Peckham, and Kate Peck Kent. *I Am Here: Two Thousand Years of Southwest Indian Arts and Crafts*. Santa Fe: Museum of New Mexico Press, 1989.

CHAPTER 15
SOUTH FROM THE SAHARA:
EARLY AFRICAN ART

Bassani, Ezio, and William Fagg. *Africa and the Renaissance: Art in Ivory*. New York: Center for African Art, 1988.

Ben-Amos, Paula. *The Art of Benin*. New York: Thames & Hudson, 1980.

Blier, Suzanne P. *Royal Arts of Africa: The Majesty of Form*. New York: Abrams, 1998.

Bourgeois, Jean-Louis, and Carollee Pelos. *Spectacular Vernacular: The Adobe Tradition*. New York: Aperture, 1989.

Campbell, Alec, and David Coulson. *African Rock Art: Paintings and Engravings on Stone*. New York: Abrams, 2001.

Connah, Graham. *African Civilizations*. 2nd ed. Cambridge: Cambridge University Press, 2001.

Dark, Philip J. C. *An Introduction to Benin Art and Technology*. Oxford: Clarendon Press, 1973.

Dewey, William J. *Legacies of Stone: Zimbabwe Past and Present*. Tervuren: Royal Museum for Central Africa, 1997.

Drewal, Henry J., John Pemberton, and Rowland Abiodun. *Yoruba: Nine Centuries of African Art and Thought*. New York: Center for African Art, in association with Abrams, 1989.

Eyo, Ekpo, and Frank Willett. *Treasures of Ancient Nigeria*. New York: Knopf, 1980.

Ezra, Kate. *Royal Art of Benin: The Perls Collection in the Metropolitan Museum of Art*. New York: Metropolitan Museum of Art, 1992.

Fagg, Bernard. *Nok Terracottas*. Lagos: Ethnographica, 1977.

Garlake, Peter. *Early Art and Architecture of Africa*. Oxford: Oxford University Press, 2002.

———. *Great Zimbabwe*. London: Thames & Hudson, 1973.

Huffman, Thomas N. *Snakes and Crocodiles: Power and Symbolism in Ancient Zimbabwe*. Johannesburg: Witwatersrand University Press, 1996.

Lajoux, Jean-Dominique. *The Rock Paintings of Tassili*. Cleveland: World Publishing, 1963.

Phillips, Tom, ed. *Africa, the Art of a Continent*. New York: Prestel, 1995.

Phillipson, D. W. *African Archaeology*. 2nd ed. New York: Cambridge University Press, 1993.

———. *Ancient Ethiopia: Aksum, Its Antecedents and Successors*. London: British Museum Press, 1998.

Prussin, Labelle. *Hatumere: Islamic Design in West Africa*. Berkeley and Los Angeles: University of California Press, 1986.

Schädler, Karl-Ferdinand. *Earth and Ore: 2500 Years of African Art in Terra-Cotta and Metal*. Munich: Panterra Verlag, 1997.

Shaw, Thurstan. *Nigeria: Its Archaeology and Early History*. London: Thames & Hudson, 1978.

———. *Unearthing Igbo-Ukwu: Archaeological Discoveries in Eastern Nigeria*. New York: Oxford University Press, 1977.

Vallées du Niger. Paris: Editions de la Réunion des Musées Nationaux, 1993.

Willett, Frank. *Ife in the History of West African Sculpture*. New York: McGraw-Hill, 1967.

CHAPTER 16
EUROPE AFTER THE FALL OF ROME:
EARLY MEDIEVAL ART IN THE WEST

Alexander, Jonathan J. G. *Insular Manuscripts, Sixth to the Ninth Century*. London: Miller, 1978.

The Art of Medieval Spain, A.D. 500–1200. New York: Metropolitan Museum of Art, 1993.

Backhouse, Janet, D. H. Turner, and Leslie Webster, eds. *The Golden Age of Anglo-Saxon Art, 966–1066*. Bloomington: Indiana University Press, 1984.

Barral i Altet, Xavier. *The Early Middle Ages: From Late Antiquity to A.D. 1000*. Cologne: Taschen, 1997.

Brown, Katharine Reynolds, Dafydd Kidd, and Charles T. Little, eds. *From Attila to Charlemagne*. New York: Metropolitan Museum of Art, 2000.

Collins, Roger. *Early Medieval Europe, 300–1000*. New York: St. Martin's, 1991.

Conant, Kenneth J. *Carolingian and Romanesque Architecture, 800–1200*. 4th ed. New Haven: Yale University Press, 1992.

Davis-Weyer, Caecilia. *Early Medieval Art, 300–1150: Sources and Documents*. Toronto: University of Toronto Press, 1986. Reprint of 1971 ed.

Diebold, William J. *Word and Image: An Introduction to Early Medieval Art*. Boulder, Colo.: Westview Press, 2000.

Dodwell, Charles R. *Anglo-Saxon Art: A New Perspective*. Ithaca, N.Y.: Cornell University Press, 1982.

———. *The Pictorial Arts of the West, 800–1200*. New Haven: Yale University Press, 1993.

Harbison, Peter. *The Golden Age of Irish Art: The Medieval Achievement 600–1200*. New York: Thames & Hudson, 1999.

Henderson, George. *Early Medieval*. New York: Penguin, 1972.

———. *From Durrow to Kells: The Insular Gospel-Books, 650–800*. London: Thames & Hudson, 1987.

Horn, Walter W., and Ernest Born. *The Plan of Saint Gall*. 3 vols. Berkeley: University of California Press, 1979.

Hubert, Jean, Jean Porcher, and Wolfgang Fritz Volbach. *The Carolingian Renaissance*. New York: Braziller, 1970.

———. *Europe of the Invasions*. New York: Braziller, 1969.

Klindt-Jensen, Ole, and David M. Wilson. *Viking Art*. 2nd ed. Minneapolis: University of Minnesota Press, 1980.

Mayr-Harting, Henry. *Ottonian Book Illumination: An Historical Study*. 2 vols. London: Miller, 1991–1993.

Megaw, Ruth, and John Vincent Megaw. *Celtic Art: From Its Beginning to the Book of Kells*. New York: Thames & Hudson, 1989.

Mütherich, Florentine, and Joachim E. Gaehde. *Carolingian Painting*. New York: Braziller, 1976.

Nees, Lawrence J. *Early Medieval Art*. New York: Oxford University Press, 2002.

Nordenfalk, Carl. *Celtic and Anglo-Saxon Painting: Book Illumination in the British Isles, 600–800*. New York: Braziller, 1977.

O'Brien, Jacqueline, and Peter Harbison. *Ancient Ireland: From Prehistory to the Middle Ages*. New York: Oxford University Press, 2000.

Richardson, Hilary, and John Scarry. *An Introduction to Irish High Crosses*. Dublin: Mercier, 1996.

Stalley, Roger. *Early Medieval Architecture*. New York: Oxford University Press, 1999.

Treasures of Early Irish Art, 1500 B.C. to 1500 A.D. New York: Metropolitan Museum of Art, 1977.

Wilson, David M. *Anglo-Saxon Art: From the Seventh Century to the Norman Conquest*. London: Thames & Hudson, 1984.

CHAPTER 17
THE AGE OF PILGRIMAGES:
ROMANESQUE ART

Armi, C. Edson. *Masons and Sculptors in Romanesque Burgundy: The New Aesthetics of Cluny III*. 2 vols. University Park: Pennsylvania State University Press, 1983.

Barral i Altet, Xavier. *The Romanesque: Towns, Cathedrals and Monasteries*. Cologne: Taschen, 1998.

Cahn, Walter. *Romanesque Bible Illumination*. Ithaca, N.Y.: Cornell University Press, 1982.

———. *Romanesque Manuscripts: The Twelfth Century*. 2 vols. London: Miller, 1998.

Conant, Kenneth J. *Carolingian and Romanesque Architecture, 800–1200*. 4th ed. New Haven: Yale University Press, 1992.

Demus, Otto. *Romanesque Mural Painting*. New York: Thames & Hudson, 1970.

Dodwell, Charles R. *The Pictorial Arts of the West, 800–1200*. New Haven: Yale University Press, 1993.

Fergusson, Peter. *Architecture of Solitude: Cistercian Abbeys in Twelfth-Century Europe*. Princeton, N.J.: Princeton University Press, 1984.

Forsyth, Ilene H. *The Throne of Wisdom: Wood Sculptures of the Madonna in Romanesque France*. Princeton, N.J.: Princeton University Press, 1972.

Grabar, André, and Carl Nordenfalk. *Romanesque Painting*. New York: Skira, 1958.

Grape, Wolfgang. *The Bayeux Tapestry: Monument to a Norman Triumph*. New York: Prestel, 1994.

Hearn, Millard F. *Romanesque Sculpture: The Revival of Monumental Stone Sculpture in the Eleventh and Twelfth Centuries*. Ithaca, N.Y.: Cornell University Press, 1981.

Kahn, Deborah, ed. *The Romanesque Frieze and Its Spectator*. London: Miller, 1992.

Kauffmann, Claus M. *Romanesque Manuscripts, 1066–1190*. Boston: New York Graphic Society, 1975.

Male, Émile. *Religious Art in France: The Twelfth Century*. Rev. ed. Princeton, N.J.: Princeton University Press, 1978.

Minne-Sève, Viviane, and Hervé Kergall. *Romanesque and Gothic France: Architecture and Sculpture*. New York: Abrams, 2000.

Nichols, Stephen G. *Romanesque Signs: Early Medieval Narrative and Iconography*. New Haven: Yale University Press, 1983.

Nordenfalk, Carl. *Early Medieval Book Illumination*. New York: Rizzoli, 1988.

Petzold, Andreas. *Romanesque Art*. New York: Abrams, 1995.

Prache, Anne. *Cathedrals of Europe*. Ithaca, N.Y.: Cornell University Press, 1999.

Schapiro, Meyer. *The Sculpture of Moissac*. New York: Thames & Hudson, 1985.

Stalley, Roger. *Early Medieval Architecture*. New York: Oxford University Press, 1999.

Swarzenski, Hanns. *Monuments of Romanesque Art: The Art of Church Treasures in North-Western Europe.* 2nd ed. Chicago: University of Chicago Press, 1967.

Tate, Robert B., and Marcus Tate. *The Pilgrim Route to Santiago.* Oxford: Phaidon, 1987.

Toman, Rolf. *Romanesque: Architecture, Sculpture, Painting.* Cologne: Könemann, 1997.

Zarnecki, George, Janet Holt, and Tristram Holland, eds. *English Romanesque Art, 1066–1200.* London: Weidenfeld & Nicolson, 1984.

Chapter 18
The Age of Great Cathedrals:
Gothic Art

Alexander, Jonathan J. G., and Paul Binski, eds. *Age of Chivalry: Art in Plantagenet England, 1200–1400.* London: Royal Academy, 1987.

Bony, Jean. *The English Decorated Style: Gothic Architecture Transformed, 1250–1350.* Ithaca, N.Y.: Cornell University Press, 1979.

———. *French Gothic Architecture of the Twelfth and Thirteenth Centuries.* Berkeley: University of California Press, 1983.

Branner, Robert. *Manuscript Painting in Paris during the Reign of St. Louis.* Berkeley: University of California Press, 1977.

———. *St. Louis and the Court Style in Gothic Architecture.* London: Zwemmer, 1965.

———, ed. *Chartres Cathedral.* New York: Norton, 1969.

Brown, Sarah, and David O'Connor. *Glass-Painters (Medieval Craftsmen).* Toronto: University of Toronto Press, 1991.

Camille, Michael. *Gothic Art: Glorious Visions.* New York: Abrams, 1996.

———. *The Gothic Idol: Ideology and Image-Making in Medieval Art.* New York: Cambridge University Press, 1989.

Courtenay, Lynn T., ed. *The Engineering of Medieval Cathedrals.* Aldershot: Scolar, 1997.

Erlande-Brandenburg, Alain. *The Cathedral: The Social and Architectural Dynamics of Construction.* New York: Cambridge University Press, 1994.

———. *Gothic Art.* New York: Abrams, 1989.

Favier, Jean. *The World of Chartres.* New York: Abrams, 1990.

Fitchen, John. *The Construction of Gothic Cathedrals: A Study of Medieval Vault Erection.* Chicago: University of Chicago Press, 1981.

Frankl, Paul, and Paul Crossley. *Gothic Architecture.* New Haven: Yale University Press, 2000.

———. *The Gothic: Literary Sources and Interpretations during Eight Centuries.* Princeton, N.J.: Princeton University Press, 1960.

Frisch, Teresa G. *Gothic Art 1140–c. 1450: Sources and Documents.* Toronto: University of Toronto Press, 1987. Reprint of 1971 ed.

Gerson, Paula, ed. *Abbot Suger and Saint-Denis.* New York: Metropolitan Museum of Art, 1986.

Gimpel, Jean. *The Cathedral Builders.* New York: Grove, 1961.

Grodecki, Louis. *Gothic Architecture.* New York: Electa/Rizzoli, 1985.

Grodecki, Louis, and Catherine Brisac. *Gothic Stained Glass, 1200–1300.* Ithaca, N.Y.: Cornell University Press, 1985.

Jantzen, Hans. *High Gothic: The Classic Cathedrals of Chartres, Reims, Amiens.* Princeton, N.J.: Princeton University Press, 1984.

Male, Émile. *Religious Art in France: The Thirteenth Century.* Rev. ed. Princeton, N.J.: Princeton University Press, 1984.

Minne-Sève, Viviane, and Hervé Kergall. *Romanesque and Gothic France: Architecture and Sculpture.* New York: Abrams, 2000.

Nussbaum, Norbert. *German Gothic Church Architecture.* New Haven: Yale University Press, 2000.

Panofsky, Erwin. *Abbot Suger on the Abbey Church of St. Denis and Its Art Treasures.* 2nd ed. Princeton, N.J.: Princeton University Press, 1979.

———. *Gothic Architecture and Scholasticism.* New York: New American Library, 1985. Reprint of 1951 ed.

Prache, Anne. *Cathedrals of Europe.* Ithaca, N.Y.: Cornell University Press, 1999.

Radding, Charles M., and William W. Clark. *Medieval Architecture, Medieval Learning.* New Haven: Yale University Press, 1992.

Rudolph, Conrad. *Artistic Change at St-Denis: Abbot Suger's Program and the Early Twelfth-Century Controversy over Art.* Princeton, N.J.: Princeton University Press, 1990.

Sauerländer, Willibald, and Max Hirmer. *Gothic Sculpture in France, 1140–1270.* New York: Abrams, 1973.

Simson, Otto G. von. *The Gothic Cathedral: Origins of Gothic Architecture and the Medieval Concept of Order.* 3rd ed. Princeton, N.J.: Princeton University Press, 1988.

Toman, Rolf, ed. *The Art of Gothic: Architecture, Sculpture, Painting.* Cologne: Könemann, 1999.

Williamson, Paul. *Gothic Sculpture, 1140–1300.* New Haven: Yale University Press, 1995.

Wilson, Christopher. *The Gothic Cathedral: The Architecture of the Great Church, 1130–1530.* London: Thames & Hudson, 1990.

CREDITS

The authors and publisher are grateful to the proprietors and custodians of various works of art for photographs of these works and permission to reproduce them in this book. Sources not included in the captions are listed here.

Introduction–© Guggenheim Museum Bilbao: 1; Aerofilms Limited: 2; akg-images/Rabatti-Dominige: 3; © 2001 The Georgia O'Keefe Foundation/Artist Rights Society (ARS), NY: 4; © 2001 Ben Shahn/Licensed by VAGA, NY, NY: 5; www.bednorz-photo.de: 6; DY/Art Resource, NY: 07; Photograph © M.M.A.: 8; Saskia: 9; © National Gallery, London: 11; MOA Art Museum, Shizuoka-ken, Japan: 12; Joachim Blauel/Arthothek: 13; Jürgen Liepe, Berlin: 14; Nimatallah/Art Resource, NY: 15; Photograph © 1983 M.M.A.: 16; Scala: 17

Chapter 1–Photo: Paul G. Bahn: 1; With permission: Namibia Archaeological Trust: 2; © Ulmer Museum. Photo: Thomas Stephan: 03; © Archivio Iconografico, S.A./Corbis: 4; Index/Alberti: 5; Jean Dieuzaide: 06; Jean Vertut: 7; R.M.N.: 8; Jean Vertut: 9; Hans Hinz: Jean Vertut: 10; 11; Eurelios/French Ministry of Culture and Communication, Regional Direction for Cultural Affairs-Rhône-Alpes region-Regional department of archaeology: 12; Jean Vertut: 13; Archivio e Studio Folco Quilici, Roma: 14; Department of Antiquities, Amman, Jordan, by P. Dorrell and S. Laidlaw, with permission of the "Ain Ghazal Archaeological Project": 15; James Mellaart: 16; © Gianni Dagli Orti/Corbis: 17; James Mellaart: 18; Pubbli Aer Foto: 19

Chapter 2–© Nik Wheeler/Corbis: 1; From E.S. Piggott, Ed., *The Dawn of Civilization*, London, Thames and Hudson, 1961, pg. 70: 2; Erwin Böhm: 03; Erwin Böhm: 04; Lessing: 5; Hir: 6; R.M.N.: 7, 13, 15, 16, 19; © Copyright the Trustees of the British Museum: 8, 11, 23, 24; University of Pennsylvania Museum (Neg. #T35-2256c.2): 9; University of Pennsylvania Museum (Neg. #T4-848c.): 10; Joseph Scherschel/National Geographic Society: 12; Erwin Böhm: 14; Gir: 17; photo Henri Stierlin: 18; © 1975 The Royal Institute of British Architects and the University of London, Athlone Press. Reprinted by permission of The Continuum International Publishing Group: 20; Saskia: 21; Klaus Göken, 1992/Bildarchiv Preussischer Kulturbesitz: 25; The Art Archive/Dagli Orti: 26; David Poole/Robert Harding Picture Library: 27; Archivio e Studio Folco Quilici, Roma: 28; M.M.A., Fletcher Fund, 1965 (65.126). Photograph © 1982 By M.M.A.: 29; Sassoon/Robert Harding Picture Library: 30

Chapter 3–J. E. Quibell and F.W. Green, *Hierakonpolis* vol. 2 (London 1902) p. 76: 1; Jürgen Liepe, Berlin: 2, 15, 40; Hir: 3; Carolyn Brown/PRI: 4; From K. Lange and M. Hirmer, *Agypten. Architectur, Plastik, Malerei in drei Jahrtausenden*, Munich, 1957. Used by permission of Phaidon Press and Hir: 5; Ancient Art & Architecture Collection Ltd.: 06; Lessing: 7; Simon Harrus/Robert Harding Picture Library: 8; Harvard University Semitic Museum: 10; Robert Harding Picture Library: 11; © Araldo de Luca: 12; 32; Courtesy, Museum of Fine Arts, Boston. Reproduced with permission. © 2000 Museum of Fine Arts, Boston. All Rights Reserved: 13; R.M.N.: 14; Jean Vertut: 16; Hirmer: 17; M.M.A.: 18; Marburg/Art Resource, NY: 19; akg-images/Francois Guenet: 20; Getty Research Library, Wim Swaan Photograph Collection, 96.P.21: 21; M.M.A., Rogers Fund, 1929 (29.3.1). Photograph by Schecter Lee. Photograph © 1986 M.M.A.: 22; John P. Stevens/AA&A: 23; Marco Casiraghi: 24; J. Jackson/Robert Harding Picture Library: 26; M.M.A., Purchase, 1890, Levi Hale Willard Bequest (90.35.1): 27; Ronald Sheridan/AA&A: 28; Jürgen Liepe/Bildarchiv Preussischer Kulturbesitz: 29; Margarete Büsin/Bildarchiv Preussischer Kulturbesitz: 33, 34; Bildarchiv Preussischer Kulturbesitz/Art Resource, NY: 35; Boltin Picture Library: 36; Robert Harding Picture Library: 37, 38

Chapter 4–The Art Archive/National Archaeological Museum, Athens/Dagli Orti: 1, 2; Hir: 4, 23, 24; Getty Research Library, Wim Swaan Photograph Collection, 96.P.21: 5; Saskia: 6; Studio Kontos: 7, 26; photo Henri Stierlin: 8, 9; Hans Hinz: 10; Studio Kontos: 11; Nimatallah/Art Resource, NY: 12; Alison Franz Collection, American School of Classical Studies at Athens: 13; © Archivio Iconografico, S.A./Corbis: 14; © British School at Athens: 15; Photo by Raymond V. Schoder, © 1987 by Bolchazy-Carducci Publishers, Inc.: 16; Lessing: 17, 20; © Vanni Archive/Corbis: 21, 22; Archaeological Receipts Fund: 25

Chapter 5–© Archivio Iconografico, S.A./Corbis: opener; M.M.A., Rogers Fund, 1914 (14.130.14). Photograph © 1996 M.M.A.: 1; M.M.A., Gift of J. Pierpont Morgan, 1917 (17.190.2072). Photograph © 1996 M.M.A.: 2; Museum of Fine Arts, Boston, Francis Bartlett Collection: 3; © Copyright the Trustees of the British Museum: 4, 46, 52; From J.G. Pedley, *Greek Art and Archaeology*, Prentice-Hall, 1993, Fig. 5.15: 5; Alison Frantz: 6; R.M.N.: 7, 21, 57, 82, 83; M.M.A., Fletcher Fund, 1932 (32.11.1). Photograph © 1993 M.M.A.: 8; Nimatallah/Art Resource, NY: 9; © Giovanni Dagli Orti/Corbis: 10; Studio Kontos: 11, 42, 64, 68, 77, 84; Saskia: 12, 27, 28, 53, 55, 71, 73, 85; Summerfield: 13; From Marvin Trachtenberg and Isabelle Hyman, *Architecture from Prehistoric to Post-Modernism/The Western Tradition*, Englewood Cliffs, NJ: Prentice Hall, 1986, p. 86, p. 293. Used by permission: 14; Vanni/Art Resource, NY: 15; photo Henri Stierlin: 24, 49; Canali: 18, 29, 65, 69; Scala: 18, 50, 56; Photo Vatican Museums: 19; Museum of Fine Arts, Boston: 20; Colorphoto Hans Hinz: 22; Musees royaux d'Art et d'Histoire: 23; From H. Berve and G. Gruben, *Greek Temples, Theaters, and Shrines*, Harry N. Abrams, Inc., Fig. 41: 25; Ancient Art & Architecture Collection Ltd.: 26; Studio Kontos: 30, 33; photo Paul M.R Maeyaert: 32; Scala: 34; Lessing: 35; Nimatallah/Art Resource, NY: 36, 54; Araldo de Luca: 37; Scala: 38; Photo by Raymond V. Schoder, © 1987 by Bolchazy-Carducci Publishers, Inc.: 40; American School of Classical Studies at Athens: Agora Excavations: 41; Hilda Westervelt: 45; Ancient Art & Architecture Collection Ltd.: 47; Scala: 48, 60, 66; From H. Berve and G. Gruben, *Greek Temples, Theaters, and Shrines*, Harry N. Abrams, Inc., Fig. 66: 51; © 1981 M. Sarri/Photo Vatican Museums: 58; Archivio I.G.D.A., Milano: 59; Photograph © 2003 Museum of Fine Arts, Boston, Gift of Nathaniel Thayer: 10.70: 61; © Archivio Iconografico, S.A./Corbis: 62; Archaeological Receipts Fund: 63; Art Resource, NY: 67; Photo by Raymond V. Schoder, © 1987 by Bolchazy-Carducci Publishers, Inc.: 70; Vanni/Art Resource, NY: 72; Bildarchiv Preussischer Kulturbesitz: 75; Bildarchiv Preussischer Kulturbesitz/Art Resource, NY 78; Bildarchiv Preussischer Kulturbesitz/Art Resource, NY: 79; Photo Giovanni Lattanzi: 80; Summerfield: 81; © Gianni Dagli Orti/Corbis: 86; Ny Carlsberg Glyptotek: 88; © 1988 T. Okamura/Photo Vatican Museums: 89; akg-images: 90

Chapter 6–Diego Lezama Orezzoli/Corbis: 1; John C. Huntington: 2, 12; SCP57227 Steatite Pasupati seal, Mohenjodaro, 2300-1750 bce, National Museum of India, New Delhi, India/Bridgeman Art Library: 3; Benoy K. Behl: 4; Edifice/Corbis: 5; Robert Harding Picture Library: 7, 20; © ephotocorp.com: 8a, 11; © The Trustees of the National Museums of Scotland: 9; Freer Gallery of Art, Smithsonian Institution, Washington, D.C.: Purchase, F1949.9: 10; Lindsay Hebberd/Corbis: 13; Douglas Dickins FRPS: 14, 21; Borromeo/Art Resource, NY: 15; Alison Wright/Corbis: 17; ACSAA Slide #3101 ©AAUM: 18; ACSAA Slide #3103 ©AAUM: 19; Robert L. Brown: 22a, 23, 24; Stephanie Colasanti/Corbis: 25; Charles & Josette Lenars/Corbis: 26; Luca I. Tettoni/Corbis: 27, 31; Paul John Miller/Stockphoto: 29

Chapter 7–Cultural Relics Publishing House, Beijing: 1, 3, 5, 12, 13, 19; A.A.M., B60B105. Used by permission: 2; The Nelson-Atkins Museum of Art, Kansas City, Missouri (Purchase: Nelson Trust) 33-81. Photo: E. G. Schempf: 4; © Imaginechina: 5; The Nelson-Atkins Museum of Art, Kansas City, Missouri (Purchase: Nelson Trust) 33-521. Photo: Robert Newcombe: 8; A.A.M., B60B1034. Used by permission: 9; Heritage Images/British Museum: 10; R.M.N.: 11; Photograph © 2003 Museum of Fine Arts, Boston. Attributed to: Yan Liben, died in 673. The Thirteen Emperors. Chinese, Tang dynasty, Second half of the 7th century (with later replacement). Object Place: China. Handscroll; ink and color on silk. 51.3 × 531cm (20 3/16 × 209 1/16 in.) Museum of Fine Arts, Boston. Denman Waldo Ross Collection. 31.643" (Photograph © 2003 Museum of Fine Art, Boston): 15; Victoria & Albert Museum, London/Art Resource, NY: 17; Collection of the National Palace Museum, Taiwan, Republic of China: 18, 23; A.A.M., B60B161. Used by permission: 20; Liu Liqun/Corbis: 21; Photograph © 2003 Museum of Fine Art., Zhou Jichang, Chinese, second half of 12th century. Lohans Bestowing Alms on Suffering Human Beings. Chinese, Southern Song Dynasty, about 1178. Object Place: China. Ink and color on silk. 111.5 × 53.1cm (43 7/8 × 20 7/8 in.) Museum of

Fine Arts, Boston. General Funds. 95.4" (Photograph © 2003 Museum of Fine Art, Boston): 24; Tokyo National Museum. Image TNM Image Archives. Source: http://TnmArchives.jp: 25; Archivio Iconografico, S.A./Corbis: 27

Chapter 8–Tokyo National Museum. Image TNM Image Archives. Source: http://TnmArchives.jp: 1, 2, 11; Tomb of Emperor Nintoku. (Nintoku-ryo Tumulus) Sakai, Osaka Prefecture: 5; Jingu Administration Office: 5; Sakamoto Photo Research Laboratory/Corbis: 6, 12, 15; Archivio Iconografico, S.A./Corbis: 7; D.Carrasco/jonarnold.com: 10; The Gotoh Museum, Tokyo: 13; Photograph © 2003 Museum of Fine Art, Boston. Artist Unknown, Japanese. Night Attack on the Sanjo Palace, from the Illustrated Scrolls of the Events of the Heiji Era (Heiji monogatari emaki). Japanese, Kamakura period, second half of the 13th century. Object Place: Japan. Handscroll; ink and color on paper. 41.3 × 699.7 cm (16 1/4 × 275 1/2 in.) Museum of Fine Arts, Boston. Fenollosa-Weld Collection. 11.4000" (Photograph © 2003 Museum of Fine Art, Boston): 16

Chapter 9–Hir: 1; David Lees: 2; Canali: 3; © Mike Andrews/Ancient Art & Achitecture Collection Ltd.: 4; Archivio e Studio Folco Quilici, Roma: 5; Archivio I.G.D.A., Milano: 7; Ancient Art & Architecture Collection Ltd.: 8; Hirmer: 9; © Araldo de Luca/Corbis: 10; Saskia: 11; © Gianni Dagli Orti/Corbis: 12, 14; Scala: 13; © Archivio Iconografico, S.A./Corbis: 15

Chapter 10–K. Koskimies: 1; photo Henri Stierlin: 2, 13, 32, 50, 52; Scala: 3, 12, 15, 17, 23, 44, 46, 51, 53, 58, 72, 78; From Robert Furneaux Jordan, *A Concise History of Western Architecture*, © 1969 by Harcourt Brace Jovanovich. Reproduced by permission of the publisher: 4; Éditions Citadelles et Mazenod, Paris: 4; © Bettmann/Corbis: 5; AL: 6, 45; German Archaeological Institute, Rome: 7, 8; The American Numismatic Society, NY.: 9, 82; The Whittlesey Foundation/Aristide D. Caratzas, Publisher: 10; White Star: 11; Photo Archives Skira, Geneva, Switzerland: 14; M.M.A., Rogers Fund, 1903 (03.14.13). Photograph by Schecter Lee. Photograph © 1986 M.M.A.: 16; Copyright © Biblioteca Apostolica Vaticana: 19; Canali: 20, 21, 24, 42, 74; Madeline Grimoldi: 22; © M. Sarri/Photo Vatican Museums: 25; Ny Carlsberg Glyptotek: 26; Saskia: 27, 28, 29, 37, 80, 81; Gir: 30; Oliver Benn/Tony Stone Images: 31; From J. B. Ward-Perkins, *Roman Architecture*, Adapted by permission of Electra Editrice, Milan: 33; Roy Rainford/Robert Harding Picture Library: 34; Ny Carlsberg Glyptotek: 35; © Araldo de Luca/Corbis: 36, 71; Werner Forman/Art Resource, NY: 38; Scala: 39, 62; Courtesy James E. Packer and John Burge: 41; Photo Marcello Bertinetti/White Star: 43; Collection of Israel Antiquities Authority. Exhibited & photo © Israel Museum: 47; Pubbli Aer Foto: 48; Ernani Orcorte/UTET: 54; © Morton Beebe/Corbis: 55; Lessing: 56; Photo Vatican Museums: 57; De Masi/Canali: 59; German Archaeological Institute, Rome: 60; *Sarcophagus*, Italy, Roman, early 2nd century. Greek marble, L. 210 cm. © The Cleveland Museum of Art, 2003. Gift of the John Huntington Art and Polytechnic Trust, 1928.856: 61; Peter Muscato: 63; Bildarchiv Preussischer Kulturbesitz: 64; M.M.A., Samuel D. Lee Fund, 1940 (40.11.1a). Photograph by Schecter Lee. Photograph © 1986 M.M.A.: 65; Araldo de Luca: 66, 69; From Sir Banister Fletcher, *A History of Architecture on the Comparative Method*, 17th ed., rev. by R. A. Cordingly, 1961. Used by permission of Athlone Press of the University of London and the British Architectural Library, Royal Institute of British Architects: 67; Fototeca: 68; M.M.A., Rogers Fund, 1905. (05.30) Photograph © 1983 M.M.A.: 70; German Archaeological Institute, Rome: 75; Index/Artphoto: 76; Istituto Centrale per il Catalogo e la Documentazione, (ICCD): 77

Chapter 11–The Jewish Museum, NY/Art Resource, NY: 1; Madeline Grimoldi: 2; Hirmer: 4, 18; Foto Archivio Fabbrica di San Pietro in Vaticano: 5; Saskia: 6, 8; Scala: 9, 13, 15, 16, 17; Hir: 10; Canali: 11; Andre Held: 12; Vanni/Art Resource, NY: 14; Österreichische Nationalbibliothek, Vienna: 19; Scala, 20

Chapter 12–R.M.N.: 1, 26; Yann Arthus-Bertrand/Corbis: 3; photo Henri Stierlin: 5; Archivio e Studio Folco Quilici, Roma: 6; Hir: 7, 33; Canali: 8, 10, 11; Scala: 9, 12, 24; Ronald Sheridan/Ancient Art & Architecture: 13, 16; Firenze, Biblioteca Medicea Laurenziana, Ms. Laur. Plut. 1.56, c. 13v Su concessione del Ministero per i beni e le attività culturali E' vietata ogni ulteriore riproduzione con qualsiasi mezzo: 15; Lessing: 17; Studio Kontos: 18; Vanni/Art Resource, NY: 20; The Art Archive/Dagli Orti: 21; Studio Kontos: 22; Ricciarini/Visconti: 23; Ricciarini, Milano: 25; Josephine Powell: 27; Sovfoto/Eastfoto: 29; Studio Kontos: 30; Andre Held: 31; Sovfoto/Eastfoto: 34; State Historical Cultural Museum "Moscow Kremlin": 35

Chapter 13–Yoram Lehmann, Jerusalem: 1; Lessing: 2; photo Henri Stierlin: 3, 9, 18, 20, 22, 23, 24; Photo Archives Skira, Geneva, Switzerland: 4; adapted from Stierlin, p. 74: 5; Bildarchiv Preussischer Kulturbesitz/Art Resource, NY: 6; © Yann Arthus-Bertrand/Corbis: 7; © E. Simanor/Robert Harding Picture Library: 10; www.bednorz-photo.de: 11, 12; © Adam Woolfitt/Robert Harding Picture Library: 13; © Musée Lorrain, Nancy/photo G. Mangin: 14; The State Hermitage Museum: 15; Reproduced by kind permission of the Trustees of the Chester Beatty Library, Dublin: 16; C. Rennie/Robert Harding Picture Library: 17; Photographer: Daniel McGrath: 26; Collection Prince Sadruddin Aga Khan: 27; Topkapi Palace Museum: 28; R.M.N.: 29

Chapter 14–Danny Lehman/Corbis: 1; Werner Forman/Art Resource, NY: 2; Los Angeles County Museum of Art, The Proctor Stafford Collection, purchased with funds provided by Mr and Mrs Allan C Balch: 3; Yann Arthus-Bertrand/Corbis: 4; Gianni Dagli Orti/Corbis: 5; © Philip Baird www.anthroarchart.org: 7, 8, 14, 17, 21; Enzo and Paolo Ragazzini/Corbis: 9; National Museum of Anthropology, Mexico City: 10; Peabody Museum, Harvard University, Cambridge: 11; Heritage Images/The British Museum: 12; Dumbarton Oaks, Pre-Columbian Collection, Washington, DC/© Justin Kerr: 13; Jonathan Blair/Corbis: 15; M.M.A., Jan Mitchell & Sons Collection, Gift of Jan Mitchell, 1991 (1991.419.31): Photo-graph by Jan Mitchell,1991. Photograph © 1984 M.M.A.: 16; Instituto Nacional de Cultura, Lima: 18; Photograph © 2003 Museum of Fine Arts, Boston: 19; The Art Institute of Chicago: 20, 30; Museo Arqueologico Rafael Larco Herrera, Lima: 22; Bruning Archaeological Museum, Lambeyeque: 23; © Hubert Stadler/Corbis: 24; National Museum of Archaeology, Anthropology and History of Peru, Lima: 25; American Museum of Natural History, NY: 26; Ohio Historical Society: 27; Superstock, Inc.: 28; Courtesy, National Museum of the American Indian, Smithsonian Institution T150853, Photo by David Heald: 29; Tom Bean/Corbis: 31

Chapter 15–Jean-Dominique Lajoux: 1; Photograph © 1980 Dirk Bakker: 2, 4, 6; IZIKO Museums of Cape Town: 3; National Museum of American Art: 5; Great Zimbabwe Site Museum, Great Zimbabwe: 8; Roger Woods/Corbis: 9; M.M.A., The Michael C Rockefeller Memorial Collection, Gift of Nelson A Rockefeller, 1972 (1978.412.323). Photograph © 1995 M.M.A.: 10; Heritage Images/British Museum: 11; Museo Nazionale Preistorico e Etnografico Luigi Pigorini, Rome: 12

Chapter 16–R.M.N.: 1, 11; University Museum of National Antiquities, Oslo, Norway. Eirik Irgens Johnsen: 3; © Artur/Dieter Leistner: 4; The Board of Trinity College, Dublin, Ireland/Bridgeman Art Library: 5, 8; Saskia: 9; © Kunsthistorischen Museums, Wien: 12; University Library, Utrecht: 14; ©The Pierpont Morgan Library/Art Resource, NY: 15; www.bednorz-photo.de: 17, 20, 21, 22; Hir: 18; Photo: Dom-Museum, Hildesheim (Frank Tomio): 24, 25; Rheimisches Bildarchiv: 26

Chapter 17–www.bednorz-photo.de: 3, 7, 8, 22, 23, 25, 26, 27, 28, 34; Jean Dieuzaide: 4; Conant, Kenneth J., *A Brief Commentary On Early Medieval Church Architecture, with Especial Reference to Lost Monuments; Lectures Given November 7, 8, 9, 14, 15, 16, 1939 at the JHU.* © 1942. The Johns Hopkins University Press: 5, 16; akg-images/Stefan Drechsel: 6; © Florian Monheim: 9, 24; Pubbli Aer Foto: 10; Canali: 11, 33; Anthony Kersting: 15; Scala: 17; akg-images/Rabatti-Dominigie: 18; Takashi Okamura/Abbeville Press, NY: 19; photo Paul M.R. Maeyaert: 20, 29; The Art Archive/Dagli Orti: 21; M.M.A., Gift of J. Pierpont Morgan, 1916 (16.32.194). Photograph © 1990 M.M.A.: 30; Photograph Speldoorn © Musées Royaux d'Art et d'Histoire, Bruxelles. (MRAH): 31; Museum of Fine Arts, Boston: 32; Abtei St. Hildegard: 35; Master and Fellows of Corpus Christi College, Cambridge: 37; Trinity MS R.17.1.f.283, Eadwine the Scribe: 38; By special permission of the City of Bayeux: 39, 40

Chapter 18–www.bednorz-photo.de: 1, 3, 6, 7, 15, 20, 21, 24, 27, 45, 46, 47, 48, 49, 50, 56; Pubbli Aer Foto: 4, 26; Index, Firenze: 5; © Uwe Dettmar: 8; Hir: 10, 17, 19, 54; photo Paul M.R Maeyaert: 12; Gir: 13; © Angelo Hornak Library: 14; Clarence Ward, Photographic Archives, National Gallery of Art, Washington, D.C.: 16; © photo Jean Mazenod, *L'art gothique*, éditions Citadelles & Mazenod, Paris: 22; © Robert G. Calkins: 28; Österreichische Nationalbibliothek, Vienna: 30; © The Pierpont Morgan Library/Art Resource, NY: 31; cliché Bibliothèque nationale de France: 33; R.M.N.: 35; The Walters Art Gallery, Baltimore: 36; Aerofilms Limited: 37; © Florian Monheim: 39, 41; © Angelo Hornak Library: 42; The Dean and Chapter of Hereford Cathedral and The Hereford Mappa Mundi Trust: 43; Pubbli Aer Foto: 44; Lessing: 51, 52, 53; Canali: 55; Archivio e Studio Folco Quilici, Roma: 57; From Ernest Gall, *Gotische Kathedralen*, 1925. Used by permission of Klinkhardt and Biermann, publishers: 59

INDEX

Boldface names refer to artists. Pages in italics refer to illustrations